Front and rear cover and front and rear internal flyleaf images
The Top Sale of the 2016-2017 season
1956 Aston Martin DBR1
US$ 22.550.000
RM Sotheby's, Monterey CA (USA) 18 August 2017
All images copyright and courtesy of RM Sotheby's

Who brings classic car lovers together?

Whether it is the Goodwood Revival, or the Grand Prix de Monaco Historique, Credit Suisse is at the heart of the world's best loved classic car events.

Listen to racing legends share their thoughts on these events at credit-suisse.com/classiccars

ADOLFO ORSI   RAFFAELE GAZZI

CLASSIC CAR AUCTION
YEARBOOK 2016 2017

Sponsored by

Classic Car Auction 2016-2017 Yearbook

Published by:
Historica Selecta srl
Via Paussolo 14/a
41012 Carpi (Modena)
Italy

Edited by:
Adolfo Orsi
Raffaele Gazzi

Data processing by:
Historica Selecta srl

Iconography:
Historica Selecta srl
Archivio Adolfo Orsi

Historica Selecta thanks for their help:
Guido Aggazzotti Cavazza, Fausto Busato, Giovanni Gasperini, Katie Hellwig

© Copyright 2017 Historica Selecta

This book is copyrighted under the Berne Convention

All rights reserved. No part of this publication may be reproduced, stored, in a retrieval system, or transmitted in any form or by any mean, electronic, electrical, chemical, mechanical, optical, photocopying, recording or otherwise without prior written permission of Historica Selecta, Carpi.

The publisher refuses all responsibility about the data reported in this catalogue, directly coming from Auction Houses. Moreover, the publisher apologizes for any mistakes or omissions incurred in the laying-out of this catalogue. We shall be pleased to include any additions in the next edition.

Printing
Grafiche Zanini - Bologna - October 2017

Printed in Italy

978-88-96232-09-5

Introduction

Dear reader,

In 1986 when I decided to specialise in the field of collector's cars, I realized that a method for analysing market prices was missing. When from 1988 to 1991, I organized auctions of cars and automobilia in Modena, I started to gather data on the most important international sales.

In 1993 Raffaele Gazzi and I collaborated with Alberto Bolaffi in producing a yearbook, the Bolaffi Catalogue, which listed the data of cars offered for sale at international auctions, complete with prices in the leading currencies, with in-depth data on every single car. This became an essential tool for auction house managers, traders, specialized journalists and collectors alike, as well as for enthusiasts keen to be up-to-date with market values.

From the 2006-2008 edition, our company Historica Selecta took over the publishing of the Classic Car Auction Yearbook, which we increased every year with more data and graphics. This edition is the 22th (covering the 24th season) and it is the most comprehensive ever.

We are honoured to have Credit Suisse as our main sponsor and to count upon the faithful support of our advertisers, who understand the "raison d'être" of our publication.

Adolfo Orsi
President Historica Selecta

Dear Classic Car Enthusiast

It is with great pleasure that we are sponsoring the prestigious Classic Car Auction Yearbook for the ninth time. Our congratulations go to Adolfo Orsi and Raffaele Gazzi for having meticulously put together another reference book of facts, figures, and trends from the world of classic car auctions.

Our sponsorship of the Classic Car Auction Yearbook ties in with our long-term partnerships with the Goodwood Revival Meeting and the Grand Prix de Monaco Historique. In addition, we will be organizing another "Monaco Classics" rally in 2018. Thanks to our sponsorship of the Grand Prix de Monaco Historique, this biennial rally offers a real highlight – a rally parade in between the races, giving our guests the opportunity to drive three laps on the legendary race track.

There are a lot of events to look forward to and now we wish you much enjoyment reading this year's Classic Car Auction Yearbook.

Best regards

Felix Baumgartner
Credit Suisse

Index

The 22th edition of the "Classic Car Auction Yearbook", edited by Adolfo Orsi and Raffaele Gazzi, and sponsored by Credit Suisse, covers the last classic car auction season, from 1st September 2016 to 31st August 2017, and will give the reader further information and useful data for a better comprehension of this important area of the antique market.

9 Market analysis of the 2016-2017 season

12 Authors' comment

24 Graphs of the prices achieved by cars offered and sold in earlier time

28 The Top 195 cars of the 2016-2017 season

32 Top 100 for make and country statistics

34 Statistics for make

36 Average price achieved graphs

45 The 2016-2017 season "TOP TEN"

63 The 2016-2017 season case

65 Auction results from 1st September 2016 until 31st August 2017

392 24 years of TOP FIVE

404 24 years of TOP FIVE for Makes

410 TOP TWENTY of the last 24 seasons

412 Advertisers

413 Photo credits

414 Previous Yearbooks

416 About the authors

Market analysis of the 2016-2017 season

This chapter reports the classic car market analysis of the last auction season, carried out by the classic car department heads of Artcurial, Bonhams, Gooding & Company, RM Sotheby's and by the authors.

At a time when the authorities in many countries around the world are calling for the end of combustion-engine powered vehicles by 2040, or even 2030 according to some, the collectors' car market has never seen so many clients enamoured with the biggest invention of the 20th century. The invention that changed our relationship with distance, and allowed us to travel independently. It is good to report that, after years of strong price increases, the market has regulated itself and ironed out price inconsistencies for models that had shot up in value without any real explanation. I am talking about cars such as Porsche 911, Maserati and Ferrari models that had been changing hands for around 50 000€. These figures increased suddenly, crossing the 100 000€ barrier, and in some cases the 200 000€ mark, bringing in speculators, attracted by a quick and easy profit. In these speculators, I include the new auction houses, with no experience in this field, no legitimacy, and who thought it would be easy to sell cars. I am also speaking about the « collector-dealers » who left behind their intrinsic love of the automobile. The seller set the price for their car. Good news: with this regulation and the return to more realistic and sustainable prices, the speculators have disappeared and been replaced by lifelong enthusiasts.

And so today, the market is returning to more realistic prices. The cars supposedly well-restored but that in reality have had little more than a layer of make-up applied, are being sanctioned. The period for approximation is over. The current market is moving towards a growing selectivity, fuelled through knowledge and research carried out before making a purchase. This is benefitting three categories of cars : 1/ Perfectly restored cars that have a complete file of invoices and a photographic record of the restoration...2/ cars in original condition, that have never been restored, with full history.3/ exceptional and very rare cars that have earned a place in motoring history, such as the prototype Dino 206 Speciale that was sold by Artcurial Motorcars at Rétromobile 2017 for €4.4M, or a race car such as the Porsche RSR that we sold for €1.8M in Monaco, or the 1956 24H Le Mans-winning Jaguar C-Type that sold for USD 22M by RM in Monterey in 2016. Cars in these three categories, more and more difficult to find, tend to see their prices rise year on year, unlike the rest. Authenticity and racing provenance with a competition car provides the secret of success in its sale. As soon as a query appears in the history, the car either sells very poorly, or not at all.

This current trend of selectivity in the market demonstrates how mature and sustainable it has become. There is now no need to question the state of the market. If you want to buy the car of your dreams, do the research, compare, take your time, select and buy. If one buys with reflection and good judgement, there is no longer a fear of losing money. There is no longer any room in the market for 'nearly right', or for amateurism, thank heavens. Following two years when the valiant Frenchmen of Artcurial Motorcars made the cover of the Classic Car Auction Yearbook, we have let another auction house take our place this year! While not being World Champions this year, we are very happy with the prices achieved for the splendid line-up of cars we presented. The secret? Strong international marketing, widespread communication, and above all, automobiles in long term ownership that are new to the market. The great French collector Hervé Ogliastro entrusted us with his collection, we treated it like a jewel and achieved very high prices. The key is in making discoveries, by covering hundreds and thousands of kilometres every year (at the expense of spending time with our wives and children), and finding rarities and interesting cars with transparent histories. And that's what gives our job its magic. An automobile, a story, an owner, a new adventure, and a world of memories!

And then, we must mention the new generation of buyers arriving at a fast pace and interested in newer cars. The 1980s/1990s/2000s have a great future as collectors' items. The collectors' car remains and will remain, an object of fascination and passion. This industrial art, our heritage, that we continue to promote in our sales, is not ready to leave our roads or our lives! No, the electric car will not kill off the old car, it will complement it!

MATTHIEU LAMOURE
Managing Director
Artcurial Motorcars

As another twelve months have passed since the last publication of the Yearbook we have clearly witnessed a far more realistic approach to the market.

Buyers will no longer run after the cars that they are afraid to miss at any price. To the contrary different elements have to be present for sales to materialize or even for there to be bidding on a car.

Cars must be estimated realistically and attractively; if they have the right ingredients they will then perform very well as we are dealing with a finite product. The descriptions must be totally transparent and continuous history will be indispensable in order to obtain a good result for vendors. Originality or top concours level restorations by reputed companies will always attract a premium and raise interest before the car crosses the block. In short 'sanity' has returned to a market which is still commanding high prices for top items just like in the art world.

This stabilization is truly good news not only for real enthusiasts but also the market in the long term. Opportunist speculators are in many cases panicking and unless they accept to take a loss on their relatively recent purchase they are stuck with it. No reserve lots are more frequent than ever in auctions guaranteeing a sale and leaving it up to the market to decide on the price on the day. More and more frequently lots are hammered below the estimate range as buyers want to leave the venue with the feeling of having made a purchase that was good deal.

As for Bonhams we started the year at our Scottsdale Auction where the trend decades ago had always been for American muscle cars but today this has changed and good results were achieved for two great European racers which oozed pedigree and history in the Ex-Bob Jane 1963 Australian GT Championship Winning, 1963 Jaguar E-Type Lightweight making US$ 7,370,000 and the Ex-Scuderia Ferrari 1952 Ferrari 340 America Spider Competizione making US$ 6,380,000 respectively.

Moving to Europe our 'Les Grandes Marques du Monde au Grand Palais' auction during Retromobile week saw the 1936 Aston Martin Ulster Sports Two-Seater from long term private ownership sell for €2,012,500. The car was fresh on the market and the model is eligible for a multitude of events, not forgetting that the marque itself is alive and flourishing. It sold to a young Continental enthusiast, clearly substantiating the fact that sexy, sporty and interesting prewar cars are not linked to generational nostalgia. In the same sale we achieved €86,850 for a 1962 Facel Vega Facellia F2B Cabriolet double its pre-sale estimate of €30,000-40,000, simply because it was beautifully presented.

At our Spa Classic auction the no reserve 'Castle Find' collection kept its promise by attracting worldwide interest in view of the above two factors, the former Rhodesian delivered 1958 Mercedes-Benz 300SL Roadster in need of a restoration to make it perfect again making a very respectable €1,127,000 for a car from that year of production.

Only a short while later at The Goodwood Festival of Speed Sale a 1973 Porsche 911 RS Lightweight achieved a strong £830,300; recently similar cars whether Touring or Lightweight have either failed to sell or sold for far lesser amounts. 'Stories' cars are today difficult at just about any level.

At Quail Lodge during Pebble Beach week we achieved a world record for the 1995 McLaren F1 making US$ 15,620,000. So what does one retain from the last 12 months? Great cars will always remain great cars

RICHARD MILLE
A RACING MACHINE ON THE WRIST

CALIBER RM 11-03

but there is a definite generational trend from affluent new young players in the market sometimes from emerging economies with different priorities and requisites for their potential purchases.

To conclude for all of the above reasons it has been a good year for the market, sanity has prevailed and sometimes emotion has produced exceptional but justified results for very special motor cars. All of the major actors should however retain that too many auctions with the arrival of many new provincial auction houses can kill a market and with the ever rising number of new motoring events and venues we should all be careful not to overload a market that may at a certain point reach saturation.

Meanwhile we should all enjoy our classic cars to the fullest and put the purely financial investment aspect back in the 'also ran' category behind emotion, pleasure and wonderful memories our machines leave us with. We look forward to being of assistance across the globe, in sharing our knowledge and passion with all enthusiasts and particularly the readers of the Classic Car Auction Yearbook.

PHILIP KANTOR
Head of Department Bonhams Motor Cars Europe
and Director European Board

Gooding & Company achieved more than $155 million for 285 lots sold and posted a strong 82% sale rate from our three esteemed auction events. Our clients recognized the quality offerings, as 40 collector cars sold above the $1 million mark and 42 new world records were established. Our events have become a destination for enthusiasts from around the world and this year, thousands tuned in from over 60 nations to witness the Gooding & Company auctions live via our HD webcast.

Our annual Scottsdale Auctions in January kickoff our auction events and this year we realized over $33 million in two days. Nine new benchmarks were set and nine cars sold for over $1 million. The most notable sales were the highly original 1925 Bugatti Type 35 Grand Prix, which sold for a world-record price of $3,300,000 and the stunning 1965 Ferrari 500 Superfast, which sold for a strong $2,915,00. Paddles were also flying for rare-to-auction sports cars, with the illustrious 1969 AMC AMX/3 selling for $891,000, a world record price for the AMC marque. Additional best-of-category sports cars sold included: the 2011 Ferrari 599 SA Aperta (sold for $1,485,000), a record price for the model, and the 1964 Shelby 289 Cobra (sold for $1,100,00). Also, the 1955 Mercedes-Benz 300 SL Gullwing (sold for $1,457,500) from single family ownership "could be a preservation-class trophy winner at major concours events" stated Gary Anderson, The Star.

Following in March, The Amelia Island Auction at the Omni Plantation Racquet Park, Gooding & Company realized over $30 million in a single day from 69 lots sold. An impressive number of nine cars sold over the $1 million mark, with the star of the day, the exotic 1998 Porsche 911 GT1 Strassenversion selling for $5,665,000, a new world record price for the model and for the Porsche 911. Thirteen new benchmarks were set across Porsche, McLaren, Aston Martin and Mazda. Highlights included the striking 2015 McLaren P1 (sold for $2,392,500), a "mid-engine masterpiece," (Viju Matthew, Robb Report) whose sale proceeds went on to endow a chair at the Rose-Hulman Institute of Technology. Also, the 1989 Mazda 767B (sold for $1,750,000) that raced at the 1989 24 Hours of Le Mans, and the 1949 Aston Martin DB Mk II (sold for $1,540,000) that was formerly owned by company head David Brown.

Gooding & Company is the official auction house of the Pebble Beach Concours d'Elegance®, and at this year's Pebble Beach Auctions we achieved over $91 million from 110 lots sold, of which an astonishing 22 lots sold at or above $1 million mark. Our new auction schedule proved to be a windfall this year for both buyers and sellers. We experienced an increase in attendance and new registered bidders, which resulted in 20 new world record prices, including the most valuable Porsche and BMW ever sold at auction. Our 1970 Porsche 917K sold for a record-setting $14,080,000 and is "arguably the most iconic 917 of all time. And now, it's also the most expensive. Fitting." stated Brian Silvestro, Road & Track. The star of Saturday's auction, the 1966 Ferrari 275 GTB/C, also set a new world auction record for the model when it garnered $14,520,000 – the highest price achieved for the celebrated marque across all auction houses this week. One of only 12 ever built, this unrivaled offering is the ultimate evolution of the single-cam Ferrari Berlinetta and its world record price illustrated the car's historical significance.

From all of us at Gooding & Company, we look forward to seeing you at our auctions in 2018.

DAVID GOODING
President
Gooding & Company

Another year has passed and we are once again able to reflect on a market that continues to deliver results that have the capability to surprise us. Perhaps the only thing predictable in the collectible car market is that it is unpredictable, and I think 2017 has developed in a way that reflects both growth and correction depending on the sector of the market.

Loosely speaking – as the market can never been viewed in an entirely scientific context – we have seen a clear divide develop between those cars that are perceived as 'blue chip', characterized by quality and rarity often combined with great provenance, and those which are simply the staple of the market – cars that seem to be offered commonly and frequently by dealers and auction houses. Obviously, it's easiest to contextualise this trend when talking about very special, high-end cars, as those cars are still capable of making huge money and very possibly greater sums than we would have seen two or three years ago at the height of the market. It's impossible not to highlight the 1956 Aston Martin DBR1, chassis no. 1, which we sold for $22,550,000 in Monterey. The car was simply unrepeatable, boasted the finest provenance anyone could wish for, and resulted in two eager bidders pushing it to a world record sum for any British car sold at auction and entering it in the top ten most valuable cars ever sold at auction. In my view, the sum achieved is probably higher than the car would have made a few years ago when most commentators would suggest the market was more robust. No year has passed in the last decade when we haven't seen records tumble at the very pinnacle of the market, proving that buyers with very deep pockets are still happy to invest in the best.

But the same is true in other, far less exotic areas of the market, too. A Series 1 E-Type Jaguar is a staple of the auction scene and a good indicator of market trends. In London this year, we sold a very nice flat-floor Roadster for £195,000, a figure which is absolutely on the money but which does not represent growth in value for such a car, when viewed year-over-year. Yet at Villa Erba in May, a similar early roadster sold for €582,400. Why? Because the car had successful period race history, whilst being presented in fully restored, original specification. This perfectly highlights the difference in performance between very good but unremarkable cars, and those which have the X-factor so sought-after by collectors. Buyers have become very select and very demanding in a market which they currently control.

There is a buyer for everything – so long as the price is realistic and fair. Where a car offers genuine rarity and provenance, we continue to witness results that can surprise and delight the market, and which fly in the face of the doom-mongers. In a year when our Monterey sale can still generate $133 million in sales with an 88 percent sell-through rate, and our recent Ferrari auction in Maranello can generate €63 million from just 38 cars, it's clear that there is still plenty of activity and energy in the market.

As with all markets (e.g. stocks, bonds, currencies, oil, livestock, corn, etc.) in which psychology – more specifically the interplay between greed and fear – create cycles, the collector car market, in our view, is also experiencing a cycle in which fear has played a bigger role in the past twelve months than it has in recent years, as I am sure this Yearbook will reflect. However, there is no question in my mind that there is strong long-term secular growth in the collector car market, and history has taught us that it is precisely when fear permeates the market that great opportunities arise. Furthermore, unlike other markets such as stocks or bonds, it is our passion for cars, the underlying assets, that drives us (no pun intended) and we have seen no shortage of passion for owning 'blue chip' cars over the last year.

AUGUSTIN SABATIÉ-GARAT
Car Specialist
RM Sotheby's

Authors' comment

Dear Readers,
the current Yearbook presents several new features, including new graphs and statistics, as well as a different layout that improves reading and comparisons of results and comments.
The 2016-2017 Season, which closed in August with the usual "star" auctions in Monterey, makes for a complex reading of light and shadows.
Before proceeding further with our interpretation, let us compare the current numbers with those of the previous season: the turnover of 2016-2017 [1] decreased to $1.086 billion or

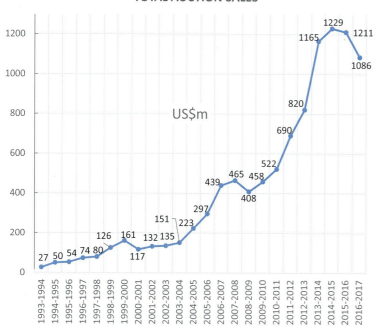

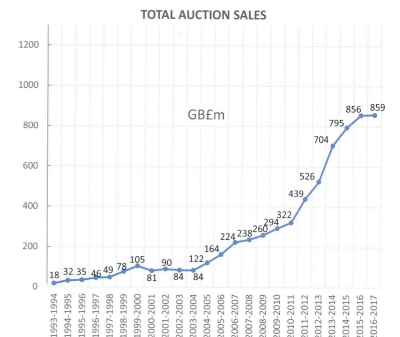

For the second season in a row we observe a decline from the historical high of $1.230 bn in 2014-2015, however, the total value of the market is still up +32% from 2012-2013, the last season when all currencies were below the threshold of a billion dollars. As the US Dollar remains the currency of reference in this market, we will from now on refer to these statistics in USD.
The other index of the market's health is traditionally the percentage of lots sold [2]: in this last season, it reached 75%, the third highest value ever, up (+3%) from the 2015-2016 season.

979 million Euro (-10% from the previous season), while it remained practically unchanged at 859 million when we compare the values in British Pounds (£), due to the relative weakness of this currency.

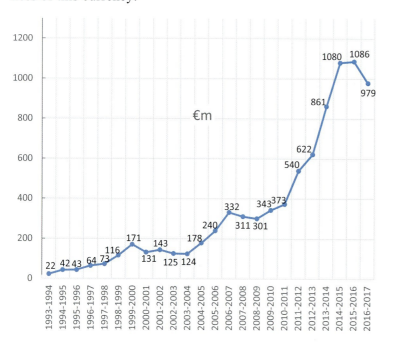

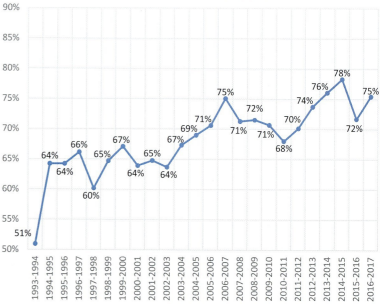

(1) Please note, as we always recall for the benefit of new readers, that we only take into consideration most of the traditional format sales organized by the most important international auction houses. We do not register data of cars for which we do not have adequate information. We highlight that the increase in prices of collector cars, heavily promoted by specialized and financial press, has attracted many non-specialized auction houses with an exponential number of sales and, therefore, a further offering of cars. Following our usual policy, we took into account the sales organized with a presentation of a catalogue including identifying chassis numbers, and organized by companies that have had a continuous and long-term presence within this field and that we continue to honor auctions with a physical auction presence rather than online.

(2) We are afraid to note that many auction houses, in the last year, have lost the habit of signaling as "post auction sales" the sales of cars unsold during the auction that are however sold by private treaty in the minutes, hours or days following the sale. In the past such sales were reported as "PA", allowing a more correct and truthful information.

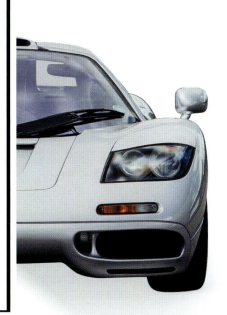

[Where the historic and modern are equally valued.]

Decades of experience in this unique market sector enables us to be at one with the industry from key selling venues to client service. It's you we value.

Bonhams

bonhams.com/motoring

London - Paris - New York - Los Angeles - Sydney - Hong Kong

The number of cars offered (5,659) remained virtually unchanged (+15 units), while the number of cars sold (4,269) increased significantly (+ 225 units). Interestingly, the absolute number of cars sold has been growing constantly in the past four seasons, thus signaling an expansion of the boundaries of the auction market.

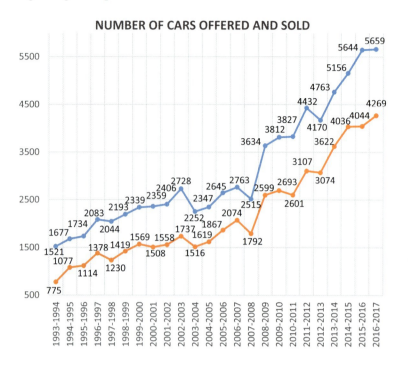

The average value fell by 15% to $254,000 (it was $299,000 in 2015-2016).

This year, we provide more new statistics to improve our understanding of the market, such as: the number of cars offered "without reserve price", the number of cars previously presented at auction in the past 24 seasons, and the average age.

The cars offered "without reserve" increased significantly: 1,461 (+ 412 units compared to the previous season), about 26% of the total number of vehicles offered. Therefore, about a quarter of the cars offered were pretty much already sold prior to the auction. When we consider only the cars presented with a reserve price, thus subject to remain unsold with only 2,737 vehicles having changed hands, the percentage sold decreases to 65% (noting a 10% difference from the overall statistic mentioned above).

The percentage of cars offered without reserve on the overall turnover rose to 21% (compared with only 9% of the previous season). This selling strategy was not restricted to the mid- and low-end market as in the past: 14 no-reserve cars (represented by an asterisk) made it in to the Top 100, up from just one last year. Therefore, the growth of the number of sold lots is due to the positive change of strategy of the auction houses in favor of presenting more cars "without reserve", rather than face the risk of spending time and resources for an uncertain outcome, a wise approach that stimulates the psychology of buyers, always looking for a bargain.

This effect is clearly demonstrated by the famous "Duemila Ruote" auction held in Milan by RM Sotheby's in November 2016 (see chapter "Season case"), a judiciary sale where nearly 430 cars (of which 272 registered in our database) were offered without reserve and generally estimated much lower than the market value. The mix of these three strategies of presenting cars fresh-to-the-market, at no-reserve and with a low estimate, proved to be explosive. This auction will long remain in the memory of those present for the extraordinary frenzy of bidders and for the incredible results achieved in relation to the low quality of the cars offered.

The increased importance of no-reserve lots is representative of a shift to a "buyers' market" as we already highlighted in 2014-2015 (which some of our loyal readers have named our "Platinum Edition" because of the color of the cover); therefore, the limited competition amongst buyers, sometimes with a single buyer bidding against the reserve price, determines this season's prices that are no longer representative of a seller's expectations, as they are during boom years.

Current prices always incorporate expectations of the future, but the direction of tomorrow's trend has changed from upward to downward, thus today's buyers are willing to wait for the next opportunity when asking prices may not be unrealistically high.

A key feature of our data is the identification of cars by their chassis, engine or registration number. This allows us to identify repeated sales of the same car over the past 24 years, mining our database of more than 75,000 cars. In the last season we observed 1,143 cars returning to the market, accounting for 20% of the lots offered. While this percentage is naturally expected

to grow over time, it is interesting to note that in the past there have been times, specifically when the market is down, when this value was higher (as in 2008-2009).

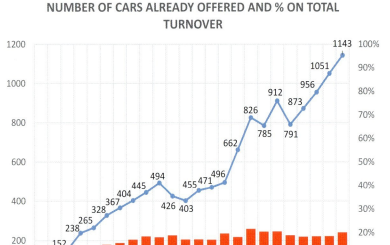

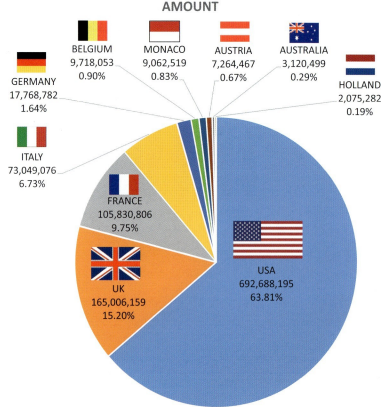

The geographical market segmentation confirms the leading role of the United States with 78% of lots sold, followed by the European auctions at 76% (an all-time record, influenced by the exceptional RM Sotheby's sale in Milan), while British auctions climb to 72% (the second best result in history). Since 16 seasons ago, the American market has remained the strongest.

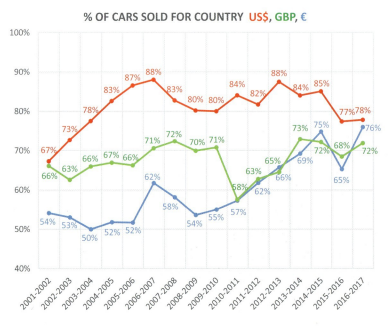

As far as overall turnover is concerned, the United States remains the market leader with 64%, followed by England at 15%, France at 10%, Italy at 7%, and six other nations combined make up the final 4.5%. This figure does not reflect the geographical distribution of buyers as many countries do not offer auction sales for the category.

This year we added a chart showing the seasonality of the sales for the last 10 seasons: it emerges that an overwhelming percentage of sales is concentrated in August (with Monterey and Pebble Beach), followed by January (Scottsdale) and then March (Amelia Island). The auctions organized around these three events account for more than 50% of the total value of the market.

This year we have a new marque seizing the Top Sale Classic Car Auction Yearbook Award: Aston Martin. The cover photograph shows the Aston Martin DBR1/1, a car with a brilliant racing history that culminated in its victory at the 1000 km of Nürburgring of 1959, sold by RM-Sotheby's on the 18th of August in Monterey for $22,550,000. Prior to this year's August auctions in California, the ranking of the Top Ten of the 2016-2017 season was led by the Bugatti Type 57S Van Vooren Cabriolet sold for $7.7 million by RM-Sotheby's in Amelia Island; now the Type 57S ranks seventh place in the final Top Ten.

Further emphasizing this point, 13 cars of the Top 25 of the 2016-2017 season were sold in August in Monterey. From this data, we can understand how the auction companies had not proposed cars of

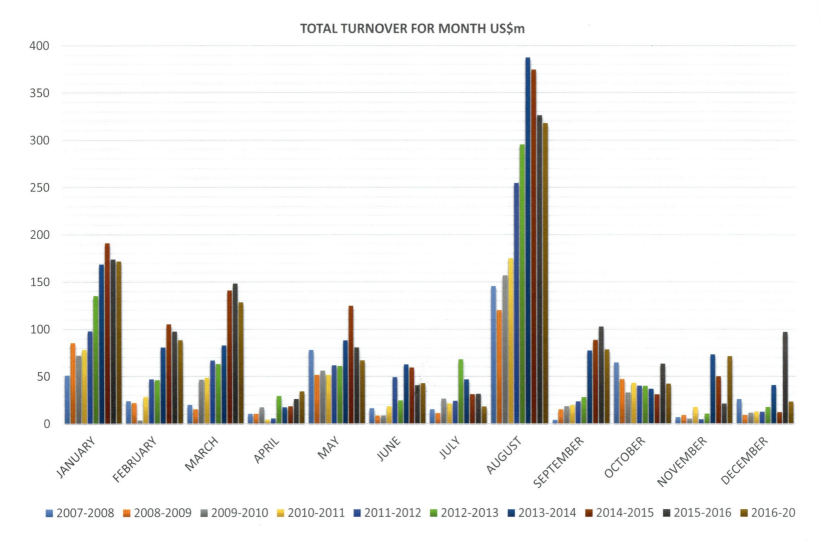

TOTAL TURNOVER FOR MONTH US$m

particular importance (at least from a monetary point of view) from September through July and how the auctions in Monterey, paired with the influence of a late offering of unexpected yet important cars, have significantly improved the result of an otherwise weak season. The value of the 100th lot by price dropped to $1,540,000 from last season's $1,650,000 and $1,898,000 in 2013-2014 and 2014-2015, thus confirming the general decrease of prices, even at the top end of the market.

The cars sold above the $1 million mark fell to 195 from 201 last year (the historical record is the 2013-2014 season with 245 cars). We notice also a smaller number of cars sold beyond the threshold of $10 million: only 4 this year compared to 12 of the 2015-2016 season and 8 of the 2014-2015 season. The market share of cars sold for more than one million dropped to 45% of the total turnover compared to 51% of the previous season.

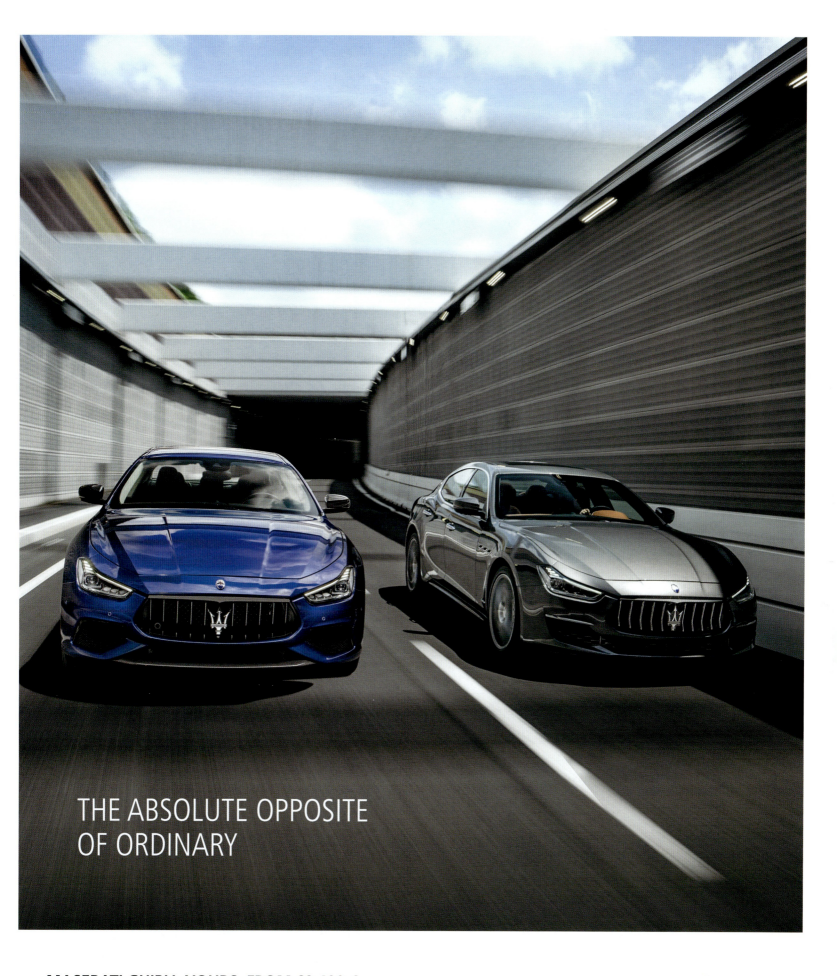

THE ABSOLUTE OPPOSITE OF ORDINARY

MASERATI GHIBLI. YOURS. FROM 69.400 €

Introducing the New Ghibli GranSport and GranLusso.

Ghibli S Q4 - Engine: V6 60° 2979 cm³ - max power: 430 HP at 5750 rpm - max torque: 580 Nm at 2250 rpm - max speed: 286 km/h - 0 - 100 km/h acceleration: 4.7 secs fuel consumption (combined cycle): 9.7 l/100 km - CO_2 emissions (combined cycle): 226 g/km. **Ghibli Diesel** - Engine: V6 60° 2987 cm³ - max power: 275 HP at 4000 rpm max torque: 600 Nm at 2000 rpm - max speed: 250 km/h - 0 - 100 km/h acceleration: 6.3 secs - fuel consumption (combined cycle): 5.9 l/100 km - CO_2 emissions (combined cycle): 158 g/km.
The data may not refer to the model represented.

maserati.com

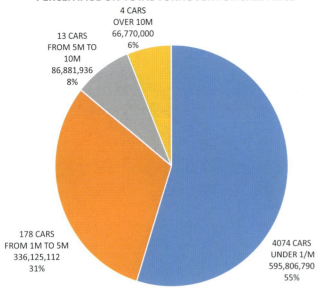

PERCENTAGE ON TOTAL TURNOVER FOR SALE PRICE

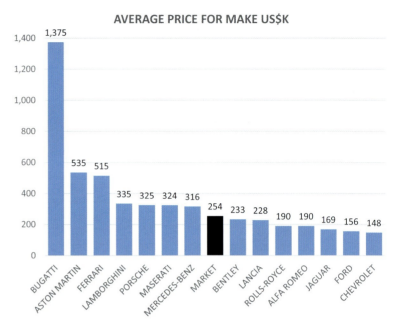

AVERAGE PRICE FOR MAKE US$k

When we consider the highest average price for Make, Bugatti wins for the second consecutive year with an average value of $1,375,000, with Aston Martin in second place, Ferrari and Lamborghini third and fourth, Porsche fifth.

When examining the weight of the individual makes in relation to the total, Ferrari has lost some of its sparkle: currently, it represents 25.03% versus 30.24% of the 2015-2016 season and 33.92% of 2014-2015.

Ferrari fell from a third to a quarter of total turnover, but managed to keep 48 cars in the Top 100, the second highest result ever. Porsche's market share grew reaching almost 15% of the total (the highest value ever for cars manufactured in Stuttgart), placing 11 cars in the Top 100.

Aston Martin, thanks to the sale of highly important cars such as the DBR1 and of the DB4 GT prototype, has taken the third place away from Mercedes-Benz; the German company has nonetheless increased its weight on the market, gaining almost one percentage point. There is a new entry in the ranking of the "Top 14 Manufacturers": Lancia, with an Astura Cabriolet "Bocca" in the Top 100 and another 5 (of which 4 are B24 Spiders) in the "million dollar club".

The percentage of lots sold by brand is led by Ford at 88%. It is worth underlining that despite our effort to include in the database all the significant car sales worldwide, sometimes coverage can only be partial. This somehow surprising statistic regarding Ford may have been partly influenced by a less-then-complete coverage of American auctions, as well as by the high percentage of sales of various models such as Mustang, Shelby Mustang GT 350 and GT 500, Boss 302 and 429, and by the recent Ford GT. In second place, we find Lancia at 81%, followed by Jaguar with 80%.

Ferrari at 65% and Lamborghini at 60% are considerably lower than the average value of 75%, a situation already arising last year with Ferrari at 60% and Lamborghini at 52%. Both values, however, have increased and are now closer to the market average, which might suggest that the discrepancy between the seller's asking price and the buyers' evaluation is closing. Those who would like to understand the dynamic of the individual Makes should go to pages 34-35 and study the historical statistics available since our first Yearbook of 1993-1994.

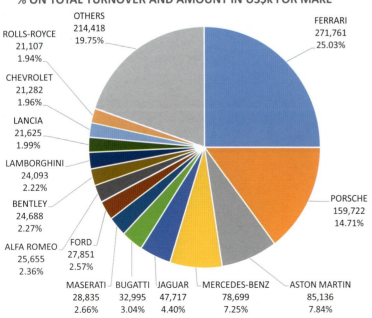

% ON TOTAL TURNOVER AND AMOUNT IN US$k FOR MAKE

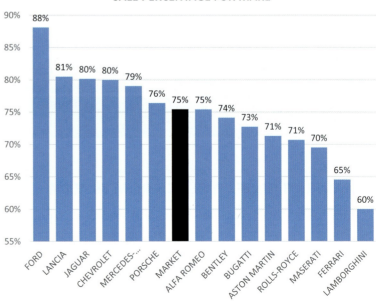

SALE PERCENTAGE FOR MAKE

CARS
Classic Automotive Relocation Services

TRADITIONAL VALUES
MODERN THINKING

- Sea and Air Freight
- Worldwide Customs Brokerage
- Race and Rally Transportation
- International Storage
- UK and European Trucking
- UK Registration

DUBAI	JAPAN	NEW YORK	EUROPE	LOS ANGELES
+971 (0) 4882 1334	+81 (0) 45 306 7043	+1 516 210 6868	+44 (0) 1284 850 950	+1 310 695 6403
info@carsmiddleeast.com	info@carsjp.net	info@carsusa.com	info@carseurope.net	info@carsusa.com
www.carsmiddleeast.com	www.carsjp.net	www.carsusa.com	www.carseurope.net	www.carsusa.com

Moving on to examine the types of vehicles offered and sold in the season in relation to their period of construction, we notice how more than 86% of the cars offered are post-war (versus 83% of the 2015-2016 season) and that they represent 85% of the total turnover. The contemporary period has increased both in numbers (a physiological phenomenon) and turnover, from 8% to almost 12%. This trend is confirmed by the presence of 15 cars built from 2000 onwards in the Top 100 (compared to 12 in the last season and 5 in the previous one). Of these, 12 have left the production of Ferrari, Bugatti, Pagani, McLaren and Porsche from 2012 onwards. Coming from a traditional perspective, we are astonished to see cars with a few months of life and with a few hundred kilometres on the speedometer change hands at prices sometimes multiple of the original list prices.

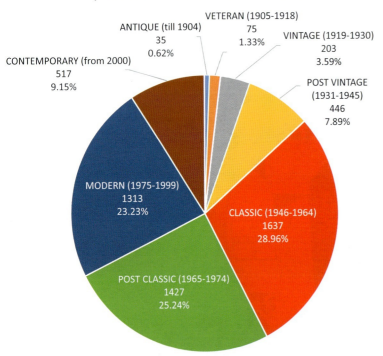

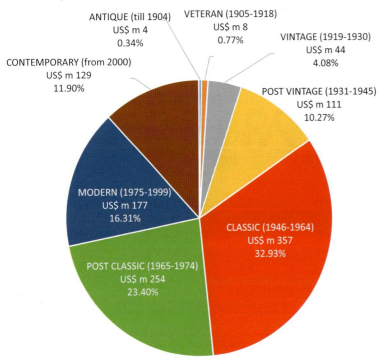

Excluding the lots bought at charity sales, we should ask what drives this phenomenon: purely speculative investments or new collecting attitudes?

We recommend to all these lucky buyers of "dreams on four wheels" to use their 'jewels' and enjoy them, waiting to see if, with time, they will also become good investments with a positive financial return.

This rejuvenation of the cars being offered is confirmed by the new chart indicating 1966 as the average year of construction, with a jump of 5 years from two seasons ago. This figure should normally increase from year to year. Interestingly, in the first three seasons we considered (from 1993-1994 to 1995-1996) the average year of construction was still in the fourth decade of the last century, then we experienced 18 seasons (from 1996-1997 to 2013-2014) in which the average year of the cars offered was from the 1950s and only the last 3 seasons this average moved to the 1960s. Will the 1960s maintain leadership for the 15 next seasons? We will return to this topic in coming years.

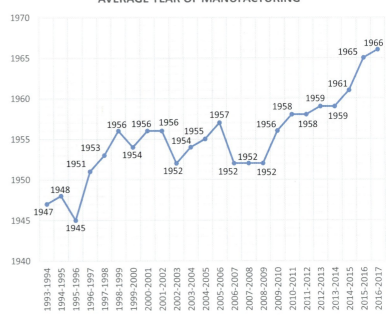

We modified and expanded the chapter "average price achieved" (from page 36) with additional data that we hope will be useful to readers to better understand the evolution of prices for some iconic models. We included the number of cars offered, sold, and the respective percentage of sales, in addition to turnover from the last 24 seasons for some key models, such as Mercedes 300SL, Ferrari F40 and Aston Martin DB4.

In conclusion, the 2016-2017 season demonstrated a good grip of the market and saw numerous "record prices". The number of cars sold and the percentage of sales were mostly increased by the strong increase of lots offered without reserve.

The average age of cars offered has increased, as has the presentation and sale of cars with very few years of life, which, during the preceding boom of the late 1980s, had been defined as "instant classics".

Turnover has declined, as well as the average value of lots sold. We are witnessing a "soft landing", a correction of collector car values that have grown abnormally in recent years, which is a healthy pause after a wild ride. This correction was not only anticipated, it was also desired by all those who work in, and love, this world. Enjoy reading!

Adolfo Orsi
Raffaele Gazzi

O ur database contains approximately 70,000 files regarding cars offered at the most important classic car auctions worldwide, beginning with the 1993-1994 sale season, together with a few cars offered from earlier years.

Reading each car's description (in italics), you will notice that, several times at the end of the description, there are [in brackets] references to previous offerings of the same car (auction, date and lot number and results price achieved in US$).

The following graphs give an overall view of the results achieved by a specific car in different years in an effort to provide the most meaningful data.

For a correct interpretation of the statistics, one should consider that a car offered twice at auctions in a span of several years could be in different condition with respect to the previous sale. The car could be in "better" condition, because it has been restored, or it might be "worse" because it has been damaged or not well maintained. It could also be that additional history has become known. One might also consider that the car may have been sold one or more times in different countries and customs/import taxes may have already been paid in some instances.

Last but not least, keep in mind the actual financial return to the seller. The reported price includes the buyer's commission retained by the auction house. The seller pays additional fees as well as various taxes and transportation fees. The actual sum paid to the seller is, therefore, often much lower than one might otherwise assume from the numbers reported.

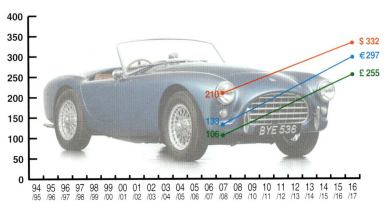

1959 AC ACE BRISTOL Chassis #BE1059

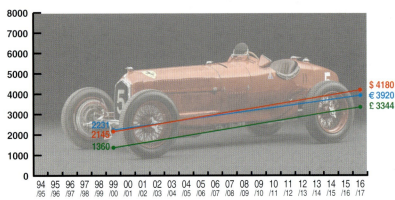

1935 ALFA ROMEO TIPO B (P3) Chassis #50006

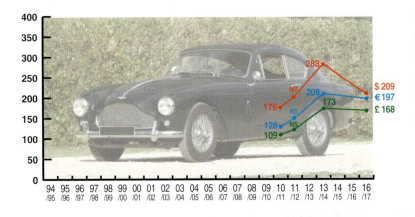

1957 ASTON MARTIN DB MARK III COUPÉ Chassis #AM30031341

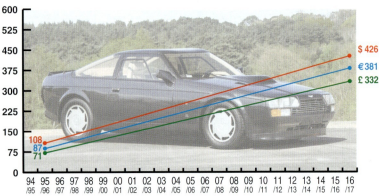

1987 ASTON MARTIN VANTAGE ZAGATO Chassis #20043

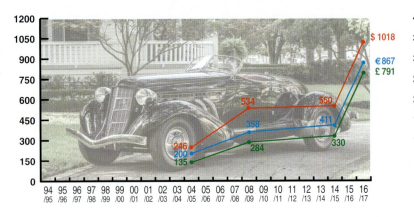

1936 AUBURN 8-852 SC BOATTAIL SPEEDSTER Chassis #35209E

1959 AUSTIN-HEALEY 3000 Chassis #HBT7L1428

* The sale price was recorded originally in Italian Lire at the exchange rate on the day of the auction. This amount was converted later to an approximate Euro equivalent using the official value of the Lire/Euro exchange at the time of the introduction of the European Union's new currency.

YOUR DREAMS ARE OUR PROJECTS.

Introducing the Zerouno: designed and built by Italdesign around your dreams.

1931 BENTLEY 8L SEDANCA DE VILLE (H.J.MULLINER) Chassis #YM5034

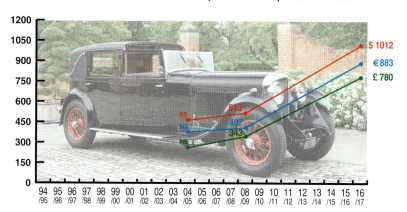

1993 BUGATTI EB 110 Chassis #39034

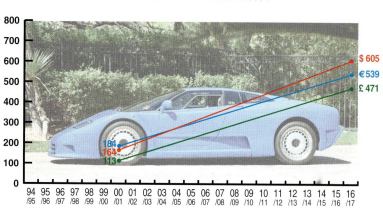

1931 CADILLAC SERIES 370 V-12 CONVERTIBLE (FLEETWOOD) Chassis #1002411 (ENGINE)

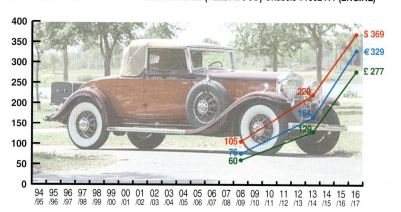

1970 CHEVROLET CHEVELLE SS CONVERTIBLE Chassis #136670B161703

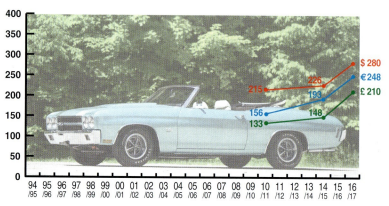

1946 CHRYSLER TOWN & COUNTRY CONVERTIBLE Chassis #7400604

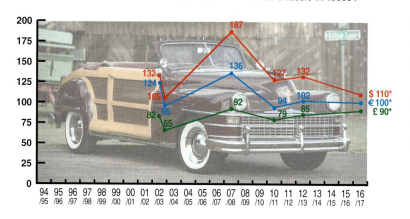

1937 CORD 812 SC PHAETON Chassis #81232013H

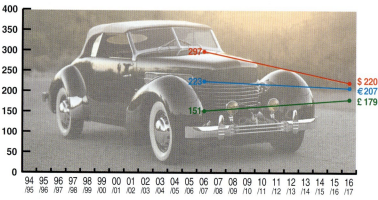

1959 FERRARI 250 GT CABRIOLET (PF) Chassis #1475GT

1965 FERRARI 275 GTB (PF/SCAGLIETTI) Chassis #07927

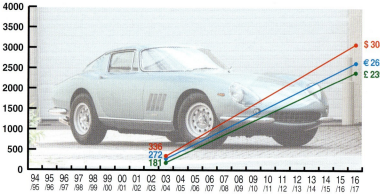

* The sale price was recorded originally in Italian Lire at the exchange rate on the day of the auction. This amount was converted later to an approximate Euro equivalent using the official value of the Lire/Euro exchange at the time of the introduction of the European Union's new currency.

1963 JAGUAR E-TYPE 3.8 LIGHTWEIGHT ROADSTER Chassis #S850667

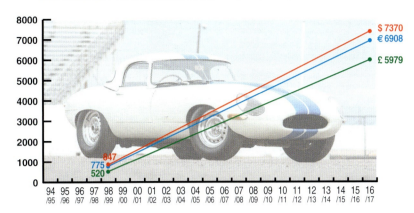

1989 LAMBORGHINI COUNTACH 25° (BERTONE) Chassis #12550

1959 MASERATI 3500 GT SPYDER (FRUA) Chassis #101.268

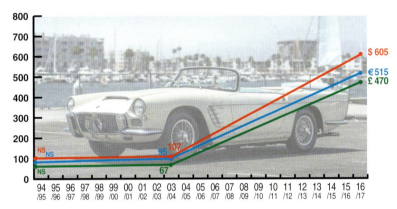

1939 MERCEDES-BENZ 540K SPEZIAL ROADSTER Chassis #408383

1988 PORSCHE 959 Chassis #900149

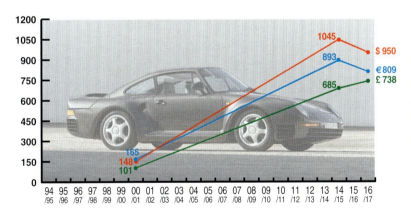

1998 PORSCHE GT1 EVOLUTION Chassis #396005

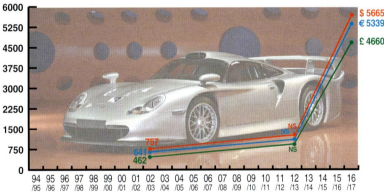

1930 ROLLS-ROYCE NEW PHANTOM NEWMARKET PHAETON (BREWSTER) Chassis #S126PR

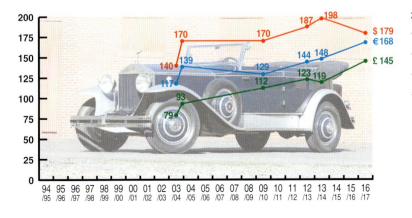

1929 STUTZ MODEL M SUPERCHARGED COUPÉ (LANCEFIELD) Chassis #MC31312

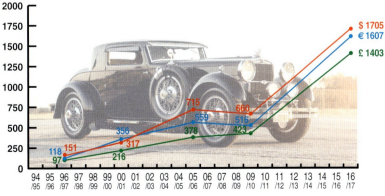

* The sale price was recorded originally in Italian Lire at the exchange rate on the day of the auction. This amount was converted later to an approximate Euro equivalent using the official value of the Lire/Euro exchange at the time of the introduction of the European Union's new currency.

The Top 195 cars of the 2016-2017 season

This chapter is dedicated to the 195 cars which, in the sales covered in the last auction season, achieved the highest prices up to $ 1.000.000. The cars are listed in descending order according to their hammer price.

We took into consideration only the highest 100 results for the update of the usual statistics given at the end of the list, which should help one to interpret trends in the classic car market.

AUCTION RESULTS IN DESCENDING ORDER (IN US$)
2016 – 2017

No.	Year	Make	Model	Bodybuilder	Hammer price	Lot	Auction House	Date
1	1956	ASTON MARTIN	DBR1		22.550.000	148	RMS	18-08-17
2	1995	McLAREN	F1		15.620.000	73	Bon	18-08-17
3	1966	FERRARI	275 GTB Competizione	PF/Scaglietti	14.520.000	120	G&Co	19-08-17
4	1970	PORSCHE	917K		14.080.000	44	G&Co	18-08-17
5	1961	FERRARI	250 GT Berlinetta Lusso	PF/Scaglietti	8.305.000*	220	RMS	19-08-17
6	1963	JAGUAR	E-Type 3.8 Lightweight roadster		8.000.000	52	Bon	18-08-17
7	1937	BUGATTI	Type 57S cabriolet	Vanvooren	7.700.000	232	RMS	11-03-17
8	1963	JAGUAR	E-Type 3.8 Lightweight roadster		7.370.000	24	Bon	19-01-17
9	2016	FERRARI	LaFerrari	Ferrari Styling Center	7.000.000	NA	RMS	04-12-16
10	1959	ASTON MARTIN	DP199/DB4 GT prototype		6.765.000	147	RMS	18-08-17
11	1939	MERCEDES-BENZ	540 K Spezial Roadster		6.600.000	258	RMS	20-01-17
12	1952	FERRARI	340 America spider	Vignale	6.380.000	44	Bon	19-01-17
13	1956	PORSCHE	550 Spyder		6.120.839	140	Bon	10-09-16
14	1935	MERCEDES-BENZ	500 K Roadster		5.921.097	16	Bon	03-09-16
15	1955	FERRARI	121 LM	Scaglietti	5.720.000	140	RMS	18-08-17
16	1998	PORSCHE	911 GT1 Evolution		5.665.000	42	G&Co	10-03-17
17	1959	FERRARI	410 Superamerica coupé	Pinin Farina	5.335.000	249	RMS	19-08-17
18	1959	FERRARI	250 GT cabriolet	Pinin Farina	4.840.000	36	G&Co	18-08-17
19	1928	MERCEDES-BENZ	S tourenwagen	Erdmann/Rossi	4.812.500	54	Bon	19-01-17
20	1965	FERRARI	Dino 206 S Berlinetta Speciale	Pininfarina	4.666.556	87	Art	10-02-17
21	1950	FERRARI	166 MM/212 Export "Uovo"	Fontana	4.500.000	152	RMS	18-08-17
22	1956	MASERATI	A6G/54 berlinetta	Zagato	4.400.000	27	G&Co	18-08-17
23	1935	ALFA ROMEO	Tipo B (P3)		4.180.680	161	RMS	08-02-17
24	1954	FERRARI	500/735 Mondial	Pinin Farina	3.850.000	252	RMS	19-08-17
25	1937	TALBOT-LAGO	T150 C SS Goutte d'Eau	Figoni/Falaschi	3.761.856	151	RMS	27-05-17
26	2014	FERRARI	LaFerrari	Ferrari Styling Center	3.740.000	465	Lea	22-04-17
27	1966	FERRARI	275 GTB	PF/Scaglietti	3.618.227*	602	RMS	25-11-16
28	1969	FERRARI	365 GTS	Pininfarina	3.602.500	263	RMS	20-01-17
29	1965	FERRARI	275 GTB	PF/Scaglietti	3.575.000	241	RMS	19-08-17
30	1970	PORSCHE	908/3		3.575.000	256	RMS	19-08-17
31	2015	FERRARI	LaFerrari	Ferrari Styling Center	3.520.000	54	G&Co	18-08-17
32	2014	FERRARI	LaFerrari	Ferrari Styling Center	3.450.000	S102	Mec	19-08-17
33	1930	BENTLEY	6½l Speed Six sportsman's saloon	Corsica	3.410.000	133	RMS	18-08-17
34	2015	FERRARI	LaFerrari	Ferrari Styling Center	3.410.000	227	RMS	19-08-17
35	1935	BUGATTI	Type 57 Atalante		3.385.670	136	RMS	27-05-17

No.	Year	Make	Model	Bodybuilder	Hammer price	Lot	Auction House	Date
36	1925	BUGATTI	Type 35		3.300.000	22	G&Co	20-01-17
37	1960	ASTON MARTIN	DB4 GT	Touring/Tickford	3.222.386	169	RMS	07-09-16
38	2004	MASERATI	MC12		3.203.021*	601	RMS	25-11-16
39	1954	FERRARI	500 Mondial		3.162.500	33	G&Co	18-08-17
40	1948	FERRARI	166 Spider Corsa	Scaglietti	3.146.609*	125	Art	10-02-17
41	1995	FERRARI	F50	Pininfarina	3.135.000	227	RMS	20-01-17
42	1966	FERRARI	275 GTB4	PF/Scaglietti	3.086.503	129	Coy	18-05-17
43	1961	FERRARI	400 Superamerica	Pininfarina	3.080.000	231	RMS	20-01-17
44	1965	FERRARI	275 GTB	PF/Scaglietti	3.080.000	16	Bon	18-08-17
45	1967	FERRARI	275 GTB4	PF/Scaglietti	3.025.000*	218	RMS	19-08-17
46	1965	FERRARI	500 Superfast	Pininfarina	2.915.000	126	G&Co	21-01-17
47	1931	ALFA ROMEO	6C 1750 GS spider	Zagato	2.805.000	30	Bon	19-01-17
48	1958	BMW	507 roadster		2.750.000	157	G&Co	19-08-17
49	1969	FERRARI	365 GTS	Pininfarina	2.722.500	245	RMS	19-08-17
50	2003	FERRARI	Enzo	Pininfarina	2.695.000	151	RMS	19-01-17
51	1995	FERRARI	F50	Pininfarina	2.640.000	218	RMS	11-03-17
52	1965	FERRARI	275 GTB	PF/Scaglietti	2.585.000	163	G&Co	19-08-17
53	1937	MERCEDES-BENZ	540 K cabriolet A		2.585.000*	257	RMS	19-08-17
54	1972	LAMBORGHINI	Miura SV	Bertone	2.538.630	75	Art	10-02-17
55	1967	FERRARI	275 GTB4	PF/Scaglietti	2.519.000	26	Bon	18-08-17
56	1935	BUGATTI	Type 57 Atalante		2.477.832	27	Art	10-02-17
57	1967	FERRARI	330 GTS	Pininfarina	2.475.000	220	RMS	20-01-17
58	1995	PORSCHE	GT2		2.472.994	132	RMS	07-09-16
59	2014	PAGANI	Huayra Tempesta coupé		2.420.000	229	RMS	19-08-17
60	1972	FERRARI	365 GTS4 Daytona spider	PF/Scaglietti	2.410.000	65	Bon	18-08-17
61	2015	McLAREN	P1		2.392.500*	26	G&Co	10-03-17
62	1956	MASERATI	A6G/54 coupé	Frua	2.365.000*	260	RMS	11-03-17
63	2015	BUGATTI	Veyron 16.4 Grand Sport Vitesse		2.350.000	S116	Mec	19-08-17
64	1964	PORSCHE	904 Carrera GTS		2.310.000	88	Bon	19-01-17
65	1973	FERRARI	365 GTS4 Daytona spider	PF/Scaglietti	2.299.374	145	RMS	08-02-17
66	1974	PORSCHE	Carrera RSR 3.0		2.296.172	176	Art	02-07-17
67	1993	PORSCHE	Carrera RSR 3.8		2.257.114	133	RMS	27-05-17
68	1952	FERRARI	342 America cabriolet	Vignale	2.255.000	142	RMS	18-08-17
69	1955	FERRARI	250 Europa GT	Pinin Farina	2.227.500	144	Bon	09-03-17
70	1935	ASTON MARTIN	Ulster		2.172.500	150	RMS	18-08-17
71	1972	FERRARI	365 GTS4 Daytona spider	PF/Scaglietti	2.172.500	234	RMS	19-08-17
72	1935	ASTON MARTIN	Ulster		2.151.765	339	Bon	09-02-17
73	1936	LANCIA	Astura 3ª serie cabriolet "Bocca"	Pinin Farina	2.145.000*	163	RMS	10-03-17
74	1966	FERRARI	275 GTB	PF/Scaglietti	2.117.500	256	RMS	20-01-17
75	1988	PORSCHE	959		2.090.340*	131	RMS	08-02-17
76	1930	DUESENBERG	Model J dual cowl phaeton	Murphy	2.090.000	253	RMS	07-10-16
77	2013	BUGATTI	Veyron 16.4 Super Sport 300		2.090.000	228	RMS	20-01-17
78	1965	FERRARI	275 GTB	PF/Scaglietti	2.060.478	157	RMS	08-02-17
79	2003	FERRARI	Enzo	Pininfarina	2.040.500	42	Bon	18-08-17
80	1965	FERRARI	275 GTS	PF/Scaglietti	2.006.323	143	RMS	27-05-17
81	1967	CHEVROLET	Corvette Sting Ray convertible		1.980.000	32	WoA	18-01-17
82	1964	FERRARI	275 GTB	PF/Scaglietti	1.842.500*	263	RMS	11-03-17
83	2015	PORSCHE	918 Spyder		1.842.500	230	RMS	19-08-17
84	1989	MAZDA	767B		1.750.000	23	G&Co	10-03-17
85	1966	FERRARI	275 GTB	PF/Scaglietti	1.732.500*	48	Bon	19-01-17
86	1960	FERRARI	250 GT cabriolet II serie	Pinin Farina	1.723.602	134	RMS	07-09-16
87	1936	TALBOT-LAGO	T150 C		1.711.779	30	Art	10-02-17
88	1966	ASTON MARTIN	Short Chassis Volante	Touring/Tickford	1.705.000*	139	RMS	10-03-17
89	1929	STUTZ	Model M Supercharged coupé	Lancefield	1.705.000	231	RMS	11-03-17

No.	Year	Make	Model	Bodybuilder	Hammer price	Lot	Auction House	Date
90	1966	FERRARI	275 GTS	PF/Scaglietti	1.700.000	14	G&Co	18-08-17
91	1956	BENTLEY	Continental S1 cabriolet	Park Ward	1.683.000*	123	RMS	10-03-17
92	1955	MERCEDES-BENZ	300 SL gullwing		1.677.500	18	G&Co	18-08-17
93	1961	FERRARI	250 GT cabriolet II serie	Pininfarina	1.651.931	123	Coy	18-05-17
94	2012	BUGATTI	Veyron 16.4 Grand Sport		1.650.000	276	RMS	11-03-17
95	2015	PORSCHE	918 Spyder		1.630.138	142	RMS	27-05-17
96	1964	FERRARI	250 GT/L	PF/Scaglietti	1.598.789	159	RMS	27-05-17
97	1932	ALFA ROMEO	6C 1750 GS roadster	Figoni	1.595.000	136	G&Co	21-01-17
98	1951	FERRARI	212 Inter coupé	Vignale	1.595.000	152	G&Co	19-08-17
99	1966	FERRARI	275 GTS	PF/Scaglietti	1.550.000	81	Bon	18-08-17
100	**1949**	**ASTON MARTIN**	**DB2 coupé**		**1.540.000**	**31**	**G&Co**	**10-03-17**
101	1993	PORSCHE	Turbo S 3.3 coupé		1.540.000	44	G&Co	10-03-17
102	1964	PORSCHE	904 Carrera GTS		1.540.000	129	G&Co	19-08-17
103	1991	FERRARI	F40	Pininfarina	1.540.000*	222	RMS	19-08-17
104	1936	MERCEDES-BENZ	500 K offener tourenwagen		1.540.000*	246	RMS	19-08-17
105	1939	BUGATTI	Type 57C cabriolet	Letourneur/Marchan	1.512.500	143	G&Co	19-08-17
106	2011	FERRARI	SA Aperta	Ferrari & PF	1.485.000	51	G&Co	20-01-17
107	1964	ASTON MARTIN	DB5 coupé	Touring/Tickford	1.485.000	1397	B/J	21-01-17
108	1990	FERRARI	F40	Pininfarina	1.485.000	29	G&Co	10-03-17
109	1953	FIAT	8V Elaborata	Zagato	1.485.000	149	G&Co	19-08-17
110	1957	MERCEDES-BENZ	300 SL gullwing		1.485.000	239	RMS	19-08-17
111	2015	PORSCHE	918 Spyder		1.475.000	S90	Mec	19-11-16
112	1955	MERCEDES-BENZ	300 SL gullwing		1.457.500	18	G&Co	20-01-17
113	1990	FERRARI	F40	Pininfarina	1.457.500	87	Bon	18-08-17
114	1996	PORSCHE	GT2 Evo		1.450.000	F192	Mec	20-05-17
115	1995	PORSCHE	Carrera Turbo cabriolet		1.433.376	150	RMS	08-02-17
116	1960	FERRARI	250 GT cabriolet II serie	Pinin Farina	1.430.000	74	Bon	19-01-17
117	1954	ASTON MARTIN	DB2/4 cabriolet	Bertone	1.430.000	168	G&Co	19-08-17
118	1929	DUESENBERG	Model J convertible coupé	Murphy	1.430.000	248	RMS	19-08-17
119	1939	BUGATTI	Type 57C Stelvio	Gangloff	1.417.092	64	Ose	18-06-17
120	1977	PORSCHE	934/5 Turbo		1.375.000	56	G&Co	10-03-17
121	1953	FIAT	8V Supersonic	Ghia	1.375.000*	122	RMS	10-03-17
122	1974	PORSCHE	Carrera RS 3.0		1.375.000*	262	RMS	11-03-17
123	1962	FERRARI	250 GT cabriolet II serie	Pininfarina	1.375.000	25	G&Co	18-08-17
124	1960	MERCEDES-BENZ	300 SL Roadster		1.375.000	251	RMS	19-08-17
125	1954	MERCEDES-BENZ	300 SL gullwing		1.358.500*	258	RMS	11-03-17
126	1948	TUCKER	Model 48 Torpedo		1.347.500	160	RMS	19-01-17
127	1952	BENTLEY	R Type Continental fastback	H.J.Mulliner	1.347.500*	152	RMS	10-03-17
128	1958	ROLLS-ROYCE	Silver Cloud "Honeymoon"	Freestone/Webb	1.347.500*	145	RMS	10-03-17
129	1957	MERCEDES-BENZ	300 SL Roadster		1.347.500	160	G&Co	19-08-17
130	2010	LAMBORGHINI	Reventón Roadster		1.340.475	127	Coy	08-09-16
131	2008	LAMBORGHINI	Reventón		1.320.000	138	RMS	19-01-17
132	1960	CHEVROLET	CERV I		1.320.000	1390	B/J	21-01-17
133	1955	LANCIA	Aurelia B24 spider	Pinin Farina	1.320.000*	261	RMS	11-03-17
134	2006	LAMBORGHINI	Concept S		1.320.000	233	RMS	19-08-17
135	1962	FERRARI	250 GT cabriolet II serie	Pininfarina	1.313.928	151	RMS	08-02-17
136	1993	PORSCHE	Turbo S 3.3 coupé		1.303.942	129	RMS	07-09-16
137	1933	CHRYSLER	Imperial CL dual-windshield	LeBaron	1.300.000	132	RMS	19-01-17
138	1955	LANCIA	Aurelia B24 spider	Pinin Farina	1.300.000	37	G&Co	10-03-17
139	1939	ALFA ROMEO	6C 2500 S cabriolet	Pinin Farina	1.273.966	147	RMS	07-09-16
140	1963	ASTON MARTIN	DB4 cabriolet	Touring/Tickford	1.273.966	153	RMS	07-09-16
141	1955	LANCIA	Aurelia B24 spider	Pinin Farina	1.265.000	54	Bon	18-08-17
142	1955	MERCEDES-BENZ	300 SL gullwing		1.265.000	116	G&Co	19-08-17

No.	Year	Make	Model	Bodybuilder	Hammer price	Lot	Auction House	Date
143	1958	MERCEDES-BENZ	300 SL Roadster		1.259.873*	62	Bon	21-05-17
144	1948	TALBOT-LAGO	T26 Lago GS cabriolet	Franay	1.253.952	132	RMS	27-05-17
145	2017	FERRARI	F12 TdF Berlinetta	Ferrari & PF	1.250.000	S79	Mec	19-08-17
146	1963	PORSCHE	356B 2000 GS Carrera 2 cabriolet	Reutter	1.250.000	134	G&Co	19-08-17
147	1953	LANCIA	Aurelia B52 PF200 C spider	Pinin Farina	1.248.500*	150	RMS	10-03-17
148	1933	ROLLS-ROYCE	Phantom II Newmarket permanent	Brewster	1.237.500*	125	RMS	10-03-17
149	1990	FERRARI	F40	Pininfarina	1.236.497	145	RMS	07-09-16
150	1987	PORSCHE	959		1.201.077	119	Art	10-02-17
151	1963	MERCEDES-BENZ	300 SL Roadster		1.200.000	557	AA	01-04-17
152	1957	PORSCHE	356A 1500 GS Carrera Speedster	Reutter	1.193.846	218	Bon	30-06-17
153	1990	FERRARI	F40	Pininfarina	1.191.254	161	RMS	27-05-17
154	1958	MERCEDES-BENZ	300 SL Roadster		1.173.913	449	Dor	15-10-16
155	1962	MERCEDES-BENZ	300 SL Roadster		1.164.776	226	Bon	30-06-17
156	1937	HORCH	853 Spezial Roadster		1.158.476	26	Bon	03-09-16
157	1925	BUGATTI	Type 35C		1.155.000	243	RMS	19-08-17
158	1953	FERRARI	250 Europa	Pinin Farina	1.155.000	1143	R&S	19-08-17
159	1964	LOTUS	34		1.150.000	82	Bon	18-08-17
160	1957	MERCEDES-BENZ	300 SL gullwing		1.144.000*	111	RMS	10-03-17
161	1957	BENTLEY	Continental S1 cabriolet	Park Ward	1.143.509	360	Bon	09-02-17
162	1956	FERRARI	250 GT	Boano	1.133.000	77	Bon	18-08-17
163	1961	MERCEDES-BENZ	300 SL Roadster		1.127.609	63	Art	10-02-17
164	1957	MERCEDES-BENZ	300 SL Roadster		1.111.000	144	WoA	22-04-17
165	1955	LANCIA	Aurelia B24 spider	Pinin Farina	1.100.000	58	WoA	18-01-17
166	1966	SHELBY AMERICAN	Cobra 427		1.100.000	157	RMS	19-01-17
167	1930	CADILLAC	Series 452 V-16 roadster	Fleetwood	1.100.000	230	RMS	20-01-17
168	1964	SHELBY AMERICAN	Cobra 289		1.100.000	14	G&Co	20-01-17
169	1928	BENTLEY	4½l tourer	Vanden Plas	1.100.000	121	G&Co	21-01-17
170	1965	ASTON MARTIN	DB5 Vantage coupé	Touring/Tickford	1.100.000	15	G&Co	10-03-17
171	1955	ALFA ROMEO	1900 C Sprint 2ª serie	Zagato	1.100.000*	257	RMS	11-03-17
172	1960	MERCEDES-BENZ	300 SL Roadster		1.100.000	213	RMS	24-06-17
173	1964	SHELBY AMERICAN	Cobra 289		1.100.000	154	RMS	18-08-17
174	1953	CUNNINGHAM	C-3 coupé	Vignale	1.100.000*	244	RMS	19-08-17
175	1992	FERRARI	F40	Pininfarina	1.091.400*	877	RMS	25-11-16
176	1988	PORSCHE	959		1.089.000	42	G&Co	20-01-17
177	1964	SHELBY AMERICAN	Cobra 289		1.089.000	24	Bon	18-08-17
178	1955	MERCEDES-BENZ	300 SL gullwing		1.087.019	350	Bon	09-02-17
179	1973	PORSCHE	911 Carrera RS 2.7		1.077.563	245	Bon	30-06-17
180	1988	PORSCHE	959		1.067.674*	875	RMS	25-11-16
181	1988	PORSCHE	959		1.056.000	46	G&Co	18-08-17
182	1957	MERCEDES-BENZ	300 SL Roadster		1.049.149	159	RMS	07-09-16
183	1965	ASTON MARTIN	DB5 coupé	Touring/Tickford	1.045.000	149	RMS	19-01-17
184	1961	MERCEDES-BENZ	300 SL Roadster		1.034.000	112	G&Co	21-01-17
185	1957	MERCEDES-BENZ	300 SL Roadster		1.034.000	19	G&Co	18-08-17
186	1976	LAMBORGHINI	Countach LP400	Bertone	1.034.000	261	RMS	19-08-17
187	1971	LAMBORGHINI	Miura S	Bertone	1.022.619	120	Coy	29-10-16
188	1939	BUGATTI	Type 57 cabriolet	Letourneur/Marchan	1.017.500	134	RMS	19-01-17
189	1936	AUBURN	8-852 SC boattail speedster		1.017.500	124	RMS	18-08-17
190	1964	MASERATI	5000 GT	Michelotti	1.017.500	117	RMS	18-08-17
191	1951	PORSCHE	356 coupé	Reutter	1.017.500	247	RMS	19-08-17
192	1931	BENTLEY	8l sedanca de ville	H.J.Mulliner	1.012.154	237	Bon	30-06-17
193	1955	MERCEDES-BENZ	300 SL gullwing		1.005.238*	203	Coy	08-04-17
194	1950	CISITALIA	Abarth 204A spyder sport	Motto	1.001.000	40	Mot	11-03-17
195	1937	MASERATI	6CM		1.000.000	136	G&Co	19-08-17

STATISTICS FOR MAKES AND COUNTRIES
(of the Top 100 year by year)

Makes	2016/17	15/16	14/15	13/14	12/13	11/12	10/11	09/10	08/09	07/08	06/07	05/06	04/05	03/04	02/03	01/02	00/01	99/00	98/99	97/98	96/97	95/96	94/95	93/94
Ferrari	48	45	52	48	33	37	37	25	31	33	22	21	25	22	19	26	31	45	28	17	26	21	11	6
Porsche	11	9	6	5	3	9	3	1	2	2	2	3	2	1	4	=	6	5	3	6	=	3	=	=
Aston Martin	7	4	4	5	3	3	5	8	=	3	5	1	2	3	5	1	1	2	1	3	1	3	2	3
Bugatti	7	3	2	4	3	2	3	6	10	2	6	3	2	6	4	7	7	4	4	7	6	9	3	3
Mercedes-Benz	5	4	4	7	9	10	8	8	4	10	5	6	9	11	17	13	7	7	8	12	11	11	8	12
Alfa Romeo	3	2	1	3	4	4	3	6	4	5	3	1	1	2	2	4	2	3	5	6	2	4	3	1
Maserati	3	3	2	3	5	=	3	1	1	2	3	3	5	5	3	5	8	4	4	1	6	5	5	=
Bentley	2	3	1	1	4	4	1	5	2	3	3	4	5	6	5	4	1	3	2	8	11	7	16	8
Jaguar	2	2	4	3	1	=	1	2	1	1	2	4	1	=	4	2	5	5	5	3	=	1	3	7
McLaren	2	3	3	2	=	=	1	=	1	=	1	=	=	1	1	=	=	2	2	2	=	=	=	=
Talbot-Lago	2	=	1	1	3	=	3	1	2	=	1	5	=	2	=	1	=	1	=	1	2	3	=	1
BMW	1	1	=	2	=	3	1	1	=	1	=	=	2	=	=	=	=	1	=	1	2	=	=	5
Chevrolet	1	1	=	3	=	=	1	1	3	1	=	5	1	=	=	=	=	1	=	1	=	=	=	=
Duesenberg	1	4	2	2	9	5	6	10	10	8	8	9	5	7	1	9	6	3	2	2	2	=	3	=
Lamborghini	1	3	4	1	1	1	7	1	1	2	=	=	=	1	1	=	=	=	1	2	1	=	=	=
Lancia	1	1	1	=	=	=	1	=	=	=	=	2	=	=	=	=	=	=	=	=	1	=	=	=
Mazda	1	=	=	=	=	=	=	=	=	=	=	=	=	=	=	=	=	=	=	=	=	=	=	=
Pagani	1	1	=	=	=	=	1	=	1	=	=	=	=	=	=	=	=	=	=	=	=	=	=	=
Stutz	1	=	=	=	1	=	=	1	=	=	=	1	1	1	=	1	=	=	=	3	=	=	=	=
Ford (USA)	=	3	=	3	5	=	1	=	2	2	=	4	2	2	5	2	=	1	5	4	=	=	=	=
Plymouth	=	2	1	1	1	=	1	=	=	1	4	=	=	=	=	=	=	=	=	=	=	=	=	=
Shelby American	=	2	3	=	4	1	1	4	4	1	5	9	5	=	1	1	1	1	4	3	=	3	3	1
Mercedes	=	1	=	=	=	1	=	=	1	=	1	1	1	=	1	1	1	=	=	=	1	=	=	=
Packard	=	1	3	=	=	=	3	1	=	2	6	2	2	2	=	3	2	1	3	1	1	=	1	1
Pierce-Arrow	=	1	=	=	=	1	=	=	=	=	=	=	2	=	=	2	=	=	=	=	=	1	=	=
Rolls-Royce	=	1	=	1	1	2	1	8	4	13	4	1	1	7	3	4	5	3	3	6	6	16	10	14
Cadillac	=	=	1	=	=	1	=	=	=	=	1	2	1	1	3	4	1	1	1	=	=	1	5	3
General Motors	=	=	1	=	=	=	=	=	=	=	=	1	=	=	=	=	=	=	=	=	=	=	=	=
Lagonda	=	=	1	=	1	=	=	1	1	=	=	=	1	=	3	=	1	=	=	=	1	=	3	1
OM	=	=	1	=	=	=	=	=	=	=	=	=	=	=	=	=	=	=	=	=	=	=	=	=
Pontiac	=	=	1	=	=	=	=	=	=	=	=	1	=	=	=	=	=	=	=	=	=	=	=	=
Talbot (GB)	=	=	1	=	=	=	=	=	=	=	=	=	=	=	=	=	=	=	=	=	=	=	=	=
Delahaye	=	=	2	1	=	3	1	=	=	4	=	=	1	=	1	1	2	1	1	2	=	2	5	=
Commer	=	=	=	1	=	=	=	=	=	=	=	=	=	=	=	=	=	=	=	=	=	=	=	=
Mercer	=	=	=	1	=	=	=	=	=	1	=	1	=	1	1	=	=	=	1	=	=	=	1	=
Tucker	=	=	=	1	=	2	1	=	1	=	=	=	1	=	1	=	=	=	=	=	=	=	=	=
Chrysler	=	=	=	=	1	1	1	1	=	=	=	3	3	3	=	=	1	1	=	=	2	=	2	=
Daimler	=	=	=	=	1	1	=	=	1	=	=	=	=	=	=	=	=	=	=	=	=	=	=	=
FIAT	=	=	=	=	1	2	1	=	=	=	=	=	=	=	=	=	=	=	=	=	=	1	=	=
Horch	=	=	=	=	1	=	=	=	1	=	=	=	=	2	=	=	=	=	=	=	=	=	=	3
Isotta Fraschini	=	=	=	=	1	1	=	=	2	=	1	=	=	=	1	1	=	=	=	1	=	=	1	2
Lincoln	=	=	=	=	1	=	=	=	=	=	1	1	=	=	=	=	=	1	=	1	=	=	1	1
Maybach	=	=	=	=	1	=	=	=	=	=	=	=	=	=	=	=	=	=	1	=	=	=	=	=
Simplex	=	=	=	=	1	=	=	=	=	=	1	=	1	=	2	=	1	=	=	=	=	=	=	=
Austin Healey	=	=	=	=	=	1	=	=	=	=	=	=	=	1	=	=	=	=	=	=	=	=	=	=
Cord	=	=	=	=	=	1	=	1	=	1	=	=	=	1	=	=	=	=	=	=	1	=	=	=
De Dion-Bouton	=	=	=	=	=	1	=	=	=	1	=	=	=	=	=	=	=	=	=	=	=	=	=	=
DeSoto	=	=	=	=	=	1	=	=	=	=	=	=	=	=	=	=	=	=	=	=	=	=	=	=
Itala	=	=	=	=	=	1	=	=	=	=	=	=	=	=	=	=	=	=	=	=	=	=	=	=
Miller	=	=	=	=	=	1	=	=	=	1	=	=	1	=	=	=	=	=	=	=	=	=	=	=
Oldsmobile	=	=	=	=	=	1	=	=	=	1	=	1	=	1	=	=	1	=	=	=	=	=	=	=
Peugeot	=	=	=	=	=	1	1	1	=	1	=	1	=	=	=	=	1	=	1	=	=	=	=	=
SIATA	=	=	=	=	=	1	=	=	=	=	=	1	=	=	=	=	=	=	=	=	=	=	=	=
SS	=	=	=	=	=	=	1	=	=	=	=	=	=	=	=	=	=	=	=	=	2	3	1	1
Hispano-Suiza	=	=	=	=	=	=	2	1	=	2	1	1	=	=	=	=	=	=	=	2	1	1	=	4
Voisin	=	=	=	=	=	=	2	=	=	=	=	=	=	=	=	=	=	=	=	=	=	=	=	=
Delage	=	=	=	=	=	=	1	1	2	=	=	1	=	1	=	=	1	=	=	=	=	=	2	2
Dodge	=	=	=	=	=	=	1	1	1	2	1	=	=	=	=	=	=	=	=	=	=	=	=	=
Lister	=	=	=	=	=	=	1	=	=	=	=	1	=	=	1	1	=	=	=	=	1	1	=	=
Lotus	=	=	=	=	=	=	1	=	1	=	=	=	=	=	=	=	=	1	2	=	=	1	=	=
Matra	=	=	=	=	=	=	1	=	=	=	=	=	3	=	=	=	=	1	1	1	=	=	=	=
Rambler	=	=	=	=	=	=	1	=	=	=	=	=	=	=	=	=	=	=	=	=	=	=	=	=
Sunbeam	=	=	=	=	=	=	1	=	=	=	=	1	=	=	=	=	=	=	=	=	=	=	=	=
Thomas	=	=	=	=	=	=	1	=	=	=	=	=	=	=	=	=	=	=	=	=	=	=	=	=
Marmon	=	=	=	=	=	=	=	1	=	=	1	=	=	=	=	=	=	=	=	=	=	=	=	=
Reo	=	=	=	=	=	=	=	1	=	=	=	=	=	=	=	=	=	=	=	=	=	=	=	=
American Napier	=	=	=	=	=	=	=	=	1	=	=	=	=	=	=	=	=	=	=	=	=	=	=	=
Cooper	=	=	=	=	=	=	=	=	1	=	=	=	=	1	=	=	=	=	=	1	=	1	=	=

Makes	2016/17	15/16	14/15	13/14	12/13	11/12	10/11	09/10	08/09	07/08	06/07	05/06	04/05	03/04	02/03	01/02	00/01	99/00	98/99	97/98	96/97	95/96	94/95	93/94
Hummer												1	=	=	=	=	=	=	=	=	=	=	=	=
Kurtis												1	=	=	=	=	=	=	=	=	=	=	=	=
Lozier												1	=	=	=	=	1	=	=	=	=	=	=	=
Panhard et Levassor												1	=	=	=	=	1	=	=	=	=	=	=	=
Pope-Hartford												1	=	=	=	=	1	=	=	=	=	=	=	=
Renault												1	=	=	=	=	=	=	=	=	=	=	=	=
Chaparral											1	1	=	=	=	=	=	=	=	=	=	=	=	=
Auburn												2	=	=	1	=	=	=	=	=	=	=	1	1
OSCA												2	=	=	1	=	=	=	=	=	=	=	=	=
Bizzarrini												1	1	=	=	1	=	1	=	=	=	=	=	=
Buick												1	=	=	=	=	=	=	=	=	=	=	1	=
Farman												1	=	=	=	=	=	=	=	=	=	=	=	=
Invicta												1	1	=	=	1	2	1	2	1	1	=	=	=
American Underslung												1	=	=	=	=	=	=	=	=	=	=	=	=
Austro Daimler												1	=	=	=	=	=	=	=	=	=	=	=	=
Porsche-Kremer												1	=	=	=	=	=	=	=	=	=	=	=	=
Mors													2	=	=	=	2	=	=	=	=	=	=	=
Abarth													1	=	=	=	=	=	=	=	=	=	=	=
Alco													1	=	=	=	=	=	=	=	=	=	=	=
Benz													1	=	=	=	=	=	=	=	=	=	=	=
Charron													1	=	=	=	=	=	=	=	=	=	=	=
Eagle													1	=	=	=	=	=	=	=	=	=	=	=
Martini													1	=	=	=	=	=	=	=	=	=	=	=
Nardi Danese													1	=	=	=	=	=	=	=	=	=	=	=
Ghia														2	=	=	=	=	=	=	=	=	=	=
ERA														1	=	=	1	=	=	=	=	=	=	=
Mercury														1	=	=	=	=	=	=	=	=	=	=
Prost														1	=	=	=	=	=	=	=	=	=	=
Saleen														1	=	=	=	=	=	=	=	=	=	=
Watson														1	=	=	=	=	=	=	=	=	=	=
Frazer-Nash															1	=	1	=	=	1	1	2		
BRM																1	=	=	=	=	1	1		
Du Pont																3	=	=	=	=	=	=		
HWM																1	=	1	=	=	=	=		
Lola																1	1	=	=	=	=	=		
MG																1	=	1	=	=	=	=		
Vanwall																1	=	=	=	=	=	=		
Minerva																	1	=	=	=	=	=		
Tyrrell																	1	=	=	=	=	=		
Connaught																		1	=	=	=	=		
Gordini																		1	=	=	=	=		
Stevens-Duryea																		1	=	=	=	=		
Vauxhall																			3	1	=			
Spyker																			1	=	=			
Cisitalia																				1	=			
Columbia																				1	=			
Locomobile																				1	1			
Rochette																				1	=			
Amilcar																					2			
Alphi																					1			
Audi																					1			
Chenard-Walcker																					1			
Darracq																					1			
De Dietrich																					1			
Guyot																					1			
Star																					1			
Wanderer																					1			

Countries	2016/17	15/16	14/15	13/14	12/13	11/12	10/11	09/10	08/09	07/08	06/07	05/06	04/05	03/04	02/03	01/02	00/01	99/00	98/99	97/98	96/97	95/96	94/95	93/94
Italy	57	55	61	55	45	47	53	33	40	42	28	26	36	32	27	39	43	52	38	26	37	32	22	11
Germany	17	15	10	14	14	23	12	10	8	13	8	10	14	13	25	14	14	13	11	20	14	14	8	22
Great Britain	13	13	14	11	11	11	10	25	12	20	17	19	17	21	23	14	17	19	25	34	26	38	43	39
France	9	3	3	9	7	4	10	14	15	5	15	11	8	10	8	11	8	9	9	11	13	13	9	22
USA	3	14	12	11	23	15	15	18	25	20	32	34	25	23	16	22	18	7	17	8	10	2	18	6
Japan	1	=	=	=	=	=	=	=	=	=	=	=	=	=	=	=	=	=	=	=	=	=	=	=
Austria															1	=	=	=	=	=	=	=	=	=
Switzerland																1	=	=	=	=	=	=	=	=
Belgium																				1	=	=	=	=
Holland																						1	=	=

STATISTICS FOR MAKE FROM 1993-1994
(NUMBER OF CARS OFFERED AND SOLD, PERCENTAGES, TURNOVER AND AVERAGE VALUE)

ALFA ROMEO

Season	Cars offered	Cars sold	% Sale	Total US$	% Turn.	Avg value US$
1993-1994	47	11	23%	146.002	0,55%	13.273
1994-1995	57	29	51%	2.926.035	5,80%	100.898
1995-1996	46	33	72%	2.839.923	5,30%	86.058
1996-1997	51	29	57%	1.922.844	2,60%	66.305
1997-1998	123	80	65%	6.400.059	7,99%	80.001
1998-1999	81	48	59%	7.849.035	6,24%	163.522
1999-2000	84	48	57%	8.868.686	5,50%	184.764
2000-2001	83	45	54%	2.765.741	2,36%	61.461
2001-2002	63	31	49%	4.749.422	3,59%	153.207
2002-2003	52	32	62%	2.103.152	1,55%	65.724
2003-2004	48	29	60%	1.842.324	1,22%	63.528
2004-2005	61	40	66%	5.682.657	2,55%	142.066
2005-2006	81	46	57%	2.796.365	0,94%	60.791
2006-2007	67	43	64%	8.204.221	1,87%	190.796
2007-2008	62	35	56%	12.979.053	2,79%	370.830
2008-2009	78	34	44%	8.686.567	2,13%	255.487
2009-2010	72	42	58%	14.078.349	3,07%	335.199
2010-2011	72	47	65%	7.533.676	1,44%	160.291
2011-2012	88	57	65%	14.050.533	2,04%	246.501
2012-2013	122	86	70%	19.595.264	2,39%	227.852
2013-2014	188	152	81%	39.852.877	3,42%	262.190
2014-2015	135	97	72%	13.847.387	1,13%	142.757
2015-2016	168	117	70%	45.351.396	3,75%	387.619
2016-2017	179	135	75%	25.654.621	2,36%	190.034

ASTON MARTIN

Season	Cars offered	Cars sold	% Sale	Total US$	% Turn.	Avg value US$
1993-1994	76	26	34%	1.008.312	3,78%	38.781
1994-1995	48	27	56%	1.419.125	2,81%	52.560
1995-1996	80	44	55%	2.419.300	4,52%	54.984
1996-1997	82	54	66%	2.881.315	3,89%	53.358
1997-1998	101	55	54%	4.460.571	5,57%	81.101
1998-1999	71	45	63%	3.171.074	2,52%	70.468
1999-2000	115	80	70%	5.200.996	3,22%	65.012
2000-2001	118	64	54%	3.948.280	3,37%	61.692
2001-2002	130	84	65%	5.445.380	4,12%	64.826
2002-2003	88	54	61%	4.699.984	3,47%	87.037
2003-2004	92	59	64%	7.135.904	4,73%	120.948
2004-2005	123	89	72%	11.819.575	5,30%	132.804
2005-2006	94	60	64%	10.259.578	3,45%	170.993
2006-2007	107	75	70%	14.713.859	3,35%	196.185
2007-2008	98	72	73%	16.803.400	3,62%	233.381
2008-2009	139	100	72%	16.613.555	4,07%	166.136
2009-2010	176	129	73%	26.121.774	5,70%	202.494
2010-2011	235	175	74%	40.993.426	7,86%	234.248
2011-2012	188	131	70%	37.020.628	5,37%	282.600
2012-2013	161	124	77%	38.263.820	4,66%	308.579
2013-2014	165	138	84%	58.530.422	5,03%	424.133
2014-2015	188	145	77%	60.929.969	4,96%	420.207
2015-2016	187	131	70%	56.968.873	4,70%	434.877
2016-2017	223	159	71%	85.136.385	7,84%	535.449

BENTLEY

Season	Cars offered	Cars sold	% Sale	Total US$	% Turn.	Avg value US$
1993-1994	85	44	52%	3.082.572	11,55%	70.058
1994-1995	100	57	57%	5.440.384	10,78%	95.445
1995-1996	121	69	57%	3.783.230	7,07%	54.829
1996-1997	124	84	68%	6.275.445	8,47%	74.708
1997-1998	110	58	53%	5.216.491	6,51%	89.940
1998-1999	118	68	58%	3.984.259	3,17%	58.592
1999-2000	103	61	59%	3.985.014	2,47%	65.328
2000-2001	127	74	58%	4.615.602	3,94%	62.373
2001-2002	94	56	60%	4.118.799	3,11%	73.550
2002-2003	149	86	58%	6.367.080	4,70%	74.036
2003-2004	101	63	62%	12.483.773	8,27%	198.155
2004-2005	117	82	70%	7.384.094	3,31%	90.050
2005-2006	98	67	68%	13.278.631	4,47%	198.189
2006-2007	86	60	70%	12.963.436	2,95%	216.057
2007-2008	80	52	65%	12.488.352	2,69%	240.161
2008-2009	119	84	71%	10.589.499	2,59%	126.065
2009-2010	158	116	73%	12.678.371	2,77%	109.296
2010-2011	165	93	56%	19.067.235	3,65%	205.024
2011-2012	184	129	70%	42.734.606	6,19%	331.276
2012-2013	144	105	73%	27.703.352	3,38%	263.841
2013-2014	143	94	66%	18.579.097	1,60%	197.650
2014-2015	137	91	66%	24.969.541	2,03%	274.391
2015-2016	150	105	70%	26.043.521	2,15%	248.034
2016-2017	143	106	74%	24.688.170	2,27%	232.907

BUGATTI

Season	Cars offered	Cars sold	% Sale	Total US$	% Turn.	Avg value US$
1993-1994	9	5	56%	452.027	1,69%	90.405
1994-1995	13	7	54%	968.779	1,92%	138.397
1995-1996	20	12	60%	2.126.224	3,97%	177.185
1996-1997	19	12	63%	2.395.408	3,23%	199.617
1997-1998	19	14	74%	2.483.931	3,10%	177.424
1998-1999	23	13	57%	3.893.666	3,10%	299.513
1999-2000	28	13	46%	3.620.530	2,24%	278.502
2000-2001	27	19	70%	7.766.789	6,63%	408.778
2001-2002	27	12	44%	3.708.893	2,80%	309.074
2002-2003	24	8	33%	4.515.102	3,33%	564.388
2003-2004	16	7	44%	4.350.427	2,88%	621.490
2004-2005	14	8	57%	5.154.382	2,31%	644.298
2005-2006	17	12	71%	8.990.195	3,03%	749.183
2006-2007	17	14	82%	7.376.359	1,68%	526.883
2007-2008	43	29	67%	29.328.333	6,31%	1.011.322
2008-2009	31	18	58%	13.977.189	3,42%	776.511
2009-2010	21	15	71%	7.546.605	1,65%	503.107
2010-2011	23	20	87%	11.716.884	2,25%	585.844
2011-2012	23	15	65%	8.535.341	1,24%	569.023
2012-2013	31	26	84%	27.177.485	3,31%	1.045.288
2013-2014	23	19	83%	20.681.615	1,78%	1.088.506
2014-2015	23	18	78%	16.542.095	1,35%	919.005
2015-2016	27	18	67%	35.369.469	2,92%	1.964.971
2016-2017	33	24	73%	32.995.055	3,04%	1.374.794

CHEVROLET

Season	Cars offered	Cars sold	% Sale	Total US$	% Turn.	Avg value US$
1993-1994	11	6	55%	80.349	0,30%	13.392
1994-1995	15	13	87%	201.662	0,40%	15.512
1995-1996	13	10	77%	207.087	0,39%	20.709
1996-1997	19	14	74%	478.400	0,65%	34.171
1997-1998	12	7	58%	304.307	0,38%	43.472
1998-1999	28	19	68%	939.587	0,75%	49.452
1999-2000	48	32	67%	2.289.562	1,42%	71.549
2000-2001	45	36	80%	1.415.971	1,21%	39.333
2001-2002	56	39	70%	2.516.493	1,90%	64.525
2002-2003	111	91	82%	3.883.260	2,87%	42.673
2003-2004	82	57	70%	4.646.966	3,08%	81.526
2004-2005	52	38	73%	4.102.450	1,84%	107.959
2005-2006	107	91	85%	14.827.488	4,99%	162.939
2006-2007	117	91	78%	12.572.283	2,86%	138.157
2007-2008	70	50	71%	10.551.819	2,27%	211.036
2008-2009	234	187	80%	21.990.297	5,39%	117.595
2009-2010	157	120	76%	12.696.077	2,77%	105.801
2010-2011	152	122	80%	14.544.568	2,79%	119.218
2011-2012	121	88	73%	11.522.448	1,67%	130.937
2012-2013	133	105	79%	16.329.278	1,99%	155.517
2013-2014	149	118	79%	32.776.758	2,81%	277.769
2014-2015	185	151	82%	23.264.275	1,89%	154.068
2015-2016	176	144	82%	22.128.966	1,83%	153.673
2016-2017	180	144	80%	21.281.808	1,96%	147.790

FERRARI

Season	Cars offered	Cars sold	% Sale	Total US$	% Turn.	Avg value US$
1993-1994	65	14	22%	876.118	3,28%	62.580
1994-1995	79	46	58%	4.554.304	9,03%	99.007
1995-1996	100	63	63%	8.328.518	15,55%	132.199
1996-1997	144	87	60%	14.758.354	19,92%	169.636
1997-1998	133	76	57%	8.528.812	10,65%	112.221
1998-1999	226	136	60%	31.914.731	25,38%	234.667
1999-2000	277	199	72%	52.233.656	32,37%	262.481
2000-2001	253	158	62%	29.476.643	25,16%	186.561
2001-2002	253	149	59%	29.998.519	22,68%	201.332
2002-2003	250	138	55%	19.026.366	14,04%	137.872
2003-2004	263	175	67%	30.335.209	20,11%	173.344
2004-2005	232	129	56%	41.400.760	18,57%	320.936
2005-2006	250	156	62%	43.155.315	14,53%	276.637
2006-2007	261	165	63%	94.917.161	21,60%	575.256
2007-2008	315	206	65%	114.997.709	24,74%	558.241
2008-2009	304	189	62%	80.515.862	19,73%	426.010
2009-2010	248	179	72%	93.695.185	20,44%	523.437
2010-2011	287	185	64%	116.180.316	22,27%	628.002
2011-2012	278	207	74%	152.242.948	22,06%	735.473
2012-2013	333	253	76%	225.038.835	27,43%	889.482
2013-2014	420	333	79%	388.052.856	33,32%	1.165.324
2014-2015	576	451	78%	416.878.614	33,92%	924.343
2015-2016	812	486	60%	366.151.396	30,24%	753.398
2016-2017	818	528	65%	271.761.028	25,03%	514.699

FORD

Season	Cars offered	Cars sold	% Sale	Total US$	% Turn.	Avg value US$
1993-1994	34	19	56%	285.328	1,07%	15.017
1994-1995	41	30	73%	634.391	1,26%	21.146
1995-1996	24	17	71%	210.810	0,39%	12.401
1996-1997	25	16	64%	942.824	1,27%	58.927
1997-1998	38	28	74%	1.296.468	1,62%	46.302
1998-1999	53	39	74%	2.865.967	2,28%	73.486
1999-2000	46	30	65%	1.371.297	0,85%	45.710
2000-2001	49	39	80%	1.248.584	1,07%	32.015
2001-2002	70	56	80%	3.562.602	2,69%	63.618
2002-2003	89	66	74%	4.412.631	3,26%	66.858
2003-2004	55	41	75%	1.980.531	1,31%	48.306
2004-2005	77	57	74%	6.585.867	2,95%	115.542
2005-2006	128	109	85%	14.585.799	4,91%	133.815
2006-2007	129	114	88%	14.726.738	3,35%	129.182
2007-2008	92	75	82%	11.339.053	2,44%	151.187
2008-2009	230	199	87%	20.757.195	5,09%	104.308
2009-2010	177	137	77%	14.176.505	3,09%	103.478
2010-2011	172	143	83%	10.853.345	2,08%	75.898
2011-2012	200	158	79%	37.109.379	5,38%	234.869
2012-2013	166	125	75%	15.904.304	1,94%	127.234
2013-2014	151	128	85%	35.624.357	3,06%	278.315
2014-2015	258	230	89%	34.214.916	2,78%	148.761
2015-2016	230	184	80%	40.933.380	3,38%	222.464
2016-2017	202	178	88%	27.851.435	2,57%	156.469

JAGUAR

Season	Cars offered	Cars sold	% Sale	Total US$	% Turn.	Avg value US$
1993-1994	134	60	45%	2.142.185	8,03%	35.703
1994-1995	147	80	54%	2.428.611	4,81%	30.358
1995-1996	143	89	62%	2.582.455	4,82%	29.016
1996-1997	188	127	68%	5.046.269	6,81%	39.734
1997-1998	156	94	60%	4.496.584	5,61%	47.836
1998-1999	164	111	68%	7.566.548	6,02%	68.167
1999-2000	153	113	74%	10.222.156	6,33%	90.462
2000-2001	239	163	68%	6.921.557	5,91%	42.464
2001-2002	239	157	66%	9.071.743	6,86%	57.782
2002-2003	264	150	57%	9.950.638	7,34%	66.338
2003-2004	212	134	63%	6.418.753	4,25%	47.901
2004-2005	210	144	69%	13.106.030	5,88%	91.014
2005-2006	231	150	65%	14.530.452	4,89%	96.870
2006-2007	196	138	70%	10.397.184	2,37%	75.342
2007-2008	153	106	69%	17.279.213	3,72%	163.011
2008-2009	238	172	72%	14.074.286	3,45%	81.827
2009-2010	280	188	67%	19.167.672	4,18%	101.956
2010-2011	306	179	58%	14.840.791	2,84%	82.909
2011-2012	377	241	64%	21.926.146	3,18%	90.980
2012-2013	315	201	64%	22.089.768	2,69%	109.899
2013-2014	392	284	72%	46.168.134	3,96%	162.564
2014-2015	374	301	80%	59.959.346	4,88%	199.200
2015-2016	328	242	74%	62.462.142	5,16%	258.108
2016-2017	353	283	80%	47.717.421	4,40%	168.613

LAMBORGHINI

Season	Cars offered	Cars sold	% Sale	Total US$	% Turn.	Avg value US$
1993-1994	9	3	33%	98.656	0,37%	32.885
1994-1995	15	9	60%	403.488	0,80%	44.832
1995-1996	19	13	68%	922.034	1,72%	70.926
1996-1997	29	13	45%	1.483.928	2,00%	114.148
1997-1998	33	14	42%	997.056	1,25%	71.218
1998-1999	28	17	61%	1.117.927	0,89%	65.760
1999-2000	47	21	45%	1.356.657	0,84%	64.603
2000-2001	32	12	38%	472.639	0,40%	39.387
2001-2002	28	18	64%	1.549.683	1,17%	86.094
2002-2003	36	25	69%	2.132.468	1,57%	85.299
2003-2004	20	10	50%	849.928	0,56%	84.993
2004-2005	19	13	68%	845.992	0,38%	65.076
2005-2006	34	22	65%	2.905.002	0,98%	132.046
2006-2007	26	19	73%	4.478.726	1,02%	235.722
2007-2008	36	28	78%	7.651.470	1,65%	273.267
2008-2009	50	26	52%	4.665.931	1,14%	179.459
2009-2010	46	31	67%	6.753.446	1,47%	217.853
2010-2011	41	32	78%	13.047.522	2,50%	407.735
2011-2012	36	19	53%	6.296.807	0,91%	331.411
2012-2013	53	39	74%	12.633.136	1,54%	323.927
2013-2014	57	49	86%	25.273.514	2,17%	515.786
2014-2015	91	73	80%	33.378.527	2,72%	457.240
2015-2016	110	57	52%	23.367.262	1,93%	409.952
2016-2017	120	111	93%	24.093.222	2,22%	217.056

LANCIA

Season	Cars offered	sold	% Sale	Total US$	% Turn.	Avg value US$
1993-1994	24	14	58%	300.251	2,61%	21.447
1994-1995	33	21	64%	387.368	1,45%	18.446
1995-1996	37	22	59%	1.030.719	2,04%	46.851
1996-1997	40	22	55%	565.908	1,06%	25.723
1997-1998	50	26	52%	696.408	0,94%	26.785
1998-1999	36	17	47%	710.237	0,89%	41.779
1999-2000	65	43	66%	1.115.289	0,89%	25.937
2000-2001	41	24	59%	585.608	0,36%	24.400
2001-2002	31	18	58%	641.234	0,55%	35.624
2002-2003	27	17	63%	389.496	0,29%	22.912
2003-2004	22	13	59%	731.787	0,54%	56.291
2004-2005	43	35	81%	3.824.863	2,54%	109.282
2005-2006	44	22	50%	1.513.498	0,68%	68.795
2006-2007	40	27	68%	3.021.632	1,02%	111.912
2007-2008	51	26	51%	3.579.192	0,81%	137.661
2008-2009	53	31	58%	3.381.041	0,73%	109.066
2009-2010	53	30	57%	2.650.499	0,65%	88.350
2010-2011	43	17	40%	3.131.467	0,68%	184.204
2011-2012	65	42	65%	5.381.372	1,03%	128.128
2012-2013	59	46	78%	10.685.462	1,55%	232.293
2013-2014	101	66	65%	16.696.856	2,03%	252.983
2014-2015	80	56	70%	10.099.659	0,87%	180.351
2015-2016	102	68	67%	11.169.208	0,91%	164.253
2016-2017	118	95	81%	21.624.628	1,99%	227.628

MASERATI

Season	Cars offered	sold	% Sale	Total US$	% Turn.	Avg value US$
1993-1994	28	11	39%	203.643	0,76%	18.513
1994-1995	34	26	76%	2.298.227	4,56%	88.393
1995-1996	33	23	70%	2.196.980	4,10%	95.521
1996-1997	44	33	75%	3.633.429	4,90%	110.104
1997-1998	48	25	52%	2.278.829	2,85%	91.153
1998-1999	56	29	52%	3.979.110	3,16%	137.211
1999-2000	49	33	67%	5.483.546	3,40%	166.168
2000-2001	81	55	68%	5.352.932	4,57%	97.326
2001-2002	51	32	63%	3.215.069	2,43%	100.471
2002-2003	76	48	63%	3.962.999	2,92%	82.562
2003-2004	46	32	70%	2.700.539	1,79%	84.392
2004-2005	48	25	52%	5.332.416	2,39%	213.297
2005-2006	53	34	64%	7.831.878	2,64%	230.349
2006-2007	50	37	74%	7.875.414	1,79%	212.849
2007-2008	56	36	64%	6.355.611	1,37%	176.545
2008-2009	75	44	59%	5.132.233	1,26%	116.642
2009-2010	59	35	59%	10.832.616	2,36%	309.503
2010-2011	49	29	59%	3.716.910	0,71%	128.169
2011-2012	70	45	64%	10.359.009	1,50%	230.200
2012-2013	67	42	63%	23.050.704	2,81%	548.826
2013-2014	79	62	78%	25.876.341	2,22%	417.360
2014-2015	88	76	86%	26.629.444	2,17%	350.387
2015-2016	155	112	72%	35.369.745	2,92%	315.801
2016-2017	128	89	70%	28.834.981	7,25%	323.989

MERCEDES BENZ

Season	Cars offered	sold	% Sale	Total US$	% Turn.	Avg value US$
1993-1994	73	33	45%	1.487.778	5,57%	45.084
1994-1995	87	51	59%	2.118.601	4,20%	41.541
1995-1996	109	61	56%	4.060.725	7,58%	66.569
1996-1997	129	94	73%	5.172.707	6,98%	55.029
1997-1998	96	54	56%	3.607.195	4,50%	66.800
1998-1999	147	101	69%	11.776.653	9,37%	116.601
1999-2000	154	104	68%	10.696.867	6,63%	102.854
2000-2001	126	94	75%	10.763.394	9,19%	114.504
2001-2002	144	97	67%	14.213.631	10,75%	146.532
2002-2003	195	123	63%	19.222.539	14,19%	156.281
2003-2004	117	78	67%	8.485.603	5,62%	108.790
2004-2005	140	95	68%	22.526.510	10,10%	237.121
2005-2006	138	104	75%	22.841.443	7,69%	219.629
2006-2007	100	74	74%	18.741.995	4,26%	253.270
2007-2008	115	85	74%	42.904.160	9,23%	504.755
2008-2009	106	79	75%	13.230.515	3,24%	167.475
2009-2010	201	144	72%	32.453.536	7,08%	225.372
2010-2011	211	152	72%	59.079.547	11,32%	388.681
2011-2012	220	153	70%	57.454.250	8,33%	375.518
2012-2013	213	171	80%	102.083.509	12,44%	596.980
2013-2014	367	293	80%	102.753.424	8,82%	350.694
2014-2015	307	235	77%	86.143.173	7,01%	366.567
2015-2016	355	259	73%	77.105.895	6,37%	297.706
2016-2017	315	249	79%	78.698.702	7,25%	316.059

PORSCHE

Season	Cars offered	sold	% Sale	Total US$	% Turn.	Avg value US$
1993-1994	28	12	43%	249.320	0,93%	20.777
1994-1995	28	13	46%	323.341	0,64%	24.872
1995-1996	32	23	72%	1.262.196	2,36%	54.878
1996-1997	22	16	73%	385.380	0,52%	24.086
1997-1998	55	40	73%	4.805.674	6,00%	120.142
1998-1999	74	49	66%	4.641.709	3,69%	94.729
1999-2000	81	53	65%	5.318.587	3,30%	100.351
2000-2001	84	53	63%	2.753.513	2,35%	51.953
2001-2002	82	41	50%	2.005.539	1,52%	48.916
2002-2003	89	56	63%	3.953.332	2,92%	70.595
2003-2004	88	52	59%	4.129.879	2,74%	79.421
2004-2005	77	44	57%	6.263.538	2,81%	142.353
2005-2006	128	90	70%	8.328.277	2,80%	92.536
2006-2007	119	80	67%	10.926.743	2,49%	136.584
2007-2008	93	60	65%	10.477.940	2,25%	174.632
2008-2009	123	70	57%	7.731.738	1,89%	110.453
2009-2010	153	95	62%	16.048.908	3,50%	168.936
2010-2011	157	90	57%	15.353.831	2,94%	170.598
2011-2012	283	180	64%	51.855.843	7,52%	288.088
2012-2013	229	165	72%	36.650.662	4,47%	222.125
2013-2014	261	193	74%	59.306.282	5,09%	307.286
2014-2015	404	306	76%	106.029.499	8,63%	346.502
2015-2016	538	355	66%	109.789.960	9,07%	309.267
2016-2017	344	492	143%	159.721.743	14,71%	324.638

ROLLS-ROYCE

Season	Cars offered	sold	% Sale	Total US$	% Turn.	Avg value US$
1993-1994	131	66	50%	2.819.764	10,57%	42.724
1994-1995	123	78	63%	7.130.221	14,13%	91.413
1995-1996	155	97	63%	4.991.771	9,32%	51.462
1996-1997	197	115	58%	5.545.837	7,49%	48.225
1997-1998	134	70	52%	4.877.119	6,09%	69.673
1998-1999	160	105	66%	6.931.916	5,51%	66.018
1999-2000	135	82	61%	5.179.341	3,21%	63.163
2000-2001	144	101	70%	6.801.376	5,81%	67.340
2001-2002	159	101	64%	7.003.406	5,30%	69.341
2002-2003	181	111	61%	6.651.513	4,91%	59.924
2003-2004	177	135	76%	9.823.837	6,51%	72.769
2004-2005	121	74	61%	4.292.507	1,93%	58.007
2005-2006	143	97	68%	8.528.181	2,87%	87.919
2006-2007	148	105	71%	29.202.051	6,65%	278.115
2007-2008	109	81	74%	23.734.878	5,11%	293.023
2008-2009	174	119	68%	14.062.161	3,45%	118.169
2009-2010	192	134	70%	23.238.337	5,07%	173.420
2010-2011	218	133	61%	19.931.432	3,82%	149.860
2011-2012	205	125	61%	27.196.237	3,94%	217.570
2012-2013	175	111	63%	19.634.010	2,39%	176.883
2013-2014	248	173	70%	28.094.975	2,41%	162.399
2014-2015	177	130	73%	19.327.965	1,57%	148.677
2015-2016	177	118	67%	21.343.759	1,76%	180.879
2016-2017	157	111	71%	21.107.360	1,94%	190.156

TOTAL MARKET

Season	Cars offered	sold	% Sale	Total US$	% Turn.	Avg value US$
1993-1994	1521	775	51%	26.688.102	-	34.436
1994-1995	1677	1077	64%	50.452.574	-	46.845
1995-1996	1734	1114	64%	53.543.789	-	48.064
1996-1997	2083	1378	66%	74.091.707	-	53.768
1997-1998	2044	1230	60%	80.081.651	-	65.107
1998-1999	2193	1419	65%	125.725.161	-	88.601
1999-2000	2339	1569	67%	161.379.319	-	102.855
2000-2001	2359	1508	64%	117.134.292	-	77.675
2001-2002	2406	1558	65%	132.250.335	-	84.885
2002-2003	2728	1737	64%	135.493.459	-	78.004
2003-2004	2252	1516	67%	150.865.076	-	99.515
2004-2005	2347	1619	69%	222.937.471	-	137.701
2005-2006	2645	1867	71%	297.003.663	-	159.081
2006-2007	2763	2074	75%	439.456.579	-	211.888
2007-2008	2515	1792	71%	464.780.590	-	259.364
2008-2009	3634	2599	72%	408.142.058	-	157.038
2009-2010	3812	2693	71%	458.360.655	-	170.204
2010-2011	3827	2601	68%	521.740.498	-	200.592
2011-2012	4432	3107	70%	689.990.876	-	222.076
2012-2013	4170	3074	74%	820.492.634	-	266.914
2013-2014	4763	3622	76%	1.164.737.544	-	321.573
2014-2015	5156	4036	78%	1.229.091.228	-	304.532
2015-2016	5644	4044	72%	1.210.968.707	-	299.448
2016-2017	5659	4269	75%	1.085.583.838	-	254.295

AVERAGE PRICE ACHIEVED (US$, GB£, € K)

MERCEDES-BENZ 300SL "GULLWING" (1954-1957) 1.400 UNITS

CARS OFFERED, CARS SOLD AND SALE %

TURNOVER US$k

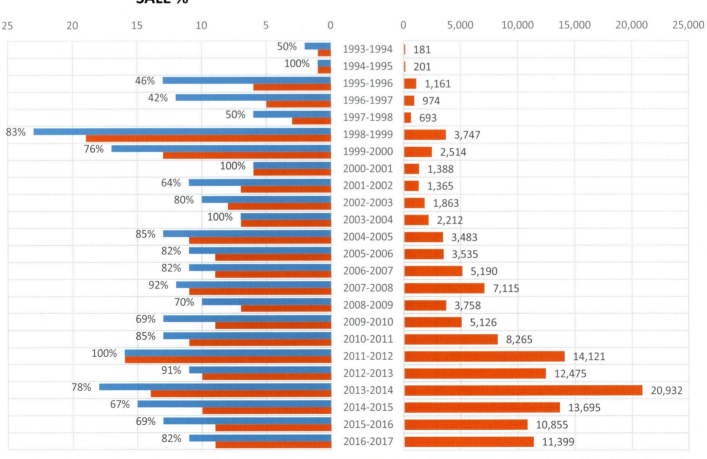

AVERAGE PRICE ACHIEVED (US$, GB£, € K)

ASTON MARTIN DB4 (1958-1963) 1.040 UNITS

CARS OFFERED, CARS SOLD AND SALE %

TURNOVER US$k

ASTON MARTIN

BEAUTIFUL HAS A NEW SOUND

EFFORTLESS GT PERFORMANCE DRIVEN BY A
NEW SPORTING V8 OR ICONIC V12 ENGINE

DB11

db11.astonmartin.com

Official government fuel consumption figures in litres/100km (mpg) for the Aston Martin DB11: urban 13.5 (20.9) – 16.6 (17); extra urban 7.9 (35.8) – 8.5 (33.2); combined 9.9 (28.5) – 11.4 (24.8). CO_2 emissions 230 – 265 g/km. Efficiency Class G. The mpg/fuel economy figures quoted are sourced from official regulated test results obtained through laboratory testing. They are for comparability purposes only and may not reflect your real driving experience, which may vary depending on factors including road conditions, weather, vehicle load and driving style.

AVERAGE PRICE ACHIEVED (US$, GB£, € K)

FERRARI F40 (1987-1992) 1.311 UNITS

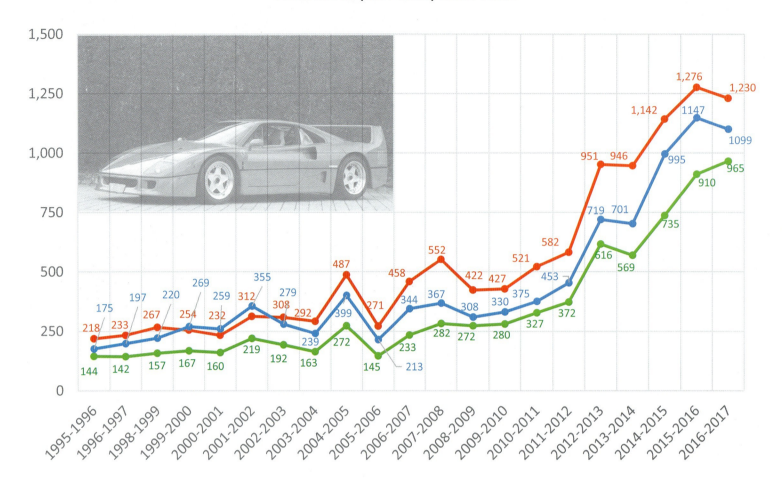

CARS OFFERED, CARS SOLD AND SALE %

TURNOVER US$k

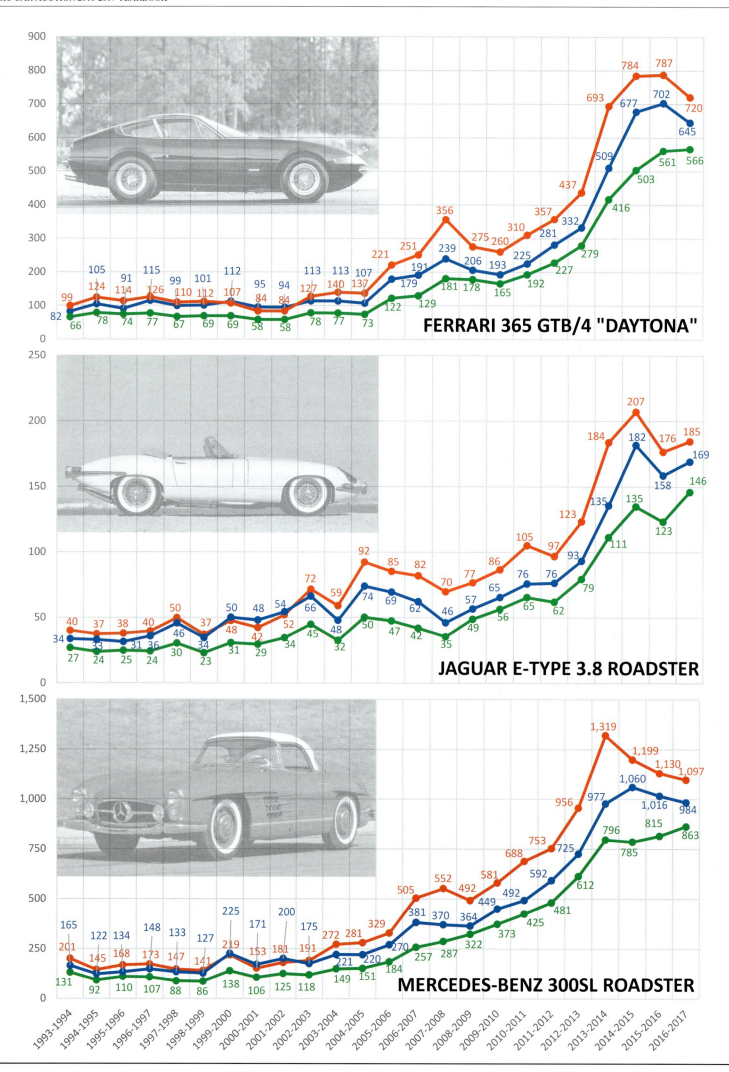

Collezione

Future technology, classic emotions.

Photo: Pirelli Stelvio Corsa limited edition exclusive for Ferrari 250GTO

Collezione, the dedicated range tyres for high value cars older than twenty years.

Only a Motorsport world leader and the preferred supplier of the most prestigious car and supercar brands could benefit from its 145 years of history and passion.

www.pirelli.com/collezione

OFFICIAL TYRE PARTNER

The 2016-2017 season "TOP TEN"

This chapter is dedicated to the 10 cars that achieved the highest hammer prices; the cars are listed in descending order according to their hammer price in US Dollars. The descriptions and photos have been taken from the relative auction house catalogue. Of course, the Top 10s are also listed in the auction results chapter, indicated as such.

1 1956 Aston Martin DBR1

Chassis: DBR1/1
Engine: RB6/300/3

The first of five DBR1s; Winner of the 1959 Nürburgring 1000 KM; Sister to the 1959 Le Mans winner; Raced by Roy Salvadori, Stirling Moss, Jack Brabham, and Carroll Shelby, among others; Fitted with correct reproduction engine for racing, offered with the original

RM Sotheby's, 18.8.2017 Monterey (USA)		Lot 148
Estimate	USD	Over 20.000.000
Hammer price	USD	22.550.000
	GBP	17.521.350
	EUR	19.212.600

...The DBR1 was the ultimate result of David Brown's dream to triumph at Le Mans, culminating in 1959 in that elusive Sarthe victory...

For 1956, Le Mans regulations stipulated a maximum 2.5-liter capacity in the sports-prototype class resulting in a 2,493cc RB6 engine with 212bhp... On its 24 Hours debut, DBR1/1 ran well for 20 hours until running its bearings and retiring. The 2nd place, courtesy of Roy Salvadori, at both the British Empire Trophy and Easter Goodwood meetings followed early in 1957.

In May that year, back to 3.0 liters, the DBR1s potential was amply demonstrated by Tony Brooks' easy win in DBR1/2 at Spa-Francorchamps with Roy Salvadori in 2nd place driving DBR1/1. Later that same month, Brooks/Noel Cunningham-Reid led the Nürburgring 1000 KM from flag to finish in DBR1/2 with Salvadori/Les Leston in DBR1/1 finishing 6th. The victory at the Nürburgring marked the first such achievement for a British sports car. It was a sign to come for the DBR1, with additional victories to follow in the coming years. For 1957, however, Le Mans again proved elusive with both DBR1/1 and DBR1/2 retiring.

Given 3.0 liters was the engine's maximum capacity, it was manna from heaven when the 1958 regulations decreed a 3,000-cc limit in the sports-prototype class. After retirements for both DBR1/1 and DBR1/2 in Sebring's 12 Hours, better fortune returned at the Nürburgring when Stirling Moss/Jack Brabham comfortably won the 1000 KM in DBR1/3... Another bitter pill to swallow followed at Le Mans, where all three DBR1s retired...

After nine years fighting to win the French classic, Aston decided that Le Mans would be the DBR1's sole 1959 event. That soon changed when DBR1/1, as all DBR1s, now with 2,992-cc, seven main bearings for greater reliability, and 50DCO Webers, realizing up to 268-bhp, ran at Sebring for Salvadori; a change rued when clutch failure caused retirement. Convinced he could replicate his victory at the Nürburgring, Moss persuaded Aston to enter again the 1000 KM where, with Jack Fairman took DBR1/1 to victory, breaking the lap record 16 times in one of his greatest drives...

The Nürburgring would be DBR1/1's last competitive outing as Works race entry. After almost a decade of racing, David Brown finally achieved his dream when DBR1/2 captured the overall victory at Le Mans.

At Goodwood's Tourist Trophy, DBR1/1 would serve as a spare car, where Aston Martin clinched the 1959 World Sportscar Championship, a feat only made possible by

DBR1/1's Nürburgring triumph.
Following Aston Martin's withdrawal from competition in August 1959, DBR1/1 would twice race for Essex Racing Stables in the Nürburgring 1000 KM, with Jim Clark/Bruce McLaren retiring from fourth in 1961 when a con-rod failed at 500 KM and McLaren/Tony Maggs finishing 4th in 1962. Shortly thereafter Aston sold DBR1/1 with 2,992-cc engine RB6/300/3, the same Works engine raced by Clark, McLaren and Maggs at Nürburgring, to the Hon. John Dawnay – later the 11th Viscount Downe and long-time Aston Martin Owners Club president – and his brother the Hon. James Dawnay… both raced the car until the latter

crashed at Silverstone in 1963, sustaining front body damage… In 1976, after laying untouched for 12 years, and using a body buck from DBR1/2, a new front section was fabricated and the remaining body refurbished; the mechanical components and engine were also rebuilt. Driven by Mike Salmon, DBR1/1 took many victories/podium in Lloyds & Scottish Historic Car Championship… In 2000 it was sold to America-based collector John McCaw.

The current owner acquired DBR1/1 from McCaw in January 2009. Deeming its last fitted Works engine, RB6/300/3, one of only seven built and raced by Aston Martin, too precious to race, RSW Ltd. produced another unit with new cylinder block and heads, now producing 302bhp. Since 2010 DBR1/1 has been successfully raced at Goodwood by Brian Redman, while in 2013 Sir Stirling Moss drove it during Aston's centenary celebrations at Nürburgring…

2 1995 McLaren F1

Chassis: 1048044
Engine: 992 61121 6070 0

Being offered by the original owner; the first McLaren F1 imported to the U.S.; the first fully federalized, U.S. road legal McLaren F1

Bonhams, 18.8.2017 Carmel (USA) Lot 73		
Estimate		Refer Dpt.
Hammer price	USD	15.620.000
	GBP	12.136.740
	EUR	13.308.240

…In total, 64 road cars were delivered to customers before production ended. McLaren F1 chassis number 044 is one of the 64 hallowed legends. This exquisitely maintained, single-owner McLaren F1 was the very first of its type to be imported to the United States, and it was the first of only 7 McLarens to be federalized by experts in the process - Ameritech. As a result of the federalization, 044 is a U.S. road legal car.

044 is the thirty-seventh F1 off the assembly line, sporting the iconic, original Base Silver paint and a black/gray Connolly leather interior, which includes McLaren's signature red colored panels for the central driver's seat. The car was purchased new by the consignor in July 1996, while on an invitational visit to the factory. Upon purchasing the ultimate road car, the consignor and two of his closest companions went on the ultimate road trip as they toured the European countryside. Beginning at the factory, the trio went to France, Germany, the Netherlands, and Belgium, before returning to the Woking based factory. The trip, which is described by the consignor as the journey of a lifetime, accounts for just about half of the 9,600 miles on the car's odometer. Upon returning to the factory, 044 was treated to its first service… From the factory, 044 was shipped to New York where Dick Fritz and the Ameritech team took delivery of the car and begun the conversion. Understanding the significance and importance of the McLaren, Ameritech went to great lengths to ensure that during the process no part of the car was physically altered in any way that could not be put back to its 100% original form. After the conversion process was completed and 044 passed all of the necessary tests to gain its compliance, the car was delivered to the consignor… All of the Ametitech conversion items have been carefully removed from the vehicle, leaving it in its original, as delivered specification. Every item that was used to federalize the car has been saved and accompanies the sale.

Throughout the car's life, it has been regularly maintained and serviced by BMW North America LLC at the National Workshop-East. In May 2002, with only 7,071 miles on the odometer, 044 received a major service which among many other things, included the replacement of its fuel cell. In October 2009, less than 2,000 miles later, 044 was brought back to BMW for its second major service where at 8,731 miles, the car received its second fuel cell replacement. In July 2017, prior to arriving in California, 044 was sent to McLaren of Philadelphia, where it has once again received a fresh service…

Accompanying the sale of 044 is its complete tool kit, including the modem used to connect to the factory, full luggage set…and major, original, components that were removed from the car during services such as the fuel cell and tires.

While many of the road cars have been returned to the factory for new aerodynamic packages or custom interiors, 044 remains unmodified and aside from the parts replaced during its scheduled services, essentially remains as it was when it left the factory…

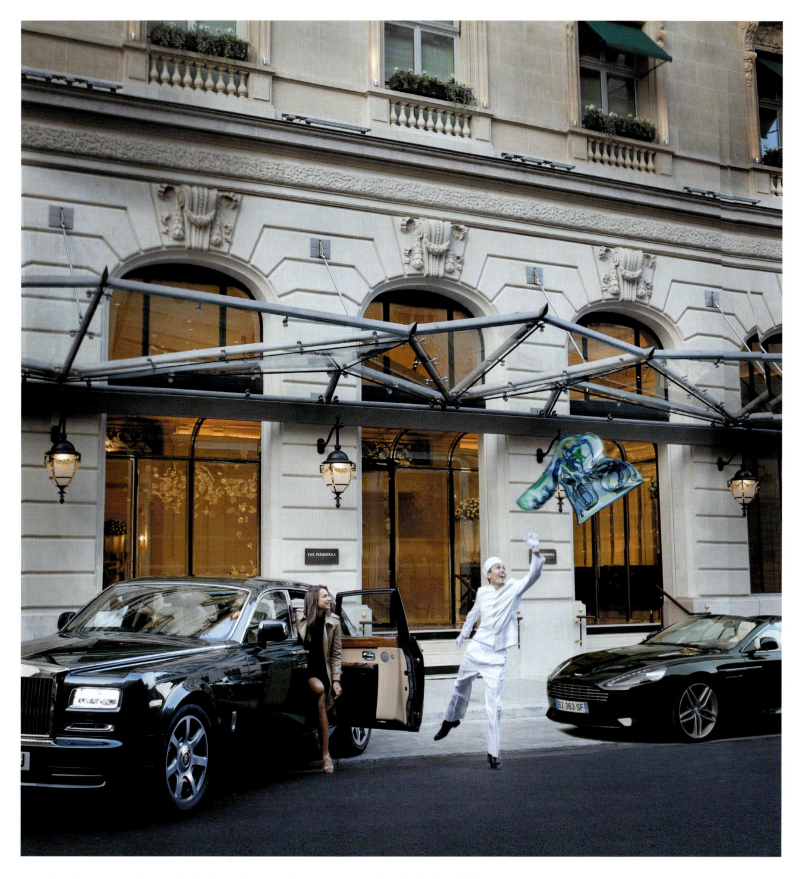

3 1966 Ferrari 275 GTB Competizione

One of only 12 GTB/Cs built; Raced in Italy between 1966 and 1970 with numerous Class and Overall wins

Body: Pininfarina/Scaglietti
Chassis: 09051
Engine: 09051

Gooding & Company, 19.8.2017 Pebble Beach (USA)		Lot 120
Estimate	USD	12.000.000-16.000.000
Hammer price	USD	14.520.000
	GBP	11.282.040
	EUR	12.371.040

…Although the factory's delivery records indicate that 09051 may have been intended for German Ferrari distributor Auto Becker, the GTB/C was instead sold to Renzo Sinibaldi, an amateur racing driver from Rome…The first race he entered with 09051 was the 500 Kilometers of Mugello in July 1966. There, he and co-driver Grana drove the GTB/C to a 1st in Class and 7th Overall finish… Sinibaldi campaigned 09051 in nine races between July and October 1966, placing 1st in Class seven times and capturing an overall win at the Tolentino-Colle Paterno Hillclimb. These results put Sinibaldi in third place in the final standings for the 1966 Italian GT Championship.
Although 09051 was technically sold to Gino di Russo in October 1966, the Ferrari remained in Sinibaldi's hands, and he continued to race it throughout the 1967 season and into 1968… In August 1968, 09051 was sold to Alberto Federici... who entered the Ferrari in the Trofeo Micangeli-Arezzo, the Catania-Etna Hillclimb, and the Trofeo Città di Orvieto, winning his class in all three events. In May 1969, Federici and co-driver Domenico Lo Coco entered 09051 in Italy's oldest open-road race – the Targa Florio…The three-year-old Ferrari retired after an accident damaged the nose…The 1969 Targa Florio is 09051's last recorded race entry; it did not qualify for the 1000 Kilometers of Monza in April 1970 and was retired from active use.
In 1971, Federici sold his GTB/C to Vittorio Roveda, an oil trader in Watford, England…That September Roveda traded 09051 to exotic car dealer Robert de la Rive Box… From there, the car was sold, via David Piper, to David Flanagan of Liverpool, England…who entered the GTB/C in the 1974 Club Ferrari France Rallye at Pierre Bardinon's Mas du Clos.
In 1978, Martin and Ian Hilton purchased 09051…In 1993 the Hilton Brothers sold 09051 and the car was exported to the USA…
In 2004, the GTB/C was sold to the current owner…In early 2007, he entrusted the car to Wayne Obry's Motion Products Inc. (MPI) in Neenah, Wisconsin…Over the next several months, 09051 was restored to show-quality standards and refinished in its 1966 livery of silver metallic with black leather upholstery. In August 2007, the GTB/C was invited to the prestigious Pebble Beach Concours d'Elegance, where it was displayed in Class M-2 for Ferrari competition cars. There, it scored 99 points and was awarded a Second in Class trophy…
In 2013, the Ferrari returned to MPI, where, in addition to a complete re-restoration of the bodywork, the car was mechanically rebuilt to exacting standards. This included a complete engine rebuild…In fall 2016, the Ferrari returned to MPI for additional fine-tuning and cosmetic attention and, in preparation for its appearance at auction, it returned once more in 2017…

1963 Ferrari 330 LM Berlinetta
Chassis: 4381SA (Factory Works)
Production run: 4

Collezione
BY MAG

YOUR KEY TO THE FINEST FERRARI AUTOMOBILES

WWW.COLLEZIONEBYMAG.COM
+1 (888) 356-7110

OFFICIAL FERRARI DEALER
Ferrari Beverly Hills
@CollezioneByMag on Instagram, Facebook, and Twitter

4 1970 Porsche 917K

Chassis: 917-024
Engine: 917-021

Documented ownership history from new includes Porsche legend Jo Siffert; Used extensively in the production of Steve McQueen's film "Le Mans"

Gooding & Company, 18.8.2017 Pebble Beach (USA)		Lot 44
Estimate	USD	13.000.000-16.000.000
Hammer price	USD	14.080.000
	GBP	10.940.160
	EUR	11.996.160

…As documented in Walter Naher's definitive work on the 917, *Porsche 917: Archive and Works Catalog 1968-1975*, it was very common for Porsche to renumber 917s during their racing careers. Porsche factory records indicate that the first 917-024 was built in 1969 and renumbered during its racing life as 002, 005 and finally 006. After months of rigorous testing work at the Nürburgring, Hockenheim. Weissach, and Zeltweg, the chassis was subsequently wrecked and scrapped in February 1970.

Porsche needed a shorttail car for the Le Mans pre-training in April 1970 and prepared a frame, numbering it 917-024…Wearing no.22, the new 917-024 was entrusted to Brian Redman and Mike Hailwood…and set the fastest times of April's test…The car would go on to further testing at the Nürburgring and at Ehra-Lessien in May 1970. On June 25, Jo Siffert purchased the car from Porsche…

With a massive budget, the finest contemporary race cars, some of the era's best professional drivers, and a star actor turned racing driver, it comes as no surprise that the 1971 film *Le Mans* is as legendary as the race it depicts…Given the film's plot, it was necessary to have several Ferrari 512s and Porsche917s as the major stars of the film. Steve McQueen's Solar Productions purchased one 917K from Porsche directly, while JWA loaned another. A third car, 917-024, was leased to Solar Productions by Jo Siffert…Today, 917-024 still retains the mounting points used to affix camera rigging to its rear frame tuber…

After the filming of *Le Mans*, 917-024 remained in Jo Siffert's ownership and returned with him to Fribourg, Switzerland…Unfortunately Siffert died on October 24, 1971…At his funeral, 917-024 led the procession… The car remained in Fribourg for a number of years, before it was sold in 1978 to Pierre Prieur from Saclay, France.

In 2001, 917-024 once again returned to the public eye when it was discovered in a warehouse outside Paris, where it had been stored during Prieur's ownership…

In early 2002 it was acquired by a Swiss gentleman…and the decision was reached to restore it…To complete the car, engine 917-021 was purchased from a private collector based in the USA…

As the owner intended to drive 917-024 in the Le Mans Classic 24 Hour after the restoration, to achieve the highest level of safety for on-track use, it was deemed prudent to build a full replacement for the original chassis…

When the time came to sell 917-024, it was decided that the original frame should be restored and installed… Swiss racing and restoration specialists Graber Sportgarage were entrusted to manage the project…Working closely with Graber was an ex-Porsche factory engineer, Walter Naher…

Unused since completion…accompanying the car at auction are the reproduction chassis built for the car's initial restoration, along with pieces of its original bodywork and sections of the original chassis tubing that were replaced for safety during the most recent restoration…

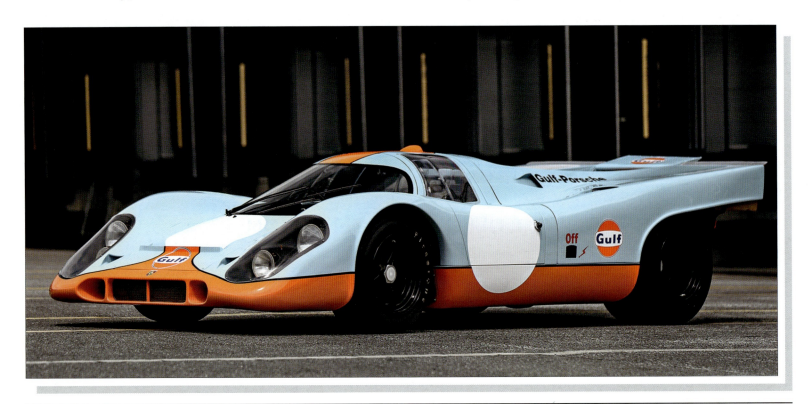

THE WORLD CLASSIC CAR SHOW

A LEAGUE OF ITS OWN!

From the absolutely authentic original up to the complete reconstruction • From the inexpensive modern classic up to the prize-winning Concours winner • From the everyday automobile, suit-able for the masses, up to the unique item for connoisseurs • From the private supplier up to the international auction house. From the manufacturer of the smallest production up to the global players in cars • From the youngster on father's shoulders up to the rally experienced professional • From the passionate do-it-yourself person up to the profit orientated investor. This all leads to the fascination of Techno-Classica. The unique variety of the show, offers so much access to the classic theme that every participant is able to follow his individual way. **Share the Passion.**

ESSEN, 21*-25 MARCH 2018

MESSE ESSEN *Wednesday, 21st March, 2 p.m. to 8 p.m.: Happy View Day / Preview
Thursday 9 a.m. to 6 p.m., Friday 9 a.m. to 7 p.m., Saturday + Sunday 9 a.m. to 6 p.m.

 50th World Show for Automobiles, Motorsport, Tuning, Classics, Show & Action World trophy Concours d'Elégance
2nd – 10th Dec. 2017

 41st National Classic Car Show for the BeNeLux-countries Concours d'Elégance BeNeLux
2nd – 4th March 2018

SIHA S.I.H.A. Ausstellungen Protmotion GmbH, Postfach 3164, 52118 Herzogenrath, Germany, Telefon: +49 (0) 24 07-1 73 00, Fax: +49 (0) 24 07-1 77 11, info@siha.de, **www.siha.de**

5 1961 Ferrari 250 GT Berlinetta Lusso

Body: Pininfarina/Scaglietti
Chassis: 2985GT

Ferrari Classiche certified; Nearly 40 years of care by renowned Ferrari collectors Charles Betz and Fred Peters; Platinum Award winner at the 2016 Cavallino Classic

RM Sotheby's, 19.8.2017 Monterey (USA)		Lot 220
Estimate	USD	8.500.000-10.000.000
Hammer price	USD	8.305.000
	GBP	6.452.985
	EUR	7.075.860

…According to the research of marque historian Marcel Massini, chassis 2985 is the 110th of 167 total examples built, including both steel and aluminum-bodied cars. It is one of approximately 90 Lusso variants… A Certificate of Origin was issued on 11 November 1961, the car was officially completed three days later.

Finished in Grigio Conchiglia and upholstered with Nero leather, this berlinetta was distributed later in November to Vincenzo Malago e Co., an official dealer in Rome. On 22 February 1962, Malago sold the Ferrari to its first owners of record, Maria Lucia del Torta and Alberto Bossa, both local residents. Just a few months later, on 19 May, the SWB was purchased by Albertina Bossa of Naples. This may have just been a formal transfer, as seven days later the car was sold yet again to Vincenzo Casillo of San Giuseppe Vesuviano in the province of Naples.

Casillo kept the Ferrari for nearly five years, and then in May 1967 he sold the car to Vincenzo Luigi Cicinelli of Riano.

…In the late 1960s, chassis number 2985 was exported to the United States and acquired by a Mr. Mordvedt, who in 1972 repainted the car. Four years later, the SWB was purchased by Charles Betz and Fred Peters, the Southern California Ferrari experts.. After being registered with California blue plates 307 UOU, the SWB was driven by Peters in several vintage racing events in Southern California as it enjoyed a refurbishment in the hands of the two owners, who have overseen the restoration of many important Ferraris over the decades.

In November 1986, Betz and Peters presented the 250 GT at the Palm Springs Concours d'Elegance… In April 1995, the owners showed the car at Skeets and Sharon Dunn's Picnic at Osuna Ranch in Rancho Santa Fe, California, and the following June, the car was displayed at the Rodeo Drive Concours d'Elegance in Beverly Hills. In October 1995, the SWB was exhibited at the Newport Beach Concours d'Elegance, while in May 1996 it returned to the Dunn's Picnic at Osuna Ranch.

In September 1999, Betz and Peters campaigned the Ferrari on the XI Colorado Grand 1000, entered as #49. Four months later, Charles Betz drove the car at two events held in conjunction with the IX Cavallino Classic in Palm Beach, Florida, the track event at Moroso raceway, and the Tour di Palm Beach. The berlinetta was then displayed at the Cavallino Classic main event, winning the prestigious Coppa SWB Award.

In September 2008, this sensational 250 GT was authenticated by Ferrari Classiche… Chassis number 2985 GT's event career then continued in stunning fashion when the car was invited by the factory for display on Ferrari Classiche's stand at the 2013 Pebble Beach Concours d'Elegance… After almost 40 years of care, Betz and Peters offered the SWB for sale. As part of their sale to the consignor, the experts agreed to oversee the restoration of the car, including a change to the current color scheme over a black leather interior. Also benefiting from a mechanical freshening that retained as much originality as possible, the Ferrari was delivered to the current owner just in time for presentation at the Cavallino Classic in January 2016, where the car won a Platinum Award…

6 1963 Jaguar E-Type 3.8 Lightweight roadster

Chassis: S850664
Engine: RA 1349-9S

Ex Team Cunningham Lightweight raced by his team at the 1963 24 Hours of Le Mans; Driven by legendary champion drivers Walt Hansgen and Augie Pabst; 11th overall and 3rd in class at the 1963 Road America 500 and 4th overall at the 1963 Bridgehampton 500

BONHAMS, 18.8.2017 Carmel (USA)		LOT 52
Estimate		Refer Dpt.
Hammer price	USD	8.000.000
	GBP	6.216.000
	EUR	6.816.000

…Officially dispatched from the factory on June 7, 1963, chassis no. S850664 was the 7th Lightweight built, and the second of the three cars sold to Briggs Cunningham…

As Brown's Lane was still working through issues with a longer-legged ZF 5-speed gearbox, the Lightweight was equipped with a Jaguar 4-speed gearbox when delivered to Cunningham for use at Le Mans. It was piloted there by Walt Hansgen and Augie Pabst, and officially entered as #14… …Unfortunately, the 4-speed gearbox failed to hold up for more than an hour, forcing S850664's early retirement after qualifying at 14th on the starting grid…

After Le Mans, S850664 was returned to the factory to replace the hood and install the desirable 5-speed ZF gearbox. In this configuration, the Lightweight was delivered to the United States and driven to an 11th-place finish for Cunningham by Hansgen and Richards at the Road America 500 in September 1963. A 4th-place finish by Richards at Bridgehampton followed a week later, and after this brief competition career the unique coupe was retired to Cunningham's well-known museum in Costa Mesa, California.

Though it is uncertain exactly how long Briggs kept the E-Type, by the early 1970s the car had come into the possession of Robert Lane…In 1973, he sold the Lightweight to Sir Anthony Bamford of Great Britain. His ownership commenced a long chain of respected English caretakers that included noted collector Paul Vestey, and Adrian Hamilton…This period featured a fair amount of vintage racing, as well as a minor accident at Silverstone during Mike Fisher's ownership circa 1975…

In the late 1980s, the Lightweight was significantly restored by Richard Freshman of California, and he took the opportunity to remove the original alloy motor and replace it with a faithful iron-block copy, in order to preserve the historically important factory motor (which was nevertheless kept with the car). S850664 was then acquired by Campbell McLaren (in his second stint of ownership), and in the early 1990s he began entrusting all mechanical maintenance and race support to the Jaguar competition specialists at Lynx Engineering. Lynx oversaw the E-Type's mechanical care and race support for the following decade (which included reinstalling the original alloy engine)…In 1995, the Lightweight was acquired by David Vine, and he presented the car at the pre-Le Mans cavalcade in June 1995, and the Goodwood Festival of Speed… Passing to dealer Andre Bloom of London in 1998, the E-Type continued to be presented at events, including the 1999 Goodwood Festival of Speed, the 2001 Louis Vuitton Classic, the 2001 Le Mans Legends, and the 2001 and 2002 Goodwood Revivals…

Around 2003, the rare E-Type was consigned to Don Williams' Blackhawk Collection and displayed at his famed Danville, California, showroom. Not long after it was purchased by a Hong Kong-based Jaguar collector… and it remained in his fine collection for many years.

S850664 desirably retains its factory-issued aluminum coachwork and matching-numbers alloy engine… It has been fastidiously maintained to highlight its 1963 Le Mans appearance, and is ready for immediate use at premium vintage racing events and concours d'elegance worldwide…

7 1937 Bugatti Type 57S cabriolet

Body: Vanvooren
Chassis: 57513

One of just 42 Type 57S chassis produced; One of four Type 57S cabriolets built by Vanvooren; One of three extant

RM Sotheby's, 11.3.2017 Amelia Island (USA)		Lot 232
Estimate	USD	8.500.000-10.000.000
Hammer price	USD	7.700.000
	GBP	6.334.020
	EUR	7.256.480

...According to the research of marque experts Pierre-Yves Laugier, David Sewell, and Bugatti SaS historian Julius Kruta, this chassis was initially sold on trade in early 1937 to Francois Labesse…On 22 March, it was completed and shipped by train to Vanvooren to be bodied…On 7 July 1937, the Type 57S was delivered to Labesse's Parisian headquarters…Though factory records are apparently inexact regarding the original color livery, Francois Labesse's nephew recalls the Bugatti being finished in black paint with a thin red line…The car was most likely sold into British ownership during the summer of 1939…to Dr. Tomas Harris (or de Tomaso by some accounts), who probably used the Bugatti strictly as a road car…During the early 1950s, the 57S was acquired by Jack Lemon Burton...

In 1954 the Bugatti was sold to Ronnie Symondson…At the BOC Members Testing Weekend at Prescott on 27 March 1954, Symondson entered the cabriolet and achieved a best time of 58.6 seconds…On 9 May, the car took second place in the Bugatti handicap class at the National Hillclimb at Prescott, setting an impressive time of 55.84 seconds.

According to Bugatti Register editor David Sewell, Symondson likely entered the car at Silverstone on 19 June, and a day later it was part of the three-car Bugatti team who excelled at Shelsley Walsh. …Later in 1954, Symondson used the 57S as a touring car for vacationing through continental Europe..While traveling the 57S was sidelined with engine problems, so he used the opportunity to visit the Molsheim factory, where a new cylinder block and pistons were fitted…He further modified and updated some mechanical elements with the addition of Koni shock absorbers, and a hydraulic brake system to replace the mechanical brakes.

In 1962 the 57S was sold to T.A. "Bob" Roberts…That winter he conducted some cosmetic work on the car, eschewing by then two-tone black over grey-blue paint for a new black over yellow, which it wears to this day. The bonnet apertures were modified with plated-steel mesh cooling grilles in place of the original louvered sides, and this round of freshening appears to have included a change in the headlamps from the original bumper-level faired-in units for the higher bullet-style components currently fitted to the coachwork…

During his ownership, Mr. Roberts removed the original engine (number 21S), retaining it as a spare, and replaced it with an unnumbered 57G competition engine that had served as an extra for the Bugatti factory team at Le Mans in 1937…

After Mr. Roberts' passing in 1990, the rare Type 57S was offered by his estate for the first time in three decades…It was sold on 10 June to Claude Decoster…He eventually commissioned Henri Novo to remove the 57G engine and re-install the original factory-equipped motor, which currently remains fitted. In 1995 the consignor, a respected collector based in New York, purchased the rare cabriolet. Since then, the Bugatti has largely been domiciled on static display, though in recent years Stu Laidlaw of Redding, Connecticut, was commissioned to return the car to a basic state of driving operation.

In early 2016, the Bugatti was submitted to RM Auto Restoration, whose technicians rebuilt the clutch, and refitted the original factory gearbox…The original engine is currently fitted with the special competition carburetor from the 57G engine…A more comprehensive overhaul is recommended for anyone who wishes to indulge in vigorous motoring or road event use.

8 1963 Jaguar E-Type 3.8 Lightweight roadster

Chassis: S850667
Engine: V682558P

Ex Bob Jane - 1963 Australian GT Championship Winning; Preserved by just 3 owners from new while accumulating less than 4,000 miles

BONHAMS, 19.1.2017 Scottsdale (USA)		LOT 24
Estimate	USD	7.500.000-8.500.000
Hammer price	USD	7.370.000
	GBP	5.979.281
	EUR	6.907.901

The story of S850667 begins with Robert "Bob" Jane, from Melbourne, Australia, who raced motorcycles and water-skied for pleasure. By the late 1950s, Mr. Jane had transitioned to sports car racing…He was a principal racing customer of Bryson's in Melbourne, the official Jaguar importer Down Under …On November 29, 1961, Jane even became an official Jaguar importer under an agreement with Jack Bryson … He sent a letter to England in the summer of 1963, inquiring about the availability of the new lightweight competition E-Type.

…The completed car shipped for Australia on October 20, 1963… On December 8, the Lightweight debuted at the Calder track in Victoria, winning the Australian GT Championship race… A few weeks later at Catalina, S850667 won the Production Sports Handicap and the New South Wales Touring Car Championships, followed by the sports and touring car races at Warwick Farm…

The Lightweight then took the checkered flag at Calder on January 26, 1964, and at the Sandown A.G.P. meeting on February 9. At the end of the month, it finished second at the Australian Tourist Trophy…Returning to Calder on March 8, the E-Type took second place, and then placed third at the New South Wales Sports Car Championship on March 29. The successful run continued at Sandown Park on April 19, where the E-Type set the fastest lap and placed third in the Victoria Sports Car Championship.

Around May 1964, Bob Jane and his brother Bill took the Lightweight to Europe, where they intended to test its mettle in long-distance continental events while stopping by the Brown's Lane factory for a few upgrades… Correspondence shows that Jane wanted to source a ZF 5-speed gearbox at Coventry, but because the ZF units were in short supply the factory declined to install one… The opportunity was taken, however, to add wider disc wheels and install a Le Mans-style 45-gallon fuel tank…

Chassis no. S850667 returned to Australia by the fall of 1964… The Lightweight's success resumed at Bathurst on February 21, 1965…On May 2, Bill Jane drove the E-Type at the One-Hour Production Car Race at Lakeside in Queensland, finishing third, and a week later the car finished first in both the preliminary and the main races at Bathurst… S850667 still managed a 4th-place finish at the Australian Tourist Trophy at Lakeside… In 1966, Jane passed driving duties to Spencer Martin, and he won the GT race at Warwick Farm on September 18…Martin then placed third at Sandown on October 16. Around this time Jane unfortunately blew out the original alloy engine block during practice… Further documentation from the McGrath archives shows that…Brown's Lane provided a correct factory alloy replacement block, no. V682558P, which continues to power the car to this day.

The end of the 1966 season basically concluded the E-Type's racing career… In November 1980 Bob Jane offered his cars publicly at the Australian Grand Prix auction.

Chassis no. S850667 was then purchased by Peter Briggs, a Jaguar enthusiast from Western Australia… The new owner commissioned a re-finish in white with large blue racing stripes down the middle, and this is the only occasion the E-Type was ever repainted. Briggs raced the Lightweight a few times and occasionally drove it to his office…

After nearly 20 years of ownership, Briggs offered the rare E-Type for sale in early 1999…

Currently displaying less than 4,000 original miles, chassis no. S850667 has been fastidiously maintained by just three caretakers over the course of 53 years…and the car has never been disassembled or restored.

9 2016 Ferrari LaFerrari

The 500th LaFerrari built; Offered from Ferrari's own collection at a charity auction

Body: Ferrari Styling Center
Chassis: NA
Engine: NA

RM Sotheby's, 4.12.2016 Daytona Beach (USA)		Sole Lot
Estimate		
Hammer price	USD	7.000.000
	GBP	5.544.700
	EUR	6.577.200

A one-of-a-kind LaFerrari, offered from Ferrari's own collection, stormed into the record books last night, commanding a staggering $7,000,000 at a charity auction in Florida. Conducted by RM Sotheby's in partnership with Ferrari, the exclusive charity sale was held as part of the Ferrari Finali Mondiali weekend at the Daytona International Speedway.

The prized LaFerrari was created as a gift from Ferrari to its home country of Italy, with proceeds from its sale benefitting the reconstruction of Central Italy in the aftermath of the devastating earthquakes of 2016. The car boasts a one-of-a-kind livery and interior, as well as a special plaque to commemorate the occasion.

The unique 949hp hypercar was the subject of a fierce bidding war at last night's sale, which lasted some 10 minutes before the car sold for an astounding $7 million. The impressive sales price not only represents a benchmark for a LaFerrari sold at auction, eclipsing the previous high sale by more than $1.8 million, but also a record as the most valuable 21st century automobile ever sold at auction.

In addition to RM Sotheby's and Ferrari working together on the special charity sale, the auction was held in collaboration with the National Italian American Foundation's Earthquake Relief Fund. The charity auction also included two official Scuderia Ferrari F1 racing suits and gloves, one autographed by Kimi Räikkönen and the other by Sebastian Vettel, which helped raise an additional $36,000 for the deserving cause.

Photo of a similar car

10 1959 Aston Martin DP199/DB4 GT Prototype

Chassis: DP199/1
Engine: 370/0184/GT

"Design Proiect" for all Aston Martin DB4 GTs; complete with original delivery engine

RM Sotheby's, 18.8.2017 Monterey (USA)		Lot 147
Estimate	USD	6.000.000-8.000.000
Hammer price	USD	6.765.000
	GBP	5.256.405
	EUR	5.763.780

It is easy to forget that when Aston Martin announced the DB4 in September 1958, it was the world's most advanced GT car; indeed, demand for the new model would vastly outstrip supply. However, such was the racing DNA in Aston Martin that, six months before the DB4 was announced, the project to create a lightweight, competition version of the DB4 was sanctioned by John Wyer. That project was DP199.

Once back from the DB4 launch in Paris, the task of designing the DB4GT began in earnest with Harold Beach and Ted Cutting as the designers. John Wyer saw it as a straightforward task and told Ted "to cut five inches out of a DB4 and produce a cheap and cheerful GT car." These inches were removed from behind the front seats, giving it shorter doors and a wheelbase of 93 inches. In fact DP199 was made by cutting a very early DB4 platform chassis in two with the floor join reinforced by a fishplate, still visible today.

The DB4GT was designed with two seats and a luggage platform in the rear. The doors were lightweight aluminum, and the boot was occupied by a 30-gallon fuel tank with the spare wheel on top. The entire body skin was in thinner 18-gauge aluminum alloy.

The first public showing of DP199 – four months before its official launch – was at Silverstone. Wyer was nervous about racing it at Silverstone so early in its development but need not have been. Moss put the car on pole position and won the race, as well as setting a lap record.

DP199 was then entered at Le Mans in June under the banner of 'Ecurie Trois Chevrons' and driven by Aston's Swiss distributor Hubert Patthey with co-driver Renaud Calderari. For this race the engine was a 3.0-liter, number RDP 5066-2. Unfortunately, a repeat of Silverstone was not to be – DP completed only 21 laps.

Following Le Mans, the car was returned to Feltham, where DP199 entered the second phase of its life as a press starlet and more significantly as a development car. It was shown at the launch of the DB4GT in London in October 1959.

DP199 was sold in June 1961 to the Hon. Gerald Lascelles, the Queen's cousin. When it was delivered, it was with at least its third engine, and was numbered as it is today 370/0184/GT. The block is the correct, very early type with the side breather mount, and the stampings on the block are authentic, with the original casting intact.

…It was then enjoyed by a handful of enthusiasts…In 1989 Aston Martin was commissioned to restore and return the car to its Le Mans 1959 guise…

VINTAGE, HISTORIC & CLASSIC CAR SERVICES

Jim Stokes Workshops has been at the forefront of Vintage, Historic and Classic race and road car restoration, maintenance and recreation for over 40 years. Our reputation for the quality of our workmanship and expertise is global, with multiple concours awards reinforcing our position. Please contact us with your requirements for our immediate attention.

- Restoration & Recreation
- Engine Building & Rebuilding
- Bespoke Servicing Packages
- Component Manufacturing
- Race Circuit Support

Styles come and go.
Quality remains.

We love that wind-in-the-hair feeling driving a roadster – experiencing classic technology with all the senses.

As a company with more than 100 years of history, we know our stuff. At ZF Tradition, we make sure that automotive icons can still roam our streets. With parts service and reproduction as well as technical support.

zf.com

The 2016-2017 season case

This year's case study is dedicated to the Duemila Ruote Collection offered by RM Sotheby's at their sale in Milan, Italy, on 25-27 November 2017.

Number of lots offered 817   **Percentage of lots sold** 100%

Total sales
US$ 54.850.000   GBP 43.664.000   EUR 51.263.000

More than 5,000 auction attendees
Record 3,000 + bidders from 57 countries
30 hours of auction action

In what can only be described as 'record-breaking', RM Sotheby's captured the attention of the global collector community during the 25-27 November weekend with incredible results at its Duemila Ruote sale in Milan. Coinciding with the Milano AutoClassica – the Classic & Sports Car Show – the RM Sotheby's event represented the largest automotive-themed collection sale ever held in Europe. During approximately 30 hours of auctioneering, 817 lots – comprising motor cars, motorcycles, bicycles, boats and automobilia, all from one single private collection – were sold before a packed house at the Fiera Milano.

For auto enthusiasts, the collection's 423 motor cars, many of which were seen on the open market for the first time in decades, presented a thrilling range of ownership opportunities at every level, driving countless bidding contests over the course of the three-day auction. In a field dominated by rare Italian machinery, top sales honours went to the 1966 Ferrari 275 GTB/6C Alloy; the first of just seven long-nose, six-carburettor, alloy body, torque tube 275 GTBs, its rarity, provenance and freshness to the market propelled it to €3.416.000. Another star of the show, the 2004 Maserati MC12, sporting less than 6,000kms, was sold at €3.024.000.

Although there are too many highlights to list individually, other notable sales included the Lancia-built, Ferrari-engined 1991 Lancia-Ferrari LC2 Group C for €851.200; a 1994 Bugatti EB110 GT for an above-estimate €616.000; and a 'project' 1952 Aston Martin DB2 DHC achieved €504.000. Worth noting, strong results were not restricted to just the top-tier vehicles, rather witnessed across all price points. As a category, rally cars of the '80s / '90s proved particularly hot, as reflected in prices for the 1992 Lancia Delta HF Integrale Group A 'Jolly Club' at €336.000 (against a pre-sale estimate of €160–€180.000) and the 1989 Lancia Delta HF Integrale 16V 'Ufficiale' at a final €246.400. Then there was the group of almost 60 Porsche 911 variants, highlighted by a 1996 Porsche 993 GT2, which exceeded estimate at €616.000, not to forget 21 Jaguar E-Types, led by a 1963 Jaguar E-Type S1 3.8 OTS, which garnered €173.600 against a pre-sale estimate of €65-€75.000.

Beyond the automobiles, phenomenal interest was also recorded for other categories included in the sale. A 2008 Ducati Desmosedici led the group of 155 motorcycles at €70.200; the 1984 CUV Lamborghini #1 Offshore Class 1 'Miura', powered by two giant Lamborghini V-12s, dominated the fleet of 55 boats at €117.000; and a Vintage Fire Service Bicycle spearheaded the docket of 140 bicycles at €10.530. The perfect holiday gift for the young enthusiast, even the Jaguar D-Type Children's Car ignited spirited bidding, selling for €30.420.

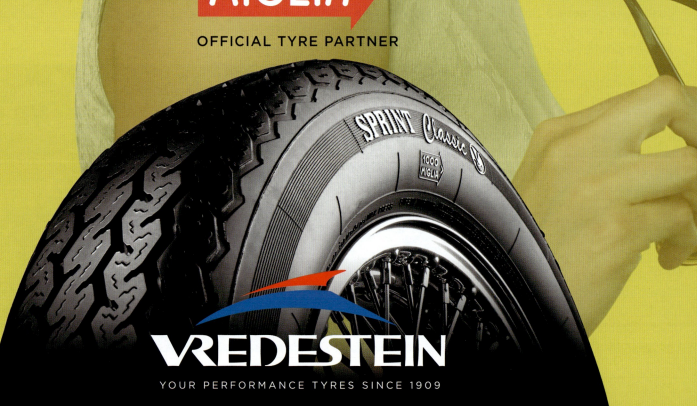

The 2016-2017 auction season results

This chapter lists, in alphabetical make order, the cars that were offered at auctions, covered by Historica Selecta, from 1st September 2016 to 31st August 2017.

5,659 cars (of 308 different makes) are listed in order of the model, presentation, year, and the date when they were auctioned.

From the first edition for the 1993-1994 season (Catalogo Bolaffi then Classic Car Auction Yearbook) forward, the technical data (year, chassis no., etc.), car condition, history, estimate and photos have been taken from the relative auction house catalogues, and the reported hammer prices are those communicated by the auction houses in their official lists. For this reason the authors cannot take any responsibility for mistakes and/or omissions.

The authors have not quoted most of the cars:
- listed in auction house sale catalogues without the indication of the chassis number or other identification number;
- of little historical interest because they were recently ceased to be produced or were replicas assembled with parts of various provenance.

N.B. The exchange rate is referred to as that of the day of the auction
The hammer prices include the buyer commission

Legenda

C	: central driver seat	F	: illustrated car
L	: left hand drive	SEASON CASE	: see chapter
M	: single-seater	TOP TEN	: see chapter
R	: right hand drive		
LWB	: long wheelbase	AUD	: Australian Dollar
SWB	: short wheelbase	EUR	: Euro
		GBP	: Pounds Sterling
NA	: not available	USD	: US Dollar
NQ	: not quoted		
UC	: unmarked chassis		
		*	: hammer price of the "no reserve" cars
NR	: no reserve	P	: price of the post auction sales
NS	: not sold		
UD	: sold for an undisclosed sum		
WD	: withdrawn	Refer Dpt.	: refer Department

List of the covered sales and auction house abbreviations

Agu - Aguttes (F)
Lyon	November 5, 2016
Lyon	March 18, 2017
Bagatelle	April 22, 2017
Lyon	June 10, 2017

Art - Artcurial (F)
* Chateau-sur-Epte	October 9, 2016
Paris	October 30, 2016
Paris	February 10, 2017
Monaco (MC)	July 2, 2017

AA - Auctions America (USA)
* Auburn, IN	September 1-4, 2016
* Hilton Head, SC	November 5, 2016
* Ft. Lauderdale, FL	March 31-April 2, 2017
* Auburn, IN	May 11-13, 2017

B/J - Barrett-Jackson (USA)
* Las Vegas, NE	October 13-15, 2016
* Scottsdale, AZ	January 14-22, 2017
* Palm Beach, FL	April 6-8, 2017
* Northeast, Uncasville, CT	June 21-24, 2017

Bon - Bonhams (GB)
Beaulieu	September 3, 2016
Chateau de Chantilly (F)	September 3, 2016
Goodwood	September 10, 2016
London	September 19, 2016
Philadelphia, PA (USA)	October 3, 2016
Knokke-Le Zoute (B)	October 7, 2016
London	November 4, 2016
London	December 4, 2016
London	December 7, 2016
Scottsdale, AZ (USA)	January 19, 2017
Paris (F)	February 9, 2017
Amelia Island, FL (USA)	March 9, 2017
Goodwood	March 19, 2017
Newport Pagnell	May 13, 2017
Spa (B)	May 21, 2017
Greenwich, CT (USA)	June 4, 2017
Goodwood	June 30, 2017
Carmel, CA (USA)	August 18, 2017

Che - Cheffins (GB)
Cambridge	July 15, 2017

CB/C - Coutau Bégarie/Coys (F)
* Paris	October 8, 2016

Coy - Coys (GB)
Fontwell Park	September 8, 2016
Ascot	October 8, 2016
London	October 29, 2016
London	December 5, 2016
Birmingham Autosport	January 14, 2017
Maastricht (H)	January 14, 2017
London	February 18, 2017
Essen (D)	April 8, 2017
* London	April 12, 2017
London	May 18, 2017
* Fontwell Park	June 29, 2017
* Blenheim Palace, Woodstock	July 15, 2017
Schloss Dyck (D)	August 5, 2017

Dor - Dorotheum (A)
* Salzburg	October 15, 2016
Wien	June 24, 2017

G&Co. - Gooding & Company (USA)
Scottsdale, AZ	January 20-21, 2017
Amelia Island, FL	March 10, 2017
Pebble Beach, CA	August 18-19, 2017

H&H - H&H (GB)
* Duxford	October 12, 2016
* Donington Park	November 16, 2016
* Chateau Impney	December 7, 2016
* Donington Park	February 23, 2017
* Duxford	March 29, 2017
* Solihull	June 2, 2017
* Woodcote Park	June 6, 2017
* Duxford	July 26, 2017

His - Historics at Brooklands (GB)
Mercedes-Benz World, Weybridge	November 26, 2016
* Brooklands	March 4, 2017
* Ascot	May 20, 2017
* Brooklands	July 8, 2017

Lea - Leake (USA)
* Dallas, TX	April 21, 2017

Mec - Mecum (USA)
* Louisville, KY	September 8-10, 2016
* Chicago, IL	October 6-8, 2016
* Dallas, TX	November 2-5, 2016
* Anaheim, CA	November 17-19, 2016
* Kansas City, KS	December 1-3, 2016
* Kissimmee, FL	January 6-15, 2017
* Los Angeles, CA	February 17-18, 2017
* Kansas City, KS	March 24-25, 2017
* Houston, TX	April 6-8, 2017
* Indianapolis, IN	May 16-20, 2017
* Monterey, CA	August 17-19, 2017

Mos - Mossgreen (AUS)
Melbourne	November 27, 2016
Melbourne	April 30, 2017
Sydney	May 28, 2017
* Mallala Motorsport Park	August 20, 2017

Mot - Motostalgia (USA)
* Amelia Island	March 11, 2017

Ose - Osenat (F)
Lyon	November 6, 2016
* Fontainebleau	March 18, 2017
Fontainebleau	March 19, 2017
* Obenheim	May 1, 2017
* Puiseux-Pontoise	May 14, 2017
Fontainebleau	June 18, 2017

RMS - RM Sotheby's (USA)
London (UK)	September 7, 2016
Hershey, PA	October 6-7, 2016
Duemila Ruote, Milan (I)	November 25-27, 2016
Daytona Beach, FL	December 4, 2016
Phoenix, AZ	January 19-20, 2017
Paris (F)	February 8, 2017
Amelia Island, FL	March 10-11, 2017
Villa Erba (I)	May 27, 2017
Santa Monica, CA	June 24, 2017
Monterey, CA	August 18-19, 2017

R&S - Russo & Steele (USA)
* Scottsdale, AZ	January 18-22, 2017
* Newport Beach, CA	June 2-4, 2017
* Monterey, CA	August 17-19, 2017

SiC - Silverstone Auctions (GB)
Salon Privé, Woodstock	September 2, 2016
* Silverstone	October 15, 2016
NEC Birmingham	November 12-13, 2016
* Stoneleigh Park	February 24-26, 2017
* Silverstone	May 13, 2017
* Silverstone	July 27-30, 2017

TFA - The Finest Automobile Auctions (USA)
* Aspen, CO	September 17, 2016
* Boca Raton, FL	February 11, 2017

WoA - Worldwide Auctioneers (USA)
* Auburn, IN	September 3, 2016
* Scottsdale, AZ	January 18, 2017
* Arlington, TX	April 21-22, 2017
* Monterey, CA	August 17, 2017

* *Partially covered sales*

PS: *The cars offered by Russo & Steele are listed with the consignment number and not with the lot number*

F1: 1953 Abarth 205 1100 Sport (Ghia)

F2: 1966 Abarth 1000 TC berlina

ABARTH (I) (1949-1981)

Year	Model (Bodybuilder)	Chassis no.	Steering	Estimate	£	$	€	Date	Place	Lot	Auc. H.
1953	**205 1100 Sport (Ghia)**	205104	R	750-1.000.000 USD	**692.307***	**891.000***	**759.132***	18-08-17	Monterey	151	**RMS** F1

One-off fitted with Fiat 1100/103 engine and gearbox, the car was exhibited at the Ghia stand at the 1953 Turin Motor Show. In 1954 it was sold to the USA to Bill Vaughn who exhibited it that same year at the New York Motor Show as the Vaughn SS Wildcat "the first overhead camshaft V-8 in the USA". No photos of the V-8 installation survive. Discovered in 1982, in 2010 it was bought by the current owner who subjected it to a restoration completed in 2015 when the car was exhibited at Pebble Beach, winning its class.

Year	Model (Bodybuilder)	Chassis no.	Steering	Estimate	£	$	€	Date	Place	Lot	Auc. H.
1956	**750 coupé (Zagato)**	110131082	L	70-80.000 GBP		NS		07-09-16	London	112	**RMS**

Red; restored at unspecified date, the car is described as in good overall condition (see lot 159 RM 31.10.12 $126,310).

| 1961 | **750 Record Monza (Zagato)** | 860214 | L | 75-90.000 GBP | | NS | | 07-09-16 | London | 172 | **RMS** |

Yellow; described as in very good overall condition. Raced in period and driven by Umberto Maglioli also (see Coys lots 254 10.5.08 NS, 130 9.8.08 NS and 204 25.10.08 NS).

| 1961 | **850 Record Monza coupé (Zagato)** | 868941 | L | 100-115.000 GBP | | NS | | 07-09-16 | London | 107 | **RMS** |

Red with black interior; 28,000 kms on the odometer. With Abarth Classiche certification.

| 1966 | **1000 TC berlina** | 110A2148946210 | L | 40-60.000 EUR | **45.750*** | **57.014*** | **53.640*** | 10-02-17 | Paris | 80 | **Art** F2 |

White with white and red chequered roof; 1,500 kms covered since the restoration carried out in 2016.

| 1967 | **595 SS** | 110F1399557 | L | 25-45.000 GBP | | NS | | 07-09-16 | London | 154 | **RMS** |

White with red vinyl interior.

| 1970 | **1300 Scorpione SS (Francis Lombardi)** | 104S1287292067 | L | 70-110.000 USD | **94.598*** | **116.600*** | **109.289*** | 19-01-17 | Scottsdale | 46 | **Bon** F3 |

Silver with black interior; full restoration completed in recent years.

| 1972 | **Formula Italia** | 025 | M | 20-25.000 GBP | | NS | | 08-09-16 | Fontwell Park | 158 | **Coy** |

Red; restored in 2006 circa. In ready to use condition.

AC (GB) (1908-)

Year	Model (Bodybuilder)	Chassis no.	Steering	Estimate	£	$	€	Date	Place	Lot	Auc. H.
1913	**10hp light car**	4383	R	25-28.000 GBP	24.150	32.078	28.661	03-09-16	Beaulieu	417	**Bon**

Light green with black wings; described as in very good driving order. Restored in Australia where it was in the same family ownership for neraly 100 years. Imported into the UK in 2015.

| 1933 | **16/56hp roadster** | 30 | R | 40-60.000 EUR | 43.694 | 54.578 | 49.200 | 06-11-16 | Lyon | 309 | **Ose** |

Dark red with black wings; built with saloon body, the car was fitted with the present body approximately in the late 1960s. Restoration completed in 1993.

| 1937 | **Ace 16/80 roadster** | L525 | R | 240-300.000 EUR | 249.374 | 307.464 | 276.000 | 07-10-16 | Zoute | 33 | **Bon** F4 |

Light metallic blue with dark blue leather interior; described as in very good overall condition. Engine rebuilt in 2012.

| 1953 | **2-litre Buckland sports tourer** | EH1984 | R | 42-52.000 GBP | | NS | | 26-11-16 | Weybridge | 179 | **His** |

Ivory; fully restored. Raced in period.

| 1948 | **2-litre cabriolet** | L930 | R | 22-27.000 GBP | 24.000 | 29.362 | 27.792 | 04-03-17 | Brooklands | 153 | **His** |

White with red leather interior; in good overall condition (see lot 204 Brooks 19.3.95 $12,838).

| 1950 | **2-litre Buckland sports tourer** | ELX1512 | L | NQ | **55.949*** | **71.500*** | **66.831*** | 22-04-17 | Arlington | 24 | **WoA** |

Black; restored at unspecified date and well maintained. From the Monical Collection (see lot 138 RM 9.10.14 $82,500).

F3: 1970 Abarth 1300 Scorpione SS (Francis Lombardi)

F4: 1937 AC Ace 16/80 roadster

F5: 1956 AC Ace Bristol

F6: 1962 AC Aceca Bristol

Year	Model	(Bodybuilder)	Chassis no.	Steering	Estimate	£	$	€	Date	Place	Lot	Auc. H.
1959	**Ace Bristol**		BE1059	R	180-220.000 GBP	**254.620**	**332.483**	**297.778**	19-09-16	London	611	**Bon**
Metallic blue with red leather interior; engine overhauled in the 1990s, body restored in 2015. From the collection of the late Robert White (see lot 518 Bonhams 11.7.08 $210,039).											
1958	**Ace**		AE414	R	120-140.000 GBP	**180.700**	**235.958**	**211.329**	19-09-16	London	614	**Bon**
Dark blue with grey interior; restored at unspecified date. Engine rebuilt in 1998 and in 2008 again. From the collection of the late Robert White.											
1959	**Ace Bristol**		BEX1099	L	275-325.000 USD	**197.085**	**242.000**	**227.601**	20-01-17	Scottsdale	65	**G&Co**
Red with black interior; bought in 1984 by Richard Riddell who had the body repainted in 1988 and drove the car in 1991 in the third running of the Colorado Grand rally. Stored for several years, the car was road-registered again in 2012 and is described as in good overall condition.											
1956	**Ace Bristol**		BEX211	L	220-280.000 EUR	**274.497**	**342.084**	**321.840**	10-02-17	Paris	11	**Art** **F5**
Blue with red interior; raced at some events in the 1950s. Restored in the 2000s (see lot 416 Artcurial 7.2.14 $380,235).											
1959	**Ace**		BEX447	L	225-275.000 USD	**170.940**	**220.000**	**188.100**	17-08-17	Monterey	33	**WoA**
Dark blue with red interior; built with Bristol engine, the car was raced at some events in period. Fitted at unspecified date with the present V8 engine, it was restored in 2000 circa and fitted with a 5-speed gearbox.											
1959	**Ace Bristol**		BEX1003	L	300-350.000 USD	**350.427**	**451.000**	**384.252**	18-08-17	Carmel	70	**Bon**
Old English white with red interior; one owner; raced in period; stored from 1972 to 1999 and subsequently fully restored.											
1963	**Aceca**		AEX796	L	75-100.000 USD	**61.639**	**77.000**	**69.408**	05-11-16	Hilton Head	140	**AA**
Bought in 1967 by the current, second owner; some restoration works carried out in 1976; following many years of storage, it requires further works prior to use.											
1962	**Aceca Bristol**		BE819	R	135-185.000 EUR	**127.082**	**158.372**	**149.000**	10-02-17	Paris	66	**Art** **F6**
Red with light brown interior; restored in Australia in 2005 and imported into Europe in 2006. 1,200 kms covered since the restoration.											
1955	**Aceca**		AE516	R	145-165.000 EUR	**141.224**	**175.890**	**165.000**	08-04-17	Essen	135	**Coy**
Blue; reimported into the UK from the USA in 2002 and subsequently restored. Engine rebuilt in 2013 in Switzerland. Swiss papers.											
1956	**Aceca Bristol**		BE573	R	100-120.000 GBP	**135.000**	**174.231**	**154.751**	06-06-17	Woodcote Park	15	**H&H**
Silver with grey leather interior; restored in 2004; some mechanical works carried out in recent years (see lot 39 H & H 17.4.13 $145,113).											
1955	**Aceca**		AE527	R	120-130.000 EUR	**114.755**	**150.854**	**127.110**	05-08-17	Schloss Dyck	232	**Coy**
Red; described as in original condition; recent mechanical works.											
1957	**Aceca Bristol**		BE603	R	175-250.000 USD	**149.573***	**192.500***	**164.010***	18-08-17	Carmel	84	**Bon**
Red with white stripes; prepared for historic racing (see lot 66 Coys 1.12.94 $52,373).											
1958	**Aceca Bristol**		BEX632	L	240-280.000 USD	**222.222**	**286.000**	**243.672**	19-08-17	Monterey	267	**RMS**
Black with red interior; sold new to the USA to Peter Sachs; with its second owner from 1965 to 2015 when it was bought by the vendor; restored in the UK by AC Cars in 2007.											
1967	**289 Sports**		COB6120	R	450-500.000 GBP		**NS**		07-09-16	London	173	**RMS**
Medium metallic blue with black interior; restoration completed in 2014. Raced at some events in the UK in the 1970s. One of the Cobras produced by AC for the British and European markets and named 289 Sports (see lot 238 Bonhams 15.5.04 NS).											

ACMA (F) *(1957-1961)*

Year	Model	(Bodybuilder)	Chassis no.	Steering	Estimate	£	$	€	Date	Place	Lot	Auc. H.
1958	**Vespa 400**		2677	L	15-20.000 GBP		**NS**		07-12-16	Chateau Impney	45	**H&H**
Yellow with yellow and white vinyl interior; restored in 2015.											

F7: 1958 Acma Vespa 400

F8: 1931 Alfa Romeo 6C 1750 GS spider (Zagato)

Where the world's greatest cars come to be sold - 14 QUEENS GATE PLACE MEWS, LONDON SW7 5BQ T: +44 (0)20 7584 3503 W: WWW.FISKENS.COM

2017 HAS SEEN FISKENS HANDLE THE SALE OF SOME OF THE WORLDS FINEST HISTORIC AUTOMOBILES. Highlights have included a 1978 Formula 1 Ferrari 312 T3, Aston Martin DB3 and DB3S, Bugatti Type 55 and a number of significant 50's & 60's sporting Jaguars. Due to this success, Fiskens are actively seeking new consignments for its refurbished central London mews showrooms. With no two negotiations ever being the same, our diverse knowledge and experience means there has never been a better time to consign. For a confidential discussion, please call Gregor, Rory or Robert.

FISKENS
FINE HISTORIC AUTOMOBILES

Year	Model	(Bodybuilder)	Chassis no.	Steering	Estimate	Hammer price £	$	€	Date	Place	Lot	Auc. H.
1958	Vespa 400		2677	L	17-22.000 EUR	11.983	14.924	14.000	08-04-17	Essen	103	Coy

See lot 45 H & H 7.12.16.

F7

ALFA ROMEO (I) *(1910-)*

Year	Model	(Bodybuilder)	Chassis no.	Steering	Estimate	£	$	€	Date	Place	Lot	Auc. H.
1932	6C 1750 GTC spider		101014946	R	300-350.000 GBP	NS			03-09-16	Beaulieu	444	Bon

Red with red interior; sold new to Australia in rolling chassis form, the car was damaged in a serious road accident in the 1940s. In the 1970s a restoration was started, using the original chassis, irreparably damaged, as a pattern for the rebuild of the present chassis. Years later the rebuilt rolling chassis was bought by a German collector who fitted it with the present, new Touring style Flying Star replica body (see lot 257 Coys 20.5.06 $182,491).

1931	6C 1750 GS spider	(Zagato)	10814358	R	2.800-3.400.000 USD	2.275.697	2.805.000	2.629.127	19-01-17	Scottsdale	30	Bon

Red with red interior; sold new to Switzerland and raced at some events. Imported into the USA in 1959; owned from 1962 to 2003 by Grant White; restored in the mid-1980s; since 2005 in the current ownership and regularly rallied and toured.

F8

| 1932 | 6C 1750 GS roadster | (Figoni) | 10814377 | R | 2.250-2.750.000 USD | 1.298.968 | 1.595.000 | 1.500.098 | 21-01-17 | Scottsdale | 136 | G&Co |

White with black wings and dark red interior; sold new to France and imported into the USA in the late 1950s. In 1974 it was bought by Gene Cesari who in the mid-1990s started the restoration and in 1997 resold the car to Sir John Venables-Llewellyn, Wales, who completed the work. Bought later by the current owner, the car has been again subjected to a concours-quality restoration completed in 2015.

F9

| 1929 | 6C 1750 Turismo cabriolet | (J.Young) | 0412061 | R | 210-250.000 EUR | NS | | | 10-02-17 | Paris | 68 | Art |

Grey with red interior; the original engine was replaced at unspecified date with a 1930 unit (see lots 720 Brooks 27.4.00 $106,144, 238 RM 29.10.08 NS, 161 Gooding & Company 16.8.09 $143,000, 151 Artcurial 9.7.10 NS, 229 RM 26.10.11 $169,953, 143 Coys 11.8.12 NA, and 454 Coys 2.12.14 NS).

| 1930 | 6C 1750 GS spider | (Sport) | 8513001 | R | 2.200-2.600.000 EUR | NS | | | 27-05-17 | Villa Erba | 141 | RMS |

Red; in very good overall condition. Raced in period.

| 1931 | 6C 1750 GS spider | | 10814349 | R | 2.000-2.500.000 USD | NS | | | 18-08-17 | Pebble Beach | 21 | G&Co |

Red with red interior; concours quality restoration carried out in the USA between 1993 and 1996; new Zagato-style body; engine rebuilt. History in Switzerland known from 1934 to 1960 when the car was imported into the USA. Since 1966 in the curren township.

| 1935 | Tipo B (P3) | | 50006 | M | 3.800-5.000.000 EUR | 3.344.348 | 4.180.680 | 3.920.000 | 08-02-17 | Paris | 161 | RMS |

Identified also by Scuderia Ferrari no.46, it is believed the car was driven also by Tazio Nuvolari and Achille Varzi, and by Antonio Brivio at the 1935 Masyrk GP in Brno. In 1936 it was sold to the UK, later in Australia and then in New Zealand and it was raced until the 1950s. In 1990 circa it was bought by Yoshiyuki Hayashi, in 2000 by Bruce McCaw and in 2007 by Umberto Rossi. Believed to be in largely original condition; included with the sale also the 3.2L SF-50-A engine from the Bimotore (see lot 235 RM 11.3.00 $2,145,000).

F10

| 1934 | 6C 2300 Pescara spider replica | | 700321 | R | 550-750.000 EUR | NS | | | 09-02-17 | Paris | 349 | Bon |

Replica of the body built in 1937 by Zagato for two 6C 2300 Pescaras of the Jacques de Rham's Scuderia Maremmana. The body, built by Dino Cognolato, is fitted to a 1934 6C 2300 Pescara chassis. Original engine rebuilt. 94 kms covered since the restoration (see lot 38 Bonhams 14.8.15 $473,000).

| 1936 | 6C 2300 Special spider | | 81301 | R | 220-300.000 GBP | 225.500 | 292.654 | 255.334 | 30-06-17 | Goodwood | 211 | Bon |

Discovered in rolling chassis form, the car was restored in the 1970s by Murray Rainey. The engine was rebuilt, fitted with twin supercharger and converted to dry sump lubrication. New two-seater sports body finished in red. Raced in the years at several historic hillclimbs. Recently recommissioned. From the Joy Rainey Collection.

| 1946 | 6C 2500 barchetta | | 913346 | R | 30-35.000 EUR | 257.590 | 320.302* | 302.400* | 25-11-16 | Milan | 623 | RMS |

Dark red with tan interior; body replica of the 412 Vignale. From the Duemila Ruote collection (see lot 200 Coys 25.10.08 NS).

| 1939 | 6C 2500 S cabriolet | (Pinin Farina) | 915019 | R | 1.000-1.200.000 GBP | 952.000 | 1.273.966 | 1.133.737 | 07-09-16 | London | 147 | RMS |

Dark brown with green leather interior; the car was discovered in 1993 in Hungary and was subsequently restored, the mechanicals in the Netherlands and the body in Czechoslovakia. Acquired later by the current owner, it received further mechanical works in Italy and the body was repainted. Three-carburettor engine. Accepted into the Registro Italiano Alfa Romeo e Registro Internazionale Touring Superleggera.

F11

| 1947 | 6C 2500 S coupé Aerlux | (Touring) | 916020 | R | 80-90.000 EUR | 195.578* | 243.192* | 229.600* | 25-11-16 | Milan | 575 | RMS |

Black; interior to be restored. From the Duemila Ruote collection.

F12

| 1949 | 6C 2500 S Freccia d'Oro | | 916431 | R | 65-75.000 EUR | 133.565* | 166.083* | 156.800* | 25-11-16 | Milan | 584 | RMS |

Dark green; the cloth interior require some attention. From the Duemila Ruote collection.

| 1948 | 6C 2500 S cabriolet | (Pinin Farina) | 916009 | R | 200-300.000 EUR | 191.106 | 238.896 | 224.000 | 08-02-17 | Paris | 135 | RMS |

Burgundy with beige interior; the car was sold new to Spain where it remained until 1987 with its first owner and was subsequently restored. In good driving order. Swiss tax paid (see lots 265 Artcurial 13.6.11 NS and 164 RM 31.10.12 $297,731).

| 1948 | 6C 2500 S cabriolet | (Pinin Farina) | 916009 | R | 300-350.000 EUR | 226.814 | 282.490 | 265.000 | 08-04-17 | Essen | 171 | Coy |

See lot 135 RM/Sotheby's 8.2.17.

| 1939 | 6C 2500 S berlinetta | (Touring) | 915005 | R | 1.800-2.400.000 USD | NS | | | 17-08-17 | Monterey | 26 | WoA |

Fitted with the three-carburettor SS engine, the car was imported after WWII in the USA where it remained in the same family ownership until the late 1980s. Reimported into Europe, it was first restored in the Netherlands in the early 1990s, and again in Italy between 2011 and 2013 by Carrozzeria Touring Superleggera (see lot 47 TSAC 15.9.90 NS).

F9: 1932 Alfa Romeo 6C 1750 GS roadster (Figoni)

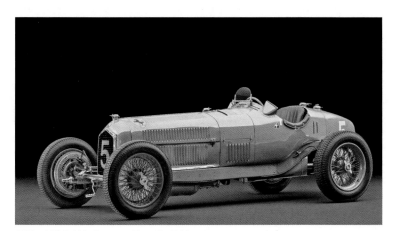

F10: 1935 Alfa Romeo Tipo B (P3)

FERRARI 125 S
MUSEO FERRARI

MERCEDES BENZ 540 K STROMLINIEN
MERCEDES-BENZ MUSEUM

BENZ PRINCE HEINRICH
LOUWMAN MUSEUM

OM SUPERBA 665 SSMM CASTAGNA
MUSEO NICOLIS

ALFA ROMEO 8C 2.3 ZAGATO
MUSEO DELLA SCIENZA E DELLA TECNOLOGIA
LEONARDO DA VINCI

Professional restorations
Full size drawings for original bodyworks
Manufacture of prototypes

DINO COGNOLATO & C. S.N.C.
CARROZZERIA NOVA RINASCENTE
VIA NOALESE, 66 - 35010 VIGONZA (PD) -ITALY-
TEL +39 049 8095482 FAX +39 049 8096298
novarinascente@cognolato.it

Year	Model	(Bodybuilder)	Chassis no.	Steering	Estimate	Hammer price £	$	€	Sale Date	Place	Lot	Auc. H.

F11: 1939 Alfa Romeo 6C 2500 S cabriolet (Pinin Farina)   F12: 1947 Alfa Romeo 6C 2500 S coupé Aerlux (Touring)

Year	Model (Bodybuilder)	Chassis no.	St.	Estimate	£	$	€	Date	Place	Lot	Auc. H.
1950	6C 2500 SS coupé (Touring)	915758	R	700-850.000 USD	723.888*	880.000*	829.312*	10-03-17	Amelia Island	162	RMS F13

Dark metallic olive green with tan leather interior; sold new in Italy, the car was imported into the USA in 1957. Concours-quality restoration completed in 2012. From the Orin Smith collection (see lot 32 Gooding & Company 17.8.13 $814,000).

1950	6C 2500 SS cabriolet (Pinin Farina)	915788	R	400-500.000 USD	376.068	484.000	412.368	18-08-17	Pebble Beach	29	G&Co

Black with green interior; sold new to Switzerland; in single ownership in France from 1957 to 2013; restored in Italy between 2006 and 2012; since 2014 with the present, fourth owner.

1949	6C 2500 SS coupé (Touring)	915831	R	700-800.000 USD		NS		19-08-17	Pebble Beach	128	G&Co

Restored in the 2000s; body recently repainted in the present two-tone livery (see lots 174 RM 16.1.09 $198,000 and 143 Gooding & Company 17.8.14 $539,000).

1956	1900 Super berlina	AR190017129	L	15-20.000 EUR	33.391*	41.521*	39.200*	25-11-16	Milan	261	RMS

Grey with blue and grey cloth interior; 17,000 kms. From the Duemila Ruote collection.

1956	1900 Super berlina	AR190012567	L	20-25.000 GBP	21.850	27.007	25.152	19-03-17	Goodwood	44	Bon F14

Dark blue with grey cloth interior; restored many years ago (see lot 215 Coys 18.5.09 NS and 39 Chevau-Légerè 3.2.11 $62,870).

1952	1900 M "Matta"	01739	L	28-32.000 GBP		NS		07-09-16	London	106	RMS

White with black interior; in off-road-ready condition.

1952	1900 M "Matta"	AR5101739	L	17-25.000 GBP	18.880	22.990	21.565	14-01-17	Birmingham	106	Coy

See lot 106 RM/Sotheby's 7.9.16.

1954	1900 M "Matta"	AR5100812	L	18-28.000 EUR	18.176	23.128	20.700	24-06-17	Wien	352	Dor

Red with black interior; restored.

1952	1900 M "Matta"	AR5100408	L	45-55.000 USD	52.137*	67.100*	57.169*	18-08-17	Pebble Beach	55	G&Co

Delivered new to Italian Army; sold to private hands in the early 1970s; restored in Italy in 2015. From the collection of Donald Osborne.

1953	1900 C Sprint (Touring)	AR1900C01247	L	160-180.000 EUR	305.292*	379.617*	358.400*	25-11-16	Milan	303	RMS

Grey/beige with brown interior. From the Duemila Ruote collection.

1952	1900 C Sprint (Touring)	AR1900C01173	R	275-325.000 EUR	224.601	288.409	257.600	27-05-17	Villa Erba	166	RMS F15

Dark green with two-tone interior; restored 10 years ago (see lot 260 Coys 18.5.09 NS).

1954	1900 C Sprint 2ª serie (Touring)	AR1900C01801	L	400-500.000 USD	291.148	357.500	336.229	21-01-17	Scottsdale	130	G&Co

Green with leather and cloth interior; sold new to the USA. The car was restored at unspecified date and is described as in very good overall condition.

1954	1900 C Sprint 2ª serie (Touring)	AR1900C02011	L	210-260.000 EUR		NS		10-02-17	Paris	67	Art

Black; restored in the 1990s, the car is in very good driving order.

1955	1900 C Sprint 2ª serie (Zagato)	AR1900C01915	L	800-1.200.000 USD	904.860*	1.100.000*	1.036.640*	11-03-17	Amelia Island	257	RMS

Metallic grey; sold new in Italy, the car was raced at some events including the 1955 and 1956 Mille Miglia editions. In 1959 it was imported into the USA where it remained from 1962 to 2002 with the same owner who stored it since 1963. Returned to running order, it was bought in 2013 by the current owner who subsequently had the body repainted to its original colour. 26.265 kms on the odometer. **F16**

1957	1900 C Super Sprint (Touring)	AR1900C10301	L	180-200.000 EUR	213.007	262.626	235.750	07-10-16	Zoute	15	Bon

Blue with red leather interior; restored between 2002 and 2006. Acquired in 2014 by the current, third owner.

1956	1900 C Super Sprint (Touring)	AR1900C10066	L	200-250.000 EUR	182.998	228.056	214.560	10-02-17	Paris	69	Art

Grey with red roof and red and white interior; restored in Belgium in 2014 (see lot 135 Coys 6.8.16 $265,474).

F13: 1950 Alfa Romeo 6C 2500 SS coupé (Touring)   F14: 1956 Alfa Romeo 1900 Super berlina

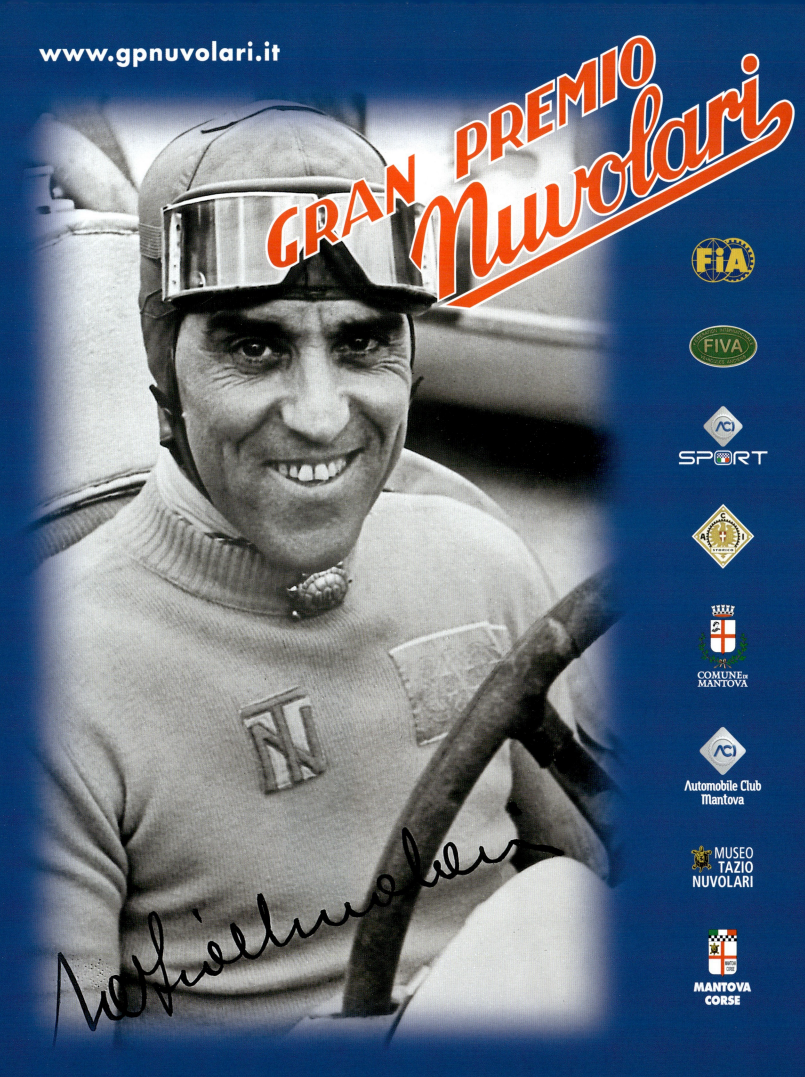

Year	Model	(Bodybuilder)	Chassis no.	Steering	Estimate	Hammer price £	Hammer price $	Hammer price €	Sale Date	Sale Place	Lot	Auc. H.

F15: 1952 Alfa Romeo 1900 C Sprint (Touring)

F16: 1955 Alfa Romeo 1900 C Sprint 2ª serie (Zagato)

Year	Model	(Bodybuilder)	Chassis no.	Steering	Estimate	£	$	€	Date	Place	Lot	Auc. H.
1957	**1900 C Super Sprint (Touring)**		AR1900C10270	L	200-250.000 USD		NS		09-03-17	Amelia Island	158	Bon

Red with black interior; in 1992 restored and prepared for the Mille Miglia Storica. Engine rebuilt on an Alfa Romeo 2000 block. In good working order.

| 1956 | **1900 C Super Sprint (Touring)** | | AR1900C10145 | L | 200-275.000 USD | 144.778* | 176.000* | 165.862* | 10-03-17 | Amelia Island | 108 | RMS |

Yellow with black roof and black Zagato-style leather seats; imported into the USA in 1969; restored in 1989; in the late 1990s prepared for historic events and fitted with the present Alfa Romeo 2000 engine and gearbox. From the Orin Smith collection.

| 1961 | **Giulietta Sprint (Bertone)** | | AR159206 | L | 50-60.000 GBP | 28.000* | 37.470* | 33.345* | 07-09-16 | London | 186 | RMS |

Light yellow with red interior; restoration completed in early 2016 (see lot 173 Coys 9.4.16 $64,278).

| 1956 | **Giulietta Sprint Veloce (Bertone)** | | AR1493E01861 | L | 45-55.000 EUR | 128.795* | 160.151* | 151.200* | 25-11-16 | Milan | 615 | RMS
F17 |

Red; for restoration. From the Duemila Ruote collection.

| 1960 | **Giulietta Sprint (Bertone)** | | AR149325759 | L | 15-20.000 EUR | 59.150* | 73.551* | 69.440* | 25-11-16 | Milan | 637 | RMS |

White; 84,186 kms. From the Duemila Ruote collection.

| 1959 | **Giulietta Sprint (Bertone)** | | AR149322221 | L | 30-40.000 GBP | 31.152 | 37.934 | 35.582 | 14-01-17 | Birmingham | 122 | Coy |

Red; raced at historic events for over 30 years. Engine rebuilt in 2014 (see lot 229 Coys 14.1.06 $12,988).

| 1960 | **Giulietta Sprint (Bertone)** | | AR149322221 | L | 32-40.000 GBP | 28.899 | 37.676 | 33.852 | 18-05-17 | London | 133 | Coy |

See lot 122 Coys 14.1.17.

| 1956 | **Giulietta Sprint Veloce (Bertone)** | | AR1493E02159 | L | 255-295.000 EUR | | NS | | 21-05-17 | SPA-Francorch. | 71 | Bon |

Blue with grey interior; sold new in Italy and never raced. Restored in the early 1990s, the car comes with Italian ASI homologation. Acquired in 2006 by the current German owner, it is described as in very good overall condition.

| 1961 | **Giulietta Spider (Pininfarina)** | | AR170384 | L | 34-40.000 GBP | 56.000 | 74.939 | 66.690 | 07-09-16 | London | 181 | RMS |

White with black interior; since new in the same family ownership.

| 1956 | **Giulietta Spider (Pinin Farina)** | | 131540883 | L | 95-115.000 USD | 49.329 | 65.000 | 57.896 | 17-09-16 | Aspen | 106 | TFA |

White with red interior; sold new to the USA. Restored a few years ago. Recently serviced.

| 1957 | **Giulietta Spider (Pinin Farina)** | | AR149501657 | L | 10-15.000 EUR | 38.162* | 47.452* | 44.800* | 25-11-16 | Milan | 238 | RMS |

Red; for restoration. From the Duemila Ruote collection.

| 1960 | **Giulietta Spider (Pinin Farina)** | | 11835 | L | 15-20.000 EUR | 47.702* | 59.315* | 56.000* | 25-11-16 | Milan | 539 | RMS |

Grey; for restoration. From the Duemila Ruote collection.

| 1955 | **Giulietta Spider (Pinin Farina)** | | AR149500016 | L | 35-40.000 EUR | 73.461* | 91.345* | 86.240* | 25-11-16 | Milan | 910 | RMS |

3rd car built; restoration in progress. From the Duemila Ruote collection.

| 1958 | **Giulietta Spider Veloce (Pinin Farina)** | | AR149505389 | L | 120-160.000 USD | 142.789 | 176.000 | 164.965 | 19-01-17 | Scottsdale | 49 | Bon
F18 |

Graphite grey with red interior; the car has covered 300 miles since a full restoration carried out in the USA. Original engine rebuilt and enlarged to 1,490cc; original gearbox rebuilt and fitted with a fifth gear.

| 1959 | **Giulietta Spider (Pinin Farina)** | | AR149506993 | L | NQ | 62.709* | 77.000* | 72.419* | 21-01-17 | Scottsdale | 824 | B/J |

Black with red interior; restored. Engine and gearbox rebuilt (see lot 107 RM 15.1.15 NS).

F17: 1956 Alfa Romeo Giulietta Sprint Veloce (Bertone)

F18: 1958 Alfa Romeo Giulietta Spider Veloce (Pinin Farina)

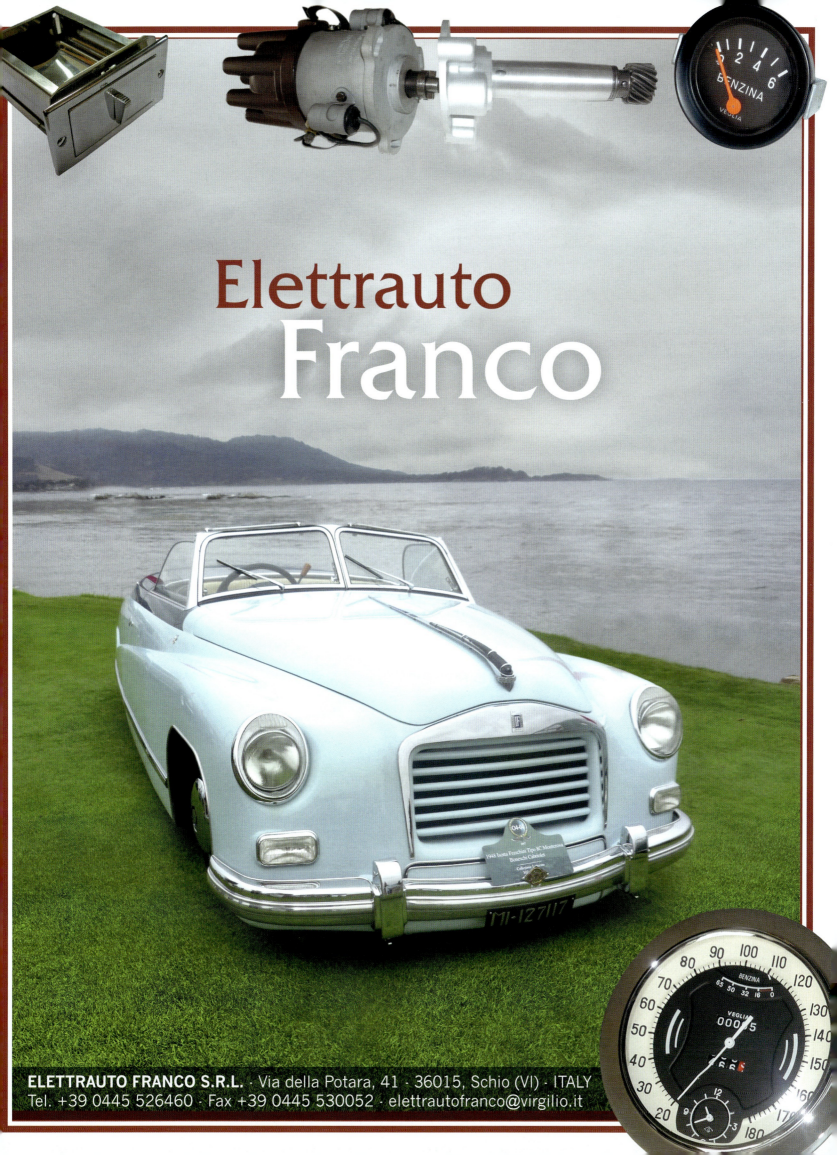

Year	Model	(Bodybuilder)	Chassis no.	Steering	Estimate	Hammer price £	$	€	Sale Date	Place	Lot	Auc. H.

F19: 1957 Alfa Romeo Giulietta Spider (Pinin Farina)

F20: 1960 Alfa Romeo Giulietta Sprint Speciale (Bertone)

1957 Giulietta Spider (Pinin Farina)   AR1495G00301   L   475-575.000 EUR   **406.099**   **507.654**   **476.000**   08-02-17   Paris   152   **RMS**
One of 24 Tipo 750-G competition examples; engine AR1315 30709. Sold new to the USA, the car was reimported into Europe in 2007 and was discovered in a neglected but complete state by the vendor in Rome in 2011. Mechanicals rebuilt in the Netherlands; "monoposto" body restored in Italy by Carrozzeria Quality Cars; electrical overhaul by Elettrauto Franco in Italy. Dutch papers; road registered; with FIVA passport.   **F19**

1962 Giulietta Spider (Pininfarina)   AR370272   L   55-75.000 EUR   **57.437**   **70.993**   **66.120**   18-03-17   Lyon   180   **Agu**
Red; restored.

1956 Giulietta Spider (Pinin Farina)   AR149500135   L   120-150.000 EUR   **89.870**   **111.930**   **105.000**   08-04-17   Essen   151   **Coy**
White with red interior; sold new to the USA; reimported into Italy in 1993. Gear lever mounted on the steering-wheel.

1961 Giulietta Spider (Pininfarina)   AR169729   L   55-65.000 GBP   **58.240**   **75.782**   **67.791**   20-05-17   Ascot   259   **His**
Red with black interior; restored.

1959 Giulietta Spider (Pinin Farina)   AR149505821   L   75-85.000 EUR   **63.228**   **82.277**   **73.600**   21-05-17   SPA-Francorch.   44   **Bon**
Dark blue with beige interior; restored in Italy between 2013 and 2014 (see lot 386 Bonhams 2.4.16 NS).

1958 Giulietta Spider (Pinin Farina)   149503466   L   55-65.000 GBP   **55.000**   **70.928**   **62.150**   08-07-17   Brooklands   135   **His**
Black with red interior; engine recently rebuilt still being run in.

1960 Giulietta Spider Veloce (Pinin Farina)   AR1495F07582   L   130-160.000 USD   **121.367**   **156.200**   **133.551**   17-08-17   Monterey   6   **WoA**
Red with light beige vinyl interior; driven until the 1970s and subsequently stored until 2009 when it received a full restoration.

1959 Giulietta Spider Veloce (Pinin Farina)   149506373   L   125-150.000 USD   **60.684***   **78.100***   **66.541***   18-08-17   Carmel   17   **Bon**
White with red interior; sold new to the USA; bought in the late 2000s by the current owner and fully restored over a two year period. Correct engine (no.131532565) not original to the car.

1961 Giulietta Sprint Speciale (Bertone)   AR102000681   L   80-90.000 EUR   **114.485***   **142.356***   **134.400***   25-11-16   Milan   560   **RMS**
White with blue and light grey interior. From the Duemila Ruote collection.

1962 Giulietta Sprint Speciale (Bertone)   AR177324   L   140-180.000 USD   **125.418***   **154.000***   **144.837***   21-01-17   Scottsdale   105   **G&Co**
Silver; sold new in Italy; restored in Belgium between 2008 and 2009; imported into the USA in 2013; engine rebuilt and enlarged to 1,430cc in 2016.

1962 Giulietta Sprint Speciale (Bertone)   AR177369   L   120-150.000 EUR   **NS**   08-02-17   Paris   104   **RMS**
Blue; in single-family ownership for over 40 years. In largely original condition.

1961 Giulietta Sprint Speciale (Bertone)   177123   L   90-130.000 USD   **69.556***   **84.700***   **80.270***   09-03-17   Amelia Island   113   **Bon**
Red with black leather interior; restored in Germany in 1990 circa. Since 2006 in the current ownership (see Coys lots 238 12.4.03 $37,685, 131a 26.4.03 $33,430, and 1119 21.6.03 $38,965).

1961 Giulietta Sprint Speciale (Bertone)   AR1012000319   L   140-180.000 USD   **104.059***   **126.500***   **119.214***   10-03-17   Amelia Island   10   **G&Co**
White with blue/grey interior; restored in the 1980s to concours condition.

1961 Giulietta Sprint Speciale (Bertone)   AR1012000334   L   90-110.000 GBP   **98.499**   **127.123**   **112.909**   06-06-17   Woodcote Park   27   **H&H**
Red with black interior; sold new to the USA; reimported into Europe in 2001 and subsequently restored.

1962 Giulietta Sprint Speciale (Bertone)   AR1012000718   L   110-130.000 EUR   **110.728**   **145.561**   **122.650**   05-08-17   Schloss Dyck   226   **Coy**
Red with black interior; restored in recent times.

1960 Giulietta Sprint Speciale (Bertone)   AR1012000177   L   125-150.000 USD   **76.923***   **99.000***   **84.348***   18-08-17   Pebble Beach   22   **G&Co**
Red; raced at several historic events since 1982; restored in 2009; 128bhp engine no.AR00530.6597 rebuilt in 2015; roll cage unbolts for road driving events. Offered with also an unassembled AR00120-series engine.

F21: 1961 Alfa Romeo Giulietta SZ coda tonda (Zagato)

F22: 1962 Alfa Romeo Giulietta SZ coda tronca (Zagato)

Pandolfini
CASA D'ASTE
dal 1924

PANDOLFINI AUCTION HOUSE

CLASSIC CARS

1935 Alfa Romeo 6C 2300T "Soffio di Satana" Carrozzeria Touring

FLORENCE
Palazzo Ramirez Montalvo
Borgo Albizi, 26 | Tel. +39 055 2340888-9
info@pandolfini.it

MILAN
Via Manzoni, 45
Tel. +39 02 65560807
milano@pandolfini.it

ROME
Via Margutta, 54
Tel. +39 06 3201799
roma@pandolfini.it

PANDOLFINI APP DOWNLOAD

FOLLOW US ON

PANDOLFINI.COM

Year	Model (Bodybuilder)	Chassis no.	Steering	Estimate	Hammer Price £	$	€	Date	Place	Lot	Auc. H.
1960	**Giulietta Sprint Speciale (Bertone)**	AR1012000338	L	125-175.000 USD	106.838*	137.500*	117.150*	18-08-17	Monterey	138	RMS **F20**
Dark blue with grey interior; restored several years ago.											
1961	**Giulietta SZ coda tonda (Zagato)**	0072	L	260-360.000 EUR	255.767	319.478	288.000	05-11-16	Lyon	248	Agu **F21**
Raced at several rallies in France in the 1960s, the car was damaged in an accident at the 1968 Criterium des Cevennes and subsequently remained unrepaired. Following some ownership changes, in 2004 it was bought by the current owner who three years ago started a restoration not yet completed.											
1961	**Giulietta SZ coda tonda (Zagato)**	AR1012600113	L	600-700.000 USD		NS		18-08-17	Pebble Beach	31	G&Co
Red; bought new by 1957 500 GP motorcycle world champion Libero Liberati and raced by him in period. In the 1980s the car was bought by Martin Swig, imported into the USA and raced at historic events. In 1997 it was acquired by the current owner and subsequently fully restored.											
1962	**Giulietta SZ coda tronca (Zagato)**	AR1012600207	L	400-500.000 USD	307.888*	379.500*	355.705*	19-01-17	Phoenix	150	RMS **F22**
Red with black interior; sold new in Italy, the car was later imported into the USA, then into Japan and in 2014 it was imported again in the USA. Restored many years ago. Currently fitted with Alfa Romeo 1750 engine, it is offered with also the 1300 Veloce engine no.AR0012000634, unrestored, believed to be original to the car (see lot 321 Bonhams 4.2.16 NS).											
1960	**2000 Berlina**	AR1020001613	L	25-35.000 USD		NS		17-09-16	Aspen	120	TFA
Light grey with blue cloth and leatherette interior; in good overall condition. Body repainted 12 years ago. Bought in 2014 by the current, third owner and imported into the USA (see lot 510 Artcurial 7.2.14 $27,506).											
1960	**2000 Spider (Touring)**	AR1020401608	L	50-70.000 EUR	61.101	77.919	69.720	10-06-17	Lyon	141	Agu
Red; in good overall condition (see lot 28 Poulain 7.10.97 $17,906).											
1962	**2600 Spider (Touring)**	AR192169	L	90-120.000 EUR	72.674	96.540	86.250	03-09-16	Chantilly	14	Bon
Blue with red leather interior; restored in Italy between 2010 and 2012.											
1963	**2600 Spider (Touring)**	AR191872	R	58-65.000 GBP	92.220	122.496	109.447	03-09-16	Beaulieu	433	Bon **F23**
White with red leather interior; body repainted, interior retrimmed (see lot 108 Coys 16.04.16 $56,720).											
1963	**2600 Spider (Touring)**	AR191782	L	50-70.000 EUR	58.613	73.214	66.000	06-11-16	Lyon	320	Ose
Red with black interior; since 1993 with the current owner who carried out several mechanical works over the years.											
1963	**2600 Spider (Touring)**	AR191496	L	70-90.000 EUR	85.998*	107.503*	100.800*	08-02-17	Paris	142	RMS
Red with black interior; sold new to the USA, the car remained in single ownership until 2013 when it was acquired by the vendor and imported into Switzerland. Stored from 1968 to 1998 when it was restored; extensive service completed in 2013.											
1965	**2600 Spider (Touring)**	AR192809	L	85-125.000 EUR	68.664	87.373	78.200	24-06-17	Wien	358	Dor
Navy blue with grey leatherette interior; sold new to the USA; imported into Germany in the early 1990s; restored in 1993-94.											
1964	**2600 Spider (Touring)**	AR192869	L	70-90.000 EUR	63.270	93.379	71.952	02-07-17	Monaco	103	Art
Red with black interior; in good overall condition. Two owners since 1969.											
1964	**2600 Spider (Touring)**	AR192801	L	100-120.000 EUR	88.583	116.449	98.120	05-08-17	Schloss Dyck	239	Coy
White with black leather interior; mechanicals rebuilt seven years ago.											
1964	**2600 Spider (Touring)**	AR192802	L	250-300.000 USD	239.316	308.000	262.416	19-08-17	Pebble Beach	139	G&Co
Sold new to the USA; in single ownership from 1972 to 2007; restored to concours condition between 2007 and 2012 and finished in the present medium grey livery with black interior; with hardtop.											
1962	**2600 Sprint (Bertone)**	AR820594	L	25-5.000 EUR	27.667*	34.403*	32.480*	25-11-16	Milan	944	RMS
White; it requires some restoration works. From the Duemila Ruote collection.											
1963	**2600 Sprint (Bertone)**	821999	L	40-50.000 EUR	32.292*	40.576*	37.950*	09-02-17	Paris	330	Bon **F24**
White with brown leather interior; restored in France between 2009 and 2014 (see Osenat lots 326 15.3.15 NS and 248 8.11.15 NS).											
1964	**2600 Sprint (Bertone)**	AR823917	L	35-45.000 EUR	50.140	61.974	57.720	18-03-17	Lyon	182	Agu
Blue; original interior; some recent mechanical works.											
1966	**2600 Sprint (Bertone)**	854543	R	18-24.000 GBP	20.720	26.721	23.414	08-07-17	Brooklands	118	His
Red with cream interior; body repainted in 2003; recently serviced.											
1963	**2600 Sprint (Bertone)**	826326	L	22-28.000 EUR	20.132	26.466	22.300	05-08-17	Schloss Dyck	269	Coy
Described as in very good mechanical condition; body restored many years ago (see lot 428 Bonhams 4.2.16 $20,619).											
1974	**Giulia Super Familiare (Giorgetti)**	AR198331	L	55-70.000 GBP	29.120*	38.968*	34.679*	07-09-16	London	178	RMS **F25**
Metallic grey with red side stripe; recent restoration and mechanical service.											
1972	**Giulia Super berlina**	1985636	L	15-25.000 EUR	18.218*	22.132*	20.264*	30-10-16	Paris	109	Art
White; for 44 years in the same ownership. With Italian ASI homologation.											
1969	**Giulia TI berlina**	AR637589	L	15-20.000 EUR	19.290*	23.434*	21.456*	30-10-16	Paris	148	Art
Italian Polizia Stradale green livery; in good condition and fitted with its original equipment.											

F23: 1963 Alfa Romeo 2600 Spider (Touring)

F24: 1963 Alfa Romeo 2600 Sprint (Bertone)

F25: 1974 Alfa Romeo Giulia Super Familiare (Giorgetti)   *F26: 1962 Alfa Romeo Giulia Spider (Pininfarina)*

Year	Model (Bodybuilder)	Chassis no.	Steering	Estimate	£	$	€	Date	Place	Lot	Auc. H.
1963	**Giulia berlina**	AR420971	L	35-45.000 EUR		NS		09-02-17	Paris	331	**Bon**
Mouse grey with light grey cloth interior; restored.											
1974	**Giulia Nuova Super 1600 berlina**	AR105260024713	L	13-15.000 GBP	**11.893**	**15.505**	**13.931**	18-05-17	London	145	**Coy**
Black with tan interior; two owners; 16,000 kms on the odometer. Gearbox rebuilt in 2016.											
1964	**Giulia TI Super berlina**	AR595241	L	90-140.000 EUR		NS		21-05-17	SPA-Francorch.	69	**Bon**
White; sold new in Italy, in 1999 the car was bought by Jurgen End and prepared for historic racing. With FIA and FIVA papers.											
1964	**Giulia Spider (Pininfarina)**	378221	L	55-75.000 EUR		NS		03-09-16	Chantilly	17	**Bon**
White with black interior; restored in 1990. Two owners and 90,000 kms covered since new.											
1963	**Giulia Spider (Pininfarina)**	AR377790	L	15-20.000 EUR	**49.610***	**61.688***	**58.240***	25-11-16	Milan	891	**RMS**
Red with red interior; it requires some restoration works. From the Duemila Ruote collection.											
1962	**Giulia Spider (Pininfarina)**	AR372823	L	80-100.000 USD	**65.942***	**80.300***	**76.100***	09-03-17	Amelia Island	114	**Bon** **F26**
Black with red interior; fully restored between 2010 and 2013.											
1964	**Giulia Spider (Pininfarina)**	AR383353	R	32-36.000 GBP	**43.700**	**54.013**	**50.303**	19-03-17	Goodwood	5	**Bon**
Red with black interior; on museum display since 1985, the car requires recommissioning and/or some restoration works prior to use.											
1963	**Giulia Spider (Pininfarina)**	AR372724	L	60-80.000 USD	**53.053**	**68.200**	**60.800**	04-06-17	Greenwich	163	**Bon**
Red with black interior; restored in the early 1990s. Recently serviced.											
1965	**Giulia Spider (Pininfarina)**	AR379851	L	65-75.000 EUR	**52.344**	**68.811**	**57.980**	05-08-17	Schloss Dyck	230	**Coy**
Red with black interior; restored between 2008 and 2011; engine rebuilt to Veloce specification.											
1965	**Giulia Sprint GT (Bertone)**	AR613513	L	4-6.000 EUR	**15.265***	**18.981***	**17.920***	25-11-16	Milan	926	**RMS**
Restoration project. From the Duemila Ruote collection.											
1963	**Giulia Sprint Speciale (Bertone)**	AR380343	L	NA		NS		02-09-16	Salon Privé	206	**SiC**
Silver; restored in 2010 (see lot 139 Bonhams 13.05.16 $97,877).											
1963	**Giulia Sprint Speciale (Bertone)**	AR352819	R	80-100.000 GBP		NS		07-12-16	London	352	**Bon**
Red with red and ivory interior; 1,075 miles covered since a long-term restoration. Recently serviced (see lot 257 Historics 11.6.16 $129,051).											
1963	**Giulia Sprint Speciale (Bertone)**	AR380106	L	90-130.000 EUR	**86.111**	**108.203**	**101.200**	09-02-17	Paris	407	**Bon** **F27**
Red with tan leather interior; recently restored in Italy. Irish papers.											
1965	**Giulia Sprint Speciale (Bertone)**	AR381311	L	100-120.000 USD		NS		01-04-17	Ft.Lauderdale	595	**AA**
Blue with beige interior; restored.											
1963	**Giulia Sprint Speciale (Bertone)**	AR10121380303	L	90-110.000 GBP		NS		29-07-17	Silverstone	445	**SiC**
Red with red and white interior; recently restored (see lot 229 RM/Sotheby's 14.5.16 $127,098).											
1963	**Giulia Sprint Speciale (Bertone)**	AR380526	L	140-180.000 USD	**128.205***	**165.000***	**140.580***	19-08-17	Pebble Beach	117	**G&Co**
Blue; sold new in Italy where it was later restored; ASI homologated. Bought by the current owner from the Artom Collection and imported into the USA.											
1965	**Giulia Sprint Speciale (Bertone)**	AR381380	L	225-275.000 USD		NS		19-08-17	Monterey	F74	**Mec**
Moss green with tobacco interior; in original, unrestored condition; 47,000 miles covered; until 2012 with its first owner. From the Colin Comer Collection.											

F27: 1963 Alfa Romeo Giulia Sprint Speciale (Bertone)   *F28: 1965 Alfa Romeo Giulia GTA (Bertone)*

Year	Model (Bodybuilder)	Chassis No.	Steering	Estimate	Hammer price £	Hammer price $	Hammer price €	Date	Place	Lot	Auc. H.
1965	**Giulia GTA (Bertone)**	AR613721	L	200-230.000 EUR	286.212*	355.891*	336.000*	25-11-16	Milan	304	RMS
	White with black interior; road version. 50,197 kms. From the Duemila Ruote collection.										
1965	**Giulia GTA (Bertone)**	AR613457	L	350-425.000 EUR		NS		08-02-17	Paris	175	RMS
	Red with black interior; sold new to Switzerland, the car was imported into Germany in 1980. Described as in original condition.										
1965	**Giulia GTA (Bertone)**	AR613526	L	250-350.000 EUR		NS		18-03-17	Lyon	181	Agu
	White; raced at some hillclimbs in France in the 1960s. Stored in 1975, it was bought in 1984 by the current owner but never used. Body repainted and mechanicals overhauled recently.										
1965	**Giulia GTA (Bertone)**	AR752675	R	225-275.000 EUR	219.719	282.139	252.000	27-05-17	Villa Erba	127	RMS F28
	Red; 40 kms covered since the restoration; for over 20 years in the current ownership. Conrero/Jolly Club team car.										
1966	**Giulia GT Veloce (Bertone)**	AR245095	L	35-40.000 EUR	41.978*	52.197*	49.280*	25-11-16	Milan	292	RMS
	White with black and grey interior; 45,841 kms. From the Duemila Ruote collection.										
1967	**Giulia GT Veloce (Bertone)**	AR249045	L	50-70.000 EUR		NS		09-02-17	Paris	311	Bon
	Yellow with black interior; restored circa 12 years ago. Mechanicals rebuilt.										
1967	**Giulia Spider Duetto (Pininfarina)**	AR663658	L	NA	25.880	34.376	30.714	02-09-16	Salon Privé	224	SiC
	Red with black interior; body repainted at unspecified date.										
1966	**Giulia Spider Duetto (Pininfarina)**	AR660062	L	45-60.000 USD		NS		05-11-16	Hilton Head	126	AA
	Red with tan interior (see lot 2008 Auctions America 18.7.15 $28,875).										
1966	**Giulia Spider Duetto (Pininfarina)**	AR660585	L	15-20.000 EUR	43.656*	54.284*	51.250*	25-11-16	Milan	270	RMS
	Red with black interior; 44,701 kms. From the Duemila Ruote collection.										
1967	**Giulia Spider Duetto (Pininfarina)**	AR665436	L	40-60.000 USD	29.810*	36.300*	34.402*	09-03-17	Amelia Island	159	Bon F29
	Red with black interior; restored.										
1966	**Giulia Spider Duetto (Pininfarina)**	663089	L	28-35.000 GBP		NS		08-07-17	Brooklands	155	His
	White with black interior; in good overall condition. Just one owner.										
1975	**Giulia 1300 Super berlina**	AR0034776	L	12-15.000 GBP		NS		08-10-16	Ascot	346	Coy
	Magenta with biscuit velour interior; in good overall condition (see Coys lots 136 16.4.16 NS and 145 2.7.16 $7,305).										
1978	**Nuova Giulia Super 1300 berlina**	AR0048337	L	105-13.500 GBP	9.800	12.357	11.516	07-12-16	Chateau Impney	50	H&H
	Black with tan interior; restored in 2014.										
1971	**Giulia GT 1300 Junior (Bertone)**	AR1264874	L	14-18.000 GBP	17.920	21.923	20.751	04-03-17	Brooklands	228	His
	Grey with brown leatherette interior in good overall condition.										
1975	**Giulia GT 1300 Junior (Bertone)**	AR105300002735	L	15-20.000 EUR		NS		05-08-17	Schloss Dyck	224	Coy
	Light blue; described as in very good mechanical order.										
1968	**Giulia GTA 1300 Junior (Bertone)**	AR775851	L	150-180.000 EUR		NS		30-10-16	Paris	149	Art
	Red; race prepared and described as in very good condition.										
1968	**Giulia GTA 1300 Junior (Bertone)**	AR775599	L	220-260.000 EUR	185.922	233.620	218.500	09-02-17	Paris	315	Bon F30
	Red; bought new by the Scuderia Monzeglio Corse; winner of the 1971 Italian Turismo 2 championship driven by Luigi Pozzo. Engine recently rebuilt and based on a Monzeglio block; offered with also a second engine based on a correct Alfa Romeo 1399 GTA block (no.00559).										
1969	**Giulia GTA 1300 Junior (Bertone)**	775403	L	290-340.000 EUR		NS		21-05-17	SPA-Francorch.	81	Bon
	White and green; ex-Autodelta official car, it was raced at numerous racing events in the 1970s. Bought in 2012 by the current German owner, it received subsequently several restoration works. Engine currently fitted with carburettors (some Spica fuel-injection parts are included with the sale).										
1969	**1750 GT Veloce (Bertone)**	AR1370772	L	45-60.000 EUR	41.795	50.774	46.488	30-10-16	Paris	150	Art
	Dark maroon; in very good condition.										
1968	**1750 GT Veloce (Bertone)**	AR1355413	L	15-20.000 EUR	40.070*	49.825*	47.040*	25-11-16	Milan	863	RMS
	Metallic grey; 73,771 kms. From the Duemila Ruote collection.										
1971	**1750 GT Veloce (Bertone)**	1391096	L	20-30.000 EUR		NS		19-03-17	Fontainebleau	206	Ose
	Red with beige interior; body restored some years ago. From the René Cocheteux collection.										
1969	**1750 GT Veloce (Bertone)**	AR130772	L	42-47.000 EUR	32.524	40.508	38.000	08-04-17	Essen	212	Coy
	See lot 150 Artcurial 30.10.16.										
1969	**1750 GT Veloce (Bertone)**	AR1452360	R	25-30.000 GBP	24.640	32.062	28.681	20-05-17	Ascot	133	His
	Red with black interior; restored in 2003.										
1968	**1750 GT Veloce (Bertone)**	AR1453161	R	28-32.000 GBP	27.000	34.846	30.950	06-06-17	Woodcote Park	7	H&H
	Red; restored in Australia in 2010, imported into the UK in 2014.										

F29: 1967 Alfa Romeo Giulia Spider Duetto (Pininfarina)

F30: 1968 Alfa Romeo Giulia GTA 1300 Junior (Bertone)

Year	Model (Bodybuilder)	Chassis No.	Steering	Estimate	£	$	€	Date	Place	Lot	Auc. H.
1971	**1750 GT Veloce (Bertone)**	AR1532603	L	26-32.000 EUR	**29.552**	**37.685**	**33.720**	10-06-17	Lyon	121	Agu
	Metallic blue with beige leatherette interior; sold new to the USA; reimported into Europe in 2007. The original Spica injection system has been replaced with carburettors.										
1970	**1750 GT Veloce (Bertone)**	AR1530818	L	32-35.000 EUR		NS		10-06-17	Lyon	142	Agu
	Red; restored between 2009 and 2012.										
1971	**1750 GT Veloce (Bertone)**	1456743	R	30-40.000 GBP	**28.000**	**36.338**	**31.704**	29-06-17	Fontwell Park	136	Coy
	Aubergine with tan interior; restored between 2014 and 2016.										
1969	**1750 GT Veloce (Bertone)**	AR1371138	L	40-60.000 EUR	**39.016***	**57.583***	**44.370***	02-07-17	Monaco	196	Art **F31**
	Red; recent restoration works carried out in Italy.										
1971	**1750 GT Veloce (Bertone)**	1456743	R	30-40.000 GBP	**27.787**	**35.912**	**31.580**	15-07-17	Blenheim Pal.	167	Coy
	See lot 136 Coys 29.6.17.										
1969	**1750 Spider Veloce (Pininfarina)**	AR1481322	L	38-45.000 EUR	**29.957**	**37.310**	**35.000**	08-04-17	Essen	126	Coy
	Red with tan interior; offered with US title and European taxes paid.										
1974	**33 TT-12**	AR11512010	R	2.400-2.800.000 USD		NS		18-08-17	Pebble Beach	48	G&Co
	Campari red livery with white front spoiler and rear wing; Works car during the 1974 and 1975 seasons, when it raced by the German Willi Kauhsen Racing Team winning the races of Spa, Zeltweg and Watkins Glen of the 1975 FIA World Sportscar Championship driven by Pescarolo/Bell. The car remained in the Autodelta ownership until 1980 when it was acquired by the current owner and subsequently raced over the years at numerous historic events.										
1973	**2000 berlina**	2349616	L	14-19.000 EUR	**9.591**	**11.980**	**10.800**	06-11-16	Lyon	313	Ose
	Described as in good working order; body repainted 10 years ago (see lot 375 Osenat 19.6.16 NS).										
1972	**2000 GT Veloce (Bertone)**	AR2410066	R	18-26.000 GBP	**18.480**	**22.649**	**20.553**	12-10-16	Duxford	81	H&H
	Yellow with black vinyl interior; some restoration works carried out in 2005. Imported into the UK from South Africa in 2016.										
1975	**2000 GT Veloce (Bertone)**	02445742	L	30-40.000 EUR	**32.504**	**40.600**	**36.600**	06-11-16	Lyon	324	Ose
	Described as in very good overall condition; since 1988 in the current ownership.										
1973	**2000 GT Veloce (Bertone)**	AR2437336	L	15-18.000 EUR	**24.805***	**30.844***	**29.120***	25-11-16	Milan	291	RMS
	Silver with black interior; 40,019 kms. From the Duemila Ruote collection.										
1972	**2000 GT Veloce (Bertone)**	AR2430821	L	15-18.000 EUR	**33.391***	**41.521***	**39.200***	25-11-16	Milan	628	RMS
	Metallic grey with tan interior; 85,054 kms. From the Duemila Ruote collection.										
1973	**2000 GT Veloce (Bertone)**	2412335	R	10-15.000 GBP	**17.920**	**22.282**	**21.036**	26-11-16	Weybridge	110	His
	Red with black interior; described as in good overall condition. Since 1985 in the current ownership.										
1974	**2000 GT Veloce (Bertone)**	2413375	R	22-24.000 GBP		NS		07-12-16	Chateau Impney	24	H&H
	Green with tan vinyl interior; stored from 1989 to 2015 and subsequently recommissioned.										
1974	**2000 GT Veloce (Bertone)**	AR3026745	L	50-75.000 USD	**67.825***	**83.600***	**78.358***	19-01-17	Scottsdale	17	Bon
	Dark blue with beige interior; restored.										
1973	**2000 GT Veloce (Bertone)**	AR2412580	R	28-34.000 GBP		NS		04-03-17	Brooklands	183	His
	White with anthracite grey interior; in good overall condition.										
1973	**2000 GT Veloce (Bertone)**	AR2436341	L	40-60.000 EUR		NS		02-07-17	Monaco	168	Art
	Amaranth with cognac interior; restored.										
1974	**2000 Spider Veloce (Pininfarina)**	AR3044025	L	19-25.000 GBP		NS		15-07-17	Blenheim Pal.	114	Coy
	Red with black interior; in good overall condition. Sold new to the USA.										
1972	**Montreal (Bertone)**	1427035	L	40-60.000 EUR	**43.605***	**57.924***	**51.750***	03-09-16	Chantilly	3	Bon
	White with black interior; described as in very good overall condition. Body repainted two years ago.										
1974	**Montreal (Bertone)**	AR1428470	L	35-50.000 GBP	**35.840**	**47.961**	**42.682**	07-09-16	London	187	RMS
	Red; recent mechanical restoration.										
1971	**Montreal (Bertone)**	AR1425356	L	NQ	**63.444***	**83.600***	**74.463***	17-09-16	Aspen	135	TFA
	Red with black interior; sold new in Italy, the car was imported into the USA in 1985 circa. In good overall condition.										
1973	**Montreal (Bertone)**	AR1428159	L	45-65.000 EUR	**50.368**	**61.189**	**56.024**	30-10-16	Paris	151	Art
	Body repainted; in good mechanical condition.										
1973	**Montreal (Bertone)**	AR1428381	L	5-10.000 EUR	**32.437***	**40.334***	**38.080***	25-11-16	Milan	652	RMS
	Orange with black interior. From the Duemila Ruote collection.										
1971	**Montreal (Bertone)**	AR1425257	L	40-45.000 EUR	**57.242***	**71.178***	**67.200***	25-11-16	Milan	895	RMS
	White with blue and black interior; 51,827 kms. From the Duemila Ruote collection.										

F31: 1969 Alfa Romeo 1750 GT Veloce (Bertone)

F32: 1973 Alfa Romeo Montreal (Bertone)

Year	Model	(Bodybuilder)	Chassis no.	Steering	Estimate	Hammer price £	$	€	Date	Place	Lot	Auc. H.
1973	**Montreal**	(Bertone)	AR1426330	L	80-100.000 EUR	66.887	83.614	78.400	08-02-17	Paris	171	**RMS** F32
	White; restored in recent years. Swiss papers (see lots 103 Gooding & Company 18.8.13 $99,000 and 209 RM/Sotheby's 14.8.15 $110,000).											
1972	**Montreal**	(Bertone)	AR1426028	L	65-70.000 EUR		NS		09-02-17	Paris	392	**Bon**
	Bronze with fawn cloth interior; restored; engine rebuilt.											
1971	**Montreal**	(Bertone)	AR1425545	L	85-100.000 USD		NS		11-02-17	Boca Raton	142	**TFA**
	Black with black and beige interior; imported into the USA in the last decade. 90,000 original kms (see lot 101 Bonhams 19.8.16 $52,800).											
1972	**Montreal**	(Bertone)	AR1427863	L	90-110.000 USD	59.721*	72.600*	68.418*	11-03-17	Amelia Island	295	**RMS**
	Metallic gold with cloth interior; described as in highly original condition. 79,866 kms on the odometer.											
1971	**Montreal**	(Bertone)	AR1425276	L	75-85.000 USD	54.764	70.400	62.762	04-06-17	Greenwich	172	**Bon**
	Metallic gold with beige interior; restoration completed before the import into the USA in 2014. Further mechanical works carried out in 2016 (see lot 371 Bonhams 16.11.11 $7,261).											
1972	**Montreal**	(Bertone)	AR1427253	L	60-80.000 EUR	61.161*	90.267*	69.554*	02-07-17	Monaco	167	**Art**
	Green; restored.											
1973	**Montreal**	(Bertone)	1427035	L	55-60.000 GBP	51.000	66.518	57.125	26-07-17	Duxford	108	**H&H**
	See lot 3 Bonhams 3.9.16.											
1976	**Giulia GT 1600 Junior**	(Bertone)	115050001858	R	20-26.000 GBP	21.185	28.299	25.051	08-09-16	Fontwell Park	106	**Coy**
	Red; 41,000 miles covered. Body repainted.											
1973	**Giulia GT 1600 Junior**	(Bertone)	AR2206022	R	14-18.000 GBP	15.120	18.531	16.816	12-10-16	Duxford	9	**H&H**
	Red with black vinyl interior; body repainted in 2008. Described as in very good mechanical condition.											
1973	**Giulia GT 1600 Junior**	(Bertone)	AR2199924	L	10-15.000 EUR	35.299*	43.893*	41.440*	25-11-16	Milan	922	**RMS**
	White; 47,240 kms. From the Duemila Ruote collection.											
1975	**Giulia GT 1600 Junior**	(Bertone)	AR0001351	L	40-50.000 EUR		NS		09-02-17	Paris	361	**Bon**
	Red with original beige vinyl interior; restored in Italy in 2016.											
1973	**Giulia 1600 Coupé Zagato**		AR3060263	L	40-60.000 EUR	53.351	70.134	59.095	05-08-17	Schloss Dyck	222	**Coy** F33
	Red; restored in the Netherlands in 2007.											
1981	**Alfetta berlina**		2176489	L	8-12.000 EUR	11.788*	14.321*	13.112*	30-10-16	Paris	147	**Art**
	Italian Polizia Stradale blue and white livery; in good overall condition. Fitted with the original equipment; movie star.											
1974	**Alfetta GT 1.8**		AR0002860	L	5-7.000 GBP	5.610	6.815	6.239	29-10-16	London	101	**Coy**
	Red with grey and black interior; in good overall condition. Recently imported into the UK from Italy.											
1983	**Alfetta GTV Production 2.0**		64810	L	14-18.000 EUR		NS		05-11-16	Lyon	223	**Agu**
	Special edition built in 300 examples; body repainted in its original grey livery; original cloth interior.											
NQ	**Alfetta GTV 2000**		10066	L	25-5.000 EUR	28.621*	35.589*	33.600*	25-11-16	Milan	224	**RMS**
	Blue and white; modified for racing, it requires several restoration works. From the Duemila Ruote collection.											
1979	**Alfetta GTV 2000**		AR116150006345	L	NQ	17.288*	22.000*	19.690*	24-06-17	Northeast	146	**B/J**
	Red with slate interior; in original condition; one owner.											
1976	**Alfetta GTV 2000**		AR116150001227	L	35-45.000 USD	18.803*	24.200*	20.618*	18-08-17	Pebble Beach	1	**G&Co**
	Red; in good overall condition; approximately 63,000 miles covered.											
1992	**Spider 1.6**	(Pininfarina)	006059	L	12-14.000 GBP		NS		26-11-16	Weybridge	208	**His**
	Yellow; in good overall condition. Fitted with LPG system.											
1984	**Spider 1.6**	(Pininfarina)	006715	L	10-15.000 EUR	8.339	10.308	9.600	18-03-17	Fontainebleau	50	**Ose**
	Red with red hardtop; from the Perinet Marquet collection.											
1985	**Spider 2.0**	(Pininfarina)	750524	L	10-12.000 EUR	19.081*	23.726*	22.400*	25-11-16	Milan	362	**RMS**
	Silver; 49,563 kms. From the Duemila Ruote collection.											
1987	**75 Alfa Corse**		AC002	L	20-30.000 EUR	47.702*	59.315*	56.000*	25-11-16	Milan	269	**RMS**
	Blue and white Italian Police livery. From the Duemila Ruote collection.											
1987	**75 Evoluzione IMSA**		AC022	L	100-120.000 EUR	286.212*	355.891*	336.000*	25-11-16	Milan	296	**RMS** F34
	Alfa Corse red livery; ex-Works car. From the Duemila Ruote collection.											
1987	**75 Turbo Evoluzione Gruppo A**		AR10	L	10-15.000 EUR	95.404*	118.630*	112.000*	25-11-16	Milan	924	**RMS**
	White. From the Duemila Ruote collection.											

F33: 1973 Alfa Romeo Giulia 1600 Coupé Zagato

F34: 1987 Alfa Romeo 75 Evoluzione IMSA

Year	Model	(Bodybuilder)	Chassis no.	Steering	Estimate	£	$	€	Date	Place	Lot	Auc. H.

F35: 1996 Alfa Romeo R.Z. (Zagato)   F36: 1951 Allard J2 competition

1988	**75 V6 3.0**		3001337	R	8-10.000 GBP	**7.627**	9.617	8.962	07-12-16	Chateau Impney	62	**H&H**

Red with grey cloth and alcantara interior; in very good overall condition.

| 1991 | **SZ (Zagato)** | | 3000507 | L | 70-90.000 EUR | | NS | | 02-07-17 | Monaco | 170 | **Art** |

Red with beige interior; 900 kms covered; recently serviced (see lot 336 Silverstone Auctions 23.5.15 NS).

| 1996 | **R.Z. (Zagato)** | | 3002206 | L | 40-50.000 GBP | **42.750** | 55.981 | 47.730 | 29-07-17 | Silverstone | 714 | **SiC** **F35** |

Yellow with black leather interior; 36,946 miles covered; recently serviced.

| 2008 | **8C Competizione** | | 38950 | L | 325-375.000 USD | **271.458** | 330.000 | 310.992 | 10-03-17 | Amelia Island | 3 | **G&Co** |

Red with tan interior; less than 2,900 miles covered.

| 2009 | **8C Spider** | | 49811 | L | 375-425.000 USD | **321.225** | 390.500 | 368.007 | 10-03-17 | Amelia Island | 80 | **G&Co** |

Red with red leather interior; two owners; less than 950 miles covered.

ALL AMERICAN RACERS (USA) *(1965-)*

| 1968 | **Indy Eagle** | | 406 | M | 350-400.000 USD | | NS | | 11-03-17 | Amelia Island | 289 | **RMS** |

Yellow and blue Sunoco livery; bought new by Roger Penske and driven by Mark Donahue at the 1968 Indianapolis 500 Miles; raced until 1975 by other owners. Restored in the early 2000s to its Indy 1968 livery and fitted with a 320cu.in. Traco-Chevrolet V8 engine.

| 1974 | **Indy Eagle** | | 7410 | M | 225-275.000 USD | **156.772*** | 192.500* | 181.046* | 21-01-17 | Scottsdale | 127 | **G&Co** |

Driven by Mario Andretti at the 1975 Indianapolis 500. Restored in 2012. 2,617cc turbocharged Offenhauser 4-cylinder engine built by Bill Akin; estimated 950bhp.

ALLARD (GB) *(1937-1959)*

| 1948 | **K1 roadster** | | 518 | R | 70-80.000 GBP | | NS | | 29-03-17 | Duxford | 75 | **H&H** |

Red with beige interior; sold in rolling chassis form, the car was fitted in 1950 probably with the present K2 body and later sold to New Zealand. Raced at several events from 1974, it was fitted in the 1990s probably with the present 235cu.in. engine. Described as in very good condition.

| 1947 | **K1 roadster** | | 161 | R | 100-120.000 EUR | **77.031** | 95.940 | 90.000 | 08-04-17 | Essen | 140 | **Coy** |

Red; restored between 2005 and 2006. Swiss papers.

| 1951 | **J2 competition** | | 99J2121 | R | 250-325.000 USD | **225.830** | 275.000 | 260.618 | 09-03-17 | Amelia Island | 135 | **Bon** **F36** |

British racing green with tan interior; in the late 1960s restored and fitted with a Shelby Cobra 289 Hi-Po engine and Ford 4-speed gearbox. In the same ownership from 1969 to 2008; fully restored again between 2008 and 2011 (see lots 6 Gooding & Company 8.3.13 $330,000 and 8 Bonhams 19.8.16 NS).

| 1950 | **K2/K1 two-seater** | | 91K1703 | L | 150-200.000 USD | **90.486*** | 110.000* | 103.664* | 10-03-17 | Amelia Island | 103 | **RMS** **F37** |

Grey with black interior; restoration completed in the 2000s. Ford V8 engine bored out to 295c.i. Ordered new with the K1 body. From the Orin Smith collection (see lot 74 Gooding & Company 11.3.11 $165,000).

| 1951 | **K2 two-seater** | | K2242 | R | 100-120.000 EUR | | NS | | 08-04-17 | Essen | 209 | **Coy** |

Green; imported into Switzerland in 1971 and subsequently restored. Swiss papers.

F37: 1950 Allard K2/K1 two-seater   F38: 1986 Alpina B6 2.7

Year	Model	(Bodybuilder)	Chassis no.	Steering	Estimate	Hammer price £	$	€	Date	Place	Lot	Auc. H.

ALPINA (D) (1961-)

Year	Model	Chassis no.	Steering	Estimate	£	$	€	Date	Place	Lot	Auc. H.
1986	B6 2.7	210040	L	50-70.000 USD	42.390*	52.250*	48.974*	19-01-17	Phoenix	108	RMS F38
1984	C1 2.3	538695	L	50-70.000 USD	42.104*	51.700*	48.624*	21-01-17	Pebble Beach	161	G&Co
1993	B10 Allroad	310013	L	15-18.000 EUR	19.653	23.932	22.448	14-01-17	Maastricht	241	Coy
1985	B10	593983	R	25-30.000 GBP	25.000	32.240	28.250	08-07-17	Brooklands	173	His
1991	B12 5.0	57526	R	45-55.000 GBP	64.688	81.209	76.545	24-02-17	Stoneleigh P.	915	SiC
1993	B12 5.7	200013	R	55-65.000 GBP	63.000	82.499	70.340	29-07-17	Silverstone	739	SiC
2003	Z8 Roadster	62126	L	295-320.000 USD		NS		17-09-16	Aspen	147	TFA
2004	Z8 Roadster	62238	L	320-380.000 EUR		NS		09-02-17	Paris	371	Bon
2003	Z8 Roadster	62392	L	275-325.000 USD	226.215	275.000	259.160	10-03-17	Amelia Island	63	G&Co
2003	Z8 Roadster	62308	L	NQ	142.194*	177.100*	166.120*	08-04-17	Palm Beach	734	B/J
2003	Z8 Roadster	62095	L	NQ		NS		08-04-17	Houston	S91.1	Mec
2003	Z8 Roadster	62504	L	225-250.000 USD	138.312	180.000	161.010	20-05-17	Indianapolis	S110	Mec
2003	Z8 Roadster	62316	L	215-245.000 USD		NS		24-06-17	Santa Monica	218	RMS
2003	Z8 Roadster	62520	L	225-275.000 USD	181.624	233.750	199.856	17-08-17	Monterey	73	WoA
2003	Z8 Roadster	62283	L	200-250.000 USD	158.120	203.500	173.382	18-08-17	Carmel	110	Bon

- 1986 B6 2.7 — One of 67 examples built with the 2.7-litre engine for the Japanese market; described as in very good original condition. 35,430 kms on the odometer.
- 1984 C1 2.3 — Blue; recently imported into the USA from Japan. Just under 65,000 kms covered. Recently serviced and detailed.
- 1993 B10 Allroad — Silver with anthracite interior; in good overall condition. 90,000 kms covered.
- 1985 B10 — Black with original black leather interior; restored.
- 1991 B12 5.0 — Blue with light grey leather interior; 39,000 miles covered.
- 1993 B12 5.7 — Dark blue with dark blue leather interior; regularly serviced, the car has covered 178,500 kms. Two owners. Manual gearbox.
- 2003 Z8 Roadster (62126) — Titanium grey with black leather interior; less than 20,000 miles covered.
- 2004 Z8 Roadster (62238) — Black with cream and black leather interior; circa 20,000 kms covered; three owners; recently serviced.
- 2003 Z8 Roadster (62392) — Black with black leather interior; less than 3,200 miles covered.
- 2003 Z8 Roadster (62308) — Silver with black interior; two owners.
- 2003 Z8 Roadster (62095) — Black with black interior; 16,100 actual miles. With hardtop. From the Emalee Burton collection.
- 2003 Z8 Roadster (62504) — Silver with black leather interior; 12,204 believed original miles.
- 2003 Z8 Roadster (62316) — Titanium grey with red interior; one owner; less than 15,000 miles covered.
- 2003 Z8 Roadster (62520) — Titanium grey with black and red leather interior; one owner; 3,998 miles covered.
- 2003 Z8 Roadster (62283) — Silver with black interior; one owner; 16,800 miles covered; with hardtop.

ALPINE (F) (1955-1980)

Year	Model	Chassis no.	Steering	Estimate	£	$	€	Date	Place	Lot	Auc. H.
1976	A110 1600 SC	20452	L	100-120.000 EUR		NA		08-10-16	Paris	181	CB/C
1972	A110 1600 S	17936	L	90-105.000 EUR	95.404*	118.630*	112.000*	25-11-16	Milan	547	RMS
1976	A110 1600 SC	20452	L	75-90.000 GBP	101.816	129.459	120.957	05-12-16	London	117	Coy
1972	A110 1600 VC Group 4	18226	L	125-175.000 EUR	254.164	316.744	298.000	10-02-17	Paris	92	Art F39
1973	A110 1600 SC	20050	L	80-110.000 EUR	93.922	116.088	108.120	18-03-17	Lyon	189	Agu
1971	A110 1600 S	17379	L	90-120.000 EUR	100.176	123.819	115.320	18-03-17	Lyon	205	Agu

- 1976 A110 1600 SC (20452) — Blue with black interior; described as in excellent overall condition.
- 1972 A110 1600 S — Blue; 87,375 kms. From the Duemila Ruote collection.
- 1976 A110 1600 SC — See lot 181 Coutau Bégarie/Coys 8.10.16.
- 1972 A110 1600 VC Group 4 — One of seven "competition client" examples sold by the factory in 1972, the car, fitted with the 1,860cc Mignolet engine, placed 14th at the 1973 Monte Carlo Rally driven by Bob Wolleck. In 1990 it was bought by the current owner, restored to its original white and red "Defense Mondiale" livery and fitted with a new 1,860cc engine. Since 2001 it is driven by Jean Ragnotti at historic events.
- 1973 A110 1600 SC — French blue; from 1976 to 2016 with the same owner who raced the car at some events in France until 1982. Recently restored.
- 1971 A110 1600 S — French blue; described as in very good original condition. Overhauled in 2016 (see lot 125 Bonhams 13.5.16 $97,877).

F39: 1972 Alpine A110 1600 VC Group 4

F40: 1964 Alpine M64

Year	Model	(Bodybuilder)	Chassis no.	Steering	Estimate	Hammer price £	Hammer price $	Hammer price €	Sale Date	Sale Place	Lot	Auc. H.
1970	A110 1600 S Group 4		16693	L	100-120.000 EUR		NS		10-06-17	Lyon	137	Agu

Blue with black interior; the car was bought new by Jean Saurel who raced it at several rallies in 1970 and 1971. Saurel bought it again in 2003 and prepared it for historic rallying. Last serviced in 2015 (see lot 163 Artcurial 5.2.16 $130,857).

1964	M64		1711	L	330-380.000 EUR	332.217	403.590	369.520	30-10-16	Paris	130	Art **F40**

Recently restored; ex-Works car. 1964 Le Mans 24 Hours class winner (see lot 156 RM 10.5.14 $432,172).

1977	A310 V6		0043955	L	20-30.000 EUR	22.215	28.268	25.300	24-06-17	Wien	338	Dor

White with black leather interior; paintwork and interior redone in recent years. Recently serviced.

ALVIS (GB) *(1920-1967)*

Year	Model	(Bodybuilder)	Chassis no.	Steering	Estimate	£	$	€	Date	Place	Lot	Auc. H.
1931	12/60 "beetleback"		9113	R	40-50.000 GBP	42.237	54.587	48.002	15-07-17	Blenheim Pal.	103	Coy

Green; from 1932 to 1975 with its first owner. Restored between 1988 and 1994.

| 1936 | Silver Eagle SG tourer | (Cross/Ellis) | 12720 | R | 115-135.000 USD | 80.606 | 99.000 | 92.832 | 18-01-17 | Scottsdale | 9 | WoA |

Red with beige interior; with its first owner in the UK until 1967 when it was exported to the USA. Restored in the 1980s, it is described as in good overall condition.

| 1933 | Firefly tourer | (Cross/Ellis) | 10778 | R | 28-32.000 GBP | 31.360 | 38.435 | 34.879 | 12-10-16 | Duxford | 136 | H&H |

White with black wings and tan interior; restored in the 1990s (see lot 130 H & H 9.12.15 NS).

| 1936 | Speed 20 SD cabriolet | (Vanden Plas) | 13031 | R | 80-100.000 GBP | | NS | | 08-09-16 | Fontwell Park | 150 | Coy |

Dark blue; some restoration works carried out over the years. Engine rebuilt approximately 14,000 miles ago (see lot 168 Coys 2.7.16 $98,287).

| 1934 | Speed 20 SC tourer | | 11940 | R | 45-55.000 GBP | 72.800 | 89.224 | 80.968 | 12-10-16 | Duxford | 114 | H&H |

Blue with grey interior; built with Lancefield limousine body, in the same ownership from 1944 to 1988, restored in the mid-1990s and fitted with the present, new Vanden Plas style body (see lot 31 H & H 11.4.01 $63,092).

| 1935 | Speed 20 SC tourer | | 12051 | R | 62-70.000 GBP | | NS | | 26-11-16 | Weybridge | 201 | His |

The car was imported at unspecified date into East Africa where it was also raced. Later reimported into the UK. Described as in good driving order.

| 1934 | Speed 20 SB tourer | (Vanden Plas) | 11171 | R | 90-120.000 GBP | 104.540 | 131.814 | 122.845 | 07-12-16 | London | 372 | Bon **F41** |

Acquired in 2009 by the current owner and subsequently restored; 14,000 miles covered in the last seven years.

| 1935 | Speed 20 SC tourer | | 12085 | R | 120-150.000 EUR | 88.449 | 110.227 | 103.704 | 10-02-17 | Paris | 130 | Art |

Dark green with green leather interior; built with saloon body, the car was fitted in 2000 with the present, new body. In good driving order.

| 1936 | Speed 20 SD cabriolet | (Vanden Plas) | 13031 | R | 60-70.000 GBP | 64.467 | 80.094 | 75.201 | 18-02-17 | London | 361 | Coy |

See lot 150 Coys 8.9.16.

| 1936 | Crested Eagle TF saloon | (Charlesworth) | 12984 | R | 26-30.000 GBP | | NS | | 07-12-16 | Chateau Impney | 33 | H&H |

Burgundy and black with burgundy leather interior; restored in the 1980s (see lot 19 H & H 3.12.14 $41,933).

| 1936 | Firebird cabriolet | | 13632 | R | NQ | 36.729 | 45.100 | 42.417 | 21-01-17 | Scottsdale | 8286 | R&S |

Red with black fenders and black leather interior; restored.

| 1936 | 4.3 litre cabriolet | (Offord) | 13178 | R | 140-160.000 GBP | 149.340 | 184.584 | 171.905 | 19-03-17 | Goodwood | 67 | Bon **F42** |

Blue with light grey interior; fully rebuilt both in the UK and abroad. Described as in very good overall condition.

| 1938 | Silver Crest saloon | (Holbrook) | 19817 | R | 20-25.000 GBP | 18.160 | 23.686 | 20.341 | 26-07-17 | Duxford | 41 | H&H |

Maroon and black with red interior; the car received much restoration works including a mechanical overhaul and repaint.

| 1939 | 12/70 Special | | 15882 | R | 72-90.000 GBP | 70.000 | 87.038 | 82.173 | 26-11-16 | Weybridge | 219 | His |

Two-seater body finished in polished aluminium; special built on a 12/70 chassis fitted with a Silver Crest 6-cylinder 2.7-litre engine and gearbox. In the 2000s raced at several historic events and subsequently on the road (see lot 274 Historics 1.9.12 $152,764).

| 1948 | TA14 coupé | (Duncan) | 21707 | R | 28-30.000 GBP | 31.050 | 41.374 | 36.720 | 10-09-16 | Goodwood | 142 | Bon |

Silver and dark blue; fully restored between 2010 and 2012.

| 1949 | TA14 cabriolet | | 22839 | R | 15-17.000 GBP | 14.471 | 18.542 | 16.581 | 02-06-17 | Solihull | 27 | H&H |

Grey and maroon with grey interior; restored in the late 1980s.

| 1953 | TA21G coupé | (Graber) | 25089 | R | 150-165.000 AUD | | NS | | 28-05-17 | Sydney | 11 | Mos |

Bronze with tan leather interior; one-off exhibited by Graber at the 1953 Geneva Motor Show. Restored in the UK in the early 1990s. Imported into Australia in 2007. Body repainted in 2015 (see lot 268 Brooks 3.12.97 $33,715).

| 1961 | TD21 coupé | (Graber/Park Ward) | 26636 | R | 22-25.000 GBP | 33.188 | 42.013 | 38.528 | 12-11-16 | Birmingham | 645 | SiC |

Bronze with tan leather interior; restored in 2012, fitted with a Tremec T5 gearbox in 2015.

| 1962 | TD21 cabriolet | (Graber/Park Ward) | 26680 | R | 55-65.000 GBP | | NS | | 07-12-16 | London | 341 | Bon |

In the same family ownership since 1963; restored between 1995 and 2005; original leather interior; in good overall condition.

F41: 1934 Alvis Speed 20 SB tourer (Vanden Plas)

F42: 1936 Alvis 4.3 litre cabriolet (Offord)

Year	Model	(Bodybuilder)	Chassis no.	Steering	Estimate	Hammer price £	$	€	Sale Date	Place	Lot	Auc. H.
1961	TD21 cabriolet	(Graber/Park Ward)	26655	R	80-120.000 GBP	91.100	112.600	104.865	19-03-17	Goodwood	75	Bon

Light grey with blue interior; restored in 2004. Automatic transmission.

| 1960 | TD21 cabriolet | (Graber/Park Ward) | 26392 | R | 60-70.000 GBP | | NS | | 06-06-17 | Woodcote Park | 18 | H&H |

Body repainted in 2013; interior in good condition; engine recommissioned in 2014. Automatic transmission.

| 1964 | TE21 cabriolet | (Park Ward) | 27200 | R | 75-85.000 GBP | 156.800 | 204.028 | 182.515 | 20-05-17 | Ascot | 171 | His F43 |

Metallic beige with beige leather interior; bought in 2008 by the present, second owner and subjected to a long, full restoration recently completed.

AMC (USA) (1958-1986)

| 1962 | Metropolitan convertible | | E95521 | L | 15-25.000 EUR | 15.019* | 19.952* | 17.825* | 03-09-16 | Chantilly | 1 | Bon |

Light blue and white; restored in 2006.

| 1962 | Metropolitan coupé | | NK3E32705 | L | 10-15.000 GBP | 8.280* | 11.033* | 9.792* | 10-09-16 | Goodwood | 101 | Bon |

Coral red and white; restored in the 1980s, interior redone in 1990.

| 1964 | Ramber Classic Cross Country | | ZK11342 | R | 18-22.000 AUD | 11.562 | 14.890 | 12.671 | 20-08-17 | Mallala Park | 30 | Mos |

Green with white roof and tan interior; 26,664 miles on the odometer. 287 engine with automatic transmission. Assembled in Australia. From the collection of the late Clem Smith.

| 1970 | AMX fastback | | ADC397X126121 | L | 65-85.000 USD | 45.538 | 60.500 | 54.051 | 03-09-16 | Auburn | 5129 | AA |

Orange with black side stripe and black leather interior; fully restored. Performance 390 Go package V-8 engine.

| 1969 | AMX/3 | | WTDO36325555 | L | 900-1.300.000 USD | 725.630 | 891.000 | 837.986 | 21-01-17 | Scottsdale | 132 | G&Co F44 |

Engineered and developed by Giotto Bizzarrini, Italdesign, and BMW, the car was fitted with a 340bhp 390 V-8 AMC engine with 4-speed gearbox. The example offered is the AMX/3 Program Monza test car in 1969. Following the cancellation of the program the car was sold in 1971 to its first private owner in the USA. In 2014 it was bought by the current German owner and restored to concours condition. One of five examples built (Bizzarrini e Diomante built a sixth example from remaining components).

AMERICAN AUSTIN (USA) (1930-1934)

| 1930 | Roadster | | A8526 | L | 28-34.000 USD | 15.189 | 18.975 | 17.104 | 05-11-16 | Hilton Head | 124 | AA |

Two-tone red with cork leather interior; restored.

AMERICAN DE DION (USA) (1900-1901)

| 1900 | Motorette 3,5hp vis-a-vis | | 8 | R | 50-70.000 GBP | | NS | | 04-11-16 | London | 202 | Bon |

Black with tan interior; restored at date unknown. The engine is still running in. Imported into the UK three years ago.

AMILCAR (F) (1921-1939)

| 1924 | CGS | (Kellner) | CGS7385 | R | 110-125.000 USD | | NS | | 17-09-16 | Aspen | 122 | TFA |

Blue with red leather interior; imported in 2003 into the USA and subsequently fully restored. Described as in concours condition.

| 1925 | G sports | | 70532 | R | 28-34.000 AUD | 17.640 | 22.824 | 20.881 | 30-04-17 | Melbourne | 21 | Mos |

Black; discovered in rolling chassis form, the car was fitted in the 1970s with the present new body.

AMPHICAR (D) (1961-1968)

| 1966 | Modell 770 | | 106523027 | L | 65-85.000 USD | 59.793* | 73.700* | 69.079* | 19-01-17 | Phoenix | 166 | RMS F45 |

Light blue with blue and white interior; restored in the 2000s. From the Mohrschladt Family Collection.

| 1966 | Modell 770 | | 106522277 | L | NQ | 46.584* | 57.200* | 53.797* | 21-01-17 | Scottsdale | 937 | B/J |

Light blue with white interior; original condition, 5,600 original miles, one owner.

| 1966 | Modell 770 | | 106521330 | L | NQ | 42.262 | 55.000 | 49.198 | 20-05-17 | Indianapolis | S77 | Mec |

White with red and white interior; mechanicals rebuilt.

| 1966 | Modell 770 | | 106523027 | L | 60-75.000 USD | 64.103* | 82.500* | 70.290* | 18-08-17 | Monterey | 170 | RMS |

See lot 166 RM/Sotheby's 19.1.17.

ANSALDO (I) (1919-1936)

| 1926 | 4CS berlina | (Harrington) | 7384 | R | 16-20.000 GBP | 16.675 | 22.149 | 19.790 | 03-09-16 | Beaulieu | 491 | Bon F46 |

Described as in good condition mechanically, with fair bodywork and paint.

F43: 1964 Alvis TE21 cabriolet (Park Ward)

F44: 1969 AMC AMX/3

Year	Model	(Bodybuilder)	Chassis no.	Steering	Estimate	Hammer price £	$	€	Date	Sale Place	Lot	Auc. H.

F45: 1966 Amphicar Modell 770

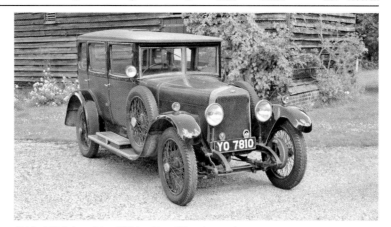

F46: 1926 Ansaldo 4CS berlina (Harrington)

APAL (B) (1961-1998)

Year	Model	Chassis no.	Steering	Estimate	£	$	€	Date	Place	Lot	Auc. H.
1963	GT	1250736	L	55-80.000 EUR	57.148	70.461	63.250	07-10-16	Zoute	24	Bon

Red; built on a 1957 Volkswagen chassis with a 90bhp 1600cc Porsche 356 (type 616/7) engine. 250 kms covered since the engine rebuild (see lot 224 Bonhams 2.2.12 $36,139).

| 1968 | Horizon GT | 2 | L | 50-70.000 EUR | 25.442 | 31.969 | 29.900 | 09-02-17 | Paris | 427 | Bon |

Silver with black interior; one of 10 examples built; 1,700cc Volkswagen engine. Never registered, the car will be registered in Belgium prior to the sale. Restored; in "as new" condition.

ARMSTRONG-SIDDELEY (GB) (1919-1960)

| 1926 | 18hp MkII tourer | 40249 | R | NQ | 16.031* | 19.944* | 18.557* | 29-03-17 | Duxford | 5 | H&H |

Restored in 1993; in need of recommissioning prior to use. From the late Sir Colin Hope's collection.

| 1928 | 20hp Ascot tourer | 8109 | R | NQ | 18.281* | 22.743* | 21.162* | 29-03-17 | Duxford | 6 | H&H |

White with black wings; in need of recommissioning prior to use. From the late Sir Colin Hope's collection.

| 1933 | 12hp saloon | 89121 | R | 8-11.000 GBP | 9.800 | 12.638 | 11.074 | 08-07-17 | Brooklands | 164 | His F47 |

Blue and black; restored many years ago. Since 1997 in the same family ownership (see lot 41 H & H 19.11.97 $8,876).

| 1935 | Special MkII touring limousine | 3418 | R | NQ | 23.062* | 28.691* | 26.697* | 29-03-17 | Duxford | 7 | H&H |

Black; in fair cosmetic condition, the car requires recommissioning prior to use. From the late Sir Colin Hope's collection.

ARNOLT (USA) (1953-1963)

| 1954 | Bristol Bolide roadster (Bertone) | 404X3000 | L | 400-500.000 USD | 266.479 | 324.500 | 307.529 | 09-03-17 | Amelia Island | 150 | Bon F48 |

Red with tan interior; first example built, the car was sold new to the USA and raced for some years. Bought in the 1990s by the current owner without engine and transmission, the car received subsequently a long restoration and was fitted again with correct, rebuilt engine and transmission.

ARNOTT (GB) (1951-1957)

| 1957 | 1100 Sports | AT121 | R | 350-425.000 USD | NS | | | 18-08-17 | Pebble Beach | 17 | G&Co |

Fitted with Climax 1100 engine and alloy body with gullwing-style doors, the car ran the 1957 Le Mans 24 Hours retiring in the fifth hour. Restored in the 1980s; imported into the USA in 1999 and later restored to Le Mans 1957 livery (see lot 19 Coys 20.9.94 NS).

ARROWS (GB) (1978-)

| 1997 | A18 | A1803 | M | 170-200.000 EUR | NS | | | 02-07-17 | Monaco | 208 | Art |

Car driven by Damon Hill in the first half of the 1997 Formula 1 season. Currently fitted with a 3-litre V10 Asiatech engine recently serviced.

F47: 1933 Armstrong-Siddeley 12hp saloon

F48: 1954 Arnolt Bristol Bolide roadster (Bertone)

F49: 1904 Aster 16/20hp rear-entrance tonneau (Renaudin Fils Besson)

F50: 1935 Aston Martin Ulster

ASA (I) *(1962-1967)*

Year	Model	Chassis no.	Steering	Estimate	£	$	€	Date	Place	Lot	Auc. H.
1963	**1000 GT** (Bertone)	01022	L	125-150.000 USD		NS		17-08-17	Monterey	12	WoA

Fifth example built; when new personal car of Oronzo De Nora; imported into the USA in the late 1960s; bought in 1990 by the current owner and subjected to a long restoration completed in 2014. Fitted with a 5-speed gearbox (the original unit is included with the sale).

ASTER (F) *(1901-1910)*

Year	Model	Chassis no.	Steering	Estimate	£	$	€	Date	Place	Lot	Auc. H.
1904	**16/20hp rear-entrance tonneau** (Renaudin Fils Besson)	9589	R	230-270.000 GBP	210.940	263.464	237.518	04-11-16	London	210	Bon

Red bonnet, black wings, black leather interior; original period wooden body fitted to the chassis prior to 2007; mechanicals overhauled in recent years (see lot 608 Bonhams 3.12.07 $457,087). **F49**

ASTON MARTIN (GB) *(1922-)*

Year	Model	Chassis no.	Steering	Estimate	£	$	€	Date	Place	Lot	Auc. H.
1928	**1.5l Standard Sports Model**	TS10	R	600-800.000 EUR		NS		09-02-17	Paris	355	Bon

Yellow with black wings and black interior; fully restored by Ecurie Bertelli Ltd in the 2000s. Engine no. ST18; new rear axle. One of the three cars displayed at the 1928 London Motor Show; sold new to India; discovered at unspecified date much modified and without its original wet-sump engine.

| 1930 | **International 1.5l tourer** | S50 | R | 110-150.000 GBP | 123.200 | 150.994 | 137.023 | 12-10-16 | Duxford | 59 | H&H |

Light blue with dark blue leather interior; in the same ownership from 1952 to 1992. Restoration completed in 1995 (see Bonhams lots 566 7.7.06 NS and 284 24.6.16 NS).

| 1935 | **Ulster** | A5537U | R | 1.600-1.800.000 EUR | 1.712.436 | 2.151.765 | 2.012.500 | 09-02-17 | Paris | 339 | Bon |

British racing green with red interior; the car did its race debut at the 1935 Le Mans 24 Hours and was subsequently raced until the 1950s. Engine rebuilt several times over the years; imported into the USA in the early 1970s and raced at numerous historic events; bought in 2003 by the current owner and driven at several events including the 2004, 2005 and 2006 editions of the Mille Miglia Storica. **F50**

| 1935 | **Ulster** | B5549U | R | 2.500-3.000.000 USD | 1.688.033 | 2.172.500 | 1.850.970 | 18-08-17 | Monterey | 150 | RMS |

The car has had a long race career and in 1935 it ran also the Mille Miglia, Le Mans 24 Hours, Targa Abruzzo and Tourist Trophy. From the 1960s until the 1990s it was owned by pre-war Aston Martin expert Derrick Edwards and subsequently it was restored to its original configuration. Always well maintained, it is described as reliable and ready to use (see lot 351 Bonhams 27.6.14 NS).

| 1935 | **1.5l Mk II tourer** | E5574L | R | 180-230.000 EUR | | NS | | 10-02-17 | Paris | 54 | Art |

Red with black interior; restored in the 1980s, the car is described as in good overall condition (see Historics lots 269 1.9.12 NS and 229 9.3.13 $150,290).

| 1934 | **1.5l Mk II tourer** | G3297L | R | 120-150.000 GBP | | NS | | 19-03-17 | Goodwood | 56 | Bon |

Dark blue with burgundy leather interior; long-wheelbase model originally fitted with a saloon body, the car was fitted with the present body in the 1960s probably. Described as in very good driving order; paintwork and interior redone in recent years (see lot 54 Bonhams 20.3.16 $123,864 and 150 Coys 6.8.16 $171,847).

| 1938 | **15/98 2l tourer** (Abbey) | D8872SO | R | 225-250.000 GBP | 198.333 | 250.078 | 233.061 | 07-12-16 | London | 363 | Bon |

Red with brown interior; described as in original condition. On display for many years at the Stratford Motor Museum. Currently registered in Sweden. **F51**

| 1938 | **15/98 2l open sports** | J8776LS | R | 400-500.000 USD | 235.264* | 286.000* | 269.526* | 10-03-17 | Amelia Island | 127 | RMS |

Built on a standard chassis and fitted with a Bertelli saloon body; in the early 1980s the chassis was shortened and fitted with the present, new body; later it was imported into the USA, restored again, converted to left-hand drive and fitted with the present Moss gearbox with synchromesh on second, third and fourth gears. From the Orin Smith collection.

| 1937 | **15/98 2l** | A40783LTSS | R | 40-60.000 GBP | 59.740 | 73.839 | 68.767 | 19-03-17 | Goodwood | 25 | Bon |

Restoration project. Long-chassis example originally fitted with a Bertelli tourer body; displayed at the 1938 Earls Court Motor Show.

F51: 1938 Aston Martin 15/98 2l tourer (Abbey)

F52: 1949 Aston Martin DB2 coupé

CLASSIC CENTER SWITZERLAND

WHERE FASCINATION
TAKES HOLD

As a leading international center of excellence for classic cars, we offer a full range of services for car enthusiasts, advising them every step of the way.

We are located halfway between Zurich and Berne in a fully renovated 19th-century factory, a unique setting that is filled with ambiance.

OUR SERVICES INCLUDE
- Purchase and sale of classic cars
- Service, maintenance and complete restorations to the highest quality standards
- Roos Engineering Ltd Aston Martin and Lagonda Heritage Specialist
- State-of-the-art classic car storage facilities
- Logistics & transport in Switzerland and abroad
- Expertise in the FIVA Vehicle ID Card
- Museum with over 70 cars from the Emil Frey Collection
- Café-Bar and shop
- Unique event space for up to 550 people
- Driving instruction in our Driving Center Safenwil

Experts for your passion

EMIL FREY CLASSICS AG | Bahnhofplatz 2 | P.O. Box 417 | 5745 Safenwil
+41 62 788 79 20 | info@emilfreyclassics.ch | www.emilfreyclassics.ch

Year	Model	(Bodybuilder)	Chassis no.	Steering	Estimate	Hammer price £	$	€	Date	Place	Lot	Auc. H.
1937	15/98 2l cabriolet	(Abbott)	A9825SC	R	275-375.000 USD		NS		18-08-17	Monterey	132	RMS

Red; short chassis; since 1993 in the current ownership; concours-quality restoration carried out between 1993 and 1998; engine rebuilt utilizing a new block supplied by Ecurie Bertelli (the original unit is included with the sale).

| 1936 | 2l Speed Model "Red Dragon" | | H6711U | R | 1.600-2.000.000 GBP | | NS | | 10-09-16 | Goodwood | 130 | Bon |

Works car at the 1936 Ards TT driven by Dick Seaman; acquired by Dutch Eddie Hertzberger it ran also the 1937 and 1938 Mille Miglia and 1937 Le Mans 24 Hours; acquired in 1947 by Dudley Folland it ran also the Spa 24 Hours in 1948 and Le Mans 24 Hours in 1949. Following some ownership changes it was bought in 1959 by Geoff Bishop who retained it until 1996. Restored in 1988-89; driven at numerous historic events; engine rebuilt in 2013.

| 1949 | 2-Litre Sports | | AMC495 | R | 1.050-1.300.000 USD | | NS | | 18-08-17 | Monterey | 149 | RMS |

Fitted with a "Spa Replica" competition engine, the car was bought new by gentleman driver Robert Lawrie who raced it, with Richard Parker, at the 1949 Le Mans 24 Hours, placing 4th in class and 11th overall. In 1953 it was fitted by the factory with the present engine no.VB6B/50/51 and was repainted in blue. Described as in highly original, never restored condition.

| 1952 | DB2 Vantage coupé | | LML50390 | R | 185-215.000 USD | | NS | | 07-09-16 | London | 166 | RMS |

Ecurie Ecosse blue with original red leather interior; sold new in the UK, the car was driven at some rallies in the 1950s. In 1974 it was exported to Canada and in 1981 it was imported into the USA. In 2002 it was acquired by the current owner and restored, the engine was rebuilt and the gearbox was replaced with a 5-speed ZF unit (the original gearbox is included with the sale). The engine has covered 2,000 miles since a recent overhaul.

| 1952 | DB2 coupé | | LML50281 | R | 150-180.000 GBP | 199.740 | 266.154 | 236.213 | 10-09-16 | Goodwood | 128 | Bon |

Green with dark green leather interior; restored between 2007 and 2008. Engine upgraded for historic rallies and hill climbs. Fitted with DB5 disc brakes (see lot 251 Bonhams 13.9.14 $310,878).

| 1949 | DB2 coupé | | LML494 | R | 1.500-2.250.000 USD | 1.266.804 | 1.540.000 | 1.451.296 | 10-03-17 | Amelia Island | 31 | G&Co F52 |

One of the development prototypes of the new model and first DB2 fitted with the 6-cylinder engine; built for personal use of David Brown; bought in 1950 by Lance Macklin and raced at the Coppa Inter-Europa at Monza and Targa Florio; returned to the factory in late 1950 and resold in 1951; in single ownership from 1965 to 1992 when it was restored by the factory at Newport Pagnell; bought in 2009 by the current owner and driven at several historic events.

| 1953 | DB2 Vantage coupé | | LML50313 | R | 100-150.000 EUR | 94.904* | 140.069* | 107.928* | 02-07-17 | Monaco | 151 | Art |

Black with beige leather interior; in original unrestored condition; working engine; since 1990 in the current ownership.

| 1952 | DB2 cabriolet | | LML50370 | R | 130-150.000 EUR | 429.317* | 533.837* | 504.000* | 25-11-16 | Milan | 567 | RMS |

Blue and red; it requires several restoration works. 36,072 miles. From the Duemila Ruote collection.

| 1953 | DB2 Vantage cabriolet | | LML50376 | L | 350-425.000 USD | 285.031* | 346.500* | 326.542* | 10-03-17 | Amelia Island | 124 | RMS F53 |

Red with grey leather interior; sold new to the USA; restored in the late 1990s; engine rebuilt in more recent years. From the Orin Smith collection (see lot 150 RM 20.1.11 NS).

| 1953 | DB2 cabriolet | | LML50394 | R | 200-250.000 GBP | 180.700 | 232.326 | 213.624 | 13-05-17 | Newp.Pagnell | 205 | Bon |

Silver; restored in the early 1980s; since 1985 in the current ownership; body repainted in 2010; in very good driving order.

| 1954 | DB2/4 coupé | | LML687 | R | 160-190.000 GBP | 183.795 | 245.513 | 217.338 | 08-09-16 | Fontwell Park | 132 | Coy |

Since 1997 in the current ownership; between 2008 and 2015 the body has been restored and finished in British racing green, and the engine has been rebuilt.

| 1954 | DB2/4 coupé | | LML664 | R | 180-220.000 GBP | 192.640 | 236.100 | 214.254 | 12-10-16 | Duxford | 50 | H&H |

Green with green interior; sold new in the UK, the car was later exported to the USA. Discovered in 2008, it was subsequently restored (see lot 148 RM 8.9.14 $198,352).

| 1954 | DB2/4 coupé | | LML555 | L | 175-225.000 USD | 169.562* | 209.000* | 195.896* | 19-01-17 | Scottsdale | 43 | Bon F54 |

White; prepared for the 1992 Carrera Panamericana Retrospective where it placed fifth. Engine rebuilt to Vantage specification; front and rear brakes from a DB4. Later it was driven at other several historic events.

| 1954 | DB2/4 coupé | | LML604 | R | 120-160.000 GBP | 152.700 | 196.326 | 180.522 | 13-05-17 | Newp.Pagnell | 231 | Bon |

Red with beige leather interior; since 1966 in the same family ownership; full restoration completed in 2000; body repainted in 2012.

| 1954 | DB2/4 coupé | | LML733 | L | NA | | NS | | 13-05-17 | Silverstone | 328 | SiC |

Dark green with beige interior; restored in 2009.

| 1954 | DB2/4 coupé | | LML846 | R | 100-150.000 GBP | 135.900 | 176.371 | 153.880 | 30-06-17 | Goodwood | 260 | Bon |

Since 1956 in the same family ownership; in original condition; 43,152 miles on the odometer; in storage for many years; engine running well.

| 1955 | DB2/4 coupé | | LML881 | R | 120-140.000 GBP | | NS | | 26-07-17 | Duxford | 98 | H&H |

Blue with grey interior; the car requires restoration. 2.9-litre engine.

| 1953 | DB2/4 Vantage coupé | (Mulliners) | LML552 | L | 300-350.000 USD | | NS | | 19-08-17 | Pebble Beach | 141 | G&Co |

Silver; sold new to France; imported into the USA in 2005, restored and driven at historic events; engine rebuilt to 2.9-litre specification; currently fitted with a 5-speed Tremec gearbox, it is offered with also a 4-speed unit (see lot 66 Gooding & Company 20.8.11 $203,500).

| 1954 | DB2/4 cabriolet | (Bertone) | LML506 | L | 1.300-1.600.000 USD | 1.111.110 | 1.430.000 | 1.218.360 | 19-08-17 | Pebble Beach | 168 | G&Co |

Blue with beige leather interior; one of two examples built by Bertone and designed by Giovanni Michelotti; sold new to the USA; reimported into Europe in 1985; restored to concours condition in the 2000s; reimported into the USA in 2011 (see lot 464 Bonhams 1.7.11 $970,946).

| 1957 | DB2/4 MkII coupé | | AM3001250 | R | 50-70.000 GBP | 54.625 | 70.231 | 64.578 | 13-05-17 | Newp.Pagnell | 202 | Bon F55 |

Restoration project.

F53: 1953 Aston Martin DB2 Vantage cabriolet

F54: 1954 Aston Martin DB2/4 coupé

F55: 1957 Aston Martin DB2/4 MkII coupé

F56: 1956 Aston Martin DBR1

Year	Model	(Bodybuilder)	Chassis no.	Steering	Estimate	£	$	€	Date	Place	Lot	Auc. H.
1956	**DBR1**		DBR11	R	Over 20.000.000 USD	**17.521.350**	22.550.000	19.212.600	18-08-17	Monterey	148	RMS **TOP TEN F56**

First of five DBR1s; raced by the factory until 1959; driven by Roy Salvadori, Stirling Moss, Jack Brabham and Carroll Shelby among others; winner of the 1959 Nürburgring 1000 KM; sold in 1961; raced by privateers until 1963 when the front end was damaged; in 1976 body restored and engine rebuilt; raced in the years at several historic events; bought in 2009 by the current owner and fitted with a reproduction engine built by R.S. Williams Ltd (the original unit no.RB6/300/3 is included with the sale).

Year	Model	(Bodybuilder)	Chassis no.	Steering	Estimate	£	$	€	Date	Place	Lot	Auc. H.
1957	**DP 193/DB Mark III prototype**		AM3003A1300	R	300-500.000 GBP	**337.500**	438.008	382.151	30-06-17	Goodwood	224	Bon **F57**

Prototype of the DB Mark III model, fitted with the 2,922cc engine redesigned by Tadek Marek and disc brake all round, and finished in grey with green leather interior. Raced at the 1958 Monte Carlo Rally, it remained in the factory ownership until June 1959. In the 1970s it was imported into Switzerland, the body resprayed in the current French blue livery and the interior re-Connollised in black. In 1984 it was bought by the current owner and imported into the USA. Original engine (rebuilt several times) and gearbox.

Year	Model	(Bodybuilder)	Chassis no.	Steering	Estimate	£	$	€	Date	Place	Lot	Auc. H.
1957	**DB MkIII coupé**		AM30031341	L	180-240.000 EUR	167.748	209.051	**196.680**	10-02-17	Paris	12	Art

Dark green with tan leather interior; restored at unspecified date (see lots 11 Chevau-Légerè 3.2.11 $176,038, 220 Bonhams 11.5.12 NS and 335 Artcurial 7.2.14 $283,154).

Year	Model	(Bodybuilder)	Chassis no.	Steering	Estimate	£	$	€	Date	Place	Lot	Auc. H.
1958	**DB MkIII coupé**		AM30031359	L	375-450.000 USD	248.837*	**302.500***	285.076*	10-03-17	Amelia Island	109	RMS

Silver metallic with dark grey leather interior; sold new to the USA. Restored at unspecified date. From the Orin Smith collection.

Year	Model	(Bodybuilder)	Chassis no.	Steering	Estimate	£	$	€	Date	Place	Lot	Auc. H.
1958	**DB MkIII coupé**		AM3003523	L	275-325.000 USD		NS		11-03-17	Amelia Island	33	Mot

Black with red leather interior; restored several years ago. The car is currently fitted with a 350 Chevrolet V8 engine with 5-speed gearbox and a correct 3-litre DB engine (to be rebuilt) is included with the sale.

Year	Model	(Bodybuilder)	Chassis no.	Steering	Estimate	£	$	€	Date	Place	Lot	Auc. H.
1958	**DB MkIII coupé**		AM30031529	R	150-200.000 GBP	**212.060**	272.646	250.697	13-05-17	Newp.Pagnell	211	Bon

Red with white leather interior; restored between 2012 and 2015 (see lots Bonhams 784 3.12.01 $29,442, and H & H 20 4.12.02 $36,346 and 16 21.2.06 $63,564).

Year	Model	(Bodybuilder)	Chassis no.	Steering	Estimate	£	$	€	Date	Place	Lot	Auc. H.
1960	**DB4 coupé**	(Touring/Tickford)	DB4312R	R	NA		NS		02-09-16	Salon Privé	216	SiC

Red with white interior; in working order. Gearbox replaced in 1960 at the factory; engine replaced in 1966 with an original DB4 unit; body repainted in the early 1980s.

Year	Model	(Bodybuilder)	Chassis no.	Steering	Estimate	£	$	€	Date	Place	Lot	Auc. H.
1959	**DB4 coupé**	(Touring/Tickford)	DB4178R	R	150-180.000 GBP	**203.100**	269.778	241.039	03-09-16	Beaulieu	422	Bon

Stored for the last 30 years; for restoration.

Year	Model	(Bodybuilder)	Chassis no.	Steering	Estimate	£	$	€	Date	Place	Lot	Auc. H.
1961	**DB4 coupé**	(Touring/Tickford)	DB4490L	L	480-520.000 GBP	**515.200**	689.441	613.552	07-09-16	London	160	RMS **F58**

Dark green with red leather interior; the car remained in the factory ownership until 1963 when it was sold to Italy where it remained in the same family ownership until 2005 when it was acquired by the present, third owner and reimported into the UK. Described as in good, highly original condition (see lot 384 Coys 19.11.05 NS).

Year	Model	(Bodybuilder)	Chassis no.	Steering	Estimate	£	$	€	Date	Place	Lot	Auc. H.
1960	**DB4 coupé**	(Touring/Tickford)	DB4474R	R	320-360.000 GBP		NS		04-12-16	London	10	Bon

Red with black leather interior; described as in good overall condition.

Year	Model	(Bodybuilder)	Chassis no.	Steering	Estimate	£	$	€	Date	Place	Lot	Auc. H.
1961	**DB4 coupé**	(Touring/Tickford)	DB4510L	L	375-475.000 USD	304.511	**374.000**	350.700	18-01-17	Scottsdale	45	WoA

Green with black interior; for 45 years in the current ownership and unused from the 1970s. For restoration.

Year	Model	(Bodybuilder)	Chassis no.	Steering	Estimate	£	$	€	Date	Place	Lot	Auc. H.
1960	**DB4 coupé**	(Touring/Tickford)	DB4211L	L	500-600.000 USD	371.774	**456.500**	429.338	20-01-17	Scottsdale	49	G&Co

Red with black interior; sold new to the USA; from 1983 for 30 years in the same family ownership who had the paintwork and interior redone and the engine rebuilt; recently serviced.

Year	Model	(Bodybuilder)	Chassis no.	Steering	Estimate	£	$	€	Date	Place	Lot	Auc. H.
1962	**DB4 coupé**	(Touring/Tickford)	DB4838L	L	425-500.000 EUR		NS		08-02-17	Paris	134	RMS

Dark green with tan leather interior; sold new to Canada and later reimported into Europe. Recently serviced (see lots 635 Barrett-Jackson 18.1.02 $78,840 and 567 Bonhams 15.8.03 $89,700).

Year	Model	(Bodybuilder)	Chassis no.	Steering	Estimate	£	$	€	Date	Place	Lot	Auc. H.
1960	**DB4 coupé**	(Touring/Tickford)	DB4287L	L	575-675.000 USD	456.954	**555.500**	523.503	10-03-17	Amelia Island	52	G&Co

Grey with red leather interior; displayed at the 1960 New York Motor Show. Restored in the 2000s. Engine rebuilt and enlarged to 4.2-litre (see Gooding & Company lots 115 19.8.12 $495,000 and 45 17.8.13 $445,500).

F57: 1957 Aston Martin DP 193/DB Mark III prototype

F58: 1961 Aston Martin DB4 coupé (Touring/Tickford)

Year	Model	(Bodybuilder)	Chassis no.	Steering	Estimate	Hammer price £	Hammer price $	Hammer price €	Date	Place	Lot	Auc. H.
1961	**DB4/DP214 replica**		DB4618R	R	600-700.000 GBP	551.666	681.859	635.023	19-03-17	Goodwood	38	Bon

Replica of the DP214 chassis 0195 built in the UK between 2010 and 2014 and based on the 1961 DB4 chassis 618/R. The mechanicals are all original DB4. Raced at several historic events. With FIA/MSA Historic Technical Passport valid to 31st December 2018.

| 1961 | **DB4 coupé** | (Touring/Tickford) | DB4748R | R | 200-300.000 GBP | 225.500 | 289.925 | 266.586 | 13-05-17 | Newp.Pagnell | 207 | Bon |

Restoration to be completed: cylinder head rebuilt in 2000, body restored and repainted in its original sage livery in 2006. Original interior. The engine last ran in 2011. Many unfitted parts. Since 1976 in the same family ownership.

| 1961 | **DB4 coupé** | (Touring/Tickford) | DB4569L | L | 350-400.000 GBP | | NS | | 13-05-17 | Newp.Pagnell | 210 | Bon |

In good mechanical order; probably original interior (see lots 18 Poulain/Sotheby's 25.5.01 $55,137 and 14 Artcurial 15.12.03 NS).

| 1960 | **DB4 coupé** | (Touring/Tickford) | DB4267R | L | 420-460.000 GBP | | NS | | 13-05-17 | Newp.Pagnell | 216 | Bon |

Grey with red interior; although it is recorded in the factory records with chassis number 267/R, the car was built in left-hand drive form and sold new to the USA. Since 1997 in the current ownership. Engine rebuilt and body repainted in the late 1990s.

| 1961 | **DB4 coupé** | (Touring/Tickford) | DB4709R | R | 360-440.000 GBP | 399.100 | 513.123 | 471.816 | 13-05-17 | Newp.Pagnell | 223 | Bon |

Aston green with fawn interior; body repainted in the late 1990s, engine rebuilt and enlarged to 4.2-litre specification in 2010.

| 1960 | **DB4 coupé** | (Touring/Tickford) | DB4744R | R | 220-260.000 GBP | 236.700 | 304.325 | 279.827 | 13-05-17 | Newp.Pagnell | 232 | Bon |

Lightweight car built in the 1980s by ADA Engineering for historic racing; in 2004 it was rebuilt by Alan Smith Motors and fitted with the present 4.5-litre engine (see lots 140 Brooks 13.5.00 NS and 345 Bonhams 9.5.09 $126,605).

| 1959 | **DB4 coupé** | (Touring/Tickford) | DB4116R | R | 380-450.000 GBP | | NS | | 13-05-17 | Newp.Pagnell | 237 | Bon |

Blue; sold new in the UK and later exported to Denmark and then to Canada. The car appears very tidy. Should the vehicle remain in the EU, local import taxes of 5% will be applied to the hammer price.

| 1960 | **DB4 coupé** | (Touring/Tickford) | DB4395R | R | 350-400.000 USD | 269.542 | 346.500 | 308.905 | 04-06-17 | Greenwich | 124 | Bon |

Dark green with black leather interior; the engine has covered 6,000 miles since the 1996 rebuild. Further cosmetic and mechanical works carried out in recent years (see lot 138 RM 3.8.14 $462,000).

| 1959 | **DB4 coupé** | (Touring/Tickford) | DB4147R | R | 300-350.000 GBP | 326.300 | 423.472 | 369.469 | 30-06-17 | Goodwood | 241 | Bon |

Grey with red interior; fitted at the factory with a Series 2 body following an accident. Since 1976 in the current ownership. Unused for 29 years and restored in 2014-15 (see Bonhams lots 223 21.5.16 NS and 267 24.6.16 NS).

| 1961 | **DB4 coupé** | (Touring/Tickford) | DB4580L | L | 650-800.000 USD | 581.196 | 748.000 | 637.296 | 18-08-17 | Monterey | 163 | RMS |

Blue with dark blue leather interior; sold new to the USA; mechanicals overhauled and interior retrimmed (see lot 320 RM/Sotheby's 15.8.15 $797,500).

| 1959 | **DP199/DB4 GT prototype** | | DP1991 | R | 6.000-8.000.000 USD | 5.256.405 | 6.765.000 | 5.763.780 | 18-08-17 | Monterey | 147 | RMS **TOP TEN** |

Prototype of the DB4 GT, the car did its race debut in 1959 at Silverstone driven by Stirling Moss who won the race. That same year in June it ran the Le Mans 24 Hours fitted with a 3-litre twin-plug engine, but was forced to retire. In June 1961 it was fitted with the present engine no.370/0184/GT and sold to private hands. In 1989 it was restored at the factory to the Le Mans 1959 specification. In recent years it has been driven at several historic events on track and road.

| 1960 | **DB4 GT** | (Touring/Tickford) | DB4GT0126R | R | 2.200-2.500.000 GBP | 2.408.000 | 3.222.386 | 2.867.687 | 07-09-16 | London | 169 | RMS **F59** |

Grey with black interior; sold new in the UK and raced only once at Brands Hatch in March 1960. Exported to the USA and later reimported into the UK. For over 10 years in the current German ownership. Never restored from the ground-up and always maintained to the highest standards. Accompanied by a history file with invoices since 1989, including an engine rebuild to 4.2-litre.

| 1963 | **DB4 cabriolet (Touring/Tickford)** | | DB4C1102R | R | 950-1.100.000 GBP | 952.000 | 1.273.966 | 1.133.737 | 07-09-16 | London | 153 | RMS **F60** |

Finished in platinum with red leather interior, the car was sold new in the UK. Exported to the USA in 1969 circa, it was reimported into the UK in 1985. In 2000 it was sold to France and later restored to concours condition (see lots 752 Brooks 18.6.99 $97,238 and 132 Bonhams 13.5.06 $315,832).

| 1964 | **DB5 coupé** | (Touring/Tickford) | DB51784R | R | 450-550.000 GBP | 455.100 | 606.421 | 538.201 | 10-09-16 | Goodwood | 139 | Bon |

Dark green with fawn interior; since 1984 in the current ownership. In good overall condition. Original engine and gearbox replaced at the factory in 1965. Interior retrimmed in the 1990s.

| 1964 | **DB5 coupé** | (Touring/Tickford) | DB51435R | R | 525-625.000 GBP | 425.000 | 516.290 | 472.685 | 29-10-16 | London | 131 | Coy |

Sage green with fawn interior; until 2016 with its first owner. Body repainted at unspecified date.

| 1964 | **DB5 coupé** | (Touring/Tickford) | DB51766L | L | 550-650.000 EUR | 600.134 | 729.065 | 667.520 | 30-10-16 | Paris | 121 | Art |

Red; original interior. Exhibited at the 1964 Paris Motor Show.

| 1963 | **DB5 coupé** | (Touring/Tickford) | DB51308R | R | 570-610.000 GBP | | NS | | 04-12-16 | London | 3 | Bon |

Green with beige interior; sold new to Australia. Restored in the UK in 1995; engine enlarged to 4.2-litre. Two owners until 2016 (see lot 259 Bonhams 24.6.16 NS).

| 1965 | **DB5 coupé** | (Touring/Tickford) | DB51990L | L | 1.000-1.200.000 USD | 847.809 | 1.045.000 | 979.479 | 19-01-17 | Phoenix | 149 | RMS **F61** |

Sage green with tan leather interior; sold new to the USA. Restored several years ago, it is described as still in very good overall condition. Several mechanical works carried out in recent years, including Harvey Bayley suspension upgrade (see lot 146 Gooding & Company 21.8.11 $687,500).

| 1964 | **DB5 coupé** | (Touring/Tickford) | DB51612L | L | 1.000-1.200.000 USD | 716.672 | 880.000 | 827.640 | 20-01-17 | Scottsdale | 26 | G&Co |

Originally finished in sand with green leather interior, the car was sold new to the USA. In the mid-1980s it was refinished in the present dark green livery with black interior. For many years in the same family ownership.

F59: 1960 Aston Martin DB4 GT (Touring/Tickford)

F60: 1963 Aston Martin DB4 cabriolet (Touring/Tickford)

Year	Model (Bodybuilder)	Chassis no.	Steering	Estimate	Hammer price £	Hammer price $	Hammer price €	Date	Place	Lot	Auc. H.
1964	DB5 coupé (Touring/Tickford)	DB51466L	L	NQ	1.209.384	1.485.000	1.396.643	21-01-17	Scottsdale	1397	B/J

Black with black leather interior; sold new to France and later imported into the USA (see lots 137 RM 15.8.14 $880,000 and 41 Gooding & Company 15.8.15 NS).

Year	Model	Chassis no.	Steering	Estimate	£	$	€	Date	Place	Lot	Auc. H.
1965	DB5 Vantage coupé (Touring/Tickford)	DB52211L	L	1.100-1.300.000 USD	904.860	1.100.000	1.036.640	10-03-17	Amelia Island	15	G&Co

Dark green with tan leather interior; sold new to France and later imported into the USA. In the early 2000s the car was fully restored and the engine was enlarged to 4.2-litre. Currently fitted with a modern 5-speed gearbox (the original unit is included with the sale).

Year	Model	Chassis no.	St.	Estimate	£	$	€	Date	Place	Lot	Auc. H.
1965	DB5 coupé (Touring/Tickford)	DB52098R	L	900-1.100.000 USD	814.374	990.000	932.976	11-03-17	Amelia Island	271	RMS

Dark blue with butterscotch leather interior; sold new in the UK, the car was exported to the USA in 1980. In 2013-14 it was fully restored and converted to left-hand drive. Engine rebuilt to 4.2-litre specification (see lot 71 Gooding & Company 8.3.13 $363,000).

1964	DB5 coupé (Touring/Tickford)	DB51666R	R	500-600.000 GBP	561.500	721.921	663.805	13-05-17	Newp.Pagnell	209	Bon

Blue with cream interior; since 1972 in the current ownership; engine rebuilt circa 25 years ago; body repainted in 2016. It requires light recommissioning prior to use.

1964	DB5 coupé (Touring/Tickford)	DB51552R	R	1.500-1.600.000 AUD		NS		28-05-17	Sydney	5	Mos

Grey with dark blue leather interior; imported into Australia from the UK in the late 1980s. Webasto sunroof.

1964	DB5 coupé (Touring/Tickford)	DB51614R	R	700-800.000 GBP		NS		06-06-17	Woodcote Park	37	H&H

Metallic blue with fawn leather interior; in single family ownership until 2005; engine overhauled in 2009 circa; interior retrimmed in 2015; last serviced in March 2016.

1965	DB5 coupé (Touring/Tickford)	DB52268L	L	1.200-1.400.000 USD		NS		18-08-17	Monterey	156	RMS

Sage green with beige leather interior; sold new to the USA; the original automatic transmission replaced with a ZF 5-speed manual gearbox at unspecified date; bought in 1987 by the current owner and later fully restored.

1966	Short Chassis Volante (Touring/Tickford)	DB5C2301L	L	1.600-2.000.000 USD	1.402.533*	1.705.000*	1.606.792*	10-03-17	Amelia Island	139	RMS

First of 37 Short Chassis Volantes built (the designation later to appear in a factory record as DBVC/2301/LN - the prefix used for the 36 Short Chassis Volantes to follow); sold new to the USA; restored in the 1990s and finished in the present Aston Martin green livery with tan interior, engine rebuilt and enlarged to 4.5-litre, original ZF gearbox replaced with a 5-speed Tremec unit. From the Orin Smith collection. **F62**

1968	DB6 Vantage coupé	DB63504R	R	200-250.000 GBP	197.500	262.339	234.393	03-09-16	Beaulieu	489	Bon

Since 1998 in the same family ownership; restoration requires completion.

1967	DB6 Vantage coupé	DB63178R	R	280-340.000 GBP	455.100	606.421	538.201	10-09-16	Goodwood	157	Bon

Light metallic green; from 1991 to 2015 with the same owner who commissioned several restoration works. Engine rebuilt to 4.2-litre in 2015.

1968	DB6 coupé	DB63342	R	240-280.000 GBP		NS		26-11-16	Weybridge	218	His

Opalescent light blue with blue leather interior; restoration completed in 2015. Automatic transmission and power steering (see lots Historics 285 7.3.15 $290,727, and Coys 115A 16.4.16 NS and 134 2.7.16 $292,204).

1967	DB6 coupé	DB63307R	R	320-350.000 GBP	359.900	453.798	422.918	07-12-16	London	333	Bon

Blue with blue leather interior; the car was restored in the late 1990s when the engine was enlarged to 4.2-litre capacity and rebuilt to Vantage specification. Top-end engine rebuilt in 2014.

1966	DB6 coupé	DB62465R	R	200-250.000 GBP	216.540	273.035	254.456	07-12-16	London	379	Bon

Silver with tan interior; mechanicals restored; automatic transmission. In good driving condition.

1966	DB6 Vantage coupé	DB62754L	L	400-500.000 USD		NS		20-01-17	Phoenix	224	RMS

Left-hand drive version sold new in the UK; upgraded at the factory at unspecified date with a Vantage-specification engine and ZF 5-speed gearbox as replacement of the original automatic unit; restored in the 2000s and finished in black with red leather interior.

1967	DB6 Vantage coupé	DB62656L	L	450-525.000 USD	389.690	478.500	450.029	21-01-17	Scottsdale	134	G&Co

Silver with red leather interior; sold new to the USA. Restored in 2003. Engine rebuilt years later. Clutch and fuel tank replaced in 2013.

1966	DB6 Vantage coupé	DB62988L	L	375-425.000 EUR	372.656	465.847	436.800	08-02-17	Paris	169	RMS

Dark green with natural leather interior; sold new to Switzerland, the car was imported into Germany in 2009. Recently serviced. Webasto sunroof. **F63**

1966	DB6 Vantage coupé	DB62666LN	L	250-350.000 EUR	233.831	291.405	274.160	10-02-17	Paris	55	Art

Dark green with beige interior; bought in 1990 by the current owner and subsequently restored in Germany. Engine block replaced with a new unit restamped with the original numbers.

1966	DB6 coupé	DB62492L	L	200-250.000 EUR	294.830	367.423	345.680	10-02-17	Paris	82	Art

Dark green with black leather interior; since 1989 in the current ownership. Stored for several years, it was returned to the road in December 2016.

1967	DB6 coupé	DB63072R	R	160-200.000 GBP	172.282	215.353	203.052	12-04-17	London	323	Coy

Since 1977 in the current ownership, the car runs and drives but requires some restoration works.

1967	DB6 Vantage coupé	DB62562R	R	280-340.000 GBP	292.700	376.324	346.030	13-05-17	Newp.Pagnell	212	Bon

Light metallic grey with blue leather interior; fitted with the present Vantage engine no.400/2313/VC possibly before delivery to its first owner. Since 1987 in the current ownership. Engine rebuilt and body repainted between 1990 and 1993.

1970	DB6 MkII Vantage coupé	DB6MK24252R	R	340-380.000 GBP	382.300	491.523	451.955	13-05-17	Newp.Pagnell	220	Bon

Blue with blue interior; restored several years ago.

F61: 1965 Aston Martin DB5 coupé (Touring/Tickford)

F62: 1966 Aston Martin Short Chassis Volante (Touring/Tickford)

Year	Model	(Bodybuilder)	Chassis no.	Steering	Estimate	Hammer price £	Hammer price $	Hammer price €	Date	Place	Lot	Auc. H.
1967	**DB6 coupé**		DB63205R	R	280-320.000 GBP		NS		13-05-17	Newp.Pagnell	225	Bon
Metallic blue with cream interior; restored during 2005-2006 (see lot 164 Coys 2.7.16 $285,563).												
1970	**DB6 Mk2 coupé**		DB64230R	R	270-310.000 GBP		NS		13-05-17	Newp.Pagnell	228	Bon
Blue with original natural leather interior; some restoration works carried out in the early 1990s; body repainted in 1999; the original automatic transmission (included with the sale) replaced with the present 5-speed ZF manual gearbox.												
1971	**DB6 Mk2 Vantage coupé**		DB6MK24286R	R	325-375.000 GBP	348.750	448.388	412.292	13-05-17	Silverstone	324	SiC
Red with tan interior; described as in very good overall condition; body repainted in the 1990s; mechanicals overhauled in recent years.												
1967	**DB6 coupé**		DB63065R	R	265-295.000 GBP		NS		13-05-17	Silverstone	327	SiC
Blue with original sand leather interior; restoration completed in 2016. Automatic transmission.												
1967	**DB6 coupé**		DB63167R	R	NQ	147.840*	192.369*	172.086*	20-05-17	Ascot	181	His
For restoration.												
1970	**DB6 Mk2 Vantage coupé**		DB6MK24240R	R	750-850.000 AUD		NS		28-05-17	Sydney	13	Mos
Silver with black leather interior; since 1978 with the current Australian owner. Stored from 1990 to 2005 when it was recommissioned and returned to road use.												
1966	**DB6 Vantage coupé**		DB62588R	R	180-220.000 GBP	249.700	322.263	286.231	06-06-17	Woodcote Park	12	H&H
Shell grey with blue leather interior; bought in 1987 by the current owner and used until 1991. Original interior. The engine is said to turn freely.												
1966	**DB6 Vantage coupé**		DB62754L	L	275-325.000 USD	267.958	341.000	305.195	24-06-17	Santa Monica	191	RMS
See lot 224 RM/Sotheby's 20.1.17.												
1966	**DB6 coupé**		DB62726R	R	160-200.000 GBP	175.100	227.245	198.266	30-06-17	Goodwood	279	Bon
Blue with light grey interior; restored in the mid-1990s; engine rebuilt in 2005 to 4.2-litre specification; the original Borg Warner automatic transmission replaced in 2006 with a ZF automatic unit.												
1967	**DB6 coupé**		DB63120R	R	290-320.000 GBP		NS		08-07-17	Brooklands	170	His
Shell grey with original red leather interior; engine recently rebuilt. 52,000 miles covered; three owners.												
1966	**DB6 coupé**		DB62465R	R	260-280.000 GBP		NS		26-07-17	Duxford	52	H&H
See lot 379 Bonhams 7.12.16.												
1970	**DB6 Volante**		DB6MK2VC3783R	R	800-1.000.000 GBP		NS		10-09-16	Goodwood	160	Bon
Silver with blue leather interior; in the same ownership from 1971 to 2014. Body repainted in 1987; some mechanical works carried out between 2010 and 2013; acquired in 2014 by the current owner who commissioned further restoration works. Automatic transmission (see lot 242 Bonhams 17.5.14 $1,273,282).												
1970	**DB6 Mk2 Volante**		DB6MK2VC3778R	R	700-800.000 GBP		NS		13-05-17	Newp.Pagnell	208	Bon
Silver with black leather interior; in the 1980s the original automatic transmission was replaced with the present ZF 5-speed manual gearbox; in very good overall condition; three owners (see lot 322 Bonhams 19.9.08 $519,858).												
1968	**DB6 Volante**		DBVC3677R	R	700-900.000 GBP		NS		13-05-17	Newp.Pagnell	221	Bon
Silver with red leather interior; body and interior restored at Aston Martin Works in 2012; some mechanical works carried out in 2014. Recently serviced.												
1968	**DB6 Volante**		DBVC3675R	R	680-750.000 GBP		NS		13-05-17	Newp.Pagnell	229	Bon
Black with black interior; restored at unspecified date; engine converted to Vantage specification at date unknown.												
1968	**DBS Vantage**		DBS5132R	R	80-90.000 GBP	80.200	107.131	94.837	08-09-16	Fontwell Park	128	Coy
Metallic olive green with original black leather interior; in good overall condition. 52,000 miles on the odometer. Since 1990 in the current ownership.												
1969	**DBS**		DBS5436RAC	R	160-180.000 GBP		NS		12-10-16	Duxford	115	H&H
Metallic olive green with red leather interior; body and interior restored, engine enlarged to 4.2-litre and rebuilt to Vantage specification, original automatic transmission replaced with a more modern Tremec T5 manual gearbox (see lot 174 Coys 10.1.15 $257,179).												
1969	**DBS**		DBS5436RAC	R	140-160.000 GBP	174.375	220.741	202.432	12-11-16	Birmingham	315	SiC
See lot 115 H & H 12.10.16.												
1971	**DBS**		DBS5634R	R	125-155.000 GBP	101.920	126.727	119.644	26-11-16	Weybridge	188	His
Olive green with tan interior; body repainted in recent years. Automatic transmission.												
1970	**DBS Vantage**		DBS5662R	R	115-130.000 GBP	114.750	144.057	135.784	24-02-17	Stoneleigh P.	521	SiC
Olive green with fawn interior; described as in very good original condition (see lot 465 Silverstone Auctions 27.7.13 $106,260).												
1972	**DBS**		DBS5796R	R	90-110.000 GBP	70.024	87.530	82.530	12-04-17	London	315	Coy
Green with tan interior; recently serviced.												
1968	**DBS**		DBS5237R	R	80-100.000 GBP	101.180	130.087	119.615	13-05-17	Newp.Pagnell	203	Bon **F64**
Restored between 2013 and 2016; just some finishing works to be done (see lot 301 Bonhams 22.5.10 $29,721).												
1969	**DBS**		DBS5266R	R	90-120.000 GBP		NS		13-05-17	Newp.Pagnell	222	Bon
Olive green with black interior; restored between 2007 and 2012. Automatic transmission; Webasto sunroof.												

F63: 1966 Aston Martin DB6 Vantage coupé

F64: 1968 Aston Martin DBS

Year	Model	(Bodybuilder)	Chassis no.	Steering	Estimate	Hammer price £	Hammer price $	Hammer price €	Sale Date	Sale Place	Lot	Auc. H.
1972	**DBS Vantage**		DBS570R	R	120-160.000 GBP	NS			20-05-17	Ascot	184	His
	Purple with cream interior; body repainted at unspecified date; always well maintained; little used in the past 10 years.											
1972	**DBS**		DBS5817RA	R	58-62.000 GBP	NS			26-07-17	Duxford	54	H&H
	Silver; running but in need of restoration. Automatic transmission; Webasto sunroof.											
1971	**DBS V8**		DBSV810165RCA	R	90-110.000 GBP	NS			08-09-16	Fontwell Park	157	Coy
	Burgundy with cream leather interior; in good overall condition (see lot 214 Coys 2.7.16 $99,283).											
1971	**DBS V8**		DBSV810165RCA	R	80-100.000 GBP	86.920	105.590	96.672	29-10-16	London	138	Coy
	See lot 157 Coys 8.9.16.											
1971	**DBS V8**		DBSV810105R	R	40-50.000 GBP	51.750	66.535	61.179	13-05-17	Newp.Pagnell	234	Bon
	Blue; restored in the late 1980s. Stored for many years, the car requires recommissioning prior to use.											
1971	**DBS V8**		DBSV810297R	R	70-90.000 GBP	82.140	105.607	97.106	13-05-17	Newp.Pagnell	239	Bon
	Red with natural leather interior; bought in 1994 by the current owner and restored in the mid-2000s.											
1971	**DBS V8**		DBSV810117RC	R	70-90.000 GBP	75.040	96.772	84.795	08-07-17	Brooklands	138	His
	Blue with blue interior; 61,500 miles covered; recently serviced.											
1973	**AM Vantage**		AM6053RA	R	75-85.000 GBP	NS			08-07-17	Brooklands	161	His
	Dark red with tan leather interior; in good overall condition. Automatic transmission (see lot 123 Bonhams 13.5.06 $34,903).											
1973	**AM V8 series 2**		V810594RCA	R	40-50.000 GBP	52.640	65.453	61.794	26-11-16	Weybridge	152	His
	Blue with natural leather interior; since 1998 in the current ownership. Fuel-injected engine; automatic transmission.											
1973	**AM V8 series 2**		V810690RCA	R	80-100.000 GBP	84.375	104.971	97.673	29-03-17	Duxford	104	H&H
	Blue with cream leather interior; recently the body has been restored and repainted, and the mechanicals have been overhauled.											
1974	**AM V8 series 3**		V811303LCA	L	80-120.000 EUR	114.297*	140.921*	126.500*	07-10-16	Zoute	14	Bon F65
	Black with tan interior; restored between 1997 and 2008. Manual gearbox.											
1978	**AM V8 series 3**		V811902LCA	L	80-120.000 EUR	82.717	101.218	92.000	15-10-16	Salzburg	442	Dor
	Red with black leather interior; in good overall condition. Automatic transmission.											
1976	**AM V8 series 3**		V811547LCA	L	130-160.000 EUR	NS			06-11-16	Lyon	332	Ose
	Body and mechanicals restored in the 2000s.											
1973	**AM V8 series 3**		V811316RCA	R	NQ	43.680*	54.312*	51.276*	26-11-16	Weybridge	163	His
	Grey with blue leather interior; engine to be rebuilt.											
1977	**AM V8 series 3**		V811606RCA	R	135-145.000 AUD	87.770	109.133	103.033	27-11-16	Melbourne	53	Mos
	Blue with cream leather interior; imported into Australia in 1982. Automatic transmission.											
1977	**AM V8 series 3**		V811649LCA	L	140-220.000 EUR	NS			09-02-17	Paris	312	Bon
	Blue with beige leather interior; in good overall condition. 15,500 miles covered. Manual gearbox.											
1974	**AM V8 series 3**		V811123RCA	R	80-100.000 GBP	65.975	82.079	76.373	29-03-17	Duxford	24	H&H
	Metallic green with cream leather interior; in good overall condition.											
1973	**AM V8 series 3**		V811046RCA	R	75-90.000 GBP	71.136	88.920	83.841	12-04-17	London	330	Coy
	Light metallic green with black leather interior; described as in very good driving order; 66,300 miles covered. Automatic transmission.											
1974	**AM V8 series 3**		V811198RCAC	R	65-75.000 GBP	70.500	91.735	82.062	20-05-17	Ascot	155	His
	Blue with blue interior; recent mechanical works (see lot 166 Bonhams 9.5.15 NS).											
1973	**AM V8 series 3**		V811051RCA	R	78-92.000 GBP	NS			08-07-17	Brooklands	167	His
	Blue with blue interior; several restoration works carried out in 2016. Manual gearbox (see lot 16 H & H 6.10.04 NS).											
1978	**AM V8 series 4 (spider/conversion)**		V812018RCAS	R	67-78.000 GBP	113.120	140.653	132.792	26-11-16	Weybridge	172	His
	Dark green with cream leather interior; one of seven examples converted by Daytona Motor Company to Volante specification, the offered car was also fitted with the Vantage kit supplied by the factory. When completed it remained for some time in the ownership of Robert Blasi, owner of Daytona Motor Company. Described as in excellent overall condition.											
1979	**AM V8 Vantage series 4**		V8VOR12072	L	350-400.000 USD	250.835	308.000	289.674	20-01-17	Phoenix	234	RMS F66
	Black with red leather interior; sold new in the UK, in 1987 the car was imported into France and converted to left-hand drive. In more recent years it has been restored in the USA. Described as in very good overall condition. Manual gearbox.											
1979	**AM V8 series 4**		V811877LCA	L	130-160.000 USD	88.264	110.000	103.488	11-02-17	Boca Raton	124	TFA
	Metallic blue with fawn interior; three owners and 66,000 original miles. Recent servicing and refurbishment works. Automatic transmission.											
1978	**AM V8 series 4**		V812017RCHS	R	85-95.000 EUR	NS			08-04-17	Essen	167	Coy
	Mistletoe with cream interior; restored 20-25 years ago. Recently serviced.											

F65: 1974 Aston Martin AM V8 series 3

F66: 1979 Aston Martin AM V8 Vantage series 4

Year	Model	(Bodybuilder)	Chassis no.	Steering	Estimate	Hammer Price £	$	€	Date	Place	Lot	Auc. H.
1978	**AM V8 "Canadian Vantage"**		V811904LCA	L	300-350.000 USD	239.316	308.000	262.416	18-08-17	Monterey	160	RMS

Burgundy with fawn leather interior; one of eight examples built for the Canadian market with Vantage-type cosmetics. Engine no.V540/1904/S with manual gearbox. Restored. Engine rebuilt in 2005 to 6-liter specification.

| 1979 | **AM V8 Volante** | | V8COR15075 | R | 160-180.000 GBP | | NS | | 12-10-16 | Duxford | 92 | H&H |

Blue with fawn interior; in recent years the original automatic transmission (included with the sale) has been replaced with a 6-speed manual unit and the body has been repainted (see lot 624 Silverstone Auctions 14.11.15 $231,215).

| 1978 | **AM V8 Volante** | | 15040 | L | 200-250.000 USD | 174.024 | 214.500 | 201.051 | 19-01-17 | Scottsdale | 6 | Bon |

Light blue with natural leather interior; less than 25,000 miles on the odometer. Manual gearbox.

| 1980 | **AM V8 Volante** | | V8COL15213 | L | 175-225.000 USD | | NS | | 19-01-17 | Scottsdale | 67 | Bon |

Red with natural leather interior; described as in largely original condition; less than 37,000 miles covered; automatic transmission (see lot 4 Gooding & Company 14.8.10 $49,500).

| 1985 | **AM V8 Volante** | | 15378 | L | 200-250.000 USD | 138.855* | 170.500* | 160.355* | 21-01-17 | Scottsdale | 139 | G&Co |

Metallic black with black leather interior; in 2016 cosmetically restored and fitted with European-style bumpers. Just over 35,000 miles covered (see lot 723 Auctions America 2.4.16 $100,000).

| 1989 | **AM V8 Volante** | | 15770 | L | 225-275.000 USD | 203.247 | 247.500 | 234.556 | 09-03-17 | Amelia Island | 151 | Bon |

British racing green with fawn interior; in very good original condition. Less than 17,500 miles covered. Manual gearbox.

| 1982 | **AM V8 Volante** | | V8COR15301 | R | 200-250.000 GBP | 197.500 | 253.926 | 233.485 | 13-05-17 | Newp.Pagnell | 215 | Bon |

Metallic green with beige interior; uprated to Vantage specification by Works Service in 1988. Last serviced in March 2017 (see lots 101 Christie's 24.3.03 $73,902 and 319 Bonhams 22.5.10 $96,917). **F67**

| 1980 | **AM V8 Volante** | | V8COL15180 | L | 90-140.000 EUR | 148.191* | 192.838* | 172.500* | 21-05-17 | SPA-Francorch. | 60 | Bon |

Metallic blue with beige interior; restored some years ago in Switzerland. From the Swiss Castle Collection.

| 1984 | **AM V8 Volante** | | 15346 | L | 210-240.000 USD | | NS | | 24-06-17 | Santa Monica | 204 | RMS |

Blue with burgundy leather interior; 3,800 miles covered; two owners. Automatic transmission (see lot 162 Artcurial 7.7.12 $81,100).

| 1988 | **AM V8 Vantage** | | 12643 | R | 240-280.000 GBP | | NS | | 07-12-16 | Chateau Impney | 63 | H&H |

Metallic blue with champagne leather interior; involved in an accident in 2001, the car was subsequently fully restored and fitted with the present Vantage engine to X-Pack specification. Described as in very good overall condition; circa 72,000 miles covered since new; last serviced in April 2016.

| 1981 | **AM V8 Vantage** | | V8VOL12319 | R | 150-180.000 GBP | | NS | | 13-05-17 | Newp.Pagnell | 242 | Bon |

Burgundy with magnolia interior; built in left-hand drive form and converted to right-hand drive in 1984 (believed by Aston Martin Works Service); engine rebuilt in 2000. Formerly owned also by actor Rowan Atkinson.

| 1985 | **Lagonda** | | 13466 | L | 65-75.000 USD | 53.818 | 71.500 | 63.878 | 03-09-16 | Auburn | 2160 | AA |

Dark grey with light grey interior; described as in very good overall condition. Car exhibited at the 1986 New York Motor Show (see lots 342 Silverstone Auctions 6.3.16 $103,523 and 146 RM/Sotheby's 30.7.16 NS).

| 1983 | **Lagonda** | | 13279 | L | 60-80.000 USD | 75.857* | 93.500* | 87.638* | 19-01-17 | Scottsdale | 8 | Bon |

Described as in highly original condition; recently serviced.

| 1981 | **Lagonda** | | L00L13083 | L | 50-80.000 EUR | 45.750* | 57.014* | 53.640* | 10-02-17 | Paris | 57 | Art |

Silver with dark blue leather interior; described as in very good original condition.

| 1984 | **Lagonda** | | 13299 | L | 65-85.000 USD | 34.778* | 42.350* | 40.135* | 09-03-17 | Amelia Island | 185 | Bon |

Red; 59,000 miles covered.

| 1979 | **Lagonda** | | LOOR13010 | R | 50-80.000 GBP | 28.750* | 36.964* | 33.988* | 13-05-17 | Newp.Pagnell | 214 | Bon |

Gold with white interior; restored in 1986; for 30 years circa in the current ownership; stored for the last 14 years, it requires recommissioning prior to use.

| 1989 | **Lagonda** | | 13588 | R | 80-100.000 GBP | 91.100 | 117.127 | 107.698 | 13-05-17 | Newp.Pagnell | 227 | Bon |

Metallic blue with magnolia interior; stored for 12 years, the car was bought in 2008 by the current owner. Body repainted. **F68**

| 1985 | **Lagonda** | | 13428 | L | 70-90.000 USD | 41.073* | 52.800* | 47.071* | 04-06-17 | Greenwich | 122 | Bon |

Metallic cranberry with grey leather interior; numerous restoration works carried out since 2013. Under 47,000 original miles.

| 1980 | **Lagonda** | | LOOR13047 | R | 50-70.000 GBP | 40.250* | 52.236* | 45.575* | 30-06-17 | Goodwood | 285 | Bon |

Light blue with blue interior; single-family ownership from new. Always maintained by Aston Martin Works and Chris Shenton Engineering. Numerous works carried out over the years.

| 1988 | **Vantage Volante "Prince of Wales"** | | 15749 | R | 600-700.000 GBP | 651.100 | 821.884 | 772.270 | 04-12-16 | London | 5 | Bon |

Green with tan leather interior; first owner the then Aston Martin CEO Victor Gauntlett, who retained it until 1990 when it was sold to Japan. Reimported into Europe in 1999. In the 2000s the engine was enlarged to 7 litres capacity, the suspension were upgraded and the brakes were swapped for superior AP Racing components. 36,143 miles on the odometer in November 2016. Recently serviced. **F69**

| 1989 | **Vantage Volante** | | 15784 | L | 375-425.000 USD | 250.835 | 308.000 | 289.674 | 20-01-17 | Phoenix | 249 | RMS |

Black with black interior; sold new to the USA. Original engine uprated to 6.3-litre factory spcification by marque English specialist Oselli. In good overall condition; circa 31,000 actual miles.

F67: 1982 Aston Martin AM V8 Volante

F68: 1989 Aston Martin Lagonda

Year	Model	(Bodybuilder)	Chassis no.	Steering	Estimate	Hammer price £	$	€	Date	Sale Place	Lot	Auc. H.

F69: 1988 Aston Martin Vantage Volante "Prince of Wales"

F70: 1986 Aston Martin Vantage Zagato

Year	Model	Chassis	Steer	Estimate	£	$	€	Date	Place	Lot	Auc
1988	**Vantage Volante**	15621	L	250-350.000 EUR	189.325	237.897	222.500	09-02-17	Paris	323	Bon

Black with black leather interior; sold new to the USA, the car was reimported into Europe in 2008. Described as in very good overall condition. Approximately 40,000 miles covered. Automatic transmission.

1988	**Vantage Volante "Prince of Wales"**	15714	L	300-500.000 EUR	406.663	506.791	476.800	10-02-17	Paris	84	Art

Blue with magnolia leather interior; sold new to the USA, the car was later reimported into Europe. 29,000 miles covered; last serviced in October 2016. Manual gearbox.

1989	**Vantage Volante**	15795	L	275-350.000 USD	271.458	330.000	310.992	10-03-17	Amelia Island	25	G&Co

Black with parchment leather interior; in very good original condition, 7,890 miles covered. Automatic transmission. First owner Greg Norman.

1989	**Vantage Volante**	15790	R	350-400.000 GBP	387.900	498.723	458.575	13-05-17	Newp.Pagnell	230	Bon

Black pearl with light tan leather interior; sold in July 1989 with the X-Pack engine, in December 1989 the car was returned to the factory where it was converted to right-hand drive and fitted with the manual gearbox as replacement of the original automatic unit. In 2012 it was bought by the current owner already restored and fitted with a new 7.0-litre R S Williams engine.

1986	**Vantage Zagato**	20013	R	250-300.000 GBP	253.500	337.789	299.789	10-09-16	Goodwood	110	Bon

Red; the car was acquired in 1998 by actor Rowan Atkinson and subsequently prepared at the factory for racing with the Aston Martin Owners Club. Raced until 2007 when it was reconverted for "fast road" use. Since 2008 in the current ownership. The Geneva Motor Show Car (see lot 316 Bonhams 17.5.08 $238,557). **F70**

1987	**Vantage Zagato**	20031	L	300-400.000 EUR	NS			13-05-17	Newp.Pagnell	219	Bon

British racing green with tan interior; front end repaired at the factory in 1996; since 1997 in the current ownership; 56,400 kms covered; automatic transmission.

1987	**Vantage Zagato**	20043	L	400-500.000 EUR	332.020	426.344	380.800	27-05-17	Villa Erba	162	RMS

Dark green with cream leather interior; just over 4,000 kms covered (see lot 28 Poulain 29.4.96 $107.889).

1989	**Volante Zagato**	30022	R	265-325.000 GBP	281.500	361.925	332.789	13-05-17	Newp.Pagnell	226	Bon

Metallic brown with magnolia interior; 3,680 miles covered; since 1998 in the current ownership.

1989	**Volante Zagato**	30028	L	450-550.000 EUR	400.376	514.120	459.200	27-05-17	Villa Erba	148	RMS

Yellow with black interior; less than 13,000 kms covered; the only left-hand drive factory example. **F71**

1989	**AMR-1**	AMR105	R	500-550.000 GBP	NS			24-02-17	Stoneleigh P.	119	SiC

Works car during the 1989 season. Raced at Group C historic events since 2001 fitted with a 6-litre engine.

1989	**AMR-1 Group C**	AMR104	R	475-675.000 USD	478.632	616.000	524.832	18-08-17	Monterey	146	RMS

One of four examples in existence; driven in period by David Leslie, Brian Redman and Michael Roe. Bought by the current owner directly from the factory. From the early 2000s raced at historic events (see lot 182 RM 10.5.14 NS). **F72**

1990	**Virage**	50010	R	28-36.000 GBP	30.800	38.297	36.156	26-11-16	Weybridge	151	His

Green with light green interior; bought in 2010 by the current owner and subsequently little used. First owner actor Rowan Atkinson (see lot 329 Bonhams 22.5.10 $26,419).

1990	**Virage**	50084	R	125-150.000 GBP	NS			13-05-17	Newp.Pagnell	204	Bon

British racing green with light grey leather interior; converted at the factory in 1993 to Vantage specification (6.3-litre engine and 6-speed manual gearbox). In 1998 the car returned at the factory where the engine was rebuilt and the rear panel and boot lid were also converted to Vantage specification.

1990	**Virage**	50019	R	40-50.000 GBP	NS			13-05-17	Newp.Pagnell	241	Bon

Blue with magnolia interior; engine partially rebuilt in 2000 (see lot 155 Bonhams/Brooks 12.5.01 NS).

1994	**Virage**	50420	R	38-44.000 GBP	38.475	50.383	42.957	29-07-17	Silverstone	422	SiC

Green with tan leather interior; in good overall condition; 45,000 miles covered; automatic transmission.

F71: 1989 Aston Martin Volante Zagato

F72: 1989 Aston Martin AMR-1 Group C

Year	Model	(Bodybuilder)	Chassis no.	Steering	Estimate	Hammer price £	$	€	Date	Place	Lot	Auc. H.
1994	**Virage Volante**		60190	L	45-55.000 EUR	57.242*	71.178*	67.200*	25-11-16	Milan	903	RMS
Blue; 47,345 kms. From the Duemila Ruote collection.												
1992	**Virage Volante**		60003	R	80-90.000 GBP	86.620	109.219	101.787	07-12-16	London	331	Bon
Green with green interior; fitted with the 6.3-litre engine as requested by its first owner the Sultan of Brunei. Displayed at the 1992 Geneva Motor Show. Since 1999 in the current ownership; 19,862 miles on the odometer.												**F73**
1994	**Virage Volante**		60108	R	150-175.000 GBP	160.000	195.744	185.280	04-03-17	Brooklands	195	His
"Widebody" finished in green with black interior; just one owner. In good overall condition. 6.3-litre engine.												
1996	**Vantage**		70132	R	175-200.000 GBP	166.666	214.282	197.033	13-05-17	Newp.Pagnell	206	Bon
Blue with parchment leather interior; described as in very good overall condition. Automatic transmission.												
1997	**Vantage**		70164	R	220-260.000 GBP	253.500	325.925	299.688	13-05-17	Newp.Pagnell	233	Bon
Dark blue with parchment leather interior; in 2000 the car was converted at the factory to the V600 package. Last serviced in February 2017.												**F74**
1996	**DB7 coupé**		100360	R	17-24.000 GBP	24.640	30.637	28.925	26-11-16	Weybridge	213	His
Silver with light grey leather interior; 27,000 miles covered. Recently serviced. Automatic transmission.												
1995	**DB7 coupé**		100063	R	28-35.000 GBP	31.220	38.017	35.659	14-01-17	Birmingham	110	Coy
Dark green; 18,400 miles covered.												
1999	**DB7 coupé Special Edition**		102631	R	35-40.000 GBP		NS		13-05-17	Newp.Pagnell	235	Bon
Black wiyh grey leather interior; in very good overall condition. Manual gearbox.												
1997	**V8 Coupé**		79072	L	65-75.000 EUR	109.714*	136.425*	128.800*	25-11-16	Milan	865	RMS
Dark green; 38,754 kms. From the Duemila Ruote collection.												
1996	**V8 Sportsman**		79007	L	300-350.000 GBP	337.500	433.924	398.993	13-05-17	Newp.Pagnell	217	Bon
British racing green with green interior; one of three shooting brake examples built by the factory. Engine rebuilt in 1999. 21,000 kms covered. Last serviced in February 2017 (see lots 23 Poulain 26.5.00 NS and 17 Bonhams 11.9.10 NS).												**F75**
2000	**DB7 V12 Vantage**		300807	R	39-44.000 GBP	52.900	66.702	62.163	07-12-16	London	351	Bon
Metallic green with magnolia leather interior; one owner and circa 20,000 miles covered.												
2003	**DB7 V12 Vantage**		303772	R	24-28.000 GBP	30.576	37.407	35.407	04-03-17	Brooklands	199	His
Blue with parchment interior; in good overall condition.												
2002	**DB7 V12 Vantage Jubilee**		303086	R	48-54.000 GBP		NS		13-05-17	Newp.Pagnell	224	Bon
Blue with magnolia leather interior; 47,099 miles from new; last serviced in 2016 (see lot 338 Bonhams 2.3.13 NS).												
2003	**DB7 V12 Vantage**		303645	L	46-52.000 GBP	55.200	70.971	65.257	13-05-17	Newp.Pagnell	238	Bon
Blue with parchment leather interior; retained by Aston Martin when new, the car was sold to its first private German owner in 2007-2008 circa. Approximately 15,000 kms covered.												
2000	**DB7 V12 Vantage**		300464	R	30-35.000 GBP		NS		29-07-17	Silverstone	744	SiC
Aston Martin racing green with green and tan interior; last serviced at 70,800 miles; manual gearbox.												
2002	**DB7 V12 Vantage Volante**		403008	L	20-30.000 EUR	49.610*	61.688*	58.240*	25-11-16	Milan	854	RMS
Dark grey; 14,951 kms. From the Duemila Ruote collection.												
2000	**Vantage Le Mans V600**		70245	R	350-450.000 GBP	354.300	472.105	418.995	10-09-16	Goodwood	124	Bon
Aston Martin racing green with magnolia leather interior; two owners and circa 17,000 miles covered. Last serviced in July 2016.												**F76**
2000	**Vantage Le Mans**		70269	R	300-400.000 GBP	309.500	397.924	365.891	13-05-17	Newp.Pagnell	236	Bon
Aston Martin racing green with tan interior; single family ownership; approximately 4,000 miles covered; manual gearbox. Example no.29 of 40 built.												
2005	**V12 Vanquish S coupé**		501733	R	NA	135.000	179.321	160.218	02-09-16	Salon Privé	237	SiC
Silver with two-tone blue leather interior; two owners and 3,892 miles covered.												
2001	**V12 Vanquish coupé**		500062	R	62-66.000 GBP	44.000	55.700	51.080	12-11-16	Birmingham	308	SiC
White with black and white interior; body originally finished in silver. 28,449 miles on the odometer. Last serviced in October 2015.												
2001	**V12 Vanquish coupé**		000022	L	65-75.000 EUR	83.955*	104.395*	98.560*	25-11-16	Milan	899	RMS
Light grey; 24,830 kms. From the Duemila Ruote collection.												
2002	**V12 Vanquish coupé**		500215	R	65-75.000 GBP	77.220	96.015	90.649	26-11-16	Weybridge	193	His
Silver with black leather interior; 13,000 miles covered.												
2003	**V12 Vanquish coupé**		500982	L	70-90.000 USD	58.008*	71.500*	67.017*	19-01-17	Scottsdale	69	Bon
In highly original condition; less than 15,000 miles covered; leather and alcantara interior.												**F77**
2007	**V12 Vanquish S coupé**		502391	R	150-180.000 GBP		NS		13-05-17	Newp.Pagnell	218	Bon
Titanium grey with parchment leather interior; one owner; 6,556 miles covered; last serviced in 2016.												

F73: 1992 Aston Martin Virage Volante

F74: 1997 Aston Martin Vantage

F75: 1996 Aston Martin V8 Sportsman

F76: 2000 Aston Martin Vantage Le Mans V600

Year	Model (Bodybuilder)	Chassis no.	Steering	Estimate	Hammer price £	$	€	Date	Sale Place	Lot	Auc. H.
2004	**V12 Vanquish coupé**	501305	R	80-90.000 GBP	91.100	117.127	107.698	13-05-17	Newp.Pagnell	240	**Bon**
	Two owners; 10,500 miles covered; cosmetically upgraded to some S specification.										
2003	**V12 Vanquish coupé**	501148	L	90-120.000 USD	69.311	89.100	79.433	04-06-17	Greenwich	174	**Bon**
	Tungsten grey with black leather and grey alcantara interior; two owners; 8,000 original miles. Converted to 6-speed manual gearbox at the factory in 2015.										
2005	**V12 Vanquish S coupé**	501689	R	160-190.000 GBP	145.000	188.181	164.184	29-06-17	Fontwell Park	145	**Coy**
	Meteorite grey; less than 20,000 miles covered; manual gearbox.										
2003	**DB AR1 Roadster** (Zagato)	800037	L	275-350.000 USD	307.888	379.500	355.705	19-01-17	Phoenix	121	**RMS** **F78**
	Tungsten grey with tan interior; one of 99 examples built. 800 actual miles.										
2003	**DB7 V12 GTA**	303817	R	50-60.000 GBP	52.312	64.114	58.181	12-10-16	Duxford	96	**H&H**
	Metallic green with black leather interior; 23,227 miles covered.										
2003	**DB7 V12 GT**	304088	L	35-40.000 EUR	71.553*	88.973*	84.000*	25-11-16	Milan	300	**RMS**
	Dark green with red interior; 6,740 kms. From the Duemila Ruote collection.										
2003	**DB7 V12 GTA**	304128	R	34-40.000 GBP	56.000	69.630	65.738	26-11-16	Weybridge	131	**His**
	Silver with black leather interior; recently serviced.										
2003	**DB7 V12 GT**	303979	R	32-38.000 GBP		NS		24-02-17	Stoneleigh P.	518	**SiC**
	Since 2006 in the current ownership; 68,000 miles covered.										
2003	**DB7 V12 GT**	304086	R	65-75.000 GBP	68.000	88.482	79.152	20-05-17	Ascot	164	**His**
	Black with burgundy interior; just over 20,000 miles covered.										
2003	**DB7 V12 GTA**	304095	R	28-35.000 GBP	33.600	43.331	37.968	08-07-17	Brooklands	208	**His**
	Blue with blue and parchment interior; recently serviced.										
2003	**DB7 Zagato**	700057	L	240-280.000 GBP	309.500	390.682	367.098	04-12-16	London	14	**Bon**
	Dark green with tan leather interior; approximately 900 kms covered. Recent Aston Martin Works service. Currently registered in Latvia.										
2003	**DB7 Zagato**	700001	L	350-400.000 EUR	334.435	418.068	392.000	08-02-17	Paris	153	**RMS** **F79**
	Black with red leather interior; example no.1 of 99 built. One owner.										
2003	**DB7 Zagato**	700040	L	300-375.000 USD	294.080*	357.500*	336.908*	10-03-17	Amelia Island	113	**RMS**
	Green with mint green leather interior; imported into the USA in 2005 after a factory conversion to left-hand drive. 513 actual miles. From the Orin Smith collection (see lot 216 RM 16.1.15 $330,000).										
2004	**DB7 Zagato**	700021	R	250-280.000 GBP	247.500	307.915	286.506	29-03-17	Duxford	110	**H&H**
	Tungsten grey with blue leather interior; last serviced in June 2016 at 4,734 miles. Two owners.										
2005	**DB9 coupé**	03323	R	25-32.000 GBP	33.600	41.106	38.909	04-03-17	Brooklands	172	**His**
	Silver with grey leather interior; one owner.										
2006	**DB9 coupé**	06636	R	45-50.000 GBP	43.313	55.688	51.205	13-05-17	Silverstone	372	**SiC**
	Tungsten grey with red leather interior; last serviced in March 2017 at 17,600 miles.										

F77: 2003 Aston Martin V12 Vanquish coupé

F78: 2003 Aston Martin DB AR1 Roadster (Zagato)

Year	Model	(Bodybuilder)	Chassis no.	Steering	Estimate	Hammer Price £	$	€	Date	Place	Lot	Auc. H.
2007	**DB9 Volante**		06755	R	40-50.000 GBP		NS		12-10-16	Duxford	55	H&H
Gunmetal grey with black leather interior; 44,800 miles on the odometer.												
2005	**DB9 Volante**		03416	L	40-45.000 EUR	59.150*	73.551*	69.440*	25-11-16	Milan	301	RMS
Light grey with burgundy interior; 9,170 kms. From the Duemila Ruote collection.												
2006	**DB9 Volante**		05076	R	28-34.000 GBP	39.200	48.741	46.017	26-11-16	Weybridge	209	His
Blue with beige interior; in good overall condition.												
2009	**DB9 Volante**		06217	L	50-60.000 GBP	61.980	78.151	72.833	07-12-16	London	360	Bon
Medium grey with tan interior; one owner and 28,331 kms on the odometer. Touchtronic semi-automatic transmission.												
2006	**DB9 Volante**		04769	L	60-80.000 USD	60.626*	73.700*	69.455*	10-03-17	Amelia Island	151	RMS **F80**
Dark green with tan leather interior; 14,718 miles covered. From the Orin Smith collection.												
2005	**DB9 Volante**		03525	L	50-70.000 EUR		NS		18-06-17	Fontainebleau	93	Ose
In very good overall condition; recently serviced.												
2006	**DBR9**		DBR99	L	275-325.000 USD	478.632*	616.000*	524.832*	18-08-17	Monterey	145	RMS **F81**
One of 10 Works cars and one of four sold to official team BMS Scuderia Italia. Raced at the FIA GT Championship until July 2007 when it was damaged in an accident at the Spa-Francorchamps 24 Hours. Rebuilt by the factory with a new chassis (the original chassis tub is included with the sale).												
2005	**V8 Vantage coupé**		00111	R	34-38.000 GBP	34.875	43.782	41.268	24-02-17	Stoneleigh P.	908	SiC
Metallic black with dark red interior; 25,000 miles covered. Last service in August 2016. Manual gearbox.												
2008	**V8 Vantage cabriolet**		08315	L	NQ	47.480*	58.300*	54.831*	21-01-17	Scottsdale	1246	B/J
Red with sand interior; 11,696 actual miles.												
2009	**V8 Vantage cabriolet**		11773	L	NQ	53.750	66.000	62.073	21-01-17	Scottsdale	8476	R&S
Black with black interior; 7,500 miles.												
2009	**DBS Volante**		11156	R	110-130.000 GBP		NS		07-09-16	London	171	RMS
Black with black interior; originally used as a factory demonstrator. 45,600 miles covered. Manual gearbox.												
2013	**V12 Vantage coupé**		01352	R	50-60.000 GBP		NS		07-12-16	Chateau Impney	82	H&H
Black; one owner and 32,500 miles covered.												
2012	**V12 Zagato**		31207	L	525-600.000 GBP	655.200	876.789	780.278	07-09-16	London	148	RMS **F82**
Blue with red leather interior; one owner and 4,200 kms covered. Number 26 of 61 road-examples built.												
2013	**V12 Zagato**		31309	L	500-600.000 GBP		NS		04-12-16	London	21	Bon
Red with leather and alcantara interior; one owner and circa 400kms covered. Recently serviced at Newport Pagnell.												
2012	**V12 Zagato**		31235	L	625-675.000 EUR	640.204	800.302	750.400	08-02-17	Paris	146	RMS
White; the car features some exclusive aesthetical details requested by the buyer and is titled "No. Zero". One of 65 examples built. One owner.												
2016	**Vantage GT12 coupé**		62485	L	350-400.000 GBP		NS		13-05-17	Newp.Pagnell	243	Bon
Viridian green with black alcantara interior; example no.74 of 100 built; new, never registered; 30 delivery kms recorded; warranty valid until June 2019. If the car remains within the EU, VAT at 20% will be added to the hammer price and buyer's premium.												
2016	**Vulcan**		11	L	2.300-2.700.000 USD		NS		19-08-17	Monterey	S108	Mec
Dark blue with black interior; example no.11 of 24 built; only for track use; less than 100 miles covered (see lot S99 Mecum 20.8.16 NS).												

ASTON-BUTTERWORTH (GB)

Year	Model	(Bodybuilder)	Chassis no.	Steering	Estimate	£	$	€	Date	Place	Lot	Auc. H.
1952	**Formula 2**		NB42	M	60-80.000 GBP		NS		10-09-16	Goodwood	152	Bon
One of two examples built by racing driver Bill Aston using a Cooper Mark I chassis and 2-litre engine built by Archie Butterworth. The present car was acquired by Robin Montgomerie-Charrington who raced it in 1952 at the Spa and Chimay GPs. Reassembled between the late 1960s-early 1970s and fitted with a later 2-litre Butterworth engine, MG gearbox and Alfa Romeo Giulietta brakes; restored between 2001 and 2004; engine rebuilt in 2015; driven at some historic events in 2015.												

AUBURN (USA) (1903-1936)

Year	Model	(Bodybuilder)	Chassis no.	Steering	Estimate	£	$	€	Date	Place	Lot	Auc. H.
1929	**8-90 Speedster**		1746	L	200-250.000 USD	140.755	187.000	167.066	03-09-16	Auburn	5155	AA
Black and red with red leather interior; concours-quality restoration completed in 2014.												
1932	**12-160A convertible sedan**		BB1856A	L	175-225.000 USD	128.969*	158.400*	148.532*	18-01-17	Scottsdale	35	WoA
Silver and burgundy with black leather interior; 800 miles covered since the restoration carried out in 2001 (see lots 3108 Auctions America 2.8.14 NS and 7003 Russo & Steele 20.8.16 NS).												
1933	**12-161A Salon phaeton (Limousine Body Co.)**		1156	L	NQ	134.376*	165.000*	155.183*	21-01-17	Scottsdale	1383	B/J
Red with tan interior; restored in the 1980s. Recently serviced.												

F79: 2003 Aston Martin DB7 Zagato

F80: 2006 Aston Martin DB9 Volante

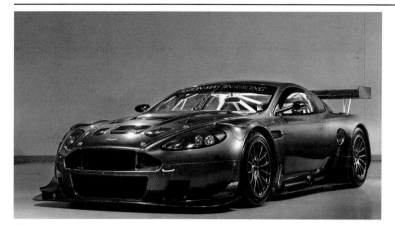

F81: 2006 Aston Martin DBR9

F82: 2012 Aston Martin V12 Zagato

Year	Model	(Bodybuilder)	Chassis no.	Steering	Estimate	£	$	€	Date	Place	Lot	Auc. H.
1935	**8-851 SC speedster**		33952E	L	900-1.200.000 USD	713.680	880.000	789.888	07-10-16	Hershey	237	**RMS**
	Light grey; discovered in Mexico in 1962, the car was bought in 1982 by a previous owner who had it restored and retained it until 2006. Later it was acquired by the current owner and subsequently restored again to concours condition.											**F83**
1935	**8-851 SC boattail speedster**		33029E	L	650-750.000 USD	564.379	693.000	651.767	21-01-17	Scottsdale	152	**G&Co**
	In the same family ownership from 1954 to 2014 and little used; body repainted in the late 1950s; in 2014 returned in running order for the first time in many years; never comprehensively restored.											
1935	**8-851 SC roadster**		33195F	L	120-150.000 EUR		NS		19-03-17	Fontainebleau	203	**Ose**
	Ivory with beige interior; restored in 1979. Since 1985 in the René Cocheteux collection.											
1936	**8-852 SC convertible sedan**		GH5265	L	NQ		NS		15-01-17	Kissimmee	S86.1	**Mec**
	Burgundy with tan leather interior.											
1936	**8-852 phaeton**		5817H	L	110-140.000 USD		NS		11-02-17	Boca Raton	118	**TFA**
	Silver and burgundy with maroon interior; restored.											
1936	**8-852 SC boattail speedster**		35209E	L	700-900.000 USD	790.598	1.017.500	866.910	18-08-17	Monterey	124	**RMS**
	Black with burgundy interior; restored at unspecified date; mechanicals rebuilt and cosmetics freshened over the past two years (see lots Christie's 29 5.6.05 $246,000, and RM 423 16.8.08 $533,500, 149 31.10.12 NS, and 146 15.8.14 $550,000).											

AUDI (D) *(1910-)*

Year	Model	(Bodybuilder)	Chassis no.	Steering	Estimate	£	$	€	Date	Place	Lot	Auc. H.
1990	**Quattro**		000668	R	NA	64.130	85.184	76.109	02-09-16	Salon Privé	204	**SiC**
	Silver; in original condition. 16,231 miles covered; last serviced in April 2016.											
1983	**Quattro**		900407	L	42-62.000 EUR	45.494	55.670	50.600	15-10-16	Salzburg	425	**Dor**
	Metallic black with beige leather interior; 77,120 kms covered. Sunroof.											
1981	**Quattro**		900146	L	100-150.000 GBP		NS		19-03-17	Goodwood	21	**Bon**
	Press and demonstrator car when new for the Volkswagen/Audi Group (UK); assigned in 1982 to David Sutton Motorsport's official Audi Rally team, converted to rally specification, and raced until 1985; subsequently sold to Spain where it was raced until 1987; back to the UK in 1990 and restored; engine rebuilt in 2009 (see lots 878 Brooks 26.10.95 NS and 229 Bonhams 24.6.16 NS).											
1985	**Quattro**		900827	R	45-55.000 GBP	47.916	59.612	55.468	29-03-17	Duxford	70	**H&H**
	Red with grey interior; in original condition; 8,200 miles covered.											
1985	**Quattro**		900735	L	40-50.000 EUR	29.101	36.244	34.000	08-04-17	Essen	181	**Coy**
	Black with grey leather interior; two owners; 111,000 kms covered; last serviced 350 kms ago.											
1986	**Quattro Sport**		905076	L	290-320.000 GBP	403.200	539.562	480.171	07-09-16	London	114	**RMS**
	Red; five owners and 32,672 miles covered. Stored since 2006, the car has been recently recommissioned. In 1988 the original aluminium-alloy engine block was replaced at the factory in Ingolstadt with a new steel block.											**F84**
1985	**Quattro Sport**		905077	L	330-400.000 EUR		NS		09-02-17	Paris	370	**Bon**
	Red with grey/beige leather interior; sold new to Switzerland; in excellent overall condition; three owners; French papers.											
1985	**Quattro Sport**		905148	L	300-350.000 EUR		NS		27-05-17	Villa Erba	124	**RMS**
	White; in preserved condition; engine block replaced in period by Audi with an iron unit (see lot 136 Coys 23.5.10 $111,638).											

F83: 1935 Auburn 8-851 SC speedster

F84: 1986 Audi Quattro Sport

Year	Model	(Bodybuilder)	Chassis no.	Steering	Estimate	Hammer price £	$	€	Date	Place	Lot	Auc. H.
1985	**Quattro Sport**		905131	L	450-550.000 USD	**376.068***	**484.000***	**412.368***	18-08-17	Carmel	23	**Bon**

White; just one owner; 18,400 kms on the odometer; in highly original condition. The car requires a full service including replacement of the timing belt prior to use.

1994	**A4 2.3E cabriolet**		004422	R	50-60.000 GBP	**54.000**	**68.359**	**62.689**	12-11-16	Birmingham	319	**SiC**

Metallic green with parchment leather interior; automatic transmission. 21,412 miles covered. When new the car was presented for personal use to Diana, Princess of Wales, who covered about 4,000 miles. Since 2013 in the current ownership (see lot 133 Coys 29.6.13 NA).

1997	**A4 Quattro Super Touring**		ST31	L	130-160.000 GBP	**112.000**	**149.878**	**133.381**	07-09-16	London	115	**RMS**

The last of 31 factory-built examples, the car was built for and raced by Emanule Pirro for most of the 1997 season. Sold to private drivers, it was raced at European Super Touring championships until 2002. Rebuilt from a bare shell in 2013.

AUSTIN (GB) *(1906-)*

Year	Model	(Bodybuilder)	Chassis no.	Steering	Estimate	£	$	€	Date	Place	Lot	Auc. H.
1930	**Seven sports**		B11010	R	8-12.000 GBP	**13.800***	**18.331***	**16.378***	03-09-16	Beaulieu	442	**Bon** **F85**

Black with light grey bonnet; in good running order. Believed Gordon England coachwork.

1929	**Seven saloon**		75452	R	10-12.000 GBP	**10.640**	**13.040**	**11.834**	12-10-16	Duxford	2	**H&H**

Black with red interior; restored several years ago.

1936	**Seven Ruby saloon**		253787	R	5-7.000 GBP	**6.048**	**7.516**	**7.024**	16-11-16	Donington Park	50	**H&H**

Yellow with black wings; in good overall condition.

1926	**Seven top hat saloon**		26731	R	10-12.000 GBP	**9.562**	**12.252**	**10.956**	02-06-17	Solihull	18	**H&H**

Maroon and black with black interior, restored many years ago, it requires recommissioning prior to use.

1940	**12/16hp saloon**		20524	R	8-10.000 GBP	**10.976**	**13.840**	**12.898**	07-12-16	Chateau Impney	1	**H&H**

Light green with tan interior; restored between 2010 and 2012. Believed to be the prototype for the 16hp model introduced immediately post-war; fitted with the 2.2-litre engine. Initially employed as a Royal Navy staff car.

1939	**Ten Four Conway cabriolet**		GCE168784	R	11-13.000 GBP	**10.360**	**13.063**	**12.174**	07-12-16	Chateau Impney	26	**H&H**

Green with black wings and green leather interior; restored in the 1990s.

1938	**12/4 Heavy LL taxi**	(J & H Ricketts)	81512	R	30-35.000 GBP		**NS**		12-10-16	Duxford	72	**H&H**

Remained in service until 1955; restored and returned to the road in 2003. One of four known survivors with Ricketts body.

1938	**12/4 Heavy LL taxi**		81512	R	24-28.000 GBP	**22.500**	**27.992**	**26.046**	29-03-17	Duxford	113	**H&H**

See lot 72 H & H 12.10.16.

1938	**20/6 Mayfair limousine**		DJN7063	R	10-12.000 GBP	**13.950**	**17.874**	**15.984**	02-06-17	Solihull	55	**H&H**

Black with black interior; restored in the 1980s. It requires recommissioning prior to use.

1950	**A90 Atlantic cabriolet**		BD251062	R	10-14.000 GBP	**17.920**	**22.387**	**21.174**	23-02-17	Donington Park	5	**H&H**

Green with cream interior; restored between 1996 and 1998.

1950	**A90 Atlantic cabriolet**		BD254029	R	20-24.000 GBP		**NS**		02-06-17	Solihull	53	**H&H**

Old English white with black interior, restored many years ago, it requires recommissioning prior to use (see lots 429 Sotheby's 3.6.95 $14,792 and 59 H & H 26.9.01 NS).

1952	**A90 Atlantic coupé**		BE2117190	R	17-22.000 GBP	**19.880**	**25.637**	**22.464**	08-07-17	Brooklands	143	**His** **F86**

Two-tone body; restored in the 1980s.

1956	**A135 Princess**	(A.Mulliner)	DH212785	R	185-260.000 GBP		**NS**		07-09-16	London	111	**RMS**

Black; described as in largely original condition. The car was acquired in 1971 by John Lennon who used it in the documentary movie "Imagine" and fitted it in the rear part with two rows of airline seats. In 1972 it was bought by William McGaw who retained it until 1987. In 2005 it was acquired by Milton Verret who presented it in 2008 to the Austin Rock & Roll Car Museum, from whom the car is offered for sale.

1956	**A135 Princess**	(A.Mulliner)	DH212785	R	NQ	**129.897***	**159.500***	**150.010***	21-01-17	Scottsdale	1380	**B/J** **F87**

See lot 111 RM/Sotheby's 7.9.16.

1954	**A70 Hereford saloon**		B53156740	R	8-9.000 GBP	**8.437**	**10.810**	**9.667**	02-06-17	Solihull	56	**H&H**

Black with light brown leather interior; in good overall condition, the car requires recommissioning prior to use.

1978	**Mini Clubman 1275 GT**		XE2D2463968A	R	130-160.000 GBP		**NS**		08-10-16	Ascot	339	**Coy**

In 1978 with financial backing from British Leyland and Patrick Motors, the racing driver Richard Longman modified and prepared the car to enter it in the British Touring Car Championship. The car won its class in 11 of 12 races in 1978 and in 10 of 12 in 1979, and won the Championship in both the years. Subsequently it went into storage and did not race for the next 30 years (see lot 198 Coys 2.7.16 NS).

1969	**Mini MkII Countryman**		AAW81340144A	R	11-13.000 GBP	**10.848**	**13.482**	**12.598**	16-11-16	Donington Park	35	**H&H**

Red; two owners over the last 30 years.

1966	**Mini Countryman**		AA257L919742A	L	15-25.000 EUR	**12.200***	**15.204***	**14.304***	10-02-17	Paris	53	**Art**

Green with green interior; restored some years ago.

F85: 1930 Austin Seven sports

F86: 1952 Austin A90 Atlantic coupé

Year	Model	(Bodybuilder)	Chassis no.	Steering	Estimate	Hammer price £	$	€	Date	Place	Lot	Auc. H.

F87: 1956 Austin A135 Princess (A.Mulliner)

F88: 1969 Austin Mini Cooper S MkII

Year	Model	Chassis no.	Steering	Estimate	£	$	€	Date	Place	Lot	Auc. H.
1960	Mini	AA25748925	R	8-10.000 GBP	12.320	15.391	14.557	23-02-17	Donington Park	60	H&H
	Grey with light blue interior; 100 miles covered since the restoration.										
1969	Mini Cooper S MkII	CA2SB1254227A	L	30-40.000 EUR	29.094*	35.871*	32.200*	07-10-16	Zoute	11	Bon F88
	Beige with black roof; prepared for historic rallying.										
1966	Mini Cooper S	CA2S7892249	R	38-50.000 GBP	48.720	60.578	57.192	26-11-16	Weybridge	176	His
	Old English white with black roof and red interior; 50 miles covered since a full restoration.										
1967	Mini Cooper S	CA257551844	R	37-46.000 GBP	33.600	41.106	38.909	04-03-17	Brooklands	198	His
	Old English white with black roof; 925 miles covered since the restoration.										
1964	Mini Cooper S hatchback	KAS2S4488266	R	70-80.000 GBP	NS			26-07-17	Duxford	69	H&H
	Almond green; Morris version built, the car was delivered to the Austin's Experimental Department where it was converted to hatchback configuration and re-badged as Austin. One of three Cooper S converted to hatchback configuration and the sole known survivor. Restored in the early 1990s. 1,071cc engine.										
1969	Mini Cooper S	U5GF165121	L	30-40.000 USD	40.598*	52.250*	44.517*	18-08-17	Carmel	12	Bon
	Red with black roof; built for the Canadian market; restored at unspecified date to the aesthetical specification of the 1964 Montecarlo Rally winning car.										
1965	Mini Moke	AAB1684814	L	25-40.000 EUR	37.962*	56.027*	43.171*	02-07-17	Monaco	120	Art F89
	Green with black interior; fully restored in France.										
1970	3-Litre saloon	ABSAD3371M	R	NA	7.952*	9.888*	9.335*	26-11-16	Weybridge	242	His
	Blue; 32,000 miles covered. Manual gearbox and power steering.										

AUSTIN-HEALEY (GB) (1953-1970)

Year	Model	Chassis no.	Steering	Estimate	£	$	€	Date	Place	Lot	Auc. H.
1954	100	BN1155919	R	55-65.000 GBP	66.460	88.558	78.596	10-09-16	Goodwood	118	Bon
	Green; sold new to Australia, the car was later stored for 30 years and was restored between 2015 and 2016. Engine rebuilt to 100M Le Mans specification.										
1955	100	BNL224927	L	50-70.000 GBP	NS			10-09-16	Goodwood	155	Bon
	Light blue; restoration completed in early 2016. For circa 50 years in the same ownership.										
1956	100	BN2L230671	L	85-125.000 EUR	109.101	134.516	120.750	07-10-16	Zoute	30	Bon F90
	Healey blue; fully restored between 2015 and 2016.										
1955	100	BN1L224877	L	80-95.000 USD	NS			05-11-16	Hilton Head	155	AA
	Ice blue; concours-quality restoration (see lot 231 Auctions America 2.4.16 $88,000).										
1954	100	BN1L159292	L	55-65.000 EUR	61.810	77.207	69.600	06-11-16	Lyon	327	Ose
	Two-colour body; restored a few years ago.										
1954	100	478102	R	60-75.000 AUD	NS			27-11-16	Melbourne	42	Mos
	Two-tone blue with blue interior; restoration completed in 2014. Currently fitted with an Austin A90 engine, it is offered with also the original Austin A70 unit.										
1955	100	BNL224927	L	48-55.000 GBP	51.750	65.252	60.811	07-12-16	London	314	Bon
	See lot 155 Bonhams 10.9.16.										

F89: 1965 Austin Mini Moke

F90: 1956 Austin-Healey 100

CLASSIC CAR AUCTION 2016-2017 YEARBOOK

Year	Model	(Bodybuilder)	Chassis no.	Steering	Estimate	Hammer price £	Hammer price $	Hammer price €	Date	Place	Lot	Auc. H.
1954	**100**		BN1156396	R	49-54.000 GBP	44.070	55.568	51.787	07-12-16	Chateau Impney	38	H&H
Green with green leather interior; an older restoration, the car is described as in good overall condition (see lot 79 H & H 9.12.15 NS).												
1953	**100**		BN1L145425	L	25-30.000 EUR	19.462	23.699	22.230	14-01-17	Maastricht	234	Coy
Restoration project.												
1955	**100**		BN1L224877	L	80-100.000 USD	66.932*	82.500*	77.327*	19-01-17	Phoenix	135	RMS
See lot 155 Auctions America 5.11.16.												
1956	**100**		BN2L229678	L	90-120.000 USD	90.332*	110.000*	104.247*	09-03-17	Amelia Island	128	Bon
The car was fully restored in 2013 in the USA to the 100M model specification. Post restoration, it was admitted to the worldwide 100M Le Mans Registry, where it is recognized as being an authentic Le Mans conversion.												
1956	**100 coupé**		BN2L231178	L	80-100.000 USD	77.818*	94.600*	89.151*	11-03-17	Amelia Island	223	RMS / F91
Red with black interior; conversion to coupé form carried out in the USA in the 1960s. Restored in 2008. Until 2013 with its first owner (see lot 44 Gooding & Company 29.1.16 $66,000).												
1955	**100**		BN2L228635	L	75-100.000 EUR	68.357*	87.777*	78.400*	27-05-17	Villa Erba	125	RMS
Red with black interior; restored in the UK.												
1955	**100**		BN2228607	R	100-140.000 GBP	113.500	147.300	128.516	30-06-17	Goodwood	221	Bon
Light green and white with light green interior; between 2010 and 2016 restored to concours condition. One of the four cars displayed by the factory at the 1955 Earls Court Motor Show.												
1954	**100**		156390	R	75-85.000 AUD	50.584	65.142	55.437	20-08-17	Mallala Park	1	Mos
Green with tan interior; restored. Since 1982 in the collection of the late Clem Smith.												
1956	**100M Le Mans**		BN2L229129	L	185-200.000 USD		NS		17-09-16	Aspen	145	TFA
Light blue with light blue interior; restored at unspecified date.												
1956	**100M Le Mans**		BN2L233030	L	180-220.000 EUR	184.210	224.318	210.410	14-01-17	Maastricht	225	Coy
Black with red leather interior; recent full restoration.												
1956	**100M Le Mans**		BN2L232274	L	190-240.000 USD	165.690	203.500	190.822	18-01-17	Scottsdale	23	WoA
Green and old English white; concours-quality restoration completed in 2013.												
1956	**100M Le Mans**		BN2L232946	L	175-225.000 USD	133.865*	165.000*	154.655*	19-01-17	Phoenix	159	RMS
Bought in the early 1980s by the current owner and restored in the early 1990s. The engine has covered circa 500 miles since a recent rebuild.												
1956	**100M Le Mans**		BN2L230813	L	170-210.000 EUR	171.995	215.006	201.600	08-02-17	Paris	106	RMS
Black and red with red interior; sold new to the USA, the car was reimported in 2014 into the UK where in 2015 the restoration was completed.												
1955	**100M Le Mans**		BN2L228388	L	200-250.000 EUR		NS		09-02-17	Paris	336	Bon
Black with red interior; sold new to the USA, the car was imported into the Netherlands in 2009 and subsequently restored to concours condition.												
1956	**100M Le Mans**		BN2L229932	L	180-240.000 EUR	161.458	202.881	189.750	09-02-17	Paris	359	Bon
Old English white with red interior; sold new to the USA. Fully restored in 2005-06. In very good overall condition. With hardtop (see RM lots 481 16.8.08 $159,500 and 144 27.10.10 $79,748).												
1956	**100M Le Mans**		BN2L233071	L	90-120.000 EUR	71.896	89.544	84.000	08-04-17	Essen	160	Coy
Old English white and blue with blue interior; raced in period in the USA. Reimported into Europe in 1990. Restoration commissioned in 1993 and recently completed.												
1956	**100M Le Mans**		BN2L232878	L	160-190.000 EUR		NS		21-05-17	SPA-Francorch.	68	Bon
Ivory with dark red interior; restored in 1992; for 18 years in the current ownership. Some works carried out in 2016 (see lots 108 Christie's 22.5.97 $48,935 and 53 Coys 26.9.98 NS).												
1956	**100M**		BN2232135	R	220-250.000 AUD	143.041	183.705	164.064	28-05-17	Sydney	17	Mos
Green and old English white; sold new to Australia and raced for many years. Bought in 2000 by the current, third owner and subsequently fully restored.												
1955	**100S**		AHS3610	R	500-800.000 USD	437.291	539.000	505.205	19-01-17	Scottsdale	68	Bon / F92
Old English white and blue; sold new to the USA where it was raced until the late 1960s; fitted with a Chevrolet V8 engine in the late 1950s; bought in 1966 by the current owner; stored from the late 1960s to the early 2000s; full restoration completed in 2007. A 100 engine block was used as the basis of the 100S motor along with a new recast 100S cylinder head plus a newly made bellhousing and gearbox.												
1957	**100-Six**		BN62363	R	30-40.000 GBP	31.360	38.435	34.879	12-10-16	Duxford	128	H&H
Red with white hardtop and black vinyl interior; reimported into the UK from Australia in 2014, the car is described as in good overall condition.												
1958	**100-Six**		BN4L049658	L	38-48.000 EUR	32.393	39.446	37.000	14-01-17	Maastricht	220	Coy
Red and white with black interior; restored in the Netherlands in 2013.												
1957	**100-Six**		BN426099	R	33-38.000 GBP	34.500	42.642	39.713	19-03-17	Goodwood	79	Bon
Light blue with light blue interior; since 1982 in the current ownership. Restored between 1991 and 2004.												
1958	**100-Six**		BN4L050888	L	40-50.000 EUR	36.485	45.095	42.000	19-03-17	Fontainebleau	222	Ose
Red with black interior; in good overall condition.												

F91: 1956 Austin-Healey 100 coupé

F92: 1955 Austin-Healey 100S

Year	Model (Bodybuilder)	Chassis No.	Steering	Estimate	Hammer Price £	$	€	Date	Place	Lot	Auc. H.
1960	**Sprite "Frogeye"** Silver with black interior; concours-quality restoration.	AN5L22187	L	NQ	26.875*	33.000*	31.037*	21-01-17	Scottsdale	856.2	B/J
1960	**Sprite "Frogeye"** White and blue with blue interior; rebuilt 1,275cc engine; front disc brakes; with hardtop.	AN5L27879	R	NA	14.694	18.700	16.737	24-06-17	Santa Monica	272	RMS **F93**
1960	**Sprite "Frogeye"** Red with black interior; restored in 2002 and fitted with a 1,275cc engine and front disc brakes.	AN539800	R	10-11.000 GBP	9.500	12.278	10.797	15-07-17	Cambridge	691	Che
1960	**3000** Light blue and ivory; in good overall condition. For 27 years in the current ownership.	HBT75485	R	40-45.000 GBP	39.880	53.272	47.158	08-09-16	Fontwell Park	134	Coy
1960	**3000** Old English white with red leather interior; restored in the early 2000s. From the Mohrschladt Family Collection.	HBN7L7809	L	55-70.000 USD	58.008*	71.500*	67.017*	19-01-17	Phoenix	169	RMS
1960	**3000** Red and black with black interior; in good overall condition. Currently fitted with a Supra 5-speed gearbox (the original unit is included with the sale).	HBT7L8739	L	36-40.000 GBP	NS			04-03-17	Brooklands	160	His
1959	**3000** Blue and white with white interior; restored at unspecified date (see lot 33 Christie's 17.8.06 $58,750).	HBT7L1428	L	50-55.000 USD	40.635	52.250	48.039	13-05-17	Auburn	3098	AA
1960	**3000** Silver grey with red leather interior; restoration completed in 2009 (see lots S67 Mecum 16.8.12 $72,500 and 190 RM/Sotheby's 12.3.16 $66,000).	HBN7L1780	L	75-100.000 USD	47.919*	61.600*	54.916*	04-06-17	Greenwich	169	Bon
1960	**3000** Blue and ivory with black leather interior; imported into France from the USA two years ago and subsequently restored.	HBN7L4346	L	65-85.000 EUR	NS			10-06-17	Lyon	148	Agu
1960	**3000** Old English white with red interior; with its second owner since 1973 for nearly 40 years; full restoration completed in 2014.	HBN7L743	L	90-120.000 USD	36.752*	47.300*	40.300*	18-08-17	Carmel	15	Bon
1962	**3000 MkII** Light blue and ivory; the engine has covered 550 miles since the rebuild.	HBJ7L19724	R	60-65.000 GBP	61.325	81.918	72.517	08-09-16	Fontwell Park	156	Coy
1963	**3000 MkII** Ice blue and white with blue interior; the car has covered 7,000 miles since the restoration completed in 2001.	HBJ723501	R	45-55.000 GBP	47.040	57.652	52.318	12-10-16	Duxford	26	H&H
1963	**3000 MkIIA** Black with tan interior; sold new to the USA; reimported into the UK in 2003; restored and converted to right-hand drive between 2005 and 2008.	HBJ7L23554	R	40-50.000 GBP	41.245	52.006	48.467	07-12-16	Chateau Impney	30	H&H
1962	**3000 MkII** Red and black with red interior; sold new to the USA, reimported into the UK in the late 1980s, restored and converted to right-hand drive in the early 1990s.	HBJ7L19521	R	40-50.000 GBP	41.000	49.926	46.830	14-01-17	Birmingham	125	Coy
1961	**3000 MkII** Ice blue with blue interior; fully restored. With hardtop.	HBT7L15506	L	80-120.000 USD	NS			19-01-17	Scottsdale	79	Bon
1963	**3000 MkII** Old English white with red leather interior; restored (see lot 223 RM 11.10.13 NS).	HBJ7L23888	L	NQ	55.990*	68.750*	64.659*	21-01-17	Scottsdale	8038	R&S
1962	**3000 MkII** Ice blue with black interior; restored about 20 years ago.	HBT7L18266	L	50-70.000 EUR	NS			19-03-17	Fontainebleau	231	Ose
1961	**3000 MkII** Red with black interior; engine recently rebuilt.	HBT7L5996	L	34-40.000 GBP	35.280	45.906	41.066	20-05-17	Ascot	183	His
1965	**3000 MkIII** One owner; in good original condition; 56,000 miles covered.	HBJ8L31945	L	50-60.000 GBP	NS			10-09-16	Goodwood	183	Bon
1966	**3000 MkIII** Red and black with black interior; restored in 1996. Recently serviced.	HBJ8L34377	L	80-100.000 USD	54.261	71.500	63.685	17-09-16	Aspen	107	TFA
1966	**3000 MkIII** Red with red interior; restored in 1997. In the same family ownership from new.	HBJ8L31113	L	60-80.000 USD	51.742*	63.800*	57.267*	07-10-16	Hershey	212	RMS **F94**
1966	**3000 MkIII** Black with red interior; sold new to the USA, in 1987 the car was reimported into the UK and then restored and converted to right hand drive. Further restoration works carried out in 2011 (see lot 100 H & H 8.10.14 NS).	HBJ8L37076	R	40-50.000 GBP	40.320	49.416	44.844	12-10-16	Duxford	73	H&H
1967	**3000 MkIII** Black with red leather interior; the car has covered circa 3,000 miles since the restoration completed in 2007.	HBJ8L40026	L	80-90.000 USD	NS			05-11-16	Hilton Head	139	AA
1965	**3000 MkIII** Red and ivory with black vinyl interior; 3,000 miles covered since the restoration.	HBJ832613	R	39-45.000 GBP	43.800	55.692	52.034	05-12-16	London	122	Coy

F93: 1960 Austin-Healey Sprite "Frogeye"

F94: 1966 Austin-Healey 3000 MkIII

Year	Model	(Bodybuilder)	Chassis no.	Steering	Estimate	Hammer price £	$	€	Date	Place	Lot	Auc. H.
1966	**3000 MkIII**		HBJ8L36173	R	54-58.000 GBP	52.640	66.374	61.857	07-12-16	Chateau Impney	54	H&H
	*British racing green with black interior; sold new to the USA, the car was reimported into the UK in 2004 and later restored and converted to right-hand drive.*
1964	**3000 MkIII**		HBJ827537	R	340-450.000 EUR		NS		08-02-17	Paris	141	RMS

Red with white hardtop and black interior; one of three Works cars prepared for the 1964 season, it won the Spa-Sofia-Liége driven by Rauno Aaltonen e Tony Ambrose. Sold to private hands at the end of the season, in 1975 it was bought by Arthur Carter and restored. In 2005 it was acquired by the current owner Peter Livanos and restored again between 2009 and 2014.

Year	Model	Chassis no.	Steering	Estimate	£	$	€	Date	Place	Lot	Auc. H.
1966	**3000 MkIII**	HBJ8L34035	L	NQ	70.655*	88.000*	82.544*	08-04-17	Palm Beach	656	B/J

Beige with tan interior; restored 10 years ago.

| 1964 | **3000 MkIII** | HBJ826449 | R | 22-30.000 GBP | 42.560 | 55.379 | 49.540 | 20-05-17 | Ascot | 209 | His |

Blue with blue interior; one owner. It requires some restoration works.

| 1967 | **3000 MkIII** | HBJ8L40966 | L | 75-95.000 USD | 39.290 | 50.000 | 44.750 | 24-06-17 | Santa Monica | 236 | RMS |

Restored in 1996.

| 1967 | **3000 MkIII** | HBJ840191 | R | 50-60.000 GBP | 56.750 | 74.018 | 63.566 | 26-07-17 | Duxford | 50 | H&H |

British racing green with black interior; body repainted in 2013.

| 1964 | **3000 MkIII** | HBJ8L27207 | L | 75-100.000 USD | 59.829* | 77.000* | 65.604* | 18-08-17 | Carmel | 48 | Bon |

Sage green with biscuit interior; restored (see lot 70 RM 17.1.14 $71,500).

| 1964 | **3000 MkIII** | HBJ8L26879 | L | 60-80.000 USD | 53.419* | 68.750* | 58.575* | 18-08-17 | Monterey | 169 | RMS |

Black with red interior; sold new to the USA; restored in 2004 (see lot 150 Gooding & Company 18.1.14 $61,600).

| 1969 | **Sprite MkIV** | HAN9U84386G | L | 25-40.000 USD | 16.260* | 19.800* | 18.764* | 09-03-17 | Amelia Island | 103 | Bon F95 |

British racing green with black interior; delivered new to the Austin-Healey dealer in Kansas City, Missouri, the car remained in his ownership until 2009 when it was sold to its first owner with 148 registered miles. In original condition; less than 4,500 kms miles.

AUTOBIANCHI (I) *(1955-1996)*

Year	Model	Chassis no.	Steering	Estimate	£	$	€	Date	Place	Lot	Auc. H.
1966	**Bianchina Panoramica**	083239	L	15-30.000 EUR	13.508*	16.654*	14.950*	07-10-16	Zoute	9	Bon

Light blue and blue with beige interior; restored in Italy in 2007. Sunroof.

| 1958 | **Bianchina Trasformabile** | 110B001835 | L | 16-20.000 GBP | 19.880 | 24.365 | 22.111 | 12-10-16 | Duxford | 135 | H&H |

Red and black; until 2016 in the same family ownership. Restored in 1996; imported into the UK in 2016 and recommissioned.

| 1967 | **Bianchina Panoramica** | 120B142281 | L | NA | 16.181* | 19.800* | 17.996* | 15-10-16 | Las Vegas | 347 | B/J |

Blue with tan interior; body repainted (see lot 1135 Auctions America 25.6.16 NS).

| 1967 | **Bianchina Cabriolet "Eden Roc"** | 110FB5008235 | L | 12-18.000 EUR | | WD | | 30-10-16 | Paris | 116 | Art |

Green and ivory; restored in 1998.

| 1965 | **Bianchina Berlina "Lutèce"** | 110DBA074330 | L | 8-14.000 EUR | 5.894* | 7.160* | 6.556* | 30-10-16 | Paris | 117 | Art |

Green.

| 1968 | **Bianchina Giadiniera** | 120236145 | L | 7-10.000 EUR | 16.219* | 20.167* | 19.040* | 25-11-16 | Milan | 646 | RMS |

Light blue with red interior; 69,258 kms. From the Duemila Ruote collection.

| 1959 | **Bianchina Trasformabile** | 110B015542 | L | 50-70.000 USD | 37.625* | 46.200* | 43.451* | 21-01-17 | Scottsdale | 101 | G&Co |

Red and white; restored between 2009 and 2012 and fitted with a Fiat 650cc engine upgraded with Abarth components.

| 1967 | **Bianchina Berlina "Lutèce"** | 110F8098382 | L | 10-15.000 EUR | 9.658* | 12.036* | 11.324* | 10-02-17 | Paris | 4 | Art F96 |

Cream; used until 1989 and then stored until 2014 when the body was repainted, the interior retrimmed and the engine replaced with a 650cc unit.

| 1958 | **Bianchina Trasformabile** | 007373 | L | 20-25.000 GBP | | NS | | 15-07-17 | Blenheim Pal. | 127 | Coy |

Two-tone light blue with cream interior; in good overall condition.

| 1959 | **Bianchina Trasformabile** | 012492 | L | 30-50.000 USD | 38.462* | 49.500* | 42.174* | 18-08-17 | Carmel | 2 | Bon F97 |

Red with white roof and red leather interior; recent cosmetic restoration. Just over 13,000 miles on the odometer.

| 1959 | **Bianchina Trasformabile** | 110B016926 | L | 75-85.000 USD | 64.103* | 82.500* | 70.290* | 19-08-17 | Pebble Beach | 121 | G&Co |

Light green with white roof; sold new to the USA; for over 50 years until 2016 in the same family ownership; just over 18,500 miles covered; in very good overall condition.

| 1965 | **Bianchina Cabriolet** | 006048 | L | 50-60.000 USD | 13.986 | 18.000 | 15.336 | 19-08-17 | Monterey | T85 | Mec |

Metallic blue with blue and white interior; 40 miles covered since the engine rebuild.

| 1984 | **A112 Abarth** | 01571907 | L | 5-10.000 EUR | 16.075* | 19.529* | 17.880* | 30-10-16 | Paris | 115 | Art |

Metallic grey; just one owner.

F95: 1969 Austin-Healey Sprite MkIV

F96: 1967 Autobianchi Bianchina Berlina "Lutèce"

Year	Model	(Bodybuilder)	Chassis no.	Steering	Estimate	Hammer price £	$	€	Date	Place	Lot	Auc. H.
1983	**A112 Abarth**		1426150	L	9-14.000 EUR	9.088	11.564	10.350	24-06-17	Wien	339	**Dor**

Red; in original condition; 70bhp engine.

AUTOCAR (USA) (1901-1911)

| 1906 | Type X runabout | | 7534 | R | 20-30.000 GBP | 13.800 | 17.057 | 15.885 | 19-03-17 | Goodwood | 24 | **Bon** |

Blue with black interior; restored in the 1960s, presumably in the USA; imported into the UK in the late 1970s; in the same family ownership since. It requires recommissioning prior to use.

AUTOKRAFT (GB) (1980-1996)

| 1989 | **AC Cobra MkIV** | | AK1280 | R | 120-150.000 GBP | 113.373 | 141.716 | 133.621 | 12-04-17 | London | 313 | **Coy** |

Red with black interior; 7,500 miles covered.

| 1989 | **AC Cobra MkIV** | | AK1280 | R | 100-120.000 GBP | 161.167 | 210.113 | 188.791 | 18-05-17 | London | 143 | **Coy** |

See lot 313 Coys 12.4.17.

BANDINI (I) (1946-1992)

| 1953 | **750 Sport** | | NQ | L | NQ | 90.480 | 111.100 | 104.490 | 21-01-17 | Scottsdale | 8667 | **R&S** |

Red; it is believed the car was sold new to the USA and raced. In 1992 it was bought by the late Raymond Milo and subsequently shipped to Italy for restoration. Crosley 750 engine (probably chassis no. 156 - see lot 29 Bonhams 19.8.16 $ 112,200).

BENEDETTI (I)

| 1950 | **750 Sport** | | 011250 | R | 250-300.000 EUR | | NS | | 09-02-17 | Paris | 345 | **Bon** |

Built by Elio Benedetti on a modified Fiat 500A Topolino chassis, the car was fitted with a Pasquale Ermini-built Fiat 1100 engine reduced to 750cc and a sport body built by Carrozzeria Lotti, Florence. It raced the 1952 Mille Miglia driven by Chiti/Cioni. Later it was fitted with the present Giannini G1 engine. Bought in the early 1990s by the current owner and subsequently restored by Carrozzeria Campana, Modena. Registered in Belgium; with FIVA/ASI papers.

BENETTON (I) (1985-2001)

| 1991 | **B191** | | B19102 | M | 750-950.000 EUR | | NS | | 21-05-17 | SPA-Francorch. | 73 | **Bon** |

Yellow and blue Camel livery; winner of the 1991 Canadian GP driven by Nelson Piquet; driven by Michael Schumacher in the last two GPs of the season in Japan and Australia; subsequently on display as a museum exhibit before to be fully restored and returned to running order.

BENTLEY (GB) (1919-)

| 1926 | **3l tourer** (Vanden Plas) | | SR1421 | R | 420-450.000 EUR | | NA | | 08-10-16 | Paris | 129 | **CB/C** |

Green with polished aluminium bonnet and green interior; mechanicals restored in 2014.

| 1924 | **3l/4.5l tourer** | | 735 | R | 250-300.000 GBP | 291.200 | 356.895 | 323.873 | 12-10-16 | Duxford | 87 | **H&H** |

Dark green with brown leather interior; discovered in 1998 in pieces and with the chassis shortened, the car was later sold to Australia where it was restored and fitted with the present, new Vanden Plas style body. The engine was rebuilt to 4.5-litre specification. Reimported into the UK in 2015 (see lot 201 Coys 2.7.16 $378,338).

| 1926 | **3l tourer** | | SR1421 | R | 360-390.000 GBP | 373.525 | 474.937 | 443.748 | 05-12-16 | London | 121 | **Coy** |

See lot 129 Coutau Bégarie/Coys 8.10.16.

| 1924 | **3l Speed Model tourer** | | 485 | R | 270-320.000 GBP | 281.500 | 347.934 | 324.035 | 19-03-17 | Goodwood | 28 | **Bon** |

Built with James Young body; fully restored in the late 1980s and fitted with the present, new Vanden Plas Le Mans tourer replica body. Engine rebuilt. Since 1990 in the current ownership.

| 1925 | **3l Speed Model tourer** (Vanden Plas) | | 893 | R | 230-270.000 GBP | 247.500 | 307.915 | 286.506 | 29-03-17 | Duxford | 41 | **H&H** |

Black with red wings; since 1958 in the same family ownership. Unused for some years, the car requires recommissioning prior to use.

| 1925 | **3l tourer** | | 777 | R | 275-325.000 USD | 211.783 | 272.250 | 242.711 | 04-06-17 | Greenwich | 158 | **Bon** |

Dark green; imported into the USA in the early 1960s; bought by the current owner in 2004, restored and fitted with the present, new, Jarvis style tourer body.

| 1929 | **6½l sedanca de ville** (H.J.Mulliner) | | KR2687 | R | 395-495.000 GBP | 358.400 | 479.611 | 426.819 | 07-09-16 | London | 163 | **RMS F98** |

Green and black; recently restored. The car was exhibited at the 1929 Olympia Motor Show. From the estate of Edward Carter (see lot 114 RM 25.5.13 NS).

| 1928 | **6½l two-seater sports** | | MD2461 | R | 320-380.000 GBP | 406.940 | 542.248 | 481.247 | 10-09-16 | Goodwood | 147 | **Bon** |

Built with Hooper saloon body, the car was rebuilt in 1992 and fitted with the present new body. Engine rebuilt on a 8-Litre cylinder block.

| 1930 | **6½l Speed Six sportsman's saloon** (Corsica) | | HM2861 | R | 3.500-5.500.000 USD | 2.649.570 | 3.410.000 | 2.905.320 | 18-08-17 | Monterey | 133 | **RMS F99** |

Black with dark red leather interior; sold new in the UK; imported into the USA in 1976; several restoration works carried out in the late 1990s.

F97: 1959 Autobianchi Bianchina Trasformabile

F98: 1929 Bentley 6½l sedanca de ville (H.J.Mulliner)

Year	Model	(Bodybuilder)	Chassis no.	Steering	Estimate	Hammer price £	Hammer price $	Hammer price €	Date	Place	Lot	Auc. H.
1926	6½l tourer		WK2662	R	650-800.000 USD	538.461	693.000	590.436	19-08-17	Pebble Beach	118	G&Co
	British racing green; built with Harrison landaulette body; fitted after WWII with the present Vanden Plas style tourer body; imported into the USA in 2000 and driven at historic events.											
1930	4½l tourer		PB3528	R	200-250.000 GBP	315.100	411.458	368.509	19-09-16	London	612	Bon
	Built with Weymann type saloon coachwork by Gurney Nutting; fitted in the late 1940s with a 4-seater tourer body; restored in the 1950s and fitted with a 3-litre engine; in the late 1980s fitted with a 4.5-litre engine; later seen in rolling chassis form with body and engine removed; currently fitted with 4.5-litre engine no.SL3057 and 4-seater Le Mans style tourer body. From the collection of the late Robert White.											
1928	4½l tourer	(Vanden Plas)	FT3221	R	1.100-1.200.000 USD	895.840	1.100.000	1.034.550	21-01-17	Scottsdale	121	G&Co F100
	British racing green with dark brown leather interior; the car was imported into the USA in 1971 and remained until 1998 with the same owner who raced it at some historic events. Restored in the 1990s; engine rebuilt in the 2000s (see lot 754 Bonhams/Brooks 6.7.01 NS).											
1927	4½l tourer	(Vanden Plas)	ST3015	R	750-900.000 USD	NS			09-03-17	Amelia Island	121	Bon
	Green with black leather interior; original body, engine replaced in the 1950s. From 1960 to 1997 in the same ownership; in 2016 imported into the USA by the current owner. Recent full service.											
1928	4½l Le Mans tourer	(Vanden Plas)	KM3088	R	6.500-7.500.000 USD	NS			11-03-17	Amelia Island	266	RMS
	Dark green with dark green interior; Works car, it raced the Le Mans 24 Hours in 1928 and 1929 when it placed third overall. In 1930 it was sold to Lauchlan Rose who resold it in 1933, reacquired it in the late 1940s and retained it for 25 years. In the 2000s the car was restored again and in 2012 it was bought by the current owner (see lots 86 Christie's 23.7.04 $2,021,573 and 20 Gooding & Company 18.8.12 $6,050,000).											
1931	8l sedanca de ville	(H.J.Mulliner)	YM5034	R	750-900.000 GBP	779.900	1.012.154	883.081	30-06-17	Goodwood	237	Bon F101
	Black with light brown leather interior; first owner Lord Brougham & Vaux; imported in 1986 in the USA where it was refurbished mechanically and cosmetically; reimported into the UK in the early 1990s; engine rebuilt in 2006; body repainted in more recent years (see lots 183 Christie's 7.12.04 NS and 651 Bonhams 1.12.08 $513,134).											
1934	3½l cabriolet	(Park Ward)	B39BN	R	90-120.000 GBP	72.500	96.302	86.043	03-09-16	Beaulieu	467	Bon
	Maroon with black wings and maroon interior; since 1972 in the same family ownership. Interior retrimmed in the late 1970s; major service in 2007.											
1934	3½l tourer		B155AE	R	100-120.000 GBP	NS			08-10-16	Ascot	322	Coy
	Dark red with black wings; built with Park Ward coupé body, the car was fitted some time ago with the present Vanden Plas style tourer body. Several mechanical works carried out in the 2000s (see lot 727 Coys 2.10.03 NS).											
1935	3½l cabriolet		B192DG	R	40-60.000 EUR	62.157*	75.510*	69.136*	30-10-16	Paris	103	Art
	In running order.											
1934	3½l tourer	(Vanden Plas)	B155AE	R	100-120.000 GBP	112.615	143.190	133.787	05-12-16	London	135	Coy
	See lot 322 Coys 8.10.16.											
1934	3½l saloon	(Park Ward)	B24CR	R	80-100.000 USD	62.470	77.000	72.172	19-01-17	Scottsdale	82	Bon F102
	Black and dark red with black leather interior; restored in the 1990s. Paintwork and interior redone in recent years. Described as in very good driving order.											
1936	3½l sedanca coupé	(Windovers)	B111FC	R	325-400.000 USD	NS			19-01-17	Phoenix	153	RMS
	One-off finished in black with dark red leather interior; restored in the early 1990s, it is described as still in good overall condition (see lot 142 RM 8.3.14 $ 374,000).											
1934	3½l tourer		B90CR	R	140-180.000 USD	53.750*	66.000*	62.073*	20-01-17	Phoenix	248	RMS
	British racing green; built with Plaxton saloon body, the car was fitted at unspecified date with the present 1920s style body. Recently serviced (see lot 505 Bonhams 18.8.06 $54,990).											
1935	3½l cabriolet	(Park Ward)	B66DG	R	250-325.000 USD	152.293*	187.000*	175.874*	21-01-17	Scottsdale	124	G&Co
	Two-tone red with brown leather interior; imported into the USA in the 1970s. Concours-quality restoration completed in 2007 (see lot 4 P.R.Group 27.11.99 $67,100).											
1936	3½l sedanca coupé	(Windovers)	B111FC	R	275-325.000 USD	157.749	200.750	179.671	24-06-17	Santa Monica	212	RMS
	See lot 153 RM/Sotheby's 19.1.17.											
1934	3½l tourer		B74BL	R	100-140.000 GBP	131.600	169.711	148.708	08-07-17	Brooklands	146	His
	Dark red with light green leather interior; originally built with Barker saloon body, in the 1990s the car was fitted with the present, new body.											
1936	4¼l saloon	(Vanvooren)	B244GA	R	60-80.000 GBP	NS			03-09-16	Beaulieu	445	Bon
	Black; restored over the course of the last 20 years.											
1937	4¼l saloon	(Thrupp/Maberly)	B214GA	R	55-65.000 GBP	59.740	79.353	70.899	03-09-16	Beaulieu	471	Bon
	Blue; body repainted in the 2000s. Recently recommissioned.											
1936	4¼l saloon	(Park Ward)	B130GA	R	72-85.000 GBP	92.960	115.586	109.126	26-11-16	Weybridge	216	His
	Black and maroon with dark red leather interior; mechanicals overhauled and body restored between 1983 and 1985. Stored from 1986 to 2010; in 2015 engine rebuilt and body repainted again.											
1937	4¼l coupé	(Park Ward)	B91JY	R	350-450.000 USD	232.861	286.000	268.182	18-01-17	Scottsdale	27	WoA
	One-off sold new in the UK and more recently imported into the USA. Some mechanical works carried out in 2010 (see lot 81 Christie's 19.8.01 NS).											
1937	4¼l saloon	(Gurney Nutting)	B119KU	R	150-180.000 USD	NS			19-01-17	Scottsdale	56	Bon
	Silver with red leather interior; in good overall condition. Exhibited at the Gurney Nutting stand at the 1937 London Motor Show.											
1936	4¼l cabriolet	(Antem)	B260GA	R	500-700.000 USD	286.669	352.000	331.056	20-01-17	Scottsdale	28	G&Co
	One-off ordered by André Embiricos who imported it in the USA in 1940 and retained it until 1945. From the early 1962 to 2002 the car was owned by R. Byron White who had it restored. Recently restored again to concours condition.											
1939	4¼l coupé	(Park Ward)	B131MX	R	175-225.000 USD	141.821	172.700	163.668	09-03-17	Amelia Island	115	Bon F103
	Red and cream with beige leather interior; sold new to the USA. Fully restored between 2004 and 2009 (see lot 654 Bonhams 1.5.04 $59,800).											
1936	4¼l Airflow saloon	(Gurney Nutting)	B118HK	R	150-200.000 USD	135.729*	165.000*	155.496*	10-03-17	Amelia Island	126	RMS
	Red with beige leather interior; one of two examples built; exhibited at the 1936 London Motor Show and sold new in the UK; imported into the USA in 1967; restored many years ago. From the Orin Smith collection.											F104
1938	4¼l saloon	(H.J.Mulliner)	B28MR	R	90-110.000 GBP	86.697	112.047	98.531	15-07-17	Blenheim Pal.	147	Coy
	Two-tone grey with grey leather interior; restored. Full perspex roof over the front seats. Exhibited at the 1938 Earls Court Motor Show (see lot 349 Bonhams 12.7.13 $113,884).											
1938	4¼l sedanca coupé	(J.Young)	B72MR	R	180-220.000 GBP	NS			26-07-17	Duxford	74	H&H
	Black with beige interior; engine overhauled in 1984; some mechanical works carried out in 1997; recently reimported into the UK and serviced.											
1949	Mk VI standard saloon		B281DZ	R	25-30.000 GBP	22.833	30.329	27.098	03-09-16	Beaulieu	465	Bon
	Black and yellow; restored between 1973 and 1975, body repainted in 1987, engine rebuilt in the 2000s. Since 1969 in the same family ownership.											
1951	Mk VI standard saloon		B310LNZ	L	NQ	62.709*	77.000*	72.419*	21-01-17	Scottsdale	972	B/J
	Blue and grey with red interior; restored in the 1980s, the car is described as in very good overall condition. Sliding sunroof.											

F99: 1930 Bentley 6½l Speed Six sportsman's saloon (Corsica)

F100: 1928 Bentley 4½l tourer (Vanden Plas)

F101: 1931 Bentley 8l sedanca de ville (H.J.Mulliner)

F102: 1934 Bentley 3½l saloon (Park Ward)

F103: 1939 Bentley 4¼l coupé (Park Ward)

F104: 1936 Bentley 4¼l Airflow saloon (Gurney Nutting)

F105: 1947 Bentley Mk VI cabriolet (Franay)

F106: 1954 Bentley R Type coupé (Abbott)

Year	Model	(Bodybuilder)	Chassis no.	Steering	Estimate	Hammer price £	$	€	Date	Place	Lot	Auc. H.
1950	Mk VI standard saloon		B161GT	R	12-14.000 GBP	17.437	22.743	19.531	26-07-17	Duxford	75	H&H
	Two-tone metallic green with brown leather interior; for 59 years with its first owner; restored at unspecified date.											
1949	Mk VI saloon		B490EY	R	NQ	13.886*	17.050*	16.036*	21-01-17	Scottsdale	8207	R&S
	Two-tone body; in good driving order. From the Missoula Auto Museum Collection.											
1947	Mk VI cabriolet	(Park Ward)	B132BH	R	90-110.000 GBP	91.840	112.559	102.144	12-10-16	Duxford	118	H&H
	Grey with blue leather interior; reimported into the UK from the USA in 1994 and later restored.											
1951	Mk VI sedanca cabriolet	(Abbott)	B118JO	R	70-90.000 GBP	136.200	173.178	161.806	05-12-16	London	130	Coy
	Royal blue with red leather interior; several restoration works carried out recently.											
1949	Mk VI cabriolet	(Pinin Farina)	B435CD	R	500-800.000 EUR		NS		10-02-17	Paris	131	Art
	Silver with blue leather interior; one-off exhibited at the 1949 Geneva Motors Show; imported into the USA at unspecified date and subjected to a long restoration completed in 1992; reimported into Europe; in very good overall condition (see lot 59 Gooding & Company 16.8.08 NS).											
1947	Mk VI cabriolet	(Franay)	B26BH	R	350-450.000 USD	325.750*	396.000*	373.190*	10-03-17	Amelia Island	106	RMS F105
	Two-tone brown with calfskin and ostrich leather interior; concours-quality restoration carried out in the 2000s. From the Orin Smith collection (see lot 1163 Sotheby's 6.12.93 $63,025).											
1952	Mk VI cabriolet	(Park Ward)	B72LNZ	L	200-275.000 USD	162.875*	198.000*	186.595*	10-03-17	Amelia Island	129	RMS
	Two-tone silver and black body; in single ownership from 1956 to 2014; restored in the 1970s. From the Orin Smith collection.											
1947	Mk VI cabriolet	(Vanden Plas)	B245AJ	R	100-120.000 GBP	105.187	130.863	121.764	29-03-17	Duxford	93	H&H
	Garnet and silver with red leather interior; stored for many years, the car was acquired in 2010 by the current owner. Body repainted; largely original interior; in good mechanical order.											
1950	Mk VI cabriolet	(Park Ward)	B425FU	R	65-75.000 GBP		NS		15-07-17	Blenheim Pal.	173	Coy
	Two-tone grey with grey leather interior (see lot 23 Historics 25.9.10 NS).											
1953	Mk VI (cabriolet/conversion)		B184MD	R	250-350.000 USD	208.118*	253.000*	238.427*	10-03-17	Amelia Island	136	RMS
	Dark green and black with tan leather interior; rolling-chassis sold to Switzerland where it was bodied by Graber to coupé form. Later the car was imported into the USA and at unspecified date the body was converted to cabriolet body. Recently restored. From the Orin Smith collection.											
1954	R Type standard saloon		B137YA	R	28-34.000 GBP	19.500	25.984	23.061	10-09-16	Goodwood	141	Bon
	Two-tone grey with red leather interior; since 1972 in the current ownership, restored in 1996. Automatic transmission.											
1953	R Type standard saloon		B427SP	L	NQ	13.357*	17.600*	15.676*	17-09-16	Aspen	160	TFA
	Grey with grey interior; in good driving order.											
1954	R Type coupé	(Abbott)	B401SP	R	15-20.000 EUR	40.070*	49.825*	47.040*	25-11-16	Milan	916	RMS F106
	For restoration. From the Duemila Ruote collection (see lot 124 Christie's 9.9.95 $30,224).											
1952	R Type Continental fastback	(H.J.Mulliner)	BC14LA	L	1.250-1.500.000 USD	1.108.454*	1.347.500*	1.269.884*	10-03-17	Amelia Island	152	RMS F107
	Dark blue with grey leather interior; sold new to the USA to William A.M. Burden Jr.; fitted at the factory in 1961 with the more powerful 4,887cc engine; in the 1990s part of the William E. "Chip" Connor collection; bought in 1999 by Erwin "Bud" Lyon who later had it fully restored by Paul Russell & Company and the engine fitted with the S1 Continental cylinder head. From the Orin Smith collection.											
1953	R Type Continental fastback	(H.J.Mulliner)	BC20A	R	1.000-1.300.000 EUR		NS		27-05-17	Villa Erba	139	RMS
	Recent mechanical works; manual gearbox. Car exhibited at the 1953 Geneva Motor Show (see lot 117 RM 15.8.14 $1,210,000).											
1956	S1 saloon	(Freestone/Webb)	B3AP	R	20-25.000 GBP	23.000	30.551	27.296	03-09-16	Beaulieu	440	Bon
	Black and blue; restored in 2011.											
1956	S1 saloon		B110EG	R	20-30.000 GBP	16.100	21.386	19.107	03-09-16	Beaulieu	475	Bon
	Black and grey; first registered to Rolls-Royce Ltd. The car incorporates numerous Radford modifications, among them a Webasto sunroof, Countryman seats, door cabinets for coffee percolator and picnic tables.											
1955	S1 saloon	(Freestone/Webb)	B202LAN	L	NQ	179.168	220.000	206.910	21-01-17	Scottsdale	1388.2	B/J
	Black with red interior; restored in the early 1990s and freshened in 2008. Hollywood producer Jack Warner was the first of just three owners.											
1956	S1 saloon		B273AP	R	15-20.000 EUR	18.909	24.121	21.600	18-06-17	Fontainebleau	68	Ose
	Black and grey; in good condition.											
1957	Continental S1 saloon	(J.Young)	BC26CH	R	130-170.000 EUR		NA		08-10-16	Paris	151	CB/C
	Pewter with tan leather interior; restored in the late 1980s.											
1957	Continental S1 saloon	(J.Young)	BC26CH	R	100-130.000 GBP	100.000	121.480	111.220	29-10-16	London	153	Coy
	See lot 151 Coutau Bégarie/Coys 8.10.16.											
1957	Continental S1 fastback	(H.J.Mulliner)	BC96LBG	L	850-1.000.000 USD	642.451*	781.000*	736.014*	10-03-17	Amelia Island	115	RMS
	Saffron with sandstone leather interior; restored in the late 1970s, interior redone in 2006. From the Orin Smith collection.											

F107: 1952 Bentley R Type Continental fastback (H.J.Mulliner)

F108: 1956 Bentley Continental S1 cabriolet (Park Ward)

Year	Model (Bodybuilder)	Chassis No.	Steering	Estimate	Hammer £	Hammer $	Hammer €	Date	Place	Lot	Auc. H.
1956	Continental S1 fastback (H.J.Mulliner)	BC94AF	R	360-400.000 GBP	NS			06-06-17	Woodcote Park	42	H&H
	Dark blue with champagne leather interior; since 1984 in the current ownership; engine overhauled in 1987; in good driving order (see lot 86 H & H 20.4.16 NS).										
1957	Continental S1 cabriolet (Park Ward)	BC30LCH	L	1.000-1.500.000 EUR	910.038	1.143.509	1.069.500	09-02-17	Paris	360	Bon
	Originally finished in sand and sable with beige leather interior, the car was acquired new by George Embiricos. In 2001 it was bought by the current, third owner and subsequently refurbished. Described as in very good overall condition.										
1956	Continental S1 cabriolet (Park Ward)	BC22LBG	L	700-900.000 USD	1.384.436*	1.683.000*	1.586.059*	10-03-17	Amelia Island	123	RMS F108
	Gunmetal grey and black with grey leather interior; sold new to the USA and retained by its first owner until 1993; restored in the 1990s; just two registered owners. From the Orin Smith collection.										
1956	Continental S1 coupé (Park Ward)	BC48LBG	L	280-340.000 EUR	247.092	328.235	293.250	03-09-16	Chantilly	19	Bon
	Shell grey with green roof and green leather interior; fully restored in 1992, the car received further works in 2011 and 2012 (see lot 347 Bonhams 05.02.11 $297,837).										
1956	Continental S1 coupé (Park Ward)	BC37AF	R	280-340.000 GBP	281.500	375.099	332.902	10-09-16	Goodwood	154	Bon
	Metallic blue with red leather interior; recent extensive refurbishment (see lot 139 Silverstone Auctions 4.9.14 NS).										
1956	Continental S1 coupé (Park Ward)	BC24AF	R	240-275.000 GBP	NS			12-11-16	Birmingham	340	SiC
	Metallic pewter green with dark green leather interior; fitted from new with automatic transmission and power steering. Engine and gearbox replaced in 1964 at 71,000 miles. Exported in 1968 to the USA. Reimported into the UK in 1988 and subsequently fully restored.										
1959	Continental S1 coupé (Park Ward)	BC24GN	R	260-330.000 GBP	NS			07-12-16	London	376	Bon
	Bought in 1999 by the current owner who subsequently had the body repainted in its original blue livery in Belgium and the engine rebuilt in Holland. Described as in very good condition.										
1957	Continental S1 coupé (Park Ward)	BC3LCH	L	350-450.000 USD	244.312	297.000	279.893	10-03-17	Amelia Island	13	G&Co
	Dark green with light brown interior; in the same family ownership since new. In the 1990s body repainted and interior restored; mechanical service in 2011.										
1958	Continental S1 coupé (Park Ward)	BC48LCH	L	450-550.000 USD	461.479*	561.000*	528.686*	10-03-17	Amelia Island	141	RMS F109
	Bronze and chocolate with tan leather interior; restored at unspecified date, the car is described as in very good overall condition. From the Orin Smith collection.										
1959	Continental S1 coupé (Park Ward)	BC23GN	R	120-160.000 GBP	NS			30-06-17	Goodwood	225	Bon
	Light blue with light blue leather interior; for 37 years in the current ownership. Stored for the last 15 years and recently recommissioned. Body and interior requiring some attention.										
1956	Continental S1 coupé (Park Ward)	BC8BG	R	250-300.000 USD	179.487	231.000	196.812	19-08-17	Pebble Beach	114	G&Co
	Black; since 1985 in the current ownership; in very good overall condition.										
1958	Continental S1 Flying Spur (H.J.Mulliner)	BC8EL	R	100-130.000 GBP	109.020	137.616	129.309	04-12-16	London	27	Bon
	Burgundy with tan leather interior; circa 48,000 miles covered. Gently recommissioned in recent months; paintwork in need of refreshment.										
1958	Continental S1 Flying Spur (H.J.Mulliner)	BC32LCH	L	NQ	NS			21-01-17	Scottsdale	1388.1	B/J
	Burgundy with tan interior; concours-quality restoration.										
1959	Continental S1 Flying Spur (H.J.Mulliner)	BC14LEL	L	175-225.000 USD	136.401	166.100	157.413	09-03-17	Amelia Island	142	Bon F110
	Silver with brown interior; several restoration works carried out between 2013 and 2015 (see lots Coys 133 9.5.14 NS and 137 9.8.14 NS, and Bonhams 386 5.2.15 NS).										
1962	S2 saloon	B298DW	R	25-30.000 GBP	18.833	25.016	22.351	03-09-16	Beaulieu	469	Bon
	Blue; single family ownership from new. In good original condition; major service in 2009.										
1960	S2 saloon	B30BS	R	13-15.000 GBP	14.000	17.158	15.571	12-10-16	Duxford	4	H&H
	Green with green interior; in the same family ownership from new. Recently recommissioned.										
1962	S2 saloon	B477LDY	L	35-40.000 EUR	57.242*	71.178*	67.200*	25-11-16	Milan	634	RMS
	Black and grey with black interior; 46,034 kms. From the Duemila Ruote collection.										
1960	S2 saloon	B257CT	R	22-28.000 GBP	24.150	30.451	28.379	07-12-16	London	324	Bon
	Grey with red leather interior; several works carried out in recent times (see lot 402 Historics 7.6.14 $41,457).										
1960	S2 saloon	B83BR	R	25-30.000 GBP	29.250	37.607	34.579	13-05-17	Silverstone	353	SiC
	Black; stored since 1991, for restoration.										
1960	S2 saloon	B271CT	R	40-50.000 EUR	NS			18-06-17	Fontainebleau	72	Ose
	Blue and grey with beige leather interior; restored some years ago.										
1962	S2 saloon	B158DW	R	25-30.000 GBP	28.000	36.109	31.640	08-07-17	Brooklands	212	His
	Two-tone green; body restored a few years ago; in very good driving order.										
1961	S2 saloon	B368BS	R	24-28.000 GBP	24.750	32.410	27.633	29-07-17	Silverstone	751	SiC
	Two-tone green with green leather interior; some mechanical works carried out in 2015; body repainted in 2016.										
1962	Continental S2 saloon (J.Young)	BC105AR	R	120-150.000 GBP	NS			19-03-17	Goodwood	58	Bon
	Blue with red leather interior; repainted and retrimmed in 2008-09. Last serviced in August 2016 (see lot 603 Coys 4.12.12 NS).										

F109: 1958 Bentley Continental S1 coupé (Park Ward)

F110: 1959 Bentley Continental S1 Flying Spur (H.J.Mulliner)

Year	Model	(Bodybuilder)	Chassis no.	Steering	Estimate	Hammer price £	Hammer price $	Hammer price €	Date	Place	Lot	Auc. H.
1961	**Continental S2 saloon**	(J.Young)	BC41LBY	L	290-340.000 USD		NS		17-08-17	Monterey	36	WoA
	Black with magnolia leather interior; imported into the USA in the 1990s; described as in excellent overall condition.											
1962	**Continental S2 cabriolet**	(Mulliner,Park Ward)	BC67BY	L	190-230.000 GBP		NS		15-07-17	Blenheim Pal.	125	Coy
	Steel grey with grey leather interior; converted at unspecified date to left-hand drive. Reimported into the UK from the USA and restored (see lot 356 Bonhams 4.5.02 NS).											
1962	**Continental S2 cabriolet**	(Mulliner,Park Ward)	BC67BY	L	200-250.000 EUR	208.371	273.919	230.805	05-08-17	Schloss Dyck	254	Coy F111
	See lot 125 Coys 15.7.17.											
1961	**Continental S2 coupé**	(Mulliner,Park Ward)	BC49BY	R	190-230.000 GBP	173.600	232.312	206.740	07-09-16	London	179	RMS F112
	Two-tone green with red leather interior; described as in very good largely original condition.											
1962	**Continental S2 coupé**	(Mulliner,Park Ward)	BC71CZ	R	240-260.000 GBP		NS		08-09-16	Fontwell Park	126	Coy
	Pewter with green leather interior; sold new to Switzerland, returned to the UK in the late 1960s, sold again to Europe in 1999 (see lot 142 Coys 2.7.16 $292,204).											
1959	**Continental S2 coupé**	(H.J.Mulliner)	BC3LAR	L	350-450.000 EUR		NS		10-02-17	Paris	65	Art
	Shell grey with dark blue leather interior; bought in 2009 by the current owner and subsequently restored. Sunroof.											
1962	**Continental S2 coupé**	(Mulliner,Park Ward)	BC71CZ	R	220-250.000 GBP	200.070	248.567	233.382	18-02-17	London	331	Coy
	See lot 126 Coys 8.9.16.											
1960	**Continental S2 Flying Spur**	(H.J.Mulliner)	BC124AR	R	140-180.000 EUR		NS		09-02-17	Paris	404	Bon
	Two-tone green with red leather interior; restored in the early 2000s (see lot 241 Bonhams 8.3.14 NS).											
1961	**Continental S2 Flying Spur**	(Mulliner,Park Ward)	BC18CZ	R	180-240.000 GBP	180.700	234.512	204.607	30-06-17	Goodwood	278	Bon
	Dark blue with tan leather interior; bought, already restored, by the current owner in Australia and reimported into the UK. The original engine was replaced with one of the new (original type) V8 units built by Bentley Motors in 2013; it carries the original engine number.											
1962	**S3 saloon**		B50CN	R	28-34.000 GBP	32.200	40.601	37.838	07-12-16	London	377	Bon F113
	Blue with grey leather interior; restored 23 years ago, the car is described as in good overall condition.											
1964	**S3 saloon**		B184EC	R	28-35.000 GBP	24.453	31.879	28.644	18-05-17	London	120	Coy
	Two-tone grey; 38,000 miles covered.											
1965	**S3 saloon**		B42HN	R	29-35.000 GBP		NS		20-05-17	Ascot	182	His
	Burgundy with black leather interior; restored many years ago; recently serviced.											
1964	**S3 saloon**		B184EC	R	28-35.000 GBP	22.000	28.552	24.911	29-06-17	Fontwell Park	114	Coy
	See lot 120 Coys 18.5.17.											
1965	**Continental S3 cabriolet**	(Mulliner,Park Ward)	BC176XC	R	180-240.000 USD	136.616*	167.750*	157.769*	20-01-17	Phoenix	244	RMS F114
	Red with beige leather interior; restored in the USA in 1995 (see lots 539 Bonhams 18.8.06 $92,430 and S191 Mecum 14.6.14 NS).											
1964	**Continental S3 cabriolet**	(Mulliner,Park Ward)	BC96XC	R	190-220.000 GBP		NS		19-03-17	Goodwood	59	Bon
	Steel blue with light blue interior; some restoration works carried out in the early 2000s. Circa 63,000 miles covered since new.											
1964	**Continental S3 coupé**	(Mulliner,Park Ward)	BC138XC	R	140-160.000 GBP		NS		12-10-16	Duxford	30	H&H
	Light metallic blue with red leathe rinterior; full-lenght Webasto sunroof. Recently serviced (see lot 126A Coys 11.7.15 $87,950).											
1965	**Continental S3 coupé**	(Mulliner,Park Ward)	BC58LXE	L	190-240.000 EUR		NS		09-02-17	Paris	357	Bon
	Dark green with beige interior; sold new to the USA. Restoration completed in 1993. Registered in the UK.											
1978	**T2 saloon**		SBH35120	R	14-17.000 GBP	13.937	17.183	15.424	08-10-16	Ascot	317	Coy
	Black with dark green interior; last serviced in 2015 at 62,694 miles (see lot 21 Bonhams 20.3.16 $16,660).											
1966	**T 2-door**	(Mulliner,Park Ward)	CBH1695	L	15-20.000 EUR	28.621*	35.589*	33.600*	25-11-16	Milan	607	RMS
	Blue; 70,796 kms. From the Duemila Ruote collection.											
1967	**T 2-door**	(Mulliner,Park Ward)	GBH1833	R	34-40.000 GBP	33.600	41.778	39.443	26-11-16	Weybridge	132	His
	White with black everflex roof.											
1971	**T 2-door**	(Mulliner,Park Ward)	CBH9242	R	35-40.000 GBP	39.100	49.301	45.946	07-12-16	London	308	Bon F115
	Dark green with black leather interior; invoices for service/maintenance dated in the 2000s (see lot 659 Brooks 27.4.95 NS).											
2012	**Mulsanne**		16596	R	215-235.000 GBP		NS		12-11-16	Birmingham	324	SiC
	Dark green; built for personal use of Her Majesty The Queen Elizabeth II, the car was used until 2014 covering less than 6,000 miles.											
1983	**Mulsanne Turbo**		07344	R	16-20.000 GBP	15.120	19.674	17.600	20-05-17	Ascot	253	His
	Beige with cream leather interior; 3,190 miles covered. Recently serviced.											
1992	**Continental cabriolet**	(Mulliner,Park Ward)	40037	L	80-90.000 EUR	90.634*	112.699*	106.400*	25-11-16	Milan	596	RMS
	Black with black interior; 63,873 kms. From the Duemila Ruote collection.											

F111: 1962 Bentley Continental S2 cabriolet (Mulliner,Park Ward)

F112: 1961 Bentley Continental S2 coupé (Mulliner,Park Ward)

Year	Model	(Bodybuilder)	Chassis no.	Steering	Estimate	Hammer price £	$	€	Date	Sale Place	Lot	Auc. H.

F113: 1962 Bentley S3 saloon

F114: 1965 Bentley Continental S3 cabriolet (Mulliner,Park Ward)

Year	Model	Chassis	St	Estimate	£	$	€	Date	Place	Lot	H.
1987	**Continental cabriolet (Mulliner,Park Ward)**	16663	L	60-70.000 GBP		NS		26-11-16	Weybridge	190	His

Black with tan leather interior; the car was sold new to the USA where it remained in the same family ownership until 2014 when it was reimported into Europe. 43,316 miles covered. Recently serviced (see lot 241 Historics 7.3.15 $74,807).

1985	**Continental cabriolet (Mulliner,Park Ward)**	10168	R	90-110.000 GBP	**83.625**	101.830	95.516	14-01-17	Birmingham	130	**Coy**

Red with beige leather interior; described as in good to excellent condition. First owner Sir Elton John (see lots 47 H & H 4.12.02 $92,517 and 419 Bonhams 5.2.15 $91,851).

1987	**Continental cabriolet (Mulliner,Park Ward)**	16663	L	70-90.000 EUR		NS		09-02-17	Paris	426	**Bon**

See lot 190 Historics 26.11.16.

1985	**Continental cabriolet (Mulliner,Park Ward)**	10168	R	90-120.000 GBP	**91.100**	118.230	103.153	30-06-17	Goodwood	217	**Bon** F116

See lot 130 Coys 14.1.17.

1988	**Continental cabriolet**	23375	L	60-70.000 GBP	**66.690**	86.190	75.793	15-07-17	Blenheim Pal.	110	**Coy**

Dark blue with cream interior; recently serviced.

1990	**Turbo R**	32912	L	20-30.000 EUR	**14.678***	18.444*	17.250*	09-02-17	Paris	338	**Bon**

Sold new to Italy; reimported into the UK in 2007; last serviced in June 2016 at 70,801 kms.

1989	**Turbo R**	27141	R	18-22.000 GBP	**22.400**	28.887	25.312	08-07-17	Brooklands	142	**His**

Dark green with cream interior; 23,000 miles covered; one owner.

1996	**Continental R Jack Barclay**	53152	R	NA	**48.380**	64.263	57.417	02-09-16	Salon Privé	214	**SiC**

Silver with black leather interior; 67,000 miles covered. One of 10 examples built (see lot 59 H & H 18.05.16 NS).

2001	**Continental T**	01503	R	45-55.000 GBP	**51.750**	68.740	61.417	03-09-16	Beaulieu	439	**Bon**

Silver with black interior; approximately 52,500 miles covered.

1999	**Continental T**	67086	L	90-105.000 EUR	**90.634***	112.699*	106.400*	25-11-16	Milan	870	**RMS**

Black with beige interior; 33,388 kms. From the Duemila Ruote collection.

1996	**Continental R**	53157	R	30-40.000 GBP	**38.080**	47.349	44.702	26-11-16	Weybridge	211	**His**

Wildberry with parchment leather interior; in very good overall condition.

2001	**Continental R Le Mans**	01771	R	80-120.000 GBP	**82.140**	103.570	96.523	07-12-16	London	330	**Bon**

Since 2012 in the current ownership; 33,313 miles covered since new.

1997	**Continental R**	63073	R	35-45.000 GBP	**46.480**	58.607	54.619	07-12-16	Chateau Impney	21	**H&H**

British racing green with cream leather interior; described as in very good overall condition.

1993	**Continental R**	42719	L	50-70.000 EUR	**49.687**	62.113	58.240	08-02-17	Paris	178	**RMS**

Dark green with beige interior; under 35,000 kms covered. Last serviced in June 2013.

2001	**Continental R Le Mans**	01754	L	80-120.000 EUR	**67.519**	84.841	79.350	09-02-17	Paris	379	**Bon**

Dark green; one owner and 145.000 kms covered. Described as in excellent overall condition. One of 46 examples built.

2000	**Continental R Mulliner**	63512	L	60-90.000 EUR	**58.712**	73.775	69.000	09-02-17	Paris	406	**Bon**

Plum with beige leather interior; in very good overall condition. Two owners and circa 59,000 kms covered.

2002	**Continental R Mulliner**	01793	L	80-100.000 USD	**135.729***	165.000*	155.496*	10-03-17	Amelia Island	153	**RMS** F117

Black with beige leather interior; 12,450 miles covered. From the Orin Smith collection.

F115: 1971 Bentley T 2-door (Mulliner,Park Ward)

F116: 1985 Bentley Continental cabriolet (Mulliner,Park Ward)

Year	Model	(Bodybuilder)	Chassis no.	Steering	Estimate	Hammer price £	$	€	Date	Place	Lot	Auc. H.

F117: 2002 Bentley Continental R Mulliner

F118: 2002 Bentley Azure (Pininfarina)

Year	Model	Chassis no.	Steering	Estimate	£	$	€	Date	Place	Lot	Auc. H.
1997	**Continental T**	53401	R	39-46.000 GBP	49.280	63.551	55.686	08-07-17	Brooklands	224	His
	Black with black and magnolia leather interior; in good overall condition.										
1998	**Brooklands R Mulliner**	66872	R	18-22.000 GBP		NS		04-03-17	Brooklands	207	His
	Pearl grey with grey interior; 59,200 miles covered. One of 100 examples built.										
1998	**Brooklands R Mulliner**	66838	R	26-28.500 GBP	15.000	19.467	16.985	29-06-17	Fontwell Park	128	Coy
	Blue with cream interior; 25,300 miles covered.										
1997	**Brooklands**	59779	R	12-15.000 GBP		NS		15-07-17	Blenheim Pal.	106	Coy
	Metallic wildberry with parchment leather interior; 27,000 miles covered.										
2001	**Azure** (Pininfarina)	62642	R	NA	79.880	106.105	94.802	02-09-16	Salon Privé	248	SiC
	Dark blue; in very good overall condition. Less than 20,000 miles covered.										
2000	**Azure** (Pininfarina)	62062	R	70-80.000 GBP	78.400	104.915	93.367	07-09-16	London	188	RMS
	Blue with tan leather interior; in excellent overall condition. 19,600 kms covered.										
1996	**Azure** (Pininfarina)	53730	L	70-80.000 EUR		NS		30-10-16	Paris	138	Art
	Black; 31,000 kms covered.										
2003	**Azure "Final Series Performance"** (Pininfarina)	01228	R	110-130.000 GBP		NS		07-12-16	London	342	Bon
	Silver with blue leather interior; one of 62 examples built. Recently serviced.										
2006	**Azure** (Pininfarina)	11667	R	135-155.000 GBP		NS		24-02-17	Stoneleigh P.	539	SiC
	Dark metallic blue with magnolia leather interior; one owner and 1,450 miles covered. Last serviced in October 2016.										
2002	**Azure** (Pininfarina)	01002	L	60-80.000 GBP	74.300	91.835	85.527	19-03-17	Goodwood	20	Bon F118
	Black with black leather interior; sold new to the USA, the car was reimported into the UK in 2007. Two owners; 9,050 miles covered.										
1997	**Azure** (Pininfarina)	61066	L	NQ	37.977*	47.300*	44.367*	08-04-17	Palm Beach	405	B/J
	Black with cream interior.										
1998	**Azure** (Pininfarina)	61617	L	NA	54.024	68.750	61.531	24-06-17	Santa Monica	268	RMS
	Blue with cream and blue interior; one owner; less than 8,000 miles covered.										
1997	**Azure** (Pininfarina)	61169	R	80-90.000 GBP	78.750	103.123	87.924	29-07-17	Silverstone	746	SiC
	Platinum with dark blue leather interior; one of 10 examples of the "Jack Barclay" limited series. Since 1997 with its second owner; 12,800 miles covered.										
1998	**Arnage Green Label**	01288	R	20-23.000 GBP	20.250	25.634	23.508	12-11-16	Birmingham	653	SiC
	Black with black interior; last serviced in September 2015 at 24,775 miles. In recent years converted to run on LPG.										
2001	**Arnage**	06353	L	35-40.000 EUR	28.621*	35.589*	33.600*	25-11-16	Milan	894	RMS
	Black; 48,766 kms. From the Duemila Ruote collection.										
2006	**Arnage RL**	19437	R	30-35.000 GBP	52.192	65.809	61.331	07-12-16	Chateau Impney	5	H&H
	Dark sapphire pearl with cream leather interior; some 4,800 miles on the odometer.										
2000	**Arnage Red Label**	04747	R	16-19.000 GBP	16.310	21.358	18.210	29-07-17	Silverstone	754	SiC
	Blue with magnolia leather interior; last serviced in September 2016 at 69,475 miles.										

F119: 1900 Benz Ideal vis-a-vis

F120: 1912 Benz 8/20 PS touring

F121: 1968 Bizzarrini 5300 GT Strada (Sports Cars/Giugiaro)

F122: 1969 Bizzarrini GT Europa

Year	Model	Chassis no.	Steering	Estimate	£	$	€	Date	Place	Lot	Auc. H.
2008	**Brooklands Coupé**	13994	R	95-110.000 GBP	101.250	128.172	117.541	12-11-16	Birmingham	633	SiC
	Silver with navy blue leather interior; 22,281 miles covered.										
2009	**Brooklands Coupé**	14062	L	135-145.000 USD	119.156	148.500	139.709	11-02-17	Boca Raton	151	TFA
	Black; 8,409 miles covered.										
2009	**Brooklands Coupé**	14079	L	140-180.000 EUR		NS		02-07-17	Monaco	154	Art
	Dark metallic grey with red leather interior; 3,600 kms covered.										

BENZ (D) (1885-1926)

1893	**Victoria**	NQ	R	20-30.000 EUR	24.463*	30.740*	28.750*	09-02-17	Paris	328	Bon
	Unknown history; it appears to have been restored at some time.										
1900	**Ideal vis-a-vis**	B170	R	120-140.000 EUR	102.746	129.106	120.750	09-02-17	Paris	324	Bon
	Black with black interior; restored in the 1950s, the car was acquired in 2005 by the current vendor's father and restored again between 2006 and 2007.										F119
1912	**8/20 PS touring**	545015537	R	175-225.000 USD	94.017	121.000	103.455	17-08-17	Monterey	30	WoA
	Burgundy with black leather interior; sold new to Australia where it was bodied; imported into the USA in the 1990s; bought some years ago by the current owner and subjected to a restoration completed in 2016.										F120

BERKELEY (GB) (1956-1961)

1959	**SE492**	74	L	25-35.000 USD	13.550*	16.500*	15.637*	09-03-17	Amelia Island	101	Bon
	Restored; 492cc Excelsior engine.										

BITTER (D) (1973-1992)

1979	**CD**	5250386	L	60-70.000 GBP	67.500	83.977	78.138	29-03-17	Duxford	55	H&H
	Red with brown interior; described as in very good overall condition, the car has covered 68,615 km. Automatic transmission. When new personal car of Erich Bitter.										

BIZZARRINI (I) (1965-1969)

1968	**5300 GT Strada (Sports Cars/Giugiaro)**	1A30309	L	600-900.000 EUR	601.806	749.982	705.600	10-02-17	Paris	34	Art
	Aluminium body finished in red with tan interior; bought in 1990 by Hervé Ogliastro and subsequently fully restored in Italy by Diomante. From the Hervé and Martine Ogliastro Collection. It appears that another example has the same chassis number (see lot 536 Bonhams 11.7.08 NS).										F121
1969	**GT Europa**	B508	L	250-350.000 EUR	260.264	324.346	305.152	10-02-17	Paris	74	Art
	Originally finished in dark metallic blue with cognac interior, the car was displayed at the 1969 Paris Motor Show. In the 1970s the engine was replaced with the present 2.4-litre Opel unit (the original engine is included with the sale). Restored by the current owner.										F122

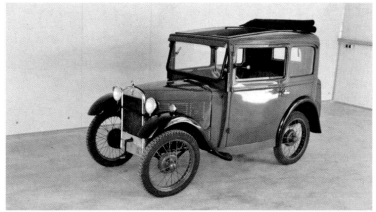

F123: 1929 BMW 3/15 DA 2 saloon

F124: 1937 BMW 327 coupé

Year	Model	(Bodybuilder)	Chassis no.	Steering	Estimate	Hammer price £	$	€	Date	Place	Lot	Auc. H.

F125: 1938 BMW 328 roadster

F126: 1940 BMW 328 roadster

BMW (D) (1929-)

Year	Model	Chassis no.	Steering	Estimate	£	$	€	Date	Place	Lot	Auc. H.
1929	3/15 DA 2 saloon	244071727	L	14-20.000 EUR	22.215*	28.268*	25.300*	24-06-17	Wien	329	Dor F123

Dark red with black wings and brown interior; restored many years ago. Sliding sunroof.

| 1936 | 319 cabriolet | 57546 | L | 60-80.000 USD | 40.171* | 51.700* | 44.048* | 18-08-17 | Carmel | 109 | Bon |

Blue and ivory with red interior; restored in the early 1990s.

| 1938 | 326 cabriolet | 84783 | R | 60-70.000 GBP | | NS | | 10-09-16 | Goodwood | 184 | Bon |

Black and red; older restoration.

| 1940 | 326 cabriolet | 115782 | L | 85-100.000 EUR | 51.759 | 63.975 | 59.584 | 19-03-17 | Fontainebleau | 211 | Ose |

Black and red; in good overall condition. Since 1987 in the current ownership.

| 1937 | 327 coupé | 74188 | L | 50-80.000 EUR | 58.942* | 71.605* | 65.560* | 30-10-16 | Paris | 131 | Art F124 |

Blue and ivory; restored.

| 1939 | 327/28 cabriolet | 74582 | L | 250-325.000 USD | | NS | | 19-01-17 | Scottsdale | 42 | Bon |

Two-tone blue with blue interior; discovered in the 1980s and subsequently subjected to a long restoration recently completed (see lot 185 Bonhams 10.3.16 NS).

| 1941 | 327 coupé | 87282 | L | 150-170.000 EUR | 119.826 | 149.240 | 140.000 | 08-04-17 | Essen | 188 | Coy |

Black and cream with deep red interior; restored at unspecified date (see Coys lots 525 12.10.13 $201,591 and 110 26.9.15 NS).

| 1939 | 327/28 cabriolet | 74582 | L | 200-250.000 USD | 171.138 | 220.000 | 196.130 | 04-06-17 | Greenwich | 140 | Bon |

See lot 42 Bonhams 19.1.17.

| 1938 | 328 roadster | 85187 | L | 700-800.000 EUR | 547.776 | 682.240 | 640.000 | 08-04-17 | Essen | 179 | Coy F125 |

White with black interior; sold new in Germany and raced before and after WWII. In 1954 it was imported into the UK and in 1971 it was bought by the current owner and reimported into Germany. Described as never restored and always well maintained; in excellent mechanical condition.

| 1940 | 328 roadster | 85133 | L | 1.500-2.000.000 USD | 470.085* | 605.000* | 517.275* | 17-08-17 | Monterey | 44 | WoA |

The current owner, who bought the car in 2007, believes that 85133 was one of five or six chassis delivered by BMW in early 1939 to Carrozzeria Touring to be bodied. From 1958 to 1970 the car was owned by Swiss Othmar Muller who fitted the body to a Simca chassis. From 1993 to 2007 the body was owned by the Grether family, Germany, who also bought later the chassis 85133 and original dry-sump engine in Switzerland. The reunited body, chassis and engine have been recently restored in the USA by Fran Roxas. **F126**

| 1957 | 502 saloon | 62941R | R | NA | 10.130 | 13.456 | 12.022 | 02-09-16 | Salon Privé | 262 | SiC |

Restored in the 1970s, the car was laid up in 1991. It needs to be restored again.

| 1956 | 502 saloon | 61595 | R | 30-35.000 GBP | | NS | | 24-02-17 | Stoneleigh P. | 517 | SiC |

Bought many years ago by the current owner and later prepared for historic racing. Currently fitted with a period-correct 2.6-litre V8 engine with 250 miles (the original block and other engine parts are included with the sale).

| 1960 | 502 Luxury | 64481 | L | 32-44.000 EUR | 38.371 | 48.826 | 43.700 | 24-06-17 | Wien | 355 | Dor F127 |

Blue with grey cloth interior; restored some years ago; in good overall condition.

| 1956 | 502 saloon | 61128 | L | 40-50.000 EUR | | NS | | 05-08-17 | Schloss Dyck | 237 | Coy |

Blue; restored several years ago, the car is described as in very good overall condition.

| 1957 | 503 coupé | 69181 | R | 120-140.000 GBP | 133.360 | 165.686 | 155.564 | 18-02-17 | London | 353 | Coy F128 |

White; described as in good mechanical order. One if two right-hand drive examples known to survive. In the same family ownership from 1961 to 2010.

F127: 1960 BMW 502 Luxury

F128: 1957 BMW 503 coupé

Year	Model	(Bodybuilder)	Chassis no.	Steering	Estimate	Hammer price £	$	€	Sale Date	Place	Lot	Auc. H.
1957	**503 cabriolet**		69090	L	550-750.000 USD	452.991	583.000	496.716	18-08-17	Carmel	90	Bon F129
Medium metallic grey with light brown leather interior; sold new to the USA and remained in the same family ownership until 2013. Concours-quality restoration completed in 2016.											
1957	**507 roadster**		70044	L	1.700-2.000.000 EUR		NS		27-05-17	Villa Erba	134	RMS
Green with black hardtop and original red leather interior; four owners and 73,000 kms covered. In single ownership for 51 years (see lot 226 RM/Sotheby's 20.8.16 NS).											
1958	**507 roadster**		70081	L	2.000-2.500.000 USD	2.136.750	2.750.000	2.343.000	19-08-17	Pebble Beach	157	G&Co F130
Metallic graphite grey with beige interior; sold new to the USA; reimported into Europe in 1995; concours-quality restoration carried out in Germany between 2013 and 2015 and subsequently reimported into the USA.											
1958	**Isetta 250**		509322	L	45-55.000 USD	34.965	45.000	38.340	19-08-17	Monterey	F7	Mec
Red with red and white interior; restored.											
1958	**Isetta 300**		508023	L	NQ	25.044*	33.000*	29.393*	17-09-16	Aspen	117	TFA
Red and white with brown interior; restored.											
1957	**Isetta 300**		425417	L	18-22.000 GBP	19.600	24.371	23.008	26-11-16	Weybridge	137	His
Beige; described as in very good overall condition.											
1957	**Isetta 300**		507290	L	25-40.000 USD	32.844	40.000	37.516	15-01-17	Kissimmee	F131	Mec
Light blue and white with brown interior; concours-quality restoration. From the Jackie and Gary Runyon collection.											
1961	**Isetta 300**		328058	R	18-25.000 GBP	17.784	22.230	20.960	12-04-17	London	329	Coy
White and red with white interior; several restoration works carried out between 2005 and 2015.											
1959	**Limousine 600**		130676	L	30-50.000 USD	33.621	42.000	37.859	04-11-16	Dallas	S165	Mec
Red with white roof; older restoration.											
1958	**Limousine 600**		124518	L	34-40.000 GBP		NS		26-11-16	Weybridge	141	His
Red and tan; in good overall condition.											
1967	**1800 saloon**		0996621	L	NQ	9.508*	12.100*	10.830*	24-06-17	Northeast	23	B/J
Blue with black interior; upgraded with a 2-liter engine and automatic transmission.											
1971	**1800 saloon**		1924901	L	10-13.000 GBP	8.960	11.555	10.125	08-07-17	Brooklands	119	His
Grey with blue interior; imported into the UK in 2013; restored in 2016.											
1967	**2000C (Karmann)**		1200046	L	25-30.000 USD	12.395	15.950	14.194	03-10-16	Philadelphia	220	Bon
Light metallic blue with blue cloth interior; engine recently fitted with the twin carburettor setup of the 2000CS model. Manual gearbox.											
1967	**Glas 3000 V8**		602001384	L	70-80.000 EUR	56.489	70.356	66.000	08-04-17	Essen	198	Coy F131
Silver; one owner; recently restored.											
1968	**2000 CS (Karmann)**		1108344	L	NA	18.877*	23.100*	20.996*	15-10-16	Las Vegas	313	B/J
Red with tan interior; since 2010 in the current, second ownership. Described as in original condition.											
1968	**2000 CS (Karmann)**		1104461	R	18-24.000 GBP		NS		07-12-16	London	317	Bon
Yellow with black roof; stored for circa 30 years, engine rebuilt a few years ago; recently serviced (see lot 310 Historics 30.8.14 $27,115).											
1966	**2000 CS (Karmann)**		1101846	L	23-26.000 GBP	23.479	30.746	26.214	29-07-17	Silverstone	454	SiC
White with blue velour interior; just over 30,000 kms on the odometer.											
1973	**2002 Tii**		2751413	R	15-20.000 GBP	20.125	26.732	23.884	03-09-16	Beaulieu	437	Bon
Red; in very good overall condition. 28,137 miles covered.											
1974	**2002 Tii**		2780147	L	45-55.000 USD	33.392	44.000	39.191	17-09-16	Aspen	134	TFA
Green with beige interior; restored. Sunroof (see lot 282 RM 13.8.10 $24,200).											
1972	**2002 cabriolet (Baur)**		2795174	L	30-40.000 EUR	47.797	58.931	52.900	07-10-16	Zoute	37	Bon F132
Dark green; fully restored.											
1969	**2002 Ti**		1681267	L	15-25.000 EUR		NS		05-11-16	Lyon	247	Agu
White with blue interior; since 1974 in the same family ownership. Repainted several years ago. Recently overhauled.											
1971	**2002**		2627731	L	10-15.000 EUR	42.932*	53.384*	50.400*	25-11-16	Milan	861	RMS
White; race prepared. From the Duemila Ruote collection.											
1972	**2002 Tii**		2760619	L	23-26.000 EUR	15.570	18.960	17.784	14-01-17	Maastricht	243	Coy
White; stored from 1988 to 2015 and subsequently subjected to several restoration works.											
1974	**2002 Tii**		02735630	L	65-85.000 EUR	57.332	71.669	67.200	08-02-17	Paris	109	RMS
Metallic garnet red; Recaro sport seats. Converted when new to Alpina A4S specification. Certified by Alpina.											

F129: 1957 BMW 503 cabriolet

F130: 1958 BMW 507 roadster

F131: 1967 BMW Glas 3000 V8

F132: 1972 BMW 2002 cabriolet (Baur)

Year	Model (Bodybuilder)	Chassis no.	Steering	Estimate	£	$	€	Date	Place	Lot	Auc. H.
1972	**2002 cabriolet (Baur)**	2795326	L	30-50.000 EUR	24.463	30.740	28.750	09-02-17	Paris	352	Bon
Yellow with blue interior; for 40 years in the current, second ownership. Restored.											
1973	**2002 Tii**	2752163	R	18-22.000 GBP	20.250	25.422	23.962	24-02-17	Stoneleigh P.	920	SiC
Orange; in good overall condition.											
1972	**2002 Tii**	27660619	L	18-20.000 EUR	14.978	18.655	17.500	08-04-17	Essen	148	Coy
See lot 243 Coys 14.1.17.											
1973	**2002 Turbo**	4291515	L	75-95.000 USD	92.139*	112.200*	106.332*	09-03-17	Amelia Island	165	Bon F133
White; described as in very good highly original condition. 16,500 believed original kms.											
1975	**2002 Turbo**	4291125	L	65-75.000 GBP	67.500	83.977	78.138	29-03-17	Duxford	94	H&H
White with black leatherette interior; described as in good original condition and 23,720 kms on the odometer.											
1975	**2002 Turbo**	4290770	L	65-75.000 GBP	70.880	92.817	79.138	29-07-17	Silverstone	712	SiC
White; well maintained; 65,000 miles covered.											
1974	**2002 Turbo**	4290443	L	90-120.000 USD	111.111*	143.000*	121.836*	18-08-17	Pebble Beach	53	G&Co
White; imported into the USA in 1985; restoration completed in 2002; original interior.											
1972	**3.0 Csi**	2263293	L	40-60.000 EUR	54.031	66.617	59.800	07-10-16	Zoute	16	Bon
Light metallic blue with blue interior; reestored between 1992 and 1995.											
1975	**3.0 CSi**	4341267	L	28-42.000 EUR	35.155	43.018	39.100	15-10-16	Salzburg	433	Dor
Fjord blue with blue leather interior; body repainted 15 years ago, interior retrimmed in more recent years.											
1973	**3.0 CSi**	2265982	R	28-32.000 GBP	49.280	61.245	57.229	16-11-16	Donington Park	41	H&H
Light blue; restored and fitted with a BMW M5 engine and gearbox (see lot 636 Silverstone Auctions 15.11.13 $57,282).											
1972	**3.0 CSi**	2263016	L	15-20.000 EUR	42.932*	53.384*	50.400*	25-11-16	Milan	627	RMS
Light blue with blue cloth interior; 38,556 kms. From the Duemila Ruote collection.											
1972	**3.0 CSi**	2261539	L	35-40.000 EUR	48.589	59.169	55.500	14-01-17	Maastricht	237	Coy
Light metallic blue with tobacco leather interior; in good overall condition. Body repainted.											
1973	**3.0 CS**	2240697	L	50-60.000 USD	53.546*	66.000*	61.862*	19-01-17	Scottsdale	90	Bon
Body and interior restored in 2013-14. Manual gearbox.											
1973	**3.0 CSi**	2265649	R	40-50.000 GBP	48.840	60.679	56.972	18-02-17	London	319	Coy
Light metallic blue with dark blue velour interior; restored some years ago.											
1972	**3.0 CSi/CSL**	2331066	R	100-125.000 GBP	105.750	132.759	125.134	24-02-17	Stoneleigh P.	128	SiC
Conversion to CSL carried out in the late 1980s; regularly raced at historic events. 379bhp engine rebuilt in 2014; that same year body modified to Group 4 specification (see lot 77 H & H 19.4.12 $215,242).											
1972	**3.0 CSi**	2260790	L	40-45.000 EUR	34.236	42.640	40.000	08-04-17	Essen	116	Coy
Blue with tan leather interior; restored in 2015-16.											
1973	**3.0 CS**	2250639	L	NA	24.203	30.800	27.566	24-06-17	Santa Monica	115	RMS
Yellow with beige interior; since 1988 with the present, second owner; engine rebuilt.											

F133: 1973 BMW 2002 Turbo

F134: 1973 BMW 3.0 CSL

119

Year	Model	(Bodybuilder)	Chassis no.	Steering	Estimate	Hammer price £	$	€	Date	Place	Lot	Auc. H.
1973	3.0 CSi		2262469	R	39-46.000 GBP		NS		08-07-17	Brooklands	139	His
Metallic fjord blue with dark blue leather interior; mechanicals restored in 2009; body repainted in 2016.												
1974	3.0 CSi		2265771	R	40-50.000 GBP		NS		26-07-17	Duxford	15	H&H
Silver with blue velour interior; body restored; recently serviced.												
1974	3.0 CSL		2285444	R	30-40.000 GBP	64.220	85.303	76.216	03-09-16	Beaulieu	431	Bon
Acquired in 1982 by the current, second owner. In storage for the last 20 years; for restoration.												
1973	3.0 CSL		2275525	L	325-375.000 USD	267.729	330.000	309.309	19-01-17	Scottsdale	40	Bon F134
"Batmobile" finished in silver with black interior; sold new to Switzerland. Fully restored, the car is described as in very good overall condition.												
1973	3.0 CSL		2285287	L	45-55.000 GBP	83.813	107.758	99.084	13-05-17	Silverstone	354	SiC
Metallic fjord blue with black interior; from the late 1970s in the same family ownership; restored many years ago; engine replaced with a new unit in 1991.												
1972	3.0 CSL		2285157	R	NQ	53.760*	69.953*	62.577*	20-05-17	Ascot	143	His
Restoration project.												
1972	3.0 CSL		2285236	R	70-85.000 GBP	78.750	103.123	87.924	29-07-17	Silverstone	430	SiC
Light green; bought in 2011 by the current owner and subsequently restored.												
1973	3.0 CSL		2285416	R	70-85.000 GBP	137.250	179.729	153.240	29-07-17	Silverstone	443	SiC
Metallic grey with black interior; restored.												
1972	3.0 CSL		2212314	L	290-330.000 USD		NS		18-08-17	Carmel	60	Bon
Orange with black interior; sold new to Italy, the car was imported into the USA in 2013. Never raced, it is described as in highly original condition (see lot 171 Bonhams 01.10.11 $100,935).												
1983	320i cabriolet	(Baur)	9129752	L	8-9.000 EUR	8.054	9.808	9.200	14-01-17	Maastricht	204	Coy
Dark blue with blue cloth interior; in good overall condition.												
1980	M1	(Italdesign)	4301096	L	575-625.000 USD	328.440	400.000	375.160	15-01-17	Kissimmee	S176	Mec
Orange with black leather and cloth interior; three owners and 36,000 original kms (see lots Mecum S194 16.8.14 NS and S65 15.8.15 NS, and Bonhams 98 28.1.16 NS).												
1979	M1	(Italdesign)	4301231	L	390-440.000 USD		NS		18-01-17	Scottsdale	67	WoA
White whit white leather interior; body modified in 1980 to Procar racing-type specification. 34.850 miles covered (see lot 600 RM 18.8.07 $121,000).												
1980	M1	(Italdesign)	4301096	L	450-550.000 USD		NS		19-08-17	Monterey	S42	Mec
See lot S176 Mecum 15.1.17.												
1986	M635 CSi		1052886	L	10-15.000 EUR	47.702*	59.315*	56.000*	25-11-16	Milan	239	RMS
Black with beige interior; 113,540 kms. From the Duemila Ruote collection.												
1983	635 CSi Group A		E24RA108	L	5-10.000 EUR	138.336*	172.014*	162.400*	25-11-16	Milan	317	RMS F135
Green and yellow. From the Duemila Ruote collection.												
1987	325i cabriolet		121343	L	10-15.000 EUR	10.717*	13.019*	11.920*	30-10-16	Paris	161	Art
Red; overhauled in 2016.												
1987	M6		2560181	L	100-120.000 USD	85.815	104.500	99.035	09-03-17	Amelia Island	140	Bon F136
Red with white leather interior; in very good original condition. Less than 7,000 miles covered.												
1988	M6		560905	L	40-50.000 USD	42.785*	55.000*	49.033*	04-06-17	Greenwich	145	Bon
Black with light grey leather interior; in very good overall condition; 75,000 miles covered; recently serviced.												
1990	M3 cabriolet		86261	L	NA	59.630	79.207	70.769	02-09-16	Salon Privé	239	SiC
Metallic black with black interior; recently serviced.												
1988	M3		913221	L	60-80.000 EUR		NA		08-10-16	Paris	126	CB/C
White with black interior; 1,000 miles covered since new.												
1988	M3 Europameister		894600	L	60-80.000 EUR	51.958	63.120	57.792	30-10-16	Paris	114	Art
Restored; sunroof.												
1994	M3 cabriolet		40215	L	15-25.000 EUR	14.920	18.636	16.800	05-11-16	Lyon	231	Agu
Blue with dark grey leather interior; major service in 2016.												
1990	M3 Sport Evolution		79160	L	95-115.000 GBP		NS		12-11-16	Birmingham	335	SiC
Red with grey interior; described as in very good overall condition. Since 2002 in the current ownership. Body repainted. In 1990 the car was fitted with a number of AC Schnitzer upgrades.												
1995	M3 Lightweight		07534	L	150-180.000 USD	119.894*	145.750*	137.355*	10-03-17	Amelia Island	28	G&Co
White; in very good original condition. 7,500 miles on the odometer.												

F135: 1983 BMW 635 CSi Group A

F136: 1987 BMW M6

Year	Model	(Bodybuilder)	Chassis No.	Steering	Estimate	Hammer Price £	$	€	Date	Place	Lot	Auc. H.
1991	M3 cabriolet		86423	L	70-90.000 USD	72.389*	88.000*	82.931*	10-03-17	Amelia Island	87	G&Co
{Metallic black; approximately 80,000 kms covered; last serviced in 2016 at the BMW Classic AG in Munich.}												
1988	M3		191322	L	60-80.000 EUR		NS		18-03-17	Lyon	198	Agu
{White with original black leather interior; restored. 194,000 kms on the odometer.}												
1990	M3		41995	L	40-50.000 GBP	52.875	67.981	62.509	13-05-17	Silverstone	330	SiC
{Red; sold new in Germany; imported into the UK in 2001; last serviced in January 2017.}												
1987	M3		842918	L	45-65.000 EUR	47.430	60.485	54.120	10-06-17	Lyon	127	Agu
{Red; in good overall condition. Recently serviced.}												
1995	M3 cabriolet		40757	L	18-26.000 EUR	24.293	30.980	27.720	10-06-17	Lyon	144	Agu
{Black with black leather interior; in good overall condition.}												
1991	M3 Group A		NQ	R	140-180.000 GBP	146.250	192.209	164.356	27-07-17	Silverstone	113	SiC F137
{Labatt's blue and white livery; one of five M3s built by Vic Lee Motorsport for the 1991 British Touring Car Championship, the car was driven by Tim Harvey.}												
1988	M3		196532	L	55-75.000 USD	46.620	60.000	51.120	19-08-17	Monterey	F18	Mec
{White with red interior; 78,450 believed original miles; electric sunroof.}												
1985	M5 Superproduction		3586317	L	85-110.000 GBP		NS		07-09-16	London	124	RMS
{The car is fitted with a 460bhp 3.5-litre dry sump engine built by Pipo Moteurs to BMW Motorsport specifications; it was driven during the 1985 season by Marc Sourd. In ready to race condition; engine rebuilt.}												
1990	Z1		02956	L	35-55.000 EUR	58.139	77.232	69.000	03-09-16	Chantilly	5	Bon
{Yellow with black interior; two owners and 23,203 kms covered.}												
1990	Z1		06057	L	72-78.000 GBP	78.400	104.915	93.367	07-09-16	London	138	RMS F138
{Red with black interior; 250 kms covered. Recently serviced.}												
1990	Z1		06359	L	30-35.000 EUR	40.070*	49.825*	47.040*	25-11-16	Milan	534	RMS
{Dark blue. From the Duemila Ruote collection.}												
1989	Z1		00171	L	40-50.000 GBP	41.400	52.201	48.649	07-12-16	London	358	Bon
{Red; professionally stored since 1996. 17,127 kms. Recently serviced.}												
1989	Z1		99762	L	40-50.000 GBP	44.360	55.113	51.746	18-02-17	London	307	Coy
{Green with grey interior; since 1993 in the current, second ownership. 14,700 miles covered. Last serviced in September 2016.}												
1989	Z1		01039	L	30-35.000 GBP	32.850	41.240	38.871	24-02-17	Stoneleigh P.	504	SiC
{Red; in the same family ownership since new. Restored in 2004 and fitted with a 33,000 mile replacement engine. Described as in very good overall condition.}												
1990	Z1		06302	L	50-70.000 EUR	49.642	61.828	58.000	08-04-17	Essen	153	Coy
{Red with grey interior; one owner; 7,000 kms covered.}												
1991	Z1		03557	L	25-30.000 GBP	26.676	33.345	31.440	12-04-17	London	326	Coy
{For 23 years with its first owner; recently serviced.}												
1989	Z1		01039	L	25-30.000 GBP	32.063	41.223	37.905	13-05-17	Silverstone	370	SiC
{See lot 504 Silverstone Auctions 24.2.17.}												
1989	Z1		00477	L	32-37.000 GBP	31.122	40.574	36.456	18-05-17	London	134	Coy
{Metallic black; in good overall condition. 85,000 kms on the odometer.}												
1989	Z1		00477	L	25-30.000 GBP		NS		15-07-17	Blenheim Pal.	160	Coy
{See lot 134 Coys 18.5.17.}												
1993	850 CSi		00684	L	26-40.000 EUR	28.951	35.426	32.200	15-10-16	Salzburg	407	Dor
{Red with black leather interior; described as in good driving order.}												
1991	850i		72189	L	25-35.000 USD	15.559	19.800	17.721	24-06-17	Santa Monica	197	RMS
{Metallic red; 55,500 miles on the odometer.}												
1996	850 CSi		88183	R	40-50.000 GBP	38.080	49.108	43.030	08-07-17	Brooklands	174	His
{Silver with black leather interior; in very good overall condition.}												
1999	Z3		23556	L	30-40.000 EUR	32.150*	39.057*	35.760*	30-10-16	Paris	158	Art
{Silver; 68,500 kms covered.}												
2003	Z3 M coupé		69227	R	45-50.000 GBP	58.500	74.055	67.913	12-11-16	Birmingham	620	SiC
{Titanium grey with red and black leather interior; 11,000 miles covered. In the same family ownership from new (see lot 291 Historics 11.6.16 $74,204).} | | | | | | | | | | | | |

F137: 1991 BMW M3 Group A

F138: 1990 BMW Z1

Year	Model	(Bodybuilder)	Chassis no.	Steering	Estimate	Hammer price £	$	€	Date	Place	Lot	Auc. H.
1998	Z3 M coupé		55408	L	20-30.000 EUR	55.334*	68.806*	64.960*	25-11-16	Milan	310	RMS
	Light grey; 14,164 kms. From the Duemila Ruote collection.											
1999	Z3M coupé		29194	R	29-34.000 GBP		NS		20-05-17	Ascot	265	His
	Yellow with black leather interior; one owner. Last serviced 3,840 miles ago.											
1998	Z3M		86177	L	NA	13.239*	14.850*	11.552*	03-06-17	Newport Beach	9143	R&S
	Silver; low mileage.											
1999	Z3M coupé		B56667	L	20-30.000 EUR	32.707	41.709	37.320	10-06-17	Lyon	145	Agu
	Silver with blue and black leather interior; engine replaced in 2012 with a used unit.											
2001	Z8		60424	L	175-200.000 USD	127.959	170.000	151.878	03-09-16	Auburn	4149	AA
	Silver with black interior; 11,000 miles on the odometer. With hardtop.											
2002	Z8		61795	L	200-225.000 USD	144.090	180.000	162.252	04-11-16	Dallas	S198	Mec
	Silver with black leather interior; 13,894 miles covered. With hardtop.											
2001	Z8		60797	L	150-180.000 GBP		NS		04-12-16	London	7	Bon
	Grey with black interior; sold new to the USA, reimported into Europe in the late 2000s, bought in 2015 by the current, fourth owner (see Silverstone Auctions lots 141 28.3.15 $184,078 and 319 20.5.16 NS).											
2002	Z8		61805	L	200-240.000 USD	138.855*	170.500*	160.355*	20-01-17	Scottsdale	33	G&Co
	Black with cream and black leather interior; sold new to the USA. 14,400 miles covered. Recently serviced.											
2000	Z8		60163	L	NQ	170.210*	209.000*	196.565*	21-01-17	Scottsdale	1370	B/J
	Titanium grey with black leather interior; 18,936 original miles.											
2000	Z8		77652	L	160-200.000 EUR	170.171	212.070	199.520	10-02-17	Paris	116	Art
	Titanium grey with red and black leather interior; three owners and 83,000 kms on the odometer. In good overall condition.											
2002	Z8		61540	L	180-220.000 USD	149.302*	181.500*	171.046*	10-03-17	Amelia Island	38	G&Co
	Titanium grey with black leather interior; two owners. Low mileage.											
2001	Z8		60892	L	150-200.000 USD	190.021*	231.000*	217.694*	10-03-17	Amelia Island	105	RMS F139
	Red with cream leather interior; 3,798 actual miles. From the Orin Smith collection.											
2001	Z8		60489	L	180-250.000 USD	153.846	198.000	168.696	18-08-17	Carmel	3	Bon
	Metallic topaz blue with black interior; sold new to the USA; 15,300 original miles.											
2003	Z8		62120	L	225-275.000 USD	341.880*	440.000*	374.880*	19-08-17	Pebble Beach	164	G&Co
	Black with black leather interior; sold new to the USA; 61 miles covered.											
2001	Z8		60405	L	250-275.000 USD	139.860	180.000	153.360	19-08-17	Monterey	F135	Mec
	Titanium grey with black leather interior; one owner; 5,640 miles covered.											
2011	M3 GTS		686128	L	195-215.000 EUR	154.062	191.880	180.000	08-04-17	Essen	136	Coy
	Orange with black cloth interior; one owner; less than 5,000 kms covered. Example no.118 out of the 150 cars built.											
2011	M3 GTS		686128	L	180-210.000 EUR	189.245	248.777	209.620	05-08-17	Schloss Dyck	238	Coy
	See lot 136 Coys 8.4.17.											

BOCAR (USA)

Year	Model	Chassis no.	Steering	Estimate	£	$	€	Date	Place	Lot	Auc. H.
1959	XP-5	XP5043	L	175-225.000 USD	131.205*	159.500*	150.313*	11-03-17	Amelia Island	267	RMS F140
	Red; raced at several historic events for 20 years. In ready to use condition. Modified Triumph chassis, 327 Chevrolet V8 engine, T-10 4-speed gearbox, front disc and rear drum brakes.										

BOND (GB) (1948-1974)

Year	Model	Chassis no.	Steering	Estimate	£	$	€	Date	Place	Lot	Auc. H.
1959	Mark F	NQ	R	5-8.000 EUR	4.796	5.990	5.400	06-11-16	Lyon	311	Ose
	Green with beige hardtop; 250cc Villiers engine.										

BORGWARD (D) (1939-1961)

Year	Model	Chassis no.	Steering	Estimate	£	$	€	Date	Place	Lot	Auc. H.
1959	Isabella coupé	348490	L	35-45.000 USD	20.870	27.500	24.494	17-09-16	Aspen	148	TFA
	White with white and red interior; fully restored a few years ago. Engine replaced in 2015 with a rebuilt unit.										
1960	Isabella coupé	369438	L	24-36.000 EUR	30.293	38.547	34.500	24-06-17	Wien	331	Dor
	The car was rediscovered about two years ago by the current owner in the Arizona desert and reimported into Austria. Chassis, mechanicals and interior restored; body in original condition.										

F139: 2001 BMW Z8

F140: 1959 Bocar XP-5

Year	Model	(Bodybuilder)	Chassis No.	Steering	Estimate	£	$	€	Date	Place	Lot	Auc. H.

BRASIER (F) (1903-1930)

Year	Model	(Bodybuilder)	Chassis No.	Steering	Estimate	£	$	€	Date	Place	Lot	Auc. H.
1906	15hp side-entrance tonneau	(Védrine)	140	R	40-60.000 GBP	59.740	79.353	70.899	03-09-16	Beaulieu	451	Bon F141

Imported into the UK from the USA in the 1980s and subsequently restored.

| 1914 | 9hp coach | | 258 | R | 20-30.000 EUR | 13.932* | 16.925* | 15.496* | 30-10-16 | Paris | 133 | Art |

Blue; older restoration.

BREGUET (F)

| 1942 | Type A2 Electrique | | 94 | L | 40-60.000 EUR | 35.583* | 44.344* | 41.720* | 10-02-17 | Paris | 20 | Art |

Blue; Paris-Rhone engine powered by six 12-volt batteries. Offered from a descendant of the manufacturer Louis Breguet. Body repainted; last used in the 1990s.

BRISTOL (GB) (1947-)

Year	Model	(Bodybuilder)	Chassis No.	Steering	Estimate	£	$	€	Date	Place	Lot	Auc. H.
1950	400 coupé		4001627	R	30-40.000 GBP	40.320	50.134	47.332	26-11-16	Weybridge	204	His
1949	400 coupé		4001637	R	75-95.000 AUD		NS		27-11-16	Melbourne	43	Mos

Silver with red leather interior; bought in 2002 by the current owner and subsequently fully restored. In the 1970s the engine was fitted with three Solex carburettors.

| 1952 | 401 coupé | (Touring) | 4011094 | R | 40-50.000 GBP | 38.080 | 48.015 | 44.748 | 07-12-16 | Chateau Impney | 37 | H&H |

Grey with dark blue interior; body repainted and mechanicals overhauled.

| 1953 | 403 coupé | | 4031385 | R | 50-70.000 GBP | 56.350 | 71.131 | 66.837 | 04-12-16 | London | 1 | Bon F142 |

Black with red leather interior; fully restored in the mid-1980s, the car is described as still in good overall condition.

| 1962 | 407 | | 4076040 | R | 33-38.000 GBP | 30.240 | 38.130 | 35.535 | 07-12-16 | Chateau Impney | 22 | H&H |

Red with beige interior; engine replaced in 2008 with "new old stock" unit.

| 1985 | Beaufighter convertible | | 4125307857180 | R | 10-13.000 GBP | 7.224 | 9.650 | 8.542 | 08-09-16 | Fontwell Park | 110 | Coy |

Red; in need of some cosmetical attention (see lot 9 Coys 25.2.97 $12,497).

| 1987 | Brigand | | 603S308525086 | R | 50-60.000 GBP | | NS | | 12-11-16 | Birmingham | 329 | SiC |

Body repainted in black pearl in recent years; engine replaced in late 2010; gearbox rebuilt.

| 1983 | Britannia sports saloon | | 603S308507032 | R | 16-18.000 GBP | 17.825 | 23.677 | 21.155 | 03-09-16 | Beaulieu | 488 | Bon |

Brown with brown leather interior; in good driving order.

| 2002 | Blenheim Series 3 sports saloon | | TTBL300471110 | R | 25-30.000 GBP | 26.450 | 35.134 | 31.391 | 03-09-16 | Beaulieu | 457 | Bon |

Blue; since 2010 in the current, second ownership. 86,489 miles covered. Automatic transmission.

BRITISH SALMSON (GB) (1934-1939)

| 1938 | 20/29 roadster | | 110 | R | 130-180.000 EUR | 116.279 | 154.463 | 138.000 | 03-09-16 | Chantilly | 18 | Bon F143 |

Black with black interior; one of six examples known to survive of 12 built, the car remained in the factory ownership until 1947. Fully restored at unspecified date.

BRITON (GB) (1909-1928)

| 1909 | Little | | HH47 | R | 16-20.000 GBP | | NS | | 03-09-16 | Beaulieu | 420 | Bon |

Dark blue with black interior; stored for 40 years, the car was recommissioned in 2015. One of five twin-cylinder examples known to survive.

BROUGH SUPERIOR (GB) (1935-1940)

| 1935 | 4-litre dual purpose cabriolet | | 546069 | R | 12-1.800 GBP | 6.900* | 9.165* | 8.189* | 03-09-16 | Beaulieu | 507 | Bon |

Restoration project; the chassis is rotten and will need to be replaced.

BSA (GB) (1907-1939)

| 1935 | Scout roadster | | 15406 | R | 10-14.000 GBP | 12.320 | 15.099 | 13.702 | 12-10-16 | Duxford | 8 | H&H |

White with red wings and red interior; restoration completed in 2005.

F141: 1906 Brasier 15hp side-entrance tonneau (Védrine)

F142: 1953 Bristol 403 coupé

F143: 1938 British Salmson 20/29 roadster

F144: 1923 Bugatti Type 27 "Brescia" torpedo

BUGATTI (F) *(1909-1956)*

Year	Model (Bodybuilder)	Chassis no.	Steering	Estimate	£	$	€	Date	Place	Lot	Auc. H.
1923	Type 23 Brescia Modifié torpedo (Lavocat/Marsaud)	1709	R	550-650.000 GBP	NS			30-06-17	Goodwood	249	Bon

Dark blue with dark red interior; sold new in France, the car had several owners until the early 1930s when it was bought by Marcel Apied in whose family it remained until 1970. Restored in the 1980s and in the 1990s again, in 2009 it was bought by the current Italian owner and restored to concours condition between 2009 and 2010. Matching chassis, engine and body.

| 1923 | Type 27 "Brescia" torpedo | 1693 | R | 380-540.000 EUR | 430.555 | 541.015 | 506.000 | 09-02-17 | Paris | 333 | Bon |

Blue with black wings; body by Lavocat et Marsaud probably. Ownership chain known since new; stored from 1934 to 1959 when it was returned to the road; mechanicals restored by Laurent Rondoni in the 2000s. In 2014 the car won the Preservation Class at the Schloss Bensberg Concours d'Elegance. **F144**

| 1925 | Type 35 | 4487 | R | 2.600-3.200.000 USD | 2.687.520 | 3.300.000 | 3.103.650 | 20-01-17 | Scottsdale | 22 | G&Co |

Bought new by Wallis C. Bird and imported into the USA, the car was raced just one time at the Roosevelt Raceway in 1937. In 1962 it was acquired by its second owner Henry Austin Clark Jr. who had it recommissioned and resold it in 1981 to the current, third owner. Subjected to a restoration completed between 2003 and 2004, the car was used at some historic events until 2007. Original chassis, engine and body, finished in France blue. **F145**

| 1925 | Type 35C | 4572 | R | 1.100-1.300.000 USD | 897.435 | 1.155.000 | 984.060 | 19-08-17 | Monterey | 243 | RMS |

Believed to be one of at least four GP Bugattis driven out of the factory under the same chassis number for tax reasons, all of which were owned and raced by Elizabeth Junek. Discovered in the USA, in 1959 it was bought by J.B. Nethercutt who subsequently sold it to "Bunny" Phillips who in the late 1960s fitted it with the present new body. From 1972 to 2011 it was owned by Richard Riddell who raced it at numerous historic events. In a letter on file, historian David Sewell noted that all of the car's major components are authentic period Type 35 and 35C pieces and that the chassis plate is a Bugatti Owners Club replacement issued by Hugh Conway in 1985.

| 1926 | Type 37 | 37140 | R | 400-600.000 GBP | NA | | | 15-07-17 | Blenheim Pal. | 158 | Coy |

Blue with black interior; restored between 2002 and 2008. Engine rebuilt on a new block (the original unit is included with the sale). Sold new to the UK, the car was raced in period. In the 1930s it received several mechanical modifications including the fitting of a supercharger, AMAC motorcycle carburettors and telescopic shock absorbers. In single ownership from 1940 to 1997 when it was bought by the present vendor.

| 1930 | Type 40 Spéciale | 37700 | R | 250-300.000 EUR | 246.484 | 299.438 | 274.160 | 30-10-16 | Paris | 134 | Art |

Light blue; car built using original Bugatti parts and known in this form since 1962. Restored.

| 1928 | Type 40 roadster | 40657 | R | 200-300.000 EUR | 291.346 | 372.290 | 348.000 | 01-05-17 | Obenheim | 305 | Ose |

Blue; originally built with Gangloff berline body, the car was fitted with the present new body in 1957. Described as in good driving order.

| 1930 | Type 44 berline (Alin/Liautard) | 441177 | R | 180-230.000 EUR | 252.124 | 321.610 | 288.000 | 18-06-17 | Fontainebleau | 60 | Ose |

Black and blue; probably restored in the 1970s. Since 1974 in the Jacques Liscourt collection.

| 1929 | Type 44 berline (Vanvooren) | 44667 | R | 200-240.000 GBP | 196.875 | 256.780 | 220.520 | 26-07-17 | Duxford | 89 | H&H |

Red and black with fawn interior; bought in 1990 by the current owner, the car was restored between 1990 and 1994 and fitted with the present engine, coming from chassis 441192, and body, previously fitted to chassis 44694. **F146**

| 1928 | Type 52 Baby | 245A | M | 65-75.000 USD | 71.667* | 88.000* | 82.764* | 20-01-17 | Scottsdale | 23 | G&Co |

Long-wheelbase version; since 1973 in the current ownership. Not operated in decades, remaining in static display. Restored many years ago and recently detailed.

| 1930 | Type 52 Baby | 388A | M | 30-50.000 EUR | 77.170 | 96.171 | 90.480 | 10-02-17 | Paris | 25 | Art |

From the early 1990s in the Hervé and Martine Ogliastro Collection.

| 1927 | Type 52 Baby | 188 | C | 50-70.000 EUR | 72.669 | 92.859 | 86.800 | 01-05-17 | Obenheim | 10 | Ose |

Blue; in very good condition; for many years in the same family ownership.

F145: 1925 Bugatti Type 35

F146: 1929 Bugatti Type 44 berline (Vanvooren)

BRUNO VENDIESSE

LILLE - FRANCE
TÈL +33 687 75 69 60
BRUNO.VENDIESSE@WANADOO.FR

Year	Model	(Bodybuilder)	Chassis no.	Steering	Estimate	Hammer price £	$	€	Date	Place	Lot	Auc. H.
1930	Type 46 sportsman's coupé		46219	R	160-200.000 GBP	281.500	365.331	318.742	30-06-17	Goodwood	244	Bon F147

Weyman patents body finished in black and yellow with beige interior; in good overall condition. For 42 years in the same family ownership.

| 1932 | Type 49 roadster | | 49369 | R | 550-700.000 USD | | NS | | 17-09-16 | Aspen | 140 | TFA |

Black with red leather interior; built with a Gangloff "conduit interieur" body, the car was fitted after 1955 with a 1930s Marsaud two-door body. Imported into the USA, in 1973 it was bought by William Serri and in 1980 by the current owner, Gene Cesari. Subjected to a long restoration completed in 2014, it is currently fitted with a new 1930s Murphy style roadster body. Also the original driveshaft was replaced with a more modern unit. The Marsaud body and the original driveshaft are included with the sale.

| 1932 | Type 49 roadster (Labourdette) | | 49534 | R | 650-850.000 USD | 526.249 | 676.500 | 603.100 | 04-06-17 | Greenwich | 178 | Bon F148 |

Believed to be an one-off, the car was sold new in France. In 1983 it was imported into the USA and in 1995 it was bought by the current owner who commissioned a full restoration completed in 2016. Currently finished in red with black fenders.

| 1937 | Type 57 berline (Graber) | | 57443 | R | 500-600.000 USD | | NS | | 19-01-17 | Scottsdale | 33 | Bon |

Red and white with tan interior; sold new to Switzerland, in 1960 circa the car was imported into the Netherlands where it was fitted with the present, correct engine renumbered with the car's chassis number. In the same ownership from 1962 to 2008; in the mid-1980s brakes converted to hydraulic system and engine rebuilt; body repainted in recent years (see lot 34 H & H 8.6.08 $279,822).

| 1939 | Type 57 cabriolet (Letourneur/Marchand) | | 57587 | R | 1.250-1.500.000 USD | 825.498 | 1.017.500 | 953.703 | 19-01-17 | Phoenix | 134 | RMS F149 |

Black and red; sold new in France and retained by its first owner until 1956; imported into the USA in 1957; restored to concours condition in the early 2000s; interior recently re-upholstered (see lot 62 Gooding & Company 21.8.05 NS).

| 1934 | Type 57 coach (Gangloff) | | 57106 | R | 430-530.000 EUR | | NS | | 10-02-17 | Paris | 40 | Art |

Black and red; the car spent all its life in France and has had several owners. In the early 2000s it was restored by Lecoq and in 2004 it was bought by the current owner.

| 1937 | Type 57S cabriolet (Vanvooren) | | 57513 | R | 8.500-1.000.000 USD | 6.334.020 | 7.700.000 | 7.256.480 | 11-03-17 | Amelia Island | 232 | RMS TOP TEN |

Black and yellow with beige interior; one of four cabriolets bodied by Vanvooren and one of three known to survive, the car was acquired by the current, sixth owner in 1995 and imported into the USA. Original chassis, body, engine and gearbox. In recent years the car remained in static display. The clutch has been rebuilt in 2016. The car requires a more comprehensive overhaul before an extensive use.

| 1937 | Type 57 cabriolet | | 57156 | R | 1.200-1.500.000 USD | 444.444 | 572.000 | 487.344 | 18-08-17 | Monterey | 123 | RMS |

Sold new to Belgium with Galibier body, the car was later taken back by the factory and sold again in 1936 with a new chassis of the same number and a new engine (no.280). The present body was probably built by d'Ieteren or Paul Nee. Imported into the USA in 1955, the car remained in the same family ownership from 1958 to the 2000s. Restored in recent years; redesigned fenders; two-tone body.

| 1939 | Type 57C cabriolet (Letourneur/Marchand) | | 57841 | R | 1.500-2.000.000 USD | 1.175.213 | 1.512.500 | 1.288.650 | 19-08-17 | Pebble Beach | 143 | G&Co F150 |

Sold by the factory in 1941 in rolling chassis form, the car was fitted in the 1950s with the present body previously on chassis 57645. In 1957 it was bought by D. Glockner who later imported it into the USA. Since 1986 in the current ownership. Little used in recent years.

| 1935 | Type 57 Atalante | | 57330 | R | 1.000-1.500.000 EUR | 1.988.280 | 2.477.832 | 2.331.200 | 10-02-17 | Paris | 27 | Art |

Brown and cream with brown leather interior; the car was displayed at the 1935 Paris Motor Show and subsequently sold in France where it remained for all its life. Following several ownership changes, in 1986 it was bought by Hervé Ogliastro who had it fully restored to its original colours by André Lecoq. Currently fitted with engine no.548. From the Hervé and Martine Ogliastro Collection.

| 1935 | Type 57 Atalante | | 57254 | R | 2.800-3.200.000 EUR | 2.636.626 | 3.385.670 | 3.024.000 | 27-05-17 | Villa Erba | 136 | RMS F151 |

(see lots G.Gersaint NQ 12.6.98 $333,209 and Christie's 58 29.8.99 NS).

| 1939 | Type 57C Stelvio (Gangloff) | | 57836 | R | 500-700.000 EUR | 1.110.921 | 1.417.092 | 1.269.000 | 18-06-17 | Fontainebleau | 64 | Ose F152 |

Ivory with original brown leather interior; bought in 1977 by the current owner and subsequently restored.

BUGATTI (F) (1998-)

| 2008 | Veyron 16.4 | | 795164 | L | 1.000-1.200.000 USD | | NS | | 19-08-17 | Monterey | S72 | Mec |

White and blue; last serviced in December 2016.

| 2011 | Veyron 16.4 Grand Sport | | 795088 | L | NQ | | NS | | 21-01-17 | Scottsdale | 1372.1 | B/J |

Pearl white with white and red interior; 1,668 miles covered.

| 2012 | Veyron 16.4 Grand Sport | | 795051 | L | 1.500-1.800.000 USD | 1.357.290 | 1.650.000 | 1.554.960 | 11-03-17 | Amelia Island | 276 | RMS |

Black and red with tan interior; sold new to the USA. 538 miles covered.

| 2009 | Veyron 16.4 Grand Sport | | 795040 | L | 1.400-1.600.000 EUR | | NS | | 02-07-17 | Monaco | 124 | Art |

Red and black with red interior; used by the factory until 2014 and serviced in 2010, 2012, 2013 and 2014. 33,764 kms covered. Recently serviced.

| 2015 | Veyron 16.4 Grand Sport Vitesse | | 795080 | L | 2.700-3.000.000 USD | 1.825.950 | 2.350.000 | 2.002.200 | 19-08-17 | Monterey | S116 | Mec |

Black with black and orange leather interior.

| 2013 | Veyron 16.4 Super Sport 300 | | 795300 | L | 2.100-2.300.000 USD | 1.702.096 | 2.090.000 | 1.965.645 | 20-01-17 | Phoenix | 228 | RMS F153 |

White; less than 400 miles covered. Last serviced in May 2016. Exhibited at the Bugatti stand at the 2015 Geneva Motor Show in a celebration of the Veyron's 10-year production run (see lot 112 RM/Sotheby's 13.8.15 $2,310,000).

BUGATTI AUTOMOBILI (I) (1987-1996)

| 1994 | EB110 | | 39068 | L | 275-325.000 EUR | 524.721* | 652.467* | 616.000* | 25-11-16 | Milan | 588 | RMS F154 |

Blue with grey interior; 31,047 kms. From the Duemila Ruote collection.

| 1995 | EB110 | | 39093 | L | 750-850.000 USD | | NS | | 18-01-17 | Scottsdale | 12 | WoA |

Blue; recently imported into the USA from Belgium. One owner and 14,600 kms covered. Recently serviced (see lot 29 Poulain/Sotheby's 25.5.01 NS).

| 1993 | EB110 | | 39034 | L | 500-700.000 USD | 470.630 | 605.000 | 539.358 | 04-06-17 | Greenwich | 181 | Bon |

Blue with grey leather interior; sold new to the UK and later imported into the USA (see lot 1971 Brooks 4.12.00 $164,022).

BUICK (USA) (1903-)

| 1922 | Series 40 Model 22-45 touring | | 786958 | L | 25-30.000 USD | 19.543* | 24.750* | 22.127* | 06-10-16 | Hershey | 112 | RMS |

Two-tone brown with tan vinyl interior; restored some years ago.

| 1923 | Series 30 sport roadster | | 1017868 | L | NQ | 27.323* | 33.550* | 31.554* | 21-01-17 | Scottsdale | 8183 | R&S |

In good driving order; from the Missoula Auto Museum Collection.

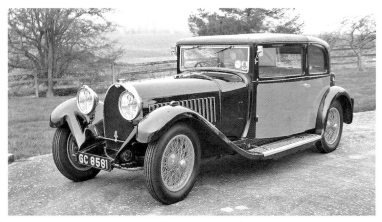
F147: 1930 Bugatti Type 46 sportsman's coupé

F148: 1932 Bugatti Type 49 roadster (Labourdette)

F149: 1939 Bugatti Type 57 cabriolet (Letourneur/Marchand)

F150: 1939 Bugatti Type 57C cabriolet (Letourneur/Marchand)

F151: 1935 Bugatti Type 57 Atalante

F152: 1939 Bugatti Type 57C Stelvio (Gangloff)

F153: 2013 Bugatti Veyron 16.4 Super Sport 300

F154: 1994 Bugatti Automobili EB110

Year	Model	(Bodybuilder)	Chassis No.	Steering	Estimate	Hammer Price £	$	€	Date	Place	Lot	Auc. H.
1927	**Series 128 Master roadster**		1682253	L	40-50.000 USD	30.377*	39.050*	34.813*	04-06-17	Greenwich	117	**Bon**
	Yellow with black fenders and burgundy leather interior; in good overall condition.											
1929	**Series 121 Master coupé**		152377	L	20-25.000 USD	8.557*	11.000*	9.807*	04-06-17	Greenwich	131	**Bon**
	Red with black roof and fenders; an older restoration.											
1930	**Series 60 roadster**		2598695	L	65-75.000 USD	52.576	69.850	62.404	03-09-16	Auburn	4063	**AA**
	Dark green and yellow cream with maroon interior; older restoration.											
1930	**Series 60 roadster**		2598695	L	NQ	44.792*	55.000*	51.728*	21-01-17	Scottsdale	1275.1	**B/J**
	See lot 4063 Auctions America 3.9.16.											
1935	**Series 60 sedan**		54689079	L	50-60.000 USD	27.655*	34.100*	30.608*	07-10-16	Hershey	261	**RMS**
	Dark blue with brown cloth interior; 4,500 miles covered since the restoration.											
1939	**Special series 40 sedan**		35970	L	8-12.000 EUR	19.776*	24.383*	21.888*	07-10-16	Chateau-sur-Epte	21	**Art**
	Grey; in good overall condition. From the Andre Weber Collection.											
1939	**Special series 40 convertible**		13569650	L	NA	33.260*	40.700*	36.992*	15-10-16	Las Vegas	402	**B/J**
	Sequoia cream with tan interior; restored between 1984 and 1994.											
1937	**Special series 40 sedan**	(Fisher)	3113161	L	19-27.000 EUR	16.661	21.201	18.975	24-06-17	Wien	343	**Dor**
	Black with brown cloth interior; body repainted many years ago, original interior.											
1939	**Special series 40 sedan**		13566422	L	21-27.000 GBP	22.960	29.609	25.945	08-07-17	Brooklands	130	**His**
	Fully restored.											
1941	**Super series 50 convertible**		14215399	L	85-100.000 USD	65.688	80.000	75.032	15-01-17	Kissimmee	S141	**Mec**
	Cream with red interior; fully restored.											
1941	**Super series 50 convertible**		54160263	L	75-100.000 USD	48.951	63.000	53.676	19-08-17	Monterey	S87	**Mec**
	Cream with red leather interior; restored in 2004. Engine rebuilt.											
1940	**Roadmaster series 70 sport phaeton**		74017319	L	80-100.000 USD		NS		03-09-16	Auburn	2119	**AA**
	Grey with red interior; described as in excellent overall condition.											
1941	**Special series 40B sedanet**		34187515	L	40-50.000 USD	24.087*	29.700*	26.659*	07-10-16	Hershey	255	**RMS**
	Dark maroon with tan cloth interior; recently serviced.											
1942	**Special series 40B estate wagon**		14364415	L	225-275.000 USD	117.632*	143.000*	134.763*	10-03-17	Amelia Island	51	**G&Co**
	Green with wooden panels and dark green leather interior; concours-quality restoration completed in 2001.											
1948	**Super series 50 convertible**		34947096	L	NA	38.034*	48.950*	41.705*	19-08-17	Monterey	1053	**R&S**
	Green with cloth and leather interior; in good overall condition. From the Art Astor Collection.											
1948	**Roadmaster series 70 sedanet**		14862969	L	40-50.000 USD	33.008*	40.700*	36.532*	07-10-16	Hershey	217	**RMS**
	Two-tone body, cloth interior. Older restoration; recent service.											
1946	**Roadmaster series 70 sedanet**		46814467	L	40-50.000 USD	44.605*	55.000*	49.368*	07-10-16	Hershey	241	**RMS** **F155**
	Black with grey cloth interior; described as in largely original condition, 4,734 miles on the odometer (see lot 731 RM 26.3.10 $44,000).											
1948	**Roadmaster series 70 convertible**		24936085	L	70-80.000 USD	31.080	40.000	34.080	19-08-17	Monterey	F47	**Mec**
	Green with black interior; restored in 1982; automatic transmission.											
1953	**Super series 50 Riviera 2-door hardtop**		26771819	L	NA	24.271*	29.700*	26.994*	15-10-16	Las Vegas	163	**B/J**
	Red with black roof and red and black interior; restored. Automatic transmission.											
1950	**Super series 50 convertible**		15878249	L	NQ	45.926*	57.200*	53.654*	08-04-17	Palm Beach	760	**B/J**
	Dark grey with red leather interior; in good overall condition. Automatic transmission.											
1949	**Super series 50 convertible**	(Fisher)	15344685	L	70-95.000 USD	43.512	56.000	47.712	19-08-17	Monterey	F42	**Mec**
	Black with red leather interior; restored; automatic transmission.											
1956	**Special series 40 convertible**		4C3055286	L	NQ		NS		03-12-16	Kansas City	F122	**Mec**
	Burgundy and cream with burgundy interior; 1,000 miles covered since the restoration. Automatic transmission.											
1953	**Roadmaster Skylark convertible**		16833256	L	150-175.000 USD	89.007	118.250	105.645	03-09-16	Auburn	4103	**AA**
	Red with red and white interior; restored.											
1953	**Roadmaster Skylark convertible**		16913888	L	NA	130.343*	159.500*	144.970*	15-10-16	Las Vegas	693	**B/J**
	Red with white interior; fully restored many years ago (see RM lots 224 8.3.08 $124,300 and NR41 6.2.09 $121,000).											

F155: 1946 Buick Roadmaster series 70 sedanet

F156: 1954 Buick Skylark Sport convertible

Year	Model (Bodybuilder)	Chassis no.	Steering	Estimate	Hammer price £	Hammer price $	Hammer price €	Date	Place	Lot	Auc. H.
1953	**Roadmaster Skylark convertible**	17144095	L	175-225.000 USD	107.474	132.000	123.776	18-01-17	Scottsdale	7	WoA
Blue with two-tone leather interior; restored at unspecified date (see lot 4131 Auctions America 8.5.14 NS).											
1953	**Roadmaster Skylark convertible**	17144095	L	NQ	108.048	137.500	123.063	24-06-17	Northeast	683	B/J
See lot 7 Worldwide Auctioneers 18.1.17.											
1953	**Roadmaster Skylark convertible**	17057172	L	125-150.000 USD	89.744*	115.500*	98.406*	18-08-17	Carmel	62	Bon
Red with red and white interior; restored to concours condition at unspecified date.											
1954	**Skylark Sport convertible**	A1049473	L	130-150.000 USD	105.566	140.250	125.299	03-09-16	Auburn	5141	AA F156
White with red leather interior; fully restored.											
1958	**Limited series 700 convertible**	8E4012620	L	80-100.000 USD	73.598	90.750	81.457	07-10-16	Hershey	243	RMS
Blue with blue and white leather interior; restored some years ago (see lot 144 RM/Sotheby's 25.7.15 $71,500).											
1959	**Le Sabre hardtop**	4F1063589	L	NA	17.529*	21.450*	19.496*	15-10-16	Las Vegas	50.3	B/J
Black and silver with original multicolour interior; 44,000 original miles.											
1959	**Le Sabre convertible**	4F5006982	L	NQ	44.792*	55.000*	51.728*	21-01-17	Scottsdale	804	B/J
Pace Car tribute finished in white with red interior; in very good original condition. 33,007 original miles (see lots S732 Russo & Steele 20.1.12 $77,000 and 7001 Barrett-Jackson 17.1.15 $93,500).											
1960	**Le Sabre convertible**	4G3015967	L	NQ	51.507	64.000	60.090	18-02-17	Los Angeles	S83	Mec
Silver with grey and red interior; 364 engine with automatic transmission.											
1963	**Special Skylark convertible**	3J1570911	L	NQ	11.481*	14.300*	13.413*	08-04-17	Palm Beach	608.1	B/J
Blue; 46,000 original miles. Automatic transmission.											
1971	**Riviera GS hardtop**	494871H910923	L	NQ	32.192	40.000	37.556	18-02-17	Los Angeles	F128.1	Mec
White with black vinyl top and black interior; 455 engine with automatic transmission.											
1965	**Riviera Gran Sport**	494475H921426	L	30-50.000 USD	37.036*	45.100*	42.741*	09-03-17	Amelia Island	110	Bon
White with saddle leather interior; body repainted and engine rebuilt at unspecified date.											
1966	**Skylark Gran Sport convertible**	446676H162515	L	NQ		NS		21-01-17	Scottsdale	8491	R&S
Red with black interior; 325bhp 400 engine with manual gearbox (see lot 1238 Barrett-Jackson 19.1.07 $ 84,700).											
1970	**Gran Sport GS 455 convertible**	446670H292998	L	NQ	76.146*	93.500*	87.937*	21-01-17	Scottsdale	1293	B/J
Blue with white interior; 455 Stage 1 engine with automatic transmission (see lot S119 Mecum 16.4.16 NS).											
1970	**Gran Sport GS 455 coupé**	446370H193675	L	NQ	120.938*	148.500*	139.664*	21-01-17	Scottsdale	1306	B/J
White with black interior; restored. Two owners. 455 Stage 1 engine with manual gearbox.											
1970	**Gran Sport GS 455 convertible**	446670H217559	L	175-200.000 USD	130.628	170.000	152.065	20-05-17	Indianapolis	S116	Mec F157
Red with white interior; fully restored. 360 bhp 455 Stage1 engine with manual gearbox.											
1970	**GSX hardtop**	446370H255253	L	150-175.000 USD	115.260	150.000	134.175	20-05-17	Indianapolis	S109	Mec
Yellow with black stripes and black interior; two times GSCA Nationals winner. 455 Stage 1 engine with dealer-installed Stage II package; automatic transmission (see lot S36 Mecum 9.7.16 $115,000).											
1987	**GNX**	1G4GJ1171HP453619	L	175-250.000 USD	180.642	220.000	206.338	15-01-17	Kissimmee	F155	Mec
Black with grey interior; no. 547 of 547 examples built. Two owners and 68 original miles. From the Colts Neck Collection.											

CADILLAC (USA) *(1903-)*

Year	Model (Bodybuilder)	Chassis no.	Steering	Estimate	£	$	€	Date	Place	Lot	Auc. H.
1912	**Model 30 touring**	39039	R	90-110.000 USD	71.368	88.000	78.989	07-10-16	Hershey	244	RMS F158
Dark green with black fenders; in good overall condition.											
1909	**Model 30 demi-tonneau**	17108	R	90-120.000 USD	61.695	75.000	70.680	11-03-17	Amelia Island	42	Mot
Dark green with black leather interior and ivory wooden wheels; the car remained with its first owner for a number of years and for 75 years with the second owner. Restored several decades ago; recent mechanical freshening.											
1912	**Model 30 touring**	46462	R	NQ	28.405*	36.300*	33.930*	22-04-17	Arlington	13	WoA
Described as in original condition, the car has had two owners since 1935. Mechanicals to be rebuilt. From the Monical collection (see lot 211 Worldwide Group 30.4.10 $46,200).											
1910	**Model 30 touring**	45042(engine)	R	100-130.000 USD	81.197*	104.500*	89.034*	18-08-17	Carmel	97	Bon
Dark red with dark red leather interior; restoration completed in 2011.											
1926	**Series 314 phaeton (Fisher)**	122354	L	100-125.000 USD		NS		03-09-16	Auburn	7039	AA
Two-tone green with tan interior; restored.											

F157: 1970 Buick Gran Sport GS 455 convertible

F158: 1912 Cadillac Model 30 touring

Year	Model	(Bodybuilder)	Chassis no.	Steering	Estimate	Hammer price £	Hammer price $	Hammer price €	Date	Place	Lot	Auc. H.
1929	Series 341B roadster	(Fisher)	335195	L	135-155.000 USD	92.677	115.500	108.662	11-02-17	Boca Raton	145	TFA
	Grey and pale green with ligth tan leather interior; an older restoration, the car is described as in excellent mechanical condition.											
1929	Series 341B roadster	(Fleetwood)	416235	L	NA	49.270	62.700	56.117	24-06-17	Santa Monica	225	RMS
	Silver and burgundy with burgundy interior; cosmetically restored.											
1932	Series 452 V-16 sedan	(Fleetwood)	1400238(engine)	L	170-210.000 USD	173.712	220.000	196.680	06-10-16	Hershey	151	RMS
	Dark maroon with grey cloth interior; fully restored between 2007 and 2014.											
1930	Series 452 V-16 roadster	(Fleetwood)	702604(engine)	L	1.000-1.250.000 USD	895.840	1.100.000	1.034.550	20-01-17	Phoenix	230	RMS F159
	Grey and blue; full concours-quality restoration carried out between 1997 and 1999.											
1931	Series 452 V-16 convertible victoria	(Lancefield)	702873	R	600-900.000 EUR		NS		10-02-17	Paris	51	Art
	Black and green with light brown interior; only example of the model bodied by Lancefield in the UK, the car remained in the same family ownership until the 1990s when it was imported into the USA where it was later restored.											
1930	Series 452 V-16 convertible	(Fleetwood)	700898(engine)	L	300-350.000 USD	303.128	368.500	347.274	11-03-17	Amelia Island	216	RMS
	Red and maroon with black leather interior; restored many years ago, the car is described as still in very good overall condition.											
1930	Series 452 V-16 club sedan	(Fleetwood)	700537(engine)	L	175-225.000 USD	156.239	195.250	182.617	01-04-17	Ft.Lauderdale	553	AA F160
	Maroon and black with beige interior; in concours condition.											
1930	Series 452 V-16 roadster	(Fleetwood)	701070(engine)	L	450-550.000 USD	626.676	797.500	713.763	24-06-17	Santa Monica	187	RMS
	Dark green and black with brown leather interior; first restored in the 1960s when the car was fitted with the present engine. In 1972 it was bought by William Gannet who retained it for over 30 years and had it restored again.											
1930	Series 452 V-16 coupé	(Fleetwood)	702089(engine)	L	350-450.000 USD	139.860*	180.000*	153.360*	19-08-17	Monterey	S104	Mec
	Burgundy and red with red leather interior; restored.											
1930	Series 353 convertible	(Fisher)	509146	L	NQ	58.210*	72.500*	68.005*	08-04-17	Houston	S36.1	Mec
	Black with green leather interior. From the Laquay Automobile Collection.											
1930	Series 353 convertible		509146	L	100-130.000 USD	72.261	93.000	79.236	19-08-17	Monterey	S119	Mec
	See lot S36.1 Mecum 8.4.17.											
1931	Series 355 roadster	(Fleetwood)	809893	L	100-125.000 USD	115.916	154.000	137.584	03-09-16	Auburn	4164	AA
	Two-tone green with brown interior; restored.											
1931	Series 355 convertible	(Fleetwood)	809471	L	80-90.000 EUR		NA		08-10-16	Paris	148	CB/C
	Liveried in real 23 carat gold leaf with white leather interior, the car is believed to have been formerly owned by pianist Liberace. Recently serviced.											
1931	Series 355 convertible	(Fleetwood)	809471	L	40-50.000 GBP	46.600	56.745	53.227	14-01-17	Birmingham	121	Coy
	See lot 148 Coutau Bégarie/Coys 8.10.16.											
1935	Series 355D town sedan	(Fleetwood)	3105172(engine)	L	50-60.000 USD	22.622*	27.500*	25.916*	11-03-17	Amelia Island	235	RMS F161
	Black with grey cloth interior; in good driving order. Displayed at the 1935 Boston Motor Show (see lot 114 RM 9.3.13 $60,500).											
1931	Series 370 V-12 convertible	(Fleetwood)	1002411(engine)	L	200-250.000 USD	277.370	368.500	329.218	03-09-16	Auburn	4146	AA F162
	Two-tone crimson with tan leather interior; for 32 years since 1982 in the same ownership. Restored in the early 2000s (see lots 537 Bonhams 4.10.08 $105,300 and 140 RM 26.7.14 $220,000).											
1933	Series 370C V-12 sedan	(Fisher)	400043	L	60-80.000 USD		NS		05-11-16	Hilton Head	158	AA
	Two-tone green; in good running order. Body repainted many years ago.											
1931	Series 370A V-12 coupé	(Fisher)	1001141	L	NA		NS		03-06-17	Newport Beach	9124	R&S
	Winner of numerous awards at Concours d'Elegance events in 2012 and 2013 (see lot S106 Mecum 22.11.13 NS).											
1938	Series 90 V-16 convertible		5270045(engine)	L	NQ	98.542*	121.000*	113.801*	21-01-17	Scottsdale	1344	B/J
	Black with tan interior.											
1938	Series 90 V-16 convertible	(Fleetwood)	5270250(engine)	L	325-375.000 USD		NS		11-03-17	Amelia Island	220	RMS
	Red with brown leather interior; restored many years ago. Recently serviced (see lot 260 RM/Sotheby's 29.1.16 $325,000).											
1938	Series 90 V-16 convertible sedan	(Fleetwood)	3271143	L	NQ	25.693	32.000	30.016	08-04-17	Houston	F189	Mec
	Black with black interior; body repainted.											
1938	Series 90 V-16 Imperial sedan	(Fleetwood)	5270245	L	80-130.000 USD	64.103*	82.500*	70.290*	18-08-17	Carmel	27	Bon
	Dark blue with black leather interior to the front compartment and grey-blue cloth to the rear; restored in the mid-1980s. Since 1992 in the T.J. Day Collection.											
1938	Series 90 V-16 convertible		5270289(engine)	L	275-325.000 USD		NS		18-08-17	Carmel	86	Bon
	Cream with red interior; built with limousine body, the car was fitted in the 1980s with the present body coming from a Series 75 chassis.											
1937	Series 75 town sedan	(Fleetwood)	3130404	L	25-35.000 USD	16.258*	20.900*	18.632*	04-06-17	Greenwich	156	Bon
	Dark blue with tan cloth interior; restored many years ago; in good driving order.											

F159: 1930 Cadillac Series 452 V-16 roadster (Fleetwood)

F160: 1930 Cadillac Series 452 V-16 club sedan (Fleetwood)

F161: 1935 Cadillac Series 355D town sedan (Fleetwood)

F162: 1931 Cadillac Series 370 V-12 convertible (Fleetwood)

Year	Model (Bodybuilder)	Chassis no.	Steering	Estimate	£	$	€	Date	Place	Lot	Auc. H.
1939	Series 75 convertible sedan (Fleetwood)	29836	L	70-90.000 USD	49.573*	63.800*	54.358*	18-08-17	Carmel	14	Bon
	Green; bought in 2011 by the current owner and subsequently subjected to several restoration works. Engine rebuilt (see lot 92 Bonhams 28.1.16 NS).										
1941	Series 60 Special sedan (Fleetwood)	6340590(engine)	L	35-45.000 USD	40.145*	49.500*	44.431*	07-10-16	Hershey	249	RMS
	Two-tone grey with grey interior; in good overall condition.										
1940	Series 60 Special sedan	6320726	L	NA	36.495	45.000	40.392	08-10-16	Chicago	S159	Mec
	Dark red with grey roof; restored.										
1940	Series 60 Special sedan (Fleetwood)	6322178	L	NQ	19.234	24.000	22.210	25-03-17	Kansas City	S49	Mec
	Maroon with brown interior; tune-up September 2016										
1941	Series 62 sedan	8350452	L	12-15.000 EUR	14.283*	17.610*	15.808*	07-10-16	Chateau-sur-Epte	25	Art
	Red; imported into France from Canada in 1994 and then restored. From the Andre Weber Collection.										
1941	Series 62 coupé	8346440	L	18-24.000 EUR	30.214*	37.252*	33.440*	07-10-16	Chateau-sur-Epte	65	Art
	Blue; body and interior redone 20 years ago. From the Andre Weber Collection.										
1940	Series 62 convertible	8325106	L	NA	89.892*	110.000*	99.979*	15-10-16	Las Vegas	735	B/J F163
	Black with red interior; concours-quality restoration (see lot 300 Brooks 10.3.00 NS).										
1942	Series 62 convertible	8382552	L	100-120.000 USD	63.991	79.750	75.029	11-02-17	Boca Raton	144	TFA
	Dark green with green leather interior; restored at unspecified date. Automatic transmission recently overhauled.										
1952	62 convertible	526282784	L	44-48.000 GBP	56.000	68.634	62.283	12-10-16	Duxford	125	H&H
	White with red interior; restored. Imported from the USA in 2013.										
1947	62 convertible	8443511	L	40-60.000 EUR	35.227	44.265	41.400	09-02-17	Paris	430	Bon
	Black with cloth interior; recent mechanical works (see lot 427 Bonhams 6.2.14 $74,492).										
1947	62 convertible	8421976	L	NQ	49.270*	62.700*	56.117*	24-06-17	Northeast	747.1	B/J
	Black with red interior; recently restored. Automatic transmission.										
1952	62 coupé	52627564	L	30-40.000 USD	25.293*	30.800*	29.189*	09-03-17	Amelia Island	107	Bon F164
	Dark metallic green with two-tone grey vinyl interior; in good driving order.										
1951	62 sedan	5162108512	L	14-18.000 EUR	12.086*	14.901*	13.376*	07-10-16	Chateau-sur-Epte	4	Art
	Metallic green with blue cloth interior; paintwork and interior redone. Since 1981 in the Andre Weber Collection.										
1952	75 Fleetwood limousine	527531504	L	65-95.000 USD	28.739	35.000	32.827	15-01-17	Kissimmee	S230.1	Mec
	Black with white roof; personal car of the USA President Dwight D. Eisenhower. Exhibited at the 1953 Paris Motor Show.										
1955	62 convertible	556227233	L	180-220.000 USD	71.667*	88.000*	82.764*	20-01-17	Phoenix	237	RMS
	Red with red and white leather interior; full restoration completed in 2000.										
1953	62 Coupé de Ville	536256294	L	10-15.000 EUR	30.529*	37.962*	35.840*	25-11-16	Milan	931	RMS
	Light blue with black roof. From the Duemila Ruote collection.										
1953	62 Eldorado convertible	536274198	L	200-250.000 USD	165.594	220.000	196.548	03-09-16	Auburn	4101	AA
	Red with red interior; restored.										

F163: 1940 Cadillac Series 62 convertible

F164: 1952 Cadillac 62 coupé

Year	Model	(Bodybuilder)	Chassis no.	Steering	Estimate	Hammer Price £	$	€	Sale Date	Place	Lot	Auc. H.
1954	**62 Eldorado convertible**		546268909	L	50-60.000 GBP	58.899	78.819	70.143	07-09-16	London	180	RMS
	White with red and white leather interior; in good driving order, some recent cosmetic works. Imported into Italy several years ago.											
1954	**62 Eldorado convertible**		546272302(engine)	L	80-100.000 USD		NS		03-10-16	Philadelphia	208	Bon
	Black with red leather interior; restored approximately 12 years ago.											
1955	**62 Eldorado convertible**		556250969	L	180-220.000 USD	89.584*	110.000*	103.455*	20-01-17	Phoenix	245	RMS **F165**
	White with original white and red leather interior; body repainted. Just over 32,000 miles on the odometer.											
1956	**62 Biarritz convertible**		5662063516	L	180-210.000 USD	127.632	159.500	149.180	01-04-17	Ft.Lauderdale	576	AA
	Maroon with maroon and white leather interior; fully restored.											
1956	**62 convertible**		5662045126	L	70-80.000 USD	56.185	71.500	63.993	24-06-17	Santa Monica	171	RMS
	Ivory; restored.											
1956	**62 convertible**		5662142142	L	100-150.000 USD	68.376*	88.000*	74.976*	19-08-17	Pebble Beach	153	G&Co
	Green with green and white leather interior; in original, unrestored condition; 35,000 miles covered.											
1956	**62 Coupé de Ville**		5662107684	L	20-25.000 EUR	23.073*	28.447*	25.536*	07-10-16	Chateau-sur-Epte	39	Art
	Red with white roof; in good overall condition. From the Andre Weber Collection.											
1959	**62 convertible**		59F003499	L	125-150.000 USD		NS		03-09-16	Auburn	4093	AA
	Black with black and white interior; originally finished in white (see lot 433 Barrett-Jackson 18.4.15 $165,000).											
1957	**62 convertible**		5762025012	L	40-60.000 USD	23.935*	30.800*	27.409*	03-10-16	Philadelphia	227	Bon
	Light green; in good driving order.											
1958	**62 convertible**		58F030075	L	125-150.000 USD	82.513	104.500	93.423	06-10-16	Hershey	133	RMS
	White with blue and white interior; restoration completed in 2015.											
1959	**62 convertible**		59F095900	L	85-125.000 EUR	80.649	98.688	89.700	15-10-16	Salzburg	440	Dor
	Red with red and white leather interior; restored 25 years ago. Engine rebuilt in 2013.											
1959	**62 convertible**		59F011939	L	80-120.000 EUR	108.782*	135.567*	127.544*	10-02-17	Paris	16	Art
	Light blue with red interior; fully restored in the early 1990s by André Lecoq in France. From 1988 to 2012 it was owned by Asterix cartoonist Albert Uderzo.											
1960	**62 convertible**		60F013455	L	40-50.000 USD	38.033	48.400	43.318	24-06-17	Santa Monica	125	RMS
	Red; in the same ownership from the 1980s.											
1959	**62 convertible**		59F109615	L	70-90.000 USD	46.244	58.850	52.671	24-06-17	Santa Monica	243	RMS
	Red with red leather interior; restored.											
1958	**Eldorado Biarritz convertible**		58E043554	L	140-175.000 USD	133.303	177.100	158.221	03-09-16	Auburn	4157	AA
	Black with red interior; described as in showroom condition.											
1957	**Eldorado Biarritz convertible**		5762042133	L	NA	88.993*	108.900*	98.979*	15-10-16	Las Vegas	692	B/J
	White with white interior; body restored in 1997, engine and automatic transmission rebuilt in 2000.											
1959	**Eldorado Biarritz convertible**		59E022620	L	200-225.000 USD		NS		04-11-16	Dallas	S126	Mec
	Argyle blue with white interior; only example known to exist in this colour. One of 99 examples produced with bucket seats.											
1957	**Eldorado Biarritz convertible**		5762110253	L	85-115.000 USD	72.045	90.000	81.126	04-11-16	Dallas	S153.1	Mec
	White with red and white interior.											
1957	**Eldorado Biarritz convertible**		5762015428	L	NA	89.221	110.000	103.488	19-11-16	Anaheim	F97.1	Mec
	Burgundy with black leather interior; body repainted. Recently serviced.											
1959	**Eldorado Biarritz convertible**		59E101397	L	175-250.000 USD	134.343	165.000	154.721	18-01-17	Scottsdale	36	WoA
	Green with white leather interior; described as in excellent condition (see lot 533 Auctions America 14.3.14 NS).											
1957	**Eldorado Biarritz convertible**		5762050027	L	NQ	136.168*	167.200*	157.252*	21-01-17	Scottsdale	1340	B/J
	Black with red leather interior; restored 13 years ago (see lot 127 RM 31.7.04 $55,000).											
1957	**Eldorado Biarritz convertible**		5762100582	L	NQ	160.960	200.000	187.780	18-02-17	Los Angeles	S116.1	Mec
	Black with red leather interior; concours-quality restoration completed in 2016.											
1959	**Eldorado Biarritz convertible**		59E004429	L	125-150.000 USD	98.291	126.500	107.778	18-08-17	Carmel	36	Bon **F166**
	Red with white interior; an older restoration.											
1961	**Eldorado Biarritz convertible**		61E015185	L	70-90.000 USD	41.026*	52.800*	44.986*	19-08-17	Pebble Beach	112	G&Co
	Topaz; restored at unspecified date.											

F165: 1955 Cadillac 62 Eldorado convertible

F166: 1959 Cadillac Eldorado Biarritz convertible

Year	Model	(Bodybuilder)	Chassis no.	Steering	Estimate	Hammer price £	$	€	Sale Date	Place	Lot	Auc. H.
1957	**Eldorado Biarritz convertible**		5762063087	L	200-250.000 USD	151.515	195.000	166.140	19-08-17	Monterey	S69	Mec
Blue with blue leather interior; fully restored.												
1958	**Eldorado Brougham**		58P060521	L	100-150.000 USD	138.327*	170.500*	159.810*	19-01-17	Phoenix	167	RMS **F167**
Blue with blue leather and cloth interior; cosmetically restored. From the Mohrschladt Family Collection (see lot 1258.1 Barrett-Jackson 29.1.16 $123,200).												
1957	**Eldorado Brougham**		5770089009	L	75-85.000 USD	56.185	71.500	63.993	24-06-17	Santa Monica	181	RMS
Dark metallic grey; in the current ownership from the 1980s.												
1959	**Broadmoor Skyview**	(Superior Coach)	59Z083683	L	175-250.000 USD		NS		09-03-17	Amelia Island	126	Bon
Red with white roof; four red leather upholstered rows of seating. One of six examples ordered to Superior Coach by the Broadmoor Hotel of Colorado Springs, Colorado, for the transport of the hotel guests. The car was in service until the early 1970s and subsequenetly it remained in a Connecticut collection from 1978 until its recent discovery. Body repainted at unspecified date; mechanicals recently rebuilt. 390 engine with automatic transmission.												
1966	**Fleetwood Brougham**		P6196942	L	40-60.000 USD	53.750*	66.000*	62.073*	20-01-17	Phoenix	204	RMS
Black; concours-quality restoration.												
1976	**Eldorado convertible**		6L67S6Q246315	L	30-40.000 USD	17.402*	21.450*	20.105*	19-01-17	Scottsdale	86	Bon
White; described as in very good overall condition.												

CAP (I)

Year	Model		Chassis no.	Steering	Estimate	£	$	€	Date	Place	Lot	Auc. H.
1971	**Fiat 500 Scoiattolo**		2745156	L	18-25.000 EUR	7.828*	9.837*	9.200*	09-02-17	Paris	308	Bon
Orange with black interior; in the ownership of Carrozzeria Arrigo Perini (CAP) until 1981. 38,000 believed-correct kms.												

CHALMERS (USA) (1908-1923)

Year	Model		Chassis no.	Steering	Estimate	£	$	€	Date	Place	Lot	Auc. H.
1911	**Thirty pony tonneau**		M5832(engine)	R	125-150.000 USD	56.456	71.500	63.921	06-10-16	Hershey	159	RMS **F168**
Light green; car restored many years ago, engine rebuilt.												
1913	**Thirty-Six Model 17 touring**		31215	R	20-25.000 GBP	29.900	39.716	35.485	03-09-16	Beaulieu	429	Bon
Blue with black fenders and black leather interior; imported into the UK in 2005 from the USA and subsequently restored.												

CHAMBERLAIN (AUS)

Year	Model		Chassis no.	Steering	Estimate	£	$	€	Date	Place	Lot	Auc. H.
1929	**8**		NQ	M	280-380.000 AUD		NS		27-11-16	Melbourne	74	Mos
One-off built by Alan Hawker Chamberlain and first fitted with an Indian engine; in the mid-1930s Chamberlain designed a 1100cc supercharged 4-cylinder two-stroke engine with 8 opposed pistons. Raced pre- and post-WWII, the car remained in the ownership of the Chamberlain family until the early 1990s. In the mid-1990s the mechanicals were recommissioned and the car was used at some historic events. In 2007 it was bought by the current owner and subjected to some restoration works.												

CHEETAH (USA)

Year	Model		Chassis no.	Steering	Estimate	£	$	€	Date	Place	Lot	Auc. H.
1964	**GT coupé**		U62065	L	NQ		NS		21-01-17	Scottsdale	1376	B/J
Silver with black interior; fully restored. Raced until the late 1960s. Ordered new with the 375bhp 327 Corvette engine, the car was upgraded in 1965 with the 425bhp 396 engine, wide body and disc brakes, and in 1967 with the 427 L88 engine still on it. Titled and licensed for street use in 1969.												

CHEVROLET (USA) (1911-)

Year	Model		Chassis no.	Steering	Estimate	£	$	€	Date	Place	Lot	Auc. H.
1916	**Series H4 touring**		N4133	L	15-20.000 USD	18.734*	23.100*	20.735*	07-10-16	Hershey	265	RMS
White with black interior; restored many years ago.												
1927	**Capitol AA touring**		3AA108824	R	15-20.000 GBP	20.700	27.496	24.567	03-09-16	Beaulieu	450	Bon
Restored in 2006.												
1931	**Independence AE coach**		563808	L	25-30.000 USD	13.028*	16.500*	14.751*	06-10-16	Hershey	115	RMS
Dark blue with black roof and fenders and grey cloth interior; older restoration. Canadian built example.												
1932	**Confederate BA DeLuxe roadster**		BA4137732	L	45-55.000 USD	35.222	44.000	39.662	05-11-16	Hilton Head	189	AA
Blue with tan leather interior; in very good condition.												
1941	**Special Deluxe convertible**		AA899308	L	60-80.000 USD	46.584*	57.200*	53.797*	21-01-17	Scottsdale	137	G&Co
Cream with red leather interior; fully restored in the early 2000s.												
1948	**Fleetline Aerosedan "Country Club"**		2FKD26378	L	40-50.000 USD	26.763*	33.000*	29.621*	07-10-16	Hershey	242	RMS **F169**
Grey with wooden panels and tan cloth interior; recently serviced.												

F167: 1958 Cadillac Eldorado Brougham

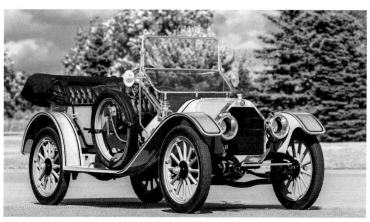

F168: 1911 Chalmers Thirty pony tonneau

Year	Model	(Bodybuilder)	Chassis no.	Steering	Estimate	Hammer price £	$	€	Date	Place	Lot	Auc. H.

F169: 1948 Chevrolet Fleetline Aerosedan "Country Club"

F170: 1953 Chevrolet Corvette roadster

Year	Model	Chassis no.	Steering	Estimate	£	$	€	Date	Place	Lot	Auc. H.
1952	Styleline DeLuxe coupé (Fisher)	14KK163683	L	15-18.000 GBP	12.880	16.015	15.120	26-11-16	Weybridge	109	His

Two-tone green with grey/green interior; restored in the USA in 1974; further cosmetical works carried out in Europe in more recent years (see lots 532 Sotheby's 20.7.98 NS and 379 Bonhams 30.4.12 $21,496).

| 1951 | Styleline 2-door sedan | 21JKL7073 | L | NQ | 5.823* | 7.150* | 6.725* | 21-01-17 | Scottsdale | 8210 | R&S |

Blue with cloth interior; automatic transmission. From the Missoula Auto Museum Collection.

| 1953 | Bel Air Six convertible | C53F100178 | L | NA | 34.775 | 46.200 | 41.275 | 03-09-16 | Auburn | 5 | WoA |

Brown with white and tan interior; restored in the 2000s.

| 1954 | Special 150 4-door station wagon | A54L023557 | L | 30-35.000 USD | 19.626* | 24.200* | 21.722* | 07-10-16 | Hershey | 258 | RMS |

White with tan and brown interior; in good overall condition.

| 1953 | Corvette roadster | E53F001214 | L | 180-220.000 USD | 136.615 | 181.500 | 162.152 | 03-09-16 | Auburn | 4100 | AA F170 |

White with red interior; since 1980 in the same ownership, restored in the early 1990s. Automatic transmission (see lot 507 Auctions America 2.4.16 NS).

| 1954 | Corvette roadster | E54S001703 | L | NA | 53.935* | 66.000* | 59.987* | 15-10-16 | Las Vegas | 774 | B/J |

Black with black interior; engine rebuilt less than 500 miles ago. Automatic transmission.

| 1953 | Corvette roadster | E53F001204 | L | 200-235.000 USD | | NS | | 04-11-16 | Dallas | S138 | Mec |

White with red interior; older restoration. Automatic transmission.

| 1954 | Corvette roadster | E54S001388 | L | 80-100.000 USD | 58.230* | 71.500* | 67.246* | 20-01-17 | Phoenix | 236 | RMS |

Red with red interior; body repainted. 37,000 miles on the odometer. Automatic transmission (see lot S94 Mecum 28.2.15 $76,000).

| 1953 | Corvette roadster | E53F001200 | L | NQ | 223.960* | 275.000* | 258.638* | 21-01-17 | Scottsdale | 1353 | B/J |

White with red interior; restored. Automatic transmission.

| 1954 | Corvette roadster | E54S004399 | L | 90-120.000 USD | 55.990* | 68.750* | 64.659* | 21-01-17 | Scottsdale | 160 | G&Co |

Blue with beige interior; restored in the 1990s. Automatic transmission (see lot 266 RM 14.3.09 $60,500).

| 1957 | Model 150 2-door utility sedan | A57S175377 | L | 90-120.000 USD | 74.535* | 97.000* | 86.767* | 20-05-17 | Indianapolis | T192 | Mec F171 |

Black and ivory with black and white interior; fully restored. 283 fuel-injected engine with 3-speed manual gearbox.

| 1955 | Corvette V8 roadster | VE55S001022 | L | 80-100.000 EUR | 71.665 | 89.586 | 84.000 | 08-02-17 | Paris | 113 | RMS |

Copper with tan interior; fully restored. Automatic transmission.

| 1955 | Corvette V8 roadster | VE55S001316 | L | 125-155.000 USD | 101.010 | 130.000 | 110.760 | 19-08-17 | Monterey | S73 | Mec |

White with red interior; restored in 1982. Automatic transmission.

| 1957 | Bel Air Nomad | VC57S137970 | L | 115-145.000 USD | 102.638 | 125.000 | 117.238 | 15-01-17 | Kissimmee | S208 | Mec |

Dark gold with beige roof and black and white interior; full restoration completed in 2010. 220bhp 283 engine with automatic transmission.

| 1957 | Bel Air hardtop | VC57N133682 | L | NQ | 52.312 | 65.000 | 61.029 | 18-02-17 | Los Angeles | S125.1 | Mec |

Red with black and red interior; restored. 283bhp 283 fuel-injected engine with 3-speed manual gearbox.

| 1957 | Bel Air hardtop | VC57N249176 | L | NQ | 52.991* | 66.000* | 61.908* | 08-04-17 | Palm Beach | 650.1 | B/J |

Ivory with red and black interior; restored. 220bhp 283 engine with automatic transmission.

F171: 1957 Chevrolet Model 150 2-door utility sedan

F172: 1955 Chevrolet Bel Air Nomad

Year	Model	(Bodybuilder)	Chassis no.	Steering	Estimate	Hammer price £	Hammer price $	Hammer price €	Sale Date	Sale Place	Lot	Auc. H.
1957	**Bel Air Nomad**		VC57J144378	L	NQ	34.430*	44.000*	41.127*	22-04-17	Arlington	21	WoA
	Ivory and red with red and black interior; in good overall condition. 283 engine with automatic transmission. Upgraded with power steering and power braking. From the Monical collection.											
1957	**Bel Air 4-door hardtop**		VC57B181885	L	NQ	18.937*	24.200*	22.620*	22-04-17	Arlington	23	WoA
	White with white and dark grey interior; in good driving order. 283 engine with 3-speed manual gearbox. From the Monical collection.											
1955	**Bel Air Nomad**		VC55N063561	L	45-55.000 USD	35.872*	45.650*	40.857*	24-06-17	Santa Monica	106	RMS F172
	Two-tone green; mostly original; automatic transmission rebuilt in 2015.											
1956	**Bel Air Nomad**		VC56K098934	L	NA	45.299*	58.300*	49.672*	19-08-17	Monterey	1011	R&S
	Black and white; older restoration.											
1957	**Bel Air convertible**		VC57L173489	L	95-110.000 USD	84.453	112.200	100.239	03-09-16	Auburn	5122	AA
	Blue with blue interior; less than 1,000 miles covered since the restoration carried out many years ago. 250bhp fuel-injected engine with automatic transmission (see lot 137 RM/Sotheby's 30.7.16 NS).											
1957	**Bel Air convertible**		VC57B163762	L	NA	60.782	81.000	71.879	10-09-16	Louisville	S126	Mec
	Silver with silver and red interior; restoration completed in 2016. 283 engine with automatic transmission.											
1957	**Bel Air convertible**		VC57B132527	L	70-90.000 USD	60.799	77.000	68.838	06-10-16	Hershey	164	RMS
	Yellow with yellow and grey interior; acquired in 2006 by the current owner who subsequently rebuilt the 283 engine. Automatic transmission.											
1955	**Bel Air convertible**		VC55F151300	L	NA	29.196	36.000	32.314	08-10-16	Chicago	S183	Mec
	White and beige with beige interior; automatic transmission.											
1957	**Bel Air convertible**		VC57J254732	L	150-175.000 USD	106.743	130.000	121.927	15-01-17	Kissimmee	F170.1	Mec
	Black with red and silver interior; restored. 283bhp 283 fuel-injected engine with 3-speed manual gearbox.											
1957	**Bel Air convertible**		VC57L139902	L	110-140.000 USD	80.626*	99.000*	93.110*	20-01-17	Phoenix	213	RMS F173
	Black with red and white interior; 600 miles covered since a full restoration. 250bhp 283 fuel-injected engine with 3-speed manual gearbox (see lots 138 RM 10.3.12 $99,000 and 2061 Auctions America 18.7.15 NS).											
1956	**Bel Air convertible**		VC56L020258	L	50-70.000 USD	51.511*	63.250*	59.487*	20-01-17	Phoenix	270	RMS
	Red and ivory with red and white vinyl interior; restored in the early 2000s- 205bhp 265 engine with automatic transmission.											
1957	**Bel Air convertible**		VC57L105514	L	NQ	78.834*	96.800*	91.040*	21-01-17	Scottsdale	1124	B/J
	Ivory with red and silver interior; in very good overall condition. 250bhp 283 fule-injected engine with automatic transmission.											
1957	**Bel Air convertible**		VC57N226609	L	NA	53.936	60.500	47.063	03-06-17	Newport Beach	9062	R&S
	Blue; 283 engine with automatic transmission.											
1957	**Bel Air convertible**		VC57S302368	L	75-100.000 USD	54.764*	70.400*	62.762*	04-06-17	Greenwich	154	Bon
	Ivory and red with red and silver vinyl interior; restored at unspecified date. 283bhp 283 fuel-injected engine with automatic transmission (see lot 116 RM 27.7.13 $74,250).											
1957	**Corvette convertible**		E57S105073	L	500-700.000 USD	369.495	450.000	422.055	15-01-17	Kissimmee	F101	Mec F174
	Black with red interior; fully restored in 2007. Raced by its first owner until 1962. Fitted with the "Airbox" and "Big Brake" packages. 283bhp 283 fuel-injected engine with 4-speed manual gearbox. From the Jackie and Gary Runyon collection.											
1957	**Corvette convertible**		E57S101903	L	NQ	82.110	100.000	93.790	15-01-17	Kissimmee	F62.1	Mec
	Red with beige coves and beige interior; concours-quality restoration. 283bhp 283 fuel-injected engine with 3-speed manual gearbox.											
1957	**Corvette convertible**		E57S100815	L	60-80.000 USD	71.667*	88.000*	82.764*	20-01-17	Phoenix	271	RMS
	Red with ivory coves and red interior; restored and fitted with a 4-speed manual gearbox as replacement of the original automatic unit. 245bhp 283 engine.											
1957	**Corvette convertible**		E57S105176	L	100-120.000 USD	79.492	96.800	91.737	09-03-17	Amelia Island	132	Bon
	Red with white coves and red interior; restoration completed in 2010. 283bhp 283 fuel-injected engine with 4-speed manual gearbox (see lots 29 Christie's 3.6.07 $99,000, and Bonhams 414 6.6.10 NS and 46 18.8.11 NS).											
1957	**Corvette convertible**		E57S105073	L	450-600.000 USD		NS		20-05-17	Indianapolis	F166	Mec
	See lot F101 Mecum 15.1.17.											
1957	**Corvette convertible**		E57S102098	L	NA		NS		03-06-17	Newport Beach	9126	R&S
	Red with white coves and red interior; restoration completed in 2015. For 35 years in the current ownership. Manual gearbox.											
1957	**Corvette convertible**		E57S102281	L	275-325.000 USD		NS		18-08-17	Pebble Beach	52	G&Co
	Light blue with white coves and red interior; restored in the 1980s and described as still in very good overall condition. 283bhp 283 fuel-injected engine with 3-speed manual gearbox; fitted with hardtop and RPO 684 option package.											
1957	**Corvette convertible**		57S102098	L	NA	70.513	90.750	77.319	19-08-17	Monterey	1097	R&S
	See lot 9126 Russo & Steele 3.6.17.											

F173: 1957 Chevrolet Bel Air convertible

F174: 1957 Chevrolet Corvette convertible

Year	Model	(Bodybuilder)	Chassis no.	Steering	Estimate	Hammer price £	Hammer price $	Hammer price €	Date	Place	Lot	Auc. H.
1958	**Bel Air Impala convertible**		F58J118998	L	NA		NS		10-09-16	Louisville	S130.1	Mec
	Turquoise with turquoise interior; fully restored. 348 Tri-Power engine with automatic transmission.											
1958	**Bel Air Impala convertible**		F58J235064	L	100-125.000 USD	131.139*	161.700*	145.142*	07-10-16	Hershey	235	**RMS F175**
	Cay coral with matching interior; concours-quality restoration carried out between 2004 and 2005. 280bhp 348 Tri-Power engine with 3-speed manual gearbox.											
1963	**Biscayne 2-door sedan**		31211B163051	L	NQ	36.063	45.000	41.643	25-03-17	Kansas City	S82.1	Mec
	Black with fawn interior; 340bhp 409 engine with automatic transmission.											
1961	**Corvette convertible**		10867S107559	L	NA	67.536	90.000	79.866	10-09-16	Louisville	S97	Mec
	Black with black interior; restored at unspecified date. 315bhp 283 fuel-injected engine with 4-speed manual gearbox.											
1959	**Corvette convertible**		J59S105082	L	75-90.000 USD	73.828*	93.500*	83.589*	06-10-16	Hershey	128	RMS
	White with silver coves and red vinyl interior; freshly restored. 230bhp 283 engine with 4-speed manual gearbox.											
1959	**Corvette convertible**		J59S103059	L	65-85.000 EUR	59.970	73.383	66.700	15-10-16	Salzburg	418	Dor
	Red with white coves and white interior; restored at unspecified date. 4-speed manual gearbox (see lot 345 Bonhams 19.9.08 $47,827 and 225 Historics 6.6.15 $72,117).											
1958	**Corvette convertible**		J58S10385	L	65-75.000 GBP	67.580	82.096	75.162	29-10-16	London	149	Coy
	Yellow with white coves and black interior; described as in very good overall condition. Fuel-injected engine.											
1960	**Corvette convertible**		00867S106083	L	NA	80.050	100.000	90.140	04-11-16	Dallas	S98.1	Mec
	Red with white coves and red interior; restored. 270bhp 283 engine with 4-speed manual gearbox.											
1961	**Corvette convertible**		10867S108514	L	NA	56.777	70.000	65.856	19-11-16	Anaheim	S128	Mec
	White with red interior; mostly unrestored; believed to be 46,000 original miles; 270bhp 283 engine with 4-speed manual gearbox.											
1959	**Corvette convertible**		J59S101605	L	55-65.000 EUR	62.012*	77.110*	72.800*	25-11-16	Milan	349	RMS
	Blue with white coves and blue interior; 87,898 kms. From the Duemila Ruote collection.											
1962	**Corvette convertible**		20867S102395	L	NQ	59.408	75.000	70.470	03-12-16	Kansas City	S88.1	Mec
	Silver with red interior; restored. 340bhp 327 engine with 4-speed manual gearbox.											
1962	**Corvette convertible**		20867S113986	L	60-80.000 GBP	63.100	79.563	74.149	07-12-16	London	362	Bon
	Beige; concours-quality restoration carried out in the USA in 2014-15. 360bhp fuel-injected engine with 4-speed manual gearbox.											
1960	**Corvette convertible**		00867S109727	L	NQ	131.376	160.000	150.064	15-01-17	Kissimmee	S73	Mec
	Black with black interior; restored. 290bhp 283 fuel-injected engine with 4-speed manual gearbox.											
1962	**Corvette convertible**		20867S104187	L	NQ	94.063*	115.500*	108.628*	21-01-17	Scottsdale	1327	B/J
	Silver with black interior; in show condition. 360bhp 327 fuel-injected engine with 4-speed manual gearbox; fitted with the RPO-687 race package.											
1958	**Corvette convertible**		J58S103004	L	NQ	84.209	103.400	97.248	21-01-17	Scottsdale	8337	R&S
	Silver blue with silver coves and light blue interior; 20 miles covered since the restoration. 270bhp 283 engine with 4-speed manual gearbox.											
1962	**Corvette convertible**		20867S109669	L	NQ	76.456	95.000	89.196	18-02-17	Los Angeles	S148.1	Mec
	Black with black interior; 360bhp 327 engine with 4-speed manual gearbox.											
1961	**Corvette convertible**		10867S104046	L	60-80.000 USD	58.816*	71.500*	67.382*	10-03-17	Amelia Island	104	**RMS F176**
	Red with white coves and red vinyl interior; 270bhp 283 engine with 4-speed manual gearbox. From the Orin Smith collection.											
1960	**Corvette convertible**		00867S109963	L	NQ	52.091	65.000	60.151	25-03-17	Kansas City	F133	Mec
	Red with white coves and red interior; with hardtop. 270bhp 283 engine with 4-speed manual gearbox.											
1962	**Corvette convertible**		20867S112333	L	NQ	46.882	58.500	54.136	25-03-17	Kansas City	F81	Mec
	Red with red interior; with hardtop. 300bhp 327 engine with 4-speed manual gearbox.											
1962	**Corvette convertible**		20867S103973	L	300-350.000 USD	273.504	352.000	299.904	19-08-17	Pebble Beach	124	G&Co
	Silver with black interior; one owner from 1970 to 2004; acquired in 2005 by the vendor and restored to concours condition. Ordered with the 360bhp 327 fuel-injected engine, 4-speed manual close-ratio T10 gearbox, big brake and 24-gallon fuel tank.											
1969	**Corvair 4-door sedan**		596779019	L	4-6.000 GBP	2.300*	3.055*	2.730*	03-09-16	Beaulieu	463	Bon
	White with red interior; in good running order.											
1964	**Corvair Monza convertible**		40667W176559	L	NQ	7.615*	9.350*	8.794*	21-01-17	Scottsdale	8495	R&S
	Light blue with light blue interior; in good driving order.											
1962	**Corvair Monza Spyder**		209270160994	L	NQ	5.165*	6.600*	6.169*	22-04-17	Arlington	9	WoA
	Metallic green with green interior; older restoration. From the Monical collection.											
1960	**Impala hardtop**		01837N130498	L	NQ	27.724	35.000	32.886	03-12-16	Kansas City	S90.1	Mec
	Red with red and white interior; 348 engine with automatic transmission.											

F175: 1958 Chevrolet Bel Air Impala convertible

F176: 1961 Chevrolet Corvette convertible

F177: 1963 Chevrolet Impala Z11 hardtop

F178: 1964 Chevrolet Impala SS convertible

Year	Model	(Bodybuilder)	Chassis no.	Steering	Estimate	£	$	€	Date	Place	Lot	Auc. H.
1963	**Impala Z11 hardtop**		31847F164836	L	750-850.000 USD	431.078	525.000	492.398	15-01-17	Kissimmee	S103	Mec F177
White with black interior; one of 57 RPO Z11 Lightweights built. Race driven in the 1960s by Dave Stickler. Restored. 430bhp 427 engine with 4-speed manual gearbox. From the Don Fezell collection.												
1963	**Impala Z11 hardtop**		31847F176794	L	375-450.000 USD	279.174	340.000	318.886	15-01-17	Kissimmee	S104	Mec
Black with black interior; one of 57 Z11 Lightweights built. Restored. 430bhp 427 engine with 4-speed manual gearbox. From the Don Fezell collection.												
1962	**Impala sedan**		21869F153163	L	100-125.000 USD	57.477	70.000	65.653	15-01-17	Kissimmee	S132	Mec
Two-tone beige with beige interior; restored. 409bhp 409 engine with 3-speed manual gearbox. Since 1991 in the Don Fezell collection.												
1962	**Impala SS sport coupé**		21847J215849	L	75-100.000 USD	53.546*	66.000*	61.862*	19-01-17	Phoenix	174	RMS
Black with red vinyl interior; 5,490 miles covered since the restoration completed in 1997. 409bhp 409 engine with 4-speed manual gearbox. From the Mohrschladt Family Collection.												
1959	**Impala 4-door hardtop**		F59L166387	L	NQ	22.474*	28.600*	25.597*	24-06-17	Northeast	624.1	B/J
Red and white with red interior; 2,200 miles covered since the restoration completed in 1998. 283 engine with automatic transmission.												
1959	**Impala convertible**		F59T226516	L	125-150.000 USD		NS		03-09-16	Auburn	5120	AA
Black with red vinyl and cloth interior; restored. 280bhp 348 engine with automatic transmission.												
1959	**Impala convertible**		F59S300871	L	NA	52.715	65.000	58.344	08-10-16	Chicago	S162	Mec
Bronze with bronze interior; restored.												
1964	**Impala SS convertible**		41467S237066	L	NA	89.892*	110.000*	99.979*	15-10-16	Las Vegas	713	B/J F178
Black with black interior; 425bhp 409 L80 engine with 4-speed manual gearbox.												
1963	**Impala SS convertible**		31867B131125	L	NQ	98.542	121.000	113.801	21-01-17	Scottsdale	8053	R&S
Black with red interior; fully restored. 409 engine with 4-speed manual gearbox.												
1966	**Impala convertible**		3A56A010281	L	40-60.000 USD	19.797*	25.300*	23.648*	22-04-17	Arlington	137	WoA
Red; 1,000 miles covered since the restoration completed in 2014. 396 engine with 4-speed manual gearbox.												
1960	**CERV I**		2152	M	NQ	1.075.008	1.320.000	1.241.460	21-01-17	Scottsdale	1390	B/J F179
Concept race car designed by Zora Arkus-Duntov. Originally fitted with a 350bhp 283 engine, it was used to develope the Chevrolet chassis and suspension systems. Later it was fitted with the present 377 engine (see lot 240 RM/Sotheby's 14.8.15 NS).												
1966	**Nova SS hardtop**		118376N165788	L	85-110.000 USD	65.688	80.000	75.032	15-01-17	Kissimmee	S255	Mec
Metallic teal green with teal interior; restoration completed in 2015. 350bhp 327 engine with 4-speed manual gearbox.												
1966	**Nova SS hardtop**		118376W167673	L	90-110.000 USD	64.103	82.500	70.290	19-08-17	Monterey	T93	Mec F180
Yellow with black interior; 292 miles covered since the restoration. 350bhp 327 L79 engine with 4-speed manual gearbox.												
1967	**Corvette Sting Ray convertible**		194677S113139	L	125-150.000 USD		NS		03-09-16	Auburn	4097	AA
Black with blue leather interior; restored. 435bhp 427 engine with manual gearbox.												
1967	**Corvette Sting Ray convertible**		194677S117941	L	NA	99.753	123.000	110.405	08-10-16	Chicago	S97	Mec
Green with green interior; restored. With hardtop. 435bhp 427 engine with manual gearbox.												
1966	**Corvette Sting Ray convertible**		194676S118084	L	100-125.000 USD	65.641	82.000	73.915	04-11-16	Dallas	S147	Mec
Blue with blue vinyl interior; restored. 425bhp 427 L72 engine with manual gearbox.												

F179: 1960 Chevrolet CERV I

F180: 1966 Chevrolet Nova SS hardtop

Year	Model	(Bodybuilder)	Chassis no.	Steering	Estimate	Hammer price £	Hammer price $	Hammer price €	Date	Place	Lot	Auc. H.
1967	Corvette Sting Ray convertible		194677S118843	L	225-275.000 USD		NS		04-11-16	Dallas	S152	Mec
Blue with blue interior; in original condition. Three owners and 15,050 miles covered. With hardtop (see Mecum lots F198 6.9.14 $210,000 and S113 23.1.16 $195,000).												
1967	Corvette Sting Ray convertible		194677S120523	L	NA		NS		19-11-16	Anaheim	S108.1	Mec
Green with white stinger and black interior; in good overall condition. 435bhp 427 engine with manual gearbox.												
1967	Corvette Sting Ray convertible		194677S113573	L	NQ	59.408	75.000	70.470	03-12-16	Kansas City	F94.1	Mec
Maroon with saddle interior; restored. 350bhp 327 engine with manual gearbox.												
1967	Corvette Sting Ray convertible		194677S120455	L	NQ	73.269	92.500	86.913	03-12-16	Kansas City	S127.1	Mec
Blue with black interior; 435bhp 427 engine with manual gearbox.												
1963	Corvette Sting Ray convertible		30867S105931	L	52-58.000 GBP	55.200	69.602	64.866	07-12-16	London	320	Bon
Blue with tan interior; restored at unspecified date. 340bhp 327 engine with 4-speed manual gearbox (see lot 76 H & H 16.10.13 NS).												
1967	Corvette Sting Ray convertible		194677S108606	L	Refer Dpt.	636.353	775.000	726.873	15-01-17	Kissimmee	S146.1 F181	Mec
The only 1967 example finished with black body with blue stinger, bright blue interior, side exhausts and 435bhp 427 L71 engine. In 1990-1992 restored to concours condition.												
1963	Corvette Sting Ray convertible		30867S109076	L	NQ	82.110	100.000	93.790	15-01-17	Kissimmee	S259	Mec
Red with red interior; 100 miles covered since the restoration. 360bhp 327 fuel-injected engine with 4-speed manual gearbox.												
1967	Corvette Sting Ray convertible		194677S115484	L	1.900-2.600.000 USD	1.612.116	1.980.000	1.856.646	18-01-17	Scottsdale	32	WoA
One of 10 427 L88 Corvette convertibles built in 1967 and the only one finished in silver pearl; 4-speed manual gearbox; side exhausts. Raced when new at some drag races. Engine block replaced with a correct unit in the 1970s. Restored to concours condition in 2012. In the past it was part of the Otis Chandler collection also.												
1966	Corvette Sting Ray convertible		194676S106766	L	220-260.000 USD		NS		18-01-17	Scottsdale	70	WoA
Black with black vinyl interior; 427 L72 engine with 4-speed manual gearbox.												
1966	Corvette Sting Ray convertible		194676S112013	L	200-240.000 USD	116.459*	143.000*	134.492*	20-01-17	Scottsdale	31	G&Co
Black with black interior; concours-quality restoration. With hardtop. 425bhp 427 L72 engine with manual gearbox.												
1967	Corvette Sting Ray convertible		194677S112839	L	NQ	143.334*	176.000*	165.528*	21-01-17	Scottsdale	1395	B/J
Maroon with black interior; in original condition, 17,900 original miles. 435bhp 427 engine with manual gearbox.												
1967	Corvette Sting Ray convertible		194677S118227	L	NQ	76.133	95.000	87.913	25-03-17	Kansas City	S49.1	Mec
Maroon with black interior; fully restored. 350bhp 327 engine with manual gearbox.												
1967	Corvette Sting Ray convertible		194677S102306	L	NA	80.911	103.400	96.648	22-04-17	Dallas	2501	Lea
Red with red interior; in good overall condition. 390bhp 427 engine with manual gearbox.												
1967	Corvette Sting Ray convertible		194677S106384	L	400-500.000 USD	238.204	310.000	277.295	20-05-17	Indianapolis	F113	Mec
Black with black vinyl interior; in original, unrestored condition; 24,000 original miles. 435bhp 427 L71 engine with manual gearbox.												
1966	Corvette Sting Ray convertible		194676S113131	L	275-325.000 USD		NS		20-05-17	Indianapolis	S108	Mec
Black with black interior; in original, unrestored condition; 45,897 original miles; two owners. 425bhp 427 L72 engine with manual gearbox.												
1967	Corvette Sting Ray convertible		194677S103677	L	350-450.000 USD	184.416	240.000	214.680	20-05-17	Indianapolis	S126.1	Mec
Black with red stinger and black interior; cosmetically restored six years ago. 400bhp 427 engine with manual gearbox.												
1967	Corvette Sting Ray convertible		194677S118843	L	175-250.000 USD	153.680	200.000	178.900	20-05-17	Indianapolis	T205	Mec
See lot S152 Mecum 4.11.16.												
1967	Corvette Sting Ray convertible		194677S102584	L	100-125.000 USD	70.085*	90.200*	76.850*	18-08-17	Carmel	50	Bon
Dark green with black interior; restored. 390bhp 427 engine with manual gearbox.												
1965	Corvette Sting Ray coupé		194375S105905	L	NA	60.750	80.694	72.098	02-09-16	Salon Privé	246	SiC
Blue; imported into the UK in 2015 in restored condition. Side exhaust pipes. 300bhp 327 engine with 4-speed manual gearbox.												
1963	Corvette Sting Ray coupé		30837S107716	L	NA	105.152	139.700	124.808	03-09-16	Auburn	22	WoA
Silver with dark blue interior; restored. 340bhp 327 engine with 4-speed manual gearbox.												
1967	Corvette Sting Ray coupé		194377S103009	L	NA	98.881*	121.000*	109.977*	15-10-16	Las Vegas	767	B/J
Red with black stinger hood and black interior; fully restored in 2007. 435bhp 427 L71 engine with manual gearbox.												
1967	Corvette Sting Ray coupé		194377S113899	L	250-300.000 USD		NS		04-11-16	Dallas	S119	Mec
Black with red stinger and black interior; concours-quality restoration. 435bhp 427 L71 engine with manual gearbox.												
1963	Corvette Sting Ray coupé		30837S116851	L	100-120.000 USD	88.055	110.000	99.154	05-11-16	Hilton Head	164	AA
Silver blue with blue vinyl interior; in largely original condition. 300bhp 327 L75 engine with automatic transmission (see lot 222 RM 1.12.12 $101,750).												
1963	Corvette Sting Ray coupé		30837S100759	L	NQ	67.329	85.000	79.866	03-12-16	Kansas City	F133.1	Mec
Red with black interior; 340bhp 327 engine with 4-speed manual gearbox.												
1963	Corvette Sting Ray coupé		30837S106717	L	NQ	63.368	80.000	75.168	03-12-16	Kansas City	S102	Mec
Black with black interior; 300bhp 327 engine with 4-speed manual gearbox.												
1967	Corvette Sting Ray coupé		194377S109446	L	NQ	102.973	130.000	122.148	03-12-16	Kansas City	S142	Mec
Yellow with black interior; restored in 2014. 400bhp 427 Tri-power engine with manual gearbox.												
1967	Corvette Sting Ray coupé		194377S108852	L	350-450.000 USD		NS		15-01-17	Kissimmee	F102	Mec
Black with red stinger and red interior; first restored in the early 1990s and between 2010 and 2013 again. Raced at some events when new. 435bhp 427 L71 engine with manual gearbox. From the Jackie and Gary Runyon collection.												
1965	Corvette Sting Ray coupé		194375S109778	L	165-185.000 USD	123.165	150.000	140.685	15-01-17	Kissimmee	S138	Mec
Black with silver interior; full restoration completed in 2016. 375bhp 327 L84 fuel-injected engine with 4-speed manual gearbox.												
1967	Corvette Sting Ray coupé		194377S113899	L	250-300.000 USD	201.170	245.000	229.786	15-01-17	Kissimmee	S164	Mec
See lot S119 Mecum 4.11.16.												
1964	Corvette Sting Ray coupé		40837S107999	L	350-400.000 USD		NS		15-01-17	Kissimmee	S235	Mec
Red with white interior; raced at SCCA events in 1964 and 1965. 36 gallon fuel tank. Restored; period-correct 327 engine rebuilt to original specification (see lot F131 Mecum 23.1.16 NS).												
1967	Corvette Sting Ray coupé		194377S119257	L	60-80.000 USD	58.230*	71.500*	67.246*	20-01-17	Scottsdale	47	G&Co
In good overall condition; 350bhp 327 L79 engine with manual gearbox.												

Year	Model	(Bodybuilder)	Chassis no.	Steering	Estimate	Hammer price £	$	€	Date	Place	Lot	Auc. H.
1963	**Corvette Sting Ray coupé**		30837S102280	L	NQ	75.251*	92.400*	86.902*	21-01-17	Scottsdale	8009	**R&S**
	Black with black interior; described as in very good overall condition. 300bhp 327 engine with automatic transmission.											
1966	**Corvette Sting Ray coupé**		194376S109204	L	50-80.000 EUR	81.333*	101.358*	95.360*	10-02-17	Paris	102	**Art**
	Yellow with black leatherette interior; imported into France in 2010, engine overhauled in 2011, body repainted in 2016. 425bhp 427 engine with manual gearbox.											
1963	**Corvette Sting Ray coupé**		30837S114581	L	NQ	112.406	140.000	131.320	08-04-17	Houston	S130	**Mec**
	Red with black interior; full restoration. 360bhp 327 fuel-injected engine with 4-speed manual gearbox. Upgraded with Z06 brakes.											
1967	**Corvette Sting Ray coupé**		194377S109577	L	100-125.000 USD	74.854	96.250	88.492	13-05-17	Auburn	3091	**AA**
	Marlboro red with black stinger and black vinyl interior; described as in original condition; 26,129 miles on the odometer. 390bhp 427 engine with manual gearbox.											
1967	**Corvette Sting Ray coupé**		194377S103475	L	Refer Dpt.	518.670	675.000	603.788	20-05-17	Indianapolis	S111	**Mec** F182
	Blue with blue interior; in the same family ownership since new; in original, unrestored condition; 8,533 miles covered. 435bhp 427 L71 engine with manual gearbox.											
1963	**Corvette Sting Ray coupé**		30837S110436	L	170-200.000 USD		NS		20-05-17	Indianapolis	S114	**Mec**
	Black with saddle leather interior; raced in period; restored to concours condition. 360bhp 327 L84 fuel-injected engine with manual gearbox.											
1963	**Corvette Sting Ray coupé**		30837S105895	L	100-130.000 USD	64.957*	83.600*	71.227*	18-08-17	Carmel	89	**Bon**
	Blue with black vinyl interior; restored at unspecified date. Currently fitted with a 5-speed Tremec manual gearbox (the original 4-speed unit is included with the sale).											
1963	**Corvette Sting Ray Z06 coupé**		30837S115727	L	225-250.000 USD		NS		03-09-16	Auburn	4180	**AA**
	Black with black interior; fully restored. In the 1970s the car was involved in an accident of enough degree to require the replacing of the frame. Ordered new with the 36-gallon fuel tank and Kelsey-Hayes knock-off wheels.											
1963	**Corvette Sting Ray Z06 coupé**		30837S108672	L	500-650.000 USD		NS		04-11-16	Dallas	S142	**Mec**
	Silver with black interior; restored several years ago. 36-gallon fuel tank (see lot S116 Mecum 16.4.16 NS).											
1963	**Corvette Sting Ray Z06 coupé**		30837S108672	L	400-500.000 USD		NS		15-01-17	Kissimmee	F177	**Mec**
	See lot S142 Mecum 4.11.16.											
1963	**Corvette Sting Ray Z06 coupé**		30837S120377	L	500-600.000 USD		NS		15-01-17	Kissimmee	S174	**Mec**
	Red with white stripes and black interior; in unrestored, original condition. 39,000 original miles. For 43 years with its first owner.											
1963	**Corvette Sting Ray Z06 coupé**		30837S116946	L	225-275.000 USD		NS		15-01-17	Kissimmee	S180	**Mec**
	Silver blue with black interior; restored some years ago. 36 gallon fuel tank.											
1963	**Corvette Sting Ray Z06 coupé**		30837S109324	L	550-650.000 USD		NS		18-01-17	Scottsdale	48	**WoA**
	Saddle with saddle leather interior; when new raced at some events. 36-gallon fuel tank. Restored in the 1990s. Formerly in the Otis Chandler collection (see lot 17 Gooding & Company 21.10.06 $330,000).											
1963	**Corvette Sting Ray Z06 coupé**		30837S106844	L	NQ	201.564*	247.500*	232.774*	21-01-17	Scottsdale	1363	**B/J**
	White with black interior; restored. 36-gallon fuel tank. When new personal car of Mickey Thompson (see lots 152 RM 15.8.03 NS and S150 Mecum 24.1.15 NS).											
1963	**Corvette Sting Ray Z06 coupé**		30837S109046	L	NQ	313.544*	385.000*	362.093*	21-01-17	Scottsdale	1393	**B/J**
	Silver with black interior; restored. 36-gallon fuel tank.											
1963	**Corvette Sting Ray Z06 coupé**		30837S108672	L	400-500.000 USD	315.044	410.000	366.745	20-05-17	Indianapolis	T166	**Mec**
	See lot F177 Mecum 15.1.17.											
1963	**Corvette Sting Ray Z06 coupé**		30837S109324	L	400-500.000 USD	277.778*	357.500*	305.663*	17-08-17	Monterey	19	**WoA**
	See lot 48 Worldwide Auctioneers 18.1.17.											
1963	**Corvette Sting Ray Z06 coupé**		30837S118180	L	340-380.000 USD	240.870	310.000	264.120	18-08-17	Carmel	43	**Bon**
	Silver with black interior; restoration completed in 2015. Big tank.											
1965	**Chevelle Malibu SS hardtop**		138375A142596	L	100-125.000 USD		NS		04-11-16	Dallas	F110	**Mec**
	Yellow with black interior; restored between 2008 and 2014 when it was acquired by the current, second owner. 350bhp 327 L79 engine with 4-speed manual gearbox.											
1965	**Chevelle Malibu convertible**		136675B141891	L	NQ	58.230*	71.500*	67.246*	21-01-17	Scottsdale	975	**B/J**
	Green with tan interior; show-quality restoration. 350bhp 327 L79 engine with 4-speed manual gearbox.											
1970	**Chevelle SS convertible**		136670B125389	L	NA	84.302	112.000	100.061	03-09-16	Auburn	35	**WoA**
	Blue with white stripes and white vinyl interior; recently restored. 454 LS6 engine with 4-speed manual gearbox.											
1970	**Chevelle SS convertible**		136670B161703	L	NA	210.112	280.000	248.472	10-09-16	Louisville	S115	**Mec**
	Turquoise with white interior; fully restored. 450bhp 454 LS6 engine with 4-speed manual gearbox (see RM lots 244 13.11.10 $214,500 and 148 15.1.15 $225,500).											
1968	**Chevelle SS convertible**		138678B194045	L	NQ	89.584*	110.000*	103.455*	21-01-17	Scottsdale	1162	**B/J**
	Blue with blue interior; restored. 396 engine with manual gearbox.											
1970	**Chevelle SS convertible**		136670B180798	L	NQ	116.459*	143.000*	134.492*	21-01-17	Scottsdale	1319	**B/J**
	Black with black interior; restored. 454 LS5 engine with manual gearbox.											

F181: 1967 Chevrolet Corvette Sting Ray convertible

F182: 1967 Chevrolet Corvette Sting Ray coupé

Year	Model	(Bodybuilder)	Chassis no.	Steering	Estimate	Hammer price £	$	€	Date	Place	Lot	Auc. H.
1970	**Chevelle SS convertible**		136670B175703	L	400-450.000 USD	295.834	385.000	344.383	20-05-17	Indianapolis	S113	Mec **F183**
Red with black stripes and red vinyl interior; concours-quality restoration. 450bhp 454 LS6 engine with manual gearbox.												
1970	**Chevelle SS convertible**		136670B184926	L	35-45.000 USD	24.387*	31.350*	27.949*	04-06-17	Greenwich	167	Bon
Red with white stripes and ivory vinyl interior; restored. 360bhp 454 LS5 engine with automatic transmission.												
1969	**Chevelle COPO coupé**		136379B404367	L	NA		NS		08-10-16	Chicago	S125	Mec
Red with white vinyl roof and parchment interior; restored in 1998. 425bhp 427 L72 engine with manual gearbox.												
1970	**Chevelle SS coupé**		136370F143626	L	NQ	43.566	55.000	51.678	03-12-16	Kansas City	F136	Mec
Black with red interior; 454 engine with manual gearbox.												
1969	**Chevelle Yenko coupé**		136379B387778	L	275-375.000 USD		NS		15-01-17	Kissimmee	F155.1	Mec
Yellow with black interior; unrestored, two owners, 1,200 original miles. 450bhp 427 engine with 4-speed manual gearbox. The original 427 L72 engine is included with the sale. From the Colts Neck Collection.												
1970	**Chevelle SS coupé**		136370A121939	L	NQ	215.002*	264.000	248.292*	21-01-17	Scottsdale	1301	B/J
Red with black stripes, black roof and black interior; just test miles covered since the restoration completed in 2013. 454 LS6 engine with manual gearbox.												
1970	**Chevelle SS coupé**		136370A162905	L	NQ	90.760*	115.500	103.373*	24-06-17	Northeast	700	B/J
Black with saddle interior; restored. 454 LS6 engine with manual gearbox.												
1968	**Camaro Yenko RS/SS coupé**		124378N459913	L	350-500.000 USD		NS		04-11-16	Dallas	S107	Mec
Red with black vinyl top and black interior; restored at unspecified date. 450bhp 427 L72 engine with manual gearbox (see lot B4 Mecum 12.4.14 $450,000).												
1969	**Camaro Yenko coupé**		124379N663684	L	275-325.000 USD	253.572	330.000	295.185	20-05-17	Indianapolis	F124	Mec **F184**
Blue with black interior; fully restored. 425bhp 427 L72 engine with manual gearbox.												
1969	**Camaro SS coupé**		124379N575390	L	NA	36.284	40.700	31.661	03-06-17	Newport Beach	9040	R&S
Silver with black roof and black interior; restored. 375bhp 396 L78 engine with manual gearbox.												
1967	**Camaro SS convertible**		124677N221699	L	60-80.000 USD	34.228*	44.000	39.226*	04-06-17	Greenwich	180	Bon
Red with black vinyl interior; restoration completed in 2014. 325bhp 396 engine with manual gearbox.												
1967	**Camaro Z/28 coupé**		124377N217951	L	95-115.000 USD	75.541	92.000	86.287	15-01-17	Kissimmee	F149	Mec
White with blue stripes and blue interior; restored. 18,047 actual miles.												
1969	**Camaro Z/28 coupé**		124379N558135	L	NA	41.316	52.800	49.352	22-04-17	Dallas	191	Lea
Red with black interior; body repainted.												
1969	**Camaro Z/28 coupé**		124379N584708	L	NA	70.513	90.750	77.319	19-08-17	Monterey	1064	R&S
Blue with white stripes and black interior; fully restored. Manual gearbox.												
1969	**Camaro ZL-1**		124379N609510	L	500-675.000 USD		NS		20-05-17	Indianapolis	S147	Mec
Blue with black interior; raced at some events in period. First restored in 1988 and in 2000 again. One of 69 examples built. 427 ZL-1 engine with manual gearbox (see Mecum lots X20 14.10.05 $840,000 and F107 23.1.16 NS).												
1969	**El Camino SS**		136809K394125	L	150-200.000 USD	114.954	140.000	131.306	15-01-17	Kissimmee	F159	Mec
Black with black interior; 18,264 miles covered. 375bhp 396 L89 engine with 4-speed manual gearbox. From the Colts Neck Collection.												
1968	**Corvette convertible**		194378S413494	L	NA	87.195*	106.700*	96.980*	15-10-16	Las Vegas	703	B/J
Blue with medium blue interior; restored. 435bhp 427 engine with manual gearbox.												
1968	**Corvette convertible**		194678S404741	L	NA	67.419*	82.500*	74.984*	15-10-16	Las Vegas	768	B/J
Blue with dark blue interior; fully restored. 435bhp 427 L71 engine with manual gearbox.												
1968	**Corvette convertible**		194678S422575	L	NQ	43.000*	52.800*	49.658*	21-01-17	Scottsdale	962	B/J
Bronze with brown interior; 390bhp 426 engine with manual gearbox.												
1968	**Corvette convertible**		194678S411010	L	NQ		NS		18-02-17	Los Angeles	S135	Mec
Dark green with tan interior; restored. 430bhp 427 L88 engine with manual gearbox (see lot S106 Mecum 26.1.11 $174,900).												
1968	**Corvette Sunray-DX race car**		194678S402351	L	950-1.250.000 USD		NS		17-08-17	Monterey	59	WoA
Built for racing by Don Yenko with a L-88 engine and Muncie M-22 4-speed gearbox, in 1968 the car, sponsored by Sunray-DX, placed 2nd in class at the Daytona 24 Hours driven by Yenko and Peter Revson, and set the fastest GT-Class lap at the Sebring 12 Hours driven by Yenko and Pedro Rodriguez. Sunsequently it was bought by Robert Luebbe and raced until the 1970s. Bought by the current owner, in 2008 it was restored to its Sebring 1968 livery.												
1968	**Corvette coupé**		194378S413494	L	NA	36.431	48.400	43.241	03-09-16	Auburn	20	WoA
Blue with blue vinyl interior; restored. 435bhp 427 engine with 4-speed manual gearbox.												
1968	**Corvette coupé**		194378S413002	L	NQ	89.584*	110.000*	103.455*	21-01-17	Scottsdale	1288.4	B/J
Silver with dark blue interior; bought in 2013 by the current, second owner. In very good original condition; 620 original miles. 390bhp 427 engine with manual gearbox.												

F183: 1970 Chevrolet Chevelle SS convertible

F184: 1969 Chevrolet Camaro Yenko coupé

Year	Model	(Bodybuilder)	Chassis no.	Steering	Estimate	Hammer price £	$	€	Date	Place	Lot	Auc. H.
1968	**Corvette coupé**		194378S417431	L	NQ		NS		21-01-17	Scottsdale	8281	R&S
Silver with original black interior; restored in 1987. 430bhp 427 L88 engine with manual gearbox.											
1968	**Corvette coupé**		194378S417431	L	500-700.000 USD		NS		20-05-17	Indianapolis	S143	Mec
See lot 8281 Russo & Steele 21.1.17.											
1968	**Corvette coupé**		194378S410684	L	NA		NS		03-06-17	Newport Beach	9222	R&S
Red with black interior; two owners; 66,278 miles covered. 435bhp 427 L71 engine with manual gearbox.											
1969	**Corvette Stingray convertible**		194679S710546	L	NA	96.184*	117.700*	106.978*	15-10-16	Las Vegas	778	B/J
Gold with black leather interior; described as in original condition. 435bhp 427 engine with automatic transmission (see lot 18 Gooding & Company 29.1.16 $99,000).											
1969	**Corvette Stingray convertible**		194679S731301	L	160-185.000 USD	123.165	150.000	140.685	15-01-17	Kissimmee	F180.1	Mec F185
Red with red vinyl interior; 435bhp 427 L71 engine with the optional L89 aluminium heads. Automatic transmission.											
1969	**Corvette Stingray convertible**		194679S710170	L	550-650.000 USD		NS		19-01-17	Scottsdale	20	Bon
Burgundy with black interior; restored in the late 2000s. 427 L88 with manual gearbox. It comes with two hardtops, one white and one black, vinyl-covered (see lot 1111 Auctions America 25.6.16 NS).											
1969	**Corvette Stingray convertible**		194679S730244	L	NQ	167.522*	205.700*	193.461*	21-01-17	Scottsdale	1069	B/J
Gold with original saddle vinyl interior; 100 miles covered since the restoration. 435bhp 427 L89 engine with manual gearbox.											
1969	**Corvette Stingray convertible**		194679S721263	L	650-750.000 USD	482.020	616.000	575.775	22-04-17	Arlington	132	WoA
Blue with black vinyl-covered hardtop and black vinyl interior; described as in very good original condition, the car has covered less than 20,000 miles. 560bhp (est.) 427 L88 engine with manual gearbox (see lot 128 Gooding & Company 19.1.13 $825,000).											
1970	**Corvette Stingray convertible**		194670S410101	L	NQ	43.219*	55.000*	49.225*	24-06-17	Northeast	630	B/J
Marlboro maroon with black interior; 26,420 original miles. With hardtop. 370bhp 350 LT-1 engine with manual gearbox.											
1969	**Corvette Stingray convertible**		194679S705266	L	NQ	72.608*	92.400*	82.698*	24-06-17	Northeast	679	B/J
Dark green with black interior; restored. 48,310 original miles. 435bhp 427 L89 engine with manual gearbox.											
1972	**Corvette Stingray convertible**		1Z67W2S507664	L	85-105.000 USD	34.188*	44.000*	37.488*	18-08-17	Carmel	47	Bon
Metallic green with saddle interior; restored. 270bhp 454 LS5 engine with automatic transmission.											
1973	**Corvette Stingray coupé**		1Z37J3S410290	L	18-25.000 USD	9.554*	12.100*	10.817*	06-10-16	Hershey	165	RMS
Red with black vinyl interior; 190bhp 350 engine with manual gearbox.											
1971	**Corvette Stingray coupé**		194371S118678	L	125-150.000 USD	119.060	145.000	135.996	15-01-17	Kissimmee	S108	Mec
Silver with black interior; body repainted, 44,932 original miles. 425bhp 454 LS6 engine with manual gearbox. From the Don Fezell collection.											
1969	**Corvette Stingray coupé**		194379S737301	L	400-500.000 USD		NA		15-01-17	Kissimmee	S140.1	Mec
Dark green with saddle leather interior; concours-quality restoration. 430bhp 427 L88 engine with 4-speed manual gearbox (see lots 5042 Barrett-Jackson 19.1.13 $280,500 and S1301 Mecum 7.9.13 NS).											
1969	**Corvette Stingray coupé**		194379S718301	L	NQ		NS		21-01-17	Scottsdale	1369	B/J
Blue with black interior; fully restored. 16,482 original miles. 427 L88 engine with manual gearbox.											
1971	**Corvette Stingray ZR-1 coupé**		194371S118742	L	250-300.000 USD		NS		20-05-17	Indianapolis	S130.1	Mec
Silver with black interior; 35,671 believed original miles. 330bhp 350 LT1 engine with manual gearbox.											
1972	**Corvette Stingray ZR-1 coupé**		1Z37L2S514058	L	NQ		NS		24-06-17	Northeast	672.1	B/J
Silver with saddle interior; restored. Less than 25,000 original miles. 255bhp 350 engine with manual gearbox.											
1978	**Corvette coupé LE Indy Pace Car**		1Z8748S906502	L	50-75.000 USD	84.524*	110.000*	98.395*	20-05-17	Indianapolis	T127	Mec F186
Black and silver with silver interior; 52 miles covered. 220bhp 350 engine with manual gearbox.											

CHEVRON (GB) (1966-1978)

Year	Model	(Bodybuilder)	Chassis no.	Steering	Estimate	£	$	€	Date	Place	Lot	Auc. H.
1968	**B10 Formula 2**		B10681	M	20-30.000 EUR	64.875*	80.669*	76.160*	25-11-16	Milan	281	RMS
Black. From the Duemila Ruote collection.											

CHRYSLER (USA) (1923-)

Year	Model	(Bodybuilder)	Chassis no.	Steering	Estimate	£	$	€	Date	Place	Lot	Auc. H.
1929	**Series 75 dual-cowl phaeton**		R272037(engine)	L	50-60.000 USD	30.331*	37.400*	33.570*	07-10-16	Hershey	232	RMS
Two-tone blue with blue leather interior; in good overall condition.											
1931	**Imperial CG dual-cowl phaeton**		7980022	L	175-200.000 USD	125.941	159.500	142.593	06-10-16	Hershey	154	RMS
Two-tone red with tan leather interior; built in Canada, the car was imported after WWII into Australia, where it was restored and fitted with the present, new, LeBaron style coachwork. Imported into the USA at unspecified date.											

F185: 1969 Chevrolet Corvette Stingray convertible

F186: 1978 Chevrolet Corvette coupé LE Indy Pace Car

Year	Model	(Bodybuilder)	Chassis no.	Steering	Estimate	Hammer price £	Hammer price $	Hammer price €	Date	Place	Lot	Auc. H.
1931	**Imperial CG dual-cowl phaeton**	(LeBaron)	7802580	L	325-375.000 USD		NS		19-01-17	Phoenix	148	RMS

Yellow with dark green leather interior; first restored between the 1950s and 1960s and between the 1980s and 1990s again. Described as still in very good overall condition (see lot 232 RM 18.8.12 $363,000).

Year	Model	(Bodybuilder)	Chassis no.	Steering	Estimate	£	$	€	Date	Place	Lot	Auc. H.
1931	**Imperial CG dual-cowl phaeton**		5P291CG	L	NQ		NS		21-01-17	Scottsdale	8081	R&S

Two-tone maroon with light grey leather interior; restored several years ago.

| 1933 | **Imperial CL sedan** | | CL1312 | L | NA | 94.387* | 115.500* | 104.978* | 15-10-16 | Las Vegas | 691 | B/J |

Maroon with tan interior; restored many years ago.

| 1933 | **Imperial CL dual-windshield phaeton** | (LeBaron) | 7803657 | L | 1.400-1.800.000 USD | 1.054.690 | 1.300.000 | 1.218.490 | 19-01-17 | Phoenix | 132 | RMS F187 |

One-off finished in dark blue with tan interior; until 1942 personal car of LeBaron designer Ralph Roberts. First restored in the 1960s and in the mid-1990s again. Formerly also in the Otis Chandler and Milhous collections (see lot 805 RM 25.2.12 $1,210,000).

| 1933 | **Imperial CL dual-cowl phaeton** | (LeBaron) | CL1313 | L | 350-400.000 USD | 210.522 | 258.500 | 243.119 | 20-01-17 | Phoenix | 233 | RMS |

Scarlet with brown interior; bought new by Lou Fageol who in 1934 circa fitted it with a 1930 Cadillac V-16 engine. First restored between 1985 and 1987, the car has been recently cosmetically restored and fitted with a period-correct Chrysler Imperial CH engine.

| 1932 | **Imperial CL cabriolet** | (De Villars) | 7803694 | L | 120-160.000 EUR | 281.452 | 347.879 | 324.000 | 19-03-17 | Fontainebleau | 202 | Ose |

Black and red; described as in very good overall condition. From the René Cocheteux collection.

| 1932 | **Imperial CL convertible sedan** | (LeBaron) | 7803380 | L | 220-260.000 USD | 141.189 | 181.500 | 161.807 | 04-06-17 | Greenwich | 121 | Bon |

Creamy white with beige interior; first restored in the 1970s and in the early 1980s again, the car is described as in good overall condition.

| 1933 | **Royal CT sedan** | | 7006588 | L | NQ | 15.229* | 18.700* | 17.587* | 21-01-17 | Scottsdale | 8193 | R&S |

Maroon and black; restored six years ago. From the Missoula Auto Museum Collection.

| 1937 | **Airflow sedan** | | C172000(engine) | L | 50-75.000 USD | 44.792* | 55.000* | 51.728* | 20-01-17 | Phoenix | 205 | RMS F188 |

Dark burgundy with black fenders and grey cloth interior; restored in the early 2000s.

| 1941 | **Royal Town & Country station wagon** | | 7712738 | L | 450-550.000 USD | 358.974 | 462.000 | 393.624 | 19-08-17 | Pebble Beach | 140 | G&Co |

Dark blue with wooden panels and red leather interior; in the same ownership from the mid-1970s to 2010 and subsequently fully restored; semi-automatic transmission.

| 1941 | **New Yorker convertible** | | 6630275 | L | 60-70.000 USD | 52.634* | 64.900* | 58.254* | 07-10-16 | Hershey | 228 | RMS |

Green with brown and tan interior; 100 miles covered since the restoration.

| 1948 | **New Yorker coupé** | | 7076630 | L | 14-18.000 EUR | 15.382* | 18.965* | 17.024* | 07-10-16 | Chateau-sur-Epte | 43 | Art |

Black; in good overall condition. From the Andre Weber Collection.

| 1949 | **Town and Country convertible** | | 7410001 | L | 65-75.000 USD | 48.660 | 60.000 | 53.856 | 07-10-16 | Hershey | 256 | RMS |

Tan with red leather and tan cloth interior; an older restoration, the car is described as in good overall condition.

| 1946 | **Town and Country convertible** | | 7400604 | L | NA | 89.892* | 110.000* | 99.979* | 15-10-16 | Las Vegas | 736 | B/J |

Maroon with wooden panels and maroon and tan interior; concours-quality restoration. Automatic transmission (see RM lots 77 17.1.03 $132,000, 119 8.3.03 $104,500, 239 4.8.07 $187,000, 238 21.1.11 $126,500 and 106 27.4.13 $132,000).

| 1948 | **Town and Country convertible** | | 7408273 | L | 125-150.000 USD | | NS | | 18-01-17 | Scottsdale | 3 | WoA |

Grey with wooden panels and leather and cloth interior; restoration completed in 1991.

| 1946 | **Town and Country convertible** | | 7400026 | L | 120-160.000 USD | 64.701* | 79.750* | 74.750* | 19-01-17 | Scottsdale | 51 | Bon |

Maroon with wooden panels; retained by its first owner for just under 70 years. Restored in the late 1980s.

| 1948 | **Town and Country convertible** | | 7405725 | L | 120-140.000 USD | 62.709* | 77.000* | 72.419* | 21-01-17 | Scottsdale | 120 | G&Co |

Beige with wooden panels and burgundy leather interior; restored in the 1990s.

| 1948 | **Town and Country convertible** | | 7404999 | L | 110-130.000 USD | 81.437* | 99.000* | 93.298* | 10-03-17 | Amelia Island | 12 | G&Co |

Metallic green with wooden panels and two-tone cream interior; restored about 10 years ago.

| 1947 | **Town and Country convertible** | | 7404990 | L | 140-160.000 USD | 85.962* | 104.500* | 98.481* | 11-03-17 | Amelia Island | 253 | RMS F189 |

Yellow with original wooden panels; in very good driving order. 44,000 original miles. Semi-automatic transmission (see lots 687 Auctions America 28.3.15 NS and 176 RM/Sotheby's 8.10.15 NS).

| 1948 | **Town and Country convertible** | | 7407063 | L | 90-120.000 USD | | NS | | 04-06-17 | Greenwich | 189 | Bon |

Blue with wooden panels and brown leather and cloth interior; restored in the late 1990s (see lot 33 Christie's 29.8.99 $123,500).

| 1948 | **Town and Country convertible** | | 5971503 | L | 100-140.000 USD | 52.727 | 67.100 | 60.055 | 24-06-17 | Santa Monica | 188 | RMS |

Green with wooden panels and green and tan leather interior; original woodwork, repainted body. 64,556 believed original miles. Automatic transmission.

| 1947 | **Town and Country convertible** | | 7404990 | L | 90-120.000 USD | 111.111 | 143.000 | 121.836 | 18-08-17 | Carmel | 111 | Bon |

See lot 253 RM/Sotheby's 11.3.17.

F187: 1933 Chrysler Imperial CL dual-windshield phaeton (LeBaron)

F188: 1937 Chrysler Airflow sedan

Year	Model	(Bodybuilder)	Chassis no.	Steering	Estimate	Hammer price £	$	€	Date	Sale Place	Lot	Auc. H.

F189: 1947 Chrysler Town and Country convertible

F190: 1961 Chrysler 300G hardtop

Year	Model	(Bodybuilder)	Chassis no.	Steering	Estimate	£	$	€	Date	Place	Lot	Auc. H.
1953	New Yorker DeLuxe coupé		7232585	L	12-15.000 EUR	15.382*	18.965*	17.024*	07-10-16	Chateau-sur-Epte	1	Art
	White with black roof; imported into France from Canada 10 years ago. Interior retrimmed. From the Andre Weber Collection											
1953	Special	(Ghia)	7231533	L	550-750.000 USD		NS		18-08-17	Carmel	55	Bon
	Two-tone blue with blue interior; sold new to France where it was discovered in the 1990s and subjected to a full restoration completed in 2001 (see lot 114 RM 10.5.14 $463,042).											
1961	300G hardtop		841315S588	L	65-75.000 USD	57.958	77.000	68.792	03-09-16	Auburn	4079	AA
	White with beige interior; fully restored. Automatic transmission.											
1961	300G hardtop		8413159853	L	90-115.000 USD	82.110	100.000	93.790	15-01-17	Kissimmee	F185	Mec F190
	Black with tan interior; engine rebuilt, body repainted. Automatic transmission (see lot S640 Russo & Steele 16.8.14 $61,600).											
1955	C-300		3N552563	L	100-120.000 USD	105.261*	129.250*	121.560*	20-01-17	Scottsdale	52	G&Co
	Red with tan interior; in good overall condition. Mechanically upgraded with front disc brakes, Koni adjustable shocks and heavy-duty front stabilizer bar.											
1958	300D hardtop		LC41735	L	90-120.000 USD	68.376*	88.000*	74.976*	19-08-17	Pebble Beach	144	G&Co
	Black with tan leather interior; less than 400 miles covered since a full restoration completed in 2012.											
1957	300C convertible		3N571621	L	NQ	85.105*	104.500*	98.282*	21-01-17	Scottsdale	1442	B/J
	White with tan interior; fully restored.											
1961	300G convertible		8413149400	L	125-150.000 USD	84.501	105.600	98.768	01-04-17	Ft.Lauderdale	535	AA
	Black with white interior (see lots Mecum F292 6.10.06 $127,050, and Auctions America 5109 1.9.13 $167,750 and 2104 18.7.15 NS).											
1955	New Yorker DeLuxe St.Regis hardtop		N5531900	L	NQ	38.521*	47.300*	44.486*	21-01-17	Scottsdale	972.1	B/J
	White with green roof and white interior; restored at unspecified date. 48,754 miles on the odometer (see lot 271 RM 4.8.07 $60,500).											
1956	New Yorker convertible		N5631956	L	100-125.000 USD	80.050	100.000	90.140	04-11-16	Dallas	S129	Mec F191
	Rose and white with black and white leather interior; restored between 2007 and 2009. 354 Hemi engine with automatic transmission.											
1956	Windsor convertible		W5613682	L	NQ	61.970	77.000	72.295	18-02-17	Los Angeles	S129.1	Mec
	Red with red interior; 250bhp 331 Spitfire engine with automatic transmission.											
1960	New Yorker convertible		8303117389	L	55-75.000 USD	59.167	77.000	68.877	20-05-17	Indianapolis	F169	Mec
	Red with red and white interior; concours-quality restoration. 413 engine with automatic transmission (see lot 33 RM 18.1.02 NS).											
1972	VH Valiant Charger R/T E38 coupé		VH7S29BL150808	R	120-150.000 AUD	86.715	111.672	95.034	20-08-17	Mallala Park	19	Mos F192
	Restored; 265ci 6-cylinder engine with 3.speed manual gearbox. From the collection of the late Clem Smith.											

CISITALIA (I) (1946-1965)

Year	Model	(Bodybuilder)	Chassis no.	Steering	Estimate	£	$	€	Date	Place	Lot	Auc. H.
1947	202 SC cabriolet	(Vignale)	054SC	R	525-625.000 USD	452.430	550.000	518.320	10-03-17	Amelia Island	59	G&Co
	Dark burgundy with brown interior; imported into the USA from Argentina in 2003, the car was subsequently subjected to a concours-quality restoration completed in 2016.											
1950	Abarth 204A spyder sport	(Motto)	04	R	Refer Dpt.	823.423	1.001.000	943.342	11-03-17	Amelia Island	40	Mot
	One of the examples bought by Carlo Abarth who restamped it as chassis 08. The car was driven by Tazio Nuvolari in 1950 at the Targa Florio and Palermo-Monte Pellegrino hillclimb. In the 1960s it was imported into Argentina where in 1978 it was bought by Sergio Lugo who had it fully restored between 2009 and 2011 and retained it until 2013 when it was sold to the USA. With FIVA passport (see lot 145 Coys 9.5.14 NS).											

F191: 1956 Chrysler New Yorker convertible

F192: 1972 Chrysler VH Valiant Charger R/T E38 coupé

Year	Model	(Bodybuilder)	Chassis no.	Steering	Estimate	Hammer price £	$	€	Date	Place	Lot	Auc. H.

CITROËN (F) *(1919-)*

Year	Model	(Bodybuilder)	Chassis no.	Steering	Estimate	£	$	€	Date	Place	Lot	Auc. H.
1924	Type C3		46380	L	5-10.000 EUR	16.219*	20.167*	19.040*	25-11-16	Milan	338	RMS
Red with black wings. From the Duemila Ruote collection.											
1930	AC4 berline		825052	L	8-10.000 GBP	5.600	6.851	6.485	04-03-17	Brooklands	106	His
Restored approximately 30 years ago, the car is described as in good overall condition.											
1934	8 Rosalie		517039	R	4-6.000 GBP	3.937	5.044	4.511	02-06-17	Solihull	15	H&H
Maroon and black with maroon interior; restored many years ago, it requires recommissioning prior to use (see H&H lots 56 12.1.99 $12,563 and 34 13.9.06 $11,618).											
1934	10A Rosalie berline		267353	L	6-8.000 EUR	8.790*	10.837*	9.728*	07-10-16	Chateau-sur-Epte	59	Art
Restored many years ago, the car is described as in good overall condition. Since 1964 in the Andre Weber Collection.											
1934	7 Sport roadster		021208	L	90-120.000 EUR	103.699*	129.232*	121.584*	10-02-17	Paris	21	Art F193
White with red interior; bought in 1979 by the current owner and subsequently restored.											
1937	7C faux-cabriolet		099436	L	60-100.000 EUR	73.199	91.222	85.824	10-02-17	Paris	28	Art
Plum with light beige interior; fully restored in 1992 by André Lecoq. From the Hervé and Martine Ogliastro Collection.											
1935	7C berline		064114	L	12-15.000 EUR	11.467	14.173	13.200	18-03-17	Fontainebleau	45	Ose
Blue with light grey cloth interior; from the Perinet Marquet collection.											
1936	11AL légère		355027	L	9-13.000 EUR	12.788	15.974	14.400	06-11-16	Lyon	312	Ose
Beige; restored in 1997. Since 1999 fitted with an ID 19 engine.											
1949	11BL légère berline		2491385	L	20-30.000 USD	18.734*	23.100*	20.735*	07-10-16	Hershey	254	RMS
Black with grey cloth interior; in good overall condition.											
1938	11B cabriolet		11B142788	L	100-140.000 EUR	101.666	126.698	119.200	10-02-17	Paris	142	Art
Burgundy and black with biscuit interior; restored some years ago.											
1938	11 BL cabriolet (Tonneline)		407485	L	100-120.000 EUR		NS		10-02-17	Paris	49	Art
Burgundy and ivory with burgundy leather interior; the car requires some mechanical attention prior to use. The original engine was replaced with a 11D unit.											
1939	11 BL cabriolet		437937	L	90-120.000 EUR	85.394	109.120	102.000	01-05-17	Obenheim	368	Ose
Ivory with dark red interior; restored at unspecified date (see lot 310 Artcurial 6.2.16 $93,469).											
1951	15 Six D berline		703122	L	24-38.000 EUR	29.985	36.692	33.350	15-10-16	Salzburg	416	Dor
Black with grey-brown cloth interior; restored in 1995-96.											
1952	15 Six D		718175	L	20-30.000 EUR	26.792*	32.548*	29.800*	30-10-16	Paris	123	Art F194
Black; since 1973 in the same ownership.											
1955	15 Six H berline		727596	L	30-35.000 EUR	29.188	36.076	33.600	18-03-17	Fontainebleau	46	Ose
Black; from the Perinet Marquet collection.											
1955	2CV pickup		853012	R	28-33.000 GBP	33.288	44.466	39.363	08-09-16	Fontwell Park	135	Coy
Sand; since 1977 in the current ownership, restored in 2006. One of two examples known to exist.											
1990	2CV Charleston		371815	L	8-12.000 EUR	9.216*	11.196*	10.251*	30-10-16	Paris	122	Art
Black; in original condition. Just one owner.											
1956	2CV AZ		269368	L	7-13.000 EUR	8.526	10.649	9.600	05-11-16	Lyon	221	Agu
Grey; restored between 2011 and 2013.											
1987	2CV6 Dolly		288537	R	NA	4.592*	5.710*	5.391*	26-11-16	Weybridge	240	His
Ivory and red; in good condition.											
1990	2CV Dolly		352008	L	20-30.000 EUR	36.600*	45.611*	42.912*	10-02-17	Paris	144	Art
Grey and red with grey cloth interior; one owner and 30 kms covered.											
1990	2CV Charleston		356503	L	20-30.000 EUR	45.750*	57.014*	53.640*	10-02-17	Paris	145	Art
Red and black with grey cloth interior; one owner and 40 kms covered.											
1956	2CV AZ		253480	L	15-25.000 EUR	27.450*	34.208*	32.184*	10-02-17	Paris	35	Art
Grey; restored and prepared for classic car rallies. 69 kms covered since the restoration.											
1987	2CV6 AZKA		213239	L	20-30.000 EUR	22.061	28.141	25.200	18-06-17	Fontainebleau	82	Ose
Grey; 640 kms covered.											

F193: 1934 Citroën 7 Sport roadster

F194: 1952 Citroën 15 Six D

Year	Model	(Bodybuilder)	Chassis no.	Steering	Estimate	Hammer price £	$	€	Date	Place	Lot	Auc. H.
1960	**2CV**		2268282	L	9-11.000 GBP	7.500	9.734	8.492	29-06-17	Fontwell Park	124	Coy
	*Blue; restored.*
1962	**DS 19 Concorde coupé**	(Chapron)	4200344	L	100-150.000 EUR	134.199	167.241	157.344	10-02-17	Paris	42	Art **F195**
	*Metallic gold with light grey roof and tan interior; fully restored. The car was displayed at the Chapron stand at the 1962 Geneva Motor Show.*
1972	**DS 21ie**		03FA1350	L	15-25.000 EUR	17.147*	20.830*	19.072*	30-10-16	Paris	125	Art
	*Light blue with leather interior; one owner. Automatic transmission.*
1968	**DS 21 Pallas**		4618086	L	15-25.000 EUR	11.788*	14.321*	13.112*	30-10-16	Paris	176	Art
	*Black with black vinyl roof and black leather interior; in good condition.*
1973	**DS 23 Pallas**		00FE7084	L	40-60.000 USD	44.622*	55.000*	51.552*	19-01-17	Phoenix	105	RMS
	*Described as in very good original condition; approximately 40,000 kms covered. 5-speed manual gearbox.*
1975	**DS 23ie Pallas**		DSFG02FG2232	L	35-45.000 EUR	NS			09-02-17	Paris	424	Bon
	*Copper metallic with beige roof and brown leather interior; restored in 2009-10. Manual gearbox; sliding sunroof (see lot 4 Bonhams 11.9.10 $29,268).*
1974	**DS 23ie Pallas**		02FG5131	L	22-26.000 GBP	30.240	36.996	35.018	04-03-17	Brooklands	145	His
	*Blue with black roof and blue cloth interior; restored in 2012. Semi-automatic transmission.*
1973	**DS 23 Break**		00FF2228	L	15-20.000 EUR	12.509	15.461	14.400	18-03-17	Fontainebleau	36	Ose
	*Blue with light grey roof; from the Perinet Marquet collection.*
1974	**DS 23ie**		1FG7580	L	30-40.000 EUR	32.315	39.942	37.200	19-03-17	Fontainebleau	242	Ose
	*White with black roof; restored.*
1965	**ID 19**		3670404	L	19-23.000 EUR	NS			14-01-17	Maastricht	246	Coy
	*White with red interior; in good driving order.*
1967	**ID 19**		3734176	L	12-18.000 EUR	12.196	15.075	14.040	18-03-17	Fontainebleau	34	Ose
	*White with black roof and red interior; sliding sunroof. From the Perinet Marquet collection.*
1973	**D Super 5**		4537095	R	NA	73.130	97.139	86.791	02-09-16	Salon Privé	209	SiC
	*White with red interior; described as in concours condition.*
1964	**DS 19 cabriolet**	(Chapron)	4272091	L	135-175.000 EUR	164.171	202.414	181.700	07-10-16	Zoute	32	Bon
	*Since 1999 in the current, third ownership; restored between 1999 and 2002; engine overhauled in 2015.*
1965	**DS 21 cabriolet**	(Chapron)	4460041	L	180-200.000 EUR	NA			08-10-16	Paris	131	CB/C
	*Sahara grey with black leather interior; mechanicals overhauled in recent years.*
1963	**ID 19 cabriolet**	(Chapron)	3281504	L	200-240.000 EUR	184.888	225.144	211.185	14-01-17	Maastricht	221	Coy
	*Metallic grey with red leather interior; restored.*
1964	**DS 19 cabriolet**	(Chapron)	4407056	L	170-210.000 EUR	176.136	221.324	207.000	09-02-17	Paris	369	Bon
	*Light metallic blue; restored in 2008 circa.*
1962	**DS 19 cabriolet**		4200446	L	120-160.000 EUR	137.249	171.042	160.920	10-02-17	Paris	143	Art **F196**
	*Metallic grey with burgundy interior; restored in 2006.*
1965	**DS 19 cabriolet**		4294050	L	130-160.000 EUR	137.249	171.042	160.920	10-02-17	Paris	19	Art
	*Blue with tan interior; in good overall condition (see lot 26 Bonhams 11.10.13 NS).*
1965	**DS 19 cabriolet**		4294071	L	40-60.000 EUR	86.416*	107.693*	101.320*	10-02-17	Paris	43	Art
	*Restoration project.*
1969	**DS 21 cabriolet**		4638784	L	110-150.000 EUR	104.242	128.844	120.000	18-03-17	Fontainebleau	30	Ose
	*White with black interior; from the Perinet Marquet collection (see lot 23 Chevau-Légerè 3.2.11 NS).*
1963	**ID 19 cabriolet**	(Chapron)	3281504	L	170-190.000 EUR	NS			08-04-17	Essen	169	Coy
	*See lot 221 Coys 14.01.17.*
1968	**Ami 6 break**		232388	L	6-8.000 EUR	6.394	7.987	7.200	06-11-16	Lyon	314	Ose
	*Red with red interior; in good overall condition.*
1980	**Mehari 4x4**		CE0098	L	28-38.000 EUR	26.642	33.279	30.000	06-11-16	Lyon	348	Ose
	*Two owners; 44,650 kms on the odometer; body recently repainted; engine overhauled.*
1982	**Mehari 4x4**		1124521	L	30-40.000 EUR	NS			18-03-17	Lyon	211	Agu
	*Green; restored about 10 years ago. 43,000 kms on the odometer.*

F195: 1962 Citroën DS 19 Concorde coupé (Chapron)

F196: 1962 Citroën DS 19 cabriolet

Year	Model	(Bodybuilder)	Chassis no.	Steering	Estimate	Hammer Price £	$	€	Date	Place	Lot	Auc. H.
1982	**Mehari 4x4**		CE2332	L	25-35.000 EUR	39.016*	57.583*	44.370*	02-07-17	Monaco	102	Art
Light green; 1,000 kms covered since the restoration completed in 2013.												
1971	**SM**		SB3895	L	NA		NS		02-09-16	Salon Privé	259	SiC
White; body restored in the past. Recently serviced.												
1971	**SM**		00SB6121	L	20-30.000 GBP	17.250	22.913	20.472	03-09-16	Beaulieu	481	Bon
Pale green with tan leather interior; sold new to the USA, the car was acquired in 1981 by the current owner and reimported into Europe. Manual gearbox.												
1972	**SM**		SB9720	L	12-18.000 EUR	13.184*	16.255*	14.592*	07-10-16	Chateau-sur-Epte	55	Art
Grey with blue cloth interior; in original condition. From the Andre Weber Collection.												
1972	**SM**		SB6477	L	35-50.000 EUR	37.508	45.567	41.720	30-10-16	Paris	124	Art
Recommissioned; three owners.												
1971	**SM**		00SB1867	L	28-34.000 GBP	32.480	40.386	38.128	26-11-16	Weybridge	159	His
In good overall condition; engine rebuilt.												
1972	**SM**		01SB0160	L	60-80.000 USD	28.558*	35.200*	32.993*	19-01-17	Scottsdale	5	Bon
Champagne with tobacco leather interior; described as in good original condition. 41,000 miles on the odometer.												
1973	**SM**		00SD0265	L	75-100.000 USD	66.292*	81.400*	76.557*	20-01-17	Scottsdale	63	G&Co
For 30 years with its first owner; mechanically sorted in 2004; recently serviced.												
1974	**SM**		00SC3639	L	40-60.000 EUR	30.500	38.009	35.760	10-02-17	Paris	106	Art
Gold; sold new to Italy. Two owners. Engine rebuilt 10,000 kms ago.												
1973	**SM**		00SC1288	L	30-35.000 GBP		NS		24-02-17	Stoneleigh P.	528	SiC
Gold; leather interior; described as in good overall condition.												
1972	**SM**		SB6787	L	15-20.000 EUR	23.976	29.634	27.600	18-03-17	Fontainebleau	43	Ose
Metallic grey with brown leather interior; from the Perinet Marquet collection.												
1971	**SM**		00SB1584	L	12-18.000 EUR	20.431	25.253	23.520	19-03-17	Fontainebleau	234	Ose
Grey with black interior; in good driving order.												
1979	**CX 2400 Prestige**		00ML6642	L	30-50.000 EUR	21.350*	26.607*	25.032*	10-02-17	Paris	44	Art
Three owners; 60,000 kms covered; recently serviced. Semi-automatic transmission.												
1986	**BX 4TC**		00KL3026	L	50-80.000 EUR	54.413*	67.811*	63.798*	10-02-17	Paris	105	Art **F197**
White; 220 kms covered. First owner Franco Sbarro.												

CLEMENT & CIE. (F) *(1895-1903)*

Year	Model	(Bodybuilder)	Chassis no.	Steering	Estimate	£	$	€	Date	Place	Lot	Auc. H.
1903	**Type B voiturette**		941	R	40-60.000 EUR	93.817	115.960	108.000	19-03-17	Fontainebleau	207	Ose
Described as in original condition; complete engine.												
1903	**12/16hp rear-entrance tonneau**		4186	R	250-300.000 GBP	281.500	347.934	324.035	19-03-17	Goodwood	23	Bon **F198**
Car imported into the UK from Australia 15-18 years ago and subjected to a full restoration completed in 2006. New body.												

CLYDE (GB) *(1899-1930)*

Year	Model	(Bodybuilder)	Chassis no.	Steering	Estimate	£	$	€	Date	Place	Lot	Auc. H.
1908	**8/10hp light roadster**		BC1058(registration)	R	20-30.000 GBP		NS		03-09-16	Beaulieu	472	Bon
One of three known survivors with a White & Poppe twin-cylinder engine; from 1952 to 1956 owned by George Wait, founder of the make. Restored in the USA in the early 1960s and on display in a motor museum in Kansas from 1962 to 2003.												

CONNAUGHT (GB) *(1948-1959)*

Year	Model	(Bodybuilder)	Chassis no.	Steering	Estimate	£	$	€	Date	Place	Lot	Auc. H.
1948	**L2**		7048	R	75-90.000 GBP		NS		26-07-17	Duxford	55	H&H
British racing green with green interior; raced in period; fitted at unspecified date with the present 2,496cc engine. Restored.												

COOPER (GB) *(1947-1971)*

Year	Model	(Bodybuilder)	Chassis no.	Steering	Estimate	£	$	€	Date	Place	Lot	Auc. H.
1937	**T1**		C1	R	30-50.000 GBP	48.300	64.360	57.120	10-09-16	Goodwood	163	Bon
The car was built by Charles Cooper for his son John's 14th birthday, using modified chassis and engine from an Austin Seven. Discovered in 1992 it was fully restored with the assistance of John Cooper and later displayed at the Cooper factory.												

F197: 1986 Citroën BX 4TC

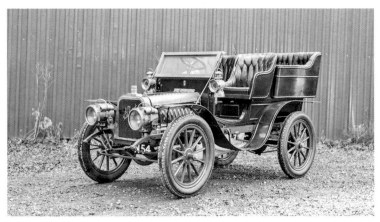

F198: 1903 Clement & Cie. 12/16hp rear-entrance tonneau

Year	Model	(Bodybuilder)	Chassis No.	Steering	Estimate	Hammer Price £	$	€	Date	Place	Lot	Auc. H.
1954	Mark VIII		MK4254	M	28-32.000 GBP		NS		26-11-16	Weybridge	203	His

Light green; raced in period. Restored in 2005. Jap engine (see lot 304 Bonhams 12.9.15 $40,794).

CORD (USA) (1929-1937)

Year	Model	(Bodybuilder)	Chassis No.	Steering	Estimate	£	$	€	Date	Place	Lot	Auc. H.
1932	L-29 convertible		2930287	L	250-300.000 USD	191.872	236.500	221.671	19-01-17	Phoenix	128	RMS

Cream with blue leather interior; restored by its previous owner who retained it from 1950 to the early 2000s. Described as still in very good overall condition.

| 1930 | L-29 convertible sedan | | FD3007A | L | NQ | 111.980* | 137.500* | 129.319* | 21-01-17 | Scottsdale | 1361 | B/J |

White with blue beltline and tan leather interior; older restoration (see lot 5141 Auctions America 5.9.15 $137,500).

| 1930 | L-29 Brougham | | FDA1785 | L | NQ | 244.320* | 300.000* | 282.150* | 21-01-17 | Scottsdale | 3005 | B/J |

Cream and brown with tan interior. 100% of hammer price to benefit Loma Linda University Children's Hospital.

| 1931 | L-29 convertible | | 2928916 | L | 220-260.000 USD | 153.826 | 187.000 | 176.229 | 11-03-17 | Amelia Island | 272 | RMS F199 |

Red with black leather interior; recently restored in Germany. Engine rebuilt.

| 1936 | 810 Westchester sedan | | 1206A | L | 35-40.000 GBP | 43.912 | 58.658 | 51.926 | 08-09-16 | Fontwell Park | 116 | Coy |

Red with grey interior; stored for 55 years and then fully restored between 2010 and 2014.

| 1936 | 810 Phaeton | | 2361H | L | 150-175.000 USD | 124.894 | 154.000 | 138.230 | 07-10-16 | Hershey | 251 | RMS |

Cigarette cream with dark red leather interior; restoration recently refreshed. Fitted with 1937-style side exhausts (see lot 129 RM 13.3.10 $170,500).

| 1936 | 810 Westchester sedan | | 1717A | L | NQ | 17.469* | 21.450* | 20.174* | 21-01-17 | Scottsdale | 8047 | R&S |

Black; cloth interior; "barn-find".

| 1936 | 810 Phaeton | | 6166907SPB65040 | L | NQ | 89.584 | 110.000 | 103.455 | 21-01-17 | Scottsdale | 8048 | R&S |

Cream with brown interior; restored.

| 1936 | 810 Phaeton | | 8102247H | L | 170-220.000 USD | 135.729* | 165.000* | 155.496* | 10-03-17 | Amelia Island | 116 | RMS |

Black with black interior; restoration carried out in the 1990s and refreshed in more recent years. From the Orin Smith collection.

| 1936 | 810 Beverly sedan | | 81017944 | L | NQ | 25.823* | 33.000* | 30.845* | 22-04-17 | Arlington | 39 | WoA |

Originally finished in maroon and repainted in cream many years ago. In good working order. From the Monical collection.

| 1937 | 812 SC Phaeton | | 32374H | L | 250-300.000 USD | 178.014 | 236.500 | 211.289 | 03-09-16 | Auburn | 4159 | AA |

Black with dark red interior; described as in very good, highly original condition (see lots Russo & Steele S644 14.8.09 NS, and Gooding & Company 36 22.1.10 $198,000 and 24 20.08.11 $198,000).

| 1936 | 812 SC Sportsman | | 32226F | L | 70-100.000 GBP | 100.060 | 132.910 | 118.751 | 03-09-16 | Beaulieu | 426 | Bon |

Yellow with red interior; since 1977 in the same family ownership. Recently recommissioned, it is described as in good driving order.

| 1937 | 812 Westchester sedan | | 81231874A | L | 40-60.000 USD | 44.605* | 55.000* | 49.368* | 07-10-16 | Hershey | 234 | RMS |

Blue with blue cloth interior believed original; built with supercharged engine, at unspecified date the car was fitted with the present, correct Cord engine no.FB375. In good driving order (see lot 33 Christie's 15.6.96 $24,725).

| 1937 | 812 SC Phaeton | | 81232013H | L | 225-275.000 USD | 179.168 | 220.000 | 206.910 | 20-01-17 | Phoenix | 268 | RMS |

Black with brown interior; restored many years ago, the car is described as still in very good overall condition (see lot 224 RM 9.6.07 $297,000).

| 1937 | 812 SC Sportsman | | 81231762F | L | 300-350.000 USD | 248.837 | 302.500 | 285.076 | 11-03-17 | Amelia Island | 249 | RMS F200 |

Rich maroon with red interior; concours-quality restoration completed in 2007. Original supercharged engine and gearbox replaced with correct rebuilt units (engine no.FC2575, gearbox no.T3061).

| 1937 | 812 SC Phaeton | | FC2284 | L | NQ | 137.720* | 176.000* | 164.507* | 22-04-17 | Arlington | 32 | WoA |

Black with red leather interior; in very good overall condition. From the Monical collection and previously owned by the same family for 50 years.

CROSLEY (USA) (1939-1952)

| 1951 | Series CD station wagon | | CD305972 | L | NA | 6.742* | 8.250* | 7.498* | 15-10-16 | Las Vegas | 26.1 | B/J |

Cream and brown with brown interior; since 1977 in the current ownership.

| 1950 | Series CD Hot Shot roadster | | VC20070 | L | 12-16.000 USD | 5.801* | 7.150* | 6.702* | 19-01-17 | Scottsdale | 75 | Bon |

Red with red vinyl interior; restored some years ago.

F199: 1931 Cord L-29 convertible

F200: 1937 Cord 812 SC Sportsman

Year	Model	(Bodybuilder)	Chassis no.	Steering	Estimate	Hammer Price £	$	€	Date	Place	Lot	Auc. H.

CROSSLE' (GB) (1957-)

| 1964 | C7S | | C7S6418 | R | 65-80.000 GBP | 66.375 | 87.233 | 74.592 | 27-07-17 | Silverstone | 123 | SiC |

Blue; raced in period. Restored in 2014; Ford 1600 Twin-Cam engine; in ready to race condition (see lot 45 Artcurial 9.2.08 NS).

CUNNINGHAM (USA) (1950-1957)

| 1953 | C-3 coupé (Vignale) | | 5223 | L | 750-950.000 USD | 854.700* | 1.100.000* | 937.200* | 19-08-17 | Monterey | 244 | RMS F201 |

Black with red leather interior; until 2014 in the ownership of the Cunningham family; paintwork and interior redone in 2003; 10,097 miles covered since new.

DAF (NL) (1958-1976)

| 1962 | 750 Daffodil | | 303047757 | L | 20-30.000 USD | 7.139* | 8.800* | 8.248* | 19-01-17 | Phoenix | 177 | RMS |

Maroon; restored in 1995. Variomatic automatic transmission. From the Mohrschladt Family Collection.

DAIMLER (GB) (1896-1983)

1897	4hp wagonette (Stirling)	1197	R	220-220.000 GBP	236.700	295.638	266.524	04-11-16	London	209	Bon F202

Red with red wheels and interior; described as in good working order, the car was driven at several London to Brighton Run editions. Since 1996 in the same family ownership.

| 1905 | 30/40hp tourer | 3127 | R | 55-65.000 GBP | 57.500 | 72.502 | 67.568 | 07-12-16 | London | 373 | Bon |

Built with Rothschild (Paris) landaulette body, the car was fitted in 1911 with a ten-seat station wagon body. In the late 1940s it was fitted with a two-seat body from a Martini of contemporary age and probably in the early 1970s it was fitted with the present tourer body, described as sound and finished in light green. Good mechanical order.

| 1939 | Light Straight 8 saloon (Vanden Plas) | 47820 | R | 50-70.000 EUR | 49.022 | 61.233 | 55.200 | 06-11-16 | Lyon | 308 | Ose |

Two-tone brown with original beige leather interior; restored in 2008.

| 1951 | DB18 Special Sports (Barker) | 59032 | R | 24-28.000 GBP | 25.300 | 33.712 | 29.920 | 10-09-16 | Goodwood | 175 | Bon |

Burgundy and cream; restored in 1992.

| 1950 | DB18 Special Sports (Barker) | 53798 | R | 17-20.000 GBP | | NS | | 19-03-17 | Goodwood | 35 | Bon |

Recent cosmetic restoration; described as in good mechanical order (see lot 317 Bonhams 20.4.09 $12,068).

| 1957 | Conquest saloon | 98108 | R | 14-16.000 GBP | 8.960 | 11.298 | 10.529 | 07-12-16 | Chateau Impney | 64 | H&H |

Silver and blue with blue leather interior; 21,500 miles on the odometer. Automatic transmission.

| 1955 | Conquest Century Roadster | 90470 | R | 32-38.000 GBP | 37.950 | 50.409 | 45.039 | 03-09-16 | Beaulieu | 493 | Bon |

Old English white with red leather interior; restored in 1988, engine overhauled in 2014. Since 1990 in the current ownership.

| 1956 | Conquest Century cabriolet | 90511 | R | 28-34.000 GBP | 31.360 | 38.366 | 36.315 | 04-03-17 | Brooklands | 185 | His |

Maroon and cream with matching interior; restored (see lot 328 Historics 7.6.14 $48,994).

| 1955 | Conquest Century Roadster | 90476 | R | 60-80.000 USD | 28.906* | 35.200* | 33.359* | 09-03-17 | Amelia Island | 164 | Bon |

Silver; bought in 2012 by the current owner and subsequently restored in Italy.

| 1955 | Conquest cabriolet | 87737 | R | 18-22.000 GBP | 19.040 | 23.294 | 22.048 | 04-03-17 | Brooklands | 159 | His |

In good overall condition; original red leather interior.

| 1963 | SP250 | 104178 | L | NA | 45.538 | 60.500 | 54.051 | 03-09-16 | Auburn | 21 | WoA |

British racing green with tan interior; restored at unspecified date. With roll bar.

| 1960 | SP250 retractable hardtop | 101354 | R | 50-70.000 GBP | 39.500 | 52.634 | 46.713 | 10-09-16 | Goodwood | 123 | Bon F203 |

Silver grey; sole example fitted with a retractable hardtop roof patented by Anthony H. Croucher Precision & Prototype Engineering Co Ltd (AHC) and with a body converted to four-seater. Since new in the Croucher family ownership. Recently recommissioned.

| 1961 | SP250 | 102749 | R | 30-40.000 GBP | 28.343 | 35.429 | 33.405 | 12-04-17 | London | 341 | Coy |

Old English white with blue interior; never fully restored and always well maintained. Engine and gearbox rebuilt.

| 1961 | SP250 | 102683 | R | 50-60.000 GBP | 43.348 | 54.185 | 51.090 | 12-04-17 | London | 346 | Coy |

Opalescent grey with dark red interior; fully restored. Automatic transmission.

| 1960 | SP250 | 100670 | R | 34-38.000 GBP | 33.600 | 43.720 | 39.110 | 20-05-17 | Ascot | 271 | His |

Red with tan leather interior; restored 10 years ago.

| 1961 | SP250 | 102526 | R | 40-50.000 GBP | 48.937 | 63.158 | 56.096 | 06-06-17 | Woodcote Park | 17 | H&H |

Gunmetal grey with grey leather interior; in very good overall condition. Engine overhauled in 2016.

F201: 1953 Cunningham C-3 coupé (Vignale)

F202: 1897 Daimler 4hp wagonette (Stirling)

Year	Model	(Bodybuilder)	Chassis no.	Steering	Estimate	Hammer price £	$	€	Sale Date	Place	Lot	Auc. H.
1964	2.5l V8		1A6388BW	R	16-18.000 GBP	14.560	17.845	16.194	12-10-16	Duxford	85	H&H
Grey with blue leather interior; restored in the late 1990s. Engine overhauled in more recent years.											
1965	2.5l V8		1A9601BW	R	13-19.000 GBP	14.690	18.352	17.358	23-02-17	Donington Park	79	H&H
Gunmetal grey with red interior.											
1964	2.5l V8 (cabriolet/conversion)		1A7045BW	R	70-100.000 GBP	74.300	96.427	84.130	30-06-17	Goodwood	235	Bon
Black with red leather interior; conversion carried out by Vicarage in the early 2000s. Circa 6,500 miles covered since the conversion (see Bonhams lots 375 22.6.07 $145,781 and 250 24.6.16 NS).												F204
1967	Sovereign		1A31884BW	R	10-15.000 GBP	5.575	6.873	6.170	08-10-16	Ascot	343	Coy
Green with red interior; restored in 2013. The interior require some attention.											
1966	Sovereign		1A70042DN	L	5-7.000 EUR	9.063*	11.270*	10.640*	25-11-16	Milan	945	RMS
Dark blue with light brown interior; 66,165 kms. From the Duemila Ruote collection.											
1968	Sovereign		1A33542BW	R	8-10.000 GBP	7.080	8.796	8.259	18-02-17	London	345	Coy
Old English white with red interior; body repainted in 2016. Recently serviced.											
1968	V8 250		P1K3031BW	R	18-20.000 GBP		NS		12-10-16	Duxford	21	H&H
Light green; several works carried out to the body and mechanicals between late 1990s-early 2000s (see lot 41 H & H 25.2.15 $30,347).											
1968	V8 250		P1K3281BW	R	12-16.000 GBP	13.440	16.711	15.777	26-11-16	Weybridge	214	His
Dark blue with red leather interior; in good condition. Two owners. Automatic transmission.											
1976	Sovereign 4.2 coupé		2H1811BW	R	24-28.000 GBP	30.800	38.297	36.156	26-11-16	Weybridge	162	His
White with black Everflex roof and biscuit velour interior; in very good original condition. 24,153 miles covered. Three owners all from the same family.											
1976	Sovereign 4.2 coupé		2H1441BW	R	14-18.000 GBP	15.680	20.403	18.252	20-05-17	Ascot	255	His
White with black everflex roof and dark blue interior; cosmetic restoration completed in 2011.											
1974	Double Six saloon		201106BW	R	18-25.000 GBP	11.150	13.747	12.340	08-10-16	Ascot	305	Coy
Purple with black vinyl roof and cream leather interior; described as in very good original condition. 47,000 miles covered. Recommissioned in 2016.											
1977	Double Six coupé		2F1274BW	R	24-28.000 GBP	32.062	41.985	35.797	29-07-17	Silverstone	431	SiC
Red with black vinyl roof and biscuit leather interior; in largely original condition, the car has covered just over 33,300 miles.											
2001	V8 Super saloon		F35595	R	50-60.000 GBP		NS		12-11-16	Birmingham	321	SiC
British racing green with beige and green interior; car built to the personal specification of Her Majesty Queen Elizabeth II, who travelled in it for more than 11,000 of the approximately 15,000 miles covered by the car. From 2007 to 2009 it was part of the Jaguar Daimler Heritage Trust (see lots 327 Bonhams 25.7.09 $23,588 and 241 Historics 31.8.13 $70,299).											
2001	V8 Super saloon		F35595	R	45-55.000 GBP	42.750	55.758	47.884	26-07-17	Duxford	60	H&H
See lot 321 Silverstone Auctions 12.11.16.											

DALLARA (I) (1978-)

Year	Model	(Bodybuilder)	Chassis no.	Steering	Estimate	£	$	€	Date	Place	Lot	Auc. H.
1982	382 Formula 3		008	M	5-10.000 EUR	25.759*	32.030*	30.240*	25-11-16	Milan	887	RMS
Blue with yellow and red stripes. From the Duemila Ruote collection.											

DARRACQ (F) (1896-1920)

Year	Model	(Bodybuilder)	Chassis no.	Steering	Estimate	£	$	€	Date	Place	Lot	Auc. H.
1903	12hp tonneau		3777	R	100-140.000 GBP		NS		04-11-16	London	211	Bon
Grey with black leather interior; restoration completed in 2013.											

DB (F) (1938-1962)

Year	Model	(Bodybuilder)	Chassis no.	Steering	Estimate	£	$	€	Date	Place	Lot	Auc. H.
1958	HBR5 coupé		1051	L	55-65.000 EUR		NS		03-09-16	Chantilly	6	Bon
Blue; in working order, the car requires servicing. Sold new to Venezuela and raced in period, it was imported into Italy in 1967. Driven at the 1991 Mille Miglia Storica.											

DE DION-BOUTON (F) (1883-1948)

Year	Model	(Bodybuilder)	Chassis no.	Steering	Estimate	£	$	€	Date	Place	Lot	Auc. H.
1900	Type E 3.5hp vis-a-vis		664	R	65-75.000 GBP	69.416	86.360	80.356	29-03-17	Duxford	96	H&H
Black with black interior; restored in the 1990s and fitted with the present 1901 4.5hp engine. Imported into the UK in 2009, the car is described as in very good condition (see lot 461 Bonhams 26.9.09 $91,260).											
1901	Type G 4.5hp vis-a-vis		1389	R	60-100.000 EUR	91.499	114.028	107.280	10-02-17	Paris	26	Art
Described as in largely original condition and good working order. Three owners since new. Since 2009 in the Hervé and Martine Ogliastro Collection.												F205

F203: 1960 Daimler SP250 retractable hardtop

F204: 1964 Daimler 2.5l V8 (cabriolet/conversion)

Year	Model	(Bodybuilder)	Chassis no.	Steering	Estimate	Hammer price £	$	€	Date	Place	Lot	Auc. H.
1908	Type BI 15/18hp double phaeton		105	R	30-60.000 EUR	66.083	82.353	77.480	10-02-17	Paris	32	Art
	Green; fully restored by André Lecoq in 1990-91. Little used in the last years. From the Hervé and Martine Ogliastro Collection.											
1909	Type BN double phaeton		174	R	25-35.000 EUR	26.263	33.501	30.000	18-06-17	Fontainebleau	51	Ose
	White with red interior; restored.											

DE LOREAN (GB) (1976-1982)

Year	Model	(Bodybuilder)	Chassis no.	Steering	Estimate	£	$	€	Date	Place	Lot	Auc. H.
1981	DMC 12 (Italdesign)		7184	L	NA	29.250	38.853	34.714	02-09-16	Salon Privé	238	SiC
	In very good overall condition; just over 33,000 miles covered.											
1981	DMC 12 (Italdesign)		6940	L	NA	29.664*	36.300*	32.993*	15-10-16	Las Vegas	390	B/J
	Grey interior; less than 900 actual miles; 5-speed manual gearbox.											
1981	DMC 12 (Italdesign)		4921	L	NQ	16.010	20.000	18.028	04-11-16	Dallas	S81.1	Mec
	Stainless with grey interior; automatic transmission.											
1981	DMC 12 (Italdesign)		4526	L	28-32.000 GBP	35.438	45.563	41.895	13-05-17	Silverstone	362	SiC
	Imported into the UK in 2016; 26,000 miles covered; recently serviced.											
1981	DMC 12 (Italdesign)		6482	L	30-40.000 GBP	31.122	40.574	36.456	18-05-17	London	131	Coy
	In original condition; two owners; approximately 9,000 miles covered.											
1981	DMC 12 (Italdesign)		6870	L	26-32.000 GBP	24.640	32.062	28.681	20-05-17	Ascot	208	His
	Imported into Europe from the USA; in good overall condition.											
1981	DMC 12 (Italdesign)		5175	L	30-35.000 GBP	36.800	47.759	41.669	30-06-17	Goodwood	202	Bon F206
	Sold new to the USA where it has had just one owner. Stored for many years, in 2016 the car was bought by the present, second owner, imported into the UK and recommissioned. 8,834 miles covered since new.											

DE SANCTIS (I) (1958-1972)

Year	Model	(Bodybuilder)	Chassis no.	Steering	Estimate	£	$	€	Date	Place	Lot	Auc. H.
1959	Formula Junior		003	M	20-30.000 GBP	33.350*	44.439*	39.440*	10-09-16	Goodwood	102	Bon F207
	Red; restored in 1999 (see lots 302 RM 1.5.10 $41,010 and 9 Besch 14.6.15 NS).											
1969	Formula 850		80269	M	15-3.000 EUR	13.357*	16.608*	15.680*	25-11-16	Milan	831	RMS
	Red. From the Duemila Ruote collection.											

DE TOMASO (I) (1961-2004)

Year	Model	(Bodybuilder)	Chassis no.	Steering	Estimate	£	$	€	Date	Place	Lot	Auc. H.
1968	Vallelunga (Ghia)		807DT0126	L	300-350.000 USD		NS		19-08-17	Pebble Beach	156	G&Co
	Yellow with black interior; concours-quality restoration carried out in 2004 (see lot 116 Bonhams 13.5.16 NS).											
1977	Deauville (Ghia)		01472	R	22-26.000 GBP		NS		29-03-17	Duxford	118	H&H
	Metallic red with beige leather interior; the car is described as in average overall condition.											
1972	Pantera (Ghia)		02320	L	90-100.000 USD	70.377	93.500	83.533	03-09-16	Auburn	5077	AA
	Yellow with black interior; restored.											
1973	Pantera (Ghia)		05410	L	70-90.000 EUR		NA		08-10-16	Paris	170	CB/C
	Yellow with black interior; described as in very good overall condition.											
1972	Pantera (Ghia)		03544	L	60-70.000 GBP	64.125	81.176	74.443	12-11-16	Birmingham	357	SiC
	Dark blue with black leather interior; currently fitted with a Ford 6.5-litre V8 engine, the car is offered with also the original Ford Cobra Jet 5.8-litre unit (see lot 307 Coys 12.7.14 $106,623).											
1982	Pantera GT5 (Ghia)		09186	L	15-20.000 EUR	114.485*	142.356*	134.400*	25-11-16	Milan	284	RMS
	White with tan interior; 65,688 kms. From the Duemila Ruote collection.											
1974	Pantera (Ghia)		07350	L	100-125.000 USD		NS		15-01-17	Kissimmee	S217	Mec
	Red with black interior; in original condition, 10,926 miles covered, two owners (see Mecum lots S165.1 18.6.16 $100,000 and F136 19.8.16 NS).											
1972	Pantera (Ghia)		04214	L	140-180.000 USD	82.104*	101.200*	94.855*	19-01-17	Scottsdale	39	Bon
	Yellow with black interior; described as in very good overall condition. Less than 21,000 (believed original) miles.											
1971	Pantera (Ghia)		01992	L	130-160.000 USD	120.938*	148.500*	139.664*	20-01-17	Scottsdale	27	G&Co
	Lime green; from 1981 to 2016 in the same ownership; less than 12,000 miles since new; body repainted. Some mechanical works carried out in 2016 (see lot 155 Bonhams 10.3.16 $112,200).											
1972	Pantera (Ghia)		02591	L	NQ	70.771*	86.900*	81.729*	21-01-17	Scottsdale	1042.1	B/J
	Red with original black interior; described as in very good overall condition.											

F205: 1901 De Dion-Bouton Type G 4.5hp vis-a-vis

F206: 1981 De Lorean DMC 12 (Italdesign)

Year	Model	(Bodybuilder)	Chassis no.	Steering	Estimate	£	$	€	Date	Place	Lot	Auc. H.
1984	Pantera GT5	(Ghia)	09318	L	160-200.000 EUR		NS		10-02-17	Paris	140	Art
	White with dark red leather interior; one owner and 22,000 kms covered. Displayed at the 1984 Paris Motor Show.											
1973	Pantera	(Ghia)	05658	L	NQ	68.119	85.000	78.659	25-03-17	Kansas City	S71	Mec
	Red with black interior; believed to be 10,450 original miles. 351 Cleveland engine.											
1984	Pantera GT5	(Ghia)	09298	L	175-225.000 USD		NS		01-04-17	Ft.Lauderdale	606	AA
	Black with burgundy interior; restored. Circa 21,000 kms on the odometer.											
1972	Pantera	(Ghia)	04154	L	70-90.000 EUR	61.625	76.752	72.000	08-04-17	Essen	192	Coy
	Red; described as in very good overall condition; less than 16,000 miles covered (see lot 123 Coys 18.4.15 $100,024).											
1972	Pantera	(Ghia)	04014	L	85-100.000 EUR		NS		01-05-17	Obenheim	314	Ose
	Yellow; restored in the late 1990s.											
1971	Pantera	(Ghia)	01227	L	120-150.000 EUR		NS		01-05-17	Obenheim	356	Ose
	Blue with black interior; in good original condition; 52,000 kms covered.											
1974	Pantera	(Ghia)	07350	L	100-125.000 USD	80.682	105.000	93.923	20-05-17	Indianapolis	T165.1	Mec
	See lot S217 Mecum 15.1.17.											
1978	Pantera GTS	(Ghia)	09040	L	55-85.000 EUR	56.313	73.278	65.550	21-05-17	SPA-Francorch.	87	Bon
	Blue with grey leather interior; 18,200 kms covered since the restoration carried out in 1987; for 27 years in the current ownership; registered in Switzerland.											
1990	Pantera GT5-S	(Ghia)	06555	L	140-180.000 GBP		NS		30-06-17	Goodwood	238	Bon
	Dark metallic blue with black leather interior; in original condition; 14,000 kms covered; in single ownership for 20 years; imported into the UK in 2016; recently serviced.											
1972	Pantera	(Ghia)	05073	L	90-110.000 EUR		NS		02-07-17	Monaco	222	Art
	Blue; sold new to the USA; reimported into Europe in 2009; recently restored in Italy.											
1971	Pantera	(Ghia)	02122	L	150-200.000 USD	97.125	125.000	106.500	19-08-17	Monterey	F73	Mec
	Yellow with black interior; in original, unrestored condition; 7,076 miles covered; with its first owner the Indy Car driver Bob Lazier until 2011. From the Colin Comer Collection.											
1974	Pantera L	(Ghia)	07380	L	125-175.000 USD	158.120*	203.500*	173.382*	19-08-17	Monterey	263	RMS F208
	Orange; in very good original condition; 16,905 miles covered.											

DECAUVILLE (F) (1898-1911)

Year	Model	Chassis no.	Steering	Estimate	£	$	€	Date	Place	Lot	Auc. H.
1901	8hp rear-entrance tonneau	163	R	100-120.000 GBP	149.340	186.526	168.157	04-11-16	London	212	Bon F209
	Restored in the 1950s; since 1998 in the current ownership; driven at numerous historic events.										

DEEP SANDERSON (GB) (1960-1969)

Year	Model	Chassis no.	Steering	Estimate	£	$	€	Date	Place	Lot	Auc. H.
1963	301 GT	1003	R	70-80.000 EUR		NA		08-10-16	Paris	118	CB/C
	The car raced the 1963 Le Mans 24 Hours driven by its designer Chris Lawrence and by Chris Spender. Subsequently it was sold to France and raced until the early 1980s. Reimported into the UK, it was rediscovered in 2002 and later fully restored.										

DELAGE (F) (1905-1953)

Year	Model	(Bodybuilder)	Chassis no.	Steering	Estimate	£	$	€	Date	Place	Lot	Auc. H.
1925	Type DI torpedo		DI17976	R	28-34.000 GBP	31.050	41.244	36.850	03-09-16	Beaulieu	454	Bon
	Yellow with black wings; restored between 1970 and 1980 and fitted with the present, new body.											
1923	Type DI torpedo		13897	L	25-30.000 EUR		NS		19-03-17	Fontainebleau	201	Ose
	Restored many years ago, the car requires mechanical recommissioning prior to use. From the René Cocheteux collection.											
1923	Type DI torpedo		13897	L	20-25.000 EUR	31.515	40.201	36.000	18-06-17	Fontainebleau	54	Ose
	See lot 201 Osenat 19.3.17.											
1930	Type D8 C cabriolet	(Chapron)	34738	R	NQ	268.752	330.000	310.365	21-01-17	Scottsdale	1379	B/J F210
	Aubergine with black wings and light grey leather interior; imported into the USA in 1960 circa. Restored between 1992 and 1994. Body repainted more recently (see lot 183 RM/Sotheby's 12.3.16 $176,000).											
1930	Type D8 cabriolet	(Figoni)	33783	R	350-450.000 EUR		NS		09-02-17	Paris	326	Bon
	Green-grey with black wings and brown leather interior; body restyled in the late 1930s circa. Restored between 2004 and 2006; since 2009 in the current ownership (see lots Artcurial 14 28.6.08 NS and 7 13.7.09 NS, and RM 165 4.2.15 NS).											

F207: 1959 De Sanctis Formula Junior

F208: 1974 De Tomaso Pantera L (Ghia)

Year	Model	(Bodybuilder)	Chassis no.	Steering	Estimate	Hammer price £	$	€	Date	Place	Lot	Auc. H.

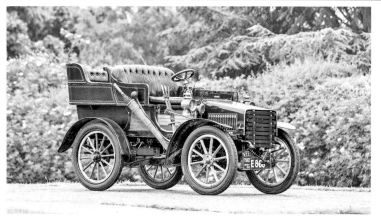

F209: 1901 Decauville 8hp rear-entrance tonneau

F210: 1930 Delage Type D8 C cabriolet (Chapron)

Year	Model	(Bodybuilder)	Chassis no.	Steering	Estimate	£	$	€	Date	Place	Lot	Auc. H.
1933	Type D8 S coupé	(Letourneur/Marchand)	38186	R	700-800.000 USD	504.273	649.000	552.948	18-08-17	Carmel	95	Bon F211

Probably the car exhibited at the 1934 Paris Motor Show; discovered in France in the 1950s; sold to Spain in 1999 and subsequently restored; bought five years ago by the current owner and restored again.

| 1934 | Type D6-11 roadster | | 38697 | R | 10-20.000 EUR | 20.875 | 25.738 | 23.104 | 07-10-16 | Chateau-sur-Epte | 58 | Art |

Blue with black wings; restored in the 1990s and fitted with the present, new body. From the Andre Weber Collection.

| 1937 | Type D6-60 sport biplace | | 50490 | R | 60-80.000 EUR | 52.866* | 65.883* | 61.984* | 10-02-17 | Paris | 39 | Art |

Bought in 1949 by the AGACI racing school, based at Montlhéry, which fitted it with the present new body and used it until the early 1960s. Stored for 37 years, it was restored in the 2000s and finished in France blue with red interior (see lots 15 Artcurial 28.6.08 NS and 355 Osenat 22.6.14 NS).

DELAHAYE (F) (1894-1954)

| 1923 | Type 87 torpedo | | 18216 | L | 45-65.000 EUR | 29.101 | 36.244 | 34.000 | 08-04-17 | Essen | 133 | Coy |

White with red wings and interior; discovered in France in 1989 and subsequently restored.

| 1934 | Type 134 berline (Sical) | | 44232 | L | 60-75.000 USD | NS | | | 11-02-17 | Boca Raton | 132 | TFA |

Black and grey with blue/grey cloth interior; cosmetically restored in 1997, mechanicals overhauled in more recent years. Imported into the USA in 2014.

| 1938 | Type 134 berline | | 45304 | R | 10-15.000 EUR | 12.509 | 15.461 | 14.400 | 19-03-17 | Fontainebleau | 216 | Ose |

Two-tone body; in good overall condition. For 32 years in the current ownership.

| 1936 | Type 135 Competition cabriolet (Figoni/Falaschi) | | 46837 | R | 1.200-1.800.000 EUR | NS | | | 10-02-17 | Paris | 29 | Art |

Originally built with a 3-seat coupé body, the car was sold new in France and raced at some events prior and after WWII. In 1946 it was bought by André Bith who in 1948 had the body modified to cabriolet form respecting the Figoni et Falaschi design. In the late 1980s it was acquired by Roger Tainguy who had it restored and finished in the present blue livery. Since 1992 in the Hervé and Martine Ogliastro Collection.

| 1946 | Type 135 M coach (Guilloré) | | 800410 | R | 110-140.000 USD | 60.799 | 77.000 | 68.838 | 06-10-16 | Hershey | 145 | RMS |

Two-tone grey with red leather interior; fully restored in 1993. Since 1960 in the current ownership (see lot 194 Bonhams 10.3.16 NS).

| 1949 | Type 135 M cabriolet (Chapron) | | 801023 | R | 150-180.000 EUR | 213.139 | 266.232 | 240.000 | 06-11-16 | Lyon | 310 | Ose F212 |

Two-tone green with light brown leather interior; restored in the late 2000s.

| 1951 | Type 135 M Gascogne coach (Dubos) | | 801641 | R | 70-100.000 EUR | 101.666* | 126.698* | 119.200* | 10-02-17 | Paris | 22 | Art F213 |

Black with two-tone brown leather interior; since 1959 in the same family ownership. Restored in the late 1990s and subsequently little used, it requires servicing prior to use.

| 1938 | Type 135 M coupé sport (Chapron) | | 60127 | R | 400-600.000 EUR | NS | | | 10-02-17 | Paris | 46 | Art |

Black with red side stripe and brown leather interior; body repainted. Formerly part of the Peter Kaus Rosso Bianco Collection (see lot 166 Bonhams 20.5.06 NS).

| 1947 | Type 135 M cabriolet (Guilloré) | | 801339 | R | 190-240.000 EUR | 173.338 | 227.866 | 192.000 | 05-08-17 | Schloss Dyck | 243 | Coy |

Restored in the 1980s; cosmetically refreshed in more recent years; in very good running condition.

| 1937 | Type 135 M coupé (Dubos) | | 47633 | R | 1.700-2.100.000 USD | NS | | | 17-08-17 | Monterey | 53 | WoA |

One-off finished in black and white with red leather interior, the car was sold new to a German diplomat living in Barcelona. It remained in Spain until the late 2000s when it was imported into the USA and subjected to a full restoration completed three years ago circa.

| 1946 | Type 135 M cabriolet (Graber) | | 800320 | R | 450-650.000 USD | NS | | | 18-08-17 | Monterey | 157 | RMS |

Sold new to Switzerland, the car remained with its first owner until 1995; restored in the USA in the late 1990s (see lot 18 P.R.Group 27.11.99 $170,500).

| 1938 | Type 135 M coupé (Van Leersum) | | 49349 | R | 550-750.000 USD | NS | | | 19-08-17 | Monterey | 260 | RMS |

Maroon and cream with red leather interior; one-off bodied in the Netherlands with Saoutchik-style lines; cosmetically and mechanically well maintained; European papers.

| 1938 | Type 135 MS cabriolet | | 601011 | R | 180-220.000 EUR | NS | | | 05-11-16 | Lyon | 245 | Agu |

Two-tone metallic blue; sold new to Argentina, restored at unspecified date, reimported into France in 1990. The hydraulic brake system, which replaced the original cable-operated unit, has been recently overhauled.

| 1939 | Type 135 MS cabriolet (Figoni/Falaschi) | | 60173 | R | 1.200-1.600.000 EUR | NS | | | 10-02-17 | Paris | 50 | Art |

Light grey with dark blue interior; body modernized in the 1950s and returned to its original specification during the restoration carried out between 2012 and 2016 (see lot 257 RM 20.8.11 NS).

| 1947 | Type 135 MS cabriolet (Guilloré) | | 801339 | R | 200-250.000 EUR | 160.909 | 200.408 | 188.000 | 08-04-17 | Essen | 199 | Coy F214 |

Black with red leather interior; restored in the1980s; paintwork and interior replaced in more recent years (see lots Bonhams 528 18.8.06 $194,000, Artcurial 13 9.2.08 NS and 25 8.2.09 NS, and Chevau-Légerè 12 3.2.11 $196,471).

| 1950 | Type 148 L coach (Saoutchik) | | 801566 | R | 700-1.000.000 EUR | NS | | | 10-02-17 | Paris | 41 | Art |

Blue with beige leather interior; one-off displayed at the Saoutchik stand at the 1950 Paris Motor Show. Described as in original condition (the body was refinished in the present livery in 1951 probably), the car has had two owners and has covered less than 30,000 kms. In 2015 the fuel tank and exhausts were replaced.

| 1953 | Type 235 coach (Chapron) | | 818080 | R | 20-25.000 EUR | 71.166* | 88.688* | 83.440* | 10-02-17 | Paris | 1 | Art |

Complete, for restoration. From the Roger Baillon Collection (see lot 12 Artcurial 6.2.15 $136,448).

F211: 1933 Delage Type D8 S coupé (Letourneur/Marchand)

F212: 1949 Delahaye Type 135 M cabriolet (Chapron)

DELLOW (GB) (1949-1957)

Year	Model	Chassis no.	Steering	Estimate	£	$	€	Date	Place	Lot	Auc. H.
1947	Mark I	283803	R	16-20.000 GBP	**16.800**	**20.889**	**19.722**	26-11-16	Weybridge	117	**His**

Green; described as one of the three prototypes of the model, the car was built on a 1937 Austin Seven chassis. Raced in period, it was acquired in 1977 by the current owner and subsequently restored. Currently fitted with a 1172cc Ford 100E engine and 3-speed gearbox.

DESOTO (USA) (1929-1961)

Year	Model	Chassis no.	Steering	Estimate	£	$	€	Date	Place	Lot	Auc. H.
1929	Series K touring	K24298	R	12-14.000 GBP	NS			07-12-16	Chateau Impney		**H&H**
1935	Airflow sedan	9603496	L	45-60.000 USD	**33.392**	**44.000**	**39.191**	17-09-16	Aspen	116	**TFA**
1934	Airflow coupé	5072977	L	80-100.000 USD	**55.542***	**68.200***	**64.142***	20-01-17	Scottsdale	19	**G&Co**
1934	Airflow SE coupé	SE11863	L	NQ	**34.042***	**41.800***	**39.313***	21-01-17	Scottsdale	996	**B/J** **F215**

1929 – White with brown interior; brakes recently overhauled (see lot 514 Sotheby's 28.2.94 $10,086).
1935 – Cream and brown with two-tone brown interior; restored in 2013-2014 (see lot 1147 Barrett-Jackson 29.1.16 $35,200).
1934 Airflow coupé – Taupe with art deco tan interior; restored.
1934 Airflow SE coupé – Grey with brown interior; oder restoration.

DEVIN (USA) (1954-1964)

Year	Model	Chassis no.	Steering	Estimate	£	$	€	Date	Place	Lot	Auc. H.
1959	D Porsche Special	DD512	L	70-90.000 USD	**72.389***	**88.000***	**82.931***	11-03-17	Amelia Island	213	**RMS** **F216**

Bought in 2003 from the estate of Bill Devin, who had started the restoration with the building of a new body using the origial body molds. Later the restoration was completed and the car was fitted with a Type 616/7 1600cc Porsche 356B engine.

DFP (F) (1906-1935)

Year	Model	Chassis no.	Steering	Estimate	£	$	€	Date	Place	Lot	Auc. H.
1920	Type A2000 torpedo	4288	R	4-6.000 EUR	**19.285**	**23.836**	**22.200**	19-03-17	Fontainebleau	208	**Ose**
1925	Type V torpedo	20854	L	13-18.000 EUR	NS			06-11-16	Lyon	303	**Ose**

1920 – In original condition; engine in need of recommissioning.
1925 – Body and interior in original, never restored condition; mechanicals recently restarted. The car requires recommissioning prior to use.

DINA (MEX)

Year	Model	Chassis no.	Steering	Estimate	£	$	€	Date	Place	Lot	Auc. H.
1974	Dinalpin A110 1300	9980987	L	110-140.000 USD	NS			17-08-17	Monterey	2	**WoA**

Built in Mexico and imported into the USA in 2016; body refinished in red; believed to be just 8,839 kms since new.

DKW (D) (1928-1966)

Year	Model	Chassis no.	Steering	Estimate	£	$	€	Date	Place	Lot	Auc. H.
1956	3=6 two-door saloon	68550799	L	5-10.000 EUR	**6.074**	**7.588**	**6.840**	06-11-16	Lyon	355	**Ose**

Engine rebuilt two years ago.

F213: 1951 Delahaye Type 135 M Gascogne coach (Dubos)

F214: 1947 Delahaye Type 135 MS cabriolet (Guilloré)

Year	Model	(Bodybuilder)	Chassis no.	Steering	Estimate	Hammer price £	$	€	Sale Date	Place	Lot	Auc. H.

F215: 1934 Desoto Airflow SE coupé

F216: 1959 Devin D Porsche Special

DODGE (USA) (1914-)

Year	Model	Chassis no.	Steering	Estimate	£	$	€	Date	Place	Lot	Auc. H.
1925	**Series 116 roadster**	A358029	L	18-24.000 USD	13.028*	16.500*	14.751*	06-10-16	Hershey	166	RMS
	Green with black fenders and black leather interior; restored.										
1933	**Series DP convertible**	TO17215	L	18-24.000 GBP	22.425*	29.787*	26.614*	03-09-16	Beaulieu	418	Bon
	Red; gearbox and brakes overhauled.										
1937	**Series D5 convertible**	4588293	L	NA	38.462*	49.500*	42.174*	19-08-17	Monterey	1048	R&S
	Light yellow with red leather interior; recently serviced. From the Art Astor Collection.										
1949	**Wayfarer convertible**	48002247	L	NQ	26.796*	34.100*	30.520*	24-06-17	Northeast	439.1	B/J
	Red with red interior; restored.										
1949	**Wayfarer roadster**	37039364	L	24-28.000 GBP		NS		26-07-17	Duxford	67	H&H
	Red with beige interior; restored in 2011.										
1956	**Coronet Sierra D500 station wagon**	35147634	L	20-30.000 EUR	17.283*	21.539*	20.264*	10-02-17	Paris	13	Art
	Two-tone body; imported into the UK from the USA in 2003 and subsequently restored. Automatic transmission.										
1959	**Custom Royal convertible**	M352106156	L	NQ	172.876	220.000	196.900	24-06-17	Northeast	691	B/J F217
	Yellow and black with yellow and black interior; restored in 2005. Recently serviced. 383 engine with automatic transmission.										
1960	**Phoenix Dart hardtop**	5305106874	L	80-110.000 USD	57.477	70.000	65.653	15-01-17	Kissimmee	F119	Mec
	Red with red interior; restored. 330bhp 383 engine with automatic transmission. From the Jackie and Gary Runyon collection.										
1960	**Phoenix hardtop**	5307121322	L	NQ	35.834	44.000	41.382	21-01-17	Scottsdale	8302	R&S
	Red with white roof; restored. 225bhp 318 engine with automatic transmission.										
1962	**Phoenix sedan**	S318182942(engine)	R	25-35.000 AUD	15.898	20.473	17.423	20-08-17	Mallala Park	4	Mos
	White with red interior; from new to 2013 with its first owner. Engine reconditioned in 1980. Model built in Australia. From the collection of the late Clem Smith.										
1963	**Polara hardtop**	6332133686	L	60-80.000 USD	42.552*	52.250*	49.141*	20-01-17	Phoenix	273	RMS
	White with blue vinyl interior; restored in 2006. Circa 4,000 believed original miles on the odometer. 425bhp 426 Max Wedge engine with automatic transmission.										
1967	**Dart GT convertible**	LP27D72334831	L	NA		NS		03-06-17	Newport Beach	9167	R&S
	Fitted with a 283 V8 engine with automatic transmission.										
1963	**330 Series Lightweight hardtop**	6132174418	L	NA		NS		19-11-16	Anaheim	S154	Mec
	White with red cloth and vinyl interior; as-raced condition; believed to be 490 miles; 426 Max Wedge engine with automatic transmission (see lot F106 Mecum 19.8.16 NS).										
1964	**330 Series Lightweight hardtop**	6142223146	L	275-350.000 USD	188.853	230.000	215.717	15-01-17	Kissimmee	S116	Mec F218
	White with red interior; raced in period. 426 Hemi engine. From the Don Fezell collection.										
1963	**330 Series Lightweight hardtop**	6132170287	L	180-260.000 USD	89.584*	110.000*	103.455*	20-01-17	Phoenix	242	RMS
	Red with red cloth and vinyl interior; restored in 2006. 425bhp 426 Max Wedge engine with automatic transmission.										
1969	**Charger Daytona**	XX29L9B409047	L	250-400.000 USD	194.121	242.500	218.590	04-11-16	Dallas	S91	Mec
	Red with black rear wing and black vinyl interior; restored. 16,000 original miles. 375bhp 440 engine with automatic transmission.										
1970	**Charger R/T hardtop**	XS29V0G184803	L	NQ		NS		03-12-16	Kansas City	S33	Mec
	Black with black interior; restoration completed in 2016. 390bhp 440 Six Pack engine with automatic transmission.										
1969	**Charger Daytona**	XX29J9B409076	L	900-1.100.000 USD		NS		15-01-17	Kissimmee	F167	Mec
	Metallic green with black vinyl interior; 21,126 original miles. One of 70 1969 examples fitted with the 425bhp 426 Hemi engine; automatic transmission. From the Tom Lembeck Collection.										
1971	**Charger R/T hardtop**	WS23R1G120747	L	200-225.000 USD	180.642	220.000	206.338	15-01-17	Kissimmee	S147	Mec F219
	Blue with black roof and black interior; 9,800 original miles. In original condition except for the paintwork redone in 2016. 425bhp 426 Hemi engine with manual gearbox.										
1969	**Charger 500 hardtop**	XX29J9B133989	L	NQ	106.743	130.000	121.927	15-01-17	Kissimmee	S90.1	Mec
	Red with black interior; restored. 425bhp 426 Hemi engine with manual gearbox.										
1969	**Charger 500 hardtop**	XX29J9B164192	L	NQ	120.938*	148.500*	139.664*	21-01-17	Scottsdale	1339	B/J
	Copper with black wraparound stripe and tan interior; recently restored. 14,523 original miles. 426 Hemi engine with automatic transmission.										
1969	**Charger Daytona**	XX29L9B410786	L	200-275.000 USD	172.890	225.000	201.263	20-05-17	Indianapolis	S163	Mec
	White with red rear wing and red interior; concours-quality restoration. Currently fitted with a 426 Hemi engine with manual gearbox. 37,950 believed original miles (see lot 9126 Russo & Steele 19.1.11 $112,200).										

Year	Model	(Bodybuilder)	Chassis no.	Steering	Estimate	Hammer price £	$	€	Date	Sale Place	Lot	Auc. H.

F217: 1959 Dodge Custom Royal convertible   *F218: 1964 Dodge 330 Series Lightweight hardtop*

Year	Model	Chassis no.	Steering	Estimate	£	$	€	Date	Place	Lot	Auc. H.
1969	**Coronet Super Bee hardtop**	WM23J9A134034	L	125-150.000 USD	**121.112**	**147.500**	**138.340**	15-01-17	Kissimmee	S111	**Mec**
	Red with white vinyl roof and red interior; restored. 426 Hemi engine with automatic transmission. From the Don Fezell collection.										
1966	**Coronet 500 hardtop**	WP23H67268107	L	65-85.000 USD	**41.944***	**51.700***	**48.458***	19-01-17	Phoenix	171	**RMS**
	Metallic bronze with gold vinyl interior; restored at unspecified date. 425bhp 426 Hemi engine with automatic transmission. From the Mohrschladt Family Collection.										
1966	**Coronet 500 convertible**	WP27H67258164	L	175-225.000 USD	**143.334***	**176.000***	**165.528***	20-01-17	Phoenix	243	**RMS** F220
	Red with white vinyl interior; restored between 1997 and 2003. One of 12 examples built in 1966 with the 425bhp 426 Hemi engine and 4-speed manual gearbox.										
1965	**Coronet Super Stock Lightweight hardtop**	W051207356	L	140-180.000 USD	**89.584***	**110.000***	**103.455***	20-01-17	Phoenix	247	**RMS**
	Red with beige vinyl interior; restored at unspecified date. Just over 1,000 believed original miles on the odometer. 425bhp 426 engine with automatic transmission.										
1967	**Coronet 440 Super Stock hardtop**	W023J71206306	L	100-130.000 USD	**60.021***	**73.700***	**69.315***	20-01-17	Phoenix	276	**RMS**
	White with black interior; restored in 2004. 425bhp 426 engine with automatic transmission.										
1968	**Coronet Super Bee coupé**	WM21J8G244328	L	NQ	**67.188***	**82.500***	**77.591***	21-01-17	Scottsdale	1032.1	**B/J**
	Red with black interior; restored. 426 Hemi engine with automatic transmission.										
1968	**Dart hardtop**	L023M8B297890	L	250-275.000 USD	NS			15-01-17	Kissimmee	S126	**Mec**
	Red with black interior; raced in Super Stock until 1988. Restored. 426 Hemi engine with 4-speed manual gearbox. From the Don Fezell collection.										
1970	**Challenger R/T hardtop**	JS23N0E114670	L	70-90.000 USD	**80.050**	**100.000**	**90.140**	04-11-16	Dallas	S92	**Mec**
	Plum with white side stripe and white interior; 250 miles covered since the restoration completed some years ago. 335bhp 383 engine with manual gearbox.										
1971	**Challenger R/T hardtop**	JS23R1B324673	L	750-850.000 USD	NS			15-01-17	Kissimmee	F170	**Mec**
	Blue with black vinyl interior; unrestored, 11,479 miles on the odometer. One of 71 1971 examples built with the 425bhp 426 Hemi engine; 4-speed manual gearbox. From the Tom Lembeck Collection.										
1970	**Challenger R/T convertible**	JS27V0B100021	L	400-600.000 USD	NS			15-01-17	Kissimmee	F186	**Mec**
	Red with white vinyl interior; restored in 2004. 390bhp 440 Six Pack engine with manual gearbox (see lot F114 Mecum 23.1.16 $450,000).										
1970	**Challenger R/T convertible**	JS27V0B203932	L	210-250.000 USD	NS			15-01-17	Kissimmee	S165.1	**Mec**
	Orange with black leather interior; concours-quality restoration. 390bhp 440 Six Pack engine and manual gearbox (see lot 7057 Russo & Steele 20.8.16 NS).										
1971	**Challenger R/T hardtop**	JS23R1B383597	L	350-380.000 USD	NS			15-01-17	Kissimmee	S210	**Mec**
	Yellow with black vinyl interior; unrestored. Believed to be 17,000 original miles. 425bhp 426 Hemi engine with manual gearbox.										
1970	**Challenger R/T hardtop**	JS23R0B279423	L	NQ	**102.638**	**125.000**	**117.238**	15-01-17	Kissimmee	S67.1	**Mec**
	Red with white vinyl roof and white interior; restored. 425bhp 426 Hemi engine with automatic transmission.										
1971	**Challenger R/T hardtop**	JS23R1B242313	L	NQ	NS			21-01-17	Scottsdale	8419	**R&S**
	Black with black interior; in original, unrestored condition. 426 Hemi engine (see lots RM 173 18.1.13 NS, and Mecum S147 17.8.13 NS and S129 23.1.16 NS).										
2003	**Viper GTS-R**	16315C45	L	15-20.000 EUR	**205.118***	**255.055***	**240.800***	25-11-16	Milan	234	**RMS**
	White; not road registered. From the Duemila Ruote collection.										
2000	**Viper GTS**	1B3ER69E5YV602566	L	NQ	**42.554**	**53.000**	**49.714**	08-04-17	Houston	F135.1	**Mec**
	Black with silver stripes and black and grey leather interior; 9,465 miles covered. From the Emalee Burton collection.										

F219: 1971 Dodge Charger R/T hardtop   *F220: 1966 Dodge Coronet 500 convertible*

Year	Model	(Bodybuilder)	Chassis no.	Steering	Estimate	£	$	€	Date	Place	Lot	Auc. H.

F221: 1958 Dual-Ghia Convertible

F222: 1927 Duesenberg Model A/Y prototype phaeton (McFarlan)

DUAL-GHIA (USA) (1956-1958)

1957	Convertible		DG154	L	450-525.000 USD		NS		21-01-17	Scottsdale	123	G&Co

Aquamarine with cognac leather interior; fully restored to concours condition (see lot 25 Gooding & Company 17.8.13 $495,000).

| 1957 | Convertible | | DG128 | L | 275-325.000 USD | 190.021* | 231.000* | 217.694* | 10-03-17 | Amelia Island | 32 | G&Co |

Dark blue with cream leather interior; in very good overall condition. Dodge "Red Ram" 315 D500 engine with automatic transmission (see lots RM 74 8.3.03 $84,700, Bonhams 415 17.8.07 $199,500, 644 13.8.10 NS, and 320 12.9.10 NS, and Auctions America 584 4.3.11 NS).

| 1958 | Convertible | | 191 | L | NQ | 211.773 | 269.500 | 241.203 | 24-06-17 | Northeast | 699 | B/J |

Plum with red and cream interior; concours-quality restoration (see lots 63 Worldwide Group 1.11.08 $319,000, 254 RM 14.3.09 $209,000, 79 Gooding & Company 9.3.12 $214,500, 230 RM 16.1.15 NS, 488 Auctions America 28.3.15 $225,500, and 107 Bonhams 19.8.16 $368,500).

| 1956 | Convertible | | D63392893 | L | 450-650.000 USD | 294.872 | 379.500 | 324.473 | 17-08-17 | Monterey | 27 | WoA |

First production car numbered 101, it was registered from new under its engine number D63392893. Two owners until 2015. Restoration completed in October 2016.

| 1958 | Convertible | | 197 | L | 300-375.000 USD | 311.966 | 401.500 | 342.078 | 18-08-17 | Carmel | 10 | Bon |

Dark blue with tan interior; concours-quality restoration carried out in the 2000s. Dodge D-500 engine (see lots 52 Gooding & Company 7.3.14 NS and S675 Russo & Steele 15.8.15 $412,500). **F221**

DUESENBERG (USA) (1920-1937)

| 1927 | Model A/Y prototype phaeton (McFarlan) | | 912 | L | 450-550.000 USD | 275.740 | 340.000 | 305.184 | 07-10-16 | Hershey | 252 | RMS |

One of two prototypes, named Model Y, built using chassis and engine (evolved to 412c.i.) from the Model A. In 1932 the prototype with the phaeton body was sold to August Duesenberg on the condition that he destroyed the prototype chassis. This he did, after moving the engine into a racing car. Later he installed the phaeton body on the used Model A chassis no.912, with engine of 260c.i., and resold the car in this form. Restored in the early 1950; since 1957 in the same family ownership (see lot 65 Worldwide Group 5.9.09 NS). **F222**

| 1923 | Model A sport phaeton | | 977 | L | 350-400.000 USD | 316.239 | 407.000 | 346.764 | 19-08-17 | Monterey | 236 | RMS |

Dark green with green leather interior; bought in rolling chassis form by Karl Killorin, former Duesenberg test driver, and then fitted with the present Cadillac body of the 1920s. Retained by the Killorin family until 2015; restored at unspecified date after 1989 (see lot 161 RM/Sotheby's 8.10.15 $374,000).

| 1930 | Model J berline (Franay) | | 2385 | L | 750-950.000 USD | 538.181 | 715.000 | 638.781 | 03-09-16 | Auburn | 4155 | AA |

Magenta with beige interior; engine J-365. Built with Kellner town car body, the car was later fitted with the present body and exhibited at the 1931 and 1932 Paris Motor Shows. After some ownership changes, in 1971 it was imported into the USA where it was subsequently restored (see lots 17 Christie's 19.8.01 $380,000, 581 Cox Auctions 17.4.09 $777,600 and 65 Kruse Cla. 15.9.12 $1,650,000). **F223**

| 1931 | Model J convertible sedan (Murphy) | | 2363 | L | 800-1.000.000 USD | 662.376 | 880.000 | 786.192 | 03-09-16 | Auburn | 4160 | AA |

Red with black fenders and tan leather interior; engine J-420. An older restoration, the car is described as in good overall condition. Recently serviced (see lot 249 RM 13.8.10 $693,000).

| 1930 | Model J dual-cowl phaeton (Murphy) | | 2366 | L | 1.600-2.000.000 USD | 1.694.990 | 2.090.000 | 1.875.984 | 07-10-16 | Hershey | 253 | RMS |

Dark purple with red leather interior; original engine J-347. Discovered in Mexico in 1962 in original condition and showing 43,832 miles, the car was reimported into the USA and restored. For 54 years in the same family ownership (see lot 77 Christie's 16.8.98 $717,500). **F224**

| 1933 | Model J convertible (Bohman/Schwartz) | | 2421 | L | 3.500-4.000.000 USD | | NS | | 20-05-17 | Indianapolis | S122.1 | Mec |

Ivory with red interior; engine J-386. Originally built with LeBaron convertible sedan body and later fitted with the present body. Formerly in the Harrah, Blackhawk and Imperial Palace collections (see lot S114 Mecum 20.8.16 NS).

F223: 1930 Duesenberg Model J berline (Franay)

F224: 1930 Duesenberg Model J dual-cowl phaeton (Murphy)

Year	Model	(Bodybuilder)	Chassis no.	Steering	Estimate	Hammer price £	$	€	Date	Sale Place	Lot	Auc. H.

F225: 1929 Duesenberg Model J convertible coupé (Murphy)

F226: 1961 Emeryson F1

| 1929 | **Model J convertible berline (Murphy)** | | 2208 | L | 800-950.000 USD | 691.504 | 880.000 | 787.600 | 24-06-17 | Santa Monica | 189 | RMS |

Mustard with brown interior; engine J-259. Body modified in 1934 by Bohman & Schwartz. Until 1959 with its first owner, Arthur K. Bourne. Bought in 1980 by Richard Gold who resold it after over 30 years to the current, fifth owner. Never fully restored, only cosmetically refinished as-needed over the years.

| 1929 | **Model J convertible coupé (Murphy)** | | 2168 | L | 1.400-1.700.000 USD | 1.111.110 | 1.430.000 | 1.218.360 | 19-08-17 | Monterey | 248 | RMS |

Silver with green leather interior; engine J-147 rebuilt probably after WWII utilizing parts coming from engine J-245. Built with LeBaron dual-cowl phaeton body and not long thereafter fitted with the present body from another Model J. Restored to concours condition between 2007 and 2009 (see lots RM 239 21.1.00 NS and 245 5.8.00 $550,000, Brooks 319 6.10.00 $530,500, H&H 55 24.5.06 $621,093, and Auctions America 5142 5.9.15 $1,402,500).   **F225**

ECHIDNA (USA)

| 1959 | **Sports Racer** | | 2 | L | NQ | | NS | | 21-01-17 | Scottsdale | 8317 | R&S |

Blue; one of three examples built. Fuel-injected Chevrolet engine and T-10 4-speed manual gearbox. Raced at historic events (see lot S727 Russo & Steele 17.1.15 $162,800).

EDSEL (USA) (1957-1959)

| 1959 | **Corsair convertible** | | W9UR705682 | L | NQ | 27.972 | 36.000 | 30.672 | 19-08-17 | Monterey | T186 | Mec |

Yellow with black and silver interior; recently restored; engine rebuilt.

| 1958 | **Pacer convertible** | | W8UR717178 | L | NQ | 32.056 | 40.000 | 37.016 | 25-03-17 | Kansas City | S108 | Mec |

Yellow with black and white interior; 1,000 miles covered since the restoration carried out five years ago.

| 1958 | **Station Wagon** | | W8RV700777 | L | NA | 44.946* | 55.000* | 49.990* | 15-10-16 | Las Vegas | 418 | B/J |

Red and white with brown and tan interior; restoration completed in 2013.

| 1959 | **Station Wagon Villager** | | B9UT733580 | L | NQ | 38.521* | 47.300* | 44.486* | 21-01-17 | Scottsdale | 751 | B/J |

Black with white roof and red interior; described as in good original condition. Sold as a lot with lots 751.1 1959 Fleetform Runabout boat with 35hp Evinrude Lark engine, and 751.2 1993 MITMV boat trailer.

EMERYSON (GB) (1946-1965)

| 1961 | **F1** | | 1004 | M | 150-180.000 GBP | 174.380 | 218.917 | 206.344 | 24-02-17 | Stoneleigh P. | 112 | SiC |

Raced at several Formula 1 events in 1961 and 1962; only survivor; restored in the 1990s and regularly raced at historic events. 4-cylinder 1.5-litre Coventry Climax FPF engine.   **F226**

EMF (USA) (1909-1912)

| 1911 | **Model 30 speedster** | | 43364 | R | 30-50.000 USD | 28.993* | 35.750* | 32.089* | 07-10-16 | Hershey | 218 | RMS |

Cream with red leather interior; mechanicals overhauled (see lot 111 RM 9.10.14 $30,250).

ESSEX (USA) (1917-1939)

| 1931 | **Super Six boattail speedabout (Murray)** | | 1267966 | L | 40-60.000 USD | 28.558* | 35.200* | 32.993* | 19-01-17 | Scottsdale | 63 | Bon |

Beige and brown; restored at unspecified date (see lot 54 Gooding & Company 20.8.11 $66,000).   **F227**

F227: 1931 Essex Super Six boattail speedabout (Murray)

F228: 1958 Facel Vega FV4

F229: 1960 Facel Vega Excellence

F230: 1948 Ferrari 166 Spider Corsa (Scaglietti)

FACEL VEGA (F) (1954-1964)

Year	Model	(Bodybuilder)	Chassis no.	Steering	Estimate	£	$	€	Date	Place	Lot	Auc. H.
1958	FV4		FV457H41	L	200-275.000 USD	201.564	247.500	232.774	20-01-17	Phoenix	222	RMS

Beige with maroon leather interior; sold new to the USA, the car was disassembled in 1968 for a restoration never started. Sold still apart, it was later subjected to a concours-quality restoration completed in 2012 (see lots 139 RM 16.8.13 $302,500 and 210 RM/Sotheby's 14.8.15 $187,000). **F228**

| 1958 | FV3B | | FV3B58357 | L | 190-240.000 EUR | | NS | | 09-02-17 | Paris | 317 | Bon |

Silver with original red leather interior; body repainted in 1978. Bought new by driver Maurice Trintignant. In single ownership from 1985 circa to 2015 (see lot 121 Artcurial 6.2.15 $225,735).

| 1960 | HK500 | | HK1BP5 | R | 90-130.000 GBP | | NS | | 14-01-17 | Birmingham | 145 | Coy |

Red with black leather interior; restored in the past and between 2013 and 2016 again. Automatic transmission.

| 1959 | HK500 | | HKL1 | R | 150-200.000 EUR | | NS | | 09-02-17 | Paris | 395 | Bon |

White with red leather interior; restored in France in 2011-12; Pont-à-Mousson manual gearbox.

| 1960 | HK500 | | HK1BQ6 | L | 150-180.000 EUR | 132.165 | 164.707 | 154.960 | 10-02-17 | Paris | 24 | Art |

Ivory with red leather interior; bought in 1985 by the current two owners and subsequently restored. Described as in good overall condition.

| 1961 | HK500 | | HK1BR6X | L | 225-275.000 USD | 119.658* | 154.000* | 131.208* | 19-08-17 | Pebble Beach | 147 | G&Co |

Dark blue with red leather interior; in the same ownership from 1970 to 2010 when it was bought by the vendor and subjected to a full restoration completed in 2015.

| 1960 | Excellence | | EX1B118 | L | 80-120.000 EUR | | NS | | 30-10-16 | Paris | 127 | Art |

Described as in good original condition; since 1979 in the same ownership.

| 1960 | Excellence | | EX1B118 | L | 60-100.000 EUR | 76.249* | 95.023* | 89.400* | 10-02-17 | Paris | 23 | Art |

See lot 127 Artcurial 30.10.16. **F229**

| 1962 | Facellia cabriolet | | F2B109B | L | 30-40.000 EUR | 73.390 | 92.219 | 86.250 | 09-02-17 | Paris | 319 | Bon |

Since 1968 in the same family ownership; body restored in the 1990s; interior retrimmed in 2013-14; engine rebuilt.

FERRARI (I) (1947-)

| 1948 | 166 Spider Corsa (Scaglietti) | | 014I | R | Refer Dpt. | 2.524.925* | 3.146.609* | 2.960.400* | 10-02-17 | Paris | 125 | Art |

Originally built with a 2,420mm chassis and Ansaloni body with cycle wings; raced by the factory in 1948 and then sold to Giampiero Bianchetti who retained it until 1952; in 1950 at the factory chassis shortened to 2,254mm and engine enlarged to 2,340cc; in 1955-56 fitted on Ferrari order with the present 500 TR style body; imported into the USA in 1959; mechanicals restored in 2008; reimported into Europe in 2013 and fully restored (see lots RM 303 17.8.01 NS, and Gooding & Company 54 18.8.07 $1,045,000 and 38 20.8.11 NS). **F230**

| 1950 | 166 MM barchetta (Touring) | | 0058M | R | 8.000-10.000.000 USD | | NS | | 11-03-17 | Amelia Island | 278 | RMS |

Red with beige leather interior; sold new in Italy; bought in 1951 by Eugenio Castellotti; raced at several events including the 1951 and 1953 Mille Miglia; imported into the USA in 1953 and subsequently raced; from 1977 to 1998 owned by Ed Gilbertson and from 1998 to 2010 by Lorenzo Zambrano; in 2007 certified by Ferrari Classiche. Original body, engine and gearbox. Over the years displayed at numerous concours d'elegances.

| 1950 | 166 MM/212 Export "Uovo" (Fontana) | | 024MB | R | 5.000-7.000.000 USD | 3.496.500 | 4.500.000 | 3.834.000 | 18-08-17 | Monterey | 152 | RMS |

One-off built by Carrozzeria Fontana on a Franco Reggiani design for Giannino Marzotto. Bought new by the Marzotto brothers, the car was damaged at the 1950 MM and then repaired at the factory. In 1951 it was fitted with the present body and raced until 1952. In late 1953 it was sent to Mexico for the Carrera but did not participate in the race. The car remained in Mexico and was then sold to California where it was raced at some events. Subjected to a restoration completed in the UK in 1986, in 1987 it was acquired by the current Italian owner. **F231**

F231: 1950 Ferrari 166 MM/212 Export "Uovo" (Fontana)

F232: 1952 Ferrari 340 America spider

Year	Model	(Bodybuilder)	Chassis no.	Steering	Estimate	Hammer price £	$	€	Date	Place	Lot	Auc. H.

F233: 1951 Ferrari 212 Inter coupé (Vignale)

F234: 1952 Ferrari 342 America cabriolet (Vignale)

| 1952 | 340 America spider | | 0196A | R | 7.500-9.000.000 USD | 5.176.094 | 6.380.000 | 5.979.974 | 19-01-17 | Scottsdale | 44 | Bon |

Built with Vignale spider body, the car was entered by the factory in the early 1952 at the MM, Berne GP, Le Mans 24 Hours and Targa Florio. Sold to Piero Scotti in July 1952, it was raced at several events until the end of the season and then returned to the factory. In 1954 it was fitted with a Vignale coupé body and in 1955 it was sold to the USA. After some ownership changes, in 1999 it was bought by Lord Bamford, imported into the UK, restored and fitted with the present new body built to its original 1952 specification. F232

| 1951 | 212 Inter coupé (Vignale) | | 0175E | R | 1.500-1.800.000 USD | 1.239.315 | 1.595.000 | 1.358.940 | 19-08-17 | Pebble Beach | 152 | G&Co |

Two-tone body with green leather interior; sold new in Italy; imported into the USA in the late 1950s; 100 miles covered since a full restoration (see lots 441 RM 27.8.99 NS and 345 Bonhams 6.5.06 NS). F233

| 1952 | 342 America cabriolet (Vignale) | | 0232AL | L | 2.250-3.000.000 USD | 1.752.135 | 2.255.000 | 1.921.260 | 18-08-17 | Monterey | 142 | RMS |

Metallic green and white with green and white leather interior; one of three examples of the model built in cabriolet form. Sold new to Switzerland and later exported to the USA. Bought in 2007 by the current owner and subsequently fully restored. F234

| 1953 | 250 Europa (Pinin Farina) | | 0321EU | L | NA | 897.435 | 1.155.000 | 984.060 | 19-08-17 | Monterey | 1143 | R&S |

Dark blue with beige leather interior; sold new in Italy; imported into the USA in the 1960s; recently restored; fitted with a Ferrari 330 GT engine and Tremec 5-speed gearbox; engine and drum brakes recently rebuilt. A Ferrari 250 transmission is included with the sale (see lot 3098 Auctions America 2.8.14 $1,017,500).

| 1955 | 250 Europa GT (Pinin Farina) | | 0389GT | L | 2.300-2.600.000 USD | 1.829.223 | 2.227.500 | 2.111.002 | 09-03-17 | Amelia Island | 144 | Bon |

Two-tone blue with caramel interior; one of two examples with alloy body; factory equipped with competition features for the 1955 MM although not completed in time for the start; sold new in Italy; imported into the USA in 1960 and fitted with Corvette transmission and rear axle; cosmetic refurbishment in the early 1980s; body repainted in 2002 and engine rebuilt in the same period; fitted again with Europa GT transmission and rear axle (see lots 19 Orion 10.11.90 $885,230 and 152 Bonhams 15.1.15 NS). F235

| 1954 | 250 Europa GT (Pinin Farina) | | 0377GT | L | 2.000-2.800.000 USD | NS | | | 18-08-17 | Monterey | 128 | RMS |

Originally finished in light blue with grey roof and beige interior; imported into the USA in 1970; restored in the 1980s and finished in the present burgundy livery with tan interior; described as still in good overall condition. Original engine.

| 1954 | 500 Mondial | | 0468MD | R | 3.000-3.800.000 USD | 2.457.263 | 3.162.500 | 2.694.450 | 18-08-17 | Pebble Beach | 33 | G&Co |

Sold new in Italy to Guido Petracchi who imported it in Ethiopia and raced it at some events. Discovered in 1970, the car was imported into the UK where in 1982 it was restored and fitted with the present, new body. Raced at several historic events, in 1997 it was bought by Jon Shirley who in 2007 had it restored again this time by Ferrari Classiche. Since 2009 in the current ownership. Certified by Ferrari Classiche. Offered with also a spare 3-liter engine built by Hall & Hall to 750 specification (see lot 892 Brooks 20.6.97 NS). F236

| 1954 | 500/735 Mondial (Pinin Farina) | | 0448MD | R | 4.000-5.500.000 USD | 2.991.450 | 3.850.000 | 3.280.200 | 19-08-17 | Monterey | 252 | RMS |

Red with tan interior; sold to the USA to Anthony Parravano, the car is believed to have been fitted with the 735 engine before leaving the factory. Raced in period and sold to Mexico in 1960. Reimported into the USA in the early 1970s and bought in 1999 by the current owner. F237

| 1955 | 121 LM (Scaglietti) | | 0546LM | R | 6.500-7.500.000 USD | 4.444.440 | 5.720.000 | 4.873.440 | 18-08-17 | Monterey | 140 | RMS |

One of two 118 LMs converted by the factory to 121 LM specification and raced in 1955 at the Mille Miglia and Le Mans 24 Hours. Subsequently the car was sold to William Doheny and imported into the USA where it was raced by Arnie McAfee until April 1956 when the driver lost his life in an accident while racing at Pebble Beach. The car was repaired and remained in Doheny ownership for 20 years before to be sold to Bill Ziering, who retained it for 20 years and used it at several historic events and concours. Since 1997 in the current ownership. F238

| 1956 | 250 GT (Boano) | | 0543GT | L | 1.100-1.400.000 USD | 880.341 | 1.133.000 | 965.316 | 18-08-17 | Carmel | 77 | Bon |

Black with red interior; raced at some events in the USA in period; restored in the 2000s and later reimported into Europe where the car received further cosmetical works and the engine was rebuilt. Certified by Ferrari Classiche (see lots 50 Worldwide Group 5.5.07 $550,000, 9 Gooding & Company 18.8.07 NS, 355 RM 14.8.10 $440,000, 144 Bonhams 20.5.11 NS, and 359 Artcurial 3.2.12 $628,361). F239

| 1958 | 250 GT Berlinetta TdF (P.F./Scaglietti) | | 0899GT | L | Refer Dpt. | NS | | | 18-08-17 | Carmel | 85 | Bon |

Sold new to Italian racing driver Edoardo Lualdi Gabardi and raced in period; acquired in 1960 by Frenchman Paul Mounier; damaged in a road accident in 1961 and not repaired; restored by Ferrari Classiche in 2012 and fitted with a newly cast correct-specification type 128 C engine supplied by the factory; certified by Ferrari Classiche in 2014 (see Coys lots 124 14.8.10 NS and 750 7.12.10 NS).

F235: 1955 Ferrari 250 Europa GT (Pinin Farina)

F236: 1954 Ferrari 500 Mondial

Year	Model	(Bodybuilder)	Chassis no.	Steering	Estimate	Hammer price £	$	€	Date	Place	Lot	Auc. H.

F237: 1954 Ferrari 500/735 Mondial (Pinin Farina)

F238: 1955 Ferrari 121 LM (Scaglietti)

| 1959 | **410 Superamerica coupé (Pinin Farina)** | | 1305SA | L | 5.500-6.500.000 USD | 4.145.295 | 5.335.000 | 4.545.420 | 19-08-17 | Monterey | 249 | **RMS** |

British racing green with yellow striping; body with covered headlamps and unique rear fenders with one-off taillights. Imported into the USA in the 1970s; restored in mid-1970s; bought in the late 1990s by the current owner. **F240**

| 1959 | **250 GT cabriolet (Pinin Farina)** | | 1475GT | L | 5.000-700.000 USD | 3.760.680 | 4.840.000 | 4.123.680 | 18-08-17 | Pebble Beach | 36 | **G&Co** |

Last example built, without side vents and with open headlamps; originally finished in yellow with brown leather interior; delivered new to US citizen Eric Don Pam then living in Monaco; imported into the USA in the mid-1960s; since 1974 for over 35 years owned by Hilary A. Raab Jr.; engine rebuilt in 1989; bought in 2014 by the current owner, cosmetically restored and finished in dark blue with tan interior (see lot 133 Gooding & Company 17.08.14 $5,610,000). **F241**

| 1960 | **250 GT cabriolet II serie (Pinin Farina)** | | 1881GT | L | 1.000-1.300.000 GBP | 1.288.000 | 1.723.602 | 1.533.879 | 07-09-16 | London | 134 | **RMS** |

Steel grey with red interior; several restoration works carried out in 2014 in Switzerland. Sold new in Italy to Angelo Moratti. Certified by Ferrari Classiche (see lots 125 Christie's 16.5.96 $125,779 and 21 Artcurial 18.6.07 NS). **F242**

| 1960 | **250 GT cabriolet II serie (Pinin Farina)** | | 1967GT | L | 1.400-1.800.000 USD | 1.160.159 | 1.430.000 | 1.340.339 | 19-01-17 | Scottsdale | 74 | **Bon** |

Light blue with tan interior; sold new in Italy and later exported to the USA; first restored in the 1980s; restored again in 2015 and refinished in its original colour; last serviced in July 2016 (see lot 41 Gooding & Company 29.1.16 NS).

| 1962 | **250 GT cabriolet II serie (Pininfarina)** | | 3803GT | L | 980-1.200.000 EUR | 1.051.081 | 1.313.928 | 1.232.000 | 08-02-17 | Paris | 151 | **RMS** |

Originally finished in white with blue interior; sold new in Italy; imported into the USA in 1972; reimported into Europe in 1990; bought by the current owner in 2001. Currently finished in silver with black interior; engine rebuilt in 2014; certified by Ferrari Classiche (see lots 745 Sotheby's 11.12.95 $123,769 and 023 Bonhams 6.12.15 NS).

| 1960 | **250 GT cabriolet II serie (Pininfarina)** | | 2139GT | L | 1.300-1.600.000 EUR | | NS | | 10-02-17 | Paris | 122 | **Art** |

Smoke grey with light beige leather interior; bought in 1990 by the current owner and reimported into Italy. Later the car was subjected to a full restoration completed in 2008. Currently fitted with engine no.1893GT.

| 1961 | **250 GT cabriolet II serie (Pininfarina)** | | 1783GT | L | Refer Dpt. | 1.267.110 | 1.651.931 | 1.484.293 | 18-05-17 | London | 123 | **Coy** |

Dark blue with black interior; fully restored in the 1990s. Bought in 2000 by the current owner and subsequently little used, the car requires recommissioning prior to use (see lots 18 Poulain 26.5.00 WD and 212 Brooks 27.5.00 $147,747).

| 1962 | **250 GT cabriolet II serie (Pininfarina)** | | 3459GT | L | 1.400-1.600.000 EUR | | NS | | 02-07-17 | Monaco | 114 | **Art** |

Shell grey with black leather interior; bought in 2006 by the current owner and subsequently restored in Italy. Certified by Ferrari Classiche.

| 1962 | **250 GT cabriolet II serie (Pininfarina)** | | 3783GT | L | 800-1.000.000 USD | 1.068.375 | 1.375.000 | 1.171.500 | 18-08-17 | Pebble Beach | 25 | **G&Co** |

Finished in grey with black leather and vinyl interior, the car was sold new to the USA. Dismantled in the mid-1980s for restoration, it is offered with many of the major components reassembled for presentation purposes and many boxes of original components and spares. Original engine. With hardtop.

| 1959 | **250 GT Coupé (Pinin Farina)** | | 1365GT | L | 160-180.000 EUR | 333.913* | 415.206* | 392.000* | 25-11-16 | Milan | 611 | **RMS** |

Restoration to be completed; engine no.1589GT. From the Duemila Ruote collection.

| 1959 | **250 GT Coupé (Pinin Farina)** | | 1247GT | L | 450-550.000 EUR | 371.843 | 467.240 | 437.000 | 09-02-17 | Paris | 348 | **Bon** |

Red with black interior; restored in France in 2012-13 and subsequently driven at some historic events.

| 1958 | **250 GT Coupé/Spyder California lwb** | | 1241GT | L | 600-800.000 GBP | 567.975 | 706.618 | 657.488 | 29-03-17 | Duxford | 45 | **H&H** |

Red with tan interior; conversion carried out in the UK in the 2000s. Type 128D inside plug engine of unknown origin (internal number 094C or perhaps 0944C); period correct gearbox upgraded with a fifth gear.

| 1960 | **250 GT Coupé (Pinin Farina)** | | 1617GT | L | 550-700.000 EUR | 527.325 | 677.134 | 604.800 | 27-05-17 | Villa Erba | 163 | **RMS** |

Light metallic grey with red interior; restored (see lot 304 Christie's 17.2.07 $152,607). **F243**

F239: 1956 Ferrari 250 GT (Boano)

F240: 1959 Ferrari 410 Superamerica coupé (Pinin Farina)

OFFICIAL FERRARI & FERRARI CLASSICHE DEALER

Niki Hasler AG

In 2017, Ferrari celebrates its 70th anniversary as the most illustrious specialist car manufacturer in history.

In 2017, Niki Hasler celebrates its 35th year as a family business which has developed into a major official Ferrari dealer having shared half the journey with the prestigious Italian marque. Since this year, we are also delighted to be appointed an Officina Ferrari Classiche.

We offer

- Sale of new Ferrari models, pre-owned and classic
- Restoration, service, maintenance
- Ferrari Classiche Certification
- Spare parts service
- Racing team "Scuderia Niki"
- Lifestyle and race track events

We are looking forward to seeing you in our brand new Ferrari Showroom in the city center of Basel.

Niki Hasler AG
Hardstrasse 15 - 4052 Basel
Switzerland
Tel: 0041 61 375 92 92
Fax: 0041 61 375 92 99
niki.hasler@nikihasler.ch
www.nikihasler.com

Year	Model	(Bodybuilder)	Chassis no.	Steering	Estimate	Hammer price £	$	€	Sale Date	Place	Lot	Auc. H.

F241: 1959 Ferrari 250 GT cabriolet (Pinin Farina)

F242: 1960 Ferrari 250 GT cabriolet II serie (Pinin Farina)

Year	Model	Chassis no.	St.	Estimate	£	$	€	Date	Place	Lot	Auc. H.
1959	250 GT Coupé (Pinin Farina)	1433GT	L	700-900.000 USD	**473.970**	**610.000**	**519.720**	18-08-17	Monterey	136	**RMS**

Blue with silver roof and natural leather interior; the car features numerous bespoke details, including a 410 Superamerica style air intake on the hood. Sold new in Italy; in single ownership from 1961 to 1986; restored in the late 1980s; imported into the USA in recent years. Certified by Ferrari Classiche.

| 1959 | 250 GT Coupé (Pinin Farina) | 1275GT | L | 500-600.000 USD | **380.342** | **489.500** | **417.054** | 19-08-17 | Pebble Beach | 104 | **G&Co** |

Blue with tan leather and vinyl interior; sold new to the USA; restored many years ago; recently serviced.

| 1961 | 250 GT Coupé (Pininfarina) | 1659GT | L | NA | | **NS** | | 19-08-17 | Monterey | 1015 | **R&S** |

Silver with black interior; body recently repainted.

| 1960 | 250 GT Spyder California swb (Scaglietti) | 2277GT | L | Refer Dpt. | | **NS** | | 19-01-17 | Scottsdale | 64 | **Bon** |

Open headlight version originally finished in hazelnut with tobacco leatherette interior and exhibited at the 1961 Brussels Motor Show; sold new in Italy; imported in late 1968 in the USA where the body was refinished in red, the interior re-upholstered in black and the bumpers were removed; following some ownership changes in 2006 bought by the current London-based owner; several cosmetic and mechanical restoration works carried out between 2007 and 2013.

| 1961 | 250 GT Berlinetta Lusso (PF/Scaglietti) | 2639GT | L | 9-10.000.000 USD | | **NS** | | 11-03-17 | Amelia Island | 254 | **RMS** |

Originally finished in silver grey with black leather interior, the car was sold new in Italy and imported into the USA in the late 1960s. In the 1980s the gearbox and clutch were rebuilt, the body was refinished in red and the interior were retrimmed in tan leather. In 1986 the car was imported into Switzerland and in 2001 it was reimported into the USA. In 2011 it was bought by the current owner and subjected to several works including the engine rebuild in 2015. Certified by Ferrari Classiche.

| 1961 | 250 GT Berlinetta Lusso (PF/Scaglietti) | 2985GT | L | 8.500-10.000.000 USD | **6.452.985*** | **8.305.000*** | **7.075.860*** | 19-08-17 | Monterey | 220 | **RMS** TOP TEN F244 |

Finished in shell grey with black leather interior, the car was sold new in Italy. In the late 1960s it was imported into the USA and in the mid-1970s it was bought by Charles Betz and Fred Peters who retained it for nearly 40 years and used it in vintage races, road events, concours and shows. In 2008 it was certified by Ferrari Classiche. As part of their sale to the consignor, Betz and Peters oversaw the restoration of the car completed in January 2016. From the Ferrari Performance Collection.

| 1961 | 400 Superamerica (Pininfarina) | 2841SA | L | 3.250-3.850.000 USD | **2.508.352** | **3.080.000** | **2.896.740** | 20-01-17 | Phoenix | 231 | **RMS** F245 |

Built on the short-wheelbase chassis, the car was originally finished in smoke grey with red interior and sold new to Switzerland. In the 1970s it was imported into the USA and from 1980 to 1999 it was owned by Greg Garrison. Between 2003 and 2006 it was restored to concours-condition and finished in the present dark blue livery with saddle leather interior. Certified by Ferrari Classiche (see RM lots 452 16.8.08 $1,650,000 and 115 16.8.13 $2,750,000).

| 1963 | 400 Superamerica coupé (Pininfarina) | 5029SA | L | Refer Dpt. | | **NS** | | 18-08-17 | Carmel | 63 | **Bon** |

Coupé Aerodinamico with covered headlamps finished in silver with red leather interior; long-wheelbase chassis. Sold new in Italy, in 1970 the car was imported into the USA where it remained in the same family ownership until 1997 when it was bought by a Swiss collector who had it restored in Italy in 2001. In 2005 it was reimported into the USA. Certified by Ferrari Classiche (see lots 214 Bonhams 17.12.05 $558,813, 14 Gooding & Company 19.1.08 $1,320,000 and 196 RM/Sotheby's 2.5.15 $2,860,000).

| 1961 | 250 GTE 2+2 (Pininfarina) | 3081 | L | 55-65.000 EUR | **138.336*** | **172.014*** | **162.400*** | 25-11-16 | Milan | 263 | **RMS** |

Blue; for restoration. From the Duemila Ruote collection.

| 1962 | 250 GTE 2+2 (Pininfarina) | 3925 | L | 55-65.000 EUR | **66.783*** | **83.041*** | **78.400*** | 25-11-16 | Milan | 616 | **RMS** |

Restoration project. From the Duemila Ruote collection.

| 1962 | 250 GTE 2+2 (Pininfarina) | 3983 | L | 45-55.000 EUR | **52.472*** | **65.247*** | **61.600*** | 25-11-16 | Milan | 904 | **RMS** |

Restoration project; lot including body and chassis only. From the Duemila Ruote collection.

| 1963 | 250 GTE 2+2 (Pininfarina) | 4139GT | L | 430-480.000 EUR | **401.322** | **501.682** | **470.400** | 08-02-17 | Paris | 137 | **RMS** F246 |

Dark grey with red leather interior; the car was imported in the 1960s in the USA where in 1969 it was dismantled for a restoration never started. In 2011 it was reimported into Europe and fully restored over a three year period. Just over 29,000 genuine kms. Certified by Ferrari Classiche.

| 1962 | 250 GTE 2+2 (Pininfarina) | 3271GT | L | 350-450.000 EUR | | **NS** | | 10-02-17 | Paris | 60 | **Art** |

Dark grey with red leather interior; sold new to Switzerland, the car was later exported to the USA and in 2010 reimported into Europe. Recently restored.

F243: 1960 Ferrari 250 GT Coupé (Pinin Farina)

F244: 1961 Ferrari 250 GT Berlinetta Lusso (PF/Scaglietti)

LUKAS HÜNI AG

Established some 40 years ago, we handle with excellence and a passion for detail all aspects of collecting historic automobiles. Our services include:

- buying and selling historic motorcars, both on our own account and for clients
- looking after our collector clients and their collections all around the world
- repair work and full restorations, using only the leading specialists and restorers
- maintenance, storage in our Zurich facilities, and transport world-wide

We concentrate in the high end of pre-war and Fifties/Sixties automobiles and specialise in the models that were market leaders and successful in their day. Our preferred marques include Bugatti, Alfa Romeo, Aston Martin, Bentley, Rolls-Royce, Lancia, Ferrari and Maserati.

New cars are available on request.

Ferrari 250 GT Berlinetta Short Wheelbase „Shark Nose" 1962 – Design Giorgio Giugiaro for BERTONE

We always have a selection of outstanding automobiles in stock which are either in excellent original condition or restored to perfection. We look forward to talking to you about our current stock, or the car that you are looking for. Please contact Yves Boitel.

If you wish to sell an important car, we would be happy to discuss your car and your requirements.

Visits to our showroom are by appointment only.

Lindenstrasse 26 · CH-8008 Zürich · Switzerland · Tel (+41) 44-384 84 00 · Fax (+41) 44-380 74 11 · cars@lukashuniag.ch

Year	Model	(Bodybuilder)	Chassis No.	Steering	Estimate	Hammer Price £	Hammer Price $	Hammer Price €	Date	Place	Lot	Auc. H.
1961	250 GTE 2+2	(Pininfarina)	2889GT	L	400-475.000 EUR	390.611	501.581	448.000	27-05-17	Villa Erba	149	RMS
Metallic grey; fully restored in Italy (see lot 138 RM 2.4.15 $288,439).												
1961	250 GTE 2+2	(Pininfarina)	2525GT	L	275-325.000 USD	213.675*	275.000*	234.300*	19-08-17	Monterey	S44	Mec
Blue and grey with red interior; body repainted. Fitted with a 5-speed Daytona gearbox. From the J. Geils Collection (see lot 544 Osenat 17.6.06 NS).												
1963	330 America	(Pininfarina)	5049	L	400-500.000 USD	339.323	412.500	388.740	11-03-17	Amelia Island	247	RMS
Medium metallic grey with maroon leather interior; sold new to the USA. From 1971 to 2006 with the same owner who had it restored.												
1964	250 GT/L	(PF/Scaglietti)	5681	L	1.400-1.600.000 EUR	1.245.073	1.598.789	1.428.000	27-05-17	Villa Erba	159	RMS F247
Dark brown with beige interior; formerly in the Aldo Cudone collection (see lots 35 Artcurial 28.6.08 NS and 248 RM/Sotheby's 14.5.16 NS).												
1964	330 GT 2+2	(Pininfarina)	6265	L	240-280.000 EUR		NS		03-09-16	Chantilly	20	Bon
White with black interior; sold new in Italy, the car was later exported to the USA. In the mid-1990s it was reimported into Italy and subsequently restored. Imported into the UK in 2014. First series with twin headlamps.												
1966	330 GT 2+2	(Pininfarina)	8075	L	170-200.000 GBP	207.200	277.275	246.754	07-09-16	London	109	RMS
Originally finished in smoke grey with beige leather interior, the car was sold new in Italy. In the 1970s it was imported into the USA where later it was repainted in the present dark blue livery. In the early 2000s reimported into Europe. Second series with single headlamp.												
1964	330 GT 2+2	(Pininfarina)	6155	R	220-260.000 GBP		NS		10-09-16	Goodwood	177	Bon
Red with beige leather interior; since 2005 in the current ownership. 38,310 miles since new. First series with twin headlamps (see lot 704 Brooks 18.6.99 $26,166).												
1964	330 GT 2+2	(Pininfarina)	6239	L	275-375.000 USD		NS		17-09-16	Aspen	150	TFA
Burgundy with red interior; originally finished in light blue, sold new to France, body repainted in the 1990s, imported into the USA in 2007. First series with twin headlamps (see lot 26 Poulain 29.4.96 $33,446).												
1964	330 GT 2+2	(Pininfarina)	6265	L	230-250.000 EUR		NA		08-10-16	Paris	163	CB/C
See lot 20 Bonhams 3.9.16.												
1967	330 GT 2+2	(Pininfarina)	8975	L	180-220.000 EUR	182.183	221.323	202.640	30-10-16	Paris	129	Art
Red; for nearly 20 years in the same ownership. Second series with single headlamp.												
1964	330 GT 2+2	(Pininfarina)	5923	L	160-180.000 EUR	214.659*	266.918*	252.000*	25-11-16	Milan	569	RMS
Silver with black interior; 23,244 kms. First series with twin headlamps. From the Duemila Ruote collection.												
1967	330 GT 2+2	(Pininfarina)	10029	L	65-75.000 EUR	219.429*	272.850*	257.600*	25-11-16	Milan	855	RMS
Metallic grey with black interior; it requires some restoration works. Second series with single headlamp. From the Duemila Ruote collection.												
1965	330 GT 2+2	(Pininfarina)	5933	L	200-220.000 EUR		NS		14-01-17	Maastricht	228	Coy
Metallic gold with black leather interior; engine rebuilt at unspecified date. First series with twin headlamps (see lot 127 Coys 6.8.16 $261,729).												
1966	330 GT 2+2	(Pininfarina)	7901	L	375-450.000 USD		NS		19-01-17	Scottsdale	38	Bon
Black with red leather interior; recent restoration and service. Second series with single headlamp (see lot 665.1 Barrett-Jackson 24.6.16 $330,000).												
1966	330 GT 2+2	(Pininfarina)	8485	L	250-300.000 USD	205.259	253.000	237.137	19-01-17	Phoenix	118	RMS
Blue with cream interior; sold new in Italy and imported into the USA in the early 1970s. 30,000 miles covered since the restoration carried out at unspecified date. Second series with single headlamp (see lots RM 27 16.8.02 WD, 133 15.8.03 $51,500 and 233 13.8.04 $60,500, and RM/Sotheby's 150 30.7.16 NS).												
1966	330 GT 2+2	(Pininfarina)	8183	L	270-330.000 EUR	234.848	295.099	276.000	09-02-17	Paris	367	Bon
Originally finished in light blue, the car was sold new in Italy and was imported into the USA in the late 1960s. In 1995 it was reimported into Europe already repainted in the present red livery. Original orange leather interior. Second series with single headlamp.												
1964	330 GT 2+2	(Pininfarina)	6215	L	200-240.000 GBP	211.185	262.376	246.347	18-02-17	London	346	Coy
Red; recently imported into the UK from Austria. First series with twin headlamps.												
1964	330 GT 2+2	(Pininfarina)	5923	L	320-385.000 USD	262.409	319.000	300.626	11-03-17	Amelia Island	21	Mot
See lot 569 RM/Sotheby's 25.11.16.												
1966	330 GT 2+2	(Pininfarina)	8421	L	180-220.000 GBP	203.100	251.032	233.788	19-03-17	Goodwood	37	Bon
Silver with red interior; restored many years ago; imported into the UK in the 2000s; engine rebuilt in 2010. Second series with single headlamp (see lots Coys 326 6.3.12 $158,549, 134 12.5.12 $127,053, and 130 14.7.12 $151,821, and Silverstone Auctions 155 4.9.14 $254,610).												
1964	330 GT Nembo Spider		5805	R	NQ	596.250*	741.795*	690.219*	29-03-17	Duxford	36	H&H F248
Light metallic blue with tan leather interior; aluminium body built by Giorgio Neri in Modena between the late 1980s-early 1990s in the style of the bodies built by Neri & Bonacini in the 1960s. The car was completed in the UK in 1998. Original engine, shortened chassis.												
1965	330 GT 2+2	(Pininfarina)	6685	L	200-240.000 GBP	196.875	244.932	227.903	29-03-17	Duxford	44	H&H
Red with light tan leather interior; sold new to the USA, the car was imported into the UK in 1988. Bought in 2006 by the current owner and subsequently restored. First series with twin headlamps.												

F245: 1961 Ferrari 400 Superamerica (Pininfarina)

F246: 1963 Ferrari 250 GTE 2+2 (Pininfarina)

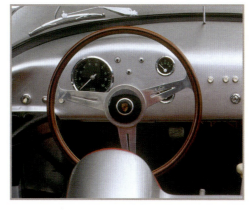

Offering restoration, preservation, maintenance, and sales and brokerage services, on pre-war through 1960s Mercedes-Benz, Ferrari, Porsche, Bugatti, Alfa Romeo, and other fine European collectibles, for over 40 years

Paul Russell and Company
Passionately Dedicated to the Preservation of Fine Automobiles since 1978

(+1) 978.768.6919   inquire@paulrussell.com   paulrussell.com

Year	Model	(Bodybuilder)	Chassis no.	Steering	Estimate	Hammer price £	Hammer price $	Hammer price €	Sale Date	Sale Place	Lot	Auc. H.

F247: 1964 Ferrari 250 GT/L (PF/Scaglietti)

F248: 1964 Ferrari 330 GT Nembo Spider

Year	Model	Chassis	Steer	Estimate	£	$	€	Date	Place	Lot	Auc.
1964	**330 GT 2+2 (Pininfarina)**	4085	L	NA	**161.807**	**181.500**	**141.189**	03-06-17	Newport Beach	9175	**R&S**

White; restored in 2007-2009. First series with twin headlamps.

| 1966 | **330 GT 2+2 (Pininfarina)** | 9209 | L | 275-350.000 USD | | NS | | 24-06-17 | Santa Monica | 216 | **RMS** |

Red with black interior; older restoration. Second series with single headlamp (see lot 271 Bonhams 15.8.14 $231,000).

| 1967 | **330 GT 2+2 (Pininfarina)** | 9419 | L | 340-380.000 EUR | **337.438** | **498.023** | **383.744** | 02-07-17 | Monaco | 161 | **Art** |

Dark metallic blue with original red leather interior; restored in Italy in 2014. Second series with single headlamp. Certified by Ferrari Classiche. **F249**

| 1966 | **330 GT 2+2 (Pininfarina)** | 9315 | L | 180-200.000 GBP | | NA | | 15-07-17 | Blenheim Pal. | 156 | **Coy** |

Black with tan interior; imported into the UK from the USA in 2015 and subsequently subjected to the interior retrimming and some mechanical works. Second series with single headlamp (see lots Russo & Steele S670 28.3.08 $111,100 and F454 15.8.08 $112,200).

| 1966 | **330 GT 2+2 (Pininfarina)** | 8871 | L | 325-375.000 USD | | NS | | 17-08-17 | Monterey | 47 | **WoA** |

Sold new to the USA; body repainted in red in 1980s circa; in single ownership from 1984 to 2012; several works carried out in recent years. Second series with single headlamp.

| 1967 | **330 GT 2+2 (Pininfarina)** | 9213 | L | 350-450.000 USD | | NS | | 18-08-17 | Pebble Beach | 3 | **G&Co** |

Smoke grey with red leather interior; first owner Chris Amon; 500 miles covered since a recent full restoration. Second series with single headlamp. Ferrari Classiche certification in progress.

| 1965 | **330 GT 2+2 shooting brake (Vignale)** | 7963 | L | 700-900.000 USD | | NS | | 19-08-17 | Pebble Beach | 173 | **G&Co** |

One-off designed by Luigi "Coco" Chinetti Jr and Bob Peak; built on an used 330 chassis and exhibited at the Vignale stand at the 1968 Turin Motor Show; sold by Chinetti in the 1970s; restored in the 1990s; paintwork redone about three years ago; in good mechanical order (see lots 225 Coys 10.5.08 NS and 344 Bonhams 15.8.08 NS).

| 1966 | **330 GT 2+2 (Pininfarina)** | 8551 | L | 300-350.000 USD | **186.480** | **240.000** | **204.480** | 19-08-17 | Monterey | S134 | **Mec** |

Metallic pine green with red leather interior; imported into the USA in 1971; restored in the 1990s; second series with single headlamp (see lot 107 Gooding & Company 18.1.14 $297,000).

| 1965 | **330 GT 2+2 (Pininfarina)** | 6813 | L | 200-225.000 USD | **91.298*** | **117.500*** | **100.110*** | 19-08-17 | Monterey | S70 | **Mec** |

Dark red with black leather interior.

| 1965 | **500 Superfast (Pininfarina)** | 5989SF | L | 2.800-3.200.000 USD | **2.373.976** | **2.915.000** | **2.741.558** | 21-01-17 | Scottsdale | 126 | **G&Co** |

Originally finished in light blue with blue cloth interior, the car was sold new to the USA. Between 2005 and 2007 it was restored and finished in the present light metallic blue livery with dark red leather interior. Since 2011 in the current ownership. In recent years the body has been repainted again and the engine and gearbox were rebuilt (see lot 268 RM 21.1.11 $935,000). **F250**

| 1965 | **275 GTB (PF/Scaglietti)** | 06901 | R | 1.100-1.500.000 GBP | | NS | | 10-09-16 | Goodwood | 115 | **Bon** |

Red with tan leather interior; sold new to the UK, restored in the 1990s, since 2001 in the current ownership. Originally the car was fitted with a Webasto sunroof. Certified by Ferrari Classiche (see Coys lots 58A 3.12.96 $178,346, 50 10.5.99 NS, 225 15.1.00 $181,752 and 72 15.5.00 $154,851).

| 1966 | **275 GTB (PF/Scaglietti)** | 08311 | L | 2.400-2.800.000 EUR | **2.909.817*** | **3.618.227*** | **3.416.000*** | 25-11-16 | Milan | 602 | **RMS** |

"Long nose" version with alloy body finished in red with black interior; six carburettor engine. Sold new in Italy, the car was sold to the USA in 1973 and reimported into Italy in 1975. Since 1980 in the current ownership. Recently serviced. From the Duemila Ruote collection. **F251**

| 1966 | **275 GTB (PF/Scaglietti)** | 08973 | L | 2.500-3.500.000 USD | **1.405.577*** | **1.732.500*** | **1.623.872*** | 19-01-17 | Scottsdale | 48 | **Bon** |

"Long nose" version finished in silver with black interior; sold new in Italy. Engine and gearbox replaced under warranty in the late 1960s probably; imported into Canada in the 1970s; restored in the USA between 1989 and 1991; bought in 2009 by the current Swiss owner; body repainted to its original colour and interior redone in late 2016. Certified by Ferrari Classiche (see lot 335 Bonhams 4.2.16 $2,319,642).

| 1966 | **275 GTB (PF/Scaglietti)** | 08431 | L | 2.400-2.800.000 USD | **1.724.492** | **2.117.500** | **1.991.509** | 20-01-17 | Phoenix | 256 | **RMS** |

"Long nose" version finished in yellow with black leather interior; described as in original condition. Six-carburettor engine. Sold new to the USA. Bought in 1997 by the current, fourth owner. Mechanicals restored. Just over 21,000 covered since new.

F249: 1967 Ferrari 330 GT 2+2 (Pininfarina)

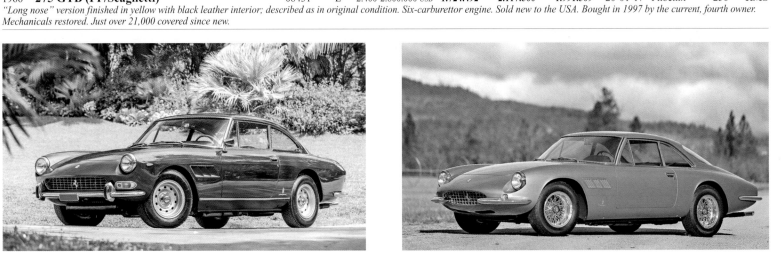

F250: 1965 Ferrari 500 Superfast (Pininfarina)

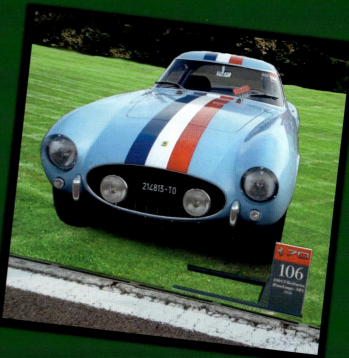

TRASMETTIAMO PASSIONE DAL 1996

www.carrozzeriaqualitycars.com

TALACREST

THE WORLD'S

OVER $1 BILLION IN SALES
INCLUDING 8 FERRARI GTO'S

THE QUEEN'S AWARDS
FOR ENTERPRISE:
INTERNATIONAL TRADE
2016

Talacrest are the biggest and most experienced dealers of classic Ferrari in the world and have sold over $1 billion worth of classic cars including eight Ferrari 250 GTO's many prototypes and numerous other desirable road and race cars. We are also very proud to have received The Queen's Award for Enterprise International Trade 2016. Our international customers represent a significant proportion of our business and we have sold many cars to overseas clients often without them even visiting our showrooms. Hopefully this award should reaffirm to customers old and new that our position as the leading and most trusted brand in the classic Ferrari market worldwide is unparalleled. If you are seriously considering to buy or sell your classic Ferrari then make Talacrest your number one choice.

NUMBER ONE

MANY FERRARI PROTOTYPES AND NUMEROUS CLASSIC CARS

WWW.TALACREST.COM

NUMBER ONE IN THE CLASSIC FERRARI MARKET

T + 44 (0)1344 308178 | M +44 (0) 7860 589855 | E john@talacrest.com

Year	Model	(Bodybuilder)	Chassis no.	Steering	Estimate	Hammer price £	$	€	Sale Date	Place	Lot	Auc. H.

F251: 1966 Ferrari 275 GTB (PF/Scaglietti)   F252: 1966 Ferrari 275 GTB Competizione (PF/Scaglietti)

1966 275 GTB (PF/Scaglietti) 08117 L 2.900-3.200.000 USD NS 21-01-17 Scottsdale 146 **G&Co**
Alloy "long nose" body finished in silver with black interior; sold new in Italy; imported into the USA in 1972; in 1990 imported into Switzerland and in 1993 into South Africa; between 1996 and 1998 body restored in Italy and engine fitted with the six-carburettor setup; in 2000 imported into Austria; in 2009 certified by Ferrari Classiche (see lot 69 TSAC 15.9.90 NS).

1965 275 GTB (PF/Scaglietti) 07341 L 1.800-2.200.000 EUR **1.648.286** **2.060.478** **1.932.000** 08-02-17 Paris 157 **RMS**
"Short nose" finished in pine green with beige leather interior; sold new to Spain, the car went later to Switzerland, then returned to Spain and is currently registered in the UK. Certified by Ferrari Classiche.

1964 275 GTB (PF/Scaglietti) 06681 L 1.800-2.000.000 USD **1.515.641*** **1.842.500*** **1.736.372*** 11-03-17 Amelia Island 263 **RMS**
"Short nose" version finished in red with black interior; sold new to the USA; restored in the early 2000s; engine rebuilt in 2013; certified by Ferrari Classiche (see lot 221 RM 18.8.12 $1,182,500).

1965 275 GTB (PF/Scaglietti) 07927 L 2.700-3.000.000 USD **2.393.160** **3.080.000** **2.624.160** 18-08-17 Carmel 16 **Bon**
Long nose version with alloy body finished in light blue with light blue interior; used by the factory for several months as a test car; sold in May 1966; imported into the USA in 1970; imported into Switzerland in 1992 and restored in Italy in 1999; reimported into the USA in 2005; restored again between 2011 and 2013 and finished in its original colours. Red Book Certification will be available once it has been issued by Ferrari (see Bonhams lots 356 18.5.02 NS and 120A 8.3.04 $335,599).

1965 275 GTB (PF/Scaglietti) 07075 L 2.000-2.400.000 USD **2.008.545** **2.585.000** **2.202.420** 19-08-17 Pebble Beach 163 **G&Co**
Originally finished in red with black interior; equipped from new with roll bar and engine with six carburettors; sold in Italy and raced at several events; imported into the USA in 1968; reimported into Europe in 1990 and later restored; acquired in 2014 by the current owner and restored again in Italy; interior retrimmed in tan leather; certified by Ferrari Classiche.

1965 275 GTB (PF/Scaglietti) 06943 L 1.900-2.200.000 USD NS 19-08-17 Monterey S78 **Mec**
Red with black interior; since 1970 for 47 years with its second owner. Built with "short nose" body, in 1981 the car was damaged in an accident and then repaired and fitted with a "long nose" front end acquired directly from Scaglietti. Restored by the owner over the years.

1965 275 GTB (PF/Scaglietti) 07933 L 2.900-3.400.000 USD **2.777.775** **3.575.000** **3.045.900** 19-08-17 Monterey 241 **RMS**
"Long nose" model with alloy body and six-carburettor engine; silver with navy blue leather interior. Sold new to the USA. Bought in 2010 by the current owner. Cosmetic restoration in 2015. Certified by Ferrari Classiche (see RM lots 305 17.8.01 $204,955 and 263 1.5.10 $1,043,896).

1966 275 GTB Competizione (PF/Scaglietti) 09051 L 12-16.000.000 USD **11.282.040** **14.520.000** **12.371.040** 19-08-17 Pebble Beach 120 **G&Co** **TOP TEN F252**
Silver with black leather interior; one of 12 examples built for the 1966 season; sold new in Italy and raced until 1970; sold to the UK in 1971; imported into the USA in 1993; bought by the current owner in 2004; restored to concours condition in 2007; body restored again and engine rebuilt in 2013.

1965 275 GTS (PF/Scaglietti) 07007 L 1.400-1.800.000 USD NS 22-04-17 Arlington NA **WoA**
Red with tan leather interior; sold new to the USA; restored in Italy between the late 1980s/early 1990s; described as in very good overall condition (see lot 194 RM 16.1.09 $385,000).

1965 275 GTS (PF/Scaglietti) 06819 L 1.600-1.800.000 EUR **1.562.445** **2.006.323** **1.792.000** 27-05-17 Villa Erba 143 **RMS F253**
Black with light blue interior; in single ownership for over 30 years. Certified by Ferrari Classiche (see Bonhams lots 221 19.12.07 $693,779 and 221 20.12.08 $557,683).

1966 275 GTS (PF/Scaglietti) 08335 L 1.850-2.200.000 USD **1.204.350** **1.550.000** **1.320.600** 18-08-17 Carmel 81 **Bon**
Light metallic blue with black leather interior; for 20 years with its first owner; restored in the late 1990s by Paul Russell & Co.; less than 35,000 miles covered since new. With hardtop. Ferrari Classiche certification in progress.

1966 275 GTS (PF/Scaglietti) 08621 L 1.700-2.000.000 USD **1.320.900** **1.700.000** **1.448.400** 18-08-17 Pebble Beach 14 **G&Co**
Black with white leatherette interior; sold new to the USA; until 2005 with its first owner; bought in 2014 by the current, third owner; 42,140 miles covered; in largely original, unrestored condition; recent mechanical works.

1965 Dino 206 S Berlinetta Speciale (Pininfarina) 0840 R 4.000-8.000.000 EUR **3.744.572** **4.666.556** **4.390.400** 10-02-17 Paris 87 **Art**
One-off built on a competition chassis finished in red with red and cream interior, the car was exhibited in 1965 and 1966 at the Turin, Paris, New York and London Motor Shows. Retained by Pininfarina, in 1967 it was presented by Sergio Pininfarina to the Automobile Club de l'Ouest (ACO) to be displayed at the Le Mans Museum. In original, not working condition; the 2-litre engine no.222/N1/0834 is not complete, the gearbox case appears to be empty and the clutch is missing. Offered by ACO. **F254**

F253: 1965 Ferrari 275 GTS (PF/Scaglietti)   F254: 1965 Ferrari Dino 206 S Berlinetta Speciale (Pininfarina)

ARTCURIAL
// Motorcars

1965 Dino 206 P Berlinette Speciale #0840
Sold for 4 390 400 €, Rétromobile February 2017

YOUR CAR COULD BE OUR NEXT RECORD

Contact :
+33 (0)1 42 99 20 73
motorcars@artcurial.com

artcurial.com/motorcars

Year	Model	(Bodybuilder)	Chassis No.	Steering	Estimate	Hammer Price £	Hammer Price $	Hammer Price €	Date	Place	Lot	Auc. H.
1967	275 GTB4	(PF/Scaglietti)	10563	L	3.000-3.400.000 USD		NS		20-01-17	Scottsdale	46	G&Co
	*Pine green with orange leather interior; sold new to the USA; engine and transaxle rebuilt in the 1970s; paintowrk and interior redone at unspecified date; 42,398 miles on the odometer.*
1966	275 GTB4	(PF/Scaglietti)	08769	L	Refer Dpt.	2.367.495	3.086.503	2.773.284	18-05-17	London	129	Coy
	*Red with black leather interior; first example built of the model, the car was exhibited at the Ferrari stand at the 1966 Paris Motor Show and subsequently sold to the USA. In the late 1980s it was part of the Albert Obrist's collection in Switzerland. Bought in 2004 by the current owner and subsequently little used, it requires recommissioning prior to use (see lot 427 Coys 15.5.04 $426,361).* **F255**
1967	275 GTB4	(PF/Scaglietti)	10507	L	2.500-3.000.000 USD	1.957.263	2.519.000	2.146.188	18-08-17	Carmel	26	Bon
	*Red with beige leather interior; Borrani wire wheels. The engine has covered 500 miles since the rebuild carried out many years ago. Three owners. Since 1992 in the T.J. Day Collection.*
1967	275 GTB4	(PF/Scaglietti)	10291	L	3.000-3.500.000 USD		NS		18-08-17	Pebble Beach	41	G&Co
	*Originally finished in black with dark beige interior; sold new in Italy and later exported to the USA; in single ownership from 1976 circa to 2014; engine rebuilt in 2009; cosmetically restored in 2015 with interior retrimmed in red leather.*
1967	275 GTB4	(PF/Scaglietti)	10147	L	2.750-3.250.000 USD	2.350.425*	3.025.000*	2.577.300*	19-08-17	Monterey	218	RMS
	*Red with black leather interior; sold new to Switzerland; imported into the USA in 1970; engine rebuilt in the early 1970s; interior retrimmed in the mid-1990s; in 1998 engine rebuilt and body repainted; cosmetically restored between 2010 and 2011. 82,577 kms on the odometer. Certified by Ferrari Classiche. From the Ferrari Performance Collection (see lot 76 Gooding & Company 11.3.11 $1,155,000).*
1967	330 GTC	(Pininfarina)	9955	L	650-700.000 USD		NS		04-11-16	Dallas	S136.1	Mec
	*Red with tan interior; the engine has covered approximately 1,000 miles since the rebuild. Interior redone in 2013 (see lot T206 Mecum 23.1.16 NS).*
1968	330 GTC	(Pininfarina)	11329	L	550-600.000 GBP	584.200	742.810	694.030	05-12-16	London	126	Coy
	*Silver with red leather interior; sold new in Italy, the car was later exported to the USA where it remained in single ownership for 33 years until 2010. In 2011 it was imported into the UK and subsequently subjected to a full restoration completed in late 2015. Certified by Ferrari Classiche.*
1967	330 GTC	(Pininfarina)	9911	L	575-675.000 USD		NS		18-01-17	Scottsdale	51	WoA
	*Silver with black leather interior; sold new in Italy, imported into the USA nel 1972, from 1979 to 2016 in the same ownership. Unused for several years, it received recently some mechanical works.*
1967	330 GTC	(Pininfarina)	10267	L	650-750.000 USD	615.305	748.000	704.915	11-03-17	Amelia Island	241	RMS
	*Dark blue with claret leather interior; restored to concours condition at unspecified date. Certified by Ferrari Classiche (see lot 234 RM 16.8.14 $1,023,000).* **F256**
1968	330 GTC	(Pininfarina)	11257	L	550-600.000 EUR	445.068	554.320	520.000	08-04-17	Essen	168	Coy
	*Red with black leather interior; 28,287 miles on the odometer. Interior retrimmed.*
1968	330 GTC	(Pininfarina)	11257	L	475-525.000 GBP	477.945	623.097	559.865	18-05-17	London	138	Coy
	*See lot 168 Coys 8.4.17.*
1966	330 GTC	(Pininfarina)	8969	L	575-650.000 EUR	527.325	677.134	604.800	27-05-17	Villa Erba	135	RMS
	*Hazelnut with beige interior; mechanicals serviced and interior retrimmed; certified by Ferrari Classiche (see lot 168 Bonhams 15.1.15 NS).*
1968	330 GTC	(Pininfarina)	11257	L	500-600.000 EUR	487.205	640.468	539.660	05-08-17	Schloss Dyck	240	Coy
	*See lot 138 Coys 18.5.17.*
1968	330 GTC	(Pininfarina)	11251	L	700-800.000 USD	705.128	907.500	773.190	18-08-17	Pebble Beach	16	G&Co
	*Metallic brown with black interior; sold new in Italy; imported into the USA in 1972; 150 miles covered since the restoration recently completed; Ferrari Classiche certification in progress.*
1967	330 GTC	(Pininfarina)	9874	L	550-650.000 USD	435.897*	561.000*	477.972*	19-08-17	Monterey	262	RMS
	*Black with red interior; sold new in Italy and imported into the USA in 1973; paintwork and interior redone in the 1990s; mechanicals overhauled in 2016. Just over 26,600 miles covered since new.*
1967	330 GTS	(Pininfarina)	10869	L	2.200-2.500.000 USD	2.015.640	2.475.000	2.327.738	20-01-17	Phoenix	220	RMS
	*Originally finished in medium green with beige interior, the car was sold new to the USA. Restored in the 1980s and finished in black with red interior. Bought in 2007 by the current owner. Restored again in 2013 e refinished in the present medium grey with black interior. Certified by Ferrari Classiche.* **F257**
1968	365 GT 2+2	(Pininfarina)	12043	L	180-220.000 EUR		WD		30-10-16	Paris	128	Art
	*Light blue; certified by Ferrari Classiche.*
1967	365 GT 2+2	(Pininfarina)	11487	L	300-350.000 USD		NS		04-11-16	Dallas	S141	Mec
	*Silver with beige interior; imported into the USA in 1980. Recently serviced. 27,200 believed original miles.*
1968	365 GT 2+2	(Pininfarina)	11794	L	130-150.000 EUR	128.795*	160.151*	151.200*	25-11-16	Milan	550	RMS
	*Blue with beige interior; for restoration. Largely complete. From the Duemila Ruote collection.*
1969	365 GT 2+2	(Pininfarina)	12831	L	80-90.000 EUR	85.863*	106.767*	100.800*	25-11-16	Milan	851	RMS
	*Blue; for restoration. From the Duemila Ruote collection.*
1969	365 GT 2+2	(Pininfarina)	12167	L	180-220.000 USD	162.868*	200.750*	188.163*	19-01-17	Scottsdale	62	Bon
	*Red with black interior; cosmetically restored. 48,017 kms covered. Last serviced in 2016 (see lot 7031 Russo & Steele 20.8.16 NS).*

F255: 1966 Ferrari 275 GTB4 (PF/Scaglietti)

F256: 1967 Ferrari 330 GTC (Pininfarina)

For more than 30 years JD Classics has been restoring, racing and supplying the most significant road and race cars.

Restored in England. Driven around the world.

Ferrari 275 GTB/4 LHD

jdclassics@jdclassics.com www.jdclassics.com

WYCKE HILL BUSINESS PARK, WYCKE HILL, MALDON, ESSEX, CM9 6UZ, U.K. +44 (0)1621 879579
MAYFAIR SHOWROOM, 26-28 MOUNT ROW, MAYFAIR, LONDON, W1K 3SQ, U.K. +44 (0) 207 125 1400
CALIFORNIA SHOWROOM, 4040 CAMPUS DRIVE, NEWPORT BEACH, CA, 92660 +1 949 500 0585

Year	Model	(Bodybuilder)	Chassis no.	Steering	Estimate	Hammer price £	Hammer price $	Hammer price €	Sale Date	Place	Lot	Auc. H.

F257: 1967 Ferrari 330 GTS (Pininfarina)   *F258: 1970 Ferrari 365 GT 2+2 (Pininfarina)*

Year	Model	(Bodybuilder)	Chassis no.	Steering	Estimate	£	$	€	Date	Place	Lot	Auc. H.
1970	365 GT 2+2	(Pininfarina)	13659	L	250-300.000 USD		NS		21-01-17	Scottsdale	154	G&Co
	Dark blue; sold new in Italy and later imported into the USA; body repainted in recent years; original engine replaced with a correct-type unnumbered unit (see lots Mecum S117 18.8.11 $81,461 and 170 16.8.12 NS, and Russo & Steele S653 16.8.14 $233,750).											
1969	365 GT 2+2	(Pininfarina)	12573	L	NQ	170.210	209.000	196.565	21-01-17	Scottsdale	8167	R&S
	Light metallic blue with black leather interior; in single ownership since 2005. Partial engine rebuild in 2006.											
1970	365 GT 2+2	(Pininfarina)	13339	L	160-200.000 EUR	193.165	240.726	226.480	10-02-17	Paris	56	Art F258
	Light grey with original black leather interior; in good overall condition.											
1970	365 GT 2+2	(Pininfarina)	13047	L	275-325.000 USD	226.215	275.000	259.160	10-03-17	Amelia Island	53	G&Co
	Gold with black leather interior; Borrani wire wheels. Certified by Ferrari Classiche.											
1968	365 GT 2+2	(Pininfarina)	11749	L	195-275.000 USD	158.351*	192.500*	181.412*	11-03-17	Amelia Island	29	Mot
	Blue with tan interior; in driving condition.											
1970	365 GT 2+2	(Pininfarina)	12793	L	200-225.000 USD		NS		01-04-17	Ft.Lauderdale	533	AA
	Red with black leather interior; last serviced in September 2016. One owner until 2016 (see lot 1106 Auctions America 25.6.16 NS).											
1968	365 GT 2+2	(Pininfarina)	11611	L	160-200.000 USD	157.447	202.400	180.440	04-06-17	Greenwich	150	Bon
	Silver with black leather interior; restored in the late 1980s; engine rebuilt in 2010-11; transmission rebuilt in more recent years.											
1968	365 GT 2+2	(Pininfarina)	11317	L	210-260.000 EUR		NS		02-07-17	Monaco	160	Art
	Red with beige interior; in good original, unrestored condition. One owner.											
1969	365 GT 2+2	(Pininfarina)	13269	L	250-300.000 USD	170.940	220.000	187.440	18-08-17	Carmel	102	Bon
	Dark metallic grey with beige leather interior; some restoration works carried out over the years. Engine rebuilt (see Coys lots 393 19.11.05 NS, 221 2005.06 NS and 222 22.7.06 $99,903).											
1969	365 GT 2+2	(Pininfarina)	13045	L	250-300.000 USD	188.034	242.000	206.184	18-08-17	Pebble Beach	56	G&Co
	Dark blue with black leather interior; sold new to the USA; recent cosmetic restoration.											
1969	365 GT 2+2	(Pininfarina)	12957	L	275-325.000 USD	222.222	286.000	243.672	19-08-17	Pebble Beach	162	G&Co
	Blue with black interior; in largely original condition; mechanicals overhauled in 2016.											
1968	Dino 206 GT	(PF/Scaglietti)	00238	L	475-575.000 EUR	449.098	561.406	526.400	08-02-17	Paris	166	RMS F259
	Silver with black and blue interior; sold new in Italy, the car was imported into the UK in 1978. First restored in the 1980s when the original engine block was replaced with a correct 2-litre unit; restored again in the late 1990s. Certified by Ferrari Classiche.											
1969	Dino 206 GT	(PF/Scaglietti)	00332	L	500-600.000 USD	384.566	467.500	440.572	10-03-17	Amelia Island	11	G&Co
	Light red; sold new in Italy, subsequently the car has had owners in Canada and Japan and in 2011 it was imported into the USA. Engine rebuilt in recent years.											
1968	Dino 206 GT	(PF/Scaglietti)	00152	L	750-900.000 USD		NS		10-03-17	Amelia Island	65	G&Co
	Red with black interior; owned by Eric Clapton in 1970; in the same family ownership from 1977 to 2006; subsequently subjected to a concours-quality restoration. Certified by Ferrari Classiche.											
1969	Dino 206 GT	(PF/Scaglietti)	00390	L	550-600.000 EUR		NS		27-05-17	Villa Erba	137	RMS
	Blue; in largely original condition with one repaint. Formerly owned by tenor Mario Del Monaco.											
1969	Dino 206 GT	(PF/Scaglietti)	00362	L	650-750.000 USD	487.179*	627.000*	534.204*	19-08-17	Monterey	216	RMS
	Originally finished in yellow with black leatherette interior; imported into the USA in 1970; in the mid-1990s repainted in the present red livery; offered for sale in 2014 claiming a recent restoration that had since accrued only 900 kms. From the Ferrari Performance Collection.											
1973	Dino 246 GT	(PF/Scaglietti)	06580	L	250-350.000 EUR		NS		03-09-16	Chantilly	22	Bon
	Red with black interior; acquired in 1991 by the current owner and fully restored between 1991 and 1992 (see Bonhams lots 23 10.10.14 NS and 126 13.5.16 $326,255).											
1971	Dino 246 GT	(PF/Scaglietti)	02114	R	150-200.000 GBP	299.420	398.977	354.094	10-09-16	Goodwood	108	Bon
	Metallic gold with black vinyl interior; since 1977 in the current, second ownership. In original condition. In 1981 the car was taken off the road and since then the engine was turned over regularly by hand. 25,253 miles covered.											
1973	Dino 246 GT	(PF/Scaglietti)	06580	L	NA	218.333	290.929	258.201	10-09-16	Goodwood	134A	Bon
	See lot 22 Bonhams 3.9.16.											
1969	Dino 246 GT	(PF/Scaglietti)	00428	L	320-350.000 EUR		NA		08-10-16	Paris	143	CB/C
	Black with gold wheels; described as in very good mechanical condition.											
1974	Dino 246 GT	(PF/Scaglietti)	07046	R	280-325.000 GBP	280.000	340.144	311.416	29-10-16	London	139	Coy
	Red with tan leather interior with black inserts; restored in the early 1990s.											
1972	Dino 246 GT	(PF/Scaglietti)	02950	L	325-375.000 USD		NS		04-11-16	Dallas	S104	Mec
	Red with tan interior with black inserts.											
1972	Dino 246 GT	(PF/Scaglietti)	04924	L	175-195.000 EUR	305.292*	379.617*	358.400*	25-11-16	Milan	612	RMS
	Silver with black interior; in the same ownership since 1974. 50,201 kms. From the Duemila Ruote collection.											

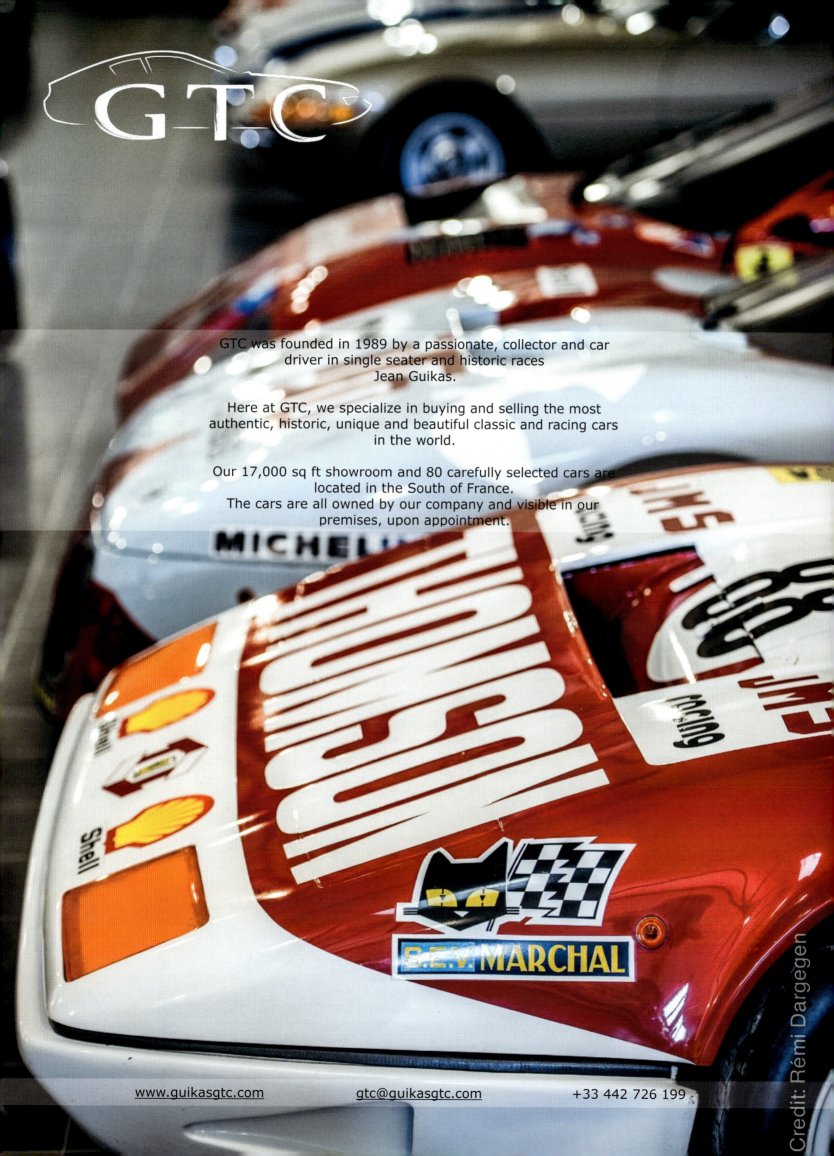

Year	Model	(Bodybuilder)	Chassis no.	Steering	Estimate	Hammer price £	Hammer price $	Hammer price €	Sale Date	Sale Place	Lot	Auc. H.

F259: 1968 Ferrari Dino 206 GT (PF/Scaglietti)

F260: 1971 Ferrari Dino 246 GT (PF/Scaglietti)

Year	Model	Chassis	Str	Estimate	£	$	€	Date	Place	Lot	Auc
1972	**Dino 246 GT** (PF/Scaglietti)	02940	R	260-300.000 GBP		NS		26-11-16	Weybridge	199	His

Red with black interior; restored in 2014. 47,111 miles on the odometer (see Coys lots 84 22.7.00 $61,878, 71 30.4.02 NS and 194 2.7.16 $345,332).

1971	**Dino 246 GT** (PF/Scaglietti)	02424	R	450-500.000 AUD	326.985	406.574	383.850	27-11-16	Melbourne	56	Mos

Red with black interior; sold new in Italy, at unspecified date the car was imported into Australia and converted to right-hand drive. Bought in 2006 by the current owner and fully restored.

1971	**Dino 246 GT** (PF/Scaglietti)	02764	R	300-350.000 GBP		NS		04-12-16	London	15	Bon

Red with beige leather interior; restored in 1989. Formerly the property of Eric Clapton.

1974	**Dino 246 GT** (PF/Scaglietti)	07246	R	270-300.000 GBP		NS		05-12-16	London	136	Coy

Red with tan interior with black inserts; restored in the early 1990s. Clutch replaced in 1997. Certified by Ferrari Classiche (see lot 422 Coys 1.12.09 $143,240).

1971	**Dino 246 GT** (PF/Scaglietti)	02524	R	300-350.000 GBP	331.900	418.493	390.016	07-12-16	London	329	Bon

White with blue interior; four owners and 52,000 miles covered. Restored in 2009-10, body recently repainted again. Displayed at the 1971 Earls Court Motor Show (see lots 722 Coys 7.12.10 NS and 337 Silverstone Auctions 24.5.14 $422,204). **F260**

1974	**Dino 246 GT** (PF/Scaglietti)	07246	R	250-280.000 GBP	273.175	332.645	312.020	14-01-17	Birmingham	131	Coy

See lot 136 Coys 5.12.16.

1972	**Dino 246 GT** (PF/Scaglietti)	03712	L	325-375.000 USD	238.119	290.000	271.991	15-01-17	Kissimmee	F182	Mec

Yellow with tan interior with black inserts; 250 miles covered since the engine rebuild (see lots 427 RM 16.8.08 $154,000 and F243 Mecum 20.5.16 $310,000).

1972	**Dino 246 GT** (PF/Scaglietti)	03978	L	275-350.000 USD	228.439	280.500	263.810	20-01-17	Scottsdale	4	G&Co

Yellow with black interior; imported into the USA in 1979, the car received in recent years some cosmetic and mechanical works (see lot 152 Gooding & Company 18.1.14 $291,500).

1970	**Dino 246 GT** (PF/Scaglietti)	00690	L	375-450.000 USD		NS		20-01-17	Phoenix	261	RMS

Red with black vinyl interior; imported into the USA in 1974. Engine and transmission rebuilt in 1981; interior restored in 2008 (see lot 12 Gooding & Company 21.1.11 $170,500).

1970	**Dino 246 GT** (PF/Scaglietti)	01004	L	375-425.000 EUR	382.211	477.792	448.000	08-02-17	Paris	108	RMS

Light metallic blue with black and blue interior; the car has covered 250 kms since a recent restoration.

1974	**Dino 246 GT** (PF/Scaglietti)	06416	L	200-250.000 EUR	229.764	286.337	269.392	10-02-17	Paris	86	Art

Red with black interior; in original condition except for the paintwork redone at unspecified date. Since 1978 in the current ownership.

1972	**Dino 246 GT** (PF/Scaglietti)	03534	L	280-300.000 GBP	355.680	441.897	414.901	18-02-17	London	354	Coy

Silver; engine rebuilt in the 1990s, body repainted in 2005. Three owners; 35,000 miles covered (see lot 127 Coys 18.4.15 $384,394).

1974	**Dino 246 GT** (PF/Scaglietti)	07336	R	300-350.000 GBP	439.875	552.219	520.504	24-02-17	Stoneleigh P.	526	SiC

Red; bought in 1995 by the current owner and restored between 2014 and 2015. 34,935 miles covered since new.

1972	**Dino 246 GT** (PF/Scaglietti)	04662	L	260-320.000 EUR	271.132	335.123	312.120	18-03-17	Lyon	190	Agu

Red with black interior; restored in Italy at unspecified date. Certified by Ferrari Classiche.

1972	**Dino 246 GT** (PF/Scaglietti)	04092	L	330-380.000 USD		NS		18-08-17	Carmel	94	Bon

Red; sold new in Italy and later imported into the USA. For 30 years in the current ownership. 4,000 miles covered since a full restoration.

1973	**Dino 246 GT** (PF/Scaglietti)	04374	L	250-325.000 USD		NS		18-08-17	Pebble Beach	9	G&Co

Red; never fully restored and always well maintained; engine rebuilt in 2014.

1972	**Dino 246 GT** (PF/Scaglietti)	01784	L	250-300.000 USD	163.170	210.000	178.920	19-08-17	Monterey	F14	Mec

Red with tan and black interior; sold new in Europe; since 1978 in the current ownership; recent engine-out service.

1969	**Dino 246 GT** (PF/Scaglietti)	00522	L	350-425.000 USD	320.513	412.500	351.450	19-08-17	Monterey	242	RMS

Rubin red with black interior with red inserts; bought in 2012 by the current owner and fully restored over a three year period.

1972	**Dino 246 GTS** (PF/Scaglietti)	06040	R	350-400.000 GBP	373.525	498.955	441.693	08-09-16	Fontwell Park	148	Coy

Red with black interior; paintwork and interior redone many years ago. Last serviced in 2016. First owner Peter Grant, manager of the Led Zeppelin.

1973	**Dino 246 GTS** (PF/Scaglietti)	06158	L	NA		NS		04-11-16	Dallas	S127.1	Mec

Red with tan interior; originally finished in metallic blue and sold new to the USA. Certified by Ferrari Classiche (see lot 141 RM 15.8.14 $440,000).

1973	**Dino 246 GTS** (PF/Scaglietti)	05338	R	280-320.000 GBP		NS		12-11-16	Birmingham	613	SiC

Red with black interior; described as in good condition. In the same ownership from 1978 to 2015. 49,303 miles covered.

1973	**Dino 246 GTS** (PF/Scaglietti)	05836	L	325-425.000 USD		NS		20-01-17	Scottsdale	32	G&Co

Red with original beige interior with black inserts; sold new to the USA. In single ownership from 1974 to 2015; body repainted; less than 16,500 miles covered; last serviced in September 2015.

1973	**Dino 246 GTS** (PF/Scaglietti)	06106	L	325-375.000 USD		NS		21-01-17	Scottsdale	138	G&Co

Red with beige interior; sold new to the USA. In the same ownership from 1975 to 2014. In original condition, just over 38,000 miles covered, recent mechanical overhaul.

1973	**Dino 246 GTS** (PF/Scaglietti)	06380	L	NQ	309.065	379.500	356.920	21-01-17	Scottsdale	8631	R&S

Black with black interior with red inserts; sold new in Italy, the car was imported into the USA in 1980. Restored between 2014 and 2016. 20,000 original miles.

We put you in the Driver's Seat.

SOME CARS RECENTLY SOLD:
500 TR • 500 TRC • 750 Monza
250 Europa GT • 375 America
250 MM Berlinetta • 250 TdF Zagato
250 PF Cab II • 250 SWB California
275 GTB/4 Alloy • 330 GTS • 365 GTC
365 GTS • F50 • 2001 Formula 1
Enzo • Porsche 550 RS Spyder
Ferrari 250 GTO

WE ARE ALWAYS SEEKING TO BUY ANY CLASSIC FERRARI OF '50s, '60s & '70s OR ANY OTHER EUROPEAN RACE OR SPORTS CARS

SOME CARS CURRENTLY AVAILABLE:
Ferrari 225S Berlinetta • Ferrari 330 GTS
Ferrari 166/MM 53 Spyder • Ferrari 512 BBi
Ferrari 365 GT4/BB • BMW 3.0 CS
Lancia B20 • Lancia B24S Spyder
Lancia Flaminia Super Sport Zagato
Maserati A6GCS
Maserati 3500 GT Vignale Spyder
Mercedes 280SE Low-Grille Cab
OSCA MT4 • Porsche 930 Turbo

For more than 35 years, Thomas Hamann has been established amongst the world's leading dealers and brokers of classic European race and sports cars as one of the most respected and experienced in the business. His primary focus is classic Ferrari from the '50s, '60s and early '70s, but he is knowledgeable and regularly works with numerous other great marques. Over the years many important classic European sports and race cars and even entire collections have changed hands with his help and involvement.

A selection of our inventory cannot be found in our advertisements or on our website. Many times buyers and sellers prefer discrete transactions away from the media hype and publicity auction sales often create. We presently have an impressive selection of vintage race and sports cars which are eligible for the world's top events. If you wish to sell or trade your classic, or if you are looking for a specific model, chances are that we know where to find it or already have a buyer. We are your reliable partner for buying, selling, or trading your classic automobiles.

Email: thomas@HamannClassicCars.com
Connecticut, USA   Tel: +1-203-813-8300   Mobile: 1-203-918-8300

HamannClassicCars.com

Year	Model	(Bodybuilder)	Chassis no.	Steering	Estimate	Hammer price £	$	€	Date	Place	Lot	Auc. H.
1973	**Dino 246 GTS**	(PF/Scaglietti)	05846	L	300-375.000 USD	262.409	319.000	300.626	10-03-17	Amelia Island	71	G&Co

Light metallic brown with tan leather interior; in very good, largely original condition, about 23,000 miles covered. Body repainted 15 years ago. In single ownership from 1974 to 2015.

1974	**Dino 246 GTS**	(PF/Scaglietti)	07798	L	350-400.000 USD		NS		11-03-17	Amelia Island	229	RMS

Metallic hazelnut with black interior; sold new to the USA and retained by its first owner until 1998. In original condition; just over 20,000 miles covered (see lot 4 Gooding & Company 15.8.15 $375,000).

1974	**Dino 246 GTS**	(PF/Scaglietti)	08278	L	275-350.000 USD		NS		04-06-17	Greenwich	173	Bon

Light metallic blue with blue interior; bought in the mid-2000s by the current, second owner and subsequently recommissioned. Under 30,000 miles covered since new.

1974	**Dino 246 GTS**	(PF/Scaglietti)	07026	L	230-260.000 GBP	253.500	328.992	287.038	30-06-17	Goodwood	246	Bon **F261**

Red with black interior; some recommissioning works carried out in UK in 2016, including a body repainting.

1974	**Dino 246 GTS**	(PF/Scaglietti)	08056	L	400-450.000 USD	324.786	418.000	356.136	19-08-17	Pebble Beach	148	G&Co

White with tan leather interior with black inserts; sold new to the USA; bought in 2014 by the current owner and restored; displaying less than 18,000 miles, believed original.

1969	**365 GTC**	(Pininfarina)	11981	L	550-650.000 EUR	629.665*	782.961*	739.200*	25-11-16	Milan	572	RMS

Blue with beige interior; in Italy since new. From the Duemila Ruote collection.

1969	**365 GTC**	(Pininfarina)	11989	L	700-800.000 USD		NS		20-01-17	Scottsdale	20	G&Co

Originally finished in silver with black leather interior, the car was sold new in Italy. In the 1970s it was imported into the USA and in the 1990s it was restored and finished in the present red livery. Paintwork redone in 2011. 43,144 kms on the odometer. Recently serviced.

1969	**365 GTC**	(Pininfarina)	12325	L	725-825.000 USD		NS		10-03-17	Amelia Island	35	G&Co

Metallic blue with original black leather interior; some mechanical works carried out over the years. Last serviced in June 2016 (see lot 278 Bonhams 18.12.01 $86,947).

1969	**365 GTC**	(Pininfarina)	12173	L	525-625.000 EUR	507.795	652.055	582.400	27-05-17	Villa Erba	126	RMS **F262**

Yellow with original black interior; 52,500 kms covered; one owner for over 40 years.

1973	**365 GTB4 Daytona**	(PF/Scaglietti)	16109	L	650-800.000 USD		NS		04-11-16	Dallas	S125	Mec

Yellow with black interior; restored in the 1990s. 48,760 miles covered since new (see Mecum lots T203 23.1.16 NS and F141 19.8.16 NS).

1969	**365 GTB4 Daytona**	(PF/Scaglietti)	12905	L	650-800.000 EUR	744.150*	925.317*	873.600*	25-11-16	Milan	876	RMS

Red with black interior; originally finished in blue, the car was sold new to the UK and was reimported into Italy in 1990. From the Duemila Ruote collection.

1972	**365 GTB4 Daytona**	(spider/conversion)	14269	R	500-600.000 GBP	529.625	673.418	629.195	05-12-16	London	118	Coy

Red with tan leather interior with black inserts; conversion carried out at unspecified date during the ownership of Bernard Fosker.

1972	**365 GTB4 Daytona**	(PF/Scaglietti)	15155	L	600-800.000 USD		NS		19-01-17	Scottsdale	11	Bon

Yellow with black leather interior; sold new to the USA; in 1989 imported into Belgium and restored; engine rebuilt in the early 2000s; recent service; recently reimported into the USA. Ferrari Classiche certification in process (see lot 64 Poulain 13.12.99 NS).

1971	**365 GTB4 Daytona**	(PF/Scaglietti)	14393	L	650-850.000 USD		NS		19-01-17	Scottsdale	66	Bon

Light red with black leather interior; sold new to the USA where it remained with its first owner until the late 1990s; body repainted in 2005; described as in largely original condition; less than 30,000 miles covered; last serviced in late 2016; certified by Ferrari Classiche.

1970	**365 GTB4 Daytona**	(PF/Scaglietti)	13183	L	700-850.000 USD		NS		19-01-17	Phoenix	120	RMS

Red with black interior; sold new in Italy and imported into the USA in the late 1970s. Older restoration recently freshened (see lot 2080 Auctions America 25.6.16 $600,000).

1971	**365 GTB4 Daytona**	(spider/conversion)	13941	L	NQ		NS		21-01-17	Scottsdale	1381	B/J

Yellow with tan interior; conversion carried out by Richard Straman in the 1980s.

1970	**365 GTB4 Daytona**	(PF/Scaglietti)	13231	L	850-950.000 USD		NS		21-01-17	Scottsdale	119	G&Co

Red with tan interior with black inserts; sold new in Italy and later imported into the USA; restored in the mid-1990s; engine rebuilt in 2010; cosmetically restored again in 2013-2014.

1969	**365 GTB4 Daytona**	(PF/Scaglietti)	12801	L	700-750.000 EUR	601.983	752.522	705.600	08-02-17	Paris	149	RMS

Red with black interior; sold new to France, the car was also owned by Pierre Bardinon, Comte Frederic Chandon and Jean Berchon. In 2015 it was bought by the current owner. Engine and gearbox rebuilt in 2009 and 2010, body repainted in 2014. US papers (see lot 152 RM 04.2.15 $807,630).

1972	**365 GTB4 Daytona**	(PF/Scaglietti)	16447	L	620-680.000 EUR		NS		09-02-17	Paris	358	Bon

Finished in silver with black leather interior, the car was sold new to the USA. Body repainted in its original colour in 2011. Gearbox overhauled in 2014. EU taxes paid (see lots Gooding & Company 39 9.3.12 $330,000 and 130 17.1.15 $698,500, and Silverstone Auctions 232 4.9.15 NS).

1970	**365 GTB4 Daytona**	(PF/Scaglietti)	13433	L	750-850.000 EUR	681.160	848.874	798.640	10-02-17	Paris	85	Art **F263**

Black with beige leather interior with black inserts; engine rebuilt. Certified by Ferrari Classiche.

1971	**365 GTB4 Daytona**	(competition conversion)	14115	L	1.250-1.500.000 USD		NS		11-03-17	Amelia Island	269	RMS

Red with NART blue and white stripes; sold new to the USA to Ferrari dealer Gordon Tatum, who prepared it for competition but never raced it. Restored in recent years to full competition specification (see lot 462 Barrett-Jackson 22.6.03 NS).

1972	**365 GTB4 Daytona**	(PF/Scaglietti)	14585	L	600-700.000 USD	542.916	660.000	621.984	11-03-17	Amelia Island	274	RMS

Originally finished in red with beige interior, the car was sold new to the USA. In the late 1980s it was restored and refinished in the present yellow livery with black interior. Certified by Ferrari Classiche.

F261: 1974 Ferrari Dino 246 GTS (PF/Scaglietti)   *F262: 1969 Ferrari 365 GTC (Pininfarina)*

Year	Model (Bodybuilder)	Chassis no.	Steering	Estimate	Hammer price £	Hammer price $	Hammer price €	Date	Place	Lot	Auc. H.
1970	365 GTB4 Daytona (PF/Scaglietti)	13319	L	650-725.000 EUR	634.743	815.069	728.000	27-05-17	Villa Erba	145	RMS

Light metallic grey with black leather interior; certified by Ferrari Classiche.

| 1971 | 365 GTB4 Daytona (spider/conversion) | 13865 | L | 550-650.000 GBP | 535.000 | 694.323 | 605.781 | 29-06-17 | Fontwell Park | 135 | Coy |

Gunmetal grey with tan interior; conversion carried out at unspecified date (see lots RM 282 10.3.07 $198,000 and 162 18.1.08 $264,000, and Coys 221 8.8.09 NS, 153 24.10.09 $375,500, and 430 2.12.14 NS).

| 1972 | 365 GTB4 Daytona (PF/Scaglietti) | 16043 | R | 500-600.000 GBP | 539.100 | 699.644 | 610.423 | 30-06-17 | Goodwood | 215 | Bon |

Sold new to the UK finished in silver with black interior. Restored in the 1990s, the car is finished at present in red with black interior with red inserts. The engine has covered 300 miles since the rebuild carried out in more recent years.

| 1972 | 365 GTB4 Daytona (PF/Scaglietti) | 15977 | R | 525-575.000 GBP | 551.250 | 721.862 | 615.471 | 29-07-17 | Silverstone | 439 | SiC |

Red with black interior; described as in very good overall condition; recently serviced. From 1973 to 1975 owned by Elton John (see Coys lots 42a 22.7.00 $92,328 and 47 11.12.00 $79,009).

| 1971 | 365 GTB4 Daytona (PF/Scaglietti) | 14207 | L | 750-1.000.000 USD | 512.820 | 660.000 | 562.320 | 18-08-17 | Carmel | 30 | Bon |

Red with black interior; Borrani wire wheels. Unrestored; 29,090 miles on the odometer. Since new in the T.J. Day Collection.

| 1971 | 365 GTB4 Daytona (PF/Scaglietti) | 14417 | L | 500-700.000 USD | 397.436 | 511.500 | 435.798 | 18-08-17 | Carmel | 83 | Bon |

Red with black and red leather interior; retained for 39 years by its first owner; described as in largely original, unrestored condition. Two owners.

| 1971 | 365 GTB4 Daytona (PF/Scaglietti) | 14169 | L | 750-900.000 USD | 534.188* | 687.500* | 585.750* | 18-08-17 | Monterey | 126 | RMS |

Originally finished in metallic copper with beige leather interior with black inserts, the car was bought new by Bill Harrah who personalized it and retained it until 1975. In 2012 it was acquired by the current owner who had the body restored and repainted and the engine rebuilt (see lot 49 Gooding & Company 20.8.06 $341,000).

| 1971 | 365 GTB4 Daytona (PF/Scaglietti) | 14229 | L | 750-850.000 USD | NS | | | 19-08-17 | Pebble Beach | 145 | G&Co |

Red with black interior; sold new to the USA, the car remained with its first owner until 2009 and was subsequently restored. Body repainted in 2016 (see lot 33 Gooding & Company 16.8.14 $627,000).

| 1971 | 365 GTB4 Daytona | 14049 | L | 1.250-1.650.000 USD | NS | | | 19-08-17 | Monterey | S111 | Mec |

Silver; sold new to France, the car was modified to racing specification and was raced at the 1972 Le Mans 24 Hours where it placed 8th overall. The next owner had it converted to the spider configuration in which it remained for the next 30 years. In 2007 it was bought by Michael Sheehan who had it restored in the USA to the Le Mans configuration and had the engine rebuilt to racing specification.

| 1972 | 365 GTB4 Daytona (PF/Scaglietti) | 15757 | L | 850-1.050.000 USD | NS | | | 19-08-17 | Monterey | S136 | Mec |

Red with tan interior with black inserts; concours-quality restoration; 19,981 original miles. Certified by Ferrari Classiche (see lot S89 Mecum 15.8.15 NS).

| 1972 | 365 GTB4 Daytona (PF/Scaglietti) | 16445 | L | 700-750.000 USD | 555.555 | 715.000 | 609.180 | 19-08-17 | Monterey | 226 | RMS |

Red with beige leather interior; sold new to the USA; bought in 2015 by the current owner and fully restored. Certified by Ferrari Classiche.

| 1973 | 365 GTS4 Daytona spider (PF/Scaglietti) | 16801 | L | 1.800-2.400.000 EUR | 1.839.391 | 2.299.374 | 2.156.000 | 08-02-17 | Paris | 145 | RMS |

Red with black interior; sold new to the USA; restored in the late 1980s; imported into Switzerland in the early 2000s; described as in very good overall condition; 20,314 miles on the odometer. F264

| 1972 | 365 GTS4 Daytona spider (PF/Scaglietti) | 16573 | L | 2.700-3.000.000 USD | 1.872.570 | 2.410.000 | 2.053.320 | 18-08-17 | Carmel | 65 | Bon |

Maroon with beige leather interior with black inserts; sold new to the USA, the car was exhibited at the 1973 Miami Motor Show and was delivered to its first private owner in February 1974. Concours-quality restoration carried out in 2008/09.

| 1972 | 365 GTS4 Daytona spider (PF/Scaglietti) | 15007 | L | 1.600-2.000.000 USD | 1.688.033 | 2.172.500 | 1.850.970 | 19-08-17 | Monterey | 234 | RMS |

Red with tan leather interior; sold new to the USA and exhibited at the 1972 Los Angeles Auto Show. Paintwork and interior redone in 1977. Since 1983 in the same family ownership. 36,513 miles covered. Stored for many years, it has been recently fully serviced in preparation for the sale.

| 1969 | 365 GTS (Pininfarina) | 12489 | L | 2.900-3.500.000 USD | 2.933.876 | 3.602.500 | 3.388.151 | 20-01-17 | Phoenix | 263 | RMS |

Dark blue with cream leather interior; one of 20 examples built. Sold new to Canada and later imported into the USA. Concours-quality restoration carried out between 1994 and 1996. Bought in 2007 by the current owner. Certified by Ferrari Classiche.

| 1969 | 365 GTS (Pininfarina) | 12163 | L | 2.800-3.200.000 USD | 2.115.383 | 2.722.500 | 2.319.570 | 19-08-17 | Monterey | 245 | RMS |

Ivory with black interior; exhibited at the 1969 Brussels Motor Show and then sold to Belgium; bought over 10 years ago by the current owner and subsequently fully restored. The original engine was replaced with the unit no.245C- A1450 built by Ferrari Classiche (see lot 179 Brooks 19.12.98 $231,351).

| 1974 | 365 GT4 BB (Pininfarina) | 18259 | R | 295-345.000 GBP | NS | | | 26-11-16 | Weybridge | 183 | His |

Blue with black interior; stored for many years, the car has been recently overhauled and the body has been repainted. 4,092 miles on the odometer (see lot 38 Coys 29.7.95 $90,152).

| 1975 | 365 GT4 BB (Pininfarina) | 18227 | L | 375-400.000 USD | NS | | | 19-01-17 | Scottsdale | 52 | Bon |

Red with original black leather interior; 35,552 kms covered. Recent engine-out service. Sold new to Germany; imported into Japan in 1977; imported into the USA in 2016.

| 1974 | 365 GT4 BB (Pininfarina) | 18001 | L | 350-400.000 USD | 282.190 | 346.500 | 325.883 | 20-01-17 | Phoenix | 250 | RMS |

Black with black interior; sold new to France, the car was imported in 1984 into the USA where it remained for nearly 30 years in the same ownership. Major service including cam belt in December 2015 (see lots 54 Gooding & Company 13.3.15 $401,500 and 214 RM/Sotheby's 14.5.16 NS). F265

| 1972 | 365 GTC4 (Pininfarina) | 15615 | L | 230-270.000 EUR | NA | | | 08-10-16 | Paris | 167 | CB/C |

Silver with original black leather interior, body repainted some years ago (see lot 364 Bonhams 4.2.16 NS).

F263: 1970 Ferrari 365 GTB4 Daytona (PF/Scaglietti)

F264: 1973 Ferrari 365 GTS4 Daytona spider (PF/Scaglietti)

Year	Model	(Bodybuilder)	Chassis No.	Steering	Estimate	Hammer Price £	$	€	Date	Place	Lot	Auc. H.
1972	365 GTC4	(Pininfarina)	15993	L	175-195.000 EUR	262.361*	326.234*	308.000*	25-11-16	Milan	859	RMS
	Silver with black interior; 45,249 kms. From the Duemila Ruote collection.											
1972	365 GTC4	(Pininfarina)	15357	L	275-325.000 USD		NS		19-01-17	Scottsdale	77	Bon
	Metallic brown with tan interior; sold new to the USA; in single ownership for 42 years; in largely original condition; less than 47,000 miles covered.											
1972	365 GTC4	(Pininfarina)	15989	R	230-260.000 GBP		NS		13-05-17	Silverstone	319	SiC
	Blue with saddle leather interior; bought in 1998 by the current owner and subjected to a long, full restoration completed in 2008.											
1972	365 GTC4	(Pininfarina)	15621	L	250-300.000 USD	183.973	236.500	210.840	04-06-17	Greenwich	113	Bon F266
	Metallic blue with tan leather interior; less than 40,000 miles covered. In single ownership from 1977 to early 2017. Body repainted in 2007.											
1972	365 GTC4	(Pininfarina)	15359	L	240-280.000 USD		NS		04-06-17	Greenwich	165	Bon
	Red with black leather interior; restored at unspecified date; 51,000 miles on the odometer; recently serviced (see Russo & Steele lots F651 18.8.11 $95,590 and S671 15.8.15 NS).											
1972	365 GTC4	(Pininfarina)	15359	L	225-275.000 USD	159.285	205.000	175.275	17-08-17	Monterey	41	WoA
	See lot 165 Bonhams 4.6.17.											
1972	365 GTC4	(Pininfarina)	15783	L	325-375.000 USD	273.504	352.000	299.904	19-08-17	Pebble Beach	171	G&Co
	Orange with black leather interior; since 1984 in the current ownership; showing less than 7,500 miles (see lot 247 Bonhams 12.8.10 NS).											
1973	365 GT4 2+2	(Pininfarina)	17261	L	60-80.000 EUR		NA		08-10-16	Paris	114	CB/C
	Light blue with black interior; in good overall condition. In 2003 the car was used in a film on the Enzo Ferrari life (see lot 145 Coys 6.8.16 NS).											
1974	365 GT4 2+2	(Pininfarina)	17811	L	35-40.000 EUR	76.323*	94.904*	89.600*	25-11-16	Milan	543	RMS
	Light blue; 63,034 kms. From the Duemila Ruote collection.											
1976	365 GT4 2+2	(Pininfarina)	19603	R	50-60.000 GBP	53.520	68.051	63.582	05-12-16	London	113	Coy
	Blue with black interior; engine rebuilt in 1999, carburettors and clutch replaced in 2014, brakes and suspension rebuilt in 2016.											
1973	365 GT4 2+2	(Pininfarina)	17175	R	55-70.000 GBP	55.750	70.886	66.231	05-12-16	London	131	Coy
	Red with biscuit leather interior; in good overall condition. Manual gearbox. Formerly owned by boxer Sir Henry Cooper OBE (see lot 322 Silverstone Auctions 14.11.15 $47,100).											
1976	365 GT4 2+2	(Pininfarina)	19603	R	50-60.000 GBP	47.794	62.309	55.986	18-05-17	London	121	Coy
	See lot 113 Coys 5.12.16.											
1973	365 GT4 2+2	(Pininfarina)	17311	R	35-50.000 GBP	28.750	37.312	32.554	30-06-17	Goodwood	275	Bon
	Dark green with beige interior; for restoration.											
1974	365 GT4 2+2	(Pininfarina)	17481	L	90-130.000 EUR	89.632	132.287	101.932	02-07-17	Monaco	162	Art F267
	Light blue with black leather interior; restored a few years ago.											
1976	365 GT4 2+2	(Pininfarina)	19603	R	50-60.000 GBP	40.014	51.714	45.476	15-07-17	Blenheim Pal.	123	Coy
	See lot 121 Coys 18.5.17.											
1974	365 GT4 2+2	(Pininfarina)	17279	L	75-90.000 EUR	68.450	89.983	75.820	05-08-17	Schloss Dyck	225	Coy
	Red with original black leather interior; described as in very good overall condition. Two owners; 102,000 kms covered.											
1979	308 GT4	(Bertone)	15220	L	65-75.000 USD	44.878	57.750	51.392	03-10-16	Philadelphia	236	Bon
	Brown with tan interior; less than 15,000 miles covered. Full engine service with belt change at 12,400 miles.											
1977	308 GT4	(Bertone)	13006	L	55-75.000 EUR		NA		08-10-16	Paris	177	CB/C
	Red with black interior; 38,000 kms on the odometer. Last serviced in 2016.											
1977	308 GT4	(Bertone)	13446	L	35-55.000 EUR	37.508	45.567	41.720	30-10-16	Paris	112	Art
	Silver and black.											
1976	308 GT4	(Bertone)	12314	R	40-50.000 GBP		NS		26-11-16	Weybridge	215	His
	Dark green with tan interior; restored betwen 1994 and 1996. Body recently repainted (see lot 309 Silverstone Auctions 6.3.16 $47,382).											
1976	308 GT4	(Bertone)	12868	R	105-125.000 AUD	66.085	82.171	77.578	27-11-16	Melbourne	44	Mos
	Red with original black leather interior; in good overall condition. Body repainted. Sunroof.											
1981	308 GT4	(Bertone)	15584	L	55-60.000 EUR	56.626	68.955	64.680	14-01-17	Maastricht	226	Coy
	Metallic brown with beige leather interior; 74,000 kms on the odometer. Recently serviced (see lot 206 Coys 9.4.16 NS).											
1975	308 GT4	(Bertone)	09848	L	90-100.000 USD		NS		01-04-17	Ft.Lauderdale	605	AA
	Red with original black interior; in very good condition.											
1980	308 GT4	(Bertone)	15450	R	38-43.000 GBP		NS		12-04-17	London	304	Coy
	Sold new to the UK finished in metallic maroon with beige leather interior; 44,000 miles on the odometer; last serviced in 2016.											

F265: 1974 Ferrari 365 GT4 BB (Pininfarina)

F266: 1972 Ferrari 365 GTC4 (Pininfarina)

Year	Model	(Bodybuilder)	Chassis no.	Steering	Estimate	Hammer price £	$	€	Date	Place	Lot	Auc. H.
1979	308 GT4	(Bertone)	15016	L	NA		NS		22-04-17	Dallas	470	Lea
	Black with black interior; described as in original condition; 16,022 miles on the odometer.											
1980	308 GT4	(Bertone)	15358	L	60-70.000 EUR		NS		18-06-17	Fontainebleau	80	Ose
	Red; engine recently rebuilt.											
1979	308 GT4	(Bertone)	14672	L	70-90.000 EUR		NS		02-07-17	Monaco	171	Art
	Dark metallic blue with beige leather interior; body and interior restored. Recently serviced.											
1976	308 GT4	(Bertone)	12248	L	85-95.000 EUR	87.523	129.175	99.534	02-07-17	Monaco	203	Art F268
	Black with beige leather interior; in good overall condition; recently serviced. Sunroof.											
1977	308 GT4	(Bertone)	12698	R	40-45.000 GBP		NS		29-07-17	Silverstone	435	SiC
	Yellow with cream cloth interior; body repainted in the late 1990s; clutch replaced in 2014.											
1979	308 GT4	(Bertone)	9726	L	33-45.000 EUR	44.686	58.743	49.497	05-08-17	Schloss Dyck	206	Coy
	Red; restored. Sold new to France.											
1975	308 GT4	(Bertone)	10668	L	60-80.000 USD	31.080	40.000	34.080	19-08-17	Monterey	F11	Mec
	Green with red interior; paintwork and interior redone.											
1975	208 GT4	(Bertone)	10698	L	30-50.000 GBP	32.480	43.465	38.680	07-09-16	London	184	RMS
	Silver; since 1983 in the current, second ownership. In original condition; 36,000 kms on the odometer; engine rebuilt in 2016.											
1980	308 GTB	(PF/Scaglietti)	29295	R	NA		NS		02-09-16	Salon Privé	256	SiC
	Metallic blue with sand interior; recommissioned in October 2015.											
1977	308 GTB	(PF/Scaglietti)	22449	L	85-90.000 EUR		NA		08-10-16	Paris	117	CB/C
	Red with black interior; in good overall condition.											
1977	308 GTB	(PF/Scaglietti)	22215	L	85-125.000 EUR		NS		15-10-16	Salzburg	446	Dor
	Black with cream leather interior; in the same family ownership from new to 2007. 50,719 kms covered. Last serviced in 2015.											
1978	308 GTB	(PF/Scaglietti)	26001	L	55-65.000 GBP	61.325	74.498	68.206	29-10-16	London	133	Coy
	Red with black interior; recently imported into the UK from the USA. Body repainted. Recently serviced.											
1977	308 GTB	(PF/Scaglietti)	20687	L	150-180.000 EUR	138.245	167.945	153.768	30-10-16	Paris	154	Art F269
	Red; recently restored. Fiberglass body.											
1983	308 GTB 4V	(PF/Scaglietti)	44737	L	70-90.000 EUR		NS		30-10-16	Paris	173	Art
	Red; sold new to France.											
1980	308 GTB	(PF/Scaglietti)	31139	L	90-105.000 EUR	100.174*	124.562*	117.600*	25-11-16	Milan	869	RMS
	White with tan interior. From the Duemila Ruote collection.											
1976	308 GTB	(PF/Scaglietti)	19267	L	100-120.000 EUR	138.336*	172.014*	162.400*	25-11-16	Milan	880	RMS
	Fiberglass body finished in red with brown interior; 36,753 kms. From the Duemila Ruote collection (see lot 155 Brooks 27.5.00 NS).											
1975	308 GTB	(PF/Scaglietti)	18265	L	155-175.000 EUR	166.957*	207.603*	196.000*	25-11-16	Milan	897	RMS
	Fiberglass body finished in red with black interior. From the Duemila Ruote collection.											
1977	308 GTB	(PF/Scaglietti)	21993	R	62-68.000 GBP	64.670	82.228	76.828	05-12-16	London	124	Coy
	Red with tan interior; 35,600 miles on the odometer.											
1978	308 GTB	(PF/Scaglietti)	24721	L	110-130.000 USD		NS		15-01-17	Kissimmee	F210	Mec
	Black with black interior; restored. 27,150 miles on the odometer (see lots F135 Mecum 14.8.15 NS, 139 Auctions America 31.10.15 $101,750 and 137 Bonhams 10.3.16 NS).											
1980	308 GTBi	(PF/Scaglietti)	32605	L	100-125.000 USD		NS		15-01-17	Kissimmee	S225	Mec
	Red with black interior; 29,000 miles on the odometer (see lot 718 Auctions America 1.8.13 $24,200).											
1978	308 GTB	(PF/Scaglietti)	22219	L	110-130.000 USD		NS		18-01-17	Scottsdale	64	WoA
	Pine green with tan leather interior; 40,000 original miles. Last serviced in December 2016.											
1977	308 GTB	(PF/Scaglietti)	22741	L	100-140.000 USD	67.825*	83.600*	78.358*	19-01-17	Scottsdale	21	Bon
	Red; restored. Last serviced in August 2016.											
1976	308 GTB	(PF/Scaglietti)	19483	L	200-240.000 USD		NS		19-01-17	Scottsdale	72	Bon
	Fiberglass body originally finished in light grey with dark blue interior; sold new in Italy; imported into the USA in the late 1970s; repainted in red and re-upholstered in black in the 1980s; 62,000 original miles; recently serviced.											

F267: 1974 Ferrari 365 GT4 2+2 (Pininfarina)

F268: 1976 Ferrari 308 GT4 (Bertone)

Year	Model	(Bodybuilder)	Chassis no.	Steering	Estimate	Hammer price £	Hammer price $	Hammer price €	Date	Place	Lot	Auc. H.
1980	308 GTB	(PF/Scaglietti)	31319	L	200-240.000 USD	120.938*	148.500*	139.664*	20-01-17	Scottsdale	39	G&Co
	*Medium metallic green with original tan leather interior; sold new in Italy, the car was imported into the USA in 2016. Body repainted; major engine and belt service in 2014. 15,953 kms on the odometer. Certified by Ferrari Classiche.*											
1979	308 GTB	(PF/Scaglietti)	30461	L	125-150.000 USD	76.146*	93.500*	87.937*	20-01-17	Phoenix	223	RMS
	*Red with black leather interior; described as in largely original condition. 23,000 miles covered. Last serviced in May 2015 (see lots 103 Bonhams 14.8.15 $126,500 and 112 The Finest Automobile Auctions 11.6.16 NS).*											
1980	308 GTB	(PF/Scaglietti)	30959	3	80-110.000 EUR		NS		09-02-17	Paris	341	Bon
	*Red with tan interior; in good overall condition.*											
1980	308 GTB	(PF/Scaglietti)	32419	L	200-300.000 EUR		NS		09-02-17	Paris	384	Bon
	*White; restored in 2015-2016 and converted to Group 4 specification. Fitted with a 297bhp race-prepared engine (the original engine is included with the sale).*											
1978	308 GTB	(PF/Scaglietti)	22545	R	65-75.000 GBP	66.690	82.856	77.794	18-02-17	London	315	Coy
	*Light blue with cream leather interior; body repainted in 1998; recently serviced (see lot 614 Silverstone Auctions 22.2.15 $94,269).*											
1978	308 GTB	(PF/Scaglietti)	26637	L	150-180.000 USD	104.059*	126.500*	119.214*	10-03-17	Amelia Island	40	G&Co
	*Metallic blue with tan leather interior; cosmetically restored in 2009. Major 30,000 mile belt service in early 2017.*											
1979	308 GTB	(PF/Scaglietti)	30397	L	95-130.000 USD		NS		11-03-17	Amelia Island	13	Mot
	*Silver with original red leather interior; body repainted. Recent engine-out service.*											
1977	308 GTB	(PF/Scaglietti)	21167	L	80-100.000 USD	68.769*	83.600*	78.785*	11-03-17	Amelia Island	230	RMS
	*Metallic iron grey with original red leather interior; body repainted; engine rebuilt in the early 2000s. Recently serviced.*											
1982	308 GTB	(PF/Scaglietti)	34883	L	60-70.000 USD		NS		01-04-17	Ft.Lauderdale	586	AA
	*Red with black interior (see lot 759 Auctions America 2.4.16 $63,250).*											
1978	308 GTB	(PF/Scaglietti)	22545	R	60-70.000 GBP	66.690	83.363	78.601	12-04-17	London	314	Coy
	*See lot 315 Coys 18.2.17.*											
1977	308 GTB	(PF/Scaglietti)	23045	L	55-65.000 GBP		NS		13-05-17	Silverstone	363	SiC
	*Yellow with black leather interior; imported into the UK from the USA in 2016; recently serviced.*											
1981	308 GTBi	(PF/Scaglietti)	37225	R	65-70.000 GBP	53.760	69.953	62.577	20-05-17	Ascot	119	His
	*Yellow with black leather interior; last serviced in October 2015 at 35,151 miles.*											
1983	308 GTB 4V	(PF/Scaglietti)	44417	R	80-90.000 GBP		NS		29-07-17	Silverstone	455	SiC
	*Red; 34,500 miles covered; major service in September 2016.*											
1977	308 GTB	(PF/Scaglietti)	22219	L	85-110.000 USD	57.265*	73.700*	62.792*	18-08-17	Carmel	88	Bon
	*See lot 64 Worldwide Auctioneers 18.1.17.*											
1978	308 GTB	(PF/Scaglietti)	25239	L	175-225.000 USD	98.291*	126.500*	107.778*	18-08-17	Pebble Beach	58	G&Co
	*Bright gold with brown leather interior; bought in 2014 by the current owner and shipped in Italy for a full restoration. Certified by Ferrari Classiche.*											
1976	308 GTB	(PF/Scaglietti)	19397	L	175-225.000 USD	149.573*	192.500*	164.010*	19-08-17	Monterey	215	RMS
	*Fiberglass body finished in red with beige leather interior; restored; 12,341 miles on the odometer; recently serviced. From the Ferrari Performance Collection (see lot 101 Gooding & Company 16.8.15 $247,500).*											
1979	308 GTS	(PF/Scaglietti)	28685	R	NA		NS		02-09-16	Salon Privé	232	SiC
	*Silver with red interior; in original condition. 23,000 miles covered.*											
1979	308 GTS	(PF/Scaglietti)	30237	L	NA		NS		10-09-16	Louisville	S106.1	Mec
	*Red with tan interior; two owners. Believed to be 24,114 original miles (see lot 4110 Auctions America 5.9.15 $74,800).*											
1978	308 GTS	(PF/Scaglietti)	24279	L	95-115.000 USD	66.783	88.000	78.382	17-09-16	Aspen	103	TFA
	*Yellow with black interior; paintwork and interior redone in 2016. Recently serviced.*											
1981	308 GTSi	(PF/Scaglietti)	36529	L	65-80.000 EUR		NA		08-10-16	Paris	145	CB/C
	*Red with beige interior; 55,000 kms on the odometer. Recently serviced.*											
1985	308 GTSi	(PF/Scaglietti)	56319	L	NA		NS		08-10-16	Chicago	S117.1	Mec
	*Red with black interior; recently serviced.*											
1984	308 GTS 4V	(PF/Scaglietti)	50657	L	45-55.000 GBP		NS		12-10-16	Duxford	65	H&H
	*Black with cream interior; body repainted in recent years.*											
1979	308 GTS	(PF/Scaglietti)	26673	L	65-85.000 EUR	66.174	80.975	73.600	15-10-16	Salzburg	426	Dor
	*Red with tan leather interior; stored from 1987 to 2006 and subsequently mechanically restored.*											
1979	308 GTS	(PF/Scaglietti)	28725	L	70-90.000 USD		NS		04-11-16	Dallas	S181	Mec
	*Yellow with black interior; 67,192 believed original miles (see lots 2052 Auctions America 25.6.16 $63,800 and F172 Mecum 19.8.16 NS).*											
1979	308 GTS	(PF/Scaglietti)	27895	L	100-120.000 USD		NS		05-11-16	Hilton Head	129	AA
	*Red with black interior; body repainted, timing belt replaced.*											
1978	308 GTS	(PF/Scaglietti)	26333	L	85-100.000 USD		NS		05-11-16	Hilton Head	183	AA
	*Black with black interior; recently serviced.*											
1981	308 GTSi	(PF/Scaglietti)	35057	R	55-65.000 GBP	65.250	82.600	75.749	12-11-16	Birmingham	356	SiC
	*Red with cream interior; clutch replaced in 2015, further works carried out in 2016.*											
1981	308 GTSi	(PF/Scaglietti)	36357	L	40-45.000 GBP	42.188	53.406	48.976	12-11-16	Birmingham	358	SiC
	*Red with tan interior; described as in good original condition. Imported into the UK from the USA.*											
1985	308 GTS 4V	(PF/Scaglietti)	58115	R	75-85.000 GBP		NS		12-11-16	Birmingham	648	SiC
	*Red with cream interior; 2,000 miles covered since a mechanical recommissioning carried out in 2011.*											
1983	308 GTSi	(PF/Scaglietti)	48313	L	NA		NS		19-11-16	Anaheim	S115	Mec
	*Red with black interior; for 22 years in the current ownership. Last serviced in July 2015.*											
1985	308 GTS 4V	(PF/Scaglietti)	55621	L	NA		NS		19-11-16	Anaheim	S120	Mec
	*Purple; last serviced in 2014; believed to be 45,000 miles.*											

Year	Model	(Bodybuilder)	Chassis no.	Steering	Estimate	Hammer price £	$	€	Sale Date	Place	Lot	Auc. H.
1982	308 GTSi	(PF/Scaglietti)	40133	L	NA	42.583	52.500	49.392	19-11-16	Anaheim	S13	Mec
Black with tan interior; 90,034 actual miles, last serviced at 88,227 miles.												
1984	308 GTS 4V	(PF/Scaglietti)	44923	L	45-55.000 EUR	65.829*	81.855*	77.280*	25-11-16	Milan	537	RMS
Red; 73,186 kms. From the Duemila Ruote collection.												
1978	308 GTS	(PF/Scaglietti)	24271	L	45-55.000 GBP	48.840	62.100	58.022	05-12-16	London	142	Coy
Yellow; 39,900 miles on the odometer. Last service carried out in Dubai. UK registered.												
1981	308 GTSi	(PF/Scaglietti)	36133	L	75-95.000 USD		NS		15-01-17	Kissimmee	F166	Mec
Grey with tan interior; 25,684 miles covered.												
1984	308 GTS 4V	(PF/Scaglietti)	51941	L	150-250.000 USD	147.251	181.500	170.120	19-01-17	Scottsdale	95	Bon
Red with tan interior; one of the cars used in the TV series "Magnum P.I.", the car was driven by actor Tom Selleck during the 1984-1985 shooting season. Subsequently it returned to Ferrari North America, was repainted and serviced, and sold as a demo car. Since 1989 in the current ownership; less than 36,000 miles covered; last serviced in the spring of 2015.												F270
1983	308 GTSi	(PF/Scaglietti)	47835	L	NQ	49.271*	60.500*	56.900*	21-01-17	Scottsdale	771.2	B/J
Black with tan interior; in original condition, 46,488 miles covered.												
1983	308 GTS 4V	(PF/Scaglietti)	46045	L	75-90.000 USD	60.173	73.150	68.937	11-03-17	Amelia Island	72	Mot
Red with black interior; described as in very good overall condition. 39,823 actual miles.												
1978	308 GTS	(PF/Scaglietti)	23705	L	75-95.000 USD	47.958	58.300	54.942	11-03-17	Amelia Island	84	Mot
Red with tan interior; recently serviced.												
1983	308 GTS 4V	(PF/Scaglietti)	45511	L	55-65.000 EUR	67.861	83.877	78.120	18-03-17	Lyon	196	Agu
Red; in good overall condition.												
1977	308 GTS	(PF/Scaglietti)	23175	L	70-80.000 EUR		NS		19-03-17	Fontainebleau	230	Ose
Red with black interior; restored between 2009 and 2012.												
1979	308 GTS	(PF/Scaglietti)	30237	L	NQ	49.687	62.000	57.375	25-03-17	Kansas City	S117.1	Mec
See lot S106.1 Mecum 10.9.16.												
1984	308 GTS 4V	(PF/Scaglietti)	50169	L	50-60.000 GBP		NS		29-03-17	Duxford	27	H&H
Black with black interior, imported into the UK in 2016. In good overall condition.												
1982	308 GTSI	(PF/Scaglietti)	40949	L	50-60.000 USD	37.849	47.300	44.240	01-04-17	Ft.Lauderdale	183	AA
Red with black interior; in largely original condition.												
1978	308 GTS	(PF/Scaglietti)	25219	L	45-60.000 GBP	42.237	52.796	49.781	12-04-17	London	338	Coy
Black with burgundy interior; imported into the UK in 2015 and immediately serviced. 34,050 miles on the odometer.												
1985	308 GTS 4V/400	(PF/Scaglietti)	55187	R	50-60.000 GBP	54.000	69.428	63.839	13-05-17	Silverstone	308	SiC
Metallic blue with white interior; in the late 1980s the car was fitted with the present 400 12-cylinder engine (see lot 36 H&H 24.7.02 NS and 270 Historics 30.11.13 NS)												
1985	308 GTS 4V	(PF/Scaglietti)	58633	R	80-90.000 GBP	87.750	112.820	103.738	13-05-17	Silverstone	320	SiC
Red with cream interior; 38,500 miles covered; last serviced in March 2016.												
1979	308 GTS	(PF/Scaglietti)	28027	L	55-65.000 GBP		NS		13-05-17	Silverstone	339	SiC
Red with tan interior; in good driving order (see lot 837 Silverstone Auctions 25.7.15 $83,565).												
1981	308 GTSi	(PF/Scaglietti)	38017	L	45-55.000 GBP	36.000	46.285	42.559	13-05-17	Silverstone	344	SiC
Red with cream interior; some mechanical works carried out over the past two years.												
1984	308 GTS	(PF/Scaglietti)	49677	L	NA	34.813	39.050	30.377	03-06-17	Newport Beach	9009	R&S
Red; timing-belt service in October 2013.												
1978	308 GTS	(PF/Scaglietti)	24527	R	70-90.000 GBP		NS		06-06-17	Woodcote Park	11	H&H
Silver with blue interior; recently restored.												
1978	308 GTS	(PF/Scaglietti)	24825	L	NA	34.575	44.000	39.380	24-06-17	Santa Monica	215	RMS
Medium metallic grey with burgundy interior.												
1981	308 GTSi	(PF/Scaglietti)	36763	L	50-60.000 GBP	48.906	63.206	55.582	15-07-17	Blenheim Pal.	111	Coy
Red with cream interior; body repainted.												
1982	308 GTSi	(PF/Scaglietti)	39035	L	45-55.000 GBP	47.670	62.175	53.395	26-07-17	Duxford	30	H&H
Red with black leather interior; in good overall condition. Imported into the UK from the USA five years ago.												
1978	308 GTS	(PF/Scaglietti)	23813	R	55-65.000 GBP	51.750	67.767	57.779	29-07-17	Silverstone	728	SiC
Red with tan interior; body repainted in 2013.												

F269: 1977 Ferrari 308 GTB (PF/Scaglietti)

F270: 1984 Ferrari 308 GTS 4V (PF/Scaglietti)

Year	Model (Bodybuilder)	Chassis No.	Steering	Estimate	Hammer Price £	$	€	Date	Place	Lot	Auc. H.
1978	308 GTS (PF/Scaglietti)	24887	R	70-80.000 GBP	65.250	85.445	72.852	29-07-17	Silverstone	734	SiC
	Red; described as in very good overall condition.										
1979	308 GTS (PF/Scaglietti)	28193	L	60-70.000 EUR		NS		05-08-17	Schloss Dyck	218	Coy
	Red with tan interior; reimported into Europe from the USA and cosmetically restored.										
1979	308 GTS (PF/Scaglietti)	28663	L	115-145.000 USD		NS		17-08-17	Monterey	17	WoA
	Red with black interior; one owner; 1,600 miles covered; professional detailing and major service in 2016 and 2017.										
1978	308 GTS (PF/Scaglietti)	26283	L	70-90.000 USD	40.793*	52.500*	44.730*	19-08-17	Monterey	T105	Mec
	Red with tan interior; 27,800 believed original miles; last serviced in May 2016.										
1978	308 GTS (PF/Scaglietti)	26311	L	NA		NS		19-08-17	Monterey	1146	R&S
	Red; 4,800 original miles.										
1980	312T5	046	M	Refer Dpt.		NS		18-08-17	Carmel	45	Bon
	Car driven by Jody Scheckter during the 1980 Formula 1 season. For 20 years in the current ownership, it is described as in ready to race condition.										
1979	400i (Pininfarina)	35097	L	55-75.000 EUR		NS		05-11-16	Lyon	259	Agu
	Brown with beige leather interior; reimported into Europe from the USA in 2010. Recently overhauled (see lots 143 Barrett-Jackson 22.6.03 $21,600, 106 Gooding & Company 19.8.07 $52,800, 369 RM 14.8.09 $30,250 and 125 Bonhams 30.4.10 NS).										
1983	400i (Pininfarina)	45663	L	30-35.000 EUR	57.242*	71.178*	67.200*	25-11-16	Milan	536	RMS
	Green; manual gearbox. 54,327 kms. From the Duemila Ruote collection.										
1981	400i (Pininfarina)	34665	L	15-20.000 EUR	62.012*	77.110*	72.800*	25-11-16	Milan	621	RMS
	Light blue; 88,354 kms. From the Duemila Ruote collection.										
1983	400i (cabriolet/conversion)	47589	R	60-70.000 GBP		NS		24-02-17	Stoneleigh P.	509	SiC
	Red with black leather interior; conversion to cabriolet carried out at date unknown.										
1978	400 GT (Pininfarina)	24537	R	25-32.000 GBP	25.760	31.515	29.830	04-03-17	Brooklands	180	His
	Red; mechanicals overhauled in recent years. Automatic transmission.										
1984	400i (Pininfarina)	50809	R	33-38.000 GBP	35.280	43.162	40.854	04-03-17	Brooklands	200	His
	Dark metallic grey with cream interior; recently serviced. Automatic transmission.										
1979	400 GT (Pininfarina)	27485	L	80-100.000 EUR	62.481	77.818	73.000	08-04-17	Essen	146 F271	Coy
	Metallic gold; in good overall condition. Manual gearbox.										
1980	400i (Pininfarina)	32017	R	22-25.000 GBP	22.500	29.464	25.121	29-07-17	Silverstone	749	SiC
	Metallic grey with dark blue leather interior; 75,145 miles on the odometer; automatic transmission.										
1980	400i (Pininfarina)	31003	L	45-55.000 EUR	39.258	51.608	43.485	05-08-17	Schloss Dyck	274	Coy
	Red with beige leather interior; paintwork and interior redone some years ago. Manual gearbox.										
1982	512 BBi (Pininfarina)	41003	L	NA	208.000	276.286	246.854	02-09-16	Salon Privé	222	SiC
	Red and black; recently recommissioned. 9,008 miles covered since new.										
1983	512 BBi (Pininfarina)	44231	L	250-300.000 USD		NS		03-09-16	Auburn	4168	AA
	Red with tan interior; described as in good original condition (see lots RM 94 2.8.03 $71,500 and 139 10.3.12 $112,750, and Auctions America 569 2.4.16 NS).										
1983	512 BBi (Pininfarina)	43937	L	320-360.000 USD		NS		03-09-16	Auburn	4179	AA
	Red with black leather interior; described as in original condition. Approximately 10,300 actual miles.										
1983	512 BBi (Pininfarina)	46511	L	220-260.000 EUR		NA		08-10-16	Paris	130	CB/C
	Red with black leather interior; 31,000 kms covered. Last serviced in 2015 (see lot 325 Bonhams 4.2.16 NS).										
1977	512 BB (Pininfarina)	22251	R	225-275.000 GBP	225.800	274.302	251.135	29-10-16	London	113	Coy
	Red with beige interior; described as in very good overall condition. 58,000 miles on the odometer. Last serviced in August 2015. Certified by Ferrari Classiche. Displayed at the 1977 London Motor Show (see lot 177 Coys 16.7.11 NA).										
1983	512 BBi (Pininfarina)	44231	L	180-220.000 USD	140.088	175.000	157.745	05-11-16	Hilton Head	173	AA
	See lot 4168 Auctions America 3.9.16.										
1977	512 BB (Pininfarina)	22401	L	275-325.000 EUR	281.441*	349.960*	330.400*	25-11-16	Milan	574	RMS
	Red with tan interior with black inserts; restored 13 years ago. 141 kms on the odometer. From the Duemila Ruote collection.										
1979	512 BB (Pininfarina)	27289	R	200-250.000 GBP	220.200	279.984	261.598	05-12-16	London	105	Coy
	Silver with red leather interior; 34,000 miles covered. Three owners. Recently serviced. Certified by Ferrari Classiche (see Coys lots 621 4.12.12 NS, 125 12.3.13 NS and 424A 27.4.13 NA).										
1983	512 BBi (Pininfarina)	43945	R	280-340.000 GBP		NS		07-12-16	London	343	Bon
	Silver with black leather interior; sold new to South Africa, imported into the UK in 2008, recently serviced. Body repainted. Circa 74,900 kms covered.										
1978	512 BB (Pininfarina)	22613	L	250-300.000 USD	190.656	235.000	220.266	19-01-17	Scottsdale	84 F272	Bon
	Black with tan interior with black inserts; sold new to Canada. Mechanicals restored in 2013-14. Circa 42,700 kms covered since new.										
1983	512 BBi (Pininfarina)	48165	L	250-325.000 USD	170.373	210.000	196.833	19-01-17	Phoenix	140	RMS
	Red with tan interior; described as in very good highly original condition (see lots 24 Christie's 17.6.00 $82,250, and RM 103 3.8.02 NS and 112 19.1.12 $96.250).										
1980	512 BB (Pininfarina)	30401	L	300-350.000 USD	228.032	280.000	263.340	20-01-17	Scottsdale	8	G&Co
	Red with black interior; largely original paintwork and interior. 23,008 kms on the odometer. Engine rebuilt in 2014.										
1982	512 BBi (Pininfarina)	42507	L	250-300.000 USD	174.689*	214.500*	201.737*	20-01-17	Phoenix	240	RMS
	Red with white interior; 7,750 miles on the odometer.										
1982	512 BBi (Pininfarina)	40897	L	290-340.000 USD	219.481	269.500	253.465	21-01-17	Scottsdale	106	G&Co
	Red with original black leather interior; stored for some years, between 2013 and 2015 the car received several restoration works to the mechanicals.										
1982	512 BBi (Pininfarina)	38833	L	275-310.000 GBP		NS		04-03-17	Brooklands	202	His
	Red with cream interior; 34,903 kms covered. Some mechanical works carried out in recent years.										
1978	512 BB (Pininfarina)	24915	L	200-300.000 EUR		NS		22-04-17	Bagatelle	190	Agu
	Red with tan leather interior; described as in good overall condition; 24,203 miles on the odometer.										

Year	Model	(Bodybuilder)	Chassis no.	Steering	Estimate	Hammer price £	$	€	Date	Place	Lot	Auc. H.
1983	512 BBi	(Pininfarina)	47411	L	225-275.000 USD	185.061	236.500	221.057	22-04-17	Arlington	126	WoA
	Sold new to the USA; one owner; in original condition; less than 21,000 kms covered; last serviced in 2017.											
1984	512 BBi	(Pininfarina)	44393	L	NA		NS		03-06-17	Newport Beach	9113	R&S
	Red; since 1985 in the current ownership; recently serviced.											
1983	512 BBi	(Pininfarina)	45055	L	260-310.000 EUR	251.656	330.821	278.750	05-08-17	Schloss Dyck	214	Coy
	Black with red leather and cloth interior; sold new to Japan and later reimported into Europe; 21,000 kms on the odometer; recently serviced.											
1984	512 BBi	(Pininfarina)	52659	L	275-350.000 USD	209.402	269.500	229.614	18-08-17	Pebble Beach	7	G&Co
	Silver with black interior; full restoration completed in 2016; certified by Ferrari Classiche.											
1984	512 BBi	(Pininfarina)	47421	L	275-350.000 USD	235.043	302.500	257.730	19-08-17	Pebble Beach	135	G&Co
	Red with black interior; in original, unrestored condition; less than 8,000 miles covered; engine-out service in 2015 (see lots S664 Russo & Steele 15.8.08 $163,900 and 3044 Auctions America 2.8.14 $253,000).											
1983	512 BBi	(Pininfarina)	47801	L	450-550.000 USD	256.410	330.000	281.160	19-08-17	Monterey	S88	Mec
	Silver with black interior; concours-quality restoration completed in 2017. 9,071 kms covered since new.											
1984	512 BBi	(Pininfarina)	48723	L	375-450.000 USD	333.333*	429.000*	365.508*	19-08-17	Monterey	221	RMS
	Red; 911 original kms; engine refurbished in late 2016. From the Ferrari Performance Collection (see lot S113 Mecum 15.8.15 NS).											
1983	512 BBi	(Pininfarina)	45929	L	275-325.000 USD	188.034*	242.000*	206.184*	19-08-17	Monterey	225	RMS
	Red; 20,458 miles on the odometer. Certified by Ferrari Classiche. From the Ferrari Performance Collection (see lot F428 Russo & Steele 14.8.09 $90,750).											
1983	512 BBi	(Pininfarina)	46545	L	NA	179.487*	231.000*	196.812*	19-08-17	Monterey	1104	R&S
	Black with black leather interior; 8,500 miles covered (see lot F442 Russo & Steele 16.8.12 $96,250).											
1987	GTS Turbo	(PF/Scaglietti)	75441	L	60-80.000 EUR		NS		05-11-16	Lyon	251	Agu
	Red; described as in very good overall condition (see lot 335 Aguttes 2.7.16 NS).											
1984	208 Turbo GTS	(PF/Scaglietti)	50379	L	50-55.000 GBP	57.375	72.631	66.607	12-11-16	Birmingham	641	SiC
	Red with black interior; in good overall condition. 33,000 kms covered.											
1985	208 GTS Turbo	(PF/Scaglietti)	53149	L	Refer Dpt.	55.000	71.379	62.277	29-06-17	Fontwell Park	121	Coy
	Red with black interior; bought, already restored, 17 years ago by the current, third owner.											
1985	208 GTS Turbo	(PF/Scaglietti)	53149	L	Refer Dpt.	66.690	86.190	75.793	15-07-17	Blenheim Pal.	119	Coy
	See lot 121 Coys 29.6.17.											
1982	Mondial 8	(PF/Scaglietti)	40529	R	24-28.000 GBP	23.000	28.189	25.581	12-10-16	Duxford	22	H&H
	Silver with red leather interior; several works carried out over the last two-three years. Recently serviced.											
1993	Mondial T	(PF/Scaglietti)	93049	R	40-50.000 GBP		NS		12-10-16	Duxford	45	H&H
	Blue with white interior; recently serviced.											
1981	Mondial 8	(PF/Scaglietti)	34461	L	24-32.000 EUR	20.162	24.672	22.425	15-10-16	Salzburg	428	Dor
	Red with cream interior; in good driving order.											
1984	Mondial 4V	(PF/Scaglietti)	49491	L	40-60.000 USD		NS		04-11-16	Dallas	S99	Mec
	Silver with black interior; with sunroof (see lot 2034 Auctions America 18.7.15 $25,850).											
1991	Mondial	(PF/Scaglietti)	79176	L	35-45.000 EUR		NS		06-11-16	Lyon	351	Ose
	Red with black leather interior; 61,300 kms on the odometer.											
1991	Mondial T	(PF/Scaglietti)	86885	L	24-28.000 GBP	32.063	40.589	37.222	12-11-16	Birmingham	360	SiC
	Red with black interior; last serviced in November 2015 at 51,749 kms (see lot 124 Artcurial 14.10.07 NS).											
1981	Mondial	(PF/Scaglietti)	37979	R	20-24.000 GBP	26.320	32.726	30.897	26-11-16	Weybridge	221	His
	Red with cream leather interior; engine rebuilt in 2010. The body requires some attention.											
1981	Mondial	(PF/Scaglietti)	37435	L	NQ	31.354*	38.500*	36.209*	21-01-17	Scottsdale	700.3	B/J
	Red with black interior; less than 19,000 miles covered (see lot 819 Kruse Cla. 7.1.05 $23,760).											
1988	Mondial 4V	(PF/Scaglietti)	74127	R	28-34.000 GBP		NS		04-03-17	Brooklands	142	His
	Red with cream interior; recently serviced.											
1982	Mondial	(PF/Scaglietti)	39647	L	35-45.000 USD	24.431*	29.700*	27.989*	11-03-17	Amelia Island	2	Mot
	Red with tan interior; just over 39,000 miles on the odometer.											
1990	Mondial T	(PF/Scaglietti)	85617	L	35-45.000 EUR	43.886	54.243	50.520	18-03-17	Lyon	183	Agu
	Red with black interior; since 1997 in the current ownership. Last serviced in April 2016.											

F271: 1979 Ferrari 400 GT (Pininfarina)

F272: 1978 Ferrari 512 BB (Pininfarina)

Year	Model (Bodybuilder)	Chassis no.	Steering	Estimate	Hammer price £	$	€	Date	Place	Lot	Auc. H.
1982	Mondial (PF/Scaglietti)	39817	R	15-17.000 GBP	23.906	29.741	27.674	29-03-17	Duxford	63	H&H
	Red with beige leather interior; since 2003 in the current ownership, unused for the past three years.										
1981	Mondial (PF/Scaglietti)	38543	R	30-35.000 GBP		NS		29-03-17	Duxford	97	H&H
	Red with black leather interior; 14,000 miles covered.										
1984	Mondial (PF/Scaglietti)	49247	L	NQ	18.547*	23.100*	21.668*	08-04-17	Palm Beach	643	B/J
	Red with black leather interior; 55,098 kms covered.										
1984	Mondial 4V (PF/Scaglietti)	49491	L	45-55.000 USD	23.240*	29.700*	27.761*	22-04-17	Arlington	108	WoA
	See lot S99 Mecum 4.11.16.										
1993	Mondial T (PF/Scaglietti)	96102	L	50-70.000 EUR		NS		02-07-17	Monaco	204	Art
	Red; in good overall condition; 3,160 kms covered two owners. Gearbox with a Valeo electro-mechanical actuator (see lot 171 RM 8.9.14 $49,588).										
1984	Mondial cabriolet (PF/Scaglietti)	49975	L	40-50.000 USD		NS		05-11-16	Hilton Head	135	AA
	Less than 26,000 miles on the odometer.										
1984	Mondial 4V cabriolet (PF/Scaglietti)	52753	L	NQ	27.096	33.000	30.951	15-01-17	Kissimmee	F78	Mec
	Red with black interior (see lot F80 Mecum 23.1.16 NS).										
1990	Mondial T cabriolet (PF/Scaglietti)	83290	R	35-40.000 GBP	38.250	48.019	45.261	24-02-17	Stoneleigh P.	926	SiC
	Red with magnolia interior; 14,100 miles on the odometer. Last serviced in 2015 when the body was repainted (see lots Historics 286 26.5.12 WD, and Coys 142 26.4.14 NS and 306 12.7.14 $37,373).										
1985	Mondial 4V cabriolet (PF/Scaglietti)	57501	R	40-50.000 GBP	42.000	51.383	48.636	04-03-17	Brooklands	197	His
	Red with white interior; in very good overall condition. Recently serviced.										
1984	Mondial 4V cabriolet (PF/Scaglietti)	49975	L	38-44.000 USD	30.808	38.500	36.009	01-04-17	Ft.Lauderdale	483	AA
	See lot 135 Auctions America 5.11.16.										
1988	Mondial 3.2 cabriolet (PF/Scaglietti)	76686	L	35-45.000 USD	19.253*	24.750*	22.065*	04-06-17	Greenwich	170	Bon
	Red with tan interior; in good overall condition.										
1989	Mondial T cabriolet (PF/Scaglietti)	82563	L	55-65.000 USD	31.982	40.700	36.427	24-06-17	Santa Monica	150	RMS F274
	Black with black interior; 19,866 miles on the odometer.										
1987	Mondial T cabriolet (PF/Scaglietti)	68847	R	35-45.000 GBP	33.345	43.095	37.897	15-07-17	Blenheim Pal.	122	Coy
	Blue; low mileage.										
1984	Mondial 4V cabriolet (PF/Scaglietti)	53355	R	30-35.000 GBP		NS		29-07-17	Silverstone	457	SiC
	Red; body repainted; 52,400 miles on the odometer.										
1984	GTO (PF/Scaglietti)	53301	L	1.900-2.200.000 USD		NS		18-08-17	Carmel	93	Bon
	Red with black leather interior; until 2017 with its first owner; 68,000 kms covered; recent full service.										
1989	Testarossa (Pininfarina)	79507	L	NA		NS		03-09-16	Auburn	14	WoA
	Red with beige interior; just over 16,000 miles covered (see lots S152 Mecum 15.8.15 $122,500 and 839 Auctions America 7.5.16 NS).										
1988	Testarossa (Pininfarina)	76899	L	150-175.000 USD	87.274	115.000	102.431	17-09-16	Aspen	113	TFA
	Black with tan interior; 19,500 miles on the odometer. Last serviced less than 1,000 miles ago (see lot 4140 Auctions America 5.9.15 $112,750).										
1987	Testarossa (Pininfarina)	73607	L	90-125.000 USD	66.675	85.800	76.353	03-10-16	Philadelphia	233	Bon
	Red with tan interior; in good original condition. Since 1992 in the current ownership. Regularly serviced.										
1988	Testarossa (Pininfarina)	81921	L	85-100.000 EUR		NA		08-10-16	Paris	172	CB/C
	Red with black leather interior; in good overall condition. One owner and 46,000 kms covered.										
1991	Testarossa (Pininfarina)	88618	L	NA	61.127*	74.800*	67.986*	15-10-16	Las Vegas	712	B/J
	Black with black interior; 17,154 actual miles.										
1991	Testarossa (Pininfarina)	88380	L	NA	54.834*	67.100*	60.987*	15-10-16	Las Vegas	731	B/J
	Black with black leather interior; recently serviced.										
1989	Testarossa (Pininfarina)	79616	L	83-93.000 GBP		NS		29-10-16	London	141	Coy
	Red with black leather interior; 31,000 kms covered (see lot 171 Coys 9.4.16 $110,188).										
1989	Testarossa (Pininfarina)	80231	L	140-160.000 EUR		NS		30-10-16	Paris	139	Art
	Red; less than 9,300 kms covered.										
1987	Testarossa (Pininfarina)	70755	L	125-150.000 USD		NS		04-11-16	Dallas	S139	Mec
	Red with black interior; 13,000 miles covered. Recently serviced.										
1990	Testarossa (Pininfarina)	83920	L	85-105.000 EUR	76.730	95.844	86.400	05-11-16	Lyon	235	Agu
	Red with black leather interior; in good overall condition. 70,500 kms covered (see lot 348 Aguttes 2.7.16 NS).										
1989	Testarossa (Pininfarina)	80111	L	110-140.000 USD		NS		05-11-16	Hilton Head	167	AA
	Metallic blue with grey leather interior; described as in original condition. Major service in late 2015 including timing belt replacement.										
1990	Testarossa (Pininfarina)	83593	L	110-130.000 USD	73.646	92.000	82.929	05-11-16	Hilton Head	182	AA
	Red with black leather interior; last major service in February 2015 (see lot 652 Auctions America 28.3.15 NS).										
1987	Testarossa (Pininfarina)	68157	L	75-85.000 GBP	82.125	103.962	95.339	12-11-16	Birmingham	346	SiC
	Red with black leather interior; last serviced, including cambelt change, in April 2016 at 51,000 kms (see lots Artcurial 28 13.7.09 $71,755 and 97 14.2.10 NS, Chevau-Légere 46 3.2.11 NS, and Silverstone Auctions 111A 17.11.12 NS and 502 30.7.16 NS).										
1987	Testarossa Koenig Competition Evolution II	76967	L	95-115.000 GBP	106.875	135.293	124.071	12-11-16	Birmingham	636	SiC
	Red; car modified in the late 1980s. Bought in 2014 by the current owner and subsequently fully serviced. 46,430 kms on the odometer (see lot 220 Artcurial 5.7.14 $161,969).										
1988	Testarossa (Pininfarina)	75836	L	NA		NS		19-11-16	Anaheim	S135	Mec
	Red with tan interior; last serviced in March 2015 at 9,937 miles (see lots S674 Russo & Steele 19.1.07 $88,000 and 436 RM 6.2.09 $66,000).										
1992	Testarossa (Pininfarina)	91201	L	80-90.000 EUR	85.863*	106.767*	100.800*	25-11-16	Milan	266	RMS
	Red with black interior. From the Duemila Ruote collection.										

Year	Model (Bodybuilder)	Chassis No.	Steering	Estimate	Hammer Price £	$	€	Date	Place	Lot	Auc. H.
1988	**Testarossa (Pininfarina)**	78091	L	90-105.000 EUR	71.553*	88.973*	84.000*	25-11-16	Milan	559	RMS
Red with black interior. From the Duemila Ruote collection.											
1986	**Testarossa (Pininfarina)**	66269	L	110-130.000 EUR	114.485*	142.356*	134.400*	25-11-16	Milan	568	RMS
Red with tan interior; 9,326 kms. From the Duemila Ruote collection.											
1988	**Testarossa (Pininfarina)**	77939	L	80-90.000 EUR	100.174*	124.562*	117.600*	25-11-16	Milan	595	RMS
Red with black interior; 47,366 kms. From the Duemila Ruote collection.											
1993	**Testarossa (Pininfarina)**	90484	R	85-105.000 GBP	107.520	133.690	126.218	26-11-16	Weybridge	189	His
Red with cream leather interior; 13,000 miles covered. Bought in 2013 by the current owner and subsequently recommissioned.											
1988	**Testarossa (Pininfarina)**	77128	L	NQ	71.846	87.500	82.066	15-01-17	Kissimmee	F278	Mec
Silver; recently serviced.											
1990	**Testarossa (Pininfarina)**	85306	L	NQ		NS		15-01-17	Kissimmee	F284	Mec
Black; 32,949 actual miles. Recently serviced.											
1991	**Testarossa (Pininfarina)**	88381	L	125-150.000 USD	82.550*	101.750*	95.370*	19-01-17	Scottsdale	100	Bon
Black with black interior; in good original condition. Less than 50,000 miles covered; last serviced in April 2016 (see lot 753 Auctions America 2.4.16 $86,900).											
1986	**Testarossa (Pininfarina)**	61481	L	130-160.000 USD	122.709*	151.250*	141.767*	19-01-17	Phoenix	113	RMS
Red with black interior; less than 8,000 miles on the odometer. Recently serviced. Certified by Ferrari Classiche.											
1988	**Testarossa (Pininfarina)**	76424	L	170-200.000 USD	111.980*	137.500*	129.319*	20-01-17	Phoenix	216	RMS
Light metallic gold with black leather interior; just under 4,300 original miles. Certified by Ferrari Classiche.											
1986	**Testarossa (Pininfarina)**	63631	L	NQ	123.626*	151.800*	142.768*	21-01-17	Scottsdale	1426	B/J
White with tan interior; used in the TV series "Miami Vice", the car remained subsequently stored from 1990 to 2015. 16,500 original miles. Certified by Ferrari Classiche (see Mecum lots S56 15.8.15 NS and S180 23.1.16 NS).											
1986	**Testarossa (Pininfarina)**	66437	L	130-150.000 EUR	119.441	149.310	140.000	08-02-17	Paris	176	RMS
Red with beige interior; three owners and 18,000 kms covered. Recently serviced.											
1987	**Testarossa (spider/conversion)**	81586	L	100-150.000 EUR	132.165	164.707	154.960	10-02-17	Paris	123	Art
Yellow with black interior; conversion carried out at unspecified date. Mechanicals recently overhauled (see lot 200 Artcurial 9.7.16 NS).											
1986	**Testarossa (Pininfarina)**	65627	L	130-160.000 EUR	142.332*	177.377*	166.880*	10-02-17	Paris	58	Art
Red with original beige leather interior; in very good overall condition. 36,710 kms covered.											
1986	**Testarossa (Pininfarina)**	60011	R	100-125.000 GBP		NS		04-03-17	Brooklands	194	His
Red with black interior; always well maintained and serviced.											
1988	**Testarossa (Pininfarina)**	78854	L	125-145.000 USD	65.942*	80.300*	76.100*	09-03-17	Amelia Island	129	Bon
Black with black interior; 24,070 miles covered. Last serviced in 2016.											
1987	**Testarossa (Pininfarina)**	70383	L	125-175.000 USD	106.321*	129.250*	121.805*	10-03-17	Amelia Island	72	G&Co
Black with tan interior; 8,973 miles covered. Last serviced in February 2016.											
1991	**Testarossa (Pininfarina)**	87750	L	275-400.000 USD	253.361	308.000	290.259	11-03-17	Amelia Island	265	RMS
Yellow with black interior; in original condition, 582 actual miles, never titled. Retained by the Ferrari dealer Auto Torino of Great Neck, New York, until 2014 when it was acquired by the current owner and subjected to a full, engine-out engine. Certified by Ferrari Classiche.										F275	
1989	**Testarossa (Pininfarina)**	82143	L	70-90.000 EUR	88.710	109.646	102.120	18-03-17	Lyon	201	Agu
Red with black interior; one owner and 81,630 kms covered. Last serviced in February 2017.											
1990	**Testarossa (Pininfarina)**	85862	L	110-125.000 USD	84.501	105.600	98.768	01-04-17	Ft.Lauderdale	505	AA
Red with tan leather interior; 30,716 miles on the odometer; recently serviced.											
1989	**Testarossa (Pininfarina)**	79616	L	80-100.000 EUR	64.193	79.950	75.000	08-04-17	Essen	156	Coy
See lot 141 Coys 29.10.16.											
1989	**Testarossa (Pininfarina)**	82237	L	NQ	130.471	162.500	152.425	08-04-17	Houston	S139.1	Mec
Red with cream interior; believed to be 1,512 miles.											
1988	**Testarossa (Pininfarina)**	77805	L	110-140.000 USD	77.468	99.000	92.535	22-04-17	Arlington	139	WoA
Black; just over 14,000 miles covered; recently serviced (see lot 716 Barrett-Jackson 18.1.02 $83,160).											
1990	**Testarossa (Pininfarina)**	87364	L	85-95.000 GBP		NS		13-05-17	Silverstone	316	SiC
Red with black interior; described as in good overall condition; major service in September 2015.											

F273: 1990 Ferrari Mondial T (PF/Scaglietti)

F274: 1989 Ferrari Mondial T cabriolet (PF/Scaglietti)

Year	Model (Bodybuilder)	Chassis no.	Steering	Estimate	Hammer price £	Hammer price $	Hammer price €	Date	Place	Lot	Auc. H.
1989	Testarossa (Pininfarina)	78749	L	69-83.000 GBP		NS		20-05-17	Ascot	201	His
	Red with black interior; imported into the UK from Japan in 2014; 15,811 kms covered (see lot 350 Historics 20.8.16 NS).										
1990	Testarossa (Pininfarina)	85027	R	105-120.000 GBP		NS		20-05-17	Ascot	233	His
	Yellow with cream leather interior; in very good overall condition. Recently serviced.										
1986	Testarossa (Pininfarina)	65725	L	220-240.000 AUD		NS		28-05-17	Sydney	20	Mos
	Red; described as in very good overall condition. Body repainted three years ago.										
1986	Testarossa (Pininfarina)	65499	L	NA	88.259	99.000	77.012	03-06-17	Newport Beach	9013	R&S
	Red with black interior; for over 25 years with the present, second owner. 15,964 miles covered. Last serviced in January 2016.										
1991	Testarossa (Pininfarina)	87769	L	NA	69.871	78.375	60.968	03-06-17	Newport Beach	9068	R&S
	Red with beige interior; described as in good overall condition.										
1990	Testarossa (Pininfarina)	87252	L	NQ	66.557*	84.700*	75.807*	24-06-17	Northeast	725	B/J
	Black with beige interior; 41,000 original miles. Major service in 2012 (see lot 426 Barrett-Jackson 28.9.13 $77.000).										
1990	Testarossa (Pininfarina)	82891	L	105-125.000 USD		NS		24-06-17	Santa Monica	203	RMS
	Black with black interior; less than 20,000 miles covered; last serviced in January 2017.										
1989	Testarossa (Pininfarina)	82009	L	70-100.000 GBP		NS		30-06-17	Goodwood	222	Bon
	Red with beige interior; imported into the UK in 2015 and subsequently recommissioned. 56,000 kms on the odometer.										
1989	Testarossa (Pininfarina)	81238	L	100-120.000 EUR		NS		02-07-17	Monaco	218	Art
	Black with red interior; 30,000 kms on the odometer; well maintained; clutch replaced in 2014.										
1989	Testarossa (Pininfarina)	81675	L	50-60.000 GBP	53.352	68.952	60.635	15-07-17	Blenheim Pal.	107	Coy
	Red with black interior; 12,000 miles on the odometer (see lot 131 Coys 2.7.16 $91,752).										
1989	Testarossa (Pininfarina)	80178	L	90-110.000 EUR	83.550	109.832	92.545	05-08-17	Schloss Dyck	253	Coy
	Red; sold new to Japan and later imported into Germany. 34,800 kms covered.										
1986	Testarossa (Pininfarina)	65813	L	180-220.000 USD	91.453*	117.700*	100.280*	18-08-17	Carmel	20	Bon
	Red with tan interior; less than 19,000 miles covered; certified by Ferrari Classiche (see lot 1051 Auctions America 25.6.16 NS).										
1987	Testarossa (Pininfarina)	70225	L	125-175.000 USD	95.726*	123.200*	104.966*	18-08-17	Carmel	28	Bon
	Red with beige leather interior; since new in the T.J. Day Collection; 4,191 miles on the odometer.										
1986	Testarossa (Pininfarina)	64253	L	120-150.000 USD	108.974*	140.250*	119.493*	19-08-17	Pebble Beach	115	G&Co
	White with red leather interior; less than 8,500 kms covered (see lot 3101 Auctions America 2.8.14 $111,100).										
1987	Testarossa (Pininfarina)	72631	L	NQ		NS		19-08-17	Monterey	F130	Mec
	Red with black interior; 23,000 original miles.										
1988	Testarossa (Pininfarina)	78728	L	125-150.000 USD	104.895	135.000	115.020	19-08-17	Monterey	S127	Mec
	Black with black interior; 9,562 miles covered; recently serviced (see lot S54 Mecum 20.8.16 NS).										
1986	Testarossa (Pininfarina)	65937	L	150-200.000 USD	113.248*	145.750*	124.179*	19-08-17	Monterey	269	RMS
	Metallic blue with cream and dark blue interior; sold new to the USA to film and television producer Michael Mann; restored in Italy in 2015; certified by Ferrari Classiche.										
1991	Testarossa (Pininfarina)	87769	L	NA	76.923	99.000	84.348	19-08-17	Monterey	1099	R&S
	See lot 9068 Russo & Steele 3.6.17.										
1988	328 GTB (PF/Scaglietti)	75912	L	140-180.000 USD	109.740*	134.750*	126.732*	21-01-17	Scottsdale	125	G&Co
	Silver with red leather interior; 33,258 miles on the odometer. Last serviced in October 2016.										
1988	328 GTB (PF/Scaglietti)	75593	L	140-160.000 USD	99.535*	121.000*	114.030*	10-03-17	Amelia Island	60	G&Co
	Red with cream interior; in very good condition. Less than 13,000 miles covered.										
1985	328 GTB (PF/Scaglietti)	61003	L	85-125.000 EUR		NS		24-06-17	Wien	361	Dor
	Red with beige leather interior; 27,090 original kms.										
1986	328 GTB (PF/Scaglietti)	68033	L	80-100.000 GBP		NS		30-06-17	Goodwood	271	Bon
	Red with black interior; 20,000 kms on the odometer; recently serviced.										
1987	328 GTS (PF/Scaglietti)	67213	L	70-90.000 GBP		NS		10-09-16	Goodwood	117	Bon
	Metallic blue with cream leather interior; sold new to the USA, the car was imported into the UK in 2014. Circa 74,500 miles from new.										
1986	328 GTS (PF/Scaglietti)	66221	R	80-100.000 GBP	86.620	115.421	102.437	10-09-16	Goodwood	127	Bon
	Red with tan interior; described as in very good overall condition. 22,214 miles covered. Last serviced in April 2016.										
1987	328 GTS (PF/Scaglietti)	68485	L	60-80.000 EUR		NA		08-10-16	Paris	132	CB/C
	Red with black interior; in good overall condition (see Artcurial lots 15 11.4.05 $46,461 and 167 6.2.15 $79,140).										
1989	328 GTS (PF/Scaglietti)	81294	L	65-85.000 EUR	62.157	75.510	69.136	30-10-16	Paris	153	Art
	Red; in good original condition (see lot 116 Artcurial 1.11.15 $101,675).										
1986	328 GTS (PF/Scaglietti)	59935	L	75-100.000 USD	38.424*	48.000*	43.267*	04-11-16	Dallas	F112	Mec
	Red with tan interior; 59,400 kms covered.										
1989	328 GTS (PF/Scaglietti)	79491	L	90-105.000 USD		NS		04-11-16	Dallas	S128	Mec
	Black with tan interior; 30,000 actual miles. Recently serviced.										
1987	328 GTS (PF/Scaglietti)	71057	L	75-100.000 USD		NS		04-11-16	Dallas	S196	Mec
	Red with tan interior; in original condition. 47,400 miles covered.										
1987	328 GTS (PF/Scaglietti)	69509	L	50-70.000 USD	47.550	59.400	53.543	05-11-16	Hilton Head	175	AA
	Gold with tan and brown interior; described as in original condition.										
1989	328 GTS (PF/Scaglietti)	78665	L	80-90.000 EUR	81.093*	100.836*	95.200*	25-11-16	Milan	309	RMS
	White with black interior; 41,924 kms. From the Duemila Ruote collection.										
1988	328 GTS (PF/Scaglietti)	76888	R	140-160.000 GBP	143.740	181.443	170.490	04-12-16	London	17	Bon
	Red with tan leather interior; since July 1988 in the present, second ownership. 2,147 miles covered. Recently recommissioned.										

F276

Year	Model	(Bodybuilder)	Chassis no.	Steering	Estimate	Hammer price £	$	€	Sale Date	Place	Lot	Auc. H.
1986	328 GTS	(PF/Scaglietti)	63241	R	90-110.000 GBP	NS			07-12-16	London	371	Bon
Red with cream leather interior; since 1989 in the current, fifth ownership; 18,875 miles coverede; recently serviced.											
1986	328 GTS	(PF/Scaglietti)	62779	L	60-70.000 GBP	NS			07-12-16	Chateau Impney	89	H&H
Red with black interior; described as in good overall condition. 41,500 miles on the odometer.											
1986	328 GTS	(PF/Scaglietti)	59995	L	45-65.000 USD	46.572*	57.200*	53.636*	18-01-17	Scottsdale	24	WoA
Stored for several years; 22,325 miles on the odometer; body repainted many years ago.											
1988	328 GTS	(PF/Scaglietti)	76919	L	90-120.000 USD	71.394*	88.000*	82.482*	19-01-17	Phoenix	112	RMS
Red with tan interior; less than 9,200 original miles.											
1987	328 GTS	(PF/Scaglietti)	73507	L	NQ	35.834*	44.000*	41.382*	21-01-17	Scottsdale	831.1	B/J
Light grey with red interior (see lot S622 Russo & Steele 16.8.14 $47,300).											
1989	328 GTS	(PF/Scaglietti)	81527	L	NQ	45.688	56.100	52.762	21-01-17	Scottsdale	8065	R&S
White; in good condition.											
1988	328 GTS	(PF/Scaglietti)	77449	L	70-90.000 EUR	66.540	83.611	78.200	09-02-17	Paris	396	Bon
Red; circa 34,000 kms covered; last serviced in September/October 2015.											
1988	328 GTS	(PF/Scaglietti)	81069	L	70-90.000 EUR	75.233*	93.756*	88.208*	10-02-17	Paris	88	Art
Red with tan interior; 28,860 kms covered. Recently serviced (see lot 14 Artcurial 20.10.13 $88,917).											
1989	328 GTS	(PF/Scaglietti)	82554	R	85-95.000 GBP	93.375	117.223	110.491	24-02-17	Stoneleigh P.	929	SiC
Red with cream interior; 22,860 miles covered. Recently serviced (see lot 651 Silverstone Auctions 26.7.14 $130,893).											
1986	328 GTS	(PF/Scaglietti)	64209	L	80-100.000 USD	54.199*	66.000*	62.548*	09-03-17	Amelia Island	167	Bon
Black with black leather interior; less than 37,000 miles covered.											
1989	328 GTS	(PF/Scaglietti)	81966	L	160-180.000 USD	113.108*	137.500*	129.580*	10-03-17	Amelia Island	49	G&Co
Red with tan interior; 12,600 miles covered. Recently serviced.											
1986	328 GTS	(PF/Scaglietti)	61001	L	60-90.000 EUR	55.352	68.416	63.720	18-03-17	Lyon	203	Agu
Red with black leather interior; sold new to the USA and later reimported into Europe. 50,000 kms on the odometer. Last serviced in 2016.											
1987	328 GTS	(PF/Scaglietti)	69729	L	80-100.000 EUR	NS			19-03-17	Fontainebleau	235	Ose
Red with black interior; since 1997 in the current ownership. Last serviced in September 2015.											
1986	328 GTS	(PF/Scaglietti)	61669	L	65-75.000 USD	40.930	51.150	47.841	01-04-17	Ft.Lauderdale	497	AA
Red with black interior; recently serviced.											
1989	328 GTS	(PF/Scaglietti)	79645	R	100-120.000 GBP	103.500	133.070	122.358	13-05-17	Silverstone	306	SiC
Red with black interior; since 1994 in the current ownership; 5,600 miles covered; last serviced in February 2017.											
1987	328 GTS	(PF/Scaglietti)	67405	R	100-120.000 GBP	NS			20-05-17	Ascot	169	His
Red with cream leather interior; last serviced in January 2016.											
1987	328 GTS	(PF/Scaglietti)	73101	L	NA	63.742	71.500	55.620	03-06-17	Newport Beach	9051	R&S
Black with beige interior; described as in very good overall condition. Last serviced in 2016.											
1989	328 GTS	(PF/Scaglietti)	81658	R	85-100.000 GBP	84.375	108.894	96.719	06-06-17	Woodcote Park	30	H&H
Red with cream interior; in very good overall condition; less than 32,900 miles covered; last serviced in May 2016.											
1987	328 GTS	(PF/Scaglietti)	74175	L	80-95.000 USD	NS			24-06-17	Santa Monica	182	RMS
Red with beige interior; 28,000 miles on the odometer.											
1988	328 GTS	(PF/Scaglietti)	78314	L	75-85.000 EUR	NS			05-08-17	Schloss Dyck	227	Coy
Red; two owners; approximately 23,000 kms covered (see lot 133 Coys 2.7.16 $91,646).											
1988	328 GTS	(PF/Scaglietti)	75109	L	80-120.000 USD	76.923*	99.000*	84.348*	18-08-17	Carmel	5	Bon
Red with tan interior; in highly original condition; less than 16,000 miles on the odometer (see lot 2095 Auctions America 25.6.16 NS).											
1988	328 GTS	(PF/Scaglietti)	78733	L	125-150.000 USD	81.197*	104.500*	89.034*	19-08-17	Pebble Beach	106	G&Co
Red with tobacco leather interior; less than 11,000 miles covered; last serviced 150 miles ago (see lots 550 Cox Auctions 19.10.07 $58,320 and 141 RM/Sotheby's 28.1.16 $99,000).											
1989	328 GTS	(PF/Scaglietti)	79638	L	90-120.000 USD	119.658*	154.000*	131.208*	19-08-17	Monterey	213	RMS
Red with black interior; less than 8,500 miles covered; certified by Ferrari Classiche. From the Ferrari Performance Collection.											
1986	328 GTS	(PF/Scaglietti)	61493	L	NA	44.872*	57.750*	49.203*	19-08-17	Monterey	1005	R&S
Blue; described as in good original condition.											

F275: 1991 Ferrari Testarossa (Pininfarina)

F276: 1988 Ferrari 328 GTS (PF/Scaglietti)

Year	Model	(Bodybuilder)	Chassis no.	Steering	Estimate	Hammer price £	$	€	Date	Place	Lot	Auc. H.
1987	328 GTS	(PF/Scaglietti)	70093	L	NA		NS		19-08-17	Monterey	1159	R&S
	Red with tan interior; one owner until 2017; body repainted; recent engine overhaul.											
1989	412	(Pininfarina)	78594	L	65-95.000 EUR	53.583*	65.095*	59.600*	30-10-16	Paris	106	Art **F277**
	Just one owner until early 2016; well maintained. Manual gearbox.											
1986	412	(Pininfarina)	63257	R	80-95.000 GBP	84.375	106.810	97.951	12-11-16	Birmingham	625	SiC
	Silver with cream leather interior; in very good original condition. Manual gearbox. 6,650 miles covered. Recommissioned in 2015 in New Zealand.											
1989	412	(Pininfarina)	78339	R	60-75.000 GBP	55.575	72.453	65.101	18-05-17	London	114	Coy
	Blue with cream interior; in good overall condition; 28,000 miles on the odometer. On display at the Ferrari stand at the 1989 Earl's Court Motor Show.											
1990	F40	(Pininfarina)	89028	L	885-1.100.000 GBP	924.000	1.236.497	1.100.392	07-09-16	London	145	RMS
	Red; one owner and less than 5,700 kms covered. Recent service including the replacement of the timing belts and fuel tanks. Certified by Ferrari Classiche.											
1992	F40	(Pininfarina)	91464	L	725-875.000 EUR	877.715*	1.091.400*	1.030.400*	25-11-16	Milan	877	RMS
	Red with red interior; sold new to Switzerland, the car was reimported into Italy in 2007. Less than 26,800 kms covered. Recently serviced. From the Duemila Ruote collection.											
1990	F40	(Pininfarina)	86678	L	1.250-1.500.000 USD		NS		20-01-17	Phoenix	219	RMS
	Red with red cloth interior; sold new to the USA. 7,614 actual miles. In very good overall condition.											
1989	F40	(Pininfarina)	80747	L	950-1.050.000 EUR		NS		08-02-17	Paris	165	RMS
	Red with red interior; sold new in Italy, the car remained in the same family ownership until 2014 when it was bought by the current owner. Certified by Ferrari Classiche; recent service carried out in the UK; interior recently retrimmed (see lot 151 RM 8.9.14 $1,226,176).											
1990	F40	(Pininfarina)	87041	L	1.300-1.600.000 USD	1.221.561	1.485.000	1.399.464	10-03-17	Amelia Island	29	G&Co
	Red with red interior; in very good overall condition; less than 1,600 miles covered; last serviced in 2013 at 1,311 miles; certified by Ferrari Classiche (see lot 446 RM 16.8.08 $753,500).											
1989	F40	(Pininfarina)	80768	L	850-1.050.000 EUR		NS		18-03-17	Lyon	202	Agu
	Red with red interior; delivered in 1989 to the French Ferrari importer Pozzi and sold in 1997 to its first owner: 25,025 kms covered. Regularly maintained over the years. Certified by Ferrari Classiche.											
1990	F40	(Pininfarina)	85749	L	850-950.000 EUR	927.702	1.191.254	1.064.000	27-05-17	Villa Erba	161	RMS **F278**
	Red with red interior; one owner; 18,600 kms covered.											
1990	F40	(Pininfarina)	84539	L	875-975.000 USD	684.552	880.000	784.520	04-06-17	Greenwich	164	Bon
	Red with red interior; sold new to Japan where it remained until 2015; 35,000 kms on the odometer; last serviced in May 2017. Ferrari Classiche certification in progress.											
1992	F40	(Pininfarina)	93065	L	900-1.100.000 USD	752.011	957.000	856.515	24-06-17	Santa Monica	229	RMS
	Red with red cloth interior; sold new to the USA. Less than 16,000 believed original miles. Recent major service including timing belts replacement.											
1988	F40	(Pininfarina)	78036	L	Refer Dpt.		NS		30-06-17	Goodwood	264	Bon
	Red with red interior; damaged by an engine bay fire in the late 2000s, the car received subsequently a full restoration recently completed. First owner the Pink Floyd guitarist David Gilmour.											
1990	F40	(Pininfarina)	87030	L	1.000-1.300.000 USD	1.132.478	1.457.500	1.241.790	18-08-17	Carmel	87	Bon
	Red with red interior; one owner; in original condition; less than 2,100 miles covered. Stored in the late 1990s, the car received recently a full major engine service.											
1991	F40	(Pininfarina)	87895	L	1.300-1.500.000 USD	1.196.580*	1.540.000*	1.312.080*	19-08-17	Monterey	222	RMS
	Red with red cloth interior; in highly original condition; two owners; 2,802 miles on the odometer; recently serviced. From the Ferrari Performance Collection.											
1989	348 tb	(Pininfarina)	82643	L	70-80.000 USD		NS		03-09-16	Auburn	3131	AA
	Red with black interior; sparingly driven.											
1992	348 tb	(Pininfarina)	94284	L	90-130.000 EUR		NS		30-10-16	Paris	108	Art
	Red; 4,240 kms covered. Recently overhauled.											
1991	348 tb	(Pininfarina)	90679	L	NQ	51.959*	63.800*	60.004*	21-01-17	Scottsdale	989.2	B/J
	Red with tan interior; last serviced in June 2016 (see lot F567 Russo & Steele 17.1.15 $42,900).											
1990	348 tb	(Pininfarina)	82135	L	90-110.000 GBP	93.375	117.223	110.491	24-02-17	Stoneleigh P.	909	SiC
	Red with tan interior; engine overhauled in 2015 in Italy. 2,500 kms covered since new (see Silverstone Auctions lots 130 28.5.16 NS and 519 30.7.16 NS).											
1991	348 tb	(Pininfarina)	88630	L	60-80.000 EUR	57.437	70.993	66.120	18-03-17	Lyon	206	Agu
	Red with black interior; in very good original condition. 19,950 kms covered (see lot 255 Aguttes 7.11.15 $73,006).											
1992	348 tb	(Pininfarina)	92157	L	65-75.000 GBP		NS		30-06-17	Goodwood	258	Bon
	Yellow with black interior; 7,250 kms on the odometer; last serviced in August 2016 (see lots 114 Silverstone Auctions 21.7.12 $37,743 and 30 H & H 16.10.13 NS).											
1990	348 tb	(Pininfarina)	82673	L	100-120.000 USD	44.444*	57.200*	48.734*	18-08-17	Carmel	39	Bon
	Medium blue with grey leather interior; for 24 years with its first owner; always well maintained; less than 11,200 miles covered (see lot 67 Gooding & Company 13.3.15 $71,500).											
1989	348 ts	(Pininfarina)	82453	L	NA		NS		02-09-16	Salon Privé	241	SiC
	Red with black interior; 3,990 miles covered. Last serviced in March 2015 (see lot 062 Bonhams 21.03.15 $78,572).											

F277: 1989 Ferrari 412 (Pininfarina)

F278: 1990 Ferrari F40 (Pininfarina)

Year	Model	(Bodybuilder)	Chassis no.	Steering	Estimate	Hammer price £	$	€	Date	Place	Lot	Auc. H.
1991	348 ts	(Pininfarina)	89411	L	NQ	41.055	50.000	46.895	15-01-17	Kissimmee	F282	Mec
	Black with black interior; 28,478 original miles.											
1992	348 ts	(Pininfarina)	94239	L	36-40.000 GBP		NS		29-03-17	Duxford	61	H&H
	Red with tan interior; in good overall condition. Sold new to the USA; imported into the UK six years ago.											
1990	348 ts	(Pininfarina)	86669	L	60-65.000 USD	36.809 P	46.000 P	43.024 P	01-04-17	Ft.Lauderdale	240	AA
	White with red interior.											
1993	348 ts	(Pininfarina)	96811	L	45-55.000 EUR	37.660	46.904	44.000	08-04-17	Essen	206	Coy
	Red with cream interior; in original condition; 23,000 kms covered; last serviced in March 2017.											
1991	348 ts	(Pininfarina)	89411	L	NQ		NS		08-04-17	Houston	F127.1	Mec
	See lot F282 Mecum 15.1.17.											
1989	348 ts	(Pininfarina)	82453	L	70-80.000 GBP		NS		13-05-17	Silverstone	337	SiC
	Red with black interior; 3,985 miles covered; last serviced in March 2015 (see lots 062 Bonhams 21.3.15 $78,572 and 241 Silverstone Auctions 9.2.16 NS).											
1990	348 ts	(Pininfarina)	87111	L	60-80.000 USD	41.494	54.000	48.303	20-05-17	Indianapolis	F189	Mec F279
	Red with black leather interior; 13,815 miles covered; belt service in June 2015.											
1991	348 ts	(Pininfarina)	91402	L	50-60.000 EUR		NS		10-06-17	Lyon	133	Agu
	Red with black interior; 41,967 kms covered. Last serviced in May 2016.											
1990	348 Challenge	(Pininfarina)	86947	L	60-90.000 USD	36.133*	44.000*	41.699*	09-03-17	Amelia Island	155	Bon
	Red with tan interior; raced at the Ferrari Challenge from 1994 to 1996. Recommissioned in 2016 (see Mecum lots S121 15.8.09 NS, S179 18.8.11 NS, and F1501 16.8.12 $35,000).											
1990	348 Challenge	(Pininfarina)	86947	L	90-120.000 USD		NS		19-08-17	Monterey	F65	Mec
	See lot 155 Bonhams 9.3.17.											
1993	348 TS Serie Speciale	(Pininfarina)	95227	L	130-160.000 USD	76.146*	93.500*	87.937*	21-01-17	Scottsdale	155	G&Co
	Red with tan interior; one of 100 examples built for the US market. Three owner and less than 18,000 miles covered. Last major service in June 2016.											
1993	348 TS Serie Speciale	(Pininfarina)	95991	L	85-115.000 USD		NS		11-03-17	Amelia Island	67	Mot
	Black with black interior; less than 24,000 miles covered. Engine-out service in 2016.											
1994	348 Spider	(Pininfarina)	97330	L	50-60.000 USD	43.882*	58.300*	52.085*	03-09-16	Auburn	5012	AA
	Blue with cream leather interior; less than 8,000 miles.											
1991	348 Spider	(Pininfarina)	87975	L	NQ		NS		15-01-17	Kissimmee	S28.1	Mec
	Red with saddle interior.											
1994	348 Spider	(Pininfarina)	98365	L	NQ	40.313*	49.500*	46.555*	21-01-17	Scottsdale	989.1	B/J
	Blue with dark blue leather interior; 34,685 miles covered. In very good overall condition.											
1993	348 Spider	(Pininfarina)	97429	R	60-70.000 GBP	66.375	85.338	78.469	13-05-17	Silverstone	312	SiC
	Yellow; 27,800 miles covered; last serviced in early 2017.											
1995	348 Spider	(Pininfarina)	99266	L	70-80.000 GBP	66.690	86.944	78.121	18-05-17	London	105	Coy
	Red; 5,800 kms on the odometer. Recommissioned in 2016 following a 15 year period in storage.											
1994	348 Spider	(Pininfarina)	99687	R	45-55.000 GBP	48.350	63.034	56.637	18-05-17	London	117	Coy F280
	Yellow with black interior; 56,500 miles covered; recently serviced.											
1994	348 Spider	(Pininfarina)	98543	L	NQ	30.352	39.500	35.333	20-05-17	Indianapolis	F275	Mec
	Red with tan interior; 30,000 believed original miles.											
1994	348 Spider	(Pininfarina)	96013	L	45-55.000 USD		NS		24-06-17	Santa Monica	145	RMS
	Red with tan interior.											
1992	512 TR	(Pininfarina)	93206	L	NA		NS		02-09-16	Salon Privé	267	SiC
	Red with black interior; 8,308 kms covered. Last serviced in September 2015 (see lot 127 Coys 08.03.16 NS).											
1992	512 TR	(Pininfarina)	93757	L	125-155.000 EUR		NS		05-11-16	Lyon	254	Agu
	Red with black leather interior; one owner and 67,717 kms covered. Body repainted some years ago; last serviced in February 2016.											
1994	512 TR	(Pininfarina)	96356	L	90-105.000 EUR	143.106*	177.946*	168.000*	25-11-16	Milan	582	RMS
	Black with black interior; 39,748 kms. From the Duemila Ruote collection.											
1993	512 TR	(Pininfarina)	96509	L	100-110.000 EUR	102.752	125.125	117.367	14-01-17	Maastricht	210	Coy
	Yellow with black interior; 29,800 kms on the odometer.											

F279: 1990 Ferrari 348 ts (Pininfarina)

F280: 1994 Ferrari 348 Spider (Pininfarina)

Year	Model	(Bodybuilder)	Chassis no.	Steering	Estimate	Hammer Price £	$	€	Date	Place	Lot	Auc. H.
1993	**512 TR**	(Pininfarina)	94762	L	250-325.000 USD	162.422*	200.200*	187.647*	19-01-17	Scottsdale	81	Bon **F281**
Blue with saddle leather interior; two owners and 8,043 miles covered. Recently serviced.											
1993	**512 TR**	(Pininfarina)	94507	L	200-250.000 USD		NS		20-01-17	Phoenix	260	RMS
Black with black interior; less than 11,000 miles covered. Last major service in November 2015.											
1994	**512 TR**	(Pininfarina)	97271	L	300-325.000 USD		NS		11-02-17	Boca Raton	137	TFA
Red with black interior; less than 30,000 kms covered. Clutch replaced in August 2015 (see lot 142 The Finest Automobile Auctions 11.6.16 NS).											
1992	**512 TR**	(Pininfarina)	94367	R	100-120.000 GBP	128.250	161.005	151.758	24-02-17	Stoneleigh P.	538	SiC
Red with cream leather interior; 71,752 miles covered. Last serviced in October 2016.											
1993	**512 TR**	(Pininfarina)	95405	R	135-155.000 GBP	146.250	181.950	169.299	29-03-17	Duxford	86	H&H
Red with cream interior; described as in very good overall condition, the car has covered 30,200 miles, Last serviced in June 2016.											
1992	**512 TR**	(Pininfarina)	94633	L	130-160.000 USD	110.028	137.500	128.604	01-04-17	Ft.Lauderdale	567	AA
Black with black interior; recently serviced. One owner.											
1993	**512 TR**	(Pininfarina)	95205	L	85-100.000 GBP		NS		13-05-17	Silverstone	325	SiC
Red with black leather interior; described as in very good overall condition, the car has covered 88,363 kms.											
1992	**512 TR**	(Pininfarina)	95421	L	130-160.000 EUR		NS		02-07-17	Monaco	211	Art
Red with black interior; two owners; 36,500 kms covered; engine-out service in 2015; body repainted.											
1992	**512 TR**	(Pininfarina)	86815	L	NA	166.667	214.500	182.754	19-08-17	Monterey	1014	R&S
Red with tan interior; described as in very good original condition. One ot two factory US specification pre-production examples.											
2000	**456M GTA**	(Pininfarina)	117689	L	75-85.000 USD		NS		05-11-16	Hilton Head	198	AA
Black leather interior; automatic transmisison.											
1994	**456 GT**	(Pininfarina)	98459	L	48-52.000 GBP	49.000	60.927	57.521	26-11-16	Weybridge	148	His
Dark blue with tan leather interior; recommissioned in 2015. 73,500 kms on the odometer.											
1998	**456 GTA**	(Pininfarina)	114507	L	45-50.000 EUR	36.978	45.029	42.237	14-01-17	Maastricht	240	Coy
Blue with blue leather interior; last serviced in 2016.											
1995	**456 GT**	(Pininfarina)	99988	L	90-120.000 USD	89.243*	110.000*	103.103*	19-01-17	Scottsdale	14	Bon
Black with caramel leather interior; in highly original condition; less than 15,000 miles covered.											
2001	**456M GT**	(Pininfarina)	124619	L	150-225.000 USD	120.938*	148.500*	139.664*	20-01-17	Phoenix	221	RMS **F282**
Blue with light blue interior; less than 4,450 miles covered. Recently serviced. Manual gearbox.											
2001	**456M GT**	(Pininfarina)	116779	L	50-60.000 EUR	56.395	69.705	64.920	18-03-17	Lyon	192	Agu
Metallic grey; in good overall condition; manual gearbox.											
1997	**456 GTA**	(Pininfarina)	105988	L	55-65.000 USD	41.610 P	52.000 P	48.636 P	01-04-17	Ft.Lauderdale	434	AA
Black with tan interior; in original condition; automatic transmission.											
1998	**456 GTA**	(Pininfarina)	114507	L	40-45.000 EUR	34.236	42.640	40.000	08-04-17	Essen	123	Coy
See lot 240 Coys 14.1.17.											
1995	**456 GT**	(Pininfarina)	99370	L	35-45.000 EUR		NS		22-04-17	Bagatelle	165	Agu
Black with tan leather interior; manual gearbox.											
2000	**456M GT**	(Pininfarina)	119224	L	67-75.000 GBP		NS		20-05-17	Ascot	151	His
Light blue with tan leather interior; in good driving order. Low mileage. Manual gearbox.											
1995	**456 GT**	(Pininfarina)	101604	R	18-24.000 GBP	33.600	43.720	39.110	20-05-17	Ascot	172	His
Dark blue; rebuilt manual gearbox.											
2003	**456M GT**	(Pininfarina)	130512	L	100-150.000 EUR	103.734	134.986	120.750	21-05-17	SPA-Francorch.	45	Bon
Black with tan interior; less than 500 kms covered; recently serviced. Manual gearbox.											
1999	**456M GT**	(Pininfarina)	116665	L	65-85.000 USD	78.723	101.200	90.220	04-06-17	Greenwich	125	Bon
Burgundy red with natural leather interior; circa 22,200 miles on the odometer. Last serviced in 2016. Manual gearbox.											
1994	**456 GT**	(Pininfarina)	99134	L	45-55.000 GBP		NS		30-06-17	Goodwood	277	Bon
Red with black interior; body partially resprayed in 2008. The brakes require attention prior to use. Manual gearbox (see lot 49 Bonhams 9.10.15 $91,464).											
1995	**456 GT**	(Pininfarina)	102122	L	47-55.000 GBP	45.281	59.059	50.719	26-07-17	Duxford	63	H&H
Blue with cream interior; 61,000 miles covered. Clutch replaced in 2011; recently serviced.											

F281: 1993 Ferrari 512 TR (Pininfarina)

F282: 2001 Ferrari 456M GT (Pininfarina)

Year	Model	(Bodybuilder)	Chassis no.	Steering	Estimate	£	$	€	Date	Place	Lot	Auc. H.
1995	F512M	(Pininfarina)	102032	L	NA		NS		02-09-16	Salon Privé	225	SiC
	Black with black leather interior; 25,395 miles covered.											
1995	F512M	(Pininfarina)	103477	L	210-290.000 GBP	235.200	314.745	280.100	07-09-16	London	116	RMS **F283**
	Red with black interior; in original condition. 3,951 kms covered. Sold new to Japan (see lot 234 RM/Sotheby's 14.5.16 NS).											
1995	F512M	(Pininfarina)	101461	L	165-185.000 EUR	190.808*	237.261*	224.000*	25-11-16	Milan	858	RMS
	Red with black interior; 38,507 kms. From the Duemila Ruote collection.											
1995	F512M	(Pininfarina)	100602	L	400-475.000 USD	266.858	325.000	304.818	15-01-17	Kissimmee	S220	Mec
	Red with beige interior; approximately 30,000 miles covered. Recent service and new clutch.											
1995	F512M	(Pininfarina)	103577	L	170-190.000 GBP		NS		29-03-17	Duxford	103	H&H
	Red with black leather interior; in very good overall condition; 26,583 kms on the odometer; imported into the UK in 2015.											
1995	F512M	(Pininfarina)	101379	L	400-500.000 USD	371.795	478.500	407.682	18-08-17	Pebble Beach	10	G&Co
	Red with beige interior; sold new to the USA; three owners; 2,302 miles covered; recent engine-out service.											
1998	F355 Berlinetta	(Pininfarina)	112742	L	85-95.000 USD		NS		17-09-16	Aspen	153	TFA
	Red with tan interior; 16,800 miles. F1 gearbox.											
1995	F355 Berlinetta	(Pininfarina)	101647	L	45-50.000 GBP	60.750	76.903	70.525	12-11-16	Birmingham	351	SiC
	Silver with burgundy interior; described as in good condition. Manual gearbox (see lot 535 Silverstone Auctions 30.7.16 NS).											
1995	F355 Berlinetta	(Pininfarina)	100206	L	55-65.000 EUR	62.012*	77.110*	72.800*	25-11-16	Milan	614	RMS
	Red with black interior; 48,149 kms. From the Duemila Ruote collection.											
1998	F355 Berlinetta	(Pininfarina)	111512	L	54-65.000 GBP		NS		26-11-16	Weybridge	206	His
	Red with black interior; body repainted. Recent service including cambelt change.											
1996	F355 Berlinetta	(Pininfarina)	105334	R	65-75.000 GBP	64.410	81.215	75.688	07-12-16	Chateau Impney	55	H&H
	Yellow with dark blue leather interior; 62,400 miles covered. Last serviced in January 2016.											
1997	F355 Berlinetta	(Pininfarina)	107043	L	NQ	68.084	83.600	78.626	21-01-17	Scottsdale	8122	R&S
	Red with tan interior; the 30.000-mile service has been done.											
1995	F355 Berlinetta	(Pininfarina)	102023	L	60-80.000 GBP	66.850	83.054	77.981	18-02-17	London	348	Coy
	Red with dark blue leather interior; 28,000 miles covered.											
1998	F355 Berlinetta	(Pininfarina)	111112	R	85-100.000 GBP	136.125	170.891	161.077	24-02-17	Stoneleigh P.	523	SiC
	Red with black leather interior; one owner and 7,017 miles covered.											
1995	F355 Berlinetta	(Pininfarina)	102023	L	50-60.000 GBP	47.794	59.743	56.330	12-04-17	London	309	Coy
	See lot 348 Coys 18.2.17.											
1998	F355 Berlinetta	(Pininfarina)	112927	L	58-65.000 GBP	57.798	75.351	67.705	18-05-17	London	108	Coy
	Titanium grey with black leather interior; 18,000 miles covered (see lot 323 Historics 20.8.16 NS).											
1997	F355 Berlinetta	(Pininfarina)	107919	L	70-90.000 EUR		NS		10-06-17	Lyon	151	Agu
	Red with black leather interior; last serviced in March 2016 at 75,500 kms.											
1998	F355 Berlinetta	(Pininfarina)	112927	L	60-70.000 GBP		NS		29-06-17	Fontwell Park	156	Coy
	See lot 108 Coys 18.5.17.											
1998	F355 Berlinetta	(Pininfarina)	109471	L	85-95.000 GBP		NS		30-06-17	Goodwood	230	Bon
	Red; two owners. Last major service, including change of cam belts, in May 2017.											
1996	F355 Berlinetta	(Pininfarina)	114864	L	47-55.000 EUR	45.140	59.340	50.000	05-08-17	Schloss Dyck	257	Coy
	Red; 51,000 kms covered; F1 gearbox (see Coys lots 310 1.12.15 NS and 219 2.7.16 NS).											
1998	F355 Berlinetta	(Pininfarina)	111485	L	90-120.000 USD	51.282*	66.000*	56.232*	18-08-17	Carmel	34	Bon **F284**
	Silver with caramel leather interior; sold new to the USA; 26,300 miles on the odometer.											
1999	F355 Berlinetta	(Pininfarina)	113463	L	NA	33.333*	42.900*	36.551*	19-08-17	Monterey	1063	R&S
	Yellow; 23,493 miles on the odometer.											
1997	F355 GTS	(Pininfarina)	107034	R	NA	70.880	94.150	84.120	02-09-16	Salon Privé	253	SiC
	Yellow with blue interior; last serviced in November 2015 at 46,646 miles.											
1999	F355 GTS	(Pininfarina)	115657	L	95-110.000 USD	68.084*	83.600*	78.626*	20-01-17	Scottsdale	15	G&Co
	Silver with black interior; 13,500 miles covered. Last serviced in February 2016.											

F283: 1995 Ferrari F512M (Pininfarina)

F284: 1998 Ferrari F355 Berlinetta (Pininfarina)

Year	Model	(Bodybuilder)	Chassis No.	Steering	Estimate	Hammer Price £	$	€	Date	Place	Lot	Auc. H.
1999	F355 GTS	(Pininfarina)	113210	L	NQ	80.626*	99.000*	93.110*	21-01-17	Scottsdale	1035	B/J
	Red with tan interior; last serviced 2,000 miles ago.											
1995	F355 GTS	(Pininfarina)	102088	L	85-95.000 USD		NS		11-02-17	Boca Raton	150	TFA
	Light blue with cream interior; 23,400 miles covered.											
1997	F355 GTS	(Pininfarina)	107693	R	65-75.000 GBP		NS		13-05-17	Silverstone	349	SiC
	Red with cream interior; 17,540 miles covered; recently serviced. In the past repaired some fire damages at the rear end.											
1995	F355 GTS	(Pininfarina)	100582	L	70-90.000 EUR	60.264	78.421	70.150	21-05-17	SPA-Francorch.	88	Bon F285
	Yellow with black leather interior; circa 37,000 kms covered; last serviced 500 kms ago (see lot 257 Bonhams 24.6.16 NS).											
1998	F355 GTS	(Pininfarina)	109092	L	70-90.000 EUR	65.378	96.491	74.350	02-07-17	Monaco	106	Art
	Red with black leather interior; in very good overall condition; just over 85,000 kms covered; major service in March 2015. First owner Jean-Paul Belmondo.											
1997	F355 Spider	(Pininfarina)	107771	L	60-70.000 USD		NS		03-09-16	Auburn	5161	AA
	Yellow with black leather interior; manual gearbox.											
1997	F355 Spider	(Pininfarina)	107908	R	85-90.000 GBP	78.050	104.259	92.294	08-09-16	Fontwell Park	105	Coy
	Yellow with black interior; 27,000 miles covered.											
1998	F355 Spider	(Pininfarina)	109753	L	NA	52.528	70.000	62.118	10-09-16	Louisville	S146	Mec
	Yellow with black interior; 15,000 mile service completed (see Auctions America lots 5059 8.5.14 $63,800 and 834 7.5.16 $55,000).											
1998	F355 Spider	(Pininfarina)	111591	L	45-55.000 GBP	51.520	63.143	57.301	12-10-16	Duxford	33	H&H
	Red with tan interior; in good overall condition. F1 gearbox.											
1995	F355 Spider	(Pininfarina)	103400	L	NA	56.632*	69.300*	62.987*	15-10-16	Las Vegas	753	B/J
	Yellow with black interior; recent major engine-out service including the clutch replacement. Manual gearbox.											
1995	F355 Spider	(Pininfarina)	104073	L	75-90.000 USD	56.035	70.000	63.098	04-11-16	Dallas	S167	Mec
	Red with tan interior; 34,700 miles on the odometer.											
2000	F355 Spider	(Pininfarina)	115696	L	60-80.000 EUR		NS		05-11-16	Lyon	257	Agu
	Metallic grey with blue leather interior; 74,500 kms covered. F1 gearbox.											
1999	F355 Spider	(Pininfarina)	116511	L	75-90.000 GBP		NS		12-11-16	Birmingham	339	SiC
	Yellow with black leather interior; example of the "Fiorano" special edition with F1 gearbox. Sold new to the USA and imported into the UK in 2014. Last serviced in June 2015 at 34,220 miles.											
1997	F355 Spider	(Pininfarina)	106429	L	NA	68.944	85.000	79.968	19-11-16	Anaheim	F141	Mec
	Red with tan interior; last serviced in January 2015 at 24,806 miles.											
1996	F355 Spider	(Pininfarina)	106479	L	65-75.000 EUR	76.323*	94.904*	89.600*	25-11-16	Milan	548	RMS
	Yellow with black interior; 40,457 kms. From the Duemila Ruote collection.											
1999	F355 Spider	(Pininfarina)	115290	L	70-80.000 GBP	69.687	88.607	82.788	05-12-16	London	103	Coy
	Blue with tan interior; three owners and 29,000 miles covered. F1 gearbox.											
1998	F355 Spider	(Pininfarina)	112320	L	100-150.000 USD	71.394*	88.000*	82.482*	19-01-17	Phoenix	126	RMS F286
	Light blue with cream interior; 6,275 original miles. Last serviced in October 2016. F1 gearbox.											
1999	F355 Spider	(Pininfarina)	114586	L	NQ	53.750*	66.000*	62.073*	21-01-17	Scottsdale	771.1	B/J
	Green with tan interior; F1 gearbox (see lot S45.1 Mecum 10.4.15 $55,000).											
1996	F355 Spider	(Pininfarina)	105459	L	100-120.000 USD	71.667*	88.000*	82.764*	21-01-17	Scottsdale	102	G&Co
	Yellow with black interior; in 2014 engine-out service and interior retrimming. 14,331 miles on the odometer. Last serviced in 2016.											
1995	F355 Spider	(Pininfarina)	103134	L	60-70.000 EUR	48.927	61.479	57.500	09-02-17	Paris	414	Bon
	Red with black interior; in good overall condition. Circa 75,000 kms covered. Last serviced in March 2015.											
1995	F355 Spider	(Pininfarina)	102481	L	65-85.000 GBP	58.920	73.202	68.730	18-02-17	London	342	Coy
	Black with black interior; described as in very good driving order. One owner and 64,000 miles covered.											
1997	F355 Spider	(Pininfarina)	107198	L	80-100.000 USD	63.340*	77.000*	72.565*	10-03-17	Amelia Island	85	G&Co
	Red with tan interior; last serviced in 2008 at 15,500 miles.											
1998	F355 Spider	(Pininfarina)	112065	L	70-80.000 USD		NS		01-04-17	Ft.Lauderdale	783	AA
	Silver with dark blue interior.											
1999	F355 Spider	(Pininfarina)	115433	L	70-90.000 EUR	50.498	62.894	59.000	08-04-17	Essen	131	Coy
	Black with cognac leather interior; two owners; 24,000 miles covered.											

F285: 1995 Ferrari F355 GTS (Pininfarina)

F286: 1998 Ferrari F355 Spider (Pininfarina)

Year	Model (Bodybuilder)	Chassis no.	Steering	Estimate	Hammer price £	$	€	Date	Place	Lot	Auc. H.
1995	**F355 Spider (Pininfarina)**	103167	L	NQ		NS		08-04-17	Houston	F178	**Mec**
Red with tan interior; believed to be 19,500 miles. Last serviced in November 2015.
1997	**F355 Spider (Pininfarina)**	108758	R	180-200.000 AUD	**111.467**	**144.228**	**131.950**	30-04-17	Melbourne	38	**Mos**
Red with black leather interior; less than 20,000 kms covered. Last serviced in April 2017.
1996	**F355 Spider (Pininfarina)**	106627	R	85-95.000 GBP	**91.125**	**117.159**	**107.728**	13-05-17	Silverstone	347	**SiC**
Yellow with black interior; 23,378 miles covered. Last serviced in March 2017.
1997	**F355 Spider (Pininfarina)**	116256	L	65-75.000 GBP		NS		13-05-17	Silverstone	355	**SiC**
Black with tan interior; 22,000 miles covered; recently serviced. F1 gearbox.
1998	**F355 Spider (Pininfarina)**	109753	L	NQ		NS		20-05-17	Indianapolis	S55.1	**Mec**
See lot S146 Mecum 10.9.16.
2000	**F355 Spider (Pininfarina)**	113764	R	75-85.000 GBP		NS		06-06-17	Woodcote Park	44	**H&H**
Red with cream leather interior; 28,050 miles covered; recently recommissioned following a period in storage. F1 gearbox.
1998	**F355 Spider (Pininfarina)**	112688	L	75-85.000 EUR	**60.397**	**79.397**	**66.900**	05-08-17	Schloss Dyck	215	**Coy**
Silver with dark blue interior; described as in very good overall condition; just over 25,000 kms covered.
1999	**F355 Spider (Pininfarina)**	115938	L	75-95.000 USD	**56.721**	**73.000**	**62.196**	19-08-17	Monterey	F17	**Mec**
Red with tan interior; 12,050 believed original miles; F1 gearbox.
1998	**F355 Spider (Pininfarina)**	112877	L	90-125.000 USD	**64.103**	**82.500**	**70.290**	19-08-17	Monterey	S141	**Mec**
Silver with black interior; 8,330 believed original miles.
1999	**F355 Spider (Pininfarina)**	115963	L	55-70.000 USD	**31.080**	**40.000**	**34.080**	19-08-17	Monterey	S164	**Mec**
Silver with black interior; 22,508 miles on the odometer; F1 gearbox (see lots 279 Mecum 28.1.10 $57,240 and 632 Auctions America 4.3.11 NS).
1999	**F355 Spider (Pininfarina)**	115427	L	175-200.000 USD		NS		19-08-17	Monterey	S75	**Mec**
Serie Fiorano finished in red with tan interior; 200 miles covered since the last service. F1 gearbox.
1996	**F355 Challenge (Pininfarina)**	104702	L	80-90.000 EUR	**100.174***	**124.562***	**117.600***	25-11-16	Milan	871	**RMS**
Red; 49,058 kms. From the Duemila Ruote collection.
1995	**F355 Challenge (Pininfarina)**	101046	L	60-80.000 EUR	**106.749***	**133.033***	**125.160***	10-02-17	Paris	98	**Art** **F287**
The car won the 1995 e 1996 Challenge Ferrari Europe West championships driven by Lucien Guitteny; later it was modified to compete in the French Championship FFSA GT. In 2010 it was bought by the current owner and raced at some hillclimb events in 2010 and 2011. The engine was replaced in 2011 with a similar unit.
1996	**F355 Challenge (Pininfarina)**	104539	L	150-200.000 EUR	**136.336**	**177.411**	**158.700**	21-05-17	SPA-Francorch.	67	**Bon**
Yellow; raced at the Ferrari Challenge from 1996 to 1998; 13,460 kms on the odometer; two owners; last serviced in 2015.
1995	**F355 Challenge (Pininfarina)**	104404	L	120-160.000 USD		NS		24-06-17	Santa Monica	233	**RMS**
Red; in the 1990s raced at the Ferrari Challenge.
1996	**F50 (Pininfarina)**	106570	L	1.100-1.200.000 GBP		NS		07-09-16	London	137	**RMS**
Red with black and red interior; last serviced in 2015. Certified by Ferrari Classiche (see lot 108 RM/Sotheby's 23.5.15 $1,375,405).
1995	**F50 (Pininfarina)**	104092	L	3.000-3.500.000 USD	**2.553.144**	**3.135.000**	**2.948.468**	20-01-17	Phoenix	227	**RMS** **F288**
Black with black and red leather and alcantara interior; less than 2,090 miles covered. Last serviced in December 2016.
1995	**F50 (Pininfarina)**	104220	L	2.200-2.400.000 USD	**2.171.664**	**2.640.000**	**2.487.936**	11-03-17	Amelia Island	218	**RMS**
Red with black and red interior; 5,694 actual miles. Several mechanical works in 2005, engine-out service in 2010, full brake system service in 2016. Certified by Ferrari Classiche. First owner boxer Mike Tyson.
1998	**550 Maranello (Pininfarina)**	110685	R	NA	**180.000**	**239.094**	**213.624**	02-09-16	Salon Privé	211	**SiC**
1,977 miles covered; last serviced in October 2015.
1997	**550 Maranello (Pininfarina)**	108775	R	NA	**93.380**	**124.037**	**110.823**	02-09-16	Salon Privé	221	**SiC**
Silver with burgundy leather interior; last serviced in February 2016 at 52,478 miles.
2000	**550 Maranello (Pininfarina)**	120150	L	195-210.000 USD	**129.013**	**170.000**	**151.419**	17-09-16	Aspen	152	**TFA**
Blue with saddle interior; in good running order (see lot 138 The Finest Automobile Auctions 11.6.16 NS).
1999	**550 Maranello (Pininfarina)**	116105	L	NA	**54.337**	**67.000**	**60.139**	08-10-16	Chicago	S109	**Mec**
Blue with tan interior; 33,741 miles. Recently serviced.
2000	**550 Maranello (Pininfarina)**	119560	L	80-110.000 EUR		NS		30-10-16	Paris	107	**Art**
Silver (see Artcurial lots 114 30.10.11 $75,913 and 112 11.11.12 $63,517).

F287: 1995 Ferrari F355 Challenge (Pininfarina)

F288: 1995 Ferrari F50 (Pininfarina)

Year	Model	(Bodybuilder)	Chassis no.	Steering	Estimate	Hammer Price £	$	€	Date	Place	Lot	Auc. H.
2000	550 Maranello	(Pininfarina)	120143	L	95-115.000 EUR		NS		05-11-16	Lyon	252	Agu
	Blue with beige leather interior; 69,000 kms covered. Last serviced in October 2016.											
1999	550 Maranello	(Pininfarina)	114367	L	NA		NS		19-11-16	Anaheim	S120.1	Mec
	Blue with tan interior; 23,389 miles on the odometer; last serviced in April 2016 (see lot S124.1 Mecum 13.11.15 NS).											
1998	550 Maranello	(Pininfarina)	111251	L	80-90.000 EUR	100.174*	124.562*	117.600*	25-11-16	Milan	577	RMS
	Blue with light grey interior; 35,349 kms. From the Duemila Ruote collection.											
1998	550 Maranello	(Pininfarina)	111488	L	59-69.000 GBP		WD		26-11-16	Weybridge	220	His
	Blue with tan interior; 29,000 miles covered. Last serviced in September 2016.											
1999	550 Maranello	(Pininfarina)	114682	R	200-240.000 GBP		NS		04-12-16	London	12	Bon
	Red with cream leather interior; just one owner. Last serviced in July 2016 at 4,042 miles.											
1998	550 Maranello	(Pininfarina)	110315	L	70-80.000 GBP	73.580	93.557	87.413	05-12-16	London	107	Coy
	Described as in good overall condition; less than 90,000 kms covered.											
2000	550 Maranello	(Pininfarina)	119581	R	60-80.000 GBP		NS		05-12-16	London	125	Coy
	Metallic grey; 37,000 miles on the odometer. Damaged in accidents in 2007 and 2011. Last serviced in 2014.											
1998	550 Maranello	(Pininfarina)	111655	L	NQ		NS		15-01-17	Kissimmee	S81.1	Mec
	Red with tan interior; for eight years in the current ownership.											
2000	550 Maranello	(Pininfarina)	120147	L	230-250.000 EUR		NS		08-02-17	Paris	112	RMS
	One of 33 examples of the World Speed Record edition; red with black interior; 40,400kms covered (see lot 242 Historics 28.11.15 NS).											
1998	550 Maranello	(Pininfarina)	111347	L	NQ		NS		18-02-17	Los Angeles	S64.1	Mec
	Black with tan interior; believed to be 13,000 actual miles.											
2000	550 Maranello	(Pininfarina)	117671	R	180-220.000 GBP	178.000	223.461	210.627	24-02-17	Stoneleigh P.	531	SiC
	Example of the World Speed Record special edition; since 2005 in the current ownership; 33,800 miles covered; recently serviced.											
1999	550 Maranello	(Pininfarina)	114954	L	125-175.000 USD		NS		11-03-17	Amelia Island	39	Mot
	Silver with black leather interior; in good overall condition.											
1998	550 Maranello	(Pininfarina)	110686	L	125-150.000 USD	135.729*	165.000*	155.496*	11-03-17	Amelia Island	212	RMS F289
	Red with beige interior; 9,350 miles covered. Last serviced in January 2016 (see lot S26 Mecum 20.8.16 $105,000).											
2001	550 Maranello	(Pininfarina)	125553	L	150-170.000 USD	140.835	176.000	164.613	01-04-17	Ft.Lauderdale	560	AA
	Red with black interior; less than 16,000 actual miles; last serviced in 2017.											
1997	550 Maranello	(Pininfarina)	108955	L	NQ		NS		08-04-17	Houston	S125.1	Mec
	Yellow with black interior; 9,800 original miles; last serviced in September 2016.											
1998	550 Maranello	(Pininfarina)	110966	L	125-150.000 USD	81.771	104.500	97.676	22-04-17	Arlington	149	WoA
	Blue with tan leather interior; just over 19,000 miles covered.											
1999	550 Maranello	(Pininfarina)	114351	L	70-90.000 GBP	83.260	108.055	94.275	30-06-17	Goodwood	286	Bon
	Red with black interior; two owners; circa 27,500 kms on the odometer; last serviced in June 2016 (see lots 253 Bonhams 24.6.16 NS and 922 Silverstone Auctions 30.7.16 NS).											
2000	550 Maranello	(Pininfarina)	120807	L	80-100.000 EUR	84.359	124.506	95.936	02-07-17	Monaco	172	Art
	Green with beige interior; 76,000 kms covered; last serviced in November 2016.											
1999	550 Maranello	(Pininfarina)	114380	R	120-140.000 GBP		NS		29-07-17	Silverstone	427	SiC
	Titanium grey with light grey leather interior; last serviced in April 2017 at 24,514 miles.											
1998	550 Maranello	(Pininfarina)	112481	L	175-225.000 USD	115.385*	148.500*	126.522*	19-08-17	Pebble Beach	142	G&Co
	Dark blue with dark blue leather interior; sold new to the USA; three owners; less than 14,500 miles covered.											
2004	360 Modena	(Pininfarina)	137981	L	130-160.000 USD	87.653	115.500	102.876	17-09-16	Aspen	108	TFA
	Titanium grey with dark grey interior; 17,004 miles on the odometer. Recently serviced.											
2001	360 Modena	(Pininfarina)	120075	L	40-50.000 GBP		NS		29-10-16	London	128	Coy
	Silver with dark blue interior; 12,620 miles covered. F1 gearbox (see lot 200 Coys 2.7.16 $54,456).											
1999	360 Modena	(Pininfarina)	117768	L	45-65.000 EUR	45.010*	54.680*	50.064*	30-10-16	Paris	105	Art
	Red; 49,800 kms covered. F1 gearbox.											
2002	360 Modena	(Pininfarina)	127579	L	70-90.000 EUR		NS		05-11-16	Lyon	255	Agu
	Grey with burgundy leather interior; last serviced in December 2014 at 31,900 kms. Manual gearbox.											
1999	360 Modena	(Pininfarina)	117046	L	55-65.000 EUR	66.783*	83.041*	78.400*	25-11-16	Milan	563	RMS
	Silver with black interior; 38,771 kms. From the Duemila Ruote collection.											
2002	360 Modena	(Pininfarina)	128219	L	48-58.000 GBP		NS		26-11-16	Weybridge	191	His
	Black with black interior; last serviced in November 2016.											
2002	360 Modena	(Pininfarina)	128305	L	NQ	54.193	66.000	61.901	15-01-17	Kissimmee	S258	Mec
	Red with black interior; believed to be 29,136 miles. F1 gearbox.											
2001	360 Modena	(Pininfarina)	126089	L	NQ		NS		15-01-17	Kissimmee	S264.1	Mec
	Yellow with black interior; manual gearbox.											
2000	360 Modena	(Pininfarina)	121727	L	NQ	49.266	60.000	56.274	15-01-17	Kissimmee	S65	Mec
	Red with natural leather interior; F1 gearbox.											
2003	360 Modena	(Pininfarina)	130753	L	85-125.000 USD	61.578*	75.900*	71.141*	19-01-17	Scottsdale	26	Bon F290
	Red with tan interior; 11,520 miles covered. Last serviced in November 2016. Sunroof.											
2001	360 Modena	(Pininfarina)	123613	L	NQ	71.667*	88.000*	82.764*	21-01-17	Scottsdale	993.1	B/J
	Silver with black leather interior; just over 21,000 miles covered. Recently serviced. Sunroof.											
2002	360 Modena	(Pininfarina)	129362	L	100-130.000 USD	67.188*	82.500*	77.591*	21-01-17	Scottsdale	143	G&Co
	Red with tan interior; one owner and 8,900 miles covered. Recently serviced. F1 gearbox.											

Year	Model (Bodybuilder)	Chassis no.	Steering	Estimate	Hammer price £	Hammer price $	Hammer price €	Date	Place	Lot	Auc. H.
2000	**360 Modena** (Pininfarina)	121762	L	NQ		NS		21-01-17	Scottsdale	8272	R&S
Blue; the engine was rebuilt under warranty at 5,000 miles and the clutch was replaced. Recently serviced.											
2004	**360 Modena** (Pininfarina)	139646	R	60-70.000 GBP		NS		18-02-17	London	365	Coy
Silver with black interior; described as in excellent overall condition. 27,800 miles on the odometer.											
2001	**360 Modena** (Pininfarina)	123187	L	75-80.000 USD		NS		01-04-17	Ft.Lauderdale	754	AA
Silver with black interior.											
2000	**360 Modena** (Pininfarina)	118508	R	60-70.000 GBP	55.575	72.453	65.101	18-05-17	London	135	Coy
Silver with dark blue leather interior; recently serviced.											
2000	**360 Modena** (Pininfarina)	122326	L	70-80.000 USD		NS		24-06-17	Santa Monica	165	RMS
Black with tan interior; one owner; less than 25,000 original miles; last serviced 1,500 miles ago. F1 gearbox.											
2000	**360 Modena** (Pininfarina)	121762	L	75-85.000 USD	53.613	69.000	58.788	19-08-17	Monterey	F132	Mec
See lot 8272 Russo & Steele 21.1.17.											
2004	**360 GTC** (Pininfarina)	2060	L	275-350.000 EUR		NS		27-05-17	Villa Erba	129	RMS
Blue; winner of the 2005 Italian and Spanish GT Championships; maintained by Michelotto; certified by Ferrari Classiche (see lot 342 RM 18.5.08 $179,002).											
2003	**360 Spider** (Pininfarina)	131109	R	65-75.000 GBP	67.000	89.499	79.228	08-09-16	Fontwell Park	125	Coy
Silver; 33,000 miles on the odometer.											
2002	**360 Spider** (Pininfarina)	129256	L	95-115.000 USD	66.783	88.000	78.382	17-09-16	Aspen	131	TFA
Light blue with blue interior; less than 11,900 miles covered. F1 gearbox.											
2003	**360 Spider** (Pininfarina)	131508	L	NA	72.813*	89.100*	80.983*	15-10-16	Las Vegas	711	B/J
Black with black interior; less than 9,500 miles covered. Last serviced 300 miles ago. F1 gearbox.											
2002	**360 Spider** (Pininfarina)	129149	L	NA	61.127*	74.800*	67.986*	15-10-16	Las Vegas	783	B/J
Silver with black interior; just over 31,000 miles covered. F1 gearbox.											
2004	**360 Spider** (Pininfarina)	139646	R	70-80.000 GBP		NS		29-10-16	London	147	Coy
Silver with black leather interior; 27,800 miles on the odometer. Cam belt replaced 400 miles ago.											
2004	**360 Spider** (Pininfarina)	136300	L	80-100.000 EUR		NS		30-10-16	Paris	168	Art
Silver; two owners. Manual gearbox.											
2001	**360 Spider** (Pininfarina)	124811	L	80-90.000 EUR	71.553*	88.973*	84.000*	25-11-16	Milan	554	RMS
Black with black interior; 16,043 kms. From the Duemila Ruote collection.											
2004	**360 Spider** (Pininfarina)	139646	R	70-80.000 GBP	72.475	88.253	82.781	14-01-17	Birmingham	127	Coy
See lot 147 Coys 29.10.16.											
2001	**360 Spider** (Pininfarina)	123818	L	NQ	45.161	55.000	51.585	15-01-17	Kissimmee	F298	Mec
Yellow with black and yellow interior; believed to be 18,350 miles. F1 gearbox.											
2004	**360 Spider** (Pininfarina)	138805	L	NQ	114.954	140.000	131.306	15-01-17	Kissimmee	S259.1	Mec
Red with tan interior; one owner and 377 miles. Recently serviced.											
2004	**360 Spider** (Pininfarina)	136806	L	130-150.000 USD	125.418*	154.000*	144.837*	20-01-17	Scottsdale	29	G&Co
Red with beige leather interior; less than 7,900 miles covered. Last serviced in March 2016.											
2004	**360 Spider** (Pininfarina)	137092	L	NQ	76.146*	93.500*	87.937*	21-01-17	Scottsdale	822.1	B/J
Yellow with black interior; less than 14,000 original miles. F1 gearbox.											
2003	**360 Spider** (Pininfarina)	130905	L	NQ		NS		21-01-17	Scottsdale	8299	R&S
Titanium grey with saddle interior; one owner and 30,000 miles covered. Manual gearbox. Last serviced in May 2016.											
2003	**360 Spider** (Pininfarina)	131124	L	NQ		NS		21-01-17	Scottsdale	8526	R&S
Titanium grey with navy blue leather interior; manual gearbox.											
2002	**360 Spider** (Pininfarina)	127192	L	80-120.000 EUR	75.347	94.678	88.550	09-02-17	Paris	409	Bon F291
Metallic black with tan interior; 8,642 kms covered. F1 gearbox. Recently serviced.											
2003	**360 Spider** (Pininfarina)	131599	L	95-110.000 USD	75.024	93.500	87.965	11-02-17	Boca Raton	128	TFA
Blue with beige interior; in very good overall condition. 5,698 miles covered. F1 gearbox.											
2001	**360 Spider** (Pininfarina)	124547	L	NQ		NS		18-02-17	Los Angeles	F163.1	Mec
Silver with black interior; manual gearbox.											

F289: 1998 Ferrari 550 Maranello (Pininfarina)

F290: 2003 Ferrari 360 Modena (Pininfarina)

Year	Model	(Bodybuilder)	Chassis no.	Steering	Estimate	£	$	€	Date	Place	Lot	Auc. H.
2002	360 Spider	(Pininfarina)	127763	L	80-90.000 GBP		NS		24-02-17	Stoneleigh P.	514	SiC
	Titanium grey with tan interior; last serviced in August 2016 at 4,546 kms; F1 gearbox.											
2001	360 Spider	(Pininfarina)	124540	R	62-68.000 GBP		NS		24-02-17	Stoneleigh P.	941	SiC
	Titanium grey with black leather interior; last serviced in April 2016 at 45,570 miles.											
2004	360 Spider	(Pininfarina)	138220	L	140-160.000 USD	90.486*	110.000*	103.664*	10-03-17	Amelia Island	47	G&Co
	Silver with black leather interior; showing 19,775 miles. Last serviced in early 2017.											
2001	360 Spider	(Pininfarina)	125058	R	85-95.000 GBP	90.000	111.969	104.184	29-03-17	Duxford	120	H&H
	Black with sand leather interior; 7,800 miles covered; recently serviced. F1 gearbox. Formerly owned by David Beckham.											
2001	360 Spider	(Pininfarina)	125790	R	68-75.000 GBP	68.500	85.221	79.296	29-03-17	Duxford	53	H&H
	Red with black interior; less than 20,000 miles covered. Last serviced in February 2017. F1 gearbox.											
2004	360 Spider	(Pininfarina)	137579	L	140-160.000 USD	121.030	151.250	141.464	01-04-17	Ft.Lauderdale	442	AA
	Red with tan interior; recently serviced; manual gearbox. One owner.											
2005	360 Spider	(Pininfarina)	140066	L	NQ		NS		08-04-17	Houston	F175	Mec
	Grey with red interior; believed to be 19,500 miles; F1 gearbox.											
2001	360 Spider	(Pininfarina)	123818	L	NQ	44.160	55.000	51.590	08-04-17	Houston	S145.1	Mec
	See lot F298 Mecum 15.1.17.											
2001	360 Spider	(Pininfarina)	123007	L	70-90.000 USD	66.851	87.000	77.822	20-05-17	Indianapolis	F212	Mec
	Metallic silver with caramel and parchment interior; 33,410 miles covered. Manual gearbox.											
2002	360 Spider	(Pininfarina)	128143	L	NQ		NS		20-05-17	Indianapolis	S42.1	Mec
	Light blue with cream interior; 13,900 original miles; recently serviced. Manual gearbox.											
2004	360 Spider	(Pininfarina)	135415	L	130-150.000 USD		NS		24-06-17	Santa Monica	223	RMS
	Metallic grey; less than 11,000 miles covered; recently serviced.											
2004	360 Spider	(Pininfarina)	136300	L	70-100.000 EUR	94.904	140.069	107.928	02-07-17	Monaco	107	Art
	See lot 168 Artcurial 30.10.16.											
2004	360 Spider	(Pininfarina)	137577	R	62-68.000 GBP	62.833	81.952	70.379	26-07-17	Duxford	91	H&H
	Blue with blue interior; last serviced in November 2016 at 16,642 miles. F1 gearbox.											
2001	360 Spider	(Pininfarina)	125088	C	95-120.000 USD		NS		19-08-17	Monterey	S154	Mec
	Red with tan interior; last serviced in June 2016 at 13,058 miles.											
2004	360 Challenge Stradale	(Pininfarina)	137059	L	185-225.000 USD		NS		17-09-16	Aspen	156	TFA
	Blue with dark blue leather interior; 25,000 miles. Recently serviced.											
2000	360 Challenge	(Pininfarina)	131424	L	45-55.000 EUR	73.938*	91.939*	86.800*	25-11-16	Milan	848	RMS
	Red. From the Duemila Ruote collection.											
2004	360 Challenge Stradale	(Pininfarina)	135696	L	145-165.000 EUR	190.808*	237.261*	224.000*	25-11-16	Milan	872	RMS
	Black with red leather interior; 16,650 kms. From the Duemila Ruote collection.											
2004	360 Challenge Stradale	(Pininfarina)	138116	L	350-450.000 USD	322.502	396.000	372.438	20-01-17	Scottsdale	59	G&Co
	Red with Tricolore racing stripe and red and black alcantara interior; two owners and 260 kms covered. Last serviced in October 2015.											
2004	360 Challenge Stradale	(Pininfarina)	138421	L	NQ	152.293*	187.000*	175.874*	21-01-17	Scottsdale	1314	B/J
	Yellow with black interior; 14,015 miles covered (see lot 761 Barrett-Jackson 28.9.13 $95,700).											
2004	360 Challenge Stradale	(Pininfarina)	139041	L	250-300.000 USD	188.126	231.000	217.256	21-01-17	Scottsdale	110	G&Co
	Red with Tricolore stripe and black leather interior; three owners and less than 10,000 kms covered.											
2004	360 Challenge Stradale	(Pininfarina)	138735	L	160-200.000 EUR	143.329	179.172	168.000	08-02-17	Paris	116	RMS F292
	Yellow with black interior; 28,000 kms on the odometer. Last serviced in April 2016 (see lot 146 Artcurial 1.11.15 $206,415).											
2005	360 Challenge	(Pininfarina)	126986	L	50-75.000 USD	49.190*	63.250*	58.152*	13-05-17	Auburn	L266	AA
	Red; raced; F1 gearbox.											
2004	360 Challenge Stradale	(Pininfarina)	138789	L	155-175.000 GBP	161.167	210.113	188.791	18-05-17	London	127	Coy
	Red with black leather interior; 24,000 kms on the odometer. Recently serviced.											
2004	360 Challenge Stradale	(Pininfarina)	136965	L	190-215.000 USD		NS		24-06-17	Santa Monica	202	RMS
	Red with red alcantara interior; 13,000 miles covered; recently serviced.											
2004	360 Challenge Stradale	(Pininfarina)	136535	L	200-250.000 EUR		NS		02-07-17	Monaco	179	Art
	Red; 16,800 kms covered; last serviced in 2016.											

F291: 2002 Ferrari 360 Spider (Pininfarina)

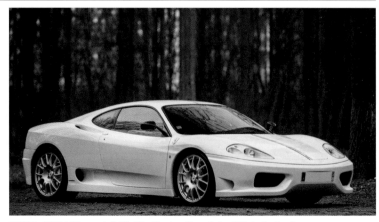

F292: 2004 Ferrari 360 Challenge Stradale (Pininfarina)

Year	Model	(Bodybuilder)	Chassis No.	Steering	Estimate	£	$	€	Date	Place	Lot	Auc. H.
2004	**360 Challenge Stradale**	(Pininfarina)	136755	L	175-200.000 USD		NS		19-08-17	Monterey	S156	**Mec**
	Black with red and black interior; 22,532 miles covered; F1 gearbox.											
2004	**360 Challenge Stradale**	(Pininfarina)	139182	L	275-325.000 USD	200.855*	258.500*	220.242*	19-08-17	Monterey	224	**RMS**
	Red; 3,847 miles on the odometer; last serviced in March 2017. From the Ferrari Performance Collection.											
2001	**550 Barchetta Pininfarina**		126233	L	380-420.000 EUR		NA		08-10-16	Paris	185	**CB/C**
	Blue with dark grey interior; one owner. Last serviced in April 2016.											
2001	**550 Barchetta Pininfarina**		124291	L	240-280.000 EUR	305.292*	379.617*	358.400*	25-11-16	Milan	604	**RMS**
	Yellow with charcoal interior; 7,931 kms. From the Duemila Ruote collection.											
2001	**550 Barchetta Pininfarina**		124279	L	375-425.000 EUR	324.880	406.123	380.800	08-02-17	Paris	118	**RMS** F293
	Red with black interior; 393 kms covered. Swiss papers.											
2001	**550 Barchetta Pininfarina**		123690	L	350-450.000 EUR		NS		10-02-17	Paris	103	**Art**
	Red with black and beige interior; three owners and 6,980 kms covered. Recently serviced.											
2001	**550 Barchetta Pininfarina**		124295	L	575-650.000 USD		NS		11-03-17	Amelia Island	226	**RMS**
	Black with beige interior with black inserts; 1,672 original miles. Last serviced in 2017.											
2001	**550 Barchetta Pininfarina**		124202	L	360-400.000 EUR	322.254	413.804	369.600	27-05-17	Villa Erba	165	**RMS**
	Red; less than 3,800 kms covered; certified by Ferrari Classiche (see lots 164 Coys 23.10.10 NA and 118 Artcurial 2.6.15 $313,831).											
2003	**Enzo**	(Pininfarina)	132648	L	1.200-1.400.000 GBP		NS		07-09-16	London	125	**RMS**
	Red with black interior; 1,471 miles on the odometer. Last serviced in October 2015. Sold new to the USA; front end damaged in a road accident and subsequently repaired. In 2008 reimported into Europe (see lot 366 Bonhams 26.6.15 $1,411,409).											
2003	**Enzo**	(Pininfarina)	132650	L	2.800-3.200.000 USD		NS		19-01-17	Scottsdale	15	**Bon**
	Yellow with black leather interior; just over 3,600 miles covered; recently serviced (see lot 564 RM 15.8.09 NS).											
2003	**Enzo**	(Pininfarina)	133026	L	2.700-3.000.000 USD	2.186.454	2.695.000	2.526.024	19-01-17	Phoenix	151	**RMS** F294
	Red with tan leather interior; last serviced in September 2016 at 3,620 miles. First and sole owner the designer Tommy Hilfiger.											
2004	**Enzo**	(Pininfarina)	135892	L	1.900-2.200.000 EUR		NS		27-05-17	Villa Erba	153	**RMS**
	Red; less than 13,500 kms covered; certified by Ferrari Classiche.											
2003	**Enzo**	(Pininfarina)	133118	L	2.000-2.500.000 USD	1.585.469	2.040.500	1.738.506	18-08-17	Carmel	42	**Bon**
	Black with saddle leather interior; since 2005 in the current second ownership; 17,302 miles covered; last serviced in July 2017. Ferrari Classiche certification in progress.											
2003	**Enzo**	(Pininfarina)	134956	L	2.700-3.000.000 USD		NS		19-08-17	Monterey	S120	**Mec**
	Red with black interior; 151 miles covered.											
2002	**575M Maranello**	(Pininfarina)	129307	R	80-100.000 GBP	134.400	179.854	160.057	07-09-16	London	164	**RMS**
	Dark green with beige leather interior; two owners and less than 16,500 miles covered. Fitted in 2004 with the Fiorano Handling Package. From the estate of Edward Carter.											
2003	**575M Maranello**	(Pininfarina)	128299	L	180-230.000 EUR		NS		07-10-16	Zoute	20	**Bon**
	Red with black leather interior; last serviced in May 2016 at 50,045 kms (see lot 136 Artcurial 9.7.16 NS).											
2002	**575M Maranello**	(Pininfarina)	130814	L	85-100.000 EUR		NA		08-10-16	Paris	191	**CB/C**
	Black with black interior; one owner and 40,000 kms covered.											
2003	**575M Maranello**	(Pininfarina)	132139	L	160-180.000 EUR	181.267*	225.398*	212.800*	25-11-16	Milan	606	**RMS**
	Blue with saddle interior; manual gearbox. 31,354 kms. From the Duemila Ruote collection.											
2002	**575M Maranello**	(Pininfarina)	129840	L	110-130.000 EUR	87.772*	109.140*	103.040*	25-11-16	Milan	879	**RMS**
	Titanium grey with charcoal interior; 20,242 kms. From the Duemila Ruote collection.											
2003	**575M Maranello**	(Pininfarina)	132937	L	130-150.000 GBP		NS		07-12-16	London	338	**Bon**
	Red with cream leather interior; sold new to Spain and imported into the UK in 2014. Last serviced in February 2016 at 9,391 kms.											
2002	**575M Maranello**	(Pininfarina)	129484	L	180-240.000 USD	129.897*	159.500*	150.010*	20-01-17	Scottsdale	48	**G&Co**
	Black with tan leather interior; less than 11,800 miles covered. Last serviced in 2015.											
2002	**575M Maranello**	(Pininfarina)	129467	L	200-250.000 USD	152.293*	187.000*	175.874*	20-01-17	Phoenix	257	**RMS** F295
	Red with black interior; 251 kms covered. Fitted with the Fiorano Handling Package (see lot S71.1 Mecum 20.8.16 NS).											
2002	**575M Maranello**	(Pininfarina)	129306	L	350-425.000 USD	250.835	308.000	289.674	21-01-17	Scottsdale	148	**G&Co**
	Titanium grey with red leather interior; in original condition; four owners and approximately 16,500 miles covered; last serviced in December 2016; manual gearbox.											
2003	**575M Maranello**	(Pininfarina)	132339	L	80-120.000 EUR	69.476	87.300	81.650	09-02-17	Paris	416	**Bon**
	Black with black interior; sold new to Japan. Circa 16,000 kms covered.											

F293: 2001 Ferrari 550 Barchetta Pininfarina

F294: 2003 Ferrari Enzo (Pininfarina)

Year	Model	(Bodybuilder)	Chassis no.	Steering	Estimate	Hammer Price £	$	€	Date	Place	Lot	Auc. H.
2003	575M Maranello	(Pininfarina)	130629	L	295-315.000 USD		NS		11-02-17	Boca Raton	123	TFA
	Titanium grey with dark blue interior; 15,000 miles covered. Recently serviced.											
2004	575M Maranello	(Pininfarina)	136922	L	NQ		NS		18-02-17	Los Angeles	S140.1	Mec
	Red; last serviced in March 2016 at 9,731 miles.											
2005	575M Maranello	(Pininfarina)	141040	L	130-150.000 GBP	146.250	183.602	173.058	24-02-17	Stoneleigh P.	922	SiC
	Red with deep red interior; one owner and 3,299 kms covered. Last serviced in June 2015 (see Silverstone Auctions lots 229 28.5.16 NS and 534 30.7.16 NS).											
2003	575M Maranello	(Pininfarina)	131554	L	NQ	120.435*	150.000*	140.700*	08-04-17	Houston	S29	Mec
	Dark blue with red interior; 10,075 original miles. Recently serviced. Fiorano Performance Handling package. From the Laquay Automobile Collection.											
2004	575M Maranello	(Pininfarina)	131566	L	120-160.000 EUR		NS		10-06-17	Lyon	136	Agu
	Black with black leather interior; in excellent overall condition. Recently serviced.											
2003	575M Maranello	(Pininfarina)	131554	L	150-175.000 USD		NS		24-06-17	Santa Monica	210	RMS
	See lot S29 Mecum 8.4.17.											
2003	575M Maranello	(Pininfarina)	133936	L	70-80.000 GBP	61.500	79.815	69.636	29-06-17	Fontwell Park	110	Coy
	Black with black leather interior; imported into the UK from Japan in 2016.											
2002	575M Maranello	(Pininfarina)	123761	L	160-200.000 GBP	120.000	155.736	135.876	29-06-17	Fontwell Park	129	Coy
	Red with beige leather interior; pre-production example used by the factory for marketing and PR purposes and sold to its first private owner in 2008. Less than 13,000 kms on the odometer (see lot 153 RM/Sotheby's 7.9.15 $111,107).											
2003	575M Maranello	(Pininfarina)	132924	L	135-145.000 GBP	100.000	129.780	113.230	29-06-17	Fontwell Park	146	Coy
	Red; described as in very good overall condition; 14,560 kms covered.											
2004	575M Maranello	(Pininfarina)	139492	L	120-150.000 EUR		NS		02-07-17	Monaco	212	Art
	Red with black leather interior; 26,500 kms covered.											
2002	575M Maranello	(Pininfarina)	123761	L	130-160.000 EUR	105.695	138.945	117.075	05-08-17	Schloss Dyck	249	Coy
	See lot 129 Coys 29.6.17.											
2007	612 Scaglietti	(Pininfarina)	155490	L	NA	85.977	106.000	99.725	19-11-16	Anaheim	S104.1	Mec
	Black with black interior; just one owner.											
2005	612 Scaglietti	(Pininfarina)	145751	L	45-55.000 EUR	81.093*	100.836*	95.200*	25-11-16	Milan	585	RMS
	Black with black interior; F1 gearbox. 29,401 kms. From the Duemila Ruote collection.											
2005	612 Scaglietti	(Pininfarina)	140444	L	NQ		NS		18-02-17	Los Angeles	S52	Mec
	Black with beige interior; 8,500 miles covered.											
2006	612 Scaglietti	(Pininfarina)	143698	L	70-90.000 EUR	68.904	85.166	79.320	18-03-17	Lyon	200	Agu F296
	Black with tan interior; last serviced in September 2016. Fitted with the HGTS package.											
2004	612 Scaglietti	(Pininfarina)	138584	R	65-75.000 GBP		NS		29-07-17	Silverstone	716	SiC
	Metallic rubin red with cream leather interior; imported into the UK from Japan in 2015; 36,200 miles covered.											
2005	612 Scaglietti	(Pininfarina)	140444	L	110-125.000 USD	66.045	85.000	72.420	19-08-17	Monterey	S35	Mec
	See lot S52 Mecum 18.2.17.											
2005	F430	(Pininfarina)	142951	L	155-175.000 USD	102.452	135.000	120.245	17-09-16	Aspen	118	TFA
	Black with black interior; last serviced in April 2016. 6-speed manual gearbox.											
2005	F430	(Pininfarina)	150500	L	75-85.000 EUR		NA		08-10-16	Paris	136	CB/C
	Red with black interior; F1 gearbox.											
2007	F430	(Pininfarina)	152947	L	60-80.000 EUR	80.649	98.688	89.700	15-10-16	Salzburg	432	Dor
	Red with black interior; in good overall condition. 34,352 kms covered. F1 gearbox.											
2007	F430	(Pininfarina)	155809	L	NQ	74.046	92.500	83.380	04-11-16	Dallas	S69.1	Mec
	Black with black interior; last serviced less than 600 miles ago. F1 gearbox.											
2005	F430	(Pininfarina)	140887	L	65-75.000 GBP		NS		05-12-16	London	134	Coy
	Red with champagne leather interior; 44,000 kms covered.											
2007	F430	(Pininfarina)	153916	L	250-350.000 USD	216.054	270.000	252.531	01-04-17	Ft.Lauderdale	569	AA
	Red with beige leather interior; less than 6,000 original miles; F1 gearbox. First owner President Donald Trump.											
2005	F430	(Pininfarina)	141978	L	150-165.000 USD		NS		01-04-17	Ft.Lauderdale	785	AA
	Red with tan interior; manual gearbox.											

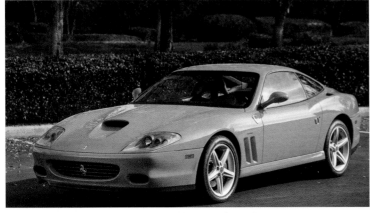

F295: 2002 Ferrari 575M Maranello (Pininfarina)

F296: 2006 Ferrari 612 Scaglietti (Pininfarina)

Year	Model (Bodybuilder)	Chassis No.	Steering	Estimate	Hammer price £	Hammer price $	Hammer price €	Sale Date	Sale Place	Sale Lot	Auc. H.
2006	F430 (Pininfarina)	148988	R	125-155.000 GBP		NS		29-07-17	Silverstone	424	SiC
	Red with black leather interior; one owner; last serviced in February 2016 at 547 miles; F1 gearbox.										
2006	F430 Challenge (Pininfarina)	147104	L	75-90.000 EUR		NA		08-10-16	Paris	119	CB/C
	Light blue; described as in very good condition.										
2006	F430 Challenge (Pininfarina)	145768	L	140-160.000 USD	96.303*	118.250*	111.214*	21-01-17	Scottsdale	131	G&Co
	Red; approximately 2,500 miles on the odometer. Recently serviced.										
2006	F430 Challenge (Pininfarina)	146816	L	130-180.000 EUR	121.999	152.037	143.040	10-02-17	Paris	100	Art
	Red and white; the car was raced at the Ferrari Challenge from 2006 to 2008, winning the European Championship in 2006 driven by Ange Barde. Described as in very good condition.										
2008	F430 GTC (Pininfarina)	2616	L	300-400.000 EUR	391.766*	489.737*	459.200*	08-02-17	Paris	154	RMS F297
	Red; bought new by the BMS Scuderia Italia, the car was raced during the 2008 and 2009 seasons, winning the 2008 Spa 24 Hours. Retired from competition it was refurbished by BMS and put into the personal collection of one of the team's benefactors. Sold on a Swiss bill of sale; documented with Ferrari Certificate of Origin.										
2006	F430 GT2 (Pininfarina)	2440	L	175-225.000 USD	175.371	225.500	207.325	13-05-17	Auburn	L246	AA
	White; in ready to race condition. Used as a spare/test car.										
2008	F430 Spider (Pininfarina)	160071	R	NA		NS		02-09-16	Salon Privé	208	SiC
	Grey with cream interior; manual gearbox. 13,100 miles covered; last serviced in July 2016.										
2006	F430 Spider (Pininfarina)	145771	L	NQ	73.646	92.000	82.929	04-11-16	Dallas	S70.1	Mec
	Medium metallic grey with black interior; 18,000 actual miles. F1 gearbox.										
2008	F430 Spider (Pininfarina)	162755	R	100-120.000 GBP	142.800	180.057	167.804	07-12-16	Chateau Impney	10	H&H
	White with red leather interior; one owner and just over 400 miles covered. F1 gearbox.										
2008	F430 Spider (Pininfarina)	163293	L	150-175.000 USD		NS		15-01-17	Kissimmee	F240	Mec
	Black with black leather interior; 5,800 actual miles.										
2006	F430 Spider (Pininfarina)	150022	L	NQ	89.584*	110.000*	103.455*	21-01-17	Scottsdale	1450	B/J
	Black with black interior; 13,047 actual miles. F1 gearbox.										
2004	F430 Spider (Pininfarina)	149655	L	80-90.000 GBP	79.900	98.756	91.973	19-03-17	Goodwood	34	Bon
	Red with tan interior; one owner; 11,920 kms covered; F1 gearbox.										
2007	F430 Spider (Pininfarina)	151470	L	NQ	101.567*	126.500*	118.657*	08-04-17	Palm Beach	745	B/J
	Yellow with black and yellow interior; less than 11,000 miles covered. F1 gearbox.										
2008	F430 Spider (Pininfarina)	162987	L	100-130.000 USD	77.794	99.000	88.605	24-06-17	Santa Monica	238	RMS
	Metallic grey with black interior; less than 28,000 miles covered.										
2005	F430 Spider (Pininfarina)	142721	L	80-90.000 EUR	72.477	95.276	80.280	05-08-17	Schloss Dyck	208	Coy
	Titanium grey with burgundy leather interior; 500 kms covered since the last service. F1 gearbox.										
2008	F430 Scuderia (Pininfarina)	163729	L	155-175.000 EUR	172.238*	214.170*	202.200*	25-11-16	Milan	873	RMS
	Silver with black alcantara interior; 1,792 kms. From the Duemila Ruote collection.										
2008	F430 Scuderia (Pininfarina)	163642	L	220-300.000 USD	150.207	182.600	172.082	11-03-17	Amelia Island	17	Mot
	Black with red leather interior; 4,343 actual miles. F1 gearbox.										
2008	F430 Scuderia (Pininfarina)	164103	L	110-130.000 GBP	112.500	147.319	125.606	29-07-17	Silverstone	451	SiC
	Red with black alcantara interior; 50,954 kms covered. Last serviced in 2016.										
2009	F430 Scuderia (Pininfarina)	167241	L	250-300.000 USD	179.487*	231.000*	196.812*	19-08-17	Monterey	214	RMS
	Red with grey alcantara interior; 3,716 miles covered. From the Ferrari Performance Collection.										
2009	F430 Scuderia Spider 16M (Pininfarina)	168947	L	325-400.000 EUR	296.214	370.289	347.200	08-02-17	Paris	140	RMS F298
	Red with black and red alcantara interior; one owner and 674 kms covered. Last serviced in October 2016. One of 499 examples built.										
2009	F430 Scuderia Spider 16M (Pininfarina)	166332	L	NQ	173.032	215.000	201.864	18-02-17	Los Angeles	F127.1	Mec
	Blue with black interior.										
2009	F430 Scuderia Spider 16M (Pininfarina)	168547	L	400-450.000 USD		NS		19-08-17	Monterey	S139	Mec
	Red fire with black interior; 2,110 original miles. Certified by Ferrari Classiche.										
2009	F430 Scuderia Spider 16M (Pininfarina)	166787	L	375-400.000 USD		NS		19-08-17	Monterey	S148	Mec
	Black with black interior; 10,062 original miles.										
2009	F430 Scuderia Spider 16M (Pininfarina)	166916	L	350-400.000 USD	286.325*	368.500*	313.962*	19-08-17	Monterey	223	RMS
	Red; 2,525 miles covered; last serviced in 2016. Three owners. From the Ferrari Performance Collection.										

F297: 2008 Ferrari F430 GTC (Pininfarina)

F298: 2009 Ferrari F430 Scuderia Spider 16M (Pininfarina)

Year	Model (Bodybuilder)	Chassis No.	Steering	Estimate	Hammer Price £	Hammer Price $	Hammer Price €	Date	Place	Lot	Auc. H.
2005	**Superamerica (Pininfarina)**	145099	L	490-550.000 USD		NS		17-09-16	Aspen	130	TFA
Red with tan seats with black inserts; less than 3,700 miles on the odometer.
2006	**Superamerica (Pininfarina)**	145394	L	220-250.000 EUR	343.454*	427.069*	403.200*	25-11-16	Milan	603	RMS
Blue with beige interior; sold new in Italy. 18,020 kms. From the Duemila Ruote collection.
2005	**Superamerica (Pininfarina)**	143339	L	375-450.000 USD	255.252	313.500	293.969	18-01-17	Scottsdale	55	WoA
Green with cream interior; in very good overall condition. Low mileage (see Russo & Steele lots 5247 30.1.16 NS and 7084 20.8.16 NS).
2005	**Superamerica (Pininfarina)**	142098	L	300-350.000 EUR		NS		08-02-17	Paris	158	RMS
Red with sand interior; two owners and 11,000 kms covered. Swiss papers.
2006	**Superamerica (Pininfarina)**	141819	L	350-450.000 EUR	326.347	406.700	382.632	10-02-17	Paris	104	Art F299
Red with black leather interior; three owners and 6,500 kms covered. Last serviced in January 2017.
2005	**Superamerica (Pininfarina)**	145099	L	400-450.000 USD		NS		09-03-17	Amelia Island	138	Bon
See lot 130 The Finest Automobile Auctions 17.9.16.
2006	**Superamerica (Pininfarina)**	146669	L	280-340.000 EUR	251.925	327.824	293.250	21-05-17	SPA-Francorch.	83	Bon
Red with beige leather interior; one owner; 21,000 kms covered.
2006	**Superamerica (Pininfarina)**	146056	L	550-600.000 EUR		NS		27-05-17	Villa Erba	131	RMS
Red with black interior; two owners; 15,000 kms covered; manual gearbox.
2005	**Superamerica (Pininfarina)**	145724	L	375-450.000 USD	329.060*	423.500*	360.822*	19-08-17	Monterey	219	RMS
Silverstone grey with black leather interior; optioned with the Fiorano Handling Package; less than 1,750 miles covered. Recently serviced. From the Ferrari Performance Collection.
2010	**599 GTB Fiorano (Pininfarina)**	169870	L	275-300.000 USD		NS		17-09-16	Aspen	159	TFA
Black with black interior; 7,829 miles. Fitted with the HGTE package.
2007	**599 GTB Fiorano (Pininfarina)**	152969	L	275-325.000 EUR	457.938*	569.426*	537.600*	25-11-16	Milan	587	RMS
Medium grey with saddle interior; manual gearbox. 2,441 kms. From the Duemila Ruote collection.
2008	**599 GTB Fiorano (Pininfarina)**	162352	L	175-225.000 USD	164.220	200.000	187.580	15-01-17	Kissimmee	F160.1	Mec
Black with tan interior; one owner and 3,621 miles covered.
2010	**599 GTB Fiorano (Pininfarina)**	175172	L	210-235.000 USD	143.693	175.000	164.133	15-01-17	Kissimmee	S187	Mec
Red with black interior; fitted with the HGTE handling package.
2007	**599 GTB Fiorano (Pininfarina)**	152365	L	700-800.000 USD		NS		10-03-17	Amelia Island	54	G&Co
Red with beige leather interior; 333 miles on the odometer. One of 20 US market examples fitted with the 6-speed manual gearbox.
2007	**599 GTB Fiorano (Pininfarina)**	150549	L	425-500.000 USD	330.083	412.500	385.811	01-04-17	Ft.Lauderdale	554	AA
Black with black leather interior; sold new to the USA; two owners, 16,582 miles covered. Manual gearbox.
2010	**599 GTB Fiorano (Pininfarina)**	172495	L	NQ	160.741	200.200	187.788	08-04-17	Palm Beach	732	B/J
Yellow with matt black roof and black leather and alcantara interior; 7,181 actual miles. HGTE package.
2007	**599 GTB Fiorano (Pininfarina)**	154019	L	NQ		NS		08-04-17	Houston	S123.1	Mec
Medium grey with saddle interior.
2007	**599 GTB Fiorano (Pininfarina)**	151574	R	100-120.000 GBP		NS		20-05-17	Ascot	137	His
Red with tan interior; 21,126 miles covered. Last serviced in April 2017.
2008	**599 GTB Fiorano (Pininfarina)**	157642	L	82-94.000 GBP	84.000	109.301	97.776	20-05-17	Ascot	207	His
Red with matt black roof and black interior; last serviced in April 2017.
2009	**599 GTB Fiorano (Pininfarina)**	166699	L	225-250.000 USD		NS		20-05-17	Indianapolis	S88.1	Mec
Red; 2,533 miles covered.
2007	**599 GTB Fiorano (Pininfarina)**	152781	L	125-175.000 USD	104.590	133.100	119.125	24-06-17	Santa Monica	164	RMS F300
Just over 12,000 miles covered.
2010	**599 GTB Fiorano (Pininfarina)**	171669	L	NQ	120.435	155.000	132.060	19-08-17	Monterey	F43	Mec
Black with black interior; with HGTE handling package.
2012	**Ferrari California (Pininfarina)**	188520	L	NA	143.827	176.000	159.966	15-10-16	Las Vegas	752	B/J
White with brown interior; 7,700 actual miles.
2012	**Ferrari California (Pininfarina)**	185151	R	90-110.000 GBP	126.560	159.580	148.721	07-12-16	Chateau Impney	75	H&H
Red with beige leather interior; one owner and just over 500 miles covered.

F299: 2006 Ferrari Superamerica (Pininfarina)

F300: 2007 Ferrari 599 GTB Fiorano (Pininfarina)

F301: 2010 Ferrari Ferrari California (Pininfarina)

F302: 2011 Ferrari 599 GTO (Ferrari & PF)

Year	Model (Bodybuilder)	Chassis no.	Steering	Estimate	£	$	€	Date	Place	Lot	Auc. H.
2011	Ferrari California (Pininfarina)	181555	L	NQ	125.418*	154.000*	144.837*	21-01-17	Scottsdale	1334	B/J
Red with tan leather interior; one owner. Recently serviced.											
2010	Ferrari California (Pininfarina)	175388	L	175-225.000 USD	143.745	185.000	157.620	19-08-17	Monterey	S114.1	Mec F301
White with white leather interior; 476 miles covered.											
2012	Ferrari California (Pininfarina)	188520	L	180-200.000 USD	139.860	180.000	153.360	19-08-17	Monterey	S123	Mec
See lot 752 Barrett-Jackson 15.10.16.											
2011	599 GTO (Ferrari & PF)	178253	L	525-600.000 EUR	383.918	479.925	450.000	08-02-17	Paris	120	RMS F302
Red with matt Silverstone grey roof; 17,000 kms covered. Recently serviced.											
2010	599 GTO (Ferrari & PF)	173507	L	500-700.000 EUR		NS		10-02-17	Paris	124	Art
Red with matt dark grey roof and bonnet and black interior; since 2015 in the current ownership. 11,700 kms covered.											
2011	599 GTO (Ferrari & PF)	177029	L	650-750.000 USD		NS		24-06-17	Santa Monica	226	RMS
White with dark blue alcantara and black cloth interior; 2,739 miles covered.											
2011	599 GTO (Ferrari & PF)	182726	L	380-440.000 GBP		NS		30-06-17	Goodwood	250	Bon
White with red and black interior; sold new to Taiwan. 5,964 kms covered. Serviced in 2011, 2013 and 2015.											
2011	599 GTO (Ferrari & PF)	175165	L	700-800.000 USD	572.649*	737.000*	627.924*	19-08-17	Monterey	217	RMS
Red with black roof and black leather interior; 511 miles covered. From the Ferrari Performance Collection.											
2013	458 Italia (Pininfarina)	194470	L	220-250.000 USD		NS		15-01-17	Kissimmee	S249	Mec
Metallic black with black and tan leather interior; 13,000 actual miles.											
2013	458 Italia (Pininfarina)	189375	L	NQ	185.104	230.000	215.947	18-02-17	Los Angeles	S107	Mec
Red with natural leather interior; 1,321 miles covered (see lot S110 Mecum 15.8.15 $215,000).											
2012	458 Italia (Pininfarina)	182705	L	175-225.000 USD	151.515	195.000	166.140	19-08-17	Monterey	F64	Mec
Red with beige leather interior; 2,200 miles covered.											
2012	458 Aperta (Pininfarina)	188774	L	225-265.000 USD		NS		11-03-17	Amelia Island	64	Mot
Red with leather and alcantara interior; less than 10,000 miles covered.											
2012	458 Challenge (Pininfarina)	195603	L	175-225.000 USD	158.440	198.000	185.189	01-04-17	Ft.Lauderdale	495	AA
Sold new to the USA, the car raced the 2014 and 2015 Ferrari Challenge series.											
2012	458 GTD (Pininfarina)	F142GT33486GAM	L	175-225.000 USD	183.926*	236.500*	217.438*	13-05-17	Auburn	L239	AA
Black; in ready to race condition. In 2014 6th in class and 23rd overall at the Daytona 24 Hours and 24th overall at the Sebring 12 Hours.											
2012	458 GTD (Pininfarina)	F142GT33484GAM	L	225-275.000 USD	359.297*	462.000*	424.763*	13-05-17	Auburn	L244	AA F303
Black; first in class and 18th overall at the 2014 Daytona 24 Hours and subsequently raced at several other events.											
2011	SA Aperta (Ferrari & PF)	181885	L	1.200-1.400.000 USD	1.209.384	1.485.000	1.396.643	20-01-17	Scottsdale	51	G&Co F304
Titanium grey with black leather interior; sold new to the USA; three owners and 2,500 miles covered; certified by Ferrari Classiche.											
2011	SA Aperta (Ferrari & PF)	182822	L	1.400-1.500.000 USD		NS		19-08-17	Monterey	S71	Mec
Red; 281 miles covered.											

F303: 2012 Ferrari 458 GTD (Pininfarina)

F304: 2011 Ferrari SA Aperta (Ferrari & PF)

Year	Model	(Bodybuilder)	Chassis no.	Steering	Estimate	Hammer Price £	Hammer Price $	Hammer Price €	Date	Place	Lot	Auc. H.
2012	FF	(Pininfarina)	186118	L	200-250.000 USD	155.400	200.000	170.400	19-08-17	Monterey	S40.1	Mec F305
White with red leather interior; 634 miles covered.												
2015	F12 Berlinetta	(Ferrari & PF)	210532	L	NQ	268.752*	330.000*	310.365*	21-01-17	Scottsdale	1374	B/J
White with black interior; 964 miles covered.												
2016	F12 TdF Berlinetta	(Ferrari & PF)	217175	L	750-800.000 EUR		NS		27-05-17	Villa Erba	156	RMS
Blu Swaters with black alcantara interior.												
2017	F12 TdF Berlinetta	(Ferrari & PF)	222794	L	1.350-1.500.000 USD	971.250	1.250.000	1.065.000	19-08-17	Monterey	S79	Mec F306
Yellow with black stripes and black alcantara interior; 84 miles covered.												
2015	458 Speciale	(Ferrari & PF)	207560	L	390-440.000 USD		NS		11-03-17	Amelia Island	50	Mot
Silver; 1,380 actual miles.												
2015	458 Speciale A	(Ferrari & PF)	213929	L	500-700.000 EUR	474.522	700.345	539.640	02-07-17	Monaco	123	Art F307
White with black stripes; one owner; 4,200 kms covered.												
2015	458 Speciale A	(Ferrari & PF)	212840	L	700-750.000 USD	481.740	620.000	528.240	19-08-17	Monterey	S126	Mec
Yellow with black and yellow leather interior; 1,207 miles covered.												
2016	LaFerrari	(Ferrari Styling Center)	TBA	L	NA	5.544.700	7.000.000	6.577.200	04-12-16	Daytona Beach	NA	RMS TOP TEN
The proceeds of the sale of the car, gifted by Ferrari factory, will benefit the reconstruction of Central Italy in the aftermath of the earthquakes of 2016. The car boasts a one-of-a-kind livery and interior, as well as a special plaque to commemorate the occasion. The auction was held in collaboration with the National Italian American Foundation's Earthquake Relief found.												
2015	LaFerrari	(Ferrari Styling Center)	210482	L	3.800-4.500.000 USD		NS		10-03-17	Amelia Island	73	G&Co
Yellow with black interior; one owner; 130 miles covered.												
2014	LaFerrari	(Ferrari Styling Center)	205216	L	NA	2.926.550	3.740.000	3.495.778	22-04-17	Dallas	465	Lea
Red with leather and alcantara interior; one owner; 569 miles covered.												
2014	LaFerrari	(Ferrari Styling Center)	201167	L	2.750-3.200.000 EUR		NS		27-05-17	Villa Erba	147	RMS
Red with black interior; 200 kms covered; sold new in Italy.												
2015	LaFerrari	(Ferrari Styling Center)	209257	L	3.300-3.900.000 USD	2.735.040	3.520.000	2.999.040	18-08-17	Pebble Beach	54	G&Co
Yellow with black leather interior; approximately 200 miles covered.												
2014	LaFerrari	(Ferrari Styling Center)	205216	L	Refer Dpt.	2.680.650	3.450.000	2.939.400	19-08-17	Monterey	S102	Mec
See lot 465 Leake 22.4.17 $3,740,000).												
2015	LaFerrari	(Ferrari Styling Center)	212349	L	4.500-4.700.000 USD		NS		19-08-17	Monterey	S80	Mec
White with red interior; 209 original miles.												
2015	LaFerrari	(Ferrari Styling Center)	211998	L	3.300-3.800.000 USD	2.649.570	3.410.000	2.905.320	19-08-17	Monterey	227	RMS F308
Black with black leather interior; one owner; 4,000 miles covered; recently serviced. Under factory warranty until July 2018.												
2017	488 Spider	(Ferrari Styling Center)	221424	L	NQ	341.430	434.500	388.878	24-06-17	Northeast	657	B/J
Red with black interior; 77 actual miles.												

FERVES (I) (1966-1971)

Year	Model		Chassis no.	Steering	Estimate	£	$	€	Date	Place	Lot	Auc. H.
1969	Ranger		11501212(engine)	L	15-30.000 EUR	14.050	18.664	16.675	03-09-16	Chantilly	2	Bon F309
Orange with black interior; it needs little work to complete the restoration.												

FIAT (I) (1899-)

Year	Model	(Bodybuilder)	Chassis no.	Steering	Estimate	£	$	€	Date	Place	Lot	Auc. H.
1913	12/15hp Tipo 1A torpedo		23117	R	40-50.000 EUR	34.249	43.035	40.250	09-02-17	Paris	410	Bon F310
Red with black wings; since 1992 in the current ownership, restored in 1993. Used in France in several movies and historic events.												
1927	509 torpedo		144591(engine)	R	20-30.000 USD	11.113*	14.300*	12.726*	03-10-16	Philadelphia	226	Bon
Imported into the USA from Italy in 1987; restored in the 1990s.												
1933	508 Balilla pickup		019240	L	18-23.000 EUR	9.785*	12.296*	11.500*	09-02-17	Paris	307	Bon
In unrestored, largely original condition.												
1935	508 Balilla van		080084	R	25-30.000 GBP	20.007	25.857	22.738	15-07-17	Blenheim Pal.	101	Coy
Restored in recent year.												
1935	508 S Berlinetta Mille Miglia		508S085264	L	45-55.000 EUR	152.646*	189.809*	179.200*	25-11-16	Milan	631	RMS F311
Blue; for restoration. From the Duemila Ruote collection.												
1937	500A Topolino		028474	R	16-20.000 GBP		NS		08-09-16	Fontwell Park	133	Coy
Burgundy with black wings and red interior; described as in very good overall condition (see lot 119 Coys 16.4.16 $20,079).												
1937	500A Topolino		028474	R	15-20.000 GBP	17.500	21.576	19.367	08-10-16	Ascot	323	Coy
See lot 133 Coys 8.9.16.												
1937	500A Topolino		013080	R	11-13.000 GBP	10.406	13.572	11.656	26-07-17	Duxford	29	H&H
Silver with black leather interior; restored in the 2000s; engine recently overhauled (see lot 15 H & H 23.7.08 $23,146).												
1947	1100 B cabriolet	(Boneschi)	261989	L	40-60.000 GBP		NS		07-12-16	London	368	Bon
Green with tan interior; known history since 1960. Restored in Italy in 1990 circa. Registered in Germany. With Italian ASI homologation.												
1948	500B Topolino		131188	L	45-55.000 USD	30.887	40.700	36.251	17-09-16	Aspen	129	TFA
Grey with tan interior; fully restored in Mexico between 2005 and 2007.												
1949	500B Topolino		136124	L	45-55.000 USD	30.892	38.500	36.221	11-02-17	Boca Raton	147	TFA
Beige with burgundy wings and brown interior; restored in Spain between 1977 and 1980. Since 1980 circa in the current, second ownership.												
1950	500C Topolino		228417	L	5-10.000 EUR	14.311*	17.795*	16.800*	25-11-16	Milan	256	RMS
Blue with tan interior. From the Duemila Ruote collection.												

F305: 2012 Ferrari FF (Pininfarina)

F306: 2017 Ferrari F12 TdF Berlinetta (Ferrari & PF)

F307: 2015 Ferrari 458 Speciale A (Ferrari & PF)

F308: 2015 Ferrari LaFerrari (Ferrari Styling Center)

F309: 1969 Ferves Ranger

F310: 1913 Fiat 12/15hp Tipo 1A torpedo

F311: 1935 Fiat 508 S Berlinetta Mille Miglia

F312: 1952 Fiat 500C Topolino

Year	Model	(Bodybuilder)	Chassis no.	Steering	Estimate	Hammer Price £	Hammer Price $	Hammer Price €	Date	Place	Lot	Auc. H.
1952	**500C Topolino**		477290	L	40-50.000 USD	38.004*	46.200*	43.539*	10-03-17	Amelia Island	161	RMS F312
	*Green with black wings; restoration completed in 2010. From the Orin Smith collection (see lot 109 RM/Sotheby's 14.3.15 $52,250).*
1950	**500C Topolino**		234195	L	12-16.000 GBP		NS		29-06-17	Fontwell Park	101	Coy
	*Burgundy with black wings; described as in good driving order (see lot 211 Coys 11.10.14 NS).*
1954	**500C Belvedere**		419714	L	6-8.000 GBP	4.460	5.431	5.094	14-01-17	Birmingham	105	Coy
	*Green with red interior; restored in Italy at unspecified date.*
1953	**500C Giardiniera**		213428	R	11-16.000 EUR	10.098	12.849	11.500	24-06-17	Wien	321	Dor
	*Beige with wooden panels and green leather interior; restored. The car ran the 2015 Mille Miglia Storica.*
1951	**500C Giardiniera**		249815	L	70-90.000 USD	64.103*	82.500*	70.290*	18-08-17	Pebble Beach	45	G&Co
	*Grey/green with wooden panels; concours-quality restoration.*
1953	**8V Supersonic**	(Ghia)	106000049	L	1.600-1.900.000 USD	1.131.075*	1.375.000*	1.295.800*	10-03-17	Amelia Island	122	RMS
	*Metallic blue-green with doeskin leather interior; believed to be the car displayed at the 1954 Geneva Motor Show; first owner Lou Fageol; early in its life fitted with a Chevrolet engine; from 1979 to 2015 with the same owner who had it restored between 2007 and 2015 and re-fitted with its original engine no.000085. From the Orin Smith collection (see lot 28 Bonhams 14.8.15 $1,815,000).* F313
1953	**8V Elaborata**	(Zagato)	106000022	L	1.400-1.800.000 USD	1.153.845	1.485.000	1.265.220	19-08-17	Pebble Beach	149	G&Co
	*Smoke grey with red leather interior; standard coupé later modified by Zagato; raced until 1958 by Anna Maria Peduzzi and then by French Jean-Claude Arifon; first restored in France; restored for the second time in the USA between 1998 and 2001; bought in 2011 by the current owner and restored again (see lots 127 Gooding & Company 21.8.11 $1,127,500 and 60 Bonhams 28.1.16 NS).* F314
1953	**1100/103 cabriolet**	(Allemano)	019195	L	275-325.000 USD		NS		20-01-17	Scottsdale	24	G&Co
	*Blue with burgundy vinyl interior; designed by Giovanni Michelotti. In the same family ownership in Italy from new to 2010. Restoration completed in 2016.*
1959	**600**	(Viotti)	100681085	L	NA	11.384*	15.000*	13.361*	17-09-16	Aspen	128	TFA
	*Grey and red with red interior; some restoration works carried out in Mexico in the 2000s.*
1963	**600D**		100D1425786	L	8-12.000 USD	5.556*	7.150*	6.363*	03-10-16	Philadelphia	251	Bon
	*Yellow; restored many years ago.*
1957	**600**		307927	L	15-20.000 USD	11.003	13.750	12.860	01-04-17	Ft.Lauderdale	416	AA
	*Blue and green with blue and green interior; restored; imported from Italy in 2016.*
1963	**600D coupé**	(Vignale)	100D1587667	L	10-12.000 GBP	9.558	12.461	11.196	18-05-17	London	102	Coy
	*Silver with red interior; just one owner in Italy until 2016 when it was imported into the UK. Interior restored in Italy. 36,000 believed original kms.*
1959	**600**	(Viotti)	100681085	L	25-35.000 USD	14.547*	18.700*	16.671*	04-06-17	Greenwich	166	Bon F315
	*See lot 128 The Finest Automobile Auctions 17.9.16.*
1958	**600 Jolly**	(Ghia)	100420901	L	80-120.000 EUR	79.087	116.724	89.940	02-07-17	Monaco	122	Art F316
	*Cream with wicker seats; in the same family ownership since new; 22,000 kns covered; in original condition except for the paintwork redone some years ago. Ordered new with Abarth 750 engine.*
1960	**600 Jolly**	(Ghia)	100610379	L	75-95.000 USD	119.658*	154.000*	131.208*	19-08-17	Pebble Beach	158	G&Co
	*Light blue with wicker seats; since new in the same family ownership in the USA; never comprehensively restored; recently serviced.*
1959	**600 Jolly**	(Ghia)	670265	L	125-150.000 USD	69.930	90.000	76.680	19-08-17	Monterey	F61	Mec
	*Light green with wicker seats; fully restored.*
1961	**600 Multipla**		095200	L	30-40.000 GBP		NS		12-10-16	Duxford	35	H&H
	*White and blue with white and red interior; body recently restored. Engine uprated to 57bhp. Two owners from new.*
1961	**600 Multipla**		095200	L	30-40.000 GBP	34.500	43.501	40.541	07-12-16	London	306	Bon
	*See lot 35 H & H 12.10.16.*
1963	**600 Multipla**		100108111611	L	25-30.000 EUR	30.577*	38.223*	35.840*	08-02-17	Paris	102	RMS
	*Light blue with white roof and tan interior; recently restored in Italy.*
1963	**600 Multipla**		100D108117630	L	30-50.000 EUR	26.433*	32.941*	30.992*	10-02-17	Paris	70	Art
	*White and light blue with blue and white leatherette interior; 169 kms covered since the restoration.*
1956	**600 Multipla**		100108006624	L	30-35.000 GBP	24.453	31.603	27.791	15-07-17	Blenheim Pal.	166	Coy
	*Dark blue and white with red interior; restoration completed in 2016.*
1959	**Nuova 500 Trasformabile**		148822	C	14-18.000 EUR	24.254*	35.796*	27.582*	02-07-17	Monaco	142	Art F317
	*Light blue with blue interior; restored three years ago.*
1963	**500 D**		110D452190	L	NA	10.435*	13.750*	12.247*	17-09-16	Aspen	127	TFA
	*Green with green interior; restored in Mexico in 2006/2007.*

F313: 1953 Fiat 8V Supersonic (Ghia)

F314: 1953 Fiat 8V Elaborata (Zagato)

F315: 1959 Fiat 600 (Viotti)   F316: 1958 Fiat 600 Jolly (Ghia)

Year	Model	(Bodybuilder)	Chassis no.	Steering	Estimate	£	$	€	Date	Place	Lot	Auc. H.
1968	500 L		110F1973625	L	8-12.000 EUR	9.645*	11.717*	10.728*	30-10-16	Paris	167	Art
Restored.												
1961	500 D		274115	L	13-18.000 EUR	15.133	18.902	17.040	05-11-16	Lyon	222	Agu
White with red and white interior; restored. Engine rebuilt five years ago and fitted with an all-synchromesh gearbox.												
1972	500 L		110F2880194	R	18-22.000 GBP	20.813	26.347	24.162	12-11-16	Birmingham	327	SiC
White with black interior; less than 15,000 miles covered. Some mechanical works carried out in 2010. In the past the car was bought by David Cameron for his wife Samantha who retained it until 2005 circa (see lot 113 Silverstone Auctions 17.11.12 $29,346).												
1969	500 F		2855540	L	25-30.000 GBP	23.000	29.001	27.027	07-12-16	London	357	Bon
White with red and white interior; restored in 2015. Offered with a Levante Graziella 300 caravan.												
1965	500 F		0962061	L	10-15.000 GBP	12.650	15.950	14.865	07-12-16	London	383	Bon
Blue with red interior; until 2012 with its first owner and subsequenly restored.												
1971	500 L		110F2777097	L	14-18.000 USD	9.840*	12.650*	11.277*	04-06-17	Greenwich	114	Bon
White with black interior; cosmetically restored. Recently imported from Italy.												
1959	500 Jolly	(Ghia)	078791	L	60-80.000 USD	57.958*	77.000*	68.792*	03-09-16	Auburn	5123	AA
Red with wicker seats.												
1957	500 Jolly	(Ghia)	110076003	L	60-80.000 USD	52.833	66.000	59.492	05-11-16	Hilton Head	161	AA
Turquoise with wicker seats; restored (see lot 261 RM 21.1.00 $24,200).												
1960	500 Jolly	(Ghia)	032743	L	80-100.000 USD	68.657	85.800	80.249	01-04-17	Ft.Lauderdale	558	AA
Light green with wicker seats with white leather covers; restored about 20 years ago (see lots RM 97 12.3.05 $29,700 and SP103 15.2.08 $70,400, and RM/Sotheby's 247 2.5.15 $77,000).												
1964	500 Jolly	(Ghia)	1100271507	L	70-100.000 GBP	77.805	101.434	91.141	18-05-17	London	116	Coy
Owned from new by President Tito of Yugoslavia. Just over 20,000 kms covered. The car has been part for many years of the Classic Automobile Museum's collection where it was refreshed in preparation for the sale.												
1958	500 Jolly	(Ghia)	110031297	L	50-70.000 USD	41.929*	53.900*	48.052*	04-06-17	Greenwich	182	Bon
Metallic blue-green with wicker seats; fitted in 2015 with a 650cc engine (the original 500cc unit is included with the sale) (see lot 462 Bonhams 6.6.10 $37,820).												
1963	500 Jolly	(Ghia)	273192	L	50-60.000 GBP		NS		15-07-17	Blenheim Pal.	145	Coy
Yellow with wicker seats; in the same family ownership until 2017; body repainted in the 1980s. It requires recommissioning prior to use.												
1968	500 Gamine	(Vignale)	1783252	L	35-45.000 USD	20.658*	26.400*	24.676*	22-04-17	Arlington	159	WoA
Burgundy with black interior just reupholstered; recently serviced.												
1957	1200 Trasformabile		103G115001850	L	85-100.000 USD		NS		17-09-16	Aspen	115	TFA
Light blue with two-tone blue interior; restored in the 1990s (see lot 465 Bonhams 6.6.10 $36,600).												
1958	1200 Trasformabile		517537	L	90-110.000 USD	37.625*	46.200*	43.451*	21-01-17	Scottsdale	118	G&Co
Black with black leather interior; restoration completed in 2016.												
1958	1200 Trasformabile		103G115002414	L	80-100.000 USD	72.389*	88.000*	82.931*	10-03-17	Amelia Island	70	G&Co
Grey beige with green leather interior; concours-quality restoration completed in 2013.												

F317: 1959 Fiat Nuova 500 Trasformabile

F318: 1964 Fiat 2300 S coupé (Ghia)

Year	Model	(Bodybuilder)	Chassis no.	Steering	Estimate	Hammer Price £	Hammer Price $	Hammer Price €	Date	Place	Lot	Auc. H.
1964	2300 S coupé	(Ghia)	114BS129460	L	50-75.000 USD	41.046*	50.400*	47.401*	20-01-17	Phoenix	211	RMS F318
	Dark blue with red interior; restoration recently completed (see lot 152 Bonhams 16.1.14 $16,500).											
1963	1100 D Taxi		1105325	L	75-10.000 GBP		NS		08-09-16	Fontwell Park	147	Coy
	Black and green; described as in good overall condition.											
1966	1500 cabriolet	(Pininfarina)	437124	L	35-45.000 USD	23.203*	28.600*	26.807*	19-01-17	Scottsdale	89	Bon F319
	Medium grey with red interior; described as in very good overall condition.											
1964	1500 cabriolet	(Pininfarina)	118H031255	L	20-25.000 EUR		NS		08-04-17	Essen	117	Coy
	Red with black interior and black hardtop; restored in the late 1990s. It comes with Italian ASI homologation (see lot 244 Coys 2.7.16 $19,923).											
1970	850 coupé		302568	L	5-10.000 EUR	12.324*	14.972*	13.708*	30-10-16	Paris	118	Art
	Red; described as in very good overall condition. Two owners.											
1971	850 Grand Prix	(Francis Lombardi)	1673714	L	30-40.000 EUR	21.090*	31.126*	23.984*	02-07-17	Monaco	195	Art F320
	Red; less than 56,000 kms on the odometer; restored five years ago in Italy.											
1972	850 Sport spider	(Bertone)	100GBS0123812	L	10-15.000 EUR	8.078	10.279	9.200	24-06-17	Wien	326	Dor
	Red with black interior; in good overall condition.											
1973	850 Sport spider	(Bertone)	100GBS10129303	R	14-16.000 GBP		NS		26-07-17	Duxford	57	H&H
	Blue with black interior; imported into the UK from the USA in 1991 and subsequently converted to right-hand drive.											
NQ	124 Sport Spider	(Pininfarina)	44477	L	18-24.000 EUR	17.147*	20.830*	19.072*	30-10-16	Paris	110	Art
	White; 103,000 kms covered. For 45 years in the same ownership.											
1981	124 Spider Turbo	(Pininfarina)	187120	L	11-14.000 GBP		NS		20-05-17	Ascot	219	His
	Imported into the UK from the USA in 2013 and subsequently restored. Turbo replaced (see lot 186 Historics 6.6.15 NS).											
1967	124 Sport Spider	(Pininfarina)	3137	L	17-20.000 EUR	17.859	22.781	20.400	18-06-17	Fontainebleau	76	Ose
	Red; described as in very good overall condition.											
1973	124 Abarth Rally	(Pininfarina)	124CS0062275	L	15-20.000 EUR	53.426*	66.433*	62.720*	25-11-16	Milan	290	RMS F321
	Some restoration works to be completed; unpainted. With hardtop. From the Duemila Ruote collection.											
1969	Dino spider	(Pininfarina)	825	L	80-120.000 EUR	87.193	111.223	99.600	18-06-17	Fontainebleau	62	Ose
	White with black interior; in good original condition. From the Jacques Liscourt collection.											
1968	Dino spider	(Pininfarina)	135AS0001011	L	100-140.000 EUR		NS		24-06-17	Wien	364	Dor
	Red with black leather interior.											
1967	Dino spider	(Pininfarina)	135AS0000556	L	90-110.000 USD	77.700*	100.000*	85.200*	19-08-17	Monterey	S46	Mec
	Silver grey with red interior; Borrani wire wheels; bumpers delete. From the J. Geils Collection.											
1967	Dino coupé	(Bertone)	0000605	L	37-45.000 GBP	30.105	40.214	35.599	08-09-16	Fontwell Park	142	Coy
	Red; the car has covered approximately 8,500 kms since the engine replacement carried out in 2010.											
1972	Dino 2400 spider	(Pininfarina)	135BS0001285	L	200-250.000 USD	129.897*	159.500*	150.010*	20-01-17	Scottsdale	58	G&Co
	Metallic silver-blue with black vinyl interior; bought in 2013 by the current owner and subsequently restored.											
1971	Dino 2400 spider	(Pininfarina)	135B0001374	L	100-180.000 EUR	82.197	103.285	96.600	09-02-17	Paris	420	Bon F322
	Blue with black interior; in good overall condition. Last serviced in November 2016.											
1972	Dino 2400 coupé	(Bertone)	135BC0005308	L	26-40.000 EUR	27.917	34.161	31.050	15-10-16	Salzburg	434	Dor
	White with grey cloth interior; stored for some years, engine serviced two years ago.											
1972	Dino 2400 coupé	(Bertone)	0005231	L	55-65.000 EUR		NS		30-10-16	Paris	152	Art
	Pale yellow; restored.											
1971	Dino 2400 coupé	(Bertone)	135BC0005397	L	10-15.000 EUR	47.702*	59.315*	56.000*	25-11-16	Milan	259	RMS F323
	Bronze with tan interior; 59,269 kms. From the Duemila Ruote collection.											
1974	130 coupé	(Pininfarina)	130BC0003254	L	10-15.000 GBP		NS		03-09-16	Beaulieu	479	Bon
	Silver with grey cloth interior; described as in very good overall condition. Automatic transmission.											
1974	130 coupé	(Pininfarina)	130BC0003254	L	15-20.000 GBP	12.822	15.808	14.190	08-10-16	Ascot	307	Coy
	See lot 479 Bonhams 3.9.16.											
1972	130 coupé	(Pininfarina)	130BC001001	L	14-20.000 EUR	11.374	13.918	12.650	15-10-16	Salzburg	409	Dor
	Metallic blue with black leather and alcantara interior; bought in 2000 by the current owner and subsequently restored.											
1974	130 coupé	(Pininfarina)	130BC0003254	L	10-15.000 GBP	8.920	10.836	9.921	29-10-16	London	152	Coy
	See lot 307 Coys 8.10.16.											
1972	130 coupé	(Pininfarina)	0000204	L	20-25.000 EUR	9.785*	12.296*	11.500*	09-02-17	Paris	309	Bon F324
	Dark blue with orange/brown velour interior; in good overall condition. 18,000 kms on the odometer. Automatic transmission.											
1974	130 coupé	(Pininfarina)	003106	L	8-10.000 GBP	8.000	10.382	9.058	29-06-17	Fontwell Park	108	Coy
	White; in good overall condition. Manual gearbox.											
1979	X1/9	(Bertone)	0107063	R	8-12.000 GBP	4.600*	6.110*	5.459*	03-09-16	Beaulieu	503	Bon
	Gold with cream interior; in good original condition (see Bonhams lots 441 18.11.09 $8,895 and 408 6.3.10 $10,557).											
1988	X1/9	(Bertone)	7164163	R	3-4.000 GBP	2.912	3.638	3.441	23-02-17	Donington Park	11	H&H
	Red with black interior; recent mechanical overhaul and body repainting.											
1977	131 Abarth Gruppo 4		92306	L	45-55.000 EUR	95.404*	118.630*	112.000*	25-11-16	Milan	327	RMS F325
	Blue and yellow. From the Duemila Ruote collection.											
1990	Panda 4x4		4153950	L	25-5.000 EUR	11.448*	14.236*	13.440*	25-11-16	Milan	889	RMS
	White; 66,548 kms. From the Duemila Ruote collection.											
1994	Coupé Turbo		14756	R	15-20.000 GBP		NS		14-01-17	Birmingham	140	Coy
	Yellow; pre-production example used when new by Pininfarina, which had designed the interior, and later part of the Pininfarina collection until a few years ago. Never registered; 825 miles covered.											

F319: 1966 Fiat 1500 cabriolet (Pininfarina)

F320: 1971 Fiat 850 Grand Prix (Francis Lombardi)

F321: 1973 Fiat 124 Abarth Rally (Pininfarina)

F322: 1971 Fiat Dino 2400 spider (Pininfarina)

F323: 1971 Fiat Dino 2400 coupé (Bertone)

F324: 1972 Fiat 130 coupé (Pininfarina)

F325: 1977 Fiat 131 Abarth Gruppo 4

F326: 1912 Fiat Type 56 touring

Year	Model	(Bodybuilder)	Chassis no.	Steering	Estimate	Hammer price £	$	€	Date	Place	Lot	Auc. H.

FIAT (USA) (1910-1918)

1912 Type 56 touring — S1547 — R — 600-700.000 USD — 384.615 — 495.000 — 423.225 — 17-08-17 — Monterey — 61 — WoA **F326**
Original body; restored in the early 2000s; interior retrimmed in more recent years. Fitted in the 1990s with a modern clutch.

FMR (D) (1957-1964)

1959 Messerschmitt KR 200 — 72963 — C — 20-24.000 GBP — 23.730 — 29.083 — 26.393 — 12-10-16 — Duxford — 132 — H&H
Light blue with red interior; restored.

1958 Messerschmitt KR 200 cabriolet — 66600 — C — 18-22.000 GBP — 19.210 — 23.544 — 21.365 — 12-10-16 — Duxford — 41 — H&H
Cream with red interior; restored over the past two years.

1959 Messerschmitt KR 200 — 70712 — C — 30-50.000 USD — 26.417 — 33.000 — 29.746 — 04-11-16 — Dallas — S164 — Mec
Rossa con interni neri.

1957 Messerschmitt KR 200 — 63410 — C — 25-35.000 EUR — 25.416* — 31.674* — 29.800* — 10-02-17 — Paris — 151 — Art **F327**
Blue; restored in the past. Since 1997 in the current ownership.

1959 Tg 500 Tiger — 20525 — C — 250-325.000 USD — NS — — — 11-02-17 — Boca Raton — 152 — TFA
Salmon with black interior; restored in Europe, the car is described as in very good overall condition.

FORD (AUS) (1925-)

1970 Falcon XW GT sedan — GJ3498C — R — 140-150.000 AUD — NS — — — 30-04-17 — Melbourne — 32 — Mos
Red with light brown vinyl interior; approximately 53,000 miles on the odometer. 351 Cleveland engine; the original automatic transmission was replaced with a 4-speed manual unit.

FORD (F) (1916-1954)

1932 AF coach — 942140 — L — 8-14.000 EUR — 9.888* — 12.192* — 10.944* — 07-10-16 — Chateau-sur-Epte — 66 — Art
Blue and black; restored many years ago, the car requires some attention prior to use. From the Andre Weber Collection.

1954 Vedette Vendome — 1055 — L — 8-12.000 EUR — 12.086* — 14.901* — 13.376* — 07-10-16 — Chateau-sur-Epte — 20 — Art
Light blue with white roof; in good overall condition. From the Andre Weber Collection.

1951 Vedette cabriolet — 57741 — L — 15-25.000 EUR — 14.283* — 17.610* — 15.808* — 07-10-16 — Chateau-sur-Epte — 29 — Art
White with red and white vinyl interior; restored many years ago. From the Andre Weber Collection.

1951 Vedette cabriolet — 44543 — L — 15-25.000 EUR — 13.734* — 16.933* — 15.200* — 07-10-16 — Chateau-sur-Epte — 33 — Art
Red with brown leather interior; restored many years ago. Cotal gearbox. Since 1978 in the Andre Weber Collection.

1953 Vedette coupé — 61887 — L — 18-22.000 EUR — 9.888* — 12.192* — 10.944* — 07-10-16 — Chateau-sur-Epte — 8 — Art
Burgundy; restored several years ago. From the Andre Weber Collection.

1952 Comète — 766 — L — 45-60.000 EUR — NS — — — 30-10-16 — Paris — 126 — Art
Black with brown interior (see lot 127 Artcurial 5.2.16 $55,948).

FORD (GB) (1911-)

1967 Anglia DeLuxe — BB22GY37775 — R — NA — 5.600* — 6.963* — 6.574* — 26-11-16 — Weybridge — 239 — His
Light green with green interior; in good condition. One owner and 38,917 miles covered.

1965 Zephyr MkIII saloon — BA54EB26265 — R — 8-10.000 GBP — 8.736 — 10.914 — 10.322 — 23-02-17 — Donington Park — 69 — H&H
Green with green interior; from the early 1970s in the current, second ownership. In highly original condition.

1955 Zephyr saloon — AAPV0240990532675 — R — 12-17.000 GBP — NS — — — 20-05-17 — Ascot — 122 — His
Two-tone green with red interior; in good overall condition.

1958 Popular 2-door saloon — 930049 — R — 4-5.000 GBP — 4.050 — 5.189 — 4.640 — 02-06-17 — Solihull — 54 — H&H
Green with light brown interior; believed but not warranted it has covered 5,209 miles since new. It requires recommissioning prior to use (see lot 626 Bonhams 12.6.04 $10,720).

1960 Zodiac MkII saloon — 206E241841 — L — 10-15.000 USD — 3.474* — 4.400* — 3.934* — 06-10-16 — Hershey — 111 — RMS
Maroon and white with red interior; restored some years ago. Automatic transmission.

1968 Zodiac MkIV saloon — BA58GP39490 — R — 7-9.000 GBP — 7.987 — 9.937 — 9.246 — 29-03-17 — Duxford — 62 — H&H
Restored in 2011; last serviced in October 2016.

F327: 1957 FMR Messerschmitt KR 200

F328: 1965 Ford Cortina GT 2-door

Year	Model	(Bodybuilder)	Chassis no.	Steering	Estimate	Hammer price £	Hammer price $	Hammer price €	Sale Date	Sale Place	Lot	Auc. H.
1963	**Consul Capri**		Z38B225065	R	12-18.000 GBP	12.600	15.415	14.591	04-03-17	Brooklands	140	His
	White with red interior; described as in very good overall condition.											
1964	**Consul Capri GT**		H39C15945J	R	18-24.000 GBP	15.680	19.183	18.157	04-03-17	Brooklands	165	His
	Two-tone body with leather interior; restored.											
1961	**Consul Classic DeLuxe 4-door**		27603	R	8-10.000 GBP		NS		07-12-16	Chateau Impney	3	H&H
	Turquoise with white roof; since 1997 in the current ownership. Restored 14 years ago.											
1965	**Cortina GT 2-door**		BA77EA40705	R	25-30.000 GBP	31.625	42.140	37.400	10-09-16	Goodwood	111	Bon F328
	White; restoration completed in 2016. Fitted with a roll cage and rally seats to the front.											
1968	**Cortina Lotus MkII**		BA91HG7738	L	40-60.000 EUR		NS		05-11-16	Lyon	229	Agu
	Dark green with yellow side stripe and original black leatherette interior; 150bhp engine prepared for historic rallying.											
1965	**Cortina Lotus**		Z74D4245305	R	35-40.000 GBP	45.000	56.493	53.249	24-02-17	Stoneleigh P.	925	SiC
	White with green side stripe and black interior; restored in 2008-09 (see Silverstone Auctions lots 147 12.4.14 NS and 624 22.2.15 $57,945).											
1963	**Cortina Lotus**		Z74C065852	R	34-42.000 GBP	47.600	58.234	55.121	04-03-17	Brooklands	163	His
	White with green side stripe; in the 1990s re-shelled and restored.											
1966	**Cortina Lotus**		BA74FJ59488	R	36-41.000 GBP	44.240	57.052	49.991	08-07-17	Brooklands	144	His
	White with green side stripe and black interior; restored in the 1980s; mechanicals recommissioned in 2014.											
1965	**Cortina Lotus**		BA74EG59595	R	45-55.000 GBP		NS		26-07-17	Duxford	72	H&H
	White with green side stripe and black interior; restored in the 1980s around a new bodyshell. Recommissioned in 2002-03 and subsequently raced at historic events (see Bonhams lots 137 5.9.03 $29,048 and 254 31.8.07 $36,035).											
1966	**Cortina Lotus**		BA74FM59709	L	70-110.000 USD	44.444*	57.200*	48.734*	18-08-17	Carmel	7	Bon
	Street car restored in the 2000s to red and gold Alan Mann Racing livery; several maintenance works carried out in 2015 and 2016 (see lot 147 Bonhams 15.1.15 $73,700).											
1972	**Escort RS1600**		ZFA141A0005230378	L	35-40.000 EUR	62.012*	77.110*	72.800*	25-11-16	Milan	619	RMS
	White with blue side stripe and black interior; 56,423 kms. From the Duemila Ruote collection.											
1970	**Escort Twin Cam**		CK49MA26689A	R	65-70.000 AUD		NS		27-11-16	Melbourne	79	Mos
	Yellow; described as in very good overall condition.											
1977	**Escort MkII Group 4**		BBATTC69901	L	80-110.000 GBP		NS		14-01-17	Birmingham	136	Coy
	White and blue; the car has had a long race career as a Works car from 1977 to 1979 and subsequently in private hands. It entered also the Monte Carlo, San Remo and Corsica Rallies and was driven also by Bjorn Waldegard. Restored to the 1977 livery (see lot 342 Coys 16.1.16 NS).											
1973	**Escort Mexico**		BFATNA70029	L	26-33.000 EUR		NS		14-01-17	Maastricht	233	Coy
	Light blue with white side stripe; in good overall condition. 10,255 kms on the odometer. Never rallied.											
1978	**Escort RS2000**		CXATUR63333	R	18-23.000 GBP	20.060	24.427	22.913	14-01-17	Birmingham	S138	Coy
	White with black cloth interior; sold new to South Africa, reimported into the UK in 2014, in good overall condition (see lot 248 Coys 2.7.16 NS).											
1968	**Escort Twin Cam**		BB48GP18167	R	200-250.000 GBP	203.100	251.032	233.788	19-03-17	Goodwood	11	Bon F329
	One of six Escorts loaned by Ford to Alan Mann Racing Team in 1968 to compete in the British and European Touring Car Championships. A spare car, it was driven on occasion by Jackie Oliver in British Championship events. Returned to Ford at the end of the 1969 season, it was sold and raced in the 1970s in the UK, Guyana and Trinidad. In 2010 it was reimported into the UK and restored between 2011 and 2014 to 1968 Group 5 specification. Fitted with a new 240bhp Geoff Richardson FVA engine.											
1985	**Escort RS Turbo**		49495	R	19-24.000 GBP	26.320	34.248	30.636	20-05-17	Ascot	161	His
	White; described as in very good original condition.											
1973	**Escort Mexico**		BFATNK00368	R	27-30.000 GBP	34.312	44.932	38.309	29-07-17	Silverstone	743	SiC
	Red with black side stripe and black interior; restored in 2002; 155bhp engine rebuilt in 2006.											
1973	**Capri RS2600**		GAECLU01517	L	5-10.000 EUR	32.437*	40.334*	38.080*	25-11-16	Milan	847	RMS
	White and blue; engine to be restored. From the Duemila Ruote collection.											
1983	**Capri 2.8**		97498	R	9-14.000 GBP	10.080	12.533	11.833	26-11-16	Weybridge	226	His
	White with grey interior; body repainted. Recently serviced.											
1987	**Capri 280 Brooklands**		11468	R	22-26.000 GBP		NS		07-12-16	Chateau Impney	56	H&H
	Green with black interior; described as in very good original condition, the car has covered 33,000 miles.											
1981	**Capri 2.8 RS Turbo**		37532	L	40-50.000 EUR	39.306	47.865	44.897	14-01-17	Maastricht	249	Coy
	Olive green; restored in 2016. One of 155 examples built, only available through Ford's German RS dealers.											
1987	**Capri 280 Brooklands**		11468	R	22-26.000 GBP	21.840	27.285	25.806	23-02-17	Donington Park	43	H&H
	See lot 56 H & H 7.12.16.											

F329: 1968 Ford Escort Twin Cam

F330: 1971 Ford Capri RS2600

Year	Model	(Bodybuilder)	Chassis no.	Steering	Estimate	£	$	€	Date	Place	Lot	Auc. H.
1979	**Capri 3.0 Group 1**		142340	R	80-90.000 GBP	88.880	111.580	105.172	24-02-17	Stoneleigh P.	122	SiC
Prepared in the 2000s by Alan Mann for historic racing, the car was driven by his son Henry. Later it was driven by Emanuele Pirro also. The engine has completed three races since the rebuild; the gearbox was rebuilt in 2016 (see lot 227 Coys 14.1.12 NA).												
1987	**Capri 2.8i Special**		91670	R	30-35.000 GBP	31.365	38.372	36.321	04-03-17	Brooklands	167	His
Black with grey leather and cloth interior; in very good overall condition. Two owners; 13,808 miles covered.												
1974	**Capri MkII 3.0 Ghia**		GAECPJ01735	R	16-20.000 GBP		NS		20-05-17	Ascot	136	His
Blue with black vinyl roof and grey interior; in good overall condition. Manual gearbox.												
1971	**Capri RS2600**		GAECKG59310	L	80-120.000 EUR	69.156	89.991	80.500	21-05-17	SPA-Francorch.	43	Bon F330
Grey with blue bonnet; prepared at Ford's competition department in Cologne, the car was sold new to French driver Francois Mazet who kept it for many years before to resell it to Clay Regazzoni. In the 2000s it was raced at several historic events, including the Tour Auto and Le Mans Classis (see Bonhams lots 24 9.11.10 $102,436 and 247 2.2.12 NS).												
1987	**Capri 280 Brooklands**		11629	R	35-45.000 GBP	55.125	72.186	61.547	29-07-17	Silverstone	417	SiC
Recently refinished; 14,680 miles covered; in very good overall condition.												
1986	**RS200 S**	(Ghia/Tickford)	00137	L	170-210.000 GBP	173.600	232.312	206.740	07-09-16	London	151	RMS
White with red seats; one of 20 S models produced. For 23 with its first owner; 4,100 kms on the odometer (see lot 380 Bonhams 6.2.14 $186,231).												
1986	**RS200 Group B**	(Ghia/Tickford)	00064	L	280-340.000 GBP	264.583	352.557	312.896	10-09-16	Goodwood	166	Bon F331
Ex-Works car, it raced the Acropolis Rally and RAC Rally during the 1986 World Rally Championship. Sold to Sweden at the end of the 1986 season; imported into Norway a few years ago; restored over the past five years.												
1986	**RS200**	(Ghia/Tickford)	00169	L	275-350.000 USD	192.606	236.500	222.428	21-01-17	Scottsdale	115	G&Co
White with red interior; 2,004 kms covered since new. Recently serviced (see lot 230 RM/Sotheby's 10.12.15 NS).												
1986	**RS200 Evolution**	(Ghia/Tickford)	00084	L	500-600.000 USD	427.350*	550.000*	468.600*	18-08-17	Carmel	18	Bon
White with blue stripes and red interior; since 1989 in the current ownership; on display for the past decades at the Auto Collections in Las Vegas; not started for the past decade; in need of mechanical recommissioning prior to use.												
1986	**RS200**	(Ghia/Tickford)	00133	L	200-300.000 USD	141.026*	181.500*	154.638*	18-08-17	Carmel	53	Bon
White with red interior; imported into the USA in the late 1980s and acquired in 1989 by the current owner who never registered it for road use. In highly original condition; circa 8,300 miles covered; in need of servicing prior to use.												
1987	**Sierra RS500 Cosworth**		38948	R	NA	50.630	67.252	60.088	02-09-16	Salon Privé	234	SiC
Described as in very good overall condition; 50,943 miles covered.												
1987	**Sierra RS500 Cosworth**		38863	R	45-55.000 GBP	47.387	58.423	52.443	08-10-16	Ascot	334	Coy
Black; recently recommissioned. Three owners and 37,000 miles covered.												
1987	**Sierra RS500 Cosworth Group A**		LR1388	L	15-20.000 EUR	95.404*	118.630*	112.000*	25-11-16	Milan	285	RMS
White and red. From the Duemila Ruote collection.												
1986	**Sierra RS Cosworth hatchback**		09643	L	10-15.000 EUR	81.093*	100.836*	95.200*	25-11-16	Milan	518	RMS
Yellow; prepared for rallying. From the Duemila Ruote collection.												
1987	**Sierra RS Cosworth hatchback**		86926	R	28-32.000 GBP	32.205	40.607	37.844	07-12-16	Chateau Impney	57	H&H
White with cloth interior; described as in very good overall condition. Last serviced in August 2016 (see lot 37 H & H 24.7.13 $28,378).												
1987	**Sierra RS500 Cosworth Group A**		A0288	L	95-115.000 GBP		NS		19-03-17	Goodwood	64	Bon
Bought new by the Italian Jolly Club racing team, the car was raced at the 1987 and 1988 European Touring Car Championships. Acquired in 2012 by the current owner and subsequently restored. In ready to race condition.												
1988	**Sierra RS Cosworth**		36522	L	45-65.000 EUR		NS		21-05-17	SPA-Francorch.	65	Bon
Described as in very good original condition; 29,307 kms covered; three owners.												
1989	**Sierra RS500 Cosworth**		ARERSC0389	R	180-220.000 GBP		NS		27-07-17	Silverstone	114	SiC
Labatt's blue and white livery; car built by Andy Rouse Engineering and driven by Tim Harvey at the 1989 and 1990 British Touring Car Championships. Later it was sold to Australia and then reimported into the UK. In ready to race condition; engine rebuilt.												
1987	**Sierra RS500 Cosworth**		39028	R	90-100.000 GBP	114.750	150.265	128.118	29-07-17	Silverstone	438	SiC F332
The car remained unused from 1991 to April 2017 when it was recommissioned and returned to the road; in very good original condition, it has covered less than 11,000 miles.												
1993	**Escort RS Cosworth Lux**		90125	R	35-40.000 GBP	40.500	51.269	47.016	12-11-16	Birmingham	348	SiC
Dark green with black leather interior; 20,600 miles covered (see lot 253 Historics 11.6.16 NS).												
1995	**Escort RS Cosworth**		98028	R	25-35.000 GBP	39.375	49.431	46.592	24-02-17	Stoneleigh P.	932	SiC
Green with black leather interior; 24,865 miles covered. In good overall condition.												

F331: 1986 Ford RS200 Group B (Ghia/Tickford)

F332: 1987 Ford Sierra RS500 Cosworth

F333: 1905 Ford Model F tonneau

F334: 1913 Ford Model T touring

FORD (USA) (1903-)

Year	Model	(Bodybuilder)	Chassis no.	Steering	Estimate	£	$	€	Date	Place	Lot	Auc. H.
1905	Model F tonneau		683	R	25-30.000 GBP	37.950	47.851	44.595	07-12-16	London	366	Bon F333
	Black with black leather interior; restored in the USA prior to be imported into the UK in 1991. Since 1992 in the current ownership. In good driving order.											
1913	Model T touring		53113(engine)	L	15-25.000 USD	11.540*	14.850*	13.215*	03-10-16	Philadelphia	247	Bon
	Black; in original condition. From the late 1930s in the Bloomington Collection.											
1913	Model T touring		253171	L	20-30.000 USD	23.195*	28.600*	25.671*	07-10-16	Hershey	214	RMS F334
	Dark blue with black fenders and black interior; restored in the 1980s.											
1919	Model T roadster		C493616(engine)	L	18-25.000 USD	13.382*	16.500*	14.810*	07-10-16	Hershey	264	RMS
	Red with black fenders and black interior; restored. Canadian built example.											
1919	Model T touring		3469684	L	13-15.000 GBP	12.093	15.045	13.999	29-03-17	Duxford	21	H&H
	Dark blue with black interior; engine overhauled in 1995.											
1928	Model A Tudor sedan		CA60425	R	12-15.000 GBP	17.250	22.913	20.472	03-09-16	Beaulieu	441	Bon
	Blue and black with grey cloth interior; manufactured in Canada and assembled in Australia. Restored in the 1990s.											
1929	Model A roadster		DMV78405CA	L	20-25.000 USD	14.532*	18.700*	16.641*	03-10-16	Philadelphia	201	Bon
	Light grey with dark blue fenders and brown interior; restored in the 1980s. On static display for many years at the Natural History Museum of Los Angeles, the car requires recommissioning prior to use.											
1931	Model AR coupé		DP96522(engine)	L	14-18.000 USD	5.556*	7.150*	6.363*	03-10-16	Philadelphia	202	Bon
	Two-tone grey with black fenders and tan interior; restored in the 1980s. From the Natural History Museum of Los Angeles.											
1931	Model A Tudor sedan		A4755319(engine)	L	15-20.000 USD	10.705*	13.200*	11.848*	07-10-16	Hershey	211	RMS
	Black; in very good overall condition. Interior redone in 2007.											
1929	Model A "woodie" station wagon		A1935462	L	25-35.000 USD	24.988*	30.800*	28.869*	19-01-17	Phoenix	176	RMS
	Two-tone brown with synthetic leather interior; described as in unrestored, original condition. Believed to have 9,580 actual miles. From the Mohrschladt Family Collection.											
1931	Model A roadster		3695	L	26-36.000 EUR	24.111	30.810	28.800	01-05-17	Obenheim	310	Ose
	Blue with black fenders and beige interior; in good driving order.											
1931	Model A DeLuxe roadster		A4828413	L	20-30.000 USD	29.949*	38.500*	34.323*	04-06-17	Greenwich	130	Bon
	Dark green with black fenders and brown leatherette interior; fully restored.											
1932	Model 18 V8 DeLuxe roadster		1874786	L	65-75.000 USD	49.942*	63.250*	56.546*	06-10-16	Hershey	146	RMS F335
	Blue with black fenders and brown leather interior; restored many years ago (see lot 133 RM/Sotheby's 30.7.16 NS).											
1932	Model 18 V8 cabriolet	(Carlton Carriage)	C18R1642	R	175-250.000 USD		NS		19-01-17	Phoenix	114	RMS
	Black with red interior; built at Ford's Canadian factory and sold in rolling-chassis form to the UK, where it was bodied. Full restoration completed in the early 2000s; engine replaced.											
1934	Model 40 V8 DeLuxe cabriolet		18741056	L	NA	57.531*	70.400*	63.987*	15-10-16	Las Vegas	774.1	B/J
	Blue with brown leather interior; a few miles covered since a full restoration.											

F335: 1932 Ford Model 18 V8 DeLuxe roadster

F336: 1940 Ford Model 01A DeLuxe station wagon

Year	Model	(Bodybuilder)	Chassis no.	Steering	Estimate	Hammer price £	$	€	Date	Place	Lot	Auc. H.
1936	Model 68 DeLuxe station wagon		182448566	L	NQ	62.709*	77.000*	72.419*	21-01-17	Scottsdale	1126.1	B/J
Body refinished in black, original wood, brown interior.												
1936	Model 68 DeLuxe club convertible		182399198	L	45-55.000 USD	30.987*	39.600*	37.014*	22-04-17	Arlington	103	WoA
Tan; restored in the early 1990s.												
1939	Model 91A DeLuxe convertible		185051763	L	NA	36.752*	47.300*	40.300*	19-08-17	Monterey	1049	R&S
Recently serviced. From the Art Astor Collection.												
1940	Model 01A DeLuxe station wagon		185851889	L	100-140.000 USD	71.368	88.000	78.989	07-10-16	Hershey	247	RMS F336
Burgundy with wooden panels; restored in the 2000s (see lot 238 RM 15.8.08 $136,400).												
1940	Model 01A DeLuxe convertible		185818608	L	40-50.000 USD	35.834*	44.000*	41.382*	20-01-17	Phoenix	207	RMS
Grey with brown leather interior; restored several years ago and later stored, it requires mechanical service prior to use. From the Jules Barsotti Collection (see lot 1545 Bonhams 13.8.04 NS).												
1940	Model 01A DeLuxe convertible		185690832	L	50-75.000 USD	48.375*	59.400*	55.866*	21-01-17	Scottsdale	103	G&Co
Maroon; leather interior; restored.												
1940	Model 022A DeLuxe convertible		85756108	L	50-70.000 USD	38.897	49.500	44.303	24-06-17	Santa Monica	186	RMS
Dark green with brown vinyl interior; restored.												
1941	DeLuxe station wagon		186301246	L	55-75.000 USD	54.292*	66.000*	62.198*	10-03-17	Amelia Island	30	G&Co
Blue with wooden panels and tan interior; for 45 years in the same family ownership; restored about 10 years ago; since 2012 in the current ownership.												
1941	DeLuxe coupé		186392328	L	NQ	14.633*	18.700*	17.479*	22-04-17	Arlington	6	WoA
Described as in good overall condition; body repainted many years ago. From the Monical collection.												
1942	GPW		50472	L	23-28.000 GBP	33.750	44.196	37.682	29-07-17	Silverstone	717	SiC
Restored in the USA and imported into the UK in 2012.												
1946	Super DeLuxe 4x4 station wagon		99A1180000LD64	L	275-350.000 USD		NS		19-08-17	Pebble Beach	166	G&Co
Burgundy with wooden panels and brown interior; one of the car modified by Marmon-Harrington; restored to concours condition in 2008 circa.												
1947	Model 79A DeLuxe Sportsman convertible		799A1934335	L	175-225.000 USD	124.940*	154.000*	144.344*	19-01-17	Phoenix	115	RMS F337
Green with wooden panels and red leather interior; body restored many years ago, interior re-upholstered in 2015.												
1947	Model 79A DeLuxe Sportsman convertible		A1684761	L	NQ	109.292*	134.200*	126.215*	21-01-17	Scottsdale	1285	B/J
Red with wooden panels and red interior.												
1951	Custom DeLuxe Country Squire s.w.		B1CH116338	L	50-60.000 USD	36.431	48.400	43.241	03-09-16	Auburn	4055	AA
Green with wooden panels; recently restored.												
1950	Custom DeLuxe station wagon		BOEG164480	L	20-25.000 GBP	12.650	15.950	14.865	07-12-16	London	359	Bon
Until 1989 with its first owner; imported into the UK in 2009; in good overall condition.												
1957	Thunderbird convertible		F7FH394780	L	175-225.000 USD	132.475*	176.000*	157.238*	03-09-16	Auburn	4147	AA F338
Black with red vinyl interior; concours-quality restoration. 300bhp 312 supercharged engine with automatic transmission.												
1957	Thunderbird convertible		F7FH394793	L	160-180.000 USD	107.260	142.500	127.310	03-09-16	Auburn	4178	AA
Black with black and white interior; restored. 312 supercharged engine with automatic transmission (see lots RM 247 10.10.14 $137,500, and Auctions America 478 28.3.15 NS and 155 31.10.15 NS).												
1962	Thunderbird convertible		2Y85Z171618	L	40-45.000 USD	52.114*	66.000*	59.004*	06-10-16	Hershey	134	RMS
White with original turquoise interior; 300bhp 390 engine with automatic transmission.												
1965	Thunderbird convertible		5Y85Z100032	L	40-50.000 USD	27.655*	34.100*	30.608*	07-10-16	Hershey	216	RMS
Red with white interior; restored. 300bhp 390 engine with automatic transmission.												
1957	Thunderbird convertible		E7FH201139	L	NA	68.935*	85.000*	76.296*	08-10-16	Chicago	S124	Mec
Gunmetal grey with red interior; restored to concours condition. 270bhp 312 engine with automatic transmission.												
1957	Thunderbird convertible		D7FH222328	L	25-30.000 GBP		NS		07-12-16	London	321	Bon
Red with red and white interior; restored in 2009, imported into the UK in 2011. 245bhp 312 engine with manual gearbox.												
1957	Thunderbird convertible		D7FH275816	L	60-70.000 USD	36.590*	45.100*	42.272*	19-01-17	Phoenix	164	RMS
Dusk rose; restored in 2005. 245bhp 312 engine with automatic transmission. From the Mohrschladt Family Collection.												
1956	Thunderbird convertible		M6FH352826	L	60-80.000 USD	27.771*	34.100*	32.071*	20-01-17	Phoenix	281	RMS
Red with red and white vinyl interior; 600 miles covered since the restoration. 202bhp 292 engine with 3-speed manual gearbox.												
1957	Thunderbird convertible		F7FH342056	L	NQ	120.938*	148.500*	139.664*	21-01-17	Scottsdale	1282	B/J
Black and red; older restoration. Supercharged 312 engine; automatic transmission (see Mecum lots F102 16.8.12 $117,000 and S173 10.4.15 NS).												

F337: 1947 Ford Model 79A DeLuxe Sportsman convertible

F338: 1957 Ford Thunderbird convertible

Year	Model	(Bodybuilder)	Chassis no.	Steering	Estimate	Hammer price £	$	€	Sale Date	Place	Lot	Auc. H.
1957	**Thunderbird convertible**		F7FH368298	L	NQ	94.341	117.500	110.215	08-04-17	Houston	S112	**Mec**
White with tan interior; restored. 300bhp 312 supercharged engine with automatic transmission.												
1957	**Thunderbird convertible**		F7FH394879	L	175-195.000 USD		NS		20-05-17	Indianapolis	S118	**Mec**
White with white and black interior; restored. 300bhp 312 supercharged engine with automatic transmission.												
1955	**Thunderbird convertible**		P5FH169216	L	35-45.000 USD	20.537*	26.400*	23.536*	04-06-17	Greenwich	146	**Bon**
Black with black and white leather interior; restored in 2014. 195bhp 292 engine with automatic transmission.												
1955	**Thunderbird convertible**		P5FH230958	L	50-70.000 USD	47.009*	60.500*	51.546*	18-08-17	Carmel	4	**Bon**
Red with red and white interior; fully restored. 193bhp 292 engine with automatic transmission.												
1957	**Thunderbird convertible**		F7FH368298	L	175-225.000 USD	135.975	175.000	149.100	19-08-17	Monterey	S122	**Mec**
See lot S112 Mecum 8.4.17.												
1957	**Thunderbird convertible**		E7FH334664	L	NA	68.376	88.000	74.976	19-08-17	Monterey	1057	**R&S**
Black; 100 miles covered since the restoration; 285bhp 312 engine with 3-speed manual gearbox.												
1955	**Fairlane Crown Victoria**		U5RW147929	L	80-100.000 USD	47.053*	57.200*	53.905*	10-03-17	Amelia Island	16	**G&Co**
Salmon and white; 500 miles covered since a full restoration carried out in the 2000s (see lots 248 RM 11.10.13 $88,000 and 122 Gooding & Company 17.1.15 $110,000).												
1955	**Fairlane Crown Victoria**		U5DW232669	L	NQ	18.076*	23.100*	21.592*	22-04-17	Arlington	11	**WoA**
White with two-tone interior; in good overall condition. From the Monical collection.												
1955	**Fairlane Crown Victoria Skyliner**		U5GF165121	L	60-80.000 USD	58.120*	74.800*	63.730*	18-08-17	Carmel	51	**Bon**
White and rose with matching vinyl interior; restored. Automatic transmission (see lot 134 RM/Sotheby's 30.7.16 NS).												
1967	**Fairlane 500 hardtop**		7H35R178811	L	150-175.000 USD	110.849	135.000	126.617	15-01-17	Kissimmee	S100	**Mec**
Red with black vinyl roof and black interior; factory original Super Stock car. In original, unrestored condition. Raced when new. Since 1989 with its current, second owner Don Fezell. 425bhp 427 engine with 4-speed manual gearbox.												
1957	**Fairlane 500 Skyliner retractable hardtop**		F7FW305543	L	140-180.000 USD	128.335*	170.500*	152.325*	03-09-16	Auburn	4148	**AA** **F339**
Black with red and white interior; concours-quality restoration. One of 13 1957 examples built with the 300bhp 312 supercharged engine. Automatic transmission.												
1957	**Fairlane 500 Sunliner convertible**		C7KC170968	L	NA	64.040	80.000	72.112	04-11-16	Dallas	S90.1	**Mec**
Rose and brown; restored. Automatic transmission.												
1957	**Fairlane 500 Sunliner convertible**		C7RC193277	L	75-85.000 USD	54.390	70.000	59.640	19-08-17	Monterey	S21	**Mec**
Red and white with red and white interior; fully restored. 212bhp 292 engine with 3-speed manual gearbox with overdrive.												
1957	**Ranchero**		C7RF143274	L	100-125.000 USD	60.438	75.500	68.056	04-11-16	Dallas	S134	**Mec**
Coral and dark grey with brown and white interior; fully restored. 292 engine with automatic transmission.												
1964	**Galaxie Lightweight hardtop**		4A66R145466	L	150-175.000 USD	82.110	100.000	93.790	15-01-17	Kissimmee	S212	**Mec**
White with red interior; restored. 425bhp 427 engine with 4-speed manual gearbox.												
1961	**Galaxie Sunliner convertible**		1G55Z181371	L	90-110.000 USD	71.394*	88.000*	82.482*	19-01-17	Phoenix	163	**RMS**
Aquamarine with blue interior; described as in very good original condition. Fewer than 19,300 believed actual miles. 401bhp 390 engine with 3-speed manual gearbox with overdrive. From the Mohrschladt Family Collection.												
1960	**Galaxie Sunliner convertible**		0R55Y100647	L	NQ	42.177*	53.900*	50.380*	22-04-17	Arlington	28	**WoA**
Black with white and black interior; restored. 360bhp 352 Interceptor Special engine with automatic transmission. From the Monical collection.												
1963	**Galaxie 500 fastback**		3N66R140581	L	65-85.000 USD	47.230*	59.000*	53.183*	04-11-16	Dallas	F93	**Mec**
Red with red vinyl interior; fully restored. 425bhp 427 engine with 4-speed manual transmission.												
1963	**Galaxie 500XL convertible**		3A69Z178218	L	40-60.000 USD	37.624*	47.000*	42.366*	04-11-16	Dallas	F95	**Mec**
Red with red interior; older restoration. 330bhp 390 engine with 4-speed manual gearbox.												
1963	**Galaxie 500 XL convertible**		3J69G109289	L	85-100.000 USD	57.477	70.000	65.653	15-01-17	Kissimmee	F99	**Mec**
Turquoise with turquoise interior; concours-quality restoration. 405bhp 406 engine with 4-speed manual gearbox.												
1963	**Galaxie 500 Lightweight hardtop**		3J66R143277	L	150-175.000 USD	123.165	150.000	140.685	15-01-17	Kissimmee	S115.1	**Mec** **F340**
White with red interior; restored. 427 engine with 4-speed manual gearbox. From the Don Fezell collection.												
1964	**Galaxie 500XL convertible**		4A69P194204	L	NQ	63.635	77.500	72.687	15-01-17	Kissimmee	S92.1	**Mec**
Yellow with black interior; 390 Police Interceptor engine with 4-speed manual gearbox.												
1962	**Galaxie 500 Club Victoria coupé**		2J63G141335	L	25-35.000 USD	32.250*	39.600*	37.244*	20-01-17	Phoenix	269	**RMS**
Blue with blue vinyl interior; in very good overall condition. 405bhp 406 engine with 4-speed manual gearbox.												
1963	**Galaxie 500XL fastback**		3E68G133987	L	NQ	85.105	104.500	98.282	21-01-17	Scottsdale	8066	**R&S**
Street Legal Drag Package; 405bhp 406 engine with 4-speed manual gearbox.												

F339: 1957 Ford Fairlane 500 Skyliner retractable hardtop

F340: 1963 Ford Galaxie 500 Lightweight hardtop

Year	Model	(Bodybuilder)	Chassis no.	Steering	Estimate	Hammer Price £	$	€	Date	Place	Lot	Auc. H.
1963	**Galaxie 500 hardtop**		3W66R125369	L	NQ	56.098	70.000	64.778	25-03-17	Kansas City	S105	Mec
Red with black interior; 425bhp 427 engine with 4-speed manual gearbox (see lot 2023 Auctions America 18.7.15 $71,500).												
1963	**Galaxie 500 convertible**		3E65X216582	L	NQ	11.669*	14.850*	13.291*	24-06-17	Northeast	33	B/J
Burgundy with black interior; body repainted. 352 engine with automatic transmission.												
1962	**Thunderbird Landau hardtop**		2Y83M160792	L	NQ	37.625*	46.200*	43.451*	21-01-17	Scottsdale	8241	R&S
Black with black interior; fully restored. 390 engine.												
1963	**Thunderbird sports roadster**		3Y89Z100064	L	NQ	55.542*	68.200*	64.142*	21-01-17	Scottsdale	855	B/J F341
Silver; four test miles since the restoration. 390 engine with automatic transmission.												
1963	**Thunderbird sports roadster**		3Y89Z119434	L	NQ	25.931*	33.000*	29.535*	24-06-17	Northeast	83	B/J
White with pearl beige interior; for 20 years in the current ownership. 390 engine with automatic transmission.												
1971	**Mustang convertible**		1F03F10144	L	18-22.000 GBP	18.400	24.441	21.837	03-09-16	Beaulieu	435	Bon
Red with black interior; restored in 2012. 351 engine with automatic transmission.												
1966	**Mustang GT convertible**		6T08K110750	L	90-110.000 USD	62.039	77.500	69.859	05-11-16	Hilton Head	141	AA
Blue with tan interior; restored in the mid-1990s. 271bhp 289 engine with 4-speed manual gearbox.												
1965	**Mustang convertible**		5F08C307139	L	20-30.000 EUR	50.564*	62.874*	59.360*	25-11-16	Milan	930	RMS
Light blue with black interior. From the Duemila Ruote collection (see lot 976 Barrett-Jackson 16.1.03 $26,460).												
1966	**Mustang convertible**		6R09C223611	L	20-25.000 GBP	17.250	21.751	20.270	07-12-16	London	325	Bon
Metallic green gold with black interior; described as in good original condition. Imported into the UK in 2014. 200bhp 289 engine with automatic transmission.												
1965	**Mustang convertible**		5F08A279509	L	NQ	17.917	22.000	20.691	21-01-17	Scottsdale	8057	R&S
Maroon with white interior; automatic transmission.												
1969	**Mustang convertible**		0F03M102045	L	35-40.000 GBP	39.880	49.547	46.520	18-02-17	London	328	Coy
Black; ordered by Henry Ford II to be used for his planned vacation to the UK subsequently cancelled. Never used by Ford, the car was later sold new to the UK. Restored in recent years. 351 engine.												
1969	**Mustang GT convertible**		9T03Q111959	L	120-150.000 USD	80.682	105.000	93.923	20-05-17	Indianapolis	S216	Mec F342
White with red interior; one of 50 examples built with the 335bhp 428 Cobra Jet engine. Automatic transmission.												
1973	**Mustang convertible**		3F03Q185515	L	10-15.000 EUR	17.783*	23.141*	20.700*	21-05-17	SPA-Francorch.	51	Bon
Red; 351 Cobra Jet V8 engine with automatic transmission. From the Swiss Castle Collection.												
1967	**Mustang convertible**		7T03C130134	L	32-38.000 EUR	30.199	39.698	33.450	05-08-17	Schloss Dyck	267	Coy
Metallic lime green with white vinyl interior; the car received light restoration works and is described as in very good overall condition. Manual gearbox.												
1965	**Mustang hardtop**		5F07C291005	L	NQ	8.958*	11.000*	10.346*	21-01-17	Scottsdale	8269	R&S
Red with black interior; 225bhp 289 engine with automatic transmission. From the Missoula Auto Museum Collection.												
1968	**Mustang GT hardtop**		8R01C156157	L	NA	24.101	30.800	28.789	22-04-17	Dallas	2521	Lea
Blue; body repainted; automatic transmission.												
1965	**Mustang hardtop 6-cylinder**		5F07U100002	L	450-650.000 USD	NS			20-05-17	Indianapolis	S125	Mec
Blue with blue vinyl interior; restored. Since 1997 in the current ownership. First Mustang hardtop to receive a VIN. 170 6-cylinder engine with 3-speed manual gearbox.												
1968	**Mustang Lightweight fastback**		8F02R135031	L	NA	NS			08-10-16	Chicago	S113	Mec
White with black interior; one of 50 examples built by the factory for the Super Stock races, fitted with the 428 Cobra Jet engine. Raced by driver Dave Lyall. Restored (see lot F180.1 Mecum 20.5.16 $140,000).												
1967	**Mustang GT fastback**		7T02C132493	R	50-55.000 GBP	60.750	76.903	70.525	12-11-16	Birmingham	637	SiC
Dark blue with black interior; restored. Automatic transmission. Imported into the UK from Australia in 2015.												
1968	**Mustang Lightweight fastback**		8F02R135046	L	275-325.000 USD	201.170	245.000	229.786	15-01-17	Kissimmee	S119	Mec
Blue and white with black interior; one of 50 examples built, raced in period, stored from 1980 to 2000 and subsequently restored. 428 Cobra Jet engine with 4-speed manual gearbox. From the Don Fezell collection..												
1967	**Mustang GT fastback**		7R02S232068	L	NQ	52.991*	66.000*	61.908*	08-04-17	Palm Beach	652.1	B/J
Blue with black interior; 400 miles covered since the restoration. 390 engine with 4-speed manual gearbox.												
1974	**Bronco**		U15GLT76652	L	NQ	49.110	62.000	58.255	03-12-16	Kansas City	S146	Mec F343
Green with white roof and green interior; 100 miles covered since the restoration completed in June 2016. Automatic transmission.												
1976	**Bronco**		U15GLC78000	L	40-60.000 USD	44.622*	55.000*	51.552*	19-01-17	Scottsdale	57	Bon
Yellow with black hardtop and black interior; less than 1,000 miles covered since the restoration. 302 engine with manual gearbox.												

F341: 1963 Ford Thunderbird sports roadster

F342: 1969 Ford Mustang GT convertible

Year	Model	(Bodybuilder)	Chassis no.	Steering	Estimate	Hammer price £	$	€	Date	Place	Lot	Auc. H.
1969	**Fairlane hardtop**		9A46R230823	L	NQ	30.459	37.400	35.175	21-01-17	Scottsdale	8060	R&S
	Black with black interior; 335bhp 428 Cobra Jet engine with automatic transmission.											
1966	**Mustang Shelby GT350 fastback**		SFM6S001	L	NA	343.608	456.500	407.837	03-09-16	Auburn	47	WoA
	White with blue stripes, blue vinyl roof and blue vinyl interior; restored in 2011. First prototype of the model.											
1966	**Mustang Shelby GT350H fastback**		SFM6S1874	L	NA	111.513	137.500	123.420	08-10-16	Chicago	S123	Mec
	Black with gold stripes and black interior; body repainted, original interior. Automatic transmission.											
1965	**Mustang Shelby GT350 fastback**		SFM5018	L	450-500.000 USD	328.205	410.000	369.574	04-11-16	Dallas	S120	Mec **F344**
	White with black interior; street model. Restored several years ago to concours condition. Manual gearbox (see lot 148 Russo & Steele 20.8.05 $324,500 and S152 Mecum 24.1.15 $445,000).											
1966	**Mustang Shelby GT350 fastback**		SFM6S2185	L	195-220.000 USD		NS		04-11-16	Dallas	S136	Mec
	Blue with white stripes and black interior; first restored in 1988 and in 2014-15 again. Manual gearbox.											
1966	**Mustang Shelby GT350H fastback**		SFM6S1555	L	72-82.000 GBP	93.240	115.935	109.454	26-11-16	Weybridge	187	His
	Black with gold stripes and black interior; imported into Europe in the early 1990s. The original automatic transmission was replaced with a 4-speed manual gearbox.											
1967	**Mustang Shelby GT350 fastback**		67200F40018	L	200-250.000 USD	192.959	235.000	220.407	15-01-17	Kissimmee	S136	Mec
	White with black interior; first used by Ford as a public relations car and later sold to Alva Bonda chairman of Avis Rent-a-Car. Concours-quality restoration. Manual geabox.											
1965	**Mustang Shelby GT350 fastback**		SFM5S391	L	375-475.000 USD	308.989	379.500	355.857	18-01-17	Scottsdale	20	WoA
	White with blue stripes; recently restored (see lot 1080 Auctions America 25.6.16 NS).											
1970	**Mustang Shelby GT350 fastback**		0F02M483090	L	70-90.000 USD	62.470*	77.000*	72.172*	19-01-17	Phoenix	131	RMS
	Blue with white interior; purchased in restored condition by the current owner in 2006 (see lot 590 Cox Auctions 19.10.06 $106,000).											
1968	**Mustang Shelby GT350H fastback**		8T02J14931501114	L	NQ	98.542*	121.000*	113.801*	21-01-17	Scottsdale	1068	B/J
	Black with black interior; 400 miles covered since the restoration carried out in 2011. Automatic transmission.											
1965	**Mustang Shelby GT350 fastback**		SFM5S219	L	NQ	362.815*	445.500*	418.993*	21-01-17	Scottsdale	1365	B/J
	White with blue stripes and black interior; restored in the late 1990s. Later the engine was fitted with a Paxton supercharger. Manual gearbox.											
1966	**Mustang Shelby GT350 fastback**		SFM6S439	L	NQ	116.459	143.000	134.492	21-01-17	Scottsdale	8260	R&S
	White with blue stripes and original black interior; 35,500 believed original miles (see lot S163 Mecum 22.11.13 NS).											
1966	**Mustang Shelby GT350H fastback**		SFM6S561	L	250-275.000 USD	184.846	231.000	216.054	01-04-17	Ft.Lauderdale	566	AA
	Black with black interior; original engine and 4-speed manual gearbox.											
1966	**Mustang Shelby GT350H fastback**		SFM6S1025	L	NQ	172.876	220.000	196.900	24-06-17	Northeast	665.1	B/J
	Green with gold stripes and black interior; restored in 2010. 72,401 miles covered since new. Automatic transmission.											
1969	**Mustang Shelby GT350 fastback**		9F02M480675	L	65-75.000 USD		NS		24-06-17	Santa Monica	179	RMS
	Silver Jade with white interior; recently serviced. Manual gearbox.											
1966	**Mustang Shelby GT350H fastback**		SFM6S1032	L	145-165.000 USD	104.701	134.750	115.211	17-08-17	Monterey	67	WoA
	Green with gold stripes; repainted several years ago; largely original interior; 4-speed manual gearbox.											
1966	**Mustang Shelby GT350H fastback**		SFM6S1183	L	150-180.000 USD	89.744*	115.500*	98.406*	18-08-17	Carmel	72	Bon
	Sapphire blue with gold stripes; restored. 4-speed manual gearbox fitted in the early 1970s (the original automatic transmission is included with the sale).											
1965	**Mustang Shelby GT350 fastback**		SFM5S111	L	300-350.000 USD	256.410	330.000	281.160	19-08-17	Pebble Beach	111	G&Co
	White with blue stripes and black interior; fitted in the mid-1970s with a Boss 351 engine and probably raced; restored in 2011-2012 and fitted again with a correct 289 engine; manual gearbox (see lot 6 Gooding & Company 17.8.13 $330,000).											
1965	**Mustang Shelby GT350 fastback**		SFM5S391	L	450-500.000 USD	299.145	385.000	328.020	19-08-17	Monterey	S36	Mec
	See lot 20 Worldwide Auctioneers 18.1.17.											
1965	**Mustang Shelby GT350 fastback**		SFM5S490	L	325-375.000 USD	350.427	451.000	384.252	19-08-17	Monterey	238	RMS
	White with blue stripes and black interior; described as in largely original condition except for the seats retrimmed some years ago. A Shelby American company car when new.											
1966	**Mustang Shelby GT350 fastback**		SFM6S853	L	NA	85.470*	110.000*	93.720*	19-08-17	Monterey	1008	R&S
	Red with white stripes; 3,000 miles covered since the restoration.											
1967	**Mustang Shelby GT350 fastback**		67200F6A00715	L	NA	82.051	105.600	89.971	19-08-17	Monterey	1026	R&S
	Blue with white stripes; restored; manual gearbox.											
1966	**Mustang Shelby GT350 fastback**		SFM6S250	L	NA	230.769	297.000	253.044	19-08-17	Monterey	1072	R&S
	White with blue stripes and black interior; restored. Fitted with a Tremec 5-speed gearbox (the original unit is included with the sale).											
1968	**Mustang Shelby GT350 convertible**		8T03J18219502878	L	110-130.000 USD	82.797	110.000	98.274	03-09-16	Auburn	4094	AA
	Blue with black interior; cosmetically restored. Manual gearbox.											

F343: 1974 Ford Bronco

F344: 1965 Ford Mustang Shelby GT350 fastback

Year	Model (Bodybuilder)	Chassis no.	Steering	Estimate	Hammer price £	$	€	Date	Place	Lot	Auc. H.
1966	**Mustang Shelby GT350 convertible**	SFM6S2377	L	NA		NS		03-09-16	Auburn	48	WoA
	Red with black vinyl; restored in 2010. One of four examples built in 1966 (see RM lots 455 18.8.00 $203,500 and 304 17.8.01 $181,500).										
1968	**Mustang Shelby GT350 convertible**	8T03J185130	L	NA	62.283	83.000	73.654	10-09-16	Louisville	S86	Mec
	Beige with beige interior; restored in 2005. 302 engine with 4-speed manual gearbox.										
1968	**Mustang Shelby GT350 convertible**	8T03J18033702981	L	90-110.000 USD	66.922	83.600	75.357	05-11-16	Hilton Head	159	AA
	Blue with black vinyl interior; some restoration works carried out in 1987. Since 1991 in the current ownership. Automatic transmission.										
1970	**Mustang Shelby GT350 convertible**	0F03M482109	L	190-220.000 USD	131.376	160.000	150.064	15-01-17	Kissimmee	S209	Mec **F345**
	Blue with white interior; concours-quality restoration. Manual gearbox; air conditioning.										
1966	**Mustang Shelby GT350 convertible**	SFM6S2377	L	800-1.100.000 USD	604.544*	742.500*	696.242*	18-01-17	Scottsdale	63	WoA
	See lot 48 Worldwide Auctioneers 3.9.16.										
1968	**Mustang Shelby GT500 fastback**	8T02S12964300551	L	NA	142.880	189.788	169.570	02-09-16	Salon Privé	258	SiC
	Red; restored in the USA at unspecified date. 4-speed manual gearbox.										
1968	**Mustang Shelby GT500 fastback**	8T02S143324	L	NA	101.304	135.000	119.799	10-09-16	Louisville	S96	Mec
	Black with black interior; 428 engine with 4-speed manual gearbox.										
1967	**Mustang Shelby GT500 fastback**	67411F9A02714	L	NA	84.420	112.500	99.833	10-09-16	Louisville	S96.1	Mec
	Red with white stripes and black interior; fully restored. 428 Police Interceptor engine with 4-speed manual gearbox. Originally fitted with automatic transmission.										
1968	**Mustang Shelby GT500KR fastback**	8T02R20528003253	L	NA	62.447	77.000	69.115	08-10-16	Chicago	S150	Mec
	Red with black interior; unrestored. Three owners and 66,000 miles covered. Automatic transmission.										
1967	**Mustang Shelby GT500 fastback**	67400F4A01016	L	110-130.000 USD	232.918*	286.000*	268.983*	20-01-17	Phoenix	225	RMS **F346**
	White with blue stripes and black interior; bought in 2005 by the current owner and subsequently restored. Manual gearbox.										
1968	**Mustang Shelby GT500KR fastback**	8T02R201783	L	NQ	107.501*	132.000*	124.146*	21-01-17	Scottsdale	1438	B/J
	Blue with black interior; restored. Automatic transmission.										
1967	**Mustang Shelby GT500 fastback**	67412F8U01331	L	NQ	88.528	110.000	103.279	18-02-17	Los Angeles	S193	Mec
	Light blue with parchment interior; rebuilt 428 engine with automatic transmission.										
1970	**Mustang Shelby GT500 fastback**	0F02R482436	L	NQ	67.318	84.000	77.734	25-03-17	Kansas City	S103	Mec
	Dark metallic green with white interior; automatic transmission.										
1967	**Mustang Shelby GT500 fastback**	67400F2A02773	L	NQ	152.551	190.000	178.220	08-04-17	Houston	F99	Mec
	Blue with black interior; in highly original condition. 428 engine with manual gearbox. From the Emalee Burton collection.										
1967	**Mustang Shelby GT500 fastback**	67400F8400819	L	170-190.000 USD	129.113	165.000	154.226	22-04-17	Arlington	135	WoA
	Restored in the 2000s; original interior; manual gearbox.										
1968	**Mustang Shelby GT500KR fastback**	8T02R203191	L	160-220.000 USD	171.094	220.000	202.268	13-05-17	Auburn	3124	AA
	Lime gold with black vinyl interior; in original condition; 22,000 original miles; manual gearbox.										
1967	**Mustang Shelby GT500 fastback**	67400F7A02720	L	185-210.000 USD	134.470	175.000	156.538	20-05-17	Indianapolis	S108.1	Mec
	Red with white stripes and black interior; restored. Manual gearbox.										
1967	**Mustang Shelby GT500 fastback**	67400F2A01926	L	170-200.000 GBP		NS		08-07-17	Brooklands	141	His
	Blue with black interior; fully restored. Imported into the UK in 1997 (see lot 175 RM/Sotheby's 7.9.15 $192,301).										
1969	**Mustang Shelby GT500 fastback**	9F02R480605	L	NA	75.214	96.800	82.474	19-08-17	Monterey	1090	R&S
	Blue with black interior; 428 Cobra Jet engine with automatic transmission.										
1968	**Mustang Shelby GT500 convertible**	8T03S174947	L	NQ	76.146*	93.500*	87.937*	21-01-17	Scottsdale	1108	B/J
	Dark blue with parchment interior; 360bhp 428 Police Interceptor engine with automatic transmission.										
1968	**Mustang Shelby GT500KR convertible**	8T03R213321	L	NQ	116.459*	143.000*	134.492*	21-01-17	Scottsdale	1338	B/J
	Red with black interior; restored by Kar Kraft. Manual gearbox.										
1968	**Mustang Shelby GT500KR convertible**	8T03R21028003664	L	NQ	143.334*	176.000*	165.528*	21-01-17	Scottsdale	1364	B/J
	Black with black interior; concours-quality restoration. 42,000 original miles. Manual gearbox (see lot 1088.1 Barrett-Jackson 19.1.13 $209,000).										
1968	**Mustang Shelby GT500KR convertible**	8T03R21322403949	L	160-200.000 USD	95.915*	116.600*	109.884*	10-03-17	Amelia Island	8	G&Co
	Lime gold; in largely original condition. About 71,000 miles covered. Automatic transmission.										
1968	**Mustang Shelby GT500KR convertible**	8T03R20531203312	L	NQ	176.638*	220.000*	206.360*	08-04-17	Palm Beach	718	B/J
	Blue with black interior; 1,500 miles covered since the restoration. Automatic transmison. First owner actor Lee Marvin (see lot S721 Russo & Steele 18.1.14 $165,130).										

F345: 1970 Ford Mustang Shelby GT350 convertible

F346: 1967 Ford Mustang Shelby GT500 fastback

Year	Model (Bodybuilder)	Chassis no.	Steering	Estimate	Hammer price £	Hammer price $	Hammer price €	Date	Place	Lot	Auc. H.
1969	**Mustang Shelby GT500 convertible**	9F03R481228	L	NQ	200.725	250.000	234.500	08-04-17	Houston	F97	Mec F347
	Blue with white interior; engine rebuilt 1,500 miles ago; two owners; 62,752 miles covered. Automatic transmission. From the Emalee Burton collection (see lot F261 Mecum 12.4.14 NS).										
1969	**Mustang Mach 1**	9F02R182393	L	NA	33.768	45.000	39.933	10-09-16	Louisville	S49	Mec
	Maroon with black interior; 8,000 miles covered since the restoration. 428 Cobra Jet engine with automatic transmission.										
1970	**Mustang Mach 1**	0T05R127337	L	80-100.000 USD		NS		04-11-16	Dallas	F128	Mec
	Metallic yellow with black stripe and black interior; restored. 428 Super Cobra Jet engine with automatic transmission.										
1969	**Mustang Mach 1**	9T02R162352	L	NQ	53.071	67.000	62.953	03-12-16	Kansas City	S150	Mec
	Black Jade with gold side stripe and black interior; restored. 428 Super Cobra Jet engine with manual gearbox.										
1969	**Mustang Mach 1**	9F02R213645	L	100-125.000 USD	139.587	170.000	159.443	15-01-17	Kissimmee	S123	Mec F348
	Yellow with black bonnet and black interior; restored, two owners, believed to be 18,545 original miles. 428 Super Cobra Jet engine with 4-speed manual gearbox. From the Don Fezell collection.										
1970	**Mustang Mach 1**	0F05R140209	L	NQ	80.626*	99.000*	93.110*	21-01-17	Scottsdale	1154	B/J
	Orange with black interior; restored. 428 Cobra Jet engine with manual gearbox.										
1971	**Mustang Mach 1**	1F05J221304	L	75-100.000 USD	145.996*	190.000*	169.955*	20-05-17	Indianapolis	F151	Mec
	Metallic silver blue with blue vinyl interior; restoration completed in early 2017. 375bhp 429 Super Cobra Jet engine with manual gearbox.										
1969	**Mustang Mach 1**	9F02R150734	L	55-70.000 USD		NS		24-06-17	Santa Monica	127	RMS
	Red with black bonnet; recently restored. 428 Cobra Jet engine with automatic transmission.										
1970	**Mustang Boss 302**	0F02G205416	L	75-100.000 USD	73.899	90.000	84.411	15-01-17	Kissimmee	S102	Mec
	White with black stripes and black interior; restored. Believed to be 13,313 original miles. Two owners. From the Don Fezell collection.										
1970	**Mustang Boss 302**	0F02G171817	L	90-120.000 USD	71.667*	88.000*	82.764*	20-01-17	Phoenix	266	RMS
	Orange with black vinyl interior; bought in 2006 by the current owner and subsequently restored.										
1970	**Mustang Boss 302**	0F02G146216	L	NQ	111.084*	136.400*	128.284*	21-01-17	Scottsdale	1318.1	B/J
	Yellow with black stripes and black interior; full restoration completed in 2006. From the collection of Barrett-Jackson president Steve Davis.										
1970	**Mustang Boss 429**	0F02Z120978	L	NA	191.352	255.000	226.287	10-09-16	Louisville	S118	Mec
	Green with black interior; restored. Believed to be 48,750 original miles (see lot S108 Mecum 20.5.16 $240,000).										
1970	**Mustang Boss 429**	0F02Z110422	L	NA	198.695	245.000	219.912	08-10-16	Chicago	S125.1	Mec
	Blue with white interior; Kar Kraft no.2153. Restored. Believed to be 25,000 original miles. Manual gearbox (see lot F513 Russo & Steele 15.1.09 $214,500).										
1969	**Mustang Boss 429**	9F02Z159818	L	NA	292.149*	357.500*	324.932*	15-10-16	Las Vegas	749	B/J
	Red with black interior; in original condition. One owner and 21,400 miles covered.										
1969	**Mustang Boss 429**	9F02Z198807	L	NA	144.090*	180.000*	162.252*	04-11-16	Dallas	S89.1	Mec
	Black with black interior; Kar Kraft no.1992. Manual gearbox.										
1969	**Mustang Boss 429**	9F02Z159771	L	240-280.000 USD	143.693	175.000	164.133	15-01-17	Kissimmee	F173	Mec
	Burgundy with black interior; Kar Kraft no.1454. Unrestored.										
1970	**Mustang Boss 429**	0F02Z140279	L	350-400.000 USD	242.225	295.000	276.681	15-01-17	Kissimmee	S98	Mec
	Coral red with white interior; Kar Kraft no.2433. Concours-quality restoration completed in 2015.										
1970	**Mustang Boss 429**	0F02Z110869	L	190-230.000 USD	158.525	194.700	182.570	18-01-17	Scottsdale	22	WoA
	Blue with white interior; Kar Kraft no.2176. Restored.										
1969	**Mustang Boss 429**	9F02Z198914	L	NQ	313.544	385.000	362.093	21-01-17	Scottsdale	1400	B/J
	Black with black interior; from the Reggie Jackson Collection.										
1969	**Mustang Boss 429**	0F02Z150467	L	NQ	273.231	335.500	315.538	21-01-17	Scottsdale	8795	R&S
	White with black interior; Kar Kraft no.1272. Restored in 2003. 32,445 miles since new.										
1969	**Mustang Boss 429**	9F02Z198782	L	190-220.000 USD	184.846	231.000	216.054	01-04-17	Ft.Lauderdale	564	AA
	Burgundy with black interior; Kar Kraft no.1885. Recently restored.										
1969	**Mustang Boss 429**	9F02Z192861	L	NQ	234.045	291.500	273.427	08-04-17	Palm Beach	729	B/J
	White with black interior; Kar Kraft no.1717. Restored. Engine rebuilt in August 2016.										
1969	**Mustang Boss 429**	9F02Z173034	L	200-230.000 EUR	164.333	204.672	192.000	08-04-17	Essen	154	Coy
	White; restored (see lot 430 Coys 16.1.16 NS)										
1969	**Mustang Boss 429**	9F02Z198927	L	NQ	260.943*	325.000*	304.850*	08-04-17	Houston	S46	Mec F349
	Maroon with black interior; Kar Kraft no.2014. In highly original condition. From the Laquay Automobile Collection.										

F347: 1969 Ford Mustang Shelby GT500 convertible

F348: 1969 Ford Mustang Mach 1

Year	Model (Bodybuilder)	Chassis no.	Steering	Estimate	Hammer price £	Hammer price $	Hammer price €	Sale Date	Sale Place	Lot	Auc. H.
1969	**Mustang Boss 429**	9F02Z187777	L	275-325.000 USD		NS		13-05-17	Auburn	3126	AA
	Maroon with black vinyl interior; Kar Kraft no.1692. Body repainted; 36,000 actual miles.										
1969	**Mustang Boss 429**	9F02Z192872	L	350-400.000 USD	169.048	220.000	196.790	20-05-17	Indianapolis	S177	Mec
	White with black interior; Kar Kraft no.1746. Concours-quality restoration.										
1970	**Mustang Boss 429**	0F02Z120964	L	350-400.000 USD	257.414	335.000	299.658	20-05-17	Indianapolis	S222	Mec
	Pastel blue with black vinyl interior; 100 miles covered since the restoration completed in 2008. Mechanicals detailed in 2017 (see Russo & Steele lots 6015 20.1.10 NA and 9143 19.1.11 NS).										
1970	**Mustang Boss 429**	0F02Z129405	L	NQ		NS		24-06-17	Northeast	650	B/J
	Blue with white interior; 10 miles covered since a recent full restoration.										
1969	**Mustang Boss 429**	9F02Z195405	L	NQ	319.821	407.000	364.265	24-06-17	Northeast	709	B/J
	Burgundy with black interior; in original condition. 2,000 miles covered.										
1969	**Torino Talladega**	9A46Q207116	L	NQ	33.561*	41.800*	39.208*	08-04-17	Palm Beach	399	B/J
	Burgundy with black interior; restored. 428 Cobra Jet engine with automatic transmission.										
1969	**Torino 2-door hardtop**	9A45Q255003	L	40-50.000 USD	24.816	31.000	27.943	04-11-16	Dallas	F167 **F350**	Mec
	White with black interior; 428 Cobra Jet engine with automatic transmission.										
1971	**Torino fastback**	1H38J115313	L	75-100.000 USD		NS		15-01-17	Kissimmee	S125.1	Mec
	Yellow with black bonnet and black interior; unrestored, two owners, believed to be 30,289 original miles. 429 Cobra Jet engine with 4-speed manual gearbox. From the Don Fezell collection.										
1969	**Torino GT**	9A42Q211769	L	NQ	43.896*	53.900*	50.693*	21-01-17	Scottsdale	1040	B/J
	"Richard Petty" edition finished in blue with blue vinyl interior; one of five examples fitted with the 428 Cobra Jet engine and automatic transmission. In original condition.										
2005	**GT**	401276	L	250-300.000 GBP		NS		10-09-16	Goodwood	167	Bon
	White with blue stripes; four owners and circa 8,000 miles covered. Last serviced in December 2015. First owner Jensen Button.										
2005	**GT**	401201	L	NA	187.600	250.000	221.850	10-09-16	Louisville	S147	Mec
	White with blue stripes and black interior; one owner and 1,259 actual miles (see lot S110.1 Mecum 23.7.16 NS).										
2006	**GT**	401107	L	285-325.000 USD	244.353	305.250	275.152	05-11-16	Hilton Head	142	AA
	Heritage Edition; one owner and 34,000 original miles. Regularly serviced.										
2006	**GT**	401261	L	NA	198.720*	245.000*	230.496*	19-11-16	Anaheim	S104	Mec
	Red with black interior; 2,500 miles covered.										
2005	**GT**	400165	L	220-250.000 EUR	286.212*	355.891*	336.000*	25-11-16	Milan	305	RMS
	Blue with white stripes; 4,607 miles covered. From the Duemila Ruote collection.										
2005	**GT**	400788	L	NQ		NS		03-12-16	Kansas City	S95.1	Mec
	Red with black interior; one owner and 4,800 miles covered (see lot F92 Mecum 19.8.16 $237,500).										
2006	**GT**	400986	L	250-280.000 USD	229.908	280.000	262.612	15-01-17	Kissimmee	F144	Mec
	Yellow with black stripes and black leather interior; 2,560 actual miles.										
2006	**GT**	401761	L	375-450.000 USD	268.910	327.500	307.162	15-01-17	Kissimmee	F156	Mec
	Blue and orange Heritage Edition livery with black interior; one owner and 1,828 miles. From the Colts Neck Collection.										
2005	**GT**	401654	L	280-330.000 USD	223.905	275.000	257.868	18-01-17	Scottsdale	10	WoA
	Black with black interior; one owner and 2,600 miles covered.										
2006	**GT**	401580	L	300-350.000 USD	248.596*	305.250*	287.088*	20-01-17	Phoenix	255	RMS
	Red with white stripes; 195 miles covered.										
2005	**GT**	400862	L	NQ	243.668*	299.200*	281.398*	21-01-17	Scottsdale	1373	B/J
	Silver with black leather interior; 281 miles covered.										
2005	**GT**	400117	L	NQ	201.564*	247.500*	232.774*	21-01-17	Scottsdale	1394	B/J
	Red; second full-production example off the assembly line, the car was originally used by the factory for test. Later it was returned to fully road legal specification. 42,839 actual miles.										
2006	**GT**	401511	L	NQ	212.762	261.250	245.706	21-01-17	Scottsdale	8303	R&S
	White with blue stripes; less than 1,100 miles covered.										
2004	**GT**	400004	L	NQ		NS		21-01-17	Scottsdale	8418	R&S
	First fully-functional prototype (CP-1) built; its body and engine compartment feature several exclusive, non-standard components and many design features. Sold on a bill of sale (see lot 654 Barrett-Jackson 24.6.16 NS).										
2006	**GT**	401580	L	NQ	245.464	305.000	286.365	18-02-17	Los Angeles	S114.1	Mec
	See lot 255 RM/Sotheby's 20.1.17.										

F349: 1969 Ford Mustang Boss 429

F350: 1969 Ford Torino 2-door hardtop

Year	Model	(Bodybuilder)	Chassis no.	Steering	Estimate	Hammer Price £	$	€	Date	Place	Lot	Auc. H.
2005	GT		401276	L	250-300.000 GBP	264.375	331.896	312.835	24-02-17	Stoneleigh P.	530	SiC
See lot 167 Bonhams 10.9.16.												
2006	GT		400445	L	250-300.000 USD	226.215	275.000	259.160	10-03-17	Amelia Island	57	G&Co
Tungsten grey with white stripes and ebony interior; less than 1,450 miles covered. In 2013 the car was bought by designer Chip Foose and slightly personalized. All replaced components are included with the sale.												
2005	GT		400136	L	250-300.000 USD	262.409*	319.000*	300.626*	10-03-17	Amelia Island	149	RMS
Red with white stripes and black interior; 2,453 miles covered. From the Orin Smith collection.												
2005	GT		400372	L	300-350.000 USD	298.604*	363.000*	342.091*	11-03-17	Amelia Island	259	RMS F351
Metallic blue with black interior; one owner; 1,850 miles covered.												
2006	GT		401372	L	250-300.000 GBP		NS		19-03-17	Goodwood	57	Bon
Yellow with black stripes and black interior; about 5,000 miles covered. Recently serviced.												
2005	GT		400413	L	NQ	240.420	300.000	277.620	25-03-17	Kansas City	S112.1	Mec
Black with silver stripes; 4,590 actual miles.												
2005	GT		400599	L	300-350.000 USD		NS		01-04-17	Ft.Lauderdale	542	AA
White with blue stripes and black interior; less than 1,500 miles covered (see lot TH320 Russo & Steele 15.1.09 $151,250).												
2005	GT		401026	L	270-295.000 USD	224.456	280.500	262.352	01-04-17	Ft.Lauderdale	552	AA
Blue with white stripes; less than 4,000 miles on the odometer.												
2006	GT		400619	L	300-350.000 USD	230.520	300.000	268.350	20-05-17	Indianapolis	F155	Mec
Tungsten grey with white stripes and black interior; one owner; 1,285 original miles.												
2005	GT		401219	L	275-325.000 USD		NS		24-06-17	Santa Monica	222	RMS
Black; less than 5,800 miles covered.												
2005	GT		401500	L	300-350.000 EUR	305.803	451.333	347.768	02-07-17	Monaco	207	Art
Light grey with black stripes and black interior; one owner; 7,750 miles covered. Registered in France.												
2006	GT		401412	L	270-320.000 USD	217.094	279.400	238.887	17-08-17	Monterey	55	WoA
White with blue stripes and black interior; one owner; 3,730 miles covered.												
2006	GT		400150	L	275-350.000 USD		NS		18-08-17	Carmel	13	Bon
Metallic tungsten grey with white stripes; less than 4,300 miles covered.												
2006	GT		400417	L	275-325.000 USD	222.222*	286.000*	243.672*	18-08-17	Pebble Beach	11	G&Co
Black with black leather interior, just over 1,100 miles covered.												
2006	GT		401583	L	275-350.000 USD	294.872*	379.500*	323.334*	18-08-17	Monterey	131	RMS
Dark blue with white stripes; 60 miles covered.												
2005	GT		401647	L	350-400.000 USD		NS		19-08-17	Monterey	F100	Mec
Dark blue with black leather interior; 2,100 original miles.												
2006	GT		401761	L	475-500.000 USD	326.340	420.000	357.840	19-08-17	Monterey	S77	Mec
See lot F156 Mecum 15.1.17.												
2006	GT		401705	L	325-350.000 USD	221.445	285.000	242.820	19-08-17	Monterey	S84	Mec
Red with white stripes and black interior; 1,805 original miles.												
2005	GT		400862	L	NA		NS		19-08-17	Monterey	1148	R&S
See lot 1373 Barrett-Jackson 21.1.17.												
2006	GTX1		400454	L	NA	322.364	401.500	376.607	08-04-17	Palm Beach	706	B/J
Dark blue with black interior; 14,970 actual miles. One of about 30 examples modified by the Ford authorized coachbuilder Genaddi Design Group.												

FRANKLIN (USA) (1902-1934)

Year	Model	(Bodybuilder)	Chassis no.	Steering	Estimate	£	$	€	Date	Place	Lot	Auc. H.
1925	Model 10-C touring		E96704	L	NA	24.839	33.000	29.482	03-09-16	Auburn	39	WoA
Dark blue with black fenders and black interior; restored many years ago.												
1926	Model 11-A victoria coupé		16356716	L	25-35.000 USD	14.547*	18.700*	16.671*	04-06-17	Greenwich	177	Bon F352
Dark blue with black fenders; restored many years ago; in good overall condition.												

F351: 2005 Ford GT

F352: 1926 Franklin Model 11-A victoria coupé

Year	Model (Bodybuilder)	Chassis no.	Steering	Estimate	Hammer Price £	$	€	Sale Date	Place	Lot	Auc. H.

FRAZER-NASH (GB) (1924-1957)

Year	Model (Bodybuilder)	Chassis no.	Steering	Estimate	£	$	€	Date	Place	Lot	Auc. H.
1935	TT Replica	9371022	R	100-150.000 GBP	105.660	140.348	125.397	03-09-16	Beaulieu	427	Bon

Black with black interior; car built in the 1980s on a Frazer Nash/GN chassis fitted with original Frazer Nash front and rear axles, Meadows engine and new body. Later it was fitted with the present BMW 6-cylinder 315 engine bored out to 1,971cc. Driven at several historic events; with VSCC "Buff Form" dated March 2016.

| 1939 | BMW 328 sports two-seater (Leacroft) | 85427 | R | 500-700.000 USD | 641.025 | 825.000 | 702.900 | 18-08-17 | Monterey | 162 | RMS F353 |

Imported into the UK in rolling chassis form and sold after WWII to its first owner who had it bodied and raced it at the 1949 Spa 24 Hours. In 1988 the car was bought by the Rosso Bianco Collection of Peter Kaus who had it fully restored. Since 2006 in the current ownership (see lot 245 Bonhams 1.9.06 $474,345).

| 1954 | Le Mans Replica | 421200210 | R | 250-350.000 GBP | 257.600 | 344.720 | 306.776 | 07-09-16 | London | 162 | RMS |

Dark blue with black interior; retained by Frazer Nash, the car was sold as a rolling chassis in 1964 and subsequently was fitted with a coupé body. In 1982 it was rebodied with the present Le Mans Replica style body. Offered from the estate of Edward Carter, who had bought it in 2012 and had it subsequently fully restored.

| ==== | Le Mans Replica recreation | 4001566 | R | 150-175.000 GBP | NS | | | 10-09-16 | Goodwood | 105 | Bon |

British racing green; one of six replicas built in the 1970s by Crosthwaite & Gardiner. Raced in the USA at VSCCA Hill Climb events (see lot 48 Bonhams 14.8.15 $220,000).

| 1950 | Le Mans Replica | 421100127 | R | 580-640.000 GBP | 603.333 | 803.941 | 713.502 | 10-09-16 | Goodwood | 170 | Bon F354 |

The car was acquired new by Anthony Baring who in 1951 resold it to Roy Salvadori who raced it at several events and retained it until late 1952. Following a long race career, the car was bought in 1972 by the current, eighth owner. Rebuilt in late 1951 following an accident at Silverstone; several works to the mechanicals and body carried out over the years.

FRISKY (GB) (1957-1964)

| 1959 | Family Three | 20446 | R | 10-12.000 GBP | 16.800 | 20.889 | 19.722 | 26-11-16 | Weybridge | 143 | His |

White with yellow roof; in good working order; two-stroke 197cc Villiers engine.

GARDNER (USA) (1919-1931)

| 1930 | Model 140 Sport Roadster | GR30580 | L | 200-250.000 USD | 102.564* | 132.000* | 112.464* | 19-08-17 | Pebble Beach | 123 | G&Co |

Black and silver with red leather interior; full restoration completed in 2016. One of two examples known to survive.

GEORGES IRAT (F) (1921-1948)

| 1936 | Type MN roadster | 1042 | L | 20-30.000 EUR | 26.060 | 32.211 | 30.000 | 19-03-17 | Fontainebleau | 209 | Ose F355 |

White with black interior; restored in 1998.

GHIA (I) (1926-)

| 1955 | Streamline X Gilda | 9967 | L | NQ | NS | | | 21-01-17 | Scottsdale | 1389.1 | B/J |

Concept car commissioned by Chrysler and designed by Giovanni Savonuzzi, it should have been fitted with a turbine engine. First exhibited at the 1955 Turin Motor Show without engine, it was subsequently imported into the USA where remained on display at the Henry Ford Museum until 1969. Formerly in the Harrah and Blackhawk collections also, it was fitted by the current owner with a AiResearch turbine engine (see lots 15 Blackhawk 12.10.01 $35,200 and 153 Gooding & Company 16.8.09 NS).

| 1961 | L6.4 coupé | 0302 | L | 300-375.000 USD | 324.786 | 418.000 | 356.136 | 18-08-17 | Monterey | 158 | RMS F356 |

Black with black leather interior; bought in 2006 by the current owner and subsequently restored. First owner Peter Lawford.

| 1967 | 450 SS convertible | 4016 | L | NA | NS | | | 19-11-16 | Anaheim | S91.1 | Mec |

Yellow with black interior; restored 10 years ago circa; automatic transmission (see lot 7088 Russo & Steele 20.8.16 NS).

GLADIATOR (F) (1896-1920)

| 1903 | 10hp rear-entrance tonneau | 61108 | R | 130-160.000 GBP | 141.500 | 174.894 | 162.881 | 19-03-17 | Goodwood | 48 | Bon F357 |

Since 1990 in the current ownership; in good driving order; requiring only some cosmetic attention.

GLAS (D) (1951-1969)

| 1961 | Goggomobil T-250 saloon | 01169530 | L | 3-6.000 EUR | 4.645* | 5.911* | 5.290* | 24-06-17 | Wien | 309 | Dor |

Red with red leatherette interior; deregistered in 2003 and subsequently refurbished and exhibited in a museum.

| 1959 | Goggomobil Dart roadster | 0112854 | R | 30-40.000 USD | 26.196* | 31.900* | 30.232* | 09-03-17 | Amelia Island | 102 | Bon F358 |

White; described as in good original condition. 35,462 miles covered. Goggomobil rolling-chassis bodied in Australia by Bill Buckle.

| 1959 | Goggomobil TS-400 coupé | 02105796 | L | NA | 20.870* | 27.500* | 24.494* | 17-09-16 | Aspen | 104 | TFA |

White with red interior; mechanicals restored several years ago. Engine rebuilt in 2016.

| 1957 | Goggomobil TS-400 cabriolet | 0267173 | L | 12-18.000 EUR | NS | | | 24-06-17 | Wien | 323 | Dor |

Red with black and grey interior.

GODSAL (GB)

| 1935 | Sports tourer (Corsica) | 001 | R | 225-275.000 USD | 176.147 | 214.500 | 203.282 | 09-03-17 | Amelia Island | 163 | Bon F359 |

One-off designed by Charles Godsal and built by Research Engineers Ltd. of London; contemporary Ford V8 engine with 4-speed pre-selector transmission. Resurfaced in 1969 when it was used in the movie "Mosquito Squadron", in 1977 it was bought by Jerry Old who imported it in the USA and retained it until 2016. Finished in red with tan interior.

GORDINI (F) (1935-1957)

| 1948 | Type 15 GP | 010GC | M | 250-350.000 USD | 188.034 | 242.000 | 206.910 | 17-08-17 | Monterey | 24 | WoA F360 |

Finished in the Argentine National Racing Team livery; 1,460cc Gordini engine; in working order but not race-prepared. The car was raced in Europe and subsequently in late 1948 it was sent to Argentina to run in the Temporada series. Driven in period among others by Prince Bira, Raymond Sommer, Harry Schell and Jean-Pierre Wimille.

F353: 1939 Frazer-Nash BMW 328 sports two-seater (Leacroft)

F354: 1950 Frazer-Nash Le Mans Replica

F355: 1936 Georges Irat Type MN roadster

F356: 1961 Ghia L6.4 coupé

F357: 1903 Gladiator 10hp rear-entrance tonneau

F358: 1959 Glas Goggomobil Dart roadster

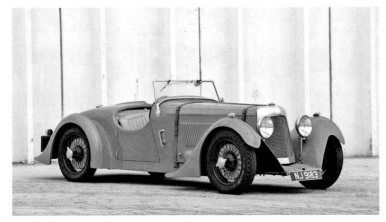

F359: 1935 Godsal Sports tourer (Corsica)

F360: 1948 Gordini Type 15 GP

Year	Model	(Bodybuilder)	Chassis no.	Steering	Estimate	Hammer Price £	$	€	Sale Date	Place	Lot	Auc. H.

GRAHAM (USA) (1930-1941)

1935	Model 68 sedan		13558013	R	10-12.000 GBP	NS			03-09-16	Beaulieu	496	Bon

Burgundy; restored in 2011.

1935	Model 68 sedan		13558013	R	10-15.000 GBP	6.250	8.111	7.077	29-06-17	Fontwell Park	106	Coy

See lot 496 Bonhams 3.9.16.

1938	Model 97 Supercharged cabriolet (Saoutchik)	141747	L	600-900.000 USD	633.402	770.000	725.648	11-03-17	Amelia Island	243	RMS F361

Light ivory with dark blue interior; example with parallel opening doors exhibited at the Saoutchik stand at the 1938 Paris Motor Show. Used as a staff car by the French Army in Algeria during WWII, it was imported into the USA in 1944. Concours-quality restoration completed by RM Auto Restoration in 2015.

HART STEAM (USA)

1897	Victoria dos-a-dos		NQ	R	60-80.000 GBP	60.860	76.014	68.528	04-11-16	London	206	Bon

Only example built; dated 1897 circa; fitted with a twin-cylinder steam engine; in the ownership of the Hart family until 1946 when it was presented to the Automobile Old Timers Museum, New York, where it remained until 1990; later imported into the UK and restored between 2002 and 2004. It requires recommissioning prior to use.

HEALEY (GB) (1946-1971)

1950	Silverstone E-Type		E69	R	250-300.000 USD	NS			20-01-17	Scottsdale	40	G&Co

Red with tan interior; full restoration completed in 2002. Original engine replaced in the 1960s with a correct unit (see lot 128 RM 20.1.11 $192,500).

1950	Silverstone		E64	R	165-185.000 GBP	NS			29-07-17	Silverstone	725	SiC

Bought in 1998 by the current owner and subjected to a restoration completed in 2003. Recently serviced.

1953	Alvis 3l Sports Convertible (Panelcraft)	G516	R	35-40.000 AUD	23.159	29.743	26.563	28-05-17	Sydney	10	Mos

Restoration project.

HEINE-VELOX (USA) (1921-1923)

1921	V12 limousine		0005	L	175-200.000 USD	NS			03-09-16	Auburn	7034	AA

Red with black interior; fully restored. In the past in the Blackhawk Collection. Displayed at the Shangai Automobile Museum from 2006 to 2015. Believed to be one of two survivor examples (see lot 1397 Barrett-Jackson 29.1.16 $99,000).

HEINKEL (D) (1955-1958)

1958	Kabine		1531519	L	20-25.000 EUR	15.406	19.188	18.000	08-04-17	Essen	109	Coy

Blue with red interior; in good condition.

HILLMAN (GB) (1907-1978)

1936	Minx tourer		M69348	R	NQ	5.062*	6.486*	5.800*	02-06-17	Solihull	9	H&H

Cream and brown with blue interior; subjected to a restoration and not run since. From a museum collection.

1967	Imp		B412016381HSOT	R	30-35.000 GBP	33.600	44.159	37.760	27-07-17	Silverstone	116	SiC

Ex-Works car, it raced in 1967 the Monte Carlo, Tulip and Alpine Rallies and the RAC Rally where it was driven by Rosemary Smith. In 1968 it was converted to Group 6 specification. In 1969 Chrysler withdrew from official rallying and the car was kept by Rootes for a number of years. The engine has been verified as the one prepared for Rosemary Smith.

HISPANO-SUIZA (E) (1903-1944)

1928	T49 cabriolet		7137	R	80-100.000 EUR	68.497	86.071	80.500	09-02-17	Paris	332	Bon F362

Pale yellow with black wings; recently restored.

HOLDEN (AUS) (1948-)

1953	Model FX sedan		100460(engine)	R	13-18.000 AUD	10.839	13.959	11.879	20-08-17	Mallala Park	12	Mos

Blue with blue vinyl interior; 39,470 miles on the odometer. From the collection of the late Clem Smith.

F361: 1938 Graham Model 97 Supercharged cabriolet (Saoutchik)

F362: 1928 Hispano-Suiza T49 cabriolet

Year	Model	(Bodybuilder)	Chassis no.	Steering	Estimate	Hammer Price £	Hammer Price $	Hammer Price €	Date	Place	Lot	Auc. H.
1977	Torana A9X hatchback		NQ	R	850-1.050.000 AUD	408.689	524.873	468.755	28-05-17	Sydney	7	Mos F363

White, green and blue; campaigned from 1978 to 1980 by the Ron Hodgson Team in the Australian Touring Car Championship and driven by Bob Morris. Later on display at the York Motor Museum; recommissioned in recent times.

HOLSMAN (USA) (1903-1910)

Year	Model	Chassis no.	Steering	Estimate	£	$	€	Date	Place	Lot	Auc. H.
1907	Highwheeler Model 3 runabout	NQ	R	NQ	10.170	12.464	11.311	12-10-16	Duxford	88	H&H

Black; restored in the USA many years ago.

HONDA (J) (1948-)

Year	Model	Chassis no.	Steering	Estimate	£	$	€	Date	Place	Lot	Auc. H.
1972	Z600 coupé	AZ6001017050	L	NA	17.978*	22.000*	19.996*	15-10-16	Las Vegas	60	B/J

Yellow with new black vinyl interior; mechanicals rebuilt (see lot 50 Barrett-Jackson 18.1.10 $27,500).

| 1967 | S800 coupé | 1003184 | R | 25-28.000 GBP | 19.040 | 23.335 | 21.176 | 12-10-16 | Duxford | 24 | H&H |

Red with black interior; restored between 2014 and 2015.

| 1967 | S800 coupé | 1003811 | L | 20-30.000 EUR | 33.550* | 41.810* | 39.336* | 10-02-17 | Paris | 2 | Art F364 |

Grey with black interior; since 2003 in the current ownership. Recently restored.

| 1968 | S800 roadster | 1005908 | L | 23-28.000 EUR | 29.292 | 36.205 | 33.720 | 18-03-17 | Lyon | 178 | Agu |

Yellow with black leatherette interior; restored in the 1990s.

| 1967 | S800 coupé | 1000884 | L | 15-25.000 EUR | 16.262 | 20.100 | 18.720 | 18-03-17 | Lyon | 179 | Agu |

The car requires some attention to the mechanicals and body; original leatherette interior.

| 1977 | Civic CVCC | SGE352853 | L | 15-25.000 USD | 12.494* | 15.400* | 14.434* | 19-01-17 | Scottsdale | 9 | Bon |

Sold new to the USA; until 2010 with its first owner; original yellow paint; re-upholstered interior.

| 2005 | NSX | 000085 | L | 140-160.000 USD | 108.464 | 144.100 | 128.739 | 03-09-16 | Auburn | 5158 | AA F365 |

Black with black interior; 4,600 original miles. Dealer installed/factory authorized Comptech supercharger.

| 2004 | NSX-T | 000030 | L | 140-160.000 USD | | NS | | 05-11-16 | Hilton Head | 178 | AA |

Yellow pearl with black leather interior; 3,500 actual miles. Manual gearbox.

| 1991 | NSX | NA11004303 | R | 23-29.000 GBP | 26.320 | 32.726 | 30.897 | 26-11-16 | Weybridge | 174 | His |

Silver with black interior; in very good overall condition. 61,000 miles covered. Bought in Japan by the current owner. Recently serviced.

| 2003 | NSX-T | 00001 | L | 110-130.000 USD | 82.110 | 100.000 | 93.790 | 15-01-17 | Kissimmee | S254 | Mec |

Red with black interior; 8,500 actual miles.

| 1991 | NSX | 001586 | L | 70-90.000 USD | 53.750* | 66.000* | 62.073* | 20-01-17 | Scottsdale | 61 | G&Co |

Black with ivory interior; 7,385 miles on the odometer. Recently serviced.

| 1995 | NSX | 001128 | L | 50-70.000 EUR | 46.398 | 68.478 | 52.765 | 02-07-17 | Monaco | 181 | Art |

Red with black leather interior; in good overall condition; manual gearbox.

HORCH (D) (1899-1940)

Year	Model	(Bodybuilder)	Chassis no.	Steering	Estimate	£	$	€	Date	Place	Lot	Auc. H.
1934	780 B cabriolet	(Glaser)	78380	L	600-900.000 EUR	532.945	707.957	632.500	03-09-16	Chantilly	25	Bon F366

Royal blue with grey leather interior; acquired in 2005 by Horch Classic and subsequently fully restored over a seven year period. Fitted with a Getrag 5-speed manual gearbox.

| 1939 | 930 V phaeton | | 931591 | L | 150-200.000 USD | 79.487* | 102.300* | 87.160* | 18-08-17 | Carmel | 11 | Bon |

Imported into the USA in the mid-1970s; refreshed in 1982; for 36 years in the same family ownership.

| 1938 | 853A Sportcabriolet | (Glaser) | 854126 | L | 700-900.000 EUR | 532.945 | 707.957 | 632.500 | 03-09-16 | Chantilly | 23 | Bon |

Black with beige leather interior; found in Ukraine in 2012 and subsequently fully restored over a four year period by Horch Classic. Currently fitted with a 5-speed Getrag manual gearbox.

| 1937 | 853 stromlinien coupé | | 853433 | L | 600-900.000 EUR | | NS | | 03-09-16 | Chantilly | 24 | Bon |

Black with black leather interior; acquired in 2005 by Horch Classic and subsequently fully restored. New body. ZF 5-speed manual gearbox.

| 1937 | 853 Spezial Roadster | | 853177 | L | 1.000-1.300.000 EUR | 872.091 | 1.158.476 | 1.035.000 | 03-09-16 | Chantilly | 26 | Bon F367 |

Silver and red with red leather interior; acquired in Ukraine in 2009 by Horch Classic and subsequently fully restored over a seven year period. Converted at date unknown to pick-up form, the car was fitted with the present, new Spezial Roadster replica body during the restoration.

| 1938 | 853 cabriolet | (Glaser) | 853400 | L | 450-550.000 EUR | | NS | | 08-02-17 | Paris | 156 | RMS |

Two-tone blue with grey interior; restored in the 2000s. Further mechanical works carried out in 2015-16 (see lots 340 Artcurial 3.2.12 $538,068 and 347 Bonhams 5.2.15 $433,010).

| 1938 | 853A cabriolet | | 854192A | L | 500-700.000 EUR | 508.328 | 633.488 | 596.000 | 10-02-17 | Paris | 132 | Art |

Two-tone red with red interior; fully restored in Germany at unspecified date. Described as in very good overall condition.

| 1938 | 853 Sport Cabriolet | | 853427 | L | 370-470.000 EUR | 435.337 | 553.957 | 495.800 | 24-06-17 | Wien | 369 | Dor |

Navy blue and cream with blue leather interior; bought in 1998 by the current owner; about 10,000 kms covered since the restoration completed in 2001.

HOTCHKISS (F) (1903-1970)

Year	Model	(Bodybuilder)	Chassis no.	Steering	Estimate	£	$	€	Date	Place	Lot	Auc. H.
1908	T Roi des Belges torpedo	(Descoins & Fils)	1219	R	80-100.000 GBP	163.900	212.709	185.584	30-06-17	Goodwood	274	Bon F368

Maroon with dark red leather interior; full restoration completed in 1998. In good driving order.

| 1911 | AB torpedo | | 3558 | R | 75-90.000 AUD | 41.303 | 51.357 | 48.486 | 27-11-16 | Melbourne | 49 | Mos |

Dark green with brown interior; restored at unspecified date, the car is described as in very good overall condition.

| 1930 | AM.2 Chantilly berline | | AM222814 | R | 12-15.000 GBP | 12.650 | 16.803 | 15.013 | 03-09-16 | Beaulieu | 415 | Bon |

Burgundy and black; acquired in 1988 by the present, second owner. Several mechanical and cosmetical works carried out over the years.

| 1925 | AM.2 torpedo | (La Savoisienne) | 21404 | R | 20-30.000 EUR | 22.061 | 28.141 | 25.200 | 18-06-17 | Fontainebleau | 59 | Ose |

Well preserved; from the Jacques Liscourt collection.

F363: 1977 Holden Torana A9X hatchback

F364: 1967 Honda S800 coupé

F365: 2005 Honda NSX

F366: 1934 Horch 780 B cabriolet (Glaser)

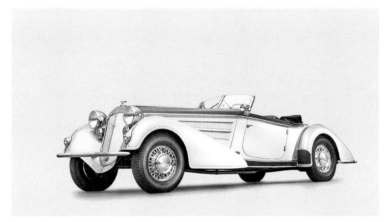

F367: 1937 Horch 853 Spezial Roadster

F368: 1908 Hotchkiss T Roi des Belges torpedo (Descoins & Fils)

F369: 1949 Hotchkiss 686.S.49 Gascogne berline

F370: 1938 HRG 1500 Airline coupé (Crofts)

Year	Model	(Bodybuilder)	Chassis no.	Steering	Estimate	Hammer price £	$	€	Date	Place	Lot	Auc. H.
1937	680 Chantilly limousine		65949	R	5-8.000 EUR	8.790*	10.837*	9.728*	07-10-16	Chateau-sur-Epte	12	Art
	Black; paintwork and interior redone many years ago. Since 1968 in the Andre Weber Collection.											
1949	686.S.49 Gascogne berline		85472	L	30-50.000 EUR	32.533*	40.543*	38.144*	10-02-17	Paris	48	Art **F369**
	From the early 1950s in the same family ownership; fully restored in 2010.											
1950	864.S.49 Artois berline		75810	R	20-30.000 EUR	20.781	25.958	23.400	06-11-16	Lyon	304	Ose
	Dark grey with red leather interior; restored circa 15 years ago.											
1952	1350 Anjou berline		3096	R	10-15.000 EUR	7.691*	9.482*	8.512*	07-10-16	Chateau-sur-Epte	11	Art
	Black; in good overall condition. From the Andre Weber Collection.											

HRG (GB) *(1935-1965)*

Year	Model	(Bodybuilder)	Chassis no.	Steering	Estimate	£	$	€	Date	Place	Lot	Auc. H.
1947	1500		W118	R	70-80.000 GBP	76.160	93.342	84.705	12-10-16	Duxford	131	H&H
	Green; acquired new by John Gott who raced it at numerous events until 1954. Since 1961 in the same family ownership. Several restoration works carried out in the late 1980s; interior retrimmed in 1999; driven at some historic events in recent years.											
1938	1500 Airline coupé	(Crofts)	WT68	R	225-275.000 USD	144.778*	176.000*	165.862*	10-03-17	Amelia Island	119	RMS **F370**
	White with green interior; only example built. With its first owner fo 23 years; in single ownership from 1965 to 2013; restored between 2000 and 2010. From the Orin Smith collection (see lot 58 Gooding & Company 08.3.13 $253,000).											
1948	1500		W169	R	38-50.000 GBP	68.906	85.726	79.766	29-03-17	Duxford	26	H&H
	Green with green leather interior; raced in period. Bought in 1983 circa by the current owner and subjected to a restoration completed in 1994.											
1951	1500 four-seater tourer		W185	R	50-60.000 GBP		NS		26-07-17	Duxford	19	H&H
	Green with red interior; sold in rolling chassis form to Australia where it was fitted with the present body. Raced at some rallies in period. In single ownership from 1956 to 2009. Reimported into the UK five years ago. Mechanicals overhauled; body and interior restored.											
1948	Bristol prototype		WB50	R	95-125.000 AUD	57.668	74.617	68.265	30-04-17	Melbourne	29	Mos
	Experimental chassis designed for a 2-litre Bristol engine. The project was later abandoned and the chassis, axles, springs, brakes and some front suspension parts were sold to Australia in the mid.1950s. Between the late 1990s and 2005 the car was rebuilt and fitted with the present sports 2-seater body finished in blue and the "-litre Bristol engine no.400/75/1065.											
1956	1.5 Twin-Cam roadster	(St. Leonards)	WS231	R	130-160.000 USD	99.535*	121.000*	114.030*	10-03-17	Amelia Island	132	RMS **F371**
	Black with burgundy leather interior; at unspecified date the car was fitted with the present 1,798cc BMC engine (the original 1-5-litre Singer engine is included with the sale). Restoration completed in 2014. From the Orin Smith collection.											

HUDSON (USA) *(1909-1957)*

Year	Model	(Bodybuilder)	Chassis no.	Steering	Estimate	£	$	€	Date	Place	Lot	Auc. H.
1937	DeLuxe Eight series 74 coupé		744238	L	35-45.000 USD	31.652	40.700	37.420	13-05-17	Auburn	3070	AA
	Beige with beige interior; in good overall condition.											
1954	Hornet brougham convertible		7283978	L	140-180.000 USD	53.546*	66.000*	61.862*	19-01-17	Scottsdale	3	Bon
	Green gold with maroon leather interior; fully restored between 2013 and 2015. Automatic transmission.											
1953	Hornet Club Coupé		236797	L	NQ	26.875*	33.000*	31.037*	21-01-17	Scottsdale	741.1	B/J
	Cream with green interior; 3-speed manual gearbox.											
1951	Hornet brougham convertible		7A109578	L	140-180.000 USD	128.205*	165.000*	140.580*	18-08-17	Carmel	22	Bon **F372**
	Black with maroon leather interior; bought in 2012 by the current owner and subsequently restored.											
1952	Hornet club coupé		164816	L	38-44.000 AUD	34.686	44.669	38.014	20-08-17	Mallala Park	24	Mos
	Tan with white roof; automatic transmission. From the collection of the late Clem Smith.											
1955	Hornet sedan		7385	L	20-28.000 AUD	18.066	23.265	19.799	20-08-17	Mallala Park	28	Mos
	Red with cream roof and green interior; automatic transmission. From the collection of the late Clem Smith.											
1955	Italia	(Touring)	IT10010	L	400-500.000 USD		NS		17-08-17	Monterey	15	WoA
	For 44 years with its first owner; recent concours-quality restoration.											

HUMBER (GB) *(1901-1976)*

Year	Model	(Bodybuilder)	Chassis no.	Steering	Estimate	£	$	€	Date	Place	Lot	Auc. H.
1903	Olympia tandem		100070	C	35-40.000 GBP	36.800	45.963	41.437	04-11-16	London	214	Bon **F373**
	Blue with grey fuel tank and blue leather upholstery; it requires recommissioning prior to use (see lot 201 Bonhams 3.11.06 $42,782).											

F371: 1956 HRG 1.5 Twin-Cam roadster (St. Leonards)

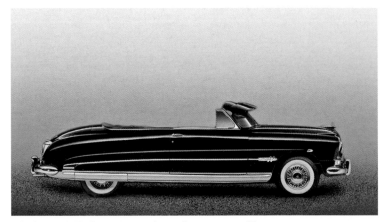

F372: 1951 Hudson Hornet brougham convertible

Year	Model	(Bodybuilder)	Chassis no.	Steering	Estimate	£	$	€	Date	Place	Lot	Auc. H.

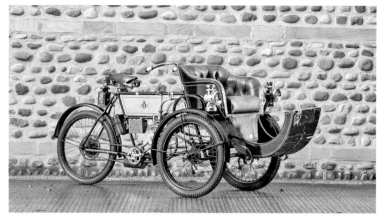

F373: 1903 Humber Olympia tandem

F374: 1933 Hupmobile Series B-216 roadster (Raulang)

Year	Model	Chassis no.	Steering	Estimate	£	$	€	Date	Place	Lot	Auc. H.
1904	**8.5hp two-seater**	2411	R	135-165.000 USD		NS		18-08-17	Carmel	68	Bon

Dark blue and white; in the same ownership in the UK from 1950 to 2000 when it was sold to the USA where it was restored. Recently recommissioned; entered for the 2017 London to Brighton run (see lots 1890 Brooks 4.12.00 $94,784 and 133 Bonhams 15.1.15 $148,500).

| 1904 | **Royal Humberette 6.5hp limousine** | 2109 | R | 50-60.000 GBP | 57.500 | 71.818 | 64.745 | 04-11-16 | London | 208 | Bon |

Known ownership history from new; restored in the 1950s; driven at several London to Brighton Run editions (see lot 209 Bonhams 2.11.12 $76,944).

| 1921 | **11.4hp doctor's coupé** | M8031A | R | 10-12.000 GBP | 11.475 | 14.703 | 13.148 | 02-06-17 | Solihull | 24 | H&H |

Blue and black with beige interior; restored in the past, the car requires recommissioning prior to use (see lot 61 H & H 7.11.15 $27,616).

| 1929 | **16/50hp Tickford saloon (Salmons)** | 17735 | R | 10-12.000 GBP | 11.250 | 14.415 | 12.890 | 02-06-17 | Solihull | 17 | H&H |

Dark blue and black with brown interior; restored in 1979 the mechanicals require recommissioning prior to use (see H&H lots 45 12.4.02 $19,825 and 75 6.8.05 $15,614).

| 1963 | **Super Snipe saloon** | B8282213VVS0 | R | 9-11.000 GBP | 8.792 | 10.927 | 10.210 | 16-11-16 | Donington Park | 87 | H&H |

Grey; in unrestored condition. Three owners.

HUMMER (USA) (1980-)

| 1980 | **H1** | 1372A8431WE179008 | L | 40-50.000 GBP | | NS | | 08-10-16 | Ascot | 342 | Coy |

Described as in very good overall condition; restored in 2002.

HUPMOBILE (USA) (1909-1940)

| 1933 | **Series B-216 roadster (Raulang)** | B8832 | L | 50-60.000 USD | 40.145 | 49.500 | 44.431 | 07-10-16 | Hershey | 219 | RMS F374 |

Red and white; restoration completed five years ago.

IMPERIAL (USA) (1946-1975)

| 1953 | **Crown Imperial limousine** | 7773649 | L | 40-50.000 USD | 35.697* | 44.000* | 41.241* | 19-01-17 | Scottsdale | 99 | Bon |

Black with light green interior; restored circa 20 years ago. The original automatic transmission was replaced with a more modern 727 Chrysler unit (see lot 38 Gooding & Company 17.1.14 $66,000 and 24 Bonhams 14.8.15 NS).

| 1951 | **Imperial convertible** | 7746232 | L | NQ | 43.896* | 53.900* | 50.693* | 21-01-17 | Scottsdale | 1079 | B/J |

Tan with red interior; restored.

| 1951 | **Imperial convertible** | 7746661 | L | 90-110.000 USD | 66.082 | 86.000 | 76.927 | 20-05-17 | Indianapolis | S207 | Mec |

Light grey with blue leather interior; fully restored. Automatic transmission (see lot 856 Auctions America 7.5.16 $70,000).

| 1956 | **Imperial Southampton two-door hardtop** | C5611508 | L | 70-80.000 USD | | NS | | 03-09-16 | Auburn | 5139 | AA |

White with turquoise roof and turquoise cloth and white leather interior; concours-quality restoration.

| 1960 | **Crown Imperial convertible** | 9204106018 | L | 120-150.000 USD | 110.028 | 137.500 | 128.604 | 01-04-17 | Ft.Lauderdale | 568 | AA F375 |

Mauve with mauve leather interior; restored (see lot S230 Mecum 20.5.16 $97,500).

F375: 1960 Imperial Crown Imperial convertible

F376: 1963 Innocenti Spider S

Year	Model	(Bodybuilder)	Chassis no.	Steering	Estimate	Hammer price £	Hammer price $	Hammer price €	Sale Date	Sale Place	Lot	Auc. H.
1958	**Crown Imperial convertible**		LY16947	L	NA	**55.949**	**71.500**	**66.831**	22-04-17	Dallas	2505	**Lea**
	Black with red interior; restored some years ago (see lot TH250 Russo & Steele 18.8.11 $95,590).											
1961	**Imperial sedan**		9313193379	L	35-50.000 USD	**15.356***	**18.700***	**17.722***	09-03-17	Amelia Island	160	**Bon**
	Metallic bronze with tan interior; in good driving order.											
1964	**Imperial Crown convertible**		9243105242	L	20-30.000 USD	**16.573***	**20.350***	**19.139***	20-01-17	Phoenix	282	**RMS**
	Blue with blue leather interior; in good overall condition.											

INNOCENTI (I) *(1961-1996)*

Year	Model	(Bodybuilder)	Chassis no.	Steering	Estimate	£	$	€	Date	Place	Lot	Auc. H.
1963	**Spider S**		300421	L	9-12.000 GBP		**NS**		26-11-16	Weybridge	171	**His**
	White with red interior; imported into the UK from Italy in 2015. Mechanical rebuild carried out in 2010 probably. 1100cc engine.											
1963	**Spider S**		300421	L	8-10.000 GBP	**9.000**	**11.711**	**10.476**	20-05-17	Ascot	261	**His** F376
	See lot 171 Historics 26.11.16.											
1971	**Mini Cooper Mk3**		146212	L	8-12.000 EUR	**9.109***	**11.066***	**10.132***	30-10-16	Paris	136	**Art**
	Red with black roof; restored.											
1974	**Mini Cooper**		557390	L	7-10.000 EUR	**12.402***	**15.422***	**14.560***	25-11-16	Milan	213	**RMS**
	Brown with white roof; 91,812 kms. From the Duemila Ruote collection.											
1975	**Mini Cooper**		560452	L	8-12.000 EUR	**9.507**	**11.751**	**10.944**	19-03-17	Fontainebleau	243	**Ose**
	Dark green; in good driving order.											

INTERMECCANICA (I) *(1959-1975)*

Year	Model	(Bodybuilder)	Chassis no.	Steering	Estimate	£	$	€	Date	Place	Lot	Auc. H.
1967	**Torino coupé**		40052	L	70-80.000 GBP	**69.750**	**91.338**	**77.876**	29-07-17	Silverstone	730	**SiC**
	Red; imported into the UK from the USA in 2015 and subsequently restored. Ford 289 Hi-Po engine with 4-speed manual gearbox.											
1970	**Italia Spyder**		50377414	L	110-130.000 USD	**105.626**	**132.000**	**123.460**	01-04-17	Ft.Lauderdale	529	**AA** F377
	Grey with red interior; restored; 4-speed manual gearbox.											
1970	**Italia Spyder**		59248314	L	120-150.000 USD	**102.986**	**128.700**	**120.373**	01-04-17	Ft.Lauderdale	614	**AA**
	Black with red interior; for 30 years in the same family ownership. The engine has covered less than 1,000 miles since the rebuild. Body recently repainted (see lot 200 Auctions America 31.10.15 $93,000).											
1972	**Indra spider**		81002414	L	75-85.000 EUR		**NS**		08-04-17	Essen	121	**Coy**
	Yellow with black interior.											

INVICTA (GB) *(1925-1950)*

Year	Model	(Bodybuilder)	Chassis no.	Steering	Estimate	£	$	€	Date	Place	Lot	Auc. H.
1932	**12/45 1.5l/S-Type 4.5l replica**		L40	R	200-250.000 GBP	**214.300**	**285.555**	**253.431**	10-09-16	Goodwood	121	**Bon**
	Green with polished aluminium bonnet; replica built between 1999 and 2010 on an original 12/45hp Invicta chassis. 4,5l Meadows marine engine. New body built to Carbodies style. 750 miles covered since completion.											

ISO (I) *(1953-1979)*

Year	Model	(Bodybuilder)	Chassis no.	Steering	Estimate	£	$	€	Date	Place	Lot	Auc. H.
1965	**Rivolta GT IR300 (Bertone)**		410495	L	10-15.000 EUR	**52.472***	**65.247***	**61.600***	25-11-16	Milan	624	**RMS**
	Red; race prepared. From the Duemila Ruote collection.											
1964	**Rivolta GT/A3C Competition recreation**		IR360262	L	220-260.000 GBP		**NS**		07-12-16	London	340	**Bon**
	Dark metallic red with black interior; recreation built on a shortened Rivolta GT chassis. Completed two years ago. 5.3-litre V8 engine.											
1965	**Rivolta GT IR340 (Bertone)**		IR410481	L	26-35.000 GBP	**41.100**	**50.047**	**46.944**	14-01-17	Birmingham	111	**Coy**
	Red with black interior; for restoration. Working engine.											
1963	**Rivolta GT IR340 (Bertone)**		IR340075	L	80-120.000 USD	**75.857***	**93.500***	**87.638***	19-01-17	Scottsdale	22	**Bon** F378
	Silver with maroon leather interior; restored at unspecified date. Currently fitted with a 1969 Chevrolet small block engine.											
1967	**Rivolta GT IR300 (Bertone)**		410389	L	80-120.000 EUR	**78.283**	**98.366**	**92.000**	09-02-17	Paris	405	**Bon**
	Light metallic blue with black vinyl interior; restored two years ago. Chevrolet 327 engine with manual gearbox (see lot 416 Bonhams 4.2.16 $103,095).											
1965	**Rivolta GT IR300 (Bertone)**		350198	L	80-100.000 USD	**59.415**	**74.250**	**69.446**	01-04-17	Ft.Lauderdale	514	**AA**
	Red with grey interior; automatic transmission.											

F377: 1970 Intermeccanica Italia Spyder

F378: 1963 Iso Rivolta GT IR340 (Bertone)

Year	Model (Bodybuilder)	Chassis No.	Steering	Estimate	Hammer price £	$	€	Date	Place	Lot	Auc. H.

F379: 1971 Iso Grifo IR 9 Can Am (Bertone)   F380: 1975 Iso Lele Sport (Bertone)

Year	Model (Bodybuilder)	Chassis No.	Steering	Estimate	£	$	€	Date	Place	Lot	Auc. H.
1967	**Grifo GL (Bertone)**	GL640064D	R	30-50.000 GBP	128.800*	172.360*	153.388*	07-09-16	London	108	**RMS**
	Complete, for restoration. Original 327 engine and gearbox.										
1966	**Grifo GL (Bertone)**	GL650082	L	275-350.000 USD	235.043	302.500	257.730	19-08-17	Monterey	231	**RMS**
	Medium grey with habana leather interior; imported into the USA in 2013 and subsequently restored. Engine rebuilt.										
1971	**Grifo IR 9 Can Am (Bertone)**	120342	L	280-360.000 EUR	376.163	468.781	441.040	10-02-17	Paris	73	**Art** F379
	Red with original black leather interior; since 1987 in the current ownership, the car has covered 7,000 kms since the restoration carried out in 2011.										
1970	**Grifo GL (Bertone)**	GL050336	L	400-500.000 USD	217.166*	264.000*	248.794*	11-03-17	Amelia Island	228	**RMS**
	Silver with original blue interior; originally finished in white and displayed at the 1970 Turin Motor Show; subsequently Piero Rivolta personal car. ZF 5-speed gearbox. Imported into the USA in 1982.										
1973	**Grifo (Bertone)**	FAGL310395	L	200-250.000 GBP	208.700	270.851	236.311	30-06-17	Goodwood	232	**Bon**
	Red with camel leather interior; 43,435 kms on the odometer. Automatic transmission. California title (see lot 128 Bonhams 13.5.16 NS).										
1973	**Fidia (Ghia)**	B310179D	R	50-60.000 GBP		NS		05-12-16	London	130A	**Coy**
	Blue with champagne leather interior; 51,500 miles on the odometer. Fitted in recent years with a more modern automatic transmission (see lots 162 Historics 6.6.15 NS and 158 Coys 2.7.16 $69,066).										
1969	**Lele (Bertone)**	500087	L	NQ	57.334	70.400	66.211	21-01-17	Scottsdale	8271	**R&S**
	White; sold new in Italy. Imported into the USA in 1984. 350 Chevrolet engine with manual gearbox.										
1969	**Lele (Bertone)**	500087	L	NA	55.556	71.500	60.918	19-08-17	Monterey	1132	**R&S**
	See lot 8271 Russo & Steele 21.1.17.										
1975	**Lele Sport (Bertone)**	239D	R	58-65.000 GBP	53.520	71.492	63.287	08-09-16	Fontwell Park	112	**Coy**
	Red with black interior; 35,000 miles covered. Recently serviced. Clutch replaced.										
1973	**Lele Sport (Bertone)**	500263D	R	28-32.000 GBP	28.560	35.003	31.764	12-10-16	Duxford	28	**H&H**
	Red with black interior; engine overhauled three years ago.										
1975	**Lele Sport (Bertone)**	239D	R	48-58.000 GBP	48.906	63.759	57.288	18-05-17	London	113	**Coy** F380
	See lot 112 Coys 8.9.16.										
1975	**Lele Sport (Bertone)**	239D	R	45-55.000 GBP		NS		15-07-17	Blenheim Pal.	143	**Coy**
	See lot 113 Coys 18.5.17.										

ISOTTA FRASCHINI (I) (1900-1949)

Year	Model (Bodybuilder)	Chassis No.	Steering	Estimate	£	$	€	Date	Place	Lot	Auc. H.
1924	**Tipo 8A landaulette (C.Sala)**	655	R	675-775.000 USD	353.857	434.500	408.647	20-01-17	Phoenix	232	**RMS**
	Blue with brown interior; Cesare Sala body with some additions by Carrozzeria Riva in 1926. Used when new by the factory as a demonstrator and before WWII stored at a warehouse, offsite of the factory. In 1993 the Isotta Fraschini name was revived by a partnership between Audi and Carrozzeria Fissore who later sold the name and the car to Finmeccanica. The current owner bought the car directly from Finmeccanica and imported it into the USA in 2016. Described as in original condition; cleaned and mechanically serviced.										F381
1933	**Tipo 8A dual-cowl phaeton (Castagna)**	1664	R	800-1.100.000 USD	741.985	902.000	850.045	11-03-17	Amelia Island	236	**RMS**
	Two-tone burgundy with beige interior; believed to be the 1933 Paris Motor Show car; sold new to the USA; bought in the 1940s by the Pacific Auto Rentals and rented for several movies. Restored some years ago, it is described as in very good overall condition (see lots 99 Christie's 17.8.97 NS and 43 Gooding & Company 17.1.09 $1,089,000).										F382

 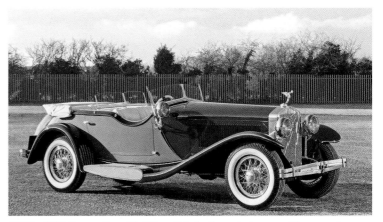

F381: 1924 Isotta Fraschini Tipo 8A landaulette (C.Sala)   F382: 1933 Isotta Fraschini Tipo 8A dual-cowl phaeton (Castagna)

F383: 1948 Jaguar 3.5l saloon *F384: 1951 Jaguar Mk V 3.5l cabriolet*

JAGUAR (GB) (1945-)

Year	Model	Chassis no.	Steering	Estimate	£	$	€	Date	Place	Lot	Auc. H.
1947	1.5l SE saloon	412220	R	NA		NS		02-09-16	Salon Privé	252	SiC
	Black with ivory interior; 50 miles covered since the engine rebuild (see lot 243 Historics 29.11.14 $28,860).										
1948	3.5l saloon	612197	R	55-65.000 GBP	69.440	84.953	80.412	04-03-17	Brooklands	203	His F383
	Black with pigskin leather interior; restoration completed in the early 2000s. In excellent overall condition. Sunroof.										
1948	3.5l saloon	SL3470	L	55-65.000 USD	36.519	47.000	40.044	19-08-17	Monterey	S57	Mec
	Burgundy and champagne with brown leather interior; sunroof.										
1948	3.5l cabriolet	637332	L	15-25.000 EUR	34.293*	41.661*	38.144*	30-10-16	Paris	102	Art
	Since 1965 in the same family ownership; for restoration.										
1948	3.5l cabriolet	637237	L	120-140.000 USD	102.638	125.000	117.238	15-01-17	Kissimmee	F216	Mec
	Burgundy and black with burgundy interior; 1,050 miles covered since a concours-quality restoration completed in 2000 (see lots 191 RM 12.3.11 $137,500 and 205 RM/Sotheby's 14.3.15 $137,500).										
1951	3.5l cabriolet	640220	R	70-80.000 GBP	68.000	84.599	78.717	29-03-17	Duxford	88	H&H
	Black with red leather interior; sold new to New Zealand, the car was discovered in 1994 and subsequently fully restored. Reimported into the UK in 2011.										
1950	Mk V 3.5l saloon	624565	R	24-26.000 GBP		NS		26-07-17	Duxford	9	H&H
	Ivory white with original tan leather interior; in good overall condition (see lots 239 Historics 8.3.14 NS and 162 Coys 11.7.15 NS).										
1951	Mk V 3.5l cabriolet	S647465	L	110-130.000 USD	60.712	80.000	71.256	17-09-16	Aspen	139	TFA
	Dark red with beige interior; the car has covered less than 1,000 miles since the restoration carried out in the 2000s (see lots 8 Gooding & Company 13.3.15 $94,600 and 181 RM/Sotheby's 8.10.15 $93,500).										
1951	Mk V 3.5l cabriolet	647505	L	60-80.000 EUR		NS		19-03-17	Fontainebleau	204	Ose
	Black with beige leather interior; from the René Cocheteux collection.										
1950	Mk V 3.5l cabriolet	647205	L	70-80.000 EUR		NS		18-06-17	Fontainebleau	67	Ose
	Restored many years ago, the car is described as in good overall condition.										
1951	Mk V 3.5l cabriolet	647505	L	40-60.000 EUR	54.627	69.682	62.400	18-06-17	Fontainebleau	71	Ose F384
	See lot 204 Osenat 19.3.17.										
1950	XK 120 alloy roadster	670111	L	300-400.000 USD	256.410	330.000	281.160	18-08-17	Monterey	135	RMS
	Red with biscuit leather interior; sold new to Venezuela; imported into the USA in 1979; restored to concours condition in the late 1980s; recently refreshed. Cylinder head replaced with an unstamped unit (see Barrett-Jackson lots 969 20.1.00 $111,300 and 654 18.1.02 $129,600).										F385
1953	XK 120 SE roadster	S673219	R	90-110.000 GBP	112.000	149.878	133.381	07-09-16	London	165	RMS
	Metallic grey with brown leather interior; sold new to the USA, the car was reimported into the UK in the 1990s and fully restored. Fitted with a XK 140 engine, Getrag 5-speed gearbox and four-wheel disc brakes. Further restoration works carried out in recent years. From the estate of Edward Carter.										
1952	XK 120 roadster	672675	R	60-70.000 GBP	54.166	72.176	64.057	10-09-16	Goodwood	164	Bon
	Red; sold new to the USA, the car was reimported into the UK in 1992 and fully restored and converted to right hand drive circa 16 years ago.										

F385: 1950 Jaguar XK 120 alloy roadster *F386: 1953 Jaguar XK 120 coupé*

INTERNATIONAL VALUERS AND AUCTIONEERS

COYS
FOUNDED 1919

› MOTOR CARS › MOTORCYCLES › SPORTING GUNS › AUTOMOBILIA ›
› AERONAUTICA › RARE MECHANICAL COMPONENTS ›
› MASCOTS & BADGES › PRECISION TOYS & MODELS ›
› BOOKS & LITERATURE › 19TH & 20TH CENTURY POSTERS & MOTORING ART ›
›› FINE CLOCKS & WATCHES › FORMULA 1 › NAUTICAL ›

UNITED KINGDOM • MONACO • FRANCE • ITALY • HOLLAND • BELGIUM • GERMANY • USA
OFFICES AND CONSULTANTS WORLDWIDE

COYS LONDON
Manor Court, Lower
Mortlake Road, Richmond,
TW9 2LL, United Kingdom
Tel. +44 (0) 208 614 7888
Fax +44 (0) 208 614 7889
auctions@coys.co.uk
www.coys.co.uk

COYS EUROPE
Michael Haag
Elisabethstr. 4,
D-68165 Mannheim,
Germany
Tel: +49 (0) 621 412004
Fax: +49 (0) 621 415551
coyseurope@web.de

COYS FRANCE
Jacques Morabito
34, avenue des Champs-
Élysées
75008 Paris
+33 (0)1 4076 5798
+33 (0)6 0203 6792
jacques.morabito@coys.co.uk

COYS ITALIA
Giuliano Fazi
+39 335 148 8303
giuliano.fazi@coys.co.uk

Year	Model	(Bodybuilder)	Chassis no.	Steering	Estimate	Hammer Price £	$	€	Date	Place	Lot	Auc. H.
1950	XK 120 roadster		660214	R	60-90.000 USD	64.111	82.500	73.417	03-10-16	Philadelphia	235	Bon

White; imported new into Australia by Bib Stillwell and raced in period. Upgraded over the years and fitted with disc brakes. Since 2005 in the current ownership and driven at historic events; unused since 2010 (see Bonhams lots 1037 19.8.05 $46,000 and 611 13.8.10 NS).

| 1951 | XK 120 roadster | | 660587 | R | 75-95.000 GBP | 62.500 | 77.713 | 73.369 | 26-11-16 | Weybridge | 153 | His |

Cream with black leather interior; since 1985 in the same family ownership. Several mechanical works carried out in 1988 including the engine replacement with the present 3.8-litre unit.

| 1950 | XK 120 roadster | | 660065 | R | 150-200.000 GBP | 169.500 | 213.960 | 201.044 | 04-12-16 | London | 26 | Bon |

White with red leather interior; restored in 1999. Last serviced in 2015 (see lot 361 Bonhams 26.6.15 $204,910).

| 1954 | XK 120 roadster | | 661145 | R | 90-110.000 GBP | 89.200 | 113.418 | 105.970 | 05-12-16 | London | 108 | Coy |

British racing green with beige leather interior; in good overall condition.

| 1952 | XK 120 roadster | | 672627 | L | 65-80.000 GBP | NS | | | 07-12-16 | Chateau Impney | 28 | H&H |

Pastel green; for 48 years with the present, third owner. Unrestored; in good mechanical order; recently recommissioned.

| 1953 | XK 120 roadster | | 673222 | L | 100-150.000 EUR | NS | | | 09-02-17 | Paris | 419 | Bon |

Black and red with red leather interior; in largely original condition. In good working order.

| 1952 | XK 120 roadster | | 672220 | L | 90-120.000 EUR | 127.082* | 158.372* | 149.000* | 10-02-17 | Paris | 10 | Art |

Grey with red leather interior; fully restored in the early 1990s (see lot 130 Artcurial 7.7.12 $140,082).

| 1954 | XK 120 roadster | | 661145 | R | 90-110.000 GBP | NS | | | 18-02-17 | London | 333 | Coy |

See lot 108 Coys 5.12.16.

| 1954 | XK 120 SE roadster | | S675382 | R | 85-100.000 GBP | 128.800 | 157.574 | 149.150 | 04-03-17 | Brooklands | 206 | His |

Silver with red and parchment interior; reimported into the UK from the USA in 2011 and subsequently restored and converted to right-hand drive. Engine rebuilt and fitted with a 5-speed gearbox; uprated to disc brakes all-round (see lots 293 Historics 18.2.12 NS, 128 Coys 21.4.12 NA, and 256 Historics 11.6.16 NS).

| 1954 | XK 120 roadster | | 661145 | R | 90-110.000 GBP | 92.254 | 115.318 | 108.731 | 12-04-17 | London | 324 | Coy |

See lot 333 Coys 18.2.17.

| 1954 | XK 120 SE roadster | | S675858 | L | 150-180.000 GBP | NS | | | 06-06-17 | Woodcote Park | 38 | H&H |

Dark blue with red leather interior; restored in the USA in the early 2000s; partial cosmetic restoration in 2011-12; registered in the UK in 2013. Described as an exact replica of the record-breaking car which attained the speed of 132.6mph at Jabbeke Belgium, 30 May, 1949 (see lot 46 Gooding & Company 20.8.06 $148,500).

| 1951 | XK 120 roadster | | 660739 | R | 100-120.000 GBP | NS | | | 15-07-17 | Blenheim Pal. | 132 | Coy |

Grey with red leather interior; recent mechanical and cosmetic works.

| 1953 | XK 120 roadster | | 661133 | R | 90-110.000 GBP | 88.920 | 114.920 | 101.058 | 15-07-17 | Blenheim Pal. | 140 | Coy |

Pastel green with original green leather interior; for 60 years in the same family ownership; raced in the 1960s and fitted with a 3.8-litre Jaguar engine; body repainted in the 1990s; recommissioned in early 2017; just over 18,000 miles covered since new.

| 1952 | XK 120 roadster | | 672274 | L | 140-180.000 USD | 94.017* | 121.000* | 103.092* | 18-08-17 | Pebble Beach | 6 | G&Co |

Pastel light blue with two-tone interior; less than 2,500 miles covered since the restoration completed in 1991.

| 1952 | XK 120 coupé | | 679368 | L | 85-105.000 GBP | 79.900 | 106.467 | 94.490 | 10-09-16 | Goodwood | 137 | Bon |

Old English white with red leather interior; restored in 2004-05.

| 1952 | XK 120 coupé | | 679274 | L | 125-150.000 USD | 68.301 | 90.000 | 80.163 | 17-09-16 | Aspen | 136 | TFA |

Dark blue with red leather interior; sold new to the USA, exported to Germany in 1987, reimported into the USA in 2008. Restored in 1991-92; 26,619 miles covered since new.

| 1953 | XK 120 coupé | | S680697 | L | 55-65.000 EUR | 78.231* | 97.277* | 91.840* | 25-11-16 | Milan | 312 | RMS |

Light blue with light beige interior. From the Duemila Ruote collection.

| 1952 | XK 120 coupé | | 679368 | L | 85-105.000 EUR | 65.904 | 82.082 | 77.000 | 08-04-17 | Essen | 115 | Coy |

See lot 137 Bonhams 10.9.16.

| 1953 | XK 120 coupé | | 680421 | L | 80-100.000 EUR | NS | | | 08-04-17 | Essen | 139 | Coy |

Light metallic green; restored, the car is described as in very good overall condition (see lots Artcurial 129 11.11.12 NS, and Coys 625 4.12.12 $89,563, 137 18.1.14 NS, 137 26.9.15 $87,770, and 105 6.8.16 $100,691).

| 1953 | XK 120 coupé | | 669035 | R | 90-120.000 GBP | 102.300 | 132.765 | 115.834 | 30-06-17 | Goodwood | 261 | Bon F386 |

Described as in very good original condition; circa 81,000 miles covered.

| 1953 | XK 120 cabriolet | | 667149 | R | 100-125.000 GBP | 111.500 | 148.942 | 131.849 | 08-09-16 | Fontwell Park | 131 | Coy |

Grey with red leather interior; recently restored. Two owners since new (see lots 352 Historics 22.10.11 $44,520 and 175 Coys 2.7.16 NS).

| 1954 | XK 120 SE cabriolet | | S667294 | R | 55-65.000 USD | 48.724 | 62.700 | 55.797 | 03-10-16 | Philadelphia | 223 | Bon |

Red with black interior; restored in the 1980s. Some mechanical works carried out in 2014 (see lot 216 Bonhams 1.9.06 $74,105).

| 1953 | XK 120 cabriolet | | 677621 | L | 70-80.000 GBP | 72.475 | 88.043 | 80.607 | 29-10-16 | London | 126 | Coy |

Black with tan interior; restored in the early 2000s and fitted with a 5-speed gearbox.

| 1953 | XK 120 cabriolet | | 667149 | R | 90-110.000 GBP | 101.480 | 123.278 | 112.866 | 29-10-16 | London | 150 | Coy |

See lot 131 Coys 8.9.16.

| 1954 | XK 120 cabriolet | | 667283 | R | 250-280.000 AUD | NS | | | 27-11-16 | Melbourne | 86 | Mos |

Ivory; for 38 years in the current ownership. Body repainted in 1990.

| 1953 | XK 120 cabriolet | | 667149 | R | 85-100.000 GBP | 104.810 | 127.627 | 119.714 | 14-01-17 | Birmingham | 129 | Coy |

See lot 150 Coys 29.10.16.

| 1954 | XK 120 SE cabriolet | | S678286 | L | 90-110.000 GBP | 100.035 | 125.044 | 117.901 | 12-04-17 | London | 1954 | Coy |

Pastel blue with blue leather interior; in good overall condition. 19,000 miles on the odometer. Sold new to the USA and reimported into the UK a few years ago.

| 1953 | XK 120 cabriolet | | 667149 | R | 90-110.000 GBP | 88.920 | 115.925 | 104.161 | 18-05-17 | London | 112 | Coy |

See lot 129 Coys 14.1.17.

| 1954 | XK SE 120 cabriolet | | S678204 | L | 72-87.000 GBP | NS | | | 20-05-17 | Ascot | 124 | His |

British racing green with light green interior; sold new to the USA; restored between 2010 and 2012; reimported into the UK in 2015.

| 1954 | XK 120 cabriolet | | 678329 | L | 90-130.000 EUR | 92.898 | 118.210 | 105.800 | 24-06-17 | Wien | 363 | Dor |

Cream yellow with burgundy leather interior; until 1980 with its first owner; restored between 1983 and 1985; mechanicals overhauled in 2000.

Year	Model	(Bodybuilder)	Chassis no.	Steering	Estimate	Hammer price £	Hammer price $	Hammer price €	Sale Date	Sale Place	Lot	Auc. H.
1953	Mk VII		717378	R	26-30.000 GBP		NS		12-10-16	Duxford	123	H&H
	Black with red leather interior; described as in good original condition.											
1955	Mk VIIM		726904DN	R	45-55.000 GBP	70.940	94.528	83.894	10-09-16	Goodwood	114	Bon F387
	Black with beige leather interior; in original condition. Three owners; believed to be 8,800 original miles.											
1955	Mk VIIM		738747DN	L	21-27.000 GBP	21.500	26.748	24.888	29-03-17	Duxford	109	H&H
	Navy blue with light blue leather interior; reimported into the UK from the USA and restored between 2011 and 2014.											
1956	XK 140 SE coupé		S815758BW	L	60-80.000 GBP	59.740	79.604	70.649	10-09-16	Goodwood	107	Bon
	White with red interior; reimported into the UK from the USA in 1992 and restored between 2002 and 2006. The original automatic transmission replaced by the present 4-speed Moss manual unit. Engine rebuilt in 2011; body repainted in 2012; full service in July 2014.											
1956	XK 140 coupé		804750DN	R	55-65.000 GBP	59.360	72.752	66.020	12-10-16	Duxford	119	H&H
	Restored in the early 1990s, the car is described as in good overall condition.											
1955	XK 140 coupé		804365DN	L	40-60.000 EUR	56.798*	69.001*	63.176*	30-10-16	Paris	104	Art
	In good overall condition.											
1955	XK 140 SE coupé		S814607	R	120-140.000 AUD		NS		27-11-16	Melbourne	41	Mos
	Sold new to the USA, later the car was imported into Australia where in 2001 it was restored and converted to right-hand drive.											
1956	XK 140 coupé		S804635DN	R	45-65.000 GBP	56.680*	72.069*	67.336*	05-12-16	London	110	Coy
	Blue with biscuit interior; in the ownership of one family for nearly 55 years. Stored since the early 1990s; recently lightly recommissioned.											
1956	XK 140 SE coupé		S815573	L	75-90.000 EUR	68.117	82.948	77.805	14-01-17	Maastricht	217	Coy
	Dark blue with grey leather interior; in good overall condition.											
1957	XK 140 MC coupé		S815909	L	NQ	80.626*	99.000*	93.110*	21-01-17	Scottsdale	1315.1	B/J
	Dark blue with grey/blue interior; bought in 1979 by the father of the present owner and fully restored over a 20 year period.											
1956	XK 140 SE coupé		S815655BW	L	100-120.000 EUR	70.455	88.530	82.800	09-02-17	Paris	365	Bon
	Finished in black with red leather interior and automatic transmission, the car was sold new to the USA. Restored in 2016. Currently fitted with a manual gearbox.											
1955	XK 140 coupé		804183	R	NQ	44.360*	55.113*	51.746*	18-02-17	London	313	Coy
	White with red interior; recently benefited from attention to the engine and gearbox (see lots 257 Historics 1.9.12 $49,293 and 331 Silverstone Auctions 15.11.13 $69,848).											
1956	XK 140 SE coupé		S815573	L	75-90.000 EUR	63.337	78.884	74.000	08-04-17	Essen	127	Coy
	See lot 217 Coys 14.1.17.											
1956	XK 140 MC coupé		S815727BW	L	80-100.000 USD	59.043	75.900	67.665	04-06-17	Greenwich	149	Bon
	Black with tan interior; some restoration works carried out in the 2000s. Automatic transmission.											
1956	XK 140 MC cabriolet		S817644	L	100-140.000 USD	135.729*	165.000*	155.496*	10-03-17	Amelia Island	130	RMS F388
	Old English white with blue interior; in 2006 the paintwork and interior were replaced, the engine was rebuilt, and the car was fitted with four-wheel disc brakes. From the Orin Smith collection (see lot 293 RM 19.1.07 $99,000).											
1955	XK 140 SE cabriolet		S817502	R	80-100.000 GBP	110.250	137.162	127.625	29-03-17	Duxford	71	H&H
	Finished in cream with red leather interior, the car was sold new to the USA. Reimported into the UK in 1988; restored in the 1990s and converted to right-hand drive; engine overhauled in 1999 and fitted with a 5-speed Getrag gearbox (see lot 39 H & H 13.9.06 $84,326).											
1957	XK 140 roadster		S813153DN	L	30-35.000 EUR	81.093*	100.836*	95.200*	25-11-16	Milan	580	RMS
	Blue; restoration to be completed. From the Duemila Ruote collection.											
1956	XK 140 roadster		812476	L	120-160.000 USD	93.705*	115.500*	108.258*	19-01-17	Phoenix	117	RMS F389
	Old English white with red interior; restored in 2008 and refreshed in 2014-15.											
1955	XK 140 roadster		S810907	L	NQ	179.168*	220.000*	206.910*	21-01-17	Scottsdale	1371	B/J
	Red; restored in recent years (see lot 4147 Auctions America 5.9.15 $181,500).											
1955	XK 140 SE roadster		S810874	L	75-85.000 GBP	121.500	156.213	143.637	13-05-17	Silverstone	322	SiC
	British racing green with green interior; reimported into the UK from the USA in 1998 and restored; several mechanical works, including an engine overhaul, carried out in 2015.											
1954	XK 140 SE roadster		S810351	R	110-135.000 GBP		NS		20-05-17	Ascot	185	His
	British racing green with beige leather interior recently retrimmed; reimported into the UK in the late 1980s, restored and converted to right-hand drive. For 26 years in the current ownership.											
1957	XK 140 SE roadster		S813038	L	90-110.000 USD	71.022	91.300	81.394	04-06-17	Greenwich	139	Bon
	Black with red leather interior; in recent times the car received new interior, four-wheel disc brakes and a Borg-Warner T-5 5-speed manual gearbox.											
1955	XK 140 roadster		810532	L	130-160.000 EUR		NS		02-07-17	Monaco	134	Art
	Grey with burgundy interior; reimported into the UK from the USA in the 2000s and subsequently restored (see Coya lots 121 13.4.13 NS and 137 9.5.14 $129,156).											

F387: 1955 Jaguar Mk VIIM

F388: 1956 Jaguar XK 140 MC cabriolet

Year	Model	(Bodybuilder)	Chassis no.	Steering	Estimate	Hammer Price £	$	€	Date	Place	Lot	Auc. H.
1956	2.4		S940324	L	10-15.000 EUR	18.127*	22.540*	21.280*	25-11-16	Milan	629	RMS
Blue with red leather interior; 372,707 kms. From the Duemila Ruote collection.												
1959	3.4 saloon		5991422	L	20-30.000 EUR	21.314	26.623	24.000	06-11-16	Lyon	316	Ose
Restored five years ago; in good working order (see lot 365 Osenat 14.6.15 NS).												
1957	3.4 saloon		S971263DN	R	70-100.000 GBP	189.660	234.420	218.318	19-03-17	Goodwood	19	Bon F390
Raced when new, the car ran also the Monte Carlo Rally in 1958 e 1960. In the 1980s it was prepared for historic racing. Sold later to Japan, it was reimported into the UK in the 2000s and prepared again for racing (see lot 52 H & H 10.10.07 $51,675).												
1956	Mk VIII		729454BW	R	15-20.000 GBP	21.850	27.007	25.152	19-03-17	Goodwood	43	Bon
Light blue; in the same family ownership since new; unused from the late 1960s; 2,020 miles covered. Automatic transmission.												
1958	Mk VIII		763851DN	R	20-25.000 GBP	31.360	40.806	36.503	20-05-17	Ascot	188	His
Medium grey with red leather interior; in good overall condition. Manual gearbox.												
1957	XKSS		XKSS716	R	16-18.000.000 USD		NS		10-03-17	Amelia Island	61	G&Co
Originally finished in British racing green with tan leather interior, the car was sold new to Canada where it was raced until late 1961. In 1980 circa it was imported into the UK, converted to D-Type specification and raced at historic events. In 1993 it was re-imported into the USA and about 10 years ago it was fully restored and returned to XKSS specification, using the original components which had been retained after the works carried out in the 1980s.												
1959	XK 150 S coupé		TS820056DN	R	NA	90.000	119.547	106.812	02-09-16	Salon Privé	255	SiC
Red with black interior; raced at historic events. Body repainted in 2015 (see lot 369 Bonhams 10.12.15 $57,399).												
1959	XK 150 coupé		T824980DN	R	35-45.000 GBP		NS		03-09-16	Beaulieu	423	Bon
Restoration project (see lot 318 Coys 04.10.08 $35,310).												
1960	XK 150 coupé		S836733DN	L	40-55.000 GBP	39.200	52.457	46.683	07-09-16	London	110	RMS
Blue with biscuit interior; for 40 years with the previous owner. Restored in Italy; with Italian ASI homologation (see lot 125 Coys 14.5.16 NS).												
1958	XK 150 SE coupé		S824581DN	R	50-60.000 GBP		NS		08-09-16	Fontwell Park	115	Coy
Old English white with red interior; several mechanical works carried out in early 2016.												
1957	XK 150 coupé		S824095BW	L	55-65.000 GBP		NS		08-10-16	Ascot	306	Coy
Maroon with tan interior; sold new in the UK, in 1988 the car was imported into Holland where it was restored and converted to left hand drive.												
1958	XK 150 SE coupé		S824581DN	R	50-60.000 GBP	46.600	56.610	51.829	29-10-16	London	114	Coy
See lot 115 Coys 8.9.16.												
1958	XK 150 coupé		S835001BW	L	10-15.000 EUR	24.805*	30.844*	29.120*	25-11-16	Milan	841	RMS
For restoration. From the Duemila Ruote collection.												
1957	XK 150 coupé		S824030DN	R	60-70.000 GBP	68.320	83.583	79.115	04-03-17	Brooklands	170	His
Dark blue with tan leather interior; restoration completed in 2015 (see lot 606 Bonhams 8.9.12 $26,595).												
1958	XK 150 coupé		S835623	L	100-125.000 USD	58.816*	71.500*	67.382*	11-03-17	Amelia Island	225	RMS F391
Black with red interior; restored in 2005. Body repainted in 2014.												
1959	XK 150 S coupé		T825029DN	R	80-100.000 GBP	113.500	140.286	130.650	19-03-17	Goodwood	16	Bon
British racing green with original red leather interior; recent mechanical recommissioning. Three owners; circa 24,000 miles covered. 3.4-litre engine (see lot 153 Historics 6.6.15 $83,278).												
1958	XK 150 SE coupé		S835556BW	L	75-85.000 EUR		NS		05-08-17	Schloss Dyck	231	Coy
Black with red leather interior; restored between 2012 and 2014.												
1959	XK 150 coupé		S836851BW	L	75-85.000 EUR	70.464	92.630	78.050	05-08-17	Schloss Dyck	262	Coy
Black with red leather interior; described as in very good overall condition.												
1959	XK 150 S cabriolet		827392DN	R	NA	189.000	251.049	224.305	02-09-16	Salon Privé	207	SiC
Pearl grey with red leather interior; restored in the 1990s. 3.4-litre engine (see lot 27 H & H 13.03.10 $105,017).												
1959	XK 150 cabriolet		S827284	R	60-70.000 GBP	51.920	69.355	61.395	08-09-16	Fontwell Park	120	Coy
Ivory with red leather interior; 39,900 miles covered since new. Restored at unspecified date (see Coys lots 118 16.4.16 $121,664 and 172 2.7.16 $76,637).												
1959	XK 150 SE cabriolet		S827388	R	135-165.000 GBP	252.000	308.851	280.274	12-10-16	Duxford	86	H&H
Light blue with grey leather interior; the car has covered 200 miles since a full restoration. Fitted with a later 4-speed gearbox with overdrive. 3.4-litre engine.												
1958	XK 150 cabriolet		S837121	L	120-150.000 GBP	144.950	176.085	161.213	29-10-16	London	106	Coy
Recently restored.												
1960	XK 150 SE cabriolet		S838862DN	L	90-110.000 GBP		NS		26-11-16	Weybridge	168	His
Reimported into the UK from the USA and subsequently fully restored. 3.8-litre engine (see Historics lots 280 31.8.13 NS and 182 12.3.16 NS).												

F389: 1956 Jaguar XK 140 roadster

F390: 1957 Jaguar 3.4 saloon

Year	Model	(Bodybuilder)	Chassis no.	Steering	Estimate	Hammer price £	$	€	Date	Sale Place	Lot	Auc. H.

F391: 1958 Jaguar XK 150 coupé

F392: 1958 Jaguar XK 150 cabriolet

Year	Model	Chassis no.	Steering	Estimate	£	$	€	Date	Place	Lot	Auc. H.
1958	XK 150 cabriolet	S827230DN	R	130-150.000 GBP	169.500	213.960	201.044	04-12-16	London	11	Bon

Finished in pearl grey with light blue interior, the car remained until 2014 with its first owner who used it until 1969. Fully restored between 2014 and 2016 and finished in black with red interior. **F392**

| 1958 | XK 150 cabriolet | S837485 | L | 90-110.000 GBP | | NS | | 05-12-16 | London | 129 | Coy |

Red with black leather interior; sold new to the USA and later imported into Italy where the body was repainted. On its arrival in the UK it received a mechanical overhaul.

| 1959 | XK 150 cabriolet | 827329 | R | 80-100.000 GBP | 79.900 | 100.746 | 93.890 | 07-12-16 | London | 315 | Bon |

In the same family ownership until 1986; body restored in 1993; engine overhauled in 1996; since 2000 in the current ownership.

| 1958 | XK 150 cabriolet | S831231 | L | NQ | 60.021* | 73.700* | 69.315* | 21-01-17 | Scottsdale | 1145 | B/J |

Black with black interior; in very good overall condition.

| 1960 | XK 150 S cabriolet | S838763DN | L | 100-120.000 EUR | 91.499 | 114.028 | 107.280 | 10-02-17 | Paris | 137 | Art |

Sold new to the USA; reimported into Europe in the late 1980s restored in the early 1990s; 3.8-litre engine overhauled in 2013.

| 1960 | XK 150 SE cabriolet | S838801BW | L | 60-70.000 GBP | 132.750 | 166.654 | 157.083 | 24-02-17 | Stoneleigh P. | 910 | SiC |

Blue with cream interior; sold new to the USA, the car was reimported into the UK in 1988 and subsequently subjected to a long restoration completed in 2013. The original automatic transmission (included with the sale) was replaced with a more modern Jaguar XJ automatic unit.

| 1959 | XK 150 cabriolet | S837836BW | L | 80-100.000 EUR | 79.087 | 116.724 | 89.940 | 02-07-17 | Monaco | 105 | Art |

Cream with blue leather interior; imported into France from the USA in the 1990s and subsequently restored. Fitted with a Tremec 5-speed gearbox and four-wheel disc brakes.

| 1960 | XK 150 S roadster | T820082DN | R | 220-280.000 GBP | 236.700 | 315.403 | 279.921 | 10-09-16 | Goodwood | 129 | Bon |

Blue with grey leather interior; between the late 1970s-early 1980s restored to concours condition. Since 1984 in the current ownership in Switzerland. Described as in very good driving order. 3.8-lire engine. **F393**

| 1960 | XK 150 SE roadster | S820090 | R | 70-90.000 GBP | 85.120 | 104.323 | 94.670 | 12-10-16 | Duxford | 90 | H&H |

Old English white with beige leather interior; sold new to Hong Kong, the car was acquired by the current owner in 1985 and restored. Subsequently it was reimported into the UK. 3.4-litre engine.

| 1958 | XK 150 S roadster | T831818DN | L | 135-170.000 USD | 100.383 | 125.400 | 113.036 | 05-11-16 | Hilton Head | 172 | AA |

Cream with black interior; 3.4-litre engine.

| 1958 | XK 150 S roadster | T831743DN | L | 20-30.000 EUR | 78.231* | 97.277* | 91.840* | 25-11-16 | Milan | 314 | RMS |

Grey; interior restoration to be completed. 3.4-litre engine. From the Duemila Ruote collection.

| 1958 | XK 150 SE roadster | S830280 | L | 90-150.000 EUR | 70.455 | 88.530 | 82.800 | 09-02-17 | Paris | 382 | Bon |

Cream with beige interior; restored in 1993-94. In 2001 fitted with power-assisted brakes, power-assisted steering and all-synchromesh overdrive gearbox. 3.4-litre engine.

| 1958 | XK 150 S roadster | T831829DN | L | 125-155.000 EUR | 117.932 | 146.969 | 138.272 | 10-02-17 | Paris | 61 | Art |

Sold new to the USA; reimported into Europe in the late 1990s; restored in 2000; body recently repainted; recent service. 3.4-litre engine.

| 1958 | XK 150 S roadster | T831226DN | L | 200-250.000 USD | 123.932* | 159.500* | 135.894* | 19-08-17 | Pebble Beach | 127 | G&Co |

Grey with red interior; in largely original condition; just under 49,000 miles covered; four owners. 3.4-litre engine.

| 1960 | Mk IX | 791772BW | L | NA | 28.389* | 35.000* | 32.928* | 19-11-16 | Anaheim | S32.1 | Mec |

Black and white with biscuit interior; restored. Automatic transmission.

| 1960 | Mk IX | 774563BW | R | 25-30.000 GBP | 30.240 | 38.998 | 34.171 | 08-07-17 | Brooklands | 206 | His |

Grey with red leather interior; in good overall condition. Upgraded brakes. **F394**

F393: 1960 Jaguar XK 150 S roadster

F394: 1960 Jaguar Mk IX

Year	Model (Bodybuilder)	Chassis no.	Steering	Estimate	Hammer Price £	Hammer Price $	Hammer Price €	Date	Place	Lot	Auc. H.
1959	Mk IX	NC34588	L	NA	25.641*	33.000*	28.116*	19-08-17	Monterey	1157	R&S
	Two-tone body; well maintained example; automatic transmission.										
1964	Mk II 2.4	117066	R	10-15.000 GBP		NS		07-12-16	London	309	Bon
	British racing green with cream leather interior; body repainted in 1989. Partially recommissioned, it requires further works to the brakes and clutch.										
1964	Mk II 3.4	P166979BW	R	NA	20.250	26.898	24.033	02-09-16	Salon Privé	244	SiC
	Primrose yellow with red leather interior; restored at unspecified date. Automatic transmission.										
1967	Mk II 3.4	181435DN	L	18-22.000 GBP		NS		26-11-16	Weybridge	229	His
	Metallic grey; in good working order (see lots 208 Coys 20.5.06 $35,291 and 129A Bonhams 5.9.15 NS).										
1967	Mk II 3.4	P181256BW	L	18-22.000 EUR	17.584	21.413	20.085	14-01-17	Maastricht	209	Coy
	British racing green with black interior; older restoration.										
1963	Mk II 3.4	64184BW	R	18-22.000 GBP	18.895	23.475	22.041	18-02-17	London	316	Coy
	Bought in 2013 by the current owner and subsequently subjected to some restoration works.										
1962	Mk II 3.4	114182DN	R	15-25.000 EUR		NS		18-03-17	Lyon	175	Agu
	Grey with red interior; restored between 1998 and 2001.										
1967	Mk II 3.4	169789DN	R	39-46.000 GBP	49.280	64.123	57.362	20-05-17	Ascot	251	His
	Gunmetal grey with red interior; 43 miles covered since a full restoration. Manual gearbox with overdrive.										
1961	Mk II 3.4	176575DN	L	60-80.000 USD	32.516*	41.800*	37.265*	04-06-17	Greenwich	109	Bon
	Dark opalescent blue with cream leather interior; restored in the mid-1990s.										
1961	Mk II 3.4	155656DN	R	29-39.000 GBP	34.875	45.010	39.977	06-06-17	Woodcote Park	5	H&H F395
	Dark grey with red leather interior; restoration completed in 2005, engine and gearbox overhauled between 2012 and 2013.										
1962	Mk II 3.8	206926DN	R	20-25.000 GBP	25.313	32.044	29.386	12-11-16	Birmingham	621	SiC
	Heather with grey leather interior; restored many years ago. Three owners.										
1967	Mk II 3.8	284540DN	R	20-24.000 GBP	24.080	30.362	28.296	07-12-16	Chateau Impney	81	H&H
	Dark blue with grey leather interior; restored in the late 1980s.										
1961	Mk II 3.8	P216150BW	L	45-55.000 GBP		NS		19-03-17	Goodwood	40	Bon
	Black with burgundy leather interior; restored in the 2000s (see lots Bonhams/Brooks 111 11.8.01 NS, and Bonhams 313 18.5.02 $29,469, 436 6.3.10 $51,054 and 408 1.12.11 $49,201).										
1960	Mk II 3.8	202161DN	R	24-28.000 GBP		NS		26-07-17	Duxford	107	H&H
	Red with magnolia leather interior; restored in the late 1980s.										
1961	Mk X	300044BW	R	NA		NS		02-09-16	Salon Privé	233	SiC
	Opalescent dark green with beige leather interior; recently restored. When new used for three years as a personal car by Sir William Lyons (see lot 341 Coys 12.07.14 $7,071).										
1963	Mk X	352122BW	L	7-9.500 GBP	7.000	9.085	7.926	29-06-17	Fontwell Park	140	Coy
	Brown with cream leather interior; sold new to Mexico and later reimported into the UK (see lot 165 Coys 26.10.13 $7,156).										
1964	E-Type 3.8 coupé	889896	L	110-140.000 USD		NS		07-10-16	Hershey	227	RMS
	Metallic blue with light grey leather interior; bought in 2003 by the current, second owner and subsequently restored. Fitted with a 5-speed gearbox (the original 4-speed unit is included with the sale).										
1964	E-Type 3.8 coupé	861574	R	35-45.000 GBP	78.400	96.087	87.196	12-10-16	Duxford	13	H&H
	Red with grey interior; in the same family ownership since 1970 and unused from 15 years. For restoration.										
1962	E-Type 3.8 coupé	886096	L	45-65.000 EUR	96.450*	117.171*	107.280*	30-10-16	Paris	120	Art
	Described as in very good original condition.										
1962	E-Type 3.8 coupé	887080	L	45-55.000 EUR	77.277*	96.091*	90.720*	25-11-16	Milan	272	RMS
	White with red interior; 93,248 kms. From the Duemila Ruote collection.										
1963	E-Type 3.8 coupé	889742	L	45-55.000 EUR	116.393*	144.729*	136.640*	25-11-16	Milan	564	RMS
	Grey with cloth and leather interior. From the Duemila Ruote collection.										
1962	E-Type 3.8 coupé	147840	L	90-105.000 EUR	125.933*	156.592*	147.840*	25-11-16	Milan	852	RMS
	Dark green with tan interior; 1,917 miles. From the Duemila Ruote collection.										
1963	E-Type 3.8 coupé	861280	R	120-150.000 GBP	169.500	213.960	201.044	04-12-16	London	16	Bon F396
	Opalescent silver grey with red leather interior; fully restored between 2012 and 2016.										
1964	E-Type 3.8 coupé	861523	R	70-90.000 GBP	88.860	112.044	104.419	07-12-16	London	365	Bon
	Blue with grey interior; subjected to a long restoration from the 1990s to the 2000s. The original engine was changed under warranty in 1965.										
1964	E-Type 3.8 coupé	889707	L	140-180.000 USD	85.105*	104.500*	98.282*	20-01-17	Scottsdale	64	G&Co
	Black with red leather interior; restored. Engine rebuilt and upgraded to a Tremec 5-speed manual gearbox.										
1963	E-Type 3.8 coupé	889189	L	70-90.000 EUR	76.326*	95.907*	89.700*	09-02-17	Paris	321	Bon
	Silver with black interior; since 1994 in the current ownership; restoration completed in 2001.										
1963	E-Type 3.8 coupé	860759	R	90-110.000 GBP		NS		18-02-17	London	343	Coy
	Metallic grey; restored and then stored for 21 years since 1995. Recently mechanically recommissioned and returned to the road.										
1963	E-Type 3.8 coupé	861395	R	80-95.000 GBP	73.370	92.109	86.819	24-02-17	Stoneleigh P.	524	SiC
	Dark grey; bought in 2013 by the current owner and subsequently restored and fitted with a 5-speed Getrag gearbox (see Coys lots 226 14.1.06 NS and 311 7.12.11 NS).										
1964	E-Type 3.8 coupé	890190	L	115-135.000 USD	70.459*	85.800*	81.313*	09-03-17	Amelia Island	111	Bon
	Red with black interior; restored several years ago. Since 1989 in the current ownership. Engine rebuilt using an earlier 3.8-litre Mark IX block; original head.										
1962	E-Type 3.8 coupé	860348	R	70-90.000 GBP	92.220	113.984	106.154	19-03-17	Goodwood	55	Bon
	In original condition and stored for the last 17 years, the car requires recommissioning prior to use.										
1963	E-Type 3.8 coupé	889742	L	145-165.000 EUR		NS		08-04-17	Essen	217	Coy
	See lot 564 RM/Sotheby's 25.11.16.										

Year	Model	(Bodybuilder)	Chassis no.	Steering	Estimate	Hammer price £	$	€	Date	Place	Lot	Auc. H.
1964	**E-Type 3.8 coupé**		889937	L	80-95.000 GBP	74.250	95.463	87.778	13-05-17	Silverstone	356	SiC
Red with black leather interior; reimported into the UK from the USA in 2014 and subjected to a restoration completed in 2016.												
1962	**E-Type 3.8 coupé**		887683	L	110-130.000 GBP	108.640	141.362	126.457	20-05-17	Ascot	138	His
Black with black leather interior; fully restored between 2013 and 2014 (see lot 126 Coys 18.4.15 $150,848).												
1964	**E-Type 3.8 coupé**		861626	R	115-130.000 GBP		NS		06-06-17	Woodcote Park	16	H&H
Dark blue with grey leather interior; restored in 2016.												
1962	**E-Type 3.8 coupé**		860826	R	50-60.000 GBP	63.000	81.308	72.217	06-06-17	Woodcote Park	26	H&H
For restoration; since 1976 in the current ownership; driven until the late 1980s.												
1961	**E-Type 3.8 coupé**		885065	L	NQ		NS		24-06-17	Northeast	678	B/J
White with red interior; full restoration completed in 2015.												
1962	**E-Type 3.8 coupé**		860759	R	100-130.000 GBP	99.500	129.131	112.664	30-06-17	Goodwood	263	Bon
See lot 343 Coys 18.2.17.												
1964	**E-Type 3.8 coupé**		889221	L	70-75.000 GBP		NS		26-07-17	Duxford	105	H&H
Primrose yellow with black interior; in good overall condition; reimported into the UK from the USA in late 2015.												
1962	**E-Type 3.8 coupé**		860709	R	100-120.000 GBP		NS		29-07-17	Silverstone	448	SiC
Red; restored many years ago; engine rebuilt in recent years; original Moss gearbox (included with the sale) replaced with a 5-speed Elite Racing unit.												
1963	**E-Type 3.8 roadster**		861436	R	200-220.000 GBP	217.400	290.403	257.076	08-09-16	Fontwell Park	137	Coy
Blue; converted in the early 2000s by M&C Wilkinson Ltd. to Semi-Lightweight specification and subsequently raced at numerous historic events. With FIA HTP papers.												
1962	**E-Type 3.8 roadster**		850336	R	200-250.000 GBP	253.500	337.789	299.789	10-09-16	Goodwood	153	Bon
Gunmetal grey with dark blue leather interior; full restoration completed in 2016.												
1962	**E-Type 3.8 roadster**		876963	L	170-200.000 EUR		NA		08-10-16	Paris	189	CB/C
Black with black leather interior; fully restored.												
1964	**E-Type 3.8 roadster**		881692	L	NA		NS		08-10-16	Chicago	S100.1	Mec
Green with tan interior.												
1962	**E-Type 3.8 roadster**		878215	R	75-95.000 GBP	72.800	89.224	80.968	12-10-16	Duxford	15	H&H
Red with black interior; sold new to the USA, the car was reimported into the UK in the early 1990s. Restored between 2012 and 2016 and converted to right hand drive.												
1962	**E-Type 3.8 roadster**		878457	L	110-130.000 GBP	107.350	131.568	119.395	12-10-16	Duxford	25	H&H
Red with black interior; restoration completed in recent times.												
1962	**E-Type 3.8 roadster**		875679	L	NA	134.838*	165.000*	149.969*	15-10-16	Las Vegas	698	B/J
White with tan interior; restored many years ago (see lot 349 Bonhams 15.8.08 NS).												
1964	**E-Type 3.8 roadster**		881875	L	90-140.000 EUR	76.513	93.627	85.100	15-10-16	Salzburg	429	Dor
Green with black leather interior; since 1975 in the current ownership. Restored in 1987.												
1962	**E-Type 3.8 roadster**		850552	R	95-110.000 GBP	171.000	216.469	198.514	12-11-16	Birmingham	635	SiC
Pearl grey with light blue leather interior; bought in 1973 by the current owner and subjected to a long restoration completed in 1990. Currently fitted with a post-1965 synchromeshed gearbox (the original Moss unit is included with the sale).												
1963	**E-Type 3.8 roadster**		876751	L	NA	93.277	115.000	108.192	19-11-16	Anaheim	F153	Mec
British racing green with tan interior; 18,716 miles believed original (see lot F104 Mecum 19.8.16 NS).												
1963	**E-Type 3.8 roadster**		878946	L	15-20.000 EUR	85.863*	106.767*	100.800*	25-11-16	Milan	330	RMS
Cream; some restoration works to be completed. From the Duemila Ruote collection.												
1963	**E-Type 3.8 roadster**		879618	L	65-75.000 EUR	147.876*	183.877*	173.600*	25-11-16	Milan	552	RMS
Black with red interior; 65,433 kms. From the Duemila Ruote collection.												
1963	**E-Type 3.8 roadster**		879361	L	65-75.000 EUR	124.025*	154.220*	145.600*	25-11-16	Milan	576	RMS
White with black interior; 36,410 kms. From the Duemila Ruote collection.												
1964	**E-Type 3.8 roadster**		850848	R	65-75.000 EUR	119.255*	148.288*	140.000*	25-11-16	Milan	632	RMS
Red with black interior; with hardtop. 14,925 miles. From the Duemila Ruote collection.												
1962	**E-Type 3.8 roadster**		877454	L	65-75.000 EUR	133.565*	166.083*	156.800*	25-11-16	Milan	868	RMS
White with red interior; 60,815 kms. From the Duemila Ruote collection.												
1962	**E-Type 3.8 roadster**		876655	R	82-95.000 GBP	94.080	116.979	110.441	26-11-16	Weybridge	167	His
Red; sold new to Canada, the car was reimported into the UK in 1990 and subsequently restored and converted to right-hand drive. Currently fitted with a 5-speed Getrag gearbox (the original 4-speed Moss unit is included with the sale).												

F395: *1961 Jaguar Mk II 3.4*

F396: *1963 Jaguar E-Type 3.8 coupé*

Year	Model	(Bodybuilder)	Chassis no.	Steering	Estimate	Hammer Price £	Hammer Price $	Hammer Price €	Date	Place	Lot	Auc. H.
1962	E-Type 3.8 roadster		850396	R	200-250.000 GBP	219.900	277.580	260.823	04-12-16	London	25	Bon
Dark opalescent green with tan leather interior; fully restored in 2015/2016 and fitted with a 5-speed manual gearbox (see lot 385 Historics 7.6.14 NS).												
1963	E-Type 3.8 roadster		878878	L	100-120.000 GBP	137.880	175.314	163.801	05-12-16	London	115	Coy
Red with beige interior; sold new to the USA and recently reimported into the UK and restored.												
1961	E-Type 3.8 roadster		875771	L	165-185.000 USD	110.849	135.000	126.617	15-01-17	Kissimmee	S185.1	Mec
Blue with black interior; recent full restoration (see lots 38 Gooding & Company 7.3.14 $129,250 and 3090 Auctions America 2.8.14 NS).												
1963	E-Type 3.8 roadster		878845	L	40-60.000 USD	47.468*	58.300*	54.668*	18-01-17	Scottsdale	4	WoA
Stored for the past 30 years.												
1964	E-Type 3.8 roadster		881399	L	150-200.000 USD	113.785*	140.250*	131.456*	19-01-17	Scottsdale	78	Bon
Black with red leather interior; sold new to the USA; concours-quality restoration completed in 2012.												
1962	E-Type 3.8 roadster		877169	L	150-180.000 EUR		NS		08-02-17	Paris	117	RMS
Red with original tan interior; since 1981 in the current Swiss ownership. 20,420 kms covered (see lot 136 TSAC 6.10.07 NS).												
1961	E-Type 3.8 roadster		876464	L	180-230.000 EUR		NS		09-02-17	Paris	346	Bon
Sold new to the USA, the car was bought in 2003 by the current owner and subsequently fully restored in Italy.												
1963	E-Type 3.8 roadster		879328	R	50-60.000 GBP	75.040	93.747	88.667	23-02-17	Donington Park	75	H&H
Restoration project.												
1964	E-Type 3.8 roadster		881806	L	115-130.000 GBP	123.750	155.356	146.433	24-02-17	Stoneleigh P.	522	SiC
Opalescent silver blue with dark blue leather interior; reimported into the UK from the USA in 2004 and fully restored between 2007 and 2011.												
1962	E-Type 3.8 roadster		850548	R	90-110.000 GBP	145.600	178.127	168.605	04-03-17	Brooklands	147	His
Red with red interior; stored a number of years ago; in original, unrestored condition; working engine to be checked.												
1961	E-Type 3.8 roadster		875053	L	350-425.000 USD	268.286*	326.700*	309.614*	09-03-17	Amelia Island	125	Bon
Opalescent blue with biscuit leather interior; sold new to the USA, bought in 2011 by the current, fourth owner. The car has covered 550 miles since a full restoration carried out in the 2000s (see lot 194 RM 12.3.11 $154,000).												
1961	E-Type 3.8 roadster		876166	L	130-160.000 USD	77.686*	94.600*	89.652*	09-03-17	Amelia Island	141	Bon
Red with tan interior; since 1975 in the current ownership. Body and engine restored in the early 2000s, interior in 2016.												
1964	E-Type 3.8 roadster		880090	L	225-275.000 USD	167.399*	203.500*	191.778*	10-03-17	Amelia Island	18	G&Co
Black with red leather interior; full restoration completed in the 2000s and freshened in 2012.												
1961	E-Type 3.8 roadster		875152	L	250-325.000 USD	339.323*	412.500*	388.740*	11-03-17	Amelia Island	255	RMS
Red with black leather interior; sold new to the USA, the car remained in the same family ownership from 1966 to 2010. Subsequently it was fully restored in the UK to its original specification.												
1961	E-Type 3.8 roadster		850151	R	160-190.000 GBP		NS		19-03-17	Goodwood	22	Bon
Opalescent dark blue with light blue interior; described as in very good original, unrestored condition; since 1981 with the present, third owner. The engine is a replacement unit fitted in 1968.												
1962	E-Type 3.8 roadster		850339	R	160-200.000 GBP	180.700	223.345	208.004	19-03-17	Goodwood	61	Bon
White with red leather interior; full restoration completed in January 2017.												
1963	E-Type 3.8 roadster		880134	L	75-90.000 GBP		NS		29-03-17	Duxford	17	H&H
Primrose yellow with black interior; recently reimported into the UK from the USA. Not used in the past 12 years, it requires recommissioning prior to use.												
1963	E-Type 3.8 roadster		879680	L	220-260.000 USD	167.242	209.000	195.478	01-04-17	Ft.Lauderdale	563	AA
Black with red leather interior; 50 miles covered since a concours-quality restoration.												
1963	E-Type 3.8 roadster		878876	L	145-195.000 EUR	128.385	159.900	150.000	08-04-17	Essen	207	Coy
Opalescent maroon with beige leather interior; in largely original condition; 28,000 kms covered; in the same family ownership since new.												
1961	E-Type 3.8 roadster		876343	L	190-225.000 GBP	177.840	222.300	209.602	12-04-17	London	348	Coy
Opalescent bronze with tan interior; concours-quality restoration.												
1961	E-Type 3.8 roadster		875610	L	120-180.000 EUR	170.789	218.239	204.000	22-04-17	Bagatelle	93	Agu
White with original red leather interior; restored several years ago.												
1964	E-Type 3.8 roadster		879997	L	150-180.000 USD	116.201	148.500	138.803	22-04-17	Arlington	148	WoA
Restored several years ago and described as in very good overall condition. Recently serviced (see lot 9 Bonhams 5.6.16 NS).												
1962	E-Type 3.8 roadster		877891	R	130-150.000 GBP	136.714	178.234	160.147	18-05-17	London	122	Coy
Silver with blue leather interior; the car received some restoration works in 1994 and is described as in excellent overall condition.												
1961	E-Type 3.8 roadster		850322	R	180-220.000 GBP	216.742	282.567	253.892	18-05-17	London	137	Coy
Gunmetal grey with red leather interior; concours-quality restoration carried out over the last two years.												
1962	E-Type 3.8 roadster		877026	R	90-110.000 GBP	97.440	126.789	113.420	20-05-17	Ascot	148	His
Black with red interior; reimported into the UK in 1991 and subsequently restored and converted to right-hand drive. Engine recently rebuilt (see lots 120 Coys 21.4.12 NA and 226 Historics 26.5.12 $68,477).												
1961	E-Type 3.8 roadster		875594	L	175-205.000 GBP		NS		20-05-17	Ascot	229	His
British racing green with light tan leather interior; sold new to Italy; reimported into the UK in 2013 just after being fully restored. With hardtop.												
1961	E-Type 3.8 roadster		875807	L	250-300.000 EUR	507.795	652.055	582.400	27-05-17	Villa Erba	130	RMS F397
Raced in Angola and Portugal in period; fully restored to its original specification.												
1961	E-Type 3.8 roadster		876343	L	150-200.000 GBP		NS		29-06-17	Fontwell Park	126	Coy
See lot 348 Coys 12.4.17.												
1962	E-Type 3.8 roadster		850454	R	210-260.000 GBP	259.100	336.260	293.379	30-06-17	Goodwood	228	Bon
Opalescent grey with dark blue leather interior; 33 miles covered since a full restoration completed in 2017. Fitted with a 5-speed Tremec gearbox.												
1962	E-Type 3.8 roadster		877116	L	120-150.000 EUR		NS		02-07-17	Monaco	117	Art
Opalescent silver grey with black interior; engine rebuilt in 2005, brakes overhauled in 2013, clutch replaced in 2014. Currently fitted with a Getrag 5-speed gearbox (the original unit can be collected from the owner).												
1963	E-Type 3.8 roadster		879161	L	150-180.000 EUR	147.629	217.885	167.888	02-07-17	Monaco	133	Art
White with dark blue interior; restored in Italy in the 2000s.												

Year	Model	(Bodybuilder)	Chassis No.	Steering	Estimate	Hammer Price £	Hammer Price $	Hammer Price €	Date	Place	Lot	Auc. H.
1963	E-Type 3.8 roadster		879578	L	128-145.000 GBP		NS		08-07-17	Brooklands	168	His
	British racing green with tan interior; restored at unspecified date (see lot 270 Historics 11.6.16 $187,239).											
1962	E-Type 3.8 roadster		877026	R	125-150.000 GBP		NS		08-07-17	Brooklands	209	His
	See lot 148 Historics 20.5.17.											
1962	E-Type 3.8 roadster		878720	L	160-200.000 GBP		NS		15-07-17	Blenheim Pal.	142	Coy
	Since new in the same family ownership; in well preserved condition; 42,000 miles on the odometer.											
1961	E-Type 3.8 roadster		876192	L	180-220.000 GBP		NS		26-07-17	Duxford	65	H&H
	Red with black interior; reimported into the UK from the USA in 2014 and subsequently restored.											
1962	E-Type 3.8 roadster		876765	L	120-140.000 GBP		NS		29-07-17	Silverstone	732	SiC
	White; reimported into the UK from the USA in 2015; restored at unspecified date; recently serviced.											
1961	E-Type 3.8 roadster		876083	L	180-225.000 EUR	170.629	224.305	189.000	05-08-17	Schloss Dyck	236	Coy
	Restored; engine rebuilt; showing 69,000 believed original kms.											
1963	E-Type 3.8 roadster		879215	L	185-235.000 USD	91.880*	118.250*	101.104*	17-08-17	Monterey	54	WoA
	Red with black interior; sold new to the USA; in single ownership from 1969 to the early 2000s; fully restored.											
1962	E-Type 3.8 roadster		876540	L	175-225.000 USD	115.385*	148.500*	126.522*	18-08-17	Carmel	76	Bon
	White with red interior; until 2016 in the same family ownership; restored in the early 1980s; recently serviced (see lot 23 Gooding & Company 11.3.16 $203,500).											
1964	E-Type 3.8 roadster		880948	L	300-350.000 USD		NS		19-08-17	Monterey	S121	Mec
	Gunmetal grey with red leather interior; 100 miles covered since a full restoration.											
1963	E-Type 3.8 Lightweight roadster		S850667	R	7.500-8.500.000 USD	5.979.281	7.370.000	6.907.901	19-01-17	Scottsdale	24	Bon TOP TEN
	White with blue stripes; bought new by Australian racing driver Robert "Bob" Jane, the car was raced until late 1966. In 1964 it was fitted at the factory with the 45-gallon fuel tank and in 1966 the engine block was replaced with the present unit supplied by the factory. In 1980 it was bought by its second owner who had the body repainted and in 1999 by the current, third owner. Never fully restored; less than 4,000 miles covered since new (see lot 126 RM 20.3.99 $847,000).											
1963	E-Type 3.8 Lightweight roadster		S850664	R	Refer Dpt.	6.216.000	8.000.000	6.816.000	18-08-17	Carmel	52	Bon TOP TEN F398
	White with blue stripes; one of three Lightweights sold to Briggs Cunningham, the car did its race debut at the 1963 Le Mans 24 Hours, driven by Walt Hansgen and Augie Pabst, but was forced to retire for gearbox failure. Imported into the USA, it was raced at other two events prior to be retired to the Cunningham's museum in Costa Mesa. Sold in the 1970s, it has had several owners, also in Europe and Japan. Restored in the late 1980s, it is still fitted with the original alloy engine. Raced over the years at several historic events.											
1967	E-Type 4.2 coupé 2+2		1E50775	R	NA	66.380	88.173	78.780	02-09-16	Salon Privé	212	SiC
	Cream; restored between 2009 and 2010.											
1965	E-Type 4.2 coupé		1E20313	R	70-90.000 GBP		NS		10-09-16	Goodwood	119	Bon
	Red with beige leather interior; the body features some semi-lightweight specification, as the bonnet, front wings and side doors made of aluminium. Fully restored between 2010 and 2013.											
1967	E-Type 4.2 coupé 2+2		1E76006	L	65-75.000 USD	48.724	62.700	55.797	03-10-16	Philadelphia	224	Bon
	Grey with black interior; just one owner. Described as in original condition except for the paintwork redone at unspecified date.											
1965	E-Type 4.2 coupé		1E20313	R	60-70.000 GBP	67.200	82.360	74.740	12-10-16	Duxford	117	H&H
	See lot 119 Bonhams 10.9.16 NS.											
1967	E-Type 4.2 coupé		1E34169	L	20-30.000 EUR	57.242*	71.178*	67.200*	25-11-16	Milan	230	RMS
	Yellow with black interior; 98,557 miles. From the Duemila Ruote collection.											
1966	E-Type 4.2 coupé		1E33870	L	35-40.000 EUR	128.795*	160.151*	151.200*	25-11-16	Milan	579	RMS
	Black with red interior; 43,259 kms. From the Duemila Ruote collection.											
1965	E-Type 4.2 coupé		1E32207	L	55-65.000 EUR	114.485*	142.356*	134.400*	25-11-16	Milan	881	RMS
	Dark green with tan interior. From the Duemila Ruote collection.											
1965	E-Type 4.2 coupé		1E31636	L	125-175.000 USD	111.554*	137.500*	128.879*	19-01-17	Scottsdale	37	Bon
	Silver with black interior; fully restored between 2007 and 2009 and fitted with a more modern 5-speed manual gearbox.											
1966	E-Type 4.2 coupé		1E32500	L	110-130.000 GBP	125.000	152.925	144.750	04-03-17	Brooklands	205	His
	Opalescent grey with red interior; in very good original condition. 22,600 miles covered.											
1966	E-Type 4.2 coupé 2+2		1E76624	L	80-100.000 USD	57.911*	70.400*	66.345*	11-03-17	Amelia Island	237	RMS
	Black with red leather interior; restored in 2014 (see lot 261 RM 16.8.14 $104,500).											
1968	E-Type 4.2 coupé		1E21792	R	58-70.000 GBP	60.000	78.072	69.840	20-05-17	Ascot	244	His
	Opalescent silver grey with dark blue interior; restored circa 10 years ago and subsequently little used. Recently recommissioned.											
1968	E-Type 4.2 coupé		1R25356	L	55-65.000 EUR		NS		10-06-17	Lyon	123	Agu
	Golden sand with tobacco leather interior; imported into France from the USA in 2014 and subsequently restored.											

F397: 1961 Jaguar E-Type 3.8 roadster

F398: 1963 Jaguar E-Type 3.8 Lightweight roadster

Year	Model (Bodybuilder)	Chassis No.	Steering	Estimate	Hammer Price £	Hammer Price $	Hammer Price €	Sale Date	Sale Place	Lot	Auc. H.
1966	**E-Type 4.2 coupé**	1E32851	R	70-80.000 GBP	75.040	96.772	84.795	08-07-17	Brooklands	126	His
	Red with original black leather interior; restored between 2007 and 2011.										
1965	**E-Type 4.2 coupé**	1E20580	R	87-107.000 GBP		NS		08-07-17	Brooklands	166	His
	British racing green with black interior; restored many years ago. Three owners.										
1965	**E-Type 4.2 coupé**	1E20700	R	78-95.000 GBP	106.400	137.213	120.232	08-07-17	Brooklands	194	His
	Black with red leather interior; fully restored in recent years.										
1965	**E-Type 4.2 coupé**	1E20541	R	60-80.000 GBP	77.625	101.245	86.948	26-07-17	Duxford	99	H&H
	Black with black interior; restored between 2013 and 2015.										
1968	**E-Type 4.2 coupé**	1E21876	R	60-70.000 GBP	90.000	117.855	100.485	29-07-17	Silverstone	755	SiC
	Opalescent silver blue with dark blue leather interior; in good overall condition.										
1966	**E-Type 4.2 coupé**	1E32560	L	125-175.000 USD	132.479*	170.500*	145.266*	18-08-17	Monterey	114	RMS F399
	Opalescent silver grey with red leather interior; restored and fitted with a 5-speed gearbox, Wilwood disc brakes and modern air conditioning system. Formerly owned by Indy 500 winner Arie Luyendyk.										
1966	**E-Type 4.2 coupé 2+2**	1E76624	L	80-100.000 USD	55.556*	71.500*	60.918*	18-08-17	Monterey	165	RMS
	See lot 237 RM/Sotheby's 11.3.17.										
1965	**E-Type 4.2 roadster**	1E12309	R	100-130.000 GBP	113.500	151.239	134.225	10-09-16	Goodwood	171	Bon
	Primrose yellow with black interior; sold new to the USA. Engine rebuilt in 2014 by JD Classics.										
1966	**E-Type 4.2 roadster**	1E12944	L	190-220.000 USD		NS		17-09-16	Aspen	114	TFA
	Opalescent maroon with biscuit leather interior; restored at unspecified date.										
1967	**E-Type 4.2 roadster**	1E16067	L	NA		NS		08-10-16	Chicago	S118.1	Mec
	Red with black interior.										
1966	**E-Type 4.2 roadster**	1E1468	R	55-65.000 GBP	67.200	82.360	74.740	12-10-16	Duxford	29	H&H
	Red with black hardtop and beige interior; restored in 1980 and unused from the early 2000s, the car requires some restoration works.										
1965	**E-Type 4.2 roadster**	1E11151	L	165-185.000 USD	131.202	163.900	147.739	05-11-16	Hilton Head	169	AA
	Old English white with tan leather interior; 200 miles covered since a full restoration. 38,000 miles covered since new.										
1965	**E-Type 4.2 roadster**	1E1080	R	90-110.000 GBP	146.250	185.138	169.782	12-11-16	Birmingham	603	SiC
	Opalescent grey with dark red interior; restored in 1999, it is described as still in very good overall condition. 16,000 miles covred since the restoration.										
1965	**E-Type 4.2 roadster**	1E10844	L	15-20.000 EUR	90.634*	112.699*	106.400*	25-11-16	Milan	890	RMS
	Red with black interior; some restoration works to be completed. From the Duemila Ruote collection.										
1965	**E-Type 4.2 roadster**	1E1192	R	105-120.000 GBP	125.440	155.972	147.254	26-11-16	Weybridge	154	His
	Red with black interior; restored in 2015.										
1967	**E-Type 4.2 roadster**	1E15362	L	200-250.000 USD	142.789*	176.000*	164.965*	19-01-17	Scottsdale	10	Bon
	Opalescent maroon with black leather interior; recent full restoration; believed to be less than 39,000 original miles.										
1967	**E-Type 4.2 roadster**	1E15499	L	175-225.000 USD	111.554*	137.500*	128.879*	19-01-17	Phoenix	152	RMS
	Opalescent silver blue with navy blue leather interior; restored to concours condition between 2013 and 2015. With hardtop.										
1965	**E-Type 4.2 roadster**	1E11193	L	180-220.000 USD	143.334*	176.000*	165.528*	20-01-17	Scottsdale	21	G&Co
	Red with black leather interior; between 2009 and 2011 restored to concours condition (see lot 81 Gooding & Company 9.3.12 $123,750).										
1965	**E-Type 4.2 roadster**	1E11799	L	240-280.000 USD	250.835*	308.000*	289.674*	20-01-17	Phoenix	252	RMS F400
	Dark opalescent blue with cinnamon leather interior; full restoration recently completed. With hardtop.										
1966	**E-Type 4.2 roadster**	1E11887	L	NQ	134.376*	165.000*	155.183*	21-01-17	Scottsdale	1366	B/J
	Red with black interior; fully restored.										
1967	**E-Type 4.2 roadster**	1E13578	L	250-300.000 USD	206.043	253.000	237.947	21-01-17	Scottsdale	128	G&Co
	Black with black leather interior and black soft-top; sold new to the USA. In original condition, three owners, less than 4,000 miles on the odometer.										
1967	**E-Type 4.2 roadster**	1E15010	L	NQ	120.938	148.500	139.664	21-01-17	Scottsdale	8323	R&S
	Red; restored some years ago.										
1965	**E-Type 4.2 roadster**	1E11996	L	145-175.000 EUR	132.102	165.993	155.250	09-02-17	Paris	399	Bon
	Gunmetal grey with red interior; restored in 2016.										
1965	**E-Type 4.2 roadster**	1E1132	R	80-100.000 GBP	110.250	138.408	130.459	24-02-17	Stoneleigh P.	510	SiC
	Dark blue with red interior; bought in 1996 by the current owner; engine rebuilt in 2004; body restored and repainted in 2013.										

F399: 1966 Jaguar E-Type 4.2 coupé

F400: 1965 Jaguar E-Type 4.2 roadster

Year	Model	(Bodybuilder)	Chassis No.	Steering	Estimate	Hammer Price £	$	€	Sale Date	Place	Lot	Auc. H.
1967	**E-Type 4.2 roadster**		1E16129	L	225-275.000 USD	**115.625***	**140.800***	**133.436***	09-03-17	Amelia Island	134	**Bon**
British racing green with tan interior; bought in 1998 by the current, second owner. Restoration completed in 2016.												
1965	**E-Type 4.2 roadster**		1E11175	L	125-175.000 USD	**122.156***	**148.500***	**139.946***	10-03-17	Amelia Island	133	**RMS**
British racing green with biscuit interior; in very good driving order. 58,082 miles on the odometer. From the Orin Smith collection.												
1967	**E-Type 4.2 roadster**		1E15851	L	140-180.000 USD	**113.108***	**137.500***	**129.580***	11-03-17	Amelia Island	217	**RMS**
British racing green with black leather interior; an older restoration, the car is in good overall condition.												
1966	**E-Type 4.2 roadster**		1E12009	L	220-280.000 USD	**199.069**	**242.000**	**228.061**	11-03-17	Amelia Island	240	**RMS**
Black with tan leather interior; restored three years ago to concours condition. With hardtop (see lot 206 RM 16.8.14 $324,500).												
1967	**E-Type 4.2 roadster**		1E14813	L	NQ	**76.276**	**95.000**	**89.110**	08-04-17	Houston	F255	**Mec**
Cream with black leather interior.												
1965	**E-Type 4.2 roadster**		1E1340	R	85-100.000 GBP	**112.500**	**144.641**	**132.998**	13-05-17	Silverstone	310	**SiC**
Blue; since 1991 in the current ownership; in good overall condition.												
1967	**E-Type 4.2 roadster**		1E14660	R	70-80.000 GBP	**70.313**	**90.401**	**83.124**	13-05-17	Silverstone	352	**SiC**
Red with tan interior; sold new to the USA, the car was later reimported into the UK and converted to right-hand drive about 20 years ago. Restoration started in 2009 and recently completed.												
1967	**E-Type 4.2 roadster**		1E13881	L	95-130.000 USD	**75.301**	**96.800**	**86.297**	04-06-17	Greenwich	134	**Bon**
Deep red with black leather interior; restored in the 1980s. In recent years the car received a new interior and some mechanical works.												
1967	**E-Type 4.2 roadster**		1E15138	L	105-125.000 GBP	**NS**			06-06-17	Woodcote Park	21	**H&H**
Primrose yellow with black leather interior; several mechanical works carried out in the 2000s, body recently repainted.												
1965	**E-Type 4.2 roadster**		1E1298	R	70-100.000 GBP	**104.540**	**135.672**	**118.371**	30-06-17	Goodwood	284	**Bon**
Opalescent silver blue with blue interior; in good overall condition; one owner; circa 54,000 miles on the odometer. With hardtop.												
1967	**E-Type 4.2 roadster**		1E14619	R	70-85.000 GBP	**82.636**	**106.567**	**93.379**	08-07-17	Brooklands	197	**His**
Red; in good overall condition. Sold new to the USA and reimported into the UK in 1994.												
1966	**E-Type 4.2 roadster**		1E13757	L	225-275.000 USD	**188.034***	**242.000***	**206.184***	18-08-17	Carmel	66	**Bon**
Black with black interior; since 1979 in the current ownership; concours-quality restoration completed in 2016 (see lot S73 Mecum 20.8.16 NS).												
1966	**E-Type 4.2 roadster**		1E12009	L	220-280.000 USD	**170.940***	**220.000***	**187.440***	18-08-17	Monterey	120	**RMS**
See lot 240 RM/Sotheby's 11.3.17.												
1966	**E-Type 4.2 roadster**		1E12331	L	220-260.000 USD	**239.316***	**308.000***	**262.416***	19-08-17	Pebble Beach	167	**G&Co**
Oyster beige with beige leather interior; full restoration to original colours completed in 2017.												
1966	**E-Type 4.2 roadster**		1E14412	L	225-275.000 USD	**196.581***	**253.000***	**215.556***	19-08-17	Monterey	232	**RMS**
Dark opalescent grey with cinnamon leather interior; recent full restoration. With hardtop.												
1964	**S-Type**		IB52577BW	R	8-15.000 GBP	**10.035**	**12.372**	**11.106**	08-10-16	Ascot	335	**Coy**
Gold with brown interior; restored over the last decade. The interior require some attention.												
1966	**S-Type 3.8**		1B79842DN	L	5-7.000 EUR	**15.265***	**18.981***	**17.920***	25-11-16	Milan	251	**RMS** **F401**
Gold with light brown leather interior; 88.392 kms. From the Duemila Ruote collection.												
1968	**420G**		G1D77621BW	L	5-7.000 EUR	**8.586***	**10.677***	**10.080***	25-11-16	Milan	351	**RMS**
Medium grey with burgundy interior; 24,559 kms. From the Duemila Ruote collection.												
1969	**420G**		P1F8112BW	R	10-15.000 EUR	**6.360***	**7.992***	**7.475***	09-02-17	Paris	301	**Bon** **F402**
Described as in original condition and good running order.												
1968	**340**		1J51358DN	R	15-20.000 GBP	**21.840**	**28.418**	**25.422**	20-05-17	Ascot	214	**His**
Grey with red leather interior; 1,200 miles covered since the restoration completed five years ago.												
1970	**E-Type 4.2 coupé series II**		1R12965	L	55-65.000 GBP	**59.920**	**73.438**	**66.643**	12-10-16	Duxford	111	**H&H**
Green with tan interior; restored six-seven years ago.												
1969	**E-Type 4.2 coupé series II**		1R25781	L	45-60.000 EUR	**47.562**	**58.201**	**52.900**	15-10-16	Salzburg	412	**Dor**
Red with black leather interior; sold new to the USA, the car was acquired in 1997 by the current owner and imported into Austria. In good overall condition; body repainted.												
1969	**E-Type 4.2 coupé series II 2+2**		J691R41475	L	45-55.000 GBP	**70.875**	**89.721**	**82.279**	12-11-16	Birmingham	656	**SiC**
Silver; concours-quality restoration completed in the mid-2000s.												

F401: 1966 Jaguar S-Type 3.8

F402: 1969 Jaguar 420G

Year	Model	(Bodybuilder)	Chassis no.	Steering	Estimate	Hammer price £	Hammer price $	Hammer price €	Date	Place	Lot	Auc. H.
1969	E-Type 4.2 coupé series II		1R26441	L	15-20.000 EUR	52.472*	65.247*	61.600*	25-11-16	Milan	246	RMS
Yellow with black interior; 66,136 miles. From the Duemila Ruote collection.												
1968	E-Type 4.2 coupé series II 2+2		1R40371	L	50-75.000 USD	41.944*	51.700*	48.458*	19-01-17	Scottsdale	97	Bon
Red with black interior; restoration recently completed.												
1970	E-Type 4.2 coupé series II		1R27890	L	40-60.000 USD	27.771*	34.100*	32.071*	20-01-17	Phoenix	235	RMS
Burgundy with black leather interior; in highly original condition. Less than 57,000 miles on the odometer.												
1970	E-Type 4.2 coupé series II 2+2		1R36000BW	R	35-40.000 GBP	37.125	46.607	43.930	24-02-17	Stoneleigh P.	533	SiC
Blue with dark blue interior; repainted some years ago. Automatic transmission.												
1970	E-Type 4.2 coupé series II		1R20709	R	42-48.000 GBP	50.960	62.344	59.012	04-03-17	Brooklands	192	His
Red with original black interior; in good driving order. 52,500 miles covered (see Coys lots 431 30.9.04 NS and 248 4.12.04 $26,211).												
1970	E-Type 4.2 coupé series II		1R20870	R	40-60.000 GBP	51.750	63.963	59.569	19-03-17	Goodwood	15	Bon
Primrose yellow with black interior; bought in 1989 by the late owner and restored between 1989 and 1993. Stored since 1997.												
1970	E-Type 4.2 coupé series II 2+2		P1R44176	L	30-40.000 EUR	27.662*	35.996*	32.200*	21-05-17	SPA-Francorch.	55	Bon
British racing green with green interior; two owners; 53,224 kms on the odometer; in original condition. From the Swiss Castle Collection.												
1969	E-Type 4.2 coupé series II		1R25351	L	60-80.000 USD	57.331*	73.700*	65.704*	04-06-17	Greenwich	142	Bon F403
Primrose yellow with black leather interior; in very good original condition. Just over 33,000 miles covered.												
1969	E-Type 4.2 coupé series II 2+2		P1R43100BW	R	45-55.000 GBP	50.625	65.337	58.031	06-06-17	Woodcote Park	20	H&H
Red with biscuit leather interior; reimported into the UK from the USA in 1984 and subsequently restored and converted to right-hand drive. Described as in very good overall condition.												
1969	E-Type 4.2 coupé series II		1R25655	L	70-100.000 EUR	62.605	79.663	71.300	24-06-17	Wien	359	Dor
Dark grey with burgundy leather interior; bought in 2005 by the current owner and subjected to a full restoration completed in 2008.												
1970	E-Type 4.2 coupé series II		1R20744	R	30-40.000 GBP	55.200	71.639	62.503	30-06-17	Goodwood	210	Bon
Dark red with black interior; body repainted in 2000; engine rebuilt in 2015. Since 1972 in the Joy Rainey Collection.												
1969	E-Type 4.2 coupé series II 2+2		1R35256	R	100-150.000 GBP	NS			26-07-17	Duxford	84	H&H
Red with beige leather interior; one registered keeper and 1,733 miles on the odometer; restored in the 2000s. Last taxed for road use 40 years ago.												
1970	E-Type 4.2 coupé series II		1R20957	R	60-70.000 GBP	78.750	102.712	88.208	26-07-17	Duxford	90	H&H
Red with black interior; 68,500 miles covered; last serviced in 2015.												
1969	E-Type 4.2 roadster series II		1R9535	L	60-70.000 USD	55.588*	70.400*	62.938*	06-10-16	Hershey	141	RMS
Light green with green leather interior; described as an exceptionally well-preserved example. Two owners; 57,292 miles on the odometer.												
1969	E-Type 4.2 roadster series II		1R9681	R	50-60.000 GBP	62.720	76.870	69.757	12-10-16	Duxford	74	H&H
Dark blue with cream interior; a mild recommissioning carried out in recent years.												
1969	E-Type 4.2 roadster series II		1R10049	L	110-130.000 GBP	100.350	121.905	111.609	29-10-16	London	123	Coy
British racing green with tobacco interior; reimported into Europe from the USA in 2012 and subsequently restored in Poland and fitted with a modern 5-speed gearbox.												
1970	E-Type 4.2 roadster series II		1R11811	L	60-70.000 EUR	64.475	80.535	72.600	06-11-16	Lyon	328	Ose
Red; in good working order (see lot 376 Osenat 20.3.16 $110,444).												
1968	E-Type 4.2 roadster series II		1R7140	L	70-80.000 GBP	70.060	88.339	82.328	07-12-16	Chateau Impney	80	H&H
Yellow with black leather interior; the car was sold new to the USA where it has had one owner and was used until 1985. Mechanicals overhauled in the USA in 2014, body repainted in the UK more recently (see lot 167 Coys 14.5.16 $98,728).												
1969	E-Type 4.2 roadster series II		1R29239	L	85-100.000 EUR	75.901	92.428	86.697	14-01-17	Maastricht	238	Coy
Red with black leather interior; restored. Engine rebuilt.												
1970	E-Type 4.2 roadster series II		2R13655	L	60-80.000 EUR	53.819	67.627	63.250	09-02-17	Paris	425	Bon
Red with tan leather interior; restored. Fitted with a 5-speed gearbox; engine rebuilt in 2014.												
1971	E-Type 4.2 roadster series II		P2R14746	R	69-78.000 GBP	77.280	94.544	89.490	04-03-17	Brooklands	179	His
Black with tan leather interior; reimported into the UK from the USA in 2015 and subsequently restored and converted to right-hand drive.												
1970	E-Type 4.2 roadster series II		1R1571	R	80-100.000 GBP	72.060	89.066	82.948	19-03-17	Goodwood	45	Bon F404
Red with black interior; in good overall condition. Since 1984 with the present, second owner. Circa 52,000 miles covered.												
1971	E-Type 4.2 roadster series II		2R13690	L	70-80.000 EUR	NS			08-04-17	Essen	177	Coy
Blue with tan interior; restored.												
1969	E-Type 4.2 roadster series II		1R29239	L	80-100.000 EUR	63.337	78.884	74.000	08-04-17	Essen	213	Coy
See lot 238 Coys 14.1.17.												
1971	E-Type 4.2 roadster series II		P2R14820	L	55-65.000 GBP	57.375	73.767	67.829	13-05-17	Silverstone	350	SiC
Reimported into the UK from the USA in 1991 and subsequently restored.												
1969	E-Type 4.2 roadster series II		1R1061	R	85-98.000 GBP	NS			20-05-17	Ascot	162	His
Red with cream interior; restored and repainted in 1985. In good overall condition.												
1969	E-Type 4.2 roadster series II		1R8404	R	78-85.000 GBP	79.520	103.471	92.561	20-05-17	Ascot	175	His
Black with red interior; fully restored. Originally built in left-hand drive form (see lot 91 Bonhams 19.8.16 $88,000).												
1969	E-Type 4.2 roadster series II		1R9417	R	100-120.000 GBP	99.680	129.704	116.028	20-05-17	Ascot	252	His
Black with grey leather interior; reimported into the UK from the USA in 2005 and recently restored and converted to right-hand drive.												
1970	E-Type 4.2 roadster series II		1R13285	L	70-90.000 USD	61.610	79.200	70.607	04-06-17	Greenwich	175	Bon
British racing green with tan leather interior; for over 20 years in the current ownership; restored about 10 years ago.												
1971	E-Type 4.2 roadster series II		2R13690	L	60-70.000 GBP	60.021	77.571	68.214	15-07-17	Blenheim Pal.	134	Coy
See lot 177 Coys 8.4.17.												
1969	E-Type 4.2 roadster series II		1R9517	L	90-110.000 GBP	NS			15-07-17	Blenheim Pal.	139	Coy
Pale blue with blue interior; described as in very good overall condition.												
1970	E-Type 4.2 roadster series II		1R12154	L	100-120.000 GBP	NS			26-07-17	Duxford	42	H&H
Gunmetal grey with red leather interior; reimported into the UK from the USA in 2015 and subjected to a restoration completed in February 2017.												
1970	E-Type 4.2 roadster series II		1R1159	R	NA	75.375	98.704	84.156	29-07-17	Silverstone	416	SiC
Red with black interior; restored in 1987.												

Year	Model (Bodybuilder)	Chassis no.	Steering	Estimate	Hammer price £	Hammer price $	Hammer price €	Sale Date	Sale Place	Lot	Auc. H.
1969	E-Type 4.2 roadster series II	1R11398	L	85-100.000 EUR	85.563	112.479	94.775	05-08-17	Schloss Dyck	248	Coy
British racing green with tan leather interior; restored.											
1969	E-Type 4.2 roadster series II	1R9125	L	NA	64.957	83.600	71.227	19-08-17	Monterey	1081	R&S
Red with black interior; described as in good overall condition.											
1972	E-Type V12 5.3 coupé	1S50718	R	45-55.000 GBP		NS		29-10-16	London	143	Coy
Fawn with tan interior; in good overall condition. Engine and 5-speed manual gearbox rebuilt.											
1971	E-Type V12 5.3 coupé	1S50576	R	16-20.000 GBP	31.640	39.322	36.744	16-11-16	Donington Park	115	H&H
Red with cinnamon interior; stored since 2010. Manual gearbox.											
1972	E-Type V12 5.3 coupé	1151084	R	30-40.000 GBP	36.520	45.372	42.601	18-02-17	London	318	Coy
Red with magnolia leather interior; restored.											
1973	E-Type V12 5.3 coupé	1S74811	L	55-65.000 EUR		NS		10-06-17	Lyon	149	Agu
Old English white with dark blue leather interior; two owners; 21,000 kms covered; recently serviced. Manual gearbox.											
1973	E-Type V12 5.3 roadster	1S2392BW	R	NA	115.880	153.923	137.526	02-09-16	Salon Privé	227	SiC
Old English white with blue leather interior; described as in largely original condition. The car has received a light recommission after being stored between 2006 and 2016.											
1974	E-Type V12 5.3 roadster	UE1S24058	L	60-70.000 USD	69.549	92.400	82.550	03-09-16	Auburn	5105	AA
British racing green with tan interior; 100 miles covered since the restoration. Manual gearbox.											
1971	E-Type V12 5.3 roadster	1S50376	R	75-80.000 GBP		NS		10-09-16	Goodwood	181	Bon
Black; engine rebuilt in 2010, body restored in 2015. Manual gearbox.											
1972	E-Type V12 5.3 roadster	UC1S20687WB	L	50-70.000 USD	38.894	50.050	44.539	03-10-16	Philadelphia	216	Bon
Sable with beige interior; since 1980 in the same family ownership. Stored from 1998 to 2006 when it was recommissioned.											
1973	E-Type V12 5.3 roadster	UD1522243	L	60-70.000 GBP	61.325	75.608	67.868	08-10-16	Ascot	318	Coy
Primrose yellow with black leather interior; sold new to the USA and recently reimported into the UK. Recent service.											
1973	E-Type V12 5.3 roadster	UE1S23611BW	L	65-75.000 GBP	63.720	78.095	70.869	12-10-16	Duxford	27	H&H
Primrose yellow with cinnamon leather interior; two owners and 20,000 miles covered. In highly original condition.											
1973	E-Type V12 5.3 roadster	1S23070	L	65-75.000 GBP	81.760	100.205	90.933	12-10-16	Duxford	91	H&H
Silver with dark blue interior; sold new to the USA, restored to concours condition in the early 2000s, recently registered in the UK. Manual gearbox.											
1974	E-Type V12 5.3 roadster	1S23635	L	70-90.000 EUR	66.174	80.975	73.600	15-10-16	Salzburg	423	Dor
White with beige interior; in good overall condition. Recently serviced. Manual gearbox.											
1972	E-Type V12 5.3 roadster	1S1406	R	85-105.000 GBP	119.250	150.959	138.437	12-11-16	Birmingham	611	SiC
Primrose yellow with black leather interior; restored in 2007-08 (see Coys lots 336 12.1.13 $116,306 and 112 12.3.13 NS).											
1971	E-Type V12 5.3 roadster	1S1104	R	45-65.000 GBP	65.340	82.387	76.781	07-12-16	London	337	Bon
Dark red with black interior; one owner and circa 63,000 miles covered. In very good overall condition; bonnet repainted two years ago. Manual gearbox.											
1973	E-Type V12 5.3 roadster	1S2536	R	65-75.000 GBP	73.180	92.273	85.994	07-12-16	London	345	Bon
Lavender blue with blue interior; in good overall condition. Manual gearbox (see H&H lots 32 23.7.08 NS and 110 8.10.14 NS).											
1974	E-Type V12 5.3 roadster	UE1S26054	L	165-185.000 USD	100.585	122.500	114.893	15-01-17	Kissimmee	S177	Mec
British racing green with brown leather interior; in original condition, 6,534 original miles, for 30 years with its first owner. Manual gearbox.											
1974	E-Type V12 5.3 roadster	UE1S24562BW	L	75-100.000 USD	61.131*	75.350*	70.626*	19-01-17	Scottsdale	76	Bon F405
Silver with black interior; in highly original condition; less than 12,000 miles covered; automatic transmission.											
1972	E-Type V12 5.3 roadster	UD1S21059	L	60-70.000 EUR	58.712	73.775	69.000	09-02-17	Paris	429	Bon
Silver with original black leather interior; body repainted. 19,474 miles covered. With hardtop (see lot 243 Bonhams 2.2.12 $78,302).											
1973	E-Type V12 5.3 roadster	1S2429BW	R	65-75.000 GBP	76.840	95.466	89.634	18-02-17	London	352	Coy
Red; always well maintained. Automatic transmission (see lot 46 H & H 19.4.12 $62,779).											
1974	E-Type V12 5.3 roadster	UE1S24373	L	75-100.000 USD	38.843*	47.300*	44.826*	09-03-17	Amelia Island	145	Bon
Silver with deep red interior; in good overall condition.											
1973	E-Type V12 5.3 roadster	1S2316	R	80-120.000 GBP	85.500	105.678	98.419	19-03-17	Goodwood	27	Bon
Red with red interior; in good overall condition; since 2002 in the current ownership; circa 25,000 miles covered since new.											
1973	E-Type V12 5.3 roadster	IS74814	R	170-225.000 GBP	166.725	208.406	196.502	12-04-17	London	360	Coy
Primrose yellow with chocolate interior; bought in 1990 by the current owner and restored. 2,500 miles covered since new.											

F403: 1969 Jaguar E-Type 4.2 coupé series II

F404: 1970 Jaguar E-Type 4.2 roadster series II

Year	Model	(Bodybuilder)	Chassis no.	Steering	Estimate	Hammer price £	Hammer price $	Hammer price €	Date	Place	Lot	Auc. H.
1972	E-Type V12 5.3 roadster		UC1S20336	L	NA	51.645	66.000	61.690	22-04-17	Dallas	2510	Lea
	Red with black interior; restored some years ago.											
1974	E-Type V12 5.3 roadster		1S2708	R	85-95.000 GBP	85.500	109.927	101.078	13-05-17	Silverstone	318	SiC
	Red with black interior; in good overall condition. Manual gearbox; black hardtop.											
1973	E-Type V12 5.3 roadster		IS74814	R	120-160.000 GBP	144.495	188.378	169.261	18-05-17	London	104	Coy
	See lot 360 Coys 12.4.17.											
1973	E-Type V12 5.3 roadster		UD1S21981	L	NQ	64.960*	84.526*	75.613*	20-05-17	Ascot	225	His
	Silver grey with blue interior; restoration completed in March 2017.											
1972	E-Type V12 5.3 roadster		7S7474SB	L	40-70.000 EUR	55.325*	71.993*	64.400*	21-05-17	SPA-Francorch.	52	Bon
	Metallic blue with original dark blue interior; restored in Switzerland. From the Swiss Castle Collection.											
1973	E-Type V12 5.3 roadster		UD1S21087	L	70-120.000 EUR	71.132	92.562	82.800	21-05-17	SPA-Francorch.	76	Bon
	British racing green with tan interior; two owners; approximately 43,700 miles covered.											
1974	E-Type V12 5.3 roadster		UE1S23641BW	R	68-85.000 GBP	81.720	105.468	93.676	06-06-17	Woodcote Park	36	H&H
	White with red interior; sold new to the USA, the car was reimported into the UK in 2015, restored and converted to right hand drive. Automatic transmission.											
1972	E-Type V12 5.3 roadster		UC1S20266	L	60-70.000 GBP		NS		26-07-17	Duxford	68	H&H
	Silver with black interior; described as in very good overall condition. Body repainted. Manual gearbox.											
1972	E-Type V12 5.3 roadster		1S1322	R	65-75.000 GBP	69.750	91.338	77.876	29-07-17	Silverstone	705	SiC
	Red with black interior; 17,428 miles on the odometer at April 2017; some recommissioning and light detailing required.											
1973	E-Type V12 5.3 roadster		UD1S22901BW	L	60-70.000 EUR	52.344	68.811	57.980	05-08-17	Schloss Dyck	250	Coy
	Sable brown with cream interior; sold new to the USA and reimported into Europe in 2016. Last serviced in 2016; interior refurbished in 2017.											
1976	XJ6 4.2 saloon		2T64270BW	L	5-7.000 GBP	5.000	6.089	5.711	14-01-17	Birmingham	144	Coy
	Green with green interior; in good overall condition. 85,000 kms covered. Automatic transmission.											
1978	XJ6C		2J53564BW	L	15-3.000 EUR	26.713*	33.217*	31.360*	25-11-16	Milan	947	RMS
	Black with beige interior; automatic transmission. 70,927 kms. From the Duemila Ruote collection.											
1977	XJ12C		2G1442BW	R	30-35.000 GBP	43.875	55.541	50.934	12-11-16	Birmingham	311	SiC F406
	Red with black roof; three owners and 42,300 miles covered. Restored in 1990 (see lot 149 Silverstone Auctions 21.7.12 $51,787).											
1978	XJ12C		2G15688BW	R	26-30.000 GBP		NS		13-05-17	Silverstone	303	SiC
	Blue with black roof and blue interior; in good overall condition.											
1984	XJ-S Eventer (Lynx)		113109	L	70-110.000 EUR	59.108	78.519	70.150	03-09-16	Chantilly	12	Bon F407
	Black with beige interior; first restored in 1999 and in 2010 again. Recently converted to left-hand drive. Automatic transmission (see lots 309 Silverstone Auctions 22.02.15 NS and 441 Bonhams 20.06.15 $39,595).											
1992	XJ-S coupé		179745	L	15-25.000 EUR	19.290*	23.434*	21.456*	30-10-16	Paris	172	Art
	Black with black leather interior.											
1992	XJ-S coupé		179845	R	NQ	14.000*	17.128*	16.212*	04-03-17	Brooklands	112	His
	Red with white interior in good overall condition.											
1991	XJ-S coupé Le Mans		177667	R	24-28.000 GBP		NS		08-07-17	Brooklands	216	His
	British racing green with magnolia leather interior; in very good overall condition. Limited edition built in 280 examples.											
1988	XJ-SC 3.6 cabriolet		140406	L	15-25.000 EUR	20.248	25.292	22.800	05-11-16	Lyon	1988	Agu
	Beige with beige interior; described as in very good overall condition. 26,500 kms covered.											
1984	XJ-SC V12 HE cabriolet		180088	L	10-15.000 EUR	29.575*	36.775*	34.720*	25-11-16	Milan	527	RMS
	White; 37,969 kms. From the Duemila Ruote collection.											
1992	XJ-SC V12 HE cabriolet		194754	L	15-18.000 EUR	27.667*	34.403*	32.480*	25-11-16	Milan	914	RMS
	Dark green; 49,644 miles. From the Duemila Ruote collection.											
1987	XJ-S V12 HE convertible		140223	R	10-12.000 GBP	11.500	15.275	13.648	03-09-16	Beaulieu	482	Bon
	Metallic blue with blue leather interior; in good overall condition.											
1990	XJ-S V12 HE convertible		168440	R	NQ	10.080*	12.354*	11.211*	12-10-16	Duxford	1	H&H
	Metallic red with cream leather interior; in good overall condition. Automatic transmission (see lot 62 H & H 18.4.07 $15,435).											
1989	XJ-S V12 HE convertible		162255	L	18-23.000 EUR	16.518	20.633	18.600	05-11-16	Lyon	224	Agu
	Black with white leather interior; in good overall condition. Automatic transmission.											

F405: 1974 Jaguar E-Type V12 5.3 roadster

F406: 1977 Jaguar XJ12C

Year	Model	(Bodybuilder)	Chassis no.	Steering	Estimate	£	$	€	Date	Place	Lot	Auc. H.

F407: 1984 Jaguar XJ-S Eventer (Lynx)

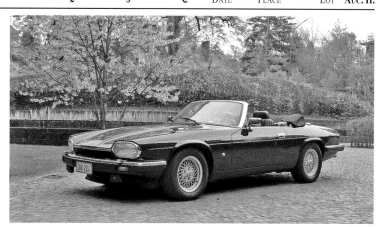

F408: 1992 Jaguar XJ-S V12 HE convertible

Year	Model	Chassis no.	Steering	Estimate	£	$	€	Date	Place	Lot	Auc. H.
1990	XJ-S V12 HE convertible	165410	R	9-12.000 GBP	15.400	19.148	18.078	26-11-16	Weybridge	228	His
Blue with grey leather interior; last serviced in April 2015.											
1990	XJ-S V12 HE convertible	170098	L	NQ	18.913	23.500	22.064	18-02-17	Los Angeles	F61	Mec
Red with tan interior; believed to be 39,765 miles.											
1992	XJ-S V12 HE convertible	184908	L	28-36.000 EUR	22.723	29.568	26.450	21-05-17	SPA-Francorch.	64	Bon F408
In original condition; one owner; 81,500 kms covered.											
1990	XJR-S	164145	R	14-16.000 GBP		NS		16-11-16	Donington Park	117	H&H
Since 1995 in the same ownership; 38,150 miles covered. 6.0-litre engine.											
1990	XJR-S 6.0	164145	R	14-16.000 GBP	14.750	18.427	17.429	23-02-17	Donington Park	57	H&H
See lot 117 H & H 16.11.16.											
1992	XJ-S 4.0 coupé	185602	R	10-14.000 GBP	10.080	12.999	11.390	08-07-17	Brooklands	127	His
Red with beige interior; recently recommissioned following a period in storage. Automatic transmission.											
1994	XJ-S 4.0 cabriolet	195831	L	7-10.000 EUR	25.759*	32.030*	30.240*	25-11-16	Milan	846	RMS
Dark blue with light grey interior. From the Duemila Ruote collection.											
1997	XJ220	220704	L	325-375.000 GBP		NS		20-05-17	Ascot	231	His
Yellow; converted to S specification by Don Law Racing. Engine producing over 680bhp; upgraded braking system. In very good overall condition.											
1993	XJ220	220672	L	350-450.000 USD	324.786	418.000	356.136	18-08-17	Monterey	125	RMS F409
Dark red; one owner; 3,390 kms covered; last serviced in 2012.											
1998	XK8 coupé	22840	L	8-12.000 EUR	12.725	16.228	14.520	10-06-17	Lyon	117	Agu
Light metallic brown with beige leather interior; in good overall condition. Automatic transmission recently overhauled.											

JENSEN (GB) *(1935-1976)*

Year	Model	Chassis no.	Steering	Estimate	£	$	€	Date	Place	Lot	Auc. H.
1960	541 S	JMEXP101	R	NA	42.750	56.785	50.736	02-09-16	Salon Privé	260	SiC
Maroon with burgundy interior; in good overall condition. Probably the car shown at the Jensen stand at the 1960 London Motor Show (see lot 653 Brooks 27.04.95 $9,266).											
1958	541 DeLuxe	5412113848	R	60-65.000 GBP	60.210	73.143	66.966	29-10-16	London	140	Coy F410
Red with tan leather interior; acquired in 2012 by the current owner and subsequently restored.											
1956	541	5411315803	R	45-55.000 GBP		NS		12-11-16	Birmingham	605	SiC
Metallic blue with red leather interior; restored at unspecified date.											
1956	541	5411315803	R	45-55.000 GBP	44.460	55.237	51.863	18-02-17	London	320	Coy
See lot 605 Silverstone Auctions 12.11.16.											
1960	541R	4616011	R	NA		NS		19-08-17	Monterey	1182	R&S
Red; two owners; fully restored.											
1963	C-V8	1042031	R	60-70.000 AUD	26.503	32.954	31.112	27-11-16	Melbourne	83	Mos
Blue with original beige interior; the car requires some cosmetical attention.											

F409: 1993 Jaguar XJ220

F410: 1958 Jensen 541 DeLuxe

Year	Model	(Bodybuilder)	Chassis no.	Steering	Estimate	Hammer price £	Hammer price $	Hammer price €	Date	Place	Lot	Auc. H.
1969	**Interceptor**		1153053	R	34-40.000 GBP	**40.880**	**50.830**	**47.989**	26-11-16	Weybridge	122	His
	Stored from 1991 to 2015 and subsequently recommissioned.											
1968	**Interceptor**		1152774	R	30-35.000 GBP	**30.240**	**37.600**	**35.499**	26-11-16	Weybridge	155	His
	Light blue; restored in Belgium in 2014-15 (see lot 524 Silverstone Auctions 30.7.16 NS).											
1968	**Interceptor**		1152900	R	35-40.000 GBP	**32.480**	**42.263**	**37.807**	20-05-17	Ascot	149	His F411
	Bronze with beige leather interior.											
1972	**Interceptor MkIII**		13315625	L	20-25.000 GBP	**22.400**	**27.453**	**24.913**	12-10-16	Duxford	133	H&H
	White with tan interior; body repainted in recent years.											
1976	**Interceptor MkIII**		1850	R	20-30.000 GBP	**34.500**	**42.642**	**39.713**	19-03-17	Goodwood	31	Bon
	Grey with vinyl roof and blue interior; in good driving order. Since 1993 in the current ownership.											
1972	**Interceptor MkIII**		1284520	R	20-30.000 GBP	**40.320**	**52.464**	**46.932**	20-05-17	Ascot	204	His
	Grey with red interior; restored in 2005.											
1974	**Interceptor MkIII cabriolet**		23111666	R	75-90.000 GBP	**67.200**	**82.360**	**74.740**	12-10-16	Duxford	20	H&H
	Metallic blue with black leather interior; described as in very good overall condition. Automatic transmission replaced in recent times. 25,000 miles on the odometer.											
1974	**Interceptor MkIII cabriolet**		23401030	R	40-50.000 GBP		NS		18-02-17	London	327	Coy
	Yellow with black leather interior; 26,000 miles covered. Stored for the last 20 years, the car is described as in good driving order.											
1975	**Interceptor MkIII cabriolet**		23111623	L	80-100.000 USD	**31.080**	**40.000**	**34.080**	19-08-17	Monterey	F50	Mec
	Red with tan leather interior; restored (see lots 244 Bonhams 31.5.15 $53,900 and 707 Auctions America 2.4.16 $59,400).											
1975	**Healey GT**		30072	R	14-18.000 GBP	**15.680**	**20.221**	**17.718**	08-07-17	Brooklands	111	His
	Blue with beige interior; in 2017 engine rebuilt and body repainted.											

JORDAN (GB) (1980-)

Year	Model	(Bodybuilder)	Chassis no.	Steering	Estimate	£	$	€	Date	Place	Lot	Auc. H.
1997	**F1 197**		19703	M	20-25.000 GBP	**94.080**	**115.097**	**108.945**	04-03-17	Brooklands	158	His
	Yellow; car driven by Giancarlo Fisichella at some events of the 1997 F1 season. Offered without engine and gearbox.											

JULIEN & BOYLER (F)

Year	Model	(Bodybuilder)	Chassis no.	Steering	Estimate	£	$	€	Date	Place	Lot	Auc. H.
1996	**Land Speed Record Car**		PC26E2013412	C	30-45.000 AUD	**24.782**	**30.814**	**29.092**	27-11-16	Melbourne	45	Mos
	Carbon-fiber and epoxy resin body finished in blue; one-off fitted with a twin-cylinder 499cc Honda engine. In 1997 in France the car set the new land speed one-hour record for non-supercharged cars with displacement between 351 and 500cc (see lot 267 RM 31.10.07 $31,907).											

KAISER (USA) (1946-1955)

Year	Model	(Bodybuilder)	Chassis no.	Steering	Estimate	£	$	€	Date	Place	Lot	Auc. H.
1954	**Darrin 161**		161001026	L	NA	**94.387***	**115.500***	**104.978***	15-10-16	Las Vegas	695	B/J
	Red with black leather interior; older restoration. Engine with McCullough supercharger.											
1954	**Darrin 161**		3495168	L	NQ	**87.792***	**107.800***	**101.386***	21-01-17	Scottsdale	1297	B/J
	Champagne white with red leather interior; 3-speed manual gearbox (see lot 2079 Auctions America 18.7.15 $90,220).											
1954	**Darrin 161**		161001188	L	70-90.000 USD	**70.167**	**90.200**	**80.413**	04-06-17	Greenwich	148	Bon F412
	Yellow with tan vinyl interior; restored several decades ago and always regularly serviced.											

KLEINSCHNITTGER (D) (1949-1957)

Year	Model	(Bodybuilder)	Chassis no.	Steering	Estimate	£	$	€	Date	Place	Lot	Auc. H.
1954	**F-125**		641818	L	20-30.000 USD	**24.188***	**29.700***	**27.933***	20-01-17	Phoenix	203	RMS
	Red with black vinyl interior; restored in 1996. Body repainted and engine overhauled in 2016 (see lot 179 Christie's 6.3.97 $22,251).											

KNOX (USA) (1900-1914)

Year	Model	(Bodybuilder)	Chassis no.	Steering	Estimate	£	$	€	Date	Place	Lot	Auc. H.
1904	**16/18hp Tudor touring**		312	L	200-225.000 USD	**240.283**	**292.600**	**277.297**	09-03-17	Amelia Island	153	Bon F413
	Dark green with black interior; first restored in 1941, the car received further works over the years. Mechanical overhauled for the 2016 London-Brighton Run (see lots 46 Gooding & Company 18.8.12 $109,000 and 34 Bonhams 14.8.15 $192,500).											

F411: 1968 Jensen Interceptor

F412: 1954 Kaiser Darrin 161

Year	Model	(Bodybuilder)	Chassis no.	Steering	Estimate	Hammer price £	$	€	Date	Place	Lot	Auc. H.

F413: 1904 Knox 16/18hp Tudor touring

F414: 1928 Lagonda 2-litre Speed Model tourer

LAGONDA (GB) (1908-1974)

Year	Model	Chassis no.	Steering	Estimate	£	$	€	Date	Place	Lot	Auc. H.
1928	2-litre Speed Model tourer	8942	R	50-70.000 GBP	54.625	72.558	64.829	03-09-16	Beaulieu	446	Bon F414

Grey with red interior; since 1949 in the same family ownership. In recent times the engine was rebuilt and the interior were retrimmed (see lots 29 H & H 4.12.13 $60,984 and 279 Bonhams 24.6.16 NS).

| 1932 | 2-litre Continental tourer | OH10117 | R | 75-85.000 GBP | NS | | | 30-06-17 | Goodwood | 216 | Bon |

Green with green leather interior; fully restored between 2005 and 2007.

| 1933 | 3-litre tourer | Z10441 | R | 120-150.000 GBP | NS | | | 20-05-17 | Ascot | 223 | His |

Black with red leather interior; restored between late 1960s/early 1970s. Engine rebuilt in more recent years (see lot 384 Historics 6.7.14 $176,663).

| 1934 | 16/80 Special 6 saloon | S11040 | R | 35-40.000 GBP | 39.675 | 52.700 | 47.086 | 03-09-16 | Beaulieu | 414 | Bon |

Red with black roof and wings; restored in 1996, ENV pre-selector gearbox overhauled in 2002, further mechanical works carried out in 2012.

| 1934 | M45 tourer | Z10681 | R | 175-225.000 GBP | 291.200 | 389.684 | 346.790 | 07-09-16 | London | 161 | RMS F415 |

Dark green; engine and gearbox rebuilt in 2012. The car was driven on the RAC Rally and Monte Carlo Rally in 1936. From the estate of Edward Carter.

| 1935 | M45A tourer | Z11408 | R | 110-130.000 GBP | 116.480 | 142.758 | 129.549 | 12-10-16 | Duxford | 93 | H&H |

Green with black interior; built with saloon body, the car was fitted with the present, new body in the 1970s probably. Described as in good overall condition (see lot 95 H & H 20.4.16 NS).

| 1934 | M45 Rapide tourer | Z11212 | R | 250-290.000 AUD | 130.794 | 162.630 | 153.540 | 27-11-16 | Melbourne | 75 | Mos |

Imported into Australia in 1935, the car remained in the same family ownership since and was regularly used. In 2005 following an irreparable damage to the original Meadows 4.5-litre engine, the car was fully restored and fitted with a 4.2-litre Jaguar engine with gearbox, and the brakes and steering were modified to power assist.

| 1937 | LG45 saloon | 12221G10 | R | 60-70.000 GBP | 62.540 | 83.072 | 74.222 | 03-09-16 | Beaulieu | 468 | Bon |

Dark red; described as in original condition. Since 1968 in the current ownership. 68,288 miles covered.

| 1936 | LG45 (Freestone/Webb) | 12146 | R | Refer Dpt. | 84.168 | 104.570 | 98.182 | 18-02-17 | London | 357 | Coy |

Black; sold new to the USA, after WWII the car was imported into China at Shanghai. In the early 1950 it was bought by an English business man who in 1985 reimported it into the UK.

| 1937 | LG45 cabriolet | 12224G10 | R | 275-325.000 USD | 162.393 | 209.000 | 178.695 | 17-08-17 | Monterey | 46 | WoA |

Chassis and engine restored in the USA, body restored in the UK. Restoration completed in 1991. Engine from chassis 12241, body from chassis 12232.

| 1938 | V12 cabriolet | 14050 | R | 235-285.000 GBP | NS | | | 07-09-16 | London | 174 | RMS |

Blue with brown leather interior; body repainted in 1970, engine rebuilt in 2008 (see lot 22 RM 5.2.14 $341,284).

| 1953 | DB 2.6 cabriolet (Tickford) | LAG50506 | R | 100-150.000 GBP | 113.500 | 151.239 | 134.225 | 10-09-16 | Goodwood | 125 | Bon F416 |

Dark red with cream leather interior; fully restored between 2015 and 2016. The car was fitted at the factory in November 1953 with the 3-litre engine. Formerly the property of Rob Walker (see Bonhams lots 100 4.6.05 $35,556 and 563 6.12.10 $45,066).

| 1950 | DB 2.6 cabriolet | LAG50335 | R | 12-16.000 GBP | 19.550 | 25.135 | 23.112 | 13-05-17 | Newp.Pagnell | 201 | Bon |

Restoration project.

| 1953 | DB 2.6/3.0 cabriolet | LAG50536 | R | 70-90.000 GBP | NS | | | 26-07-17 | Duxford | 28 | H&H |

Blue with grey leather interior; bought new by Peter Ustinov who retained it for 12 years; fitted in 1954 at the factory with the 3-litre engine; since 1968 in the same family ownership; interior retrimmed in the 1970s; engine overhauled in the late 1990s.

F415: 1934 Lagonda M45 tourer

F416: 1953 Lagonda DB 2.6 cabriolet (Tickford)

Year	Model	(Bodybuilder)	Chassis No.	Steering	Estimate	Hammer Price £	$	€	Date	Place	Lot	Auc. H.
1957	DB 3l saloon		LB2901209	R	16-20.000 GBP	14.833	18.179	16.497	12-10-16	Duxford	82	H&H

Unused for over 20 years, the car requires recommissioning prior to use (see lot 2 H & H 20.4.16 $30,175).

| 1963 | Rapide | (Touring) | LR133R | R | 170-220.000 GBP | | NS | | 07-12-16 | London | 327 | Bon |

Blue with white leather interior; body repainted in 1996, major refurbishment carried out in more recent years. Automatic transmission (see lots Bonhams 229 11.5.02 NS, and H & H 34 7.5.03 $20,701 and 63 3.10.05 $32,465).

LAMBORGHINI (I) (1963-)

Year	Model	(Bodybuilder)	Chassis No.	Steering	Estimate	£	$	€	Date	Place	Lot	Auc. H.
1966	350 GT	(Touring)	0335	L	600-800.000 EUR		NS		07-10-16	Zoute	23	Bon

Light blue with blue leather interior; restored eight years ago.

| 1965 | 350 GT | (Touring) | 0232 | L | 600-750.000 USD | | NS | | 11-03-17 | Amelia Island | 252 | RMS |

Black with original tobacco leather interior; never restored, the car is described as in very good driving order. Paintwork redone some 20 years ago and recently detailed. Fewer than 60,000 kms covered since new. Recently serviced. From the Adam Carolla collection.

| 1968 | Miura | (Bertone) | 3646 | L | 800-1.000.000 EUR | 757.409 | 943.898 | 888.040 | 10-02-17 | Paris | 120 | Art F417 |

Red with black leather interior; bought in 1989 in the USA by the current Italian owner and later fully restored. Described as in very good overall condition.

| 1971 | Miura S | (Bertone) | 4863 | R | 800-900.000 GBP | 841.800 | 1.022.619 | 936.250 | 29-10-16 | London | 120 | Coy |

Blue with black leather interior; for the last 20 years with the present owner who had it converted to Sv specification and later in 2013 had it restored. First owner the rock legend Rod Stewart (see lot 33 RM 5.2.14 $705,319).

| 1971 | Miura SV | (Bertone) | 4946 | L | 2.300-2.600.000 USD | | NS | | 19-01-17 | Phoenix | 139 | RMS |

Red with blue leather interior; sold new to the USA. Recent cosmetic restoration. Mechanicals described as in very good condition.

| 1972 | Miura SV | (Bertone) | 5050 | L | 2.200-2.600.000 EUR | 2.037.066 | 2.538.630 | 2.388.400 | 10-02-17 | Paris | 75 | Art F418 |

Originally finished in metallic brown with mustard interior, the car was sold new to France; in 1976 it was bought by its third owner who retained it for 37 years and had it repainted in the early 1980s in the present red livery. Engine overhauled in 2014 and in 2016 again. Original interior. Four owners and 42,580 kms covered.

| 1966 | 400 GT "interim" | (Touring) | 0427 | L | 650-750.000 EUR | | NS | | 27-05-17 | Villa Erba | 155 | RMS |

Grey with beige interior; restored in Italy.

| 1967 | 400 GT "interim" | (Touring) | 0568 | L | 550-750.000 EUR | | NS | | 02-07-17 | Monaco | 183 | Art |

Dark blue with beige leather interior; sold new to the USA where it was restored in 1990. Bought five years ago by the current owner and subsequently recommissioned in Italy. Last serviced in June 2016.

| 1967 | 400 GT 2+2 | (Touring) | 1036 | L | 580-660.000 EUR | | NS | | 10-02-17 | Paris | 83 | Art |

Silver with tobacco leather interior; the car has covered less than 1,000 kms since the restoration completed in 2013.

| 1967 | 400 GT 2+2 | (Touring) | 0622 | L | 475-550.000 USD | | NS | | 10-03-17 | Amelia Island | 21 | G&Co |

Red with tan interior; the engine has covered 200 miles since the rebuild carried out two years ago. Approximately 13,000 believed original miles covered since new.

| 1967 | 400 GT 2+2 | (Touring) | 01174 | L | 450-550.000 USD | 370.993 | 451.000 | 425.022 | 11-03-17 | Amelia Island | 239 | RMS F419 |

Silver grey with beige leather interior; body repainted in recent years. Recently serviced.

| 1974 | Espada 400 GT | (Bertone) | 9414 | R | 60-80.000 GBP | 57.000 | 75.953 | 67.408 | 10-09-16 | Goodwood | 165 | Bon |

Red with black interior; restored in the late 1980s following a road accident and fitted with a Lamborghini Jarama GTS engine and new gearbox. Engine top-end rebuilt in 2008; body repainted in recent times.

| 1971 | Espada 400 GT | (Bertone) | 8296 | L | 170-220.000 EUR | | NS | | 05-11-16 | Lyon | 230 | Agu |

Blue with fawn interior; bought in 1991 by the current, second owner and restored in the mid-1990s. 73,000 kms covered since new.

| 1975 | Espada 400 GT | (Bertone) | 9566 | L | 90-120.000 USD | 55.331* | 68.200* | 63.924* | 19-01-17 | Scottsdale | 58 | Bon |

Red with tan interior; mechanicals refurbished in recent years.

| 1969 | Espada 400 GT | (Bertone) | 7189 | L | 240-280.000 EUR | 228.748 | 285.070 | 268.200 | 10-02-17 | Paris | 78 | Art F420 |

Silver with black leather interior; sold new in Italy, the car was restored in 2013.

| 1971 | Espada 400 GT | (Bertone) | 8346 | L | 70-110.000 EUR | 71.132* | 92.562* | 82.800* | 21-05-17 | SPA-Francorch. | 59 | Bon |

Metallic blue with beige leather interior; restored in Switzerland some years ago. From the Swiss Castle Collection.

| 1968 | Islero 400 GT 2+2 | (Marazzi) | 6318 | L | 250-300.000 USD | 203.247 | 247.500 | 234.556 | 09-03-17 | Amelia Island | 168 | Bon |

Silver with tobacco leather interior; sold new in Italy and imported into the USA in 1984. Mechanicals overhauled and body repainted in 2011-12. Recently serviced.

| 1969 | Islero 400 GT 2+2 | (Marazzi) | 6267 | L | 250-300.000 USD | 199.069 | 242.000 | 228.061 | 11-03-17 | Amelia Island | 284 | RMS F421 |

Dark blue with pigskin leather interior; never fully restored, the car is described as in good condition (see lot 21 Gooding & Company 16.8.08 $203,500).

| 1969 | Islero 400 GT 2+2 | (Marazzi) | 6342 | L | 250-300.000 EUR | | NS | | 02-07-17 | Monaco | 182 | Art |

Light blue with light beige interior; restored in the USA some years ago.

F417: 1968 Lamborghini Miura (Bertone)

F418: 1972 Lamborghini Miura SV (Bertone)

F419: 1967 Lamborghini 400 GT 2+2 (Touring)

F420: 1969 Lamborghini Espada 400 GT (Bertone)

Year	Model	(Bodybuilder)	Chassis no.	Steering	Estimate	£	$	€	Date	Place	Lot	Auc. H.
1968	**Islero 400 GT 2+2**	**(Marazzi)**	6327	L	300-375.000 USD		NS		19-08-17	Pebble Beach	177	G&Co
	Metallic blue; sold new in Italy; imported into the USA in the 1980s; bought in 2013 by the current owner and subsequently restored.											
1974	**Jarama 400 GTS 2+2**	**(Bertone)**	10608	R	NA	129.380	171.855	153.548	02-09-16	Salon Privé	217	SiC
	Grey with black interior; 2,000 miles covered since the restoration carried out in Australia (see lot 480 Coys 20.11.97 NS).											
1973	**Jarama 400 GT S 2+2**	**(Bertone)**	10378	L	90-105.000 EUR	114.485*	142.356*	134.400*	25-11-16	Milan	565	RMS
	Blue with white interior; 87,432 kms. From the Duemila Ruote collection.											
1971	**Jarama 400 GT 2+2**	**(Bertone)**	10066	L	175-225.000 USD	94.063*	115.500*	108.628*	20-01-17	Phoenix	267	RMS
	Metallic brown with mustard interior; sold new to the USA. Since 1984 with the current, second owner. Less than 30,000 miles covered (see lot 433 Auctions America 28.3.15 NS).											
1970	**Jarama 400 GT 2+2**	**(Bertone)**	10018	L	130-175.000 EUR	109.886	137.365	128.800	08-02-17	Paris	105	RMS
	Described as in very good and largely original condition; 77,000 kms on the odometer. Recently serviced. Swiss papers (see lot 44 Poulain 13.12.99 WD).											
1971	**Jarama 400 GT 2+2**	**(Bertone)**	10160	L	180-240.000 EUR	177.915	221.721	208.600	10-02-17	Paris	79	Art **F422**
	Dark green with red interior; the car has covered approximately 200 kms since the restoration carried out in Germany in 2014 (see lot 204 Artcurial 5.2.16 NS).											
1972	**Jarama 400 GT 2+2**	**(Bertone)**	10348	L	200-250.000 USD	108.583*	132.000*	124.397*	10-03-17	Amelia Island	24	G&Co
	Metallic bronze with mustard interior; sold new to the USA and retained by its first owner until 2009; unrestored; about 5,200 miles covered (see lot 19 Gooding & Company 16.8.14 $176,000).											
1973	**Jarama 400 GTS 2+2**	**(Bertone)**	10442	L	180-250.000 EUR	166.045	206.804	194.000	08-04-17	Essen	158	Coy
	Silver with black leather interior; body repainted, interior retrimmed. 9,000 miles covered. Recently serviced.											
1972	**Jarama 400 GT 2+2**	**(Bertone)**	10180	L	110-170.000 EUR	110.810	141.003	126.200	24-06-17	Wien	366	Dor
	Dark red with black leather interior; interior restored; engine overhauled in 2012-13.											
1974	**Jarama 400 GTS 2+2**	**(Bertone)**	10608	R	120-150.000 GBP	135.900	176.371	153.880	30-06-17	Goodwood	233	Bon
	See lot 217 Silverstone Auctions 2.9.16.											
1973	**Jarama 400 GTS 2+2**	**(Bertone)**	10442	L	160-220.000 EUR		NS		02-07-17	Monaco	184	Art
	See lot 158 Coys 8.4.17.											
1972	**Jarama 400 GT 2+2**	**(Bertone)**	10228	L	130-170.000 USD		NS		17-08-17	Monterey	9	WoA
	Sold new to the USA; body recently repainted; original interior.											
1974	**Urraco P250**	**(Bertone)**	15868	R	75-85.000 GBP		NS		08-10-16	Ascot	309	Coy
	Red with champagne interior; stored in 2006 for nine years and subsequently restored. 27,200 miles on the odometer.											
1974	**Urraco P250**	**(Bertone)**	15868	R	60-70.000 GBP	65.640	83.461	77.980	05-12-16	London	138	Coy
	See lot 309 Coys 8.10.16.											
1973	**Urraco P250 S**	**(Bertone)**	15420	L	120-140.000 EUR	116.916	145.702	137.080	10-02-17	Paris	77	Art **F423**
	Metallic blue; the car was sold new to Switzerland where it remained with its first owner until 2014 when it was resold to the Netherlands. Original condition; recently serviced.											
1975	**Urraco P250S**	**(Bertone)**	15858	R	60-80.000 GBP		NS		19-03-17	Goodwood	65	Bon
	Silver; described as in very good overall condition. Colin Clarke replacement engine.											
1975	**Countach LP400**	**(Bertone)**	1120062	L	900-1.100.000 EUR	712.865*	915.385*	817.600*	27-05-17	Villa Erba	160	RMS **F424**
	Yellow with tobacco interior; less than 6,000 kms covered.											

F421: 1969 Lamborghini Islero 400 GT 2+2 (Marazzi)

F422: 1971 Lamborghini Jarama 400 GT 2+2 (Bertone)

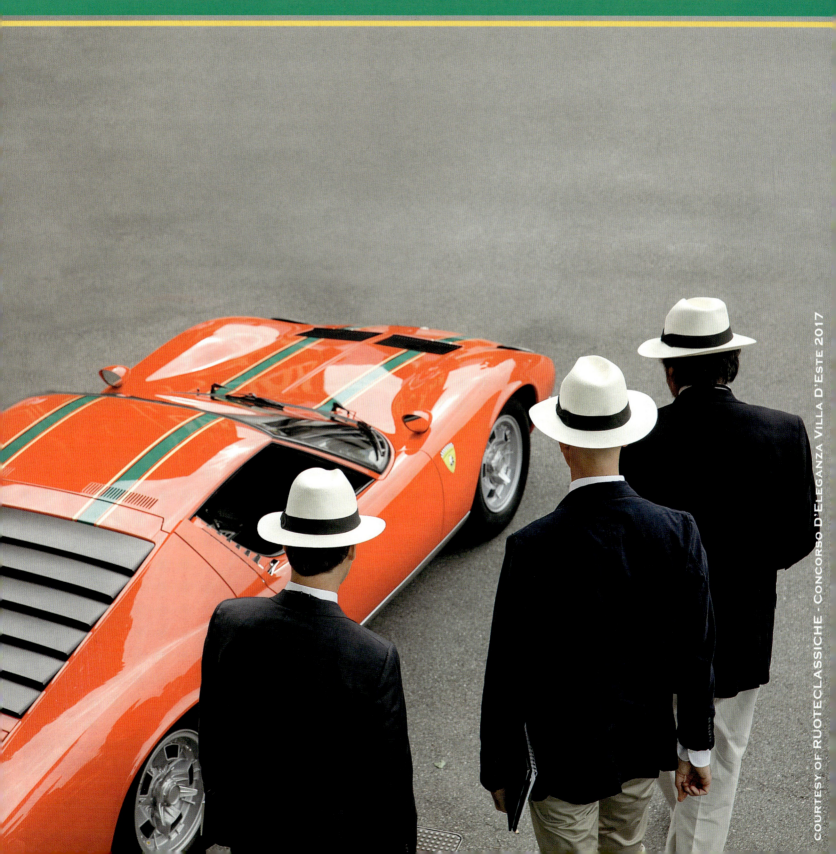

MODENA
WWW.CREMONINICLASSIC.IT

1° CLASSE F - MIURA P 400 COUPÉ BERTONE 1968

COURTESY OF RUOTECLASSICHE · CONCORSO D'ELEGANZA VILLA D'ESTE 2017

F423: 1973 Lamborghini Urraco P250 S (Bertone)

F424: 1975 Lamborghini Countach LP400 (Bertone)

Year	Model (Bodybuilder)	Chassis no.	Steering	Estimate	Hammer price £	$	€	Date	Place	Lot	Auc. H.
1976	**Countach LP400 (Bertone)**	1120172	L	900-1.200.000 USD	803.418	1.034.000	880.968	19-08-17	Monterey	261	RMS
Blue with tobacco leather interior; two owners; restored in the 1990s and subsequently stored; recommissioned in 2013; described as in very good overall condition (see lot 326 RM/Sotheby's 15.8.15 $1,320,000).											
1981	**Countach S LP400 (Bertone)**	1121298	L	350-400.000 GBP		NS		12-11-16	Birmingham	626	SiC
White with red leather interior; restoration just completed.											
1979	**Countach S LP400 (Bertone)**	1121094	L	600-700.000 USD	348.048	429.000	402.102	19-01-17	Phoenix	137	RMS
Black with natural leather interior; sold new to Germany. Body refinished in the present colour in the early 1980s. Engine rebuilt in 2002 and overhauled in 2014; clutch replaced in 2016. For 22 years in the current ownership.											
1981	**Countach S LP400 (Bertone)**	1121252	L	600-700.000 USD		NS		20-01-17	Phoenix	265	RMS
Metallic grey with black interior; the car has covered 200 miles since the restoration recently completed. 34,640 kms on the odometer.											
1984	**Countach 5000 S (Bertone)**	12661	L	NQ	168.105	210.000	189.294	04-11-16	Dallas	F183	Mec
Black with black interior; restoration completed in September 2015. Engine rebuilt.											
1984	**Countach 5000 S (Bertone)**	12661	L	225-275.000 USD	184.748	225.000	211.028	15-01-17	Kissimmee	S166.1	Mec
See lot F183 Mecum 4.11.16.											
1987	**Countach 5000 4V (Bertone)**	12086	L	325-375.000 USD		NS		20-01-17	Scottsdale	6	G&Co
Red with mustard leather interior; sold new to the USA, the car is described as in good original condition. 22,000 kms covered.											
1987	**Countach 5000 4V (Bertone)**	12197	L	275-350.000 USD	215.002*	264.000*	248.292*	20-01-17	Phoenix	241	RMS
White with white interior; 6,209 kms on the odometer.											
1983	**Countach 5000S (Bertone)**	12550	R	325-350.000 GBP		NS		24-02-17	Stoneleigh P.	519	SiC
Red; stored for the previous 10 years, the car was bought in 2014 by the current owner and recommissioned. Body repainted in 2016.											
1986	**Countach 5000 S (Bertone)**	12927	L	340-380.000 USD	275.513	335.500	317.953	09-03-17	Amelia Island	112	Bon F425
Red with white leather interior; imported into the USA from Switzerland in 2014. In largely original condition.											
1987	**Countach 5000 4V (Bertone)**	12123	L	275-325.000 USD		NS		10-03-17	Amelia Island	84	G&Co
Red with mustard leather interior; in the same ownership from 1991 to 2016; 10,450 kms covered; last serviced in early 2017.											
1988	**Countach 5000 4V (Bertone)**	12218	L	350-400.000 USD		NS		01-04-17	Ft.Lauderdale	503	AA
Yellow with white leather interior; 13,860 kms on the odometer; recently serviced.											
1988	**Countach 5000 4V (Bertone)**	12232	L	NQ	189.886	236.500	221.837	08-04-17	Palm Beach	748	B/J
White with red and black interior; restored. 18,997 actual kms.											
1988	**Countach 5000 4V (Bertone)**	12340	L	NQ	195.942	255.000	228.098	20-05-17	Indianapolis	F115.1	Mec
White with red interior; 13,749 original kms (see lot 135 RM/Sotheby's 28.1.16 NS).											
1987	**Countach 5000 4V (Bertone)**	12110	L	475-575.000 EUR		NS		27-05-17	Villa Erba	164	RMS
White with white interior; restored by Lamborghini Polo Storico.											
1988	**Countach 5000 4V (Bertone)**	12261	L	NA		NS		19-08-17	Monterey	1160	R&S
Black with white interior; less than 5,500 kms on the odometer; engine-out service.											

F425: 1986 Lamborghini Countach 5000 S (Bertone)

F426: 1989 Lamborghini Countach 25° (Bertone)

Year	Model	(Bodybuilder)	Chassis no.	Steering	Estimate	Hammer price £	$	€	Date	Place	Lot	Auc. H.
1990	**Countach 25°**	(Bertone)	12031	L	340-380.000 GBP	312.200	417.037	369.177	08-09-16	Fontwell Park	151	Coy
Red; two owners and 625 kms covered. Recently serviced (see lot 162 Coys 2.7.16 $484,793).											
1990	**Countach 25°**	(Bertone)	12815	R	200-250.000 GBP	225.500	300.479	266.676	10-09-16	Goodwood	116	Bon
Black with red interior; four owners and 10,800 miles covered. Body repainted in 2016 (see lot 271 Bonhams 29.6.12 $177,117).											
1989	**Countach 25°**	(Bertone)	12987	L	220-250.000 EUR	372.075*	462.659*	436.800*	25-11-16	Milan	589	RMS
Red with beige interior; 34,369 kms. From the Duemila Ruote collection.											
1990	**Countach 25°**	(Bertone)	12939	L	230-260.000 GBP	238.560	296.626	280.046	26-11-16	Weybridge	158	His
Red with tan interior; 7,081 kms on the odometer. Last serviced in October 2016.											
1990	**Countach 25°**	(Bertone)	12060	R	225-250.000 GBP	NS			04-12-16	London	19	Bon
Black with black interior; circa 39,500 kms covered. Four owners. Last serviced in August 2016.											
1989	**Countach 25°**	(Bertone)	12651	L	250-350.000 USD	NS			15-01-17	Kissimmee	S234	Mec
Red with ivory leather interior; 10,565 kms since new, clutch replaced in 2009, serviced in 2014 (see Mecum lots S169 24.1.15 $350,000, S60 15.8.15 NS, and T212 23.1.16 NS).											
1989	**Countach 25°**	(Bertone)	12699	L	250-325.000 USD	151.713*	187.000*	175.275*	19-01-17	Scottsdale	53	Bon
Red with black interior; described as in very good overall condition. Showing just over 10,000 kms (see lot 24 Bonhams 5.6.16 NS).											
1989	**Countach 25°**	(Bertone)	12550	L	300-350.000 USD	245.418	302.500	283.533	19-01-17	Phoenix	141	RMS F426
White with red leather interior; sold new to the USA. 3,620 kms covered. Last serviced in 2012 (see lot 233 RM 13.8.10 $101,750).											
1989	**Countach 25°**	(Bertone)	12711	L	NQ	210.522*	258.500*	243.119*	21-01-17	Scottsdale	1389	B/J
Black with black interior; in original condition. 3.710 actual kms. Recently serviced (see lot S133 Mecum 15.8.15 $270,000).											
1989	**Countach 25°**	(Bertone)	12820	L	285-350.000 EUR	284.664	354.754	333.760	10-02-17	Paris	59	Art
Blue with white leather interior; 34,500 kms covered (see lot 38 Bonhams 9.10.15 NS).											
1989	**Countach 25°**	(Bertone)	12478	L	325-350.000 USD	NS			11-02-17	Boca Raton	138	TFA
Red with tan interior; in good overall condition. Body recently repainted.											
1989	**Countach 25°**	(Bertone)	12846	R	190-240.000 GBP	200.000	257.920	226.000	08-07-17	Brooklands	198	His
Black with cream leather interior recently retrimmed; 27,500 miles covered.											
1989	**Countach 25°**	(Bertone)	12694	L	225-275.000 USD	NS			17-08-17	Monterey	58	WoA
Black with cream leather interior; sold new to the USA; one owner until 2015; major service in 2015 (see lot S132 Mecum 12.12.15 NS).											
1990	**Countach 25°**	(Bertone)	12923	L	300-350.000 USD	222.222	286.000	243.672	18-08-17	Carmel	96	Bon
Red with black interior; 2,700 kms on the odometer; imported into the USA in 2014 (see lots 119 RM 8.9.14 $360,640 and 125 Bonhams 10.3.16 NS).											
1989	**Countach 25°**	(Bertone)	12651	L	275-325.000 USD	202.020	260.000	221.520	19-08-17	Monterey	S151	Mec
See lot S234 Mecum 15.1.17.											
1984	**Jalpa 3500**	(Bertone)	12165	L	70-90.000 USD	58.116	72.600	65.442	05-11-16	Hilton Head	144	AA F427
Red with tan interior; cosmetically restored. Approximately 63,000 kms on the odometer.											
1988	**Jalpa 3500**	(Bertone)	12381	L	110-125.000 USD	NS			11-02-17	Boca Raton	135	TFA
Black with black interior; in very good running condition. 25,378 original miles (see lot 514 Auctions America 28.3.15 $88,000).											
1988	**Jalpa 3500**	(Bertone)	12386	L	NQ	59.415	74.000	69.412	08-04-17	Houston	S118	Mec
White with white interior; repainted seven years ago; recently serviced.											
1988	**LM002**		12108	L	200-300.000 USD	151.713	187.000	175.275	19-01-17	Scottsdale	7	Bon F428
Sold new to the USA; described as in very good overall condition; less than 19,000 miles on the odometer.											
1990	**LM002**		12194	L	250-300.000 USD	239.860	299.750	280.356	01-04-17	Ft.Lauderdale	496	AA
Red with tan interior; 17,253 kms on the odometer (see lot S53 Mecum 15.8.15 $240,000).											
1991	**LM002**		12236	L	140-180.000 GBP	161.167	201.459	189.951	12-04-17	London	342	Coy
Light metallic grey with red leather interior; overhauled in 2005 and in 2007 again. 27,975 miles on the odometer (see lots 348 Coys 20.10.07 NS and 507 Bonhams 11.7.08 NS).											
1999	**Diablo GT**	(Gandini)	12309	L	375-425.000 GBP	515.200	689.441	613.552	07-09-16	London	135	RMS F429
Grey with black and blue leather interior; one owner and 11,000 kms covered. Last serviced in May 2014. One of 80 examples built.											
1993	**Diablo VT**	(Gandini)	12958	L	130-170.000 GBP	151.200	202.336	180.064	07-09-16	London	149	RMS
Grey with beige leather interior; less than 15,600 kms covered. Recently serviced (see lot 373 Bonhams 4.2.16 NS).											
1997	**Diablo SV**	(Gandini)	12872	R	200-250.000 GBP	NS			10-09-16	Goodwood	134	Bon
Dark blue with snowcorn leather interior; 50,605 kms on the odometer. Last major service in August 2015 (see lot 223 Silverstone Auctions 4.9.15 $281,700).											

F427: 1984 Lamborghini Jalpa 3500 (Bertone)

F428: 1988 Lamborghini LM002

Year	Model	(Bodybuilder)	Chassis no.	Steering	Estimate	Hammer price £	$	€	Sale Date	Place	Lot	Auc. H.
1991	Diablo	(Gandini)	12624	L	95-125.000 GBP	107.900	143.777	127.603	10-09-16	Goodwood	145	Bon
Yellow with black leather interior; in good overall condition. 36,200 kms covered.												
1995	Diablo VT	(Gandini)	12341	L	220-260.000 USD		NS		17-09-16	Aspen	149	TFA
Silver with black interior; 20,388 kms.												
1995	Diablo VT	(Gandini)	12324	L	165-185.000 EUR		NS		30-10-16	Paris	169	Art
Yellow; since 2003 in the same ownership.												
1997	Diablo VT Roadster	(Gandini)	12751	L	235-255.000 USD		NS		05-11-16	Hilton Head	170	AA
Red; one owner and 4,700 original miles.												
1998	Diablo SV	(Gandini)	12883	L	130-150.000 EUR	200.348*	249.124*	235.200*	25-11-16	Milan	605	RMS
Titanium grey with black alcantara interior; 40,174 kms. From the Duemila Ruote collection.												
1998	Diablo VT	(Gandini)	12939	R	160-180.000 GBP		NS		07-12-16	London	328	Bon
Yellow with white leather interior; two owners, 13,675 kms covered, last serviced in September 2016.												
1998	Diablo VT Roadster	(Gandini)	12865	L	NQ		NS		15-01-17	Kissimmee	S61	Mec
Black with tan interior; 15,790 actual kms.												
1999	Diablo VT	(Gandini)	12246	L	250-300.000 USD		NS		19-01-17	Phoenix	155	RMS
Red with beige leather interior; two owners, 7,300 original miles. Engine-out service in 2003.												
2001	Diablo VT 6.0	(Gandini)	12647	L	300-375.000 USD	237.398	291.500	274.156	20-01-17	Phoenix	251	RMS
Grey with black interior; less than 9,300 miles covered.												
1999	Diablo VT	(Gandini)	12319	L	NQ	179.168*	220.000*	206.910*	21-01-17	Scottsdale	1352	B/J
Platinum Edition; tobacco leather interior; 30.000-mile engine-out service recently carried out.												
1998	Diablo VT Roadster	(Gandini)	12924	L	NQ		NS		21-01-17	Scottsdale	8468	R&S
Yellow with black and yellow leather interior; 47,620 kms covered. Recent service including a new clutch.												
1997	Diablo VT Roadster	(Gandini)	12762	L	200-250.000 EUR		NS		09-02-17	Paris	378	Bon
Silver with black interior; approximately 33,000 kms covered.												
1997	Diablo VT Roadster	(Gandini)	12717	L	225-250.000 USD	151.654	189.000	177.811	11-02-17	Boca Raton	148	TFA
Light blue with black interior; 26,800 kms covered. Recently serviced.												
1997	Diablo VT Roadster	(Gandini)	12626	L	260-335.000 USD		NS		11-03-17	Amelia Island	25	Mot
Yellow with champagne leather interior; 5,800 kms on the odometer.												
1999	Diablo VT Roadster	(Gandini)	12228	L	240-280.000 USD		NS		01-04-17	Ft.Lauderdale	492	AA
Titanium grey; 18,000 miles on the tachometer.												
1997	Diablo VT Roadster	(Gandini)	12626	L	220-240.000 USD	169.442	211.750	198.050	01-04-17	Ft.Lauderdale	510	AA F430
See lot 25 Motostalgia 11.3.17.												
1992	Diablo	(Gandini)	12537	L	150-175.000 USD	103.426	129.250	120.888	01-04-17	Ft.Lauderdale	578	AA
Red with tan interior; described as in very good overall condition; 43,000 kms covered.												
1994	Diablo VT	(Gandini)	12930	L	NQ	112.165	139.700	131.039	08-04-17	Palm Beach	744	B/J
Red with black interior; 23,801 actual miles. Body originally finished in black.												
1994	Diablo SE30	(Gandini)	12020	L	370-450.000 EUR		NS		27-05-17	Villa Erba	150	RMS
36,000 kms covered; one of 150 examples built.												
1991	Diablo	(Gandini)	12300	L	NQ		NS		24-06-17	Northeast	661	B/J
Yellow with black interior; 11,832 actual miles.												
2001	Diablo VT SE 6.0	(Gandini)	12711	L	300-400.000 EUR		NS		02-07-17	Monaco	173	Art
Gold; 55,000 kms covered. Chassis 01 of the Special Edition built in 42 examples, the car was exhibited at the 2001 Geneva Motor Show.												
1991	Diablo	(Gandini)	12446	L	180-240.000 EUR		NS		02-07-17	Monaco	209	Art
Yellow with black interior; 5,500 kms covered. Bought new by Keke Rosberg who retained it until early 2016 (see lot 210 Artcurial 5.2.16 $226,997).												
2000	Diablo GTR	(Gandini)	12492	L	580-780.000 USD		NS		19-08-17	Monterey	258	RMS
Car no.19 of 30 built; raced for some years; restored in 2012-13 and finished in the present orange livery.												
2010	Murciélago LP 670-4 SV		04024	L	325-375.000 GBP		NS		07-09-16	London	182	RMS
Yellow with black interior; one owner and less thab 4,100 kms covered. Last serviced in September 2015.												

F429: 1999 Lamborghini Diablo GT (Gandini)

F430: 1997 Lamborghini Diablo VT Roadster (Gandini)

Year	Model	(Bodybuilder)	Chassis no.	Steering	Estimate	Hammer Price £	$	€	Date	Place	Lot	Auc. H.

F431: 2008 Lamborghini Murciélago LP640 Roadster
F432: 2008 Lamborghini Gallardo Spyder

Year	Model	Chassis no.	Steering	Estimate	£	$	€	Date	Place	Lot	Auc. H.
2009	**Murciélago LP 670-4 SV**	03758	R	300-350.000 GBP		NS		08-10-16	Ascot	332	Coy
	Yellow with black alcantara interior; 15,900 miles covered.										
2008	**Murciélago LP640**	03353	R	120-140.000 GBP	140.625	178.017	163.252	12-11-16	Birmingham	316	SiC
	Black with black interior; two owners and 15,600 miles covered.										
2001	**Murciélago**	12026	L	90-110.000 GBP	94.167	119.206	109.318	12-11-16	Birmingham	652	SiC
	Yellow; pre-production example, it was used by the factory at the Nard Circuit and set new production car world records for one hour, 100 kms and 100 miles. Sold to private hands in 2002 (see lot 152 RM/Sotheby's 7.9.15 $145,294).										
2002	**Murciélago**	12051	L	145-165.000 EUR	143.106*	177.946*	168.000*	25-11-16	Milan	571	RMS
	Black with white and black interior; manual gearbox. 16,044 kms. From the Duemila Ruote collection.										
2002	**Murciélago**	12140	L	NQ	125.218	152.500	143.030	15-01-17	Kissimmee	F276.1	Mec
	Orange with black interior; 14,966 kms on the odometer.										
2010	**Murciélago LP 670-4**	04021	R	240-280.000 GBP	249.750	313.536	295.529	24-02-17	Stoneleigh P.	916	SiC
	Orange with black alcantara interior; 14,000 kms covered; imported into the UK from Singapore in 2015.										
2008	**Murciélago LP640 Roadster**	02631	L	NQ	136.493	170.000	159.460	08-04-17	Houston	S136.1	Mec
	Black with black leather interior; less than 1,400 original miles.										
2008	**Murciélago LP640 Roadster**	02631	L	225-275.000 USD	142.154	185.000	165.483	20-05-17	Indianapolis	S175	Mec **F431**
	See lot S136.1 Mecum 8.4.17.										
2002	**Murciélago**	12185	L	NQ		NS		24-06-17	Northeast	702	B/J
	Orange with black leather interior; recently serviced.										
2008	**Gallardo Spyder**	06676	L	100-140.000 USD	83.479	110.000	97.977	17-09-16	Aspen	125	TFA
	Green with black and white interior; one owner and 8,854 miles covered.										
2004	**Gallardo**	01093	L	NQ	61.784	78.000	73.289	03-12-16	Kansas City	S96.1	Mec
	Yellow with black interior; recently serviced.										
2008	**Gallardo Spyder**	06764	L	NQ	80.290	100.000	93.800	08-04-17	Houston	S137.1	Mec **F432**
	Black with black and yellow interior.										
2007	**Gallardo Spyder**	05525	L	NQ	108.048	137.500	123.063	24-06-17	Northeast	720	B/J
	Black with black and yellow interior; one owner and less than 3,300 actual miles.										
2004	**Gallardo**	00567	L	90-110.000 USD	70.015	89.100	79.745	24-06-17	Santa Monica	209	RMS
	Black with black interior; 4,019 miles on the odometer.										
2006	**Gallardo**	3047	R	58-68.000 GBP	55.575	71.825	63.161	15-07-17	Blenheim Pal.	172	Coy
	Grey with black interior; just over 48,000 miles covered. Clutch replaced.										
2006	**Concept S**	LA00001	L	1.500-2.500.000 USD	1.025.640	1.320.000	1.124.640	19-08-17	Monterey	233	RMS **F433**
	White with black interior; non-running concept car first presented at the 2005 Geneva Motor Show. In 2006 this fully functional example was built on a Gallardo platform and it remains the only example produced. 180 kms covered (see lot 212 RM/Sotheby's 10.12.15 NS).										

F433: 2006 Lamborghini Concept S
F434: 2008 Lamborghini Reventòn

F435: 1913 Lancia Theta speedster (Hayes/Miller)

F436: 1938 Lancia Astura berlina convertibile (Pinin Farina)

Year	Model (Bodybuilder)	Chassis no.	Steering	Estimate	£	$	€	Date	Place	Lot	Auc. H.
2010	**Reventòn Roadster**	NQ	R	900-1.000.000 GBP	**1.003.500**	1.340.475	1.186.639	08-09-16	Fontwell Park	127	Coy
One of 15 examples built of which just three in right-hand drive form; one owner and 1,050 miles covered.											
2008	**Reventòn**	03148	L	1.000-1.400.000 USD	1.070.916	**1.320.000**	1.237.236	19-01-17	Phoenix	138	RMS F434
Example no. 3 of 20 built: four owners and less than 1,000 miles covered. Last serviced in June 2015 (see lot 60 Bonhams 19.8.16 NS).											
2016	**Aventador SV Roadster**	05066	L	NA		NS		02-09-16	Salon Privé	228	SiC
Grey with black and red interior; 59 kms covered.											
2015	**Aventador Roadster**	03155	L	NQ		NS		08-04-17	Houston	S121.1	Mec
Black with cream interior; 18,000 actual miles; one owner (see lot S159.1 Mecum 16.4.16 NS).											

LANCIA (I) (1906-)

Year	Model (Bodybuilder)	Chassis no.	Steering	Estimate	£	$	€	Date	Place	Lot	Auc. H.
1913	**Theta speedster (Hayes/Miller)**	2182	R	225-250.000 USD	177.954	**216.700**	205.367	09-03-17	Amelia Island	183	Bon F435
Red with black fenders; described as in largely original condition, never fully restored. Engine replaced a few years back (the original unit is included with the sale).											
1938	**Astura berlina convertibile (Pinin Farina)**	412984	R	200-250.000 AUD	130.794	162.630	153.540	27-11-16	Melbourne	48	Mos F436
Dark green with tan interior; imported into Australia from the UK at unspecified date, the car was bought in 1972 by the current owner, who in 1973 started a long restoration completed in 2005. 12,000 miles covered since.											
1936	**Astura 3ª serie cabriolet "Bocca" (Pinin Farina)**	335313	R	2.000-2.600.000 USD	1.764.477*	**2.145.000***	2.021.448*	10-03-17	Amelia Island	163	RMS F437
Built on the short-wheelbase chassis and finished in pale grey with blue interior, the car was exhibited at the Pinin Farina stand at the 1936 Milan Motor Show. Sold new in Italy, it was exported prior to WWII to Germany, and in 1947 it was imported into the USA where it remained with the same owner until 1980. In 2011 it was bought by Orin Smith for his collection and restored to concours condition.											
1936	**Augusta cabriolet**	343662	R	50-80.000 EUR	54.899*	68.417*	**64.368***	10-02-17	Paris	47	Art
Cabriolet body originally built probably by Pinin Farina and modified and modernized during WWII by Langenthal in Switzerland. Restored in 2010, the car is described as in very good overall condition.											
1946	**Aprilia cabriolet (Pinin Farina)**	43911844	R	400-450.000 USD		NS		18-08-17	Monterey	134	RMS
Light blue with red interior; the car was driven by Pinin Farina to Paris and exhibited in front of the entrance of the 1946 Motor Show closed that year to the Italian manufacturers and coachbuilders. Later the car was sold to France where it was discovered in 2010 and subsequently fully restored in Italy (see lot 308 Artcurial 5.7.14 NS).											
1950	**Ardea**	12313	R	15-25.000 USD	11.447	**14.300**	12.890	05-11-16	Hilton Head	105	AA
Grey; in good working order.											
1949	**Ardea**	25015592	R	2-5.000 EUR	28.621*	35.589*	**33.600***	25-11-16	Milan	645	RMS F438
The car requires some restoration works. From the Duemila Ruote collection.											
1953	**Aurelia B22 berlina**	B221267	R	10-15.000 GBP	**17.250**	21.005	19.703	14-01-17	Birmingham	117	Coy
For restoration. First owned by Giovanni Bracco.											
1953	**Aurelia B52 PF200 C spider (Pinin Farina)**	B521052	R	1.100-1.400.000 USD	1.027.016*	**1.248.500***	1.176.586*	10-03-17	Amelia Island	150	RMS F439
Burgundy with light brown leather interior; exhibited at the 1953 Geneva and Turin Motor Shows and subsequently sold in Italy; imported into the USA in the 1960s; in single ownership from 1968 to 2014; concours-quality restoration completed in 2013. Original engine replaced with the present unit no.B214843 coming from the PF200 coupé formerly owned by Kjell Qvale. From the Orin Smith collection (see lot 219 RM 16.8.14 $1,100,000).											

F437: 1936 Lancia Astura 3a serie cabriolet "Bocca" (Pinin Farina)

F438: 1949 Lancia Ardea

Year	Model	(Bodybuilder)	Chassis no.	Steering	Estimate	Hammer price £	$	€	Sale Date	Place	Lot	Auc. H.

F439: 1953 Lancia Aurelia B52 PF200 C spider (Pinin Farina) *F440: 1952 Lancia Aurelia B52 coupé (Vignale)*

Year	Model (Bodybuilder)	Chassis no.	Steering	Estimate	£	$	€	Date	Place	Lot	Auc. H.
1952	**Aurelia B52 coupé (Vignale)**	B521054	R	250-350.000 EUR	**244.132**	**313.488**	**280.000**	27-05-17	Villa Erba	123	RMS F440
	Blue with light grey roof and red interior; one-off; 2-litre engine.										
1955	**Aurelia B20 4ª serie (Pinin Farina)**	3279	R	100-150.000 EUR		NS		03-09-16	Chantilly	27	Bon
	Red with grey cloth interior; prepared for historic rally (see lot 242 Bonhams 23.01.10 $66,647).										
1951	**Aurelia B20 Speciale 1ª serie (Pinin Farina)**	B201346	R	80-120.000 GBP	**173.600**	**232.312**	**206.740**	07-09-16	London	113	RMS
	Black and amaranth; the car presents several special features as the original leather interior, nonstandard bumpers and a dashbord layout similar to later-series B20s. It is believed, but not confirmed, that the car was exhibited at the Pinin Farina stand at the 1952 Paris Motor Show. Body repainted in 2010 in its original colors.										
1958	**Aurelia B20 6ª serie (Pinin Farina)**	1771	L	120-150.000 EUR		NA		08-10-16	Paris	128	CB/C
	Metallic grey with grey cloth and blue leather interior; it comes with Italian ASI homologation.										
1954	**Aurelia B20 4ª serie (Pinin Farina)**	B203162	R	100-140.000 EUR	**112.459**	**137.613**	**125.080**	15-10-16	Salzburg	444	Dor
	Black with green cloth interior; since 1997 in the current ownership. Engine overhauled in 1999.										
1956	**Aurelia B20 5ª serie (Pinin Farina)**	B20S1286	L	20-30.000 EUR	**62.012***	**77.110***	**72.800***	25-11-16	Milan	319	RMS
	For restoration. From the Duemila Ruote collection.										
1951	**Aurelia B20 1ª serie (Pinin Farina)**	B201246	R	80-90.000 EUR	**286.212***	**355.891***	**336.000***	25-11-16	Milan	566	RMS F441
	Black with red interior; 53,535 kms. From the Duemila Ruote collection.										
1952	**Aurelia B20 2ª serie (Pinin Farina)**	B201569	R	140-180.000 EUR	**129.421**	**157.600**	**147.829**	14-01-17	Maastricht	213	Coy
	Amaranth with grey cloth interior; restored in Italy circa 10 years ago (see lot 422 Bonhams 4.2.16 $161,086).										
1952	**Aurelia B20 2ª serie (Pinin Farina)**	B201824	R	130-160.000 EUR	**119.441**	**149.310**	**140.000**	08-02-17	Paris	110	RMS
	Dark red with black interior; the car was restored in the UK in the 1970s, fitted with a later 2.5-litre engine and raced at historic events. Engine fully overhauled in 2015. Swiss papers (see lot 220 RM 1.5.10 $134,215).										
1957	**Aurelia B20 5ª serie (Pinin Farina)**	B20S1276	L	130-150.000 EUR	**141.888**	**178.289**	**166.750**	09-02-17	Paris	375	Bon F442
	Burgundy with leather and cloth interior; restored between 2005 and 2007. In the same family ownership since new (see lot 398 Artcurial 7.2.14 $145,622).										
1958	**Aurelia B20 6ª serie (Pinin Farina)**	B20S1832	L	110-140.000 USD	**83.105**	**101.200**	**95.907**	09-03-17	Amelia Island	148	Bon
	Silver; largely original interior. The car requires a light recommissioning.										
1953	**Aurelia B20 3ª serie (Pinin Farina)**	B202848	R	120-140.000 GBP	**130.300**	**161.051**	**149.988**	19-03-17	Goodwood	29	Bon
	Black with cloth and vinyl interior; four owners; sold in 1953 to Mrs Ingrid Lindblad who kept it in Italy before to import it into Sweden in 1959, and resold it in 2002. Imported into the UK, in 2012 it was bought by the current owner and subsequently restored.										
1954	**Aurelia B20 4ª serie (Pinin Farina)**	B202991	R	105-125.000 GBP	**123.750**	**153.957**	**143.253**	29-03-17	Duxford	35	H&H
	Grey with blue interior; restoration started in the USA and completed in the UK in 2012.										
1953	**Aurelia B20 3ª serie (Pinin Farina)**	B202389	R	90-110.000 GBP	**102.375**	**132.125**	**117.352**	06-06-17	Woodcote Park	39	H&H
	Green with beige cloth interior; imported into the UK in 1965; engine replaced with a 4th series unit in 1967; since 1987 in the current ownership; restored between 1989 and 1991 (see lot 55 H & H 10.7.16 NS).										
1958	**Aurelia B20 6ª serie (Pinin Farina)**	B203941	R	120-150.000 GBP		NS		30-06-17	Goodwood	227	Bon
	Black with beige interior; bought in 1997 by the current owner and imported into the UK. Well maintained; 89,768 kms on the odometer.										

F441: 1951 Lancia Aurelia B20 1a serie (Pinin Farina) *F442: 1957 Lancia Aurelia B20 5a serie (Pinin Farina)*

CHRISTOPH GROHE
FINE CLASSIC CARS

ALVIS GRABER SUPER, 1962

CHRISTOPH GROHE SA
RTE D'ALLAMAN 10
CH-1173 FÉCHY
SWITZERLAND

T +41 21 807 35 65
F +41 21 807 34 23

INFO@CHRISTOPHGROHE.COM
WWW.CHRISTOPHGROHE.COM

Year	Model	(Bodybuilder)	Chassis no.	Steering	Estimate	Hammer price £	$	€	Sale Date	Place	Lot	Auc. H.

F443: 1955 Lancia Aurelia B24 spider (Pinin Farina)

F444: 1958 Lancia Aurelia B24 convertibile (Pinin Farina)

Year	Model (Bodybuilder)	Chassis	St.	Estimate	£	$	€	Date	Place	Lot	Auc. H.
1958	**Aurelia B20 6ª serie (Pinin Farina)**	1732	L	165-185.000 EUR		NS		02-07-17	Monaco	199	Art
	Medium grey with blue leather and beige cloth interior; restored in Italy in the 1990s.										
1952	**Aurelia B20 2ª serie (Pinin Farina)**	B201580	R	220-260.000 USD	175.214	225.500	192.126	18-08-17	Carmel	107	Bon
	Dark blue; full restoration completed in 2016. In very good working order.										
1959	**Appia berlina 2ª serie**	C10S28548	L	20-30.000 USD	15.387*	19.800*	17.620*	03-10-16	Philadelphia	231	Bon
	Black with grey cloth interior; in running order.										
1955	**Aurelia B24 spider (Pinin Farina)**	B24S1177	L	1.200-1.500.000 USD	895.620	1.100.000	1.031.470	18-01-17	Scottsdale	58	WoA
	Black with tan leather interior; sold new in Italy, the car remained with its first owner until 1987. Restored in the 1980s. Recently serviced. With wire wheels and hardtop (see lot 249 Bonhams 15.8.14 $1,100,000).										
1955	**Aurelia B24 spider (Pinin Farina)**	B241013	R	900-1.200.000 EUR		NS		10-02-17	Paris	121	Art
	Red with beige leather interior; bought in the 1990s by the current Italian owner and subsequently fully restored. The engine has been fitted with the Nardi carburettor kit. The car ran also the 2006 and 2007 editions of the Mille Miglia Storica.										
1955	**Aurelia B24 spider (Pinin Farina)**	B24S1009	L	1.500-1.700.000 USD	1.069.380	1.300.000	1.225.120	10-03-17	Amelia Island	37	G&Co
	Metallic grey with tan leather interior; concours-quality restoration completed in 2014. Recently serviced (see lot 110 Gooding & Company 17.8.14 $1,347,500).										
1955	**Aurelia B24 spider (Pinin Farina)**	B24S1072	L	1.400-1.800.000 USD	1.085.832*	1.320.000*	1.243.968*	11-03-17	Amelia Island	261	RMS F443
	Light grey with red leather interior; Borrani wire wheels. Concours-quality restoration carried out between 2010 and 2012.										
1955	**Aurelia B24 spider (Pinin Farina)**	B24S1110	L	1.200-1.500.000 USD	982.905	1.265.000	1.077.780	18-08-17	Carmel	54	Bon
	Light grey with dark red leather interior; full restoration completed in 2013 (see lot 141 RM 10.5.14 $1,080,430).										
1958	**Aurelia B24 convertibile (Pinin Farina)**	B24S1697	L	300-350.000 EUR		NS		08-02-17	Paris	172	RMS
	Red with tan interior; bought in 2006 by the current owner and subsequently restored by Dino Cognolato.										
1956	**Aurelia B24 convertibile (Pinin Farina)**	B24S1188	L	380-480.000 EUR		NS		09-02-17	Paris	327	Bon
	Described as in very good overall condition; sold new in Italy; from 1970 to 2013 in the Guido Artom's collection; since 2015 in the current owner ownership. With hardtop.										
1958	**Aurelia B24 convertibile (Pinin Farina)**	B24S1565	L	220-280.000 EUR	205.626	303.483	233.844	02-07-17	Monaco	131	Art F444
	Light pastel blue with natural leather interior; since 1968 in the same family ownership; restored in the 2000s; recently serviced.										
1958	**Aurelia B24 convertibile (Pinin Farina)**	B24S1678	L	350-450.000 USD	264.957	341.000	290.532	18-08-17	Carmel	101	Bon
	Black with original red leather interior; in largely original condition; body repainted; full service in 2016. Since 1983 for 34 years in the same ownership.										
1957	**Appia GT (Zagato)**	812011874	L	180-200.000 EUR	162.440	203.062	190.400	08-02-17	Paris	119	RMS F445
	Light metallic grey; recently restored. The car competed in the 2015 Mille Miglia Storica.										
1959	**Flaminia berlina**	813002298	L	4-6.000 EUR	16.219*	20.167*	19.040*	25-11-16	Milan	248	RMS
	Black and grey with beige cloth interior; 47,558 kms. From the Duemila Ruote collection.										
1961	**Flaminia Gran Turismo (Touring)**	824001690	L	35-40.000 EUR	104.944*	130.493*	123.200*	25-11-16	Milan	893	RMS
	Grey with light brown interior. From the Duemila Ruote collection.										
1962	**Flaminia 3C GT (Touring)**	824103476	L	15-3.500 EUR	28.621*	35.589*	33.600*	25-11-16	Milan	354	RMS
	Restoration project. From the Duemila Ruote collection.										

F445: 1957 Lancia Appia GT (Zagato)

F446: 1967 Lancia Flaminia 3C 2.8 GT (Touring)

CLAIM YOUR HISTORY

LANCIA CLASSICHE CERTIFICATION AND RESTORATION SERVICES

Heritage

PASSIONE SENZA TEMPO

www.fcaheritage.com | Toll Free Number 00800 52624200

Year	Model (Bodybuilder)	Chassis No.	Steering	Estimate	Hammer Price £	$	€	Date	Place	Lot	Auc. H.
1963	**Flaminia 3C GT** (Touring)	3805	L	45-55.000 EUR	119.255*	148.288*	140.000*	25-11-16	Milan	561	RMS
	Blue with beige interior; 35,149 kms. From the Duemila Ruote collection.										
1964	**Flaminia 3C GT** (Touring)	3785	L	60-75.000 EUR	50.331	66.164	55.750	05-08-17	Schloss Dyck	233	Coy
	Ivory white with light brown leather interior; described as in very good original condition.										
1966	**Flaminia 3C 2.8 GT** (Touring)	8261381120	L	85-100.000 EUR		NA		08-10-16	Paris	142	CB/C
	Metallic grey with tan leather interior; restored many years ago, the car is in good driving order. With sunroof.										
1963	**Flaminia 3C 2.8 GT** (Touring)	8261381083	L	135-165.000 AUD	115.305	143.371	135.358	27-11-16	Melbourne	54	Mos
	Blue with biscuit leather interior; in good overall condition. Sold new to Europe and later imported into Australia.										
1966	**Flaminia 3C 2.8 GT** (Touring)	8261381120	L	85-100.000 EUR		NS		08-04-17	Essen	175	Coy
	See lot 142 Coutau Bégarie/Coys 8.10.16.										
1967	**Flaminia 3C 2.8 GT** (Touring)	8261381157	L	150-175.000 USD	186.480*	240.000*	204.480*	19-08-17	Monterey	S45	Mec F446
	Blue with tan interior; from the J. Geils Collection.										
1964	**Flaminia 3C 2.8 GTL** (Touring)	1112	L	20-30.000 EUR	57.242*	71.178*	67.200*	25-11-16	Milan	280	RMS
	Grey with red interior; 81,737 kms. From the Duemila Ruote collection.										
1961	**Flaminia Convertibile** (Touring)	824041355	L	115-125.000 GBP		NS		30-06-17	Goodwood	262	Bon
	Dark blue with tan leather interior; circa 2,000 kms covered since a full restoration. With hardtop.										
1963	**Flaminia 3C Convertibile** (Touring)	824142244	L	220-260.000 USD	160.339	195.250	185.038	09-03-17	Amelia Island	116	Bon F447
	Silver with red interior; paintwork and interior redone at unspecified date, engine rebuilt recently.										
1963	**Flaminia 3C 2.8 Convertibile** (Touring)	8261341019	L	175-195.000 EUR		NS		14-01-17	Maastricht	239	Coy
	Silver; restored in the 2000s.										
1968	**Flaminia 3C 2.8 Convertibile** (Touring)	8261341013	L	100-200.000 EUR	100.177	147.851	113.924	02-07-17	Monaco	113	Art
	Green with original red leather interior; body repainted; engine in need of recommissioning.										
1963	**Flaminia 3C 2.8 Convertibile** (Touring)	8261341019	L	120-140.000 EUR	120.608	158.548	133.593	05-08-17	Schloss Dyck	246	Coy
	See lot Coys 14.1.17.										
1961	**Flaminia Sport** (Zagato)	824031843	L	130-150.000 EUR	248.050*	308.439*	291.200*	25-11-16	Milan	878	RMS F448
	Grey with beige interior; 32,458 kms. From the Duemila Ruote collection.										
1962	**Flaminia 3C Sport** (Zagato)	824133107	L	240-300.000 EUR		NS		09-02-17	Paris	363	Bon
	Silver with yellow stripe; bought in 1998 by the current owner already prepared fo historic racing and fitted with a 2.8-litre engine of the Super Sport model. Raced over the years at numerous events, the car is described as in very good overall condition.										
1958	**Flaminia 3C 2.8 Sport** (Zagato)	8261321011	L	180-240.000 EUR		NS		02-07-17	Monaco	198	Art
	Car already offered by Bonhams on 9.2.2017 lot 363 and identified as a 1962 Flaminia 3C Sport, chassis 824133107.										
1967	**Flaminia 3C 2.8 Super Sport** (Zagato)	826232002121	L	275-325.000 USD	201.564	247.500	232.774	20-01-17	Scottsdale	10	G&Co
	Metallic grey with red leather interior; paintwork and interior restored in 2008, mechanicals and engine rebuilt recently (see lot 178 RM 9.3.13 $192,500).										
1965	**Flaminia 3C 2.8 Super Sport** (Zagato)	826232002024	L	325-425.000 USD		NS		11-02-17	Boca Raton	143	TFA
	Brown with tan interior; full restoration completed in May 2016 in the Netherlands.										
1965	**Flaminia 3C 2.8 Super Sport** (Zagato)	826232002045	L	350-425.000 USD	264.957	341.000	290.532	18-08-17	Pebble Beach	20	G&Co
	White with red leather interior; believed to have been in the same family ownership in Italy from new to 2012; body repainted in 2008; imported into the USA in 2013; last serviced in spring 2017 (see lot 400 Artcurial 8.2.13 $207,132).										
1964	**Flavia Coupé** (Pininfarina)	008172	L	20-30.000 EUR		NS		06-11-16	Lyon	318	Ose
	White; described as in very good condition. Body repainted some years ago (see lot 378 Osenat 19.6.16 $33,222).										
1967	**Flavia Coupé 1.8 Iniezione** (Pininfarina)	015329	L	10-12.000 EUR	23.851*	29.658*	28.000*	25-11-16	Milan	641	RMS
	Metallic grey with red leather interior; 75,708 kms. From the Duemila Ruote collection.										
1963	**Flavia Coupé** (Pininfarina)	8151312370	R	10-15.000 GBP	15.580	19.061	18.042	04-03-17	Brooklands	174	His F449
	Dark blue with dark red interior; in good overall condition (see lot 331 Historics 30.8.14 $22,286).										
1964	**Flavia Coupé** (Pininfarina)	008172	L	20-25.000 EUR	19.088	24.391	22.800	01-05-17	Obenheim	354	Ose
	See lot 318 Osenat 6.11.16.										
1963	**Flavia Coupé 1.8** (Pininfarina)	8153305590	L	15-20.000 EUR		NS		05-08-17	Schloss Dyck	228	Coy
	White with blue interior; 50 kms covered since the restoration.										
1963	**Flavia Sport** (Zagato)	1048815132	L	4-6.000 EUR	28.621*	35.589*	33.600*	25-11-16	Milan	530	RMS
	For restoration. From the Duemila Ruote collection.										

F447: 1963 Lancia Flaminia 3C Convertibile (Touring)

F448: 1961 Lancia Flaminia Sport (Zagato)

F449: 1963 Lancia Flavia Coupé (Pininfarina)

F450: 1966 Lancia Flavia Sport 1.8 (Zagato)

Year	Model (Bodybuilder)	Chassis no.	Steering	Estimate	Hammer price £	$	€	Date	Sale Place	Lot	Auc. H.
1965	**Flavia Sport (Zagato)**	815533001583	R	19-29.000 GBP	28.125	36.683	31.503	26-07-17	Duxford	17	H&H
White with black interior; since 1993 in the current ownership; restored between 1995 and 1998.											
1966	**Flavia Sport 1.8 (Zagato)**	001602	L	65-80.000 EUR	57.377	75.427	63.555	05-08-17	Schloss Dyck	216	Coy **F450**
Silver blue with black interior; restored in 2012. Fuel-injected engine (see lots 174 Bonhams/Brooks 11.8.01 NS, 20 Artcurial 20.6.05 NS, and 158 Coys 25.10.08 $30,470).											
1975	**Fulvia Coupé Safari**	071024	L	10-15.000 EUR	14.311*	17.795*	16.800*	25-11-16	Milan	840	RMS
Red with black and grey interior; 56,138 kms. From the Duemila Ruote collection.											
1972	**Fulvia Coupé Montecarlo 1.3S**	818630030192	L	25-30.000 EUR	17.614*	22.132*	20.700*	09-02-17	Paris	302	Bon
Dark green with matt black bonnet; recently restored.											
1966	**Fulvia Coupé**	818130011773	L	17-22.000 EUR	13.699*	17.214*	16.100*	09-02-17	Paris	337	Bon
Blue with light grey cloth interior; in the same family ownership from 1966 to 2003. Partially restored in the 1990s.											
1971	**Fulvia Coupé 1.3S**	818630012337	L	38-45.000 USD	35.440	45.100	40.365	24-06-17	Santa Monica	120	RMS
Restored and finished in the red and white Marlboro livery.											
1974	**Fulvia Coupé 1.3S**	818630069499	L	7-9.000 GBP	6.669	8.619	7.579	15-07-17	Blenheim Pal.	102	Coy
Red; 22,000 kms on the odometer.											
1966	**Fulvia Coupé HF**	818140001480	L	15-20.000 EUR	66.783*	83.041*	78.400*	25-11-16	Milan	638	RMS
Red with black interior; 48,484 kms. From the Duemila Ruote collection.											
1971	**Fulvia Coupé HF**	818740001757	L	35-45.000 EUR	35.342	44.971	40.250	24-06-17	Wien	337	Dor
Red with black bonnet and black interior; restored about 10 years ago to the aesthetical specification of the Fulvia Coupé Rallye 1.6 HF "Fanalona" winner of the 1972 Monte Carlo Rally.											
1968	**Fulvia Coupé Rallye 1.3 HF**	818340001861	L	10-15.000 EUR	28.621*	35.589*	33.600*	25-11-16	Milan	250	RMS
Red with black interior; 92,148 kms. From the Duemila Ruote collection.											
1968	**Fulvia Coupé Rallye 1.3 HF**	001984	L	30-35.000 EUR	40.070*	49.825*	47.040*	25-11-16	Milan	541	RMS
Burgundy; 8,956 kms. From the Duemila Ruote collection.											
1970	**Fulvia Coupé Rallye 1.6 HF**	818540002218	L	35-40.000 EUR	54.380*	67.619*	63.840*	25-11-16	Milan	276	RMS
Red with black interior; roll-cage and external fuel cap. From the Duemila Ruote collection.											
1970	**Fulvia Coupé Rallye 1.6 HF**	818540001891	L	35-40.000 EUR	66.783*	83.041*	78.400*	25-11-16	Milan	323	RMS
Red with black interior; 28,525 kms. From the Duemila Ruote collection.											
1970	**Fulvia Coupé Rallye 1.6 HF**	001849	L	45-55.000 EUR	47.702*	59.315*	56.000*	25-11-16	Milan	618	RMS
Red; 26,852 kms. From the Duemila Ruote collection.											
1969	**Fulvia Coupé Rallye 1.6 HF**	8185411276	R	90-120.000 AUD		NS		27-11-16	Melbourne	51	Mos
Red with black bonnet; sold new to the UK, the car remained with its first owner for nearly 30 years. Bought by Max Atkin in 1999 it was prepared for historic events. Acquired in 2008 by the current owner and imported into Australia (see lot 793 Brooks 12.6.98 $10,325).											
1970	**Fulvia Coupé 1600 HF**	818740001060	L	37-45.000 GBP	29.000	38.738	34.293	08-09-16	Fontwell Park	122	Coy
Red; about 36,000 kms on the odometer. It comes with Italian ASI homologation.											

F451: 1971 Lancia Fulvia Coupé 1600 HF

F452: 1967 Lancia Fulvia Sport 1.3 (Zagato)

Year	Model	(Bodybuilder)	Chassis no.	Steering	Estimate	Hammer price £	$	€	Date	Place	Lot	Auc. H.
1971	**Fulvia Coupé 1600 HF**		818740002524	L	30-40.000 EUR	27.863*	33.849*	30.992*	30-10-16	Paris	111	Art **F451**
Blue; three owners.												
1972	**Fulvia Sport 1.3S**	(Zagato)	818650001962	L	25-30.000 EUR	31.078	37.755	34.568	30-10-16	Paris	174	Art
Red; restored.												
1972	**Fulvia Sport 1.3 S**	(Zagato)	003367	L	25-35.000 EUR		NS		06-11-16	Lyon	317	Ose
Red with black interior; restored 10 years ago.												
1967	**Fulvia Sport 1.3**	(Zagato)	818332001340	L	20-30.000 EUR	138.336*	172.014*	162.400*	25-11-16	Milan	613	RMS **F452**
Orange with yellow stripe on the nose; race prepared. From the Duemila Ruote collection.												
1970	**Fulvia Sport 1.3**	(Zagato)	818363002233	R	16-19.000 GBP		NS		07-12-16	London	316	Bon
Red with black interior; restored some years ago.												
1972	**Fulvia Sport 1.6**		818751001308	R	15-20.000 GBP	22.400	28.887	25.312	08-07-17	Brooklands	129	His
Silver with black interior; mechanicals overhauled. In need of a cosmetic restoration (see lot 318 Coys 12.1.13 NS).												
1971	**Stratos**	(Bertone)	829ARO001544	L	290-335.000 GBP	308.000	412.166	366.797	07-09-16	London	120	RMS **F453**
Road version finished in red-orange; approximately 70,000 kms covered and two owners. Described as in highly original condition.												
1975	**Stratos**	(Bertone)	829ARO001948	L	500-600.000 USD	367.294	451.000	424.166	20-01-17	Scottsdale	55	G&Co
Road version finished in light blue with black alcantara interior; sold new to Germany, the car was part of the Bianco Rosso Collection from 1981 to 2006. Imported into the USA in 2007, it was bought in 2011 by the previous owner who had it fully restored to its original colours (see Bonhams lots 163 20.5.06 NS and 446 17.8.07 $131,300).												
1977	**Stratos**	(Bertone)	829ARO001744	L	350-400.000 EUR	318.024	399.614	373.750	09-02-17	Paris	314	Bon
Body repainted in 2015; original interior; mechanicals refurbished in 2015. Sold new to Austria; imported into the UK in 2001.												
1976	**Stratos Gruppo 4**	(Bertone)	829ARO001827	L	350-450.000 EUR		NS		09-02-17	Paris	390	Bon
Finished in the white/red/green Alitalia livery; sold new to Switzerland; bought in 1998 by the current, third owner; driven at numerous historic events; engine rebuilt 4,000 kms ago.												
1975	**Stratos**	(Bertone)	000008	L	400-550.000 USD	282.051*	363.000*	309.276*	18-08-17	Carmel	69	Bon
Road version finished in turquoise with white rear spoiler, hoop and wheels; one of the cars left unfinished when Lancia ended production and completed by Scuderia Jolly Club. Since 1989 in the current ownership; 12,700 kms on the odometer; in need of a full service prior to use.												
1974	**Beta 1.8 coupé**		828AC1001050	L	5-7.000 EUR	47.702*	59.315*	56.000*	25-11-16	Milan	842	RMS
Black; prepared for rallying. From the Duemila Ruote collection.												
1983	**Montecarlo**	(Pininfarina)	004004	L	15-20.000 EUR		NS		06-11-16	Lyon	319	Ose
Light metallic grey; recently serviced.												
1990	**Delta Integrale 16V**		505191	L	90-120.000 USD	64.507	85.000	75.710	17-09-16	Aspen	138	TFA
White; the car was sold new in Italy where it was immediately put into storage after covering just 127 kms. In 2015 it was acquired by the current owner and imported into the USA.												
1992	**Delta Integrale Evoluzione**		562931	L	33-40.000 GBP	30.105	36.572	33.483	29-10-16	London	129	Coy
Metallic red with green alcantara interior; restored in 2011, engine rebuilt in 2015 (see lots 363 Bonhams 9.12.13 $21,288 and 124 Coys 2.7.16 NS).												
1992	**Delta Integrale Evoluzione**		580689	L	70-90.000 EUR	94.307*	114.567*	104.896*	30-10-16	Paris	113	Art **F454**
Martini livery; 57,500 kms covered. Two owners.												
1992	**Delta Integrale Evoluzione**		568054	L	50-70.000 EUR	85.256	106.493	96.000	05-11-16	Lyon	232	Agu
Martini 5 Special Edition; described as in very good overall condition. Since 2005 in the current ownership.												
1993	**Delta Integrale Evoluzione II**		583064	L	28-32.000 GBP	43.875	55.541	50.934	12-11-16	Birmingham	304	SiC
Metallic red with beige interior; described as in very good overall condition. 41,000 kms on the odometer. Recently serviced.												
1988	**Delta HF Integrale**		425337	L	15-20.000 EUR	34.345*	42.707*	40.320*	25-11-16	Milan	328	RMS
Red with cloth and alcantara interior; 15,100 kms. From the Duemila Ruote collection.												
1986	**Delta HF 4WD**		365835	L	15-18.000 EUR	40.070*	49.825*	47.040*	25-11-16	Milan	519	RMS
White; prepared for rallying. From the Duemila Ruote collection.												
1989	**Delta HF Integrale 4V Gruppo A**		501630	L	130-150.000 EUR	209.888*	260.987*	246.400*	25-11-16	Milan	549	RMS
Ex-Works car; finished in the 1990 Corsica livery. From the Duemila Ruote collection.												
1991	**Delta Integrale Evoluzione**		552942	L	30-35.000 EUR	52.472*	65.247*	61.600*	25-11-16	Milan	578	RMS
Red with grey interior; 18,187 kms. From the Duemila Ruote collection.												
1992	**Delta HF Integrale Gruppo A**		556754	L	160-180.000 EUR	286.212*	355.891*	336.000*	25-11-16	Milan	594	RMS
Ex-Jolly Club; finished in the 1993 Monte Carlo Rally livery (14th driven by Sainz-Moya). From the Duemila Ruote collection.												
1989	**Delta Integrale 16V**		501576	L	15-20.000 EUR	36.253*	45.080*	42.560*	25-11-16	Milan	839	RMS
Red; 10,648 kms. From the Duemila Ruote collection.												

F453: 1971 Lancia Stratos (Bertone)

F454: 1992 Lancia Delta Integrale Evoluzione

Year	Model	(Bodybuilder)	Chassis no.	Steering	Estimate	Hammer price £	$	€	Date	Place	Lot	Auc. H.

F455: 1983 Lancia 037 (Pininfarina)

F456: 1991 Lancia LC2 Gruppo C

Year	Model	Chassis no.	Steering	Estimate	£	$	€	Date	Place	Lot	Auc. H.
1993	**Delta Integrale Evoluzione II**	583203	L	38-44.000 GBP	40.320	50.134	47.332	26-11-16	Weybridge	200	His
	Dark blue with tan alcantara interior; sold new to Japan and imported into the UK in 2011. Described as in good overall condition.										
1991	**Delta Integrale Evoluzione**	493606	R	68-78.000 AUD	44.057	54.780	51.719	27-11-16	Melbourne	50	Mos
	Red; in good overall condition, approximately 70,000 kms covered. Sold new in Italy, later the car was imported into Australia and converted to right-hand drive.										
1992	**Delta Integrale Evoluzione**	576058	L	50-60.000 GBP		NS		07-12-16	London	361	Bon
	Gifted to Alberto Tomba by the Agnelli family; imported into the UK in 2014; 11,459 kms covered.										
1994	**Delta Integrale Evoluzione II**	583705	L	50-55.000 GBP	53.100	66.662	62.833	24-02-17	Stoneleigh P.	536	SiC
	Metallic red; in original condition, 13,540 kms covered. Imported into the UK from Japan in 2014 and recommissioned.										
1993	**Delta Integrale Evoluzione II**	582788	L	26-30.000 GBP	41.063	52.795	48.545	13-05-17	Silverstone	361	SiC
	Red with beige interior; in good overall condition. Since 1998 in the current ownership.										
1995	**Delta Integrale Evoluzione II**	586166	L	55-65.000 EUR	59.051	87.154	67.155	02-07-17	Monaco	180	Art
	"Dealers Collection" special edition finished in red with cream leather Recaro seats; 82,590 kms covered; last serviced in December 2015.										
1990	**Delta Integrale Gruppo A**	500836	L	120-150.000 GBP	225.000	295.706	252.855	27-07-17	Silverstone	107	SiC
	Martini livery; a Works car driven by Juha Kankkunen at the 1990 1,000 Lakes Rally. Subsequently it was used by Jolly Club and in 1991 it was sold to HF-Grifone Srl and driven by Tabaton. In 1992 it was converted to Evoluzione specification. In late 1994 it was imported into the UK and driven at several rallies (see lot 237 Coys 15.1.11 NS).										
1994	**Delta Integrale Evoluzione II**	582708	L	30-35.000 GBP	42.190	55.248	47.105	29-07-17	Silverstone	710	SiC
	Red; engine rebuilt in January 2017.										
1983	**037 (Pininfarina)**	0111	L	200-300.000 EUR	210.974	269.590	252.000	22-04-17	Bagatelle	73	Agu
	Red; the car has been driven at some historic rallies (see lot 139 Artcurial 7.7.12 $135,658).										
1983	**037 (Pininfarina)**	000159	L	300-400.000 USD	205.128*	264.000*	224.928*	18-08-17	Carmel	78	Bon F455
	Road version finished in red; since 1990 in the current ownership; in largely original condition; 9,342 kms on the odometer. It requires a full service prior to use.										
1991	**LC2 Gruppo C**	0009	R	240-280.000 EUR	725.069*	901.591*	851.200*	25-11-16	Milan	599	RMS F456
	Red; offered with an assortment of spare parts. It raced also at Le Mans, Nürburgring and Magny Cours. From the Duemila Ruote collection.										
1985	**Delta S4**	000119	L	450-550.000 EUR	429.672	551.739	492.800	27-05-17	Villa Erba	146	RMS F457
	Road version finished in red; less than 1,600 kms covered.										
1985	**Delta S4**	000005	L	350-450.000 USD	341.880*	440.000*	374.880*	18-08-17	Carmel	46	Bon
	Black with leather and alcantara interior; in highly original condition; just one owner; less than 8,900 kms covered.										
1994	**Hyena (Zagato)**	579320	L	150-200.000 EUR	136.995	172.141	161.000	09-02-17	Paris	343	Bon
	Green with black leather interior; sold new to Germany, the car has covered circa 8,000 kms. Last serviced in October 2015. One of 24 examples built.										

LASALLE (USA) *(1927-1940)*

Year	Model	Chassis no.	Steering	Estimate	£	$	€	Date	Place	Lot	Auc. H.
1930	**Series 340 roadster**	607852	R	180-260.000 EUR		NS		10-02-17	Paris	136	Art
	Silver and red with brown interior; sold new to India, the car was imported into Europe in 1951. In 2006 it was sold to Italy and subsequently fully restored.										
1939	**Series 39-50 convertible**	SH3272PA	L	NQ	31.354*	38.500*	36.209*	21-01-17	Scottsdale	849.1	B/J
	Burgundy with tan interior; recent mechanical update.										

F457: 1985 Lancia Delta S4

F458: 1949 Lea-Francis 2.5l sports

269

Year	Model	(Bodybuilder)	Chassis no.	Steering	Estimate	Hammer price £	$	€	Sale Date	Place	Lot	Auc. H.

LE ZEBRE (F) (1908-1931)

| 1919 | Type D torpedo | | D206744 | R | 10-12.000 GBP | 13.800 | 18.331 | 16.378 | 03-09-16 | Beaulieu | 409 | Bon |

Imported into the UK in 1976 and subsequently restored; described as in good overall condition.

LEA-FRANCIS (GB) (1903-1960)

| 1949 | 2.5l sports | | 5158 | R | 100-140.000 USD | 67.865* | 82.500* | 77.748* | 10-03-17 | Amelia Island | 144 | RMS **F458** |

Light metallic blue with red leather interior; imported into the USA in the mid-2000s and subsequently restored. From the Orin Smith collection (see lot 13 Bonhams 14.8.15 $110,000).

| 1950 | 2.5l sports | | 5200 | R | 55-75.000 EUR | | NS | | 18-03-17 | Lyon | 195 | Agu |

Burgundy with tan interior; restoration completed in 2006.

| 1949 | 2.5l sports | | 5200 | R | 38-48.000 GBP | 50.400 | 64.996 | 56.952 | 08-07-17 | Brooklands | 204 | His |

See lot 195 Aguttes 18.3.17.

LENHAM (GB)

| 1967 | Sprite GT coupé | | GAN454417 | R | 20-25.000 GBP | 20.070 | 24.439 | 22.924 | 14-01-17 | Birmingham | 123 | Coy |

Red; prepared for historic racing.

LEXUS (J)

| 2012 | LFA | | 100085 | L | 335-375.000 USD | 252.525 | 325.000 | 276.900 | 19-08-17 | Monterey | S126.1 | Mec **F459** |

Dark pearl grey with tan interior; 465 original miles.

LINCOLN (USA) (1920-)

| 1925 | Model L convertible | | 29368 | L | 75-100.000 USD | 55.060 | 73.150 | 65.352 | 03-09-16 | Auburn | 7043 | AA |

Two-tone green with black fenders and grey cloth interior; in good overall condition. Stated to be bodied by LeBaron.

| 1930 | Model L touring | | K63515 | L | 55-65.000 USD | 56.417* | 72.600* | 64.607* | 03-10-16 | Philadelphia | 238 | Bon |

Two-tone green with brown leather interior; a two family owner car from new. Restored many years ago. From the estate of Richard Hopeman.

| 1925 | Model L limousine | (Brunn) | 34686 | L | 50-60.000 USD | 21.714* | 27.500* | 24.585* | 06-10-16 | Hershey | 123 | RMS |

Burgundy and black; restored and fitted with a period-correct rebuilt engine and four-wheels brakes.

| 1925 | Model L roadster | (Brunn) | 27771 | L | 125-175.000 USD | 121.598 | 154.000 | 137.676 | 06-10-16 | Hershey | 149 | RMS **F460** |

Grey and black with grey leather interior; until 1977 in the same family ownership. Acquired in 2008 by the current, fifth owner and fully restored (see lot 126 Gooding & Company 16.8.15 NS).

| 1929 | Model L brougham | (Brunn) | 61375 | L | 40-50.000 USD | 31.224* | 38.500* | 34.558* | 07-10-16 | Hershey | 222 | RMS |

Described as in original, unrestored condition. Believed to have been originally delivered to gangster Jack "Legs" Diamond.

| 1930 | Model L sport phaeton | | 64272 | L | 70-90.000 USD | 49.976* | 61.600* | 57.738* | 19-01-17 | Phoenix | 106 | RMS |

Maroon; an older restoration, the car is described as still in good overall condition. Since 1981 in the current ownership.

| 1930 | Model L roadster | (LeBaron) | 64754 | L | 90-120.000 USD | 50.586* | 61.600* | 58.378* | 09-03-17 | Amelia Island | 175 | Bon |

Two-tone green with green interior; restored in the 1970s, the car is described as in good overall condition. Recently serviced (see lot 19 Bonhams 19.8.16 $66,000).

| 1930 | Model L convertible roadster | (LeBaron) | 64277 | L | 75-100.000 USD | 51.282* | 66.000* | 56.232* | 18-08-17 | Carmel | 108 | Bon |

Grey and black with brown interior; older restoration (see lots 189 RM 16.1.09 NS, S45.1 Mecum 7.10.11 $62,500, and 127 RM/Sotheby's 30.7.16 NS).

| 1931 | Model K V8 convertible | (LeBaron) | K69029 | L | 90-110.000 USD | 61.546* | 79.200* | 70.480* | 03-10-16 | Philadelphia | 237 | Bon |

Two-tone blue; restored many years ago, the car requires servicing prior to use. From the estate of Richard Hopeman.

| 1932 | Model KB V12 boattail speedster | | KB1411(engine) | L | 200-275.000 USD | 477.708 | 605.000 | 540.870 | 06-10-16 | Hershey | 144 | RMS |

Body designed in the mid-1990s for Greg Bilpuch by David Holls, retired Vice President of Design at General Motors. Built by Marcel DeLay of Corona, CA, the body was fitted to a Lincoln Model KA chassis, with a Model KB engine. Completed over a three year period, the car was exhibited at the 1999 Pebble Beach Concours d'Elegance.

| 1932 | Model KB V12 sedan | | KB1291 | L | 70-90.000 USD | | NS | | 05-11-16 | Hilton Head | 179 | AA |

Two-tone blue with tan interior; engine and gearbox recently rebuilt (see lot 106 The Finest Automobile Auctions 11.6.16 $75,900).

| 1933 | Model KA V12 town sedan | (Murray) | KA775 | L | 30-40.000 GBP | 32.915 | 42.930 | 36.868 | 26-07-17 | Duxford | 13 | H&H |

Black and red with beige cloth interior; restored between the 1970s and 1990s.

F459: 2012 Lexus LFA

F460: 1925 Lincoln Model L roadster (Brunn)

Year	Model	(Bodybuilder)	Chassis no.	Steering	Estimate	Hammer Price £	$	€	Date	Place	Lot	Auc. H.
1938	**Series K V12 limousine**	(Willoughby)	K9125	L	75-85.000 USD	48.030*	60.000*	54.084*	04-11-16	Dallas	S117	**Mec**
Blue with black fenders and tan interior; restoration completed in 2006.													
1935	**Series K V12 convertible**	(LeBaron)	K3533	L	275-325.000 USD	264.273	324.500	305.192	20-01-17	Scottsdale	53	**G&Co**
Stored in a barn from 1948 to 2003 when it was discovered with 10,163 miles on the odometer; bought in 2011 by the current owner and subsequently restored to concours-condition and finished in light metallic green with tan leather interior.													
1936	**Series K V12 convertible sedan**	(Brunn)	K5686	L	NQ	42.152	52.500	49.245	08-04-17	Houston	F158.1	**Mec**
Tan with brown interior (see lot 67 RM 6.8.05 $50,600).													
1937	**Series K V12 sedan**	(Judkins)	K8375	L	NQ	73.472*	93.500*	83.683*	24-06-17	Northeast	407	**B/J**
Green with black fenders and black leather roof; beige cloth interior. Fully restored at unspecified date (see lot 1338 Barrett-Jackson 29.1.16 $66,000).													
1939	**Zephyr coupé**		AA461181816300198	L	80-120.000 EUR		NS		03-09-16	Chantilly	29	**Bon**
Dark green with beige interior; restored in the USA in the early 1990s.													
1937	**Zephyr coupé**		H22236	L	125-175.000 USD	147.655	187.000	167.178	06-10-16	Hershey	147	**RMS**
Black cherry with brown interior; restored more than 10 years ago, the car is in very good overall condition.													
1939	**Zephyr coupé**		H71701	L	175-200.000 USD	156.175*	192.500*	180.430*	19-01-17	Phoenix	142	**RMS F461**
Black with grey cloth interior; in very good overall condition.													
1941	**Zephyr coupé**		H122174	L	NQ	24.636*	30.250*	28.450*	21-01-17	Scottsdale	8203	**R&S**
Maroon; restored. Engine rebuilt. From the Missoula Auto Museum Colelction.													
1939	**Zephyr coupé**		H66822	L	175-225.000 USD	126.680*	154.000*	145.130*	11-03-17	Amelia Island	248	**RMS**
Red with tan cloth interior; restored (see lot 63 Bonhams 19.8.16 NS).													
1939	**Zephyr convertible**		H84568	L	75-85.000 USD		NS		24-06-17	Santa Monica	152	**RMS**
Black with burgundy interior; older restoration (see lot 126 Auctions America 31.10.15 $63,250).													
1941	**Zephyr coupé**		H120055	L	225-250.000 USD	119.658*	154.000*	131.208*	18-08-17	Pebble Beach	47	**G&Co**
Black with cloth interior; restored to concours condition (see lot 52 Gooding & Company 11.3.16 $214,500).													
1941	**Continental coupé**		H111814	L	NQ	8.510*	10.450*	9.828*	21-01-17	Scottsdale	8202	**R&S**
White; well maintained.													
1941	**Continental convertible**		16H5692	L	NQ	24.636*	30.250*	28.450*	21-01-17	Scottsdale	8332	**R&S**
Black with red leather interior; restored 12 years ago.													
1941	**Continental convertible**		H107729	L	NQ	66.239*	82.500*	77.385*	08-04-17	Palm Beach	661.1	**B/J**
Burgundy with burgundy interior; restored.													
1942	**Continental convertible**		H133783	L	130-150.000 USD	66.822	86.000	73.272	19-08-17	Monterey	F53	**Mec**
Blue with blue leather interior; concours-quality restoration.													
1948	**V12 Continental club coupé**		8H180954	L	40-50.000 USD	22.583*	28.600*	25.568*	06-10-16	Hershey	143	**RMS**
Burgundy with burgundy leather and cloth interior; restored many years ago.													
1949	**Model 9-EL convertible**		9EL026403	L	NA	25.141	31.000	27.826	08-10-16	Chicago	S91	**Mec**
Blue with grey and blue interior; older restoration. 3-speed manual gearbox.													
1956	**Continental MkII coupé**		C5601637	L	10-15.000 USD	22.225*	28.600*	25.451*	03-10-16	Philadelphia	239	**Bon**
Black with two-tone grey leather interior; restoration to be completed. From the estate of Richard Hopeman.													
1956	**Continental MkII coupé**		C56C2516	L	200-250.000 USD	156.772*	192.500*	181.046*	21-01-17	Scottsdale	111	**G&Co**
Dark blue with two-tone blue leather interior; between 2009 and 2015 restored to concours condition.													
1956	**Continental MkII coupé**		C5601637	L	75-95.000 USD	40.649*	49.500*	46.911*	09-03-17	Amelia Island	161	**Bon F462**
See lot 239 Bonhams 3.10.16. Restauro completato.													
1956	**Continental MkII coupé**		C56P3557	L	160-180.000 USD	56.554*	68.750*	64.790*	10-03-17	Amelia Island	76	**G&Co**
Light blue with blue and white leather interior; restoration completed in 2012.													
1956	**Continental MkII coupé**		C56C2392	L	45-55.000 USD	20.745*	26.400*	23.628*	24-06-17	Santa Monica	270	**RMS**
Dark red; restored many years ago and offered from long-term storage, the car requires recommissioning prior to use.													
1956	**Continental MkII coupé**		C5613262	L	100-150.000 USD		NS		18-08-17	Carmel	32	**Bon**
White with light blue leather interior; 19,964 miles on the odometer. From the T.J. Day Collection.													
1957	**Continental MkII coupé**		C56R3803	L	225-275.000 USD	145.299*	187.000*	159.324*	19-08-17	Pebble Beach	119	**G&Co**
White with white and red leather interior; concours quality restoration.													

F461: 1939 Lincoln Zephyr coupé

F462: 1956 Lincoln Continental MkII coupé

Year	Model	(Bodybuilder)	Chassis no.	Steering	Estimate	Hammer price £	$	€	Sale Date	Place	Lot	Auc. H.
1956	**Premiere sedan**		56WA31779L	L	30-40.000 USD	**18.240***	**23.100***	**20.651***	06-10-16	Hershey	148	**RMS**
Amethyst with pink leather and grey cloth interior; restored several years ago.												
1957	**Premiere convertible**		57WA30027L	L	50-60.000 USD	**53.526**	**66.000**	**59.242**	07-10-16	Hershey	229	**RMS**
Yellow with tan and white interior; in good overall condition.												
1957	**Premiere convertible**		57WA39088L	L	55-65.000 USD		NS		24-06-17	Santa Monica	247	**RMS**
Blue; restored.												
1958	**Continental MkIII convertible**		H8YG418810	L	90-120.000 USD	**45.243***	**55.000***	**51.832***	10-03-17	Amelia Island	4	**G&Co**
White; in largely original, unrestored condition. Body repainted.												
1959	**Continental MkIV convertible**		H9YC419424	L	80-100.000 USD	**44.792***	**55.000***	**51.728***	20-01-17	Scottsdale	5	**G&Co**
White with black and white interior; restored approximately five years ago (see lot 61 Gooding & Company 12.3.10 $79,200).												
1959	**Continental MkIV convertible**		H9YC406833	L	35-55.000 EUR	**25.442**	**31.969**	**29.900**	09-02-17	Paris	431	**Bon**
Blue with black and white interior; restored between 2012 and 2016.												
1960	**Continental MkV convertible**		0Y85H408884	L	60-75.000 USD	**53.546***	**66.000***	**61.862***	19-01-17	Phoenix	170	**RMS** F463
Fully restored in the mid-1990s; 35,618 miles on the odometer. From the Mohrschladt Family Collection.												
1963	**Continental convertible sedan**		3Y86N430130	L	60-80.000 USD	**53.546***	**66.000***	**61.862***	19-01-17	Phoenix	146	**RMS**
Black with black interior; described as in very good original condition, except for the paintwork redone four years ago.												
1967	**Continental convertible sedan**		7Y86G820527	L	NQ	**53.750***	**66.000***	**62.073***	21-01-17	Scottsdale	8544	**R&S**
Black with black interior; in good overall condition.												
1963	**Continental convertible limousine**	(Hess/Eisenhardt)	3Y82N420576	L	50-60.000 GBP	**52.240**	**65.300**	**61.570**	12-04-17	London	339	**Coy**
Dark blue with blue leather interior; 700 kms covered since the engine, gearbox and brakes overhaul. Formerly in the Musée automobile des voitures de chefs d'Etat (see lots 37 Bonhams 11.10.13 NS and 241 Coys 11.10.14 NS).												
1964	**Continental convertible sedan**		4Y86N425715	L	NA	**23.536**	**26.400**	**20.537**	03-06-17	Newport Beach	9025	**R&S**
White; new blue interior.												

LISTER (GB) *(1953-)*

Year	Model	(Bodybuilder)	Chassis no.	Steering	Estimate	£	$	€	Date	Place	Lot	Auc. H.
1958	**Lister-Jaguar**		BHL102	R	Refer Dpt.		NS		19-08-17	Monterey	F75	**Mec**
White with blue stripes; one of two examples bought by the Briggs Cunningham Team and raced from 1958 to 1960; driven by Cunningham Stirling Moss, John Fitch and Walt Hangsen among others; acquired in 1960 by racing driver Chuck Daigh; restored in 1984 and subsequently raced at numerous historic events. With FIA Technical Passport.												
1989	**XJ-S Le Mans convertible**		158784	R	50-70.000 GBP	**57.500**	**74.624**	**65.107**	30-06-17	Goodwood	269	**Bon** F464
Red with beige leather interior; standard XJ-S bought new by the current owner and subsequently modified by Lister and fitted with the 7-litre engine. Circa 3,970 miles covered.												

LLOYD (D) *(1950-1963)*

Year	Model	(Bodybuilder)	Chassis no.	Steering	Estimate	£	$	€	Date	Place	Lot	Auc. H.
1954	**LP 400**		55549	L	30-35.000 USD		NS		17-09-16	Aspen	158	**TFA**
Two-tone green; restored in Germany several years ago. Imported into the USA, it was part of the Bruce Weiner's collection also (see lot 611 RM 15.2.13 $31,050).												

LOCOMOBILE (USA) *(1899-1929)*

Year	Model	(Bodybuilder)	Chassis no.	Steering	Estimate	£	$	€	Date	Place	Lot	Auc. H.
1899	**Steam Style 2 stanhope**		1270(car no.)	R	45-65.000 USD		NS		03-10-16	Philadelphia	243	**Bon**
Black and red with black interior; since 1930 in the same ownership. Restored in the 1950s; boiler replaced. Not used in recent times.												
1901	**Style 5 locosurrey**		4507	R	40-60.000 USD	**94.029***	**121.000***	**107.678***	03-10-16	Philadelphia	248	**Bon** F465
In original, unrestored condition. From the late 1930s in the Bloomington Collection.												
1907	**Model E**		NQ	R	40-50.000 USD	**52.143***	**67.100***	**59.712***	03-10-16	Philadelphia	203	**Bon**
The car was dismantled in the late 1970s for restoration; engine restored; ready to be reassembled. From the Natural History Museum of Los Angeles.												

LOLA (GB) *(1959-)*

Year	Model	(Bodybuilder)	Chassis no.	Steering	Estimate	£	$	€	Date	Place	Lot	Auc. H.
1966	**T70 MkII spyder**		SL7129	R	250-350.000 EUR		NS		10-02-17	Paris	97	**Art**
The car was raced at some events of the 1966 CanAm Championship. Damaged by fire, it was stored and later restored and driven at some historic events in the USA in 2009 and 2010. Imported into France, it was raced at some Classic Endurance Racing events in 2014. Finished in yellow and black and fitted with a 350 Chevrolet engine (see lot 185 Artcurial 7.7.12 NS).												

F463: 1960 Lincoln Continental MkV convertible

F464: 1989 Lister XJ-S Le Mans convertible

Year	Model	(Bodybuilder)	Chassis No.	Steering	Estimate	Hammer price £	$	€	Date	Place	Lot	Auc. H.
1965	T70 spyder		SL702	R	200-300.000 GBP	270.300	334.091	311.142	19-03-17	Goodwood	18	Bon F466

Car raced when new by David Hobbs in events in Europe and the USA, where it was subsequently acquired by Monte Shelton and raced in SCCA National and Can-Am events. In 2001 it was reimported into the UK, fully restored, fitted with a Chevrolet V8 engine and raced at historic events.

Year	Model		Chassis No.	Steering	Estimate	£	$	€	Date	Place	Lot	Auc. H.
1967	T70 MkIIIB spyder		SL75122	R	500-600.000 USD		NS		19-08-17	Monterey	S135	Mec

Dark blue; driven by Dan Gurney at the 1967 Can-Am Championship; raced at Can-Am and SCCA events until 1970; converted to coupé form in 1971; damaged in an accident in 1996; bought in 1998 by the current owner along with a new tub; restoration completed in 2010 to 1967 Spyder configuration; Ford 351 engine (see lot S126 Mecum 15.8.15 NS).

| 1969 | T70 MkIIIB coupé | | SL76142 | R | 400-600.000 EUR | | NS | | 10-02-17 | Paris | 96 | Art |

The car was bought new by James Nicoll Cuthbert and was driven at several 1969 races by Paul Hawkins who died that same year for an accident at the Tourist Trophy. The damaged car remained in the Cuthbert's ownership until 2007 when it was bought, via marque historian John Starkey, by Louis Beuzieron who subsequently had it restored in the USA. Finished in yellow and black livery and fitted with a 5-litre TRACO Chevrolet engine.

| 1971 | T212 | | HU37 | R | 140-160.000 GBP | | NS | | 27-07-17 | Silverstone | 119 | SiC |

Cream and blue; sold new to Canada, the car was raced at some events in period. In the 1980s and 1990s it was driven at historic events and later reimported into the UK. Restored in 2006; Richardson FVC (Ford Cosworth 1,790cc) engine.

LORRAINE-DIETRICH (F) (1905-1930)

| 1929 | B 3/6 Sport cabriolet (Gangloff) | | 133643 | R | 500-700.000 EUR | | NS | | 01-05-17 | Obenheim | 355 | Ose |

Blue; raced at some events by its first owner who retained it until 1951. Restored in the early 1990s.

LOTUS (GB) (1948-)

| 1970 | Seven S3 | | SB2596 | R | 25-30.000 GBP | 31.360 | 38.435 | 34.879 | 12-10-16 | Duxford | 14 | H&H F467 |

One owner from new; Holbay engine overhauled in 1989. The car requires some mechanical and cosmetic attention.

| 1961 | Seven S2 | | SB1188 | R | 22-26.000 GBP | 26.600 | 33.058 | 30.891 | 16-11-16 | Donington Park | 118 | H&H |

Yellow with polished aluminium bonnet; restored.

| 1961 | Elite | | 1998 | R | 58-68.000 GBP | 59.000 | 78.812 | 69.768 | 08-09-16 | Fontwell Park | 139 | Coy |

Dark metallic blue with silver roof; mechanicals rebuilt prior to the 2016 Rally Monte Carlo Classique.

| 1962 | Elite S2 Super 95 | | 1959 | R | 65-75.000 GBP | 103.420 | 137.807 | 122.304 | 10-09-16 | Goodwood | 109 | Bon F468 |

Dark green with grey leather interior; engine rebuilt 700 miles ago, interior retrimmed in 2013. Believed to be the 1962 Earls Court Motor Show car.

| 1958 | Elite | | MYH1009P | R | 75-100.000 GBP | 121.500 | 153.807 | 141.049 | 12-11-16 | Birmingham | 309 | SiC |

Light green; fully restored in 2016, it is described as in ready to race condition. First production series example; displayed at the 1958 London Motor Show; bought new by jazz legend Chris Barber; raced from 1958 to 1963 (see lot 509 Silverstone Auctions 30.7.16 WD).

| 1962 | Elite | | EB2181718 | R | 60-80.000 GBP | 73.180 | 92.273 | 85.994 | 07-12-16 | London | 374 | Bon |

Primrose yellow with silver roof and black leather interior; restored 10 years ago. Engine rebuilt to 1,460cc FWB specification; Type 5-speed gearbox.

| 1960 | Elite | | 1187 | R | 75-85.000 EUR | | NS | | 08-02-17 | Paris | 115 | RMS |

Red; bought in 2003 by the current owner. Prepared for historic racing, it is fitted with a zero kilometre "ultimate specification" 1,216cc engine and ZF gearbox.

| 1961 | Elite | | 1753 | L | 70-90.000 EUR | 80.371 | 102.701 | 96.000 | 22-04-17 | Bagatelle | 65 | Agu |

Metallic grey; prepared for historic racing.

| 1961 | Elite | | 1471 | R | 75-90.000 GBP | | NS | | 26-07-17 | Duxford | 53 | H&H |

Metallic blue with black interior; raced at some events in period; restoration completed in 2014. Ford Type 9 5-speed gearbox.

| 1962 | Elite S2 | | EB2311585 | R | 60-70.000 GBP | | NS | | 29-07-17 | Silverstone | 415 | SiC |

Yellow with blue leather interior; 879 miles covered since the restoration.

| 1962 | Elite S2 Super 95 | | 1334 | L | 90-125.000 USD | 61.538* | 79.200* | 67.478* | 18-08-17 | Carmel | 59 | Bon |

Yellow; restored in the late 1980s.

| 1962 | 23 | | 23S8 | R | 200-250.000 USD | | NS | | 19-08-17 | Monterey | F119 | Mec |

Green; restored; 1,600cc engine. Raced in period. Imported into the USA in 1994. Recently raced at historic events.

| 1967 | Elan S3 coupé | | 366740 | L | 35-45.000 USD | 24.090 | 31.000 | 27.587 | 03-10-16 | Philadelphia | 215 | Bon |

Red; acquired by the vendor in 1986, just following a restoration. Mechanicals overhauled circa 5,000 miles ago.

| 1968 | Elan Plus 2 | | 500418 | R | NQ | 23.520* | 29.245* | 27.610* | 26-11-16 | Weybridge | 169 | His |

Originally finished in silver, the car was registered to the factory and given to Graham Hill for personal use. Bought in 1976 by the current owner, it is currently finished in yellow. Engine replaced many years ago. Stored for 37 years, it requires restoration.

F465: 1901 Locomobile Style 5 locosurrey

F466: 1965 Lola T70 spyder

Year	Model	(Bodybuilder)	Chassis No.	Steering	Estimate	Hammer Price £	Hammer Price $	Hammer Price €	Date	Place	Lot	Auc. H.
1969	Elan S4 roadster		459463	R	25-30.000 GBP	22.400	27.984	26.468	23-02-17	Donington Park	80	H&H
\multicolumn{13}{l}{Yellow and green with black interior.}
1964	Elan S2 roadster		CHN0263915	R	34-39.000 GBP	26.000	31.808	30.108	04-03-17	Brooklands	178	His F469
\multicolumn{13}{l}{Red with black interior; 8,000 miles covered since the restoration (see lot 220 Historics 28.11.15 $41,300).}
1967	Elan Plus 2		501438	R	40-48.000 AUD	24.424	31.602	28.912	30-04-17	Melbourne	22	Mos
\multicolumn{13}{l}{Yellow with black interior; for 48 in the current ownership; approximately 61,000 miles on the odometer. Recently serviced.}
1968	Elan S3 coupé		367807	R	27-32.000 GBP	24.453	31.879	28.644	18-05-17	London	130	Coy
\multicolumn{13}{l}{Blue; for 40 years until 2016 with the previous owner. Restored some years ago.}
1967	Elan S3 roadster		TW14154	R	28-35.000 GBP	27.787	35.912	31.580	15-07-17	Blenheim Pal.	113	Coy
\multicolumn{13}{l}{British racing green with black interior; restored over the years (see lot 407 Bonhams 22.11.05 $12,185).}
1971	Elan S4 coupé		368751	R	30-40.000 GBP	33.345	43.095	37.897	15-07-17	Blenheim Pal.	149	Coy
\multicolumn{13}{l}{White with black interior; stored for 38 years, in 2012 the car was bought by the current owner and restored over a two and half year period.}
1970	Elan Sprint		7006140170G	R	NA	47.250	61.874	52.755	29-07-17	Silverstone	426	SiC
\multicolumn{13}{l}{Red and white; one of the Elan S4s converted at the factory to Sprint specification before being sold. Bought in 2014 by the current owner and restored around a genuine galvanised Lotus replacement chassis.}
1964	34		2	M	1.800-2.500.000 USD	893.550	1.150.000	979.800	18-08-17	Carmel	82	Bon F470
\multicolumn{13}{l}{Pearl white, red and blue; raced until the end of the 1966 season, driven by A.J. Foyt, Parnelli Jones, Dan Gurney and Jim Clark, winner of four USAC events, and on the pole position at the 1965 Indy 500 driven by Foyt. The car remained in the Foyt's ownership until 1992 when it was bought by the current owner. Recently restored to original specification and running condition (see lot 23 Christie's 19.8.01 NS).}
1974	Europa Twin-Cam Special		743814R	L	40-60.000 USD	23.526*	28.600*	26.953*	10-03-17	Amelia Island	6	G&Co
\multicolumn{13}{l}{Maroon; in good original condition. Approximately 30,000 miles covered (see lot 127 Gooding & Company 17.1.15 $33,000).}
1973	Europa Twin-Cam Special		1184Q	L	20-25.000 EUR	13.831*	17.998*	16.100*	21-05-17	SPA-Francorch.	40	Bon
\multicolumn{13}{l}{Red; restored in 2010. Mechanicals overhauled in 2014 (see lot 8 Bonhams 25.5.13 $30,504).}
1992	Esprit Turbo SE	(Italdesign)	60175	R	NA	48.380	64.263	57.417	02-09-16	Salon Privé	218	SiC
\multicolumn{13}{l}{Black with cream leather interior; in very good overall condition. 1,800 miles covered.}
2001	Esprit V8 GT	(Italdesign)	10211	L	40-60.000 EUR	41.716	50.678	46.400	30-10-16	Paris	170	Art
\multicolumn{13}{l}{Dark green; in very good condition. Two owners.}
1990	Esprit Turbo SE	(Italdesign)	65347	R	10-14.000 GBP	20.440	25.415	23.995	26-11-16	Weybridge	150	His
\multicolumn{13}{l}{Silver with blue leather interior; in very good overall condition. Exhibited at the 1989 London Motor Show.}
1995	Esprit S4S	(Italdesign)	63075	L	40-50.000 USD	32.127*	39.600*	37.117*	19-01-17	Scottsdale	70	Bon
\multicolumn{13}{l}{British racing green with magnolia leather interior; in very good original condition; 22,000 miles covered.}
1983	Esprit Turbo	(Italdesign)	60363	L	50-60.000 USD	35.697*	44.000*	41.241*	19-01-17	Phoenix	156	RMS F471
\multicolumn{13}{l}{Silver with red leather interior; 32,000 original miles. Recently serviced (see lot 16 Bonhams 28.1.16 $46,200).}
1990	Esprit Turbo SE	(Italdesign)	65517	R	30-40.000 USD	26.196*	31.900*	30.232*	09-03-17	Amelia Island	109	Bon
\multicolumn{13}{l}{British racing green with tan leather interior; in good overall condition. Less than 9,500 original miles.}
1979	Esprit JPS	(Italdesign)	79030689G	R	30-40.000 GBP	38.250	47.587	44.278	29-03-17	Duxford	52	H&H
\multicolumn{13}{l}{World Championship Commerative Model (John Player Special) finished in black and gold; one of 99 UK market right-hand drive examples. Mechanicals overhauled in 2007.}
1979	Elite		79071566A	R	4-5.000 GBP	8.550	11.152	9.577	26-07-17	Duxford	2	H&H
\multicolumn{13}{l}{Silver with black leather interior; 33,500 miles covered; one owner; recently serviced.}

LUCCHINI (I)

Year	Model	(Bodybuilder)	Chassis No.	Steering	Estimate	£	$	€	Date	Place	Lot	Auc. H.
1985	SN85		016	L	15-20.000 EUR	24.805*	30.844*	29.120*	25-11-16	Milan	929	RMS
\multicolumn{13}{l}{Yellow. From the Duemila Ruote collection.}

MARCH (GB) (1969-)

Year	Model	(Bodybuilder)	Chassis No.	Steering	Estimate	£	$	€	Date	Place	Lot	Auc. H.
1975	753		12	M	5-10.000 EUR	23.851*	29.658*	28.000*	25-11-16	Milan	610	RMS
\multicolumn{13}{l}{Red. From the Duemila Ruote collection.}
1979	792		NQ	M	10-15.000 EUR	90.634*	112.699*	106.400*	25-11-16	Milan	608	RMS
\multicolumn{13}{l}{White BMW livery with blue and red stripes. From the Duemila Ruote collection.}
1982	82G		82G001	R	195-250.000 USD	143.693	175.000	164.133	15-01-17	Kissimmee	S210.1	Mec F472
\multicolumn{13}{l}{Red with white stripe; first example built, driven by Bobby Rahal at the 1982 IMSA Championship. Restored in 2010. 650bhp 358 "small block" Chevrolet engine.}
1984	84G Group C		84G03	R	500-700.000 EUR	304.997	380.093	357.600	10-02-17	Paris	93	Art F473
\multicolumn{13}{l}{Bought new by South Africa Kreepy Krauly Team and fitted with a Porsche 956 engine, the car was raced at several IMSA events until 1986 and also raced the Le Mans 24 Hours in 1985 and 1986. Restored in the early 2000s it has been driven at historic events. Described as in ready to race condition.}
1990	90C Indy		90CA001	M	20-30.000 EUR	81.093*	100.836*	95.200*	25-11-16	Milan	287	RMS
\multicolumn{13}{l}{Black and gold. From the Duemila Ruote collection.}
1991	CG 911B		CG911B05	M	15-20.000 EUR	40.070*	49.825*	47.040*	25-11-16	Milan	609	RMS
\multicolumn{13}{l}{Light blue. From the Duemila Ruote collection.}

MARCOS (GB) (1959-)

Year	Model	(Bodybuilder)	Chassis No.	Steering	Estimate	£	$	€	Date	Place	Lot	Auc. H.
1964	GT 1800		4008	R	45-50.000 GBP		NS		29-10-16	London	110	Coy
\multicolumn{13}{l}{Silver with blue stripe; raced in period. Later the car was prepared for historic racing and raced at numerous events until April 2016.}

F467: 1970 Lotus Seven S3

F468: 1962 Lotus Elite S2 Super 95

F469: 1964 Lotus Elan S2 roadster

F470: 1964 Lotus 34

F471: 1983 Lotus Esprit Turbo (Italdesign)

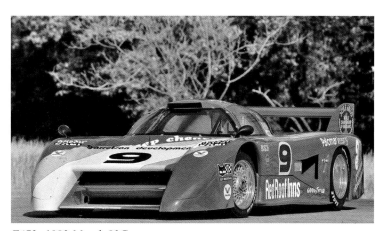
F472: 1982 March 82G

F473: 1984 March 84G Group C

F474: 1928 Marmon Series 68 roadster (Murray)

F475: 1937 Maserati 6CM

F476: 1956 Maserati A6G/54 coupé (Frua)

MARMON (USA) (1902-1933)

Year	Model	(Bodybuilder)	Chassis no.	Steering	Estimate	£	$	€	Date	Place	Lot	Auc. H.
1928	Series 68 roadster	(Murray)	E2YC74	L	70-90.000 USD	23.885*	30.250*	27.044*	06-10-16	Hershey	125	RMS

Blue with black fenders; described as in original condition except for the front seats which have been re-upholstered. Three owners and 38,000 miles from new. F474

MASERATI (I) (1914-)

Year	Model	(Bodybuilder)	Chassis no.	Steering	Estimate	£	$	€	Date	Place	Lot	Auc. H.
1937	6CM		1540	M	1.000-1.400.000 USD	777.000	1.000.000	852.000	19-08-17	Pebble Beach	136	G&Co

Sold new in Italy and raced by Giovanni Rocco and Giuseppe Negro; after WWII it was imported into the UK and raced at some events; in single ownership from 1969 to 2000 when it was bought by Sam Mann who had it restored in the UK prior to import it in the USA where it was raced at historic events; bought in 2006 by the current owner and refinished in the present silver livery (see lot 55 Gooding & Company 20.8.06 $726,000). F475

| 1949 | A6 1500 (Pinin Farina) | | 078 | L | 600-700.000 USD | | NS | | 20-01-17 | Scottsdale | 30 | G&Co |

Dark blue with red leather and cloth interior; sold new in Italy, the car was imported in the 1950s into the USA where it remained in single ownership from 1963 to 2003 when it was re-imported into Italy and subsequently subjected to a full restoration completed in 2011. In 2013 it was re-imported into the USA (see lot 130 The Finest Automobile Auctions 11.6.16 NS).

| 1956 | A6G/54 coupé (Frua) | | 2181 | L | 1.600-2.000.000 USD | 1.945.449* | 2.365.000* | 2.228.776* | 11-03-17 | Amelia Island | 260 | RMS |

Red with black roof and black stinger; tan leather interior. Displayed at the 1956 Turin Motor Show and subsequently sold new to the USA, where over the years it was fitted first with an American V8 engine and later with a Maserati 3500 GT engine and gearbox. In 2007 it was sold to Germany, restored in Italy and fitted with the present A6G/54 engine no.2104 and a correct gearbox. In 2012 it was bought by the current owner, of Chicago, and shipped to the UK where McGrath Maserati rebuilt the engine. F476

| 1956 | A6G/54 cabriolet (Frua) | | 2180 | L | 3.200-3.600.000 USD | | NS | | 18-08-17 | Carmel | 61 | Bon |

Red with ivory hood stripe and ivory leather interior; sold new to France, the car was later imported into the USA. In the 1970s it was fitted with a Ford 289 V8 engine and in 1999 it was acquired by the current owner who in 2002 fitted it with the present engine (no.2146) and gearbox. In 2003 it was sent to Italy and fully restored to concours condition over a five year period.

| 1956 | A6G/54 berlinetta (Zagato) | | 2186 | L | 4.000-5.000.000 USD | 3.418.800 | 4.400.000 | 3.748.800 | 18-08-17 | Pebble Beach | 27 | G&Co |

Sold new to the USA and raced in period; retired from competition and fitted in the 1960s with a Buick V8 engine; restored between the late 1980s and 1990s and fitted with a correct Maserati engine no.2175; bought in 2007 by Argentinian Claudio Scalise and later fully restored in Italy by Quality Cars; finished in red and fitted again with its original engine no.2186. F477

| 1956 | 300S | | 3069 | R | 6.000-7.000.000 USD | | NS | | 18-08-17 | Carmel | 38 | Bon |

Red with red interior; engine no.3058. Believed a Works car for the 1956 season; bought in 1957 by Giambertone for Fangio and raced by the Argentinian driver in Europe and South America; later sold to Brazil and raced in South America until the 1970s; bought by Colin Crabbe in 1978, imported into the UK and restored in the early 1980s; acquired in 1998 by the current owner, raced at several events, including those of the Ferrari/Maserati Shell Historic Challenge, and restored again (see lot 19 Poulain 29.4.96 $280,517).

| 1960 | 3500 GT (Touring) | | AM101954 | R | 150-175.000 GBP | 117.600 | 157.372 | 140.050 | 07-09-16 | London | 117 | RMS |

Red; since 1964 with the current owner. The paintwork and interior are original but require some attention; the engine was rebuilt in 2009 by Bill McGrath

| 1959 | 3500 GT (Touring) | | AM101326 | L | 60-90.000 GBP | 135.900 | 181.087 | 160.715 | 10-09-16 | Goodwood | 159 | Bon |

Sold new in Italy, the car was later exported to the USA and in the 1990s it was imported into the UK. Restoration to be completed; engine rebuilt in 2013.

| 1962 | 3500 GTI (Touring) | | AM1012290 | L | 200-300.000 EUR | 187.031 | 230.598 | 207.000 | 07-10-16 | Zoute | 18 | Bon |

Restored some 8-9 years ago; the original Lucas injection replaced with Weber carburettors. Described as in very good overall condition.

| 1960 | 3500 GT (Touring) | | AM1011038 | L | 275-375.000 USD | 178.311 | 222.750 | 200.787 | 05-11-16 | Hilton Head | 146 | AA |

Maroon with black leather interior; 42,300 kms on the odometer.

F477: 1956 Maserati A6G/54 berlinetta (Zagato)

F478: 1960 Maserati 3500 GT (Touring)

MASERATI
CLASSICHE

The Importance of Origins

MASERATI CLASSICHE OPENS THE DOORS TO THE MASERATI HISTORICAL ARCHIVE

As of today, you will have the possibility to receive historical documents of your Trident-branded classic vehicle simply requesting them. The Vehicle's sales orders, technical characteristics, historical and aesthetic features and the Vehicle's technical and test documents are just a few examples of the items you may request. For information and orders: maserati.classiche@maserati.com

WWW.MASERATI.COM – MASERATI PASSION/MASERATI CLASSIC section

Timeless Emotions

Year	Model	(Bodybuilder)	Chassis no.	Steering	Estimate	Hammer price £	Hammer price $	Hammer price €	Date	Place	Lot	Auc. H.
1962	3500 GTi	(Touring)	AM1012310	L	155-175.000 EUR	171.727*	213.535*	201.600*	25-11-16	Milan	874	RMS
\multicolumn{13}{l}{Green with beige leather interior; 22,530 kms. From the Duemila Ruote collection.}
1961	3500 GT	(Touring)	AM1011804	L	35-40.000 EUR	114.485*	142.356*	134.400*	25-11-16	Milan	905	RMS
\multicolumn{13}{l}{For restoration. From the Duemila Ruote collection.}
1961	3500 GT	(Touring)	AM1011580	L	160-180.000 USD	126.725	156.200	146.406	19-01-17	Scottsdale	96	Bon
\multicolumn{13}{l}{Red with black interior; sold new in Italy and later imported into the USA. Paintwork and interior redone over 30 years ago. Mechanicals restored in recent years (see lot 108 Gooding & Company 17.8.14 $154,000).}
1963	3500 GTI	(Touring)	AM1012716	L	180-220.000 EUR	151.673	190.585	178.250	09-02-17	Paris	377	Bon
\multicolumn{13}{l}{Red with beige leather interior; delivered new in Italy, the car was later resold to the USA where it was restored in 2003. Mechanicals rebuilt between 2010 and 2014. Currently fitted with a correct three-carburettor Maserati 3500 GT engine restamped as the original fuel-injected unit (see lots 332 Bonhams 6.5.06 NS, 152 RM 8.9.14 $234,416, and 254 Bonhams 24.6.16 NS).}
1960	3500 GT	(Touring)	AM1011154	L	220-260.000 EUR		NS		10-02-17	Paris	141	Art
\multicolumn{13}{l}{Black with white interior; sold new in Italy, in the past the car was prepared for historic events. Bought in 2015 by the current owner, it has been subsequently restored to its original configuration (see lot 240 Coys 16.5.15 $172,799).}
1964	3500 GT	(Touring)	AM1012646	L	230-250.000 EUR	173.748	216.398	203.000	08-04-17	Essen	178	Coy
\multicolumn{13}{l}{Metallic grey with cognac interior; fully restored between 2012 and 2016.}
1963	3500 GT	(Touring)	AM1012660	L	200-250.000 EUR	149.783	186.550	175.000	08-04-17	Essen	190	Coy
\multicolumn{13}{l}{Gunmetal grey with red interior; restored in the 2000s (see lot 44 Coys 11.8.90 $95,456).}
1963	3500 GT	(Touring)	AM1012660	L	150-175.000 GBP	161.167	210.113	188.791	18-05-17	London	128	Coy
\multicolumn{13}{l}{See lot 190 Coys 8.4.17.}
1963	3500 GT	(Touring)	AM1012660	L	150-180.000 GBP	148.000	192.074	167.580	29-06-17	Fontwell Park	122	Coy
\multicolumn{13}{l}{See lot 128 Coys 18.5.17.}
1960	3500 GT	(Touring)	AM1011120	R	200-250.000 GBP	214.300	278.119	242.652	30-06-17	Goodwood	219	Bon F478
\multicolumn{13}{l}{Red with black interior; since 1993 in the current ownership; restored in the 1990s by Bill McGrath; cylinder head overhauled in 2008; body restored again in 2013.}
1959	3500 GT	(Touring)	AM101742	L	180-220.000 EUR		WD		02-07-17	Monaco	159	Art
\multicolumn{13}{l}{Grey with red leather; restored over a 20 year period circa; engine rebuilt in 2007.}
1963	3500 GT	(Touring)	AM1012660	L	150-180.000 GBP		NS		15-07-17	Blenheim Pal.	109	Coy
\multicolumn{13}{l}{See lot 122 Coys 29.6.17.}
1964	3500 GT	(Touring)	AM1012646	L	150-180.000 EUR	136.165	178.999	150.825	05-08-17	Schloss Dyck	212	Coy
\multicolumn{13}{l}{See lot 178 Coys 8.4.17.}
1963	3500 GT	(Touring)	AM1012660	L	160-200.000 EUR	160.053	210.402	177.285	05-08-17	Schloss Dyck	263	Coy
\multicolumn{13}{l}{See lot 109 Coys 15.7.17.}
1962	3500 GT	(Touring)	AM1012360	L	250-325.000 USD		NS		18-08-17	Pebble Beach	32	G&Co
\multicolumn{13}{l}{Grey with brown leather interior; sold new in Italy to Carlo Dusio, son of Piero Dusio founder of Cisitalia; imported into the USA in 1975; previously stored for 10 years when bought by the current owner and subjected to some mechanical works. It requires further works for optimal running condition.}
1962	3500 GT Spyder	(Vignale)	AM1011365	L	750-850.000 EUR		NS		08-02-17	Paris	160	RMS
\multicolumn{13}{l}{Silver with blue interior; restored in the USA in 2014 and subsequently bought by the current Italian owner. The original Lucas fuel-injection system was replaced by a previous owner with three Weber carburetors still on the car (see lot 214 RM 16.8.14 $764,500).}
1961	3500 GT Spyder	(Vignale)	AM1011129	L	750-950.000 EUR	732.396	940.464	840.000	27-05-17	Villa Erba	140	RMS F479
\multicolumn{13}{l}{Black with black interior; restored (see lot 202 Artcurial 2.6.15 $982,427).}
1961	3500 GT Spyder	(Vignale)	AM1011285	L	800-900.000 EUR		NS		02-07-17	Monaco	132	Art
\multicolumn{13}{l}{Dark green with black interior; sold new in Italy and later imported into the UK. For 30 years until 2012 with the same German owner who had it restored. The engine is currently fitted with a unnumbered replacement block (the original unit is included with the sale).}
1959	3500 GT Spyder	(Frua)	AM101268	L	650-1.000.000 USD	470.085	605.000	515.460	18-08-17	Monterey	155	RMS F480
\multicolumn{13}{l}{Pastel yellow with turquoise and white leather interior; one-off; sold new to France; restored in the 1980s and fitted with a new 3500 GT engine supplied by the factory, 5-speed gearbox and disc brakes. Restoration freshened in the USA between 1998 and 2000 (see lots 51 Christie's 11.9.93 NS, 41 Poulain 13.6.94 NS, and 444 RM 15.8.03 $106,701).}
====	Tipo 61 Birdcage replica		2473	R	600-650.000 AUD		NS		28-05-17	Sydney	9	Mos
\multicolumn{13}{l}{Replica built in the UK by Crosthwaite & Gardiner between the late 1980s-early 1990s and commissioned by American Don Orosco. Imported into Australia in 2008. With FIA Historic Technical Passport (see lot 34 Manheim 28.10.12 NS).}
1964	5000 GT	(Michelotti)	AM103016	L	1.100-1.400.000 USD	790.598	1.017.500	866.910	18-08-17	Monterey	117	RMS F481
\multicolumn{13}{l}{Silver; restored in the early 1990s. One-off ordered by Briggs Cunningham. Formerly in the Alfredo Brener Collection (see lot 445 RM 15.8.03 $302,500).}

F479: 1961 Maserati 3500 GT Spyder (Vignale)

F480: 1959 Maserati 3500 GT Spyder (Frua)

GALLERY AALDERING

EXQUISITE CLASSIC AUTOMOBILES

A DIFFERENT PERSPECTIVE ON A SOLID RETURN ON INVESTMENT

VISIT US TO POWER UP YOUR EQUITY PORTFOLIO

Arnhemsestraat 47 | 6971 AP Brummen | The Netherlands | T. 0031 (0)575 56 40 55 | E. info@gallery-aaldering.com

www.gallery-aaldering.com

Year	Model	(Bodybuilder)	Chassis no.	Steering	Estimate	Hammer price £	$	€	Date	Place	Lot	Auc. H.

F481: 1964 Maserati 5000 GT (Michelotti)

F482: 1966 Maserati Sebring 3500 GTI (Vignale)

Year	Model	Chassis no.	Steering	Estimate	£	$	€	Date	Place	Lot	Auc. H.
1966	**Sebring 3700 GTI (Vignale)**	AM101S10425	L	NA		NS		02-09-16	Salon Privé	240	SiC
	Silver with deep blue leather interior; restored many years ago (see lot 248 Bonhams 24.06.16 NS).										
1967	**Sebring 3700 GTI (Vignale)**	AM101S10535	L	125-160.000 GBP	110.000	147.202	130.999	07-09-16	London	167	RMS
	Silver; in the same ownership from 1974 to 2006. Some cosmetical works carried out in the mid-2000s. In 2011 reimported into Europe from the USA (see lot 247 RM 21.1.11 $77,000).										
1963	**Sebring 3500 GT (Vignale)**	AM10102105	L	260-320.000 EUR	218.202	269.031	241.500	07-10-16	Zoute	34	Bon
	Dark grey with red leather interior; in 2015 paintwork and interior redone and engine overhauled. One of four examples completed with carburettor induction.										
1964	**Sebring 3500 GTI (Vignale)**	AM10110153	L	90-105.000 EUR	171.727*	213.535*	201.600*	25-11-16	Milan	583	RMS
	White with black interior; 69,250 kms. From the Duemila Ruote collection.										
1965	**Sebring 3500 GTI (Vignale)**	AM10102019	L	15-20.000 EUR	136.632*	169.896*	160.400*	25-11-16	Milan	860	RMS
	For restoration. From the Duemila Ruote collection.										
1962	**Sebring 3500/A6GCS-53 replica**	AM10101507	L	70-90.000 EUR		NS		14-01-17	Maastricht	230	Coy
	Red; replica built by Giovanni Giordanengo in 1989-90. Shortened chassis; engine in need of recommissioning.										
1966	**Sebring 3700 GTI (Vignale)**	AM10101077	L	290-340.000 USD		NS		18-01-17	Scottsdale	43	WoA
	Silver with black and red interior; paintwork and interior redone.										
1966	**Sebring 3500 GTI (Vignale)**	AM10110419	L	200-250.000 EUR	193.165	240.726	226.480	10-02-17	Paris	107	Art **F482**
	Grey with cognac leather interior; since 1970 in the same family ownership. Body repainted in 1984, brakes overhauled in 1988, gearbox overhauled in 1989, engine rebuilt in 2011.										
1963	**Sebring 3500 GTI (Vignale)**	AM10101577	L	250-280.000 EUR		NS		02-07-17	Monaco	216	Art
	Blue with beige leather interior; sold new to Switzerland; imported into Sweden in 1989 and subsequently restored; sold to Germany in 2004. Over the past two years the mechanicals have been overhauled and the interior redone.										
1966	**Sebring 3700 GTI (Vignale)**	AM101S10403	L	300-400.000 USD		NS		18-08-17	Carmel	98	Bon
	Red with white leather interior; sold new to Spain, the car has had probably one owner until 2014 when it was imported into the USA. Less than 34,000 kms covered; in highly original condition.										
1966	**Sebring 3700 GTI (Vignale)**	AM10110107	L	30-50.000 USD	62.160*	80.000*	68.160*	19-08-17	Monterey	S48	Mec
	Restoration project. From the J. Geils Collection.										
1967	**Quattroporte 4.2 (Frua)**	AM1072152	L	15-20.000 EUR	52.472*	65.247*	61.600*	25-11-16	Milan	350	RMS
	Burgundy with tan interior; 86,432 kms. From the Duemila Ruote collection.										
1968	**Quattroporte (Frua)**	AM1072170	L	40-70.000 EUR	54.337*	70.707*	63.250*	21-05-17	SPA-Francorch.	54	Bon **F483**
	Metallic blue with beige leather interior; restored in Switzerland. From the Swiss Castle Collection.										
1965	**Quattroporte 4.7 (Frua)**	AM107504	L	80-100.000 GBP		NS		06-06-17	Woodcote Park	33	H&H
	Black with red leather interior; restored in 2012-2013. Described as the first Quattroporte fitted with the 4.7-liter engine, the car was ordered new by dott. Enrico Wax, who later had the engine fitted with carburettors in place of the Lucas fuel injection system.										
1967	**Mistral 4.0 coupé (Frua)**	AM109A11304	L	170-230.000 EUR		NS		03-09-16	Chantilly	10	Bon
	Silver grey with black leather interior; described as in highly original condition, the car has had two owners and has covered 78,000 kms.										
1963	**Mistral 3.5 coupé (Frua)**	AM101960	L	195-235.000 GBP		NS		07-09-16	London	118	RMS
	Silver with red interior; one of the prototypes of the new model, the car was built with chassis numer 109.004 and was later renumbered as 101.960 (3500 GT numering) prior to be exported to South Africa. In the early 2000s it was reimported into Europe and subsequently received extensive recommissioning (see lot 109 Christie's 2.12.03 NS).										

F483: 1968 Maserati Quattroporte (Frua)

F484: 1967 Maserati Mistral 4.0 coupé (Frua)

M^CGRATH MASERATI

SERVICE, RESTORATION & PARTS

MODERN SERVICE
TRADITIONAL CRAFT

MCGRATHMASERATI.CO.UK

Year	Model	(Bodybuilder)	Chassis no.	Steering	Estimate	Hammer price £	$	€	Sale Date	Place	Lot	Auc. H.

F485: 1967 Maserati Mistral 4.0 Spider (Frua)

F486: 1968 Maserati Mexico 4.2 (Vignale)

Year	Model	Chassis no.	Steering	Estimate	£	$	€	Date	Place	Lot	Auc. H.
1967	**Mistral 4.0 coupé (Frua)**	AM109A11152	L	90-140.000 EUR	103.397	126.523	115.000	15-10-16	Salzburg	437	Dor
	Silver with original cognac leather interior; since 1976 in the current ownership. In the mid-1970s the body was repainted and the mechanicals were overhauled.
1965	**Mistral 3.7 coupé (Frua)**	AM109432	L	100-120.000 EUR	104.944*	130.493*	123.200*	25-11-16	Milan	297	RMS
	White with black interior; 79,780 kms. From the Duemila Ruote collection.
1968	**Mistral 4.0 coupé (Frua)**	AM109A11580	L	90-105.000 EUR	133.565*	166.083*	156.800*	25-11-16	Milan	598	RMS
	Gold with red interior; 38,371 kms. From the Duemila Ruote collection.
1967	**Mistral 4.0 coupé (Frua)**	AM109A11374	L	155-175.000 EUR	190.808*	237.261*	224.000*	25-11-16	Milan	898	RMS F484
	Silver with brown interior; 74,267 kms. From the Duemila Ruote collection.
1967	**Mistral 4.0 coupé (Frua)**	AM109A11158	L	175-225.000 USD		NS		18-01-17	Scottsdale	61	WoA
	Restored several years ago; recently uncovered following years of garage storage.
1965	**Mistral 3.7 coupé (Frua)**	AM109232	R	115-130.000 GBP		NS		24-02-17	Stoneleigh P.	529	SiC
	Blue; 2,500 miles covered since the restoration completed in 2015.
1967	**Mistral 4.0 Spider (Frua)**	AM109SA1657	L	600-650.000 GBP	739.200	989.197	880.313	07-09-16	London	136	RMS F485
	Metallic grey with original red leather interior; sold new to Switzerland, the car was later imported into New Zealand. In 2002 it was reimported into Europe and subsequently restored.
1968	**Mistral 4.0 Spider (Frua)**	AM109SA1707	L	520-580.000 GBP		NS		04-12-16	London	20	Bon
	Silver with original leather interior; 26,000 miles covered. Three owners. Sold new to South Africa; imported into the UK in 2016.
1964	**Mistral 3.5 Spider (Frua)**	AM109S033	L	600-700.000 USD		NS		20-01-17	Scottsdale	36	G&Co
	Red with tan leather interior; sold new to Germany, the car was imported into the USA in 1997. The original Lucas fuel-injection system was replaced with three carburettors. It requires mechanical attention prior to use.
1967	**Mistral 4.0 Spider (Frua)**	AM109SA1673	L	350-450.000 USD	393.614	478.500	450.938	10-03-17	Amelia Island	17	G&Co
	Finished in red with black interior, the car was sold new to the USA. Last road-registered in 1983, it requires a full restoration.
1965	**Mistral 3.7 Spider (Frua)**	AM109S057	L	730-830.000 EUR		NS		02-07-17	Monaco	118	Art
	Silver with black interior; sold new in Italy, later exported to the USA and then reimported into Italy where it was restored in the early 2000s. With its original black hardtop.
1968	**Mistral 4.0 Spider (Frua)**	AM109SA1691	L	750-900.000 USD		NS		18-08-17	Carmel	67	Bon
	Silver with red leather interior; sold new in Italy, the car was imported into the USA in the early 1970s. Bought in 2005 by the current owner; 7,000 miles covered since the restoration.
1968	**Mexico 4.2 (Vignale)**	AM112326	L	15-20.000 EUR	81.093*	100.836*	95.200*	25-11-16	Milan	311	RMS F486
	Blue with white interior; 29,578 kms. From the Duemila Ruote collection.
1968	**Mexico 4.7 (Vignale)**	AM1121292	L	15-20.000 EUR	76.323*	94.904*	89.600*	25-11-16	Milan	315	RMS
	White with black interior; 71,183 kms. From the Duemila Ruote collection.
1967	**Mexico 4.7 (Vignale)**	AM1121118	L	130-160.000 USD	111.953	137.500	128.934	18-01-17	Scottsdale	38	WoA
	Metallic burgundy with black leather interior; in good overall condition. Wire wheels and air conditioning.
1967	**Mexico 4.2 Speciale (Frua)**	AM112001	L	450-550.000 USD	282.190	346.500	325.883	20-01-17	Phoenix	262	RMS F487
	Amaranth with natural leather interior; one-off sold new in Italy and later imported into the USA. From 1980 to 1999 it was owned by Frank Mandarano who restored first the body and interior and in 1999 the mechanicals (see lots RM 428 18.8.00 $102,300 and 449 15.8.03 $77,000, and Gooding & Company 10 22.1.10 $187,000).

F487: 1967 Maserati Mexico 4.2 Speciale (Frua)

F488: 1972 Maserati Ghibli SS coupé (Ghia)

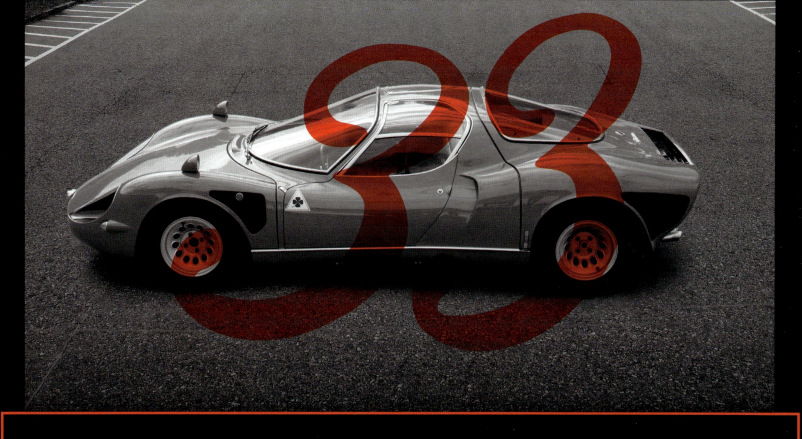

www.zweimuellercars.com

Year	Model	(Bodybuilder)	Chassis no.	Steering	Estimate	Hammer price £	$	€	Sale Date	Place	Lot	Auc. H.
1970	**Ghibli coupé**	(Ghia)	AM1151407	L	230-280.000 EUR	213.139	266.232	240.000	05-11-16	Lyon	244	**Agu**
	*Black with magnolia leather interior; restored at unspecified date. Recently checked.*
1971	**Ghibli coupé**	(Ghia)	AM1151742	L	35-40.000 EUR	152.646*	189.809*	179.200*	25-11-16	Milan	265	**RMS**
	*Blue; interior to be restored. From the Duemila Ruote collection.*
1970	**Ghibli coupé**	(Ghia)	AM1151574	L	90-105.000 EUR	157.416*	195.740*	184.800*	25-11-16	Milan	321	**RMS**
	*Light blue with black interior; 73,964 kms. From the Duemila Ruote collection.*
1968	**Ghibli (spider/conversion)**		AM115778	L	280-320.000 EUR	226.814	282.490	265.000	08-04-17	Essen	143	**Coy**
	*Yellow with original black leather interior; conversion carried out in period.*
1967	**Ghibli coupé**	(Ghia)	AM115082	L	150-200.000 USD	113.807*	146.300*	130.426*	04-06-17	Greenwich	184	**Bon**
	*The car remained stored for decades; the body is in fair condition and finished in metallic graphite grey; the seats have been retrimmed with cloth covers; the mechanicals require recommissioning prior to use.*
1972	**Ghibli SS coupé**	(Ghia)	AM115492472	R	240-280.000 GBP	309.800	376.345	344.560	29-10-16	London	118	**Coy**
	*Red with black leather interior; described as in very good overall condition. Formerly owned by the U2 drummer, Adam Clayton (see lot 225 Bonhams 08.03.09 $58,623).*
1971	**Ghibli SS coupé**	(Ghia)	AM115492184	L	10-12.000 EUR	100.174*	124.562*	117.600*	25-11-16	Milan	219	**RMS**
	*Ivory; restoration project. From the Duemila Ruote collection.*
1970	**Ghibli SS coupé**	(Ghia)	AM115491780	L	200-230.000 EUR	257.590*	320.302*	302.400*	25-11-16	Milan	324	**RMS**
	*Red with black interior, recently restored. 6,087 kms. From the Duemila Ruote collection.*
1971	**Ghibli SS coupé**	(Ghia)	AM115492130	L	200-230.000 EUR	257.590*	320.302*	302.400*	25-11-16	Milan	573	**RMS**
	*Silver with black interior; 34,611 kms. From the Duemila Ruote collection.*
1971	**Ghibli SS coupé**	(Ghia)	AM115491956	L	220-260.000 GBP	203.100	256.373	240.897	04-12-16	London	23	**Bon**
	*Cordoba red with cream leather interior; the car was acquired in 1989 by the current owner, Alexander Fyshe, who had it fully restored over the next four years. Described as still in very good overall condition.*
1972	**Ghibli SS coupé**	(Ghia)	NQ	R	240-280.000 GBP	265.000	336.948	314.820	05-12-16	London	116	**Coy**
	*Sold new to the UK, in 1988 the car was bought by collector Ian Wade who retained it until 2011. Restored in the 1990s and finished in the present blue livery.*
1972	**Ghibli SS coupé**	(Ghia)	AM115492008	L	300-350.000 USD	232.032	286.000	268.068	19-01-17	Phoenix	147	**RMS** F488
	*Red with tan leather interior; in very good mechanical condition. Cosmetic restoration of the engine compartment in late 2016.*
1972	**Ghibli SS coupé**	(Ghia)	AM115492372	L	375-450.000 USD		NS		21-01-17	Scottsdale	142	**G&Co**
	*Gold with black leather interior; sold new to the USA, the car remained with its first owner until 2011 and was subsequently shipped to Italy for restoration. Described as in very good overall condition; three owners.*
1971	**Ghibli SS coupé**	(Ghia)	AM115492302	L	270-320.000 EUR	184.019	229.190	215.000	08-04-17	Essen	197	**Coy**
	*Dark blue with mustard leather interior; sold new to the USA, later the car was reimported into Europe and restored.*
1972	**Ghibli SS coupé**	(Ghia)	AM115492316	L	300-350.000 USD		NS		22-04-17	Arlington	NA	**WoA**
	*Sold new to the USA; in the same ownership from 1980 to 2016; mechanicals rebuilt between 2012 and 2015.*
1969	**Ghibli SS coupé**	(Ghia)	AM115491082	L	100-150.000 EUR	150.167*	195.409*	174.800*	21-05-17	SPA-Francorch.	61	**Bon**
	*Metallic blue with beige leather interior; restored in Switzerland. From the Swiss Castle Collection.*
1969	**Ghibli SS Spider**	(Ghia)	AM115S1005	L	900-1.100.000 USD		NS		04-11-16	Dallas	S107.1	**Mec**
	*Yellow with black leather interior; restored in recent years (see lots 328 Artcurial 7.2.14 $1,017,398 and S121 Mecum 20.8.16 NS).*
1969	**Ghibli SS Spider**	(Ghia)	AM115S1005	L	800-1.000.000 USD	755.412	920.000	862.868	15-01-17	Kissimmee	S185	**Mec**
	*See lot S107.1 Mecum 4.11.16.*
1970	**Ghibli 4.7 Spider**	(Ghia)	AM115S1161	L	500-700.000 EUR	477.829	595.479	560.240	10-02-17	Paris	108	**Art** F489
	*Originally finished in gold with mustard interior, the car was sold new to the USA. The mechanicals were rebuilt between 2003 and 2010 and the original automatic transmission was replaced with a manual unit. Currently finished in blue. The interior appear original (see lot 146 RM 31.10.12 $415,019).*
1970	**Ghibli 4.7 Spider**	(Ghia)	AM115S1079	L	975-1.100.000 EUR		NS		27-05-17	Villa Erba	154	**RMS**
	*Black with black interior; less than 50,000 kms covered (see lot 226 RM 13.8.04 $125,400).*
1970	**Indy 4.2**	(Vignale)	AM116670	L	35-40.000 GBP	43.680	53.534	48.581	12-10-16	Duxford	97	**H&H**
	*Dark red with beige interior; some restoration works carried out in the 1990s. Engine overhauled in more recent years.*
1970	**Indy 4.2**	(Vignale)	AM116272	L	70-100.000 EUR	72.378	88.566	80.500	15-10-16	Salzburg	439	**Dor**
	*Dark metallic grey with black leather interior; overhauled at unspecified date.*
1974	**Indy 4.9**	(Vignale)	AM116492044	L	35-40.000 EUR	97.312*	121.003*	114.240*	25-11-16	Milan	244	**RMS**
	*Light blue with black interior; 69,819 kms. From the Duemila Ruote collection.*

F489: 1970 Maserati Ghibli 4.7 Spider (Ghia)

F490: 1971 Maserati Indy America 4.2 (Vignale)

Year	Model	(Bodybuilder)	Chassis no.	Steering	Estimate	Hammer price £	Hammer price $	Hammer price €	Date	Place	Lot	Auc. H.
1972	Indy 4.7	(Vignale)	AM116471228	L	80-100.000 USD		NS		22-04-17	Arlington	NA	WoA
{colspan 13} Originally finished in maroon with white leather interior, the car was sold new in Italy and later exported to the USA. The body was refinished in the present blue livery in the 1990s. Recently serviced.
| 1971 | Indy America 4.2 | (Vignale) | AM1161056 | L | 50-80.000 EUR | 46.433* | 60.422* | 54.050* | 21-05-17 | SPA-Francorch. | 56 | Bon F490 |
Metallic blue with beige interior; paintwork and interior redone. From the Swiss Castle Collection.
| 1971 | Indy 4.9 | (Vignale) | AM116491208 | L | 175-225.000 USD | | NS | | 19-08-17 | Monterey | F135.1 | Mec |
Restored in 2017.
| 1973 | Bora | (Italdesign) | AM117660 | L | 170-250.000 EUR | 143.676 | 175.812 | 159.800 | 15-10-16 | Salzburg | 447 | Dor |
Green with tan interior; sold new to the USA and imported into Germany in 2003 by its sole owner. 33,000 kms covered. In original condition except for the paintwork redone at unspecified date.
| 1975 | Bora 4.9 | (Italdesign) | AM11449US930 | L | 160-190.000 USD | | NS | | 04-11-16 | Dallas | S145 | Mec |
Dark blue with light grey interior; sold new to the USA. Recently serviced.
| 1973 | Bora 4.7 | (Italdesign) | AM117286 | L | 155-175.000 EUR | 171.727* | 213.535* | 201.600* | 25-11-16 | Milan | 326 | RMS |
Silver with dark brown interior. From the Duemila Ruote collection.
| 1975 | Bora 4.9 | (Italdesign) | AM11749US916 | L | 175-225.000 USD | 129.402* | 159.500* | 149.499* | 19-01-17 | Phoenix | 129 | RMS |
Dark metallic blue with blue leather interior; 38,690 miles covered. Body repainted and interior re-upholstered.
| 1974 | Bora 4.9 | (Italdesign) | AM11749764 | L | 180-220.000 USD | 107.501* | 132.000* | 124.146* | 21-01-17 | Scottsdale | 153 | G&Co |
Gold with tan interior; sold new to the USA; major service in 2016.
| 1973 | Bora 4.9 | (Italdesign) | AM11749562 | L | 170-200.000 EUR | 152.884 | 191.117 | 179.200 | 08-02-17 | Paris | 148 | RMS F491 |
Black with red leather interior; sold new to the USA, the car was recently reimported into Europe (see lots 26 Gooding & Company 29.1.16 $187,000 and 125 Coys 6.8.16 NS).
| 1973 | Bora 4.9 | (Italdesign) | AM117634 | L | 185-225.000 EUR | | NS | | 02-07-17 | Monaco | 165 | Art |
Yellow with original black interior; sold new to the USA, in 1992 the car was imported into the Netherlands and subsequently restored.
| 1974 | Bora 4.9 | (Italdesign) | AM11749US762 | L | 130-170.000 USD | 108.974 | 140.250 | 119.493 | 18-08-17 | Carmel | 9 | Bon |
Metallic gold with saddle leather interior; described as in very good overall condition; last serviced in 2016.
| 1974 | Bora 4.9 | (Italdesign) | AM11749US766 | L | 175-225.000 USD | 145.299* | 187.000* | 159.324* | 19-08-17 | Monterey | 266 | RMS |
Metallic copper with bone interior; sold new to the USA; in largely original condition except for the bumpers replaced with European market items; 15,129 original miles.
| 1975 | Khamsin | (Bertone) | AM120192 | L | 90-120.000 EUR | | NS | | 30-10-16 | Paris | 171 | Art |
White; automatic transmission.
| 1975 | Khamsin | (Bertone) | AM120096 | L | 90-105.000 EUR | 95.404* | 118.630* | 112.000* | 25-11-16 | Milan | 544 | RMS |
Grey with black interior; 38,191 kms. According to the sale catalogue the chassis number stamp does not appear to be original. Furthermore, another Khamsin claims this serial number. This car is believed to be chassis AM120 032. From the Duemila Ruote collection.
| 1978 | Khamsin | (Bertone) | AM120US1258 | L | 130-160.000 EUR | 141.888 | 178.289 | 166.750 | 09-02-17 | Paris | 403 | Bon F492 |
Silver with red leather interior; sold new to the USA, the car was reimported into Italy in 1999 and returned to European aesthetical specification. Engine rebuilt in 2016.
| 1979 | Khamsin | (Bertone) | AM120334 | L | 135-185.000 EUR | 113.470 | 141.408 | 133.040 | 10-02-17 | Paris | 139 | Art |
Metallic blue with blue leather interior; since 1983 in the current ownership; in good overall condition; just over 68,000 kms on the odometer.
| 1979 | Khamsin | (Bertone) | AM120US1058 | L | 160-180.000 EUR | 144.448 | 189.888 | 160.000 | 05-08-17 | Schloss Dyck | 242 | Coy |
Black with tobacco leather interior; sold new to the USA and later reimported into Europe and converted to European specification.
| 1978 | Khamsin | (Bertone) | AM1201224 | L | 140-180.000 USD | 115.385* | 148.500* | 126.522* | 18-08-17 | Carmel | 103 | Bon |
Tobacco with light brown interior; sold new to the USA; 23,332 miles covered. In recent years body repainted and fitted with European bumpers. Recently serviced.
| 1976 | Khamsin | (Bertone) | AM120210 | L | 175-225.000 USD | 115.385* | 148.500* | 126.522* | 18-08-17 | Carmel | 71 | Bon |
Bronze with maroon interior; European market version; one owner; 28,000 original kms.
| 1973 | Merak 3.0 | (Italdesign) | AM1220526 | L | 75-85.000 EUR | 62.344 | 76.866 | 69.000 | 07-10-16 | Zoute | 40 | Bon |
Gold with black leather interior; restored in Italy in 2013. Engine serviced (see lot 128 Coys 14.5.16 $79,663).
| 1978 | Merak SS | (Italdesign) | AM122A1718 | L | 20-40.000 GBP | 36.563 | 46.285 | 42.446 | 12-11-16 | Birmingham | 331 | SiC |
Red with blue and black interior; described as in highly original condition. 15,298 kms on the odometer. It requires servicing prior to use.
| 1978 | Merak SS | (Italdesign) | AM122AUS2284 | L | NA | 41.366 | 51.000 | 47.981 | 19-11-16 | Anaheim | F166 | Mec |
Red with black interior; believed to have only 32,000 original kms.
| 1975 | Merak SS | (Italdesign) | AM122A1238 | L | 45-55.000 EUR | 62.012* | 77.110* | 72.800* | 25-11-16 | Milan | 590 | RMS |
Dark blue with beige interior; 47,420 kms. From the Duemila Ruote collection (see lot 790 Brooks 4.12.97 NS).
| 1973 | Merak | (Italdesign) | AM1220116 | L | 10-15.000 EUR | 87.772* | 109.140* | 103.040* | 25-11-16 | Milan | 650 | RMS |
Dark blue; Group 4 prepared. From the Duemila Ruote collection.

F491: 1973 Maserati Bora 4.9 (Italdesign)

F492: 1978 Maserati Khamsin (Bertone)

Year	Model	(Bodybuilder)	Chassis no.	Steering	Estimate	Hammer price £	$	€	Date	Place	Lot	Auc. H.
1980	**Merak SS**	(Italdesign)	AM122AUS2668	L	60-70.000 EUR	**48.786**	**60.762**	**57.000**	08-04-17	Essen	202	Coy
Dark blue with cream interior; 46,000 miles on the odometer. Recently serviced.												
1984	**Quattroporte III 4.9**	(Italdesign)	AM330493520	L	20-30.000 EUR	**14.678***	**18.444***	**17.250***	09-02-17	Paris	351	Bon
Blue with habana leather interior; 95,000 kms covered. Automatic transmission.												
1986	**Quattroporte III 4.9**	(Italdesign)	305830	L	50-60.000 USD	**34.575**	**44.000**	**39.380**	24-06-17	Santa Monica	154	RMS F493
Black; body repainted (see lot 101 Bonhams 28.1.16 $39,600).												
1983	**Quattroporte III 4.9**	(Italdesign)	330493140	L	20-30.000 EUR		**NS**		02-07-17	Monaco	164	Art
In good overall condition; 26,000 kms covered.												
1978	**Kyalami 4.9**	(Frua)	AM129490094	L	20-30.000 EUR	**71.553***	**88.973***	**84.000***	25-11-16	Milan	273	RMS
Grey with white interior; 49,617 kms. From the Duemila Ruote collection.												
1978	**Kyalami 4.9**	(Frua)	AM129490190	L	65-90.000 EUR	**61.161**	**90.267**	**69.554**	02-07-17	Monaco	166	Art
Dark red; restored in the late 1980s; major service in 2014-2015.												
1988	**Biturbo 2.5l**		180242	R	6-8.000 GBP		**NS**		08-10-16	Ascot	310	Coy
Ivory with tan interior; in good overall condition. 29,700 miles covered (see lot 102 Coys 16.4.16 NS).												
1989	**Spyder**	(Zagato)	102031	L	8-12.000 EUR	**8.979**	**11.098**	**10.336**	19-03-17	Fontainebleau	240	Ose
Red; since 1996 in the current ownership. Engine overhauled in 2006.												
1990	**Shamal**		300060	L	125-175.000 USD		**NS**		18-08-17	Carmel	80	Bon
Black with black leather interior; since 1994 in the current ownership; 6,200 kms on the odometer; recently serviced.												
1999	**Ghibli GT**		400235	R	10-12.000 GBP	**16.240**	**19.904**	**18.062**	12-10-16	Duxford	51	H&H
Blue with red leather interior; 2.8-litre engine with automatic transmission. Recently serviced (see lot 38 H & H 11.7.15 $15,641).												
1994	**Ghibli 2.0**		360313	L	18-26.000 EUR		**NS**		05-11-16	Lyon	225	Agu
Metallic blue with grey leather interior; in good overall condition.												
2001	**3200 GTA**	(Italdesign)	001659	L	45-65.000 EUR		**NS**		22-04-17	Bagatelle	134	Agu
Grey with biscuit leather interior; 5,600 kms covered. Automatic transmission.												
2004	**4200 GT Cambiocorsa**		13419	R	14-18.000 GBP	**15.680**	**19.183**	**18.157**	04-03-17	Brooklands	220	His
Described as in very good overall condition; recently serviced.												
2004	**4200 Spyder Cambiocorsa**		13513	L	NQ	**14.425**	**18.000**	**16.657**	25-03-17	Kansas City	S67.1	Mec
Blue with tan leather interior; 52,000 actual miles.												
2004	**4200 Spyder**		11697	L	NQ	**23.846***	**29.700***	**27.859***	08-04-17	Palm Beach	461	B/J
Red with black interior; 32,580 actual miles. Automatic transmission.												
2004	**4200 Spyder Cambiocorsa**		11054	L	NQ	**18.105***	**22.550***	**21.152***	08-04-17	Palm Beach	54	B/J
Silver with black interior; 25,600 actual miles.												
2004	**MC12**		12100	L	1.100-1.300.000 EUR	**2.575.904***	**3.203.021***	**3.024.000***	25-11-16	Milan	601	RMS F494
Pearl white and blue with blue and black interior; sold new in Italy. Less than 6.000 kms covered. Recently serviced. From the Duemila Ruote collection.												
2007	**MC12 Corsa**		29630	L	2.300-2.500.000 USD		**NS**		19-08-17	Monterey	S85	Mec
Blue with blue interior; one of 12 examples built.												

MATFORD (F) (1934-1940)

Year	Model		Chassis no.	Steering	Estimate	£	$	€	Date	Place	Lot	Auc. H.
1937	**V8 72 cabriolet**		799	L	18-24.000 EUR	**16.480***	**20.319***	**18.240***	07-10-16	Chateau-sur-Epte	30	Art
Restored many years ago and fitted with a later engine probably from a Vedette. Body built by Antem probably. From the early 1960s in the Andre Weber Collection.												

MATHIS (F) (1910-1950)

1933	**TY berline**		651569	R	12-17.000 EUR		**NS**		01-05-17	Obenheim	303	Ose
Black and red; restored. Engine rebuilt.												

MATRA (F) (1965-1983)

1966	**Bonnet Djet V Luxe**		10476	L	35-55.000 EUR	**34.416***	**41.809***	**38.280***	30-10-16	Paris	119	Art
Blue; 23,000 kms on the odometer. Two owners. Sunroof.												

F493: 1986 Maserati Quattroporte III 4.9 (Italdesign)

F494: 2004 Maserati MC12

Year	Model	(Bodybuilder)	Chassis no.	Steering	Estimate	Hammer price £	Hammer price $	Hammer price €	Sale Date	Sale Place	Lot	Auc. H.
1966	**Bonnet Djet VS**		20042	L	30-40.000 EUR	**32.315**	**39.942**	**37.200**	19-03-17	Fontainebleau	228	**Ose**
	Light grey with red interior; engine rebuilt in 2016.											
1970	**M530 LX**		008584	L	15-3.000 EUR	**17.173***	**21.353***	**20.160***	25-11-16	Milan	522	**RMS**
	Yellow with black interior; 74,474 kms. From the Duemila Ruote collection.											

MAXWELL (USA) (1904-1925)

Year	Model	(Bodybuilder)	Chassis no.	Steering	Estimate	£	$	€	Date	Place	Lot	Auc. H.
1923	**Model 25 touring**		60622	L	25-35.000 USD	**8.921***	**11.000***	**9.874***	07-10-16	Hershey	262	**RMS**
	Blue with black fenders; older restoration.											

MAYBACH (D) (1921-1941)

Year	Model	(Bodybuilder)	Chassis no.	Steering	Estimate	£	$	€	Date	Place	Lot	Auc. H.
1939	**SW38 Spezial Four Door Cabriolet (Petera & Sohne)**		2240	L	750-950.000 EUR	**572.443**	**719.304**	**672.750**	09-02-17	Paris	368	**Bon** **F495**
	Imported into the USA after WWII, the car was formerly owned by the Imperial Palace Museum Collection which had it restored and finished in the present blue livery.											

MAZDA (J) (1960-)

Year	Model	(Bodybuilder)	Chassis no.	Steering	Estimate	£	$	€	Date	Place	Lot	Auc. H.
1970	**Cosmo Sport 110S coupé**		L10A10512	R	65-95.000 USD	**35.306**	**44.000**	**41.395**	11-02-17	Boca Raton	166	**TFA**
	White with black interior; described as in largely original condition.											
1967	**Cosmo Sport 110S coupé**		L10A10055	R	65-95.000 EUR	**76.072***	**98.990***	**88.550***	21-05-17	SPA-Francorch.	84	**Bon**
	White; full restoration recently completed in Japan.											
1968	**Cosmo Sport 110S coupé**		L10A10322	R	110-130.000 USD		**NS**		24-06-17	Santa Monica	177	**RMS**
	White with black and chequered interior.											
1969	**Cosmo Sport L10B**		L10B10618	R	110-130.000 USD	**79.060***	**101.750***	**86.691***	18-08-17	Pebble Beach	8	**G&Co**
	White with black and white houndstooth cloth interior; for over 40 years with its first owner in Japan; imported into the USA in 2014; 28,400 believed original kms.											
1979	**RX7**		539851	L	15-18.000 EUR		**NS**		14-01-17	Maastricht	247	**Coy**
	Red; one owner and 25,000 miles covered. Wankel rotary engine.											
1989	**767B**		767003	R	1.800-2.400.000 USD	**1.439.550**	**1.750.000**	**1.649.200**	10-03-17	Amelia Island	23	**G&Co** **F496**
	Ex-Works car, it raced the Le Mans 24 Hours in 1989 (12th overall and 3rd in the GTP class) and 1990 (20th overall and 1st in the IMSA GTP class). Prepared in the UK in 2014 for the Spa Classic; restored in Germany in 2015-16 to 1990 specification. In ready to race condition.											

McFARLAN (USA) (1910-1928)

Year	Model	(Bodybuilder)	Chassis no.	Steering	Estimate	£	$	€	Date	Place	Lot	Auc. H.
1927	**Line 8 boattail**		4H18568(engine)	L	70-90.000 USD	**45.305***	**58.300***	**51.881***	03-10-16	Philadelphia	205	**Bon**
	Black and yellow; restored in the early 1970s and fitted with the present new body. From the Natural History Museum of Los Angeles.											

McLAREN (GB) (1963-)

Year	Model	(Bodybuilder)	Chassis no.	Steering	Estimate	£	$	€	Date	Place	Lot	Auc. H.
1966	**M1B**		3012	R	275-325.000 USD		**NS**		10-03-17	Amelia Island	39	**G&Co**
	Raced in period by Peter Revson and Skip Barber at Can-Am and USRRC events. Returned to race-ready specification in the early 2000s. Built with Ford engine, the car is currently fitted with a 358 Chevrolet engine.											
1965	**M1B**		3004	R	200-250.000 GBP		**NS**		30-06-17	Goodwood	248	**Bon**
	Red with white stripes; raced at several Can-Am events until 1970. First restored in the late 1980s and raced at historic events; restored again in the 2000s and fitted with a new "small block" engine; bought in 2015 by the current owner, restored and fitted with a new Hewland LG500 gearbox and a 5.7-litre wet-sump Chevrolet V8 engine. In ready to race condition.											
1979	**M24B Indy**		001	M	300-400.000 USD	**166.667***	**214.500***	**182.754***	18-08-17	Monterey	122	**RMS**
	One of two Works cars (chassis 001 and 002) driven by Johnny Rutherford during the 1979 CART season. Backup car at Indy 500. Later it was used for promotional purpose and then sold to private hands. In the 2000s it was bought by Rutherford and restored to 1979 Indy Budweiser livery. In need of appropriate preparation for vintage racing events.											
1995	**F1**		1048044	C	Refer Dpt.	**12.136.740**	**15.620.000**	**13.308.240**	18-08-17	Carmel	73	**Bon** **TOP TEN**
	Silver with black and grey leather interior; one owner; 9,600 miles on the odometer. Last serviced in July 2017. The first fully federalized, U.S. road legal McLaren F1 (all of the Ameritech conversion items have been removed from the vehicle, leaving it in its original specification. Every item that was used to federalize the car has been saved and accompanies the sale).											
2012	**MP4-12C High Sport**		001505	L	950-1.200.000 USD	**677.408**	**825.000**	**773.768**	15-01-17	Kissimmee	F183.1	**Mec**
	Finished in the silver, black and red Vodafone livery; alcantara and leather interior. 208 miles. One of 10 examples built (see lot S148 Mecum 23.1.16 NS).											
2012	**MP4-12C**		001763	L	135-165.000 USD		**NS**		11-03-17	Amelia Island	18	**Mot**
	Silver with grey leather interior; two owners; 11,000 actual miles.											

F495: 1939 Maybach SW38 Spezial Four Door Cabriolet (Petera & Sohne)

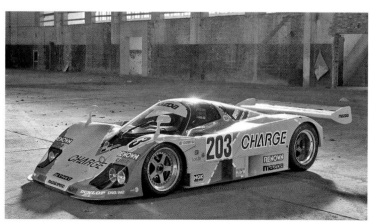

F496: 1989 Mazda 767B

Year	Model	(Bodybuilder)	Chassis no.	Steering	Estimate	Hammer price £	$	€	Date	Place	Lot	Auc. H.

F497: 2015 McLaren P1   F498: 1911 Mercedes 28/50 PS tourer

Year	Model	Chassis no.	Steering	Estimate	£	$	€	Date	Place	Lot	Auc. H.
2012	MP4-12C	1555	R	90-110.000 GBP	96.750	126.694	108.021	29-07-17	Silverstone	409	SiC
	Blue with red leather interior; one owner; 22,880 miles covered; recently serviced.										
2012	MP4-12C High Sport	001505	L	950-1.200.000 USD		NS		19-08-17	Monterey	S128	Mec
	See lot F183.1 Mecum 15.1.17.										
2015	P1	000209	L	2.000-2.300.000 USD	1.968.071*	2.392.500*	2.254.692*	10-03-17	Amelia Island	26	G&Co F497
	Blue and black with red seats with black inserts; just over 1,100 miles covered. Consignor's proceeds for the benefit of the Rose-Hulman Institute of Technology in Terre Haute, Indiana.										
2016	P1 GTR	100033	L	3.200-3.600.000 EUR		NS		27-05-17	Villa Erba	157	RMS
	Black; one owner and 360 kms covered. Converted to road-legal specification by Lanzante.										
2015	P1	00308	L	2.000-2.200.000 USD		NS		19-08-17	Pebble Beach	165	G&Co
	Ice silver with black alcantara interior; one owner; 1,800 miles covered.										
2015	P1	00291	L	2.200-2.500.000 USD		NS		19-08-17	Monterey	S97	Mec
	Silver with black interior; less than 1,000 miles covered.										
2014	650S Chantilly Edition coupé	004072	L	230-330.000 EUR		NS		03-09-16	Chantilly	21	Bon
	Metallic pearl white and matt black with black alcantara interior; one-off. One owner and 28 kms covered.										
2016	675LT	675290	L	335-375.000 USD		NS		24-06-17	Santa Monica	205	RMS
	Grey; 730 original miles; one of 500 examples built.										

MERCEDES (D) (1886-1926)

Year	Model	Chassis no.	Steering	Estimate	£	$	€	Date	Place	Lot	Auc. H.
1911	28/50 PS tourer	11138	R	300-400.000 GBP	359.900	467.078	407.515	30-06-17	Goodwood	220	Bon F498
	White with red interior; in running condition. Originally bodied in France by Million-Guiet and sold to the UK in 1912. Since 1957 in the same family ownership. Restored in the early 1960s and fitted with the present new body built by Robinson's of Norwich, UK.										
1926	24/100/140 PS phaeton (Erdmann/Rossi)	36010	L	275-375.000 USD	564.102	726.000	618.552	18-08-17	Pebble Beach	12	G&Co F499
	Pale yellow with red interior; delivered new to the USA to the German actor Emil Jannings; cosmetic restoration carried out in the 1950 or 1960s; from the mid-1960 for over 30 years in the same ownership; stored for many years; not running.										

MERCEDES-BENZ (D) (1926-)

Year	Model	Chassis no.	Steering	Estimate	£	$	€	Date	Place	Lot	Auc. H.
1928	S tourenwagen (Erdmann/Rossi)	35323	L	5.000-6.000.000 USD	3.904.381	4.812.500	4.510.756	19-01-17	Scottsdale	54	Bon F500
	Red with black leather interior; sold new to the USA. Restored to concours condition in the mid-1990s and later reimported into Europe. Interior refurbished in recent years.										
1928	S 680 torpedo-sport (Saoutchik)	35949	L	6.500-8.000.000 EUR		NS		27-05-17	Villa Erba	144	RMS
	Car displayed at the 1929 New York Motor Show; fully restored in the USA by Paul Russell & Company; the 2012 Pebble Beach Best of Show winner(see lots 52 Christie's 17.8.06 $3,645,000 and 155 Bonhams 2.9.08 $3,363,388).										
1928	S 26/120/180 tourer	35947	L	3.500-4.000.000 USD		NS		18-08-17	Monterey	121	RMS
	Cream with red leather interior; bought new by Al Jolson who retained it until 1947 when it was acquired by Brooks Stevens in whose collection it remained until 1990. Restored in the early 1990s. Recent mechanical and cosmetic freshening.										

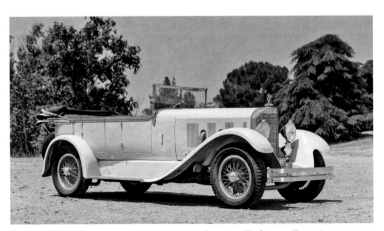

F499: 1926 Mercedes 24/100/140 PS phaeton (Erdmann/Rossi)   F500: 1928 Mercedes-Benz S tourenwagen (Erdmann/Rossi)

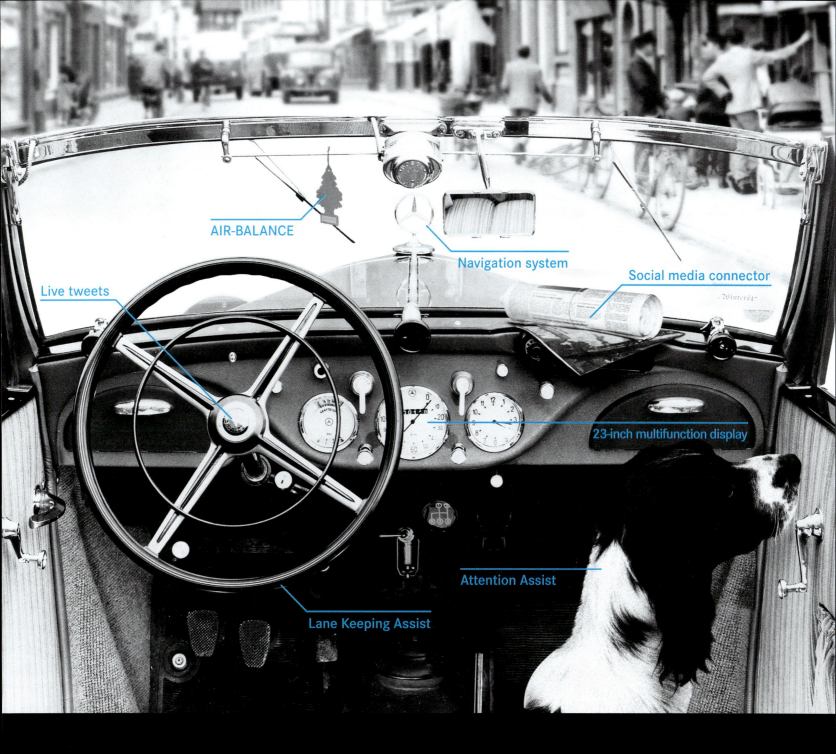

Always at the cutting edge.

Year	Model	(Bodybuilder)	Chassis no.	Steering	Estimate	Hammer price £	$	€	Sale Date	Place	Lot	Auc. H.

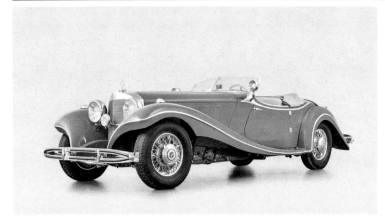

F501: 1935 Mercedes-Benz 500 K Roadster

F502: 1936 Mercedes-Benz 500 K offener tourenwagen

1928 S sports tourer (Glaser) — 35920 — R — 5.000-6.000.000 USD — NS — 19-08-17 Pebble Beach 154 **G&Co**
Believed to be a one-off example, the car was sold new in Germany. In the late 1930s it was imported into the UK and probably in the 1950s into the USA. Since 1964 in the same family ownership, it was first restored in the late 1960s and finished in the present yellow and black livery with black leather interior. Restored again between 2013 and 2015.

1931 370 S Mannheim sport cabriolet — U87058 — L — 350-450.000 USD — 268.752* — 330.000* — 310.365* — 20-01-17 Phoenix 210 **RMS**
White with black interior; restored in the 1970s. Stored for several years it requires mechanical service prior to use. Since 1966 in the Jules Barsotti family ownership.

1934 380K cabriolet C — U953429736 — L — 650-750.000 USD — NS — 17-08-17 Monterey 56 **WoA**
Sold new in Germany and later imported into the USA; well-maintained restoration.

1938 200 V roadster — 189478 — L — 50-70.000 USD — 143.334* — 176.000* — 165.528* — 20-01-17 Phoenix 208 **RMS**
Two tone grey with red leather interior; bought in 1979 by the current owner Jules Barsotti and subsequently restored. Stored for several years, it requires recommissioning prior to use. Only known survivor of 31 examples built.

1935 500 K Roadster — 105380 — L — 5.000-7.000.000 EUR — 4.457.354 — 5.921.097 — 5.290.000 — 03-09-16 Chantilly 16 **Bon**
Red with tan leather interior; cosmetically restored in 1991 in the USA. Exhibited at the 1935 Berlin Motor Show and sold new to Hans Friedrich Prym, at unspecified date the car was stolen overnight from the Prym premises and resurfaced in the USA in the 1970s. Following some ownership changes, in 2012 it was exhibited at the Techno Classica Essen show where it was seen by the Prym family heirs who later were able to get back it. Offered from the Prym family (see RM lots 69 8.3.03 NS and 247 20.8.11 $3,767,500). **F501**

1936 500 K offener tourenwagen — 123724 — L — Refer Dpt. — 1.196.580* — 1.540.000* — 1.312.080* — 19-08-17 Monterey 246 **RMS**
Medium green with tan leather interior; imported into the USA in 1951 and remained in the same family ownership until 2014 when it was bought by the current owner. Recent full restoration. **F502**

1938 170 V cabriolet A — 414843 — L — 130-160.000 USD — 90.486* — 110.000* — 103.664* — 11-03-17 Amelia Island 246 **RMS**
Black and red with red interior; restored in the 1990s.

1940 230 cabriolet B — 446561 — L — 180-210.000 USD — 127.626 — 156.750 — 146.984 — 18-01-17 Scottsdale 42 **WoA**
Aqua green and cream with beige leather interior; restoration completed in 2009 (see lot 420 Barrett-Jackson 9.4.16 $145,200).

1938 230 saloon — 409306 — R — 130-160.000 GBP — NS — 18-02-17 London 362 **Coy**
Maroon with light brown leather interior; stored in 1972, the car has recently undergone a full five-year restoration.

1937 230N roadster — 155124 — L — 200-250.000 USD — NS — 24-06-17 Santa Monica 178 **RMS**
Two-tone blue with light grey leather interior; restored.

1939 540 K Spezial Roadster — 408383 — L — 7.400-8.400.000 USD — 5.375.040 — 6.600.000 — 6.207.300 — 20-01-17 Phoenix 258 **RMS**
One-off originally finished in black and sold new to Rolf Horn, Berlin; discovered after WWII in East Berlin, it was moved to Russia in 1953 circa. In 1964 it was bought by Al Johansson and imported into Sweden. Imported into the USA in the mid-1970s. Restored between 2011 and 2012 and finished in the present dark blue livery with blue leather interior (see RM lots 232 20.8.11 $4.620.000 and 132 16.8.13 $7.480.000). **F503**

1936 540 K cabriolet B — 130921 — L — 600-750.000 USD — 574.586* — 698.500* — 658.266* — 10-03-17 Amelia Island 135 **RMS**
Red with tan leather interior; cosmetically restored some years ago. From the Orin Smith collection.

1941 540 K cabriolet B — 408429 — L — 900-1.300.000 USD — 722.222 — 929.500 — 791.934 — 18-08-17 Carmel 29 **Bon**
Red with light grey leather interior; imported into the USA soon after WWII; bought in 1985 by T.J. Day and subjected to a full restoration completed in 1988.

1937 540 K cabriolet A — 154146 — L — Refer Dpt. — 2.008.545* — 2.585.000* — 2.202.420* — 19-08-17 Monterey 257 **RMS**
Burgundy with biscuit leather interior; delivered new in Germany and subsequently imported into the USA; acquired a few years ago by the current owner and subjected to a restoration completed in 2014. Engine previously rebuilt in Germany (see lots 121 Coys 12.5.12 NS, 139 RM 15.1.15 NS, and 31 Bonhams 5.6.16 NS). **F504**

F503: 1939 Mercedes-Benz 540 K Spezial Roadster

F504: 1937 Mercedes-Benz 540 K cabriolet A

CELEBRATING **30** YEARS

My customers and I have shared passion and enthusiasm for the world's most exciting and beautiful cars for 30 years. Our clients appreciate our expertise, discretion and dependability in buying and selling their classic automobiles. Please feel free to contact us and trust in our experience and global network.

Yours, Axel Schuette

AXEL SCHUETTE FINE CARS

best cars. best expertise. best service. since 1987

Aston Martin DB4GT Zagato, Le Mans 1961, sold by **AXEL SCHUETTE** FINE CARS

BENTLEY // BMW // FERRARI // LAMBORGHINI // MASERATI // MERCEDES-BENZ // PORSCHE

AXEL SCHUETTE FINE CARS • Germany • Fon +49 5202 72000 • www.axelschuette.de • info@axelschuette.de

F505: 1938 Mercedes-Benz 320 cabriolet B

F506: 1953 Mercedes-Benz 300 saloon

Year	Model (Bodybuilder)	Chassis no.	Steering	Estimate	Hammer price £	$	€	Sale Date	Place	Lot	Auc. H.
1938	**320 cabriolet B**	435053	L	350-450.000 EUR	**303.346**	**381.170**	**356.500**	09-02-17	Paris	374	**Bon** F505
Metallic blue with black wings and beige leather interior; concours-quality restoration carried out in 2010 (see lot 120 Bonhams 19.3.16 NS).											
1938	**320 cabriolet A**	191150	L	525-650.000 USD	**286.325**	**368.500**	**313.962**	18-08-17	Carmel	49	**Bon**
Dark blue with grey interior; reimported into Germany in 2007 and subsequently restored. New body (see Bonhams lots 252 15.8.14 $517,000 and 172 10.3.16 NS).											
1951	**170 S cabriolet B**	13604332451	L	100-120.000 GBP		**NS**		12-10-16	Duxford	130	**H&H**
Black and cream with cream interior; restored at unspecified date.											
1953	**220 saloon**	1870110223453	L	80-100.000 USD	**66.932***	**82.500***	**77.327***	19-01-17	Phoenix	122	**RMS**
Light blue with grey wings; bought in the early 1960s by its second owner who completed in 2012 a 20-year period restoration (see lot 103 Bonhams 28.1.16 $66,000).											
1959	**300d saloon**	1890104120011696	L	50-70.000 USD	**29.918**	**38.500**	**34.261**	03-10-16	Philadelphia	209	**Bon**
Black with grey cloth interior; in good driving order. Automatic transmission.											
1958	**300d saloon**	1890108500366	L	45-60.000 USD	**23.885***	**30.250***	**27.044***	06-10-16	Hershey	135	**RMS**
Black with red leather interior; in original condition. Automatic transmission.											
1956	**300c saloon**	1860176500835	L	75-100.000 USD	**45.243***	**55.000***	**51.832***	10-03-17	Amelia Island	68	**G&Co**
Strawberry red; restored in the 1980s, the car is in good overall condition. Full-lenght sliding sunroof; automatic transmission (see lot 62 Gooding & Company 16.1.15 $85,250).											
1953	**300 saloon**	1860110030853	L	40-60.000 EUR	**60.106***	**88.710***	**68.354***	02-07-17	Monaco	201	**Art** F506
Olive green; in good driving order.											
1956	**300c cabriolet**	A1860336500040	L	120-150.000 USD	**81.891**	**102.300**	**92.213**	05-11-16	Hilton Head	187	**AA**
Blue with tan interior; from the 1970s in the same family ownership. Several restoration and maintenance works carried out over the years.											
1954	**300 cabriolet**	1880103500280	L	NQ	**344.898**	**423.500**	**398.302**	21-01-17	Scottsdale	8171	**R&S**
Black with dark red leather interior; restored many years ago. Sold new to the USA.											
1953	**300b cabriolet D**	W186014	L	130-150.000 EUR	**127.210**	**159.845**	**149.500**	09-02-17	Paris	402	**Bon**
Imported into Spain from the USA in 2004 and subjected to a full restoration completed in 2004. 1,500 kms covered since the rebuild.											
1953	**300 S coupé**	0019653	L	200-250.000 GBP	**292.700**	**388.793**	**347.376**	03-09-16	Beaulieu	476	**Bon** F507
Silver with red leather interior; restored circa 15 years ago. First owner King Hussein of Jordan; since 1999 with the current, third owner (see lot 177 Brooks 7.8.99 $105,156).											
1954	**300 S coupé**	1880113500356	L	NA	**430.544**	**572.000**	**511.025**	03-09-16	Auburn	45	**WoA**
Grey beige with green leather interior; an older restoration, it is described as still in very good overall condition. Sold new to the USA (see lot 145 Bonhams 10.3.16 $429,000).											
1955	**300 S coupé**	1880115500037	L	250-300.000 USD	**246.356***	**302.500***	**284.501***	20-01-17	Phoenix	209	**RMS**
Metallic strawberry with tan leather interior; bought in 1979 by the current owner Jules Barsotti and restored in the 1980s. Stored for several years, it requires some mechanical works prior to use.											
1955	**300 S coupé**	1880115500020	L	400-550.000 USD		**NS**		09-03-17	Amelia Island	123	**Bon**
Black with red leather interior; cosmetically restored in the 2000s, engine rebuilt within the past 18 months (see lots 129 Bonhams 9.2.08 $216,969, 156 Coys 9.8.08 NS and 34 H & H 5.12.12 NS).											
1953	**300 S coupé**	1880113500337	L	340-440.000 EUR	**268.156**	**341.223**	**305.400**	24-06-17	Wien	367	**Dor**
White with green-grey leather interior; sold new to the USA; bought in 1992 by the current owner and reimported into Germany; restored between 1993 and 1996. It ran the 2013 Mille Miglia Storica.											

F507: 1953 Mercedes-Benz 300 S coupé

F508: 1953 Mercedes-Benz 300 S roadster

Nothing but the best.

Engine overhaul, bodywork repair or upholstery, our specialists face every job. Engine dynamometer and frame straightener ensure perfection down to the last detail, because Kienle-restored vehicles are compared with the best - with Mercedes-Benz.

KIENLE
Automobiltechnik

The World Of Classic Cars - Restoration And Trading

Main Sponsor of the Mille Miglia

D-71254 Heimerdingen/Stuttgart · Max-Planck-Str. 4 · Germany
Tel. (49) 71 52 / 901 63-0 · Fax (49) 71 52 / 901 63-115
www.kienle.com · email: info@kienle.com

Please ask for a portrait of our company available as brochure or DVD for € 10,- each.
Hours of business: Weekdays 8 am - 6 pm and Saturdays 9 am - 2 pm

As the leading specialist for the restoration of Mercedes-Benz vehicles we have been setting quality standards for partial and complete restorations, repairs and maintenance for over three decades now.
In addition, we own one of the world's largest stock of original parts and high-quality re-manufactured parts, and prepare expert appraisals for Mercedes-Benz vehicles.

We are looking for classic Mercedes-Benz vehicles. Offer us your vintage car, we guarantee a professional brokerage service or buy directly.

Visit our large showroom with over 50 classic cars for sale!
e.g. 300 SL Coupé and Roadster, 320 Cabriolet A, 300 S Cabriolet

Year	Model	(Bodybuilder)	Chassis No.	Steering	Estimate	Hammer Price £	Hammer Price $	Hammer Price €	Date	Place	Lot	Auc. H.
1955	**300 Sc coupé**		1880145500018	L	400-500.000 USD	333.333	429.000	365.508	18-08-17	Pebble Beach	34	G&Co
	Originally finished in silver with black interior; sold new to J. Paul Getty; since 1964 for over 50 years with its second owner; unrestored; less than 75,000 miles on the odometer; to be recommissioned prior to use.											
1953	**300 S cabriolet**		1880100018053	L	550-700.000 EUR	586.753	717.991	652.600	15-10-16	Salzburg	448	Dor
	Ivory yellow with original red leather interior; restored between 2002 and 2004. For over 50 years with its previous owner in Austria.											
1953	**300 S roadster**		1880120017053	L	400-500.000 USD	416.236*	506.000*	476.854*	10-03-17	Amelia Island	118	RMS **F508**
	Ivory with brown leather interior; restored many years ago and subsequently always well maintained. From the Orin Smith collection.											
1954	**220 coupé**		1870124500254	L	90-120.000 GBP	95.000	127.129	113.136	07-09-16	London	119	RMS **F509**
	Black with burgundy interior; since 1955 in the same family ownership. Restored over a 25 year period beginning in 1977.											
1955	**300 SL gullwing**		1980405500626	L	1.350-1.500.000 USD		NS		19-01-17	Phoenix	158	RMS
	Originally finished in metallic blue with red leather interior and Rudge knock-off wheels, the car was sold new to the USA. Three owners; original interior; body repainted in the present graphite grey in 1995; engine rebuilt at unspecified date.											
1955	**300 SL gullwing**		1980405500098	L	900-1.100.000 USD	1.186.988	1.457.500	1.370.779	20-01-17	Scottsdale	18	G&Co
	Red with beige vinyl and red tartan interior; offered from over 60 years of single family ownership. Last road registered in 1976 and last run 15 years ago, the car requires recommissioning prior to use. Evidence of paint repair at the front and rear of the car, original interior showing some use damage. For preservation or concours restoration.											
1955	**300 SL gullwing**		198405500823	L	1.100-1.300.000 EUR	865.081	1.087.019	1.016.666	09-02-17	Paris	350	Bon
	Originally finished in light metallic green with red leather interior; the car was sold new to the USA. Restored between 2000 and 2004, it was reimported into Europe in 2005. Currently finished in red with tan interior. Engine overhauled in 2015 (see lot 73 RM 9.3.02 $214,500).											
1956	**300 SL gullwing**		1980406500071	L	1.200-1.400.000 EUR		NS		10-02-17	Paris	114	Art
	Ivory with black leather interior; sold new to France, the car was later exported to the USA and in 1997 it was reimported into Europe. Since 2001 in the current ownership, the car ran the 2005 Mille Miglia Storica and was restored in 2009-10.											
1957	**300 SL gullwing**		1980407500077	L	950-1.050.000 USD	941.054*	1.144.000*	1.078.106*	10-03-17	Amelia Island	111	RMS
	Red with black leather interior; sold new to the USA. Body repainted some years ago; last serviced in 2010 including brake rebuild. From the Orin Smith collection.											
1954	**300 SL gullwing**		1980404500116	L	1.200-1.400.000 USD	1.117.502*	1.358.500*	1.280.250*	11-03-17	Amelia Island	258	RMS **F510**
	Dark blue with tan leather interior and Rudge wheels; sold new in Germany and later imported into the USA; bought in 2005 by the current owner; cosmetically restored in 2007; engine rebuild completed in 2015.											
1955	**300 SL gullwing**		1980404500158	L	950-1.100.000 EUR	807.114	1.005.238	943.000	08-04-17	Essen	203	Coy
	Light grey with blue plaid and vinyl interior; sold new to the USA, the car was imported into the UK in the late 2013 and subsequently restored. 52,480 miles recorded since new.											
1955	**300 SL gullwing**		1980405500771	L	900-1.100.000 USD	714.529	919.600	783.499	18-08-17	Carmel	91	Bon
	Red with black interior; raced in period and later at numerous historic events until the late 1980s. In the 1960s fitted at the factory with a new aluminium engine complete with sports cam. Restored many years ago.											
1955	**300 SL gullwing**		1980405500080	L	1.000-1.300.000 USD	1.303.418	1.677.500	1.429.230	18-08-17	Pebble Beach	18	G&Co
	Dark green with tan interior; sold new to the USA; in single family ownership since new; in original condition; just over 16.300 miles covered.											
1955	**300 SL gullwing**		1980405500512	L	1.250-1.500.000 USD	982.905	1.265.000	1.077.780	19-08-17	Pebble Beach	116	G&Co
	Silver with red leather interior; sold new to the USA; concours-quality restoration completed in 2001. Rudge knock-off wheels.											
1957	**300 SL gullwing**		1980407500069	L	1.250-1.500.000 USD	1.153.845	1.485.000	1.265.220	19-08-17	Monterey	239	RMS
	Black with red leather interior and Rudge knock-off wheels; sold new to the USA; three owners; fully restored.											
1957	**300 SL Roadster**		1980427500239	L	900-1.000.000 GBP	784.000	1.049.149	933.666	07-09-16	London	159	RMS
	Metallic strawberry red with tan leather interior; the car was imported into the USA from Japan in 2005 and later it was subjected to a two-year period restoration completed in 2014 (see lot 13 Gooding & Company 16.8.14 $1,705,000).											
1957	**300 SL Roadster**		1980427500397	L	900-1.100.000 USD	651.420	825.000	737.550	06-10-16	Hershey	142	RMS
	Red with tan interior; sold new to the USA. Recent engine rebuild.											
1958	**300 SL Roadster**		1980428500271	L	950-1.250.000 EUR	959.340	1.173.913	1.067.000	15-10-16	Salzburg	449	Dor
	Red with black leather interior; when new used as a demonstrator by Mercedes-Benz. For over 30 years with its last owner. 14,000 kms covered since the restoration carried out between 1995 and 1998.											
1957	**300 SL Roadster**		1980427500432	L	1.000-1.200.000 GBP		NS		04-12-16	London	22	Bon
	Originally finished in light blue with white leather interior, the car was sold new to the USA. In 1989 it was reimported into Germany and later restored. Currently finished in anthracite grey with cognac leather interior.											
1961	**300 SL Roadster**		19804210002930	L	1.100-1.300.000 USD	842.090	1.034.000	972.477	21-01-17	Scottsdale	112	G&Co
	Red with tan interior; fully restored in the 1990s. Always well maintained; interior retrimmed. Fitted with hardtop and luggage set (see Christie's lots 77 28.8.94 $200,500 and 50 18.8.02 NS).											

F509: 1954 Mercedes-Benz 220 coupé

F510: 1954 Mercedes-Benz 300 SL gullwing

Year	Model	(Bodybuilder)	Chassis No.	Steering	Estimate	Hammer Price £	Hammer Price $	Hammer Price €	Date	Place	Lot	Auc. H.
1961	300 SL Roadster		19804210002734	L	900-1.100.000 EUR	904.825	1.127.609	1.060.880	10-02-17	Paris	63	Art **F511**
	Graphite grey with original beige interior; since 1979 with the present, third owner; body repainted in 1980; fitted with front disc brakes in 1981 (the original drums are included with the sale); clutch and water and oil radiators replaced in 2011.											
1958	300 SL Roadster		1980428500286	L	900-1.050.000 USD	787.228*	957.000*	901.877*	10-03-17	Amelia Island	148	RMS
	Metallic silver blue with tan leather interior; sold new to the USA and restored several years ago. Fitted with a later alloy engine block, Rudge knock-off wheels, and medium blue hardtop. From the Orin Smith (see lot 119 RM 9.3.13 $792,000).											
1963	300 SL Roadster		19804210002994	L	1.250-1.500.000 USD	960.240	1.200.000	1.122.360	01-04-17	Ft.Lauderdale	557	AA
	Silver with red leather interior; recent restoration.											
1957	300 SL Roadster		1980427500378	L	1.200-1.400.000 USD	869.358	1.111.000	1.038.452	22-04-17	Arlington	144	WoA
	Silver with deep red leather interior; for 42 years with the previous owner who had it fully restored. Recently detailed (see lot 138 RM/Sotheby's 12.3.16 NS).											
1958	300 SL Roadster		1980428500327	L	600-800.000 EUR	968.183*	1.259.873*	1.127.000*	21-05-17	SPA-Francorch.	62	Bon
	Silver with red interior; sold new to the USA and later reimported into Germany; restored at unspecified date. For some 20 years in the Swiss Castle Collection.											
1960	300 SL Roadster		1980421000061	L	1.100-1.300.000 USD	864.380	1.100.000	984.500	24-06-17	Santa Monica	213	RMS
	Light green with dark green interior; concours-quality restoration completed in early 2017.											
1962	300 SL Roadster		19804210003042	L	850-950.000 GBP	897.500	1.164.776	1.016.239	30-06-17	Goodwood	226	Bon
	Red with red hardtop and black leather interior; sold new to the USA; bought in 1989 by the current, third owner and imported into the UK; recently recommissioned. 70,500 covered since new.											
1957	300 SL Roadster		1980427500299	L	1.000-1.200.000 USD	543.900	700.000	596.400	18-08-17	Carmel	21	Bon
	Silver with red leather interior; sold new to the USA; restored in 1989 by its then-German owner; sold in 1999 to the current owner in the UK; engine rebuilt in 2011 by German specialist Kienle (see lot 165 Brooks 7.8.99 $132,338).											
1957	300 SL Roadster		1980427500180	L	800-1.000.000 USD	803.418	1.034.000	880.968	18-08-17	Pebble Beach	19	G&Co
	Light metallic blue with light grey leather interior; sold new to the USA; in the same family ownership since 1957; in original condition; just under 38,000 miles covered.											
1957	300 SL Roadster		1980427500211	L	1.200-1.500.000 USD	1.047.008	1.347.500	1.148.070	19-08-17	Pebble Beach	160	G&Co
	Silver with red interior; fitted with Rudge knock-off wheels and hardtop. Restored in the early 1990s, the car is described as still in good overall condition.											
1960	300 SL Roadster		19804210002607	L	1.250-1.500.000 USD	1.068.375	1.375.000	1.171.500	19-08-17	Monterey	251	RMS
	Medium blue with beige interior; sold new to Panama and later imported into the USA. Bought about 10 years ago by the current owner and subsequently restored. With hardtop (see lots 171 RM 13.3.04 WD and 1565 Bonhams 13.8.04 NS).											
1957	190 SL		1210427500616	L	145-165.000 USD	87.274	115.000	102.431	17-09-16	Aspen	112	TFA
	Light blue with blue leather interior; restored between 1986 and 1992, the car received further works since 2007. Described as in excellent overall condition.											
1960	190 SL		12104010016863	L	140-160.000 EUR		NA		08-10-16	Paris	139	CB/C
	White with red interior; acquired in 2009 by the current, third owner and restored in 2015 (see lot 21 Artcurial 16.11.09 $67,069).											
1958	190 SL		1210408500148	L	75-95.000 EUR	77.160	93.737	85.824	30-10-16	Paris	141	Art
	Silver; restored. For 36 years in the same ownership. With hardtop.											
1961	190 SL		12104010019368	L	100-140.000 EUR	94.847	118.473	106.800	05-11-16	Lyon	249	Agu
	Red with beige leather interior; restored in California in 2011 and later imported into France.											
1962	190 SL		12104010025586	L	140-160.000 USD		NS		05-11-16	Hilton Head	166	AA
	Black with red leather interior; body repainted.											
1960	190 SL		12104220015135	R	100-120.000 GBP	109.688	138.854	127.337	12-11-16	Birmingham	332	SiC
	Black with red leather interior; some mechanical works carried out in late 2015, body repainted in early 2016 (see Historics lots 62 2.6.10 $33, 716 223 24.11.12 $86,612 and 265 30.11.13 $89,701).											
1958	190 SL		1210427503282	L	110-130.000 GBP		NS		05-12-16	London	132	Coy
	Silver with red leather interior; recently restored.											
NQ	190 SL		12104210024129	L	90-120.000 GBP		NS		07-12-16	London	323	Bon
	Black with cream interior; recently imported into the UK from South Africa where it was restored at unspecified date.											
1955	190 SL		1210425501389	L	125-150.000 USD	98.167*	121.000*	113.413*	19-01-17	Scottsdale	102	Bon **F512**
	Silver with red leather interior; fully restored in 2016.											
1959	190 SL		121040109502307	L	125-150.000 USD	80.319*	99.000*	92.793*	19-01-17	Phoenix	110	RMS
	White with black interior; restored. With hardtop.											
1959	190 SL		121040109500447	L	NQ	85.105*	104.500*	98.282*	21-01-17	Scottsdale	1090	B/J
	Red with red interior; cosmetically restored. With hardtop.											

F511: 1961 Mercedes-Benz 300 SL Roadster

F512: 1955 Mercedes-Benz 190 SL

Year	Model (Bodybuilder)	Chassis no.	Steering	Estimate	Hammer Price £	$	€	Date	Place	Lot	Auc. H.
1955	**190 SL**	1210455500559	L	NQ	**111.980***	**137.500***	**129.319***	21-01-17	Scottsdale	1283	B/J
	Black with parchment interior; restored.										
1962	**190 SL**	190SL023143C	L	NQ	**125.418**	**154.000**	**144.837**	21-01-17	Scottsdale	8262	R&S
	White; recent concours-quality restoration. With hardtop.										
1956	**190 SL**	1210426502351	L	80-100.000 EUR	**73.390**	**92.219**	**86.250**	09-02-17	Paris	394	Bon
	Black; currently registered in the UK.										
1961	**190 SL**	1210426502393	L	90-120.000 EUR	**101.666***	**126.698***	**119.200***	10-02-17	Paris	62	Art
	Grey with red interior; restored in Germany in 2006.										
1960	**190 SL**	12104010016968	L	60-75.000 USD	**56.458***	**68.750***	**65.154***	09-03-17	Amelia Island	172	Bon
	Silver with dark blue leather interior; in good driving order.										
1961	**190 SL**	12104010025444	L	200-225.000 USD		NS		11-03-17	Amelia Island	238	RMS
	Beige with black leather interior and black hardtop; concours-quality restoration carried out in Germany.										
1961	**190 SL**	12104210015477	L	100-150.000 EUR		NS		18-03-17	Lyon	193	Agu
	Black with burgundy interior; imported into France from the USA a few years ago; mechanicals overhauled.										
1960	**190 SL**	12104010019122	L	80-100.000 GBP	**105.750**	**131.564**	**122.416**	29-03-17	Duxford	98	H&H
	White with red interior; circa 8,900 miles covered since the restoration carried out in the 1990s.										
1957	**190 SL**	1210406504032	L	100-130.000 EUR	**85.590**	**106.600**	**100.000**	08-04-17	Essen	129	Coy
	Red with beige leather interior; recently restored.										
1960	**190 SL**	12104010018238	L	100-120.000 EUR	**68.472**	**85.280**	**80.000**	08-04-17	Essen	183	Coy
	Black with red leather interior; sold new to the USA; imported into the UK in 2016 and recommissioned.										
1962	**190 SL**	12104210024577	L	90-120.000 GBP	**116.480**	**151.564**	**135.583**	20-05-17	Ascot	152	His
	Light metallic blue with cream leather interior; fully restored (see lot 271 Historics 11.06.16 $145,182).										
1957	**190 SL**	1210427502597	L	200-220.000 AUD		NS		28-05-17	Sydney	16	Mos
	Silver with navy blue interior; restored circa 15 years ago.										
1961	**190 SL**	12104010023541	L	90-120.000 USD	**63.788**	**82.000**	**73.103**	04-06-17	Greenwich	168	Bon
	Ivory with black leather interior; bought in 2012 by the current, third owner and subsequently restored (see lot 19 Bonhams 28.1.16 $115,500).										
1957	**190 SL**	1210427502033	L	NA	**99.404**	**126.500**	**113.218**	24-06-17	Santa Monica	160	RMS
	Black with tan leather interior; restored.										
1958	**190 SL**	1210427503282	L	80-100.000 GBP	**80.000**	**103.824**	**90.584**	29-06-17	Fontwell Park	148	Coy
	See lot 132 Coys 5.12.16.										
1962	**190 SL**	12104220023634	R	60-80.000 GBP	**75.420**	**97.880**	**85.398**	30-06-17	Goodwood	206	Bon
	Ivory with red interior; since 1995 in the same family ownership; stored in 1996 and recently recommissioned.										
1961	**190 SL**	12104210023475	L	82-95.000 GBP	**89.600**	**115.548**	**101.248**	08-07-17	Brooklands	152	His
	Silver with red leather interior; restored over a 10 year period (see lot 39 H & H 6.6.01 $8,842).										
1960	**190 SL**	12104010018238	L	65-85.000 GBP		NS		15-07-17	Blenheim Pal.	108	Coy
	See lot 183 Coys 8.4.17.										
1960	**190 SL**	1210422001540	R	NQ	**56.250***	**73.366***	**63.006***	26-07-17	Duxford	64	H&H
	Unused for the past 30 years; for restoration.										
1955	**190 SL**	1210425500514	L	105-120.000 GBP	**129.375**	**169.417**	**144.447**	29-07-17	Silverstone	745	SiC
	Silver with blue leather and tartan interior; sold new to the USA, the car was later imported into the UK and subjected to a full restoration completed in 2005 (see lot 340 Silverstone Auctions 23.5.15 $150,144).										
1961	**190 SL**	12104010021564	L	100-130.000 EUR	**95.629**	**125.712**	**105.925**	05-08-17	Schloss Dyck	207	Coy
	Silver; reimported into Germany from the USA in 1992 and restored. Further restoration works carried out in the 2000s.										
1958	**190 SL**	7501727	L	125-175.000 USD		NS		17-08-17	Monterey	3	WoA
	Dark green with tan interior; restored between 2009 and 2012 (see lot 25 Bonhams 14.8.15 $121,000).										
1955	**190 SL**	1210425500064	L	200-250.000 USD	**106.838***	**137.500***	**117.150***	18-08-17	Pebble Beach	26	G&Co
	Silver with olive green interior; restored to concours condition between 2014 and 2016. With hardtop (see lot 102 RM/Sotheby's 19.8.16 WD).										
1957	**190 SL**	1210407500167	L	175-225.000 USD	**76.923***	**99.000***	**84.348***	18-08-17	Monterey	167	RMS
	Light metallic blue; two owners; 80 miles covered since the restoration.										
1960	**190 SL**	12104010016880	L	120-150.000 USD	**89.744***	**115.500***	**98.406***	19-08-17	Pebble Beach	109	G&Co
	Blue with black interior; from 1963 to 2011 in the same family ownership; several restoration works carried out starting in 1999; fitted with a period Judson supercharger rebuilt in 2014.										
1959	**190 SL**	9502306	L	150-200.000 USD	**93.240**	**120.000**	**102.240**	19-08-17	Monterey	S133.1	Mec
	Black with tan interior; 24,500 miles on the odometer.										
1958	**190 saloon**	1210108500458	L	18-28.000 EUR	**22.215**	**28.268**	**25.300**	24-06-17	Wien	354	Dor
	White grey with grey cloth interior; bought in 1994 by the current owner and subsequently restored.										
1959	**220 S saloon**	180010N8519521	R	NQ	**20.720***	**25.763***	**24.323***	26-11-16	Weybridge	114	His
	Black with red leather interior; restored in Germany in 1991-92; engine overhauled in 1996 (see lot 301 Brooks 18.4.98 $10,824).										
1959	**220 S saloon**	180010109502992	L	30-40.000 USD	**19.907***	**24.200***	**22.806***	10-03-17	Amelia Island	22	G&Co
	Black with red leather interior; described as in very good original condition. Engine rebuilt in the early 2000s.										
1959	**220 S saloon**	8517504	R	15-18.000 AUD		NS		28-05-17	Sydney	2	Mos
	Bought in 1975 by the current owner and subsequently restored. Engine and gearbox replaced.										
1957	**220 S cabriolet**	1800307506175	R	NA		NS		02-09-16	Salon Privé	254	SiC
	White; interior retrimmed in red leather.										

Year	Model	(Bodybuilder)	Chassis no.	Steering	Estimate	Hammer price £	$	€	Date	Place	Lot	Auc. H.
1957	**220 S cabriolet**		10921N7506764	L	100-120.000 EUR	**85.359**	**103.945**	**97.500**	14-01-17	Maastricht	216	**Coy**
Light grey with red leather interior; described as in good overall condition.												
1958	**220 S cabriolet**		8512711	L	60-90.000 USD	**66.846***	**81.400***	**77.143***	09-03-17	Amelia Island	181	**Bon F513**
Light blue with cream interior and white leather interior; in original, unrestored condition. First owner Rodman Rockefeller. Since 2011 in the current, third ownership.												
1957	**220 S cabriolet**		1800307506195	R	55-65.000 GBP	**57.000**	**74.168**	**66.348**	20-05-17	Ascot	224	**His**
White with red interior; in single ownership from 1973 to 2015; paintwork and interior redone in recent years (see lot 136 Coys 10.10.15 $73,198).												
1958	**220 S cabriolet**		180030Z8509592	L	140-180.000 USD	**123.932***	**159.500***	**135.894***	19-08-17	Pebble Beach	125	**G&Co**
Blue with grey leather interior; bought in 2003 by the current owner and subsequently restored.												
1960	**220 SE coupé**		12803010002524	L	130-150.000 USD		**NS**		07-10-16	Hershey	231	**RMS**
Black with parchment leather interior; described as in very good original, unrestored condition. Recently serviced.												
1961	**220 S coupé**		8507907	L	50-60.000 GBP		**NS**		19-03-17	Goodwood	42	**Bon**
Ivory and dark grey with tan interior; restored. Sunroof.												
1960	**220 SE coupé**		12803710003528	L	65-75.000 EUR		**NS**		08-04-17	Essen	196	**Coy**
Ivory with red leather interior; restored. Recently serviced.												
1958	**220 S coupé**		1800377516490	L	65-75.000 EUR	**48.786**	**60.762**	**57.000**	08-04-17	Essen	216	**Coy**
Dark blue with red leather interior; restored some years ago. Sliding sunroof (see lot 129 Bonhams 19.3.16 $82,365).												
1960	**220 SE coupé**		1280371000274	L	45-65.000 EUR	**50.232**	**64.188**	**60.000**	01-05-17	Obenheim	363	**Ose**
Metallic blue grey with cream leather interior; recently restored.												
1962	**220 Sb saloon**		A1110126000239	R	15-18.000 GBP		**NS**		03-09-16	Beaulieu	478	**Bon**
Ivory with red leather interior; restored in 2014.												
1965	**220SE cabriolet**		11102310029958	L	18-24.000 USD	**23.935***	**30.800***	**27.409***	03-10-16	Philadelphia	217	**Bon**
For restoration; just one owner.												
1963	**220 SEb cabriolet**		11102320047097	R	40-50.000 GBP	**55.200**	**69.602**	**64.866**	07-12-16	London	354	**Bon**
Cream with red leather interior; in good overall condition. Body repainted (see lots Coys 310 12.7.14 NS and 267 11.10.14 NS, and Historics 291 7.3.15 $76,507).												
1962	**220 SEb cabriolet**		11102310031980	L	70-90.000 GBP	**69.820**	**86.298**	**80.370**	19-03-17	Goodwood	50	**Bon F514**
Brown with light brown interior; restored many years ago. Imported into the UK from the USA in 2014. Recently serviced.												
1964	**220 SE cabriolet**		11102322067822	R	70-80.000 GBP	**72.000**	**92.570**	**85.118**	13-05-17	Silverstone	359	**SiC**
Red; restored in 1986; automatic transmission.												
1962	**220 SE cabriolet**		11102310032086	L	85-100.000 USD		**NS**		24-06-17	Santa Monica	163	**RMS**
White; imported into the USA by the current owner in 1976.												
1963	**220 SE cabriolet**		11102320046511	R	50-60.000 GBP	**56.250**	**73.659**	**62.803**	29-07-17	Silverstone	456	**SiC**
Green with beige leather interior; until 2014 in the same family ownership; just over 77,000 miles on the odometer (see lot 213 Coys 16.5.15 $76,723).												
1965	**220 SE coupé**		11102010079804	L	40-50.000 USD	**21.714***	**27.500***	**24.585***	06-10-16	Hershey	162	**RMS**
Ivory yellow with black roof and brown leather interior; restored at unspecified date. Manual gearbox.												
1963	**220 SE coupé**		11102122048082	R	24-28.000 GBP	**32.200**	**40.037**	**37.800**	26-11-16	Weybridge	120	**His**
White with black leather interior; body and interior restored in 2008. Automatic transmission (see lot 157 Coys 10.10.15 NS).												
1964	**220 SEb coupé**		11102120034337	R	22-26.000 GBP		**NS**		07-12-16	Chateau Impney	46	**H&H**
Silver with black roof and red leather interior; restored in 2010.												
1965	**220 SE coupé**		11102122065801	R	60-70.000 AUD	**36.379**	**47.071**	**43.064**	30-04-17	Melbourne	27	**Mos**
White with red leather interior; since 1985 in the current ownership. In very good overall condition.												
1963	**220 SEb coupé**		11102110042201	L	30-40.000 EUR		**NS**		05-08-17	Schloss Dyck	251	**Coy**
Light metallic blue with red leather interior; 850 kms covered since the last service. Sunroof.												
1965	**300 SE saloon**		11201422008407	R	15-18.000 GBP	**28.320**	**35.185**	**33.035**	18-02-17	London	364	**Coy**
Beige with turquoise leather interior; stored for 18 years, the car is described as in good overall condition. 55,000 miles on the odometer. Automatic transmission.												
1965	**300 SE cabriolet**		11202310007784	L	150-200.000 GBP		**NS**		07-09-16	London	183	**RMS**
White with original red leather interior; acquired in 1966 by actor James Mason and since then in his family ownership. Recently serviced.												
1967	**300 SE cabriolet**		11202312009474	L	275-375.000 USD	**223.960**	**275.000**	**258.638**	20-01-17	Scottsdale	12	**G&Co**
Dark maroon with cognac leather interior; between 2010 and 2015 fully restored to concours condition.												

F513: 1958 Mercedes-Benz 220 S cabriolet

F514: 1962 Mercedes-Benz 220 SEb cabriolet

Year	Model (Bodybuilder)	Chassis no.	Steering	Estimate	Hammer price £	Hammer price $	Hammer price €	Date	Place	Lot	Auc. H.
1965	**300 SE cabriolet**	11202320007273	R	175-225.000 USD		NS		01-04-17	Ft.Lauderdale	585	AA
	Finished in black with red leather interior, the car was sold new to Sierra Leone. Imported into the USA at unspecified date. Restored. Manual gearbox.										
1967	**300 SE cabriolet**	11202312009516	L	240-280.000 USD		NS		24-06-17	Santa Monica	221	RMS
	Dark blue; restored at unspecified date and recently refreshed.										
1965	**300 SE cabriolet**	11202312009027	L	120-180.000 EUR	112.783	166.456	128.260	02-07-17	Monaco	108	Art **F515**
	Metallic blue with dark blue leather interior; reimported into Europe from the USA in 1994 and later restored.										
1963	**300 SE coupé**	11202112004862	L	10-15.000 EUR	40.070*	49.825*	47.040*	25-11-16	Milan	340	RMS
	Beige with black interior; 47,160 kms. From the Duemila Ruote collection.										
1964	**300 SE coupé**	11202112006596	L	80-100.000 EUR	76.978	113.612	87.542	02-07-17	Monaco	202	Art **F516**
	Gold; restored between 2015 and 2017. First owner King Hussein of Jordan.										
1967	**230 SL**	11304222018032	R	58-68.000 GBP	55.000	73.288	65.043	10-09-16	Goodwood	106	Bon
	For 10 years in the current ownership; engine rebuilt in 1986, body restored in 1997. Recently serviced. Automatic transmission (see lot 264 Coys 11.10.14 NS).										
1967	**230 SL**	11304020018904	R	80-100.000 GBP	79.900	106.467	94.490	10-09-16	Goodwood	126	Bon
	White with black leather interior; restored between 2010 and 2014. One owner; 33,600 miles on the odometer; manual gearbox.										
1965	**230 SL**	11304210015581	L	NA	53.036*	64.900*	58.988*	15-10-16	Las Vegas	635	B/J
	Ivory with red interior; described as in original condition. Two owners; 53,000 original miles.										
1967	**230 SL**	016103	L	70-75.000 USD	46.669	58.300	52.552	05-11-16	Hilton Head	197	AA
	Light beige with red interior; in original, never restored condition. One owner.										
1966	**230 SL**	11304212017127	L	NA		NS		19-11-16	Anaheim	S49	Mec
	Red with black interior; in the same ownership since 1979, body repainted in 2014. Automatic transmission.										
1966	**230 SL**	11304212018110	R	67-74.000 GBP	69.440	86.342	81.516	26-11-16	Weybridge	210	His
	Old English white with black leather interior; several restoration works carried out over the last 10 years (see lot 366 Historics 7.6.14 $86,682).										
1965	**230 SL**	OOO88D(registr.no.)	R	75-85.000 GBP	87.740	110.754	104.068	04-12-16	London	2	Bon **F517**
	Silver with red leather interior; restored. Fitted with hardtop and automatic transmission.										
1967	**230 SL**	017661	L	50-60.000 GBP		NS		07-12-16	London	348	Bon
	Red with black interior; sold new to the USA, engine rebuilt in 1988, imported into the UK in 2005, body repainted in 2007, automatic transmission rebuilt in 2016.										
1966	**230 SL**	11304210015475	L	45-65.000 EUR	56.755*	71.316*	66.700*	09-02-17	Paris	320	Bon
	White; sold new to the USA and later reimported into Europe; older restoration (see lot 116 Coys 10.8.13 NA).										
1964	**230 SL**	11304212015122	L	130-140.000 EUR		NS		08-04-17	Essen	132	Coy
	Light grey with cream interior; recently restored. Automatic transmission.										
1967	**230 SL**	11304210017122	L	80-110.000 USD	42.785*	55.000*	49.033*	04-06-17	Greenwich	160	Bon
	Dark red with parchment interior; in very good overall condition; interior retrimmed in 2016.										
1965	**230 SL**	11304210009206	L	80-110.000 EUR	80.781	102.792	92.000	24-06-17	Wien	356	Dor
	Red with beige leather interior; restored in Austria in the early 2000s.										
1966	**230 SL**	11304212018110	R	62-68.000 GBP	55.468	71.532	62.679	08-07-17	Brooklands	165	His
	See lot 210 Historics 26.11.16.										
1964	**230 SL**	1130421003626	L	75-100.000 USD	41.880*	53.900*	45.923*	18-08-17	Carmel	19	Bon
	Red; restored; fitted at unspecified date with a 2.8-litre engine.										
1967	**600**	100122000952	R	30-40.000 GBP	24.530	30.243	27.147	08-10-16	Ascot	337	Coy
	Since 1986 in the current ownership; for restoration. Working engine.										
1966	**600**	10001212000580	L	NA		NS		08-10-16	Chicago	S151	Mec
	Maroon with grey interior.										
1965	**600**	10001212000382	L	20-30.000 EUR	66.783*	83.041*	78.400*	25-11-16	Milan	557	RMS
	Blu with light brown interior; 16,679 kms. From the Duemila Ruote collection.										
1978	**600**	10001222001901	R	70-80.000 GBP		NS		07-12-16	London	332	Bon
	Blue with blue velour interior; in good overall condition. Circa 49,000 miles on the odometer.										
1965	**600**	10001212000297	L	70-95.000 EUR		NS		08-02-17	Paris	174	RMS
	Dark blue with beige velour interior; in good driving order. Just over 56,000 miles covered.										

F515: 1965 Mercedes-Benz 300 SE cabriolet

F516: 1964 Mercedes-Benz 300 SE coupé

F517: 1965 Mercedes-Benz 230 SL

F518: 1971 Mercedes-Benz 600 Pullman

Year	Model	(Bodybuilder)	Chassis no.	Steering	Estimate	£	$	€	Date	Place	Lot	Auc. H.
1979	600		10001212002570	L	100-140.000 EUR	91.499	114.028	107.280	10-02-17	Paris	64	Art
	Armoured body finished in blue with white interior; sold new to Africa; recently imported into France and subjected to some restoration works. Two owners; 29,900 kms covered.
1966	600		10001212000790	L	80-110.000 USD	61.610	79.200	70.607	04-06-17	Greenwich	143	Bon
	Dark red with original black leather interior; bought five years ago by the current owner and subsequently subjected to several mechanical works.
1970	600		10001212001667	L	120-160.000 USD	89.744*	115.500*	98.406*	18-08-17	Pebble Beach	4	G&Co
	Metallic anthracite grey with cognac leather interior; recently restored; less than 80,000 miles covered since new.
1968	600 Pullman		10001412001065	L	90-120.000 USD	120.938*	148.500*	139.664*	20-01-17	Phoenix	246	RMS
	Black with original beige leather interior; body repainted. Just over 71,000 miles on the odometer.
1971	600 Pullman		10001612001500	L	240-320.000 EUR	289.747	361.088	339.720	10-02-17	Paris	113	Art F518
	Black; approximately 67,500 miles covered. Full service carried out in 2015.
1967	230 S Universal		11100162104739	R	35-40.000 GBP	39.375	51.562	43.962	29-07-17	Silverstone	429	SiC F519
	Blue with blue interior; engine enlarged to 2.8-litre at unspecified date. Described as in good overall condition. One of the cars delivered by the factory to IMA of Mechelen, Belgium, to be converted to station wagon form.
1968	250 SE cabriolet		1102312089063	L	80-100.000 EUR		NS		06-11-16	Lyon	330	Ose
	In good overall condition; automatic transmission replaced.
1966	250 SE cabriolet		11102312086963	L	110-130.000 EUR	88.158	109.798	103.000	08-04-17	Essen	208	Coy
	Silver with black leather interior; restored.
1965	250 SE coupé		11102112083265	L	30-50.000 EUR	31.438	39.269	35.400	05-11-16	Lyon	228	Agu
	Ivory with red leather interior; described as in good original condition. In the same family ownership since 1968.
1966	250 SE coupé		11102110086353	L	17-22.000 GBP	22.960	28.548	26.953	26-11-16	Weybridge	227	His
	Silver; imported into the UK from California and restored.
1967	250 SE coupé		12998122000346	R	32-38.000 AUD	18.659	24.143	22.087	30-04-17	Melbourne	31	Mos
	Burgundy with cream vinyl interior; in good driving order. Automatic transmission.
1966	250 SE coupé		11102122083312	R	NA	37.125	48.615	41.450	29-07-17	Silverstone	419	SiC
	Dark blue; restored at unspecified date.
1969	280 SE cabriolet		11102512004350	L	130-160.000 EUR	114.297	140.921	126.500	07-10-16	Zoute	22	Bon
	Metallic green with tan leather interior; acquired in 2010 by the current owner and subsequently restored (see lot 371 Bonhams 12.9.10 $64,350).
1969	280 SE cabriolet		11102512002523	L	NQ	63.225	77.000	72.218	15-01-17	Kissimmee	S278	Mec
	Gold with tan interior; for 34 years in the same family ownership. Automatic transmission.
1970	280 SE cabriolet		11202512004367	L	NQ	111.980*	137.500*	129.319*	21-01-17	Scottsdale	1425	B/J
	Tobacco with tan leather interior; recently restored. Automatic transmission.
1969	280 SE coupé		11102412000351	L	45-65.000 EUR	45.010	54.680	50.064	30-10-16	Paris	142	Art
	Described as in very good condition.

F519: 1967 Mercedes-Benz 230 S Universal

F520: 1970 Mercedes-Benz 280 SE coupé

Year	Model	(Bodybuilder)	Chassis no.	Steering	Estimate	Hammer price £	$	€	Date	Place	Lot	Auc. H.
1970	280 SE coupé		11102410004380	L	35-40.000 EUR	44.840*	55.756*	52.640*	25-11-16	Milan	906	RMS
	Grey with black interior. From the Duemila Ruote collection.											
1970	280 SE coupé		11102412004911	L	70-90.000 EUR	46.800	58.806	55.000	09-02-17	Paris	418	Bon
	Silver with red leather interior; restored in 2004-05. Automatic transmission; electric sunroof (see lot 74 Bonhams 18.5.14 $85,052).											
1970	280 SE coupé		11102412003888	L	35-45.000 USD	28.238	36.300	32.361	04-06-17	Greenwich	112	Bon F520
	Ivory with brown interior; since 1988 in the current ownership. Always well maintained. Automatic transmission.											
1969	280 SE saloon		1081810020506	L	15-20.000 USD	7.817*	9.900*	8.851*	06-10-16	Hershey	116	RMS
	Brown with original brown interior; body restored years ago. Manual gearbox.											
1971	280 SE 3.5 cabriolet		11102712001412	L	325-375.000 USD		NS		03-09-16	Auburn	4099	AA
	Silver with black leather interior; restored, the car is described as in very good overall condition.											
1970	280 SE 3.5 cabriolet		11102722000818	R	220-240.000 GBP	249.750	316.159	289.935	12-11-16	Birmingham	334	SiC
	Navy blue with magnolia leather interior; the car has covered circa 9,000 miles since a full restoration carried out in 2000-01 (see lots H&H 29 26.9.01 $88,429 and 82 19.4.12 NS, and Bonhams 208 14.9.13 $259,437).											
1971	280 SE 3.5 cabriolet		11102712001412	L	350-400.000 USD	240.956*	297.000*	278.378*	19-01-17	Scottsdale	83	Bon F521
	See lot 4099 Auctions America 3.9.16.											
1971	280 SE 3.5 cabriolet		11102712002786	L	350-400.000 USD	304.586	374.000	351.747	21-01-17	Scottsdale	108	G&Co
	Tobacco brown with cognac leather interior; engine rebuilt in 2009. 59,000 miles on the odometer. Recent cosmetic and mechanic freshening.											
1971	280 SE 3.5 cabriolet		11102712003785	L	275-325.000 USD		NS		09-03-17	Amelia Island	133	Bon
	Silver with royal blue leather interior; bought 20 years ago by the current, second owner and imported into the USA. Restored over the years; body repainted in 2016.											
1971	280 SE 3.5 cabriolet		11102712003444	L	350-425.000 USD	271.458	330.000	310.992	10-03-17	Amelia Island	9	G&Co
	Dark green with tan interior; fully restored at unspecified date.											
1971	280 SE 3.5 cabriolet		11102712003179	L	400-450.000 USD		NS		01-04-17	Ft.Lauderdale	561	AA
	Black with cognac interior; recently cosmetically restored.											
1971	280 SE 3.5 cabriolet		11102712004080	L	300-400.000 EUR	246.986	321.396	287.500	21-05-17	SPA-Francorch.	89	Bon
	Green with tan leather interior; restored in 2010.											
1971	280 SE 3.5 cabriolet		11102712001589	L	240-280.000 USD		NS		24-06-17	Santa Monica	240	RMS
	White; three owners.											
1971	280 SE 3.5 cabriolet		11102712002921	L	320-360.000 USD		NS		17-08-17	Monterey	43	WoA
	Silver with blue leather interior; described as in very good overall condition; two owners (see lot 1110 Auctions America 25.6.16 NS).											
1971	280 SE 3.5 cabriolet		11102712003813	L	300-350.000 USD	282.051	363.000	309.276	19-08-17	Pebble Beach	107	G&Co
	Silver with black leather interior; body repainted many years ago; several mechanical works carried out in 2010; interior retrimmed.											
1970	280 SE 3.5 coupé		11102622002520	R	45-55.000 GBP	53.320	71.225	63.051	08-09-16	Fontwell Park	121	Coy
	Ivory with black leather interior; engine rebuilt (see lot 196 Coys 2.7.16 $62,983).											
1970	280 SE 3.5 coupé		11102612001948	L	90-130.000 EUR	67.539	83.272	74.750	07-10-16	Zoute	38	Bon
	Dark aubergine metallic with rose metallic roof and tan leather interior; restored several years ago (see lot 86 Artcurial 14.2.10 $43,657).											
1971	280 SE 3.5 coupé		11102612001771	L	100-125.000 USD	66.041	82.500	74.366	05-11-16	Hilton Head	180	AA
	Metallic grey blue with original black leather interior; restored in 2012.											
1971	280 SE 3.5 coupé		11102610002752	L	55-65.000 EUR	57.242*	71.178*	67.200*	25-11-16	Milan	633	RMS
	Champagne with dark blue interior; 72,511 kms. From the Duemila Ruote collection.											
1971	280 SE 3.5 coupé		11102612004007	L	50-60.000 GBP	89.600	111.409	105.181	26-11-16	Weybridge	198	His
	Sold new to the Royal Qatar Family and delivered to the USA; later the car was moved to London where it remained unused for many years; sold in 2007 and subsequently recommissioned and repainted; 8,385 miles covered since new.											
1970	280 SE 3.5 coupé		11102612001051	L	130-160.000 USD		NS		19-01-17	Scottsdale	104	Bon
	Metallic silver grey with cognac leather interior; restored in 1995-96. Described as in very good overall condition.											
1970	280 SE 3.5 coupé		11102612000655	L	120-140.000 USD	82.865*	101.750*	95.696*	20-01-17	Scottsdale	50	G&Co
	Sold new in Europe and later exported to Japan; recently imported into the USA; in good overall condition.											
1971	280 SE 3.5 coupé		11102622003550	R	65-75.000 GBP	70.313	88.271	83.201	24-02-17	Stoneleigh P.	917	SiC
	Silver with black leather interior; in good overall condition; just over 46,500 miles covered.											
1971	280 SE 3.5 coupé		11102622002008	R	100-120.000 GBP		NS		29-07-17	Silverstone	433	SiC
	For 38 years in the same ownership; in good overall condition. Sunroof.											
1967	250 SL		11304322001490	R	48-55.000 GBP	55.560	68.500	61.488	08-10-16	Ascot	313	Coy
	Silver with red leather interior; in good overall condition.											
1967	250 SL		11304322001658	R	38-44.000 GBP	48.300	60.901	56.757	07-12-16	London	375	Bon
	White; since 1986 in the current ownership; body restored in 2000; in driving order; automatic transmission.											
1967	250 SL		113043220011092	R	30-40.000 GBP	74.600	92.683	87.021	18-02-17	London	305	Coy
	White with black interior; described as in very good overall condition. 64,000 miles covered.											
1967	250 SL California		11304312004029	L	60-80.000 USD		NS		09-03-17	Amelia Island	147	Bon
	Graphite grey with tan interior; body repainted at some point. Automatic transmission.											
1967	250 SL		11304322004189	R	90-110.000 GBP		NS		18-05-17	London	139	Coy
	Black with red interior; restored at unspecified date. Recently serviced.											
1967	250 SL		11304322002643	R	80-90.000 GBP		NS		06-06-17	Woodcote Park	40	H&H
	Red with black interior; restored at unspecified date; described as in very good overall condition. Automatic transmission (see lot 50 H & H 25.2.15 $75,789).											
1967	250 SL California		1130432202441	R	50-60.000 GBP	55.125	72.186	61.547	29-07-17	Silverstone	447	SiC
	Metallic beige; restored in recent years; automatic transmission (see lot 95 H & H 8.10.14 NS).											

Year	Model	(Bodybuilder)	Chassis no.	Steering	Estimate	Hammer price £	$	€	Date	Place	Lot	Auc. H.
1970	280 SL		11304412020448	L	80-100.000 GBP		NS		03-09-16	Beaulieu	438	Bon
Silver with black interior; sold new to the USA, the car was imported into Poland in 2015 and restored. Automatic transmission.												
1968	280 SL		11304422000315	R	85-95.000 GBP		NS		08-09-16	Fontwell Park	113	Coy
Light blue with tan leather interior; cosmetically restored at unspecified date. Tan leather reconnolised.												
1969	280 SL		11304412001530	L	140-165.000 USD	91.827	121.000	107.775	17-09-16	Aspen	123	TFA
Red with light tan interior; recent restoration. Automatic transmission (see lot 20 Gooding & Company 29.1.16 $99,000).												
1970	280 SL		11304410014571	L	75-100.000 USD		NS		03-10-16	Philadelphia	219	Bon
Red with cognac interior; restored. Manual gearbox.												
1969	280 SL		11304410006445	L	200-300.000 EUR	207.812	256.220	230.000	07-10-16	Zoute	26	Bon
Red with cognac interior; described as in very good original condition, except for the paintwork redone in the 2000s. 5-speed manual gearbox.												
1968	280 SL		13098312028787	L	50-60.000 GBP	50.175	61.861	55.529	08-10-16	Ascot	326	Coy
Silver with black interior; restored in 2015.												
1968	280 SL		11304412001135	L	55-65.000 GBP	59.890	73.401	66.610	12-10-16	Duxford	38	H&H
Red with brown interior; described as in good overall condition. Imported into the UK from the USA in 2015. Automatic transmission.												
1969	280 SL		11304412010658	L	38-45.000 GBP	48.720	60.578	57.192	26-11-16	Weybridge	130	His
Metallic blue/grey; body repainted in the USA. Imported into the UK in 2013. Automatic transmission.												
1970	280 SL		11304412015555	L	120-140.000 EUR		NS		14-01-17	Maastricht	205	Coy
Silver grey with black leather interior; fully restored. Automatic transmission.												
1968	280 SL		113044100007040	L	55-70.000 EUR	59.570	72.541	68.043	14-01-17	Maastricht	218	Coy
Red with black interior; in good overall condition. Manual gearbox.												
1968	280 SL		11304412000592	L	NQ	68.151	83.000	77.846	15-01-17	Kissimmee	S267	Mec
Burgundy; new paintwork and interior. Believed to be 33,000 original miles. Automatic transmission.												
1969	280 SL		11304412014788	L	80-100.000 USD	47.032*	57.750*	54.314*	20-01-17	Phoenix	238	RMS F522
Red with tan interior; body repainted. Automatic transmission.												
1971	280 SL		11304410021087	L	160-180.000 USD	80.626*	99.000*	93.110*	21-01-17	Scottsdale	129	G&Co
Red with black interior; major refurbishment in 2016. Manual gearbox.												
1970	280 SL		1130441002545	L	70-90.000 EUR	60.669	76.234	71.300	09-02-17	Paris	340	Bon
Grey with blue interior; sold new to the USA, the car was later reimported into Europe. Described as in good overall condition.												
1971	280 SL		11304410020160	L	90-120.000 EUR	80.240	100.826	94.300	09-02-17	Paris	400	Bon
Described as in highly original condition; with hardtop; engine replaced many years ago with a new unstamped unit.												
1968	280 SL		11304422004944	R	90-110.000 GBP	97.812	122.265	115.281	12-04-17	London	333	Coy
Blue with cognac leather interior; body repainted, interior retrimmed. Automatic transmission.												
1971	280 SL		11304412019017	L	80-100.000 USD	55.620	71.500	63.742	04-06-17	Greenwich	152	Bon
Grey-beige with bamboo interior; restored in the late 2000s. Automatic transmission (see lot 16 Bonhams 14.8.15 $99,000).												
1969	280 SL		1130441209625	L	55-75.000 EUR	78.979	100.718	90.120	10-06-17	Lyon	140	Agu
Cream with blue interior; in very good overall condition. Automatic transmission; hardtop.												
1968	280 SL		11304412001599	L	80-100.000 GBP	92.960	119.881	105.045	08-07-17	Brooklands	193	His
Red with tan leather interior; fully restored (see lot 125 Coys 10.10.15 $62,890).												
1968	280 SL		11304410002504	L	65-75.000 EUR	61.404	80.720	68.015	05-08-17	Schloss Dyck	266	Coy
In good overall condition; original beige interior; manual gearbox.												
1970	280 SL		11304412016875	L	125-175.000 USD		NS		17-08-17	Monterey	8	WoA
Restored to concours condition between 2012 and 2013; automatic transmission (see lot 1 Gooding & Company 13.3.15 $143,000).												
1968	280 SL		11304410002826	L	100-120.000 USD		NS		18-08-17	Carmel	56	Bon
Red with cognac interior; body repainted in 2003, interior retrimmed in more recent years. Manual gearbox.												
1971	280 SL		11304410019355	L	140-170.000 USD	158.120*	203.500*	173.382*	18-08-17	Pebble Beach	40	G&Co
Silver with blue leather interior; body repainted two years ago; interior recently retrimmed; manual gearbox.												
1970	280 SL		11304412015640	L	60-80.000 USD	68.376*	88.000*	74.976*	19-08-17	Pebble Beach	170	G&Co
White; in largely original condition; since new in the same family ownership; automatic transmission.												

F521: 1971 Mercedes-Benz 280 SE 3.5 cabriolet

F522: 1969 Mercedes-Benz 280 SL

Year	Model	(Bodybuilder)	Chassis no.	Steering	Estimate	Hammer price £	$	€	Date	Place	Lot	Auc. H.
1970	300 SEL 6.3 saloon		1090812003690	L	23-27.000 GBP	24.080	29.941	28.268	26-11-16	Weybridge	217	His
	Metallic gold with beige velour interior; described as in good original condition. Recently serviced (see lots 205 Coys 27.2.07 NS and 50 Historics 2.6.10 NS).											
1971	300 SEL 6.3 saloon		10901812004785	L	50-75.000 USD	40.159*	49.500*	46.396*	19-01-17	Scottsdale	106	Bon F523
	Described as in largely original condition; less than 45,000 miles covered. Body repainted a few years ago.											
1969	300 SEL 6.3 saloon		10901812002441	L	150-180.000 USD	104.059*	126.500*	119.214*	10-03-17	Amelia Island	45	G&Co
	Silver with black leather interior; fully restored in 1993. Recently updated mechanically and cosmetically.											
1971	300 SEL 6.3 saloon		10901812003251	L	10-20.000 EUR	20.953	25.898	24.120	18-03-17	Lyon	174	Agu
	Metallic beige with beige cloth interior; for restoration.											
1970	300 SEL 6.3 saloon		10901812004825	L	50-60.000 USD	37.601	47.850	42.826	24-06-17	Santa Monica	158	RMS
	Blue; restored; original interior.											
1970	300 SEL 6.3 saloon		1091812003385	L	NA	32.846	41.800	37.411	24-06-17	Santa Monica	206	RMS
	White with brown leather interior; several mechanical and aesthetical works carried out in recent times.											
1971	300 SEL 6.3 saloon		10901812005304	L	140-160.000 USD	68.376*	88.000*	74.976*	19-08-17	Pebble Beach	155	G&Co
	Metallic beige with vinyl roof and dark brown leather interior; in original condition; 45,000 miles covered; three owners.											
1972	250 C coupé		11402112002221	L	9-14.000 EUR	10.857	13.285	12.075	15-10-16	Salzburg	404	Dor
	Metallic blue with brown leather interior; body restored and repainted in 2014. Automatic transmission and electric sunroof.											
1970	300 SEL 3.5 saloon		10905612000816	L	16-30.000 GBP	21.280	28.477	25.342	07-09-16	London	144	RMS
	Grey with black interior; in good original condition, 63,380 kms covered. Since new in the same family ownership.											
1979	350 SL		10704322014740	R	9-14.000 GBP	15.680	19.497	18.407	26-11-16	Weybridge	112	His
	Navy blue with cream interior; 59,000 miles covered; since 1991 in the current, second ownership.											
1972	350 SL		10704412004899	L	12-18.000 EUR		NS		10-06-17	Lyon	118	Agu
	Garnet with tan leather interior; in good driving order. Body repainted.											
1973	450 SL		10704412012163	L	40-60.000 USD	26.773*	33.000*	30.931*	19-01-17	Scottsdale	31	Bon
	Olive green wirh bamboo interior; described as in very good condition. Less than 40,000 miles covered. Body repainted in its original colour.											
1979	450 SL		10704412052062	L	65-75.000 USD	67.188*	82.500*	77.591*	20-01-17	Scottsdale	45	G&Co
	Silver with black leather interior; in very good original condition; 743 miles covered; recently serviced.											
1973	450 SL		10704412009777	L	20-25.000 EUR	26.420*	33.199*	31.050*	09-02-17	Paris	329	Bon F524
	Metallic maroon with black leather interior; sold new to the USA; imported into the UK in 2015; approximately 50,000 miles covered.											
1978	350 SLC		10702312013042	L	10-15.000 EUR	14.641*	18.631*	16.675*	24-06-17	Wien	306	Dor
	Metallic brown with beige leather interior; body repainted. Automatic transmission.											
1976	450 SLC		10702412012145	L	16-18.000 GBP	12.265	16.384	14.503	08-09-16	Fontwell Park	102	Coy
	Silver with dark olive green interior; in good original condition.											
1979	450 SLC		10702412026803	L	10-15.000 USD	11.540*	14.850*	13.215*	03-10-16	Philadelphia	221	Bon
	Anthacite grey with grey interior; one long term owner. 32,000 miles covered.											
1979	450 SLC		10702412027545	L	30-40.000 USD	22.248*	28.600*	25.497*	04-06-17	Greenwich	135	Bon F525
	Metallic grey-blue with blue interior; in highly original condition. Under 32,000 miles covered.											
1977	280 SL		10704210002420	L	25-35.000 EUR	26.883	32.896	29.900	15-10-16	Salzburg	419	Dor
	Silver with leather and cloth interior; from new in the same ownership. Last serviced in 2015. Manual gearbox.											
1983	280 SL		12014105	L	12-15.000 EUR	18.909	24.121	21.600	18-06-17	Fontainebleau	85	Ose
	White with original red interior; in good overall condition.											
1979	450 SEL 6.9 saloon		11603612005879	L	18-24.000 USD	11.967*	15.400*	13.704*	03-10-16	Philadelphia	222	Bon
	Anthacite grey with black interior; in working order. Two owners.											
1980	450 SEL 6.9 saloon		WDB11603622007224	R	NQ	14.000*	18.054*	15.820*	08-07-17	Brooklands	137	His
	Light metallic green with brown leather interior; in good mechanical order; body recently repainted.											
1980	280 CE coupé		12305322017053	R	NQ	11.768*	14.632*	13.814*	26-11-16	Weybridge	118	His
	In good overall condition.											
1980	450 SLC 5.0		10702612001429	L	40-60.000 USD	40.171*	51.700*	44.204*	17-08-17	Monterey	23	WoA
	Silver blue with blue leather interior; in very good overall condition.											

F523: 1971 Mercedes-Benz 300 SEL 6.3 saloon

F524: 1973 Mercedes-Benz 450 SL

Year	Model	(Bodybuilder)	Chassis no.	Steering	Estimate	Hammer price £	$	€	Date	Place	Lot	Auc. H.
1982	**380 SL**		WDB10704512014429	L	17-19.000 EUR	21.722	26.451	24.811	14-01-17	Maastricht	236	Coy
	Silver with dark red leather interior; paintwork and interior redone. In good mechanical order.											
1985	**380 SL**		WDBBA45CFA02795	L	40-50.000 USD	30.090	37.500	35.280	11-02-17	Boca Raton	169	TFA
	Metallic grey with blue leather interior; in very good original condition. Bought in 2015 by the current, second owner; 7,845 miles since new (see lot 11 Bonhams 19.8.16 $33,000).											
1985	**380 SL**		WDBBA45C6FA035420	L	50-70.000 USD	37.939*	46.200*	43.784*	09-03-17	Amelia Island	108	Bon
	Light blue with grey leather interior; in very good original condition, just over 1,400 miles covered. Automatic transmission.											
1985	**500 SL**		WDB1070461A035721	L	45-65.000 EUR	53.583*	65.095*	59.600*	30-10-16	Paris	143	Art
	Burgundy; 34,800 kms covered. Recently serviced.											
1984	**500 SL**		WDB1070461A009317	L	30-40.000 USD	16.354*	20.900*	19.535*	22-04-17	Arlington	104	WoA
	Red with tan leather interior; European market version; three owners; 31,500 miles covered.											
1987	**500 SL**		107461A069449	L	35-45.000 EUR	31.614	41.139	36.800	21-05-17	SPA-Francorch.	74	Bon
	White with blue interior; some 52,000 kms on the odometer; recently serviced.											
1982	**500 SL**		WDB10704622001240	R	24-28.000 GBP	34.720	44.775	39.234	08-07-17	Brooklands	220	His
	White with dark red leather interior; 31,685 miles on the odometer; some mechanical works carried out in 2017.											
1981	**380 SLC**		WDB10702522000856	R	15-20.000 GBP	17.780	23.283	19.851	29-07-17	Silverstone	747	SiC
	Light green with olive green leather interior; 17,083 miles covered; recently serviced.											
1981	**500 SLC**		10702612002730	L	20-30.000 EUR	45.445*	59.137*	52.900*	21-05-17	SPA-Francorch.	53	Bon
	Metallic blue with beige leather interior; one owner; 45,000 kms covered. From the Swiss Castle Collection.											
1981	**300 GD 4-door lwb wagon**		WDB46033317014557	L	25-40.000 GBP	42.000	56.204	50.018	07-09-16	London	142	RMS **F526**
	Agave green with black interior; in original condition, 12,985 kms covered. One owner. Recently serviced.											
1988	**300 E AMG saloon**		12417216011	L	25-5.000 EUR	71.553*	88.973*	84.000*	25-11-16	Milan	217	RMS
	Black; 54,800 kms. From the Duemila Ruote collection.											
1989	**560 SEC 6.0 AMG**		WDB1260451A429238	L	125-140.000 USD		NS		19-01-17	Scottsdale	92	Bon
	Smoke silver with black leather interior; sold new to Japan, the car remained with its first owner for 25 years before arriving in the USA. Described as in largely original condition; 68,000 miles on the odometer.											
1987	**560 SEC**		WDB1260451A332951	L	20-25.000 EUR	14.819*	19.284*	17.250*	21-05-17	SPA-Francorch.	95	Bon
	Metallic black with grey leather interior; sunroof.											
1985	**190E 2.3-16**		WDB2010341F161733	L	25-35.000 EUR	22.859*	28.184*	25.300*	07-10-16	Zoute	10	Bon
	Described as in very good overall condition; recently serviced.											
1986	**300 SL**		WDB1070412A047079	R	18-25.000 GBP	28.175	37.425	33.438	03-09-16	Beaulieu	411	Bon
	White with leather and cloth interior; described as in very good overall condition. 49,750 miles covered. Automatic transmission.											
1989	**300 SL**		WDB1070412A093000	R	10-12.000 GBP	17.250	22.913	20.472	03-09-16	Beaulieu	497	Bon
	Light green with cream leather interior; in good overall condition. Automatic transmission.											
1989	**300 SL**		WDB1070411A246144	L	10-15.000 EUR	42.932*	53.384*	50.400*	25-11-16	Milan	651	RMS
	Black with cream interior; 90,099 kms. From the Duemila Ruote collection.											
1987	**300 SL**		WDB1070412A067624	R	25-35.000 GBP	39.656	51.723	44.419	26-07-17	Duxford	21	H&H
	Red with black interior; in good overall condition; 24,400 miles covered (see lot 56 H & H 10.10.07 $33,701).											
1989	**420 SL**		WOB1070472A099206	R	18-24.000 GBP	19.550	24.651	22.973	07-12-16	London	318	Bon
	White with red leather interior; 71,000 miles on the odometer. Automatic transmission.											
1989	**560 SL**		WDBBA48D0KA094543	L	55-75.000 USD	42.552*	52.250*	49.141*	21-01-17	Scottsdale	104	G&Co
	Blue green; bought in 2016 by the current, second owner. Less than 13,200 miles covered. Recently serviced.											
1988	**560 SL**		WDBBAH8D0JA087770	L	22-28.000 GBP	24.000	31.229	27.936	20-05-17	Ascot	247	His
	Silver with blue interior; one owner; in good overall condition.											
1989	**560 SL**		WDBBA48D3KA101453	L	22-28.000 EUR	30.603	39.027	34.920	10-06-17	Lyon	150	Agu
	Dark grey with light grey leather interior; body repainted (see lot 342 Aguttes 12.3.16 $38,593).											
1986	**560 SL**		WDBBA48DGA051735	L	23-28.000 GBP	22.230	28.730	25.264	15-07-17	Blenheim Pal.	115	Coy
	Red with tan interior; sold new to the USA where it has had just one owner until 2015 when it was reimported into Germany. 42,000 miles covered.											
1989	**560 SL**		WDBBA48D8KA100623	L	45-65.000 USD	51.282*	66.000*	56.232*	18-08-17	Carmel	74	Bon
	Dark metallic grey with black interior; in very good original condition; less than 27,000 miles covered.											

F525: 1979 Mercedes-Benz 450 SLC

F526: 1981 Mercedes-Benz 300 GD 4-door lwb wagon

Year	Model (Bodybuilder)	Chassis no.	Steering	Estimate	Hammer price £	Hammer price $	Hammer price €	Sale Date	Sale Place	Lot	Auc. H.
1996	**320 SL**	WDB129063F124532	R	30-35.000 GBP	31.500	39.876	36.568	12-11-16	Birmingham	623	SiC
	Example of the "Mille Miglia" special edition finished in silver with red and black leather interior; in excellent overall condition, 9,806 miles covered.										
1996	**500 SL**	WDB1290672F141053	R	45-55.000 GBP	53.352	66.690	62.881	12-04-17	London	305	Coy
	Red with mushroom leather interior; one owner; 81 miles covered; just recommissioned.										
1995	**SL60 AMG**	WDB1290672F123805	R	NA	56.250	74.717	66.758	02-09-16	Salon Privé	245	SiC
	Red with mushroom leather interior; in very good overall condition. 13,500 miles covered; last serviced in June 2015.										
1995	**SL72 AMG**	115979	L	70-100.000 GBP	74.300	96.427	84.130	30-06-17	Goodwood	255	Bon F527
	Silver with black leather interior; three owners; last serviced in March 2016 (see lot 108 Coys 26.9.15 $87,446).										
1991	**190E 2.5-16**	WDB2010351F747407	L	30-40.000 EUR	11.742*	14.755*	13.800*	09-02-17	Paris	354	Bon
	Circa 184,000 kms covered; well maintained.										
1990	**190E 2.5-16 Evolution II**	WDB2010361F742442	R	NA	202.500	268.981	240.327	02-09-16	Salon Privé	257	SiC
	Black with black interior; 885 miles covered.										
1990	**190E 2.5-16 Evolution II**	WDB2010361F736047	L	60-70.000 GBP	90.720	111.186	100.899	12-10-16	Duxford	40	H&H
	Blue/black with black leather interior; since 2003 in the current ownership. Some recommissioning works carried out in 2012 and 2013.										
1990	**190E 2.5-16 Evolution II**	WDB2010361F735498	L	100-115.000 GBP	120.375	152.383	139.743	12-11-16	Birmingham	310	SiC
	Metallic blue/black with black anthracite leather interior; five owners and 41,000 kms on the odometer. Some cosmetical works carried out recently (see lot 848 Silverstone Auctions 25.7.15 $155,815).										
1990	**190E 2.5-16 Evolution II**	WDB2010361F7435730	L	150-200.000 USD	127.617*	157.300*	147.437*	19-01-17	Scottsdale	87	Bon
	Sold new to Italy; imported into the USA in 2013; in very good original condition; less than 56,000 kms covered.										
1990	**190E 2.5-16 Evolution II**	WDB2010361F734005	L	225-275.000 USD	179.168	220.000	206.910	20-01-17	Phoenix	214	RMS F528
	5,000 kms covered; upgraded with DTM specification, including a Motec engine management system and OZ DTM wheels.										
1990	**190E 2.5-16 Evolution II**	WDB2010361F740617	L	80-120.000 EUR	162.665*	202.716*	190.720*	10-02-17	Paris	112	Art
	Since 1996 in the current, second ownership; just over 54,000 kms covered. Recently serviced.										
1990	**190E 2.5-16 Evolution II**	WDB2010361F741504	L	190-220.000 EUR	136.944	170.560	160.000	08-04-17	Essen	210	Coy
	Black with black leather interior; in very good original condition; 8,700 miles covered. Sold new in Germany and imported into Japan in 2005, the car is currently registered in the UK (see lot 289 Historics 20.8.16 NS).										
1990	**190E 2.5-16 Evolution II**	WDB2010361F742667	L	50-80.000 EUR	121.267	178.977	137.908	02-07-17	Monaco	175	Art
	Black with black interior; since 1997 in the current ownership; 168,000 kms covered; regularly serviced.										
1995	**500E Limited saloon**	WDB1240361C213789	L	35-45.000 EUR	45.013*	56.561*	52.900*	09-02-17	Paris	391	Bon F529
	Black; three owners; 83,000 kms covered.										
1993	**AMG E60**	WDB1240361C036814	L	90-120.000 EUR	122.798	156.598	140.120	10-06-17	Lyon	146	Agu
	Blue with blue leather interior; in very good original condition. 74,000 kms covered.										
2011	**SLR McLaren roadster**	001685	L	290-375.000 GBP	347.200	464.623	413.480	07-09-16	London	143	RMS
	Metallic palladium grey with red leather interior; one owner and 3,583 kms covered. Recently serviced.										
2008	**SLR McLaren roadster**	001809	L	395-425.000 USD		NS		04-11-16	Dallas	S114	Mec
	Black with black interior; 2,047 miles covered.										
2006	**SLR McLaren coupé**	000955	L	260-300.000 USD		NS		15-01-17	Kissimmee	S93	Mec
	Silver with red and black interior; 4,666 miles since new.										
2009	**SLR McLaren 722 S roadster**	001940	L	725-850.000 USD	549.720	675.000	634.838	20-01-17	Phoenix	253	RMS F530
	Grey with black interior; just over 1,900 miles covered. Last serviced in November 2016.										
2007	**SLR McLaren 722 coupé**	001313	L	450-550.000 USD	340.419	418.000	393.129	20-01-17	Phoenix	254	RMS
	Grey with black interior; two owners and 3,200 miles covered. Last serviced in December 2016.										
2006	**SLR McLaren coupé**	000693	L	275-350.000 USD		NS		10-03-17	Amelia Island	5	G&Co
	Silver with light grey leather interior; less than 4,600 miles covered. Last serviced in January 2017.										
2006	**SLR McLaren coupé**	001016	L	300-350.000 USD	226.215*	275.000*	259.160*	11-03-17	Amelia Island	221	RMS
	Silver with red and black interior; 1,379 original miles.										
2004	**SLR McLaren coupé**	000036	L	130-160.000 GBP	191.900	237.188	220.896	19-03-17	Goodwood	54	Bon
	Silver with red interior; two owners; 8,600 kms covered; last serviced in February 2017.										
2008	**SLR McLaren roadster**	001562	L	340-380.000 USD		NS		01-04-17	Ft.Lauderdale	199	AA
	Black with red interior; 5,500 kms covered; one owner.										

F527: 1995 Mercedes-Benz SL72 AMG

F528: 1990 Mercedes-Benz 190E 2.5-16 Evolution II

F529: 1995 Mercedes-Benz 500E Limited saloon

F530: 2009 Mercedes-Benz SLR McLaren 722 S roadster

Year	Model (Bodybuilder)	Chassis no.	Steering	Estimate	£	$	€	Date	Place	Lot	Auc. H.
2004	**SLR McLaren coupé**	000818	L	300-350.000 EUR	198.569	247.312	232.000	08-04-17	Essen	155	Coy
	Silver with red interior; 1,945 kms covered.										
2004	**SLR McLaren coupé**	000818	L	200-250.000 GBP	205.627	268.076	240.871	18-05-17	London	126	Coy
	See lot 155 Coys 8.4.17.										
2005	**SLR McLaren coupé**	000495	L	260-290.000 USD	207.451	264.000	236.280	24-06-17	Santa Monica	214	RMS F531
	Silver with red interior; less than 8,000 miles covered.										
2009	**SLR McLaren 722S roadster**	001940	L	900-1.100.000 USD	NS			19-08-17	Monterey	S82	Mec
	See lot 253 RM/Sotheby's 20.1.17.										
2008	**SLR McLaren roadster**	001619	L	NA	273.504	352.000	299.904	19-08-17	Monterey	1151	R&S
	Silver with black leather interior; 6,500 miles covered.										
2006	**CLK DTM AMG**	WDB2093422F165862	R	210-250.000 GBP	NS			26-11-16	Weybridge	164	His
	Silver; 9,940 miles covered. Sold new to Singapore; currently registered in the UK.										
2005	**CLK DTM AMG**	WDB2093421F132322	L	350-425.000 USD	NS			18-08-17	Pebble Beach	57	G&Co
	One of 100 examples built; imported into the USA in 2016; just over 4,900 miles covered; recently serviced.										
2013	**C63 AMG Black Series**	005494	L	115-150.000 GBP	121.520	162.618	144.718	07-09-16	London	140	RMS
	Red with black leather and alcantara interior; one owner and 2,533 kms covered. Recently serviced.										
2011	**SL65 AMG Black Series coupé**	159978	L	145-205.000 GBP	240.800	322.239	286.769	07-09-16	London	141	RMS
	Silver with black leather and alcantara interior; one owner and 2,360 kms covered. Recently serviced.										
2009	**SL65 AMG Black Series coupé**	157951	L	235-265.000 USD	166.958	220.000	195.954	17-09-16	Aspen	143	TFA
	Diamond white metallic with black leather interior with white inserts; 18,910 miles covered. Recently serviced.										
2009	**SL65 AMG Black Series coupé**	157951	L	NQ	132.396*	165.000*	155.232*	11-02-17	Boca Raton	158	TFA
	See lot 143 The Finest Automobile Auctions 17.9.16.										
2009	**SL65 AMG Black Series coupé**	158062	L	150-200.000 USD	147.607	189.750	169.162	04-06-17	Greenwich	190	Bon
	Black with black leather interior; just over 13,000 miles covered.										
2014	**SLS AMG Black Series coupé**	011284	L	320-415.000 GBP	386.400	517.080	460.164	07-09-16	London	139	RMS F532
	Yellow with black interior; one owner and 848 kms covered. Recently serviced.										
2011	**SLS AMG coupé**	006144	R	180-240.000 GBP	153.820	194.167	182.446	04-12-16	London	28	Bon
	Black with red leather interior; two owners and circa 13,000 miles covered.										
2014	**SLS AMG GT3**	135	L	450-550.000 USD	NS			15-01-17	Kissimmee	S139	Mec
	White; it raced partial season of the 2015 Pirelli World Challenge.										
2014	**SLS AMG Black Series coupé**	011179	L	320-380.000 EUR	401.322	501.682	470.400	08-02-17	Paris	111	RMS
	Yellow with black interior; sold new to France. One owner and 9,350 kms covered.										
2013	**SLS AMG Roadster**	008195	L	200-220.000 EUR	NS			08-04-17	Essen	137	Coy
	Silver with black interior; one owner; 1,600 kms covered. Recently serviced.										

F531: 2005 Mercedes-Benz SLR McLaren coupé

F532: 2014 Mercedes-Benz SLS AMG Black Series coupé

Year	Model	(Bodybuilder)	Chassis no.	Steering	Estimate	Hammer price £	$	€	Date	Place	Lot	Auc. H.

F533: 1922 Mercer Series 5 Sporting F534: 1941 Mercury Series 19A station wagon

Year	Model	Chassis no.	Steering	Estimate	£	$	€	Date	Place	Lot	Auc. H.
2013	SLS AMG roadster	008195	L	180-220.000 EUR	191.258	251.424	211.850	05-08-17	Schloss Dyck	258	Coy

See lot 137 Coys 8.4.17.

MERCER (USA) (1910-1925)

Year	Model	Chassis no.	Steering	Estimate	£	$	€	Date	Place	Lot	Auc. H.
1922	Series 5 Sporting	16210	L	90-120.000 USD	53.526*	66.000*	59.242*	07-10-16	Hershey	239	RMS F533

Pale yellow with black fenders; described as in largely original condition. Mechanicals reconditioned in recent years (see Bonhams lots 343 2.6.13 $121,000 and 120 12.3.15 NS).

| 1923 | Series 6 Sporting | 20239 | L | NQ | 80.626* | 99.000* | 93.110* | 21-01-17 | Scottsdale | 1360 | B/J |

Pale blue with black fenders and brown leather interior; restored in the late 1980s (see lot 144 RM/Sotheby's 8.10.15 $82,500).

MERCURY (USA) (1939-2010)

Year	Model	Chassis no.	Steering	Estimate	£	$	€	Date	Place	Lot	Auc. H.
1939	Series 99A coupé	99A93297	L	NA	22.222*	28.600*	24.367*	19-08-17	Monterey	1050	R&S

Tan with tan cloth interior; in good overall condition. From the Art Astor Collection.

| 1941 | Series 19A station wagon | 99A380723 | L | 90-115.000 USD | 63.248* | 81.400* | 69.353* | 18-08-17 | Carmel | 1 | Bon F534 |

Light green with wooden panels; restored in 2000.

| 1948 | Series 89M convertible | 899A2155227 | L | 60-80.000 USD | 35.825* | 44.000* | 41.259* | 18-01-17 | Scottsdale | 71 | WoA |

Red; 200 miles covered since a full restoration (see lot 1121 Auctions America 25.6.16 NS).

| 1949 | Series 9CM 2-door station wagon | 9CM262504 | L | NQ | 33.569* | 42.900* | 40.099* | 22-04-17 | Arlington | 22 | WoA |

Black with wooden panels and tan vinyl interior; restored. From the Monical collection.

| 1949 | Series 9CM coupé | 9CM290057 | L | 45-50.000 USD | 36.357 | 46.750 | 42.982 | 13-05-17 | Auburn | 3109 | AA |

Green with beige interior; described as in original, unrestored condition. 63,000 believed original miles on the odometer (see lot 246 RM 8.5.06 $41,250).

| 1951 | Series 1CM convertible | 51DA20714M | L | NQ | 36.152* | 46.200* | 43.183* | 22-04-17 | Arlington | 33 | WoA |

Yellow with brown interior; older restoration. From the Monical collection (see lot 54 H & H 16.4.09 $50,809).

| 1951 | Series 1CM sport coupé | 51SL124801M | L | 30-40.000 USD | 20.745* | 26.400* | 23.628* | 24-06-17 | Santa Monica | 129 | RMS |

Tan; restored. Automatic transmission.

| 1964 | Comet Lightweight hardtop | 4H23551848 | L | 250-275.000 USD | 160.115 | 195.000 | 182.891 | 15-01-17 | Kissimmee | S118 | Mec F535 |

White with red interior; restored. One of 22 A/FX lightweight cars built. Raced in period. 425bhp 427 engine with 4-speed manual gearbox. From the Don Fezell collection.

| 1964 | Parklane Super Maurader hardtop | 4Z67R513249 | L | 100-125.000 USD | 76.840* | 100.000* | 89.450* | 20-05-17 | Indianapolis | S98.1 | Mec |

Turquoise with white interior; fully restored. 425bhp 427 engine with 4-speed manual gearbox. One of three examples known to survive.

| 1967 | Monterey S-55 convertible | 7Z45Q515421 | L | 35-50.000 USD | 27.217* | 34.000* | 30.648* | 04-11-16 | Dallas | F96 | Mec |

Turquoise with white interior; 345bhp 428 engine with automatic transmission.

| 1970 | Cougar Eliminator hardtop | 0F91G544281 | L | 150-175.000 USD | | NS | | 03-09-16 | Auburn | 5132 | AA |

Gold with black stripe and black interior; restored. Fitted with the factory Super Drag Pak. Boss 302 engine with manual gearbox.

| 1970 | Cougar XR-7 convertible | 0F94Q537182 | L | NQ | 123.165 | 150.000 | 140.685 | 15-01-17 | Kissimmee | S36 | Mec |

Blue with black interior; less than 200 miles covered since the restoration. Since 1979 in the same family ownership. 428 Cobra Jet engine with manual gearbox.

F535: 1964 Mercury Comet Lightweight hardtop F536: 1970 Mercury Cougar XR-7 convertible

Year	Model	(Bodybuilder)	Chassis no.	Steering	Estimate	Hammer price £	$	€	Date	Place	Lot	Auc. H.

F537: 1912 Metallurgique 12hp cabriolet (Van den Plas)

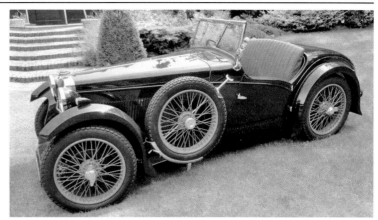

F538: 1932 MG F Magna threesome sports tourer

Year	Model	Chassis no.	Steering	Estimate	£	$	€	Date	Place	Lot	Auc. H.
1970	**Cougar Eliminator**	0F91G511824	L	NQ	89.584*	110.000*	103.455*	21-01-17	Scottsdale	1082	B/J
Orange with black interior; recent full restoration. Boss 302 engine with manual gearbox.												
1969	**Cougar XR-7 convertible**	9F94Q557106	L	NQ	67.188*	82.500*	77.591*	21-01-17	Scottsdale	981.1	B/J
Maroon with white interior; restored. 428 Cobra Jet engine with automatic transmission.												
1968	**Cougar GT-E hardtop**	8F93W537798	L	NQ	72.261*	90.000*	84.420*	08-04-17	Houston	S50	Mec
White with black interior; 390bhp 427 engine with automatic transmission. From the Laquay Automobile Collection.												
1970	**Cougar XR-7 convertible**	0F94Q536901	L	180-200.000 USD	138.312	180.000	161.010	20-05-17	Indianapolis	S132	Mec **F536**
Silver with black leather interior; restored in the late 1990s. 428 Cobra Jet engine with manual gearbox.												

MESSERSCHMITT (D) *(1953-1956)*

1955	**KR 175**	9190	C	40-50.000 USD		NS		24-06-17	Santa Monica	143	RMS
White and light blue.												

METALLURGIQUE (B) *(1901-1927)*

1912	**12hp cabriolet (Van den Plas)**	15149	R	22-28.000 GBP	36.800	46.401	43.244	07-12-16	London	356	Bon **F537**
Imported into the UK in 1913, since 1988 in the same family ownership. Little used in recent years, it runs and drives well.												

MG (GB) *(1924-1980)*

1930	**M Midget**	2M359	R	28-33.000 EUR		NS		19-03-17	Fontainebleau	213	Ose
Restored (see lot 209 Osenat 9.11.14 $43.000).												
1932	**F Magna threesome sports tourer**	F1286	R	65-75.000 GBP	64.750	80.555	74.955	29-03-17	Duxford	43	H&H **F538**
Dark blue with grey interior; fully restored between 2002 and 2010. Engine recently overhauled.												
1932	**J2 Midget**	J2087	R	30-35.000 GBP	27.000	34.714	31.919	13-05-17	Silverstone	340	SiC
Black with green interior; restored.												
1933	**L Magna roadster**	L0317	R	150-200.000 USD	64.103*	82.500*	70.290*	18-08-17	Monterey	168	RMS
British racing green with green leather interior; built with 4-seater tourer body, the car was fitted with the present 2-seater body at unspecified date. Imported into the USA a few years ago (see lot 119 RM/Sotheby's 28.1.16 $99,000).												
1934	**N Magnette**	NA0448	R	70-80.000 GBP	73.920	90.596	82.214	12-10-16	Duxford	75	H&H **F539**
Black with apple green interior; bought new by driver Ken Crawford and raced in period. Acquired in 1987 by the current owner and fully restored over a nearly 30 years period.												
1934	**P Midget tourer**	PA0711	R	60-90.000 USD	26.773*	33.000*	30.931*	19-01-17	Scottsdale	105	Bon
British racing green; described as in good overall condition.												
1936	**PB Midget**	PB0540	R	40-60.000 EUR	44.733*	55.747*	52.448*	10-02-17	Paris	52	Art
Green; restored in 2011-12. Last serviced in December 2016.												

F539: 1934 MG N Magnette

F540: 1938 MG TA Tickford cabriolet (Salmons)

Year	Model	(Bodybuilder)	Chassis no.	Steering	Estimate	Hammer price £	$	€	Date	Place	Lot	Auc. H.
1934	**P Midget**		PA01011	R	30-35.000 GBP	25.416	31.620	29.422	29-03-17	Duxford	60	H&H
Green with black interior; restored at unspecified date. Some recent mechanical works.												
1934	**PA Midget**		PA1438	R	NA	22.474	28.600	25.597	24-06-17	Santa Monica	244	RMS
Two-tone blue with blue interior.												
1937	**SA saloon**		SA1857	R	18-22.000 GBP		NS		29-03-17	Duxford	119	H&H
Partially restored: body finished in primer.												
1938	**TA Tickford cabriolet**	**(Salmons)**	TA2566	R	75-110.000 USD	62.447	77.000	69.115	07-10-16	Hershey	221	RMS
Pale yellow with red leather interior; 28 miles covered since the restoration. The factory 1,275cc engine has been replaced with a more powerful 1,750cc unit.												
1939	**TA**		TA2931	R	28-32.000 GBP	38.080	46.671	42.353	12-10-16	Duxford	19	H&H
Red with red interior; restored some years ago (see lot 82 H & H 21.9.11 $44,673).												
1938	**TA Tickford cabriolet**	**(Salmons)**	TA2736	R	100-140.000 USD	70.127*	85.250*	80.340*	10-03-17	Amelia Island	134	RMS **F540**
Black with red leather interior; 287 miles covered since the restoration completed in 1994. From the Orin Smith collection (see lots Barrett-Jackson 633 20.1.00 $74,200, RM 452 15.8.03 $70,400 and 127 12.3.11 $112,750, and RM/Sotheby's 161 14.3.15 $115,500).												
1936	**TA**		TA0778	R	27-33.000 AUD		NS		30-04-17	Melbourne	20	Mos
Green with tan interior; restored at unspecified date.												
1937	**TA**		TA1400	R	36-40.000 GBP		NS		26-07-17	Duxford	22	H&H
Two-tone metallic green with red leather interior; reimported from Australia into the UK in 2000 and subsequently restored (see lots 354 Coys 28.7.03 NS, 20 H & H 17.2.10 NS, and 136 Coys 14.8.10 NS).												
1947	**TC Special replica**		3798	R	80-100.000 GBP	66.666	88.832	78.839	10-09-16	Goodwood	135	Bon
Replica of the car modified in period by George Phillips and raced at several events including the 1949 Le Mans 24 Hours. Built on an original 1947 TC chassis; engine built to period racing specification. Driven at some historic events including the 2014 Goodwood Revival Meeting and the 2016 Le Mans Classic. With FIA HTP papers.												
1946	**TC**		TC1370	R	25-30.000 GBP	23.520	28.826	26.159	12-10-16	Duxford	37	H&H
Dark green with green interior; in good overall condition (see lot 68 H & H 15.4.15 $28,963).												
1949	**TC**		XPAG7496	R	34-38.000 USD	23.335	29.150	26.276	05-11-16	Hilton Head	196	AA
Green with black interior; restored.												
1949	**TC**		TC9506	R	30-40.000 AUD	22.717	28.246	26.667	27-11-16	Melbourne	40	Mos
British racing green; since 1966 in the current ownership. Fully restored between 1966 and 1971. TF (XPAG) 1500cc block engine. A 1250cc engine block and the original BMC engine crate included with the sale.												
1947	**TC**		TC3781	R	50-75.000 USD	49.084*	60.500*	56.707*	19-01-17	Scottsdale	29	Bon **F541**
Dark blue with red interior; fully restored. Engine upgraded with supercharger.												
1945	**TC**		TC0421	R	19-22.000 GBP	19.000	24.428	22.462	13-05-17	Silverstone	341	SiC
Cream and lime green; restored. Reimported into the UK from the USA in 2015.												
1947	**TC**		XAG3796	R	19-25.000 GBP	21.674	28.256	25.389	18-05-17	London	110	Coy
Yellow with brown interior; restored.												
1950	**TD**		TD2494	R	15-20.000 GBP	14.950*	19.858*	17.743*	03-09-16	Beaulieu	473	Bon
Two-tone green with green interior; described as in good overall condition.												
1953	**TD**		TD23515	R	18-22.000 GBP	16.500	20.887	19.155	12-11-16	Birmingham	644	SiC
Green with tan leather interior; it requires some attention to the mechanicals and paintwork.												
1952	**TDC MkII**		XPAGGTD213826	L	35-50.000 USD	18.076*	23.100*	21.592*	22-04-17	Arlington	157	WoA
First restored in 1969 and restored again in recent times.												
1953	**TD**		26932	R	20-30.000 EUR	21.010	26.801	24.000	18-06-17	Fontainebleau	65	Ose
In good overall condition; interior replaced; mechanicals overhauled.												
1955	**TF**		TF6880	L	18-22.000 GBP		NS		03-09-16	Beaulieu	502	Bon
Red; repainted in 2015.												
1954	**TF**		HDA165324	R	23-28.000 GBP	24.780	33.101	29.302	08-09-16	Fontwell Park	149	Coy
Restored in the 1990s.												
1954	**TF**		HDH553391	R	19-23.000 GBP	21.280	26.081	23.668	12-10-16	Duxford	53	H&H
Red with red interior; in the 2000s fitted with a modern 5-speed gearbox (see lot 215 Coys 11.7.09 $32,293).												
1954	**TF**		HDB463078	L	NQ	22.971	29.000	27.248	03-12-16	Kansas City	S133	Mec **F542**
Yellow with tan interior; restored.												

F541: 1947 MG TC

F542: 1954 MG TF

Year	Model	(Bodybuilder)	Chassis no.	Steering	Estimate	£	$	€	Date	Place	Lot	Auc. H.
1955	TF		HDA466538	L	22-28.000 GBP	24.080	29.917	28.089	18-02-17	London	304	Coy
	Black with green leather interior; mechanicals overhauled. Recently imported into the UK from the USA where it remained in the same family ownership since new (see lot 3 Bonhams 5.6.16 $13,750).
1955	TF		HDA466538	L	19-25.000 GBP	17.784	22.230	20.960	12-04-17	London	306	Coy
	See lot 304 Coys 18.2.17.
1955	TF		HAD466538	L	18-25.000 GBP	19.000	24.658	21.514	29-06-17	Fontwell Park	109	Coy
	See lot 306 Coys 12.4.17.
1955	TF		HDB269985	R	30-35.000 GBP	NS			26-07-17	Duxford	20	H&H
	Red with cream interior; restored between 2009 and 2011 and converted to right hand drive. 5-speed gearbox.
1960	Magnette MkIII		GHS1L11036	L	5-7.000 EUR	7.632*	9.490*	8.960*	25-11-16	Milan	844	RMS
	Grey and green with red interior. From the Duemila Ruote collection.
1959	MGA roadster		HDA4355438	L	30-35.000 GBP	NS			03-09-16	Beaulieu	509	Bon
	Restored in 2014.
1956	MGA roadster		HDC4312827	L	26-30.000 GBP	29.500	37.509	35.046	05-12-16	London	141	Coy
	The car has covered less than 300 miles since the restoration completed in 2016.
1959	MGA roadster		650880548	R	20-25.000 GBP	16.240	20.477	19.084	07-12-16	Chateau Impney	12	H&H
	White with black interior; described as in good overall condition.
1956	MGA roadster		HDA4315756	L	35-50.000 USD	25.979*	31.900*	30.002*	20-01-17	Scottsdale	1	G&Co
	Iris blue with navy blue interior; one owner until 2010. Recently restored and fitted with more recent front disc brakes (see lot 1 Gooding & Company 29.1.16 $41,800).
1957	MGA roadster		15706	L	25-30.000 EUR	NS			19-03-17	Fontainebleau	220	Ose
	Primrose yellow; restored five years ago. 5-speed gearbox (see lot 343 Osenat 15.3.15 $33,492).
1958	MGA roadster		HDA4352352	L	30-40.000 EUR	29.192	38.375	32.335	05-08-17	Schloss Dyck	203	Coy
	British racing green with beige leather interior; in good overall condition.
1959	MGA Twin Cam roadster		YD3734	L	100-120.000 USD	40.303*	49.500*	46.416*	18-01-17	Scottsdale	52	WoA
	Old English white with red leather interior; fully restored (see lot 207 RM/Sotheby's 14.3.15 $82,500).
1959	MGA Twin Cam roadster		YD3617	L	65-85.000 USD	47.032*	57.750*	54.314*	21-01-17	Scottsdale	151	G&Co
	Old English white with black leather interior; restored in the UK in the 1980s; described as in very good overall condition.
1959	MGA Twin Cam roadster		YD3734	L	75-100.000 USD	64.103*	82.500*	70.290*	19-08-17	Pebble Beach	176	G&Co
	See lot 52 Worldwide Auctioneers 18.1.17.
1959	MGA Twin Cam coupé		YM11893	R	28-34.000 GBP	25.645	32.608	30.466	05-12-16	London	137	Coy F543
	Blue; restored 10-15 years ago.
1958	MGA Twin Cam coupé		YM3873	L	30-40.000 EUR	NS			08-04-17	Essen	187	Coy
	Red with black roof and black interior; rallied when new. Engine recently overhauled.
1960	MGA 1600 roadster		GHNL77386	L	30-40.000 EUR	NS			06-11-16	Lyon	326	Ose
	Green; in good working order (see lot 231 Osenat 9.11.14 $32,250).
1960	MGA 1600 roadster		GHN89619	R	14-16.000 GBP	15.960	19.835	18.534	16-11-16	Donington Park	70	H&H
	Red; older restoration.
1960	MGA 1600 roadster		GHNL80925	L	25-35.000 EUR	23.107	29.526	27.600	22-04-17	Bagatelle	124	Agu
	Green; restored some years ago.
1959	MGA 1600 roadster		GHNL80102	R	22-27.000 GBP	31.360	40.806	36.503	20-05-17	Ascot	189	His
	Iris blue with black leather interior; reimported into the UK from the USA in 2011 and restored.
1961	MGA 1600 roadster		88054	L	30-40.000 USD	17.969*	23.100*	20.594*	04-06-17	Greenwich	171	Bon F544
	Red with tan interior; 7,000 miles covered since the restoration completed in 1988.
1960	MGA 1600 coupé		GHDL77155	L	35-45.000 USD	21.519*	27.500*	25.704*	22-04-17	Arlington	162	WoA
	Finished in blue with black interior, the car was sold new to the USA. Described as in good overall condition.
1962	MGA 1600 MkII roadster		GHNL2105523	L	28-38.000 EUR	29.985	36.692	33.350	15-10-16	Salzburg	436	Dor
	Iris blue with black interior; imported in 2005 into Germany from the USA where the body and interior had been restored. Engine serviced 1,000 miles ago.
1962	MGA 1600 MkII roadster		GHNL2108626	L	37-45.000 EUR	35.442	43.807	40.800	19-03-17	Fontainebleau	212	Ose
	Grey with red leather interior; engine overhauled in recent years.

F543: 1959 MG MGA Twin Cam coupé

F544: 1961 MG MGA 1600 roadster

Year	Model	(Bodybuilder)	Chassis no.	Steering	Estimate	Hammer price £	$	€	Date	Place	Lot	Auc. H.
1963	**MGB roadster**		A015558BG13	L	18-22.000 EUR	17.147*	20.830*	19.072*	30-10-16	Paris	140	Art
White; in good working order.												
1966	**MGB GT**		GHD3191354	R	10-15.000 GBP	18.975	23.453	21.842	19-03-17	Goodwood	32	Bon
Red with original black leather interior; less than 1,000 miles covered since the restoration completed in 2006. Since 1989 in the current ownership.												
1968	**MGB MkII roadster**		GHN4U169796G	L	16-23.000 EUR	17.051	21.299	19.200	06-11-16	Lyon	322	Ose
Green with beige leather interior redone a few years ago.												
1967	**MGB MkII roadster**		GHN3U133548G	L	30-40.000 USD	31.670*	38.500*	36.282*	11-03-17	Amelia Island	292	RMS
Blue with black leather interior; sold new to the USA, the car remained with its first owner until 2004 when it was bought by the present vendor. 6,000 miles covered since the restoration completed in 2011.												
1972	**MGB MkII roadster**		GHN5239123G	L	17-23.000 EUR		NS		19-03-17	Fontainebleau	237	Ose
White; acquired in 2015 by the current, second owner. 147,000 miles on the odometer.												
1979	**MGB MkII roadster**		GHN5UL4716G	L	12-18.000 EUR	30.580*	45.134*	34.777*	02-07-17	Monaco	104	Art **F545**
Blue; fully restored between 2014 and 2016.												
1972	**MGB GT MkII**		GHD5298277G	R	48-5.200 GBP	7.006	8.753	8.278	23-02-17	Donington Park	41	H&H
Red with cream interior; some restoration works carried out in the past.												
1970	**MGB GT MkII**		GHD5192234	R	10-14.000 GBP	12.320	15.888	13.922	08-07-17	Brooklands	122	His
Red; recently restored.												
1970	**MGC roadster**		GCN12962G	R	20-24.000 GBP	20.440	25.051	22.733	12-10-16	Duxford	52	H&H
Old English white with black interior; described as in very good overall condition. Body restored in 2003 circa.												
1968	**MGC roadster**		GCN1522	R	NQ	20.720*	25.349*	23.994*	04-03-17	Brooklands	218	His
British racing green with black interior; in good overall condition.												
1968	**MGC roadster**		GCN12940G	R	18-22.000 GBP	19.968	24.842	23.115	29-03-17	Duxford	49	H&H
Dark blue with black interior; restored and fitted with power steering and 5-speed gearbox.												
1968	**MGC roadster**		GCN1U8139G	L	30-35.000 USD	20.109	25.850	23.045	04-06-17	Greenwich	115	Bon
British racing green with black interior; restored.												
1968	**MGC GT**		GCD1U3792G	R	10-12.000 GBP	10.304	12.806	11.966	16-11-16	Donington Park	17	H&H
Primrose yellow with black interior; body restored.												
1970	**Midget MkIII**		GAN592713	R	NQ	8.960*	11.659*	10.429*	20-05-17	Ascot	111	His
See lot 325 Historics 6.11.16.												
1975	**MGB GT V8**		GD2D11350G	R	15-20.000 GBP	14.160	17.202	15.749	29-10-16	London	156	Coy
Black; described as in good overall condition. Body repainted. Upgraded with power steering.												
1974	**MGB GT V8**		GD2D11076G	R	NQ	11.872*	15.310*	13.415*	08-07-17	Brooklands	233	His
Black with black leather interior; in good overall condition.												
1977	**Midget 1500**		GAN6192798G	R	33-5.300 GBP	3.416	4.245	3.967	16-11-16	Donington Park	26	H&H
Dark green; restored in 2009.												
1979	**Midget 1500**		GAN6229488G	R	10-15.000 GBP	28.750	37.312	32.554	30-06-17	Goodwood	242	Bon **F546**
Limited edition model from the final year of production; black with black interior; retained by a MG dealer and never registered; 35 miles covered.												

MILWAUKEE STEAM (USA) (1900-1902)

Year	Model		Chassis no.	Steering	Estimate	£	$	€	Date	Place	Lot	Auc. H.
1901	**Stanhope**		316	R	50-70.000 GBP		NS		12-10-16	Duxford	110	H&H
Black and green; restored in the 1950s in the USA and fitted with new boiler and water tank. Restored again in the 2000s.												
1900	**Stanhope**		NQ	R	70-90.000 EUR		NS		01-05-17	Obenheim	304	Ose
Black and red; fully restored. New burner and boiler.												

MINERVA (B) (1899-1939)

Year	Model		Chassis no.	Steering	Estimate	£	$	€	Date	Place	Lot	Auc. H.
1930	**Type AM convertible sedan**		57804	L	500-700.000 USD	376.068	484.000	412.368	19-08-17	Pebble Beach	122	G&Co **F547**
Tan with green leather interior to the front compartment and beige cloth to the rear; known history from the 1940s in the USA; in single ownership from 1974 to 2016; discovered following a long period in storage in largely original condition; 62,310 miles on the odometer; returned to running status.												

F545: 1979 MG MGB MkII roadster

F546: 1979 MG Midget 1500

Year	Model	(Bodybuilder)	Chassis no.	Steering	Estimate	Hammer price £	$	€	Date	Sale Place	Lot	Auc. H.

F547: 1930 Minerva Type AM convertible sedan

F548: 1957 Molina Monza Holden

MITSUBISHI (J) (1917-)

1992	3000 GT		22565	L	15-25.000 EUR	15.666	19.568	17.640	05-11-16	Lyon	261	Agu

Black with beige leather interior; described as in very good overall condition. Clutch and timing belt replaced in 2015.

| 1996 | 3000 GT | | 22565 | L | 15-25.000 EUR | 13.777 | 17.569 | 15.720 | 10-06-17 | Lyon | 132 | Agu |

See lot 261 Aguttes 5.11.16.

MOLINA (AUS)

| 1957 | Monza Holden | | NQ | R | 250-350.000 AUD | 144.562 | 179.748 | 169.702 | 27-11-16 | Melbourne | 46 | Mos |

Red; fitted with a supercharged Holden "Grey" engine, the car was raced in Australia until the 1960s. In the 1990s it was first restored, saving some 60% of the original tubular chassis, and subsequently raced at historic events. In 2013 it was acquired by the current owner and restored again; engine rebuilt.
F548

MONTEVERDI (CH) (1959-1984)

| 1971 | 375L High Speed (Fissore) | | 2052 | L | 110-130.000 GBP | 156.800 | 209.830 | 186.733 | 07-09-16 | London | 170 | RMS |

The car was exhibited at the 1971 Geneva Motor Show where it was acquired by the current and sole owner. Described as in very good original condition; 51,043 kms covered. 375bhp 440 Chrysler V8 engine with automatic transmission.
F549

| 1980 | Safari | | 5074 | L | 15-25.000 EUR | 15.509 | 18.978 | 17.250 | 15-10-16 | Salzburg | 422 | Dor |

Light metallic brown with brown interior; since 1985 in the same ownership. Unused for some time and mildly recommissioned in recent years. Automatic transmission.

MORETTI (I) (1945-1984)

| 1969 | 500 Coupé | | 1898816 | L | 8-12.000 EUR | 8.861 | 10.952 | 10.200 | 19-03-17 | Fontainebleau | 233 | Ose |

Red with black interior; in good overall condition (see lot 107 Artcurial 11.11.12 $15,879).
F550

| 1976 | 128 coupé | | 1871040 | L | 9-14.000 EUR | 6.204 | 7.591 | 6.900 | 15-10-16 | Salzburg | 408 | Dor |

Red with black interior; in good overall condition. Since 1976 in the same family ownership.

| 1970 | 126 Minimaxi | | 2741029 | L | 18-22.000 USD | 14.089 | 17.600 | 15.865 | 05-11-16 | Hilton Head | 205 | AA |

Red with black interior.

MORGAN (GB) (1910-)

| 1933 | Super Sport | | 452D | R | 18-24.000 GBP | 37.950 | 49.252 | 42.971 | 30-06-17 | Goodwood | 209 | Bon |

Red with black interior; since 1965 in the same family ownership; restored in 1967; in good driving order. From the Joy Rainey Collection.
F551

| 1947 | F Super | | 761 | R | 35-40.000 USD | 32.575* | 39.600* | 37.319* | 11-03-17 | Amelia Island | 210 | RMS |

Light green; bought in 2005 by the current owner and subsequently restored.

| 1949 | 4/4 | | G1874 | R | 10-15.000 GBP | 10.925 | 14.512 | 12.966 | 03-09-16 | Beaulieu | 501 | Bon |

Red with black interior; reimported into the UK in 2014 and never used (see lot 150 Coys 10.1.15 NS).

F549: 1971 Monteverdi 375L High Speed (Fissore)

F550: 1969 Moretti 500 Coupé

Year	Model	(Bodybuilder)	Chassis no.	Steering	Estimate	Hammer Price £	$	€	Date	Place	Lot	Auc. H.
1936	4/4 roadster		096	R	50-70.000 USD	35.939	46.200	41.187	04-06-17	Greenwich	133	Bon F552
Dark green; restored in the early 1980s, engine rebuilt in 1986. Last serviced in July 2016.													
1963	Plus 4 four-seater		5301	L	28-42.000 EUR	27.917	34.161	31.050	15-10-16	Salzburg	414	Dor
Grey with original leather interior; body repainted. 2-litre Triumph engine.													
1962	Plus 4 cabriolet		5104	L	40-50.000 USD	27.771*	34.100*	32.071*	21-01-17	Scottsdale	133	G&Co
Black with black leather interior; in driving order. TR4 Triumph engine.													
1954	Plus 4		P3069	L	60-75.000 USD		NS		19-08-17	Monterey	S18	Mec
White with black interior.													
1960	4/4		A644	R	18-22.000 GBP	18.563	23.866	21.945	13-05-17	Silverstone	373	SiC
Red with cream leather interior; restored. Ford engine.													
1967	4/4 roadster		B1448	L	40-60.000 USD	45.352*	58.300*	51.974*	04-06-17	Greenwich	138	Bon
Blue with tan interior; restoration completed in 2009.													
1985	Plus 8		R9438	R	NA	36.560	48.563	43.389	02-09-16	Salon Privé	251	SiC
Nutmeg with black ambra interior; in original condition. Two owners and less than 7,500 miles covered.													
1970	Plus 8 Sports Roadster		R7285	R	40-50.000 GBP		NS		03-09-16	Beaulieu	425	Bon
Brilliant green with black interior; in good overall condition. Exhibited at the Morgan stand at the 1970 London Motor Show.													
1993	Plus 8 Sports Roadster		R10910	R	20-25.000 GBP	31.050	41.244	36.850	03-09-16	Beaulieu	466	Bon
Aluminium coachwork recently repainted.													
1971	Plus 8		R7351	R	35-40.000 GBP		NS		08-10-16	Ascot	333	Coy
Red with black leather interior; described as in good overall condition. Bought over 40 years ago by the current owner directly from Peter Morgan and raced at some events in the 1970s.													
1993	Plus 8 Sports Roadster		R10910	R	27-32.000 GBP	25.000	32.445	28.308	29-06-17	Fontwell Park	112	Coy
See lot 466 Bonhams 3.9.16.													
1964	Plus 4 Plus coupé		A5558	L	120-140.000 GBP	128.800	172.360	153.388	07-09-16	London	104	RMS F553
Black and red with red leather interior; sold new to the USA. Restored to concours condition in the 2000s and later reimported into the UK by the current, fifth owner (see lots 106 Bonhams 16.8.13 NS and 112 RM 8.9.14 $207,368).													
1963	Plus 4 Plus coupé		A5504	R	175-225.000 USD	72.650*	93.500*	79.943*	17-08-17	Monterey	57	WoA
Red with grey vinyl interior; the 1963 Earls Court Motor Show display car; sold new in the UK; exported to the USA in the 1970s; bought in 2007 by Allen Smith and subsequently fully restored on a new chassis supplied by Morgan (the original is also available).													

MORRIS (GB) *(1912-1983)*

Year	Model	(Bodybuilder)	Chassis no.	Steering	Estimate	£	$	€	Date	Place	Lot	Auc. H.
1926	Cowley "bullnose" tourer		154507	R	9-11.000 GBP	11.648	14.552	13.763	23-02-17	Donington Park	22	H&H
Khaki with khaki interior; since 1973 in the same family ownership; restored in 1984; in running order.													
1926	Cowley "bullnose" tourer		145174	R	13-15.000 GBP	14.175	18.488	15.877	26-07-17	Duxford	8	H&H
Blue and black with dark blue interior; restored several years ago; in good working order. Since 1978 in the current ownership.													
1930	Minor saloon		M29355	R	10-12.000 GBP	9.225	12.032	10.333	26-07-17	Duxford	7	H&H
Maroon and black with brown leatherette interior; several restoration works carried out many years ago.													
1940	Ten saloon		SMTN84075	L	12-16.000 USD	8.921*	11.000*	9.874*	07-10-16	Hershey	266	RMS
Dark green with brown interior; in good overall condition.													
1933	Ten Special coupé		12369	R	9-11.000 GBP		NS		12-10-16	Duxford	6	H&H
Two-tone grey with light blue interior; in good overall condition.													
1934	Ten Special Coupé		14823	R	8-10.000 GBP	9.000	11.532	10.312	02-06-17	Solihull	21	H&H F554
Green and black with green leather interior; restored at unspecified date, the car requires recommissioning prior to use (see lot 34 H & H 15.4.15 $21,680).													
1958	Minor Traveller		FLA4625082	L	50-60.000 USD	37.099*	45.100*	42.502*	10-03-17	Amelia Island	159	RMS F555
Dark green with wooden panels; restored. From the Orin Smith collection.													
1970	Minor 1000 Traveller		302032	L	14-20.000 EUR	19.690	25.055	22.425	24-06-17	Wien	313	Dor
Green with wooden panels and beige interior; in 2010 restored and converted to left-hand drive in the UK.													
1970	Minor 1000 saloon		MA2S5D1284282M	R	5-8.000 GBP	14.375	18.656	16.277	30-06-17	Goodwood	208	Bon
Blue; prepared in 2003 for the 2004 London-to-Sydney Marathon. Engine enlarged to 1,275cc; front disc brakes. Engine rebuilt (it still requires running in). From the Joy Rainey Collection.													

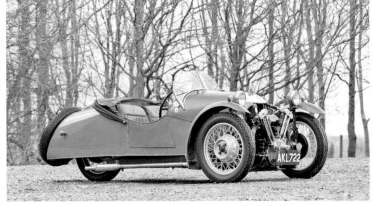

F551: 1933 Morgan Super Sport

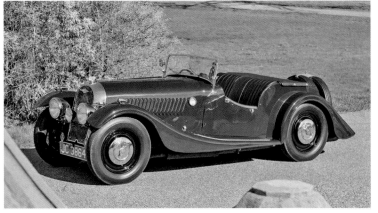

F552: 1936 Morgan 4/4 roadster

F553: 1964 Morgan Plus 4 Plus coupé

F554: 1934 Morris Ten Special Coupé

Year	Model	(Bodybuilder)	Chassis no.	Steering	Estimate	£	$	€	Date	Place	Lot	Auc. H.
1959	**Minor 1000 convertible**		FCA47577349	L	NQ	13.240*	16.500*	15.523*	11-02-17	Boca Raton	133	TFA
	Red with tan interior; in good running condition. 35,908 miles on the odometer.											
1962	**Mini**		MA254124536	R	12-16.000 GBP		NS		10-09-16	Goodwood	185	Bon
	Grey with dark grey interior; described as in good original condition (see lot 389 Bonhams 26.6.15 NS).											
1959	**Mini**		MA2541290	R	45-55.000 GBP		NS		08-10-16	Ascot	321	Coy
	One of the first press cars used for press car races also. Bought in 1960 directly from the factory by journalist John Bolton and later by the current, second owner who restored it (see lot 227 Coys 2.7.16 $55,784).											
1969	**Mini Traveller**		MAW61256221A	R	9-14.000 GBP	14.560	17.813	16.860	04-03-17	Brooklands	138	His
	Red with red interior; body restored in 2014, original wooden. Automatic transmission. Since new in the same family ownership.											
1968	**Mini Traveller MkII**		1114069	L	12-18.000 EUR	10.549	13.479	12.600	22-04-17	Bagatelle	164	Agu
	Champagne with black interior; body repainted about 15 years ago.											
1966	**Mini Cooper S**		850926	R	100-150.000 GBP		NS		08-09-16	Fontwell Park	140	Coy
	Red with white roof; Works car from 1966 to 1968, it was driven by Timo Makinen and Paddy Hopkirk at several rallies. For more than 30 years in the current ownership, it is described as in ready to use condition (see lot 332 Coys 1.12.15 $172,103).											
1971	**Mini Cooper S MkIII**		XAD1312155A	R	22-25.000 GBP	28.688	36.316	33.304	12-11-16	Birmingham	354	SiC
	Red with black roof and blue vinyl interior; restoration completed in 2014 (see lot 258 Historics 28.11.15 $26,971).											
1971	**Mini Cooper S MkIII**		265157	L	10-12.000 EUR	22.897*	28.471*	26.880*	25-11-16	Milan	901	RMS
	Red with white roof; 77,350 kms. From the Duemila Ruote collection.											
1966	**Mini Cooper S**		850926	R	40-60.000 GBP	51.080	62.200	58.344	14-01-17	Birmingham	151	Coy **F556**
	See lot 140 Coys 8.9.16.											
1965	**Mini Cooper S**		KA254550919	R	50-58.000 GBP	56.000	68.510	64.848	04-03-17	Brooklands	168	His
	Grey with white roof; fully restored. 970cc engine.											
1964	**Mini Cooper S**		KA2S4L553414	L	50-60.000 GBP		NS		19-03-17	Goodwood	69	Bon
	Red with white roof; modified in 1966 by Broadspeed for the Swedish championship and fitted with a 971cc engine. Restored between 1983 and 1985, fitted with a 1,293cc engine built by Richard Longman and raced at historic events. Engine recently rebuilt.											
1964	**Mini Cooper S**		KA2S4488434	R	39-46.000 GBP	47.600	61.937	55.406	20-05-17	Ascot	243	His
	Blue with old English white roof and blue and gold original interior; restored between 2003 and 2006. 1071cc engine.											
1965	**Mini Cooper S**		KA2S4L732883	L	34-40.000 GBP		NS		08-07-17	Brooklands	201	His
	Red with black roof; full restoration recently completed. 1,275cc engine.											
1970	**Mini Cooper S Margrave**	(Wood & Pickett)	KA2S61321285	R	40-50.000 GBP		NS		26-07-17	Duxford	83	H&H
	Blue with original black leather interior; restored in the 2000s; engine and gearbox overhauled in more recent years (see lot 398 Historics 7.6.14 $67,838).											
1964	**Mini Cooper S**		KA2S4550846	R	43-50.000 GBP		NS		29-07-17	Silverstone	425	SiC
	Light green with old English white roof; the 970cc engine has covered some 3,000 miles since the rebuild.											
1967	**Mini Moke**		MAB1996586	R	17-20.000 GBP	19.688	24.923	22.856	12-11-16	Birmingham	649	SiC
	White; restored. Used when new by the BMC Publicity Department.											

F555: 1958 Morris Minor Traveller

F556: 1966 Morris Mini Cooper S

313

Year	Model	(Bodybuilder)	Chassis No.	Steering	Estimate	Hammer Price £	Hammer Price $	Hammer Price €	Sale Date	Sale Place	Lot	Auc. H.

NAPIER (GB) (1900-1924)

| 1913 | 15hp doctor's coupé | | 12165 | R | 35-45.000 GBP | 36.800 | 48.881 | 43.674 | 03-09-16 | Beaulieu | 490 | Bon **F557** |

Blue and black with blue leather interior; for 30 years in the same family ownership. Driven at several events.

NASH (USA) (1917-1957)

| 1934 | Ambassador V-8 lwb brougham | | 522564 | L | 20-25.000 USD | 14.532* | 18.700* | 16.641* | 03-10-16 | Philadelphia | 210 | Bon |

In highly original condition; working engine.

| 1932 | Ambassador V-8 convertible sedan | | 108316 | L | NQ | 57.407* | 71.500* | 67.067* | 08-04-17 | Palm Beach | 432 | B/J |

Red with cream interior; restored many years ago and well maintained.

| 1950 | Rambler Custom convertible | | D5980 | L | NA | 18.653 | 23.000 | 20.645 | 08-10-16 | Chicago | S176 | Mec |

Blue with blue interior; restored.

| 1950 | Rambler Custom convertible | | D5980 | L | 40-50.000 USD | 24.589 | 32.000 | 28.624 | 20-05-17 | Indianapolis | T225 | Mec |

See lot S176 Mecum 8.10.16.

| 1952 | Healey roadster | (Pinin Farina) | AZ124140 | L | NA | 56.632* | 69.300* | 62.987* | 15-10-16 | Las Vegas | 649 | B/J |

Red with red interior; older restoration (see lot 1262 Barrett-Jackson 18.1.14 $77,000).

| 1953 | Healey roadster | (Pinin Farina) | NHA1453 | L | 80-100.000 USD | 84.692 | 108.900 | 100.123 | 13-05-17 | Auburn | 3129 | AA **F558** |

Red with saddle leather interior; cosmetically restored.

| 1956 | Metropolitan convertible | | E22593 | L | 15-20.000 USD | 20.359* | 24.750* | 23.324* | 10-03-17 | Amelia Island | 101 | RMS |

Yellow and white; in very good overall condition. From the Orin Smith collection (see lot 201 RM 22.1.10 $28,600).

NISSAN (J) (1933-)

| 1973 | Datsun 240Z | | HS30100376 | R | 45-55.000 GBP | 48.375 | 61.238 | 56.159 | 12-11-16 | Birmingham | 630 | SiC |

One of 75 Super Samuri examples built by Spike Anderson; recently restored.

| 1970 | Fairlady Z 432 | | PS3000166 | R | 150-200.000 USD | 140.253* | 170.500* | 160.679* | 11-03-17 | Amelia Island | 244 | RMS **F559** |

Red with matt black hood; imported into the USA in 2013 after a restoration carried out in Japan. One of 420 examples built for the Japanese market.

| 1982 | Datsun 280ZX | | 966709 | L | 12-16.000 EUR | 9.109* | 11.066* | 10.132* | 30-10-16 | Paris | 177 | Art |

Blue; described as in very good original condition.

| 1980 | Datsun 280ZX | | HGS130164010 | L | 14-20.000 EUR | 23.224 | 29.553 | 26.450 | 24-06-17 | Wien | 341 | Dor |

Metallic red with beige interior; one owner; 26,991 kms covered.

| 1983 | 240 RS Group B | | 432688 | L | 100-120.000 EUR | 71.896 | 89.544 | 84.000 | 08-04-17 | Essen | 141 | Coy |

Red, blue and white; the car participated in the Acropolis Rally from 1983 to 1987. With FIA Historic Technical Passport.

| 1989 | Skyline R32 GT-R | | BNR32002354 | R | 50-70.000 USD | 49.271* | 60.500* | 56.900* | 20-01-17 | Phoenix | 264 | RMS |

Recently imported into the USA from Japan, the car is described as in very good original condition. 23,360 kms covered.

| 1991 | Skyline R32 GT-R | | BNR32015996 | R | 35-55.000 USD | 17.949* | 23.100* | 19.751* | 17-08-17 | Monterey | 74 | WoA |

Imported from Japan and registered for road use. Body recently repainted.

| 1992 | Skyline R32 GT-R | | BNR32221085 | R | 75-85.000 USD | 67.521* | 86.900* | 74.039* | 18-08-17 | Carmel | 40 | Bon |

Light grey; bought a few years ago by the current owner; 6,700 kms on the odometer.

NORTHERN (USA) (1902-1908)

| 1903 | Runabout | | 1512 | R | 60-70.000 USD | 31.584 | 40.000 | 35.760 | 06-10-16 | Hershey | 157 | RMS **F560** |

Dark green with red chassis; restored many years ago, cosmetically refreshed several years ago (see lot 236 RM 10.10.08 $46,200).

NSU (D) (1905-1977)

| 1965 | Spider Wankel | (Bertone) | 5601389 | R | 18-24.000 GBP | 15.525 | 20.622 | 18.425 | 03-09-16 | Beaulieu | 480 | Bon |

Red with black hardtop; bought in 1980 by the current owner and subsequently fully restored over a period of many years.

| 1969 | 1200 TT | | 3670614619 | R | 14-16.000 GBP | 12.500 | 15.761 | 14.689 | 07-12-16 | Chateau Impney | 36 | H&H **F561** |

Red with black cloth interior; engine recently overhauled.

OAKLAND (USA) (1907-1931)

| 1912 | Model 30 touring | | 7500 | R | 40-50.000 USD | 35.684* | 44.000* | 39.494* | 07-10-16 | Hershey | 236 | RMS **F562** |

Dark green and black with black interior; mechanicals restored (see lot 221 RM 11.10.13 $49,500).

| 1918 | Model 34-B touring | | C6829(engine) | L | 10-15.000 USD | 10.750* | 13.200* | 12.415* | 20-01-17 | Phoenix | 206 | RMS |

Blue with black fenders and black interior; restored many years ago. From the Jules Barsotti Collection.

OLDSMOBILE (USA) (1896-2004)

| 1903 | Model R curved dash runabout | | 19240 | R | 40-60.000 USD | 39.085* | 49.500* | 44.253* | 06-10-16 | Hershey | 119 | RMS **F563** |

Black and maroon with black interior; older, recently refreshed restoration.

| 1903 | Model R curved dash runabout | | 16232 | R | 40-45.000 GBP | | NS | | 12-10-16 | Duxford | 63 | H&H |

Black with black interior; restored in Australia in the 1980s. Registered in the UK in 2010.

| 1911 | Autocrat roadster | | 65877 | R | 650-750.000 USD | 470.085 | 605.000 | 515.460 | 19-08-17 | Monterey | 254 | RMS **F564** |

Yellow with black seats; known as "Yellow Peril". Bought new by John Greenway Albert, the car was raced in period and remained in the ownership of the Albert family until the early 1970s. First restored in the 1970s, it was restored again in 2008 (see lots 325 Christie's 19.3.99 $100,000, 260 RM 14.3.09 $660,000, and 262 RM/Sotheby's 9.10.15 $698,500).

F557: 1913 Napier 15hp doctor's coupé

F558: 1953 Nash Healey roadster (Pinin Farina)

F559: 1970 Nissan Fairlady Z 432

F560: 1903 Northern Runabout

F561: 1969 NSU 1200 TT

F562: 1912 Oakland Model 30 touring

F563: 1903 Oldsmobile Model R curved dash runabout

F564: 1911 Oldsmobile Autocrat roadster

Year	Model	(Bodybuilder)	Chassis no.	Steering	Estimate	Hammer price £	$	€	Date	Place	Lot	Auc. H.
1913	Series 53 touring	(Rothschild)	81402	R	200-250.000 USD		NS		06-10-16	Hershey	124	RMS
Green with black fenders and black interior; retained by its first owner until 1949, the car was acquired in 1995 by the current, fifth owner. Engine recently rebuilt. The sole known survivor of 500 examples built.												
1941	Series 78 coupé		7814570	L	18-24.000 EUR	15.382*	18.965*	17.024*	07-10-16	Chateau-sur-Epte	27	Art
Black; automatic transmission. From the Andre Weber Collection.												
1948	Futuramic S.98 convertible		98C13007	L	NQ	33.146	40.700	38.278	21-01-17	Scottsdale	8403	R&S
Red with leather and cloth interior; restored.												
1955	Classic 98 2-door DeLuxe Holiday hardtop		559M24633	L	NA	26.763	33.000	29.621	08-10-16	Chicago	S109.1	Mec
White and red; restored. 245bhp 324 engine with automatic transmission.												
1953	Classic 98 convertible		539M33713	L	NQ	60.917*	74.800*	70.349*	21-01-17	Scottsdale	1473	B/J
White with two-tone leather interior; restored.												
1953	Fiesta 98 convertible		539M39753	L	120-160.000 USD	126.265	167.750	149.868	03-09-16	Auburn	4102	AA **F565**
White and red with red and white leather interior; cosmetically restored (see lots 267 RM 19.1.07 $187.000 and E695 Auctions America 2.9.10 $148,500).												
1953	Fiesta 98 convertible		539M40417	L	125-175.000 USD	122.944*	160.000*	143.120*	20-05-17	Indianapolis	T124	Mec
Red and white with red and white interior; 187 miles covered since a full restoration.												
1959	Series Super 88 Holyday hardtop		598B01047	L	NQ	16.423*	20.900*	18.706*	24-06-17	Northeast	429	B/J
Light blue with two-tone blue interior; fully restored.												
1956	Series 98 Starfire convertible		569C8219	L	NA	46.227	57.000	51.163	08-10-16	Chicago	S146.1	Mec
White and brown with black and white interior.												
1957	Series 98 Starfire convertible		579C02688	L	NQ	116.459*	143.000	134.492*	21-01-17	Scottsdale	1289.2	B/J
Black with red and white interior; full restoration completed in 2015.												
1957	Series 98 Starfire convertible		579A02453	L	NQ	48.375*	59.400*	55.866*	21-01-17	Scottsdale	8553	R&S
Light blue; restored. 300bhp J2 engine.												
1957	Series 98 Starfire convertible		579M18085	L	100-120.000 USD		NS		24-06-17	Santa Monica	245	RMS
Green with green and white interior; restored (see lot 227 RM 20.1.12 $126,500).												
1964	F-85 Cutlass 442 Holiday coupé		824M227837	L	40-50.000 USD	31.235*	38.500*	36.086*	19-01-17	Phoenix	175	RMS
White with blue interior; in original condition. 46,142 miles on the odometer. 310bhp 330 engine with 4-speed manual gearbox. From the Mohrschladt Family Collection.												
1965	Starfire convertible		366675M423640	L	15-18.000 EUR	21.974*	27.092*	24.320*	07-10-16	Chateau-sur-Epte	49	Art
White with light blue interior; in good overall condition. From the Andre Weber Collection.												
1964	Starfire convertible		864M060795	L	NQ	19.234	24.000	22.210	25-03-17	Kansas City	S56	Mec
Black with black interior; believed to be 61,000 original miles. 394 engine with automatic transmission.												
1970	442 convertible		344670M309086	L	350-400.000 USD		NS		15-01-17	Kissimmee	F150.1	Mec
Black with black interior; restored. 370bhp 455 W-30 engine with manual gearbox. From the Tom Lembeck Collection.												
1970	442 convertible		344670M283717	L	170-200.000 USD	119.060	145.000	135.996	15-01-17	Kissimmee	S222	Mec
Silver with black interior; restored to concours condition. 455 W-30 engine with manual gearbox.												
1970	442 convertible		344670M266164	L	225-275.000 USD	144.075	187.500	167.719	20-05-17	Indianapolis	F162	Mec **F566**
Red with white interior; fully restored. 370bhp 455 engine with automatic transmission (see lot 1256.1 Barrett-Jackson 20.1.12 $220,000).												
1970	442 convertible		344670M369764	L	NQ	103.726	132.000	118.140	24-06-17	Northeast	680	B/J
Red with black interior; fully restored. 370bhp 455 W30 engine with automatic transmission.												
1970	442 coupé		344870M277583	L	NA	68.318*	83.600*	75.984*	15-10-16	Las Vegas	700	B/J
Red with black interior; restored. 455 W30 engine with 4-speed manual gearbox.												
1970	442 coupé		344870M182832	L	100-125.000 USD	80.050	100.000	90.140	04-11-16	Dallas	S94	Mec
Blue with blue interior; described as in original condition. 370bhp 455 W30 engine with manual gearbox.												

OPEL (D) (1898-)

Year	Model	(Bodybuilder)	Chassis no.	Steering	Estimate	Hammer price £	$	€	Date	Place	Lot	Auc. H.
1950	Olympia saloon		OLY51L20613425	L	60-80.000 USD	21.418*	26.400*	24.745*	19-01-17	Scottsdale	34	Bon **F567**
The Opel Olympia is offered together with an Egon Brütsch half size Maserati child's car. Both cars are described as in ready to use condition.												
1971	GT		792454767	L	14-20.000 EUR	18.611	22.774	20.700	15-10-16	Salzburg	411	Dor
Red with black leatherette interior; restored in 2015.												

F565: 1953 Oldsmobile Fiesta 98 convertible

F566: 1970 Oldsmobile 442 convertible

Year	Model	(Bodybuilder)	Chassis no.	Steering	Estimate	Hammer price £	$	€	Date	Place	Lot	Auc. H.

F567: 1950 Opel Olympia saloon

F568: 1957 Osca Tipo S-273 1100

Year	Model	(Bodybuilder)	Chassis no.	Steering	Estimate	£	$	€	Date	Place	Lot	Auc. H.
1979	**Kadett C coupé**		3292567957	L	15-20.000 EUR	40.070*	49.825*	47.040*	25-11-16	Milan	640	**RMS**

Yellow and black; race prepared. From the Duemila Ruote collection.

1976	**Manta GT/E**		5865230111	L	7-10.000 EUR	15.265*	18.981*	17.920*	25-11-16	Milan	509	**RMS**

White with black, yellow and grey stripes; prepared for rallying. From the Duemila Ruote collection.

1980	**Ascona 400**		81050445539	L	10-15.000 EUR	57.242*	71.178*	67.200*	25-11-16	Milan	531	**RMS**

White; prepared for rallying. From the Duemila Ruote collection.

OSCA (I) (1947-1967)

1954	**MT4 1500 (Frua)**		1142	L	975-1.175.000 EUR	NS			08-02-17	Paris	168	**RMS**

Black with yellow and red stripes; sold new in Italy to Giulio Cabianca, the car was later acquired by Alfonso de Portago and then by Giannino Parravicini (there is some speculation that this was for tax purposes). Raced until 1956, in 1954 it ran also the Mille Miglia and Carrera Panamericana. In 1987 it was bought by Peter Kaus for the Rosso Bianco Collection and in 2003 by the current owners and subsequently restored. Fitted with a Hall & Hall-built engine stamped to match the original with a correct cylinder head.

1957	**Tipo S-273 1100**		1187S	L	500-800.000 EUR	493.079	614.484	578.120	10-02-17	Paris	33	**Art** F568

Red with black interior; sold new in Italy, the car was raced until 1965. Discovered without engine and gearbox in 2003, it was subsequently bought by Hervé Ogliastro, restored and fitted with correct Type S273 engine and ZF gearbox. From the Hervé and Martine Ogliastro Collection.

1964	**1600 GT coupé (Zagato)**		011	L	280-330.000 EUR	247.162	328.327	293.332	03-09-16	Chantilly	9	**Bon** F569

Gunmetal grey with red interior; sold new in Italy, it was raced at some events in 1964 e 1965 driven by Fausto Mariani. Described as in excellent overall condition.

1961	**1600 GT (Touring)**		0019	L	325-375.000 USD	264.957	341.000	290.532	19-08-17	Pebble Beach	132	**G&Co**

Light blue; one of two examples bodied by Touring; exhibited at the 1961 Turin Motor Show; sold new in Italy where at unspecified date it received a restoration overseen by Carlo Felice Bianchi Anderloni; most recently it was repainted and retrimmed again (see lot 10 Bonhams 5.9.15 NS).

OSELLA (I) (1974-)

1986	**FA1G**		01	M	90-120.000 EUR	NS			21-05-17	SPA-Francorch.	90	**Bon**

Car driven by Piercarlo Ghinzani in the 1986 F1 season. Bought in 2015 by the current owner and restored to running condition.

OSI (I) (1960-1968)

1965	**Fiat 1200 S spider**		040550	L	35-55.000 EUR	21.090*	31.126*	23.984*	02-07-17	Monaco	128	**Art** F570

Red with black interior; in good overall condition.

OVERLAND (USA) (1903-1926)

1912	**Model 61 touring**		611191	R	90-110.000 USD	NS			06-10-16	Hershey	122	**RMS**

Grey and red with black interior; first restored in the 1960s, the car was acquired in 2008 by the current owner and restored again.

F569: 1964 Osca 1600 GT coupé (Zagato)

F570: 1965 Osi Fiat 1200 S spider

Year	Model	(Bodybuilder)	Chassis No.	Steering	Estimate	£	$	€	Date	Place	Lot	Auc. H.

PACKARD (USA) (1899-1958)

Year	Model (Bodybuilder)	Chassis No.	Steering	Estimate	£	$	€	Date	Place	Lot	Auc. H.
1906	Model S touring	2425	R	275-350.000 USD		NS		20-05-17	Indianapolis	S209	Mec

Dark blue with black fenders and black leather interior; described as in excellent overall condition (see Mecum lots S108.1 10.4.15 $300,000 and S56 20.8.16 NS).

1912	Thirty phaeton	20237	R	250-325.000 USD	222.222	286.000	243.672	19-08-17	Pebble Beach	151	G&Co

Dark blue with black fenders and black leather interior; in the same family ownership from 1918 to 1978 when it was acquired by the current owner and restored between 1979 and 1984; further works carried out in 2016.

1910	Eighteen touring	12578	R	125-175.000 USD	104.227*	132.000*	118.008*	06-10-16	Hershey	155	RMS F571

Black and red with brown leather interior; since 1958 in the current ownership, the car has been restored in recent years. New coachwork.

1920	Twin Six 3-35 touring	160466	L	135-150.000 USD		NS		09-03-17	Amelia Island	184	Bon

Blue and black; described as in largely original condition. 8,000 miles covered.

1927	Single Six 426 runabout	98292	L	75-100.000 USD	82.519	101.750	91.331	07-10-16	Hershey	223	RMS

Black and yellow; acquired in 1997 by the current owner and subsequently subjected to a long restoration completed in 2005.

1928	Single Six 5th series runabout	143707	L	95-105.000 USD		NS		24-06-17	Santa Monica	183	RMS

Maroon and white with maroon interior; restored at unspecified date.

1926	Eight 243 touring	200346	L	70-90.000 USD	72.659	93.500	83.206	03-10-16	Philadelphia	225	Bon

Green with black fenders; restored at unspecified date, the car is described as in very good overall condition (see lot 61 Bonhams 5.6.16 NS).

1928	Custom Eight 443 convertible sedan (Murphy)	227594	L	125-175.000 USD	98.404	126.500	112.775	04-06-17	Greenwich	141	Bon

Deep red with brown leather interior; for nearly 40 years in the current ownership. Fully restored.

1929	DeLuxe Eight 645 roadster (Dietrich)	174037	L	55-75.000 USD	48.639*	61.600*	55.070*	06-10-16	Hershey	114	RMS

Mechanicals in working order; car in original condition, body and interior requiring restoration. Missing windshield.

1929	Eight 626 convertible	259300	L	110-130.000 USD	82.908	105.000	93.870	06-10-16	Hershey	129	RMS

Black with tobacco interior; restored some years ago.

1929	Custom Eight 640 runabout	178382	L	160-200.000 USD	151.838	189.750	177.473	01-04-17	Ft.Lauderdale	550	AA

Black with saddle leather interior; restored in the late 1990s; bought in 2002 by the current owner and later restored again (see lot 166 RM 18.1.08 $148,500).

1929	Eight 645 dual-cowl sport phaeton	177879	L	300-400.000 USD	247.863	319.000	271.788	19-08-17	Pebble Beach	159	G&Co

Dark green with cinnamon leather interior; concours-quality restoration carried out in the 1990s.

1930	Eight 734 boattail speedster	184006	L	350-450.000 EUR		NS		10-02-17	Paris	133	Art

Black and orange with brown leather interior; fitted at unspecified date with the present new body. Imported into Europe in recent years (see lot E726 Auctions America 2.9.10 $99,000).

1930	DeLuxe Eight 745 phaeton	187403	L	160-200.000 USD	124.031	155.000	144.972	01-04-17	Ft.Lauderdale	570	AA

Red with black fenders and black interior; recently serviced.

1930	DeLuxe Eight 745 convertible victoria (Proux)	179021	L	400-600.000 USD	233.100	300.000	255.600	18-08-17	Carmel	25	Bon

Indian yellow and Siena with beige leather interior; imported into the USA in the early 1980s and subjected to a restoration completed in 1984; bought in 1999 by T.J. Day and restored again in 2000 (see lot 151 RM 20.3.99 $181,500).

1931	DeLuxe Eight 845 convertible (LeBaron)	189744	L	250-325.000 USD		NS		07-10-16	Hershey	245	RMS

Tan; restored at unspecified date. Recently serviced (see lot 123 RM/Sotheby's 25.7.15 NS).

1931	DeLuxe Eight 840 convertible victoria (Dietrich)	188700	L	250-300.000 USD	156.175	192.500	180.430	19-01-17	Phoenix	116	RMS F572

Black with black leather interior; exhibited at the New York Motor Show in 1930 and 1931. For many years from 1952 in the ownership of the Packard historian Edward J. Blend, who had it restored over a nearly 14 year period from the mid-1960s.

1931	Eight 840 roadster	47233	L	275-300.000 USD		NS		11-02-17	Boca Raton	164	TFA

Silver and maroon with maroon interior; restored in 1978 and recently refreshed.

1931	DeLuxe Eight 840 dual-cowl phaeton	190397	L	225-325.000 USD	205.128	264.000	224.928	18-08-17	Carmel	31	Bon

Beige with grey fenders and orange beltine accent; orange leather interior. Restored to concours condition in the 1970s; bought in 1984 by T.J. Day and subjected to further works.

1932	Standard Eight 902 roadster	509129	L	80-100.000 USD	86.980	107.250	96.268	07-10-16	Hershey	240	RMS

Two-tone red with red leather interior; restored about 1980.

1932	DeLuxe Eight 903 phaeton	194335	L	225-275.000 USD	208.118*	253.000*	238.427*	10-03-17	Amelia Island	137	RMS

Black with burgundy leather interior; first restored in the mid-1950s and between 2007 and 2010 again. From the Orin Smith collection (see lot 166 RM 9.3.13 $242,000).

1932	Standard Eight 902 roadster	345801	L	NA	61.966	79.750	67.947	19-08-17	Monterey	1045	R&S

Maroon; recently serviced.

F571: 1910 Packard Eighteen touring

F572: 1931 Packard DeLuxe Eight 840 convertible victoria (Dietrich)

Year	Model (Bodybuilder)	Chassis no.	Steering	Estimate	Hammer price £	$	€	Sale Date	Place	Lot	Auc. H.
1933	**Super Eight 1004 convertible**	558392	L	NA		NS		03-09-16	Auburn	40	WoA
	Maroon with black fenders and burgundy leather interior; restored in the 1990s.										
1933	**Eight 1004 roadster**	558392	L	300-350.000 USD	250.774	308.000	288.812	18-01-17	Scottsdale	53	WoA
	See lot 40 Worldwide Auctioneers 3.9.16.										
1934	**Super Eight 1104 coupé**	753291	L	120-140.000 USD	97.713	123.750	110.633	06-10-16	Hershey	136	RMS F573
	Red with black fenders; older restoration.										
1934	**Super Eight 1105 hunting car (McAvoy & Son)**	110515	L	75-100.000 USD	44.605	55.000	49.368	07-10-16	Hershey	225	RMS
	Built with LeBaron town car body, the car was converted to the present body at unspecified date and kept on the road until 1948. For restoration.										
1934	**Super Eight 1104 roadster**	752604	L	225-275.000 USD	197.085	242.000	227.601	20-01-17	Phoenix	217	RMS
	Green; fully restored in the mid-1990s, the car is described as still in very good overall condition.										
1934	**Eight 11th series coupé**	718142	L	NQ	192.606*	236.500*	222.428*	21-01-17	Scottsdale	1386	B/J
	Silver with grey and blue pinstriping; restoration completed in 2005.										
1934	**Eight 1101 convertible sedan**	72329	L	140-180.000 USD	99.535*	121.000*	114.030*	10-03-17	Amelia Island	34	G&Co
	Three-tone light grey, tangerine and black; restored in the late 1990s.										
1934	**Super Eight 1104 roadster**	753642	L	180-200.000 USD	162.875	198.000	186.595	11-03-17	Amelia Island	268	RMS
	Green with black fenders and brown interior; the car has covered 600 miles since the restoration carried out many years ago. Recently serviced (see lot 283 RM 24.7.10 $154,000).										
1934	**Super Eight 1104 roadster**	753642	L	NQ	146.945	187.000	167.365	24-06-17	Northeast	698	B/J
	See lot 268 RM/Sotheby's 11.3.17.										
1935	**Eight 1202 convertible sedan**	863227	R	80-100.000 USD	60.799	77.000	68.838	06-10-16	Hershey	127	RMS
	Yellow with brown interior; restored some time ago. 16,657 on the odometer, likely the mileage since the restoration.										
1938	**Eight 1601 convertible sedan**	D303801A(engine)	L	70-80.000 USD	52.918	65.250	58.568	07-10-16	Hershey	230	RMS
	Cream with red interior; in good overall condition.										
1939	**Eight 120 1701 convertible victoria (Darrin)**	17012098	L	225-300.000 USD	176.448*	214.500*	202.145*	10-03-17	Amelia Island	143	RMS
	Cream with red leather interior; restored in the early 2000s. From the Orin Smith collection.										
1940	**Eight One-Twenty 1801 convertible victoria (Darrin)**	18012022	L	425-500.000 USD		NS		19-01-17	Phoenix	130	RMS
	Maroon with tan leather interior; concours-quality restoration completed in the mid-1990s.										
1941	**Custom Super Eight 180 sport brougham (LeBaron)**	CD502599(engine)	L	90-120.000 USD		NS		07-10-16	Hershey	238	RMS
	Silver and blue; acquired in 2006 by the current owner and restored, the car has covered about 2,500 miles since the restoration.										
1941	**Eight 180 touring sedan**	13322132	L	40-60.000 USD	29.810*	36.300*	34.402*	09-03-17	Amelia Island	131	Bon
	Black with cloth interior; several restoration works carried out in recent years.										
1941	**Super Eight 180 1906 convertible victoria (Darrin)**	NQ	L	NQ	279.972	360.000	330.984	13-05-17	Auburn	3112	AA
	Cream with saddle leather interior; restored, the car is described as in excellent driving condition.										
1932	**Twin Six 906 Custom convertible sedan (Dietrich)**	900245	L	Refer Dpt.		NS		20-01-17	Scottsdale	38	G&Co
	Dark grey with brown interior; one of two examples built; first owned by Al Jolson. After some ownership changes in 1959 it was bought by Harold Crosby who had it restored, displayed it at Pebble Beach and retained it until 1968. In single ownership from 1972 to 2011. Restored again in 2011-12 and displayed at Pebble Beach in 2012.										
1933	**Twelve 1005 convertible victoria (Dietrich)**	901136	L	475-550.000 USD	429.809	522.500	492.404	11-03-17	Amelia Island	233	RMS F574
	Black with dark red leather interior; in single ownership from 1941 to 2012. Bought by the current, fourth owner and restored to concours-condition (see lot 190 RM 12.10.12 $357,500).										
1934	**Twelve 1107 roadster (Rollston)**	DRF73303	L	NA	114.163	139.700	126.973	15-10-16	Las Vegas	734	B/J
	Engine overhauled many years ago. Recently serviced.										
1934	**Twelve 1107 club sedan**	73637	L	185-225.000 USD		NS		24-06-17	Santa Monica	211	RMS
	Black with tan interior; concours-quality restoration.										
1934	**Twelve 1107 phaeton**	901630	L	450-550.000 USD	273.504*	352.000*	299.904*	18-08-17	Monterey	118	RMS
	Green; restored to concours condition at unspecified date, the car is described as still in good overall condition.										
1935	**Twelve 1207 convertible victoria**	827218	L	225-275.000 USD		NS		06-10-16	Hershey	139	RMS
	Dark maroon with burgundy interior; acquired in recent years by the current, third owner following a long period in storage. In well-preserved "barn find" condition and good mechanical order.										
1936	**Twelve 14th series dual-cowl phaeton**	904502(engine)	L	600-800.000 USD	529.914	682.000	581.064	18-08-17	Monterey	141	RMS F575
	Dark blue; in the 1990s fully restored to concours condition.										
1937	**Twelve 1508 convertible sedan**	1073232	L	175-200.000 USD	217.140	275.000	245.850	06-10-16	Hershey	156	RMS
	Grey with red leather interior; restored 10 years ago, the car is described as in excellent overall condition.										

F573: 1934 Packard Super Eight 1104 coupé

F574: 1933 Packard Twelve 1005 convertible victoria (Dietrich)

Year	Model	(Bodybuilder)	Chassis no.	Steering	Estimate	Hammer price £	$	€	Sale Date	Place	Lot	Auc. H.
1937	**Twelve 1507 convertible victoria**		905736A	L	275-350.000 USD	201.515	247.500	232.081	18-01-17	Scottsdale	25	WoA
	Black with burgundy leather interior; restored, the car is described as in very good overall condition.											
1937	**Twelve 1507 roadster**		1039228	L	350-425.000 USD	241.877	297.000	279.329	20-01-17	Scottsdale	16	G&Co
	Creamy yellow with red leather interior; restored several years ago, the car is described as still in very good overall condition.											
1937	**Twelve dual-cowl phaeton**		1035288	L	500-700.000 EUR		NS		10-02-17	Paris	135	Art
	Dark blue with white interior; originally built with limousine body, the car was bought at unspecified date in the USA by the current German owner and shipped to the UK for the restoration. New LeBaron-style body.											
1937	**Twelve 1507 roadster**		906694	L	450-550.000 USD	363.248	467.500	399.713	17-08-17	Monterey	38	WoA
	The car has covered 100 miles since the full restoration completed in 2013.											
1938	**Twelve 1608 convertible victoria**	(Derham)	A600130(engine)	L	650-750.000 USD		NS		19-08-17	Pebble Beach	126	G&Co
	Maroon and black; bought in 2006 by the current owner and subsequently fully restored.											
1939	**Twelve 1708 convertible sedan**		12532017	L	170-200.000 USD	138.276	170.500	153.041	07-10-16	Hershey	248	RMS
	Silver metallic with red leather interior; restored, the car is described as in very good overall condition (see lots 17 Gooding & Company 12.3.10 $170,500, 237 Bonhams 31.5.15 $160,600 and 7068 Auctions America 05.9.15 NS).											
1940	**One-Ten 1800 Six cabriolet**		F7991	R	40-45.000 AUD		NS		28-05-17	Sydney	12	Mos
	White; sold new to Australia; a few miles covered since the restoration carried out in the 1990s.											
1940	**One-Ten 1800 Six club coupé**		13859061	L	NQ	18.584*	23.650*	21.167*	24-06-17	Northeast	39.1	B/J
	Blue; restored.											
1941	**One-Ten 1900 Six 2-door sedan**		14843026	L	NA	22.650*	29.150*	24.836*	19-08-17	Monterey	1052	R&S
	Two-tone grey; recently serviced. From the Art Astor collection.											
1948	**Eight 2201 station sedan**		22933287	L	60-80.000 USD	37.348	47.300	42.286	06-10-16	Hershey	152	RMS
	Green with wooden panels and beige vinyl and cloth interior; restored some years ago.											
1949	**Eight 22nd series station sedan**		23932856	L	60-80.000 USD	58.008*	71.500*	67.017*	19-01-17	Phoenix	109	RMS
	Fully restored, the car is described as in very good overall condition. 3-speed manual gearbox with overdrive.											
1948	**Eight 2201 station sedan**		22933982	L	60-80.000 USD	57.911*	70.400*	66.345*	10-03-17	Amelia Island	110	RMS
	Brown with wooden panels and vinyl and cloth interior; an older restoration. From the Orin Smith collection.											
1949	**Custom Eight convertible victoria**		225993221	L	55-65.000 USD	46.780	62.150	55.525	03-09-16	Auburn	4080	AA
	White with red and white interior; restored. Automatic transmission (see lot NR104 RM 6.2.09 $70,400).											
1949	**Eight Series 2301 station sedan**		239353428	L	NA	24.839	33.000	29.482	03-09-16	Auburn	46	WoA
	Dark red with wooden panels; restored many years ago											
1952	**200 2-door sedan**		25953686	L	NQ	8.510*	10.450*	9.828*	21-01-17	Scottsdale	8213	R&S
	Blue with cloth interior; in good driving order. From the Missoula Auto Museum Collection.											
1952	**200 cabriolet**	(Saoutchik)	246220259A	L	50-70.000 EUR		NS		01-05-17	Obenheim	359	Ose
	Cream and light brown; built with sedan body, the car was converted to cabriolet by Saoutchik in the early 1950s. Fully restored.											
1951	**250 convertible**		24693877	L	45-55.000 USD	35.939*	46.200*	41.187*	04-06-17	Greenwich	162	Bon
	Pale yellow with burgundy and white interior; restored; 3-speed manual gearbox.											
1952	**Patrician 400 sedan**		25522759	L	30-40.000 USD	41.209*	50.600*	47.589*	20-01-17	Scottsdale	37	G&Co
	Black; in original condition, the car has covered 1,314 miles. In the same family ownership from new to 2016, recently it has been serviced and returned to running order.											
1951	**Patrician 400 sedan**		256222218	R	20-24.000 GBP	15.400	20.038	17.926	20-05-17	Ascot	174	His
	Blue with grey roof; restored.											
1954	**8 Caribbean convertible**		54782165	L	NA	61.127*	74.800*	67.986*	15-10-16	Las Vegas	724	B/J
	Red and sand with red and white leather interior; 2,500 miles covered since the restoration.											
1953	**8 Caribbean convertible**		26782574	L	115-135.000 USD	84.163	102.500	96.135	15-01-17	Kissimmee	S169	Mec **F576**
	Black with green and black leather interior; concours-quality restoration.											
1953	**8 Caribbean convertible**		L410304	L	60-80.000 EUR	47.489*	59.182*	55.680*	10-02-17	Paris	14	Art
	Burgundy with burgundy and white interior; restored about 10 years ago. Automatic transmission (see lot 344 Bonhams 5.2.11 NS).											
1953	**8 Caribbean convertible**		L411958	L	100-110.000 USD		NS		13-05-17	Auburn	3111	AA
	Metallic maroon with maroon and white leather interior; restored.											

F575: 1936 Packard Twelve 14th series dual-cowl phaeton

F576: 1953 Packard 8 Caribbean convertible

F577: 1948 Paganelli Lancia siluro

F578: 2014 Pagani Huayra Tempesta coupé

Year	Model (Bodybuilder)	Chassis no.	Steering	Estimate	£	$	€	Date	Place	Lot	Auc. H.
1953	**8 Caribbean convertible**	26792395	L	NA	42.735*	55.000*	46.860*	19-08-17	Monterey	1054	**R&S**
	Yellow with red leather interior; restored. From the Art Astor Collection.										
1954	**Deluxe Clipper hardtop**	54673464	L	NQ	9.406*	11.550*	10.863*	21-01-17	Scottsdale	8215	**R&S**
	White with red roof and red leather and black cloth interior; described as in good overall condition. From the Missoula Auto Museum Collection.										
1955	**400 HardTop**	55876182	L	NQ	21.610*	27.500*	24.613*	24-06-17	Northeast	102	**B/J**
	Two-tone blue with blue and white interior; fully restored between 1998 and 2000.										
1956	**Caribbean convertible**	56991113	L	80-100.000 USD	55.888*	74.250*	66.335*	03-09-16	Auburn	4106	**AA**
	White, blue and copper with tri-color matching interior; restored.										
1956	**Caribbean convertible**	56991266	L	80-100.000 USD	55.310*	68.200*	61.216*	07-10-16	Hershey	246	**RMS**
	Three-tone white, green and black body; described as in very good overall condition.										
1955	**Caribbean convertible**	55881269	L	80-100.000 USD	62.447	77.000	69.115	07-10-16	Hershey	259	**RMS**
	White and two-tone blue; recently restored.										
1955	**Caribbean convertible**	55881185	L	NA	47.449*	58.500*	55.037*	19-11-16	Anaheim	S167.1	**Mec**
	White, red and blue.										

PAGANELLI (I)

1948	**Lancia siluro**	0053751	L	45-55.000 EUR	209.888*	260.987*	246.400*	25-11-16	Milan	630	**RMS** F577
	Polished aluminium body. From the Duemila Ruote collection.										

PAGANI (I) *(1999-)*

2014	**Huayra Tempesta coupé**	76059	L	2.200-2.800.000 USD	1.880.340	2.420.000	2.061.840	19-08-17	Monterey	229	**RMS** F578
	Matt dark grey with beige leather interior; one owner; 640 miles covered. After its delivery, the car was fitted with the "Tempesta" package.										

PANHARD ET LEVASSOR (F) *(1891-1967)*

1902	**A 7hp voiturette (Clement/Rothschild)**	5139	R	210-250.000 EUR	215.278	270.508	253.000	09-02-17	Paris	325	**Bon**
	France blue with black wings and black leather interior; owned by only two families between 1903 and 2007; fully restored at unspecified date; mechanicals rebuilt again in 2007 (see lot 312 Christie's 17.2.07 $200,393).										F579
1911	**X8 limousine decouverte**	72092	R	80-110.000 EUR	60.669	76.234	71.300	09-02-17	Paris	401	**Bon**
	Probably sold new in France, the car was discovered in the 1950s in the Netherlands where it is believed the present period body, attributed to Carrosserie Schutter & Van Bakel, was fitted. In the past the car was part also of the Louwman Collection. Imported later in the UK where the non-period front doors, scuttle and wings were removed and replaced. Some mechanical works carried out by the present owner.										F580
1938	**X73 Panoramique berline**	99605	R	8-12.000 EUR	24.171*	29.802*	26.752*	07-10-16	Chateau-sur-Epte	61	**Art**
	Two-tone body; restored many years ago. From the Andre Weber Collection.										

F579: 1902 Panhard Et Levassor A 7hp voiturette (Clement/Rothschild)

F580: 1911 Panhard Et Levassor X8 limousine decouverte

Year	Model	(Bodybuilder)	Chassis no.	Steering	Estimate	Hammer price £	$	€	Date	Place	Lot	Auc. H.
1939	X80 Dynamic limousine		222538	L	40-50.000 EUR		NS		05-08-17	Schloss Dyck	244	Coy
Ivory with cloth interior; restored.												
1955	Dyna berline		18258	L	9-13.000 EUR	7.460	9.318	8.400	06-11-16	Lyon	321	Ose
Since 1977 in the same family ownership; described as in good original condition.												
1964	24 CT		2308765	L	9-11.000 EUR		NA		08-10-16	Paris	168	CB/C
Red; in good overall condition.												

PEEL (GB) *(1962-1967)*

Year	Model	(Bodybuilder)	Chassis no.	Steering	Estimate	£	$	€	Date	Place	Lot	Auc. H.
1964	P50		D536	R	90-120.000 USD	108.974*	140.250*	119.493*	18-08-17	Monterey	144	RMS **F581**
White; fully restored.												
1965	Trident		E185	R	80-100.000 USD	94.017*	121.000*	103.092*	18-08-17	Monterey	143	RMS
Red; fully restored.												

PEERLESS (USA) *(1900-1931)*

Year	Model	(Bodybuilder)	Chassis no.	Steering	Estimate	£	$	€	Date	Place	Lot	Auc. H.
1927	6-80 Taxicab		A36032	L	25-30.000 GBP		NS		10-09-16	Goodwood	186	Bon
Black and light yellow; imported from the USA at unspecified date. Restored in the 1990s; in good driving order.												

PEGASO (E) *(1951-1958)*

Year	Model	(Bodybuilder)	Chassis no.	Steering	Estimate	£	$	€	Date	Place	Lot	Auc. H.
1955	Z-102B coupé (Saoutchik)		01021500146	L	600-800.000 USD		NS		10-03-17	Amelia Island	46	G&Co
Red with red and black leather interior; sold new in France, the car was later imported into the USA where in 1964 it was bought by Bill Harrah who subsequently had it restored. Later it was part also of the Imperial Palace and Blackhawk collections. Restored again between 2006 and 2008 (see lot 655 Barrett-Jackson 21.1.99 NS).												
1954	Z-102 coupé (Saoutchik)		01021500161	R	725-900.000 USD	598.290	770.000	656.040	19-08-17	Monterey	265	RMS **F582**
Black with cream roof and red leather interior; sold new in Spain, the car was later imported into the USA, then sold to the Netherlands and reimported into the USA in 2005. Restored to concours condition.												

PETERSEN ENGINEERING (GB)

Year	Model	(Bodybuilder)	Chassis no.	Steering	Estimate	£	$	€	Date	Place	Lot	Auc. H.
====	Bentley "Blue Train" Special		32TC	R	750-950.000 USD	361.944*	440.000*	414.656*	10-03-17	Amelia Island	114	RMS
One of five Specials produced, the offered car was built in recent years on a 1931 Rolls-Royce Phantom II chassis fitted with a Bentley B81 inline 8-cylinder engine with Petersen supercharger. Black with black interior. From the Orin Smith collection.												
2011	Bentley "Embiricos" coupé recreation		B119MX	R	750-950.000 USD	551.965*	671.000*	632.350*	10-03-17	Amelia Island	154	RMS
Recreation built in 2011 on a 1939 Bentley 4.1/4 chassis (as the original car) fitted with its original engine with the 4-speed manual gearbox with overdrive. From the Orin Smith collection.												

PEUGEOT (F) *(1889-)*

Year	Model	(Bodybuilder)	Chassis no.	Steering	Estimate	£	$	€	Date	Place	Lot	Auc. H.
1910	Lion Type VC2C spider		4211	R	30-40.000 GBP	20.666	27.451	24.526	03-09-16	Beaulieu	448	Bon
Yellow with black wings; restored in Australia before coming to the UK in 2003. Originally built with a four-seater body (see lot 8 Bonhams 2.12.07 NS).												
1929	Type 190 S spider		405247	L	6-8.000 EUR	8.120	10.441	9.600	14-05-17	Puiseux-Pontoise	700	Ose
Blue with black wings; described as in good original condition.												
1929	Type 190 S spider		407360	L	10-15.000 EUR		NS		18-06-17	Fontainebleau	57	Ose
Blue with black wings and black interior; in good condition.												
1935	Type 201 D coach		514526	L	6-8.000 EUR	9.455	12.060	10.800	18-06-17	Fontainebleau	56	Ose
Black; in good overall condition.												
1934	Type 601 roadster		712071	L	175-225.000 USD	134.343	165.000	154.721	18-01-17	Scottsdale	60	WoA
Dark blue with red leather interior; 100 kms covered since the restoration carried out in the Netherlands in the mid-1990s (see lot 104 RM/Sotheby's 3.2.16 $91,837).												
1937	Type 402 berline		690787	L	12-16.000 EUR	6.592*	8.128*	7.296*	07-10-16	Chateau-sur-Epte	15	Art
Restored in the 1960s; in running condition. From the Andre Weber Collection.												
1938	Type 402 DS Darl'mat roadster (Pourtout)		705551	L	400-460.000 EUR		NS		10-02-17	Paris	45	Art
French blue with black interior; fully restored by Lecoq many years ago, the car is described as still in very good overall condition. Since 1997 in the current ownership, it ran several editions of the Le Mans Classic (see lot 16 Poulain 7.10.97 $ 471,129).												

F581: 1964 Peel P50

F582: 1954 Pegaso Z-102 coupé (Saoutchik)

CLASSIC CAR AUCTION 2016-2017 YEARBOOK

F583: 1938 Peugeot Type 402 DS Darl'mat roadster (Pourtout)

F584: 1949 Peugeot 203 Luxe Export berline

Year	Model (Bodybuilder)	Chassis no.	Steering	Estimate	Hammer price £	$	€	Date	Place	Lot	Auc. H.
1938	**Type 402 DS Darl'mat roadster (Pourtout)**	400248	L	700-900.000 USD	576.923	742.500	632.610	18-08-17	Pebble Beach	28	G&Co F583
	Raced until 1948; in single ownership from 1960 to 2009 when it was bought by the current, fourth owner and fully restored.										
1958	**203 berline**	1882581	L	6-8.000 EUR	8.790*	10.837*	9.728*	07-10-16	Chateau-sur-Epte	16	Art
	Body repainted, vinyl interior. From the Andre Weber Collection.										
1949	**203 Luxe Export berline**	112088	L	15-25.000 EUR	30.500*	38.009*	35.760*	10-02-17	Paris	38	Art F584
	Light beige with beige leather interior; the car has covered 200 kms since a full restoration.										
1958	**203 berline**	1876159	L	6-8.000 EUR	5.282	6.528	6.080	19-03-17	Fontainebleau	218	Ose
	Restored in the early 1990s; mechanicals in need of recommissioning prior to use.										
1952	**203 cabriolet**	1252624	L	80-90.000 EUR	NA			08-10-16	Paris	187	CB/C
	Green; restored.										
1967	**404 cabriolet (Pininfarina)**	6801707	L	10-15.000 EUR	33.758	43.050	38.520	10-06-17	Lyon	138	Agu
	For 33 years in the current ownership and stored for several decades; for restoration.										
1963	**404 berline**	4307757	L	6-10.000 EUR	5.170	6.326	5.750	15-10-16	Salzburg	403	Dor
	Blue with red cloth interior; bought by the current owner and prepared for the 1997 Beijing-Paris where it placed 15th. Overhauled three years ago.										
1968	**404 station wagon**	6838975	L	15-3.000 EUR	11.448*	14.236*	13.440*	25-11-16	Milan	643	RMS
	Burgundy with tan interior. From the Duemila Ruote collection.										
1972	**304 S cabriolet**	3365471	L	10-12.000 EUR	9.590	11.854	11.040	18-03-17	Fontainebleau	57	Ose
	Metallic grey with black interior; from the Perinet Marquet collection.										
1980	**504 2.0 cabriolet (Pininfarina)**	463728	L	25-35.000 EUR	30.580*	45.134*	34.777*	02-07-17	Monaco	112	Art F585
	White with beige leather interior; in original condition; less than 57,000 kms covered; one owner.										
1986	**205 GTI**	383216	L	10-15.000 EUR	15.539*	18.878*	17.284*	30-10-16	Paris	157	Art
	Described as in very good original condition.										
1987	**205 GTI 1.9**	784761	L	14-18.000 EUR	23.037	28.475	26.520	18-03-17	Lyon	186	Agu
	Described as in very good original condition; two owners; 68,636 kms covered.										
1988	**205 GTI 1.9**	652981	R	28-32.000 GBP	38.480	50.390	42.963	29-07-17	Silverstone	704	SiC
	White with red and grey interior; described as in very good original condition; 5,726 miles covered. Until 2012 with its first owner.										
1985	**205 Turbo 16**	5100012	L	140-180.000 EUR	147.415	183.712	172.840	10-02-17	Paris	94	Art F586
	Raced at the 1985 Tour de Corse and at some rallies until the late 1980s. Bought in 2004 by the current owner, it received several mechanical works in 2009 and has covered circa 2000 kms since.										
1985	**205 Turbo 16**	5100009	L	275-325.000 EUR	NS			02-07-17	Monaco	192	Art
	Pearl white; 248 kms covered; car owned by André de Cortanze, Technical Director of Peugeot Sport between 1984 and 1992.										
1985	**205 Turbo 16**	5100014	L	230-280.000 EUR	NS			02-07-17	Monaco	210	Art
	Road version converted in France in 1985 to Group B specification using factory parts. Raced at some rallies in France in 1985 and 1986. Restored in the UK in 2002 and subsequently raced at historic rallies.										
1985	**205 Turbo 16**	100127	L	225-275.000 USD	153.846*	198.000*	168.696*	18-08-17	Carmel	44	Bon
	Metallic grey; in highly original condition; since 1997 in the current ownership; 1,113 kms on the odometer. The car requires a full service prior to use.										

F585: 1980 Peugeot 504 2.0 cabriolet (Pininfarina)

F586: 1985 Peugeot 205 Turbo 16

323

Year	Model	(Bodybuilder)	Chassis no.	Steering	Estimate	Hammer price £	$	€	Sale Date	Place	Lot	Auc. H.

PHEBUS (F) (1899-1903)

1899 • 2¼hp Forecar — 46 — C — 50-60.000 GBP — NS — 12-10-16 — Duxford — 46 — H&H
Green and black with black interior; in good overall condition (see lot 143 Bonhams 18.7.09 $79,461).

PIERCE-ARROW (USA) (1901-1938)

1911 • Model 48 touring — 9079 — R — 550-750.000 USD — 451.660 — 550.000 — 521.235 — 09-03-17 — Amelia Island — 180 — Bon **F587**
Restored at unspecified date, the car is described as in very good overall condition. For several decades in the current ownership.

1915 • Model 66-A-3 touring — 67145 — R — 600-750.000 USD — NS — 06-10-16 — Hershey — 153 — RMS
Red with black fenders and black leather interior; fully restored. New aluminium coachwork.

1916 • Model 66-A-4 touring — 67219 — R — 400-500.000 USD — NS — 07-10-16 — Hershey — 250 — RMS
Two-tone grey with black interior; restored many years ago and fitted with a new body, the car was restored again in the 2000s (see lot 263 RM 22.1.10 $325,000).

1924 • Model 33 touring — 339177 — L — 70-80.000 USD — 41.929* — 53.900* — 48.052* — 04-06-17 — Greenwich — 137 — Bon
(Crimson with black fenders and black leather interior; restored some years ago. Formerly in the Barney Pollard collection (see lot 122 RM/Sotheby's 30.7.16 $60,500).

1923 • Model 33 sedan — 337585 — L — 50-70.000 USD — 83.761* — 107.800* — 91.846* — 18-08-17 — Carmel — 6 — Bon
Light grey with black fenders and black leather interior to the front compartment and beige cloth to the rear; fully restored.

1927 • Model 80 sedan — 8016115 — L — 15-25.000 USD — 5.984* — 7.700* — 6.852* — 03-10-16 — Philadelphia — 249 — Bon
Highly original example; unrestored. In the Bloomington Collection prior to WWII.

1926 • Model 80 roadster — 8013647 — L — NQ — 47.526 — 60.000 — 56.376 — 03-12-16 — Kansas City — S125 — Mec
Tan and brown; older restoration.

1927 • Model 36 coupé (Judkins) — 362026 — L — 100-150.000 USD — 35.825* — 44.000* — 41.259* — 18-01-17 — Scottsdale — 44 — WoA
Restored in the 2000s; only known example.

1931 • Model 41 convertible victoria (LeBaron) — 3050235 — L — 400-475.000 USD — 370.222 — 456.500 — 409.754 — 07-10-16 — Hershey — 233 — RMS **F588**
Brown and burgundy with maroon leather interior; concours-quality restoration carried out in the early 2000s. Only example of the Model 41 known to survive with this kind of body, it is believed the car exhibited at the 1931 New York Motor Show (see lot 245 RM 18.8.12 $385,000).

1931 • Model 41 convertible sedan (LeBaron) — 3050251 — L — 180-220.000 USD — 124.940* — 154.000* — 144.344* — 19-01-17 — Phoenix — 154 — RMS
Two-tone brown with orange pinstriping; concours-quality restoration carried out in the late 1990s. Formerly in the Matt and Barbara Browning Collection (see lots 26 Christie's 20.8.00 $138,000, 41 Worldwide Group 18.2.11 $137,500, and 133 RM 19.8.11 NS).

1933 • Model 1247 convertible sedan (LeBaron) — 355091 — L — 450-550.000 EUR — NS — 10-02-17 — Paris — 134 — Art
Bought new by actress Carole Lombard; in the same family ownership from 1944 to 1998 and subsequently restored (see RM lots 76 23.1.04 $374,000, 167 11.3.06 $418,000, and 372 14.8.10 $302,500).

1933 • Model 836 limousine — 15500247 — L — 40-50.000 USD — 49.958* — 61.600* — 55.292* — 07-10-16 — Hershey — 226 — RMS
Blue and black; in good driving order (see lots Bonhams 340 15.8.08 NS and 529 4.10.08 $76,050, RM 218 24.7.10 NS, Bonhams 336 12.9.10 $68,445, and RM 149 10.10.13 $60,500).

PININFARINA (I) (1930-)

1985 • Spidereuropa Volumex — 5511735 — L — 28-42.000 EUR — 38.371 — 48.826 — 43.700 — 24-06-17 — Wien — 327 — Dor
Black with beige leather interior; in very good original condition; one owner; 26,000 kms covered.

PLYMOUTH (USA) (1928-2001)

1941 • P12 Special DeLuxe station wagon — 3290410 — L — 75-100.000 USD — 59.156 — 72.045 — 67.571 — 15-01-17 — Kissimmee — F129 — Mec **F589**
Beige with wooden panels and brown interior; fully restored. From the Jackie and Gary Runyon collection.

1949 • Special DeLuxe sedan — 20351568 — L — 6-8.000 EUR — 10.657* — 13.140* — 11.795* — 07-10-16 — Chateau-sur-Epte — 72 — Art
Described as in largely original condition; from the Andre Weber Collection.

1947 • Special DeLuxe convertible — 25010767 — L — NQ — 44.792* — 55.000* — 51.728* — 21-01-17 — Scottsdale — 949 — B/J
Black with maroon interior; recently restored.

1953 • Cambridge 2-door sedan — 13134190 — L — NA — 7.949* — 9.900* — 9.286* — 08-04-17 — Palm Beach — 50 — B/J
Two-tone green with grey interior; since 1967 in the same family ownership. Older cosmetic restoration.

1952 • Cranbrook Belvedere coupé — 13025569 — L — 35-45.000 USD — NS — 11-02-17 — Boca Raton — 105 — TFA
White and grey with grey interior; in very good running order.

F587: 1911 Pierce-Arrow Model 48 touring

F588: 1931 Pierce-Arrow Model 41 convertible victoria (LeBaron)

F589: 1941 Plymouth P12 Special DeLuxe station wagon

F590: 1966 Plymouth Belvedere Satellite convertible

Year	Model	(Bodybuilder)	Chassis no.	Steering	Estimate	£	$	€	Date	Place	Lot	Auc. H.
1964	**Belvedere Race Hemi hardtop**		3241257503	L	125-175.000 USD	42.552*	52.250*	49.141*	20-01-17	Phoenix	274	RMS
	Red with red vinyl interior; restored in 2004. "Transitional" model fitted with the 425cv 426 Hemi engine with automatic transmission.											
1965	**Belvedere hardtop**		R051188807	L	650-750.000 USD		NS		15-01-17	Kissimmee	F107	Mec
	White and blue; one of 12 "altered-wheelbase" (AWB) examples built at the factory for drag racing. Driven in period by Lee Smith. Restored at unspecified date. 426 Hemi engine with manual gearbox. From the Jackie and Gary Runyon collection.											
1966	**Belvedere Satellite convertible**		RP27H67271660	L	125-175.000 USD	100.585	122.500	114.893	15-01-17	Kissimmee	F117	Mec **F590**
	Red with black interior; one of 27 examples built with the 426 Hemi engine of whom just 11 with the 4-speed manual gearbox. From the Jackie and Gary Runyon collection.											
1965	**Belvedere Lightweight hardtop**		R051194863	L	250-350.000 USD		NA		15-01-17	Kissimmee	S127	Mec
	Bronze with brown interior; raced in period, 1967 Super Stock World Champion. 426 Hemi engine with 4-speed manual gearbox. Since 1997 in the Don Fezell collection.											
1966	**Belvedere II hardtop**		RH23H61238755	L	100-135.000 USD	59.119	72.000	67.529	15-01-17	Kissimmee	S128	Mec
	Silver with black interior; restored. 426 Hemi engine with 4-speed manual gearbox. From the Don Fezell collection.											
1965	**Belvedere Lightweight hardtop**		R0511991722	L	160-200.000 USD	98.542*	121.000*	113.801*	20-01-17	Phoenix	239	RMS
	White with tan interior; restored in 2002. 425bhp 426 Hemi engine with 4-speed manual gearbox.											
1967	**Belvedere II Super Stock hardtop**		R023J71206021	L	100-140.000 USD	56.438*	69.300*	65.177*	20-01-17	Phoenix	278	RMS
	White with black interior; used at drag-race when new. Restored. Believed to have 367 original miles. 425bhp 426 Hemi engine with automatic transmission.											
1966	**Belvedere hardtop**		RH23H7199174	L	NQ	52.855	64.900	61.038	21-01-17	Scottsdale	8244	R&S
	Metallic bronze; fully restored. 426 Hemi engine with 4-speed manual gearbox.											
1971	**Barracuda convertible**		BH27N1B172724	L	85-95.000 USD	82.741	103.400	96.710	01-04-17	Ft.Lauderdale	523	AA
	White with white interior; 300bhp 383 engine with automatic transmission. Sold new to Sweden.											
1968	**GTX convertible**		RS27J8G146479	L	125-150.000 USD	147.798	180.000	168.822	15-01-17	Kissimmee	F247	Mec **F591**
	Metallic blue with black interior; 19,000 miles on the odometer. 425bhp 426 Hemi engine with manual gearbox.											
1968	**GTX convertible**		RS27J8G186893	L	NQ	143.693	175.000	164.133	15-01-17	Kissimmee	F32	Mec
	Black with red vinyl interior; 425bhp 426 Hemi engine with automatic transmission.											
1970	**Road Runner hardtop**		RM23N0A101284	L	NA	26.968	30.250	23.531	03-06-17	Newport Beach	9077	R&S
	Lime green; restored; 34,000 original miles.											
1970	**Road Runner Super Bird**		RM23U0A175691	L	140-180.000 USD	113.846*	151.250*	135.127*	03-09-16	Auburn	4104	AA
	Red with black vinyl roof and original black interior; body repainted. Believed to have 4,000 original miles. 440 engine with automatic transmission.											
1970	**Road Runner Super Bird**		RM23V0A167083	L	NA	139.333	170.500	154.967	15-10-16	Las Vegas	770	B/J
	Red with black roof and black interior; restored. 390bhp 440 Six Pack engine with automatic transmission (see lot 259 RM 19.4.08 $104,500).											
1970	**Road Runner Super Bird**		RM23R0A172595	L	375-450.000 USD	246.330	300.000	281.370	15-01-17	Kissimmee	F157	Mec **F592**
	Orange with black roof and black vinyl interior; two owners. 425bhp 426 Hemi engine with automatic transmission. From the Colts Neck Collection.											
1970	**Road Runner Super Bird**		RM23R0A179732	L	600-750.000 USD		NS		15-01-17	Kissimmee	F191	Mec
	Orange with black vinyl roof and black interior; restoration completed in 2016. 425bhp 426 Hemi engine with manual gearbox.											

F591: 1968 Plymouth GTX convertible

F592: 1970 Plymouth Road Runner Super Bird

Year	Model	(Bodybuilder)	Chassis no.	Steering	Estimate	Hammer Price £	$	€	Date	Place	Lot	Auc. H.
1970	**Road Runner Super Bird**		RM23V0A169498	L	NQ		NS		15-01-17	Kissimmee	F90	**Mec**
	Blue with white vinyl interior; in original, unrestored condition. 440 Six Pack engine with manual gearbox.											
1970	**Road Runner Super Bird**		RM23U0A175651	L	100-140.000 USD	89.584*	110.000*	103.455*	20-01-17	Phoenix	275	**RMS**
	Orange with black roof and black vinyl interior; restored. 375bhp 440 engine with automatic transmission (see lot 226 RM 1.12.12 $110,000).											
1970	**Road Runner Super Bird**		RM23U0A163487	L	NQ	176.480*	216.700*	203.806*	21-01-17	Scottsdale	1320	**B/J**
	Blue with black roof and white interior; in very good overall condition. 14,800 original miles. 440 Super Commando engine with automatic transmission.											
1970	**Road Runner Super Bird**		RM23V0A166159	L	NQ	179.168*	220.000*	206.910*	21-01-17	Scottsdale	1440	**B/J**
	Yellow with black roof and black vinyl interior; 21,000 original miles. 440 engine with manual gearbox.											
1970	**Road Runner Super Bird**		RM23R0A166207	L	300-375.000 USD	176.732	230.000	205.735	20-05-17	Indianapolis	F174	**Mec**
	Red with black vinyl top and black interior; in original, unrestored condition; 9,809 original miles. 425bhp 426 Hemi engine with automatic transmission (see lot 711 Barrett-Jackson 16.1.03 $145,800).											
1970	**Road Runner Super Bird**		RM23U0A164599	L	140-160.000 USD	119.658	154.000	131.208	18-08-17	Carmel	104	**Bon**
	Orange with black roof and black interior; little distance covered since the restoration. 375bhp 440 Super Commando engine with automatic transmission.											
1970	**'Cuda hardtop**		BS23R0B179117	L	160-185.000 USD	90.056	112.500	101.408	04-11-16	Dallas	S131	**Mec**
	Metallic blue with blue interior; fully restored. 425bhp 426 Hemi engine with automatic transmission.											
1970	**'Cuda hardtop**		BS23R0B272440	L	300-400.000 USD	208.130	260.000	234.364	04-11-16	Dallas	S93	**Mec**
	Red with black interior; described as in original condition. 36,000 original miles. 425bhp 426 Hemi engine with manual gearbox.											
1970	**'Cuda hardtop**		BS23J0B282264	L	125-150.000 USD	160.115	195.000	182.891	15-01-17	Kissimmee	F118	**Mec**
	Red with black bonnet, black vinyl roof and black vinyl interior; restored in the 2000s. 275bhp 340 Six Pack engine with 4-speed manual gearbox. From the Jackie and Gary Runyon collection (see lot F186 Mecum 23.1.15 $ 140,000).											
1970	**'Cuda hardtop**		BS23R0B145107	L	250-300.000 USD	157.651	192.000	180.077	15-01-17	Kissimmee	S110.1	**Mec**
	White with black interior; restored. 425bhp 426 Hemi engine with automatic transmission. From the Don Fezell collection.											
1970	**'Cuda hardtop**		BS23R0B146392	L	NQ	246.356*	302.500*	284.501*	21-01-17	Scottsdale	1350	**B/J** **F593**
	Purple; just test miles covered since a concours-quality restoration. 426 Hemi engine with manual gearbox (see lots X2 Mecum 14.10.05 $ 267,750, and 5136 Steele & Russo 30.1.16 $ 148,500).											
1970	**'Cuda hardtop**		BS23VOB207703	L	NQ	48.375*	59.400*	55.866*	21-01-17	Scottsdale	8554	**R&S**
	Plum with black roof and black interior; 440 Six-Pack engine.											
1970	**'Cuda hardtop**		BS23R0B179117	L	NQ	112.196	140.000	129.556	25-03-17	Kansas City	S118	**Mec**
	See lot S131 Mecum 4.11.16.											
1970	**'Cuda hardtop**		BS23R0B172798	L	NQ	144.522*	180.000*	168.840*	08-04-17	Houston	S52	**Mec**
	Blue with black vinyl roof and black interior; 425bhp 426 Hemi engine with manual gearbox. From the Laquay Automobile Collection.											
1970	**'Cuda hardtop**		BS23R0B202497	L	350-400.000 USD	226.678	295.000	263.878	20-05-17	Indianapolis	F130.1	**Mec**
	Yellow with black vinyl roof and interior; in original, unrestored condition; 6,130 believed original miles. 425bhp 426 Hemi engine with automatic transmission.											
1970	**'Cuda hardtop**		BS23R0B242053	L	NQ	159.910	203.500	182.133	24-06-17	Northeast	670	**B/J**
	Blue with white interior; 426 Hemi engine with manual gearbox.											
1971	**'Cuda hardtop**		BS23R1B227275	L	400-500.000 USD	236.985	305.000	259.860	19-08-17	Monterey	F90	**Mec**
	Red with black vinyl roof and black leather interior; restored; three owners. 425bhp 426 Hemi engine and manual gearbox (see lot F127 Mecum 19.8.16 NS).											
1970	**'Cuda convertible**		BS27N0B242420	L	NA		NS		10-09-16	Louisville	S98	**Mec**
	Red with white interior; restored. 335bhp 383 engine with 4-speed manual gearbox.											
1970	**'Cuda convertible**		BS27V0B100004	L	400-600.000 USD		NS		15-01-17	Kissimmee	F187	**Mec**
	White with black leather interior; restored in 2005. 390bhp 440 Six Pack engine with manual gearbox (see lot F113 Mecum 23.1.16 $ 475,000).											
1970	**'Cuda convertible**		BS27V0B201063	L	1.000-1.250.000 USD		NS		15-01-17	Kissimmee	F98	**Mec**
	Black with blue vinyl interior; fully restored. 8,160 miles covered since new. 390bhp 440 Six Pack engine with manual gearbox. From the Tom Lembeck Collection.											
1970	**'Cuda convertible**		BS27N0B161634	L	90-120.000 USD	55.990*	68.750*	64.659*	20-01-17	Phoenix	277	**RMS**
	Plum with black vinyl interior; restoration completed in 2013. 440 engine modified to Six-Pack specification with 390bhp; automatic transmission.											
1970	**'Cuda convertible**		BS27N0B160329	L	NQ	95.855*	117.700*	110.697*	21-01-17	Scottsdale	1043	**B/J**
	Yellow with black interior; fully restored. 383 engine with automatic transmission.											
1970	**'Cuda convertible**		BS27R0B159521	L	NQ		NS		21-01-17	Scottsdale	1392	**B/J**
	Black with black interior; described as one of 14 examples built, the car is fitted with the 426 Hemi engine with automatic transmission. Raced in the 1970s. Discovered in 1989, it was restored and the engine was replaced with a date-code-correct unit that has been restamped (see lot 48 Worldwide Group 30.4.11 NS).											

F593: 1970 Plymouth 'Cuda hardtop

F594: 1928 Pontiac Model 6-27 coupé

Year	Model	(Bodybuilder)	Chassis No.	Steering	Estimate	Hammer Price £	$	€	Date	Place	Lot	Auc. H.

PONTIAC (USA) (1926-2009)

Year	Model	Chassis No.	Steering	Estimate	£	$	€	Date	Place	Lot	Auc. H.
1928	Model 6-27 coupé	P411887	L	18-25.000 USD	10.857*	13.750*	12.293*	06-10-16	Hershey	113	RMS F594
Light brown with black fenders and grey cloth interior; restored some years ago.											
1929	Model 6-29 convertible	486693	L	NA	20.226*	24.750*	22.495*	15-10-16	Las Vegas	371	B/J
Tan with black fenders and black interior; three owners in two families since new. In good running order. 26,000 original miles.											
1937	DeLuxe Model 6CA station wagon (Hercules)	6CA100563	L	NQ	34.042*	41.800*	39.313*	21-01-17	Scottsdale	1267	B/J
Black with wooden panels; from the late 1970s un the current, second ownership. Body restored, original wood.											
1947	Streamliner sedan coupé	P8MB33800	L	12-16.000 EUR	10.987*	13.546*	12.160*	07-10-16	Chateau-sur-Epte	5	Art
Two-tone green; in fair overall condition. Sold new to Belgium. From the Andre Weber Collection.											
1951	Streamliner DeLuxe station wagon	L8UH15614	L	35-45.000 USD	18.670*	24.000*	21.396*	04-06-17	Greenwich	108	Bon
Light green with burgundy vinyl interior; restored in 1988. Body repainted in 2005. Automatic transmission.											
1950	Streamliner Silver Streak sedan coupé	A8TS1176	L	NQ	25.931*	33.000*	29.535*	24-06-17	Northeast	348	B/J
Dark blue with grey interior; fully restored at unspecified date.											
1958	Chieftain convertible	K558H1839	L	NQ	36.950	45.000	42.206	15-01-17	Kissimmee	F86	Mec
White with blue side stripe and blue interior; 370 Tri-Power engine with automatic transmission.											
1957	Star Chief Catalina coupé	P857H36749	L	80-90.000 USD		NS		03-09-16	Auburn	2121	AA
Black with white interior; restoration completed in 2015. Automatic transmission.											
1957	Star Chief Custom Catalina coupé	P857H39166	L	65-80.000 USD	28.558*	35.200*	32.993*	19-01-17	Phoenix	165	RMS
Red with ivory roof and red and ivory interior; restored at unspecified date. 290bhp 347 Tri-Power engine with automatic transmission. From the Mohrschladt Family Collection.											
1958	Bonneville convertible	C558H1257	L	135-185.000 USD	101.010	130.000	110.760	19-08-17	Monterey	F91	Mec
Light blue with blue and white leather interior; concours-quality restoration completed in 2008.											
1958	Bonneville hardtop	C558H1699	L	NQ	175.585*	215.600*	202.772*	21-01-17	Scottsdale	1289.1	B/J
Copper with white roof and white and copper interior; restored. Fuel-injected engine with 4-speed automatic transmission.											
1963	Catalina "Swiss Cheese" hardtop	363P104314	L	500-650.000 USD	353.073	430.000	403.297	15-01-17	Kissimmee	F108	Mec F595
Silver with blue interior; sponsored by Packer Pontiac of Detroit and driven by Howard Maselles. Discovered in the late 1970s by Randy Williams and restored in 2000. One of 14 examples built by the factory. 405bhp 421 Super Duty engine with 3-speed manual gearbox. From the Jackie and Gary Runyon collection (see Mecum lots S112 6.10.06 $462,000 and S158 17.5.14 $530,000).											
1962	Catalina hardtop	362R32201	L	250-450.000 USD	164.220	200.000	187.580	15-01-17	Kissimmee	S115	Mec
Red with ivory roof and red interior; restored. Raced in period. 421 Super duty engine with 4-speed manual gearbox. From the Don Fezell collection.											
1959	Catalina convertible	159W15942	L	100-115.000 USD	55.014	67.000	62.839	15-01-17	Kissimmee	S239	Mec
Black with red and ivory interior; restored to concours condition. 345bhp 389 Tri Power engine with 4-speed manual gearbox.											
1963	Tempest convertible	163K2635	L	14-18.000 GBP		NS		07-12-16	London	307	Bon
Red with white interior; in good original condition. Imported into the UK in 2016.											
1965	Le Mans GTO convertible	237675P266411	L	NA	48.660	60.000	53.856	08-10-16	Chicago	S153	Mec
Blue with black interior; restored. 335bhp 389 engine with automatic transmission.											
1964	Le Mans GTO coupé	824M9010	L	75-100.000 USD	49.271*	60.500*	56.900*	21-01-17	Scottsdale	141	G&Co
Red with black interior; concours-quality restoration carried out at unspecified date. 348bhp 389 engine with 4-speed manual gearbox.											
1969	GTO Judge hardtop	242379Z119153	L	90-120.000 USD	59.125*	72.600*	68.280*	20-01-17	Scottsdale	9	G&Co
Red; recently restored. 366bhp 400 Ram-Air III engine with manual gearbox.											
1969	GTO Judge hardtop	242379P334364	L	NQ	116.459*	143.000*	134.492*	21-01-17	Scottsdale	1295	B/J
Yellow with black vinyl roof and black interior; fresh restoration. 370bhp 430 Ram Air IV engine with manual gearbox.											
1966	GTO hardtop	242176P297432	L	NQ	46.481	58.000	53.673	25-03-17	Kansas City	S75	Mec
Red with black interior; restoration completed in 2013. 360bhp 389 Tri-Power engine with 4-speed manual gearbox.											
1969	GTO Judge hardtop	242379B176476	L	NQ	112.369	143.000	127.985	24-06-17	Northeast	669	B/J
Orange with black interior; fully restored. 370bhp 400 Ram Air IV engine with manual gearbox.											
1970	GTO Judge convertible	242670P262941	L	NA	99.428	132.500	117.581	10-09-16	Louisville	S98.1	Mec F596
White with red interior; 366bhp 400 engine with 4-speed manual gearbox (see lot 133 RM 1.5.04 WD).											
1970	GTO Judge convertible	242670P255726	L	NA	103.376*	126.500*	114.976*	15-10-16	Las Vegas	722	B/J
Blue with black interior; fully restored. 400 Ram Air III engine with manual gearbox (see lot 64 Worldwide Group 31.8.13 $214,500).											

F595: 1963 Pontiac Catalina "Swiss Cheese" hardtop

F596: 1970 Pontiac GTO Judge convertible

Year	Model	(Bodybuilder)	Chassis no.	Steering	Estimate	Hammer price £	$	€	Date	Place	Lot	Auc. H.
1969	GTO convertible		242679B169050	L	300-400.000 USD	NS			15-01-17	Kissimmee	S189	Mec
	Red with parchment interior; recent mechanical sorting. 370bhp 400 Ram Air IV engine with automatic transmission (see lot S95 Mecum 5.10.07 $330,000).											
1969	GTO Judge convertible		242679B170503	L	NQ	138.855*	170.500*	160.355*	21-01-17	Scottsdale	1439	B/J
	Light green with green interior; restored to concours condition. 366bhp 400 Ram Air III engine with automatic transmission.											
1970	GTO convertible		242670P177509	L	NQ	101.132	128.700	115.187	24-06-17	Northeast	710	B/J
	Metallic blue with black interior; restored. 455 engine with automatic transmission.											
1969	Firebird coupé		223379L100001	L	NA	134.838*	165.000*	149.969*	15-10-16	Las Vegas	699	B/J
	Green with black interior; only test miles covered following a full restoration. 400 engine with automatic transmission.											
1967	Firebird convertible		223677U100001	L	NA	NS			15-10-16	Las Vegas	747	B/J
	Red with red interior; restored. First Firebird convertible built, the car was first used by the factory for auto show and advertising purposes. 326 engine with automatic transmission. Offered as a pair with lot 747.1 (first Firebird coupé built).											
1967	Firebird coupé		223377U100002	L	NA	NS			15-10-16	Las Vegas	747.1	B/J
	Silver with black interior; restored. First Firebird coupé built, the car was first used by the factory for auto show and advertising purposes. 326 engine with 4-speed manual gearbox. Sold as a pair with lot 747 (first Firebird convertible built).											
1968	Firebird hardtop		223378L107568	L	NA	NS			19-11-16	Anaheim	S92	Mec
	Dark green with black interior; restored between 2002 and 2004. 340bhp 400 Ram Air II engine with manual gearbox.											
1974	Firebird TransAm		2V87X4N167500	L	NA	46.744*	57.200*	51.989*	15-10-16	Las Vegas	464	B/J
	White with white interior; body repainted in the 1990s. 455 Super Duty engine with automatic transmission.											
1974	Firebird TransAm		2V87X4N160905	L	NA	105.174*	128.700*	116.975*	15-10-16	Las Vegas	699.1	B/J
	Blue with black interior; recently rebuilt 455 Super Duty engine with 4-speed manual gearbox.											
1976	Firebird TransAm SE		2W87W6N601918	L	NQ	55.447	70.000	65.772	03-12-16	Kansas City	S132.1	Mec
	Black with gold stripes and black interior; until 2014 with its first owner. 455 HO engine with manual gearbox.											
1979	Firebird TransAm		2W87K9L133169	L	NQ	89.584*	110.000*	103.455*	21-01-17	Scottsdale	1403	B/J
	Black with tan interior; one owner and 4,341 miles. In very good condition. Automatic transmission.											
1975	Grand Ville Brougham convertible		2R67S5P170996	L	12-15.000 EUR	15.382*	18.965*	17.024*	07-10-16	Chateau-sur-Epte	53	Art
	White with white interior; in good overall condition. From the Andre Weber Collection.											

PORSCHE (D) (1948-)

Year	Model	(Bodybuilder)	Chassis no.	Steering	Estimate	£	$	€	Date	Place	Lot	Auc. H.
1953	356 coupé		50894	L	230-290.000 EUR	NA			08-10-16	Paris	184	CB/C
	Silver with blue and white interior; recent full restoration. 1500 S engine (see lot 165 Coys 6.8.16 $290,441).											
1953	356 coupé (Reutter)		50451	L	130-160.000 USD	80.050	100.000	90.140	04-11-16	Dallas	S153	Mec
	Silver with blue and grey interior; restored in the 1990s. The engine has covered 150 miles since a recent rebuild.											
1953	356 coupé		51009	L	15-20.000 EUR	113.531*	141.170*	133.280*	25-11-16	Milan	313	RMS
	Black; some restoration works to be completed. 1100 engine. From the Duemila Ruote collection.											
1955	356 Continental coupé (Reutter)		53846	L	275-475.000 EUR	244.634	307.395	287.500	09-02-17	Paris	373	Bon
	Jade green with beige leatherette interior; sold new to the USA, the car was reimported into Europe in recent years. Restored, it is described as in very good overall condition. Original engine.											
1952	356 coupé (Reutter)		11976	L	140-160.000 GBP	144.860	187.999	164.025	30-06-17	Goodwood	251	Bon
	Blue with beige leather interior; several restoration works to the body and mechanicals carried out in the USA before the import in 2014 into the UK, where further mechanical works were completed (see lot 285 Historics 30.8.14 $195,004).											
1955	356 Continental coupé (Reutter)		54215	L	190-260.000 USD	223.931	288.200	245.546	18-08-17	Carmel	92	Bon
	Graphite grey with garnet red leather interior; fully restored. 1500 engine.											
1951	356 coupé (Reutter)		11111	L	600-700.000 USD	790.598	1.017.500	866.910	19-08-17	Monterey	247	RMS **F597**
	Black with grey-green leather interior; sold new in Germany and imported into the USA in 1952. Concours quality restoration carried out between 2006 and 2010. Original 1500 engine no.30069.											
1955	356 cabriolet		60898	L	240-270.000 EUR	NA			08-10-16	Paris	123	CB/C
	Graphite grey with red leather interior; fully restored. Engine replaced in 1959 with an unit supplied by the factory.											
1953	356 cabriolet (Reutter)		60115	L	300-400.000 USD	223.905*	275.000*	257.868*	18-01-17	Scottsdale	57	WoA
	Light blue with grey interior; approximately 100 miles covered since a recent full restoration. 1500 engine.											
1953	356 cabriolet (Reutter)		60157	L	225-300.000 USD	182.948	225.500	211.361	19-01-17	Scottsdale	47	Bon **F598**
	Light grey with red interior; sold new to the USA. Fully restored and fitted with a 1960 1600 Super engine.											

F597: 1951 Porsche 356 coupé (Reutter)

F598: 1953 Porsche 356 cabriolet (Reutter)

LADENBURGER AUTOMOBILIA AUKTION
17./18. NOVEMBER 2017

CONSINGNMENTS NOW ACCEPTED!

Automobilia Auktion Ladenburg - Tel.0049 (0)6203 957777
www.autotechnikauktion.de - info@autotechnikauktion.de

F599: 1955 Porsche 356 Speedster

F600: 1956 Porsche 550 Spyder

Year	Model	(Bodybuilder)	Chassis no.	Steering	Estimate	Hammer price £	$	€	Date	Place	Lot	Auc. H.
1954	356 cabriolet	(Reutter)	60568	L	250-350.000 USD		NS		10-03-17	Amelia Island	74	G&Co

Red with black interior; less than 1,500 miles covered since the restoration carried out at unspecified date. Since 1984 in the current ownership.

| 1955 | 356 Speedster | (Reutter) | 80945 | R | 150-180.000 GBP | 229.600 | 307.251 | 273.431 | 07-09-16 | London | 157 | RMS |

Originally finished in red, the car was sold new to Hong Kong fitted with the present 1600 Type 616/1 engine. In 1990 it was imported into the UK where it remained in storage for some 25 years. Currently finished in white, it requires some restoration works. Later gearbox. With Porsche Certificate of Authenticity.

| 1955 | 356 Speedster | | 80926 | L | 350-550.000 EUR | 529.920 | 653.361 | 586.500 | 07-10-16 | Zoute | 28 | Bon |

White with black interior; sold new to Belgium, the car has had four owners. Fully restored between 2012 and 2014. Fitted with its original 1600 engine no.P60004, rebuilt. With Porsche Certificate of Authenticity.

| 1955 | 356 Speedster | (Reutter) | 81066 | L | 350-450.000 USD | 241.817* | 297.000* | 278.497* | 18-01-17 | Scottsdale | 37 | WoA |

Red with black interior; concours-quality restoration completed in 2016. 1600 engine.

| 1955 | 356 Speedster | (Reutter) | 81009 | L | 275-325.000 USD | 227.570* | 280.500* | 262.913* | 19-01-17 | Phoenix | 124 | RMS |

Ivory white with red leatherette interior; restored approximately 10 years ago. 1600 engine (see RM lots 486 19.8.06 $137,500 and 130 30.7.11 NS).

| 1955 | 356 Speedster | (Reutter) | 80861 | L | 300-400.000 EUR | 315.324* | 394.178* | 369.600* | 08-02-17 | Paris | 121 | RMS |

Silver with black interior; in good overall condition. From a Swiss Porsche collection.

| 1955 | 356 Speedster | | 80363 | L | 350-550.000 EUR | 313.131 | 393.466 | 368.000 | 09-02-17 | Paris | 347 | Bon |

Yellow with brown interior; sold new to the USA, the car was reimported into Europe in 1991. Restored in the Netherlands some years ago; 1500S engine rebuilt just over a year ago.

| 1955 | 356 Speedster | | 80994 | L | 380-520.000 EUR | 335.497 | 418.102 | 393.360 | 10-02-17 | Paris | 18 | Art F599 |

Silver; sold new to the USA. Fully restored between 1999 and 2001. Imported into the UK in 2009. 1600 engine.

| 1955 | 356 Speedster | (Reutter) | 80879 | L | 275-325.000 USD | 204.651 | 255.750 | 239.203 | 01-04-17 | Ft.Lauderdale | 225 | AA |

White with tan interior; restored; 1600 engine. Formerly owned by actor Nicholas Cage (see lot 42 Gooding & Company 12.3.10 $137,500).

| 1954 | 356 Speedster | (Reutter) | 80075 | L | 330-360.000 EUR | 292.958 | 376.186 | 336.000 | 27-05-17 | Villa Erba | 128 | RMS |

Black; fully restored; 356C 1600 engine.

| 1955 | 356 Speedster | (Reutter) | 80773 | L | 250-300.000 GBP | 303.900 | 394.401 | 344.106 | 30-06-17 | Goodwood | 223 | Bon |

Silver with black interior; bought by John Coombs in the USA in 2004, imported into the UK in 2005 and subjected to a full restoration completed in 2007. New 1600 engine.

| 1954 | 356 Speedster | (Reutter) | 80052 | L | 275-350.000 USD | 273.504 | 352.000 | 299.904 | 19-08-17 | Pebble Beach | 108 | G&Co |

Red; for 47 years in the same family ownership; stored in 1998; original 1500 S engine.

| 1956 | 550 Spyder | | 5500090 | L | 4.700-6.200.000 GBP | 4.593.500 | 6.120.839 | 5.432.273 | 10-09-16 | Goodwood | 140 | Bon F600 |

Silver with blue stripes on the rear wings; sold new to the USA, the car was never raced and is in original, unrestored condition. FIVA Postwar award-winning at the 2010 Pebble Beach Concours.

| 1957 | Type 597 Jagdwagen | | NQ | L | 170-200.000 GBP | 175.100 | 233.321 | 207.073 | 10-09-16 | Goodwood | 138 | Bon F601 |

One of 49 examples built for civilian use; in good overall condition.

| 1958 | 356A coupé | | 103435 | L | 120-140.000 EUR | 105.108 | 131.393 | 123.200 | 08-02-17 | Paris | 173 | RMS |

Black; restored. With sunroof. Used as a press car by Porsche when new.

| 1959 | 356A coupé | | 107238 | L | 75-95.000 EUR | 73.390 | 92.219 | 86.250 | 09-02-17 | Paris | 334 | Bon F602 |

Black with dark red leather interior; with its second owner from 1960 to 2015; body repainted circa 20 years ago. Approximately 800,000 miles covered since new. Currently fitted with a 356C 1600 engine.

F601: 1957 Porsche Type 597 Jagdwagen

F602: 1959 Porsche 356A coupé

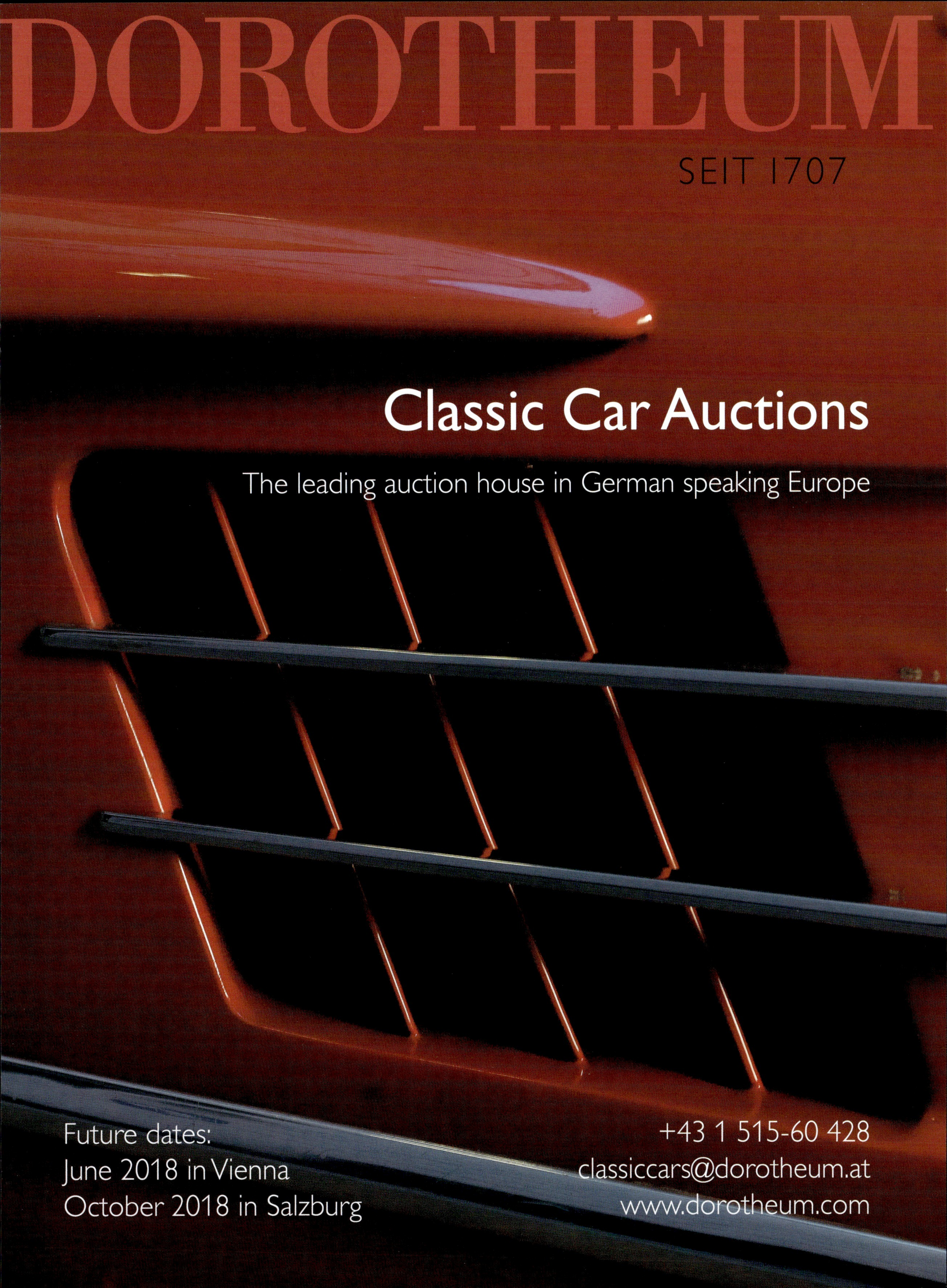

DOROTHEUM
SEIT 1707

Classic Car Auctions

The leading auction house in German speaking Europe

Future dates:
June 2018 in Vienna
October 2018 in Salzburg

+43 1 515-60 428
classiccars@dorotheum.at
www.dorotheum.com

Year	Model (Bodybuilder)	Chassis No.	Steering	Estimate	Hammer Price £	Hammer Price $	Hammer Price €	Date	Place	Lot	Auc. H.
1957	356A coupé (Reutter)	100288	L	100-120.000 USD		NS		09-03-17	Amelia Island	187	Bon
	Black with black interior; described as in highly original condition. Recently serviced.										
1958	356A coupé (Reutter)	104499	L	70-80.000 GBP	76.500	98.356	90.438	13-05-17	Silverstone	348	SiC
	Black with grey leather interior; restored many years ago; imported into the UK from the USA in 2009; gearbox rebuilt in 2010.										
1959	356A coupé	107004	R	170-185.000 AUD		NS		28-05-17	Sydney	4	Mos
	Black; described as in highly original condition, even if the 1600 engine is not its original unit.										
1959	356A coupé	107429	L	NQ	77.794*	99.000*	88.605*	24-06-17	Northeast	704	B/J
	Blue with tan leather interior; 300 miles covered since a full restoration. 1600 engine.										
1959	356A coupé (Reutter)	108804	L	85-125.000 EUR	101.959	129.741	116.120	24-06-17	Wien	362	Dor
	Light metallic grey with red leatherette interior; imported into Italy in 2011 and subsequently restored.										
1958	356A coupé	102310	L	75-95.000 GBP	78.220	101.514	88.569	30-06-17	Goodwood	281	Bon
	Red with caramel leather interior; imported into the UK in 2014 and subjected to a restoration completed in 2016.										
1959	356A cabriolet	151610	L	80-100.000 USD		NS		03-09-16	Auburn	5125	AA
	Ivory with black interior; for 20 years in the current ownership. Body repainted 30 years ago circa.										
1958	356A cabriolet (Reutter)	150531	L	160-190.000 EUR		NA		08-10-16	Paris	152	CB/C
	Red with beige leather interior; sold new to the USA, the car was reimported into Europe in 2012. Mechanicals restored in 2013.										
1958	356A cabriolet (Reutter)	150730	L	180-240.000 USD	160.637*	198.000*	185.585*	19-01-17	Phoenix	145	RMS
	Black with light brown leather interior; 250 miles covered since the restoration. 1600 S engine (see Barrett-Jackson lots 743 17.1.06 $135,000 and 725 19.1.07 $99,000).										
1959	356A cabriolet (Reutter)	151769	L	80-120.000 USD	74.072*	90.200*	85.483*	09-03-17	Amelia Island	177	Bon
	Red with red interior; 1961 1600 engine. In running order.										
1959	356A convertible D (Drauz)	85879	L	180-220.000 USD	125.387*	154.000*	144.406*	18-01-17	Scottsdale	8	WoA
	Finished in red with beige leatherette interior, the car was sold new to the USA. Paintwork redone several years ago, interior reupholstered in recent years.										
1959	356A convertible D (Drauz)	85720	L	175-200.000 USD	132.033	165.000	154.325	01-04-17	Ft.Lauderdale	532 F603	AA
	Red with light brown interior; currently fitted with a later 1600 engine (the original engine block is included with the sale).										
1959	356A convertible D (Drauz)	86410	L	210-260.000 EUR		NS		21-05-17	SPA-Francorch.	80	Bon
	Aquamarine blue with tan leather interior; sold new to the USA, the car was reimported into Germany in the mid-1990s. Restored some years ago; fitted with a Type 612/2 1600 S engine.										
1959	356A convertible D (Drauz)	86018	L	180-220.000 USD	166.667*	214.500*	182.754*	19-08-17	Pebble Beach	174	G&Co
	Ivory with black leather interior; from the early 1980s in the current ownership; restoration recently completed.										
1959	356A convertible D (Drauz)	85720	L	250-300.000 USD		NS		19-08-17	Monterey	S140	Mec
	See lot 532 Auctions America 1.4.17.										
1957	356A Speedster (Reutter)	83643	L	200-250.000 USD	269.254*	341.000*	304.854*	06-10-16	Hershey	140	RMS
	Orange; in the same family ownership since 1967. Stored in a Texas garage for more than 40 years, virtually complete and largely original (except for the paintwork), for restoration. Original 1600 engine. With a black fiberglass hardtop.										
1958	356A Speedster	84466	L	270-320.000 EUR		NA		08-10-16	Paris	115	CB/C
	Ivory with red interior; fully restored.										
1957	356A Speedster	83119	L	200-250.000 USD	532.733	665.500	599.882	05-11-16	Hilton Head	184	AA
	Metallic aquamarine with beige leatherette interior; in original condition. The car remained in the same family ownership from new to 2016 and was last used on the road in 1975 when it was put in storage having covered about 25,000 miles. 1600 engine.										
1957	356A Speedster (Reutter)	83099	L	280-320.000 GBP	306.563	388.078	355.889	12-11-16	Birmingham	634	SiC
	Black; imported into the UK from the USA and subsequently restored.										
1956	356A Speedster (Reutter)	82601	L	425-525.000 USD	428.366	528.000	494.894	19-01-17	Scottsdale	27	Bon
	Metallic aquamarine blue with dark red interior; sold new to the USA. Full restoration to concours condition completed in September 2016.										
1958	356A Speedster (Reutter)	84274	L	200-275.000 USD	277.710*	341.000*	320.711*	20-01-17	Scottsdale	62	G&Co
	Originally finished in blue and fitted with the 1600 S engine, the car was sold new to the USA. In 1970 it was bought by the current, third owner who drove it until 1974 when he put it into long term storage. For restoration.										
1957	356A Speedster (Reutter)	83456	L	340-380.000 USD	268.752	330.000	310.365	20-01-17	Phoenix	229	RMS
	Black with black leather interior; restored in 1989, the car is described as still in very good overall condition.										
1958	356A Speedster (Reutter)	84282	L	400-500.000 USD	277.710	341.000	320.711	21-01-17	Scottsdale	158	G&Co
	Black with black interior; sold new to the USA, the car has had three owners. Body repainted in 1975. In more recent years some mechanical and cosmetic attention. Never fully restored. With unrestored hardtop.										
1957	356A Speedster	83375	L	330-400.000 EUR	288.668	362.726	339.250	09-02-17	Paris	376	Bon
	Finished in red and sold new to the USA, the car remained until 2007 with its first owner. Reimported into Europe by the current, third owner. Unrestored; body repainted; original interior; 60bhp engine and gearbox in good working order.										
1958	356A Speedster (Reutter)	84708	L	475-550.000 USD	389.090	473.000	445.755	10-03-17	Amelia Island	67	G&Co
	Light blue with red interior; sold new to the USA; acquired in 2013 by the current owner and subsequently fully restored.										
1958	356A Speedster	84518	L	300-350.000 USD	215.188	275.000	257.043	22-04-17	Arlington	120	WoA
	Silver with black leatherette interior; sold new to the USA; in single ownership from 1970 to 2009; fully restored between 2009 and 2011; 1600 engine (see lot 75 Worldwide Group 4.5.13 $231,000).										
1958	356A Speedster	84185	L	300-400.000 EUR	276.624	359.964	322.000	21-05-17	SPA-Francorch.	46	Bon
	Silver with black interior; restored in 2003 in the USA and fitted with a 1600SC engine tuned to 110bhp. Reimported into Europe in 2015.										
1958	356A Speedster	84308	L	375-475.000 USD	279.720	360.000	307.800	17-08-17	Monterey	20	WoA
	One owner since new; bought in Germany and imported into the USA in early 1958; original 1600 engine and gearbox; restored at unspecified date.										
1957	356A Speedster (Reutter)	83366	L	475-550.000 USD		NS		18-08-17	Carmel	35	Bon
	White with red interior; sold new to Switzerland and later imported into the USA. Bought in 2009 by the current owner and subsequently restored. Less than 30,000 kms covered since new.										
1956	356A Speedster (Reutter)	81216	L	275-325.000 USD	230.769*	297.000*	253.044*	18-08-17	Carmel	64	Bon
	White with black interior; in the same ownership from 1978 to early 2017. Stored in 1999; in working order. 1957 1600 engine no.66322 fitted in the 1990s probably.										

Year	Model (Bodybuilder)	Chassis no.	Steering	Estimate	Hammer price £	$	€	Date	Place	Lot	Auc. H.
1956	356A Speedster (Reutter)	82435	L	250-300.000 USD	217.949	280.500	238.986	18-08-17	Pebble Beach	5	G&Co
	White; since 1957 in the same ownership; used until 1986 and recently returned to running condition.										
1958	356A Speedster (Reutter)	84683	L	350-400.000 USD	213.675	275.000	234.300	19-08-17	Monterey	S115	Mec
	Silver with black leatherette interior; recently restored. 1600 engine.										
1958	356A Speedster (Reutter)	83895	L	325-425.000 USD	247.863	319.000	271.788	19-08-17	Monterey	259	RMS
	Light blue with navy blue interior; fitted with a 912 engine at unspecified date; restored in the early 1990s; paintwork and interior redone in more recent years; engine and gearbox rebuilt in 2016 (see lots 444 RM 16.8.08 NS and 253 RM/Sotheby's 29.1.16 $295,000).										
1957	356A 1500 GS Carrera Speedster (Reutter)	83727	R	900-1.000.000 GBP	919.900	1.193.846	1.041.603	30-06-17	Goodwood	218	Bon F604
	Sold new to Australia finished in red with black interior. In the 1960s it was fitted with a 1600N engine; in the 1980s it was restored and fitted with engine number P90897 coming from GT Carrera Speedster chassis 83794. Between 2012 and 2014 it was restored again in the UK.										
1963	356B coupé	123345	R	NA	146.250	194.264	173.570	02-09-16	Salon Privé	231	SiC
	Grey with red leatherette interior; recent full restoration. In the 1990s the car was raced at three editions of the Monte-Carlo Historique Rallye.										
1961	356B coupé	118029	L	60-80.000 GBP		NS		10-09-16	Goodwood	149	Bon
	Champagne yellow with black leather interior; restored in 2010.										
1961	356B coupé	116133	L	62-76.000 EUR		NS		15-10-16	Salzburg	430	Dor
	Green with beige interior; overhauled some years ago. Imported into Austria from the USA.										
1959	356B coupé	109072	R	45-55.000 GBP	45.560	55.747	50.672	15-10-16	Silverstone	308	SiC
	Red; until 1997 with its first owner. In working order, the car requires recommissioning prior to use.										
1962	356B coupé	120352	R	60-65.000 GBP	63.000	77.087	70.069	15-10-16	Silverstone	321	SiC
	Silver; restored at unspecified date. Super 90 engine.										
1961	356B coupé	113404	L	55-75.000 EUR		NS		06-11-16	Lyon	340	Ose
	Restored in the USA approximately 20 years ago and imported into France four years ago; recently overhauled.										
1963	356B coupé	123765	L	65-75.000 EUR	85.863*	106.767*	100.800*	25-11-16	Milan	882	RMS
	Black with red interior. From the Duemila Ruote collection.										
1963	356B coupé	214319	L	68-74.000 GBP		NS		26-11-16	Weybridge	207	His
	Medium grey with red interior; imported into the UK from the USA in 2013 and subsequently restored. Gearbox recently replaced (see Coys lots 157 6.9.15 NS and 142 10.10.15 NS).										
1961	356B coupé	118029	L	60-80.000 GBP	74.300	93.685	87.310	07-12-16	London	349	Bon
	See lot 149 Bonhams 10.9.16.										
1963	356B coupé	120709	L	58-70.000 EUR	52.529	63.966	60.000	14-01-17	Maastricht	244	Coy
	Red; restored in 2006 in France.										
1961	356B coupé (Reutter)	116839	L	90-120.000 USD	84.781*	104.500*	97.948*	19-01-17	Scottsdale	98	Bon F605
	Grey con red interior; restoration completed in 2015. Upgraded with a period, Outlaw performance look.										
1961	356B coupé (Reutter)	117294	L	90-110.000 USD	73.907*	90.750*	85.350*	20-01-17	Scottsdale	17	G&Co
	Black with red interior; 100 miles covered since the recent restoration. Fitted with a 1,750cc engine with estimated 125bhp.										
1962	356B coupé	118461	L	NQ	58.230*	71.500*	67.246*	21-01-17	Scottsdale	1155	B/J
	Blue with original red interior; Super 90 engine.										
1960	356B coupé	110545	L	55-65.000 EUR		NS		05-08-17	Schloss Dyck	241	Coy
	Red; restored many years ago; engine rebuilt in 2015.										
1962	356B hardtop coupé (Karmann)	201982	L	90-120.000 AUD	57.898	74.357	66.407	28-05-17	Sydney	8	Mos F606
	Metallic grey with original red leather interior; imported into Australia from the USA in 2010 by its current, second owner. Rebuilt 1600 engine.										
1961	356B cabriolet (Reutter)	154828	L	130-160.000 EUR	126.765	156.294	140.300	07-10-16	Zoute	39	Bon
	Blue with grey interior; sold new to the USA, the car was imported in 2013 into the UK where it was restored. Further restoration works carried out in Germany between 2014 and 2016 (see lots 111 Coys 18.1.14 $115,464 and 35 Bonhams 10.10.14 $156,964).										
1963	356B cabriolet	157788	L	NQ		NS		15-01-17	Kissimmee	S70.1	Mec
	Black with red interior; stored for over 30 years and subsequently restored. 1600 engine (see lot 2127 Auctions America 8.5.15 NS).										
1960	356B cabriolet (Reutter)	154251	L	150-175.000 USD	124.940	154.000	144.344	19-01-17	Scottsdale	61	Bon F607
	Silver blue with blue interior; sold new to the USA. A few years ago the body was repainted, the interior re-upholstered, and the original 1600 engine rebuilt to Super 90 specification (see lots S642 Russo & Steele 18.8.11 $105,270, S91 Mecum 16.8.12 NS, 145 RM 27.4.13 $148,500, 2126 Auctions America 18.7.15 NS, and 124 RM/Sotheby's 28.1.16 $167,750).										

F603: 1959 Porsche 356A convertible D (Drauz)

F604: 1957 Porsche 356A 1500 GS Carrera Speedster (Reutter)

Year	Model (Bodybuilder)	Chassis no.	Steering	Estimate	Hammer price £	$	€	Date	Place	Lot	Auc. H.

F605: 1961 Porsche 356B coupé (Reutter)   F606: 1962 Porsche 356B hardtop coupé (Karmann)

Year	Model (Bodybuilder)	Chassis no.	Steering	Estimate	£	$	€	Date	Place	Lot	Auc. H.
1963	356B cabriolet	158009	L	130-150.000 EUR	109.555	136.448	128.000	08-04-17	Essen	122	Coy
	Black with red leather interior; full restoration recently completed.										
1963	356B cabriolet	158052	L	135-145.000 EUR	102.708	127.920	120.000	08-04-17	Essen	157	Coy
	Silver with black interior; the car received several restoration works including a repaint.										
1960	356B cabriolet	153606	L	NQ		NS		08-04-17	Houston	S99.1	Mec
	Red with new black interior.										
1961	356B cabriolet	155510	R	100-120.000 GBP	123.750	159.105	146.297	13-05-17	Silverstone	309	SiC
	Ivory with red leather interior; since 1965 in the same family ownership. Body repainted in the early 2000s.										
1961	356B cabriolet	154668	L	130-170.000 EUR	147.629	217.885	167.888	02-07-17	Monaco	110	Art
	Silver with red interior; restored in the early 2000s. Super 90 engine.										
1962	356B cabriolet	155628	L	100-120.000 GBP		NS		29-07-17	Silverstone	722	SiC
	Silver with dark blue leather interior; sold new to the USA and later reimported into Europe; restored in 2006 (see lot 137 Silverstone Auctions 4.9.14 $184,828).										
1963	356B cabriolet (Reutter)	157310	L	175-225.000 USD	158.120*	203.500*	173.382*	18-08-17	Pebble Beach	51	G&Co
	Champagne yellow with beige leather interior; restored in 1992 in California (see lot 19 Gooding & Company 11.3.16 $187,000).										
1960	356B roadster (Drauz)	87746	L	NQ	100.600	125.000	117.363	18-02-17	Los Angeles	S103	Mec
	Red with tan interior; less than 450 miles covered since the restoration completed in 2014. 1600 Super engine (see Mecum lots S11 15.8.15 $170,000 and S62 20.8.16 NS).										
1960	356B roadster (Drauz)	88222	L	NA	133.979	170.500	152.598	24-06-17	Santa Monica	224	RMS
	Red with light brown interior; restored in recent years (see lots 54 Worldwide Group 31.8.13 $182,600 and 115 RM 17.1.14 $198,000).										
1961	356B roadster (D'Ieteren)	89353	L	140-180.000 EUR	126.539	186.759	143.904	02-07-17	Monaco	137	Art F608
	Red with burgundy interior; 1600 S engine recently rebuilt.										
1961	356B roadster (Drauz)	88579	L	200-250.000 USD	136.752*	176.000*	149.952*	18-08-17	Pebble Beach	35	G&Co
	Red with grey leather interior; in original, unrestored condition; some mechanical works performed this year; believed to have had just one owner prior to 2017. Super 90 engine.										
1962	356B roadster (D'Ieteren)	89663	L	400-500.000 USD	393.162	506.000	431.112	19-08-17	Pebble Beach	146	G&Co
	Black with green leather interior; sold new to the USA; concours-quality restoration carried out between 2007 and 2010; engine rebuilt and enlarged to 1,720cc.										
1962	356B roadster (D'Ieteren)	89748	L	300-400.000 USD	112.665*	145.000*	123.540*	19-08-17	Monterey	S143	Mec
	Red with black interior; in the same ownership from 1975 to 2017; stored many years ago. Super 90 engine.										
1962	356B 2000 GS Carrera 2 coupé (Reutter)	120995	L	500-600.000 USD		NS		10-03-17	Amelia Island	77	G&Co
	Green with light green interior; sold new to Switzerland and later imported into the USA. Restoration completed in 2001 (see lot 15 Gooding & Company 22.1.10 $203,500).										
1963	356B 2000 GS Carrera 2 coupé (Reutter)	121298	L	600-750.000 USD		NS		11-03-17	Amelia Island	281	RMS
	Blue with light brown leatherette interior; electric sunroof. Sold new in Germany and imported into the USA in 1966. Restored between 1998 and 2005. Engine Type 587/1 no. 97079 recently rebuilt. Sunroof (see lots 323 Bonhams 6.5.06 NS and S160 Mecum 16.8.14 NS).										
1963	356B 2000 GS Carrera 2 cabriolet (Reutter)	157116	L	1.250-1.500.000 USD	971.250	1.250.000	1.065.000	19-08-17	Pebble Beach	134	G&Co
	Silver with red leather interior; sold new in Germany; imported into the USA in the 1970s; concours-quality restoration carried out between 2015 and 2017.										

F607: 1960 Porsche 356B cabriolet (Reutter)   F608: 1961 Porsche 356B roadster (D'Ieteren)

Year	Model	(Bodybuilder)	Chassis No.	Steering	Estimate	Hammer price £	Hammer price $	Hammer price €	Date	Place	Lot	Auc. H.
1964	356SC coupé		216758	L	85-125.000 EUR	103.397	126.523	115.000	15-10-16	Salzburg	438	Dor
	Blue; body repainted, interior retrimmed, mechanicals serviced.											
1963	356C coupé		215963	L	35-40.000 EUR	71.553*	88.973*	84.000*	25-11-16	Milan	293	RMS
	Grey with black interior; 66,398 kms. From the Duemila Ruote collection.											
1963	356C coupé		126183	L	45-55.000 EUR	59.150*	73.551*	69.440*	25-11-16	Milan	524	RMS
	Grey; 1600 engine. 86,424 kms. From the Duemila Ruote collection.											
1964	356C coupé		131661	L	10-15.000 EUR	59.150*	73.551*	69.440*	25-11-16	Milan	639	RMS
	Yellow with blue stripe: race prepared. From the Duemila Ruote collection.											
1964	356SC coupé		108264	L	100-125.000 EUR	NS			14-01-17	Maastricht	215	Coy
	Blue with silver stripe and black interior; restored in 2006.											
1964	356C coupé		220321	L	NQ	52.855*	64.900*	61.038*	21-01-17	Scottsdale	1034.1	B/J
	Red with black interior; body repainted.											
1965	356C coupé (Karmann)		221823	L	65-85.000 USD	36.133*	44.000*	41.699*	09-03-17	Amelia Island	105	Bon
	Ivory with black interior; fitted with a 912 engine enlarged to 1,730cc.											
1964	356C coupé (Karmann)		216431	L	70-90.000 USD	75.879*	92.400*	87.567*	09-03-17	Amelia Island	162	Bon
	Red with black interior; the car has covered about 7,500 miles since the restoration carried out in the 2000s.											
1963	356C coupé		131863	R	95-105.000 GBP	NS			12-04-17	London	308	Coy
	Blue with blue interior; body repainted in 2010. The engine has covered 25 miles since the rebuild.											
1965	356SC coupé		219526	L	NA	88.259	99.000	77.012	03-06-17	Newport Beach	9160	R&S
	Grey.											
1964	356SC coupé		218092	L	85-125.000 EUR	96.937	123.350	110.400	24-06-17	Wien	353	Dor
	Irish green with red leatherette interior; in the same family ownership until late 2016. Paintwork and interior restored some years ago.											
1964	356C coupé (Reutter)		129361	L	100-125.000 USD	101.132	128.700	115.187	24-06-17	Santa Monica	176	RMS
	Blue; since 1980 in the current ownership; restored. Electric sunroof.											
1964	356SC coupé		216233	L	40-60.000 EUR	34.799*	51.359*	39.574*	02-07-17	Monaco	143	Art
	For restoration.											
1965	356SC coupé (Reutter)		131727	L	130-160.000 USD	61.538*	79.200*	67.478*	18-08-17	Carmel	33	Bon
	Irish green with saddle interior; the car received much restoration and maintenance work over the years.											
1964	356C coupé		128265	L	NA	94.872	122.100	104.029	19-08-17	Monterey	1098	R&S
	Blue; restored; engine rebuilt. Sunroof.											
1965	356C cabriolet (Reutter)		161242	L	125-150.000 USD	118.247*	145.750*	136.611*	19-01-17	Phoenix	111	RMS F609
	Red with black interior; from 1971 for 42 years in the same ownership. Cosmetic restoration carried out five years ago; mechanical overhaul in 2013.											
1965	356SC cabriolet (Reutter)		161043	L	225-275.000 USD	156.772*	192.500*	181.046*	20-01-17	Scottsdale	43	G&Co
	Champagne yellow with black leatherette interior; sold new to the USA; in the same family ownership from 1969 circa for 46 years; recently serviced.											
1965	356SC cabriolet (Reutter)		160079	L	125-160.000 USD	103.866	129.800	121.402	01-04-17	Ft.Lauderdale	226	AA
	White with black leather interior; well maintained restoration.											
1964	356SC cabriolet (Reutter)		159378	L	190-230.000 USD	NS			18-08-17	Carmel	100	Bon
	Red with black leather interior; restored in the 1990s.											
1965	356C cabriolet (Reutter)		162126	L	120-150.000 USD	112.820*	145.200*	123.710*	18-08-17	Carmel	106	Bon
	Irish green with black leather interior; bought new by actor Christopher Lloyd who retained it until 2011. In largely original condition. Engine rebuilt.											
1963	356C 2000 GS Carrera coupé		123909	L	400-600.000 EUR	467.662	582.809	548.320	10-02-17	Paris	17	Art F610
	Slate grey with red leatherette interior; sold new to Italy, the car has had subsequent owners in Austria, France and Germany. Fitted in the 1970s probably with the present engine no.97089. Restored in the 1990s. Mechanicals overhauled in more recent years.											
1964	356C 2000 GS Carrera coupé		129913	L	550-650.000 USD	425.284	517.000	487.221	10-03-17	Amelia Island	27	G&Co
	Red with black interior; sold new in Germany, imported into Canada in 1967, into New Zealand in 1988 and into the USA in 1998; body repainted in 1998-99; interior and original engine restored in 2000 (see lot S182 Mecum 16.8.14 NS).											
1964	904 Carrera GTS		904098	L	2.000-2.500.000 USD	1.874.103	2.310.000	2.165.163	19-01-17	Scottsdale	88	Bon F611
	Blue with white stripe and original blue interior; originally finished in light ivory, the car was sold new to the USA and raced during the 1964 and 1965 seasons. Subsequently the original Type 587/3 engine was sold and the car fitted with a Type 547/4 unit previously on a 550 Spyder. Retained by one owner from 1969 to 1989 when it was osld to the present vendor and imported into Denmark. In 1992 it was reunited with its original engine no.99090. In largely original condition; low mileage.											

F609: 1965 Porsche 356C cabriolet (Reutter)

F610: 1963 Porsche 356C 2000 GS Carrera coupé

Year	Model	(Bodybuilder)	Chassis no.	Steering	Estimate	Hammer Price £	$	€	Date	Place	Lot	Auc. H.
1964	904 Carrera GTS		904042	L	1.500-1.800.000 USD	1.196.580	1.540.000	1.312.080	19-08-17	Pebble Beach	129	G&Co

Red and silver; sold new to the USA and raced in period. In 1983 it was bought by the previous owner, restored and raced at historic events. Over the last two years it received some mechanical works.

Year	Model	(Bodybuilder)	Chassis no.	Steering	Estimate	£	$	€	Date	Place	Lot	Auc. H.
1964	901 cabriolet	(Karmann)	13360	L	850-1.000.000 EUR	554.206	692.798	649.600	08-02-17	Paris	159	RMS

Red with black interior; only known cabriolet prototype of the car which would become the 911. In 1967 it was sold by the factory to German collector Manfred Freisinger who saved it from being destroyed and retained it until 2001 when it was bought by American Myron Vernis. The car was fitted with a 2-litre engine of the correct type with an early case number; the body and interior remained original. Vernis drove it, exhibited it at 2013 Pebble Beach and resold it in 2014. Currently registered in the UK. **F612**

| 1967 | 911S coupé | | 308181 | L | 150-200.000 USD | NS | | | 03-09-16 | Auburn | 4170 | AA |

White with white interior; described as in very good original condition. 5-speed manual gearbox.

| 1965 | 911coupé | | 301153 | L | 200-250.000 EUR | NS | | | 03-09-16 | Chantilly | 15 | Bon |

Red with black interior; fully restored between 2014 and 2016 by the Porsche Classic Brussels.

| 1968 | 911 coupé | | 11835259 | L | 80-100.000 GBP | 85.500 | 113.929 | 101.112 | 10-09-16 | Goodwood | 179 | Bon |

Imported new into the USA by Brumos Motors. Modified in the early 1990s by Kenny Hawkins, North Carolina, and fitted with the present RS bodywork; engine modified to 1968-period race specification. Imported into Switzerland in 2012. Currently registered in the UK. Mechanicals restored by Francis Tuthill between 2014 and 2015.

| 1968 | 911 T coupé | | 11820916 | R | 85-100.000 GBP | 84.380 | 103.247 | 93.847 | 15-10-16 | Silverstone | 327 | SiC |

Irish green; bought by the current owner in 1988 and restored in more recent years.

| 1967 | 911 S coupé | | 305306 | L | 40-60.000 EUR | 47.956 | 59.902 | 54.000 | 05-11-16 | Lyon | 227 | Agu |

White with original black leather interior; body repainted 15 years ago. Engine replaced in the past with a correct period unit.

| 1967 | 911 S coupé | | 308181 | L | 100-125.000 USD | 88.055 | 110.000 | 99.154 | 05-11-16 | Hilton Head | 191 | AA |

See lot 4170 Auctions America 3.9.16.

| 1967 | 911 S coupé | | 308175S | L | 25-5.000 EUR | 62.012* | 77.110* | 72.800* | 25-11-16 | Milan | 228 | RMS |

Red; it requires several restoration works. From the Duemila Ruote collection.

| 1965 | 911 coupé | | 302540 | L | 80-90.000 EUR | 124.025* | 154.220* | 145.600* | 25-11-16 | Milan | 322 | RMS |

White; 50,404 kms. From the Duemila Ruote collection.

| 1969 | 911 S-S/T coupé | | 119300644 | L | 700-900.000 GBP | 680.150 | 864.811 | 808.018 | 05-12-16 | London | 109 | Coy |

Built as a normal 911 S, the car was sent new to the Werks Porsche Competition Department who converted it to S/T specification using the original 2 Litre engine tuned to 242bhp. Finished in green, it was raced in Sweden until 1976 being upgraded over the years to meet the competition. Used by the current owner at numerous European events; engine recently rebuilt. **F613**

| 1967 | 911 S coupé | | 3066008 | L | 110-130.000 GBP | 111.500 | 141.772 | 132.462 | 05-12-16 | London | 128 | Coy |

Silver; sold new to the USA, the car remained with its first owner until early 2016. Engine rebuilt in the 1990s; body repainted in 2000. With UK documents.

| 1968 | 911 L coupé | | 11805973 | L | 50-65.000 EUR | NS | | | 14-01-17 | Maastricht | 248 | Coy |

Light metallic blue with black leatherette interior.

| 1966 | 911 coupé | | 304037 | L | 170-210.000 USD | 118.247* | 145.750* | 136.611* | 19-01-17 | Scottsdale | 23 | Bon |

Light ivory with black interior; less than 1,000 miles covered since a full restoration carried out between 2009 and 2013.

| 1967 | 911 S coupé | | 306058 | L | NQ | 138.855* | 170.500* | 160.355* | 21-01-17 | Scottsdale | 1367 | B/J |

Irish green with brown interior; restored in recent years (see lot 83 Bonhams 28.1.16 $139,700).

| 1969 | 911 E Targa | | 119210741 | L | NQ | NS | | | 21-01-17 | Scottsdale | 8090 | R&S |

Light green; recently serviced.

| 1965 | 911 coupé | | 302527 | L | 170-240.000 USD | 185.181* | 225.500* | 213.706* | 09-03-17 | Amelia Island | 122 | Bon |

Light ivory with black leather interior; electric sunroof. Purchased from long-term storage in 2015 by the current owner and subsequently restored.

| 1969 | 911 E coupé | | 119200650 | L | 100-125.000 USD | 80.533* | 97.900* | 92.261* | 10-03-17 | Amelia Island | 36 | G&Co |

Light grey; full restoration completed in 2010 (see Gooding & Company lots 23 20.8.11 $104,500 and 57 7.3.14 $137,500).

| 1966 | 911 coupé | | 304572 | L | 180-200.000 USD | 117.632* | 143.000* | 134.763* | 10-03-17 | Amelia Island | 58 | G&Co |

White with black interior; until the mid-2000s with its first owner. In very good condition, original except for the paintwork redone in its factory colour.

| 1968 | 911 L coupé | | 11805378 | L | 125-175.000 USD | 92.296 | 112.200 | 105.737 | 11-03-17 | Amelia Island | 24 | Mot |

White with black and red plaid interior; 27,227 believed to be original miles on the odometer. Body repainted five years ago.

| 1965 | 911 coupé | | 303058 | L | 275-325.000 USD | 158.351* | 192.500* | 181.412* | 11-03-17 | Amelia Island | 279 | RMS |

Irish green with beige interior; sold new to the USA. In single ownership from the 1980s to 2013. Recent full restoration; original engine rebuilt.

| 1968 | 911 coupé | | 11835019 | L | 225-275.000 USD | 235.264 | 286.000 | 269.526 | 11-03-17 | Amelia Island | 287 | RMS |

Silver metallic with black leatherette interior; sold new to the USA; in very good original condition; 27,726 miles covered; Sportomatic transmission. **F614**

| 1969 | 911 T coupé | | 119100214 | L | 60-80.000 EUR | NS | | | 18-03-17 | Lyon | 209 | Agu |

Tangerine with black interior; described as in good original condition. Sold new to the USA and reimported into Europe in 1996 (see lot 42 Poulain/Sotheby's 26.6.00 $12,598).

F611: 1964 Porsche 904 Carrera GTS

F612: 1964 Porsche 901 cabriolet (Karmann)

Year	Model	(Bodybuilder)	Chassis no.	Steering	Estimate	Hammer price £	$	€	Date	Sale Place	Lot	Auc. H.

F613: 1969 Porsche 911 S-S/T coupé

F614: 1968 Porsche 911 coupé

Year	Model	Chassis no.	Steering	Estimate	£	$	€	Date	Place	Lot	Auc. H.
1967	911 S coupé	308411	L	220-250.000 GBP	NS			29-03-17	Duxford	84	H&H

Sand beige with black leatherette interior; in original, unrestored condition, the car is described as in very good overall condition. Since 2014 in the current, third ownership.

| 1967 | 911 S coupé | 308114 | L | 220-240.000 GBP | NS | | | 29-03-17 | Duxford | 95 | H&H |

Sand beige with black leatherette interior; sold new to the USA; from 1979 to 2015 with its second owner; recent full restoration.

| 1968 | 911 S coupé | 119300349 | L | 130-160.000 EUR | 88.158 | 109.798 | 103.000 | 08-04-17 | Essen | 112 | Coy |

Metallic grey; restoration completed in 2015.

| 1965 | 911 coupé | 301276 | L | 180-210.000 EUR | 149.783 | 186.550 | 175.000 | 08-04-17 | Essen | 128 | Coy |

Red; full restoration recently completed in the UK.

| 1965 | 911 coupé | 302094 | L | 100-120.000 GBP | NS | | | 13-05-17 | Silverstone | 351 | SiC |

Red with black leatherette interior; imported into the UK from the USA in 2013; in good overall condition.

| 1967 | 911 S coupé | 11800138 | R | 220-250.000 GBP | 203.000 | 264.144 | 236.292 | 20-05-17 | Ascot | 202 | His |

Ivory white with black interior; retained by its first owner until 2000; bought by the current, third owner in 2011 and subsequently fully restored (see lot 47 Coys 15.5.00 $16,018).

| 1966 | 911 coupé | 303419 | L | 85-125.000 EUR | NS | | | 21-05-17 | SPA-Francorch. | 42 | Bon |

Blue with black interior; sold new to the USA, the car was imported into Holland in 1997 and prepared for historic rallying. Original engine tuned to around 180bhp.

| 1965 | 911 coupé | 301814 | L | NA | 61.781 | 69.300 | 53.908 | 03-06-17 | Newport Beach | 9010 | R&S |

Irish green; restored and fitted with a 1967 911 S engine.

| 1969 | 911 T coupé | 119122935 | L | 85-125.000 EUR | 92.898 | 118.210 | 105.800 | 24-06-17 | Wien | 357 | Dor |

Blood orange with black leatherette interior; restoration completed in 2015.

| 1967 | 911 S coupé | 306438S | L | 240-280.000 GBP | NS | | | 30-06-17 | Goodwood | 257 | Bon |

Green with black interior; concours-quality restoration carried out in the USA between 2009 and 2013.

| 1969 | 911 T coupé | 119123429 | L | 65-75.000 GBP | NS | | | 29-07-17 | Silverstone | 719 | SiC |

Beige with black interior; imported into the UK from the USA in 2015 and restored in 2016.

| 1966 | 911 coupé | 305599 | L | 200-230.000 EUR | 191.258 | 251.424 | 211.850 | 05-08-17 | Schloss Dyck | 245 | Coy |

Yellow; sold new in Germany; fully restored between 2014 and 2017.

| 1969 | 911 S coupé | 119300296 | L | 140-160.000 USD | 95.726 | 123.200 | 105.336 | 17-08-17 | Monterey | 29 | WoA |

Finished in light ivory with black leatherette interior, the car was sold new to the USA. Described as in good overall condition. Interior reupholstered in black leather.

| 1968 | 911 Targa | 11880010 | L | 175-200.000 USD | 115.385* | 148.500* | 126.522* | 18-08-17 | Pebble Beach | 15 | G&Co |

Blue with black interior; soft-window version; restoration completed in early 2017; engine rebuilt to S specification.

| 1969 | 911 S Targa | 119310373 | L | 175-250.000 USD | 106.838* | 137.500* | 117.150* | 18-08-17 | Monterey | 115 | RMS F615 |

Metallic blue with black leatherette interior; in largely original condition. Body repainted in the 1980s, engine rebuilt in 2013. For 45 years with its first owner.

| 1967 | 911 S coupé | 308377S | L | 225-275.000 USD | 145.299* | 187.000* | 159.324* | 18-08-17 | Monterey | 139 | RMS |

Grey with black leatherette interior; converted in the past to a race car and raced at several historic events. Bought in 2012 by the current owner and fully restored to its original specification.

| 1967 | 911 S Targa | 5004185 | L | 275-350.000 USD | 221.445 | 285.000 | 242.820 | 19-08-17 | Pebble Beach | 113 | G&Co |

Red; recent full restoration; soft-window version.

F615: 1969 Porsche 911 S Targa

F616: 1969 Porsche 912 Targa

337

Year	Model	(Bodybuilder)	Chassis no.	Steering	Estimate	Hammer price £	$	€	Date	Place	Lot	Auc. H.
1967	**911 S coupé**		306301S	L	200-250.000 USD	123.932*	159.500*	135.894*	19-08-17	Pebble Beach	161	G&Co
	Red with black interior; restored in the USA in 2005; modified in 2009 as a tribute to the car winner of the 1967 Monte Carlo Rally. Engine rebuilt.											
1969	**912 Targa**		129010445	L	80-120.000 EUR	83.125	102.488	92.000	07-10-16	Zoute	36	Bon F616
	Blue; sold new to the USA where it remained in the same family ownership until 2014 when it was imported into the Netherlands. Described as in very good original condition.											
1968	**912 coupé**		12800311	L	38-42.000 GBP	48.940	59.883	54.431	15-10-16	Silverstone	307	SiC
	Irish green; imported into the UK from the USA in 2015 and subsequently restored.											
1968	**912 coupé**		12803890	L	36-40.000 GBP		NS		15-10-16	Silverstone	337	SiC
	Red with black interior; sold new to the USA. Believed to have been restored in the mid-1990s (see Coys lots 319 16.1.16 NS and 107 16.4.16 $45,177).											
1969	**912 Targa**		129010279	L	20-24.000 GBP	22.500	28.483	26.120	12-11-16	Birmingham	363	SiC
	Red with black interior; imported into the UK from the USA.											
1967	**912 coupé**		460616	L	20-24.000 GBP	29.250	37.028	33.956	12-11-16	Birmingham	606	SiC
	Green with black interior; in good overall condition. Imported into the UK from the USA in early 2016.											
1967	**912 coupé**		461628	L	60-80.000 USD	93.167*	114.400*	107.593*	21-01-17	Scottsdale	107	G&Co
	Yellow with black leatherette interior; about 8,000 miles covered since the restoration carried out in 2008.											
1967	**912 Targa**		550164	L	40-50.000 EUR	41.697	51.538	48.000	19-03-17	Fontainebleau	221	Ose
	Metallic grey with red interior; engine rebuilt at unspecified date (see Osenat lots 342 16.3.14 NS and 313 22.6.14 $47,286).											
1968	**912 Targa**		129010275	L	36-44.000 EUR	30.812	38.376	36.000	08-04-17	Essen	118	Coy
	Light ivory with black vinyl interior.											
1969	**912 Targa**		129010279	L	40-60.000 EUR	46.378	59.143	52.920	10-06-17	Lyon	124	Agu
	See lot 363 Silverstone Auctions 12.11.16.											
1968	**912 coupé**		12803024	L	45-55.000 GBP		NS		29-07-17	Silverstone	750	SiC
	Ivory with black leatherette interior; imported into the UK from the USA in 1998 and restored over the last 12 months.											
1969	**912 Targa**		129010762	L	70-90.000 USD	47.009*	60.500*	51.546*	18-08-17	Pebble Beach	30	G&Co
	Burgundy with black leather interior; sold new to the USA; described as in very good, unrestored condition; engine rebuilt in 2007.											
1970	**908/3**		90803003	R	3.500-4.500.000 USD	2.777.775	3.575.000	3.045.900	19-08-17	Monterey	256	RMS F617
	Yellow; used by the factory for test and development of the model; raced only at the 1970 Nürburgring 1000 KM where it placed 2nd overall driven by Hermann/Attwood for the Porsche Salzburg team. Subsequently it was used for further developments; damaged in an accident it was sold by the factory in 1973; later it was bought by driver Siggi Brunn and restored; acquired by the current owner it has been recently restored to its 1970 Nürburgring livery.											
1970	**917/10**		91710001	R	4.600-5.500.000 EUR		NS		08-02-17	Paris	147	RMS
	First 917/10 built, the car remained in the factory ownership and was used for test and development until October 1972 when it was rebuilt and sold to Willi Kauhsen. Raced until the end of the 1974 season and driven among others by Kauhsen and Emerson Fittipaldi. Retained by Kauhsen until 2008; first restored between 1997 and 1999; restored again in 2014 and fitted with the present 600+bhp normally aspirated 12-cylinder 5-liter engine (see lot 254 Coys 20.5.06 NS).											
1970	**917K**		917024	R	13-16.000.000 USD	10.940.160	14.080.000	11.996.160	18-08-17	Pebble Beach	44	G&Co TOP TEN F618
	Used by the factory for test and development, in June 1970 the car was acquired by Jo Siffert, who in 1971 loaned it to the Steve McQueen's Solar Productions for the filming of the movie "Le Mans". After the death of the driver in October 1971, the car was bought from his estate in 1978 by Pierre Prieur, who retained it until 2002, when it was discovered, without engine, in a warehouse outside Paris and was bought by the current owner. Later it was fully restored, fitted with engine 917.021 and finished in the Gulf livery of Le Mans 1971.											
1975	**VW 914**		4752906850	L	40-50.000 USD	32.580	40.700	36.687	05-11-16	Hilton Head	137	AA
	Yellow with black leatherette interior; described as in original condition with 3,200 original miles.											
1970	**VW 914**		4702901600	L	25-35.000 USD	10.759*	13.750*	12.852*	22-04-17	Arlington	134	WoA
	Yellow with black leatherette interior; sold new to the USA; for some 40 years in the same ownership and subsequently restored.											
1974	**VW 914 2.0 Bumblebee**		4742915510	L	30-50.000 EUR	30.626*	39.853*	35.650*	21-05-17	SPA-Francorch.	34	Bon
	Black and yellow; one of 500 examples built. Restored between 2015 and 2017.											
1975	**VW 914**		4752906850	L	40-50.000 USD	72.650*	93.500*	79.662*	18-08-17	Monterey	112	RMS
	See lot 137 Auctions America 5.11.16.											
1970	**VW 914.6**		9140431688	L	85-125.000 EUR	88.921	108.810	98.900	15-10-16	Salzburg	443	Dor F619
	Yellow with black leatherette interior; sold new to the USA and later reimported into Europe. Restored in the late 1980s. Engine overhauled at unspecified date.											
1970	**VW 914.6**		9140431518	L	65-85.000 USD	49.084*	60.500*	56.707*	19-01-17	Scottsdale	35	Bon
	Yellow with black leatherette interior; less than 27,000 miles on the odometer. Body repainted several years ago.											
1970	**VW 914.6**		9140430501	L	80-100.000 USD	80.626*	99.000*	93.110*	21-01-17	Scottsdale	149	G&Co
	Red; less than 350 miles covered since a full restoration completed in 2014.											

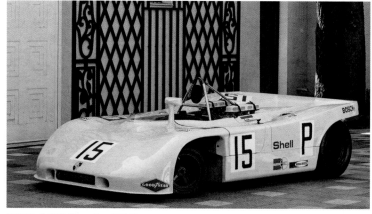

F617: 1970 Porsche 908/3

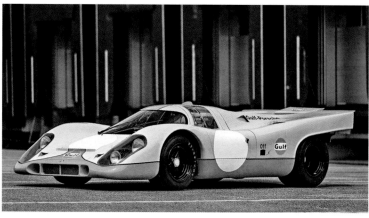

F618: 1970 Porsche 917K

Year	Model	(Bodybuilder)	Chassis no.	Steering	Estimate	Hammer Price £	$	€	Date	Place	Lot	Auc. H.
1970	VW 914.6		9140430216	L	40-60.000 EUR	49.687*	62.113*	58.240*	08-02-17	Paris	126	RMS
Black with black interior; less than 45,000 miles covered. From a Swiss Porsche collection.												
1970	VW 914.6		9140431533	L	180-240.000 EUR	156.566	196.733	184.000	09-02-17	Paris	342	Bon
Silver and black; the car was converted to GT specification by Kremer Racing in 1971 and raced until 1972. Recently restored in Belgium and fitted with a new engine built by Irmgartz (see lot 349 Bonhams 5.2.11 NS).												
1972	VW 914.6		9142430183	L	75-90.000 EUR	53.066	66.092	62.000	08-04-17	Essen	189	Coy
White with black interior; just over 52,000 kms covered. Regularly serviced.												
1971	VW 914.6		9141430383	L	NA	89.744	115.500	98.406	19-08-17	Monterey	1075	R&S
Orange; restored by the Chip Ganassi Racing Team.												
1971	911 T 2.2 coupé		9111101301	R	NA	69.750	92.649	82.779	02-09-16	Salon Privé	235	SiC
Ivory white with black leatherette interior; in recent years the body was restored and the engine and gearbox were rebuilt.												
1970	911 T 2.2 coupé		9110123533	L	NA	56.777	70.000	65.856	19-11-16	Anaheim	S165.1	Mec
Black with black interior; unrestored; believed to be 72,000 original miles.												
1971	911 S 2.2 coupé		9111300390	L	10-12.000 EUR	100.174*	124.562*	117.600*	25-11-16	Milan	363	RMS
Red with black interior; 63,333 kms. From the Duemila Ruote collection.												
1971	911 2.2 coupé		9111300541	L	45-55.000 EUR	95.404*	118.630*	112.000*	25-11-16	Milan	620	RMS
Black; 56,841 kms. From the Duemila Ruote collection.												
1970	911 S 2.2 coupé		9110300331	L	175-225.000 USD		NS		15-01-17	Kissimmee	S247	Mec
Brown with light brown interior; less than 1,000 miles covered since the restoration (see lots 29 Gooding & Company 9.3.12 NS and 105 RM 16.8.13 NS).												
1971	911 T 2.2 Targa		9111111299	L	NQ	51.959*	63.800*	60.004*	21-01-17	Scottsdale	823.1	B/J
Silver with black interior.												
1971	911 E 2.2 Targa		9111210785	L	175-225.000 USD	138.855*	170.500*	160.355*	21-01-17	Scottsdale	135	G&Co
Blue with black leatherette interior; until January 2016 with its first owner. Described as in original condition. Recently serviced.												
1970	911 E 2.2 coupé		9110200901	L	70-90.000 EUR	58.712	73.775	69.000	09-02-17	Paris	362	Bon
Silver with black vinyl interior; body repainted and engine overhauled in the 2000s.												
1970	911 E 2.2 coupé		9110220387	L	80-120.000 EUR	73.199*	91.222*	85.824*	10-02-17	Paris	89	Art
Light ivory with black leatherette interior; bought in 1971 by the current, second owner, the car has been always well maintained, is in original condition and has covered 128,423 kms.												
1970	911 E 2.2 coupé		9110220628	L	185-195.000 USD		NS		11-02-17	Boca Raton	167	TFA
Blue with tan leather interior; fully restored.												
1971	911 S 2.2 coupé		9111300100	L	180-220.000 USD	135.729*	165.000*	155.496*	10-03-17	Amelia Island	20	G&Co
Metallic green with black leatherette interior; since 1991 in the current, second ownership. Restored between 2009 and 2014.												
1971	911 S 2.2 coupé		9111301413	L	160-220.000 EUR	201.284	256.130	229.240	24-06-17	Wien	365	Dor F620
Silver with black leather interior; since 1976 in the same family ownership; body restored in 1994; engine overhauled in 2016.												
1971	911 S 2.2 coupé		911130023	L	150-180.000 USD		NS		24-06-17	Santa Monica	231	RMS
Yellow; restored.												
1970	911 S 2.2 coupé		99110300980	L	120-150.000 GBP		NS		29-07-17	Silverstone	442	SiC
Ivory white with black interior; imported into the UK from the USA in 2000; engine and gearbox overhauled in more recent years.												
1970	911 E 2.2 coupé		9110200496	L	100-120.000 USD	64.103	82.500	70.538	17-08-17	Monterey	5	WoA
Green; sold new to the USA; engine rebuilt; body repainted (see lots 50 Gooding & Company 20.1.12 $63,250, 77 RM 17.1.14 $71,500 and 115 RM/Sotheby's 30.7.16 $70,000).												
1970	911ST 2.2 Rallye		9110301383	L	750-900.000 USD		NS		10-03-17	Amelia Island	48	G&Co
Sold new in Germany and later imported into Canada. Recently the car has been fully restored to concours condition, finished in silver metallic and fitted with a correct 2.2 S engine. Documented by Production Record, Factory Correspondence, and Porsche COA.												
1973	911 S 2.4 coupé		9113301078	L	150-180.000 GBP		NS		10-09-16	Goodwood	161	Bon
Brown with black leather interior; 1,857 kms covered since the restoration (see lot 336 Bonhams 26.6.15 $231,329).												
1973	911 T 2.4 coupé		9113102002	L	50-60.000 GBP		NS		10-09-16	Goodwood	182	Bon
Brown with beige interior; sold new to the USA and imported in 2015 into the UK.												
1973	911 S 2.4 Targa		9113310416	L	150-180.000 EUR		NA		08-10-16	Paris	138	CB/C
Blue with black interior; restored in 1990.												
1971	911 S 2.4 coupé		9112300299	L	160-240.000 EUR	214.166	262.068	238.200	15-10-16	Salzburg	441	Dor
Silver metallic with black interior; in the same family ownership from new. At unspecified date body repainted, interior retrimmed, mechanicals serviced.												
1972	911 S 2.4 coupé		9112301372	R	180-220.000 GBP	200.250	245.026	222.718	15-10-16	Silverstone	330	SiC
Yellow; since 2002 in the current ownership. Restoration completed in 2007.												
1973	911 S 2.4 coupé		9113300938	L	110-130.000 EUR	157.416*	195.740*	184.800*	25-11-16	Milan	325	RMS
Black with beige interior; original engine. 35,389 kms. From the Duemila Ruote collection.												
1973	911 S 2.4 coupé		9113601163	L	35-40.000 EUR	62.012*	77.110*	72.800*	25-11-16	Milan	556	RMS
Black; restoration to be completed. Body painted. From the Duemila Ruote collection.												
1973	911 S 2.4 coupé		9113300340	L	35-40.000 EUR	85.863*	106.767*	100.800*	25-11-16	Milan	849	RMS
White with black interior; 63,006 kms. From the Duemila Ruote collection.												
1973	911 S 2.4 Targa		9113310833	R	150-180.000 GBP	147.100	185.684	174.475	04-12-16	London	18	Bon F621
Light ivory with black interior; sold new to Australia; restored between 1994 and 1999; imported into the UK in 2014.												
1973	911 S 2.4 coupé		9113300487	R	100-120.000 GBP		NS		04-12-16	London	29	Bon
Metallic blue; body restored in the mid-1990s, engine rebuilt in 2003, gearbox and suspension rebuilt in 2015.												
1972	911 S 2.4 coupé		9112301372	R	180-220.000 GBP	203.100	256.089	238.663	07-12-16	London	344	Bon
See lot 330 Silverstone Auctions 15.10.16.												

Year	Model	(Bodybuilder)	Chassis No.	Steering	Estimate	Hammer Price £	Hammer Price $	Hammer Price €	Date	Place	Lot	Auc. H.
1973	911 S 2.4 Targa		9113310416	L	75-90.000 GBP	81.395	99.115	92.969	14-01-17	Birmingham	139	Coy
See lot 138 Coutau Bégarie/Coys 8.10.16.												
1973	911 S 2.4 coupé		9113301340	L	200-250.000 USD	152.293*	187.000*	175.874*	20-01-17	Scottsdale	25	G&Co
Black with black interior; described as in very good and highly original condition. Only the paintwork was redone. Less than 55,000 miles on the odometer. Recently serviced.												
1973	911 S 2.4 Targa		9113310441	L	250-325.000 USD	NS			20-01-17	Scottsdale	57	G&Co
Silver with black leatherette interior; sold new to the USA, the car remained with its second owner from 1973 to 2016. In original condition; 35,900 miles on the odometer; recommissioned in 2015 following 20 years of storage.												
1973	911 S 2.4 Targa		9113310296	L	NQ	165.730*	203.500*	191.392*	21-01-17	Scottsdale	1424	B/J
Blue with black interior; restored. Engine and gearbox rebuilt (see lots 273 RM 20.1.12 $88,000 and 146 The Finest Automobile Auctions 11.6.16 NS).												
1973	911 T 2.4 coupé		9113100811	L	150-180.000 USD	134.376*	165.000*	155.183*	21-01-17	Scottsdale	116	G&Co
Light blue with black interior; with its second owner from 1977 to 2011 and subsequently restored (see lot S109 Mecum 20.8.16 NS).												
1973	911 S 2.4 Targa		9113310416	L	80-100.000 GBP	75.582	93.903	88.166	18-02-17	London	350	Coy
See lot 139 Coys 14.1.17.												
1972	911 T 2.4 coupé		9112501105	R	90-110.000 GBP	93.375	117.223	110.491	24-02-17	Stoneleigh P.	511	SiC
Yellow; body recently repainted; full mechanical service (see lot 393 Historics 22.10.11 NS).												
1972	911 S 2.4 Targa		9112310928	L	125-155.000 GBP	NS			04-03-17	Brooklands	176	His
Metallic blue; black Recaro seats; in good driving order.												
1973	911 S 2.4 coupé		9113300301	L	130-170.000 USD	135.498*	165.000*	156.371*	09-03-17	Amelia Island	143	Bon
Ivory with brown interior; sold new to the USA. Engine rebuilt and enlarged to 2,687cc in 1988. Since 1994 in the current ownership. Engine rebuilt again in the 1990s.												
1972	911 S 2.4 Targa		9112310456	L	130-180.000 EUR	NS			18-03-17	Lyon	204	Agu
Blue with beige leather interior; restored in recent years.												
1972	911 T 2.4 coupé		9112102587	L	89-99.000 EUR	65.048	81.016	76.000	08-04-17	Essen	144	Coy
Light ivory with black interior; sold new to Japan; imported into the UK in 2016; recently serviced.												
1973	911 S 2.4 Targa		9113310416	L	55-65.000 GBP	88.920	111.150	104.801	12-04-17	London	312	Coy
See lot 350 Coys 18.2.17.												
1973	911 S 2.4 coupé		9113300814	L	130-170.000 EUR	NS			02-07-17	Monaco	148	Art
Light ivory with black interior; prepared for historic events.												
1972	911 S 2.4 coupé		9112200948	L	90-110.000 GBP	88.920	114.920	101.058	15-07-17	Blenheim Pal.	126	Coy
Black with black interior; restored in 1988; in good overall condition (see lot 7 Coys 2.3.98 $19,426).												
1973	911 T 2.4 coupé		9113103178	L	130-150.000 USD	NS			17-08-17	Monterey	40	WoA
Until 2010 with its first owner and subsequently restored to its original colours (see lot 26 Gooding & Company 16.1.15 $115,500).												
1973	911 T 2.4 Targa		9113112280	L	140-180.000 USD	111.111*	143.000*	121.836*	19-08-17	Pebble Beach	150	G&Co
Orange with black leather interior; until 2012 in the same family ownership; described as in very good original condition; showing less than 81,000 miles.												
1972	911 E 2.4 Targa		9112210344	L	NA	47.863	61.600	52.483	19-08-17	Monterey	1183	R&S
Metallic gold; described as original and with low mileage.												
1973	911 Carrera RS 2.7		9113601418	L	450-550.000 GBP	224.000	299.757	266.762	07-09-16	London	133	RMS
Lightweight version finished in yellow with black interior; restored in the 1980s including the replacement of the engine (unstamped block) and transmission. Since 2000 in the current ownership.												
1973	911 Carrera RS 2.7		9113600435	L	450-550.000 GBP	459.200	614.501	546.861	07-09-16	London	152	RMS
Touring version finished in white; sold new to Portugal, the car was imported into France in 2011 and subsequently in 2014 in the UK. Recent major service and replacement of the interior.												
1973	911 Carrera RS 2.7		9113600305	L	495-545.000 EUR	458.653	573.350	537.600	08-02-17	Paris	164	RMS
Touring version finished in yellow with black interior; sold new in Germany, the car remained with its first owner until 1996 when it was imported into Japan and restored for the first time. In 2014 it was bought by the current owner, reimported into Europe and restored again to its original specification.												
1973	911 Carrera RS 2.7		9113601518	L	400-600.000 EUR	NS			10-02-17	Paris	117	Art
Touring version finished in yellow with black interior; recently restored, the car is described as in very good overall condition. In 2007 the engine was rebuilt and enlarged to 2.8-litre; since then it has covered less than 5,000 kms.												
1973	911 Carrera RS 2.7		9113601315	L	550-650.000 USD	NS			11-03-17	Amelia Island	250	RMS
Touring version finished in yellow with black interior; early in its life raced at some rallies in the Netherlands and subsequently imported into the USA. In the same family ownership since 1991; 50 miles covered since the restoration completed in 2015. Crankcase replaced with a correct unit stamped as the original.												
1973	911 Carrera RS 2.7		9113600336	L	800-1.000.000 USD	714.839*	869.000*	818.946*	11-03-17	Amelia Island	264	RMS
Lightweight version finished in yellow with black interior; sold new in Germany and imported into the USA in the 1980s. Described as in original condition except for the paintwork redone several years ago in its original colour. Mechanicals freshened in the 2000s.												

F619: 1970 Porsche VW 914.6

F620: 1971 Porsche 911 S 2.2 coupé

Year	Model	(Bodybuilder)	Chassis no.	Steering	Estimate	Hammer price £	$	€	Sale Date	Place	Lot	Auc. H.

F621: 1973 Porsche 911 S 2.4 Targa

F622: 1973 Porsche 911 Carrera RS 2.7

1973 911 Carrera RS 2.7 — 9113601496 — R — 750-850.000 GBP — **830.300** — **1.077.563** — **940.149** — 30-06-17 — Goodwood — 245 — **Bon**
Lightweight version finished in white with black interior; sold new to the UK and raced at several rallies in period. Restored in 1999-2000. Engine rebuilt in 2007. Bought in 2012 by the current owner and regularly maintained. **F622**

1973 911 Carrera RS 2.7 — 9113600354 — L — 875.000-950.000 USD — NS — 18-08-17 — Monterey — 129 — **RMS**
Lightweight version finished in yellow with black interior; sold new to Switzerland and raced until 1982; original engine replaced in 1976 with an unit supplied by the factory; imported into the USA in 1993 and restored. The engine case was replaced with a new-old-stock unstamped unit, subsequently stamped with the original engine number 66303509 (the replaced case is included with the sale) (see lot 60 Gooding & Company 13.3.15 NS).

1973 911 Carrera RS 2.7 — 9113600427 — L — 650-850.000 USD — **504.273** — **649.000** — **552.948** — 18-08-17 — Monterey — 159 — **RMS**
Touring version finished in yellow with black interior; sold new in Germany, the car was imported into the USA in partially restored condition about four years ago. Restoration completed in California; recent engine-out service.

1973 911 Carrera RS 2.7 — 9113600813 — L — 650-750.000 USD — NS — 19-08-17 — Pebble Beach — 131 — **G&Co**
Touring version finished in yellow; with sunroof; imported into the USA in the early 1980s; several mechanical works carried out in the 2000s; cosmetic and mechanical restoration works carried out in 2016 (see lots RM 241 17.8.01 $66,000 and 51 9.3.02 $58,200, and Gooding & Company 36 8.3.13 $550,000).

1973 911 Carrera RS 2.7 — 9113601014 — L — 1.300-1.400.000 USD — NS — 19-08-17 — Monterey — S26 — **Mec**
Lightweight version finished in tangerine with black interior; rally-racing history dating back to 1976-80.

1974 Carrera RSR 3.0 — 9114609113 — L — 1.400-1.600.000 EUR — **1.555.781** — **2.296.172** — **1.769.280** — 02-07-17 — Monaco — 176 — **Art**
White; sold new to the USA, the car raced at numerous events until 1986. It ran also eight editions of the Sebring 12 Hours, and seven of the Daytona 24 Hours. Restored some years ago (see lot 246 Bonhams 15.8.14 NS). **F623**

1976 911 2.7 Targa — 9116310919 — R — 25-30.000 GBP — **26.450*** — **35.134*** — **31.391*** — 03-09-16 — Beaulieu — 421 — **Bon**
Red; cosmetically restored in 2015-16. Built with Sportomatic transmission, the car is currently fitted with a 5-speed manual gerabox.

1976 911 2.7 coupé — 9116300556 — L — 30-40.000 GBP — **28.500** — **34.930** — **31.698** — 12-10-16 — Duxford — 116 — **H&H**
Green with black interior; in good driving order.

1977 911 2.7 Lux Targa — 9117311179 — R — 20-25.000 GBP — **24.750** — **30.284** — **27.527** — 15-10-16 — Silverstone — 335 — **SiC**
White; described as in good overall condition. Since 1983 in the current ownership. Sportomatic transmission.

1974 911 2.7 coupé — 9114102995 — L — 10-15.000 EUR — **29.677*** — **36.903*** — **34.840*** — 25-11-16 — Milan — 918 — **RMS**
Red; 28,870 kms. From the Duemila Ruote collection.

1976 911 S 2.7 coupé — 9116200180 — L — 120-140.000 USD — **76.146*** — **93.500*** — **87.937*** — 21-01-17 — Scottsdale — 122 — **G&Co**
Metallic platinum with cork interior; described as in very good overall condition. One of 200 examples of the Ferry Porsche Signature Edition.

1977 911 S 2.7 coupé — 9117200053 — L — 45-65.000 EUR — **47.948*** — **60.249*** — **56.350*** — 09-02-17 — Paris — 415 — **Bon**
Red with lobster leatherette interior; in very good overall condition. With its first owner until late 2013; 56,000 miles covered.

1976 911 S 2.7 Targa — 9116211280 — L — 55-65.000 USD — **41.058** — **52.250** — **46.764** — 24-06-17 — Santa Monica — 153 — **RMS**
White; 830 miles covered since the restoration carried out in 2015. **F624**

1975 911 S 2.7 coupé — 9115200465 — L — 90-100.000 GBP — NS — 30-06-17 — Goodwood — 267 — **Bon**
Sahara beige; sold new to the USA, the car was reimported into Europe in 2012. Described as in very good overall condition. 9,591 miles covered (see lot 226 Silverstone Auctions 25.10.15 $121,314).

F623: 1974 Porsche Carrera RSR 3.0

F624: 1976 Porsche 911 S 2.7 Targa

Year	Model	(Bodybuilder)	Chassis no.	Steering	Estimate	Hammer price £	$	€	Date	Place	Lot	Auc. H.
1975	911 S 2.7 Targa		9116210881	L	55-65.000 EUR	38.252	50.285	42.370	05-08-17	Schloss Dyck	252	Coy
	*Burgundy with beige leather interior; restored in the Netherlands in recent times.*
1974	911 Carrera 2.7 coupé		9114600269	L	180-200.000 GBP		NS		07-09-16	London	175	RMS
	*Light yellow; body repainted in 1989, original interior. Since 1988 in the current ownership.*
1974	911 Carrera 2.7 Targa		9115610125	R	150-180.000 GBP		NS		10-09-16	Goodwood	180	Bon
	*Red with original black leather interior; in good overall condition. Restored in 2014/2015.*
1976	911 Carrera 2.7 "Sondermodell" coupé		9116609034	L	175-275.000 EUR		NS		07-10-16	Zoute	31	Bon
	*Copper brown; one of 113 examples built for the German market. Restored in recent years; engine and gearbox overhauled.*
1975	911 Carrera 2.7 Targa		9115610125	R	130-160.000 GBP		NS		15-10-16	Silverstone	324	SiC
	*See lot 180 Bonhams 10.9.16.*
1975	911 Carrera 2.7 Targa		9115610195	L	150-200.000 EUR	143.869	179.707	162.000	06-11-16	Lyon	354	Ose
	*Red; restored in 2010-11. First registered to the Porsche company.*
1975	911 Carrera 2.7 coupé		9115600513	R	240-280.000 GBP		NS		12-11-16	Birmingham	333	SiC
	*Ice green; the car remained with its first owner until May 2015 and was subsequently restored (see lot 381 Silverstone Auctions 23.5.15 $228,735).*
1975	911 Carrera 2.7 coupé		9115600482	L	NA	162.220	200.000	188.160	19-11-16	Anaheim	S129.1	Mec
	*White with blue and black interior; sold new to Switzerland; imported into the USA in 2013; recently serviced (see lot 7253 Russo & Steele 20.8.16 NS).*
1975	911 Carrera 2.7 coupé		9115400268	L	120-150.000 USD	89.584*	110.000*	103.455*	20-01-17	Scottsdale	35	G&Co
	*Silver with black leather interior; just over 36,000 miles covered. Recently serviced.*
1975	911 Carrera 2.7 coupé		9115600208	L	170-200.000 EUR		NS		08-02-17	Paris	162	RMS
	*Metallic grey with black interior; sold new to France. Recently restored; engine rebuilt.*
1974	911 Carrera 2.7 coupé		9114600528	L	120-160.000 EUR		NS		09-02-17	Paris	393	Bon
	*White; sold new to Italy; since 1985 in the current ownership; serviced in October 2015.*
1975	911 Carrera 2.7 coupé		9115600180	L	150-180.000 EUR	142.356	210.103	161.892	02-07-17	Monaco	220	Art
	*Light green with black interior; restored in 2016.*
1976	911 Carrera 2.7 coupé		9116609061	L	200-250.000 EUR	211.391	277.889	234.150	05-08-17	Schloss Dyck	219	Coy
	*Black with black interior; 5-speed gearbox. Engine rebuilt in 1990 and overhauled in 2013. Body repainted in 2010 (see lot 130 Coys 18.4.15 NS).*
1974	911 Carrera 2.7 coupé		9114600298	L	225-275.000 USD	179.487*	231.000*	196.812*	19-08-17	Monterey	268	RMS
	*Sold new to Japan and for a long time stored in a museum; well maintained; 119,080 kms covered.*
1974	Carrera RS 3.0		9114609106	L	900-1.100.000 USD	1.131.075*	1.375.000*	1.295.800*	11-03-17	Amelia Island	262	RMS F625
	*White; factory demonstration car when new, it was later sold in the USA and in 1996 it was imported into Japan. In 2004 it was bought by the current owner and reimported into the USA. Described as in very good original condition; 29,279 kms covered.*
1977	911 Turbo coupé		9307700268	L	110-130.000 GBP	140.000	187.348	166.726	07-09-16	London	126	RMS
	*Metallic copper brown with tan leather interior; 83,289 kms covered. Last serviced in July 2016. Since 1996 in the current ownership.*
1977	911 Turbo coupé		9307800150	L	NA	81.110	100.000	94.080	19-11-16	Anaheim	S61	Mec
	*Beige grey with brown interior; refinished in 2011.*
1976	911 Turbo coupé		9306700102	L	55-65.000 EUR	109.714*	136.425*	128.800*	25-11-16	Milan	336	RMS
	*Black with black interior; 154,788 kms. From the Duemila Ruote collection.*
1977	911 Turbo coupé		9307800095	L	NQ	147.814*	181.500*	170.701*	21-01-17	Scottsdale	1427	B/J
	*Metallic ice green with black leather and green tartan interior; for 30 years in the current, third ownership. 106,000 actual kms.*
1976	911 Turbo coupé		9307700060	L	155-185.000 EUR	119.826	149.240	140.000	08-04-17	Essen	176	Coy
	*Metallic grey; restored several years ago.*
1976	911 Turbo coupé		9306800292	L	140-170.000 USD	119.797	154.000	137.291	04-06-17	Greenwich	151	Bon F626
	*Silver with black leather interior; restored in recent years (see lot 20 Bonhams 19.8.16 $132,000).*
1976	911 Turbo coupé		9307700060	L	130-160.000 GBP		NS		15-07-17	Blenheim Pal.	105	Coy
	*See lot 176 Coys 8.4.17.*
1976	911 Turbo coupé		9307800174	L	110-130.000 EUR	92.609	121.742	102.580	05-08-17	Schloss Dyck	275	Coy
	*Red with tan interior; described as in very good overall condition, the car received recently some renovation works.*
1976	Carrera 3.0 coupé		9117600739	L	190-260.000 EUR	203.617	247.361	226.480	30-10-16	Paris	146	Art
	*Replica, built by Jacques and Jean Marie Alméras, of the Carrera RSR driven by Fréquelin/Delaval al 1974 Tour de France. 2,000 kms covered since the rebuild. Group IV and V VHC FIA homologation.*

F625: 1974 Porsche Carrera RS 3.0

F626: 1976 Porsche 911 Turbo coupé

Year	Model	(Bodybuilder)	Chassis no.	Steering	Estimate	Hammer price £	$	€	Date	Place	Lot	Auc. H.
1977	**Carrera 3.0 coupé**		9117600834	L	100-150.000 USD	49.084*	60.500*	56.707*	19-01-17	Scottsdale	4	**Bon**
Copper metallic with cork leather interior; sold new to Belgium and later imported into the USA. In good original condition. Air conditioning.												
1977	**Carrera 3.0 Targa**		9117610110	L	175-225.000 EUR	133.774	167.227	156.800	08-02-17	Paris	170	**RMS**
Ordered new by the Frankfurt Porsche dealer Glocker with "Turbo-look" body finished in yellow with black leatherette interior. Recently restored.												
1977	**Carrera 3.0 Targa**		9117610595	L	190-210.000 USD		NS		11-02-17	Boca Raton	160	**TFA**
Ice metallic green with black leather and black tartan interior; sold new in Europe, the car was imported into the USA in 1985 and later restored.												
1977	**Carrera 3.0 coupé**		9117600816	R	40-50.000 GBP	51.129	66.657	59.893	18-05-17	London	142	**Coy**
Red; engine rebuilt and body restored at unspecified date; gearbox rebuilt in 2014.												
1977	**Carrera 3.0 Sport coupé**		9117600684	R	80-100.000 GBP	95.720	125.345	106.871	29-07-17	Silverstone	441	**SiC**
Blue with black leatherette and tartan cloth interior; 108,082 miles on the odometer; last serviced in April 2014 at 106,646 miles.												
1976	**912 E coupé**		9126001763	L	20-30.000 EUR	28.666*	35.834*	33.600*	08-02-17	Paris	122	**RMS** **F627**
Red with black interior; from a Swiss Porsche collection.												
1976	**912 E coupé**		9126000082	L	27-30.000 GBP		NS		26-07-17	Duxford	51	**H&H**
Brown with tan leather interior; recently imported into the UK from the USA. Engine overhauled.												
1981	**924**		408546	L	15-20.000 GBP	15.750	19.272	17.517	15-10-16	Silverstone	354	**SiC**
White; recently overhauled. 10,220 kms on the odometer. Stored from 1995 circa to 2015.												
1981	**924 GTR**		924004	L	250-300.000 USD	180.972	220.000	207.328	10-03-17	Amelia Island	64	**G&Co** **F628**
One of six cars built (and chassis numbered) by Al Holbert, using bodies and racing components from Porsche Motorsport. Raced until 1986 at numerous IMSA events and in 1984 also at the Daytona 24 Hours and Sebring 12 Hours. Restored in 2014; in ready to race condition.												
1987	**924 S**		452147	L	20-30.000 USD	16.287*	19.800*	18.660*	11-03-17	Amelia Island	211	**RMS**
Silver metallic with black interior; just over 43,500 miles covered. Recently serviced.												
1977	**934/5 Turbo**		DMV47012CA	L	750-1.000.000 USD		NS		15-01-17	Kissimmee	S158	**Mec**
Built with chassis 930770960 to IMSA specification, the car was heavily damaged at Daytona in 1978 and in 1979 it was rebuilt by Dan McLaughlin who fitted the mechanical parts on the new chassis DMV47012CA. Raced at numerous events in the 1980s; 3rd overall at the 1981 Sebring 12 Hours. Restored in 2007 (see lot S175 Mecum 16.8.14 NS).												
1977	**934/5 Turbo**		9307700956	L	1.400-1.600.000 USD	1.131.075	1.375.000	1.295.800	10-03-17	Amelia Island	56	**G&Co** **F629**
The car was raced in Europe until the end of the 1979 season, when it was restored at the factory and sold to Australia, where it won the 1981 National Sports Car Championship. Later it was modified for road use and converted to right-hand drive form. Restored in 1995, the car was restored again between 2014 and 2015 to its 1979 silver, blue and red "Boss" livery and returned to left-hand drive form.												
1976	**934/5 Turbo**		9306700478	L	320-400.000 EUR		NS		21-05-17	SPA-Francorch.	49	**Bon**
Bought new by the German Kremer racing team and raced at three events in 1977. Stored for many years, in 2006 it was prepared for historic racing. Finished in the Martini livery.												
1976	**934/935 Turbo**		9306700171	L	800-1.000.000 USD		NS		19-08-17	Monterey	S64	**Mec**
Gialla e blu; raced in Europe until 1977, including the 1976 and 1977 Le Mans 24 Hours, and subsequently at IMSA events until 1986. First converted to 934/5 specification, in 2007 the car was restored to 935 K3 specification and finished in the 1981 Daytona 24 Hours livery (see lots 237 Bonhams 12.8.10 NS, 223 RM 17.8.13 NS, and S174 Mecum 16.8.14 NS).												
1977	**935 Turbo**		9307700907	L	1.600-1.750.000 USD		NS		19-08-17	Monterey	S90	**Mec**
White with blue stripes; raced in period in Europe and at the 1978 Daytona 24 Hours; modified to K3 specification in the early 1980s: restored in 2015.												
1980	**911SC Targa**		91A0132933	L	30-50.000 GBP	30.240*	40.467*	36.013*	07-09-16	London	185	**RMS**
Silver with black leather interior; described as in very good original condition. Engine rebuilt 2,000 kms ago.												
1978	**911SC Targa**		9118311405	L	30-40.000 USD	24.362	31.350	27.898	03-10-16	Philadelphia	234	**Bon**
Ice green metallic; in good driving order. Body repainted.												
1981	**911SC coupé**		129588	L	35-50.000 EUR	54.031*	66.617*	59.800*	07-10-16	Zoute	17	**Bon** **F630**
Recently imported into Europe from Japan; circa 105,000 kms on the odometer. Electric sliding sunroof.												
1980	**911SC coupé**		91A0134411	L	40-50.000 EUR	40.723*	49.472*	45.296*	30-10-16	Paris	144	**Art**
Red; mechanical overhaul. Sunroof.												
1983	**911SC coupé**		102480	L	35-45.000 EUR	36.437*	44.265*	40.528*	30-10-16	Paris	155	**Art**
Recent mechanical overhaul.												
1978	**911SC Targa**		9118310074	L	33-43.000 EUR	35.168	43.928	39.600	06-11-16	Lyon	350	**Ose**
Black; gearbox redone in 2016. In good working order.												
1983	**911SC cabriolet**		150088	L	20-30.000 EUR	57.242*	71.178*	67.200*	25-11-16	Milan	538	**RMS**
White; 168,515 kms. From the Duemila Ruote collection.												

F627: 1976 Porsche 912 E coupé

F628: 1981 Porsche 924 GTR

Year	Model	(Bodybuilder)	Chassis No.	Steering	Estimate	£	$	€	Date	Place	Lot	Auc. H.
1983	911SC coupé		102659	L	30-35.000 EUR	38.162*	47.452*	44.800*	25-11-16	Milan	917	RMS
	White; 127,527 kms. From the Duemila Ruote collection.											
1977	911SC coupé		9118300714	R	27-33.000 GBP	28.750	36.251	33.784	07-12-16	London	322	Bon
	Light metallic green; engine rebuilt in 1996, body restored in 2009. Circa 92,000 covered since new.											
1979	911SC Targa		9119310891	R	27-32.000 GBP	26.676	33.142	31.118	18-02-17	London	363	Coy
	Light metallic blue with black interior; last serviced in March 2016.											
1985	911SC Targa		140427	R	27-32.000 GBP	29.120	37.891	33.896	20-05-17	Ascot	250	His
	Red with black leather interior; recently cosmetically restored and mechanically recommissioned.											
1980	911SC coupé		91A0132228	L	36-42.000 EUR	33.758	43.050	38.520	10-06-17	Lyon	126	Agu
	Beige; in good overall condition.											
1986	911SC coupé		100091	L	35-40.000 EUR	47.273	60.302	54.000	18-06-17	Fontainebleau	83	Ose
	Grey with grey and burgundy interior; one of 200 examples of the Ferry Porsche edition.											
1989	911 Turbo SE 3.3 slantnose coupé		000310	R	NA	146.250	194.264	173.570	02-09-16	Salon Privé	247	SiC
	Black with black interior; in very good overall condition. Recently serviced.											
1988	911 Turbo 3.3 coupé		000299	R	NA	171.000	227.139	202.943	02-09-16	Salon Privé	263	SiC
	White with blue and white leather interior; described as in very good original condition. 30,857 miles covered (see lot 620 Silverstone Auctions 14.11.15 $171,270).											
1989	911 Turbo 3.3 coupé		000409	L	110-130.000 GBP	106.400	142.384	126.712	07-09-16	London	127	RMS
	Black with black interior; highly original condition. 75,378 kms covered. Since 2001 in the current ownership.											
1989	911 Turbo SE 3.3 slantnose cabriolet		020243	R	100-130.000 GBP	107.900	143.777	127.603	10-09-16	Goodwood	120	Bon
	White with white interior; in very good overall condition. Circa 33,200 miles from new (see lot 326 Bonhams 28.4.14 $153,467).											
1989	911 Turbo 3.3 Targa		010073	L	250-300.000 EUR	275.351	339.492	304.750	07-10-16	Zoute	21	Bon F631
	Black with black leather interior; 79,000 kms on the odometer. Recently serviced.											
1989	911 Turbo 3.3 Sonauto coupé		000578	L	520-560.000 EUR		NA		08-10-16	Paris	178	CB/C
	Black with tricolour leather interior; one of 10 examples of the Sonauto special edition. 330bhp engine. Recently reimported into Europe from Japan.											
1988	911 Turbo 3.3 cabriolet		020143	R	55-65.000 GBP		NS		12-10-16	Duxford	31	H&H
	White with black leather interior; in good overall condition. Gearbox redone in 2007.											
1989	911 Turbo 3.3 coupé		050615	L	NA	134.838*	165.000*	149.969*	15-10-16	Las Vegas	766	B/J
	White with black interior; fitted with numerous special order features. With Porsche Certificate of Authenticity.											
1977	911 Turbo 3.3 coupé		9308800031	L	85-125.000 EUR	95.125	116.401	105.800	15-10-16	Salzburg	445	Dor
	Black with black interior; sold new to the USA, imported into Austria in 2012. Last serviced in July 2016. Sunroof.											
1986	911 Turbo SE 3.3 slantnose coupé		001126	R	100-120.000 GBP	140.630	172.075	156.409	15-10-16	Silverstone	306	SiC
	White with blue leather interior; in good overall condition. Body repainted. Recently serviced (see lot 418 Coys 22.7.02 NS).											
1989	911 Turbo 3.3 coupé		000415	R	135-155.000 GBP	151.880	185.840	168.921	15-10-16	Silverstone	339	SiC
	White; in good overall condition. Last serviced in 2015 at 24,060 miles.											
1988	911 Turbo 3.3 slantnose Targa		010115	R	57-62.000 GBP	63.000	77.087	70.069	15-10-16	Silverstone	350	SiC
	Black with black interior; converted to "slantnose" specification in 1989 using the factory option kit. In 2015 the body was repainted and the engine and gearbox were restored.											
1979	911 Turbo 3.3 coupé		9309801058	L	145-175.000 USD		NS		04-11-16	Dallas	S124	Mec
	Metallic black with cork leather interior; restoration completed in April 2016.											
1986	911 Turbo 3.3 coupé		050491	L	130-150.000 USD		NS		05-11-16	Hilton Head	128	AA
	Metallic grey with red leather interior; in original condition.											
1985	911 Turbo SE 3.3 slantnose coupé		001063	R	100-120.000 GBP	202.500	256.345	235.082	12-11-16	Birmingham	608	SiC
	Silver metallic with red leather interior; 33,864 miles on the odometer. Last serviced in April 2015. When new the car was retained by Porsche GB and used as press car (see lot 244 Silverstone Auctions 25.10.15 NS).											
1989	911 Turbo 3.3 slantnose coupé		050347	R	130-150.000 GBP	211.500	267.738	245.530	12-11-16	Birmingham	624	SiC
	Red with black interior; in very good overall condition. Last serviced in 2015 at 11,977 miles. Sunroof.											
1988	911 Turbo 3.3 slantnose coupé		050578	L	NA		NS		19-11-16	Anaheim	S123	Mec
	White with black interior; one owner; believed to be 13,590 miles.											
1986	911 Turbo 3.3 coupé		000683	L	65-75.000 EUR	81.093*	100.836*	95.200*	25-11-16	Milan	294	RMS
	White with black interior; 72,720 kms. From the Duemila Ruote collection.											

F629: 1977 Porsche 934/5 Turbo

F630: 1981 Porsche 911SC coupé

Year	Model (Bodybuilder)	Chassis no.	Steering	Estimate	Hammer price £	$	€	Sale Date	Place	Lot	Auc. H.

F631: 1989 Porsche 911 Turbo 3.3 Targa

F632: 1989 Porsche 911 Turbo 3.3 slantnose cabriolet

Year	Model	Chassis no.	Steering	Estimate	£	$	€	Date	Place	Lot	Auc. H.
1988	911 Turbo 3.3 cabriolet	070425	L	95-120.000 EUR	74.928	91.242	85.585	14-01-17	Maastricht	207	Coy
	White; 62,500 kms covered. Three owners.										
1989	911 Turbo 3.3 cabriolet	020106	L	200-225.000 USD		NS		15-01-17	Kissimmee	S199	Mec
	Black with green leather interior; mechanicals restored in 2016 (see lot S111 Mecum 23.1.16 $160,000).										
1979	911 Turbo 3.3 coupé	9309800256	L	130-160.000 USD	75.857*	93.500*	87.638*	19-01-17	Scottsdale	73	Bon
	Black with black leather interior; less than 50,000 miles on the odometer; recent engine-out service.										
1979	911 Turbo 3.3 coupé	9309700477	L	180-220.000 USD	118.699*	145.750*	137.078*	20-01-17	Scottsdale	11	G&Co
	White with black leather interior; several restoration works carried out in 2016. Sunroof.										
1989	911 Turbo 3.3 cabriolet	070239	L	125-150.000 USD	116.459*	143.000*	134.492*	20-01-17	Scottsdale	60	G&Co
	Red with beige interior; 22,000 original miles. Unnumbered engine case; recently serviced.										
1989	911 Turbo 3.3 slantnose cabriolet	070302	L	225-275.000 USD	194.845	239.250	225.015	20-01-17	Phoenix	212	RMS **F632**
	Black with black leather interior; bought in 2010 by the current, second owner. 9,300 miles on the odometer.										
1979	911 Turbo 3.3 coupé	9309800520	L	140-180.000 USD	94.063*	115.500*	108.628*	21-01-17	Scottsdale	113	G&Co
	Metallic red with original cork leather interior; 52,000 miles on the odometer. Electric sunroof.										
1986	911 Turbo 3.3 slantnose coupé	000279	L	100-130.000 EUR	119.441*	149.310*	140.000*	08-02-17	Paris	130	RMS
	Dark purple with red interior; two owners and 29,281 kms covered. From a Swiss Porsche collection.										
1984	911 Turbo 3.3 coupé	000104	L	75-110.000 EUR	76.326	95.907	89.700	09-02-17	Paris	412	Bon
	Black with black interior; circa 70,800 kms covered. Engine, gearbox and clutch checked fewer than 10,000 miles ago. Electric sunroof.										
1988	911 Turbo 3.3 coupé	000174	L	170-200.000 EUR	223.664	278.735	262.240	10-02-17	Paris	115	Art
	Red with beige leather interior; in very good original condition. 34,200 kms covered. Owned by French driver Sébastien Loeb.										
1988	911 Turbo 3.3 coupé	050438	L	NQ		NS		18-02-17	Los Angeles	S68.1	Mec
	Red with brown interior; believed to be 10,603 original miles.										
1978	911 Turbo 3.3 coupé	9308700444	L	80-120.000 USD	70.459*	85.800*	81.313*	09-03-17	Amelia Island	137	Bon
	White with black leather interior; sunroof. In very good overall condition; low mileage.										
1989	911 Turbo 3.3 coupé	000491	L	175-225.000 USD	199.069*	242.000*	228.061*	10-03-17	Amelia Island	14	G&Co
	Black with black leather interior; in very good original condition. Showing approximately 34,800 kms. 5-speed manual gearbox.										
1989	911 Turbo 3.3 slantnose cabriolet	070542	L	275-325.000 USD		NS		11-03-17	Amelia Island	283	RMS
	White with beige interior; imported into the USA in 1994; three owners; 10,500 miles since new; last serviced in 2016.										
1989	911 Turbo 3.3 slantnose cabriolet	070080	L	225-250.000 USD	154.039	192.500	180.045	01-04-17	Ft.Lauderdale	565	AA
	Red with black interior (see lot 417 Barrett-Jackson 9.4.16 $183,700).										
1985	911 Turbo 3.3 coupé	000316	L	90-110.000 EUR	70.184	87.412	82.000	08-04-17	Essen	111	Coy
	Metallic sienna with beige interior; in good driving order.										
1989	911 Turbo 3.3 coupé	000728	L	80-100.000 EUR	55.634	69.290	65.000	08-04-17	Essen	180	Coy
	Described as in good overall condition.										
1989	911 Turbo 3.3 cabriolet	070122	L	150-200.000 EUR	127.529	158.834	149.000	08-04-17	Essen	205	Coy
	Silver with black interior; in very good overall condition. Getrag G50 5-speed gearbox.										
1979	911 Turbo 3.3 coupé	9309700209	R	80-100.000 GBP	87.750	112.820	103.738	13-05-17	Silverstone	329	SiC
	White with black leather interior; in 2005 gearbox rebuilt and clutch replaced, in 2015 top-end engine rebuilt.										
1988	911 Turbo 3.3 cabriolet	020100	R	80-90.000 GBP	74.583	95.891	88.172	13-05-17	Silverstone	346	SiC
	Black with black interior; in good overall condition.										
1989	911 Turbo 3.3 cabriolet	020115	R	79-89.000 GBP	95.200	123.874	110.813	20-05-17	Ascot	190	His
	Black with black leather interior; recently serviced.										
1989	911 Turbo 3.3 Targa	010076	L	200-300.000 EUR		NS		21-05-17	SPA-Francorch.	82	Bon
	Black with wine red leather interior; described as in excellent overall condition; 109,000 kms on the odometer. 5-speed G50 gearbox.										
1983	911 Turbo 3.3 coupé	000542	R	170-190.000 AUD		NS		28-05-17	Sydney	15	Mos
	White with biscuit leather interior; body repainted in 2010; engine rebuilt at 140,000 kms.										
1982	911 Turbo 3.3 coupé	000601	R	100-120.000 GBP		NS		06-06-17	Woodcote Park	32	H&H
	Metallic bronze with brown leather interior; recently recommissioned following a long period of storage.										

Year	Model	(Bodybuilder)	Chassis no.	Steering	Estimate	Hammer price £	$	€	Date	Place	Lot	Auc. H.
1979	911 Turbo 3.3 coupé		9309801058	L	NQ	92.489*	117.700*	105.342*	24-06-17	Northeast	690	B/J
See lot S124 Mecum 4.11.16.												
1982	911 Turbo 3.3 coupé		000482	L	140-160.000 GBP	124.700	161.836	141.198	30-06-17	Goodwood	268	Bon F633
Black with black interior; in very good overall condition; three owners; circa 27,000 kms on the odometer.												
1978	911 Turbo 3.3 coupé		9308700256	R	60-80.000 GBP		NS		30-06-17	Goodwood	282	Bon
Black with black interior; since 1987 with the current owner. 143,100 miles on the odometer. Engine rebuilt in 1988; engine top-end rebuilt in 2016. First owner Peter Sellers.												
1989	911 Turbo 3.3 coupé		000513	L	130-160.000 EUR	126.539	186.759	143.904	02-07-17	Monaco	205	Art
Dark metallic grey with grey leather interior; 116,000 kms on the odometer; last serviced in 2015. Sunroof.												
1989	911 Turbo 3.3 cabriolet		020210	R	75-90.000 GBP	82.880	106.882	93.654	08-07-17	Brooklands	210	His
Black with ivory leather interior; in very good overall condition; recently serviced (see lot 172 Historics 12.3.16 $119,252).												
1986	911 Turbo 3.3 coupé		000683	L	80-90.000 GBP	62.244	80.444	70.740	15-07-17	Blenheim Pal.	155	Coy
See lot 294 RM/Sotheby's 25.11.16.												
1989	911 Turbo LE 3.3 coupé		000692	R	175-195.000 GBP		NS		29-07-17	Silverstone	432	SiC
White with cream interior; 30,500 miles covered; in very good overall condition. Sunroof (see lot 632 Silverstone Auctions 26.7.14 $150,429).												
1989	911 Turbo S 3.3 coupé		000249	L	325-400.000 USD		NS		18-08-17	Pebble Beach	13	G&Co
Metallic slate grey with black and grey interior; sold new to Japan where the car remained until 2017; 58,000 kms on the odometer.												
1979	911 Turbo 3.3 coupé		9309800573	L	200-240.000 USD	94.017*	121.000*	103.092*	18-08-17	Pebble Beach	43	G&Co
Beige with cork leather interior; in good original condition; less than 36,000 miles covered; three owners.												
1984	911 Turbo S 3.3 slantnose coupé		000486	L	275-325.000 USD		NS		19-08-17	Pebble Beach	169	G&Co
Red with cashemire interior; described as in highly original condition.												
1979	911 Turbo 3.3 coupé		9309800531	L	225-275.000 USD	179.487*	231.000*	196.812*	19-08-17	Monterey	264	RMS
Light metallic blue; in largely original condition; 11,000 believed original miles; engine and gearbox rebuilt in 2016 (see lot 51 Gooding & Company 15.8.15 $302,500).												
1994	928 GTS		800531	L	70-90.000 EUR	85.271	113.273	101.200	03-09-16	Chantilly	11	Bon
Dark blue with grey leather interior; in good overall condition. Last serviced in March 2016 at 47,000 kms. Manual gearbox.												
1987	928 Prototype Club Sport		842014	L	225-265.000 EUR	228.593	281.842	253.000	07-10-16	Zoute	27	Bon F634
White with black leather interior; one of the five prototypes of the CS series, all delivered to the Porsche's factory drivers: Derek Bell, Jochen Mass, Hans Stuck, Bob Wollek and Jacky Ickx. The car offered remained with Derek Bell until 2005. Since 2009 in the JFD Collection in Belgium.												
1985	928 S		840237	R	NA	9.560*	11.698*	10.633*	15-10-16	Silverstone	301	SiC
Blue with dark blue interior; recently imported into the UK from South Africa. Last serviced 800 kms ago.												
1991	928 GT		800626	R	22-27.000 GBP	24.750	30.284	27.527	15-10-16	Silverstone	304	SiC
Metallic black with cream leather interior; several mechanical works carrued out between 2012 and 2016. Manual gearbox (see lot 242 Bonhams 5.3.11 $14,965).												
1985	928 S		841322	L	20-30.000 EUR	18.650	23.295	21.000	05-11-16	Lyon	242	Agu
Silver with brown leather interior; 55,137 kms on the odometer. Last serviced in 2016.												
1988	928 S4		841159	L	40-45.000 GBP	49.500	62.662	57.465	12-11-16	Birmingham	622	SiC
Grey with grey leather interior; one owner, 18,500 miles on the odometer, automatic transmission.												
1993	928 GTS		800503	L	70-80.000 EUR	53.520	65.173	61.132	14-01-17	Maastricht	203	Coy
Metallic blue with grey interior; in very good overall condition. Body repainted in 2013.												
1993	928 GTS		800405	L	50-70.000 EUR	71.665*	89.586*	84.000*	08-02-17	Paris	127	RMS F635
Black; 6,206 kms covered. Automatic transmission. From a Swiss Porsche collection.												
1985	928 S3		860235	L	25-35.000 EUR	22.506	28.280	26.450	09-02-17	Paris	422	Bon
Black with black interior; restored in 2015. Manual gearbox.												
1993	928 GTS		800503	L	65-75.000 EUR	44.507	55.432	52.000	08-04-17	Essen	114	Coy
See lot 203 Coys 14.1.17.												
1994	928 GT		801349	L	60-80.000 EUR	76.175	94.874	89.000	08-04-17	Essen	170	Coy
Medium grey with black leather interior; 18,000 kms covered; recently serviced. Manual gearbox.												
1987	928 S4		841019	R	25-28.000 GBP	33.900	44.195	39.710	18-05-17	London	111	Coy
Diamond blue with blue leather interior; in very good overall condition; 44,750 miles covered.												
1988	928 S4		841639	L	25-35.000 EUR	31.614*	41.139*	36.800*	21-05-17	SPA-Francorch.	35	Bon
Metallic granite green with black leather interior; less than 145,000 kms covered; last serviced in 2016. Manual gearbox.												

F633: 1982 Porsche 911 Turbo 3.3 coupé

F634: 1987 Porsche 928 Prototype Club Sport

Year	Model	(Bodybuilder)	Chassis no.	Steering	Estimate	Hammer price £	$	€	Sale Date	Place	Lot	Auc. H.
1991	**928 GT**		801079	L	50-70.000 EUR	64.324*	94.935*	73.151*	02-07-17	Monaco	194	**Art**
	Light grey metallic; described as in good overall condition; recently repainted. First owner Johnny Hallyday.											
1993	**928 GTS**		800633	R	40-50.000 GBP		NS		08-07-17	Brooklands	190	**His**
	Black; in good overall condition (see lot 21 H & H 9.12.09 $11,134).											
1984	**928 S2**		840366	L	22-28.000 EUR	20.132	26.466	22.300	05-08-17	Schloss Dyck	278	**Coy**
	Described as in good original condition.											
1981	**924 Carrera GT**		700217	L	65-100.000 EUR	57.148*	70.461*	63.250*	07-10-16	Zoute	25	**Bon**
	Red; paintwork and engine recently redone.											
1981	**924 Carrera GT**		700218	L	70-90.000 EUR	78.353*	97.947*	91.840*	08-02-17	Paris	123	**RMS**
	Silver with black interior; recently restored. 73,000 kms covered since new. From a Swiss Porsche collection.											
1981	**924 Carrera GT**		700237	L	60-80.000 EUR	48.189*	71.122*	54.802*	02-07-17	Monaco	144	**Art** **F636**
	Silver with black and red interior; in original condition; 40,800 kms covered; since 1990 in the current ownership.											
1988	**944 Turbo S coupé**		101706	R	35-40.000 GBP	35.440	43.364	39.416	15-10-16	Silverstone	329	**SiC**
	Red; described as in very good overall condition. 47,177 miles covered.											
1990	**944 cabriolet**		430722	L	17-22.000 EUR	19.183	23.961	21.600	06-11-16	Lyon	345	**Ose**
	In good working order; clutch redone.											
1991	**944 Turbo cabriolet**		130322	R	22-25.000 GBP	24.188	30.620	28.080	12-11-16	Birmingham	647	**SiC**
	Red with black interior; in good overall condition. Last serviced in 2014.											
1989	**944 S2 coupé**		404105	L	10-15.000 EUR	22.897	28.471	26.880	25-11-16	Milan	919	**RMS**
	White; 137,192 kms. From the Duemila Ruote collection.											
1987	**944 S coupé**		452281	L	30-40.000 USD	21.418*	26.400*	24.745*	19-01-17	Scottsdale	94	**Bon**
	Silver with black interior; in highly original condition. Less than 15,000 miles covered.											
1986	**944 Turbo coupé**		151677	L	60-75.000 USD		NS		11-02-17	Boca Raton	109	**TFA**
	Red with tan interior; in very good original condition. 9,720 miles covered.											
1991	**944 Turbo coupé**		100515	R	25-30.000 GBP	32.625	40.957	38.605	24-02-17	Stoneleigh P.	906	**SiC**
	Red; fully restored in 2014.											
1991	**944 Turbo cabriolet**		130353	R	24-28.000 GBP	32.063	40.252	37.940	24-02-17	Stoneleigh P.	914	**SiC**
	Red with black leather interior; described as in very good overall condition. 72,590 miles covered.											
1991	**944 Turbo cabriolet**		130427	R	25-30.000 GBP	39.375	50.624	46.549	13-05-17	Silverstone	332	**SiC**
	Red with black leather interior; body repainted. Recently serviced.											
1984	**944 coupé**		12	L	25-30.000 EUR	26.263	33.501	30.000	18-06-17	Fontainebleau	87	**Ose**
	White; example no.12 of the 200 of the Rothmans special edition.											
1992	**944 Turbo cabriolet**		130523	R	30-35.000 GBP	31.050	40.297	35.158	30-06-17	Goodwood	289	**Bon** **F637**
	Metallic cobalt blue with blue interior; restored in 2015. 72,878 miles covered from new.											
1990	**944 S2 cabriolet**		430154	R	12-15.000 GBP	10.003	12.928	11.368	15-07-17	Blenheim Pal.	128	**Coy**
	Silver with black interior; two owners: recently serviced.											
1989	**911 Carrera 3.2 Targa**		140968	L	90-150.000 EUR	98.711*	121.705*	109.250*	07-10-16	Zoute	19	**Bon** **F638**
	White and orange; bought new by the Dutch Rijkspolitie, the car remained in service until 1991. Recently restored in Italy and subsequently imported into Belgium.											
1989	**911 Carrera 3.2 Sport cabriolet**		150891	R	50-60.000 GBP	54.880	67.261	61.038	12-10-16	Duxford	102	**H&H**
	White with blue leather interior; described as in very good overall condition.											
1989	**911 Carrera 3.2 coupé**		102429	R	50-60.000 GBP		NS		12-10-16	Duxford	95	**H&H**
	White; described as in very good overall condition. 69,000 miles covered.											
1989	**911 Carrera 3.2 cabriolet**		151109	R	26-30.000 GBP		NS		15-10-16	Silverstone	361	**SiC**
	Metallic blue with grey interior; in good overall condition. Body recently repainted.											
1986	**911 Carrera 3.2 Targa**		141945	L	35-40.000 EUR	55.334*	68.806*	64.960*	25-11-16	Milan	243	**RMS**
	White with black interior; 62,963 kms. From the Duemila Ruote collection.											
1985	**911 Carrera 3.2 cabriolet**		150193	L	35-40.000 EUR	71.553*	88.973*	84.000*	25-11-16	Milan	267	**RMS**
	Black with black interior; 135,326 kms. From the Duemila Ruote collection.											

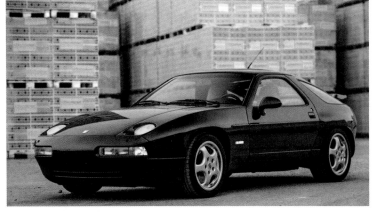

F635: 1993 Porsche 928 GTS

F636: 1981 Porsche 924 Carrera GT

Year	Model (Bodybuilder)	Chassis no.	Steering	Estimate	Hammer price £	Hammer price $	Hammer price €	Sale Date	Place	Lot	Auc. H.
1989	911 Carrera 3.2 coupé	101436	L	20-30.000 EUR	72.507*	90.159*	85.120*	25-11-16	Milan	525	RMS
Anthracite grey; 93,213 kms. From the Duemila Ruote collection.											
1987	911 Carrera 3.2 cabriolet	151336	L	45-55.000 EUR	81.093*	100.836*	95.200*	25-11-16	Milan	635	RMS
Blue; 33,902 kms. From the Duemila Ruote collection.											
1988	911 Carrera 3.2 Targa	141143	R	74-85.000 GBP	107.520	133.690	126.218	26-11-16	Weybridge	205	His
White; fully restored in 2013 by Porsche Brooklands. 302 miles covered since the restoration (see lot 269 Historics 29.8.15 $177,539).											
1988	911 Carrera 3.2 Club Sport	105099	R	180-220.000 GBP	NS			04-12-16	London	24	Bon
White; described as in excellent overall condition. 48,342 miles covered; three owners.											
1989	911 Carrera 3.2 cabriolet	170405	L	60-80.000 USD	66.292*	81.400*	76.557*	20-01-17	Scottsdale	7	G&Co
Metallic blue with linen and marine blue interior; in well-preserved condition. 30,449 miles on the odometer.											
1989	911 Carrera 3.2 coupé	120917	L	90-120.000 USD	86.001*	105.600*	99.317*	21-01-17	Scottsdale	109	G&Co
Black with black interior; described as in original condition, the car has had two owners and has covered less than 20,000 miles.											
1987	911 Carrera 3.2 Clubsport	105071	L	250-300.000 EUR	NS			10-02-17	Paris	111	Art
White; described as in good overall condition. The car remained in the factory ownership as a press car until 1989. Three private owners.											
1986	911 Carrera 3.2 cabriolet	141051	R	22-28.000 GBP	22.230	27.619	25.931	18-02-17	London	311	Coy
Body repainted in 2015; recently serviced.											
1986	911 Carrera 3.2 coupé	120808	L	60-80.000 USD	44.338*	53.900*	50.795*	10-03-17	Amelia Island	1	G&Co
Red with black interior; in good original condition. 48,952 miles on the odometer.											
1986	911 Carrera 3.2 cabriolet	150753	R	38-44.000 GBP	44.275	54.724	50.965	19-03-17	Goodwood	63	Bon
White with blue interior; in highly original condition; last serviced in June 2016.											
1987	911 Carrera 3.2 coupé	102055	L	30-40.000 EUR	41.697	51.538	48.000	19-03-17	Fontainebleau	238	Ose
Red with black interior; in good overall condition.											
1986	911 Carrera 3.2 cabriolet	171273	L	40-60.000 GBP	36.679	45.849	43.230	12-04-17	London	357	Coy
Gold with brown interior; until 2016 with its first owner. In good overall condition.											
1986	911 Carrera 3.2 cabriolet	151139	R	40-50.000 GBP	40.014	50.018	47.161	12-04-17	London	362	Coy
Blue with cream interior; body repainted in recent years. Last serviced in 2015.											
1986	911 Carrera 3.2 coupé	121261	L	40-50.000 USD	36.795*	47.300*	42.168*	04-06-17	Greenwich	144	Bon
Metallic gold with champagne leather interior; recently serviced.											
1986	911 Carrera 3.2 cabriolet	141051	R	22-28.000 GBP	NS			29-06-17	Fontwell Park	154	Coy
See lot 311 Coys 18.2.17.											
1985	911 Carrera 3.2 cabriolet	171049	L	30-40.000 EUR	34.306	45.098	38.000	05-08-17	Schloss Dyck	264	Coy
White with pearl white leather interior; sold new to the USA and later reimported into Europe. Three owners; 104,000 miles covered.											
1989	962	962108C2	R	1.500-2.000.000 USD	NS			20-05-17	Indianapolis	F145	Mec
Campaigned by Jim Busby Racing and sponsored by BF Goodrich and Miller Brewing Company, the car won, among other events, the 1989 Daytona 24 Hours driven by Derek Bell, Bob Wolleck and John Andretti. Fitted during its race career with the present honeycomb tub built by Jim Chapman. Retired from competition at the end of the 1989 season (see Mecum lots S98 23.1.16 NS and S124 20.8.16 NS).											
1988	959	900133	L	600-700.000 EUR	858.635*	1.067.674*	1.008.000*	25-11-16	Milan	875	RMS
Komfort version finished in silver with black leather interior; 29,200 kms. From the Duemila Ruote collection.											
1988	959	900182	L	1.100-1.300.000 USD	886.882	1.089.000	1.024.205	20-01-17	Scottsdale	42	G&Co
Komfort version finished in silver metallic; sold new to the UK; imported into the USA in 2000; engine rebuilt and clutch replaced in 2012-13; less than 22,000 kms covered.											
1987	959	900104	L	900-1.200.000 USD	761.464	935.000	879.368	20-01-17	Phoenix	226	RMS
Komfort version finished in red with black interior; described as in very good overall condition, the car received several mechanical works from 2012 to 2016. 13,000 kms on the odometer.											
1988	959	905011	L	1.500-2.000.000 EUR	1.672.174*	2.090.340*	1.960.000*	08-02-17	Paris	131	RMS F639
Sport version finished in white with grey cloth interior; in original condition. Sold new to Vasek Polak. From a Swiss Porsche collection.											
1987	959	900197	L	950-1.200.000 EUR	963.777	1.201.077	1.130.000	10-02-17	Paris	119	Art
Metallic graphite black with tree-tone grey leather interior; sold new to Italy, the car remained in the ownership of a Porsche dealer until 2006 when it was bought by the current, second owner. 26,000 kms covered. Last serviced 6,000 kms ago.											
1988	959	900248	L	1.000-1.250.000 USD	NS			10-03-17	Amelia Island	78	G&Co
Komfort version finished in black with black interior; approximately 10,000 kms covered. Upgraded to the Stage II power kit by the Porsche Classic Centre in Stuttgart (see lot 253 RM/Sotheby's 14.5.16 $1,016,781).											

F637: 1992 Porsche 944 Turbo cabriolet

F638: 1989 Porsche 911 Carrera 3.2 Targa

Year	Model	(Bodybuilder)	Chassis no.	Steering	Estimate	Hammer Price £	$	€	Date	Place	Lot	Auc. H.

F639: 1988 Porsche 959   F640: 1987 Porsche 959 Speedster

Year	Model	Chassis no.	Steering	Estimate	£	$	€	Date	Place	Lot	Auc. H.
1987	**959 Speedster**	900142	L	1.200-1.500.000 EUR	785.716	978.588	918.000	08-04-17	Essen	159	Coy **F640**
	White; one-off. In good mechanical condition; just over 8,000 kms covered. With hardtop.										
1988	**959**	900023	L	850-950.000 EUR	680.441	847.470	795.000	08-04-17	Essen	191	Coy
	Silver with dark grey leather interior; last serviced in 2016 in Switzerland.										
1988	**959**	900199	L	925-1.050.000 EUR		NS		27-05-17	Villa Erba	138	RMS
	Komfort version finished in silver; two owners; 12,500 kms covered; last serviced in 2015 (see lots 43 Poulain 12.9.96 NS and 123 Brooks 9.6.99 $158,435).										
1987	**959**	900087	L	950-1.050.000 EUR		NS		02-07-17	Monaco	193	Art
	Komfort version finished in silver with grey interior; 27,000 kms covered; regularly maintained.										
1988	**959**	900108	L	1.200-1.400.000 USD	820.512	1.056.000	899.712	18-08-17	Pebble Beach	46	G&Co
	Silver with dark grey leather interior; sold new in Germany; imported into the USA in 2015; less than 8,200 kms covered (see lot 19 Gooding & Company 20.8.16 $1,320,000).										
1988	**959**	900149	L	1.200-1.400.000 USD	738.150	950.000	809.400	19-08-17	Monterey	S113	Mec
	Komfort version finished in graphite grey with grey interior; sold new in Italy; imported into the USA in 2013; major service in September 2015; 21,950 kms covered since new (see lots 40 Poulain/Sotheby's 18.12.00 $148,357 and 130 RM 15.1.15 $1,045,000).										
1989	**Carrera 3.2 Speedster**	173628	L	NA	108.808	145.000	128.673	10-09-16	Louisville	S121.1	Mec
	Red with tan interior; unrestored. Believed to be 40,504 original miles.										
1989	**Carrera 3.2 Speedster**	152181	L	130-150.000 EUR	248.050*	308.439*	291.200*	25-11-16	Milan	307	RMS
	Black with black interior; 16,449 kms. From the Duemila Ruote collection.										
1989	**Carrera 3.2 Speedster**	173005	L	175-225.000 USD	119.060	145.000	135.996	15-01-17	Kissimmee	F168	Mec
	Black with black leather interior; bought new by actor Nicolas Cage, in 2002 the car was stolen and abandoned at Lake of the Ozarks where it rolled down a boat ramp into the water. Subsequently the body was restored and the engine refurbished. 2,900 miles covered since new.										
1989	**Carrera 3.2 Speedster**	173247	L	190-220.000 USD		NS		18-01-17	Scottsdale	76	WoA
	Red; 8,872 miles covered. Recently serviced (see lot S68 Mecum 20.8.16 NS).										
1989	**Carrera 3.2 Speedster**	173434	L	170-240.000 EUR	166.351	209.029	195.500	09-02-17	Paris	380	Bon
	Black with black interior; sold new to the USA, the car was reimported into Europe in 2013. In original condition; circa 19,900 miles covered.										
1989	**Carrera 3.2 Speedster**	173506	L	275-325.000 USD	223.500	271.700	256.050	10-03-17	Amelia Island	7	G&Co
	Red with black interior; in very good original interior. 474 miles covered.										
1989	**Carrera 3.2 Speedster**	173721	L	180-220.000 USD	126.680*	154.000*	145.130*	11-03-17	Amelia Island	219	RMS
	Red with beige leather interior; 8,019 original miles. "Turbo-look" wide-body.										
1989	**Carrera 3.2 Speedster**	152019	L	220-250.000 EUR	166.901	207.870	195.000	08-04-17	Essen	149	Coy
	Silver with black leather interior; 4,700 kms covered. Recently serviced.										
1989	**Carrera 3.2 Speedster**	151214	R	145-165.000 GBP	164.250	211.176	194.176	13-05-17	Silverstone	314	SiC
	Black with black interior; sold new to Australia and imported into the UK in 2014. 8,997 kms covered (see lot 227 Historics 12.3.16 $148,637).										
1989	**Carrera 3.2 Speedster**	152253	L	270-320.000 EUR	237.560	309.131	276.528	21-05-17	SPA-Francorch.	72	Bon **F641**
	Red with black leather interior; just over 20,000 kms covered. Last serviced in March 2016.										
1989	**Carrera 3.2 Speedster**	152069	L	240-260.000 EUR		NS		27-05-17	Villa Erba	122	RMS
	Silver; narrow body; less than 76,000 kms on the odometer.										
1989	**Carrera 3.2 Speedster**	152149	L	290-320.000 EUR		NS		02-07-17	Monaco	125	Art
	Silver with black interior; two owners; 41,700 kms covered; regularly serviced.										
1989	**Carrera 3.2 Speedster**	151916	L	220-260.000 EUR		NS		02-07-17	Monaco	138	Art
	Turbo-look body finished in grey with grey interior; 33,000 kms covered. Formerly owned by Olivier Panis.										
1989	**Carrera 3.2 Speedster**	151938	R	130-160.000 GBP	123.200	158.879	139.216	08-07-17	Brooklands	169	His
	Red with black interior; in very good overall condition. Turbo-look body.										
1989	**Carrera 3.2 Speedster**	151641	R	120-140.000 GBP		NA		15-07-17	Blenheim Pal.	124	Coy
	Silver with black interior; in good overall condition. Just over 55,000 miles on the odometer.										
1989	**Carrera 3.2 Speedster**	152446	L	140-180.000 EUR	150.993	198.492	167.250	05-08-17	Schloss Dyck	260	Coy
	Red with black leather interior; sold new in Germany; three owners; approximately 52,000 kms covered.										
1989	**Carrera 3.2 Speedster**	173770	L	175-250.000 USD	166.667*	214.500*	182.754*	18-08-17	Monterey	119	RMS
	Silver with black interior; in very good original condition; 7,724 kms covered.										
1989	**Carrera 3.2 Speedster**	173357	L	275-325.000 USD	230.769	297.000	253.044	19-08-17	Pebble Beach	110	G&Co
	Metallic linen grey with black interior; sold new to the USA; less than 2,400 miles covered; recently serviced.										

Year	Model	(Bodybuilder)	Chassis no.	Steering	Estimate	Hammer price £	$	€	Date	Place	Lot	Auc. H.
1989	**Carrera 3.2 Speedster**		173197	L	200-250.000 USD	**124.320**	**160.000**	**136.320**	19-08-17	Monterey	F66	Mec
White with black leather interior; 8,100 original miles.											
1991	**Carrera 4 3.6 cabriolet**		422937	R	55-65.000 GBP	**61.600**	**75.497**	**68.512**	12-10-16	Duxford	62	H&H
Red with black leather interior; in very good overall condition. 25,500 miles on the odometer.											
1992	**Carrera 4 3.6 cabriolet**		451780	R	29-33.000 GBP	**25.880**	**31.667**	**28.784**	15-10-16	Silverstone	356	SiC
White with blue interior; described as in very good original condition.											
1990	**Carrera 4 3.6 cabriolet**		420621	R	32-38.000 GBP		NS		29-10-16	London	136	Coy
Metallic grey with light grey leather interior; 49,000 miles on the odometer.											
1990	**Carrera 4 3.6 cabriolet**		422605	L	35-40.000 EUR	**57.242***	**71.178***	**67.200***	25-11-16	Milan	299	RMS
Anthracite grey with black interior; 75.531 kms. From the Duemila Ruote collection.											
1995	**Carrera 4S 3.6 coupé**		316733	L	65-75.000 EUR	**133.565***	**166.083***	**156.800***	25-11-16	Milan	545	RMS
Light blue; 42,440 kms. From the Duemila Ruote collection.											
1990	**Carrera 4 3.6 cabriolet**		406201	R	38-45.000 GBP	**38.640**	**49.830**	**43.663**	08-07-17	Brooklands	192	His
Red with ivory leather interior; last serviced in November 2015 at 79,118 miles.											
1990	**Carrera 2 3.6 Targa**		410590	R	60-70.000 GBP	**58.500**	**71.581**	**65.064**	15-10-16	Silverstone	320	SiC
Red with black leather interior; 500 miles covered since the full restoration carried out in 2014.											
1990	**Carrera 2 3.6 cabriolet**		451354	R	30-35.000 GBP		NS		15-10-16	Silverstone	362	SiC
Red with black interior; last serviced in October 2015 at 109,000 miles. Engine rebuilt in 2009 at 93,648 miles.											
1990	**Carrera 2 3.6 Targa**		411284	L	55-65.000 EUR	**71.553***	**88.973***	**84.000***	25-11-16	Milan	337	RMS
Red with black interior; 70,233 kms. From the Duemila Ruote collection.											
1993	**Carrera 2 3.6 cabriolet**		451255	L	65-75.000 EUR	**124.025***	**154.220***	**145.600***	25-11-16	Milan	593	RMS
Dark blue with black interior; "turbo-look" body. 80,129 kms. From the Duemila Ruote collection.											
1990	**Carrera 2 3.6 coupé**		403189	L	10-15.000 EUR	**36.253***	**45.080***	**42.560***	25-11-16	Milan	885	RMS
Black; 143,276 kms. From the Duemila Ruote collection.											
1991	**Carrera 2 3.6 cabriolet**		452245	L	35-40.000 EUR	**62.012***	**77.110***	**72.800***	25-11-16	Milan	909	RMS
Black; 88,199 kms. From the Duemila Ruote collection.											
1991	**Carrera 2 3.6 Cup**		409094	L	225-275.000 EUR	**191.106**	**238.896**	**224.000**	08-02-17	Paris	155	RMS
Blue; raced in the 1990s; re-shelled in 1992 with a correct factory replacement; restored in 2014 to 1991 specification; original engine rebuilt in 2016.											
1992	**Carrera 2 3.6 America Roadster**		460476	L	100-120.000 USD	**61.530***	**74.800***	**70.492***	11-03-17	Amelia Island	288	RMS
Black with black leather interior; sold new to the USA. 22,800 miles covered. Swiss papers.											
1993	**Carrera 2 3.6 coupé**		402330	L	145-165.000 EUR	**158.174**	**233.448**	**179.880**	02-07-17	Monaco	188	Art
Silver with black leather interior; one owner; 40,000 kms covered. One of 74 examples of the "Jubilee" special edition built for the Italian market.											
1991	**Carrera 2 3.6 Targa**		411090	R	40-45.000 GBP	**42.560**	**54.885**	**48.093**	08-07-17	Brooklands	162	His
Red with light linen interior; in good overall condition. Recommissioned in 2016.											
1993	**Carrera 2 Speedster**		455328	L	190-230.000 GBP		NS		10-09-16	Goodwood	136	Bon
Red with black interior; sold new to Japan, the car was registered in the UK in April 2016. Circa 7,500 miles covered.											
1994	**Carrera 2 Speedster**		465926	L	120-160.000 EUR		NA		08-10-16	Paris	162	CB/C
White with black leather interior; described as in excellent overall condition. Just one owner.											
1994	**Carrera 2 Speedster**		465385	L	NA	**77.055**	**95.000**	**89.376**	19-11-16	Anaheim	S90.1	Mec
White with black leather interior; 57,890 miles covered.											
1994	**Carrera 2 Speedster**		465313	L	120-150.000 USD	**85.962***	**104.500***	**98.481***	11-03-17	Amelia Island	280	RMS **F642**
Mint green; sold new to the USA; 20,800 miles covered. Triptronic transmission. Swiss papers.											
1993	**Carrera 2 Speedster**		455328	L	190-225.000 EUR	**145.503**	**181.220**	**170.000**	08-04-17	Essen	201	Coy
See lot 136 Bonhams 10.9.16.											
1993	**Carrera 2 Speedster**		465242	L	180-220.000 EUR		NS		02-07-17	Monaco	139	Art
Black with black interior; recently repainted; just over 87,000 miles covered. Reimported into Europe from the USA.											
1993	**Carrera RS 3.8**		497097	L	400-500.000 GBP	**716.800**	**959.222**	**853.637**	07-09-16	London	128	RMS **F643**
Silver with black and grey leather interior; one owner and 16,652 kms covered. One of 55 examples built.											

F641: 1989 Porsche Carrera 3.2 Speedster

F642: 1994 Porsche Carrera 2 Speedster

Year	Model	(Bodybuilder)	Chassis no.	Steering	Estimate	Hammer Price £	Hammer Price $	Hammer Price €	Date	Place	Lot	Auc. H.

F643: 1993 Porsche Carrera RS 3.8

F644: 1993 Porsche Turbo S 3.3 coupé

Year	Model	Chassis no.	Steering	Estimate	£	$	€	Date	Place	Lot	Auc. H.
1992	**Carrera RS**	491414	L	160-180.000 GBP	**168.000**	224.818	200.071	07-09-16	London	150	**RMS**
Blue with tri-colour black/dark blue/light blue interior; sold new to Japan. Imported in 2015 into the UK and subjected to a major service.												
1992	**Carrera RS**	491467	L	140-160.000 GBP		NS		15-10-16	Silverstone	333	**SiC**
Rubystone red with black leather interior; 41,000 kms on the odometer. Recently imported from Japan.												
1991	**Carrera RS N-GT**	499076	L	135-155.000 GBP	**157.500**	192.717	175.172	15-10-16	Silverstone	345	**SiC**
Blue; described as in good overall condition. 25,000 miles on the odometer.												
1991	**Carrera RS**	490613	L	150-200.000 EUR		NS		30-10-16	Paris	145	**Art**
In very good overall condition.												
1992	**Carrera RS**	491716	L	110-130.000 EUR	267.131*	332.165*	313.600*	25-11-16	Milan	334	**RMS**
Silver with black and grey interior; 38,179 kms. From the Duemila Ruote collection.												
1993	**Carrera RS America**	418276	L	150-200.000 USD	124.940*	154.000*	144.344*	19-01-17	Phoenix	136	**RMS**
Red with black interior; 15,380 miles on the odometer. One of 701 exmples built.												
1992	**Carrera RS**	491688	L	175-225.000 EUR	**191.106**	238.896	224.000	08-02-17	Paris	177	**RMS**
Red with black interior; one owner and 17,300 kms covered. Properly cared for.												
1991	**Carrera RS N-GT**	499076	L	150-170.000 EUR	**129.167**	162.305	151.800	09-02-17	Paris	344	**Bon**
See lot 345 Silverstone Auctions 15.10.16.												
1992	**Carrera RS**	491254	L	250-300.000 USD	**162.875**	198.000	186.595	10-03-17	Amelia Island	82	**G&Co**
Red with black and grey interior; the car has covered approximately 1,500 kms since the engine rebuild carried out in 2013 in the UK.												
1992	**Carrera RS**	491065	R	180-220.000 GBP		NS		13-05-17	Silverstone	335	**SiC**
Red with black leatherette interior and two-tone grey leather seats; last serviced in March 2016.												
1992	**Carrera RS**	491361	L	180-220.000 EUR	**171.126**	224.958	189.550	05-08-17	Schloss Dyck	213	**Coy**
One owner; 112,000 kms covered; well maintained and serviced.												
1992	**Carrera RS**	490667	L	325-375.000 USD	213.675*	275.000*	234.300*	19-08-17	Monterey	250	**RMS**
Silver with black and grey interior; 12,600 kms covered; recently imported into the USA.												
1993	**Turbo S 3.3 coupé**	479031	L	210-250.000 GBP	**974.400**	1.303.942	1.160.413	07-09-16	London	129	**RMS** **F644**
Yellow with black leather interior with grey and yellow inserts; two owners and 6,303 kms covered. One of 86 examples built.												
1991	**Turbo 3.3 coupé**	470071	R	80-100.000 GBP	**90.000**	110.124	100.098	15-10-16	Silverstone	312	**SiC**
Blue with white interior; engine rebuilt in 2012. Last serviced in 2016.												
1993	**Turbo S 3.3 coupé**	479036	L	1.300-1.600.000 USD	**1.266.804**	1.540.000	1.451.296	10-03-17	Amelia Island	44	**G&Co**
Yellow with black and grey interior with yellow inserts; in excellent original condition. Less than 2,250 kms covered. Bought in 2015 by the current, second owner and imported into the USA.												
1991	**Turbo 3.3 coupé**	480490	L	180-220.000 USD	137.539*	167.200*	157.569*	11-03-17	Amelia Island	234	**RMS**
Red with black interior; two owners; 8,950 miles covered; last serviced in October 2016.												
1993	**Turbo S 3.3 coupé**	479051	L	475-575.000 GBP	**556.875**	715.974	658.338	13-05-17	Silverstone	331	**SiC**
Black with black interior; in good overall condition. Imported into the UK in 2014.												
1991	**Turbo 3.3 coupé**	480273	L	80-110.000 USD	**71.744**	91.300	81.714	24-06-17	Santa Monica	174	**RMS**
White; less than 55,000 miles on the odometer; well-maintained.												
1992	**Turbo S 3.3 coupé**	479034	L	550-650.000 EUR	**530.260**	697.067	587.350	05-08-17	Schloss Dyck	234	**Coy**
Black; since 2011 in the current ownership.												
1993	**Carrera RSR 3.8**	496086	L	1.200-1.400.000 USD		NS		10-03-17	Amelia Island	75	**G&Co**
Yellow with black interior; approximately 4,000 kms covered. Never raced.												
1993	**Carrera RSR 3.8**	496107	L	2.000-2.200.000 EUR	**1.757.750**	2.257.114	2.016.000	27-05-17	Villa Erba	133	**RMS** **F645**
Silver with red leather interior; in original condition; 10 kms covered; one of 51 examples built.												
1993	**Carrera RSR 3.8**	496081	L	900-1.100.000 USD	**735.042**	946.000	805.992	18-08-17	Pebble Beach	50	**G&Co**
Salad Team white and red livery; winner of the 1994 IMSA GT2 Championship; raced until 2006 when it was acquired by the current UK-based owner. The latest engine and gearbox rebuilds still have 20 racing hours available on them. Original chassis.												
1993	**Turbo 3.6 coupé**	470430	L	190-240.000 EUR	**201.065**	267.093	238.625	03-09-16	Chantilly	8	**Bon**
Metallic green with green interior; approximately 50,000 kms covered, engine overhauled about two years ago.												
1994	**Turbo 3.6 coupé**	480147	L	150-170.000 GBP	**147.180**	178.794	163.694	29-10-16	London	112	**Coy**
Light metallic green with light grey leather interior; 32,770 miles on the odometer.												

Year	Model	(Bodybuilder)	Chassis no.	Steering	Estimate	Hammer price £	$	€	Date	Place	Lot	Auc. H.
1993	Turbo 3.6 coupé		470149	L	130-150.000 EUR	186.037*	231.329*	218.400*	25-11-16	Milan	331	RMS
	Dark blue with black interior; 85,231 kms. From the Duemila Ruote collection.											
1994	Turbo 3.6 coupé		480068	L	225-275.000 USD		NS		15-01-17	Kissimmee	S252	Mec
	Black with black leather interior; one owner and 28,415 actual miles.											
1994	Turbo S 3.6 coupé		480409	L	650-750.000 EUR	769.200*	961.556*	901.600*	08-02-17	Paris	125	RMS
	Black with black interior; in very good overall condition. Less than 23,000 miles covered. One of 17 "traditional nose" examples built. From a Swiss Porsche collection.											
1993	Turbo 3.6 coupé		470185	L	180-240.000 EUR	185.922	233.620	218.500	09-02-17	Paris	322	Bon
	Dark metallic blue with red leather interior; 50,000 kms covered since new.											
1994	Turbo 3.6 coupé		480107	L	180-240.000 USD	153.564	187.000	177.220	09-03-17	Amelia Island	124	Bon
	White with dark blue leather interior; bought in 2015 by the current, second owner. Less than 50,000 miles covered.											
1994	Turbo 3.6 coupé		480147	L	160-190.000 EUR	122.394	152.438	143.000	08-04-17	Essen	166	Coy
	See lot 112 Coys 29.10.16.											
1993	Turbo 3.6 coupé		470303	L	200-250.000 EUR	167.950	218.549	195.500	21-05-17	SPA-Francorch.	77	Bon
	Dark metallic blue with blue interior; sunroof. Circa 62,400 kms on the odometer.											
1993	Turbo 3.6 coupé		470239	L	250-300.000 GBP		NS		30-06-17	Goodwood	229	Bon
	Black; described as in very good overall condition. 96,500 kms covered. Last serviced in February 2017. Ordered new with the X88 package with the 380bhp engine.											
1993	Turbo 3.6 coupé		470551	R	140-180.000 GBP	138.140	179.278	156.416	30-06-17	Goodwood	231	Bon
	Amazon green metallic; regularly maintained; body repainted in 2008 (see lot 241 Silverstone Auctions 4.9.15 NS).											
1994	Turbo S 3.6 slantnose coupé		470443	L	700-900.000 USD	555.555	715.000	609.180	18-08-17	Pebble Beach	23	G&Co
	White with black leather interior; sold new to France, later exported to Japan and then imported into the USA. Approximately 47,000 kms covered.											
1994	Turbo S 3.6 coupé		480408	L	1.150-1.300.000 USD		NS		19-08-17	Monterey	S98	Mec
	Black with tan interior; 6,356 miles covered.											
1992	968 Club Sport		815295	L	45-65.000 EUR	51.953*	64.055*	57.500*	07-10-16	Zoute	12	Bon F646
	White; less than 85,000 kms covered. Last serviced in September 2016.											
1993	968 Club Sport		815668	R	25-30.000 GBP	26.440	32.352	29.407	15-10-16	Silverstone	319	SiC
	Blue; over the last two years the body was repainted and the gearbox was overhauled.											
1992	968 cabriolet		830179	L	15-20.000 EUR	27.667*	34.403*	32.480*	25-11-16	Milan	253	RMS
	Red with black interior; 108,834 kms. From the Duemila Ruote collection.											
1993	968 Club Sport		815283	L	30-35.000 EUR	62.012*	77.110*	72.800*	25-11-16	Milan	886	RMS
	White with black interior; 84,173 kms. From the Duemila Ruote collection.											
1992	968 cabriolet		830602	L	30-35.000 EUR	30.529*	37.962*	35.840*	25-11-16	Milan	902	RMS
	Blue with blue interior; 90,237 kms. From the Duemila Ruote collection.											
1992	968 cabriolet		840211	L	100-125.000 USD	36.950	45.000	42.206	15-01-17	Kissimmee	S243	Mec
	Silver with grey interior; 6,207 miles.											
1994	968 Club Sport		815134	R	16-20.000 GBP	20.000	24.468	23.160	04-03-17	Brooklands	212	His
	Silver with black interior; in very good driving order.											
1994	968 cabriolet		840597	L	NA	16.181	18.150	14.119	03-06-17	Newport Beach	9188	R&S
	Red with black interior.											
1994	968 Club Sport		815104	R	28-32.000 GBP	25.000	32.738	27.913	29-07-17	Silverstone	702	SiC
	Yellow; some restoration works carried out recently.											
1996	Carrera S coupé		310675	L	80-90.000 EUR	95.404*	118.630*	112.000*	25-11-16	Milan	546	RMS
	Silver; 85,510 kms. From the Duemila Ruote collection.											
1996	Carrera cabriolet		330328	L	55-65.000 EUR	81.093*	100.836*	95.200*	25-11-16	Milan	591	RMS
	Black with black interior; 7,921 kms. From the Duemila Ruote collection.											
1996	Carrera Targa		330942	L	65-75.000 EUR	66.783*	83.041*	78.400*	25-11-16	Milan	592	RMS
	Silver with black interior; 89,947 kms. From the Duemila Ruote collection.											
1994	Carrera "30 Jahre 911"		400084	L	80-90.000 EUR	114.485*	142.356*	134.400*	25-11-16	Milan	900	RMS
	Silver with black interior; 102,370 kms. From the Duemila Ruote collection.											

F645: 1993 Porsche Carrera RSR 3.8

F646: 1992 Porsche 968 Club Sport

Year	Model	(Bodybuilder)	Chassis No.	Steering	Estimate	Hammer Price £	$	€	Date	Place	Lot	Auc. H.
1996	**Carrera Cup**		398078	L	120-220.000 GBP	158.600	193.127	181.153	14-01-17	Birmingham	134	Coy
Blue and green; cosmetically and mechanically restored. Described as in ready to race condition.												
1995	**Carrera Turbo cabriolet**		338505	L	850-1.000.000 EUR	1.146.634	1.433.376	1.344.000	08-02-17	Paris	150	RMS
Dark metallic blue; one of 14 cabriolets built-to-order by the Porsche Exclusive Department fitting the 1995 993 series cabriolet body with the 1994 964 series turbo engine and G50/52 5-speed manual gearbox. Two owners and 18,000 kms covered.												F647
1997	**Carrera 4S coupé**		344783	L	65-75.000 EUR	66.440	80.906	75.890	14-01-17	Maastricht	214	Coy
Silver with black leather interior; sunroof.												
1996	**Carrera 4S coupé**		316012	L	70-90.000 EUR	73.073	90.320	84.120	18-03-17	Lyon	184	Agu
Grey with red leather interior; in good overall condition. 118,000 kms covered.												
1996	**Carrera 4S coupé**		315095	L	80-110.000 EUR	84.820	107.931	96.600	24-06-17	Wien	360	Dor
Silver with green leather interior; 109,008 kms; regularly serviced.												
1995	**Carrera RS Clubsport**		390250	L	220-260.000 GBP	403.200	539.562	480.171	07-09-16	London	130	RMS
Red; one owner and less than 9,000 kms covered. One of 100 examples built.												
1995	**Carrera RS**		390639	L	300-330.000 EUR		NA		08-10-16	Paris	188	CB/C
Silver with black leather interior; described as in very good overall condition.												
1995	**Carrera RS**		390556	L	160-180.000 EUR	290.982*	361.823*	341.600*	25-11-16	Milan	332	RMS
Silver with black and grey interior; 60,980 kms. From the Duemila Ruote collection.												
1995	**Carrera RS**		390115	L	65-75.000 EUR	238.510*	296.576*	280.000*	25-11-16	Milan	853	RMS
Red; 46,147 kms. From the Duemila Ruote collection.												
1995	**Carrera RS**		390669	L	450-550.000 USD	341.430	434.500	388.878	24-06-17	Santa Monica	230	RMS
White; 24,520 kms on the odometer; three owners.												
1995	**Carrera RS**		390626	L	500-600.000 USD		NS		19-08-17	Monterey	S114	Mec
White with black interior; 28,954 km covered.												
1995	**Carrera RS Clubsport**		390260	L	400-500.000 USD	316.239*	407.000*	346.764*	19-08-17	Monterey	255	RMS
Yellow with black interior; 31,417 kms covered. Sold new to Japan and later imported into Canada and then into the USA.												
1995	**GT2**		392064	L	750-850.000 GBP	1.848.000	2.472.994	2.200.783	07-09-16	London	132	RMS F648
Blue with black and grey leather interior; one owner and less than 13,000 kms covered. In excellent overall condition. One of 57 road-going examples built.												
1996	**GT2 Evo**		394062	L	1.250-1.750.000 USD		NS		04-11-16	Dallas	S130	Mec
White; approximately 7,000 kms covered. One of 11 examples built (see lot S76 Mecum 20.8.16 WD).												
1996	**GT2**		393082	L	30-35.000 EUR	524.721*	652.467*	616.000*	25-11-16	Milan	896	RMS
Silver; race prepared. From the Duemila Ruote collection.												
1996	**GT2**		392120	L	1.100-1.500.000 USD		NS		20-01-17	Phoenix	218	RMS
Yellow with black interior; sold new to Japan and recently imported into the USA. Two owners and 33,500 kms covered.												
1996	**GT2**		392139	L	1.300-1.600.000 USD		NS		21-01-17	Scottsdale	140	G&Co
Silver with black interior; sold new to Japan and imported into the USA in 2013. Approximately 36,000 kms covered. Recently serviced. One of 57 road version examples built (see lot 52 Gooding & Company 13.3.15 $973,500).												
1996	**GT2 Evo**		394062	L	1.250-1.750.000 USD	1.114.180	1.450.000	1.297.025	20-05-17	Indianapolis	F192	Mec
See lot S130 Mecum 4.11.16.												
1995	**GT2**		392127	L	1.100-1.400.000 USD		NS		18-08-17	Monterey	137	RMS
White with black leather interior; bought 13 years ago in Japan by the current owner; 11,470 kms covered; meticulously maintained.												
1996	**GT2**		392194	L	1.600-1.900.000 USD		NS		19-08-17	Monterey	S68	Mec
Yellow with black leather interior.												
1997	**911 Cup RSR 3.8**		398063	L	750-950.000 USD		NS		10-03-17	Amelia Island	33	G&Co
Red; until 2016 with its first owner, the car was never raced professionally, but only at Porsche Club and National Auto Sport Association events. Just over 8,000 miles covered. Recently serviced.												
1997	**911 Cup RSR 3.8**		398063	L	500-550.000 USD	277.778*	357.500*	304.590*	18-08-17	Monterey	164	RMS
See lot 33 Gooding & Company 10.3.17.												
1998	**Turbo S 3.6 coupé**		370536	L	200-240.000 GBP	313.600	419.660	373.466	07-09-16	London	131	RMS
Red with black leather interior; one owner and 38,992 kms covered.												

F647: 1995 Porsche Carrera Turbo cabriolet

F648: 1995 Porsche GT2

Year	Model (Bodybuilder)	Chassis No.	Steering	Estimate	Hammer Price £	Hammer Price $	Hammer Price €	Date	Place	Lot	Auc. H.
1995	Turbo 3.6 coupé	370801	R	115-130.000 GBP	112.500	137.655	125.123	15-10-16	Silverstone	323	SiC
	Black with cream leather interior; bought in 2005 by the current owner. Later the body was repainted, the interior were retrimmed, the gearbox was overhauled and the clutch was replaced.										
1995	Turbo 3.6 coupé	370828	L	90-110.000 GBP		NS		15-10-16	Silverstone	340	SiC
	Silver; imported into the UK from Japan in 2015. 77,000 kms on the odometer.										
1997	Turbo S 3.6 coupé	375941	L	425-475.000 USD		NS		05-11-16	Hilton Head	177	AA
	Arctic silver metallic with red leather interior; less than 18,800 miles covered.										
1998	Turbo 3.6 coupé	371090	R	95-115.000 GBP	108.563	137.430	126.031	12-11-16	Birmingham	350	SiC
	Silver with chestnut interior; ordered new with the X50 Power Option and Turbo S interior. Described as in very good overall condition; 64,500 miles on the odometer.										
1997	Turbo 3.6 coupé	370348	L	80-90.000 EUR	143.106*	177.946*	168.000*	25-11-16	Milan	866	RMS
	Silver; 123,915 kms. From the Duemila Ruote collection.										
1996	Turbo 3.6 coupé	376239	L	130-160.000 EUR	100.790	122.735	115.125	14-01-17	Maastricht	212	Coy
	Yellow; in very good overall condition. 84,000 kms covered. Two owners.										
1996	Turbo 3.6 coupé	372134	L	150-170.000 EUR	131.368	159.970	150.052	14-01-17	Maastricht	235	Coy
	Red with blue leather interior; 65,000 kms on the odometer. Fitted with the 430bhp power kit.										
1997	Turbo S 3.6 coupé	375783	L	425-550.000 USD	340.419	418.000	393.129	20-01-17	Phoenix	215	RMS F649
	Yellow with black interior; sold new to the USA. Just over 12,500 miles covered.										
1997	Turbo 3.6 coupé	375445	L	NQ	179.168*	220.000*	206.910*	21-01-17	Scottsdale	1323	B/J
	Silver with black leather interior; 37,000 actual miles.										
1997	Turbo S 3.6 coupé	375924	L	400-500.000 USD	322.502	396.000	372.438	21-01-17	Scottsdale	150	G&Co
	Black with cashmere leather interior; sold new to the USA; three owners; 9,372 miles on the odometer (see lot S97.1 Mecum 20.8.16 NS).										
1996	Turbo 3.6 coupé	372174	L	100-150.000 EUR	205.492	258.212	241.500	09-02-17	Paris	383	Bon
	Silver with black interior; 57,568 kms covered. Factory-fitted 430bhp Powerkit.										
1996	Turbo 3.6 coupé	375817	L	185-195.000 USD	150.049	187.000	175.930	11-02-17	Boca Raton	149	TFA
	Red with cashmere interior; in the same family ownership since new. 7,626 miles covered.										
1997	Turbo S 3.6 coupé	375859	L	300-400.000 USD	246.360	300.000	284.310	09-03-17	Amelia Island	157	Bon
	Black with black leather interior; two owners; approximately 20,000 miles covered.										
1997	Turbo S 3.6 coupé	375923	L	350-400.000 USD		NS		10-03-17	Amelia Island	19	G&Co
	Red with grey leather interior; less than 26,000 miles covered.										
1997	Turbo S 3.6 coupé	375680	L	300-350.000 USD	253.361	308.000	290.259	10-03-17	Amelia Island	86	G&Co
	Silver with red leather interior; two owners; just over 1,000 miles covered.										
1997	Turbo S 3.6 coupé	375762	L	400-450.000 USD	253.361*	308.000*	290.259*	11-03-17	Amelia Island	270	RMS
	Black with black interior; just over 18,000 miles covered. Swiss papers.										
1995	Turbo 3.6 coupé	371104	L	100-150.000 EUR	99.134	122.531	114.120	18-03-17	Lyon	207	Agu
	Grey with black leather interior; body repainted some years ago, engine overhauled in 2006.										
1995	Turbo 3.6 coupé	371090	L	95-125.000 EUR	70.184	87.412	82.000	08-04-17	Essen	172	Coy
	See lot 350 Silverstone Auctions 12.11.16.										
1996	Turbo 3.6 coupé	376230	L	165-185.000 USD		NS		24-06-17	Santa Monica	192	RMS
	Dark metallic blue with dark blue interior; 24,765 miles on the odometer.										
1997	Turbo S 3.6 coupé	375734	L	NA	172.876	220.000	196.900	24-06-17	Santa Monica	217	RMS
	Silver metallic with light grey interior; in very good overall condition; approximately 60,000 miles on the odometer.										
1997	Turbo S 3.6 coupé	375710	L	300-350.000 USD	226.496	291.500	249.233	17-08-17	Monterey	35	WoA
	Silver with black leather interior; always well maintained; low mileage; recently serviced.										
1997	Turbo S 3.6 coupé	375758	L	375-450.000 USD	279.914*	360.250*	306.933*	18-08-17	Monterey	153	RMS
	Red with black interior; 8,300 original miles; sold new to the USA.										
1997	Turbo S 3.6 coupé	375780	L	400-500.000 USD	299.145	385.000	328.020	19-08-17	Pebble Beach	138	G&Co
	Silver metallic with black leather interior; sold new to the USA; less than 9,500 miles on the odometer.										
1998	911 GT1 Evolution	396005	L	Refer Dpt.	4.660.029	5.665.000	5.338.696	10-03-17	Amelia Island	42	G&Co F650
	Silver with black leather interior; in very good original condition. 7,910 kms on the odometer. Since 2015 in the current ownership. Recently serviced (see lots 217 Bonhams 26.5.03 $756,623 and 246 RM 18.8.12 NS).										

F649: 1997 Porsche Turbo S 3.6 coupé

F650: 1998 Porsche 911 GT1 Evolution

Year	Model	(Bodybuilder)	Chassis no.	Steering	Estimate	Hammer price £	$	€	Date	Place	Lot	Auc. H.
2003	911 GT3		690667	R	55-75.000 GBP	57.500	76.619	68.000	10-09-16	Goodwood	172	Bon
Silver with black leather interior; described as in very good overall condition. Last serviced in February 2016 at 22,737 miles.											
2004	911 GT3 RS		691597	L	130-150.000 EUR	171.727*	213.535*	201.600*	25-11-16	Milan	333	RMS
White with red and black interior; 21,184 kms. From the Duemila Ruote collection.											
2004	911 GT3 RS		690879	L	200-250.000 EUR	334.435*	418.068*	392.000*	08-02-17	Paris	128	RMS F651
White; one owner and 196 kms covered. From a Swiss Porsche collection.											
2000	911 GT3 Clubsport		691351	L	100-130.000 EUR	95.553*	119.448*	112.000*	08-02-17	Paris	129	RMS
Yellow with black interior; 7,900 kms covered. From a Swiss Porsche collection.											
2003	911 GT3 RS		691767	L	125-165.000 EUR		NS		09-02-17	Paris	388	Bon
White with blue alcantara interior; engine rebuilt 2,300 kms ago at 96,700 kms.											
2003	911 GT3 Club Sport		690175	L	55-60.000 GBP	60.000	77.868	67.938	29-06-17	Fontwell Park	125	Coy
Silver; 44,000 kms on the odometer. Upgraded by Gemballa; 421bhp engine.											
2005	911 GT3 RSR		693068	L	280-340.000 EUR		NS		02-07-17	Monaco	178	Art
White; raced at the French GT FFSA Championship from 2005 to 2008. The engine and gearbox have been covered 200 kms since the overhaul.											
2001	911 GT2 Clubsport		695114	R	95-115.000 GBP	103.960	127.413	115.624	12-10-16	Duxford	129	H&H
Silver grey; described as in excellent overall condition.											
2001	911 GT2		695275	R	100-120.000 GBP		NS		15-10-16	Silverstone	346	SiC
Silver with black leather interior; 38,400 miles covered. Last serviced in May 2016.											
2002	911 GT2 Clubsport		695388	L	85-105.000 GBP	90.280	109.672	100.409	29-10-16	London	116	Coy
Silver with black leather interior; recently serviced.											
2002	911 GT2		695290	L	100-120.000 EUR	124.025*	154.220*	145.600*	25-11-16	Milan	298	RMS
Silver with black interior; 16.507 kms. From the Duemila Ruote collection.											
2002	911 GT2		695461	L	130-150.000 EUR	162.187*	201.672*	190.400*	25-11-16	Milan	570	RMS
White with black interior; 11,172 kms. From the Duemila Ruote collection.											
2001	911 GT2 Club Sport		695114	R	95-115.000 GBP	103.960	131.083	122.163	07-12-16	Chateau Impney	58	H&H
See lot 129 H & H 12.10.16.											
2004	911 GT2 Clubsport		695072	L	175-225.000 EUR	210.216*	262.786*	246.400*	08-02-17	Paris	124	RMS
Silver with black interior; just over 24,000 kms covered. From a Swiss Porsche collection.											
2004	911 GT2		695091	R	80-90.000 GBP	88.860	109.831	102.287	19-03-17	Goodwood	72	Bon
White; in very good overall condition. Circa 36,000 miles covered.											
2001	911 GT2		695439	R	90-110.000 EUR	70.184	87.412	82.000	08-04-17	Essen	138	Coy
Blue with black interior; in very good condition.											
2002	911 GT2		696171	L	140-160.000 USD		NS		24-06-17	Santa Monica	220	RMS
Black with black interior; less than 16,500 actual miles.											
2003	911 Turbo cabriolet		670244	43-49.000 GBP			NS		15-10-16	Silverstone	359	SiC
Silver; last serviced in October 2016 at 59,785 miles.											
2001	911 Turbo coupé		682299	L	28-34.000 GBP	34.720	43.171	40.758	26-11-16	Weybridge	166	His
Metallic black with grey leather interior; last serviced in October 2016. Two owners.											
2005	911 Turbo S cabriolet		675448	L	75-100.000 EUR	71.665*	89.586*	84.000*	08-02-17	Paris	133	RMS
Silver with black interior; 31,000 miles covered. From a Swiss Porsche collection.											
2005	911 Turbo S cabriolet		675716	L	70-90.000 USD	85.962*	104.500*	98.481*	11-03-17	Amelia Island	273	RMS F652
Black with black interior; recently serviced. Swiss papers.											
2008	911 Turbo S cabriolet		708263	L	NQ	73.472*	93.500*	83.683*	24-06-17	Northeast	726	B/J
Yellow with navy blue and yellow interior; 25,000 actual miles.											
2005	Carrera GT		000261	L	600-650.000 GBP		NS		07-09-16	London	146	RMS
Silver with black interior; 3,500 kms covered. Porsche Certificate of Authenticity (see lot 267 RM/Sotheby's 14.5.16 NS).											
2004	Carrera GT		001040	L	650-700.000 EUR		NA		08-10-16	Paris	171	CB/C
Black with dark grey leather interior; two owners and 1,722 miles covered. Last serviced in September 2016.											

F651: 2004 Porsche 911 GT3 RS

F652: 2005 Porsche 911 Turbo S cabriolet

Year	Model	(Bodybuilder)	Chassis No.	Steering	Estimate	£	$	€	Date	Place	Lot	Auc. H.
2004	**Carrera GT**		001068	L	440-480.000 GBP		NS		15-10-16	Silverstone	317	SiC
	Silver with black leather interior; sold new to the USA, the car was imported into the UK in 2009. Last serviced in November 2015 (see lot 423 Silverstone Auctions 26.2.16 $597,474).											
2004	**Carrera GT**		000143	L	500-600.000 EUR	500.877	625.645	564.000	05-11-16	Lyon	253	Agu
	Metallic grey with black interior; 21,000 kms covered. Clutch replaced in June 2015 at 19,550 kms; last serviced in July 2016 at 20,436 kms.											
2004	**Carrera GT**		001071	L	850-950.000 USD	640.400	800.000	721.120	05-11-16	Hilton Head	168	AA
	Silver with terracotta leather interior; one owner and 24 miles covered.											
2005	**Carrera GT**		000216	L	650-800.000 EUR	648.746*	806.687*	761.600*	25-11-16	Milan	600	RMS
	Metallic black with terracotta interior; imported into Italy in 2007 circa. 7,500 kms since new. From the Duemila Ruote collection.											
2004	**Carrera GT**		001040	L	480-540.000 GBP		NS		04-12-16	London	8	Bon
	See lot 171 Coutau Bégarie/Coys 8.10.16.											
2005	**Carrera GT**		001525	L	500-700.000 USD	513.188	625.000	586.188	15-01-17	Kissimmee	S157	Mec
	Red with black leather interior; two owners and 2,720 miles covered (see lots S190 Mecum 23.1.16 NS and 400 Barrett-Jackson 9.4.16 NS).											
2005	**Carrera GT**		001230	L	650-750.000 USD	602.390	742.500	695.945	19-01-17	Phoenix	133	RMS
	Silver with dark grey leather interior; 1,132 miles covered. Last serviced in late 2016.											
2005	**Carrera GT**		001207	L	NQ	501.670*	616.000*	579.348*	21-01-17	Scottsdale	1396	B/J
	Black with black interior; 5,448 actual miles.											
2005	**Carrera GT**		001466	L	650-750.000 USD	506.150	621.500	584.521	21-01-17	Scottsdale	156	G&Co
	Silver with dark grey leather interior; sold new to the USA. 5,150 miles covered. Last serviced in June 2016 including clutch replacement.											
2005	**Carrera GT**		001164	L	600-700.000 USD		NS		09-03-17	Amelia Island	117	Bon
	Metallic black with terracotta leather interior; one owner and less than 8,500 miles covered. Recently serviced.											
2005	**Carrera GT**		001234	L	875-1.100.000 USD		NS		10-03-17	Amelia Island	50	G&Co
	Medium grey with dark grey leather interior; less than 900 miles covered. Last serviced in January 2017.											
2005	**Carrera GT**		001514	L	750-850.000 USD	633.402*	770.000*	725.648*	11-03-17	Amelia Island	256	RMS **F653**
	Black with brown leather interior; 3,665 original miles.											
2004	**Carrera GT**		001150	L	575-650.000 USD	497.673*	605.000*	570.152*	11-03-17	Amelia Island	275	RMS
	Medium metallic grey with black interior; sold new to the USA. Less than 8,500 miles covered. Recently serviced. Swiss papers.											
2005	**Carrera GT**		001107	L	700-800.000 USD		NS		19-08-17	Monterey	S150.1	Mec
	Silver with dark grey interior; 4,900 miles covered; until 2015 with its first owner (see lots 191 Bonhams 10.3.16 NS and F133 Mecum 19.8.16 NS).											
2004	**Carrera GT**		001071	L	1.100-1.250.000 USD	765.345	985.000	839.220	19-08-17	Monterey	S83	Mec
	See lot 168 Auctions America 5.11.16.											
2005	**Carrera GT**		001207	L	NA	521.367	671.000	571.692	19-08-17	Monterey	1149	R&S
	See lot 1396 Barrett-Jackson 21.1.17.											
2007	**911 GT3 RS**		790646	L	155-175.000 EUR	181.267*	225.398*	212.800*	25-11-16	Milan	306	RMS
	Yellow with black interior; 1,426 kms covered. From the Duemila Ruote collection.											
2007	**911 GT3**		790181	L	90-105.000 EUR	124.025*	154.220*	145.600*	25-11-16	Milan	867	RMS
	White; 7,463 kms. From the Duemila Ruote collection.											
2008	**911 GT3 RS**		792127	L	250-300.000 USD		NS		15-01-17	Kissimmee	S194	Mec
	Orange with black interior; 11,630 actual miles. Recently serviced.											
2008	**911 GT3 RS**		792346	L	275-325.000 USD		NS		15-01-17	Kissimmee	S228	Mec
	Black with black interior; 6,879 original miles.											
2010	**911 GT3 RSR**		799913	L	200-300.000 EUR	401.322*	501.682*	470.400*	08-02-17	Paris	143	RMS **F654**
	Sold new to BMS Scuderia Italia, nel 2010 the car won the Spa 25 Hours and placed 3rd at the Le Mans 24 Hours. In 2011 it was raced at the Monza Trofeo where it placed 1st in class. Subsequently the car was retired from competition and restored by BMS.											
2008	**911 GT3 RS**		792265	L	275-325.000 USD		NS		18-08-17	Pebble Beach	37	G&Co
	White with black leather interior; just over 5,300 miles covered.											
2008	**911 GT2**		794669	L	130-150.000 GBP	135.000	165.186	150.147	15-10-16	Silverstone	334	SiC
	Grey with black leather and alcantara interior; 13,800 miles covered. Last serviced in September 2016.											
2008	**911 GT2**		794206	L	155-175.000 EUR	219.429*	272.850*	257.600*	25-11-16	Milan	857	RMS
	White with black interior; 4,448 kms. From the Duemila Ruote collection.											

F653: 2005 Porsche Carrera GT

F654: 2010 Porsche 911 GT3 RSR

Year	Model	(Bodybuilder)	Chassis No.	Steering	Estimate	Hammer Price £	Hammer Price $	Hammer Price €	Date	Place	Lot	Auc. H.
2008	911 GT2		796175	L	270-310.000 USD		NS		24-06-17	Santa Monica	227	RMS
	White with black interior; less than 8,000 original miles.											
2011	911 GT2 RS		778120	L	450-500.000 USD		NS		19-01-17	Phoenix	144	RMS
	White with matt black bonnet and black wheels; red and black leather interior. One owner and 4,650 miles covered. Last serviced in mid-2016.											
2011	911 GT2 RS		778189	L	550-650.000 USD	461.479	561.000	528.686	10-03-17	Amelia Island	41	G&Co
	Black with black leather and red alcantara interior; sold new to the USA. Three owners. Less than 2,900 miles covered.											
2011	911 GT2 RS		778175	L	375-450.000 USD	357.420	434.500	409.473	11-03-17	Amelia Island	227	RMS
	Silver with black front hood; one owner, 3,232 original miles.											
2010	911 GT2 RS		776186	L	290-340.000 GBP	320.700	416.204	363.129	30-06-17	Goodwood	254	Bon
	Black with red and black leather interior; circa 8,900 kms covered; two owners. Last serviced in December 2016.											
2011	911 GT2 RS		778064	L	450-500.000 USD		NS		19-08-17	Monterey	S81	Mec
	Black with red and black interior; 7,500 miles covered.											
2011	911 GT3 RS 4.0		785398	L	NA	208.130	276.459	247.009	02-09-16	Salon Privé	250	SiC
	White with black leather and alcantara interior; 27,000 miles covered.											
2010	911 GT3 RS 3.8		780358	L	150-180.000 GBP	149.666	199.430	176.995	10-09-16	Goodwood	151	Bon
	White; one owner and circa 1,600 miles covered. Major service in 2015 (see lot 209 Silverstone Auctions 25.10.15 $207,968).											
2011	911 GT3 RS 4.0		785565	L	NA		NS		19-11-16	Anaheim	S149.1	Mec
	Black with black and red interior; 7,994 miles covered.											
2011	911 GT3 RS 3.8		783202	L	225-275.000 USD	182.948	225.500	211.361	19-01-17	Phoenix	125	RMS
	Black with red wheels; 11,900 original miles.											
2011	911 GT3 RS 3.8		783483	L	225-275.000 USD	174.689*	214.500*	201.737*	20-01-17	Scottsdale	54	G&Co
	Dark grey with black interior; two owners and less than 2,900 miles covered; never raced or tracked.											
2011	911 GT3 RS 4.0		785618	L	650-750.000 USD	615.305	748.000	704.915	10-03-17	Amelia Island	43	G&Co
	Black with black and red leather and alcantara interior; sold new to the USA. Two owners. 134 miles covered.											
2011	911 GT3 RS 3.8		783220	L	175-250.000 USD	139.348*	169.400*	159.643*	10-03-17	Amelia Island	66	G&Co
	Dark grey; 16,600 miles covered. Bought new and offered for sale by Caitlyn Jenner; all proceeds to benefit the Caitlyn Jenner Foundation.											
2011	911 GT3 RS 4.0		785689	L	475-550.000 USD	475.052	577.500	544.236	11-03-17	Amelia Island	277	RMS
	White; sold new to the USA. 700 original miles.											
2011	911 GT3 RS 4.0		785072	L	320-360.000 EUR		NS		08-04-17	Essen	215	Coy
	White with leather and alcantara interior; 2,991 kms covered; Russian registered (see lot 304 Historics 11.6.16 NS)											
2012	911 GT3 Cup 4.0		798183	L	425-500.000 USD	307.360	400.000	357.800	20-05-17	Indianapolis	S219	Mec
	White with red and blue stripes; one of the last five US-specification examples built by Porsche in 2012 and offered by Brumos Porsche in Jacksonville, Florida, as Brumos Commemorative Editions.											
2011	911 GT3 RS 3.8		783602	L	475-525.000 USD		NS		18-08-17	Pebble Beach	38	G&Co
	Green with black leather interior; 30 miles covered; three owners.											
2011	911 GT3 RS 4.0		785582	L	525-475.000 USD	316.239	407.000	346.764	18-08-17	Pebble Beach	39	G&Co
	Black with red and black leather interior; sold new to the USA; just over 5,200 miles covered.											
2011	911 GT3 RS 4.0		785644	L	425-525.000 USD	324.786	418.000	356.136	19-08-17	Monterey	235	RMS
	White with black and red leather interior; bought in 2013 by the current, first private owner. Just over 4,500 miles covered. Last serviced in September 2016.											
2011	Speedster		795663	L	275-325.000 USD	223.960*	275.000*	258.638*	21-01-17	Scottsdale	145	G&Co
	White; sold new to the USA; two owners and less than 3,500 miles covered.											
2010	Speedster		795073	L	200-250.000 EUR	200.661	250.841	235.200	08-02-17	Paris	167	RMS
	Blue; just under 5,300 kms covered.											
2011	Speedster		795654	L	235-255.000 USD	197.992	246.750	232.142	11-02-17	Boca Raton	127	TFA
	Blue with blue/black interior; in very good overall condition.											
2011	Speedster		795608	L	250-300.000 USD	203.247	247.500	234.556	09-03-17	Amelia Island	166	Bon
	White; less than 5,500 miles covered.											
2011	Speedster		795579	L	275-350.000 USD	298.604	363.000	342.091	11-03-17	Amelia Island	224	RMS
	Blue with black interior; 1,881 original miles.											
2011	Speedster		795595	L	240-280.000 USD	194.449	243.000	227.278	01-04-17	Ft.Lauderdale	549	AA
	Blue with black leather interior; 7,800 actual miles.											
2011	Speedster		795562	L	225-275.000 USD	205.128*	264.000*	224.928*	19-08-17	Pebble Beach	178	G&Co
	Blue with black interior; showing less than 6,500 miles; last serviced in 2016.											
2011	Speedster		795626	L	350-400.000 USD	264.180	340.000	289.680	19-08-17	Monterey	S86	Mec
	White with black and white interior; one owner; 318 miles covered.											
2014	911 Carrera S Martini Racing Edition		114574	L	150-180.000 EUR	105.108*	131.393*	123.200*	08-02-17	Paris	132	RMS
	White version; one owner and 150 kms covered. From a Swiss Porsche collection.											
2014	911 GT3		183231	L	125-150.000 USD	119.766*	154.000*	141.588*	13-05-17	Auburn	L167.1	AA
	Black with black leather and alcantara interior; one owner; less than 900 miles covered.											
2016	911 GT3 RS		193215	L	NQ		NS		24-06-17	Northeast	689	B/J
	White with black alcantara interior; 17 actual miles.											
2015	918 Spyder		800381	L	NA	1.196.373	1.475.000	1.387.680	19-11-16	Anaheim	S90	Mec
	Ordered without paint with exposed carbon fiber with matt black plastic wrap; black and green interior; 1,957 miles covered; fitted with the Weissach package (see lot S112 Mecum 20.8.16 NS).											

Year	Model	(Bodybuilder)	Chassis no.	Steering	Estimate	Hammer price £	$	€	Date	Sale Place	Lot	Auc. H.

F655: 2015 Porsche 918 Spyder   F656: 2016 Porsche 911 R

Year	Model	Chassis no.	Steering	Estimate	£	$	€	Date	Place	Lot	Auc.H.
2015	918 Spyder	800268	L	1.300-1.500.000 USD		NS		19-01-17	Scottsdale	36	Bon

Dark metallic blue with black leather interior; one owner and 817 miles covered.

| 2015 | 918 Spyder | 800537 | L | 1.200-1.400.000 EUR | 1.269.486 | 1.630.138 | 1.456.000 | 27-05-17 | Villa Erba | 142 | RMS F655 |

Blue; one owner and less than 11,000 kms covered. Fitted with the Weissach package.

| 2015 | 918 Spyder | 800089 | L | 1.200-1.600.000 USD | 1.431.623 | 1.842.500 | 1.569.810 | 19-08-17 | Monterey | 230 | RMS |

Metallic black with black leather interior; one owner; 1,188 miles covered; last serviced in April 2017.

| 2016 | 911 Carrera GTS Rennsport Reunion Edition | 123336 | L | 250-300.000 USD | 182.948 | 225.500 | 211.361 | 19-01-17 | Phoenix | 119 | RMS |

One of the 25 examples built for the US market on the occasion of the fifth edition of the Rennsport Reunion held in Laguna Seca in 2015. One owner and 72 miles covered.

| 2016 | 911 Carrera GTS Rennsport Reunion Edition | 123404 | L | 200-250.000 USD | 176.448 | 214.500 | 202.145 | 11-03-17 | Amelia Island | 290 | RMS |

Grey with leather and alcantara interior; 1,200 original miles. One of 25 examples built fo the US market.

| 2016 | 911 R | 194097 | L | 250-350.000 EUR | 436.405 | 538.062 | 483.000 | 07-10-16 | Zoute | 35 | Bon |

White; sold new to Sweden; 52 kms covered. Example no.135 of 991 built.

| 2016 | 911 R | 194422 | L | 450-650.000 EUR | 439.543 | 549.461 | 515.200 | 08-02-17 | Paris | 136 | RMS F656 |

Slate grey with silver stripes and black interior; example no.967 of 991 built. Sold new to France. Paint to sample colours.

| 2016 | 911 R | 194133 | L | 390-440.000 EUR | 312.489 | 401.265 | 358.400 | 27-05-17 | Villa Erba | 152 | RMS |

Silver; one owner and less than 1,000 kms covered.

| 2016 | 911 R | 195265 | L | 450-500.000 USD | | NS | | 19-08-17 | Monterey | S59 | Mec |

Black with red stripes and black leather interior; 79 miles covered.

| 2016 | 911 R | 195145 | L | NA | | NS | | 19-08-17 | Monterey | 1102 | R&S |

Silver; 48 miles on the odometer.

PREMIER (USA) (1902-1926)

| 1904 | Model F 16hp rear-entrance tonneau | NQ | R | 175-250.000 USD | 264.957 | 341.000 | 290.532 | 18-08-17 | Carmel | 8 | Bon F657 |

Green; bought in the late 1980s by the current owner and subjected to a full restoration completed in 1999. New body.

PULLMAN (USA) (1905-1917)

| 1908 | Model H light touring | 902 | R | 60-80.000 USD | 40.822 | 51.700 | 46.220 | 06-10-16 | Hershey | 163 | RMS |

Light grey with deep red leather interior; restored several years ago, the car is described as in good overall condition.

| 1910 | Model O roadster | 4510 | R | 65-85.000 USD | 53.526 | 66.000 | 59.242 | 07-10-16 | Hershey | 257 | RMS F658 |

Yellow with dark brown leather interior; restoration completed in 1992. The only known surviving Model O.

QVALE (USA)

| 2004 | Mangusta GTR | 00022 | L | 40-50.000 GBP | | NS | | 14-01-17 | Birmingham | 143 | Coy |

Blue with white stripes and tan interior; one owner and 5,000 kms on the odometer (see Coys lots 134 1.8.05 NS, 210 14.1.06 NS, 210 20.5.06 $40,854, and 346 3.3.08 NS).

F657: 1904 Premier Model F 16hp rear-entrance tonneau   F658: 1910 Pullman Model O roadster

Year	Model	(Bodybuilder)	Chassis No.	Steering	Estimate	Hammer Price £	$	€	Date	Place	Lot	Auc. H.

RAILTON (GB) *(1933-1949)*

Year	Model	Chassis No.	Steering	Estimate	£	$	€	Date	Place	Lot	Auc. H.
1935	Fairmile cabriolet	546552	R	90-120.000 AUD	59.616	76.774	65.336	20-08-17	Mallala Park	6	Mos

Two-tone blue with blue interior; restored in 2013. From the collection of the late Clem Smith.

RALEIGH (GB) *(1903-1936)*

| 1934 | Safety Seven | ZP944 | R | 7-9.000 GBP | | NS | | 23-02-17 | Donington Park | 38 | H&H |

Blue with blue interior; mechanicals overhauled, body restored. The clutch requires attention.

RAMBLER (USA) *(1902-1917)*

| 1904 | Model G runabout | 4372 | R | 30-40.000 GBP | | NS | | 03-09-16 | Beaulieu | 484 | Bon |

Red with black interior; restored circa in 1990. In good running order (see lot 28 H & H 1.10.10 $63,284).

| 1905 | Type One surrey | 6372 | R | 45-65.000 USD | 57.331 | 73.700 | 65.704 | 04-06-17 | Greenwich | 155 | Bon **F659** |

Green with black leather interior; restored in the early 2000s.

| 1912 | Four Cross Country touring | 30374 | R | 80-100.000 USD | | NS | | 11-03-17 | Amelia Island | 56 | Mot |

Burgundy with black leather interior; restored many years ago. Described as in good driving order (see lots 466 Bonhams 17.8.07 $70,200, 171 RM 13.3.10 $46,750, and 351 Bonhams 1.6.14 $66,000).

RAYNAUD (F)

| 1896 | Vis-a-vis | BS8649(registr.no.) | R | 110-125.000 GBP | | NS | | 04-11-16 | London | 204 | Bon |

Probably only example built, the car is fitted with a twin-cylinder 3.8-litre engine. In the 1970s it was acquired by a Swiss collector who presented it to the Veteran Car Club of Great Britain Dating Committee which retained it completely original and certified it as built in 1896. Imported into the UK in recent years. In working order, the car requires further mechanical works prior to use.

REGAL (USA) *(1908-1918)*

| 1912 | Twenty-Five Model T touring | 5410 | R | 50-75.000 USD | | NS | | 06-10-16 | Hershey | 126 | RMS |

Dark blue with black interior; acquired in 2000 by the current owner and subsequently restored.

RELIANT (GB) *(1934-)*

| 1970 | Scimitar GTE | 450979 | R | 7-10.000 GBP | 4.025* | 5.346* | 4.777* | 03-09-16 | Beaulieu | 504 | Bon |

Blue with black leather interior; restored in the 2000s.

| 1975 | Scimitar GTE | 93X5853 | R | 4-6.000 GBP | | NS | | 02-06-17 | Solihull | 11 | H&H |

Yellow with tan interior; in good overall condition. Automatic transmission.

RENAULT (F) *(1899-)*

| 1900 | Type C rear-entrance tonneau | 1697 | R | 60-80.000 GBP | 37.083 | 46.317 | 41.755 | 04-11-16 | London | 201 | Bon |

Yellow with green leather interior; restored in the early 1980s, it is described as in very good condition. De Dion-Bouton engine.

| 1904 | Type N-B tonneau | 3388 | R | 250-280.000 GBP | 272.540 | 340.402 | 306.880 | 04-11-16 | London | 205 | Bon **F660** |

Red with black wings and black leather interior; driven at numerous historic events. In the same family ownership from the 1920s to the 1980s; in the current ownership from the 1980s.

| 1903 | Type N-C wagonette | 227 | R | 110-130.000 GBP | 124.700 | 155.750 | 140.412 | 04-11-16 | London | 207 | Bon **F661** |

Black with beige leather interior; discovered in 1969 lacking the engine and part of the wooden body. Subjected to a long restoration completed in the mid-1990s and fitted with a period correct twin-cylinder engine. Regularly driven at the London to Brighton Run. Since 1969 in the same family ownership.

| 1912 | Type AG landaulette | 11957 | R | 25-35.000 EUR | | NS | | 18-06-17 | Fontainebleau | 52 | Ose |

Red with black wings.

| 1909 | Type AX torpedo | 14561 | R | 245-28.500 GBP | 24.750 | 30.791 | 28.651 | 29-03-17 | Duxford | 14 | H&H |

White; restored in the 2000s.

| 1910 | Type BY Roy-des-Belges torpedo | 24213 | R | 65-75.000 GBP | 86.240 | 105.696 | 95.916 | 12-10-16 | Duxford | 94 | H&H |

Blue with black interior; restored in the mid-1980s, the car is described as in good overall condition. Engine overhauled in 2006. For 32 years in the current ownership.

F659: 1905 Rambler Type One surrey

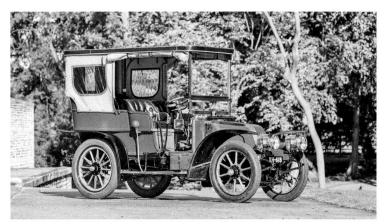

F660: 1904 Renault Type N-B tonneau

Year	Model	(Bodybuilder)	Chassis no.	Steering	Estimate	£	$	€	Date	Place	Lot	Auc. H.

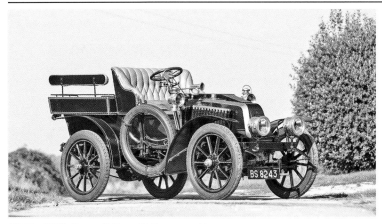

F661: 1903 Renault Type N-C wagonette

F662: 1955 Renault 4CV Police (Currus)

Year	Model	Chassis no.	Steering	Estimate	£	$	€	Date	Place	Lot	Auc. H.
1915	**Type EK spider**	58748	R	18-20.000 EUR	24.162	30.821	27.600	18-06-17	Fontainebleau	53	Ose

Black; for 38 years in the previous ownership (see lot 206 Osenat 8.11.15 $19,555).

| 1933 | **Type KZ11 Taxi** | 617537 | L | 10-15.000 EUR | | NS | | 18-06-17 | Fontainebleau | 55 | Ose |

Black and red; restored in 1990.

| 1927 | **Monasix cabriolet (Mauguy)** | 312815 | R | 10-12.000 GBP | 9.200 | 12.220 | 10.919 | 03-09-16 | Beaulieu | 410 | Bon |

Blue with black wings and grey/blue cloth interior; older restoration.

| 1932 | **Monasix RY1 coach (Chesnot)** | RY18079 | R | 10-12.000 EUR | 5.493* | 6.773* | 6.080* | 07-10-16 | Chateau-sur-Epte | 10 | Art |

Red and black with beige interior; in good overall condition except for the paintwork which requires some attention. From the Andre Weber Collection.

| 1933 | **Vivaquatre Type K II Taxi** | 617537 | L | 15-20.000 EUR | | NS | | 19-03-17 | Fontainebleau | 205 | Ose |

Black and red; restored in 1990. From the René Cocheteux collection.

| 1939 | **Viva Grand Sport cabriolet** | 930988 | L | 90-130.000 EUR | | NS | | 09-02-17 | Paris | 356 | Bon |

Dark blue; since 1969 in the same family ownership. Fully restored between 2005 and 2016; engine rebuilt in 2014.

| 1955 | **4CV Police (Currus)** | 2262123 | L | 28-34.000 EUR | 33.270 | 41.806 | 39.100 | 09-02-17 | Paris | 353 | Bon |

White and black; one of the first 15 examples built for the Prefecture de Police de Paris, the car features cutaway door windows, enabling the easy use of firearms. For 50 years in the current ownership; restored in 2000. **F662**

| 1955 | **4CV berline Sport** | R10622261180 | L | 10-20.000 EUR | 15.250* | 19.005* | 17.880* | 10-02-17 | Paris | 146 | Art |

Grey; bought in 2008 by the current owner. 860 kms covered since new. In original condition; brakes rebuilt.

| 1962 | **4CV berline** | 3665733 | L | 6-10.000 EUR | 7.270* | 9.251* | 8.280* | 24-06-17 | Wien | 307 | Dor |

Blue with grey interior; for a long time on display in the showroom of a Renault dealer in Wien.

| 1953 | **Fregate berline** | 1986649 | L | 4-6.000 EUR | 7.471* | 9.212* | 8.269* | 07-10-16 | Chateau-sur-Epte | 14 | Art |

Two-tone green; restored at unspecified date. From the Andre Weber Collection.

| 1956 | **Fregate coupé (Chapron)** | 2418230 | L | 16-21.000 EUR | 33.357 | 41.230 | 38.400 | 19-03-17 | Fontainebleau | 219 | Ose |

For restoration; since 1967 in the same family ownership. **F663**

| 1962 | **Dauphine** | R1090 | L | NQ | 3.808* | 4.911* | 4.303* | 08-07-17 | Brooklands | 203 | His |

Burgundy with red interior; in original condition; one owner.

| 1964 | **Caravelle cabriolet** | 117955 | L | 10-12.000 EUR | 10.945 | 13.529 | 12.600 | 18-03-17 | Fontainebleau | 44 | Ose |

Metallic grey with black hardtop; from the Perinet Marquet collection.

| 1983 | **R5 Alpine Turbo** | 14784 | L | 15-20.000 EUR | 18.117 | 22.630 | 20.400 | 05-11-16 | Lyon | 240 | Agu |

Blue; in good overall condition.

| 1982 | **R5 Alpine Turbo** | 19089 | L | 17-23.000 EUR | | NS | | 18-03-17 | Lyon | 185 | Agu |

White; in good overall condition.

| 1982 | **R5 Turbo Group B** | 000020 | L | 200-250.000 EUR | 219.771 | 274.730 | 257.600 | 08-02-17 | Paris | 114 | RMS |

Yellow and white; Works car at the 1981 Monte Carlo Rally, the car was subsequently sold to Greece. In 1982 it was updated at the factory to Group B specification. In 1984 it was bought by Dimitri Manolopoulos who retained it for 30 years and raced it at over 200 events in the Greek hill climb and rally Championships.

F663: 1956 Renault Fregate coupé (Chapron)

F664: 1982 Renault R5 Turbo Group 4

Year	Model	(Bodybuilder)	Chassis no.	Steering	Estimate	Hammer price £	$	€	Date	Place	Lot	Auc. H.
1983	**R5 Turbo Group B**		000016	L	200-300.000 EUR	**166.351**	**209.029**	**195.500**	09-02-17	Paris	372	**Bon**

One of 20 works cars built for Group B competition, the car was driven during the 1983 season by Jean Ragnotti. Sold by Renault in 1985, it was bought in 2010 by the current owner who had it restored to the white and yellow 1983 livery (see lot 64 Poulain 12.12.94 $37,802).

1982	**R5 Turbo Group 4**		VF1822000C0000009	L	300-500.000 EUR	**274.497**	**342.084**	**321.840**	10-02-17	Paris	95	**Art**

Works car for Jean Ragnotti for the 1982 season; driving this car he won the Corsica Rally, placed 3rd at the Criterium Alpin and was forced to retire for accident at the Ivory Coast Rally. In 1984 the car was presented by Renault Sport to Jean Ragnotti and was delivered to Bozian brothers for a long restoration completed in 1995. Finished in the Renault Sport livery at the Ivory Coast Rally (aka Bandama Rally). Owned and offered by Jean Ragnotti.

F664

1982	**R5 Turbo**		000052	L	90-120.000 EUR	**84.238**	**107.424**	**96.120**	10-06-17	Lyon	134	**Agu**

Dark blue with beige interior; described as in very good original condition.

| 1982 | **R5 Turbo Group 4** | | C0000069 | L | 110-160.000 EUR | **147.629** | **217.885** | **167.888** | 02-07-17 | Monaco | 189 | **Art** |

Competition Client version finished in yellow and sold new to Bulgaria where it was raced at numerous rallies until 1987. Bought in the early 1990s by the current, second owner in Germany. Regularly maintained.

| 1981 | **R5 Turbo** | | 1639 | L | 70-80.000 GBP | **74.250** | **97.230** | **82.900** | 29-07-17 | Silverstone | 727 | **SiC** |

Two-tone blue; in good overall condition.

| 1984 | **R5 Turbo 2** | | 000535 | L | 65-85.000 EUR | | **NS** | | 03-09-16 | Chantilly | 7 | **Bon** |

White with beige interior; engine and gearbox overhauled some years ago.

| 1984 | **R5 Turbo 2** | | 000397 | L | 50-70.000 EUR | | **NS** | | 30-10-16 | Paris | 163 | **Art** |

White; restored.

| 1984 | **R5 Turbo 2** | | 000181 | L | 60-80.000 EUR | **54.883** | **68.555** | **61.800** | 05-11-16 | Lyon | 234 | **Agu** |

White with light beige cloth interior; body recently restored and repainted. Mechanicals overhauled.

| 1984 | **R5 Turbo 2** | | 001185 | L | 90-115.000 USD | **80.319*** | **99.000*** | **92.793*** | 19-01-17 | Scottsdale | 2 | **Bon** |

Burgundy; in very good original condition. Two owners. Less than 27,000 kms covered.

| 1985 | **R5 Turbo 2** | | 000222 | L | 80-100.000 USD | **69.610*** | **85.800*** | **80.420*** | 19-01-17 | Scottsdale | 93 | **Bon** |

White and grey; body repainted, interior re-upholstere. In excellent mechanical condition.

| 1983 | **R5 Turbo 2** | | 000188 | L | 75-95.000 EUR | **76.442** | **95.558** | **89.600** | 08-02-17 | Paris | 107 | **RMS** |

White with black leather interior; 5,900 original kms.

F665

| 1986 | **R5 Maxi Turbo** | | R5T684 | L | 290-360.000 GBP | | **NS** | | 07-09-16 | London | 158 | **RMS** |

Silver and red; freshly restored. The car was driven by Giovanni Rossi, 1988 European Hill Climb Champion.

| 1989 | **GTA Turbo** | | 65054 | L | 25-35.000 EUR | **27.207** | **33.628** | **31.320** | 18-03-17 | Lyon | 187 | **Agu** |

White with black leather interior; in original condition; 41,000 kms covered; last serviced in 2014.

| 1994 | **Clio Williams Phase 2** | | 019469 | L | 20-30.000 EUR | **24.648*** | **29.944*** | **27.416*** | 30-10-16 | Paris | 156 | **Art** |

Blue; 31,428 kms covered.

| 1993 | **Clio Williams 2.0** | | 943112 | L | 12-18.000 EUR | **12.788** | **15.974** | **14.400** | 05-11-16 | Lyon | 241 | **Agu** |

Blu; in good overall condition. Engine major work in 2008.

| 2002 | **Clio V6 Phase 1** | | 607477 | L | 40-60.000 EUR | **52.789*** | **65.787*** | **61.894*** | 10-02-17 | Paris | 91 | **Art** |

Light grey with dark grey interior; two owners and 4,340 kms covered. Last serviced in 2015.

| 1997 | **Laguna Super Touring** | | 981ST41 | L | 80-120.000 GBP | | **NS** | | 07-09-16 | London | 121 | **RMS** |

The car was prepared in 1998 by the Williams team for the British Touring Car Championship and was driven by Jason Plato. Offered in ready to race condition.

RENWICK & BERTELLI (GB)

| 1925 | **1.5-litre** | | R&B1 | R | 240-280.000 GBP | | **NS** | | 10-09-16 | Goodwood | 162 | **Bon** |

Only example built by William Somerville Renwick and Augustus Cesare Bertelli using an Enfield-Allday chassis fitted with an engine designed by them and with a body built by Enrico Bertelli. Later the car became the "Buzzbox" after they, together with Lord and Lady Charnwood, took over Bamford & Martin Ltd from the receivers in 1926 and re-launched it as Aston Martin Motors Ltd. The car received a long, full restoration completed in 2015 to the original specification (see lot 460 Brooks 23.7.98 NS).

REO (USA) (1904-1936)

| 1905 | **7.5hp runabout** | | 16946 | R | 25-35.000 USD | **22.225*** | **28.600*** | **25.451*** | 03-10-16 | Philadelphia | 244 | **Bon** |

Black and red; in the same ownership from the late 1930s. Described as in largely original condition; to be recommissioned prior to use. From the Bloomington Collection.

F666

| 1933 | **Flying Cloud coupé** | | QINVAAA334001 | R | 35-40.000 AUD | | **NS** | | 28-05-17 | Sydney | 6 | **Mos** |

Red; restored in the late 1990s. Semi-automatic transmission.

F665: 1983 Renault R5 Turbo 2

F666: 1905 Reo 7.5hp runabout

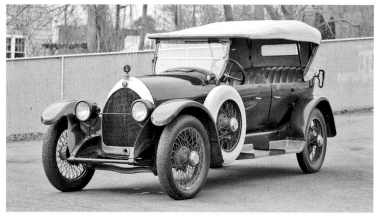

F667: 1920 Revere Model A touring

F668: 1950 Riley 2.5-litre RMC roadster

REVERE (USA) (1918-1926)

Year	Model	(Bodybuilder)	Chassis no.	Steering	Estimate	£	$	€	Date	Place	Lot	Auc. H.
1920	Model A touring		1357	L	125-175.000 USD	112.915	137.500	130.309	09-03-17	Amelia Island	174	Bon F667

For many decades in the same family ownership, the car is described as in highly original condition. The 4-cylinder Duesenberg engine received recently several works.

REYNARD (GB) (1973-)

Year	Model	Chassis no.	Steering	Estimate	£	$	€	Date	Place	Lot	Auc. H.
1993	93D	025	M	20-30.000 EUR	52.472*	65.247*	61.600*	25-11-16	Milan	295	RMS

White, blue, yellow. From the Duemila Ruote collection.

RICKENBACKER (USA) (1922-1927)

Year	Model	Chassis no.	Steering	Estimate	£	$	€	Date	Place	Lot	Auc. H.
1923	Model B coupé	10585	L	60-80.000 USD		NS		04-06-17	Greenwich	120	Bon

Dark blue and black; restored.

RILEY (GB) (1898-1969)

Year	Model	Chassis no.	Steering	Estimate	£	$	€	Date	Place	Lot	Auc. H.
1929	Nine tourer	603563	R	18-22.000 GBP	15.255	18.697	16.967	12-10-16	Duxford	89	H&H
1937	Nine Merlin saloon	67M2790	R	4-6.000 GBP	10.080	12.527	11.706	16-11-16	Donington Park	21	H&H
1936	Nine Merlin saloon	66M1917	R	16-20.000 GBP	16.800	20.553	19.454	04-03-17	Brooklands	155	His
1950	1.5-litre RMA saloon	40S18209	R	4-6.000 GBP	2.300*	3.055*	2.730*	03-09-16	Beaulieu	408	Bon
1953	2.5-litre RMB saloon	62S9845	R	105-12.500 GBP	12.320	15.391	14.557	23-02-17	Donington Park	73	H&H
1950	2.5-litre RMC roadster	59554860	R	27-32.000 GBP	25.300	33.606	30.026	03-09-16	Beaulieu	424	Bon F668

- 1929: *Dark blue and black with grey interior; since 1965 in the current ownership. Restored over the years.*
- 1937: *Blue; in the same ownership from 1937 to 1968, stored from the late 1960s to 2002, in the process of restoration since.*
- 1936: *Black and white with red leather interior; restoration recently completed.*
- 1950: *Black and yellow with original brown leather interior; it requires some works prior to use.*
- 1953: *Black and green with green interior; older restoration. Engine overhauled in 2007 circa.*
- 1950: *Two-tone blue with blue interior; described as in good overall condition. Recently reimported from Australia.*

ROAMER (USA) (1916-1929)

Year	Model	Chassis no.	Steering	Estimate	£	$	€	Date	Place	Lot	Auc. H.
1916	Six roadster	NQ	R	55-75.000 EUR		NS		01-05-17	Obenheim	308	Ose

White; sold new to Australia; imported into Europe in the 1980s; restored.

ROCHET SCHNEIDER (F) (1894-1932)

Year	Model	(Bodybuilder)	Chassis no.	Steering	Estimate	£	$	€	Date	Place	Lot	Auc. H.
1914	12hp limousine	(Allignol)	11905	R	18-22.000 GBP	17.250	22.913	20.472	03-09-16	Beaulieu	447	Bon

Blue with grey cloth interior; rebodied in 1918. Restored in the late 1990s (see Bonhams lots 719 8.9.07 $29,069, 506 21.4.08 NS and 388A 20.4.09 $20,114).

ROLLS-ROYCE (GB) (1904-)

Year	Model	Chassis no.	Steering	Estimate	£	$	€	Date	Place	Lot	Auc. H.
1926	Silver Ghost Piccadilly roadster	S295PL	L	280-320.000 GBP		NS		07-09-16	London	168	RMS
1921	Silver Ghost tourer	48CE	R	340-360.000 GBP	328.925	439.378	388.954	08-09-16	Fontwell Park	119	Coy
1926	Silver Ghost Piccadilly roadster	S295PL	L	250-280.000 GBP		NS		07-12-16	London	335	Bon
1913	Silver Ghost tourer	2371	R	750-900.000 USD	566.693	698.500	654.704	19-01-17	Scottsdale	80	Bon
1924	Silver Ghost Pall Mall tourer	404MF	R	250-300.000 USD		NS		20-01-17	Scottsdale	44	G&Co

- 1926 (168): *Red with tan interior; built with Brewster convertible body, the car was fitted in 1932 with the present body. In the late 1960s it was acquired by collector Robert Atwell who had it restored. In more recent years the car was imported into Europe and the mechanicals were restored again (see lot 39 Christie's 28.8.94 $63,000).*
- 1921: *Light grey with black leather interior; at unspecified date the car was fitted with the present, new London to Edinburgh style tourer body (see lot 163 Coys 2.7.16 NS).*
- 1926 (335): *See lot 168 RM/Sotheby's 7.9.16.*
- 1913: *Built on a London to Edilburgh chassis, the car was fitted with a Barker body and sold new to France. Rediscovered in the late 1990s, it was restored and fitted with the present 1914 engine no.K10 and with the present body built by Kenneth Neve for chassis no.1701 (the original London to Edinburgh Run car) during its 1970 restoration.*
- 1924: *Blue with black interior; described as in very good driving condition (see lot 161 Bonhams 10.3.16 $214,500).*

Year	Model	(Bodybuilder)	Chassis no.	Steering	Estimate	Hammer Price £	$	€	Date	Place	Lot	Auc. H.
1914	**Silver Ghost tourer**		35PB	R	600-800.000 USD	597.208*	726.000*	684.182*	10-03-17	Amelia Island	131	RMS
	Built with H.J. Mulliner landaulette body; sold new in the UK and later imported into the USA where in the 1920s it was fitted with a Locke coupé body; between 2000 and 2005 it was fully restored in the UK and fitted with the present, new body; in 2011 it was repainted in the present grey livery with black wings and black interior. From the Orin Smith collection (see lot 54 Gooding & Company 17.1.09 NS).											**F669**
1921	**Silver Ghost tourer**		25JG	R	320-350.000 AUD		NS		30-04-17	Melbourne	30	Mos
	Grey with black fenders and black interior; sold new to Australia in rolling chassis form, the car was fitted with several bodies over the years, including the present one which was built in the 1990s circa. In good overall condition.											
1921	**Silver Ghost tourer**		33NE	R	100-150.000 EUR	60.264*	78.421*	70.150*	21-05-17	SPA-Francorch.	58	Bon
	Sold new to Sweden in rolling chassis form; restored many years ago. From the Swiss Castle Collection (see lot 336 Sotheby's 14.6.97 $92,338).											
1921	**Silver Ghost cabriolet**		32SG	R	90-120.000 USD	85.569*	110.000*	98.065*	04-06-17	Greenwich	191	Bon
	Ivory with black wings; built with Windovers cabriolet body, the car was sold new to Denmark. Restored in the mid-1980s and fitted with the present, new body (see lot 386 Bonhams 6.2.14 $130,362).											
1914	**Silver Ghost tourer**		64AB	R	300-400.000 GBP	550.300	714.179	623.105	30-06-17	Goodwood	234	Bon
	White with dark blue interior; fitted with Hooper tourer body, the car was sold new to India to the Maharana of Udaipur. In 1979 it was reimported into the UK, where it was fully restored between 2009 and 2013 and fitted with the present new Cann & Co. style tourer body.											
1922	**Silver Ghost tourer**		12YG	R	200-240.000 GBP		NA		15-07-17	Blenheim Pal.	168	Coy
	Burgundy with black wings and maroon interior; new post-war body. In good mechanical order; recently serviced.											
1923	**Silver Ghost tourer**		55PK	R	120-150.000 GBP		NS		26-07-17	Duxford	100	H&H
	Grey with navy blue interior; built with Barker limousine body; bought by the current owner in 1988 in rolling chassis form and subsequently restored and fitted with the present, new London-Edinburgh style tourer body.											
1923	**Silver Ghost Piccadilly roadster**	(Merrimac)	367XH	R	150-225.000 USD	226.496*	291.500*	248.358*	18-08-17	Monterey	166	RMS
	Restoration completed in 2003; original chassis, engine and coachwork.											**F670**
1923	**20hp doctor's coupé**	(J.Young)	GA74	R	35-45.000 GBP	22.425	29.787	26.614	03-09-16	Beaulieu	419	Bon
	Light blue and black with black interior; long restoration conpleted in 2010 (see lot 69 Coys 26.11.98 $26,534).											**F671**
1923	**20hp tourer**	(Smith/Waddington)	83K7	R	45-55.000 GBP	39.458	49.323	46.505	12-04-17	London	351	Coy
	Sold in rolling chassis form to Australia where it was bodied. Restored in 1978; engine rebuilt in 1990. Reimported into the UK in 2013.											
1927	**New Phantom tourer**	(Windovers)	47YC	R	170-190.000 GBP		NS		03-09-16	Beaulieu	494	Bon
	Dark blue with polished aluminium bonnet and blue leather interior; sold new to India.											
1929	**New Phantom Berwick sedan**	(Brewster)	S199FR	L	20-30.000 USD	15.387*	19.800*	17.620*	03-10-16	Philadelphia	230	Bon
	For restoration; for over 50 years in the current ownership.											
1929	**New Phantom all-weather tourer**	(Park Ward)	20KR	R	60-80.000 GBP	112.000	137.267	124.566	12-10-16	Duxford	77	H&H
	Green and black with fawn interior; three owners from new. Some restoration works carried out between the late 1970s-early 1980s. Stored for 20 years, the car has been recently recommissioned.											
1928	**New Phantom tourer**		24FH	R	295-350.000 AUD		NS		27-11-16	Melbourne	85	Mos
	Red with black wings; fitted with a Weyman body, the car was sold new to Australia. Converted to an utility vehicle during WWII; bought in rolling chassis form by a panel beater who retained it for 45 years; acquired in 2012 by the current owner who later had it fully restored and fitted with the present body.											
1926	**New Phantom brougham de ville**	(Charles Clark)	76TC	R	500-700.000 GBP	561.500	708.781	665.995	04-12-16	London	9	Bon
	Black with simulated cane-work decor on the sides and rear; interior upholstered in tapestries from Aubusson, France, to the rear compartment and black leather to the front. Unique specification ordered by its first owner Clarence Warren Gasque. Known ownership history; last serviced in January 2016.											**F672**
1929	**New Phantom Ascot phaeton**	(Brewster)	S368LR	L	300-400.000 USD	223.108*	275.000*	257.758*	19-01-17	Scottsdale	41	Bon
	Brown and pewter with tah interior; several works carried out over the last decade. The engine has covered less than 3,000 miles since the rebuild (see lots 615 Bonhams 13.8.10 $403,000, 143 RM 26.7.14 NS, and 148 RM/Sotheby's 8.10.15 $302,500).											
1930	**New Phantom Newmarket phaeton**	(Brewster)	S126PR	L	175-225.000 USD	145.020	178.750	167.542	19-01-17	Scottsdale	71	Bon
	Blue with silver fenders and light blue interior; restored in the late 1990s (see lots 176 RM 1.5.04 $140,250, 1535 Bonhams 13.8.04 $170,000, 11 Gooding & Company 12.3.10 $170,000, 334 Bonhams 2.6.13 $187,000, and 54 Gooding & Company 16.8.14 $198,000).											
1929	**New Phantom Henley roadster**	(Brewster)	S303LR	L	400-500.000 USD	561.013*	682.000*	642.717*	10-03-17	Amelia Island	112	RMS
	Ivory with tan interior; restored many years ago. Built for chassis S140FR, the body was fitted to chassis S303LR in 1940. From the Orin Smith collection (see RM lots 237 23.9.00 NS, 101 18.1.02 NS, 179 15.8.03 $313,500, and 274 24.7.10 $286,000).											**F673**
1927	**New Phantom Ascot tourer**	(Brewster)	S337FM	L	350-450.000 USD	294.080*	357.500*	336.908*	10-03-17	Amelia Island	120	RMS
	Pale yellow with buff fenders and beige leather interior; built with convertible body, the car was fitted in the 1930s with the present body. Recent concours-quality restoration. From the Orin Smith collection.											
1929	**New Phantom Stratford coupé**	(Brewster)	S285FP	L	100-150.000 GBP	104.540	129.211	120.336	19-03-17	Goodwood	26	Bon
	One of six examples built; imported into the UK in 2008 following 50 years in museum storage; restored in 2008-09; bought in 2014 by the current owner and prepared for historic rallying.											**F674**
1927	**New Phantom Regent convertible**	(Brewster)	S82PM	L	275-325.000 USD	196.581	253.000	215.556	18-08-17	Carmel	79	Bon
	Black with red interior; described as in very good overall condition. Originally built with St Stephens town car body, it was later fitted at the factory with the present body.											
1929	**New Phantom Riviera town car**	(Brewster)	S390LR	L	750-950.000 USD	641.025	825.000	702.900	19-08-17	Monterey	237	RMS
	Black with canework decorating the rear quarter panels and gold-plated exterior trim; in single ownership from the mid-1960s to 1996; restored in the late 1990s preserving the original canework and gold-plated brightwork (see lot 104 RM 21.5.11 $717,545).											**F675**
1933	**Phantom II Continental sedanca de ville**	(Barker)	90MY	R	150-180.000 GBP	162.400	217.324	193.402	07-09-16	London	156	RMS
	Black with leather interior to the front compartment and cloth to the rear; from 1982 to 2003 the car was part of the collection of Sir William McAlpine and during his ownership its was fully restored (see lot 1052 Bonhams 1.12.03 $108,885).											
1930	**Phantom II limousine**	(Windovers)	116GY	R	10-15.000 EUR	62.012*	77.110*	72.800*	25-11-16	Milan	513	RMS
	Black with leather interior to the front compartment and cloth to the rear. From the Duemila Ruote collection.											
1934	**Phantom II cabriolet**	(Binder)	162SK	R	475-575.000 USD		NS		18-01-17	Scottsdale	40	WoA
	Black with red interior; built with Windovers sedanca de ville body, the car was fitted many years ago in the USA with the present body coming from chassis 103GY. In good overall condition; engine overhauled in the 2000s (see lot 251 Bonhams/Brooks 18.8.01 $158,700).											
1932	**Phantom II Continental sports saloon**	(H.J.Mulliner)	80MS	R	140-180.000 USD	89.243	110.000	103.103	19-01-17	Scottsdale	12	Bon
	Red and black with tan leather interior; restored in the 1990s; described as in very good driving order (see lot 909 Bonhams 1.8.03 NS).											

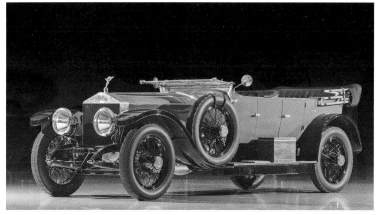
F669: 1914 Rolls-Royce Silver Ghost tourer

F670: 1923 Rolls-Royce Silver Ghost Piccadilly roadster (Merrimac)

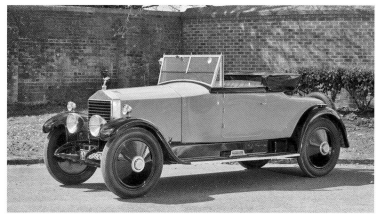
F671: 1923 Rolls-Royce 20hp doctor's coupé (J.Young)

F672: 1926 Rolls-Royce New Phantom brougham de ville (Charles Clark)

F673: 1929 Rolls-Royce New Phantom Henley roadster (Brewster)

F674: 1929 Rolls-Royce New Phantom Stratford coupé (Brewster)

F675: 1929 Rolls-Royce New Phantom Riviera town car (Brewster)

F676: 1934 Rolls-Royce Phantom II Continental sedanca coupé (Gurney Nutting)

Year	Model	(Bodybuilder)	Chassis no.	Steering	Estimate	Hammer price £	$	€	Date	Place	Lot	Auc. H.
1933	**Phantom II tourer**	(Hooper)	110MY	R	275-375.000 USD		NS		19-01-17	Phoenix	143	RMS
{British racing green with tan leather interior; full restoration completed in the late 1990s (see lot 52 Gooding & Company 17.1.09 NS).}
| 1932 | **Phantom II Henley roadster** | | 211AJS | L | NQ | 277.710* | 341.000* | 320.711* | 21-01-17 | Scottsdale | 1382 | B/J |
{Blue with tan interior; documented by the Rolls-Royce Foundation as a re-bodied Henley Roadster by Brewster. Recently restored.}
| 1933 | **Phantom II Continental saloon** | (Gurney Nutting) | 136PY | R | 240-260.000 USD | | NS | | 11-02-17 | Boca Raton | 146 | TFA |
{Maroon with tan interior; concours-quality restoration carried out in 1983 in the USA (see RM lots 235 RM 5.8.00 NS and 26 10.3.01 $82,500).}
| 1933 | **Phantom II Continental cabriolet** | (Barker) | 186MY | R | 700-950.000 USD | | NS | | 10-03-17 | Amelia Island | 69 | G&Co |
{Garnet and black with tan interior; in good overall condition (see lot 58 Gooding & Company 20.8.16 NS).}
| 1934 | **Phantom II Continental sedanca coupé** | (Gurney Nutting) | 201RY | R | 750-950.000 USD | 520.295* | 632.500* | 596.068* | 10-03-17 | Amelia Island | 117 | RMS / F676 |
{Two-tone beige with beige leather interior; sold new in the UK, the car was imported into the USA in the late 1950s. Restored to concours condition between 1970 and 1975, it is described as in excellent overall condition. From the Orin Smith collection.}
| 1933 | **Phantom II Newmarket permanent sedan** | (Brewster) | 289AJS | L | 700-1.000.000 USD | 1.017.968* | 1.237.500* | 1.166.220* | 10-03-17 | Amelia Island | 125 | RMS / F677 |
{Black with black leather roof and leather interior to the front compartment and cloth to the rear; in single ownership from 1955 to 1995 circa; restored in the early 1960s; restored again between 2010 and 2015. From the Orin Smith collection (see lots 50 Sotheby's 5.10.96 NS and 53 Christie's 29.8.99 $167,500).}
| 1934 | **Phantom II Continental sedanca coupé** | (H.J.Mulliner) | 120SK | R | 500-750.000 USD | 235.264* | 286.000* | 269.526* | 10-03-17 | Amelia Island | 138 | RMS |
{Black and grey with light grey leather interior; wing styling modernized in France probably after WWII. Imported into the USA in 1957. Cosmetically restored in the 2000s. From the Orin Smith collection (see lots 42 Christie's 18.8.02 NS, 255 RM 10.10.08 NS, 51 Worldwide Group 2.5.09 NS, 258 RM 22.1.10 $357,500, and 170 RM/Sotheby's 12.3.16 $550,000).}
| 1931 | **Phantom II Croydon convertible** | (Brewster) | 239AJS | L | 700-1.000.000 USD | 416.236* | 506.000* | 476.854* | 10-03-17 | Amelia Island | 160 | RMS |
{Black with green leather interior; concours-quality restoration completed in 2011. From the Orin Smith collection (see lot 6 Blackhawk 12.10.01 $66,000).}
| 1933 | **Phantom II Newport town car** | (Brewster) | 253AJS | L | 200-250.000 USD | 180.972 | 220.000 | 207.328 | 11-03-17 | Amelia Island | 214 | RMS |
{Two-tone grey with broadcloth interior; in single ownership from 1946 to 1994; restoration completed in the late 1990s (see lot 489 Auctions America 28.3.15 $200,000).}
| 1933 | **Phantom II roadster** | | 100PY | R | 80-120.000 EUR | 95.830* | 124.702* | 111.550* | 21-05-17 | SPA-Francorch. | 57 | Bon |
{Built with H.J. Mulliner limousine body, the car was fitted with the present body at date unknown. From the Swiss Castle Collection.}
| 1935 | **20/25hp saloon** | (Hooper) | GRF26 | R | 30-40.000 GBP | 31.050 | 41.244 | 36.850 | 03-09-16 | Beaulieu | 455 | Bon |
{Grey with black wings and grey interior; since 1959 in the same family ownership. Engine overhauled in 2005; interior retrimmed a few years ago.}
| 1934 | **20/25hp tourer** | | GXB8 | R | 50-70.000 USD | 49.066* | 60.500* | 54.305* | 07-10-16 | Hershey | 224 | RMS |
{Red with black fenders and black interior; restored. Since 1974 in the current ownership (see lot 138 RM 10.10.13 $71,500).}
| 1930 | **20/25hp saloon** | | GWP28 | R | 30-40.000 GBP | | NS | | 08-10-16 | Ascot | 319 | Coy |
{Red and cream; built with cabriolet body and later fitted with the present body. Mechanicals recently restored.}
| 1933 | **20/25hp saloon** | (Abbott) | GGA3 | R | 40-50.000 GBP | 44.800 | 56.488 | 52.644 | 07-12-16 | Chateau Impney | 29 | H&H |
{Two-tone grey; recent cosmetic and mechanical works (see lot 34 H & H 20.6.15 $75,389).}
| 1933 | **20/25hp sedanca coupé** | (Gurney Nutting) | GSY20 | R | 125-155.000 GBP | | NS | | 07-12-16 | Chateau Impney | 68 | H&H |
{Dark green and black with tan interior; restored many years ago, it is described as in very good overall condition.}
| 1933 | **20/25hp cabriolet** | (Barker) | GTZ48 | R | 165-220.000 EUR | 119.441 | 149.310 | 140.000 | 08-02-17 | Paris | 144 | RMS |
{Black with original red leather interior; displayed at the Barker stand at the 1933 Paris Motor Show and later sold in the UK. Some restoration works carried out in the 1070s; body repainted to its original colour in more recent years; last serviced in late 2016 (see lots Christie's 49 11.6.05 $117,885, and Gooding & Company 22 17.8.13 NS and 64 7.3.14 $192,500).}
| 1934 | **20/25hp coupé** | (Park Ward) | GHA29 | R | 60-80.000 GBP | 93.340 | 121.137 | 105.689 | 30-06-17 | Goodwood | 240 | Bon / F678 |
{Black with dark blue leather interior; in good overall condition. Restored in the 1990s. Believed unique coachwork.}
| 1933 | **20/25hp saloon** | (Park Ward) | GRW43 | R | 48-56.000 GBP | 51.520 | 66.440 | 58.218 | 08-07-17 | Brooklands | 145 | His |
{Two-tone blue with red leather interior; restored in the late 1990s; engine rebuilt in more recent years.}
| 1934 | **20/25hp tourer** | | GXB8 | R | 110-130.000 USD | | NS | | 17-08-17 | Monterey | 18 | WoA |
{See lot 224 RM/Sotheby's 7.10.16.}
| 1936 | **25/30hp saloon** | (Park Ward) | GGM27 | R | 40-50.000 GBP | | NS | | 12-10-16 | Duxford | 121 | H&H |
{Grey; recently reimported into the UK from the USA.}
| 1936 | **25/30hp saloon** | (Windovers) | GHL20 | R | 28-32.000 GBP | | NS | | 12-10-16 | Duxford | 39 | H&H |
{Cream and brown with brown leather interior; since 1984 in the same family ownership (see lot 94 H & H 28.7.16 NS).}
| 1935 | **25/30hp saloon** | | GHL20 | R | 18-22.000 GBP | 14.280 | 18.006 | 16.780 | 07-12-16 | Chateau Impney | 41 | H&H |
{See lot 39 H & H 12.10.16.}
| 1937 | **25/30hp limousine** | | GMP49 | R | NQ | 12.990* | 15.950* | 15.001* | 21-01-17 | Scottsdale | 8196 | R&S |
{Two-tone body; from the Missoula Auto Museum Collection.}

F677: 1933 Rolls-Royce Phantom II Newmarket permanent sedan (Brewster)

F678: 1934 Rolls-Royce 20/25hp coupé (Park Ward)

Year	Model (Bodybuilder)	Chassis No.	Steering	Estimate	Hammer price £	Hammer price $	Hammer price €	Sale Date	Place	Lot	Auc. H.
1935	25/30hp cabriolet (Caffyns)	GTL56	R	35-40.000 GBP	46.575	57.567	53.612	19-03-17	Goodwood	36	Bon
	Built with Barker saloon body, the car was fitted with the present body in the late 1940s. For 30 years in the current ownership. Restored over a number of years.										
1936	25/30hp saloon (H.J.Mulliner)	GGM10	R	120-160.000 AUD		NS		28-05-17	Sydney	14	Mos
	Blue with grey leather interior; imported into Australia in 1962.										
1937	25/30hp saloon (Lancefield)	GRO3	R	60-80.000 USD		NS		24-06-17	Santa Monica	151	RMS
	Dark green with tan interior; restored.										
1936	Phantom III landaulette (Barker)	3AX97	R	35-50.000 USD	46.160*	59.400*	52.860*	03-10-16	Philadelphia	229	Bon
	Grey and blue; in largely original condition except for the paintwork redone in the past. In working order.										
1937	Phantom III sedan (Brewster)	3BT129	R	180-250.000 USD		NS		19-01-17	Scottsdale	91	Bon
	Coffee and cream; body originally fitted to Phantom II chassis no.216AMS. In 1941 it was modernized by Inskip with their trademark sweeping fender treatment, echoing that of the French caochbuilder Saoutchik, and fitted to the offered car. Former ownership for more than 40 years. Low mileage. Well preserved interior.										
1937	Phantom III saloon (Park Ward)	3BT147	R	115-125.000 GBP		NS		18-02-17	London	344	Coy
	Black with blue leather interior; described as in very good overall condition.										
1938	Phantom III 4-door cabriolet (H.J.Mulliner)	3DL56	R	500-600.000 USD	325.750*	396.000*	373.190*	10-03-17	Amelia Island	140	RMS F679
	Pewter with grey leather interior; built with Hooper limousine body, the car was fitted after WWII with the present, more modern body. Imported into the USA in 1957, it received a concours-quality restoration between 2003 and 2006. From the Orin Smith collection (see lot 908 Bonhams 1.8.03 $79,500).										
1936	Phantom III sedanca de ville (Windovers)	3AX175	R	110-160.000 USD	61.078*	74.250*	69.973*	11-03-17	Amelia Island	20	Mot
	White with leather interior; cosmetically restored in the 1970s. Recent mechanical overhaul.										
1939	Wraith saloon (H.J.Mulliner)	WKC4	R	30-40.000 GBP	62.640	78.983	73.608	07-12-16	Chateau Impney	76	H&H
	Black and grey with grey interior; described as in very good overall condition.										
1938	Wraith sports saloon (Thrupp/Maberly)	WRB57	R	150-180.000 USD		NS		19-01-17	Scottsdale	16	Bon
	Dark blue with tan leather interior; fully restored in the USA in the late 2000s.										
1939	Wraith sports saloon (Thrupp/Maberly)	WRB57	R	110-130.000 USD	111.111*	143.000*	121.836*	19-08-17	Pebble Beach	130	G&Co
	See lot 16 Bonhams 19.1.17.										
1950	Silver Wraith saloon (Park Ward)	WGC63	R	30-40.000 USD	25.644	33.000	29.367	03-10-16	Philadelphia	213	Bon
	Red with black wings and tan interior; imported into the USA in 1971 and subsequently restored. For nearly 40 years in the current ownership.										
1958	Silver Wraith limousine (H.J.Mulliner)	LGLW23	L	160-190.000 USD		NS		06-10-16	Hershey	158	RMS
	Two-tone grey; final Silver Wraith delivered to a customer, the car is fitted with the 4.9-litre engine, automatic transmission and Lucas P100 headlamps. Recently the body has been repainted and the mechanicals overhauled.										
1951	Silver Wraith limousine (H.J.Mulliner)	WOF16	R	30-40.000 EUR	34.059*	41.993*	37.696*	07-10-16	Chateau-sur-Epte	57	Art
	Black with beige leather interior; paintwork redone circa 10 years ago. From the Andre Weber Collection.										
1951	Silver Wraith limousine (Hooper)	BLW15	R	25-30.000 GBP	17.920	22.595	21.058	07-12-16	Chateau Impney	79	H&H
	Black and pale blue with light blue leather interior; exhibited when new at the Hooper stand at the London Motor Show (see lots 173 Christie's 20.11.00 $38,520 and 48 H & H 15.6.13 NS).										
1956	Silver Wraith limousine (H.J.Mulliner)	LFLW22	R	35-55.000 EUR	45.013	56.561	52.900	09-02-17	Paris	397	Bon
	Dark burgundy with brown interior; displayed at the Rolls-Royce stand at the 1956 Paris Motor Show; sold new to France; restored in 1987-88; since 1990 in the current ownership.										
1953	Silver Wraith limousine (H.J.Mulliner)	LBLW8	L	85-110.000 USD	64.829	82.500	73.838	24-06-17	Santa Monica	161	RMS
	Black with beige interior; described as in largely original condition.										
1947	Silver Wraith cabriolet (Franay)	WVA63	R	200-300.000 USD	198.730	242.000	229.343	09-03-17	Amelia Island	120	Bon
	Black with maroon fenders and caramel leather interior; cosmetically refurbished in 2013. Displayed at the 1947 Paris Motor Show and 1948 Deauville Concours d'Elegance (see lots 205 Brooks 20.5.98 $78,154, 115 RM 20.1.11 $165,000, 5045 Barrett-Jackson 19.1.13 $220,000, 58 Worldwide Group 31.8.13 $264,000, 119 RM 8.3.14 NS, and 5077 Barrett-Jackson 17.1.15 $231,000).										
1948	Silver Wraith cabriolet (Franay)	LWAB63	L	400-500.000 USD	389.090*	473.000*	445.755*	10-03-17	Amelia Island	156	RMS F680
	Light blue with beige leather interior; one-off; in the same family ownership from new to 1999 when it was restored to concours condition. From the Orin Smith collection.										
1956	Silver Wraith cabriolet (Park Ward)	LELW94	L	380-460.000 EUR		NS		02-07-17	Monaco	135	Art
	Black and metallic grey with red leather interior; restored in the USA many years ago, the car is described as still in good overall condition (see lot 344 RM/Sotheby's 15.8.15 $297,000).										
1947	Silver Wraith cabriolet (Inskip)	WZB36	R	425-600.000 USD	435.897	561.000	477.972	18-08-17	Monterey	130	RMS
	Dark sapphire blue with red leather interior; in the same ownership from 1957 to 1996 and subsequently restored; three private owners from new (see lot 55 Sotheby's 5.10.96 $184,000).										
1954	Silver Dawn saloon	SPG11	R	30-40.000 GBP	28.000	34.317	31.142	12-10-16	Duxford		H&H
	Shell grey; restored in 1998.										
1955	Silver Dawn saloon	SVJ109	R	25-30.000 GBP	30.800	38.836	36.193	07-12-16	Chateau Impney	17	H&H
	Black and grey with grey leather interior; several works carried out in the 2000s. Automatic transmission (see lot 341 Bonhams 3.3.12 $38,331).										

F679: 1938 Rolls-Royce Phantom III 4-door cabriolet (H.J.Mulliner)

F680: 1948 Rolls-Royce Silver Wraith cabriolet (Franay)

Year	Model	(Bodybuilder)	Chassis no.	Steering	Estimate	Hammer price £	$	€	Date	Place	Lot	Auc. H.
1951	**Silver Dawn saloon**		SFC82	R	20-25.000 GBP	34.465	43.457	40.500	07-12-16	Chateau Impney	7	**H&H**
Restored several years ago; last serviced in 2013.												
1953	**Silver Dawn cabriolet**	(Park Ward)	LSLE31	L	400-500.000 USD	370.993*	451.000*	425.022*	10-03-17	Amelia Island	128	**RMS** **F681**
One-off finished in silver with red leather interior; automatic transmission. Concours-quality restoration carried out in the 2000s. From the Orin Smith collection.												
1955	**Silver Cloud saloon**		SWA86	R	20-25.000 GBP		NS		03-09-16	Beaulieu	510	**Bon**
Two-tone grey; for over 50 years in the same family ownership. Recently serviced.												
1959	**Silver Cloud estate car**	(H.J.Mulliner)	LSMH65	L	375-475.000 USD	479.576*	583.000*	549.419*	10-03-17	Amelia Island	146	**RMS** **F682**
Two-tone green with parchment leather interior; one of two examples built on the short-wheelbase chassis; bodied by H.J. Mulliner in collaboration with Harold Radford; Webasto sunroof. Four owners. Restored in recent years. From the Orin Smith collection.												
1958	**Silver Cloud Empress saloon lwb**	(Hooper)	BLC2	R	50-70.000 EUR		NS		08-04-17	Essen	211	**Coy**
Black with blue interior; in very good original condition; 25,000 miles on the odometer.												
1958	**Silver Cloud "Honeymoon Express" cabriolet**	(Freestone/Webb)	SGE270	R	1.300-1.800.000 USD	1.108.454*	1.347.500*	1.269.884*	10-03-17	Amelia Island	145	**RMS** **F683**
Black and dark green with buckskin leather interior; one of two examples built. Bought in 2012 by Orin Smith (its third owner) for his collection and subsequently restored (see lot 350 RM 12.5.12 NS).												
1959	**Silver Cloud cabriolet**	(J.Young)	LSHF169	L	750-950.000 USD	551.965*	671.000*	632.350*	10-03-17	Amelia Island	147	**RMS**
Dark blue with saddle leather interior; restored in recent years. From the Orin Smith collection (see lot 94 Gooding & Company 20.8.06 NS).												
1957	**Silver Cloud cabriolet**	(H.J.Mulliner)	L146SDD	L	650-900.000 USD		NS		18-08-17	Monterey	161	**RMS**
Dark green with biscuit leather interior; sold new to the USA; the car remained with its first owner until 1977 when it was bought by the second owner who retained it for 30 years. Subsequently bought by the third owner and restored. Automatic transmission.												
1960	**Silver Cloud II saloon**		STB72	R	275-32.500 GBP		NS		12-10-16	Duxford	42	**H&H**
Cream and silver with cream interior; some restoration works carried out in the early 2000s.												
1961	**Silver Cloud II saloon**		SYD490	R	25-40.000 EUR	33.758	41.010	37.548	30-10-16	Paris	137	**Art**
Two-tone grey; restored in 1990.												
1961	**Silver Cloud II saloon lwb**		LLCB80	L	70-90.000 EUR		NS		02-07-17	Monaco	215	**Art**
Black with beige interior; sold new to the USA; mechanicals overhauled in 2004; body repainted in 2006; imported into Europe in 2016 (see lot 6 Bonhams 5.6.16 $50,600).												
1962	**Silver Cloud II cabriolet**	(Mulliner,Park Ward)	LSAE281	L	230-270.000 GBP		NS		08-09-16	Fontwell Park	138	**Coy**
Sold new to the USA, the car was reimported into the UK in the late 1990s. Subsequently it was restored and finished in the present metallic grey livery with biscuit leather interior (see lots Historics 240 12.3.16 NS, and Coys 128 16.4.16 NS and 156 14.5.16 $480,020).												
1962	**Silver Cloud II cabriolet**	(Mulliner,Park Ward)	LSAE281	L	190-210.000 GBP	237.000	301.346	281.556	05-12-16	London	120	**Coy** **F684**
See lot 138 Coys 8.9.16.												
1962	**Silver Cloud II cabriolet**	(Mulliner,Park Ward)	LSAE583	L	335-395.000 EUR		NS		09-02-17	Paris	387	**Bon**
Ivory with blue leather interior; restored at unspecified date. In the same family ownership from new until the current vendor purchased it.												
1963	**Silver Cloud III saloon**		LSDW479	L	50-70.000 USD	42.741*	55.000*	48.945*	03-10-16	Philadelphia	206	**Bon** **F685**
Black with light grey leather interior; in original condition. Two owners and 31,142 miles covered; in need of recommissioning prior to use. From the Natural History Museum of Los Angeles.												
1965	**Silver Cloud III saloon**		LSGT449	L	30-35.000 GBP		NS		07-12-16	London	369	**Bon**
Blue; sold new to the USA and reimported into Europe in 1998. In good condition; brakes and gearbox require some attention (see lot 329 Bonhams 4.2.16 NS).												
1962	**Silver Cloud III saloon lwb**	(J.Young)	CAL5	R	65-75.000 GBP		NS		24-02-17	Stoneleigh P.	537	**SiC**
Dark green with champagne leather interior. Described as in very good overall condition; 105,000 miles covered. Some recommissioning works and partial repainting in 2015.												
1963	**Silver Cloud III saloon**		LSDW231	L	120-150.000 USD	89.744	115.500	98.753	17-08-17	Monterey	68	**WoA**
Two-tone exterior finish; sold new to the USA; fully restored.												
1965	**Silver Cloud III saloon**		LSKP109	L	120-150.000 USD	59.829*	77.000*	65.604*	19-08-17	Pebble Beach	137	**G&Co**
Shell grey with original black leather interior; recent mechanical and cosmetic freshening.												
1965	**Silver Cloud III cabriolet**	(Mulliner,Park Ward)	LCSC85B	L	160-220.000 EUR	174.418	231.695	207.000	03-09-16	Chantilly	28	**Bon**
Green with tan leather interior; sold new to the USA, the car was reimported into Europe in 2003. Recent refurbishment works (see lot 424 Bonhams 01.12.11 $178,509).												
1966	**Silver Cloud III cabriolet**	(Mulliner,Park Ward)	CSC81C	R	340-380.000 GBP		NS		07-12-16	London	334	**Bon**
Dark blue with grey leather interior; sold new to the Malaysian royal family, the car was reimported into the UK in the 2000s and subsequently restored (see lot 281 Historics 28.11.15 NS).												
1965	**Silver Cloud III cabriolet**	(Mulliner,Park Ward)	LSJR571C	L	100-180.000 EUR		NS		09-02-17	Paris	316	**Bon**
Black; sold new to Switzerland; reimported into the UK in 1987 and restored in 1989; reimported into Switzerland in 1995; exhibited at the 2011 Villa d'Este Concours d'Elegance (see lot 1699 Sotheby's 5.12.94 $82,097).												
1963	**Silver Cloud III cabriolet**	(Mulliner,Park Ward)	LSCX789	L	550-650.000 USD		NS		11-02-17	Boca Raton	153	**TFA**
Shell grey with black interior; concours-quality restoration (see lot 16 Gooding & Company 20.8.16 NS).												
1965	**Silver Cloud III cabriolet**	(Mulliner,Park Ward)	CSC11B	R	150-180.000 GBP		NS		29-03-17	Duxford	85	**H&H**
Medium metallic blue with beige leather interior; described as in good overall condition, the car has seen little use in the last years and requires recommissioning prior to use.												
1963	**Silver Cloud III cabriolet**	(Mulliner,Park Ward)	SCX361	L	750-850.000 USD	473.970	610.000	519.720	19-08-17	Monterey	S110	**Mec** **F686**
Black with white interior; fully restored and converted to left-hand drive.												
1965	**Silver Cloud III coupé**	(Mulliner,Park Ward)	LSGT641C	L	60-70.000 GBP	66.134	82.668	77.946	12-04-17	London	345	**Coy**
Mahogany with magnolia leather interior; in the same family ownership since new; in original condition (see lot 138 Coys 8.3.16 NS).												
1965	**Silver Cloud III coupé**	(Mulliner,Park Ward)	CSC65B	R	60-70.000 GBP	67.580	87.705	76.521	30-06-17	Goodwood	243	**Bon** **F687**
Red with black leather interior; restored at unspecified date.												
1964	**Phantom V**	(Mulliner,Park Ward)	5VC49	R	50-60.000 GBP	47.250	59.318	55.911	24-02-17	Stoneleigh P.	547	**SiC**
Black and blue with black leather interior to the front compartment and biscuit leather to the rear. Interior retrimmed in 2015; last serviced in 2013.												
1960	**Phantom V**	(Park Ward)	5AS69	R	80-120.000 USD	43.433*	52.800*	49.759*	10-03-17	Amelia Island	79	**G&Co**
Black; always well maintained.												
1963	**Phantom V**	(J.Young)	5LVA99	L	60-80.000 EUR	126.062	160.805	144.000	18-06-17	Fontainebleau	70	**Ose**
In very good condition; brakes rebuilt in 2005; engine rebuilt in 2008.												

F681: 1953 Rolls-Royce Silver Dawn cabriolet (Park Ward)

F682: 1959 Rolls-Royce Silver Cloud estate car (H.J.Mulliner)

F683: 1958 Rolls-Royce Silver Cloud "Honeymoon Express" cabriolet (Freestone/Webb)

F684: 1962 Rolls-Royce Silver Cloud II cabriolet (Mulliner,Park Ward)

F685: 1963 Rolls-Royce Silver Cloud III saloon

F686: 1963 Rolls-Royce Silver Cloud III cabriolet (Mulliner,Park Ward)

F687: 1965 Rolls-Royce Silver Cloud III coupé (Mulliner,Park Ward)

F688: 1970 Rolls-Royce Silver Shadow 2-door (Mulliner,Park Ward)

Year	Model	(Bodybuilder)	Chassis no.	Steering	Estimate	Hammer Price £	$	€	Date	Place	Lot	Auc. H.
1975	**Silver Shadow**		SRH22044	R	20-24.000 GBP	17.360	21.585	20.379	26-11-16	Weybridge	192	His
	Shell grey with blue interior; stored from 1984 to 2007, the car has covered 18,814 miles since new.											
1980	**Silver Shadow II**		SRX38859	L	18-26.000 EUR	18.678*	23.029*	20.672*	07-10-16	Chateau-sur-Epte	56	Art
	White with black vinyl roof and red leather interior; it requires servicing prior to use. From the Andre Weber Collection.											
1980	**Silver Shadow II**		SRL39777	L	20-30.000 EUR	18.650	23.295	21.000	06-11-16	Lyon	329	Ose
	Metallic burgundy with biscuit leather interior; in good overall condition (see lot 218 Osenat 08.11.15 $25,422).											
1969	**Silver Shadow cabriolet**	(Mulliner,Park Ward)	CRH5073	R	40-45.000 GBP	34.720	43.171	40.758	26-11-16	Weybridge	175	His
	White; described as in good overall condition. Body repainted.											
1968	**Silver Shadow cabriolet**	(Mulliner,Park Ward)	CRH5023	R	18-24.000 GBP	24.640	30.145	28.533	04-03-17	Brooklands	128	His
	Red with beige interior; in good running order (see lot 142 Bonhams 5.9.15 $42,902).											
1970	**Silver Shadow cabriolet**		DRH7612	R	28-36.000 EUR	25.345	32.321	28.920	10-06-17	Lyon	122	Agu
	Burgundy with new magnolia interior; the body requires some attention; in good mechanical condition.											
1970	**Silver Shadow 2-door**	(Mulliner,Park Ward)	CRH7260	R	20-25.000 GBP	20.700	27.496	24.567	03-09-16	Beaulieu	458	Bon **F688**
	Maroon; restored between 2013 and 2015.											
1968	**Silver Shadow 2-door**	(Mulliner,Park Ward)	CRH3827	R	22-25.000 GBP	21.840	26.767	24.290	12-10-16	Duxford	101	H&H
	Beige with black Everflex roof; body repainted in 2012, engine overhauled in 2015 (see lot 32 H & H 20.6.15 $27,495).											
1967	**Silver Shadow 2-door**	(Mulliner,Park Ward)	CRX1937	L	32-40.000 GBP		NS		12-10-16	Duxford	48	H&H
	Black with red leather interior; in very good overall condition (see lot 298 Bonhams 23.1.10 $26,008).											
1966	**Silver Shadow 2-door**	(Mulliner,Park Ward)	CRH2154	R	38-48.000 AUD	28.224	35.094	33.132	27-11-16	Melbourne	84	Mos
	Blue with grey leather interior; in good overall condition. Imported into Australia in 1989.											
1971	**Phantom VI** (Mulliner,Park Ward)		PRH4632	R	35-39.000 GBP	46.813	59.261	54.345	12-11-16	Birmingham	607	SiC
	41,000 miles on the odometer; the paintwork requires some attention. First owner the AVIS car rental company (see lot 324 Bonhams 21.6.03 NS).											
1971	**Phantom VI** (Mulliner,Park Ward)		PRH4609	R	NA		NS		19-11-16	Anaheim	S140.1	Mec
	Burgundy and white with black and green leather interior (see lot 1091 Auctions America 25.6.16 NS).											
1970	**Phantom VI** (Mulliner,Park Ward)		PRH4611	R	48-60.000 GBP	59.360	77.239	69.095	20-05-17	Ascot	228	His **F689**
	Black and blue with blue leather interior; in good overall condition.											
1971	**Phantom VI four-door cabriolet** (Frua)		PRH4643	L	400-600.000 USD	299.145	385.000	328.020	19-08-17	Monterey	228	RMS **F690**
	Burgundy with champagne leather interior; one-off completed in 1993 because of the death of Pietro Frua in 1983. Exhibited at the 1993 Geneva Motor Show. 72 miles covered (see lots 652 Brooks 5.5.97 NS and 144 Gooding & Company 21.8.16 NS).											
1989	**Corniche cabriolet** (Mulliner,Park Ward)		2908	R	35-45.000 GBP	47.725	63.393	56.640	03-09-16	Beaulieu	434	Bon
	Grey with parchment leather interior; in very good overall condition.											
1984	**Corniche cabriolet** (Mulliner,Park Ward)		09129	R	100-120.000 GBP	135.000	170.897	156.722	12-11-16	Birmingham	323	SiC
	Royal blue with magnolia leather interior; the car was delivered new to the London Embassy of Qatar for the personal use of the Emir when in the UK. Resold by the Qatar Royal Family's private collection of London cars in 2005 with an odometer reading of 11,466 miles.											
1973	**Corniche cabriolet** (Mulliner,Park Ward)		DRH14275	R	90-110.000 GBP	95.625	121.052	111.011	12-11-16	Birmingham	330	SiC
	Yellow with black interior; in the same family ownership from new to 2016. Less than 26,000 miles covered.											
1985	**Corniche cabriolet** (Mulliner,Park Ward)		10305	L	30-35.000 EUR	62.967*	78.296*	73.920*	25-11-16	Milan	535	RMS
	Blue; approximately 50,000 kms. From the Duemila Ruote collection.											
1982	**Corniche cabriolet** (Mulliner,Park Ward)		DRH0050699	R	40-50.000 GBP	76.160	96.030	89.496	07-12-16	Chateau Impney	73	H&H
	Café au lait and ivory with sandalwood leather interior; one owner and less than 11,000 miles covered (see lot 109 Christie's 7.6.04 NS).											
1976	**Corniche cabriolet** (Mulliner,Park Ward)		DRH23528	R	36-42.000 GBP	28.000	34.255	32.424	04-03-17	Brooklands	175	His
	Ivory with brown leather interior; recently serviced.											
1982	**Corniche cabriolet** (Mulliner,Park Ward)		05384	L	50-60.000 EUR		NS		19-03-17	Fontainebleau	236	Ose
	Black; 41,000 miles on the odometer.											
1990	**Corniche cabriolet** (Mulliner,Park Ward)		30109	R	50-60.000 GBP	63.562	79.077	73.579	29-03-17	Duxford	29	H&H
	Red with magnolia leather interior; 64,900 miles covered. Last serviced in July 2015.											
1972	**Corniche cabriolet** (Mulliner,Park Ward)		DRA12467	L	50-60.000 EUR	52.526	67.002	60.000	18-06-17	Fontainebleau	77	Ose
	White with beige interior; restored 10 years ago (see lot 170 Artcurial 9.7.16 $47,504).											
1988	**Corniche cabriolet** (Mulliner,Park Ward)		23510	L	55-60.000 USD	49.702	63.250	56.609	24-06-17	Santa Monica	126	RMS
	In original condition; just one owner.											

F689: 1970 Rolls-Royce Phantom VI (Mulliner,Park Ward)

F690: 1971 Rolls-Royce Phantom VI four-door cabriolet (Frua)

Year	Model	(Bodybuilder)	Chassis No.	Steering	Estimate	Hammer Price £	$	€	Date	Place	Lot	Auc. H.
1983	Corniche cabriolet	(Mulliner,Park Ward)	07088	L	NA	44.083	56.100	50.210	24-06-17	Santa Monica	199	RMS F691
Red with beige interior; one owner; 12,300 original miles; regularly serviced.												
1980	Corniche cabriolet	(Mulliner,Park Ward)	DRH50301	R	32-38.000 GBP	34.720	44.775	39.234	08-07-17	Brooklands	163	His
Blue with magnolia leather interior; in good overall condition. Later fuel-injected engine.												
1976	Corniche 2-door	(Mulliner,Park Ward)	CRX24038	L	23-28.000 EUR	39.431	49.253	44.400	05-11-16	Lyon	226	Agu
White with black vinyl roof and black leather interior; in good overall condition. Body repainted in the 1990s.												
1976	Corniche 2-door	(Mulliner,Park Ward)	CRE26154	L	60-80.000 USD	59.721*	72.600*	68.418*	10-03-17	Amelia Island	55	G&Co
Sand and brown with dark tan interior; in very good condition. Less than 27,000 miles covered (see lot 26 Bonhams 5.6.16 $50,600).												
1972	Corniche 2-door	(Mulliner,Park Ward)	CRH12347	R	25-30.000 GBP	41.400	51.170	47.656	19-03-17	Goodwood	68	Bon
Maroon with beige interior; restored in the 1990s.												
1977	Corniche 2-door	(Mulliner,Park Ward)	CRF30463	L	35-45.000 USD	21.610	27.500	24.613	24-06-17	Santa Monica	149	RMS
White; two owners; regularly serviced.												
1972	Corniche 2-door	(Mulliner,Park Ward)	13581	R	30-35.000 GBP		NS		15-07-17	Blenheim Pal.	148	Coy
Metallic claret with white roof and magnolia leather interior; described as in very good overall condition.												
1980	Camargue	(PF/Mulliner, Park Ward)	JRH50294	R	15-20.000 GBP	25.960	33.008	30.840	05-12-16	London	139	Coy
Blue with tan leather interior; in good overall condition. Body recently repainted (see lots Brooks 993 6.12.99 $16,700, Christie's 63 4.12.01 $36,766, and Coys 110 11.7.15 NS, 120 Coys 8.3.16 NS and 147 2.7.16 $30,084).												
1982	Camargue	(PF/Mulliner, Park Ward)	JRH50491	R	75-90.000 GBP		NS		04-03-17	Brooklands	177	His
Royal blue with grey leather interior; one owner; less than 5,000 miles covered.												
1977	Camargue	(PF/Mulliner, Park Ward)	JRF30980	L	38-46.000 USD	37.939*	46.200*	43.784*	09-03-17	Amelia Island	179	Bon F692
Black with black interior; 59,000 miles covered. Brakes recently serviced. First owner Sammy Davis Jr.												
1983	Camargue	(PF/Mulliner, Park Ward)	JRX50231	L	40-50.000 EUR	47.273	60.302	54.000	18-06-17	Fontainebleau	84	Ose
Red with original leather interior; body repainted; 40,000 kms on the odometer.												
1975	Camargue	(PF/Mulliner, Park Ward)	JRH18624	R	45-55.000 GBP		NS		26-07-17	Duxford	104	H&H
Blue with turquoise interior; described as in very good overall condition; 34,500 miles covered (see lots 95 Christie's 6.3.97 $69,817 and 331 Sotheby's 14.6.97 $54,504).												
1980	Silver Wraith II		LRH0039342	R	90-110.000 GBP		NS		12-11-16	Birmingham	325	SiC
Dark red with black roof; car used by HRH Princess Margaret until 2002 when it was inherited by her son who resold it later that year. Described as in very good condition; 48,000 miles covered.												
1980	Silver Wraith II		LRL41292C	L	NQ	13.240*	16.500*	15.523*	11-02-17	Boca Raton	171	TFA
White with tan interior; two owners and just over 35,000 original miles (see lot 168 RM 20.1.11 $25,300).												
1980	Silver Wraith II		LRH0039277	R	14-19.000 GBP		NS		26-07-17	Duxford	34	H&H
Metallic pewter with grey leather interior; in good overall condition. Little used in the last years and recommissioned in late 2016.												
1984	Silver Spirit		09722	R	20-25.000 GBP	21.600	27.343	25.075	12-11-16	Birmingham	337	SiC
Metallic green with champagne interior; 6,690 miles covered. Last serviced in June 2016.												
1980	Silver Spirit		01304	R	10-14.000 GBP	11.480	14.045	13.294	04-03-17	Brooklands	127	His
Claret with tan interior; one owner and 41,001 miles covered. Recently recommissioned.												
1994	Silver Spur III		55376	L	30-40.000 USD	15.814*	20.350*	18.109*	03-10-16	Philadelphia	207	Bon
White with tan leather interior; three owners and less than 23,000 miles covered.												
2000	Silver Seraph		04092	R	25-30.000 GBP	18.080	22.159	20.109	12-10-16	Duxford	34	H&H
Grey with cream interior; last serviced in May 2016.												
1998	Silver Seraph		01662	R	30-35.000 GBP	29.120	35.689	32.387	12-10-16	Duxford	61	H&H
Silver with dark blue leather interior; 45,800 miles on the odometer (see lot 105 H & H 18.5.16 $43,182).												
1999	Silver Seraph		01891	L	35-45.000 USD	34.655*	44.550*	39.716*	04-06-17	Greenwich	123	Bon
Black with black and oyster interior; under 31,000 original miles. Recently serviced.												
2002	Corniche		02008	L	80-90.000 EUR	128.795*	160.151*	151.200*	25-11-16	Milan	597	RMS
White with burgundy interior; 32,280 kms. From the Duemila Ruote collection.												
2001	Corniche		68595	L	120-150.000 EUR	107.639	135.254	126.500	09-02-17	Paris	381	Bon
Blue with beige interior; 19,470 kms covered. Last serviced in February 2015.												
2001	Corniche		68136	L	90-120.000 EUR		NS		02-07-17	Monaco	116	Art
Lime green with magnolia leather interior; less than 29,000 kms covered. Recently serviced.												

F691: 1983 Rolls-Royce Corniche cabriolet (Mulliner,Park Ward)

F692: 1977 Rolls-Royce Camargue (PF/Mulliner, Park Ward)

Year	Model	(Bodybuilder)	Chassis no.	Steering	Estimate	Hammer price £	$	€	Date	Place	Lot	Auc. H.
2005	**Phantom**		00242	R	135-155.000 GBP	123.750	156.655	143.661	12-11-16	Birmingham	322	SiC
First owner Sir Elton John; approximately 6,600 miles covered.												
2003	**Phantom**		00027	R	70-80.000 GBP	99.680	125.687	117.134	07-12-16	Chateau Impney	8	H&H
Light metallic blue with beige leather interior; approximately 5,100 miles on the odometer.												

ROVER (GB) *(1904-)*

Year	Model	(Bodybuilder)	Chassis no.	Steering	Estimate	£	$	€	Date	Place	Lot	Auc. H.
1937	**Light Six saloon**		812122	R	9-11.000 GBP	11.760	14.692	13.896	23-02-17	Donington Park	63	H&H
Black with brown interior; for 32 years in the current ownership. 10,000 miles covered since the restoration carried out in 1990.												
1936	**12 saloon**		641566	R	11-13.000 GBP	18.480	22.967	21.461	16-11-16	Donington Park	38	H&H
Black with red leather interior; less than 9,000 miles covered since the restoration carried out in the 1990s.												
1946	**P2 10 saloon**		6110831	R	9-11.000 GBP		NS		07-12-16	Chateau Impney	34	H&H
Black; in good overall condition. Refreshed in 2000. For 62 years with the previous owner.												
1947	**P2 12 tourer**		756183	R	12-16.000 GBP	12.880	16.759	14.992	20-05-17	Ascot	180	His **F693**
Blue; original leather interior; restored 15 years ago.												
1978	**Land Rover Cerimonial**		91184307C	R	20-30.000 GBP	44.850	59.763	53.040	10-09-16	Goodwood	144	Bon
Dark green; in original condition, 2,201 miles covered. Last used in November 2012; offered by the Ministry of Defence.												
1957	**Land Rover**		111703585	R	30-35.000 GBP	25.300	33.712	29.920	10-09-16	Goodwood	169	Bon
Restored in the early 1990s; in the same family ownership from 1961 to 2015 (see lot 114 Coys 10.1.15 $50,936).												
1950	**Land Rover**		R06105044	R	25-28.000 GBP	39.938	50.558	46.364	12-11-16	Birmingham	662	SiC
Light green; fully restored between 2010 and 2014.												
1958	**P4 90 saloon**		610900642	R	NQ	8.960*	11.141*	10.518*	26-11-16	Weybridge	116	His
Grey with red leather interior; restored several years ago (see lot 249 Historics 1.9.12 NS).												
1970	**P5B 3.5 saloon**		84006327D	R	8-10.000 GBP		NS		16-11-16	Donington Park	9	H&H
Ivory; automatic transmission.												
1968	**P5B 3.5 Coupé**		B600059783B	L	25-5.000 EUR	17.173*	21.353*	20.160*	25-11-16	Milan	516	RMS
Light grey with burgundy leather interior; automatic transmission. From the Duemila Ruote collection.												
1975	**Range Rover 2-door**		35816833D	L	40-60.000 EUR	33.915	45.052	40.250	03-09-16	Chantilly	4	Bon
Gold with bronze interior; restored between 2015 and 2016.												
1971	**Range Rover 2-door**		35501436A	R	7-10.000 GBP	23.000	30.551	27.296	03-09-16	Beaulieu	401	Bon
Gold with beige vinyl interior; for restoration.												
1979	**Range Rover 2-door**		35653050F	R	35-40.000 GBP		NS		10-09-16	Goodwood	168	Bon
Gold with tan cloth interior; extensive renovation works carried out in 2013. First owned by Colin Chapman.												
1975	**Range Rover 2-door**		35510719D	R	18-20.000 GBP	36.795	45.365	40.721	08-10-16	Ascot	341	Coy
Sand; in good working order. Body repainted; 50,000 miles on the odometer.												
1970	**Range Rover 2-door**		35500026A	R	80-100.000 GBP	86.024	104.502	95.676	29-10-16	London	115	Coy
Red with beige interior; built to near final production standard, the car is one of the 20 examples prepared for the press launch of the model. It remained in the factory ownership until 1973. Acquired in the early 2000s by the current owner and subsequently fully restored.												
1973	**Range Rover 2-door**		35507499B	R	24-28.000 GBP	22.960	28.548	26.953	26-11-16	Weybridge	173	His
Gold with beige interior; in very good overall condition. Several mechanical works carried out recently.												
1983	**3.5 SD1 Rally**		249998	R	40-60.000 GBP	35.650	47.504	42.160	10-09-16	Goodwood	132	Bon
Works car built by the Austin-Rover Competitions Department; sold to private hands, it was acquired by Austin-Rover's parts division, Unipart Group Ltd and prepared for the 1986 Himalayan Rally where it was driven by Philip Young. Restored in the 1990s. From the late 1990s in the collection of the late Philip Young.												
1984	**Metro Turbo**		31976	R	16-20.000 GBP		NS		24-02-17	Stoneleigh P.	903	SiC
Described as in very good original condition; for 30 years with its first owner; 7,317 miles covered.												
1985	**MG Metro 6R4 Group B**		570124	R	100-120.000 GBP	113.500	151.239	134.225	10-09-16	Goodwood	122	Bon **F694**
White and blue Rothmans Rally livery; car raced in period at hill climb events and rallies. Exported in 1997 to Australia where it was fitted with a 3.0.litre, International Specification engine from specialist Nelson Engineering Services. According to an article in Autosport in 1992, this car is built on an ex-Works shell; however this information is not verified.												
1987	**MG Metro 6R4 Clubman**		570146	R	110-160.000 EUR		NS		02-07-17	Monaco	191	Art
Road version finished in red and yellow; 6,600 miles covered; never raced.												

F693: 1947 Rover P2 12 tourer

F694: 1985 Rover MG Metro 6R4 Group B

F695: 1998 Ruf CTR2 Sport

F696: 1972 Saab Sonnett III coupé

Year	Model (Bodybuilder)	Chassis no.	Steering	Estimate	£	$	€	Date	Place	Lot	Auc. H.
1994	**Mini cabriolet**	92293	L	15-25.000 EUR	21.433*	26.038*	23.840*	30-10-16	Paris	166	Art
	Blue; 19,600 kms covered. Cooper S look.										
2000	**Mini Cooper Sport 500**	188464	R	17-20.000 GBP	23.800	29.593	27.939	26-11-16	Weybridge	181	His
	British racing green with platinum silver roof and stripes; 439 miles covered. In the same family ownership since new.										
1997	**Mini Cooper 35° Anniversary**	138826	L	40-60.000 EUR		NS		10-02-17	Paris	8	Art
	Green with white roof; two owners and 19 kms covered.										

RUF (D)

1998	**CTR2 Sport**	PR06002	L	450-550.000 EUR	449.098*	561.406*	526.400*	08-02-17	Paris	139	RMS
	Yellow with light grey interior; bought new by racing driver Steve Beddor who had placed second overall at the 1997 Pikes Peak hill climb at the wheel of another RUF CTR2. Imported into the UK in 2016; 17,647 kms on the odometer.										**F695**
1989	**CTR coupé**	PR06015	L	500-800.000 EUR		NS		02-07-17	Monaco	174	Art
	Yellow; one of 28 examples built; raced in the 1990s; 41,130 kms covered; recently serviced.										

SAAB (S) (1950-)

1976	**95 station wagon**	95763000068	R	6-8.000 EUR	6.150	7.602	7.080	18-03-17	Lyon	212	Agu
	Ivory and dark brown; in good overall condition. Original interior.										
1964	**96 Gran Turismo 850**	213962	L	NQ	23.374*	30.800*	27.434*	17-09-16	Aspen	146	TFA
	Red with red interior; restored.										
1972	**Sonnett III coupé**	97725001063	L	20-25.000 EUR	13.831*	17.998*	16.100*	21-05-17	SPA-Francorch.	41	Bon
	Black with beige interior; sold new to the USA, the car was imported into Belgium in 2005 and subsequently restored (see lot 352 Bonhams 2.6.14 $26,383).										**F696**

SAFIR (GB)

1987	**GT40 Mark V**	GT40P1119	R	180-240.000 GBP	197.500	263.169	233.564	10-09-16	Goodwood	178	Bon
	Light blue and orange Gulf Oil livery; one of 40 examples built between 1980 and mid-1990s. Since 1991 in the current ownership. Restoration completed in 2011. 302 Ford V8 engine.										

SALEEN (USA) (1983-)

2004	**S7**	0045	L	390-450.000 USD	389.090	473.000	445.755	11-03-17	Amelia Island	222	RMS
	Silver with beige interior; less than 1,500 miles covered.										
2005	**S7R**	0060	L	400-600.000 EUR	379.617	560.276	431.712	02-07-17	Monaco	190	Art
	Blue and white; sold new to Europe; raced at the GT Endurance Championship until 2009. Bought in 2011 by the current owner and restored. Engine rebuilt.										**F697**

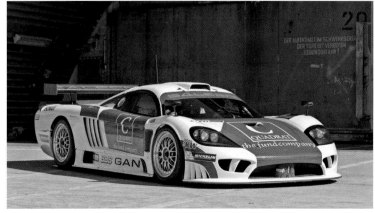

F697: 2005 Saleen S7R

F698: 1922 Salmson AL3 GSS Course

Year	Model	(Bodybuilder)	Chassis no.	Steering	Estimate	Hammer price £	Hammer price $	Hammer price €	Date	Place	Lot	Auc. H.

SALMSON (F) (1921-1957)

Year	Model	(Bodybuilder)	Chassis no.	Steering	Estimate	£	$	€	Date	Place	Lot	Auc. H.
1922	AL3 GSS Course		463	R	150-200.000 EUR	135.514	167.497	156.000	19-03-17	Fontainebleau	210	Ose F698

Dark blue; from 1965 to 1992 at the Le Mans Museum; bought in 1994 by the current owner and subsequently restored. New body.

| 1955 | 2300 Sport (Chapron) | | 85235 | R | 40-60.000 EUR | | NS | | 05-11-16 | Lyon | 246 | Agu |

Dark grey with red interior; bought in 2006 by the current owner and subsequently fully restored.

| 1955 | 2300 Sport cabriolet (Chapron) | | 85188 | R | 150-250.000 EUR | | NS | | 18-03-17 | Lyon | 194 | Agu |

Light grey with dark green interior; restored in the early 2000s. One of five examples built, the offered car was exhibited at the 1955 Paris Motor Show.

| 1955 | 2300 Sport coupé (Chapron) | | 85235 | L | 40-60.000 EUR | | NS | | 22-04-17 | Bagatelle | 191 | Agu |

Dark grey with red interior; bought in 2006 by the current owner and subsequently fully restored (see lot 246 Aguttes 11.5.16 NS).

SAXON (USA) (1913-1923)

| 1914 | Model A roadster | | 19957 | L | 10-15.000 USD | 855* | 1.100* | 979* | 03-10-16 | Philadelphia | 246 | Bon |

Complete, for restoration. From the Bloomington Collection.

SEARS (USA) (1908-1912)

| 1909 | Model J runabout | | 2938 | L | 15-20.000 EUR | | NS | | 18-06-17 | Fontainebleau | 50 | Ose |

Black.

SHELBY AMERICAN (USA) (1962-1970)

| 1965 | Cobra 289 | | CSX2442 | L | 1.000-1.150.000 USD | | NS | | 03-09-16 | Auburn | 4151 | AA |

Red with black interior; early in its life the car was damaged in the front end in a minor accident and in 1966 it was acquired, still unrepaired, by a new owner who repaired it and retained it for nearly 50 years. Stored from 1973 to the 1990s when it was restored. 25,952 miles on the odometer. With hardtop.

| 1964 | Cobra 289 | | CSX2216 | L | 825-875.000 USD | | NS | | 03-09-16 | Auburn | 4166 | AA |

Red with black interior; prepared for racing in the 1970s and raced until 1982 when it was sold with a replacement engine.

| 1963 | Cobra 289 | | CSX2082 | L | 480-520.000 GBP | 459.200 | 614.501 | 546.861 | 07-09-16 | London | 122 | RMS |

Red with black interior; sold new in the USA, the car was damaged in an accident in the 1970s and subsequently repaired. In 2003 it was acquired by the current owner and imported into the UK. Fuel tank recently replaced (see lot 697 Barrett-Jackson 16.01.03 $167,400).

| 1962 | Cobra 289 | | CSX2032 | L | 1.100-1.300.000 USD | | NS | | 15-01-17 | Kissimmee | F153 | Mec |

Nera con interni neri; ordered new by Lance Reventlow. Restored in 1978 and refreshed in the 1990s. Fitted with several competition options (see lot 150 RM 18.1.13 NS).

| 1964 | Cobra 289 | | CSX2411 | L | 900-1.100.000 USD | 895.840 | 1.100.000 | 1.034.550 | 20-01-17 | Scottsdale | 14 | G&Co F699 |

Metallic blue with black interior; first restored in the 1980s when the engine was fitted with a Weber four-carburettor setup. Restored again to its original colours between 2006 and 2007.

| 1963 | Cobra 289 "Dragonsnake" | | CSX2093 | L | 1.100-1.300.000 USD | | NS | | 22-04-17 | Arlington | NA | WoA |

Prepared to "Dragonsnake" specification by Bruce Larson and raced at drag events until 1969. In the mid-1970s it was returned to road specification and finished in light green; in the early 1990s it was restored and finished in its 1960s fuchsia livery (see lots Mecum S137 18.8.11 NS and S93.1 12.4.14 NS, and RM/Sotheby's 251 29.1.16 $990,000).

| 1964 | Cobra 289 | | CSX2328 | L | 1.050-1.250.000 USD | 846.153 | 1.089.000 | 927.828 | 18-08-17 | Carmel | 24 | Bon |

Red with black interior; fully restored by the current owner to its original specification.

| 1965 | Cobra 289 | | CSX2448 | L | 1.200-1.400.000 USD | | NS | | 18-08-17 | Pebble Beach | 24 | G&Co |

Black with black interior; independently prepared, the car was raced at SCCA events in the 1960s. Bought in 1976 by the current owner and fully restored in the 2000s. Est.420bhp rebuilt race-specification engine.

| 1964 | Cobra 289 | | CSX2344 | L | 1.200-1.400.000 USD | 854.700 | 1.100.000 | 937.200 | 18-08-17 | Monterey | 154 | RMS |

Light blue with black leather interior; in highly original condition; since new in the same family ownership; 15,500 original miles; stored in 1974; returned to running condition in 2010.

| 1965 | Cobra 289 | | CSX2588 | L | 1.000-1.200.000 USD | | NS | | 19-08-17 | Monterey | S100.1 | Mec |

Maroon with black interior; body repainted in 2006 (see lot NR98 RM 10.2.06 $342,400).

| 1963 | Cobra 289 | | CSX2075 | L | 850-950.000 USD | 623.931 | 803.000 | 684.156 | 19-08-17 | Monterey | 240 | RMS |

Black with original black interior; converted to "Dragonsnake" specification by its first owner for drag-racing. Returned to street specification in 1971 by a further owner. Restored many years ago.

| 1965 | Cobra 289 | | CSX2417 | L | NA | | NS | | 19-08-17 | Monterey | 1021 | R&S |

White with red interior; recently restored and fitted with a 5-speed gearbox.

F699: 1964 Shelby American Cobra 289

F700: 1966 Shelby American Cobra 427

Year	Model	(Bodybuilder)	Chassis No.	Steering	Estimate	Hammer Price £	$	€	Sale Date	Place	Lot	Auc. H.
1967	Cobra 427		CSX3308	L	800-1.000.000 USD	581.163	726.000	654.416	05-11-16	Hilton Head	171	AA

Red; during the early 1980s restoration the Cobra was given the competition-spec look. Raced at historic events from 1979 to 1983.

1966	Cobra 427		CSX3293	L	900-1.200.000 USD	892.430	1.100.000	1.031.030	19-01-17	Phoenix	157	RMS

Red with black interior; 427 engine rebuilt in the late 1980s to S/C specification. Cosmetic restoration carried out a few years ago. Circa 21,000 miles on the odometer (see lot 237 RM 18.8.12 $819,300).

F700

1966	Cobra 427		CSX3359	L	1.600-2.000.000 USD		NS		18-08-17	Carmel	58	Bon

Red with black interior; restored in 2004; 1,880 miles covered since new (see lot 129 RM 15.8.14 $1,705,000).

SHELBY AMERICAN (USA) (1995-)

2002	Cobra 427 SC 4000 Series		CSX4285	L	NQ	98.355*	122.500*	114.905*	08-04-17	Houston	S30	Mec

40th Anniversary edition finished in blue with black leather interior; 23,655 miles since new; two owners. From the Laquay Automobile Collection.

SIATA (I) (1926-1970)

1952	Daina 1400 Gran Sport spider	(Stabilimenti Farina)	SLO216	L	250-350.000 GBP		NS		07-12-16	London	326	Bon

Red; believed originally sold to the USA, registered in Germany in 2006 and currently registered in the UK. Fitted in the past with a Ford V8 engine, the car was restored in 2014 in the UK and fitted with the present Siata engine no. SL0209. It was accepted at the Mille Miglia Storica in 2015 and 2016.

1952	Daina 1400 Gran Sport spider	(Stabilimenti Farina)	SLO216	L	280-380.000 EUR		NS		09-02-17	Paris	364	Bon

See lot 326 Bonhams 7.12.16.

1951	Daina 1400 coupé	(Stabilimenti Farina)	SL0186	L	115-125.000 GBP		NS		30-06-17	Goodwood	280	Bon

Restoration project. Sold new in Italy, the car was early in its life exported to Mexico and reimported into Europe in 2017 (EU taxes paid).

1952	208S Speciale cabriolet	(Stabilimenti Farina)	208SL1006613	L	225-300.000 USD	162.393*	209.000*	178.068*	18-08-17	Monterey	113	RMS

Red and black with parchment leather interior; fully restored in recent years. One-off fitted with a Ford V8 engine commissioned as a promotional tool by Jimmy Mulgrew of Euclid Ford in Euclid, Ohio.

F701

SIGMA (F) (1913-1928)

1920	10hp torpedo		1340	R	14-18.000 GBP	12.226	15.283	14.410	12-04-17	London	316	Coy

Green with black wings; 1600cc Ballot engine (see lot 127 Coys 2.7.16 $15,938).

SIL (SOCIETE INDUSTRIELLE DE LIVRY) (F)

1951	Atlas Babycar		FH297	L	40-60.000 USD	24.884*	30.250*	28.508*	11-03-17	Amelia Island	293	RMS

Black and red with red interior; restored at unspecified date. Described as in very good running order. 175cc AMC four-stroke single-cylinder engine. Formerly in the Bruce Weiner Microcar Museum (see lot 271 RM 15.2.13 $60,375).

SIMCA (F) (1934-1981)

1950	Six		616806	L	4-6.000 EUR	4.568	5.873	5.400	14-05-17	Puiseux-Pontoise	701	Ose

In original condition; requiring recommissioning prior to use.

1951	8 Sport cabriolet		897700	L	60-80.000 EUR		NS		02-07-17	Monaco	129	Art

Yellow with dark green interior; restored seven years ago.

1953	9 Sport coupé	(Facel Metallon)	48771	L	35-40.000 EUR	40.071	59.141	45.570	02-07-17	Monaco	223	Art

Dark green with biscuit leather interior; older restoration.

F702

1956	Regence		134267	L	5-8.000 EUR	7.142*	8.805*	7.904*	07-10-16	Chateau-sur-Epte	18	Art

Two-tone body; restored many years ago. From the Andre Weber Collection.

1960	Plein Ciel coupé	(Facel Metallon)	1755068	L	20-30.000 EUR	17.579*	21.674*	19.456*	07-10-16	Chateau-sur-Epte	34	Art

Red with white roof; in good overall condition. From the Andre Weber Collection.

1959	Chambord		201807	L	8-12.000 EUR	7.142*	8.805*	7.904*	07-10-16	Chateau-sur-Epte	60	Art

Two-tone body; interior and engine redone. From the Andre Weber Collection.

1967	1000 coupé	(Bertone)	SB163228	L	10-15.000 EUR	9.785*	12.296*	11.500*	09-02-17	Paris	318	Bon

White with original black vinyl interior; sold new to Italy. Body repainted in 2004 (see lot 330 Bonhams 6.2.14 $17,071).

F701: 1952 Siata 208S Speciale cabriolet (Stabilimenti Farina)

F702: 1953 Simca 9 Sport coupé (Facel Metallon)

Year	Model	(Bodybuilder)	Chassis no.	Steering	Estimate	Hammer price £	Hammer price $	Hammer price €	Date	Place	Lot	Auc. H.
1971	1200 S coupé	(Bertone)	CA013289G	L	22-28.000 EUR		NS		05-08-17	Schloss Dyck	205	Coy

Grey with black roof; sold new to Italy.

SINGER (GB) *(1905-1970)*

Year	Model		Chassis no.	Steering	Estimate	£	$	€	Date	Place	Lot	Auc. H.
1939	Twelve Super saloon		J1188	R	NQ	**2.137***	**2.738***	**2.449***	02-06-17	Solihull	47	H&H

Green with green leather interior; in average overall condition.

| 1939 | Nine Sports Le Mans | | 5690 | R | 40-60.000 EUR | | NS | | 06-11-16 | Lyon | 305 | Ose |

Light blue; imported into France from Uruguay in 1995 and subsequently restored.

SNCAN (F) *(1953-1956)*

| 1956 | Inter 175A berline | | 1199 | C | 50-70.000 EUR | **66.887** | **83.614** | **78.400** | 08-02-17 | Paris | 101 | RMS **F703** |

Light green with red interior; one of an estimated 30 surviving examples. 175cc one-cylinder two-stroke Ydral engine.

SPYKER (NL) *(2000-)*

| 2010 | C8 Spyder | | 363219 | L | 225-275.000 USD | **182.543** | **225.000** | **210.893** | 19-01-17 | Scottsdale | 19 | Bon |

Dark sapphire blue with blue leather interior; less than 1,100 miles covered.

SQUIRE (GB) *(1934-1937)*

| 1936 | 1.5l tourer | (Ranalah) | 1501 | R | 1.500-2.000.000 USD | | NS | | 20-01-17 | Scottsdale | 34 | G&Co |

Maroon with dark red interior; one of two examples built on the long-wheelbase chassis. Raced at some events in the UK in 1936 and 1937; imported into the USA in 1959; bought in Europe in 2011 by the current owner and subjected to a full restoration completed in 2015.

SS (GB) *(1932-1945)*

| 1941 | Jaguar 100 2.5l | | 49061 | R | 385-445.000 EUR | | NS | | 08-02-17 | Paris | 138 | RMS |

White with red interior; sold new in the UK, the car was imported into the USA in the 1950s and remained in single ownership from 1955 to 1989 when it was reimported into the UK. Described as in good overall condition. Original engine (see lot 250 Brooks 19.3.95 NS).

| 1937 | Jaguar 100 2.5l | | 18124 | R | 400-500.000 USD | **262.409*** | **319.000*** | **300.626*** | 10-03-17 | Amelia Island | 142 | RMS |

Red with black interior; 87 miles covered since the restoration. Original engine replaced with a correct unit at unspecified date. From the Orin Smith collection.

| 1937 | Jaguar 100 2.5l | | 18106 | R | 290-390.000 EUR | **297.659** | **378.765** | **339.000** | 24-06-17 | Wien | 368 | Dor **F704** |

Grey with red leather interior; raced in period; imported into the USA in the 1960s; from 1968 to 1998 with the same owner who restored it and raced it at historic events; bought in 2008 by the current owner and imported into Austria. Fitted at date unknown with a 3.5-litre engine, the car was fitted in 2014 with a correct 2.5-litre unit (see lot 424 Coys 15.5.04 $152,497).

| 1937 | Jaguar 100 2.5l | | 49026 | R | 500-600.000 USD | **435.897** | **561.000** | **477.972** | 18-08-17 | Pebble Beach | 42 | G&Co |

Dark green with brown leather interior; imported into the USA in the early 1960s and retained for nearly 30 years by the same owner who had it restored; further restoration works and interior retrimming in the 2000s (see lot 8 Gooding & Company 20.1.12 $319,000).

| 1937 | Jaguar 100 2.5l | | 18114 | R | 400-500.000 USD | | NS | | 18-08-17 | Monterey | 127 | RMS |

Gunmetal grey with red leather interior; bought new by journalist Laurence E.W. Pomeroy; exported in the late 1950s to Malaysia where it was raced at historic events; reimported into the UK in the late 1970s and restored; imported in 2002 into Japan where it remained until 2014 after being repainted and exhibited at several concours (see lot 244 RM 16.8.14 $484,000).

| 1938 | Jaguar 100 3.5l | | 39067 | R | 450-525.000 USD | | NS | | 21-01-17 | Scottsdale | 144 | G&Co |

Originally finished in gunmetal grey with silver interior; sold new in the UK and raced at some events; imported into the USA in 1948 and bought by Dave Garroway who refinished it in the present white livery with alligator skin interior, fitted it with a Jaguar XK 120 engine, raced it and retained it until 1977; reimported into the UK in 2007; restored in 2010; offered with a correct SS 100 3.5-litre engine.

| 1939 | Jaguar 2.5l cabriolet | | 46268 | R | 175-200.000 USD | **134.376*** | **165.000*** | **155.183*** | 20-01-17 | Scottsdale | 13 | G&Co |

Gunmetal grey with black leather interior; in the same family ownership from the 1970s. Concours-quality restoration completed in 2001.

| 1937 | Jaguar 2.5l tourer | | 19098 | R | 350-550.000 USD | **256.410** | **330.000** | **282.150** | 17-08-17 | Monterey | 49 | WoA |

Originally finished in green with green interior and sold new in the UK; imported into the USA at unspecified date before 1963; recent full restoration.

STANGUELLINI (I) *(1947-1963)*

| 1957 | 1200 Spider America | (Bertone) | 121166 | L | 300-400.000 USD | **226.215** | **275.000** | **259.160** | 11-03-17 | Amelia Island | 245 | RMS **F705** |

Metallic grey with blue interior; one-off designed by Franco Scaglione; displayed at the Bertone stand at the 1957 Turin Motor Show and later at the 1960 Buenos Aires Motor Show; sold to Argentina; acquired in 1994 by the current owner and subsequently restored. Presented at the 2004 Villa d'Este Concours d'Elegance and at the 2015 Pebble Beach Concours d'Elegance.

F703: 1956 SNCAN Inter 175A berline

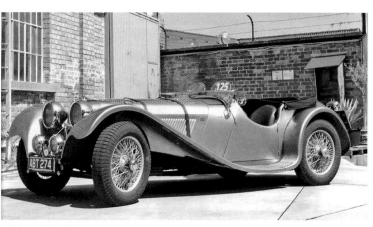

F704: 1937 SS Jaguar 100 2.5l

Year	Model	(Bodybuilder)	Chassis no.	Steering	Estimate	Hammer price £	Hammer price $	Hammer price €	Date	Place	Lot	Auc. H.

STANLEY (USA) (1895-1931)

1910 Model 61 10hp toy tonneau — 5424 — R — 190-260.000 USD — NS — 17-08-17 Monterey — 71 — **WoA**
Green with cream/yellow accents and black leather interior; since 1982 in the Allen Blazick Steam Car Collection; restored in the early 1990s; mechanicals freshened in 2017.

1924 Model 750B touring — 24098 — L — 50-60.000 GBP — NS — 07-12-16 London — 364 — **Bon**
Restored in the USA in the 1960s; since 2012 in the current ownership; fitted in 2013 with a new 30hp boiler.

STAR (GB) (1898-1932)

1899 Benz 3.5hp vis-a-vis — Y204(registrat. no.) — R — 110-130.000 GBP — NS — 04-11-16 London — 203 — **Bon**
In the same family ownership from new to 1930 circa. Since 1995 in the current ownership. Described as in good driving order.

STEARNS-KNIGHT (USA) (1912-1929)

1927 Model G-8 sedan — G309 — L — 100-140.000 AUD — NS — 20-08-17 Mallala Park — 27 — **Mos**
Red; one of two examples known to survive. From the collection of the late Clem Smith.

STEVENS-DURYEA (USA) (1901-1927)

1903 Model L runabout — 326 — R — 120-150.000 USD — NS — 06-10-16 Hershey — 160 — **RMS**
Red with leather fenders and black leather interior; retained by its first owner until 1941, restored many years ago and later acquired by the Indianapolis Motor Speedway Hall of Fame Museum, sold by the Museum in 2012, recently mechanically serviced and returned to running order (see lot 249 Bonhams 5.10.15 NS).

STEYR (A) (1920-1941)

1931 Typ 30 Standard 4-door cabriolet — 302032 — L — 26-40.000 EUR — 57.902 — 70.853 — 64.400 — 15-10-16 Salzburg — 415 — **Dor F706**
Grey with black wings and black leather interior; in recent years mechanicals overhauled and interior retrimmed.

STEYR-PUCH (A) (1941-1977)

1954 Fiat 500C Topolino — 480908 — L — 8-12.000 EUR — 11.107* — 14.134* — 12.650* — 24-06-17 Wien — 310 — **Dor**
Red with beige interior; in good overall condition. Recently serviced.

1960 Fiat 500 D — 5117289 — L — 10-16.000 EUR — 10.602 — 13.491 — 12.075 — 24-06-17 Wien — 302 — **Dor**
Red with grey interior; restored in the mid-1990s. Recently serviced.

STODDARD DAYTON (USA) (1904-1913)

1910 Model 10C raceabout/4-seat roadster — 10C214 — R — 125-175.000 USD — NS — 09-03-17 Amelia Island — 176 — **Bon**
Cream with brown interior and red chassis and wheels; 4-seat tourabout body which can be converted to 2-seat raceabout form (see lot 869 Bonhams 27.9.08 $144,500).

STUDEBAKER (USA) (1902-1966)

1906 Garford Model G touring — 841 — R — 250-350.000 USD — NS — 11-03-17 Amelia Island — 251 — **RMS**
Discovered in the 1940s by Henry Austin Clark Jr. who had it restored and retained it until 1968 when it was acquired by Bill Harrah who resold it in 1982. Later it was subjected to a second restoration completed in 2005 (see lot 129 RM 26.7.14 $275,000).

1929 President convertible — 7018939 — L — NQ — 89.584* — 110.000* — 103.455* — 21-01-17 Scottsdale — 1278 — **B/J F707**
Burgundy and white with black fenders and red interior; restored.

1931 President roadster — 7034735 — L — 170-220.000 USD — NS — 18-08-17 Carmel — 41 — **Bon**
Two-tone grey with red interior; restored in 2005 (see lot 169 RM 20.1.06 $105,600).

1937 Dictator business coupé — D165177 — L — 45-65.000 USD — 23.451* — 29.700* — 26.552* — 06-10-16 Hershey — 120 — **RMS**
White with camel vinyl interior; restored and mildly customized with a 1953 6-cylinder Studebaker engine, 3-speed synchromesh manual gearbox with overdrive and air conditioning.

1951 Champion Regal convertible — G1076582 — L — NQ — 44.792* — 55.000* — 51.728* — 21-01-17 Scottsdale — 749.1 — **B/J**
Red with red interior; in original condition except for the paintwork redone at unspecified date. Two owners and 22,300 miles covered. In good running order.

1951 Commander State convertible — 8191404 — L — 35-45.000 USD — 34.361* — 45.650* — 40.784* — 03-09-16 Auburn — 4124 — **AA**
Beige with tan interior; three-speed manual gearbox with overdrive.

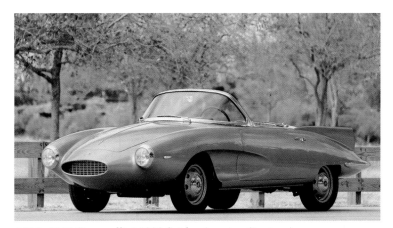

F705: 1957 Stanguellini 1200 Spider America (Bertone)

F706: 1931 Steyr Typ 30 Standard 4-door cabriolet

Year	Model	(Bodybuilder)	Chassis no.	Steering	Estimate	Hammer price £	$	€	Date	Place	Lot	Auc. H.

F707: 1929 Studebaker President convertible

F708: 1963 Studebaker Avanti R2

Year	Model	(Bodybuilder)	Chassis no.	Steering	Estimate	£	$	€	Date	Place	Lot	Auc. H.
1951	Commander State convertible		HS22043	L	NQ	15.677*	19.250*	18.105*	21-01-17	Scottsdale	8211	R&S
	Red; restored. From the Missoula Auto Museum Collection.											
1955	President Speedster		7155873	L	NQ	13.624	17.000	15.732	25-03-17	Kansas City	F99.1	Mec
	White and blue with white and blue interior; believed to be 41,347 miles. Automatic transmission.											
1957	Golden Hawk		6101001	L	60-70.000 USD	42.427	53.000	47.774	05-11-16	Hilton Head	153	AA
	Gold with white fins; in good overall condition. 23,000 believed original miles. 289 engine with McCulloch supercharger and automatic transmission.											
1963	Lark Daytona convertible		63V8546	L	90-100.000 USD	51.867	67.500	60.379	20-05-17	Indianapolis	F195	Mec
	Black with red interior; 4,768 believed original miles. 289 supercharged engine with automatic transmission.											
1963	Avanti R2		63R2687	L	75-100.000 USD	89.355	115.000	97.980	19-08-17	Monterey	F79	Mec F708
	Turquoise with fawn and black interior; body repainted in the 1980s. 290bhp 289 supercharged engine with 4-speed manual gearbox. From the Colin Comer Collection.											

STUTZ (USA) (1911-1934)

Year	Model	(Bodybuilder)	Chassis no.	Steering	Estimate	£	$	€	Date	Place	Lot	Auc. H.
1917	Series R Bearcat		2217S	R	185-250.000 USD		NS		09-03-17	Amelia Island	178	Bon
	Red with black fenders and black interior; restored in the 1960s, the car is described as in good driving condition.											
1918	Series S Bearcat		S18333	R	190-200.000 GBP	214.300	270.211	251.824	07-12-16	London	370	Bon
	Red with black fenders and black wings; from 1920 to 1959 in the same ownership; restored in the early 1960s; imported into the UK in 1989 and subsequently restored again; acquired in 2013 by the current owner; engine recently rebuilt.											
1920	Series H Bearcat		5067	R	400-500.000 USD	367.294	451.000	424.166	21-01-17	Scottsdale	117	G&Co F709
	Yellow with black fenders and brown leather interior; fully restored. Cylinder block replaced in 2014. In very good overall condition (see lot 200 Bonhams 16.1.14 $341,000).											
1920	Series H sport phaeton		7201	L	75-95.000 USD	39.125	50.000	46.735	22-04-17	Arlington	129	WoA
	Concours-quality restoration completed in 2002.											
1922	Series K roadster		13271	L	NQ	28.102*	35.000*	32.830*	08-04-17	Houston	S36	Mec
	Light grey with black fenders and black interior; believed to have been restored in the early 1950s. From the Laquay Automobile Collection.											
1923	Speedway Four roadster		13253	L	175-225.000 USD		NS		18-08-17	Carmel	105	Bon
	Red and black with black interior; restored in the 1960s; in good overall condition (see lot 276 RM 5.8.06 NS).											
1930	Model M convertible (LeBaron)		M846CD25E	L	160-200.000 USD	85.815*	104.500*	99.035*	09-03-17	Amelia Island	149	Bon
	Black; bought in 2007 by the current owner and subsequently restored in Italy. Largely original interior (see lot 89 Bonhams 19.8.16 NS).											
1929	Model M Supercharged coupé (Lancefield)		MC31312	R	1.000-1.200.000 USD	1.402.533	1.705.000	1.606.792	11-03-17	Amelia Island	231	RMS F710
	Black with red interior; one of three authentic supercharged Stutz cars known to survive, it was reimported into the USA from the UK in 1946 by A.K. Miller who retained it until 1996. First restored in the late 1990s and in 2010-11 again (see lots Christie's 36 7.9.96 $151,000, and RM 224 23.9.00 $316,800, 251 5.8.06 $715,000, and 356 14.8.10 $660,000).											
1929	Model M dual-cowl speedster (LeBaron)		M844CY25D	L	275-350.000 USD		NS		04-06-17	Greenwich	188	Bon
	Dark red with black fenders; in the AK Miller collection until 1996 and subsequently restored.											
1931	Model MA cabriolet		MA271344	L	120-140.000 USD	92.423	115.500	108.027	01-04-17	Ft.Lauderdale	531	AA
	Grey with grey leather interior; recently serviced.											
1929	Model MB sedan		32265(engine)	L	10-15.000 USD	15.387*	19.800*	17.620*	03-10-16	Philadelphia	204	Bon
	Restoration started many years ago to be completed. From the Natural History Museum of Los Angeles.											
1931	Model SV-16 convertible		MA271344	L	140-180.000 USD		NS		11-03-17	Amelia Island	78	Mot
	Grey with grey leather interior; restored many years ago, the car is described as in good driving order.											

STUTZ (USA) (1969-1985)

Year	Model	(Bodybuilder)	Chassis no.	Steering	Estimate	£	$	€	Date	Place	Lot	Auc. H.
1972	Blackhawk		2K57Y2A103298	L	45-55.000 USD		NS		04-11-16	Dallas	F158	Mec
	Black and orange with black and orange interior.											

SUBARU (J) (1958-)

Year	Model	(Bodybuilder)	Chassis no.	Steering	Estimate	£	$	€	Date	Place	Lot	Auc. H.
1996	Impreza WRC		PROWRC97001	L	175-200.000 GBP	230.625	297.645	264.365	06-06-17	Woodcote Park	34	H&H F711
	First example built, the car was used by Prodrive for test and development and subsequently it had a long race career until 2007. Later it was bought by the current owner who had it restored by Prodrive (see lots 233 Coys 10.1.09 NS and 112 H & H 14.10.15 $238,406).											
1997	Impreza STI		GC8061819	R	65-75.000 GBP	113.500	140.286	130.650	19-03-17	Goodwood	10	Bon
	First prototype of the car (type 22B) for the 1998 World Rally Championship, it was displayed at the 1997 Tokyo Motor Show. For 20 years with the present owner, it has covered 51 kms. Import VAT of 20% plus an additional 10% Import Duty subject to UK VAT at 20% is applicable to the hammer price should the car remain in the EU.											

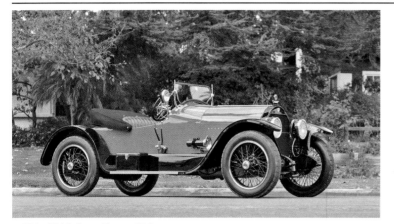

F709: 1920 Stutz Series H Bearcat

F710: 1929 Stutz Model M Supercharged coupé (Lancefield)

SUNBEAM (GB) (1901-1935)

Year	Model (Bodybuilder)	Chassis no.	Steering	Estimate	£	$	€	Date	Place	Lot	Auc. H.
1912	12/16hp two-seater tourer	4658	R	25-28.000 GBP	25.000	32.310	28.413	15-07-17	Cambridge	690	Che

Yellow with blue wings and blue interior; reimported into the UK from New Zealand in 1989 and subsequently subjected to a long restoration. New body.

SUNBEAM-TALBOT (GB) (1938-1975)

Year	Model (Bodybuilder)	Chassis no.	Steering	Estimate	£	$	€	Date	Place	Lot	Auc. H.
1954	90 MkIIa cabriolet	3015821	R	15-18.000 GBP		NS		02-06-17	Solihull	62	H&H
1954	90 MkIIa cabriolet	3015821	R	12-15.000 GBP	11.812	15.406	13.231	26-07-17	Duxford	62	H&H

See lot 62 H & H 2.6.17.

| 1954 | Alpine Special | A3015663ERO5 | R | 50-60.000 GBP | 50.175 | 61.861 | 55.529 | 08-10-16 | Ascot | 304 | Coy |

Ivory with red interior; restored. With hardtop. Used when new by the factory as a demonstrator.

| 1954 | Alpine Special | A3015937HRUS | R | 13-15.000 GBP | 12.880 | 15.786 | 14.325 | 12-10-16 | Duxford | 69 | H&H |

Red with black interior; restored in the 1970s, the car is described as in average condition.

| 1954 | Alpine Special | A3015663ERO5 | R | 50-60.000 GBP | | NS | | 29-10-16 | London | 132 | Coy |

See lot 304 Coys 8.10.16.

| 1953 | Alpine (Thrupp/Maberly) | A3013164 | L | 55-75.000 USD | 72.266* | 88.000* | 83.398* | 09-03-17 | Amelia Island | 152 | Bon |

Light blue with ivory leather interior; 800 miles covered since the restoration carried out in the USA. Fitted with a 5-speed Tremec gearbox.

| 1954 | Alpine Special | A3015663ERO5 | R | 38-50.000 GBP | 30.000 | 38.934 | 33.969 | 29-06-17 | Fontwell Park | 130 | Coy |

See lot 132 Coys 29.10.16.

| 1963 | Rapier Series IIIA cabriolet | B3064154LCX | L | 20-25.000 USD | 6.514* | 8.250* | 7.376* | 06-10-16 | Hershey | 117 | RMS |

Blue with white side stripe and light blue interior; restored some years ago.

| 1963 | Rapier MkIII saloon | B3066819HHO | R | 15-20.000 GBP | 23.063 | 28.953 | 27.290 | 24-02-17 | Stoneleigh P. | 121 | SiC |

Prepared in the early 2000s for historic rallying, in 2012 the car was prepared again for track events. Described as in good driving condition.

| 1963 | Alpine | B94102030ODLRO | L | 20-30.000 USD | 7.817* | 9.900* | 8.851* | 06-10-16 | Hershey | 130 | RMS |

Red with black interior; restored at unspecified date. With hardtop.

| 1961 | Le Mans coupé (Harrington) | B9106097 | L | 100-140.000 GBP | 109.200 | 146.131 | 130.046 | 07-09-16 | London | 155 | RMS |

Red; sold new to the USA, the car was raced at some events including the Sebring 12 Hours in 1962 (as a Rootes Group Works entry) and in 1963 (as a NART entry). Its second owner first converted it to road specifications and later between 1993 and 2002 restored it to 1963 Sebring specifications. Acquired by the current, third owner, the car has been restored again and prepared for historic racing. Offered with a spare engine believed to be the one fitted for Sebring 1963. Believed to be the only left-hand drive built. **F712**

| 1965 | Tiger V8 | B9472451HROFE | R | 25-35.000 GBP | 25.875 | 34.370 | 30.708 | 03-09-16 | Beaulieu | 470 | Bon |

Rebuilt during the 1990s and fitted with a 4.7-liter engine; recently recommissioned.

| 1965 | Tiger V8 | B9473518LRXFE | L | 95-115.000 USD | | NS | | 04-11-16 | Dallas | S144 | Mec |

Red with black interior; restoration completed in 2014 (see lot F224 Mecum 23.1.15 $94,000).

F711: 1996 Subaru Impreza WRC

F712: 1961 Sunbeam-Talbot Le Mans coupé (Harrington)

Year	Model	(Bodybuilder)	Chassis no.	Steering	Estimate	Hammer price £	$	€	Sale Date	Place	Lot	Auc. H.

F713: 1955 Swallow Doretti Doretti

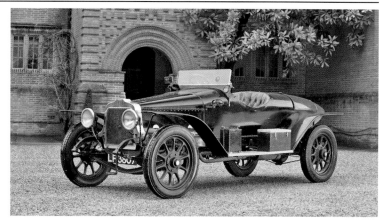

F714: 1913 Talbot 15hp 20/30

1965 **Tiger V8**   B9473614LRXFE   L   90-110.000 USD   53.546*   66.000*   61.862*   19-01-17   Scottsdale   55   Bon
Red with black interior; restored at unspecified date and fitted with a 289 engine (the original 260 unit is included with the sale).

1965 **Tiger V8**   B9473708HRO1FE   R   40-50.000 GBP   44.800   54.808   51.878   04-03-17   Brooklands   189   His
Royal blue with cream leather interior; restored many years ago. The engine has covered approximately 1,000 miles since the rebuild.

1965 **Tiger V8**   B9473518LRXFE   L   100-125.000 USD   90.379   115.500   107.958   22-04-17   Arlington   121   WoA
See lot S144 Mecum 4.11.16.

1964 **Tiger V8 GT**   B9470207LRXFE   L   130-160.000 USD   NS   24-06-17   Santa Monica   173   RMS
Black with black hardtop and black leather interior; discovered in California in the late 1990s and restored. Bought in 2015 by the current owner and restored again. 260 cu.in. believed original engine.

1966 **Tiger V8**   B382002495   L   70-80.000 USD   NS   24-06-17   Santa Monica   196   RMS
Black; body repainted. With hardtop.

1967 **Tiger V8 MkII**   B382100268   L   200-250.000 USD   NS   19-08-17   Monterey   S112   Mec
Dark green with black interior; for 28 years in the current ownership; restored; original 289 engine rebuilt.

SWALLOW DORETTI (GB) *(1954-1956)*

1955 **Doretti**   1246   L   50-70.000 EUR   62.344*   76.866*   69.000*   07-10-16   Zoute   29   Bon
Ice blue with grey/blue leather interior; described as in good overall condition.

1955 **Doretti**   1150   R   60-70.000 GBP   68.700   86.624   80.729   07-12-16   London   312   Bon
Royal blue with mulberry leather interior; 10,000 miles covered since the restoration. TR2 Triumph engine enlarged to 2138cc; Triumph TR4 rear axle and front disc brakes.   **F713**

TALBOT (F) *(1920-1935)*

1929 **M67 cabriolet**   M6771330   R   14-20.000 GBP   11.500   15.275   13.648   03-09-16   Beaulieu   443   Bon
Described as in good overall condition.

1930 **M67 berline**   66974   R   20-30.000 EUR   18.586   23.750   22.200   01-05-17   Obenheim   307   Ose
Cream yellow with beige interior; restored about 12 years ago.

TALBOT (F) *(1979-1990)*

1981 **Sunbeam Lotus**   T4DCYAL307662   L   15-20.000 EUR   38.162*   47.452*   44.800*   25-11-16   Milan   883   RMS
White with blue side stripe and blue interior; prepared for rallying. From the Duemila Ruote collection.

TALBOT (GB) *(1902-1938)*

1910 **4AB waggonette**   2757   R   NQ   19.295*   25.166*   21.612*   26-07-17   Duxford   11   H&H
Cream and brown with brown interior; in good working order; later body.

1913 **15hp 20/30**   5473   R   140-180.000 GBP   169.500   209.502   195.111   19-03-17   Goodwood   51   Bon
Retained by the factory, the car was raced until 1919 when it was acquired by Malcolm Campbell who in 1923 resold it to Australia. Damaged heavily in an accident, it was repaired many years later and fitted with a new five seater tourer body. In 1993 it was reimported into the UK, restored again and fitted with the present new body, replica of the form in which it had been campaigned by the factory at hillclimbs before the Great War. Original rebuilt engine.   **F714**

1919 **25/50 4SW tourer (Salmons)**   SW10206   R   50-70.000 GBP   46.000   61.102   54.593   03-09-16   Beaulieu   428   Bon
Blue with red wings and red interior; converted to crane truck at unspecified date, the car was rediscovered in the late 1950s and subsequently it was fitted with the present, period original body. Fully restored between 1993 and 1996 (see lot 375 Bonhams 13.09.08 $99,813).

1916 **15/20 4CY "balloon car"**   8529   R   34-42 GBP   NS   20-05-17   Ascot   187   His
Blue with red interior; discovered in Australia in the 1990s; reimported into the UK in 2001; restored and fitted with the present new body (see lots 210 Coys 30.9.06 NS and 15 H&H 12.3.14 NS).

1923 **10/23 tourer**   16448   R   18-22.000 GBP   17.833   22.575   20.702   12-11-16   Birmingham   658   SiC
Described as in good overall condition.

1929 **14/45 coupé**   26803   R   20-24.000 GBP   NS   29-03-17   Duxford   92   H&H
Black with brown interior; described as in good original condition. Mechanicals overhauled.

1929 **14/45 Type AG tourer**   25065   R   100-150.000 USD   36.752*   47.300*   40.442*   17-08-17   Monterey   28   WoA
Dark blue with black fenders and dark blue leather interior; long restoration completed in 1996 (see lots 623 Bonhams 24.4.06 $40,076 and 132 RM/Sotheby's 3.2.16 $48,980).

1930 **90 cabriolet**   30000   R   80-100.000 GBP   74.166   90.898   82.487   12-10-16   Duxford   113   H&H
Dark blue with blue interior; in the 2000s body restored, interior retrimmed and engine overhauled.

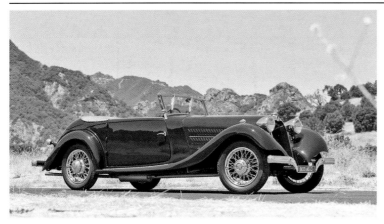

F715: 1936 Talbot-Lago T120 Baby Sport cabriolet (Figoni)   F716: 1936 Talbot-Lago T150 C

Year	Model	(Bodybuilder)	Chassis no.	Steering	Estimate	£	$	€	Date	Place	Lot	Auc. H.
1934	AW75 saloon	(Darracq)	34324	R	10-15.000 GBP	19.550	25.968	23.202	03-09-16	Beaulieu	430	Bon

For restoration; since 1963 in the same family ownership. Unused for the last 30 plus years.

TALBOT-LAGO (F) (1935-1958)

Year	Model	(Bodybuilder)	Chassis no.	Steering	Estimate	£	$	€	Date	Place	Lot	Auc. H.
1935	T120 coach		85434	R	20-30.000 EUR	31.862*	39.284*	35.264*	07-10-16	Chateau-sur-Epte	64	Art

Dark blue; restored many years ago. It seems the body was modified and modernized after WWII. From the Andre Weber Collection.

| 1938 | T120 Baby Sport coach | | 85313 | R | 35-45.000 EUR | 35.168 | 43.928 | 39.600 | 06-11-16 | Lyon | 353 | Ose |

Green with black wings; since 1983 in the current ownership. Recently body repainted, interior retrimmed, engine block and gearbox redone.

| 1936 | T120 Baby Sport cabriolet (Figoni) | | 85722 | R | 375-475.000 USD | 273.504 | 352.000 | 299.904 | 18-08-17 | Carmel | 99 | Bon F715 |

Dark green with tan leather interior; concours-quality restoration completed in 2005. Since 1962 in the same family ownership.

| 1936 | T150 C | | 82930 | R | 1.200-1.600.000 EUR | 1.373.578 | 1.711.779 | 1.610.480 | 10-02-17 | Paris | 30 | Art |

The car was raced until 1950 at numerous events, including the Le Mans 24 Hours (in 1937/38/39/49), Spa 24 Hours, Mille Miglia and Tourist Trophy, and was driven among others by Chiron, Chinetti, Levegh and Rosier. In 1947 the body was modernized. In 1983 the car was imported into the UK, restored to its original specification and driven at historic events until 2006. Since 2013 in the Hervé and Martine Ogliastro Collection (see lots 50 Barrett-Jackson/Coys 27.5.00 $681,337 and 342 Artcurial 8.2.13 $1,955,001).   F716

| 1938 | T150 C Lago Spéciale cabriolet | | 90039 | R | 1.200-1.500.000 USD | NS | | | 09-03-17 | Amelia Island | 169 | Bon |

Blue; fully restored between 2013 and 2016. Engine rebuilt on a T23 block (see lot 583 Bonhams 7.2.13 $280,402).

| 1937 | T150 C SS Goutte d'Eau (Figoni/Falaschi) | | 90110 | L | 3.200-4.200.000 EUR | 2.929.584 | 3.761.856 | 3.360.000 | 27-05-17 | Villa Erba | 151 | RMS |

Black and silver with red interior; original chassis, engine and drivetrain; restored to the original Goutte d'Eau design first fitted to this chassis; one of two examples with fully enclosed front fenders.   F717

| 1938 | T15 Baby cabriolet | | 93017 | R | 550-750.000 USD | NS | | | 18-01-17 | Scottsdale | 28 | WoA |

Restored in the early 1990s; recent cosmetic refreshing and engine rebuild.

| 1947 | T26 Lago Record cabriolet | | 100064 | R | 650-850.000 USD | 289.555* | 352.000* | 331.725* | 10-03-17 | Amelia Island | 158 | RMS |

Imported into the USA in the 1960s; restored in 2004. From the Orin Smith collection (see lots 349 Bonhams/Brooks 9.6.01 NS and 102 RM 17.8.01 NS).

| 1948 | T26 Lago GS cabriolet (Franay) | | 110121 | R | 1.200-1.500.000 EUR | 976.528 | 1.253.952 | 1.120.000 | 27-05-17 | Villa Erba | 132 | RMS F718 |

Black with black interior; concours-quality restoration. One-off.

| 1956 | T14 LS Special | | 140031 | R | 130-160.000 GBP | 135.900 | 176.371 | 153.880 | 30-06-17 | Goodwood | 252 | Bon |

Light grey with grey interior; restored in 1994. A factory demonstrator when new (see Bonhams lots 102 5.9.03 $68,358, 230 2.2.12 $210,813, and 129 13.5.16 NS).

| 1958 | T Lago America | | 140069B | L | 450-550.000 EUR | NS | | | 09-02-17 | Paris | 335 | Bon |

Blue; restored circa 15 years ago; original interior. Described as in very good overall condition. Approximately 9,000 kms covered since new. One of circa 12 examples built with the 2.5-litre 8-cylinder BMW engine.

TAMPOLLI (I)

| 1997 | RTA-1 | | 001 | R | 2.5-5.000 EUR | 38.162* | 47.452* | 44.800* | 25-11-16 | Milan | 642 | RMS |

Red; 3.0-litre Alfa Romeo engine. From the Duemila Ruote collection.

F717: 1937 Talbot-Lago T150 C SS Goutte d'Eau (Figoni/Falaschi)   F718: 1948 Talbot-Lago T26 Lago GS cabriolet (Franay)

Year	Model	(Bodybuilder)	Chassis no.	Steering	Estimate	Hammer price £	Hammer price $	Hammer price €	Date	Place	Lot	Auc. H.

TATRA (CS) (1899-1998)

1960 T603 — 798913193 — L — 35-45.000 USD — 32.846 — 41.800 — 37.411 — 24-06-17 — Santa Monica — 128 — **RMS F719**
White; 4-speed manual gearbox.

TERRAPLANE (USA) (1932-1938)

1934 Six cabriolet — 93205(engine) — R — 20-28.000 AUD — 16.620 — 21.404 — 18.215 — 20-08-17 — Mallala Park — 13 — **Mos**
White with red fenders and black interior; restored. Since 1994 in the collection of the late Clem Smith.

THOMAS (USA) (1903-1918)

1909 Model K-6-70 flyabout — K179 — R — 750-1.100.000 USD — NS — — — 18-08-17 — Carmel — 37 — **Bon**
Red with black interior; restored using the basis of a rolling chassis coming from the spares at the Harrah Collection, and engine and other period components coming from other sources. Restoration completed in 1993.

TOJEIRO (GB) (1952-1962)

1952 JAP sports — BHL1 — R — 90-110.000 GBP — NS — — — 27-07-17 — Silverstone — 118 — **SiC**
The car was raced in period and driven also by Brian Lister, Archie Scott-Brown and Peter Hughes. Bought in 2009 by the current owner and restored, it has been driven at some historical events. Fitted with a 1,100cc JAP engine and 4-speed Jowett Jupiter gearbox.

1953 Bristol sports — PHC101 — R — 400-600.000 EUR — NS — — — 02-07-17 — Monaco — 130 — **Art**
British racing green with dark green interior; bought in the late 1990s by the current owner and restored in Italy. A spare engine, rebuilt to Jaguar C-Type specification is included with the lot (see lot 42 Chevau-Légerè 25.9.11 NS).

1958 Climax coupé — TAD650 — R — 65-75.000 GBP — NS — — — 06-06-17 — Woodcote Park — 31 — **H&H**
Bought by the current owner in 2009 following a long period of inactivity, the car has been fully restored and finished in the present metallic racing green livery. 1098cc Coventry Climax FWA engine.

TOURETTE (GB) (1956-1958)

1957 Supreme — T10178S — R — 18-24.000 GBP — 31.360 — 38.993 — 36.814 — 26-11-16 — Weybridge — 142 — **His**
Red; for 55 years withits first owner; in working order; two-stroke 197cc Villiers engine.

TOYOTA (J) (1936-)

1970 FJ40 Land Cruiser — FJ4086368 — L — 65-85.000 USD — 37.928* — 46.750* — 43.819* — 19-01-17 — Phoenix — 107 — **RMS**
Red with white roof and black vinyl interior; 25 miles covered since the restoration completed in April 2016.

1977 FJ40 Land Cruiser — FJ40248509 — L — 80-100.000 USD — 55.542* — 68.200* — 64.142* — 21-01-17 — Scottsdale — 157 — **G&Co**
Red with white roof; 600 miles covered since a full restoration.

1979 BJ40 Land Cruiser convertible — BJ40042089 — L — 65-85.000 USD — 78.632* — 101.200* — 86.222* — 18-08-17 — Carmel — 75 — **Bon**
Tan; fully restored. Diesel variant with a 3-litre engine with manual gearbox.

1967 2000 GT — MF1010100 — L — 750-900.000 USD — 576.300 — 750.000 — 670.875 — 20-05-17 — Indianapolis — S202 — **Mec F720**
Red with black interior; restored. One of 62 examples built for the US market (see lot S59 Mecum 15.8.15 $925,000 and S200 Mecum 23.1.16 NS).

1985 Supra Group A — 00056255 — R — 60-80.000 GBP — NS — — — 27-07-17 — Silverstone — 121 — **SiC**
Red and white; the car was raced by Barry Sheene at the 1985 British Touring Car Championship. Restored in 2012.

1992 Celica GT-Four ST185 — 14906 — L — 180-240.000 EUR — 172.103 — 212.721 — 198.120 — 18-03-17 — Lyon — 208 — **Agu F721**
Toyota Team Europe car used at some events of the World Rally Championship and driven also by Carlos Sainz and Didier Auriol. Sold to private hands in 1993 and raced until 2007. Bought in 2009 by the current owner and restored to the 1993 Castrol livery.

TRACTA (F) (1926-1932)

1927 Type A GePhi — 13 — R — 500-700.000 EUR — 617.409 — 787.568 — 705.264 — 18-06-17 — Fontainebleau — 58 — **Ose F722**
Polished aluminium with blue wings; since 1958 in the Jacques Liscourt collection. The car raced the Le Mans 24 Hours in 1928 and 1929.

1928 Type D2 Sport — 503 — R — 60-80.000 EUR — 50.884 — 63.938 — 59.800 — 09-02-17 — Paris — 411 — **Bon**
Sold new to the UK, the car remained in the same family ownership until 1986; restored in the late 1980s. 1,600cc SCAP engine.

F719: 1960 Tatra T603

F720: 1967 Toyota 2000 GT

F721: 1992 Toyota Celica GT-Four ST185

F722: 1927 Tracta Type A GePhi

TRIUMPH (GB) (1923-1984)

Year	Model (Bodybuilder)	Chassis no.	Steering	Estimate	£	$	€	Date	Place	Lot	Auc. H.
1939	**Dolomite 14/60 cabriolet**	3061657	R	30-35.000 GBP		NS		02-06-17	Solihull	61	H&H
White with dark blue leather interior; in good overall condition, the car requires recommissioning prior to use.												
1939	**Dolomite 14/60 cabriolet**	3061657	R	25-30.000 GBP	21.937	28.612	24.572	26-07-17	Duxford	40	H&H
See lot 61 H & H 2.6.17.												
1948	**1800 Roadster**	TRD2408	R	15-20.000 GBP	11.760	14.413	13.079	12-10-16	Duxford	84	H&H
Blue; described as in fair, original condition.												
1947	**1800 Roadster**	TRD868	R	30-35.000 EUR	26.172	34.405	28.990	05-08-17	Schloss Dyck	210	Coy F723
Red; in good overall condition. Imported into Germany from the UK in 2009.												
1949	**2000 Roadster**	TRA439	R	23-26.000 GBP		NS		07-12-16	London	378	Bon
Blue; restored circa 20 years ago; described as in good overall condition.												
1953	**Mayflower saloon**	TT30589DL	R	3-4.000 GBP		NS		02-06-17	Solihull	51	H&H
Black with light brown leather interior, in fair overall condition. It requires recommissioning prior to use.												
1954	**TR2**	TS3704	R	24-28.000 GBP	40.040	48.985	46.366	04-03-17	Brooklands	148	His F724
British racing green with tan interior; restored. Until 1995 with its first owner (see lot 282 Historics 8.3.14 $56,347).												
1954	**TR2**	TS2167L	L	21-27.000 GBP	22.400	29.147	26.074	20-05-17	Ascot	153	His
British racing green with brown leather interior; reimported into the UK from the USA in 1990 and fully restored. Described as still in very good overall condition.												
1959	**TR3**	TS27087	L	NQ	22.963*	28.600*	26.827*	08-04-17	Palm Beach	609	B/J
Red with black interior; an older restoration.												
1958	**TR3A**	TS24153L	L	30-40.000 EUR		NS		06-11-16	Lyon	346	Ose
Red; restored a few years ago.												
1959	**TR3A**	TS39531L	R	20-24.000 GBP	23.800	30.009	27.967	07-12-16	Chateau Impney	60	H&H
Red with black interior; sold new to the USA, the car was reimported into the UK in 2005 and later restored and converted to right-hand drive (see lots 403 Bonhams 1.12.11 $27,535 and 39 H & H 24.2.16 $31,161).												
1961	**TR3A**	TS70697L	L	30-40.000 EUR	31.272	38.653	36.000	19-03-17	Fontainebleau	214	Ose
British racing green; in good driving order.												
1962	**TR3B**	TCF2037L	L	22-28.000 GBP		NS		03-09-16	Beaulieu	477	Bon
White with pale blue interior; restored in the USA prior to 1999 and imported into the UK in 2015.												
1963	**TR3B**	TCF2639L	L	20-35.000 USD	19.016	24.200	21.659	24-06-17	Santa Monica	133	RMS
Dark ivory; less than 500 miles covered since the restoration completed in 2007.												
1967	**Vitesse cabriolet (cabriolet/conversion)**	HC675DL	R	NQ	7.336*	9.165*	8.668*	23-02-17	Donington Park	15	H&H
Blue with beige interior; built with saloon body and converted to cabriolet between the late 1970s and early 1980s. Some recent restoration works.												
1969	**Vitesse MkII cabriolet (Michelotti)**	HC51986CVO	R	NQ	5.600*	6.851*	6.485*	04-03-17	Brooklands	111	His
In good overall condition; with hardtop. Manual gearbox with overdrive.												

F723: 1947 Triumph 1800 Roadster

F724: 1954 Triumph TR2

Year	Model (Bodybuilder)	Chassis no.	Steering	Estimate	Hammer price £	$	€	Date	Place	Lot	Auc. H.
1966	**Spitfire MkII** (Michelotti)	FC69065	R	18-20.000 GBP	17.920	22.282	21.036	26-11-16	Weybridge	111	His
Red with black interior; restored in recent years.											
1966	**Spitfire Mk II** (Michelotti)	FC76863	R	14-19.000 GBP		NS		04-03-17	Brooklands	208	His
Red with red interior; fully restored. With an old English white hardtop.											
1963	**Spitfire** (Michelotti)	FC8036	R	16-20.000 GBP		NS		08-07-17	Brooklands	147	His
Red with black interior; an older restoration, the car is described as still in good overall condition.											
1962	**TR4** (Michelotti)	CT17336L	R	18-22.000 GBP	24.188	30.366	28.622	24-02-17	Stoneleigh P.	940	SiC
Red; reimported from the USA. Recently restored and converted to right-hand drive.											
1962	**TR4** (Michelotti)	CT6468	R	17-21.000 GBP	18.480	22.608	21.400	04-03-17	Brooklands	181	His
Green with beige interior; engine recently rebuilt and increased to 2290cc.											
1964	**TR4** (Michelotti)	CT34660LO	L	22-28.000 EUR		NS		18-03-17	Lyon	177	Agu
British racing green with black interior; in original condition. In good mechanical order.											
1963	**TR4** (Michelotti)	CT21961L	L	28-32.000 EUR		NS		08-04-17	Essen	113	Coy
Red; restored in 2003. The car comes with the Italian ASI homologation.											
1967	**TR4A IRS** (Michelotti)	CTC78490	R	25-29.000 GBP	32.480	42.263	37.807	20-05-17	Ascot	230	His
Royal blue with magnolia leather interior; fully restored over a 12 year period.											
1963	**TR4** (Michelotti)	CT20726	R	17-20.000 GBP	19.320	24.915	21.832	08-07-17	Brooklands	121	His
Red with original black interior.											
1970	**GT6 MkII** (Michelotti)	KC807020	R	12-15.000 GBP	13.338	17.389	15.624	18-05-17	London	101	Coy **F725**
Blue; in good overall condition.											
1968	**TR5** (Michelotti)	CP2267	R	35-40.000 GBP	37.125	46.997	43.098	12-11-16	Birmingham	631	SiC
Light blue with black interior; restored several years ago (see lot 241 Historics 6.6.15 $51,512).											
1968	**TR250** (Michelotti)	CD7532LO	L	25-35.000 EUR		NS		06-11-16	Lyon	325	Ose
Red with black interior; described as in good original condition.											
1974	**TR6**	CF24347U	R	14-17.000 GBP	17.640	21.620	19.619	12-10-16	Duxford	10	H&H
Red with black interior; restored in 2012 (see lot 42 H & H 28.7.16 $15,853).											
1973	**TR6**	1CR5114L	L	15-20.000 EUR	24.805*	30.844*	29.120*	25-11-16	Milan	526	RMS
Dark green; 47,522 miles. From the Duemila Ruote collection.											
1969	**TR6**	CC29804L	L	10-12.000 GBP	9.800	12.185	11.504	26-11-16	Weybridge	125	His
Red; described as in good working order.											
1975	**TR6**	CF38573U	L	19-25.000 EUR	18.488	22.514	21.118	14-01-17	Maastricht	206	Coy
Red with tan vinyl interior; in good original condition. Bought in 2012 by the current, second owner.											
1973	**TR6 PI**	CR8490	R	22-25.000 GBP	23.063	29.652	27.265	13-05-17	Silverstone	305	SiC
White with black interior; fully restored between 2013 and 2015.											
1973	**TR6**	1CR117L	L	18-22.000 EUR		NS		10-06-17	Lyon	147	Agu
Burgundy with black vinyl interior; restored.											
1976	**Stag** (Michelotti)	LD41981A	R	14-18.000 GBP	12.320	15.072	14.267	04-03-17	Brooklands	113	His
Red with black interior; in very good mechanical condition. Automatic transmission.											
1972	**Stag** (Michelotti)	LD118040	R	16-20.000 GBP	18.480	24.046	21.511	20-05-17	Ascot	129	His
Red; restored in 1999-2000. Manual gearbox.											
1974	**Stag** (Michelotti)	LD31258A	R	13-18.000 GBP	22.074	28.467	24.944	08-07-17	Brooklands	132	His
Magenta with black interior; described as in very good original condition. 47,500 miles covered.											
1970	**Stag** (Michelotti)	LD12	R	40-45.000 GBP		NS		26-07-17	Duxford	48	H&H
White with black interior; pre-production car no. 9; Belgian press launch car. Stored in 1989 and restored between 2014 and 2016. Manual gearbox.											
1978	**Dolomite Sprint**	VA26549DL0	R	NQ	9.520*	12.277*	10.758*	08-07-17	Brooklands	160	His
Yellow with black roof and black interior; fully restored.											
1979	**TR7**	TCT113071UCF	L	20-30.000 USD	19.633*	24.200*	22.683*	19-01-17	Scottsdale	32	Bon
Orange with red tartan and black vinyl interior; in highly original condition. Less than 1,000 miles on the odometer.											

F725: 1970 Triumph GT6 MkII (Michelotti)

F726: 1948 Tucker Model 48 Torpedo

Year	Model	(Bodybuilder)	Chassis no.	Steering	Estimate	Hammer price £	Hammer price $	Hammer price €	Date	Place	Lot	Auc. H.
1979	TR7 V8 coupé		ACG26381	R	20-30.000 GBP	41.400	55.166	48.960	10-09-16	Goodwood	133	Bon

Red and blue; built in the 2000s as an evocation of the Tony Pond's 1980 Ypres Rally winning car. From the collection of the late Philip Young.

TUCKER (USA) (1947-1948)

Year	Model	(Bodybuilder)	Chassis no.	Steering	Estimate	£	$	€	Date	Place	Lot	Auc. H.
1948	Model 48 Torpedo		1044	L	1.600-2.100.000 USD	1.093.227	1.347.500	1.263.012	19-01-17	Phoenix	160	RMS F726

Bought in 1982 by the previous owner, the car was subsequently stored for 33 years until 2016 when it was acquired by the vendor, recommissioned and returned to the road. The paintwork was redone in 1972 and requires to be replaced again; the cloth interior were retrimmed in 1972 and are still in good condition.

TURCAT-MERY (F) (1898-1929)

Year	Model	(Bodybuilder)	Chassis no.	Steering	Estimate	£	$	€	Date	Place	Lot	Auc. H.
1927	Type VG Sport		7808	R	80-100.000 EUR	94.546	120.604	108.000	18-06-17	Fontainebleau	61	Ose

Beige with burgundy wings; restored at unspeciifed date. From the Jacques Liscourt collection.

TVR (GB) (1949-)

Year	Model	(Bodybuilder)	Chassis no.	Steering	Estimate	£	$	€	Date	Place	Lot	Auc. H.
1960	Grantura		7F145	R	30-35.000 GBP	NS			24-02-17	Stoneleigh P.	946	SiC
1970	Tuscan V8		MAL013	R	70-100.000 AUD	57.825	71.899	67.881	27-11-16	Melbourne	47	Mos F727

Silver with red leather interior; sold new to the USA, reimported into the UK in 1988, converted to right-hand drive in the early 1990s, driven at historic events, imported into Australia in 2002, body repainted, interior retrimmed, 302bhp engine.

| 1974 | 3000M | | 3893FM | R | 25-35.000 AUD | 15.833 | 19.687 | 18.586 | 27-11-16 | Melbourne | 80 | Mos |

Silver; imported new into Australia where it remained with its first owner until 2015. Recently serviced. Only 3000M modified to order of its first owner with an opening tailgate, a special feature which went into production with the new model Taimar which was lauched in 1976.

| 1989 | 420 SEAC | | 19406 | R | 22-28.000 GBP | NS | | | 20-05-17 | Ascot | 193 | His |

Light metallic green; 23,000 miles covered. Rover V8 engine rebuilt in 2009.

| 1995 | Chimera | | 11264 | L | 28-35.000 EUR | 24.159 | 31.759 | 26.760 | 05-08-17 | Schloss Dyck | 271 | Coy |

Black with red leather interior; 60,000 kms covered. Sold new to the Netherlands.

| 2006 | Tuscan 4.0 cabriolet | | 001082 | R | 75-95.000 EUR | NS | | | 21-05-17 | SPA-Francorch. | 78 | Bon |

Metallic topaz blue with blue leather and cloth interior.

| 1999 | Cerbera | | 1002 | R | 17-23.000 GBP | 22.950 | 28.536 | 26.941 | 26-11-16 | Weybridge | 134 | His |

Pearl yellow with purple leather interior; described as in very good overall condition. Recently serviced.

| 2000 | Cerbera Speed Six coupé | | 001247 | R | 11-14.000 GBP | 15.120 | 18.498 | 17.509 | 04-03-17 | Brooklands | 118 | His |

Blue with magnolia interior; last serviced in October 2016 at 32,867 miles.

UNIC (F) (1904-1940)

Year	Model	(Bodybuilder)	Chassis no.	Steering	Estimate	£	$	€	Date	Place	Lot	Auc. H.
1915	Type M1T coupé chauffeur	(Vicard)	2392	R	30-40.000 GBP	27.500	36.528	32.637	03-09-16	Beaulieu	449	Bon

Red with black wings; interior reupholstered in 2003.

VALE (GB) (1932-1936)

Year	Model	(Bodybuilder)	Chassis no.	Steering	Estimate	£	$	€	Date	Place	Lot	Auc. H.
1933	Special		VS310	R	19-25.000 GBP	23.230	28.220	25.836	29-10-16	London	144	Coy

Black; recently reimported from the USA where it was imported in the late 1980s and raced at historic events.

VALLEE (F) (1896-1901)

Year	Model	(Bodybuilder)	Chassis no.	Steering	Estimate	£	$	€	Date	Place	Lot	Auc. H.
1897	4hp vis-a-vis		NQ	R	70-90.000 GBP	85.120	113.908	101.369	07-09-16	London	105	RMS F728

Dark green; described as in original condition except for a repaint and new black canvas. With Veteran Car Club of Great Britain certificate no. 1364 issued in 1974 (see lot 114 RM/Sotheby's 3.2.16 $91,837).

VANDEN PLAS (GB) (1960-1980)

Year	Model	(Bodybuilder)	Chassis no.	Steering	Estimate	£	$	€	Date	Place	Lot	Auc. H.
1965	Princess 4-Litre R		VR531682	R	7-9.000 GBP	6.750	8.398	7.814	29-03-17	Duxford	58	H&H

Metallic grey with light grey interior; in very good original condition. Recently recommissioned.

F727: 1970 TVR Tuscan V8

F728: 1897 Vallee 4hp vis-a-vis

Year	Model	(Bodybuilder)	Chassis no.	Steering	Estimate	Hammer price £	$	€	Date	Place	Lot	Auc. H.
1973	**Princess 1300**		VAS235878M	R	9-12.000 GBP		NS		07-12-16	London	304	**Bon**
	Blue; circa 15,000 miles covered since new. In good overall condition. Automatic transmission.											
1974	**Princess 1300**		VAS239097M	R	3-4.000 GBP	10.080	12.593	11.911	23-02-17	Donington Park	35	**H&H**
	Red with dark blue interior; described as in good overall condition, the car remained unused from 1981 to January 2017 when it was recommissioned.											

VAUXHALL (GB) (1903-)

Year	Model	(Bodybuilder)	Chassis no.	Steering	Estimate	£	$	€	Date	Place	Lot	Auc. H.
1914	**25hp D-type "Prince Henry"**	(Hoskison)	C97	R	500-600.000 GBP	516.700	652.230	612.858	04-12-16	London	6	**Bon**
	White with polished aluminium bonnet; leather interior believed original. In the same ownership from new to 1945 when it was acquired by Laurence Pomeroy Jnr. who retained it for 21 years. Since 1970 in the current, fourth ownership. Driven at several events over the years. Started and run in July 2016, it requires recommissioning prior to use.											**F729**
1924	**14/40 M-Type Melton tourer**		M1696	R	30-35.000 GBP		NS		08-10-16	Ascot	338	**Coy**
	Yellow with black wings; described as in good driving order. Fitted in period at the factory with front wheel brakes (see Bonhams lots 1057 2.12.02 NS and 441 12.9.09 $27,847).											
1928	**20/60 Melton roadster**	(Holden)	R3212	R	50-60.000 GBP		NS		12-10-16	Duxford	120	**H&H**
	Two-tone grey with grey interior; restored in Australia, the car was reimported in 2007 into the UK where the body was repainted and the engine was overhauled.											
1960	**Cresta PA saloon**		BADX144429	R	8-10.000 GBP		NS		16-11-16	Donington Park	122	**H&H**
	Some recent works to the mechanicals and body.											
1979	**Chevette HS hatchback**		9B08RJY146283	R	16-20.000 GBP	14.375	19.155	17.000	10-09-16	Goodwood	131	**Bon**
	Silver with tartan interior; engine rebuilt in 2012 and body repainted in 2013. From the collection of the late Philip Young (see lot 307 Silverstone Auctions 22.2.14 $27,237).											
1979	**Chevette HSR**		9808DE7227913	R	60-80.000 GBP		NS		14-01-17	Birmingham	153	**Coy**
	Silver; ex-Works car, it won the 1979 Sedan Open Rally Championship driven by Pentti Airikkala. Offered in the 1981 HSR specification (see lot 45 H & H 26.2.11 $106,194).											
1991	**Lotus Carlton**		1250674	R	60-70.000 GBP	72.000	94.284	80.388	29-07-17	Silverstone	410	**SiC**
	Dark green; 4,500 miles covered; recently recommissioned following a storage period.											**F730**
1991	**Lotus Carlton**		249679	R	22-26.000 GBP	23.625	30.937	26.377	29-07-17	Silverstone	446	**SiC**
	Dark green; in good overall condition; 73,000 miles covered. Clutch recently replaced.											

VENTURI (F) (1985-)

Year	Model	(Bodybuilder)	Chassis no.	Steering	Estimate	£	$	€	Date	Place	Lot	Auc. H.
1990	**Transcup 210**		CH0002	L	30-40.000 EUR	26.642	33.279	30.000	05-11-16	Lyon	237	**Agu**
	Formerly owned by Gérad Godfroy, designer and co-founder of the make. Described as in good overall condition; last serviced in September 2015. 49,500 kms covered.											
1996	**260 LM**		135	L	50-60.000 EUR		NS		10-06-17	Lyon	135	**Agu**
	Silver with black leather interior; less than 17,000 miles covered.											
1992	**400 Trophy**		CE0051	L	130-180.000 EUR		NS		05-11-16	Lyon	239	**Agu**
	Silver; raced until 1995 and again in the early 2000s in Belgium. Restored in 2015-2016.											
1998	**Atlantique 300**		CE0031	L	55-75.000 EUR		NS		05-11-16	Lyon	238	**Agu**
	Dark blue; in 2004 the body was repainrted, the engine upgraded to 310bhp and the gearbox replaced with a 400 GT unit. 44,130 kms covered. Not used recently, it requires recommissioning.											

VOISIN (F) (1919-1958)

Year	Model	(Bodybuilder)	Chassis no.	Steering	Estimate	£	$	€	Date	Place	Lot	Auc. H.
1938	**C28 cabriolet**		53002	R	800-1.000.000 USD		NS		19-08-17	Monterey	253	**RMS**
	Two-tone red with tan interior; restored in the early 2000s. One of two Voisins with coachworks attributed to R. Saliot, but probably built by other coachbuilders. It is believed that the present body was fitted to the car in 1946 or 1947.											

VOLKSWAGEN (D) (1936-)

Year	Model	(Bodybuilder)	Chassis no.	Steering	Estimate	£	$	€	Date	Place	Lot	Auc. H.
1985	**Beetle Jubilee Edition**		002683	L	20-30.000 GBP	15.680*	20.983*	18.673*	07-09-16	London	177	**RMS**
	Metallic pewter with cloth interior; one 3,150 examples built. 25 kms covered. It requires recommissioning prior to use.											
1956	**Beetle**		11628654	L	NQ	11.687*	15.400*	13.717*	17-09-16	Aspen	151	**TFA**
	Black with tan interior; restored six years ago. Recently serviced.											
1956	**Beetle**		1361305	L	NA	35.957*	44.000*	39.992*	15-10-16	Las Vegas	86	**B/J**
	Grey with saddle interior; recently restored.											
1954	**Beetle**		10610151	R	15-20.000 GBP	15.340	18.635	17.061	29-10-16	London	105	**Coy**
	Grey; in good condition.											

F729: 1914 Vauxhall 25hp D-type "Prince Henry" (Hoskison)

F730: 1991 Vauxhall Lotus Carlton

Year	Model	(Bodybuilder)	Chassis no.	Steering	Estimate	Hammer price £	Hammer price $	Hammer price €	Sale Date	Place	Lot	Auc. H.
1958	Beetle DeLuxe		1754939	L	25-35.000 USD	17.912*	22.000*	20.629*	18-01-17	Scottsdale	66	WoA
	Black with red interior; restored and fitted with a 36bhp 1,585cc engine. Fabric sunroof.											
1952	Beetle		10331718	L	55-80.000 EUR	49.687	62.113	58.240	08-02-17	Paris	103	RMS F731
	Sold new to Sweden, the car remained with its first owner until 2014 when it was bought by the vendor. Stored from 1963 to 2014, it is described as in completely original condition and has covered 77,000 kms. In driving order.											
1950	Beetle DeLuxe		10195459	L	65-75.000 USD	36.194*	44.000*	41.466*	10-03-17	Amelia Island	62	G&Co
	Burgundy; a few miles covered since the restoration carried out in 2007.											
1964	Beetle 1200 Luxury		6349319	L	9-14.000 EUR	12.117	15.419	13.800	24-06-17	Wien	308	Dor
	Red with grey interior; restored 25 years ago. Recently serviced.											
1956	Beetle		1239680	L	25-35.000 EUR	16.872*	24.901*	19.187*	02-07-17	Monaco	146	Art
	Grey; since 1992 in the current ownership; restored in 2011. With sunroof.											
1956	Beetle		381002	L	55-65.000 USD	59.829*	77.000*	65.835*	17-08-17	Monterey	37	WoA
	Green; fully restored.											
1943	Typ 166 "Schwimmwagen"		1881	L	150-175.000 USD	88.412	116.500	103.767	17-09-16	Aspen	154	TFA
	Acquired in the 1990s by the current owner and subsequently restored.											
1956	Beetle cabriolet	(Karmann)	1575247	L	55-65.000 USD		NS		17-09-16	Aspen	109	TFA
	White with black interior; restored to concours condition.											
1952	Beetle cabriolet	(Karmann)	10371026	L	135-150.000 USD		NS		17-09-16	Aspen	121	TFA
	Blue with blue leather interior; acquired in 2002 by the current owner and subsequently fully restored to concours condition.											
1979	Beetle 1303 cabriolet		1592002108	L	18-28.000 EUR	23.781	29.100	26.450	15-10-16	Salzburg	413	Dor
	Metallic grey with tan leatherette interior; in good original condition. 64,951 kms covered. Since 1981 in the current ownership.											
1957	Beetle cabriolet		1479760	L	15-20.000 EUR	38.162*	47.452*	44.800*	25-11-16	Milan	838	RMS
	Light blue with light grey interior. From the Duemila Ruote collection.											
1956	Beetle cabriolet	(Karmann)	1575247	L	40-60.000 USD	28.558	35.200	32.993	19-01-17	Scottsdale	45	Bon
	See lot 109 The Finest Automobile Auctions 17.9.16.											
1956	Beetle cabriolet		1209639	L	NQ	37.536*	46.750*	43.852*	08-04-17	Palm Beach	386	B/J
	Red with beige interior; restored.											
1978	Beetle cabriolet		1582049817	L	17-22.000 EUR		NS		05-08-17	Schloss Dyck	265	Coy
	Black with black interior; restored about nine years ago.											
1959	Minibus		484771	L	NA	85.977	106.000	99.725	19-11-16	Anaheim	S91	Mec
	Red and white with two-tone grey interior; 70 miles covered since the restoration.											
1963	Minibus		1049669	L	150-200.000 USD		NS		19-01-17	Phoenix	168	RMS
	23-window version finished in grey and white with grey cloth and vinyl interior; restoration completed five years ago. From the Mohrschladt Family Collection.											
1964	Minibus		245016637	L	60-100.000 EUR	83.366*	103.892*	97.744*	10-02-17	Paris	147	Art
	21 window version; restoration completed in 2015. Sunroof.											
1961	Minibus		608038	L	NQ	234.045*	291.500*	273.427*	08-04-17	Palm Beach	711	B/J
	23 window version finished in red with light grey roof and grey interior; fully restored (see lot 1361 Barrett-Jackson 18.1.14 $148,500).											
1959	Minibus		481764	L	165-180.000 USD	101.010	130.000	110.760	19-08-17	Monterey	F86	Mec
	23-window version finished in white and red with grey and white interior; less than 200 miles covered since a full restoration.											
1968	Karmann Ghia cabriolet		149044618	L	3-6.000 EUR	15.453	19.302	17.400	05-11-16	Lyon	262	Agu
	Grey with beige interior; it requires several restoration works.											
1968	Karmann Ghia cabriolet		657645	R	40-50.000 GBP		NS		29-03-17	Duxford	74	H&H
	Black with cream leather interior; fully restored a few years ago.											
1969	Karmann Ghia cabriolet		149953166	L	33-38.000 EUR	30.199	39.698	33.450	05-08-17	Schloss Dyck	204	Coy F732
	White with dark blue leatherette interior; in good overall condition.											
1970	Karmann Ghia coupé		1402572282	L	15-20.000 EUR		NS		06-11-16	Lyon	352	Ose
	Yellow; reimported into Europe from the USA in 1991.											
1973	Modell 181 "The Thing"		1833024537	L	NA	16.630*	20.350*	18.496*	15-10-16	Las Vegas	28.1	B/J
	Cream with black interior; restored.											

F731: 1952 Volkswagen Beetle

F732: 1969 Volkswagen Karmann Ghia cabriolet

Year	Model	(Bodybuilder)	Chassis no.	Steering	Estimate	Hammer price £	$	€	Date	Place	Lot	Auc. H.
1973	Modell 181 "The Thing"		1833015183	L	20-30.000 USD	19.633*	24.200*	22.683*	19-01-17	Phoenix	179	RMS F733
	Orange; in largely original condition. From the Mohrschladt Family Collection.											
1973	Modell 181 "The Thing"		1833015461	L	NQ	10.418	13.000	12.030	25-03-17	Kansas City	F147	Mec
	White with black interior; restored.											
1973	Modell 181 "The Thing"		1833022899	L	NQ	12.911*	16.500*	15.423*	22-04-17	Arlington	44	WoA
	White; restored. From the Monical restoration.											
1975	Modell 181 "The Thing"		1842818752	L	7-10.000 EUR	10.602*	13.491*	12.075*	24-06-17	Wien	314	Dor
	White with grey and black interior; a federal army car when new. Refurbished at unspecified date..											
1974	Modell 181 "The Thing"		1842542277E	L	25-50.000 USD	27.778*	35.750*	30.566*	17-08-17	Monterey	66	WoA
	Acapulco Edition; fully restored.											
1981	Golf GTI		153098	L	28-38.000 EUR	23.577*	28.642*	26.224*	30-10-16	Paris	159	Art
	White; body recently repainted. Engine rebuilt in 2013. Oettinger version.											
1977	Golf GTI		177343398517EG1	L	18-26.000 EUR	25.577	31.948	28.800	05-11-16	Lyon	250	Agu
	Metallic grey with cloth and vinyl interior; restored between 2013 and 2016. Engine replaced in 2010 (the original unit is included with the sale).											
1977	Golf GTI		43188417EG2	L	12-18.000 EUR	13.777	17.569	15.720	10-06-17	Lyon	129	Agu
	Metallic grey with cloth and vinyl interior; restored between 2007 and 2009.											

VOLPINI (I)

Year	Model	(Bodybuilder)	Chassis no.	Steering	Estimate	£	$	€	Date	Place	Lot	Auc. H.
1959	Formula Junior		006	M	65-85.000 GBP		NS		10-09-16	Goodwood	156	Bon
	Red; sold new to the USA where it was raced in period. Reimported into Europe in the early 1980s; several restoration works carried out over the years. With FIA papers.											

VOLVO (S) (1926-)

Year	Model	(Bodybuilder)	Chassis no.	Steering	Estimate	£	$	€	Date	Place	Lot	Auc. H.
1960	PV 544 Sport		274054	L	15-20.000 USD	27.655*	34.100*	30.608*	07-10-16	Hershey	260	RMS
	Red with red and white vinyl interior; recently restored.											
1969	122S Group 2		131341T345256	L	25-35.000 EUR	21.735*	28.283*	25.300*	21-05-17	SPA-Francorch.	39	Bon F734
	White; prepared when new at the factory to Group 2 Rally specification, the car has had a long race career in Scandinavia. Restored in the late 1990s; recommissioned in 2016.											
1964	122S four-door saloon		167079	R	9-11.000 GBP	8.100	10.379	9.281	02-06-17	Solihull	46	H&H
	Cream with red interior; in largely original condition.											
1971	P1800E		184352U37Y32	R	18-24.000 GBP	24.150	32.180	28.560	10-09-16	Goodwood	112	Bon
	Blue with black leather interior; restored over the years. Recently serviced.											
1963	P1800		3655	L	8-12.000 USD	17.951*	23.100*	20.557*	03-10-16	Philadelphia	252	Bon
	One owner; original interior; body repainted; engine not running.											
1971	P1800E		184352037352	R	11-14.000 GBP	19.600	24.371	23.008	26-11-16	Weybridge	177	His
	Red with black interior; restored in 1999. The original injection system replaced by twin SU carburettors. Webasto sunroof.											
1972	P1800E		184352U	R	28-34.000 GBP		NS		07-12-16	London	319	Bon
	Yellow; fully restored (see lot 316 Silverstone Auctions 26.7.14 $39,072).											
1965	P1800S		15545	L	40-50.000 EUR	44.824	55.403	51.600	19-03-17	Fontainebleau	232	Ose F735
	200 kms covered since the restoration recently completed.											
1967	P1800S		25822	R	22-26.000 GBP	19.125	24.944	21.422	26-07-17	Duxford	61	H&H
	White with original red leather interior; some restoration works carried out in 2016.											
1965	130 Amazon 2-door saloon		125729	L	8-10.000 EUR	6.847	8.528	8.000	08-04-17	Essen	106	Coy
	Red with black interior; restored.											

WANDERER (D) (1911-1939)

Year	Model	(Bodybuilder)	Chassis no.	Steering	Estimate	£	$	€	Date	Place	Lot	Auc. H.
1938	W25K roadster		180155	L	55-70.000 USD	85.962	104.500	98.481	11-03-17	Amelia Island	46	Mot
	Restoration project.											

F733: 1973 Volkswagen Modell 181 "The Thing"

F734: 1969 Volvo 122S Group 2

F735: 1965 Volvo P1800S

F736: 1932 Willys 6-90 Silver Streak roadster

WHIPPET (USA) (1927-1931)

Year	Model	Chassis no.	Steering	Estimate	£	$	€	Date	Place	Lot	Auc. H.
1927	Model 96 touring	19071551	R	10-14.000 GBP	10.360	12.674	11.997	04-03-17	Brooklands	126	His

White with black fenders and black interior; restored approximately 10 years ago.

WILLYS (USA) (1914-1963)

Year	Model	Chassis no.	Steering	Estimate	£	$	€	Date	Place	Lot	Auc. H.
1932	6-90 Silver Streak roadster	8610	L	20-30.000 USD	35.047*	45.100*	40.134*	03-10-16	Philadelphia	211	Bon F736

Black and navy blue with black interior; restored more than 20 years ago, it is described as in good overall condition.

| 1943 | MB Jeep | MB290552 | L | NA | 24.190 | 32.132 | 28.709 | 02-09-16 | Salon Privé | 202 | SiC |

On display in a museum for 15 years until 2015; some mechanical works carried out recently.

| 1942 | MB Jeep | 140814 | L | NA | 21.560* | 26.808* | 25.309* | 26-11-16 | Weybridge | 196 | His |

Restored in 2008.

| 1950 | Jeepster phaeton | 10825 | L | 25-30.000 USD | 18.734* | 23.100* | 20.735* | 07-10-16 | Hershey | 263 | RMS |

Red and black with red interior; restored.

| 1950 | Jeepster | 651BA110104 | L | 30-35.000 USD | | NS | | 05-11-16 | Hilton Head | 162 | AA |

Yellow; 6-cylinder engine. Body repainted 12 years ago.

| 1951 | M38 Jeep | MC36583 | L | 30-50.000 USD | 30.400* | 38.500* | 34.419* | 06-10-16 | Hershey | 121 | RMS |

Restored; in good working order. Fitted with numerous accessories, including an inert .50 caliber air-cooled machine gun and an inert .30 caliber water-cooled machine gun.

| 1960 | DJ3A Gala | 5633718471 | L | 25-35.000 USD | 37.928* | 46.750* | 43.819* | 19-01-17 | Phoenix | 103 | RMS F737 |

Blue and white with blue and white vinyl interior; 45 miles covered since a full restoration.

WINTON (USA) (1897-1925)

| 1906 | Model K touring | 5399 | L | 200-250.000 USD | 126.336 | 160.000 | 143.040 | 06-10-16 | Hershey | 137 | RMS F738 |

Red with white chassis and wheels and black leather interior; acquired in 1982 by the current owner and subsequently restored over a 20 year period.

WOLFE (USA) (1907-1909)

| 1907 | Four touring | 57 | R | 50-70.000 USD | 38.462* | 49.500* | 42.174* | 19-08-17 | Pebble Beach | 133 | G&Co |

Red with black interior; restoration completed in 2010; further mechanical sorting may be necessary before serious use.

WOLSELEY (GB) (1896-1975)

| 1938 | 14/56 saloon | 21413627 | R | 11-13.000 GBP | | NS | | 23-02-17 | Donington Park | 48 | H&H |

Black with green interior; restored, the car is described as in very good overall condition.

F737: 1960 Willys DJ3A Gala

F738: 1906 Winton Model K touring

Year	Model	(Bodybuilder)	Chassis no.	Steering	Estimate	Hammer price £	$	€	Date	Place	Lot	Auc. H.

F739: 1951 Wolseley 6/80 saloon

F740: 1959 WRE Maserati Sport

1937	**Super Six 25 station wagon**		325501	R	NA		NS		19-11-16	Anaheim	S123.1	Mec

Dark green with wooden panels and green interior; built with saloon body and fitted in the 1950s with the present body; restored in the 1990s.

1951	**6/80 saloon**		AAE141861	R	8-12.000 GBP	10.350*	13.748*	12.283*	03-09-16	Beaulieu	461	Bon **F739**

Maroon with tan interior; older restoration.

| 1954 | **4/44 saloon** | | NAA1315920 | R | 7-10.000 GBP | 1.610* | 2.139* | 1.911* | 03-09-16 | Beaulieu | 407 | Bon |

Black; recently mildly recommissioned, it requires some further works.

| 1965 | **6/110 saloon** | | WBS331256 | R | 4-6.000 GBP | 4.370* | 5.805* | 5.186* | 03-09-16 | Beaulieu | 464 | Bon |

Grey; recently recommissioned.

WRE (GB) *(1959-1961)*

| 1959 | **Maserati Sport** | | 1002 | R | 750-950.000 EUR | 634.743 | 815.069 | 728.000 | 27-05-17 | Villa Erba | 158 | RMS **F740** |

Red with blue interior; one of three examples built; raced in period; for 30 years in the current ownership; restored in Italy in the 1980s (see lot 30 TSAC 10.7.06 NS).

ZAGATO (I) *(1966-)*

| 1974 | **Zele** | | Z1000183 | L | 12-14.000 GBP | 13.440 | 16.711 | 15.777 | 26-11-16 | Weybridge | 144 | His |

Orange; imported into the UK from Italy in 2016. Electric engine.

ZIMMERLI (CH)

| 1949 | **18-6 Roadster** | | LIP1454 | L | 125-175.000 USD | 58.816* | 71.500* | 67.382* | 11-03-17 | Amelia Island | 291 | RMS **F741** |

Maroon with tan interior; one-off fitted with a 2,275cc 6-cylinder Vauxhall engine. Owned by the Zimmerli family until 1966, the car was imported into the USA in 2000 circa. In 2008 it was bought by the current owner and subsequently restored (see lot 304 Bonhams 15.8.08 NS).

ZUNDAPP (D) *(1917-1958)*

| 1957 | **Janus 250** | | W2416 | L | 30-50.000 EUR | 14.233* | 17.738* | 16.688* | 10-02-17 | Paris | 152 | Art **F742** |

In good cosmetic condition; to be serviced prior to use.

F741: 1949 Zimmerli 18-6 Roadster

F742: 1957 Zundapp Janus 250

All about originality

A classic Ferrari is more than simply a collectors' car. It is a testimony to Ferrari's heritage and each model represents the pinnacle of road-car engineering of its era. When you own a Ferrari, the most important aspect is originality. Since 2003, Ferrari has provided factory support for the collector car world, introducing a programme that testifies to the authenticity of cars and supplying a comprehensive range of services dedicated to the preservation of these historically significant motor vehicles.

Ferrari Classiche has certified over 5400 cars and carried out over 95 full restorations. Recent projects include the 1954 Ferrari 500 Mondial Spider PF (chassis no. 0438 MD) originally owned Porfirio Rubirosa who drove it at Santa Barbara in September 1954, finishing eighth overall and second in its category. In the hands of subsequent owner, American John Von Neumann, the 500 Mondial went on to win two races at Santa Barbara in 1955, then took victory at Pomona before triumphing again at Santa Barbara in 1956. Now owned by Californian Tom Peck, the vehicle was sent to the Ferrari Classiche Department for a full restoration that included the installation of a factory-produced replacement for its original engine. Just a week after the restoration was finished in 2015, it arrived in Pebble Beach for the legendary Concours d'Elegance, where it dominated the scene, winning three prizes in two days.

Equally noteworthy was the Ferrari Classiche Department's efforts in restoring the engine, bodywork, suspension and running gear of a 250 GT Berlinetta passo corto Competizione (chassis no. 2321 GT) to pristine condition. The car arrived in Maranello in March 2014 and work began in the summer of the same year, finishing 14 months later. The 250 GT Berlinetta Competizione's first owner was Dorino Serafini, a GT and Scuderia Ferrari Formula 1 driver. After many changes of livery, the colour chosen by the new owner is a Pininfarina grey (with brown interior) similar to the colour sported by many Prancing Horse cars in the late 1960s.

All restoration work carried out by Ferrari Classiche is underpinned by in-depth research using Ferrari's production archive, a treasure trove of invaluable technical information on every car built at the factory. This extensive archive allows us to offer our classic car clients a Certificate of Authenticity or an Attestation for vehicles of historic interest, and to supply all major mechanical components manufactured to the original specifications.

Ferrari Classiche
via Abetone Inferiore 4
41053 Maranello - Italy
Tel +39 0536 1935914, Fax +39 0536 949335
ferrariclassiche@ferrari.com   www.ferrari.com

Twenty-four years of Top Five

1993-94

1 – 1912 ROLLS-ROYCE
Silver Ghost tourer
Sotheby's, Solvang (USA)
18.8.1993 – Lot 82
US$ 1.762.500

2 – 1927 DELAGE
1500 G.P.
Poulain Le Fur, Paris (F)
19.2.1994 – Lot 30
US$ 1.192.170

3 – 1931 BENTLEY
4½l supercharged tourer
Sotheby's, London (GB)
6.12.1993 – Lot 1152
US$ 593.662

4 – 1930 BENTLEY
4½l supercharged tourer
Sotheby's, London (GB)
16.5.1994 – Lot 560
US$ 580.403

5 – 1928 MERCEDES-BENZ
S 26/120/180 PS tourer
Sotheby's, London (GB)
6.12.1993 – Lot 1183
US$ 495.092

1994-95

1 – 1954 MASERATI
250F
Brooks, Monaco (MC)
24.5.1995 – Lot 242
US$ 884.969

2 – 1948 FERRARI
166MM barchetta
Sotheby's, Los Angeles (USA)
17.6.1995 – Lot 26
US$ 800.000

3 – 1927 DELAGE
1500 G.P.
Poulain Le Fur, Paris (F)
12.6.1995 – Lot 32
US$ 708.491

4 – 1964 FERRARI
250 LM
Coys, Silverstone (GB)
29.7.1995 – Lot 49
US$ 589.119

5 – 1931 BENTLEY
8l tourer
Coys, Silverstone (GB)
29.7.1995 – Lot 72
US$ 562.340

1995-96

1 – 1933 ALFA ROMEO
8C 2300 corto spider
Christie's, Pebble Beach (USA)
20.8.1995 – Lot 41
US$ 1.817.500

2 – 1935 ALFA ROMEO
8C-35
Brooks, London (GB)
4.12.1995 – Lot 767
US$ 1.319.763

3 – 1931 BENTLEY
4½l supercharged tourer
Christie's, Pebble Beach (USA)
20.8.1995 – Lot 44
US$ 717.500

4 – 1927 MERCEDES-BENZ
S 26/120/180 PS tourer
Brooks, Stuttgart (D)
20.4.1996 – Lot 111
US$ 710.902

5 – 1960 MASERATI
Tipo 61 Birdcage
Brooks, Monaco (MC)
15.5.1996 – Lot 152
US$ 705.032

1996-97

1 – 1949 FERRARI
166MM barchetta
Christie's, Pebble Beach (USA)
18.8.1996 – Lot 73
US$ 1.652.500

2 – 1952 FERRARI
225 Sport barchetta
Poulain Le Fur, Paris (F)
9.6.1997 – Lot 14
US$ 1.294.188

3 – 1953 FERRARI
625 TF barchetta
Christie's, Geneva (CH)
22.5.1997 – Lot 133
US$ 876.217

4 – 1956 MASERATI
300S
Christie's, London (GB)
14.7.1997 – Lot 413
US$ 745.516

5 – 1930 DUESENBERG
Model J convertible
Sotheby's, New York (USA)
5.10.1996 – Lot 59
US$ 662.500

This chapter is dedicated to the Top Five cars of the last 24 auction seasons.

REAL PASSION FOR REAL LOVERS
CLASSIC CAR INTERIOR RESTORATION

MANTOVA - ITALY
Phone: +39 0376 695 105
E-mail : maieli@inwind.it

1997-98

1 – 1938 DUESENBERG
Model SJ convertible sedan
Christie's, Tarrytown (USA)
25-04-1998 – Lot 91
US$ 1.267.500

2 – 1962 ASTON MARTIN
DB4 GT Zagato
Brooks, Goodwood (GB)
12.6.1998 – Lot 724
US$ 1.115.743

3 – 1953 FERRARI
340/375 MM spider
Christie's, Pebble Beach (USA)
17.8.1997 – Lot 95
US$ 1.080.500

4 – 1956 JAGUAR
D-Type
Christie's, Pebble Beach (USA)
17.8.1997 – Lot 54
US$ 1.014.500

5 – 1911 ROLLS-ROYCE
Silver Ghost landaulette
Sotheby's, London (GB)
24.11.1997 – Lot 526
US$ 840.575

1998-99

1 – 1967 FERRARI
275GTS/4 NART Spider
Christie's, Pebble Beach (USA)
16.8.1998 – Lot 47
US$ 2.092.500

2 – 1965 FERRARI
250 LM
Brooks, Gstaad (CH)
19.12.1998 – Lot 173
US$ 1.797.334

3 – 1935 ALFA ROMEO
8C-35
Christie's, Pebble Beach (USA)
16.8.1998 – Lot 45
US$ 1.322.500

4 – 1957 VANWALL
F1
Brooks, Nürburgring (D)
8.8.1998 – Lot 304
US$ 1.306.447

5 – 1960 MASERATI
Tipo 60 Birdcage
RM Auctions, Amelia Island (USA)
20.3.1999 – Lot 152
US$ 1.100.000

1999-2000

1 – 1937 ALFA ROMEO
8C 2900B cabriolet
Christie's, Pebble Beach (USA)
29.8.1999 – Lot 29
US$ 4.072.500

2 – 1954 FERRARI
250 Monza
RM Auctions, Monterey (USA)
27.8.1999 – Lot 452
US$ 2.970.000

3 – 1955 JAGUAR
D-Type
Christie's, London (GB)
1.11.1999 – Lot 219
US$ 2.809.496

4 – 1965 FERRARI
250 LM
RM Auctions, Amelia Island (USA)
11.3.2000 – Lot 249
US$ 2.310.000

5 – 1964 FERRARI
250 LM
Christie's, Pebble Beach (USA)
29.8.1999 – Lot 24
US$ 2.147.500

2000-01

1 – 1966 FERRARI
330 P3
Christie's, Pebble Beach (USA)
20.8.2000 – Lot 89
US$ 5.616.000

2 – 1964 SHELBY AMERICAN
Cobra Daytona Coupé
RM Auctions, Monterey (USA)
18.8.2000 – Lot 454
US$ 4.400.000

3 – 1938 ALFA ROMEO
8C 2900B berlinetta
Brooks, Carmel (USA)
19.8.2000 – Lot 336
US$ 3.082.500

4 – 1935 MERCEDES-BENZ
500K Spezial Roadster
RM Auctions, Amelia Island (USA)
10.3.2001 – Lot 61
US$ 2.970.000

5 – 1960 MASERATI
Tipo 60 Birdcage
Christie's, London (GB)
26.3.2001 – Lot 62
US$ 2.055.942

ANY CAR TELLS A STORY.

JUST FEW BECOME A CLASSIC.

Convert your Abarth in a real collector's item.
Discover our certification and restoration services.

ABARTH CLASSICHE - OFFICINE ABARTH - TORINO, ITALIA
ABARTHCLASSICHE.COM

JOIN THE COMMUNITY.
SCORPIONSHIP.ABARTH.COM

2001-02

1 – 1956 FERRARI
410 Sport
RM Auctions, Monterey (USA)
17.8.2001 – Lot 277
US$ 3.822.500

2 – 1937 MERCEDES-BENZ
540K Spezial Roadster
RM Auctions, Phoenix (USA)
18.1.2002 – Lot 73
US$ 3.630.000

3 – 1933 ALFA ROMEO
8C 2600 Monza
RM Auctions, Amelia Island (USA)
9.3.2002 – Lot 75
US$ 2.530.000

4 – 1934 DUESENBERG
Model J convertible coupé
RM Auctions, Rochester (USA)
4.8.2001 – Lot 37
US$ 1.980.000

5 – 1953 FERRARI
375 MM spider
RM Auctions, Amelia Island (USA)
9.3.2002 – Lot 118
US$ 1.925.000

2002-03

1 – 1962 FERRARI
330 TRI/LM
RM Auctions, Monterey (USA)
16.8.2002 – Lot 143
US$ 6.490.000

2 – 1929 MERCEDES-BENZ
SSK Rennwagen
Artcurial, Paris (F)
10.2.2003 – Lot 34
US$ 3.331.553

3 – 1932 BUGATTI
Type 55 roadster
Christie's, Paris (F)
8.2.2003 – Lot 51
US$ 1.812.822

4 – 1954 FERRARI
250 Monza
RM Auctions, Monterey (USA)
16.8.2002 – Lot 174
US$ 1.705.000

5 – 1963 JAGUAR
E-Type 3.8 Lightweight roadster
RM Auctions, Amelia Island (USA)
8.3.2003 – Lot 82
US$ 1.375.000

2003-04

1 – 1930 BENTLEY
6½l Speed Six tourer
Christie's, Le Mans (F)
23.7.2004 – Lot 83
US$ 5.105.896

2 – 1956 FERRARI
860 Monza
RM Auctions, Monterey (USA)
15.8.2003 – Lot 453
US$ 2.057.001

3 – 1928 BENTLEY
4½l tourer
Christie's, Le Mans (F)
23.7.2004 – Lot 86
US$ 2.021.573

4 – 2000 FERRARI
F1/2000
Bonhams, Monaco (MC)
15.5.2004 – Lot 272
US$ 1.690.637

5 – 1956 ASTON MARTIN
DB3S
Christie's, Le Mans (F)
23.7.2004 – Lot 91
US$ 1.646.090

2004-05

1 – 1929 MERCEDES-BENZ
SSK two-seater tourer
Bonhams, Goodwood (GB)
3.9.2004 – Lot 144
US$ 7.487.841

2 – 1935 DUESENBERG
Model SJ speedster special
Gooding & Company, Pebble Beach (USA)
15.8.2004 – Lot 37
US$ 4.455.000

3 – 1954 OLDSMOBILE
F-88 convertible concept car
Barrett & Jackson, Scottsdale (USA)
26.1.2005 – Lot 992
US$ 3.240.000

4 – 2004 FERRARI
F-2004
Sotheby's, Maranello (I)
28.6.2005 – Lot 133
US$ 3.205.175

5 – 1934 DUESENBERG
Model J convertible coupé
RM Auctions, Phoenix (USA)
28.1.2005 – Lot 53
US$ 2.750.000

2005-06

1 – 1940 GENERAL MOTORS
Futurliner Bus
Barrett & Jackson, Scottsdale (USA)
17.1.2006 – Lot 1307
US$ 4.320.000

2 – 1967 FERRARI
275 GTS/4 NART Spider
Gooding & Company, Pebble Beach (USA)
21.8.2005 – Lot 37
US$ 3.960.000

3 – 1938 TALBOT-LAGO
T150 C SS Goutte d'Eau
Gooding & Company, Palm Beach (USA)
22.1.2006 – Lot 29
US$ 3.905.000

4 – 1938 TALBOT-LAGO
T150 C Speciale Goutte d'Eau
RM Auctions, Monterey (USA)
20.8.2005 – Lot 251
US$ 3.685.000

5 – 1937 TALBOT-LAGO
T150 C SS Goutte d'Eau
Christie's, Monterey (USA)
18.8.2005 – Lot 85
US$ 3.535.000

2006-07

1 – 1962 FERRARI
330 TRI/LM
RM Auctions, Maranello (I)
20.5.2007 – Lot 221
US$ 9.265.438

2 – 1953 FERRARI
340/375 Mille Miglia Berlinetta
RM Auctions, Maranello (I)
20.5.2007 – Lot 233
US$ 5.707.510

3 – 1958 FERRARI
412 S
RM Auctions, Monterey (USA)
19.8.2006 – Lot 465
US$ 5.610.000

4 – 1966 SHELBY AMERICAN
Cobra 427 "Supersnake"
Barrett & Jackson, Scottsdale (USA)
19.1.2007 – Lot 1301
US$ 5.500.000

5 – 1928 MERCEDES-BENZ
S torpedo roadster
Christie's, Monterey (USA)
17.8.2006 – Lot 52
US$ 3.645.000

2007-08

1 – 1961 FERRARI
250 GT Spyder California swb
RM Auctions, Maranello (I)
18.5.2008 – Lot 328
US$ 10.910.592

2 – 1937 MERCEDES-BENZ
540 K Spezial Roadster
RM Auctions, London (GB)
31.10.2007 – Lot 225
US$ 8.090.769

3 – 1904 ROLLS-ROYCE
10HP two-seater
Bonhams, London (GB)
3.12.2007 – Lot 604
US$ 7.266.967

4 – 1964 FERRARI
250 LM
RM Auctions, Maranello (I)
18.5.2008 – Lot 339A
US$ 6.989.598

5 – 1959 FERRARI
250 GT Spyder California lwb
RM Auctions, Monterey (USA)
18.8.2007 – Lot 560
US$ 4.950.000

2008-09

1 – 1957 FERRARI
250 Testa Rossa
RM Auctions, Maranello (I)
17.5.2009 – Lot 237
US$ 12.193.236

2 – 1937 BUGATTI
Type 57SC Atalante
Gooding & Company, Pebble Beach (USA)
16.8.2008 – Lot 27
US$ 7.920.000

3 – 1960 JAGUAR
E2A
Bonhams, Carmel (USA)
15.8.2008 – Lot 364
US$ 4.957.000

4 – 1960 FERRARI
250 GT Spyder California swb
Gooding & Company, Scottsdale (USA)
17.1.2009 – Lot 78
US$ 4.950.000

5 – 1939 TALBOT-LAGO
T150 C SS Aerocoupé
Bonhams, Carmel (USA)
15.8.2008 – Lot 330
US$ 4.847.000

Hortons Books are the leading suppliers of new and out-of-print motoring literature

We are exhibiting at the following events next year:

Autosport International: The Racing Car Show, UK

Retromobile: Paris, France

Race Retro: International Historic Motorsport Show, UK

Amelia Island Concours D'Elegance: USA

Goodwood Members' Meeting: UK

Techno Classica Essen: Germany

Goodwood Festival of Speed: UK

F1 British Grand Prix: UK

Silverstone Classic: UK

Automobilia Monterey: USA

Pebble Beach RetroAuto: USA

Pebble Beach Concours D'Elegance: USA

Goodwood Revival: UK

email: contact@hortonsbooks.co.uk **tel:** +44 (0) 1672 514 777

2009-10

1 – 1965 SHELBY AMERICAN
Cobra Daytona Coupé
Mecum, Monterey (USA)
15.8.2009 – Lot S104
US$ 7.685.000

2 – 1962 FERRARI
250 GT Spyder California swb
Gooding & Company, Pebble Beach (USA)
16.8.2009 – Lot 135
US$ 5.115.000

3 – 1933 ALFA ROMEO
8C 2300 cabriolet
Gooding & Company, Pebble Beach (USA)
16.8.2009 – Lot 139
US$ 4.180.000

4 – 1955 JAGUAR
D-Type
Gooding & Company, Scottsdale (USA)
22.1.2010 – Lot 16
US$ 3.740.000

5 – 1962 FERRARI
400 Superamerica cabriolet
RM Auctions, Monaco (MC)
1.5.2010 – Lot 221
US$ 3.728.200

2010-11

1 – 1959 FERRARI
250 GT Spyder California lwb
Gooding & Company, Pebble Beach (USA)
14.8.2010 – Lot 46
US$ 7.260.000

2 – 1933 ALFA ROMEO
8C 2300 Monza
Gooding & Company, Pebble Beach (USA)
15.8.2010 – Lot 117
US$ 6.710.000

3 – 1961 FERRARI
250 GT Berlinetta Competizione
Gooding & Company, Pebble Beach (USA)
15.8.2010 – Lot 133
US$ 6.105.000

4 – 1955 FERRARI
375 MM coupé
RM Auctions, Villa d'Este (I)
21.5.2011 – Lot 120
US$ 4.783.632

5 – 1954 FERRARI
375 MM coupé
RM Auctions, Pebble Beach (USA)
14.8.2010 – Lot 351
US$ 4.620.000

2011-12

1 – 1957 FERRARI
250 Testa Rossa
Gooding & Company, Pebble Beach (USA)
20.8.2011 – Lot 18
US$ 16.390.000

2 – 1931 DUESENBERG
Model J coupé
Gooding & Company, Pebble Beach (USA)
21.8.2011 – Lot 123
US$ 10.340.000

3 – 1937 MERCEDES-BENZ
540 K Spezial Roadster
RM Auctions, Monterey (USA)
20.8.2011 – Lot 242
US$ 9.680.000

4 – 1929 BENTLEY
4½l Supercharged
Bonhams, Goodwood (GB)
29.6.2012 – Lot 204
US$ 7.867.261

5 – 1912 ROLLS-ROYCE 40/50hp
Silver Ghost double pullman limousine
Bonhams, Goodwood (GB)
29.6.2012 – Lot 272
US$ 7.342.933

2012-13

1 – 1954 MERCEDES-BENZ
W196R
Bonhams, Goodwood (GB)
12.7.2013 – Lot 320
US$ 29.598.265

2 – 1953 FERRARI
340/375 Mille Miglia Berlinetta
RM Auctions, Villa Erba (I)
25.5.2013 – Lot 130
US$ 12.752.678

3 – 1936 MERCEDES-BENZ
540 K Spezial Roadster
Gooding & Company, Pebble Beach (USA)
19.8.2012 – Lot 123
US$ 11.770.000

4 – 1960 FERRARI
250 GT Spyder California lwb
Gooding & Company, Pebble Beach (USA)
18.8.2012 – Lot 49
US$ 11.275.000

5 – 1968 FORD
GT40
RM Auctions, Monterey (USA)
17.8.2012 – Lot 139
US$ 11.000.000

2013-14

1 – 1962 FERRARI
250 GTO
Bonhams, Carmel (USA)
14.8.2014 – Lot 03
US$ 38.115.000

2 – 1964 FERRARI
275 GTB/C Speciale
RM Auctions, Monterey (USA)
16.8.2014 – Lot 239
US$ 26.400.000

3 – 1954 FERRARI
375 Plus spider
Bonhams, Goodwood (UK)
27.6.2014 – Lot 320
US$ 18.315.361

4 – 1961 FERRARI
250 GT Spyder California swb
Gooding & Company, Pebble Beach (USA)
16.8.2014 – Lot 18
US$ 15.180.000

5 – 1964 FERRARI
250 LM
RM Sotheby's, New York (USA)
21.11.2013 – Lot 141
US$ 14.300.000

2014-15

1 – 1961 FERRARI
250 GT Spyder California swb
Artcurial, Paris (F)
6.2.2015 – Lot 59
US$ 18.644.874

2 – 1964 FERRARI
250 LM
RM Sotheby's, Monterey (USA)
13.8.2015 – Lot 113
US$ 17.600.000

3 – 1961 FERRARI
250 GT Spyder California swb
Gooding & Company, Pebble Beach (USA)
16.8.2015 – Lot 129
US$ 16.830.000

4 – 1962 FERRARI
250 GT Berlinetta Speciale swb
Gooding & Company, Pebble Beach (USA)
15.8.2015 – Lot 39
US$ 16.500.000

5 – 1998 McLAREN
F1
RM Sotheby's, Monterey (USA)
13.8.2015 – Lot 107
US$ 13.750.000

2015-16

1 – 1957 FERRARI
335 S
Artcurial, Paris (F)
5.2.2016 – Lot 170
US$ 35.930.639

2 – 1956 FERRARI
290 MM
RM Sotheby's, New York (USA)
10.12.2015 – Lot 221
US$ 28.050.000

3 – 1955 JAGUAR
D-Type
RM Sotheby's, Monterey (USA)
19.8.2016 – Lot 114
US$ 21.780.000

4 – 1939 ALFA ROMEO
8C 2900B Spider
RM Sotheby's, Monterey (USA)
20.8.2016 – Lot 234
US$ 19.800.000

5 – 1959 FERRARI
250 GT Spyder California lwb
Gooding & Company, Pebble Beach (USA)
20.8.2016 – Lot 33
US$ 18.150.000

2016-17

1 – 1956 Aston Martin
DBR1
RM Sotheby's, Monterey (USA)
18.8.2017 – Lot 148
US$ 22.550.000

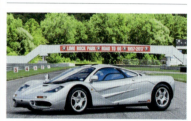

2 – 1995 McLAREN
F1
Bonhams, Carmel (USA)
18.8.2017 – Lot 73
US$ 15.620.000

3 – 1966 FERRARI
275 GTB Competizione
Gooding & Company, Pebble Beach (USA)
19.8.2017 – Lot 120
US$ 14.520.000

4 – 1970 PORSCHE
917K
Gooding & Company, Pebble Beach (USA)
18.8.2017 – Lot 44
US$ 14.080.000

5 – 1961 FERRARI
250 GT Berlinetta Lusso
RM Sotheby's, Monterey (USA)
19.8.2017 – Lot 220
US$ 8.305.000

EXCELLENT CARRIER FOR EXCLUSIVE CARS

info@menabetz.com

+39 059 822 864

EVENTI E TRASPORTI

lorenzo.menabue@menabetz.com
Mobile +39 335 603 1723

The 1st August 1993-31st August 2017 "Top Five" for Makes

Alfa Romeo | Aston Martin | Bentley | Bugatti

1 – 1939 8C 2900B Spider
RM Sotheby's, Monterey (USA)
20.8.2016 – Lot 234
US$ 19.800.000

1 – 1956 Aston Martin DBR1
RM Sotheby's, Monterey (USA)
18.8.2017 – Lot 148
US$ 22.550.000

1 – 1929 4½l Supercharged single-seater
Bonhams, Goodwood (UK)
29.6.2012 – Lot 204
US$ 7.867.261

1 – 1932 Type 55 Roadster
Gooding & Company, Pebble Beach (USA)
21.8.2016 – Lot 135
US$ 10.400.000

2 – 1933 8C 2300 Monza
Gooding & Company, Pebble Beach (USA)
21.8.2016 – Lot 128
US$ 11.990.000

2 – 1962 DB4 GT Zagato
RM Sotheby's, New York (USA)
10.12.2015 – Lot 215
US$ 14.300.000

2 – 1928 4½l Le Mans "bobtail" tourer
Gooding & Company, Pebble Beach (USA)
18.8.2012 – Lot 20
US$ 6.050.000

2 – 1937 Type 57S sports tourer
Bonhams, Amelia Island (USA)
10.3.2016 – Lot 139
US$ 9.735.000

3 – 1935 8C-35
Bonhams, Goodwood (UK)
14.9.2013 – Lot 235
US$ 9.402.426

3 – 1959 DP199/DB4 GT prototype
RM Sotheby's, Monterey (USA)
18.8.2017 – Lot 147
US$ 6.765.000

3 – 1930 6½l Speed Six tourer
Christie's, Le Mans (F)
23.7.2004 – Lot 83
US$ 5.105.896

3 – 1937 Type 57SC Atalante
Gooding & Company, Pebble Beach (USA)
18.8.2013 – Lot 123
US$ 8.745.000

4 – 1933 8C 2300 Monza
Gooding & Company, Pebble Beach (USA)
15.8.2010 – Lot 117
US$ 6.710.000

4 – 1955 DB3S
Gooding & Company, Pebble Beach (USA)
16.8.2014 – Lot 32
US$ 5.500.000

4 – 1931 4½l Supercharged Le Mans
Bonhams, Carmel (USA)
16.8.2013 – Lot 152
US$ 4.647.500

4 – 1937 Type 57SC Atalante
Gooding & Company, Pebble Beach (USA)
16.8.2008 – Lot 27
US$ 7.920.000

5 – 1948 6C 2500 Competizione
Gooding & Company, Pebble Beach (USA)
18.8.2013 – Lot 114
US$ 4.840.000

5 – 1960 DB4 GT Jet
Bonhams, Newport Pagnell (UK)
18.5.2013 – Lot 239
US$ 4.874.880

5 – 1931 4½l Supercharged 2-seater boat tail
Gooding & Company, Pebble Beach (USA)
19.8.2007 – Lot 112
US$ 4.510.000

5 – 1937 Type 57S cabriolet
RM Sotheby's, Amelia Island (USA)
11.3.2017 – Lot 232
US$ 7.700.000

ASTON MARTIN
ASSURED PROVENANCE

REST ASSURED

DISCOVER THE TRUE HERITAGE OF YOUR CAR

The Aston Martin Assured Provenance certification programme comprehensively assesses the background of its sports cars, offering a true blue riband service to owners and collectors. Drawing on the unrivalled knowledge of a committee of authoritative Aston Martin experts, the pioneering Assured Provenance certification programme is administered and run by the brand's world-renowned in-house heritage car facility – Aston Martin Works.

For further information please contact the Assured Provenance team.

EXPERIENCE MATTERS

ASTON MARTIN WORKS

Tickford Street, Newport Pagnell
Buckinghamshire MK16 9AN

Tel: +44 (0)1908 610 620
Email: enquiry@astonmartin.com

www.astonmartinworks.com

Ferrari	Ford	Jaguar	Lamborghini
 **1 – 1962 250 GTO** Bonhams, Carmel (USA) 14.8.2014 – Lot 03 **US$ 38.115.000**	 **1 – 1968 GT40 coupé** RM, Monterey (USA) 17.8.2012 – Lot 139 **US$ 11.000.000**	 **1 – 1955 D-Type** RM Sotheby's, Monterey (USA) 19.8.2016 – Lot 114 **US$ 21.780.000**	 **1 – 1972 Miura SV** Artcurial, Paris (F) 10.2.2017 – Lot 75 **US$ 2.538.630**
 **2 – 1957 335 S** Artcurial, Paris (F) 5.2.2016 – Lot 170 **US$ 35.930.639**	 **2 – 1964 GT40 coupé** Mecum, Houston (USA) 12.4.2014 – Lot S147.1 **US$ 7.000.000**	 **2 – 1953 C-Type** RM Sotheby's, Monterey (USA) 14.8.2015 – Lot 235 **US$ 13.200.000**	 **2 – 1971 MIURA SV** RM Sotheby's, Monterey (USA) 13.8.2015 – Lot 105 **US$ 2.475.000**
 **3 – 1956 290 MM** RM Sotheby's, New York (USA) 10.12.2015 – Lot 221 **US$ 28.050.000**	 **3 – 1965 GT40 roadster** RM, Monterey (USA) 15.8.2014 – Lot 134 **US$ 6.930.000**	 **3 – 1953 C-Type** Bonhams, Monaco (MC) 13.5.2016 – Lot 114 **US$ 8.221.626**	 **3 – 1972 MIURA SV** RM Sotheby's, New York (USA) 10.12.2015 – Lot 202 **US$ 2.420.000**
 **4 – 1967 275 GTB/4 NART Spider** RM Auctions, Monterey (USA) 17.8.2013 – Lot 225 **US$ 27.500.000**	 **4 – 1964 GT40 coupé** Gooding & Company, Pebble Beach (USA) 19.8.2012 – Lot 113 **US$ 4.950.000**	 **4 – 1963 E-Type 3.8 Lightweight roadster** Bonhams, Carmel (USA) 18.8.2017 – Lot 52 **US$ 8.000.000**	 **4 – 1971 MIURA SV** RM Sotheby's, Amelia Island (USA) 14.3.2015 – Lot 152 **US$ 2.310.000**
 **5 – 1964 275 GTB/C Speciale** RM Auctions, Monterey (USA) 16.8.2014 – Lot 239 **US$ 26.400.000**	 **5 – 1966 GT40 coupé** Mecum, Monterey (USA) 20.8.2016 – S103 **US$ 4.400.000**	 **5 – 1963 E-Type 3.8 Lightweight roadster** Bonhams, Scottsdale (USA) 19.1.2017 – Lot 24 **US$ 7.370.000**	 **5 – 1969 MIURA S** Mecum, Monterey (USA) 15.8.2015 – Lot S66 **US$ 2.300.000**

Maserati

1 – 1955 300 S
Bonhams, Goodwood (UK)
12.7.2013 – Lot 340
US$ 6.090.585

2 – 1956 250 F
Gooding & Company, Pebble Beach (USA)
17.8.2014 – Lot 115
US$ 4.620.000

3 – 1955 A5G/54 spider
RM Sotheby's, New York (USA)
21.11.2013 – Lot 134
US$ 4.455.000

4 – 1956 A6G/54 berlinetta
Gooding & Company, Pebble Beach (USA)
18.8.2017 – Lot 27
US$ 4.400.000

5 – 1972 Boomerang
Bonhams, Goodwood (UK)
5.9.2015 – Lot 11
US$ 3.714.523

Mercedes-Benz

1 – 1954 W196R
Bonhams, Goodwood (GB)
12.7.2013 – Lot 320
US$ 29.598.265

2 – 1936 540 K Spezial Roadster
Gooding & Company, Pebble Beach (USA)
19.8.2012 – Lot 123
US$ 11.770.000

3 – 1937 540 K Spezial Roadster
RM Sotheby's, Phoenix (USA)
29.1.2016 – Lot 242
US$ 9.900.000

4 – 1937 540 K Spezial Roadster
RM Auctions, Monterey (USA)
20.8.2011 – Lot 242
US$ 9.680.000

5 – 1928 S Torpedo Roadster
RM Auctions, Monterey (USA)
17.8.2013 – Lot 216
US$ 8.250.000

Porsche

1 – 1970 917K
Gooding & Company, Pebble Beach (USA)
18.8.2017 – Lot 44
US$ 14.080.000

2 – 1982 956
Gooding & Company, Pebble Beach (USA)
15.8.2015 – Lot 50
US$ 10.120.000

3 – 1956 550 Spyder
Bonhams, Goodwood (UK)
10.9.2016 – Lot 140
US$ 6.120.839

4 – 1998 911 GT1 Evolution
Gooding & Company, Amelia Island (USA)
10.3.2017 – Lot 42
US$ 5.665.000

5 – 1972 917/10 spyder Can-Am
Mecum, Monterey (USA)
16.8.2012 - Lot S123
US$ 5.500.000

Shelby American

1 – 1962 Cobra 260
RM Sotheby's, Monterey (USA)
19.8.2016 – Lot 117
US$ 13.750.000

2 – 1965 Cobra Daytona Coupé
Mecum, Monterey (USA)
15.8.2009 – Lot S104
US$ 7.685.000

3 – 1966 Cobra 427 "Supersnake"
Barrett & Jackson, Scottsdale (USA)
19.1.2007 – Lot 1301
US$ 5.500.000

4 – 1966 Cobra 427 "Supersnake"
Barrett & Jackson, Scottsdale (USA)
17.1.2015 – Lot 2509
US$ 5.115.000

5 – 1964 Cobra Daytona Coupé
RM Auctions, Monterey (USA)
18.8.2000 – Lot 454
US$ 4.400.000

TWO OF THE MOST PRESTIGIOUS CLASSIC CAR MEETINGS IN EUROPE
DYCK CASTLE / GERMANY

MASTERPIECES
CONCOURS D'ÉLÉGANCE
EST. 2014

THE WORLD COLLECTORS MEETING
JUNE 28TH – 30TH, 2018

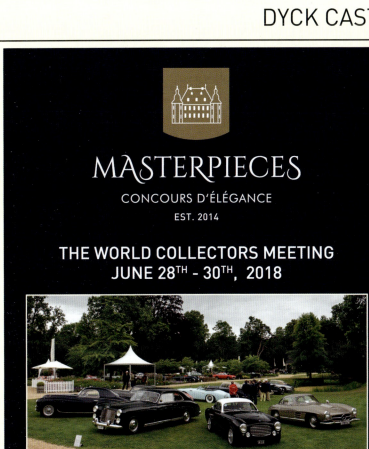

PROTOTYPES & ONE-OFFS

COACHBUILDING CLASSICS

PRIVACY WITH TOP-LIFESTYLE

ADMISSION ONLY BY PERSONALIZED BOOKING IN ADVANCE:
MASTERPIECES-CONCOURS.DE

ELEGANCE · PASSION · STYLE

CLASSIC DAYS
RACING LEGENDS · JEWELS IN THE PARK
EST. 2006

THE CLASSIC- AND MOTORFESTIVAL
AUGUST 3RD – 5TH, 2018

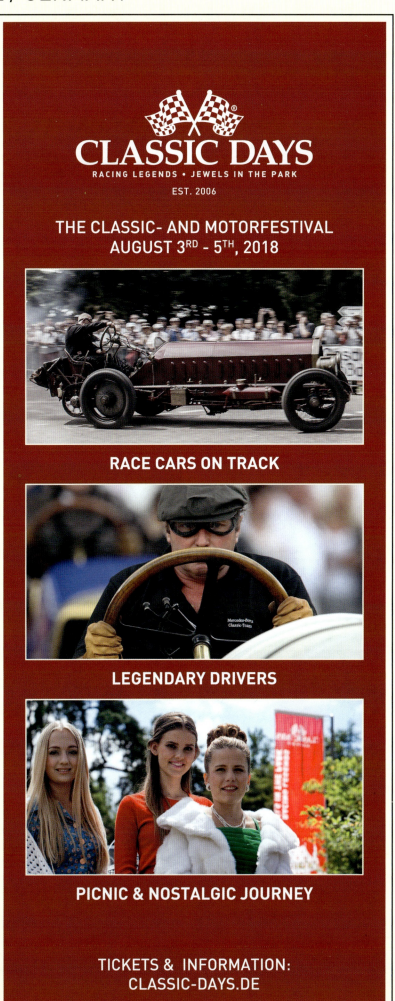

RACE CARS ON TRACK

LEGENDARY DRIVERS

PICNIC & NOSTALGIC JOURNEY

TICKETS & INFORMATION:
CLASSIC-DAYS.DE

MOTORSPORT · RETROSTYLE · FESTIVAL

CONTACT: OFFICE@CLASSIC-DAYS.DE | PHONE: +49 2165 1714692

The 1ˢᵗ August 1993 - 31ˢᵗ August 2017 "Top Twenty"

1 – 1962 FERRARI
250 GTO
Bonhams, Carmel (USA)
14.8.2014 – Lot 03
US$ 38.115.000

2 – 1957 FERRARI
335 S
Artcurial, Paris (F)
5.2.2016 – Lot 170
US$ 35.930.639

3 – 1954 MERCEDES-BENZ
W196R
Bonhams, Goodwood (GB)
12.7.2013 – Lot 320
US$ 29.598.265

4 – 1956 FERRARI
290 MM
RM Sotheby's, New York (USA)
10.12.2015 – Lot 221
US$ 28.050.000

5 – 1967 FERRARI
275 GTB/4 NART Spider
RM Auctions, Monterey (USA)
17.8.2013 – Lot 225
US$ 27.500.000

6 – 1964 FERRARI
275 GTB/C Speciale
RM Auctions, Monterey (USA)
16.8.2014 – Lot 239
US$ 26.400.000

7 – 1956 Aston Martin
DBR1
RM Sotheby's, Monterey (USA)
18.8.2017 – Lot 148
US$ 22.550.000

8 – 1955 JAGUAR
D-Type
RM Sotheby's, Monterey (USA)
19.8.2016 – Lot 114
US$ 21.780.000

9 – 1939 ALFA ROMEO
8C 2900B Spider
RM Sotheby's, Monterey (USA)
20.8.2016 – Lot 234
US$ 19.800.000

10 – 1961 FERRARI
250 GT Spyder California swb
Artcurial, Paris (F)
6.2.2015 – Lot 59
US$ 18.644.874

11 – 1954 FERRARI
375 Plus spider
Bonhams, Goodwood (UK)
27.6.2014 – Lot 320
US$ 18.315.361

12 – 1959 FERRARI
250 GT Spyder California lwb
Gooding & Company, Pebble Beach (USA)
20.8.2016 – Lot 33
US$ 18.150.000

13 – 1964 FERRARI
250 LM
RM Sotheby's, Monterey (USA)
13.8.2015 – Lot 113
US$ 17.600.000

14 – 1961 FERRARI
250 GT Spyder California swb
Gooding & Company, Amelia Island (USA)
11.3.2016 – Lot 69
US$ 17.160.000

15 – 1961 FERRARI
250 GT Spyder California swb
Gooding & Company, Pebble Beach (USA)
16.8.2015 – Lot 129
US$ 16.830.000

16 – 1962 FERRARI
250 GT Berlinetta Speciale swb
Gooding & Company, Pebble Beach (USA)
15.8.2015 – Lot 39
US$ 16.500.000

17 – 1957 FERRARI
250 Testa Rossa
Gooding & Company, Pebble Beach (USA)
20.8.2011 – Lot 18
US$ 16.390.000

18 – 1995 McLAREN
F1
Bonhams, Carmel (USA)
18.8.2017 – Lot 73
US$ 15.620.000

17 – 1961 FERRARI
250 GT Spyder California swb
Gooding & Company, Pebble Beach (USA)
16.8.2014 – Lot 18
US$ 15.180.000

20 – 1966 FERRARI
275 GTB Competizione
Gooding & Company, Pebble Beach (USA)
19.8.2017 – Lot 120
US$ 14.520.000

Advertisers:

	page
Abarth Classiche	395
Alfa Romeo	8
Artcurial Motorcars	173
Aston Martin	39
Aston Martin Works	405
Automobilia Ladenburg	329
Axel Schuette	291
BMW	117
Bonhams	13
Bruno Vendiesse	125
Carrozzeria G.A.	257
CARS	21
Christoph Grohe	263
Collezione by MAG	51
Coys	235
Credit Suisse	2
Cremonini Carrozzeria	255
Dino Cognolato Snc	71
Dorotheum	331
Egon Zweimuller	283
Elettrauto Franco	75
Emil Frey Classics	89
Ferrari Classiche	391
Fiskens	69
Gallery Aaldering	279
Girardo & Co.	55
Gooding & Company	339
Gran Premio Nuvolari	73
GTC	177
Hagerty	23
Hamann	179
Historica Selecta	6
Hortons Books	399
Interni Auto Maieli	393
Italdesign	25
J.D. Classics	175
Joe Macari	41
JSWL	61
Kienle Automobiltechnik	293
Lamborghini PoloStorico	253
Lancia Classiche	265
Lukas Huni	165
Maserati	19
Maserati Classiche	277
Masterpieces/Dyck Castle	409
McGrath Maserati	281
Mecum Auctions	15
Menabetz	403
Mercedes-AMG Motorsport	37
Mercedes-Benz Classic	289

	page
Niki Hasler	163
Pagani	17
Pandolfini Casa d'Aste	77
Paul Russell and Company	167
Pirelli Collezione	43
Quality Cars	169
René Grosse Restaurierungen	227
Retromobile	397
Richard Mille	10
RM Sotheby's	159
RPM Logistic System	407
Ruote da Sogno	401
Sport Auto Modena	161
Stefano Ricci	44
Talacrest	170-171
Techno Classica Essen	53
The Peninsula Hotels	49
Vredestein	64
ZF Friedrichshafen AG	62
Zoute Concours d'Elegance	411

Photo credits

Images copyright and courtesy of Aguttes
21, 273, 296, 721

Images copyright and courtesy of Artcurial
Season case, 2, 5, 6, 31, 39, 40, 89, 96, 121, 122, 124, 193, 194, 195, 196, 197, 205, 213, 229, 230, 249, 254, 258, 263, 267, 268, 269, 277, 287, 299, 307, 316, 317, 320, 327, 364, 369, 379, 417, 418, 422, 423, 444, 451, 454, 473, 482, 489, 506, 511, 515, 516, 518, 545, 568, 570, 584, 585, 586, 599, 608, 610, 623, 636, 664, 697, 702, 716, 742

Images copyright and courtesy of Auctions America
156, 160, 162, 170, 223, 303, 338, 339, 365, 375, 377, 427, 430, 558, 565, 603

Images copyright and courtesy of Barrett-Jackson
87, 163, 178, 179, 210, 215, 217, 341, 593, 707

Images copyright and courtesy of Bonhams
Top Ten 2, Top Ten 6, Top Ten 8, 3, 4, 8, 14, 18, 23, 24, 26, 27, 29, 30, 36, 41, 42, 46, 48, 49, 50, 51, 54, 55, 57, 64, 65, 67, 68, 69, 70, 73, 74, 75, 76, 77, 85, 88, 90, 92, 95, 97, 101, 102, 103, 110, 113, 115, 116, 118, 119, 129, 132, 133, 134, 136, 141, 142, 143, 144, 147, 148, 164, 166, 198, 202, 203, 204, 206, 207, 209, 211, 221, 227, 232, 235, 239, 260, 261, 266, 270, 272, 276, 281, 284, 285, 290, 291, 309, 310, 315, 319, 322, 324, 328, 329, 330, 331, 333, 352, 354, 357, 358, 359, 362, 366, 367, 368, 372, 373, 378, 386, 387, 390, 392, 393, 396, 398, 402, 403, 404, 405, 407, 408, 412, 413, 414, 416, 420, 425, 428, 435, 442, 447, 455, 462, 464, 465, 466, 468, 470, 478, 483, 490, 492, 495, 498, 500, 501, 505, 507, 512, 513, 514, 517, 520, 521, 523, 524, 525, 527, 529, 534, 537, 541, 544, 546, 551, 552, 557, 567, 569, 579, 580, 587, 598, 600, 601, 602, 604, 605, 607, 611, 616, 621, 622, 626, 630, 631, 633, 634, 637, 638, 641, 646, 657, 659, 660, 661, 662, 666, 667, 668, 671, 672, 674, 678, 685, 687, 688, 692, 694, 696, 713, 714, 715, 734, 736, 739
Photos by
David Traver Adolphus, Stephen Archer, Christian Baraja, Kyle Brown, Brain Buchard, David Bush, Theo Civitello, Ron Clark, Simon Clay, Jeremy Cliff, Christian Koch Photography, Mathieu Damiens, Clint Davis, Dirk De Jager, Lies De Mol, Xavier De Nombel, Jasen Delgado, Roger Dixon, Patrick Ernzen, Foto Studio Smit BV, Anthony Fraser, Neil Fraser, Gérard Gencey, Jonathan Harper, Marc Joly, Jonathan Kane, Thornley Kelham, Greg Keysar, Paul Kim, Paul Kooyman, Sergei Krishkov, Dale LaFollette, Erik Lasalle, Jerry Lee, Marco Leibetseder, Pablo Leon, James Lipman, Legacy Overland, Matthew Little, Pawel Litwinski, Juan Martinez, Bob Masters, Gabor Mayer, Calvin Miller, Zachary Minot, Motor Klassik, Motorcar Studios, Scott Nidermaier, Alessandro Onger, Bob Ouwens, Glenn Perry, Pole-Position Car Detailing, Rasy Ran, John Reid, Remco Pronk, Ken Richardson, RoyBoy Productions-Travis Scanlan, Brian Rozar, Andre Salerno, Dan Savinelli, Lucas Scarfone, Jeremy Scott, Tim Scott, Seven Gables Motor Garge, Drew Shipley, Peter Singhof, Sean Smith, Elsevier Stokmans, Joshua Sweeny, Francois Tomasi, Keith Treder, Daniele Turetta, Francis Vermeulen, Matthew Wagner, John Waugh, Randy Wells, Tom Wood, Wally Wright

Images copyright and courtesy of Coys
7, 33, 111, 125, 128, 131, 214, 255, 271, 280, 380, 410, 450, 543, 556, 613, 640, 684, 723, 725, 732

Images copyright and courtesy of Dorotheum
123, 127, 619, 620, 704, 706

Images copyright and courtesy of Gooding & Company
Photos by
Brian Henniker 100, 145, 233, 304, 314, 699
Mathieu Heurtault Top Ten 3, Top Ten 4, 9, 44, 52, 130, 236, 250, 252, 475, 477, 583, 618, 629, 650
Matt Howell 241, 496
Mike Maez 150, 499, 628, 709
Anna McGrath 497
Chip Riegel 547

Images copyright and courtesy of H & H
146, 248, 395, 467, 538, 539, 554, 561, 711

Images copyright and courtesy of Historics at Brooklands
43, 47, 86, 376, 383, 394, 411, 449, 469, 689, 693, 724

Images copyright and courtesy of Mecum Auctions
157, 171, 174, 177, 180, 181, 182, 183, 184, 185, 186, 190, 191, 218, 219, 279, 301, 305, 306, 340, 342, 343, 344, 345, 347, 348, 349, 350, 431, 432, 446, 459, 472, 535, 536, 542, 566, 576, 589, 590, 591, 592, 595, 596, 686, 708, 720

Images copyright and courtesy of Mossgreen
192, 363, 436, 548, 606, 727

Images copyright and courtesy of Osenat
152, 212, 355, 384, 550, 663, 698, 722, 735

Images copyright and courtesy of RM Sotheby's
Top Ten 1, Top Ten 5, Top Ten 7, Top Ten 9, Top Ten 10, 1, 10, 11, 12, 13, 15, 16, 17, 19, 20, 22, 25, 28, 32, 34, 37, 38, 45, 53, 56, 58, 59, 60, 61, 62, 63, 66, 71, 72, 78, 79, 80, 81, 82, 83, 84, 91, 93, 94, 98, 99, 104, 105, 106, 107, 108, 109, 112, 114, 117, 135, 138, 139, 140, 149, 151, 153, 154, 155, 158, 159, 161, 165, 167, 168, 169, 172, 173, 175, 176, 187, 188, 189, 199, 200, 201, 208, 216, 220, 222, 224, 225, 228, 231, 234, 237, 238, 240, 242, 243, 244, 245, 246, 247, 251, 253, 256, 257, 259, 262, 264, 265, 274, 275, 278, 282, 283, 286, 288, 289, 292, 293, 294, 295, 297, 298, 300, 302, 308, 311, 312, 313, 318, 321, 323, 325, 334, 335, 336, 337, 346, 351, 353, 356, 361, 370, 371, 374, 381, 382, 385, 388, 389, 391, 397, 399, 400, 401, 409, 415, 419, 421, 424, 426, 429, 433, 434, 437, 438, 439, 440, 441, 443, 445, 448, 452, 453, 456, 457, 458, 460, 461, 463, 471, 474, 476, 479, 480, 481, 484, 485, 486, 487, 488, 491, 493, 494, 502, 503, 504, 508, 509, 510, 522, 526, 528, 530, 531, 532, 533, 540, 549, 553, 555, 559, 560, 562, 563, 564, 571, 572, 573, 574, 575, 577, 578, 581, 582, 588, 594, 597, 609, 612, 614, 615, 617, 624, 625, 627, 632, 635, 639, 642, 643, 644, 645, 647, 648, 649, 651, 652, 653, 654, 655, 656, 658, 665, 669, 670, 673, 675, 676, 677, 679, 680, 681, 682, 683, 690, 691, 695, 700, 701, 703, 705, 710, 712, 717, 718, 719, 726, 728, 729, 731, 733, 737, 738, 740, 741
Photos by
Robin Adams, Ahmed Rashdi Photos, Ravi Angard, John Bazay, Chasen Bell, Bildermeister, David Bush, Simone Caldirola, Andrew Chenovick, Steve Chesler, Theo Civitello, Josh Clason, Simon Clay, Kris Clewell, Jeremy Cleef, Jeff Creech, Rémi Dargegen, Dirk De Jager, Nathan Deremer, Scott Dickey, Jason Dodd, Muhammad El-Kurdi, Patrick Ernzen, Owen Fitter, Michael Ford, Erik Fuller, Bruno des Gayets/Nikoja, Tom Gidden, Noah Golub, Phil Greatorex, Andrew Holiday, Karissa Hosek, Ned Jackson, Pieter Kamp, Greg Keysar, Stephen Kim, Nathan Leach-Proffer, Linhbergh, Matthew Eric Lit, Pawel Litwinski, James Mann, Gabor Mayer, Scott McGuigan, David McNeese, Ryan Merrill, Motorcar Studios, Jorge Nabais, Matt Odom, Dan Olivares, Andrew Olson, Khiem Pham, Teddy Pieper, Ahmed Qadri, Rasy Ran, Dom Romney, Brian Rozar, Lucas Scarfone, Darin Schnabel, Tim Scott, Drew Shipley, Jonathan Sierakowski, Corey Silvia, Ryan Sterling, Aaron Summerfield, Josh Sweeney, Cymon Taylor, Trace Taylor, Diana Varga, William Walker, Tom Wood, Don Wright, Dimitry Zaltsman, Michael Zumbrunn

Images copyright and courtesy of Silverstone Auctions
35, 137, 226, 332, 406, 519, 730

Images copyright and courtesy of Worldwide Auctioneers
120, 126, 326, 360
Photos by
Matthew Heurtault, Nathan Leach-Proffer, Pavel Litwinski, Robbie McCay, Drew Shipley, Dave Wendt Photography, Glenn Zanotti

By the same authors, previous Yearbooks still available:

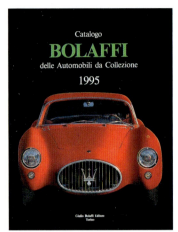

1993-1994 season
All the Makes
Italian text
p. 208 hard-bound
€ 46,00

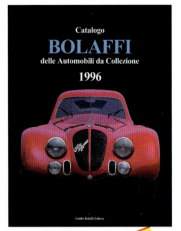

1994-1995 season
All the Makes
Italian/English text
p. 208 hard-bound
€ 46,00

1995-1996 season
All the Makes
Italian/English text
p. 206 hard-bound
€ 49,00

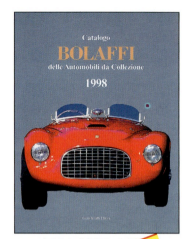

1996-1997 season
All the Makes
Italian/English text
p. 254 hard-bound
€ 57,00

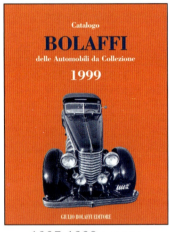

1997-1998 season
All the Makes
Italian/English text
p. 238 hard-bound
€ 46,00

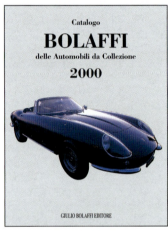

1998-1999 season
All the Makes
Italian/English text
p. 248 hard-bound
€ 46,00

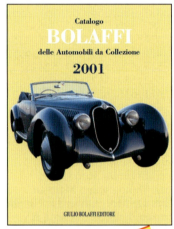

1999-2000 season
All the Makes
Italian/English text
p. 236 hard-bound

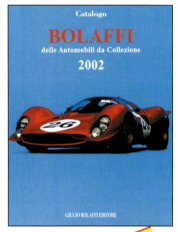

2000-2001 season
All the Makes
Italian/English text
p. 254 soft-bound

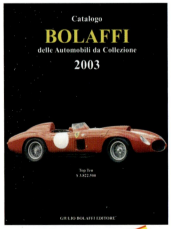

2001-2002 season
All the Makes
Italian/English text
p. 272 soft-bound
€ 46,00

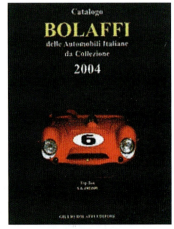

2002-2003 season
Only Italian Makes
Italian/English text
p. 102 soft-bound
€ 29,90

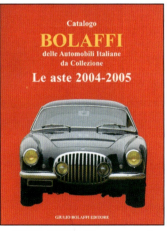

2003-2005 (2 seasons)
Only Italian Makes
Italian/English text
p. 158 soft-bound
€ 29,90

2005-2006 season
Only Italian Makes
Italian/English text
p. 126 soft-bound
€ 29,90

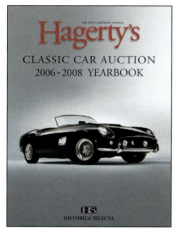
2006-2008 (2 seasons)
All the Makes
English text
p. 390 hard-bound
€ 39,90

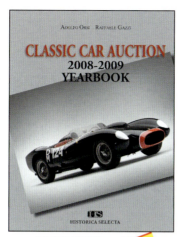
2008-2009 season
All the Makes
English text
p. 286 hard-bound
€ 39,90

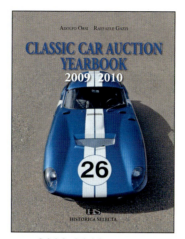
2009-2010 season
All the Makes
English text
p. 320 hard-bound
€ 39,90

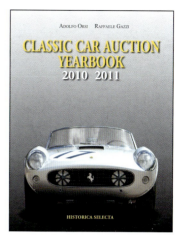
2010-2011 season
All the Makes
English text
p. 320 hard-bound
€ 44,90

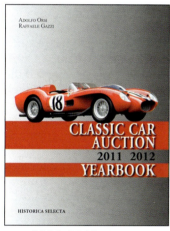
2011-2012 season
All the Makes
English text
p. 336 hard-bound
€ 44,90

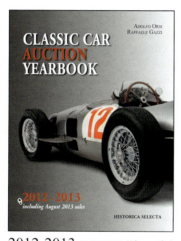
2012-2013 season (13 months)
All the Makes
English text
p. 400 hard-bound
€ 52,00

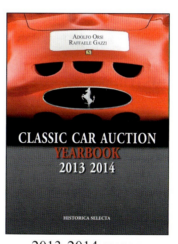
2013-2014 season
All the Makes
English text
p. 392 hard-bound
€ 60,00

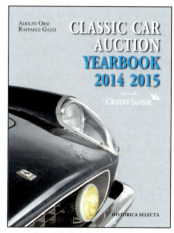
2014-2015 season
All the Makes
English text
p. 424 hard-bound
€ 70,00

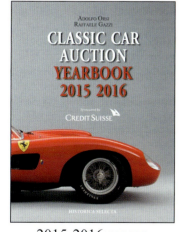
2015-2016 season
All the Makes
English text
p. 416 hard-bound
€ 70,00

HISTORICA SELECTA SRL

41012 CARPI (MODENA) - VIA PAUSSOLO, 14/A - ITALY

TEL +39 059 663955

info@historicaselecta.it

www.classiccarauctionyearbook.com

About the authors

Adolfo Orsi's passion for motorcars was honed throughout his teenage years. In fact, as the grandson of Adolfo and son of Omar Orsi, who held the reins of Maserati between 1937 and 1968, he grew up surrounded by cars.

In 1986 he decided to dedicate himself full-time to his passion and, from 1988 to 1991, he organized auctions of collector cars, motorcycles and automobilia, in association with Finarte Casa d'Aste, in Modena and Monza.

In 1990 he established the company **HISTORICA SELECTA** and Raffaele Gazzi, a long-time friend and fellow enthusiast, joined the company in 1991.

As leading specialists in the international collector car market, HISTORICA SELECTA often advises many of the world's most prestigious Manufacturers, Museums and collectors.

In detail, HISTORICA SELECTA:
- **Organizes historical exhibitions:** "*Maserati 100 – A Century of pure Italian Luxury Sports Cars*", MEF (Museo Enzo Ferrari), Modena 2014; "*The history of the automobile in Modena 1895-1970*", MEF (Museo Enzo Ferrari), Modena 2012 (still part of the Museum exhibit); "*Quando scatta Nuvolari*", Palazzo Te, Mantova, 2009-2010; "*Mitomacchina*", MART, Rovereto, 2006-2007, which had 130.000 visitors and was described by Thoroughbred & Classic Cars as "the most braintingling exhibition of cars ever assembled in the name of art"; "*Cuando el hombre es mas que el mito*" (Fangio), Modena, 2005; "*Maserati, la macchina sublime*", Modena, 1996; "*Maserati ottantanni: 1914-1994*", Motorshow Bologna, 1994; "*Lo sviluppo della tecnica automobilistica dagli inizi del secolo a oggi: Bugatti*", Fiera Bologna, 1993; "*Bugatti e Lotus*", Motorshow Bologna, 1993;
- **Advises manufacturers on Heritage collections and programs:** FCA, Lamborghini and Maserati;
- **Advises Museums** and **private collectors;**
- **Organizes celebrations and forums:** in 2017, HISTORICA SELECTA collaborated with Ferrari for the Concorso Ferrari 70 celebration (as in 2007 for the 60th); in 2014 it organized the Concorso d'Eleganza for the Maserati Centennial Gathering, in 2013 for the 50th Anniversary of Lamborghini, in 2009 it coordinated the "XI World Forum for Motor Museums" in Emilia-Romagna; and in 2001, it organized the 75th Anniversary Celebration of the Modena Automobile Club;
- **Publishes** the "*Classic Car Auction Yearbook*" from 2008; from 1994 to 2006 HISTORICA SELECTA edited the "*Catalogo Bolaffi delle automobili da collezione*".

The President of Historica Selecta is Doctor **Adolfo Orsi**, who is an:
- **Automobile historian**, one of the leading experts in the field of Italian Sports and Racing Cars;
- **Expert in the problems of the authenticity and restoration**, having coordinated the restoration of several Italian cars winning the most prestigious Awards in many Concours d'Elegance;
- **Judge in more than 100 Concours d'Elegances:** judge since 1997 at Pebble Beach, convinced of the importance of preserving cars in their original condition, in 1999 he inspired the FIVA Award for the best preserved car in the field, for which he has been chief class judge ever since; on last September he served as Chief Judge of the Ferrari 70 Concorso (as he did before for the 60th in 2007), 2014 Maserati Centennial Gathering, 2013 Concorso Lamborghini 50th, 2016 and 2017 Swiss Concours in Geneva, Uniques Special Ones in Florence and St. Petersburg; he was a member of the Louis Vuitton Classic Concours Award jury and actually of The Peninsula Classics Best of the Best Award; throughout the years, he has also judged at many other significant events including Amelia Island, Bund Classic in Shanghai, Cavallino Classic, Chantilly, Villa d'Este, Salon Privé, The Legend of Motorcycles, Schloss Dyck, Zoute, Techno Classica, Terme della Salvarola and 21 Gun Salute in New Delhi.
- **Lecturer,** in Italy and abroad, on automobile history and car collecting;
- **Writer,** for the Italian financial newspaper "Il Sole-24 Ore" (from 1989 to 2008) and for "The Official Ferrari Magazine";
- **Honorary member** of the Maserati Club UK, Maserati Club Japan, Maserati Club Italia, Gruppo Anziani Maserati, Club Castiglionese Auto e Moto d'Epoca, **charter member** of ICJAG (International Chief Judge Advisory Group), consulting member of the IAC-PFA (International Advisory Council for the Preservation of Ferrari Automobiles) and FIVA Technical Committee Advisor.

Raffaele Gazzi, a long-time enthusiast of automotive history and of vintage cars in general, was still a bank manager in 1988 when he began dedicating a few of his weekends to working with Adolfo Orsi to create the most important auctions for classic cars and memorabilia in Italy.

At the end of 1991, Raffaele joined HISTORICA SELECTA as a part owner. In addition to co-organizing numerous ongoing events and exhibitions for the company, Raffaele often serves as Secretary of Jury or Judge at various, leading Concours d'Elegance.